A-Z LANCASHIRE

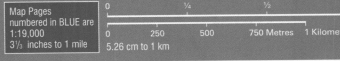

C000202326

CONTENTS

Key to Map Pages	2-3
Map Pages	4-225
Large Scale Town & City Centres	226-229
Postcode Map	230-231
Road M	232-235
Index t and selected Places of Interest	236-319
Index to Hospitals etc.	320

REFERENCE

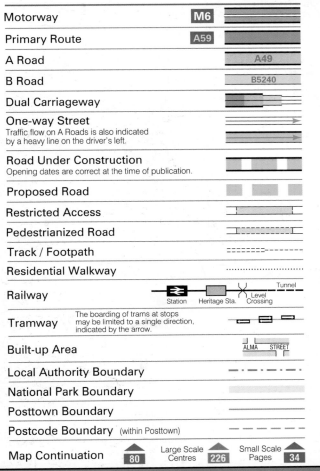

Motorway	M6
Primary Route	A59
A Road	A49
B Road	B5240
Dual Carriageway	
One-way Street Traffic flow on A Roads is also indicated by a heavy line on the driver's left.	
Road Under Construction Opening dates are correct at the time of publication.	
Proposed Road	
Restricted Access	
Pedestrianized Road	
Track / Footpath	
Residential Walkway	
Railway	Station, Heritage Sta., Level Crossing, Tunnel
Tramway The boarding of trams at stops may be limited to a single direction, indicated by the arrow.	
Built-up Area	ALMA STREET
Local Authority Boundary	
National Park Boundary	
Posttown Boundary	
Postcode Boundary (within Posttown)	
Map Continuation	80 / Large Scale Centres 226 / Small Scale Pages 34

Airport	
Car Park (selected)	P
Church or Chapel	†
Cycleway (selected)	
Fire Station	
Hospital	H
House Numbers (A & B Roads only)	13 8
Information Centre	i
National Grid Reference	360
Park & Ride	Preston Portway P+
Police Station	▲
Post Office	★
Safety Camera with Speed Limit Fixed cameras and long term road works cameras. Symbols do not indicate camera direction.	30
Toilet: without facilities for the Disabled with facilities for the Disabled Disabled use only	
Viewpoint	
Educational Establishment	
Hospital or Healthcare Building	
Industrial Building	
Leisure or Recreational Facility	
Place of Interest	
Public Building	
Shopping Centre or Market	
Other Selected Buildings	

SCALES

Map Pages numbered in BLUE are 1:19,000, 3⅓ inches to 1 mile — 5.26 cm to 1 km — 8.47 cm to 1 Mile

Map Pages numbered in RED are 1:9,500, 6 ⅔ inches to 1 mile — 0, ⅛, ¼ Mile; 0, 250, 500 Metres — 10.52 cm to 1 km — 16.94 cm to 1 mile

Map Pages numbered in GREEN are 1:38,000, 1⅔ inches to 1 mile — 0, ¼, ½, ¾, 1 Mile; 0, 500, 1 Kilometre — 2.63 cm to 1 km — 4.23 cm to 1 mile

Copyright of Geographers' A-Z Map Company Limited

Fairfield Road, Borough Green, Sevenoaks, Kent TN15 8PP
Telephone: 01732 781000 (Enquiries & Trade Sales)
01732 783422 (Retail Sales)
www.az.co.uk

Edition 3 2012

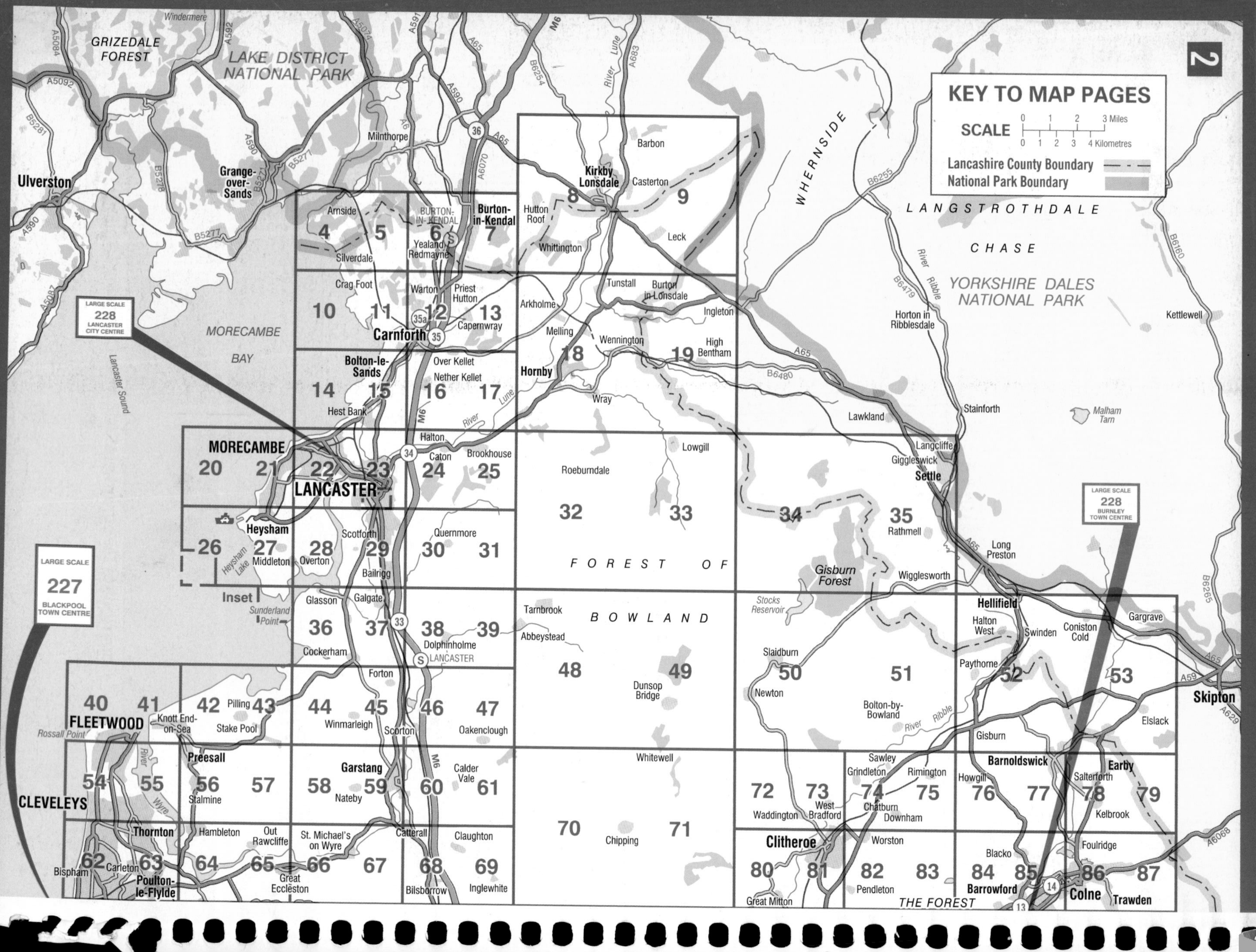

2

KEY TO MAP PAGES

SCALE

Lancashire County Boundary
National Park Boundary

0 1 2 3 4 Kilometres
0 1 2 3 Miles

LAKE DISTRICT NATIONAL PARK

GRIZEDALE FOREST

YORKSHIRE DALES NATIONAL PARK

LANGSTROTHDALE CHASE

WHERNSIDE

MORECAMBE BAY

FOREST OF BOWLAND

THE FOREST

Ulverston
Grange-over-Sands
Milnthorpe
Skipton
Gargrave
Elslack
Earby
Colne
Trawden
Kettlewell
Malham Tarn
Long Preston
Hellifield
Barnoldswick
Barrowford
Stainforth
Langcliffe
Giggleswick
Settle
Rathmell
Wigglesworth
Gisburn
Howgill
Rimington
Sawley
Grindleton
Downham
Pendleton
Worston
Blacko
Kelbrook
Foulridge
Salterforth
Coniston Cold
Swinden
Halton West
Paythorne
Bolton-by-Bowland
Slaidburn
Newton
West Bradford
Waddington
Clitheroe
Great Mitton
Stocks Reservoir
Gisburn Forest
Horton in Ribblesdale
River Ribble
Lawkland
Ingleton
High Bentham
Lowgill
Dunsop Bridge
Whitewell
Chipping
Tarnbrook
Abbeystead
Leck
Casterton
Barbon
Kirkby Lonsdale
Hutton Roof
Whittington
Burton-in-Lonsdale
Tunstall
Arkholme
Melling
Wennington
Wray
Roeburndale
Brookhouse
Caton
Halton
Quernmore
Oakenclough
Calder Vale
Claughton
Inglewhite
Bilsborrow
Catterall
Forton
Scorton
Winmarleigh
Nateby
Garstang
St. Michael's on Wyre
Out Rawcliffe
Great Eccleston
Poulton-le-Fylde
Carleton
Bispham
Thornton
Hambleton
Stalmine
Preesall
Knott End-on-Sea
Pilling
Stake Pool
Cockerham
Glasson
Galgate
Ballrigg
Scotforth
Dolphinholme
LANCASTER
MORECAMBE
Heysham
Middleton
Overton
Sunderland Point
Heysham Lake
Lancaster Sound
Rossall Point
FLEETWOOD
CLEVELEYS
Burton-in-Kendal
Warton
Yealand Redmayne
Priest Hutton
Capernwray
Over Kellet
Nether Kellet
Carnforth
Bolton-le-Sands
Hest Bank
Crag Foot
Silverdale
Amside
River Lune
River Ribble
River Wyre
River
A65
A59
A683
A65
A590
A6
A591
A5074
A590
A595
M6
A6070
A5092
A5087
A5084
A590
A5281
A5278
B5277
B5277
B5278
B5271
B5254
B6254
B6480
B6479
B6255
B6160
B6265
B6427
A629
A59
A682
Windermere

Grid squares:

4 5 6 7
8 9
10 11 12 13
14 15 16 17 18 19
20 21 22 23 24 25
26 27 28 29 30 31 32 33 34 35
36 37 38 39 40 41 42 43 44 45 46 47 48 49 50 51 52 53
54 55 56 57 58 59 60 61 62 63 64 65 66 67 68 69 70 71 72 73 74 75 76 77 78 79
80 81 82 83 84 85 86 87

3s
3a
35

14
13

LARGE SCALE 228 BURNLEY TOWN CENTRE
LARGE SCALE 228 LANCASTER CITY CENTRE
LARGE SCALE 227 BLACKPOOL TOWN CENTRE

Inset

THE FOREST OF TRAWDEN

OF PENDLE

BLACKPOOL · LYTHA M ST. ANNE'S · PRESTON · BLACKBURN · BURNLEY · NELSON · ACCRINGTON · WHALLEY · CHORLEY · SOUTHPORT · ORMSKIRK · SKELMERSDALE · WIGAN · BOLTON · BURY · ROCHDALE · OLDHAM · MANCHESTER · SALFORD · STOCKPORT · ALTRINCHAM · LEIGH · WARRINGTON · ST. HELENS · PRESCOT · HUYTON · LIVERPOOL · BOOTLE · CROSBY · LITHERLAND · MAGHULL · KIRKBY · AINTREE · WALLASEY · BIRKENHEAD

FOREST OF ROSSENDALE

| LARGE SCALE 226 | BLACKBURN TOWN CENTRE |
| LARGE SCALE 229 | PRESTON CITY CENTRE |

Grid reference numbers (selected): 89, 90, 91, 92, 93, 94, 95, 96, 97, 98, 99, 100, 101, 102, 103, 104, 105, 106, 107, 108, 109, 110, 111, 112, 113, 114, 115, 116, 117, 118, 119, 120, 121, 122, 123, 124, 125, 126, 127, 128, 129, 130, 131, 132, 133, 134, 135, 136, 137, 138, 139, 140, 141, 142, 143, 144, 145, 146, 147, 148, 149, 150, 151, 152, 153, 154, 155, 156, 157, 158, 159, 160, 161, 162, 163, 164, 165, 166, 167, 168, 169, 170, 171, 172, 173, 174, 175, 176, 177, 178, 179, 180, 181, 182, 183, 184, 185, 186, 187, 188, 189, 190, 191, 192, 193, 194, 195, 196, 197, 198, 199, 200, 201, 202, 203, 204, 205, 206, 207, 208, 209, 210, 211, 212, 213, 214, 215, 216, 217, 218, 219, 220, 221, 222, 223, 224, 225

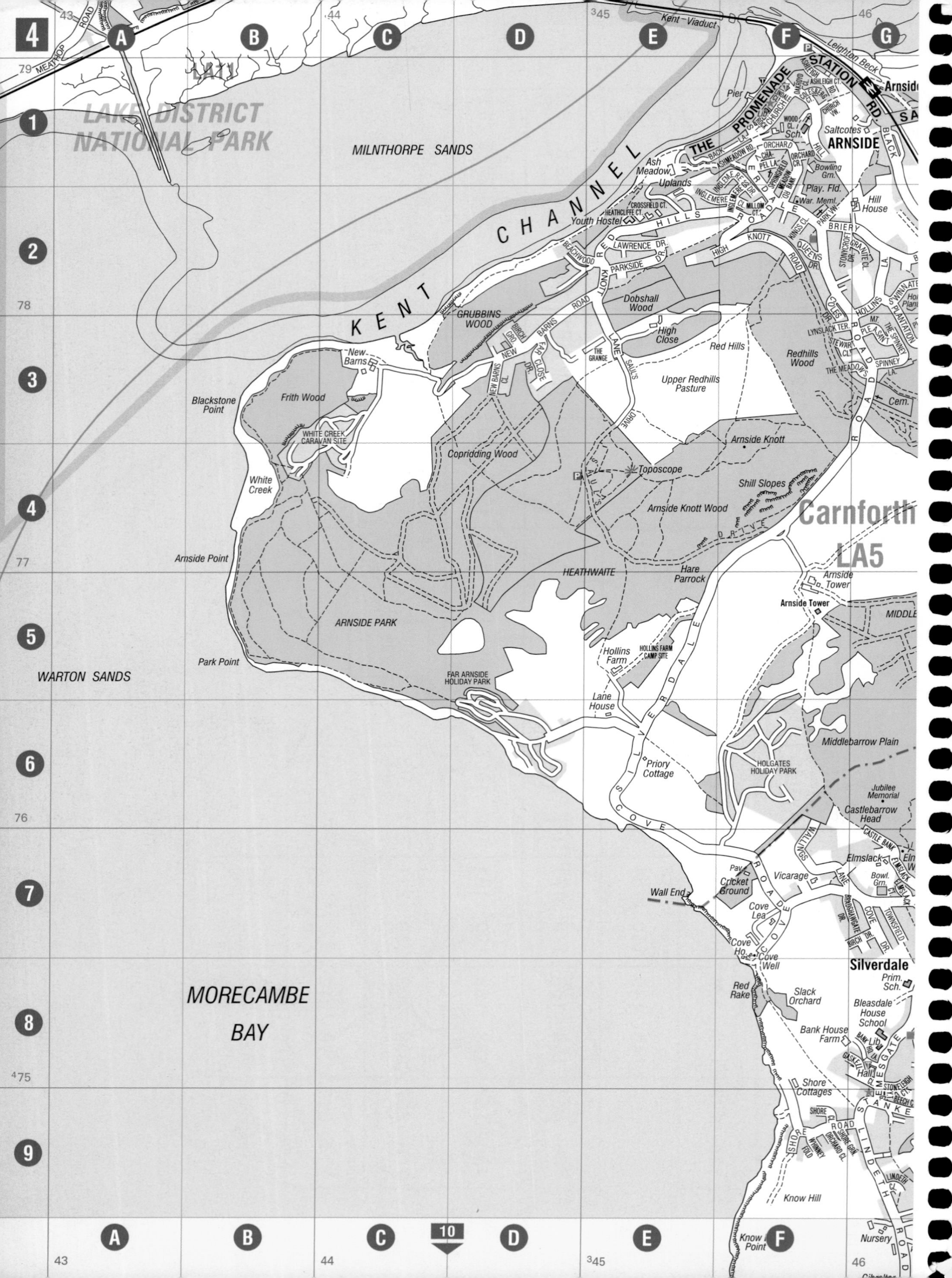
LAKE DISTRICT
NATIONAL PARK
MILNTHORPE SANDS
KENT CHANNEL
Kent Viaduct
Pier
THE PROMENADE
STATION RD.
Arnside
ARNSIDE
Saltcotes
Ash Meadow
Uplands
Youth Hostel
Bowling Grn.
Play. Fld.
War. Meml.
Hill House
GRUBBINS WOOD
Dobshall Wood
High Close
Red Hills
Redhills Wood
New Barns
Upper Redhills Pasture
Blackstone Point
Frith Wood
WHITE CREEK CARAVAN SITE
Copridding Wood
Arnside Knott
Toposcope
Shill Slopes
White Creek
Arnside Knott Wood
Carnforth
LA5
Arnside Point
HEATHWAITE
Hare Parrock
Arnside Tower
ARNSIDE PARK
Hollins Farm
HOLLINS FARM CAMP SITE
Park Point
WARTON SANDS
FAR ARNSIDE HOLIDAY PARK
Lane House
SILVERDALE
Middlebarrow Plain
Priory Cottage
HOLGATES HOLIDAY PARK
Jubilee Memorial
Castlebarrow Head
COVE
Elmslack
Vicarage
Cricket Ground
Wall End
Cove Lea
Cove Ho.
Cove Well
Silverdale
Prim. Sch.
Red Rake
Slack Orchard
Bleasdale House School
MORECAMBE BAY
Bank House Farm
Shore Cottages
Know Hill
Know Point
Nursery

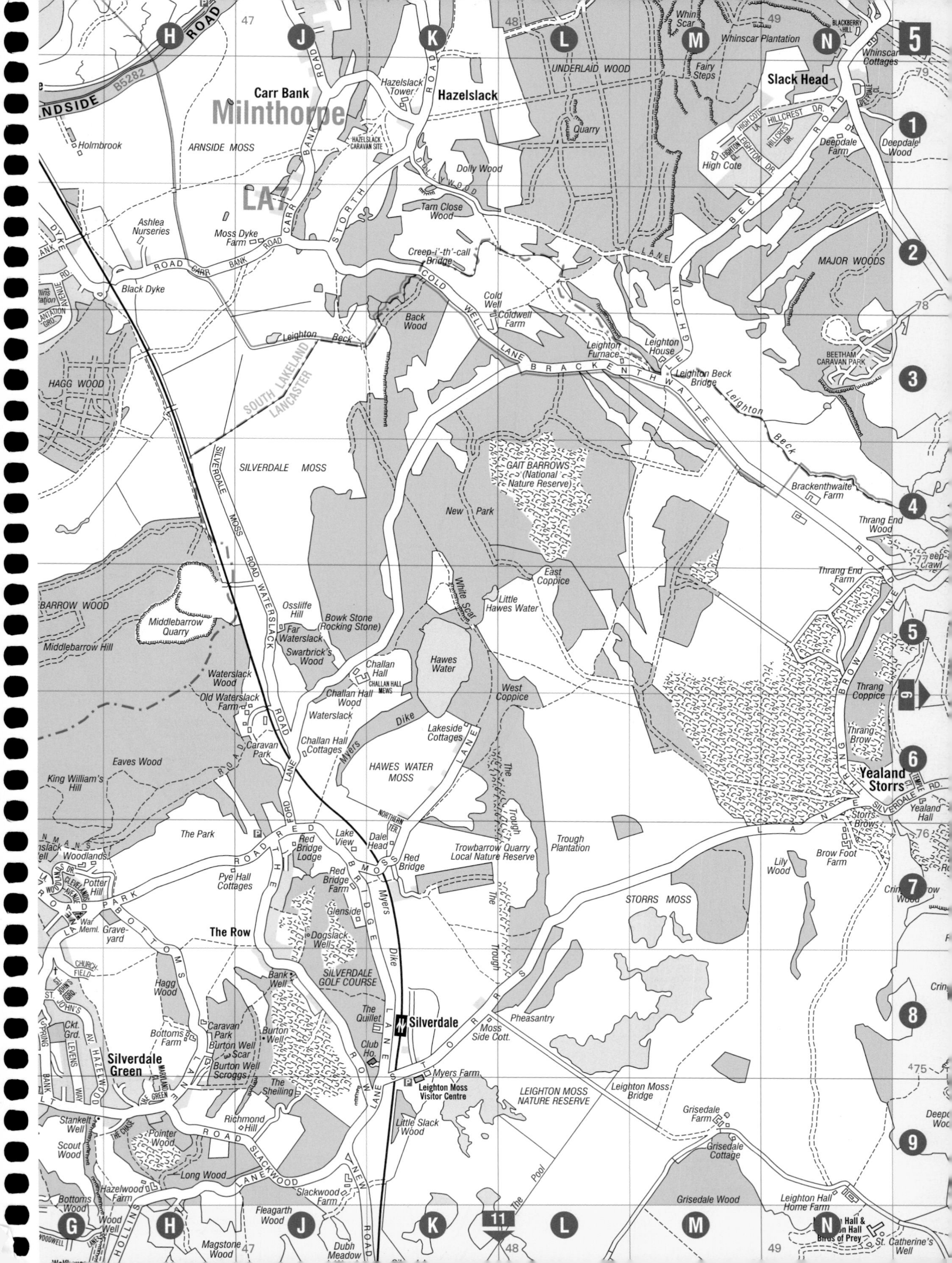

Milnthorpe
LA7
Carr Bank
Hazelslack
Hazelslack Tower
Slack Head
Whinscar Plantation
Whinscar Cottages
Underlaid Wood
Fairy Steps
Quarry
High Cote
Deepdale Farm
Deepdale Wood
Hillcrest Dr.
Leighton Dr.
Hazelslack Caravan Site
Dolly Wood
Arnside Moss
Holmbrook
Tarn Close Wood
Ashlea Nurseries
Moss Dyke Farm
Carr Bank Road
Creep-i'-th'-call Bridge
Black Dyke
Major Woods
Cold Well
Coldwell Farm
Back Wood
Leighton Beck
Leighton Furnace
Leighton House
Leighton Beck Bridge
Beetham Caravan Park
Brackenthwaite
Hagg Wood
South Lakeland
Lancaster
Silverdale Moss
Gait Barrows (National Nature Reserve)
New Park
Brackenthwaite Farm
Thrang End Wood
Thrang End Farm
East Coppice
Little Hawes Water
White Scar
Barrow Wood
Middlebarrow Quarry
Middlebarrow Hill
Ossliffe Hill
Bowk Stone (Rocking Stone)
Far Waterslack
Swarbrick's Wood
Hawes Water
Challan Hall
Challan Hall Mews
Challan Hall Wood
Waterslack Wood
Old Waterslack Farm
Waterslack
West Coppice
Thrang Coppice
Thrang Brow
Myers Dike
Lakeside Cottages
Challan Hall Cottages
Caravan Park
Hawes Water Moss
Eaves Wood
King William's Hill
Yealand Storrs
Yealand Hall
Storrs Brows
The Park
Red Bridge Lodge
Lake View
Dale Head
Northern Ter.
Red Bridge
Trowbarrow Quarry Local Nature Reserve
Trough Plantation
The Trough
Lily Wood
Brow Foot Farm
Woodlands
Potter Hill
Pye Hall Cottages
Red Bridge Farm
Glenside
Storrs Moss
War Meml.
Graveyard
The Row
Dogslack Well
Silverdale Golf Course
Bank Well
Hagg Wood
Churchfield
St. John's
The Quillet
Silverdale
Ckt. Grd.
Bottoms Farm
Caravan Park
Burton Well
Burton Well Scar
Burton Well Scroggs
Club Ho.
Moss Side Cott.
Pheasantry
Silverdale Green
Myers Farm
Leighton Moss Visitor Centre
Leighton Moss Nature Reserve
Leighton Moss Bridge
The Sheiling
Stankelt Well
Richmond Hill
Pointer Wood
Grisedale Farm
Scout Wood
Little Slack Wood
Grisedale Cottage
Long Wood
Hazelwood Farm
Slackwood Farm
Slackwood Lane
The Pool
Grisedale Wood
Leighton Hall Home Farm
Bottoms Wood
Wood Well
Fleagarth Wood
Magstone Wood
Dubh Meadow
Birds of Prey
St. Catherine's Well
Grisedale Wood
B5282
11
9

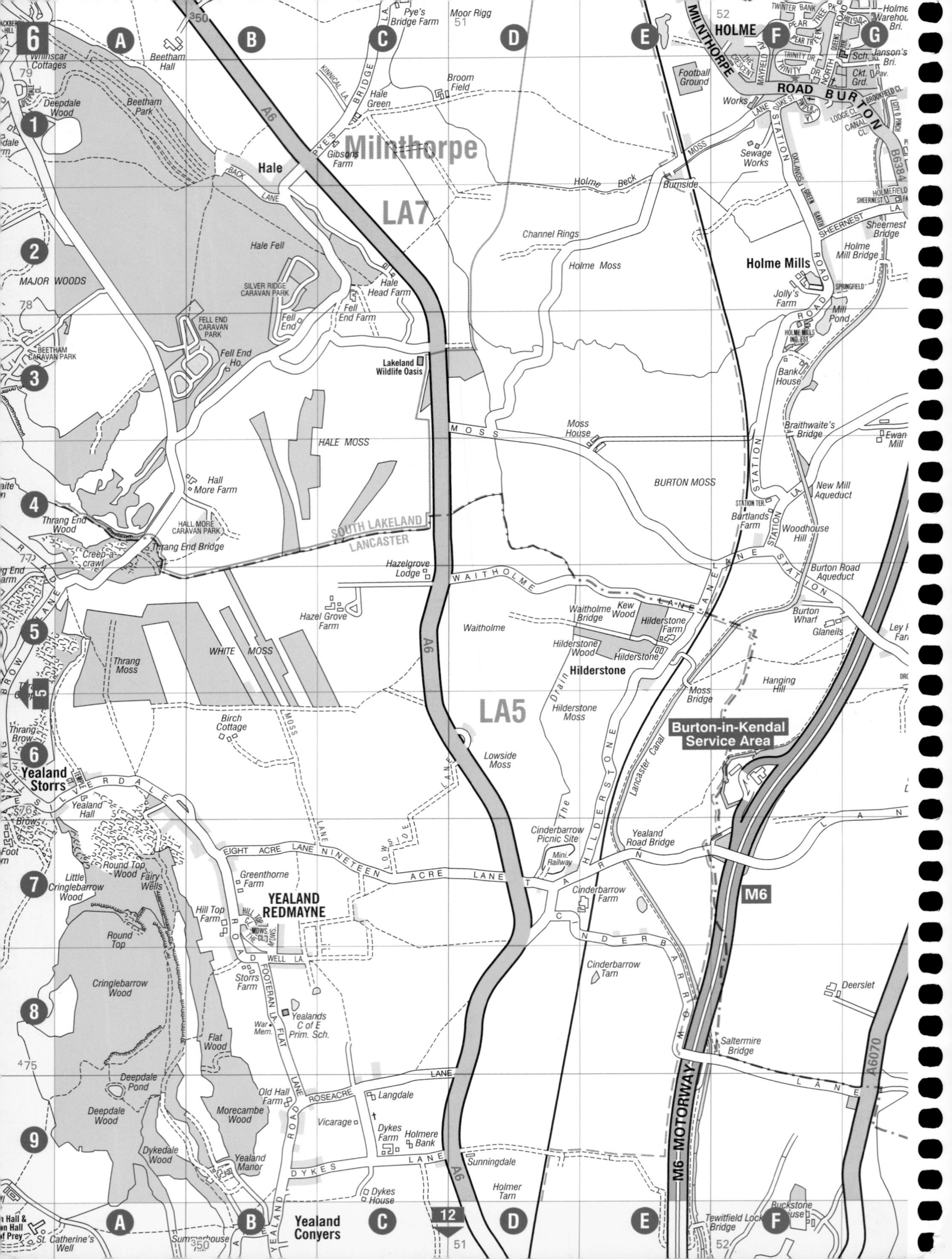
6
Milnthorpe
LA7
LA5
Hale
Hale Fell
MAJOR WOODS
Whinscar Cottages
Beetham Hall
Beetham Park
Deepdale Wood
SILVER RIDGE CARAVAN PARK
FELL END CARAVAN PARK
BEETHAM CARAVAN PARK
Fell End Ho.
Fell End
Fell End Farm
Hale Head Farm
Lakeland Wildlife Oasis
Pye's Bridge Farm
Moor Rigg
Hale Green
Broom Field
Gibsons Farm
Holme Beck
Channel Rings
Holme Moss
HOLME
MILNTHORPE ROAD
BURTON ROAD
Football Ground
Works
Sewage Works
Burnside
Holme Mills
Jolly's Farm
Mill Pond
HOLME MILLS IND. EST.
Bank House
Sheernest Bridge
Holme Mill Bridge
Janson's Bri.
Holme Warehouse Bri.
Ckt. Grd.
Sch.
Braithwaite's Bridge
Ewan Mill
New Mill Aqueduct
Moss House
BURTON MOSS
HALE MOSS
Hall More Farm
HALL MORE CARAVAN PARK
Thrang End Wood
Thrang End Bridge
Creep-a-crawl
SOUTH LAKELAND
LANCASTER
Hazelgrove Lodge
Hazel Grove Farm
WAITHOLME LANE
Waitholme
Waitholme Bridge
Kew Wood
Hilderstone Farm
Hilderstone Wood
Hilderstone
Hilderstone Moss
Burtlands Farm
Woodhouse Hill
Burton Road Aqueduct
Burton Wharf
Glaneils
Hanging Hill
Moss Bridge
Burton-in-Kendal Service Area
WHITE MOSS
Thrang Moss
Birch Cottage
Lowside Moss
Lancaster Canal
The Drain
Yealand Storrs
Yealand Hall
Thrang Brow
LIVERDALE
EIGHT ACRE LANE
NINETEEN ACRE LANE
Cinderbarrow Picnic Site
Mini. Railway
Yealand Road Bridge
Cinderbarrow Farm
CINDERBARROW LANE
Cinderbarrow Tarn
M6
M6 MOTORWAY
A6
A6070
B6384
Greenthorne Farm
YEALAND REDMAYNE
Hill Top Farm
Round Top Wood
Fairy Wells
Little Cringlebarrow Wood
Round Top
Cringlebarrow Wood
Storrs Farm
Yealands C of E Prim. Sch.
War Mem.
Flat Wood
Deepdale Pond
Deepdale Wood
Dykedale Wood
Morecambe Wood
Old Hall Farm
ROSEACRE
Langdale
Vicarage
Dykes Farm
Holmere Bank
DYKES LANE
Sunningdale
Yealand Manor
Dykes House
Holmer Tarn
Deerslet
Saltermire Bridge
Tewitfield Lock Bridge
Buckstone House
Yealand Conyers
St. Catherine's Well
Summerhouse
12
5
350
51
52
79
78
77
76
475

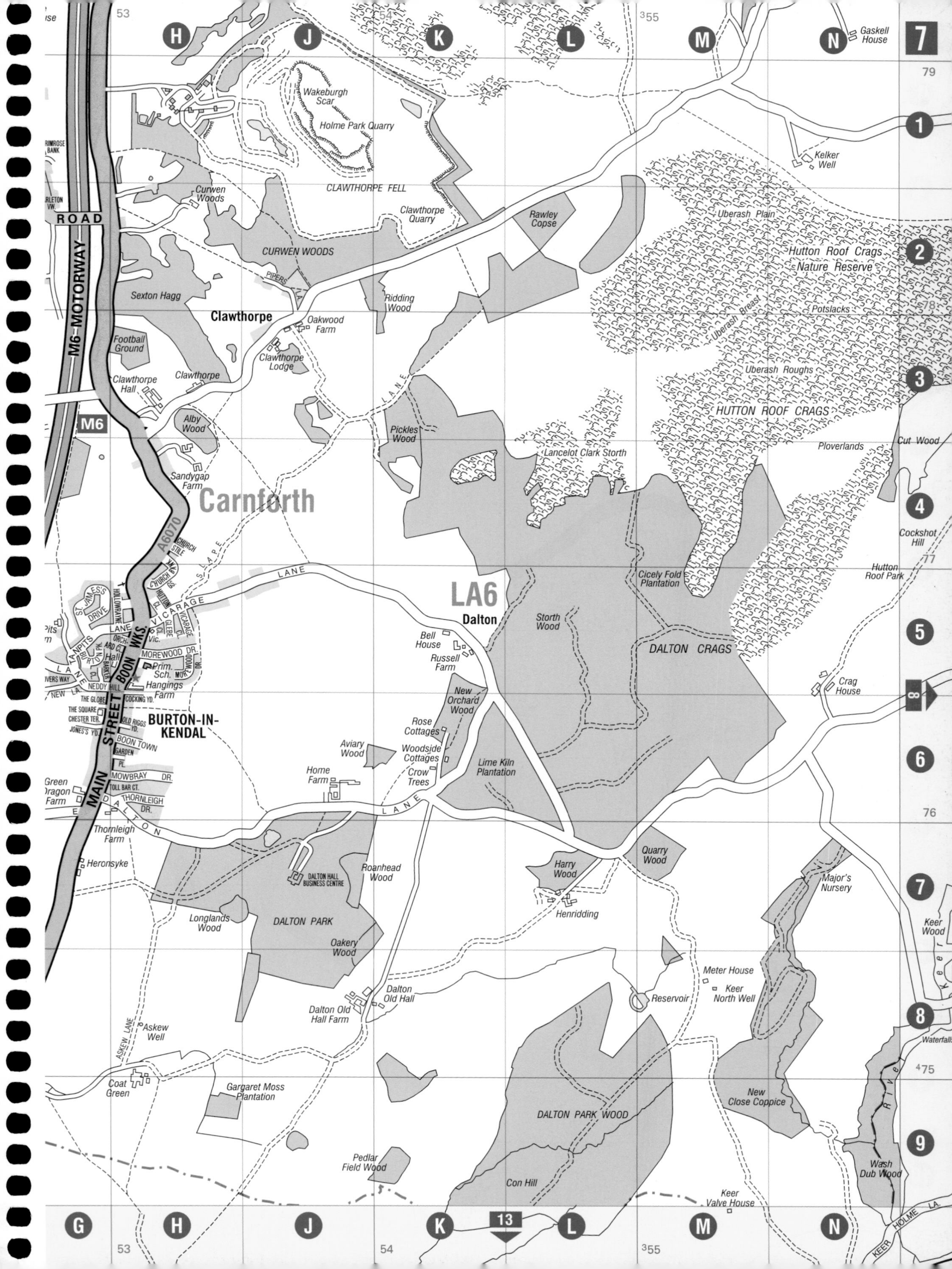

Wakeburgh Scar
Holme Park Quarry
CLAWTHORPE FELL
Curwen Woods
Clawthorpe Quarry
CURWEN WOODS
Rawley Copse
Gaskell House
Kelker Well
Uberash Plain
Hutton Roof Crags
Nature Reserve
Uberash Breast
Potslacks
Uberash Roughs
HUTTON ROOF CRAGS
Ploverlands
Cut Wood
Lancelot Clark Storth
Cockshot Hill
Hutton Roof Park
Cicely Fold Plantation
Storth Wood
DALTON CRAGS
Crag House
M6 MOTORWAY
ROAD
Sexton Hagg
PIPERS LA.
Ridding Wood
Clawthorpe
Oakwood Farm
Football Ground
Clawthorpe Lodge
Clawthorpe Hall
Clawthorpe
M6
Alby Wood
Pickles Wood
LANE
Sandygap Farm
Carnforth
A6070
CHURCH STILE
SLAPE
LANE
LA6
Dalton
Bell House
Russell Farm
New Orchard Wood
Rose Cottages
Woodside Cottages
Crow Trees
Aviary Wood
Home Farm
Lime Kiln Plantation
VICARAGE
HOLLOWRAYNE
ST. JAMES'S DRIVE
TANPITS
MOREWOOD DR.
BOON WKS.
Prim. Sch.
Hangings Farm
NEDDY HILL
NEW LA.
THE GLOBE
COCKING YD.
THE SQUARE
CHESTER TER.
JONES'S YD.
OLD RIGGS YD.
BURTON-IN-KENDAL
BOON TOWN
GARDEN
MOWBRAY DR.
TOLL BAR CT.
THORNLEIGH DR.
MAIN STREET
Green Dragon Farm
DALTON LANE
Thornleigh Farm
Heronsyke
DALTON HALL BUSINESS CENTRE
Roanhead Wood
Harry Wood
Quarry Wood
Major's Nursery
Henridding
Longlands Wood
DALTON PARK
Oakery Wood
Keer Wood
Meter House
Keer North Well
Reservoir
Dalton Old Hall
Dalton Old Hall Farm
ASKEW LANE
Askew Well
Waterfalls
River Keer
Coat Green
Gargaret Moss Plantation
New Close Coppice
DALTON PARK WOOD
Wash Dub Wood
Pedlar Field Wood
Con Hill
Keer Valve House
KEER HOLME LA.
G
H
J
K
L
M
N
1
2
3
4
5
6
7
8
9
53
54
355
79
78
77
76
475
13

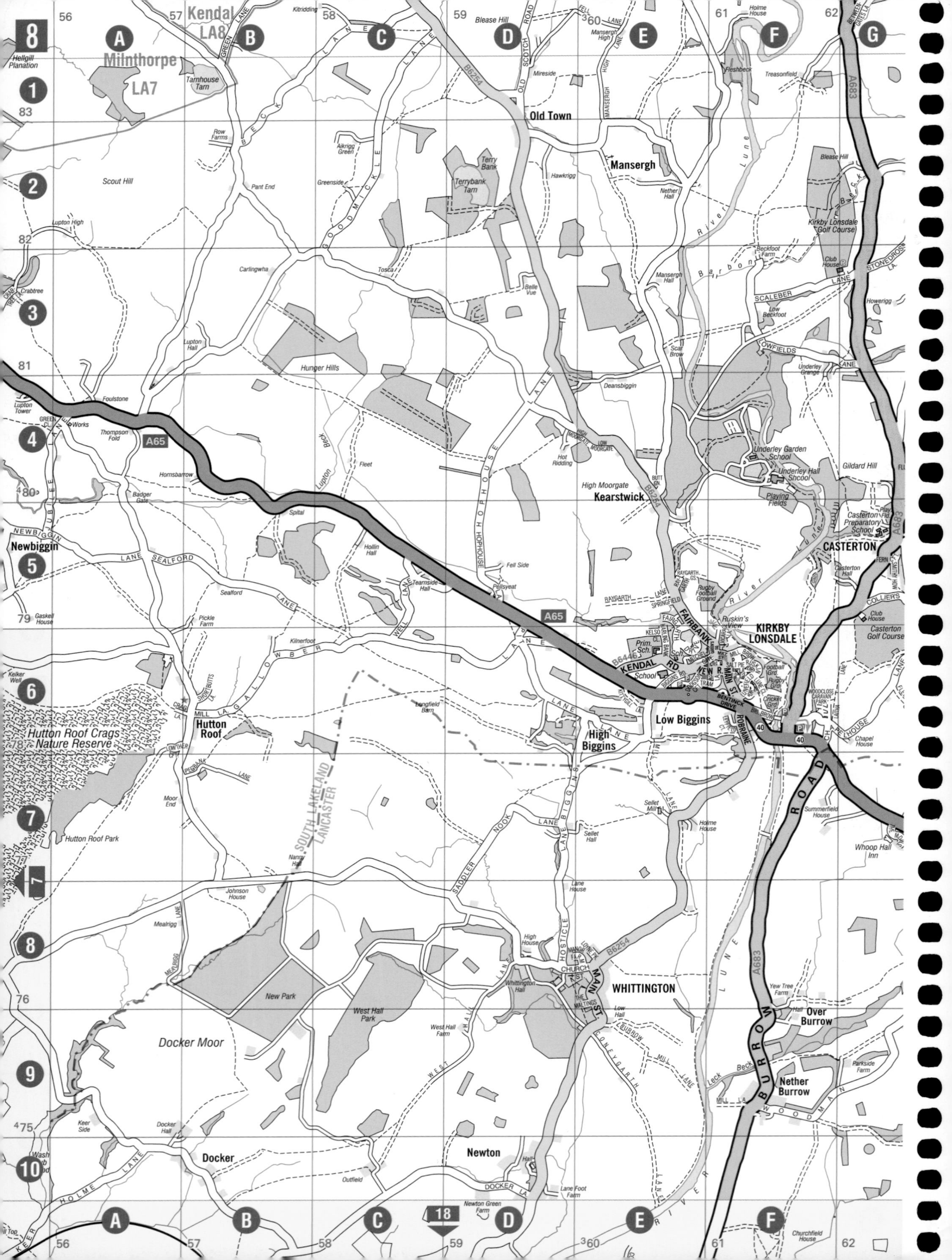

8
A
B
C
D
E
F
G
56
57
58
59
60
61
62
Kendal
LA8
Milnthorpe
LA7
Hellgill Plantation
Tarnhouse Tarn
Kitridding
Blease Hill
Holme House
Mireside
Fleshbeck
Treasonfield
Old Town
Mansergh
Mansergh High
Row Farms
Aikrigg Green
Terry Bank
Terrybank Tarn
Scout Hill
Pant End
Greenside
Hawkrigg
Nether Hall
Blease Hill
Kirkby Lonsdale Golf Course
Lupton High
Carlingwha
Tosca
Mansergh Hall
Beckfoot Farm
Club House
Crabtree
Belle Vue
Low Beckfoot
Howerigg
Lupton Hall
Hunger Hills
Scar Brow
Underley Grange
Deansbiggin
Foulstone
Lupton Tower
Works
Thompson Fold
A65
Fleet
Hot Ridding
High Moorgate
Low Moorgate
Underley Garden School
Underley Hall School
Gildard Hill
Hornsbarrow
Badger Gate
Spital
Kearstwick
Playing Fields
Casterton Preparatory School
Newbiggin
Hollin Hall
Fell Side
CASTERTON
Casterton Hall
Sealford
Teamside Hall
Pellsyeat
Rugby Football Ground
Gaskell House
Pickle Farm
Ruskin's View
KIRKBY LONSDALE
Club House
Casterton Golf Course
Kilnerfoot
Kelker Well
Hutton Roof
Longfield Barn
High Biggins
Low Biggins
Hutton Roof Crags Nature Reserve
SOUTH LAKELAND
LANCASTER
Moor End
Sellet Mill
Sellet Hall
Holme House
Summerfield House
Chapel House
Hutton Roof Park
Whoop Hall Inn
Nanny Hall
Johnson House
Lane House
Mealrigg
High House
Whittington Hall
WHITTINGTON
New Park
West Hall Park
Low Hall
Yew Tree Farm
Over Burrow
Docker Moor
West Hall Farm
Parkside Farm
Nether Burrow
Keer Side
Docker Hall
Docker
Newton
Outfield
Lane Foot Farm
Newton Green Farm
Churchfield House
18
7
76
75
79
80
81
82
83
River Lune
A683
B6254
B6446

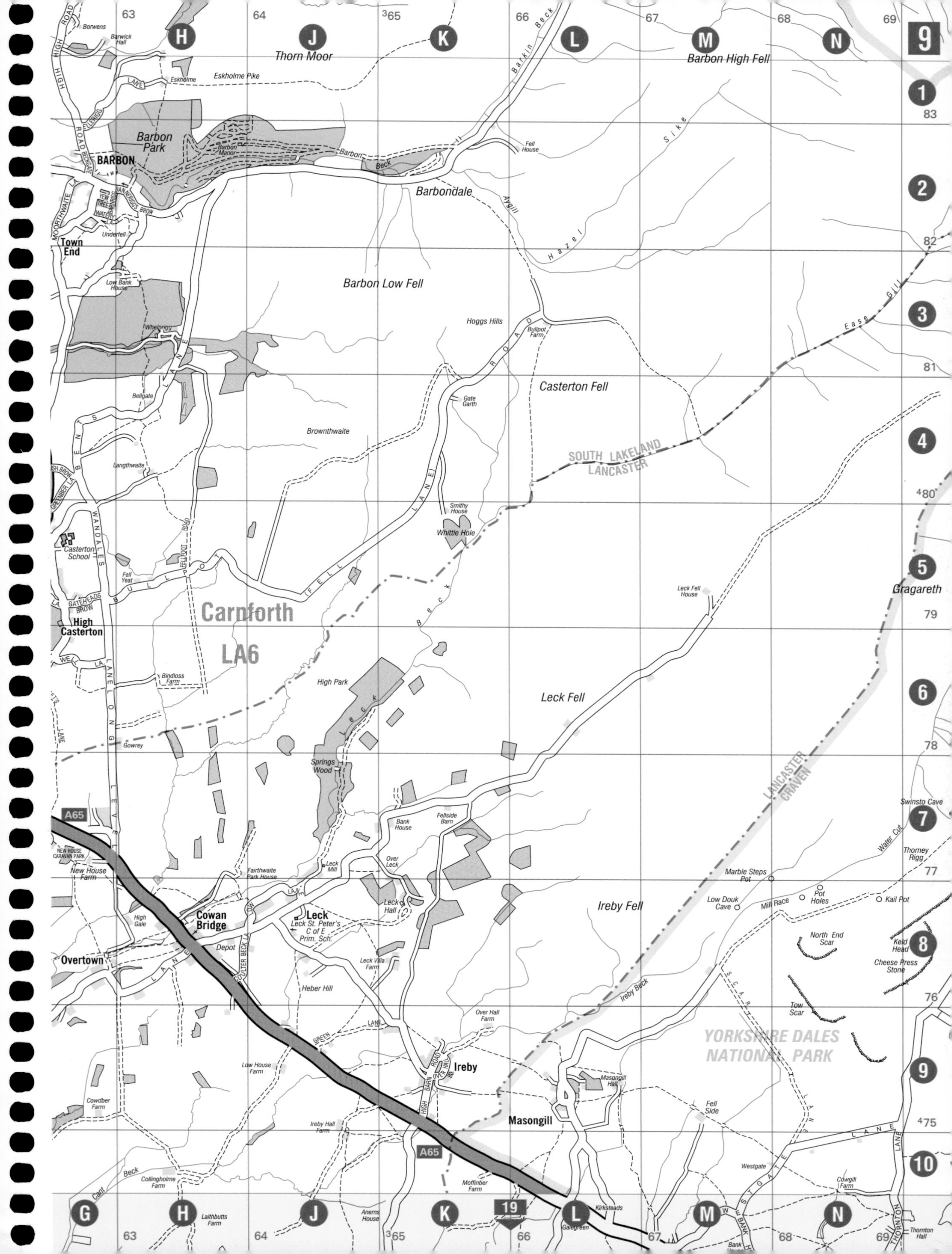
Thorn Moor
Barbon High Fell
Barbon Park
BARBON
Barbon Manor
Barbondale
Town End
Barbon Low Fell
Hoggs Hills
Bullpot Farm
Casterton Fell
Brownthwaite
SOUTH LAKELAND
LANCASTER
Smithy House
Whittle Hole
Casterton School
Carnforth
LA6
High Casterton
Leck Fell House
Gragareth
High Park
Leck Fell
Springs Wood
Bank House
Fellside Barn
LANCASTER
CRAVEN
Swinsto Cave
Thorney Rigg
Marble Steps Pot
Low Douk Cave
Pot Holes
Kail Pot
Ireby Fell
Cowan Bridge
Leck
Leck St. Peter's C of E Prim. Sch.
Leck Hall
North End Scar
Keld Head
Cheese Press Stone
Overtown
Heber Hill
Leck Villa Farm
Over Hall Farm
Tow Scar
YORKSHIRE DALES NATIONAL PARK
Ireby
Masongill Hall
Masongill
Fell Side
Low House Farm
Cowdber Farm
Ireby Hall Farm
Westgate
Cowgill Farm
Collingholme Farm
Moffinber Farm
Laithbutts Farm
Anems House
Kirksteads
Galegreen
Thornton Hall
A65

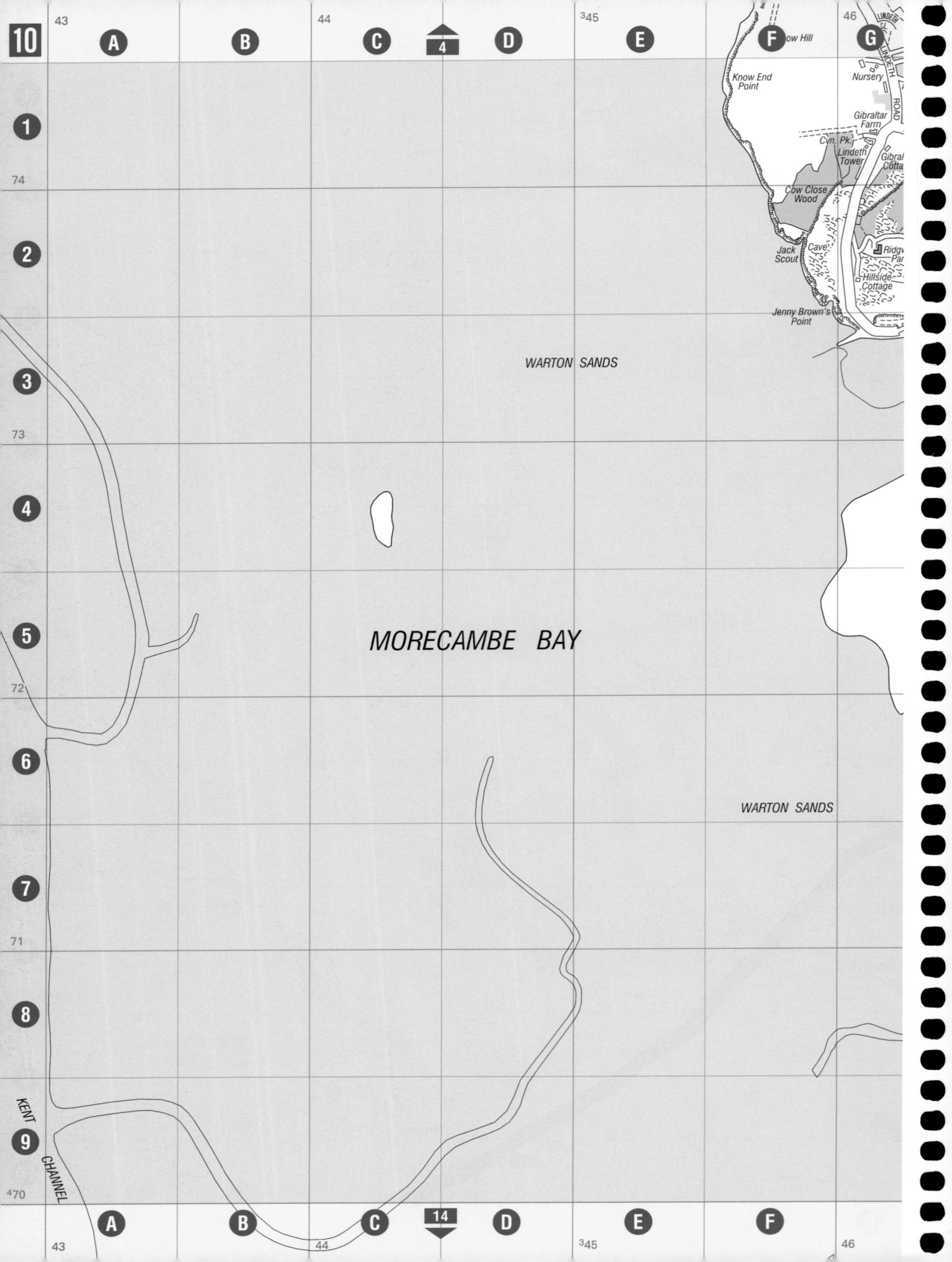

43 A B 44 C ⬆4 D ³45 E F ow Hill G 46 LINDETH

74

73

72

71

470

WARTON SANDS

Know End Point

Nursery

Gibraltar Farm

Cvn. Pk.
Lindeth Tower

Gibral Cotta

Cow Close Wood

Jack Scout

Cave

Ridgw Par

Hillside Cottage

Jenny Brown's Point

MORECAMBE   BAY

WARTON   SANDS

KENT

CHANNEL

A B C 14 D E F

43 44 ³45 46

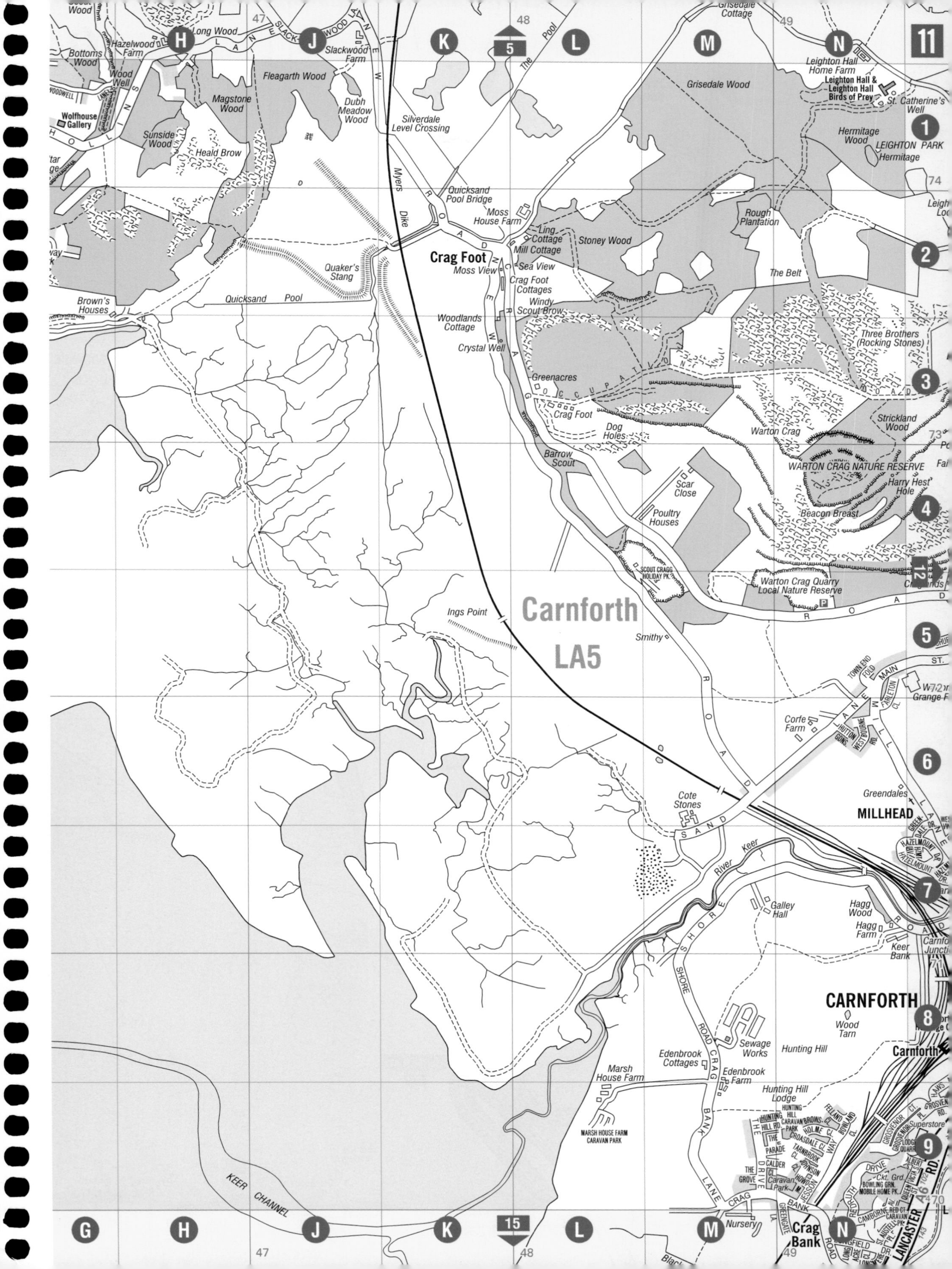

Carnforth
LA5
Crag Foot
CARNFORTH
MILLHEAD
Leighton Hall Home Farm
Leighton Hall & Leighton Hall Birds of Prey
St. Catherine's Well
Grisedale Wood
Hermitage Wood
LEIGHTON PARK
Hermitage
Long Wood
Hazelwood Farm
Bottoms Wood
Wood Well
Slackwood Farm
Fleagarth Wood
Magstone Wood
Dubh Meadow Wood
Wolfhouse Gallery
Sunside Wood
Heald Brow
Silverdale Level Crossing
Quicksand Pool Bridge
Moss House Farm
Myers Dike
Ling Cottage
Mill Cottage
Stoney Wood
Rough Plantation
The Belt
Sea View
Moss View
Crag Foot Cottages
Windy Scout Brow
Quaker's Stang
Brown's Houses
Quicksand Pool
Woodlands Cottage
Crystal Well
Greenacres
Three Brothers (Rocking Stones)
Strickland Wood
Warton Crag
WARTON CRAG NATURE RESERVE
Harry Hest' Hole
Beacon Breast
Dog Holes
Barrow Scout
Scar Close
Poultry Houses
SCOUT CRAGG HOLIDAY PK
Warton Crag Quarry Local Nature Reserve
Ings Point
Smithy
Corfe Farm
Cote Stones
Greendales
River Keer
Galley Hall
Hagg Wood
Hagg Farm
Keer Bank
Wood Tarn
Sewage Works
Hunting Hill
Edenbrook Cottages
Edenbrook Farm
Marsh House Farm
MARSH HOUSE FARM CARAVAN PARK
Hunting Hill Lodge
HUNTING HILL CARAVAN PARK
Caravan Park
BOWLING GRN. MOBILE HOME PK.
Superstore
Nursery
Crag Bank
KEER CHANNEL
SHORE ROAD
CRAG BANK LANE
SAND LANE
OCCUPATION ROAD
LANCASTER RD.
A6

5
12
15

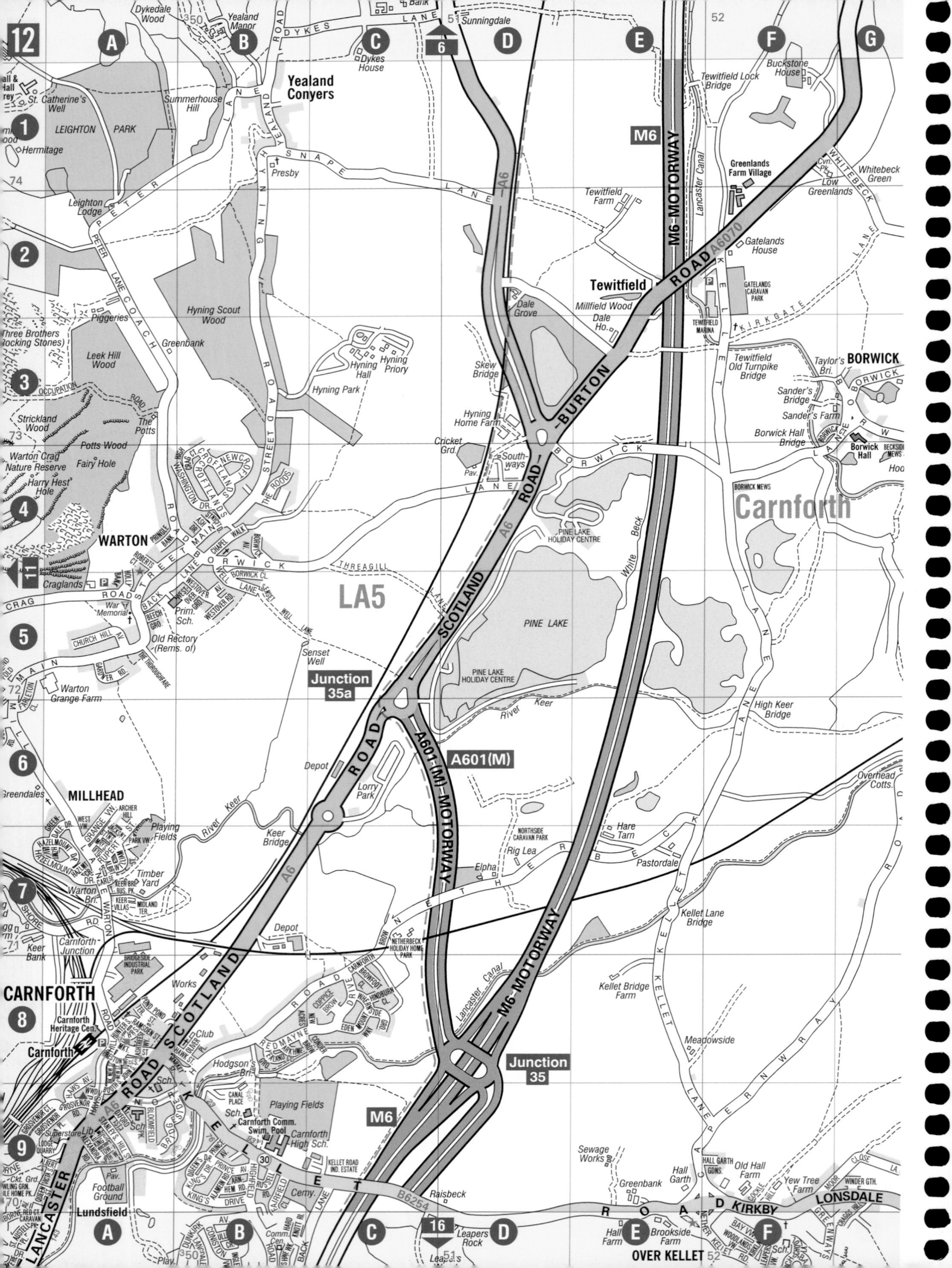
Yealand Conyers
Yealand Manor
Dykedale Wood
Sunningdale
Dykes House
LEIGHTON PARK
St. Catherine's Well
Hermitage
Summerhouse Hill
Presby
Leighton Lodge
Hyning Scout Wood
Piggeries
Three Brothers (Rocking Stones)
Greenbank
Leek Hill Wood
Hyning Hall
Hyning Priory
Hyning Park
Strickland Wood
The Potts
Potts Wood
Fairy Hole
Warton Crag Nature Reserve
Harry Hest' Hole
WARTON
Craglands
War Memorial
Prim. Sch.
Old Rectory (Rems. of)
Warton Grange Farm
Sènset Well
Junction 35a
LA5
Pine Lake
Pine Lake Holiday Centre
River Keer
High Keer Bridge
Depot
Lorry Park
Keer Bridge
MILLHEAD
Playing Fields
Timber Yard
Warton Bri.
Carnforth Junction
Keer Bank
Bridgeside Industrial Park
CARNFORTH
Carnforth Heritage Cen.
Carnforth
Works
Club
Hodgson's Bri.
Playing Fields
Carnforth Comm. Swim. Pool
Carnforth High Sch.
Kellet Road Ind. Estate
Superstore
Football Ground
Lundsfield
Cemy.
Raisbeck
Leapers Rock
Junction 35
M6
M6-MOTORWAY
A601(M)
A601(M)-MOTORWAY
SCOTLAND ROAD
BURTON ROAD
A6
A6070
B6254
Tewitfield
Tewitfield Farm
Tewitfield Lock Bridge
Buckstone House
Greenlands Farm Village
Low Greenlands
Whitebeck Green
Gatelands House
Gatelands Caravan Park
Tewitfield Marina
Millfield Wood
Dale Ho.
Dale Grove
Skew Bridge
Hyning Home Farm
Cricket Grd.
Southways
Tewitfield Old Turnpike Bridge
Taylor's Bri.
BORWICK
Sander's Bridge
Sander's Farm
Borwick Hall Bridge
Borwick Hall
Borwick Mews
Carnforth
Lancaster Canal
White Beck
Overhead Cotts.
Northside Caravan Park
Hare Tarn
Rig Lea
Pastordale
Elpha
Netherbeck Holiday Home Park
Kellet Lane Bridge
Kellet Bridge Farm
Meadowside
Sewage Works
Greenbank
Hall Garth
Old Hall Farm
Yew Tree Farm
Hall Farm
Brookside Farm
OVER KELLET
KIRKBY LONSDALE ROAD
A B C D E F G
1 2 3 4 5 6 7 8 9
6
11
16

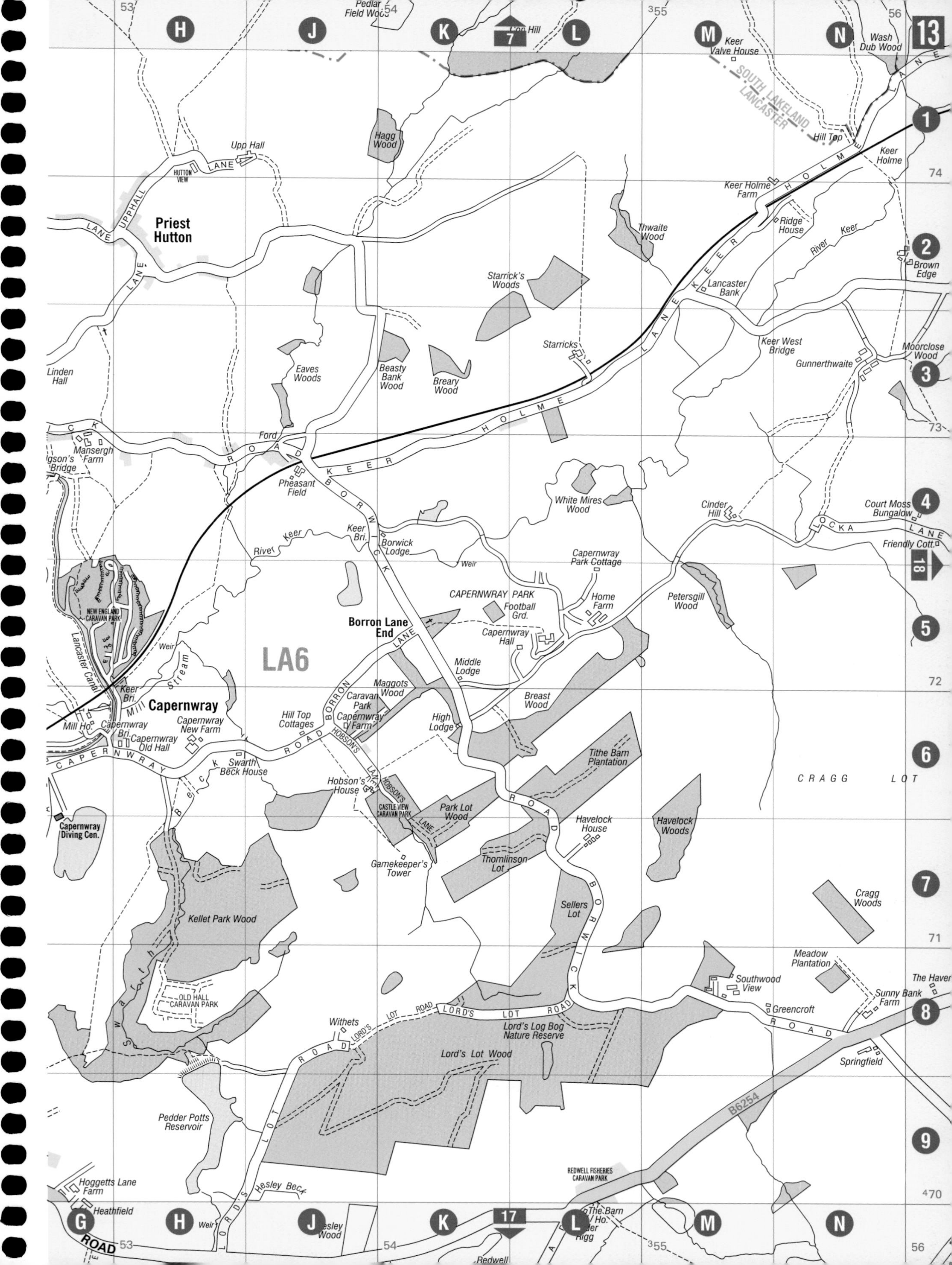
H
J
K
L
M
N
7
Keer Valve House
Wash Dub Wood
SOUTH LAKELAND
LANCASTER
Hill Top
Keer Holme
Upp Hall
HUTTON VIEW
UPPHALL LANE
Priest Hutton
Hagg Wood
Keer Holme Farm
Ridge House
Thwaite Wood
River Keer
Brown Edge
Starrick's Woods
Lancaster Bank
Keer West Bridge
Moorclose Wood
Gunnerthwaite
Starricks
Linden Hall
Eaves Woods
Beasty Bank Wood
Breary Wood
KEER HOLME LANE
Ford
Mansergh Farm
Pheasant Field
Bridge
White Mires Wood
Cinder Hill
Court Moss Bungalow
LOCKA LANE
Friendly Cott.
Keer Bri.
Borwick Lodge
River Keer
Weir
Capernwray Park Cottage
18
NEW ENGLAND CARAVAN PARK
CAPERNWRAY PARK
Football Grd.
Home Farm
Petersgill Wood
Borron Lane End
Capernwray Hall
Lancaster Canal
LA6
Middle Lodge
Mill Stream
Maggots Wood
Breast Wood
Capernwray
Caravan Park
Capernwray Farm
High Lodge
Mill Ho.
Capernwray Bri.
Capernwray New Farm
Hill Top Cottages
Capernwray Old Hall
BORRON ROAD
HOBSON'S LANE
Tithe Barn Plantation
CAPERNWRAY ROAD
Swarth Beck House
CRAGG LOT
Hobson's House
CASTLE VIEW CARAVAN PARK
Park Lot Wood
Havelock House
Havelock Woods
Capernwray Diving Cen.
Thomlinson Lot
Gamekeeper's Tower
Cragg Woods
Kellet Park Wood
Sellers Lot
BORWICK ROAD
Meadow Plantation
The Haver
Southwood View
Sunny Bank Farm
OLD HALL CARAVAN PARK
Greencroft
LORD'S LOT ROAD
Withets
Lord's Log Bog Nature Reserve
Lord's Lot Wood
Springfield
Swarth Beck
Pedder Potts Reservoir
B6254
REDWELL FISHERIES CARAVAN PARK
Hoggetts Lane Farm
Heathfield
Hesley Beck
G
Weir
Hesley Wood
17
The Barn
Rigg
ROAD
Redwell
53
54
355
56
74
73
72
71
470
1
2
3
4
5
6
7
8
9

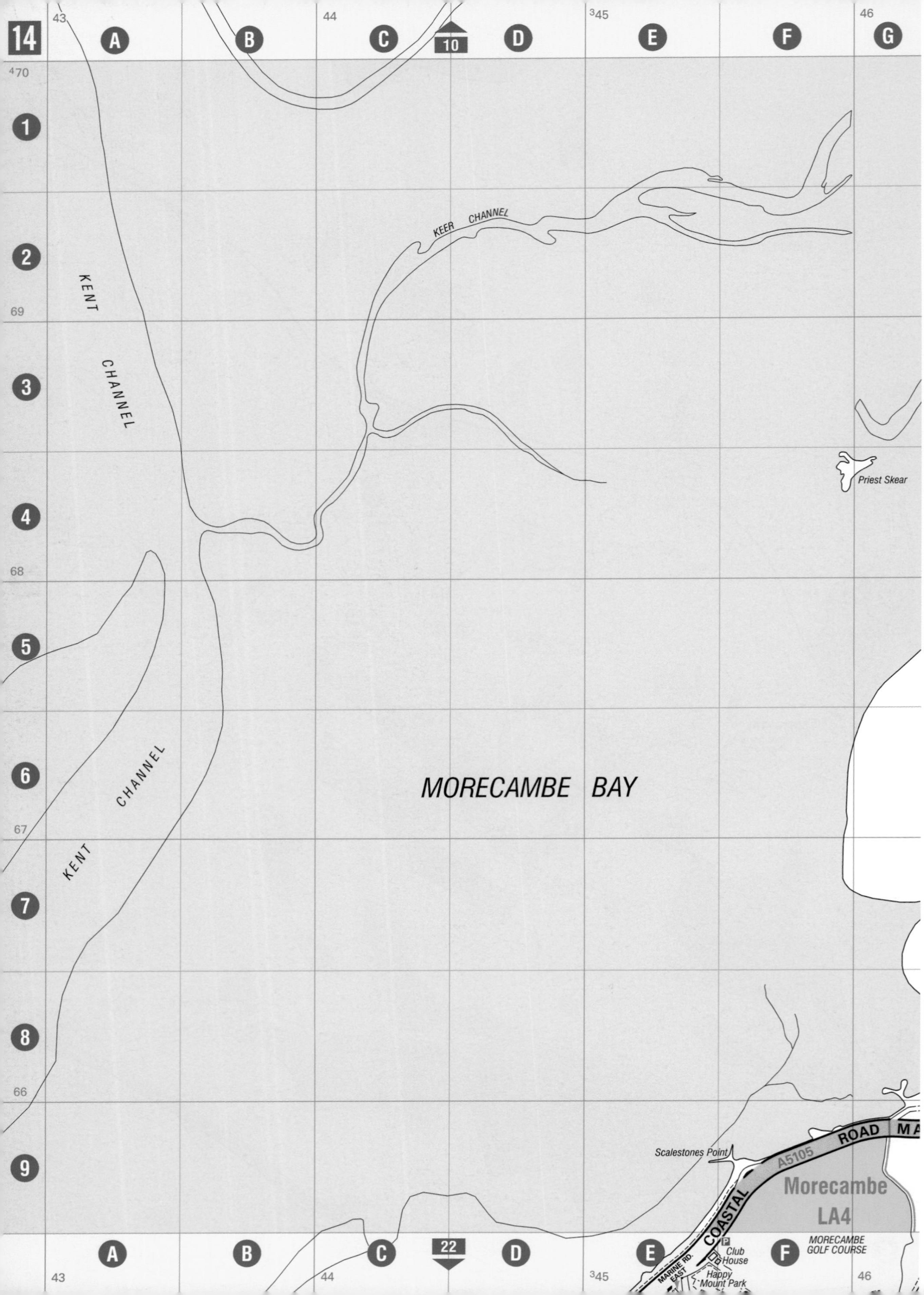

470

1

2

69

KENT

3

CHANNEL

Priest Skear

4

68

5

CHANNEL

6

MORECAMBE BAY

67

KENT

7

8

66

Scalestones Point

ROAD   MA

A5105

9

COASTAL

Morecambe

LA4

MORECAMBE
GOLF COURSE

43   44   345   MARINE RD.   Club   House   Happy   Mount Park

KEER   CHANNEL

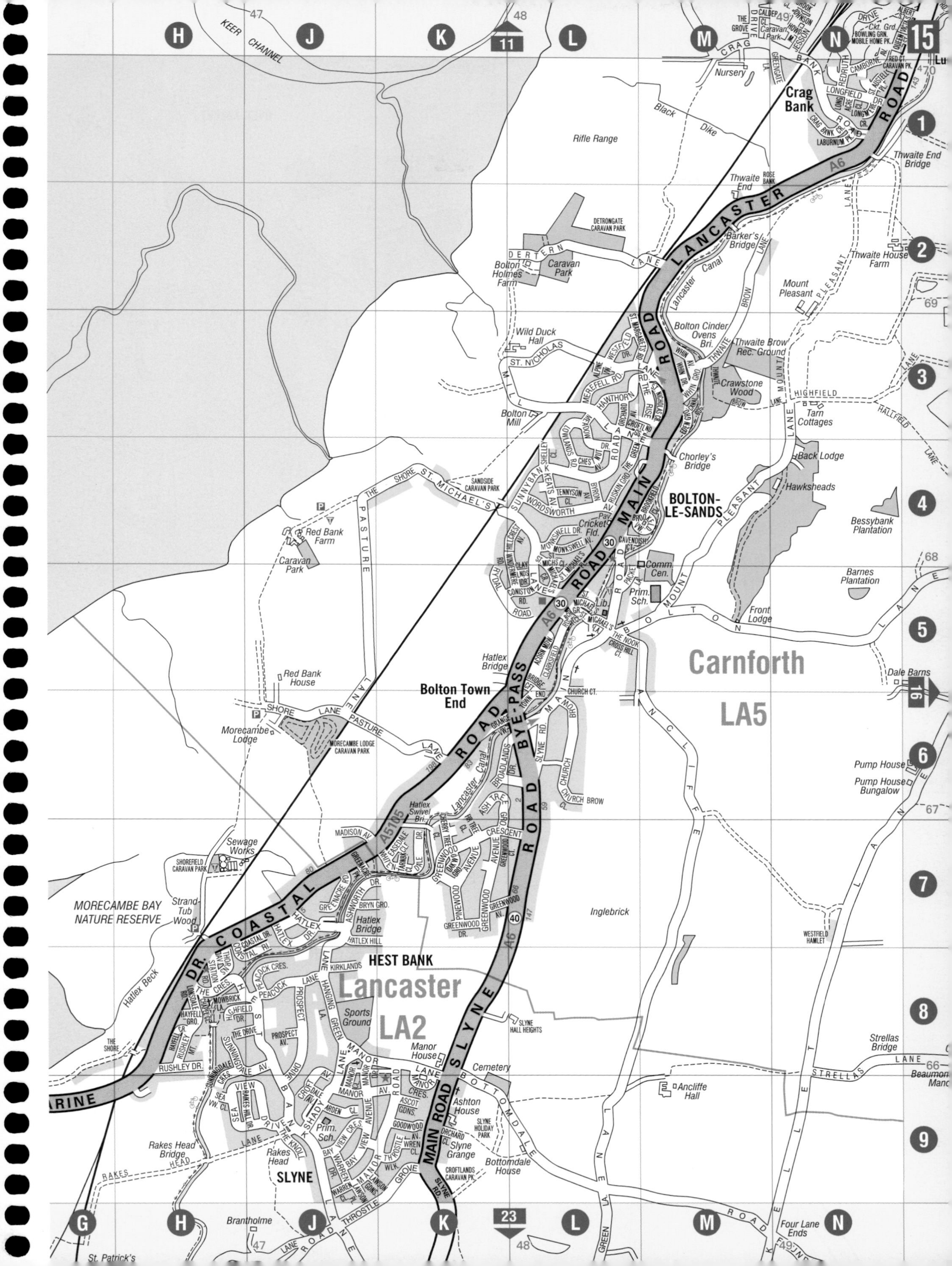

Keer Channel
Crag Bank
Rifle Range
Black Dike
Thwaite End
Thwaite End Bridge
Lancaster Road
A6
Detrongate Caravan Park
Dertern Lane
Bolton Holmes Farm
Caravan Park
Barker's Bridge
Lancaster Canal
Thwaite House Farm
Mount Pleasant
Wild Duck Hall
St. Nicholas
Bolton Cinder Ovens Bri.
Thwaite Brow Rec. Ground
Crawstone Wood
Highfield
Tarn Cottages
Bolton Mill
Chorley's Bridge
Back Lodge
Hawksheads
Sandside Caravan Park
The Shore
St. Michael's
Bolton-le-Sands
Bessybank Plantation
Red Bank Farm
Pasture
Caravan Park
Main Road
Barnes Plantation
Comm. Cen.
Prim. Sch.
Front Lodge
Bolton
Carnforth
Hatlex Bridge
Red Bank House
Bolton Town End
Dale Barns
Shore Lane
Morecambe Lodge
Morecambe Lodge Caravan Park
LA5
Ancliffe Lane
Bye-Pass
Pump House
Pump House Bungalow
Hatlex Swivel Bri.
A5105
Sewage Works
Shorefield Caravan Park
Coastal Road
Morecambe Bay Nature Reserve
Strand-Tub Wood
Inglebrick
Westfield Hamlet
Hatlex Bridge
Hest Bank
Hatlex Beck
Lancaster
Sports Ground
LA2
Slyne Road
Slyne Hall Heights
Manor House
Strellas Bridge
Cemetery
Strellas Lane
The Shore
Rushley Dr.
Marine
Bottomdale Road
Ancliffe Hall
Ashton House
Slyne Holiday Park
Prim. Sch.
Slyne Grange
Rakes Head Bridge
Rakes Head
Bottomdale House
Croftlands Caravan Pk.
Slyne
Rakes Head Lane
Brantholme
Throstle Grove
Four Lane Ends
St. Patrick's

11
16
23

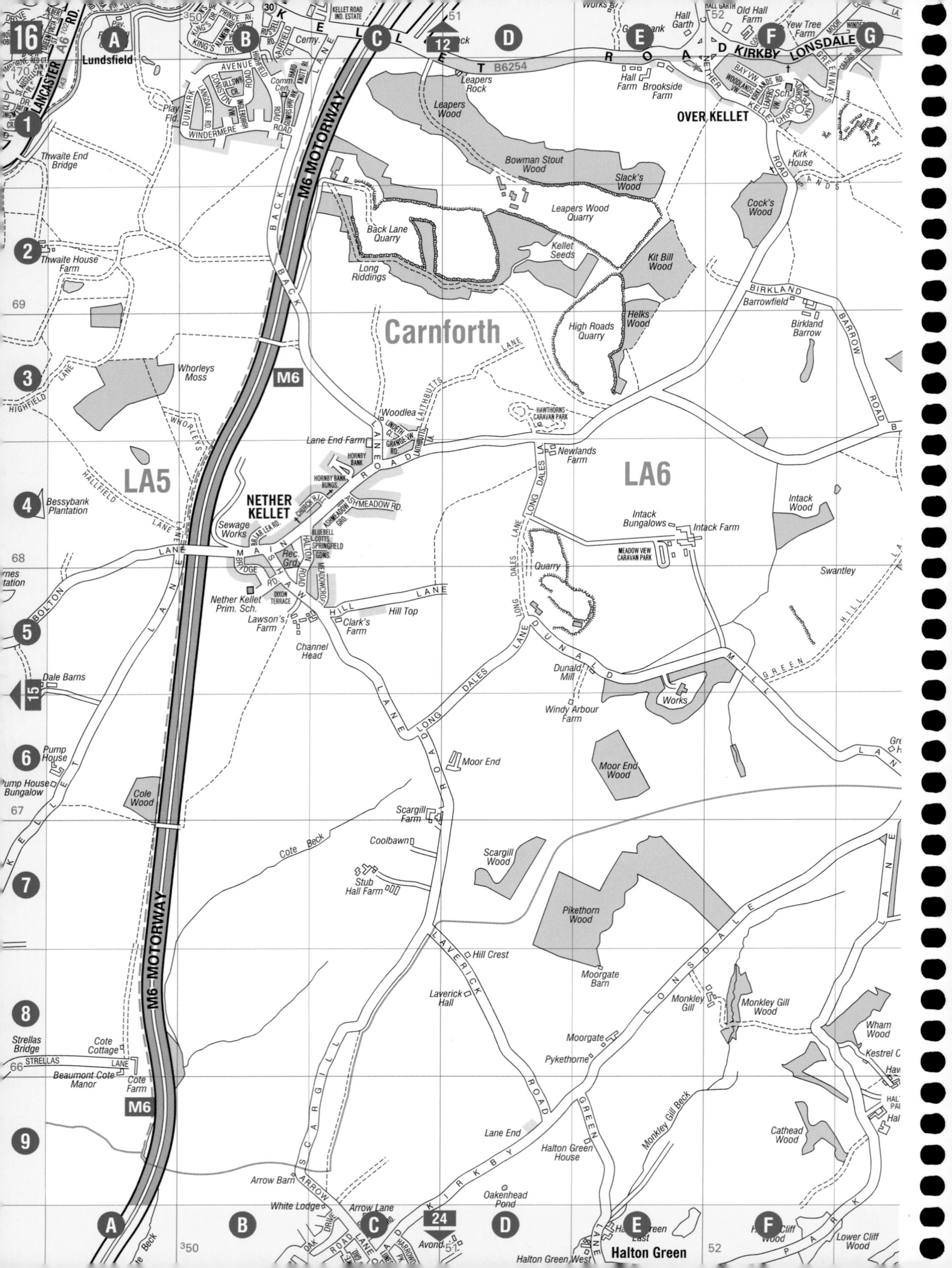

Lundsfield
LANCASTER RD.
A6
Thwaite End Bridge
Thwaite House Farm
Whorleys Moss
HIGHFIELD LANE
WHORLEYS
HALLFIELD LANE
Bessybank Plantation
LA5
Dale Barns
Pump House
Pump House Bungalow
Cole Wood
KELLET LANE
BOLTON LANE
Strellas Bridge
STRELLAS LANE
Cote Cottage
Beaumont Cote Manor
Cote Farm
M6-MOTORWAY
M6
M6 MOTORWAY
BACK LANE
Back Lane Quarry
Long Riddings
Leapers Rock
Leapers Wood
Bowman Stout Wood
Slack's Wood
Leapers Wood Quarry
Kellet Seeds
Kit Bill Wood
Helks Wood
High Roads Quarry
Carnforth
KELLET ROAD
B6254
Hall Garth
Hall Farm
Brookside Farm
Old Hall Farm
Yew Tree Farm
KIRKBY LONSDALE
OVER KELLET
Kirk House
Cock's Wood
BIRKLAND BARROW ROAD
Barrowfield
Birkland Barrow
Woodlea
LAITHBUTTS LANE
HAWTHORNS CARAVAN PARK
Lane End Farm
Newlands Farm
LA6
NETHER KELLET
Sewage Works
MAIN ROAD
Rec. Grd.
Nether Kellet Prim. Sch.
Lawson's Farm
Channel Head
HILL LANE
Hill Top
Clark's Farm
LONG DALES LANE
Quarry
Intack Bungalows
Intack Farm
MEADOW VIEW CARAVAN PARK
Intack Wood
Swantley
DUNALD MILL
Dunald Mill
Windy Arbour Farm
Works
GREEN HILL
Moor End
Moor End Wood
Scargill Farm
Coolbawn
Cote Beck
Scargill Wood
Stub Hall Farm
Pikethorn Wood
LAVERICK ROAD
Hill Crest
Laverick Hall
Moorgate Barn
Monkley Gill
Monkley Gill Wood
Wham Wood
Moorgate
Pykethorne
LONSDALE
Monkley Gill Beck
GREEN
Lane End
Halton Green House
Cathead Wood
SCARGILL
Arrow Barn
White Lodge
Arrow Lane
Oakenhead Pond
KIRKBY
Halton Green
Halton Green West
Lower Cliff Wood
PARK
12
15
24
A B C D E F G
1 2 3 4 5 6 7 8 9
69 68 67 66
350 51 52

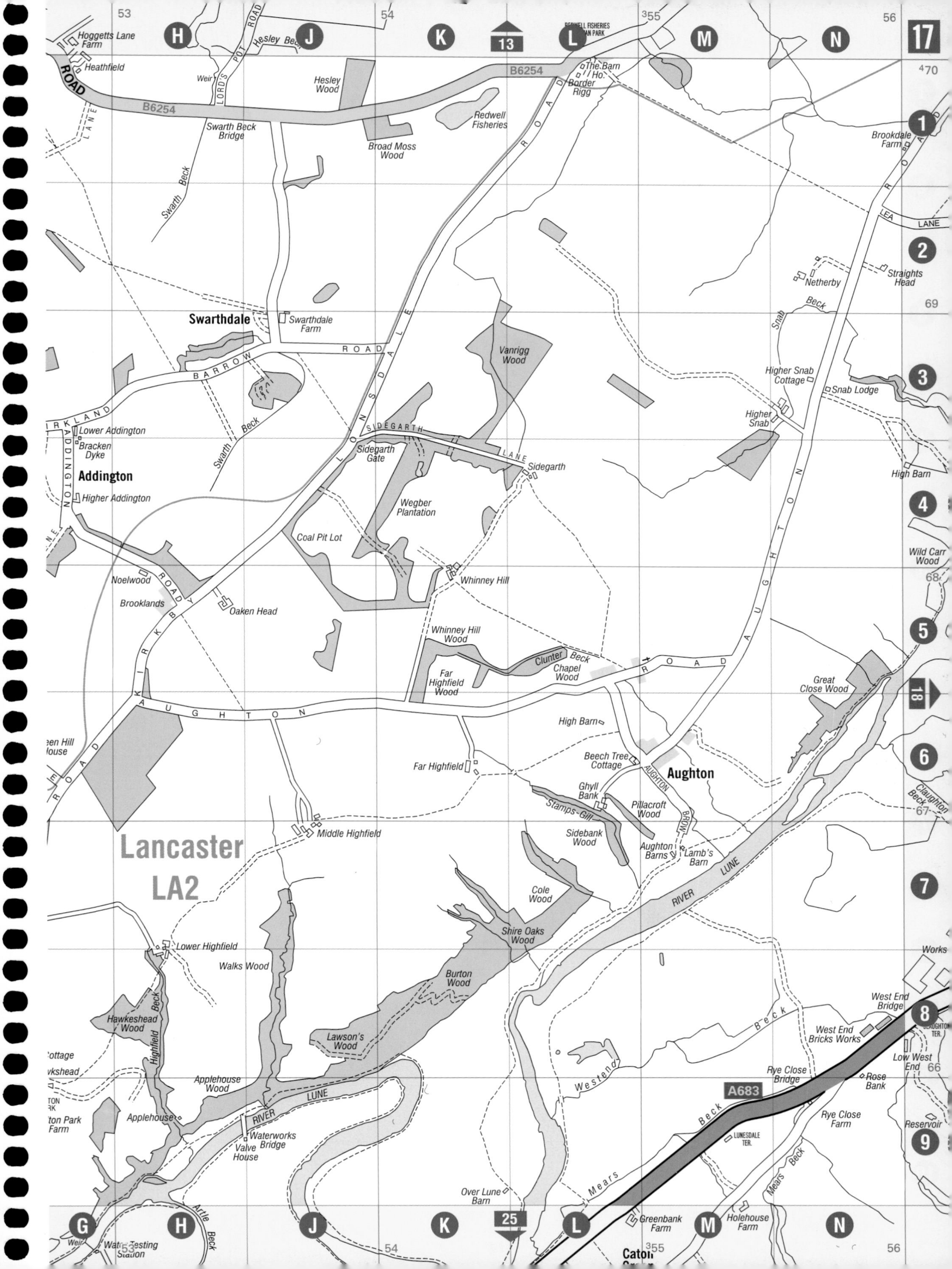
Hoggetts Lane Farm
Heathfield
ROAD
B6254
Hesley Beck
LORD'S POT ROAD
Weir
Hesley Wood
Swarth Beck Bridge
Broad Moss Wood
Redwell Fisheries
The Barn Ho.
Border Rigg
Swarth Beck
Swarthdale
Swarthdale Farm
BARROW ROAD
LONSDALE ROAD
Vanrigg Wood
SIDEGARTH LANE
Sidegarth Gate
Sidegarth
Lower Addington
Bracken Dyke
ADDINGTON
Addington
Higher Addington
Wegber Plantation
Coal Pit Lot
Noelwood
Brooklands
KIRKBY ROAD
Oaken Head
Whinney Hill
Whinney Hill Wood
Clunter Beck
Chapel Wood
Far Highfield Wood
AUGHTON ROAD
High Barn
Far Highfield
Beech Tree Cottage
Aughton
Ghyll Bank
Stamps Gill
Pillacroft Wood
Sidebank Wood
AUGHTON BROW
Aughton Barns
Lamb's Barn
Middle Highfield
Lancaster LA2
RIVER LUNE
Cole Wood
Shire Oaks Wood
Lower Highfield
Walks Wood
Burton Wood
Hawkeshead Wood
Highfield Beck
Lawson's Wood
Applehouse Wood
Applehouse
Waterworks Bridge
Valve House
Artle Beck
Weir
Water Testing Station
Brookdale Farm
LEA LANE
Netherby
Straights Head
Snab Beck
Higher Snab Cottage
Snab Lodge
Higher Snab
High Barn
Wild Carr Wood
Great Close Wood
Claughton Beck
Works
West End Bridge
West End Bricks Works
Low West End
Rye Close Bridge
Rose Bank
A683
Rye Close Farm
Reservoir
LUNESDALE TER.
Mears Beck
Westend Beck
Over Lune Barn
Greenbank Farm
Holehouse Farm
Caton
13
18
25
53
54
355
56
470
69
68
67
66
H J K L M N G
1 2 3 4 5 6 7 8 9

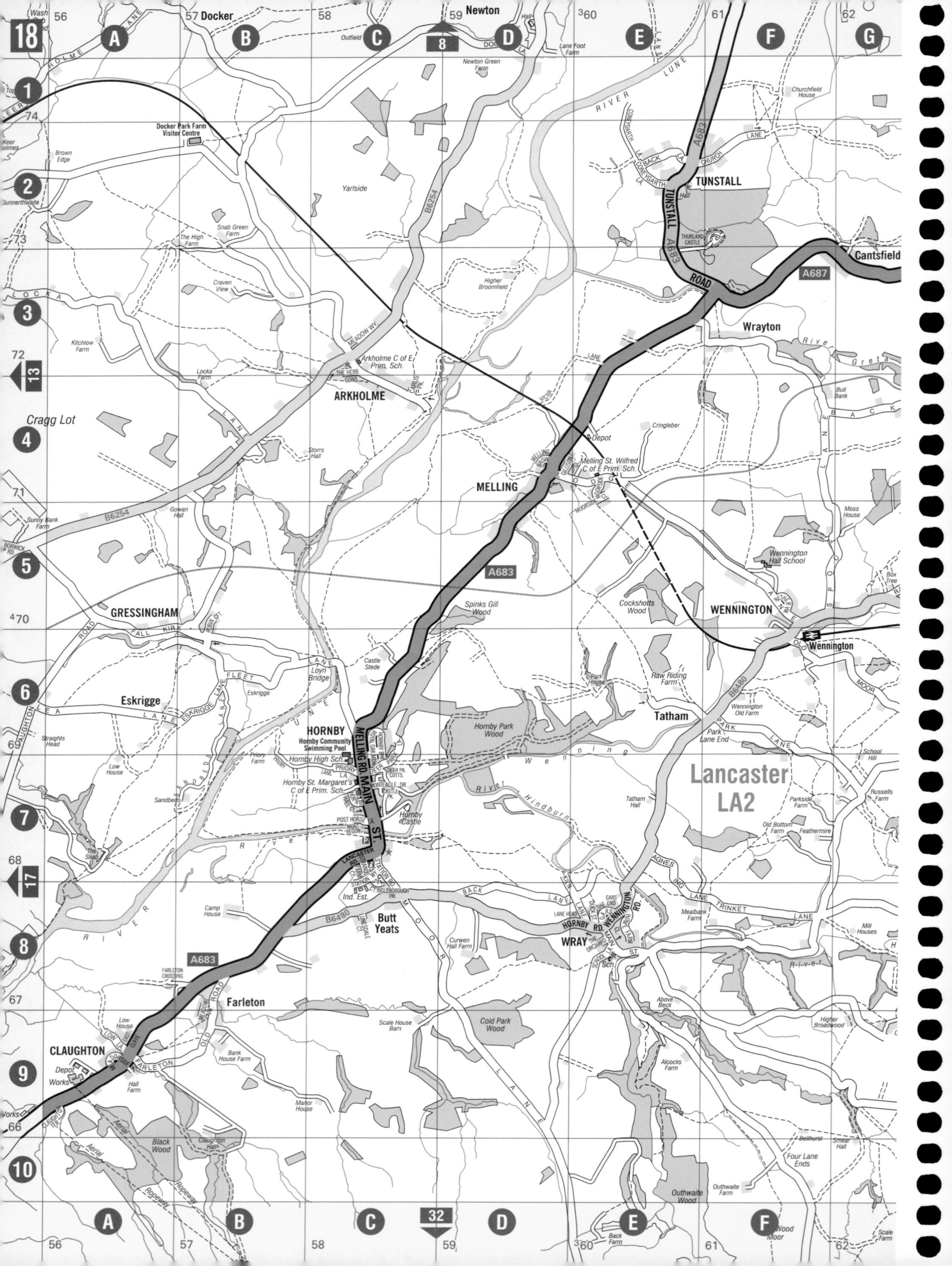

Docker
Newton
Docker Park Farm Visitor Centre
Yarlside
TUNSTALL
Cantsfield
Wrayton
ARKHOLME
Arkholme C of E Prim. Sch.
Cragg Lot
MELLING
Melling St. Wilfred C of E Prim. Sch.
GRESSINGHAM
WENNINGTON
Wennington
Wennington Hall School
Eskrigge
HORNBY
Hornby Community Swimming Pool
Hornby High Sch.
Hornby St. Margaret's C of E Prim. Sch.
Hornby Castle
Hornby Park Wood
Tatham
Lancaster LA2
Butt Yeats
WRAY
Farleton
CLAUGHTON
Cold Park Wood
Black Wood
Outhwaite Wood
A683
A687
B6254
B6480
River Lune
River Wenning
River Hindburn

8
13
17
32

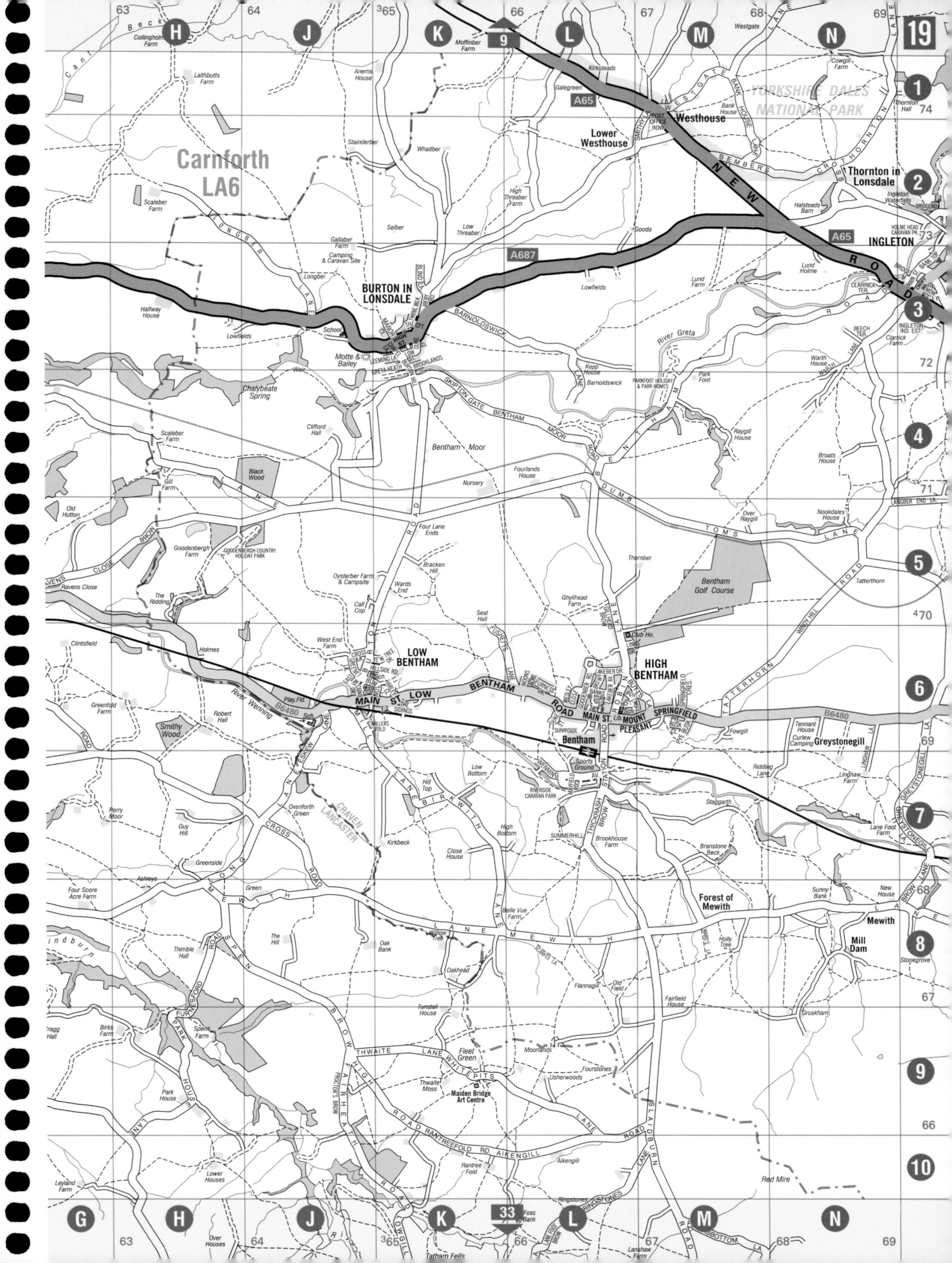

19
Carnforth
LA6
YORKSHIRE DALES
NATIONAL PARK
Collingholm Farm
Laithbutts Farm
Anems House
Moffinber Farm
Kirksteads
Galegreen
Westgate
Cowgill Farm
Thornton Hall
Westhouse
Lower Westhouse
Bank House
Thornton in Lonsdale
Ingleton Waterfalls
Halsteads Barn
INGLETON
Stainderber
Whaitber
Scaleber Farm
High Threaber Farm
Selber
Low Threaber
Gooda
Gallaber Farm
Camping & Caravan Site
Longber
BURTON IN LONSDALE
Halfway House
Lowfields
School
Motte & Bailey
Lund Farm
Lund Holme
Kepp House
Barnoldswick
PARKFOOT HOLIDAY & PARK HOMES
River Greta
Park Foot
Warth House
Chalybeate Spring
Clifford Hall
Scaleber Farm
Bentham Moor
Raygill House
Broats House
Black Wood
Gill Farm
Fourlands House
Nursery
Old Hutton
Four Lane Ends
Over Raygill
Nookdales House
Goodenbergh Farm
GOODENBERGH COUNTRY HOLIDAY PARK
Ravens Close
Bracken Hill
Thornber
Tatterthorn
Oysterber Farm & Campsite
Wards End
Bentham Golf Course
The Ridding
Calf Cop
Ghyllhead Farm
Seat Hall
Clintsfield
Holmes
West End Farm
LOW BENTHAM
Club Ho.
HIGH BENTHAM
Greenfold Farm
River Wenning
Robert Hall
Smithy Wood
Bentham
Sports Ground
Fowgill
Tennant House
Curlew Camping
Greystonegill
Low Bottom
Hill Top
RIVERSIDE CARAVAN PARK
Ridding Lane
Linghaw Farm
Staggarth
Perry Moor
Oxenforth Green
CRAVEN
LANCASTER
Guy Hill
High Bottom
SUMMERHILL
Brookhouse Farm
Branstone Beck
Lane Foot Farm
Kirkbeck
Close House
Greenside
Ashleys
Four Score Acre Farm
Green
Forest of Mewith
Sunny Bank
New House
Mewith
Belle Vue Farm
Holly Tree
Mill Dam
Stonegrove
The Hill
Thimble Hall
Oak Bank
Willow Tree
Oakhead
Flannagill
Old Field
Fairfield House
Gruskham
Cragg Hall
Birks Farm
Spens Farm
Tunstall House
Fleet Green
Moorlands
Fourstones
Usherwoods
Thwaite Moss
Maiden Bridge Art Centre
Park House
Rantree Fold
Aikengill
Red Mire
Leyland Farm
Lower Houses
Ringstones
Foss Bank
Over Houses
Tatham Fells
Lanshaw Farm
A65
A687
B6480
MAIN ST.
LOW BENTHAM ROAD
MOUNT PLEASANT
SPRINGFIELD
STATION ROAD
MEWITH LANE
THWAITE LANE
RANTREEFOLD RD
AIKENGILL
SLAIDBURN ROAD
TOM'S LANE
DUMB
NEW ROAD
9
33
G
H
J
K
L
M
N
63
64
65
66
67
68
69
74
73
72
71
70
69
68
67
66
1
2
3
4
5
6
7
8
9
10

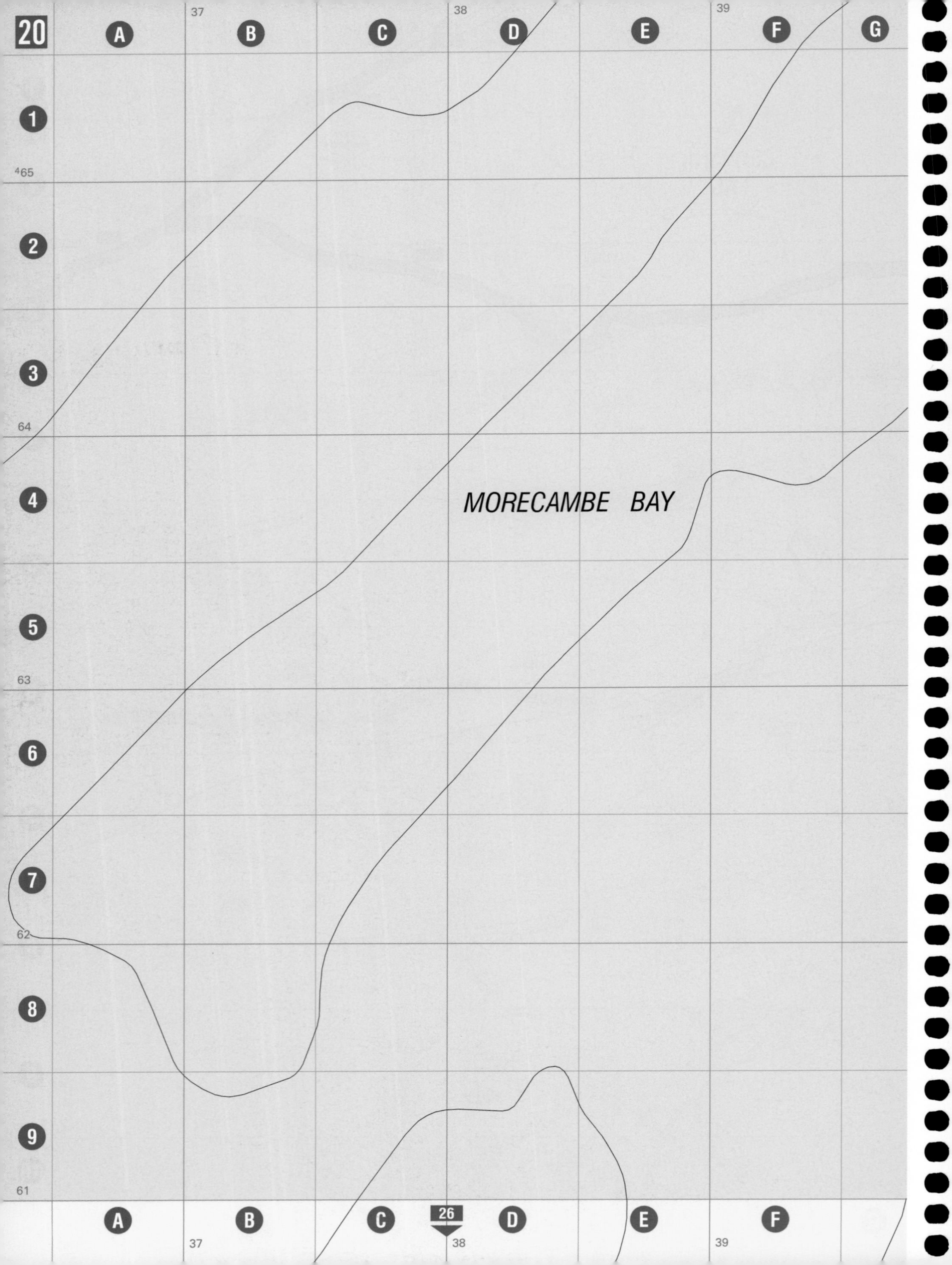

A   37   B   C   38   D   E   39   F   G

1

⁴65

2

3

64

4

MORECAMBE BAY

5

63

6

7

62

8

9

61

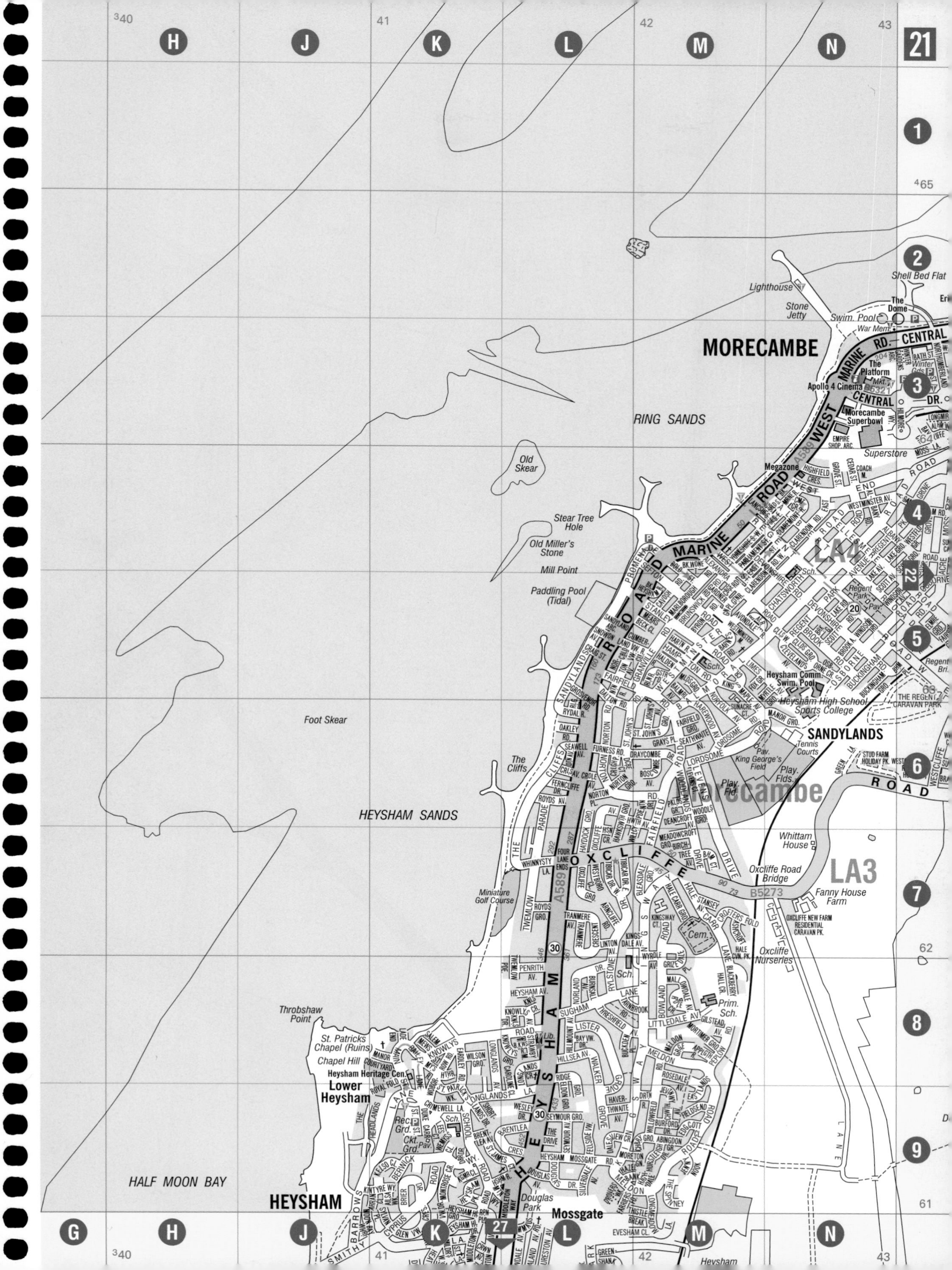
21
MORECAMBE
RING SANDS
Old Skear
Stear Tree Hole
Old Miller's Stone
Mill Point
Paddling Pool (Tidal)
Foot Skear
The Cliffs
HEYSHAM SANDS
Miniature Golf Course
Throbshaw Point
St. Patricks Chapel (Ruins)
Chapel Hill
Heysham Heritage Cen.
Lower Heysham
HALF MOON BAY
HEYSHAM
Mossgate
Douglas Park
Lighthouse
Stone Jetty
Swim. Pool
War Mem.
The Dome
Shell Bed Flat
The Platform
Apollo 4 Cinema
Morecambe Superbowl
Superstore
Megazone
LA4
LA3
Regent Park
Heysham Comm. Swim. Pool
Heysham High School Sports College
SANDYLANDS
Tennis Courts
King George's Field
Play. Flds.
Morecambe
Whittam House
Oxcliffe Road Bridge
Fanny House Farm
OXCLIFFE NEW FARM RESIDENTIAL CARAVAN PK.
Oxcliffe Nurseries
Prim. Sch.
THE REGENT CARAVAN PARK
STUD FARM HOLIDAY PK.
MARINE ROAD WEST
MARINE RD. CENTRAL
CENTRAL DR.
HEYSHAM ROAD
OXCLIFFE ROAD
A589
B5273
B5321
H J K L M N
G H J K L M N
1 2 3 4 5 6 7 8 9
340
41
42
43
465
64
63
62
61
22
27

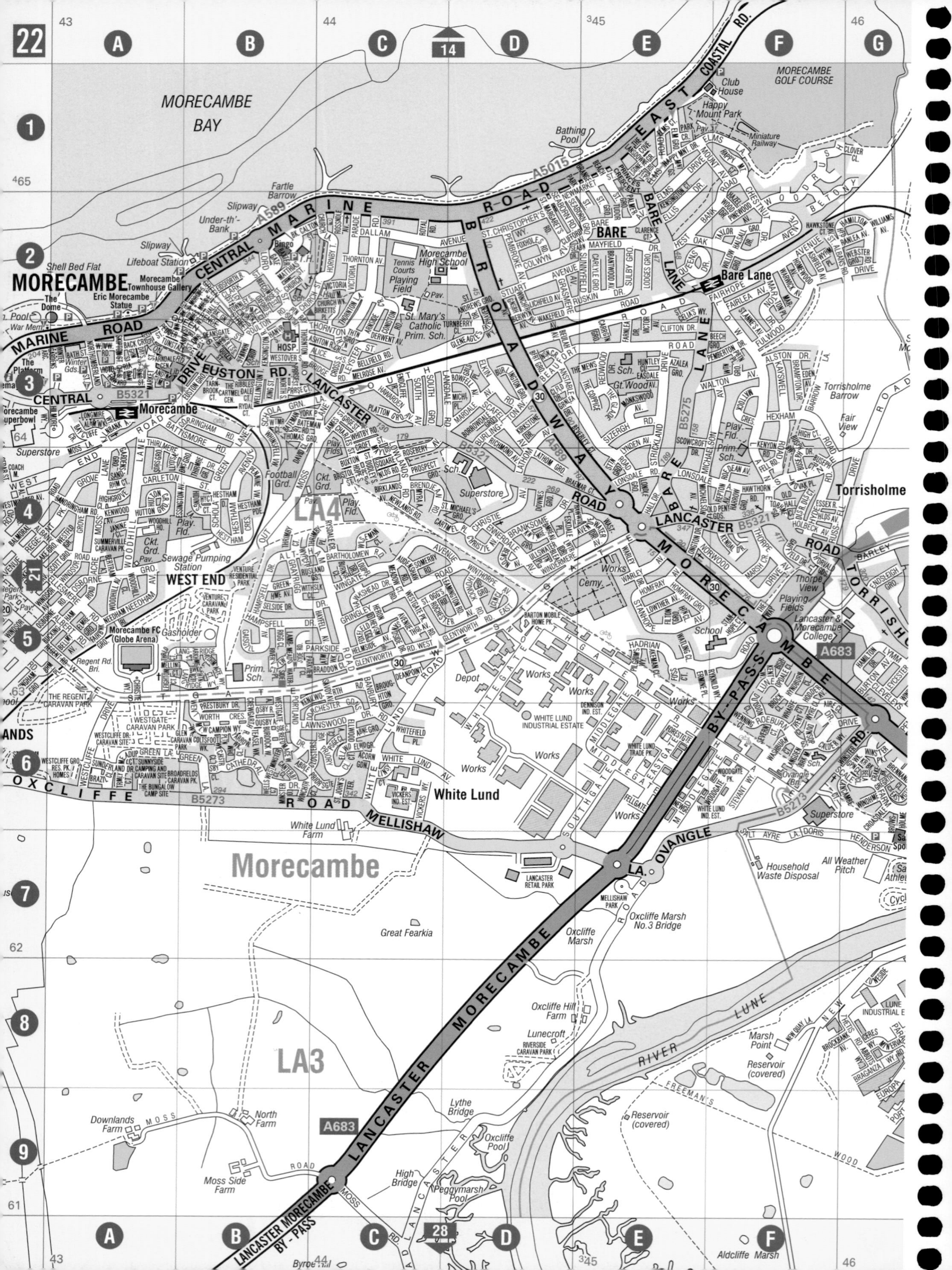
MORECAMBE BAY
MORECAMBE
MORECAMBE GOLF COURSE
Club House
Happy Mount Park
Miniature Railway
Bathing Pool
Fartle Barrow
Slipway
Under-th'-Bank
Lifeboat Station
Shell Bed Flat
Morecambe Townhouse Gallery
Eric Morecambe Statue
The Dome
The Platform
Winter Gds.
War Mem.
MARINE ROAD
CENTRAL MARINE ROAD EAST
COASTAL RD.
A5015
A589
BARE
BARE LANE
Bare Lane
Morecambe High School
Tennis Courts
Playing Field
St. Mary's Catholic Prim. Sch.
EUSTON RD.
LANCASTER ROAD
SOUTH ROAD
BROADWAY
B5321
B5275
Morecambe
Superstore
LA4
WEST END
Sewage Pumping Station
Football Grd.
Ckt. Grd.
Play. Fld.
Torrisholme
Torrisholme Barrow
Fair View
Thorpe View
Playing Fields
Lancaster & Morecambe College
A683
MORECAMBE ROAD
BY-PASS
Morecambe FC (Globe Arena)
Gasholder
Regent Rd. Bri.
THE REGENT CARAVAN PARK
WESTGATE CARAVAN PARK
Cemy.
Works
Depot
WHITE LUND INDUSTRIAL ESTATE
White Lund
OXCLIFFE ROAD
B5273
MELLISHAW
White Lund Farm
LANCASTER RETAIL PARK
OVANGLE
Household Waste Disposal
All Weather Pitch
Morecambe
Great Fearkia
Oxcliffe Marsh
Oxcliffe Marsh No.3 Bridge
Oxcliffe Hill Farm
Lunecroft
RIVERSIDE CARAVAN PARK
RIVER LUNE
Marsh Point
Reservoir (covered)
FREEMAN'S WOOD
LA3
LANCASTER MORECAMBE BY-PASS
Lythe Bridge
Oxcliffe Pool
High Bridge
Peggymarsh Pool
North Farm
Downlands Farm
MOSS ROAD
Moss Side Farm
ALDCLIFFE ROAD
Aldcliffe Marsh
Byroe Hill
LUNE INDUSTRIAL E
A B C D E F G
1 2 3 4 5 6 7 8 9
43 44 345 46
465 62 61

14
21
28

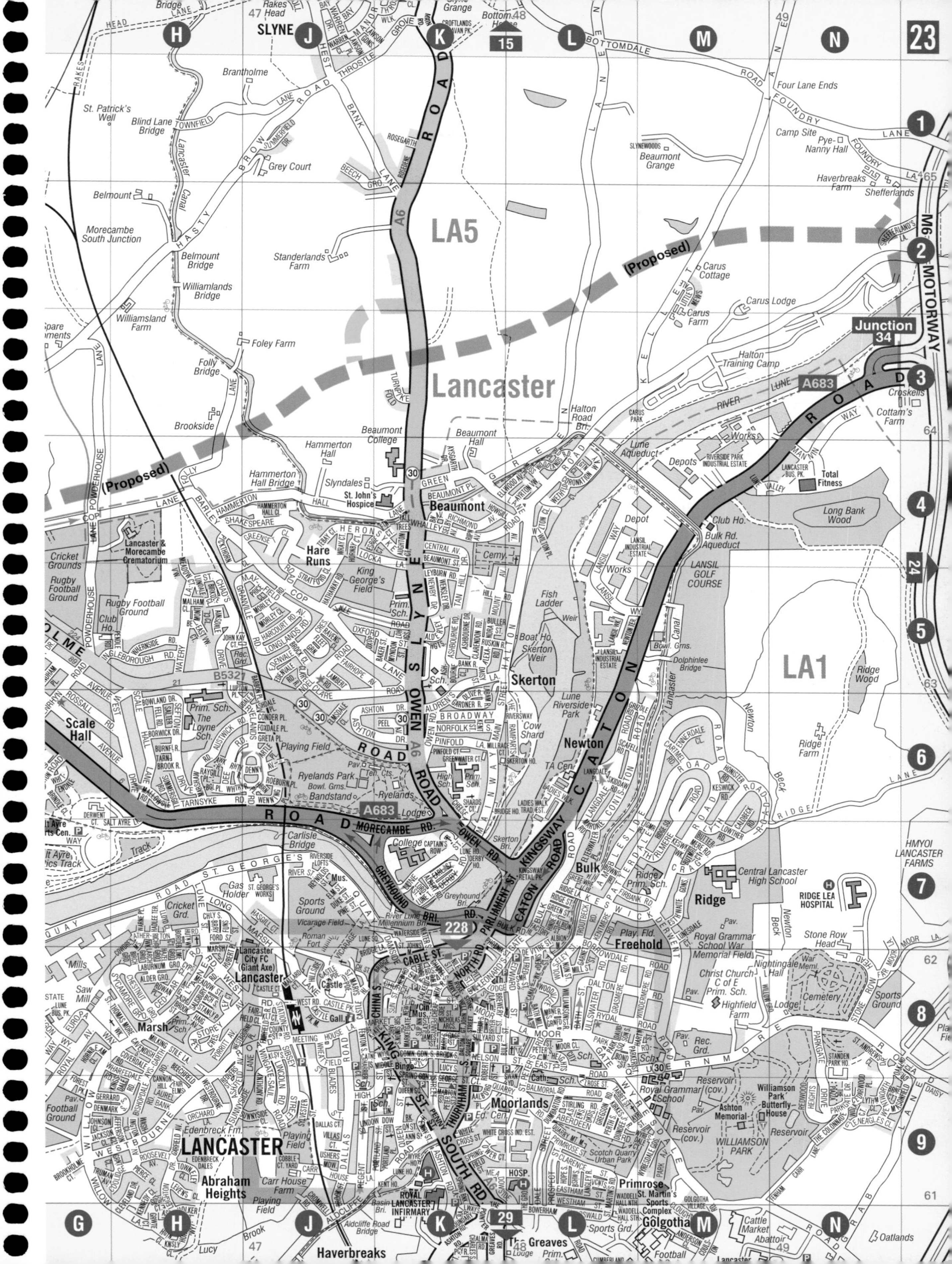

LA5
Lancaster
LA1
LANCASTER
Slyne
Beaumont
Skerton
Newton
Bulk
Ridge
Freehold
Moorlands
Primrose
Golgotha
Marsh
Abraham Heights
Scale Hall
Hare Runs
Haverbreaks
The Greaves
(Proposed)
Junction 34
M6 MOTORWAY
A6
A683
B5321
SLYNE ROAD
OWEN ROAD
CATON ROAD
MORECAMBE RD.
BOTTOMDALE ROAD
FOUNDRY LANE
KELLET LANE
HALTON ROAD
KINGSWAY
SOUTH RD.
WESTBOURNE
LANCASTER CITY FC (Giant Axe)
ROYAL LANCASTER INFIRMARY
Williamson Park
Cemetery
Royal Grammar School
Lancaster Farms
HMYOI LANCASTER FARMS
Ridge Lea Hospital
Lansil Golf Course
Lune Aqueduct
Four Lane Ends
Lancaster & Morecambe Crematorium
15
29
24
228

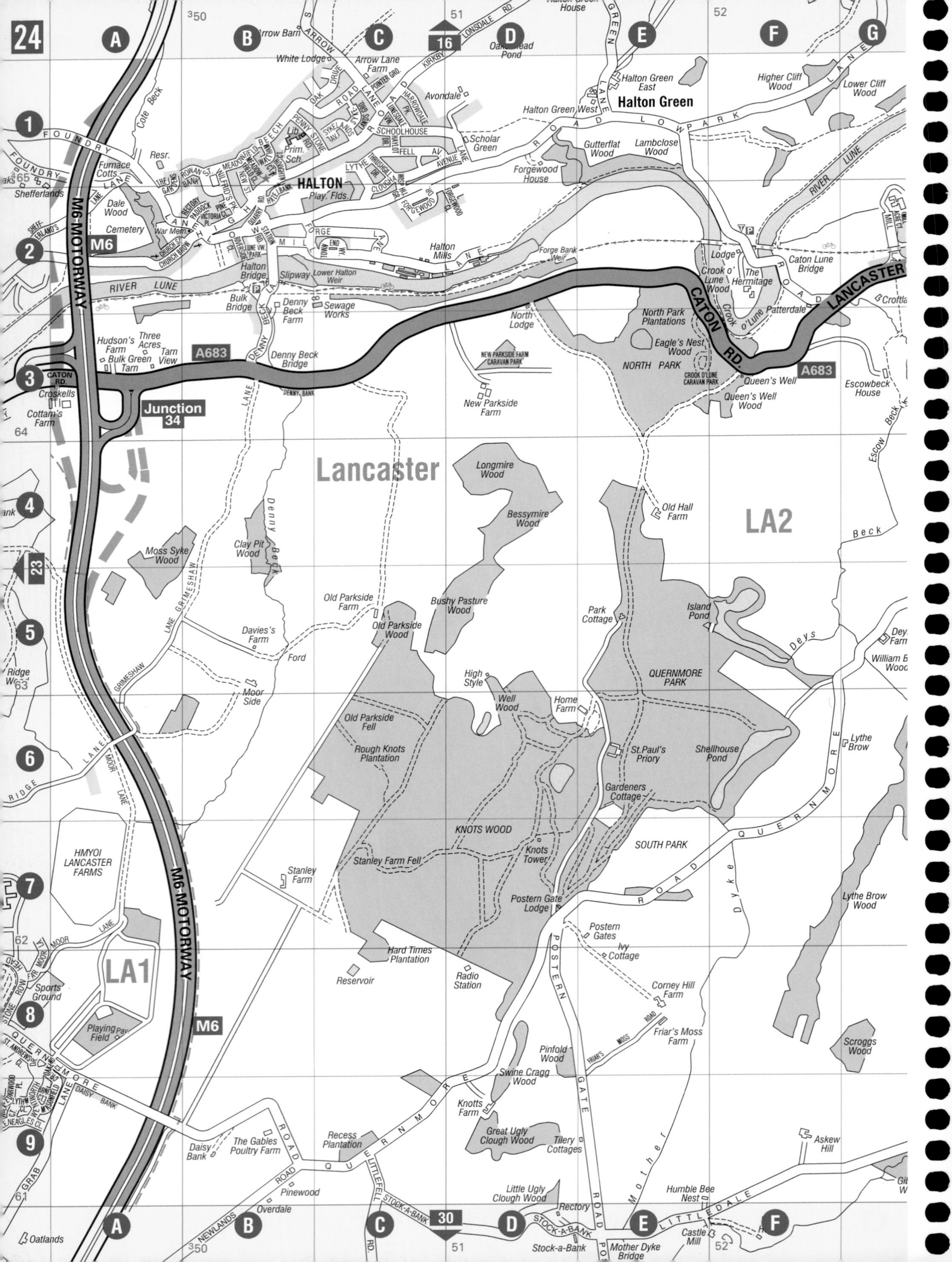

A
B
C
D
E
F
G
1
2
3
4
5
6
7
8
9
350
51
52
16
30
23
Arrow Barn
White Lodge
Arrow Lane Farm
Oaklands Pond
Halton Green East
Halton Green
Higher Cliff Wood
Lower Cliff Wood
Avondale
Halton Green West
LOW PARK LANE
Scholar Green
Gutterflat Wood
Lambclose Wood
Forgewood House
RIVER LUNE
HALTON
Play. Flds.
Prim. Sch.
Lib.
FOUNDRY LANE
Cote Beck
Resr.
Furnace Cotts
Shefferlands
Dale Wood
Cemetery
War Mem.
M6
M6 MOTORWAY
HIGH ROAD
FORGE LANE
MILL LANE
Halton Mills
Forge Bank Weir
Halton Bridge
Slipway
Lower Halton Weir
Bulk Bridge
Denny Beck Farm
Sewage Works
North Lodge
Lodge
Crook o' Lune Wood
The Hermitage
Caton Lune Bridge
LANCASTER
Croftlands
North Park Plantations
Eagle's Nest Wood
NORTH PARK
CROOK O'LUNE CARAVAN PARK
CATON RD.
Patterdale
Queen's Well
Queen's Well Wood
A683
Escowbeck House
Hudson's Farm
Three Acres
Tarn View
Bulk Green Tarn
Denny Beck Bridge
NEW PARKSIDE FARM CARAVAN PARK
New Parkside Farm
CATON RD.
Croskells
Cottam's Farm
Junction 34
DENNY BANK
Lancaster
Longmire Wood
Bessymire Wood
Old Hall Farm
LA2
Escow Beck
Moss Syke Wood
Clay Pit Wood
Denny Beck
Old Parkside Farm
Old Parkside Wood
Bushy Pasture Wood
Park Cottage
Island Pond
Deys Farm
William Bank Wood
Davies's Farm
Ford
GRIMESHAW LANE
Ridge Wood
Moor Side
High Style
Well Wood
Home Farm
QUERNMORE PARK
Old Parkside Fell
Rough Knots Plantation
St.Paul's Priory
Shellhouse Pond
Lythe Brow
MOOR LANE
RIDGE LANE
Gardeners Cottage
KNOTS WOOD
Knots Tower
SOUTH PARK
HMYOI LANCASTER FARMS
Stanley Farm
Stanley Farm Fell
QUERNMORE ROAD
Postern Gate Lodge
Lythe Brow Wood
Dyke
Postern Gates
Ivy Cottage
Hard Times Plantation
Reservoir
Radio Station
LA1
Sports Ground
Corney Hill Farm
Friar's Moss Farm
FRIAR'S MOSS ROAD
Scroggs Wood
Playing Field
Pinfold Wood
Swine Cragg Wood
POSTERN GATE ROAD
Knotts Farm
Great Ugly Clough Wood
Tilery Cottages
Mother Dyke
Askew Hill
Daisy Bank
The Gables Poultry Farm
Recess Plantation
DAISY BANK
Pinewood
Overdale
Little Ugly Clough Wood
Humble Bee Nest
Rectory
LITTLEDALE
Castle Mill
STOCK-A-BANK
Stock-a-Bank
Mother Dyke Bridge
NEWLANDS ROAD
GRAB LANE
Oatlands
LITTLEFELL RD.

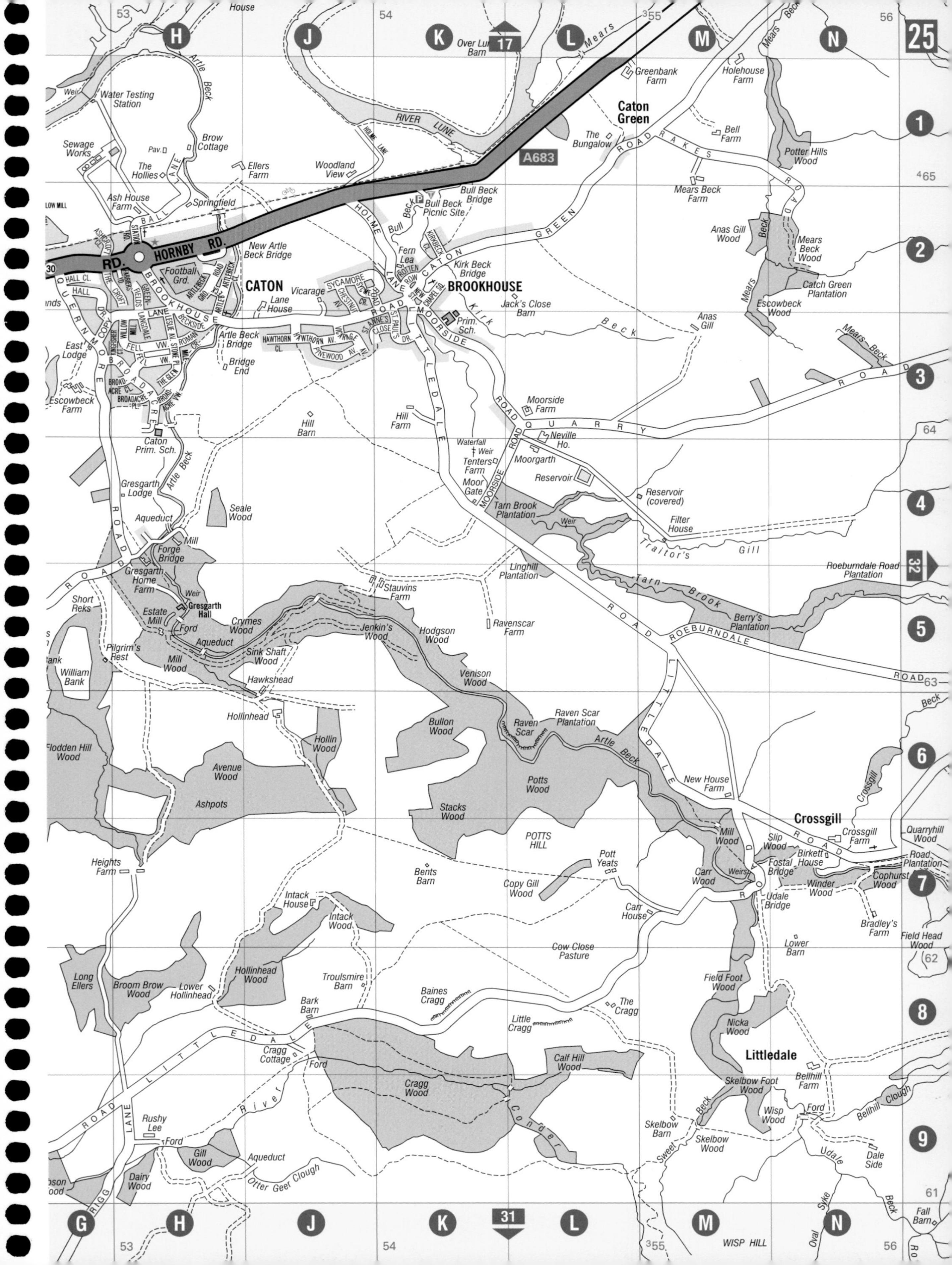
CATON
BROOKHOUSE
Caton Green
Crossgill
Littledale
A683
HORNBY RD.
RIVER LUNE
Water Testing Station
Sewage Works
Brow Cottage
The Hollies
Ellers Farm
Woodland View
Ash House Farm
Springfield
New Artle Beck Bridge
Football Grd.
Lane House
Vicarage
Bull Beck Bridge
Bull Beck Picnic Site
Fern Lea
Kirk Beck Bridge
Jack's Close Barn
Prim. Sch.
Greenbank Farm
The Bungalow
Bell Farm
Holehouse Farm
Potter Hills Wood
Mears Beck Farm
Anas Gill Wood
Mears Beck Wood
Catch Green Plantation
Escowbeck Wood
Anas Gill
Artle Beck Bridge
Bridge End
East Lodge
Escowbeck Farm
Hill Barn
Hill Farm
Moorside Farm
QUARRY ROAD
Neville Ho.
Moorgarth
Reservoir
Reservoir (covered)
Filter House
Waterfall
Weir
Tenters Farm
Moor Gate
Caton Prim. Sch.
Gresgarth Lodge
Seale Wood
Aqueduct
Mill
Forge Bridge
Tarn Brook Plantation
Traitor's Gill
Linghill Plantation
Roeburndale Road Plantation
Gresgarth Home Farm
Gresgarth Hall
Stauvins Farm
Ravenscar Farm
Short Reks
Estate Mill
Ford
Crymes Wood
Jenkin's Wood
Hodgson Wood
Berry's Plantation
ROEBURNDALE ROAD
Tarn Brook
Pilgrim's Rest
William Bank
Mill Wood
Sink Shaft Wood
Venison Wood
Hawkshead
Hollinhead
Bullon Wood
Raven Scar
Raven Scar Plantation
Artle Beck
Flodden Hill Wood
Hollin Wood
Avenue Wood
Ashpots
Potts Wood
Stacks Wood
POTTS HILL
New House Farm
Mill Wood
Slip Wood
Crossgill Farm
Quarryhill Wood
Road Plantation
Birkett House
Fostal Bridge
Cophurst Wood
Winder Wood
Heights Farm
Bents Barn
Pott Yeats
Copy Gill Wood
Carr Wood
Weirs
Udale Bridge
Intack House
Intack Wood
Carr House
Bradley's Farm
Field Head Wood
Cow Close Pasture
Lower Barn
Long Ellers
Broom Brow Wood
Lower Hollinhead
Hollinhead Wood
Troulsmire Barn
Baines Cragg
Field Foot Wood
Bark Barn
Little Cragg
The Cragg
Nicka Wood
Cragg Cottage
Ford
Cragg Wood
Calf Hill Wood
Bellhill Farm
Skelbow Foot Wood
Bellhill Clough
Rushy Lee
River Conder
Skelbow Barn
Skelbow Wood
Wisp Wood
Gill Wood
Aqueduct
Sweet Beck
Udale
Dale Side
Dairy Wood
Otter Geer Clough
LITTLEDALE ROAD
RIGG LANE
Oval Syke
Fall Barn
WISP HILL
17
32
31

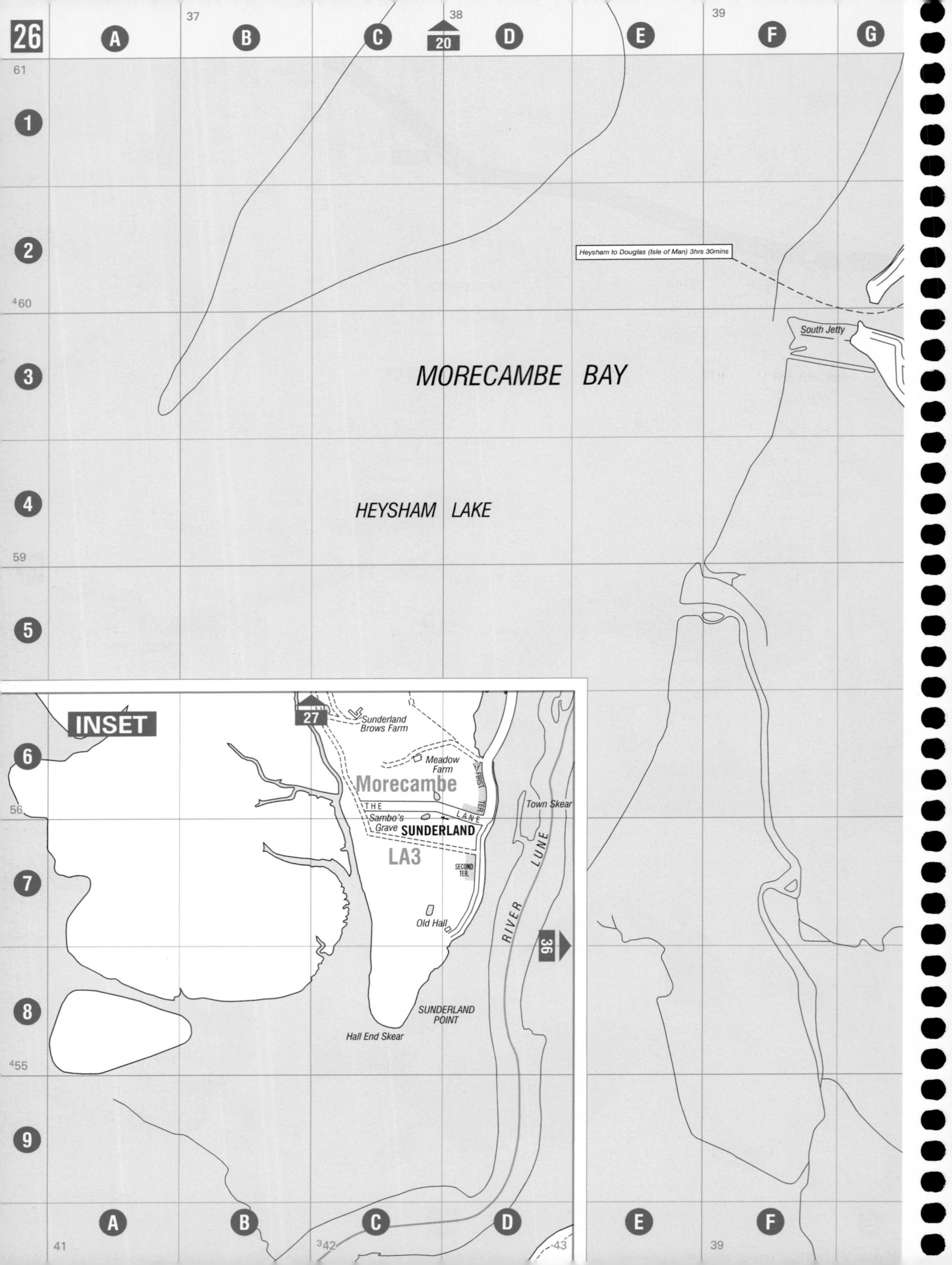

A B C **20** D E F G
37 38 39

61

1

2

⁴60

MORECAMBE BAY

3

HEYSHAM LAKE

4

59

5

Heysham to Douglas (Isle of Man) 3hrs 30mins

South Jetty

INSET

27
Sunderland Brows Farm

Meadow Farm

Morecambe

THE LANE
FIRST TER.

Town Skear

Sambo's Grave **SUNDERLAND**

6

56

LA3

SECOND TER.

7

Old Hall

RIVER LUNE

36

Hall End Skear

SUNDERLAND POINT

8

⁴55

9

A B C D E F
41 ³42 ⁴43 39

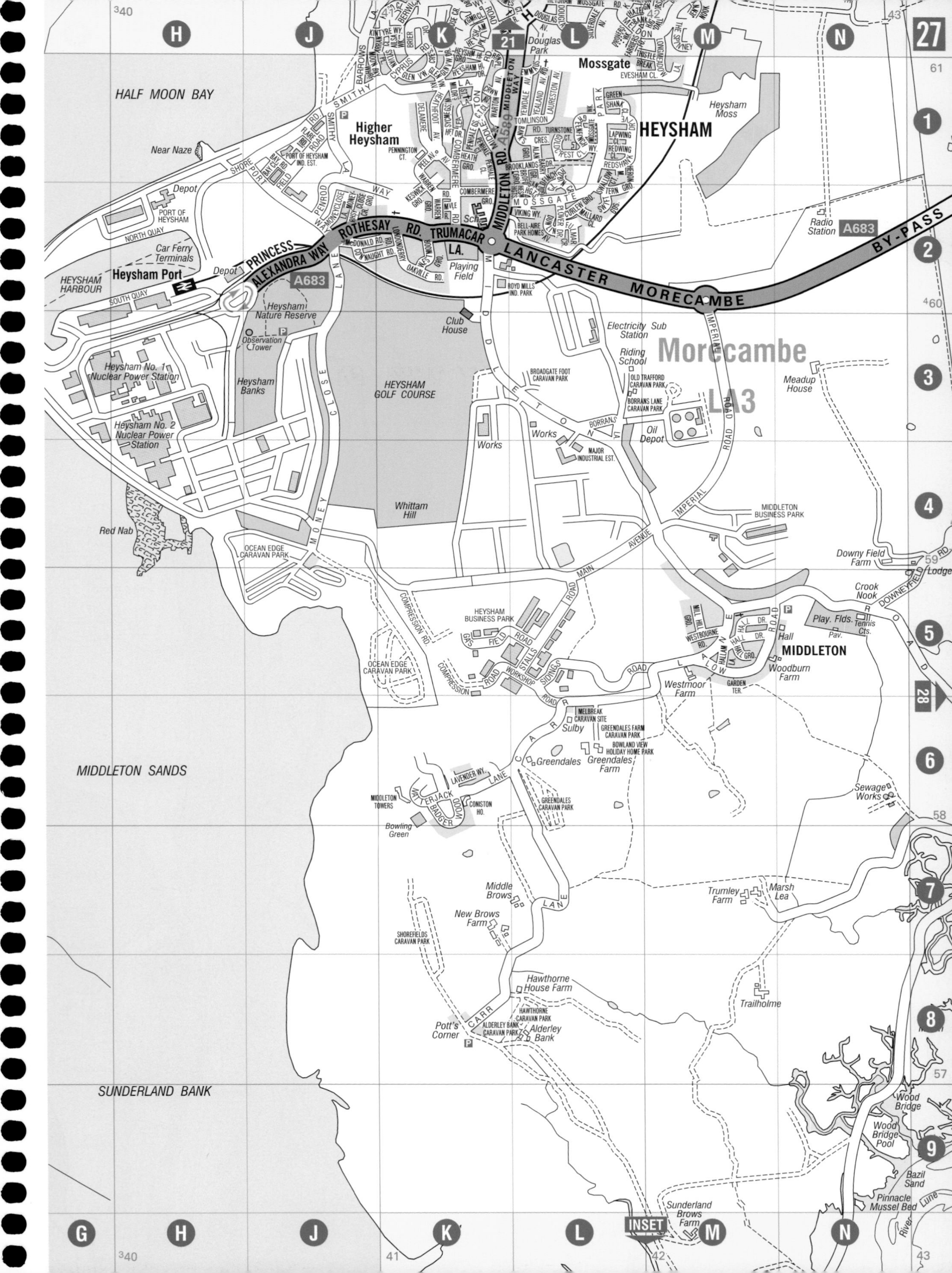
HALF MOON BAY
Near Naze
Higher Heysham
HEYSHAM
Mossgate
Douglas Park
Heysham Moss
Radio Station
A683
BY-PASS
LANCASTER
MORECAMBE
Depot
PORT OF HEYSHAM
NORTH QUAY
Car Ferry Terminals
HEYSHAM HARBOUR
Heysham Port
SOUTH QUAY
PRINCESS
ALEXANDRA WAY
ROTHESAY RD.
TRUMACAR LA.
MIDDLETON RD.
A589
Playing Field
ROYD MILLS IND. PARK
Club House
Heysham Nature Reserve
Observation Tower
Heysham No. 1 Nuclear Power Station
Heysham Banks
Heysham No. 2 Nuclear Power Station
HEYSHAM GOLF COURSE
Whittam Hill
Red Nab
OCEAN EDGE CARAVAN PARK
MONEY CLOSE LANE
Electricity Sub Station
Riding School
Morecambe
LA3
OLD TRAFFORD CARAVAN PARK
BORRANS LANE CARAVAN PARK
Oil Depot
BROADGATE FOOT CARAVAN PARK
Works
MAJOR INDUSTRIAL EST.
IMPERIAL ROAD
Meadup House
MIDDLETON BUSINESS PARK
MAIN AVENUE
Downy Field Farm
Lodge
Crook Nook
DOWNEYFIELD ROAD
HEYSHAM BUSINESS PARK
COMPRESSION RD.
GAS FIELD ROAD
STALLS
WORKSHOP
SIDINGS
Play. Flds.
Tennis Cts.
Pav.
Hall
MIDDLETON
Woodburn Farm
Westmoor Farm
GARDEN TER.
MELBREAK CARAVAN SITE
Sulby
GREENDALES FARM CARAVAN PARK
BOWLAND VIEW HOLIDAY HOME PARK
Greendales
Greendales Farm
CARR LANE
LAVENDER WY.
NATTERJACK
BADGER
MIDDLETON TOWERS
CONISTON HO.
GREENDALES CARAVAN PARK
Bowling Green
MIDDLETON SANDS
Sewage Works
Middle Brows
New Brows Farm
SHOREFIELDS CARAVAN PARK
Trumley Farm
Marsh Lea
Hawthorne House Farm
HAWTHORNE CARAVAN PARK
Pott's Corner
ALDERLEY BANK CARAVAN PARK
Alderley Bank
Trailholme
SUNDERLAND BANK
Wood Bridge
Wood Bridge Pool
Bazil Sand
Pinnacle Mussel Bed
River Lune
Sunderland Brows Farm
INSET
21
28
G H J K L M N
1 2 3 4 5 6 7 8 9
340 41 42 43
461 460 59 58 57

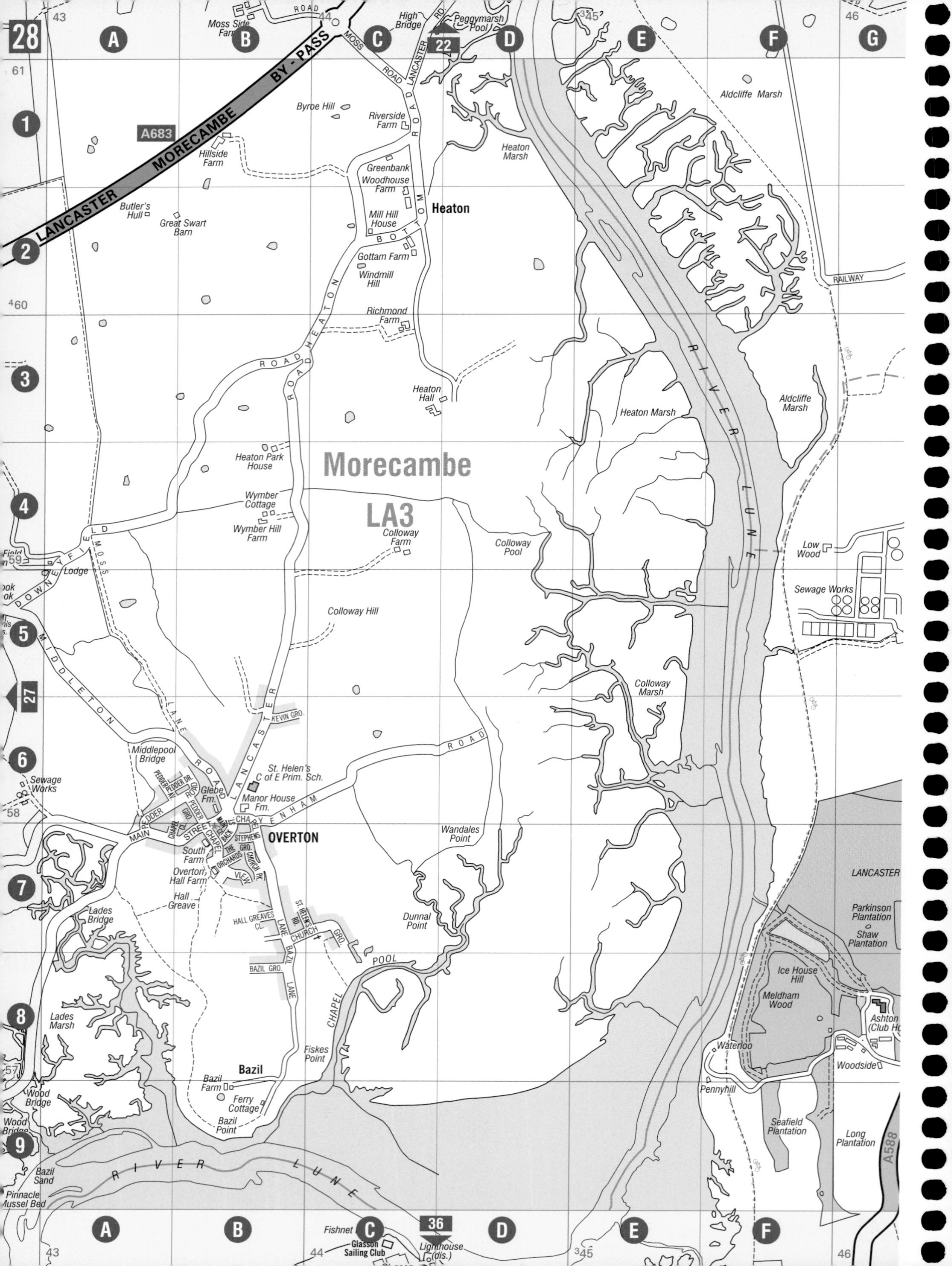

A B C 22 D E F G

43 44 45 46

LANCASTER MORECAMBE BY - PASS

A683

1

Moss Side Farm

High Bridge

Peggymarsh Pool

Aldcliffe Marsh

61

Hillside Farm

Butler's Hull

Great Swart Barn

Byroe Hill

Riverside Farm

Greenbank Woodhouse Farm

Heaton

Mill Hill House

Gottam Farm

Windmill Hill

Heaton Marsh

RAILWAY

2

460

3

Richmond Farm

ROAD HEATON

Heaton Hall

Heaton Marsh

Aldcliffe Marsh

RIVER LUNE

Heaton Park House

Morecambe

LA3

Low Wood

Sewage Works

4

Wymber Cottage

Wymber Hill Farm

Colloway Farm

Colloway Pool

Field

459

Down Lodge

DOWNFIELD

MOSS

Colloway Hill

Colloway Marsh

ook

5

27

MIDDLETON LANE

KEVIN GRO.

St. Helen's C of E Prim. Sch.

ROAD

6

Middlepool Bridge

PEDDER DR.

OLD PEDDER

GLEBE

LANCASTER ROAD

Manor House Fm.

CHA ENHAM

Wandales Point

Sewage Works

458

MAIN

CHAPEL

DIDDER

STREET

CHAPEL

BACK

STEPHENS

OVERTON

THE GRO.

ORCHARDS

VIEW

MIDDLE PK.

7

Lades Bridge

South Farm

Overton Hall Farm

Hall Greave

ST HELEN'S RD

LANE

Dunnal Point

LANCASTER

Parkinson Plantation

Shaw Plantation

8

457

Lades Marsh

HALL GREAVES CL.

BAZIL GRO.

BAZIL LANE

CHAPEL POOL

Fiskes Point

Ice House Hill

Meldham Wood

Ashton (Club Ho

Waterloo

Woodside

9

Bazil

Bazil Farm

Ferry Cottage

Bazil Point

Pennyhill

Seafield Plantation

Long Plantation

Wood Bridge

Wood Bridge

Bazil Sand

Pinnacle Mussel Bed

RIVER LUNE

A588

A B C 36 D E F

43 44 45

Fishnet

Glasson Sailing Club

Lighthouse (dis.)

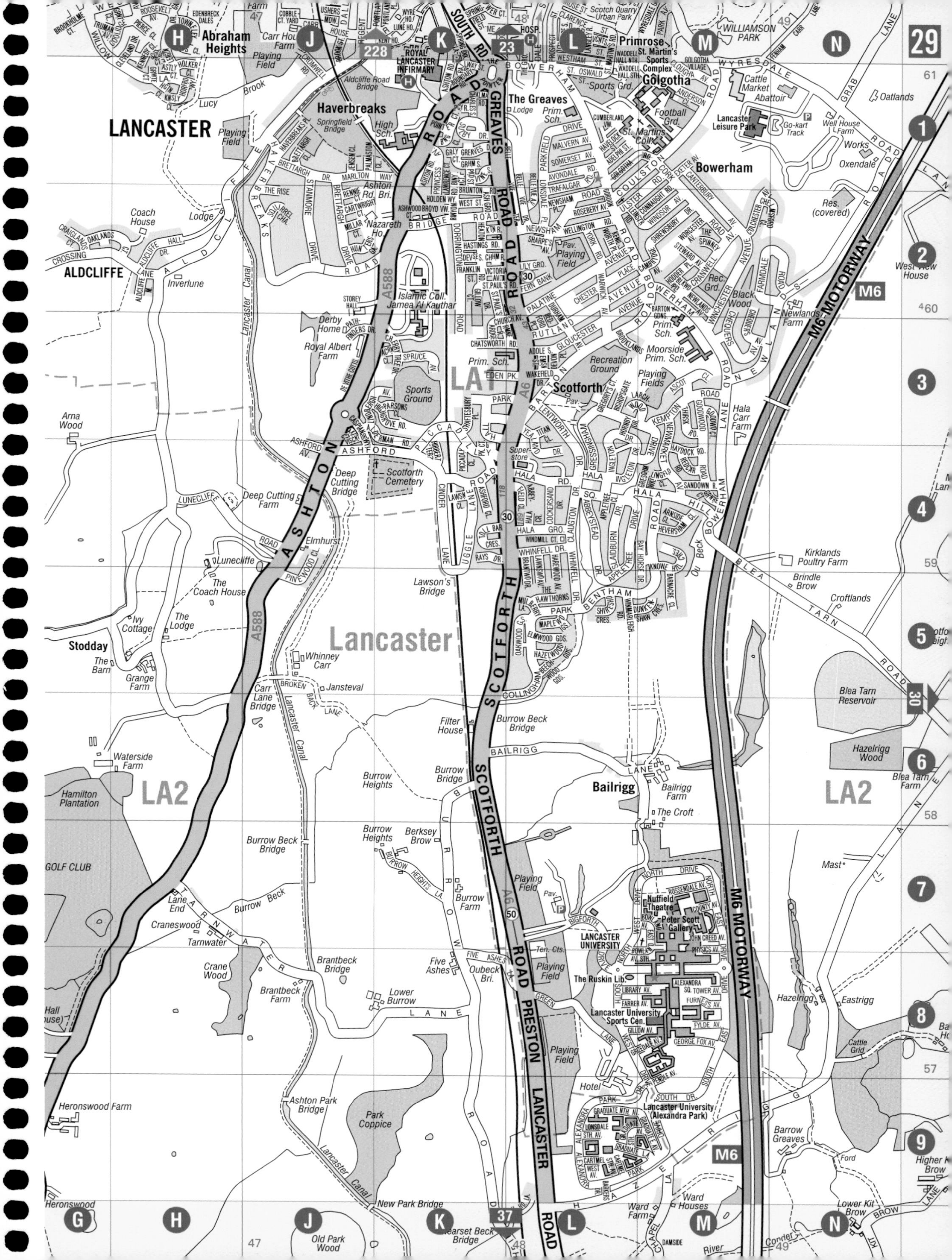
LANCASTER
Abraham Heights
Haverbreaks
ALDCLIFFE
The Greaves
Primrose
Golgotha
Bowerham
Lancaster Leisure Park
Cattle Market Abattoir
Royal Lancaster Infirmary
Scotforth
Scotforth Cemetery
Recreation Ground
Lancaster
Stodday
Bailrigg
LANCASTER UNIVERSITY
Lancaster University (Alexandra Park)
Nuffield Theatre
Peter Scott Gallery
The Ruskin Lib.
Lancaster University Sports Cen.
Blea Tarn Reservoir
Hazelrigg Wood
Hamilton Plantation
GOLF CLUB
Heronswood Farm
Park Coppice
Old Park Wood
LA1
LA2
M6 MOTORWAY
A588
A6
SCOTFORTH ROAD
LANCASTER ROAD
PRESTON ROAD
ASHTON ROAD
GREAVES ROAD
Lancaster Canal
Islamic Coll. Jamea Al Kauthar
Royal Albert Farm
Deep Cutting Bridge
Burrow Heights
Burrow Beck Bridge
Filter House
Ward Farm
Ward Houses
228
23
30
37
G H J K L M N
1 2 3 4 5 6 7 8 9
47 48 49
56 57 58 59 60 61

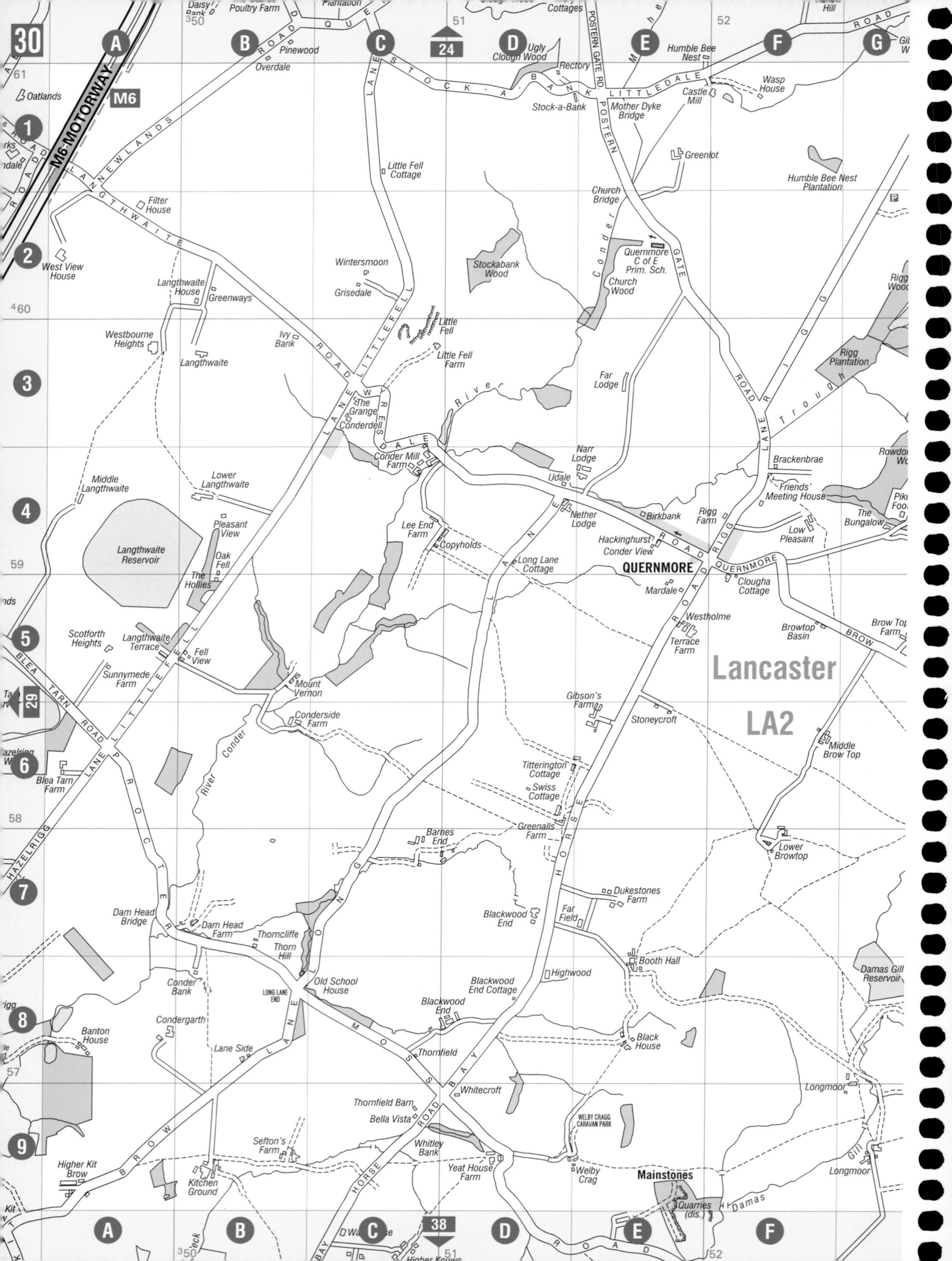

M6-MOTORWAY
M6
Oatlands
Poultry Farm
Pinewood
Overdale
NEWLANDS
LANGTHWAITE
Filter House
West View House
Langthwaite House
Greenways
Westbourne Heights
Langthwaite
Ivy Bank
Wintersmoon
Grisedale
Little Fell Cottage
Little Fell
Little Fell Farm
STOCK-A-BANK
Ugly Clough Wood
Rectory
Stock-a-Bank
POSTERN GATE RD.
POSTERN
Mother Dyke Bridge
Humble Bee Nest
LITTLEDALE
Castle Mill
Wasp House
Greenlot
Humble Bee Nest Plantation
Church Bridge
Conder
Quernmore C of E Prim. Sch.
Church Wood
Stockabank Wood
GATE
Rigg Wood
Rigg Plantation
Trough
RIGG LANE
Far Lodge
River
The Grange
Conderdell
WYRESDALE
Conder Mill Farm
Middle Langthwaite
Lower Langthwaite
Narr Lodge
Udale
Brackenbrae
Friends' Meeting House
Rowdon Wood
Langthwaite Reservoir
Pleasant View
Oak Fell
The Hollies
Lee End Farm
Copyholds
Nether Lodge
Birkbank
Rigg Farm
Low Pleasant
The Bungalow
Hackinghurst
Conder View
QUERNMORE
Long Lane Cottage
Mardale
Clougha Cottage
Westholme
Terrace Farm
Browtop Basin
Brow Top Farm
BROW
Scotforth Heights
Langthwaite Terrace
Fell View
Sunnymede Farm
Mount Vernon
LITTLEFELL LANE
BLEA TARN ROAD
Lancaster
LA2
Conderside Farm
Gibson's Farm
Stoneycroft
Middle Brow Top
Blea Tarn Farm
River Conder
Titterington Cottage
Swiss Cottage
HORSE
Greenalls Farm
Barnes End
Lower Browtop
HAZELRIGG
PROCTER
LONG
Dukestones Farm
Blackwood End
Far Field
Dam Head Bridge
Dam Head Farm
Thorncliffe
Thorn Hill
Booth Hall
Highwood
Damas Gill Reservoir
Conder Bank
LONG LANE END
Old School House
Blackwood End Cottage
Blackwood End
Banton House
Condergarth
Lane Side
MOSS
Black House
Thornfield
Longmoor
Whitecroft
Thornfield Barn
Bella Vista
WELBY CRAGG CARAVAN PARK
Sefton's Farm
Whitley Bank
Higher Kit Brow
BROW
BAY
HORSE ROAD
Yeat House Farm
Welby Crag
Mainstones
Kitchen Ground
Quarries (dis.)
Damas
Gill
ROAD
24
29
38
A
B
C
D
E
F
G
1
2
3
4
5
6
7
8
9
350
51
52
461
460
59
58
57

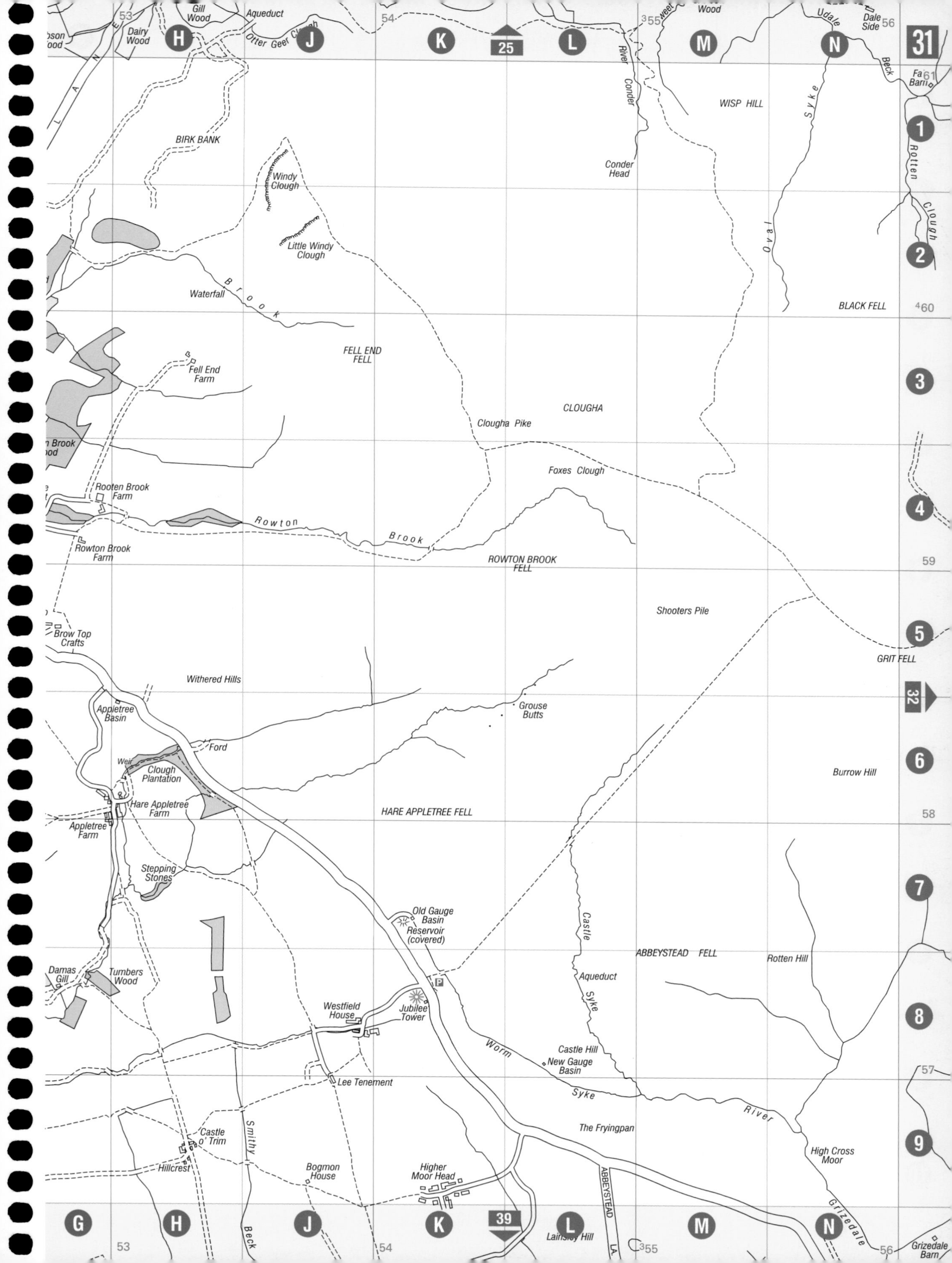
Gill Wood
Aqueduct
Dairy Wood
Otter Geer Clough
25
Wood
Udale
Dale Side
River Conder
Beck
WISP HILL
Syke
BIRK BANK
Windy Clough
Conder Head
Rotten Clough
Oval
Little Windy Clough
Waterfall
Brook
BLACK FELL
FELL END FELL
Fell End Farm
CLOUGHA
Clougha Pike
Foxes Clough
Rooten Brook Farm
Rowton Brook
Rowton Brook Farm
ROWTON BROOK FELL
Shooters Pile
Brow Top Crafts
GRIT FELL
Withered Hills
32
Grouse Butts
Appletree Basin
Ford
Weir
Clough Plantation
Burrow Hill
Hare Appletree Farm
HARE APPLETREE FELL
Appletree Farm
Stepping Stones
Old Gauge Basin
Reservoir (covered)
Castle
Damas Gill
Tumbers Wood
ABBEYSTEAD FELL
Rotten Hill
Aqueduct
Syke
Westfield House
Jubilee Tower
Worm
Castle Hill
New Gauge Basin
Lee Tenement
Syke
River
Castle o' Trim
Smithy
The Fryingpan
High Cross Moor
Hillcrest
Bogmon House
Higher Moor Head
ABBEYSTEAD LA.
Grizedale
39
Beck
Lainsley Hill
Grizedale Barn

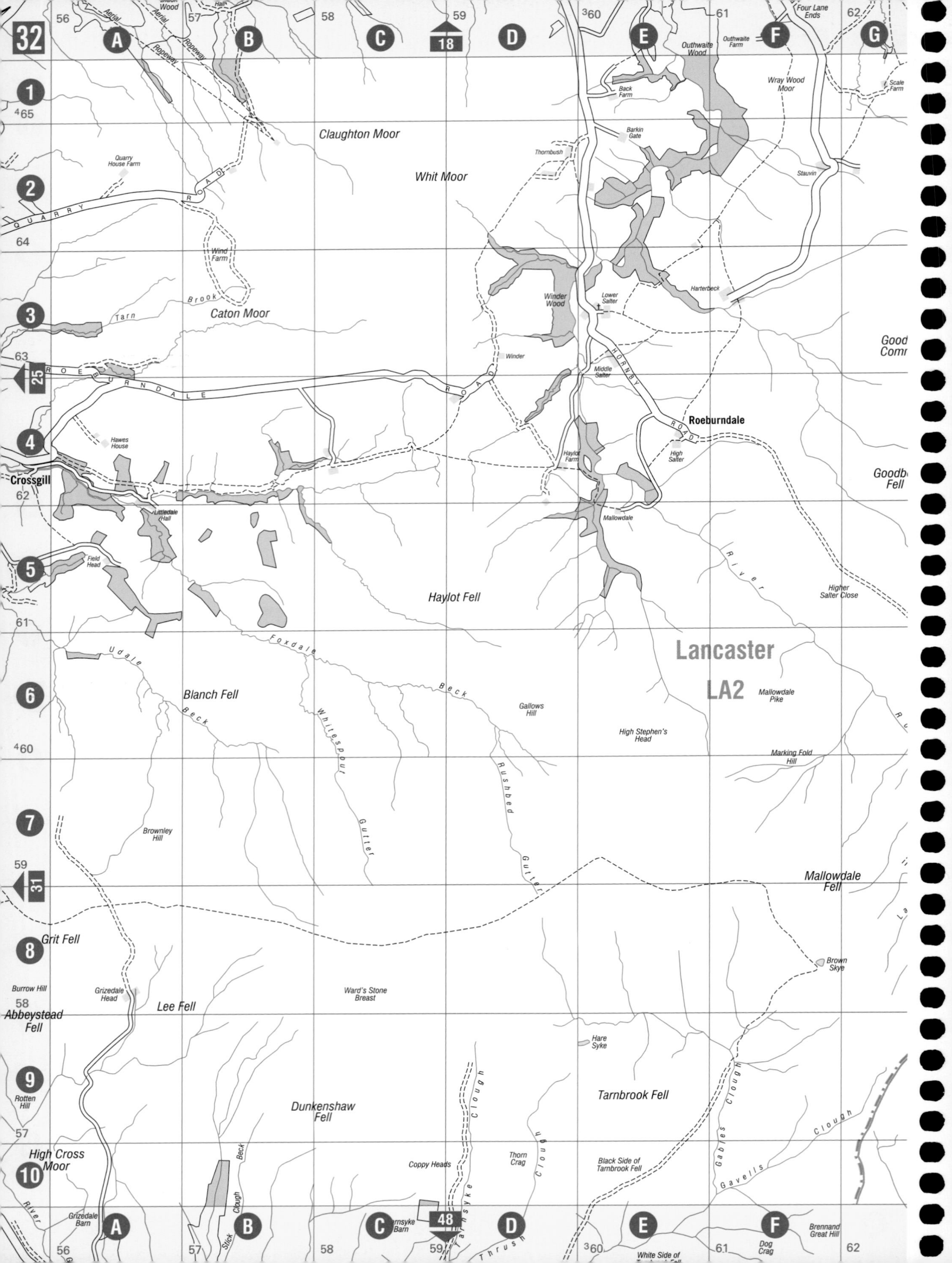

32
Claughton Moor
Whit Moor
Caton Moor
Quarry House Farm
Wind Farm
Quarry Road
Roeburndale Road
Hornby Road
Roeburndale
Crossgill
Hawes House
Littledale Hall
Field Head
Back Farm
Barkin Gate
Thornbush
Outhwaite Wood
Outhwaite Farm
Wray Wood Moor
Scale Farm
Stauvin
Harterbeck
Four Lane Ends
Winder Wood
Lower Salter
Winder
Middle Salter
Haylot Farm
High Salter
Mallowdale
Haylot Fell
Blanch Fell
Foxdale Beck
Udale Beck
Whitespout Gutter
Rushbed Gutter
Gallows Hill
High Stephen's Head
Lancaster LA2
Mallowdale Pike
Marking Fold Hill
Higher Salter Close
River
Goodber Fell
Brownley Hill
Mallowdale Fell
Grit Fell
Burrow Hill
Grizedale Head
Abbeystead Fell
Lee Fell
Ward's Stone Breast
Brown Skye
Hare Syke
Tarnbrook Fell
Dunkenshaw Fell
Rotten Hill
High Cross Moor
Coppy Heads
Thorn Crag
Black Side of Tarnbrook Fell
Gables Clough
Gavells Clough
Brennand Great Hill
Dog Crag
Grizedale Barn
Stick Clough
Beck
Tarnsyke
Clough
Aerial Ropeway
18
25
31
48

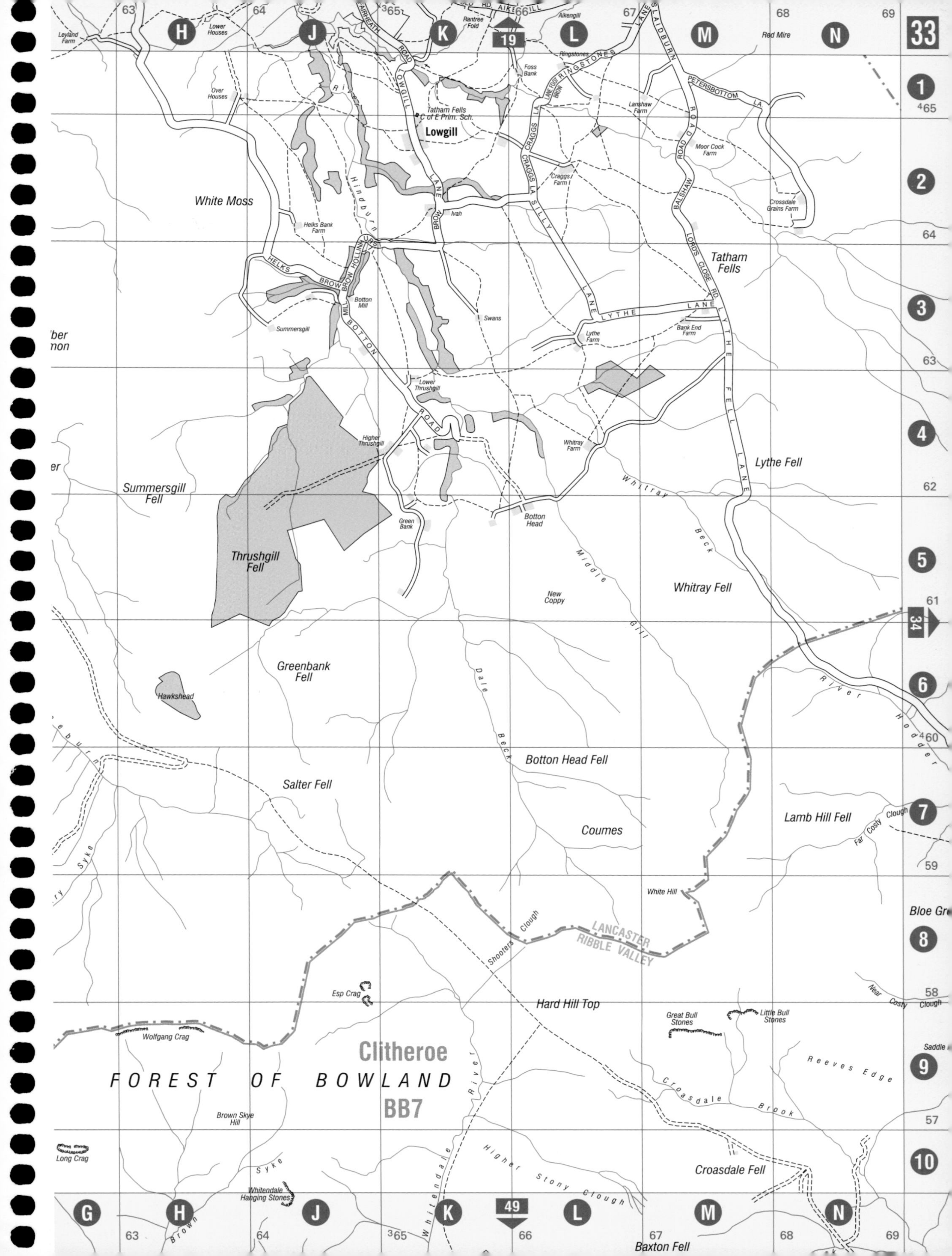

H
J
K
L
M
N
19
Lower Houses
Leyland Farm
Rantree Fold
Aikengill
Red Mire
Ringstones
Foss Bank
Over Houses
Tatham Fells C of E Prim. Sch.
Lowgill
Lanshaw Farm
Moor Cock Farm
Craggs Farm
Crossdale Grains Farm
White Moss
Helks Bank Farm
Ivah
Tatham Fells
Botton Mill
Swans
Summersgill
Lythe Farm
Bank End Farm
Lower Thrushgill
Higher Thrushgill
Whitray Farm
Lythe Fell
Summersgill Fell
Green Bank
Botton Head
Thrushgill Fell
New Coppy
Whitray Fell
Whitray Beck
Middle Gill
34
River Hodder
Greenbank Fell
Hawkshead
Dale Beck
Botton Head Fell
Salter Fell
Lamb Hill Fell
Far Costy Clough
Coumes
White Hill
Bloe Gr
Shooters Clough
LANCASTER
RIBBLE VALLEY
Esp Crag
Hard Hill Top
Great Bull Stones
Little Bull Stones
Near Costy Clough
Wolfgang Crag
Clitheroe
Saddle
Reeves Edge
FOREST OF BOWLAND
BB7
River Whitendale
Croasdale Brook
Brown Skye Hill
Long Crag
Higher Stony Clough
Croasdale Fell
Whitendale Hanging Stones
Syke
49
G
Baxton Fell
1
2
3
4
5
6
7
8
9
10
63
64
365
66
67
68
69
465
64
63
62
61
460
59
58
57

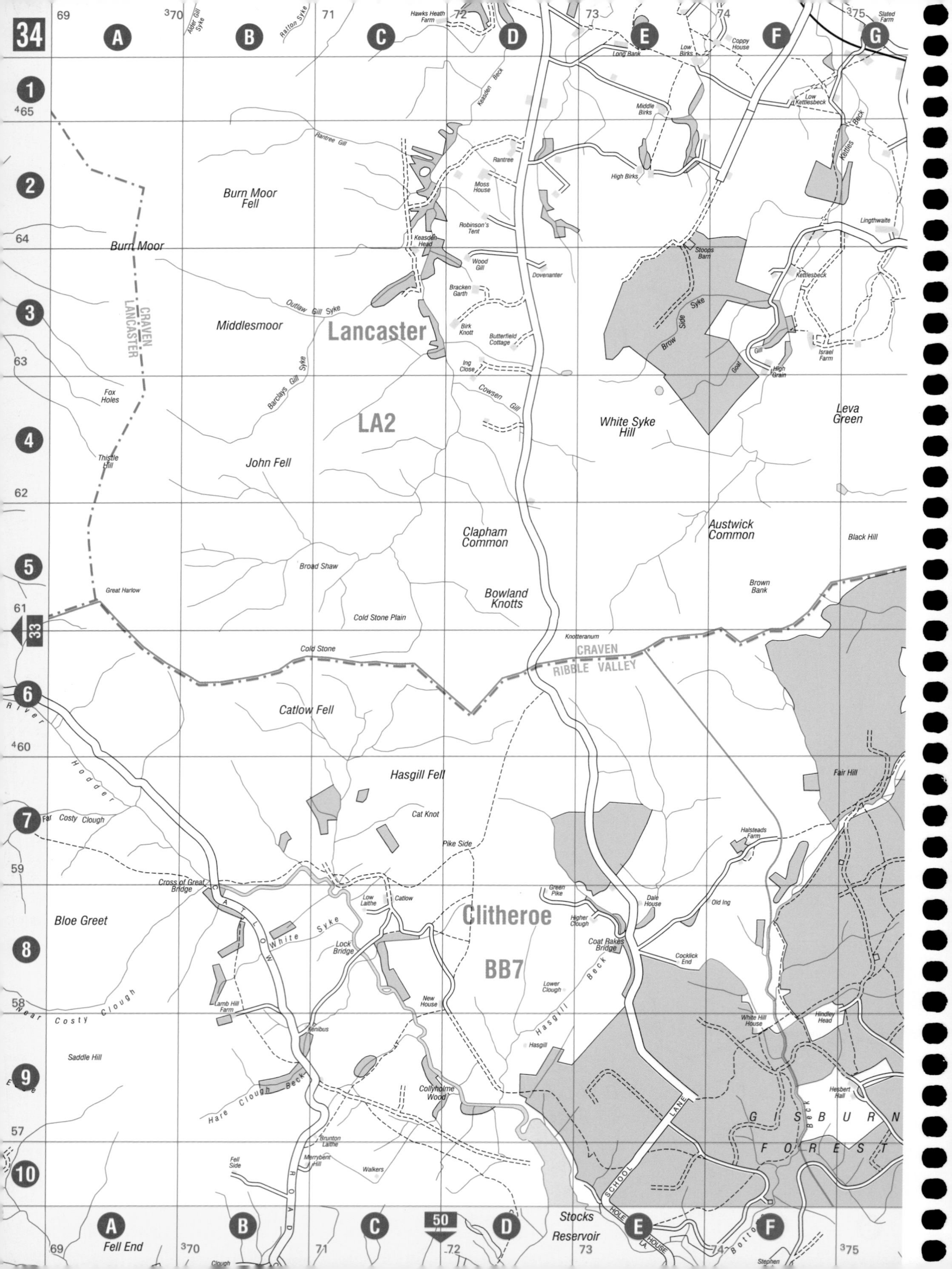
Burn Moor Fell
Burn Moor
Middlesmoor
Lancaster
LA2
John Fell
Clapham Common
Bowland Knotts
White Syke Hill
Austwick Common
Leva Green
Black Hill
Broad Shaw
Cold Stone Plain
Cold Stone
Catlow Fell
Hasgill Fell
Cat Knot
Pike Side
Clitheroe
BB7
Bloe Greet
Saddle Hill
Collyholme Wood
Fair Hill
Stocks Reservoir
Fell End
CRAVEN
LANCASTER
RIBBLE VALLEY
Keasden Head
Robinson's Tent
Moss House
Rantree
Dovenanter
Wood Gill
Bracken Garth
Birk Knott
Butterfield Cottage
Ing Close
Stoops Barn
Kettlesbeck
Israel Farm
High Grain
Lingthwaite
High Birks
Middle Birks
Long Bank
Low Birks
Coppy House
Low Kettlesbeck
Hawks Heath Farm
Slated Farm
Fox Holes
Thistle Hill
Great Harlow
Knotteranum
Brown Bank
Halsteads Farm
Cross of Great Bridge
Low Laithe
Catlow
Lock Bridge
Green Pike
Higher Clough
Coat Rakes Bridge
Dale House
Old Ing
Cocklick End
Lower Clough
New House
Lamb Hill Farm
Kenibus
Hasgill
White Hill House
Hindley Head
Hesbert Hall
Brunton Laithe
Merrybent Hill
Fell Side
Walkers
GISBURN FOREST
SCHOOL LANE
HOLE HOUSE LA
CATLOW ROAD
River Hodder
Far Costy Clough
Near Costy Clough
Hare Clough Beck
White Syke
Hasgill Beck
Brow Side Syke
Goat Gill
Cowsen Gill
Barclays Gill Syke
Outlaw Gill Syke
Rantree Gill
Keasden Beck
Kettles Beck
Ratton Syke
Alder Gill Syke
33
50

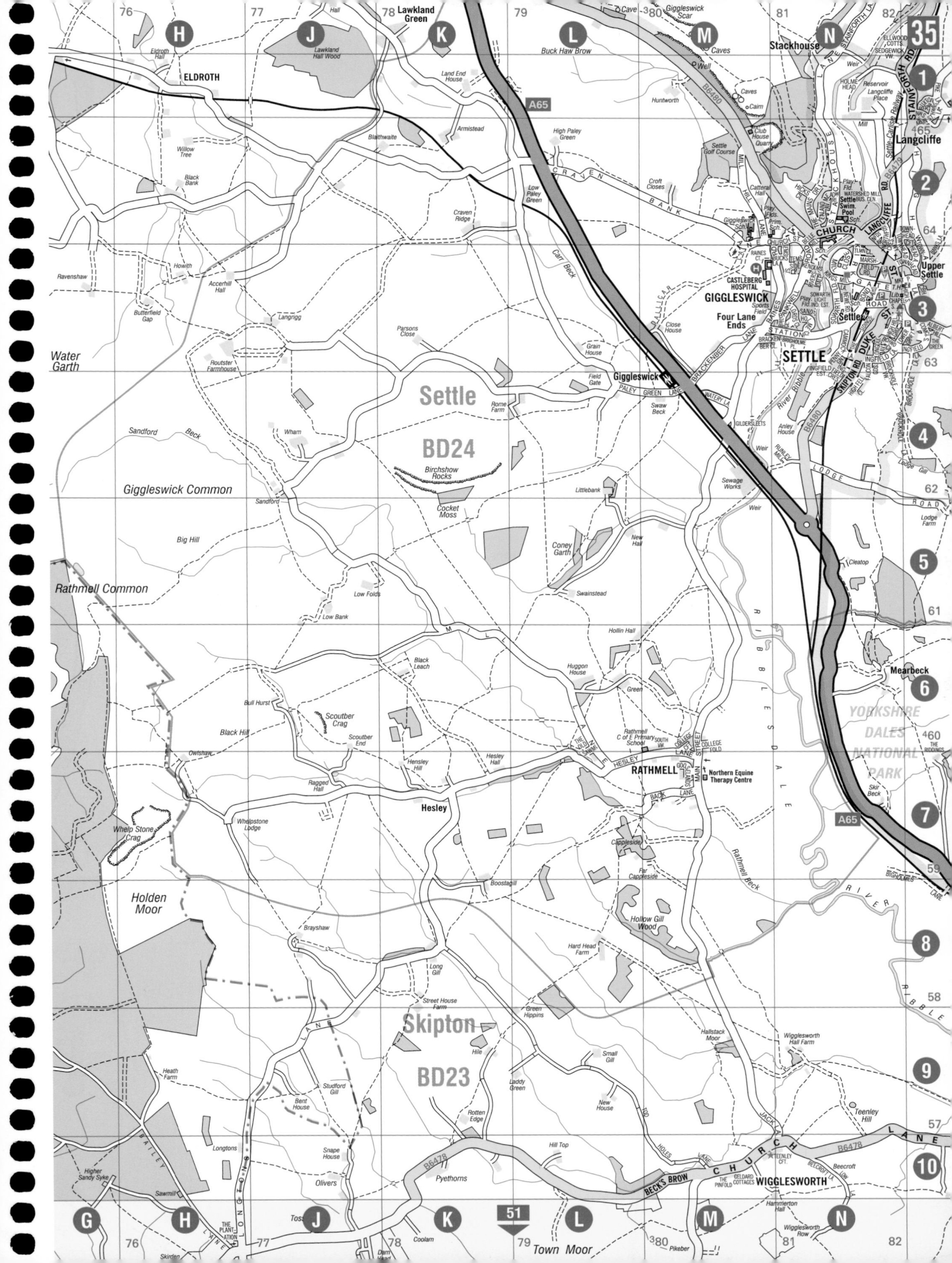
Lawkland Green
Eldroth Hall
ELDROTH
Lawkland Hall Wood
Land End House
Buck Haw Brow
Giggleswick Scar
Stackhouse
Caves
Huntworth
A65
Armistead
Blaithwaite
Willow Tree
High Paley Green
Settle Golf Course
Club House Quarry
Langcliffe
Black Bank
CRAVEN BANK
Croft Closes
Low Paley Green
Craven Ridge
Carr Beck
CASTLEBERG HOSPITAL
GIGGLESWICK
Four Lane Ends
SETTLE
Upper Settle
Ravenshaw
Howith
Accerhill Hall
Butterfield Gap
Langgrig
Parsons Close
Water Garth
Routster Farmhouse
Grain House
Field Gate
Giggleswick
PALEY GREEN LANE
Settle
BD24
Rome Farm
Swaw Beck
Sandford Beck
Wham
Birchshow Rocks
Giggleswick Common
Sandford
Cocket Moss
Littlebank
Sewage Works
Weir
Lodge Farm
Big Hill
New Hall
Coney Garth
Cleatop
Rathmell Common
Low Folds
Swainstead
Low Bank
MILL
Hollin Hall
Black Leach
Huggon House
Mearbeck
Green
Bull Hurst
Scoutber Crag
Scoutber End
YORKSHIRE DALES NATIONAL PARK
Black Hill
Rathmell C of E Primary School
Owlshaw
Hensley Hill
Hesley Hall
HESLEY LANE
RATHMELL
Northern Equine Therapy Centre
Ragged Hall
Hesley
BACK LANE
Skir Beck
Whelpstone Lodge
A65
Whelp Stone Crag
Cappleside
Far Cappleside
Rathmell Beck
Holden Moor
Boostagill
RIVER RIBBLE
Hollow Gill Wood
Brayshaw
Hard Head Farm
Long Gill
Street House Farm
Green Hippins
Skipton
BD23
Hallstack Moor
Wigglesworth Hall Farm
Heath Farm
Hile
Small Gill
Studford Gill
Laddy Green
Bent House
New House
Teenley Hill
Rotten Edge
Longtons
Hill Top
B6478
Snape House
Higher Sandy Syke
Pyethorns
BECK'S BROW
CHURCH LANE
WIGGLESWORTH
Beecroft
Sawmill
Olivers
Hammerton Hall
Toss
51
Coolam
Town Moor
Pikeber
Wigglesworth Row
Skirden

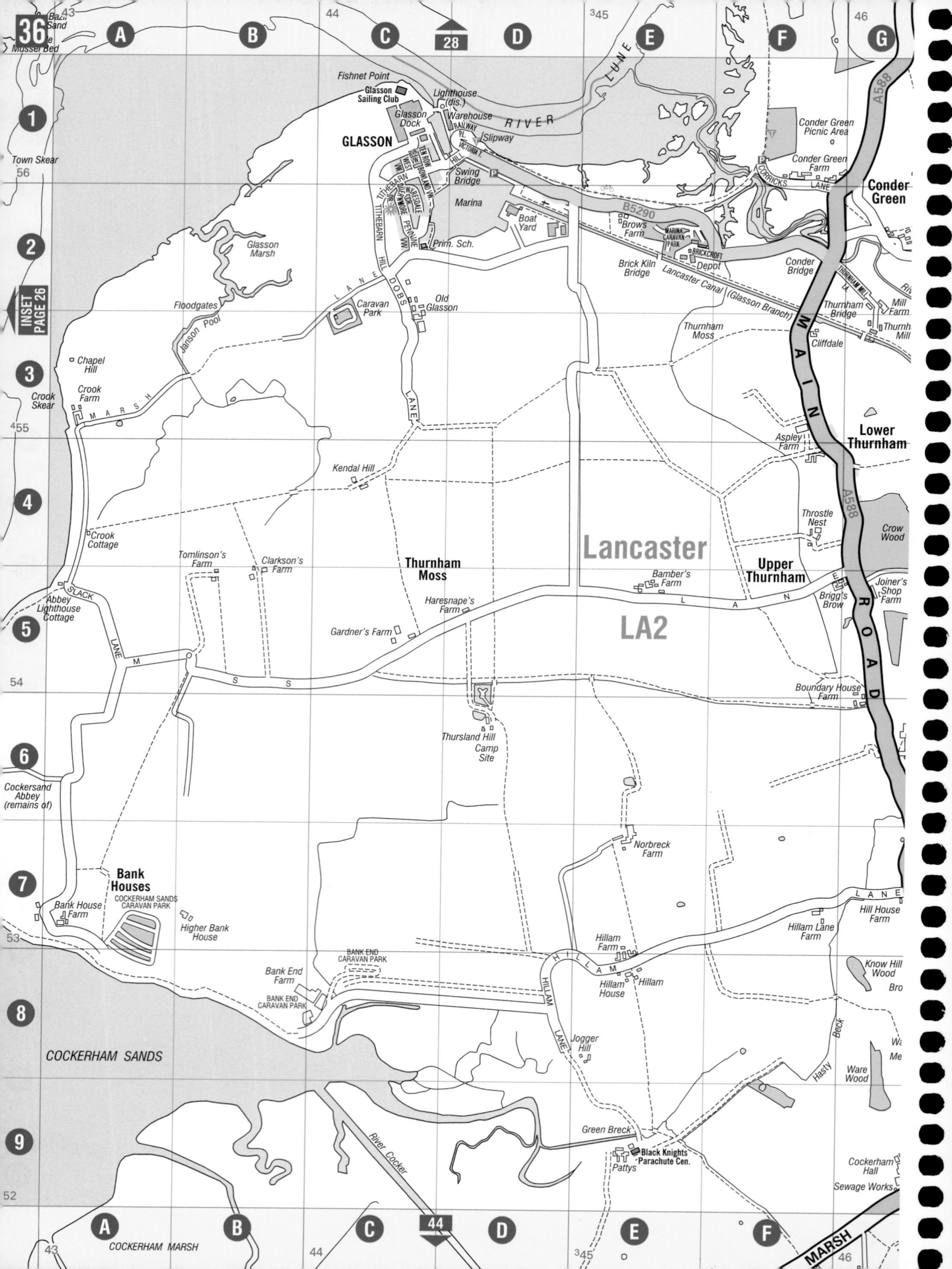

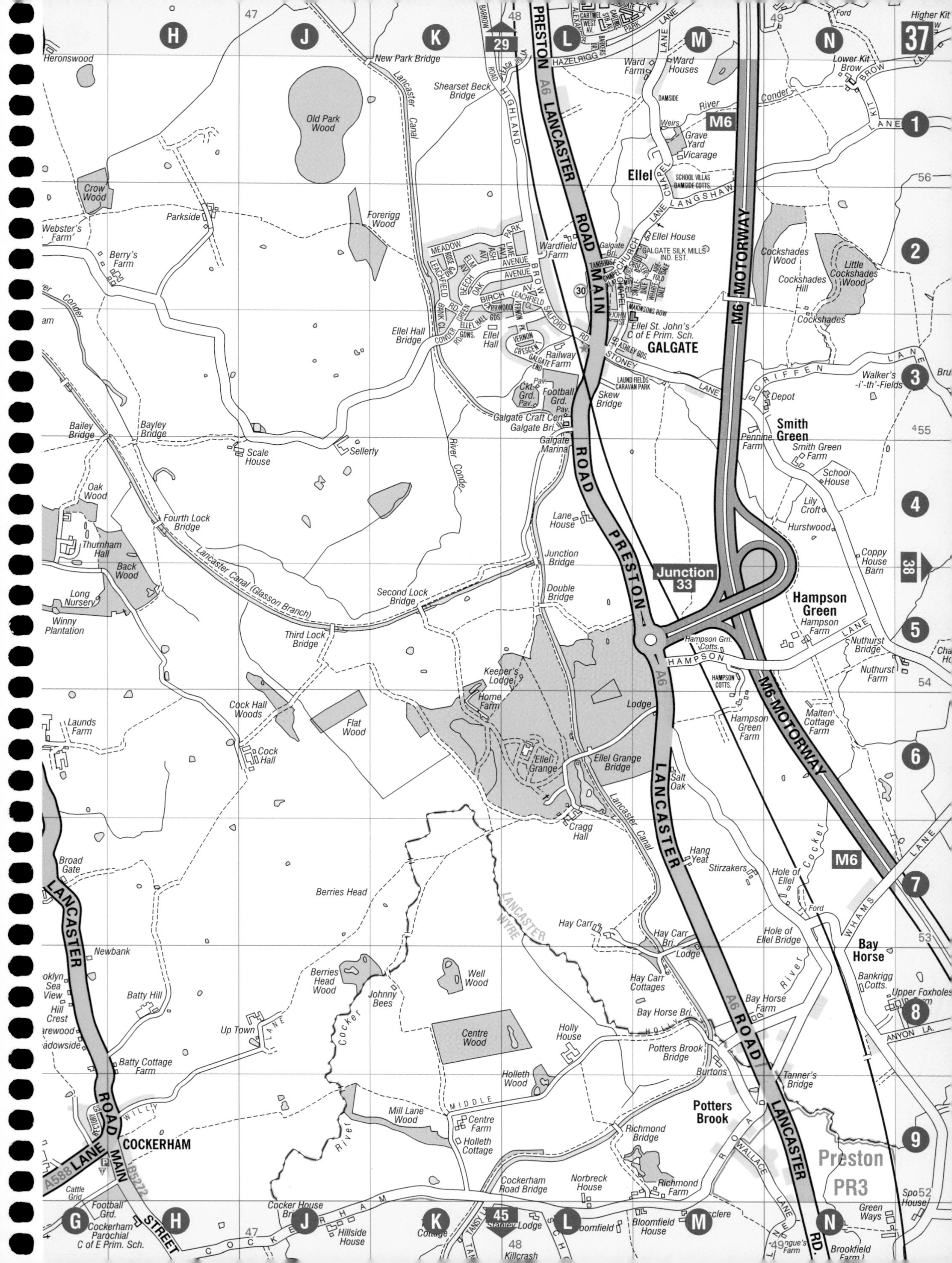

H
J
K
L
M
N
29
45
38
Heronswood
New Park Bridge
Old Park Wood
Shearset Beck Bridge
Lancaster Canal
Crow Wood
Parkside
Webster's Farm
Berry's Farm
Forerigg Wood
Ward Farm
Ward Houses
Damside
River Conder
Weirs
Grave Yard
Vicarage
M6
Ellel
School Villas
Damside Cotts.
Langshaw
Ellel House
Galgate Silk Mills Ind. Est.
Cockshades Wood
Little Cockshades Wood
Cockshades Hill
Cockshades
M6 Motorway
Wardfield Farm
Galgate
Ellel St. John's C of E Prim. Sch.
Ellel Hall Bridge
Ellel Hall
Railway Farm
Laund Fields Caravan Park
Skew Bridge
Scriffen Lane
Depot
Walker's -i'-th'-Fields
Smith Green
Pennine Farm
Smith Green Farm
School House
Lily Croft
Hurstwood
Coppy House Barn
Bailey Bridge
Bayley Bridge
Scale House
Sellerly
Galgate Craft Cen.
Galgate Bri.
Galgate Marina
River Conder
Oak Wood
Fourth Lock Bridge
Thurnham Hall
Back Wood
Lancaster Canal (Glasson Branch)
Long Nursery
Winny Plantation
Second Lock Bridge
Third Lock Bridge
Lane House
Junction Bridge
Double Bridge
Junction 33
Hampson Green
Hampson Farm
Nuthurst Lane
Nuthurst Bridge
Nuthurst Farm
Hampson Grn. Cotts.
Hampson
Hampson Cotts.
Keeper's Lodge
Home Farm
Flat Wood
Cock Hall Woods
Cock Hall
Launds Farm
Lodge
Hampson Green Farm
Malten Cottage Farm
Ellel Grange
Ellel Grange Bridge
Salt Oak
Cragg Hall
Lancaster Canal
Broad Gate
Berries Head
Hang Yeat
Stirzakers
Hole of Ellel
M6
Lancaster Wyre
Hay Carr
Hay Carr Bri.
Lodge
Ford
Hole of Ellel Bridge
Whams Lane
Bay Horse
Bankrigg Cotts.
Upper Foxholes
Newbank
Berries Head Wood
Johnny Bees
Well Wood
Hay Carr Cottages
River Cocker
Batty Hill
Up Town
Centre Wood
Holly House
Bay Horse Bri.
Bay Horse Farm
Anyon La.
Potters Brook Bridge
Burtons
Tanner's Bridge
Batty Cottage Farm
Holleth Wood
Middle
Mill Lane Wood
Centre Farm
Holleth Cottage
Potters Brook
Richmond Bridge
Cockerham
Lancaster Road
Main Street
A588
B5272
Cattle Grid
Football Grd.
Cockerham Parochial C of E Prim. Sch.
Cockerham Road Bridge
Norbreck House
Richmond Farm
Wallace Lane
Preston PR3
Cocker House Bri.
Hillside House
Cottage
Lodge
Bloomfield House
Green Ways
Brookfield Farm
Killcrash
A6 Lancaster Road
Preston Road
Main Road
Hazelrigg
Highland Brow
Salford Rd.
Stoney Lane
Kit Brow Lane
Lower Kit Brow
Higher Kit
G
1
2
3
4
5
6
7
8
9
47
48
49
52
53
54
55
56

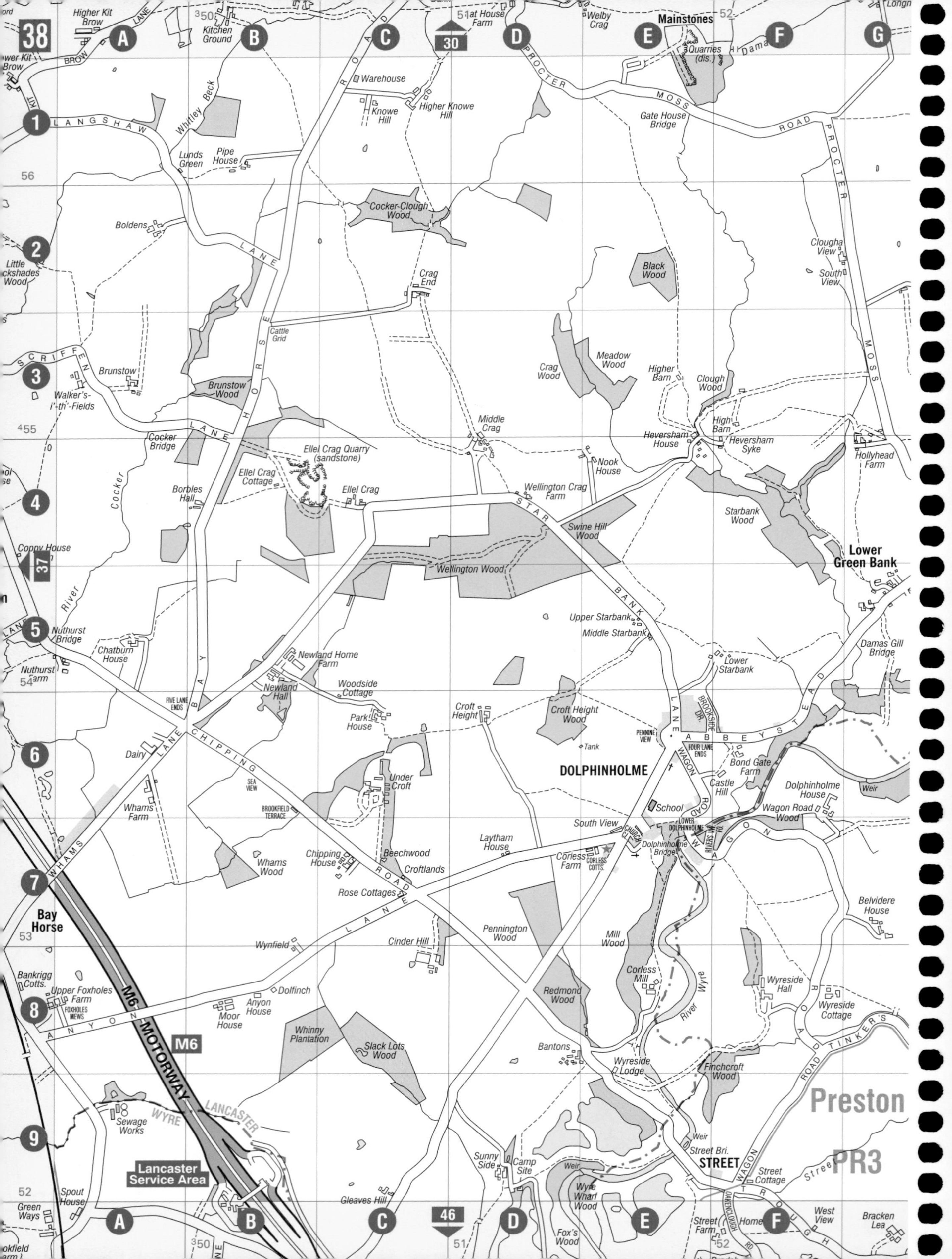
Higher Kit Brow
Kitchen Ground
Flat House Farm
30
Welby Crag
Mainstones
Quarries (dis.)
Lower Kit Brow
Warehouse
Knowe Hill
Higher Knowe Hill
PROCTER MOSS ROAD
Gate House Bridge
LANGSHAW LANE
Whitley Beck
Lunds Green
Pipe House
Cocker-Clough Wood
Boldens
Little Crookshades Wood
Crag End
Black Wood
Clougha View
South View
Cattle Grid
SCRIFFEN LANE
Brunstow
Walker's-i'-th'-Fields
Brunstow Wood
Meadow Wood
Crag Wood
Higher Barn
Clough Wood
Middle Crag
High Barn
Heversham House
Heversham Syke
Hollyhead Farm
Cocker Bridge
Ellel Crag Quarry (sandstone)
Ellel Crag Cottage
Ellel Crag
Nook House
Wellington Crag Farm
Borbles Hall
Swine Hill Wood
Starbank Wood
STAR BANK
Coppy House
37
Wellington Wood
Lower Green Bank
River Cocker
Upper Starbank
Middle Starbank
Nuthurst Bridge
Chatburn House
Newland Home Farm
Nuthurst Farm
Woodside Cottage
Newland Hall
Lower Starbank
Damas Gill Bridge
FIVE LANE ENDS
BAY HORSE LANE
Croft Height
Park House
Croft Height Wood
BROOKSIDE DR.
PENNINE VIEW
ABBEYSTEAD
FOUR LANE ENDS
Tank
DOLPHINHOLME
Bond Gate Farm
Dairy
SEA VIEW
Under Croft
Castle Hill
Dolphinholme House
Weir
BROOKFIELD TERRACE
School
Whams Farm
Wagon Road Wood
South View
LOWER DOLPHINHOLME
RIVERSIDE
Laytham House
Dolphinholme Bridge
CHURCH
Chipping House
Beechwood
Whams Wood
Corless Farm
CORLESS COTTS.
WHAMS LANE
CHIPPING ROAD
Croftlands
Rose Cottages
Belvidere House
Bay Horse
Pennington Wood
Mill Wood
Cinder Hill
Wynfield
Corless Mill
River Wyre
Wyreside Hall
Bankrigg Cotts.
Upper Foxholes Farm
FOXHOLES MEWS
Dolfinch
Redmond Wood
Wyreside Cottage
ANYON LANE
Anyon House
Moor House
M6 MOTORWAY
M6
Whinny Plantation
Slack Lots Wood
Bantons
Wyreside Lodge
TINKER'S ROAD
Finchcroft Wood
Sewage Works
WYRE
LANCASTER
Preston
Weir
Street Bri.
Lancaster Service Area
Sunny Side
Camp Site
STREET
WAGON ROAD
PR3
Street Cottage
Spout House
Green Ways
Gleaves Hill
Wyre Wharf Wood
46
Street Farm
Home
West View
Bracken Lea
OAKENCLOUGH RD
TROUGH
Fox's Wood
A
B
C
D
E
F
G
1
2
3
4
5
6
7
8
9
350
51
52
56
455
54
53
52

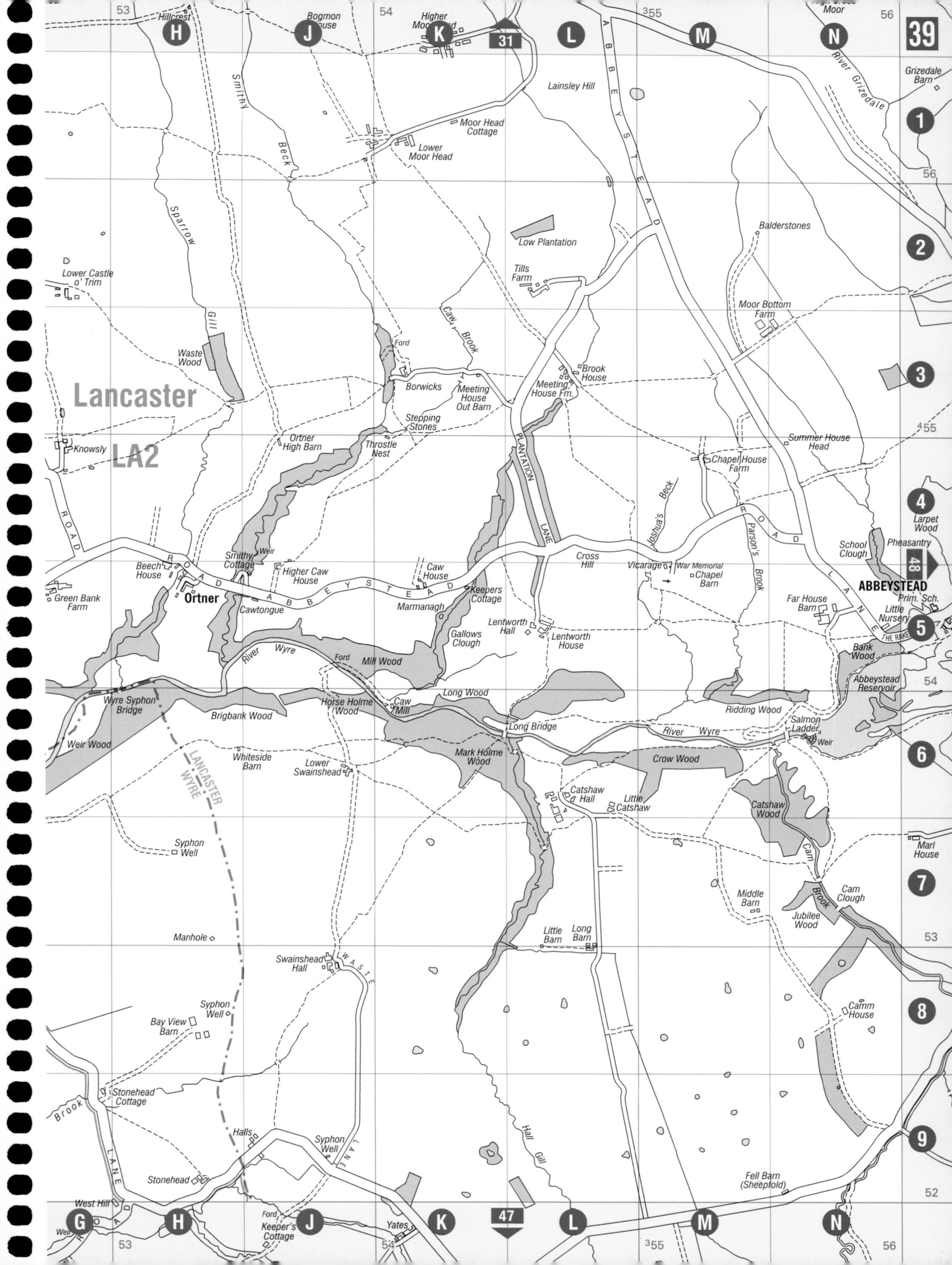

Hillcrest
Bogmon House
Higher Moor Head
31
Lainsley Hill
River Grizedale
Grizedale Barn
Smithy Beck
Moor Head Cottage
Lower Moor Head
ABBEYSTEAD
Sparrow
Balderstones
Low Plantation
Lower Castle o' Trim
Tills Farm
Moor Bottom Farm
Gill
Caw Brook
Ford
Waste Wood
Brook House
Lancaster
Borwicks
Meeting House Out Barn
Meeting House Fm.
Stepping Stones
Knowsly
LA2
Ortner High Barn
Throstle Nest
PLANTATION LANE
Summer House Head
Chapel House Farm
Joshua's Beck
ROAD
Parson's Brook
Larpet Wood
School Clough
Pheasantry
48
Smithy Cottage
Weir
Cross Hill
Beech House
Higher Caw House
Caw House
Vicarage
War Memorial
Chapel Barn
ABBEYSTEAD
Green Bank Farm
Ortner
ABBEYSTEAD ROAD
Keepers Cottage
Far House Barn
Prim. Sch.
Little Nursery
Cawtongue
Marmanagh
Lentworth Hall
Lentworth House
THE RAKE
LANE
Gallows Clough
River Wyre
Ford
Mill Wood
Bank Wood
Abbeystead Reservoir
Long Wood
Wyre Syphon Bridge
Horse Holme Wood
Caw Mill
Ridding Wood
Brigbank Wood
Long Bridge
River Wyre
Salmon Ladder
Weir
Weir Wood
LANCASTER WYRE
Whiteside Barn
Lower Swainshead
Mark Holme Wood
Crow Wood
Catshaw Hall
Little Catshaw
Catshaw Wood
Syphon Well
Marl House
Cam
Cam Clough
Brook
Middle Barn
Jubilee Wood
Little Barn
Long Barn
Manhole
Swainshead Hall
WASTE
Camm House
Syphon Well
Bay View Barn
Brook
Stonehead Cottage
Hall Gill
Halls
Syphon Well
LANE
Stonehead
Fell Barn (Sheepfold)
West Hill
Weir
ROAD
Ford
Keeper's Cottage
Yates
47
G
H
J
K
L
M
N
1
2
3
4
5
6
7
8
9
53
54
355
56
455
54
53
52

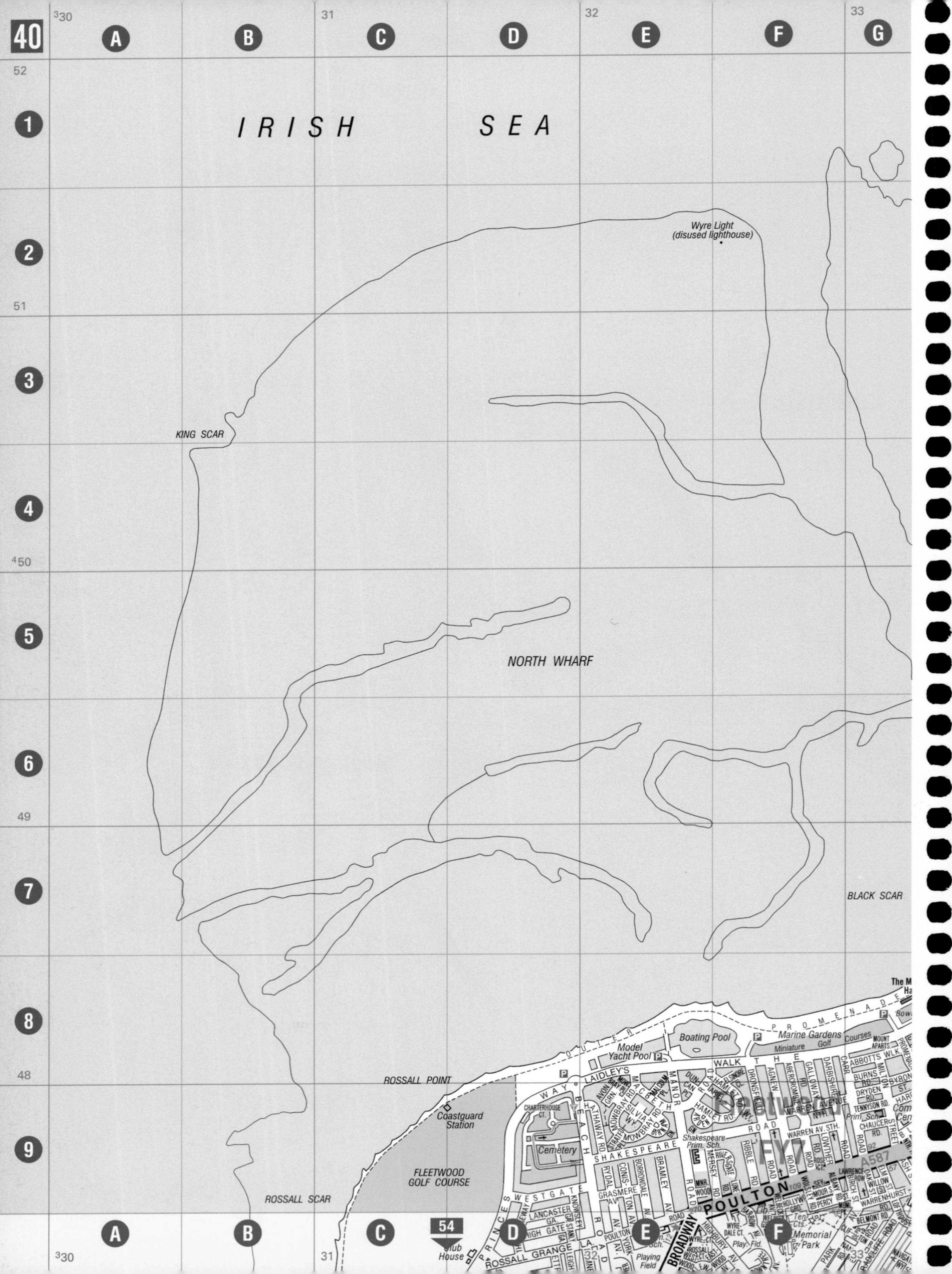

³30   A   B   31   C   D   32   E   F   33   G

52

1

IRISH   SEA

2

51

3

KING SCAR

Wyre Light
(disused lighthouse)

4

⁴50

5

NORTH WHARF

6

49

7

BLACK SCAR

8

The M
Ha

P R O M E N A D E

P   Bow

Marine Gardens   MOUNT
Boating Pool   Miniature Golf   Courses   APARTS.

Model   P
Yacht Pool

WALK

THE

48

LAIDLEY'S

ROSSALL POINT

Fleetwood
FY7

9

Coastguard
Station

Cemetery

Shakespeare
Prim. Sch.

POULTON
A587

54

FLEETWOOD
GOLF COURSE

ROSSALL SCAR

W E S T G A T E

Memorial
Park

A   B   C   D   E   F

³30   31   Club
House

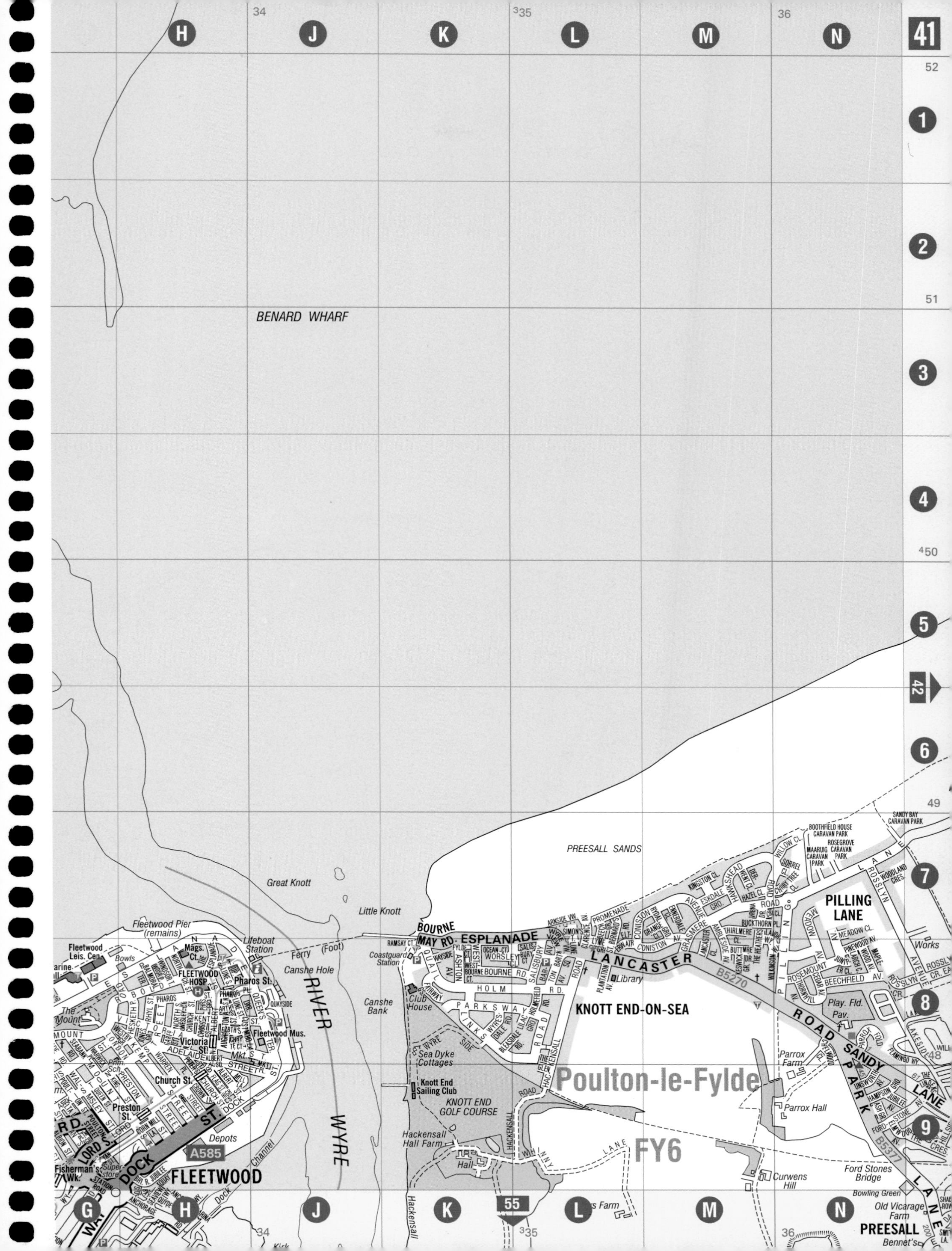
BENARD WHARF
PREESALL SANDS
Great Knott
Little Knott
Fleetwood Pier (remains)
Fleetwood Leis. Cen.
Lifeboat Station
Ferry (Foot)
Canshe Hole
Canshe Bank
RIVER WYRE
Coastguard Station
Club House
Sea Dyke Cottages
Knott End Sailing Club
KNOTT END GOLF COURSE
Hackensall Hall Farm
Hall
KNOTT END-ON-SEA
Poulton-le-Fylde
FY6
Library
ESPLANADE
LANCASTER ROAD
B5270
PILLING LANE
Play. Fld. Pav.
Parrox Farm
Parrox Hall
Curwens Hill
Ford Stones Bridge
Bowling Green
Old Vicarage Farm
PREESALL
SANDY BAY CARAVAN PARK
BOOTHFIELD HOUSE CARAVAN PARK
ROSEGROVE CARAVAN PARK
MAARUIG CARAVAN PARK
Works
FLEETWOOD
FLEETWOOD HOSP
Fleetwood Mus.
Pharos St.
Victoria St.
Church St.
Preston St.
Fisherman's Wk.
Depots
A585
DOCK ST.
Mags. Ct.
The Mount
B5377
SANDY LANE
PARK LANE
Hackensall
55
42

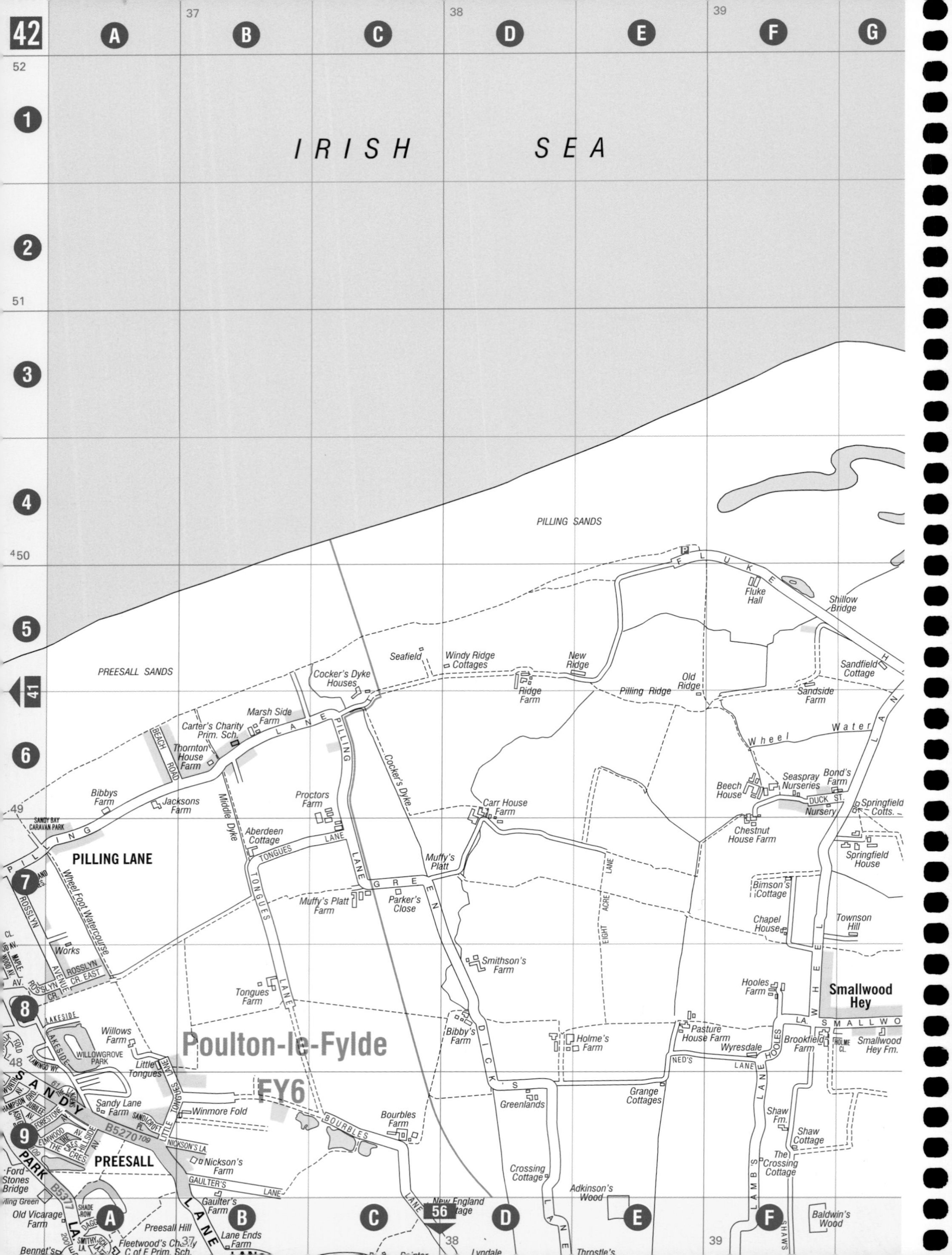
IRISH SEA
PILLING SANDS
PREESALL SANDS
Fluke Hall
Shillow Bridge
Seafield
Windy Ridge Cottages
New Ridge
Old Ridge
Pilling Ridge
Ridge Farm
Sandfield Cottage
Sandside Farm
Cocker's Dyke Houses
Marsh Side Farm
Carter's Charity Prim. Sch.
Thornton House Farm
Wheel Water
Beech House
Seaspray Nurseries
Bond's Farm
Springfield Cotts.
Duck St.
Nursery
Carr House Farm
Chestnut House Farm
Springfield House
Bibbys Farm
Jacksons Farm
Middle Dyke
Cocker's Dyke
Proctors Farm
Aberdeen Cottage
Sandy Bay Caravan Park
PILLING LANE
Muffy's Platt
Muffy's Platt Farm
Parker's Close
Bimson's Cottage
Chapel House
Townson Hill
Eight Acre Lane
Wheel Foot Watercourse
Works
Rosslyn Cr. East
Smithson's Farm
Tongues Farm
Tongues Lane
Hooles Farm
Smallwood Hey
Lakeside
Willows Farm
Willowgrove Park
Poulton-le-Fylde
FY6
Little Tongues
Bibby's Farm
Holme's Farm
Pasture House Farm
Wyresdale
Brookfield Farm
Smallwood Hey Fm.
Ned's Lane
Hooles Lane
Sandy Lane Farm
Winmore Fold
Sandy Lane
B5270
Greenlands
Grange Cottages
Bourbles Farm
Bourbles Lane
Shaw Fm.
Shaw Cottage
The Crossing Cottage
Preesall
Nickson's Farm
Nickson's La.
Gaulter's Lane
Gaulter's Farm
Crossing Cottage
Adkinson's Wood
Ford Stones Bridge
Park Lane
B5377
Old Vicarage Farm
Preesall Hill
Lane Ends Farm
Fleetwood's Charity C of E Prim. Sch.
New England Cottage
Dick's Lane
Lamb's Lane
Baldwin's Wood
Bennet's
Lyndale
Throstle's
Pilling Lane
Fluke Hall Lane
41
56

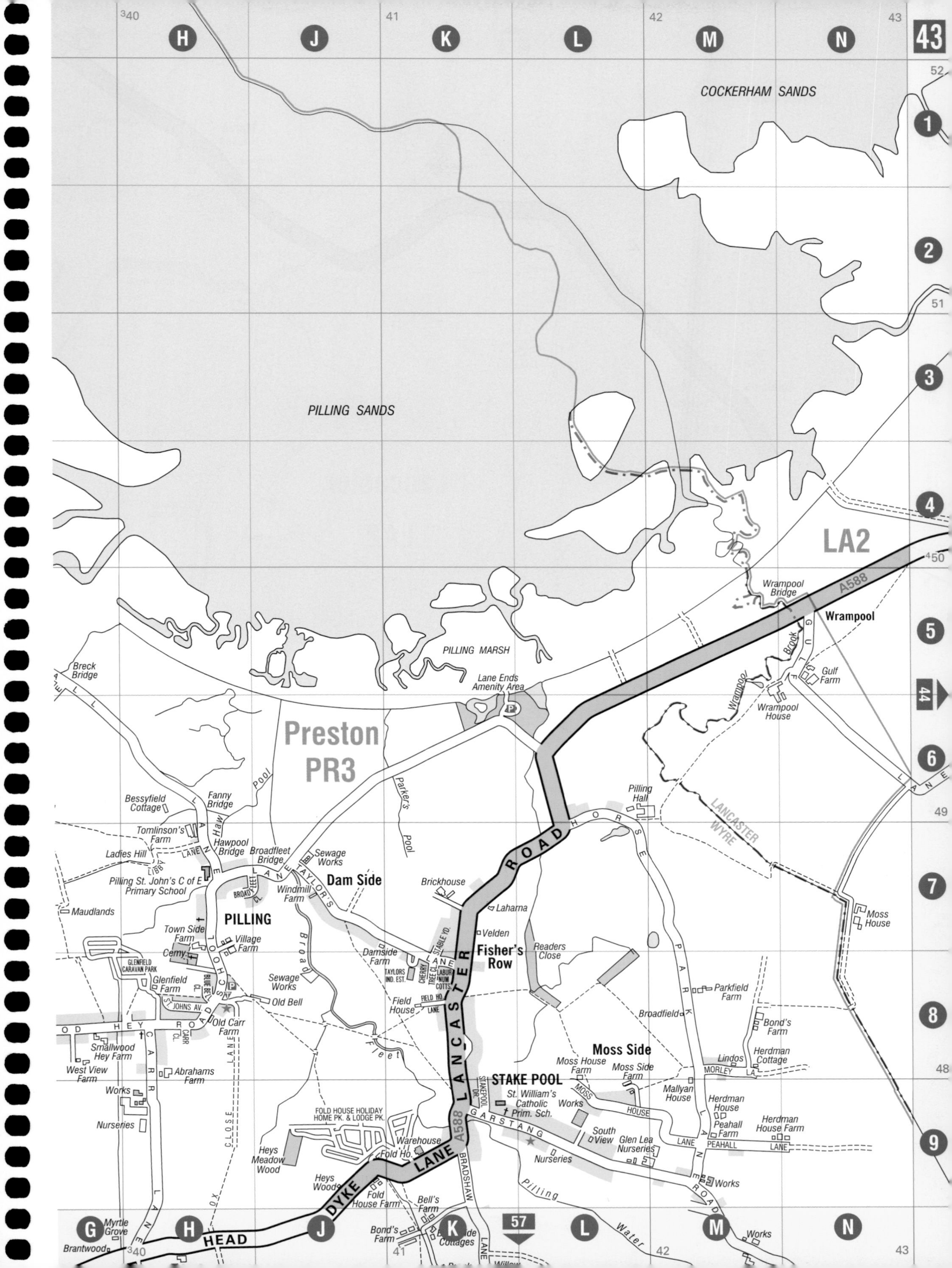
COCKERHAM SANDS
PILLING SANDS
PILLING MARSH
LA2
A588
Wrampool Bridge
Wrampool
Gulf Farm
Wrampool House
Wrampool Brook
Lane Ends Amenity Area
Breck Bridge
Preston PR3
Bessyfield Cottage
Fanny Bridge
Haw Pool
Parker's Pool
Pilling Hall
LANCASTER WYRE
Tomlinson's Farm
Hawpool Bridge
Broadfleet Bridge
Ladies Hill
Sewage Works
Dam Side
Brickhouse
Laharna
Velden
Pilling St. John's C of E Primary School
Maudlands
PILLING
Windmill Farm
Town Side Farm
Village Farm
Cemy.
GLENFIELD CARAVAN PARK
Glenfield Farm
Damside Farm
TAYLORS IND. EST.
Fisher's Row
Readers Close
Moss House
Parkfield Farm
Sewage Works
Old Bell
Field House
Broadfield
Bond's Farm
Old Carr Farm
Smallwood Hey Farm
West View Farm
Abrahams Farm
Moss Side
Moss House Farm
Moss Side Farm
Lindos
Herdman Cottage
STAKE POOL
St. William's Catholic Prim. Sch.
Works
Mallyan House
Herdman House
Peahall Farm
Herdman House Farm
Works
Nurseries
FOLD HOUSE HOLIDAY HOME PK. & LODGE PK.
Warehouse
Fold Ho.
South View
Glen Lea Nurseries
Nurseries
Heys Meadow Wood
Heys Wood
Fold House Farm
Bell's Farm
Works
Myrtle Grove
Brantwood
Bond's Farm
Bankside Cottages
Works
Pilling Water
LANCASTER ROAD
HORSE PARK LANE
GARSTANG ROAD
DYKE LANE
HEAD DYKE LANE
TAYLORS LANE
BROAD FLEET CL.
SCHOOL LANE
HEY ROAD
CARR LANE
CLOSE LANE
MOSS HOUSE LANE
MORLEY LA.
PEAHALL LANE
BRADSHAW LANE
STAKEPOOL DR.
STABLE YD.
CHERRY TREE CL.
LABURNUM COTTS.
FIELD HO. LANE
GULF LANE
ST. JOHNS AV.
BLUE BELL CL.
CARR CL.
LIBB LANE
Broad Fleet
Fleet
57
44
H J K L M N G
1 2 3 4 5 6 7 8 9
340 41 42 43
52 51 450 49 48

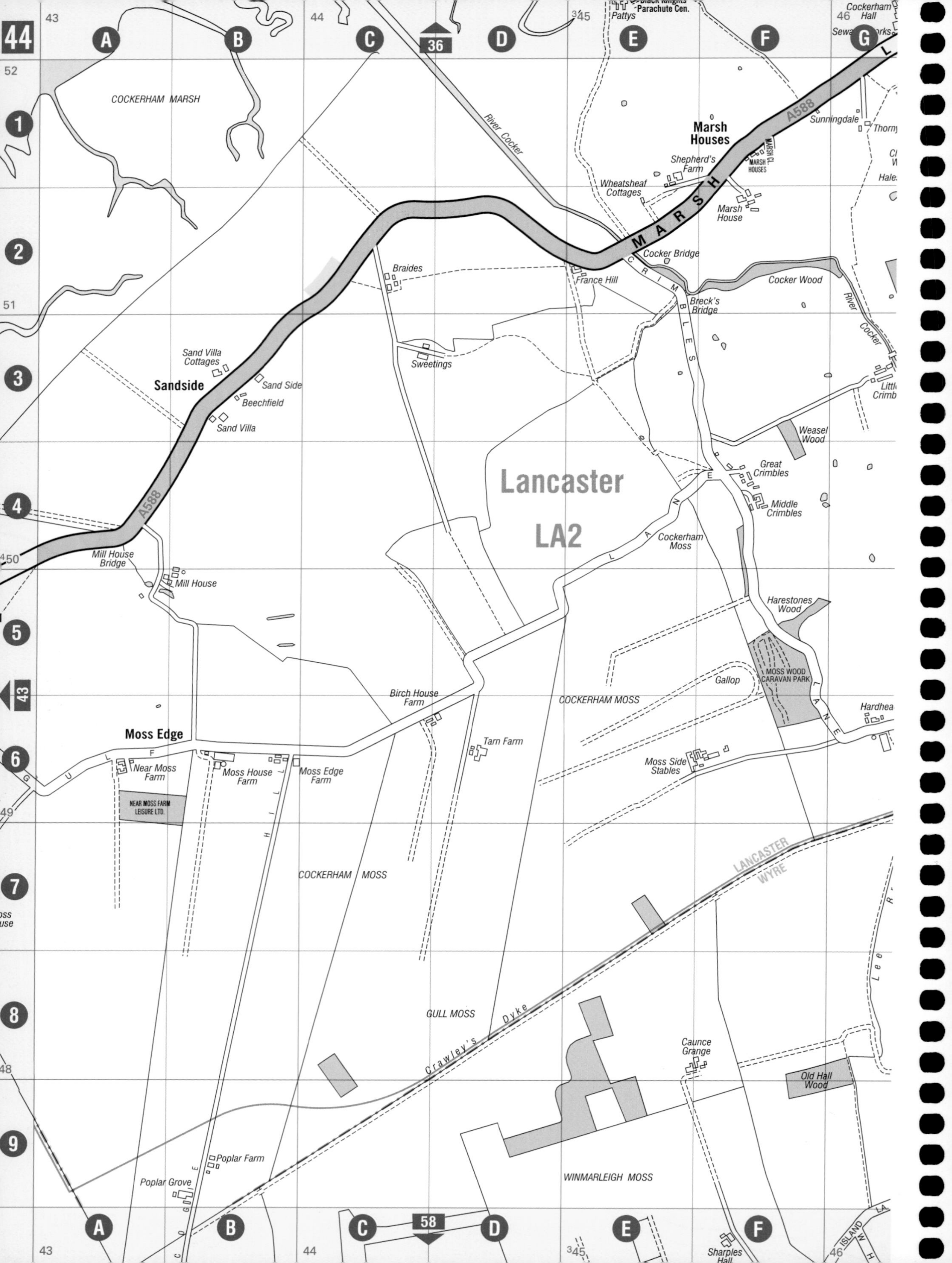
COCKERHAM MARSH
Marsh Houses
Shepherd's Farm
Wheatsheaf Cottages
Marsh House
Sunningdale
A588
MARSH
River Cocker
Cocker Bridge
Braides
France Hill
Cocker Wood
Breck's Bridge
CRIMBLES
Sand Villa Cottages
Sandside
Sand Side
Beechfield
Sand Villa
Sweetings
Lancaster
LA2
Weasel Wood
Great Crimbles
Middle Crimbles
Cockerham Moss
Mill House Bridge
Mill House
Harestones Wood
MOSS WOOD CARAVAN PARK
Gallop
COCKERHAM MOSS
Birch House Farm
Tarn Farm
Moss Edge
Near Moss Farm
Moss House Farm
Moss Edge Farm
Moss Side Stables
NEAR MOSS FARM LEISURE LTD.
LANCASTER
WYRE
GULL MOSS
Crawley's Dyke
Caunce Grange
Old Hall Wood
Poplar Farm
Poplar Grove
WINMARLEIGH MOSS
Sharples Hall
Black Knights Parachute Cen.
Pattys
Cockerham Hall
Sewage Works
36
58
43

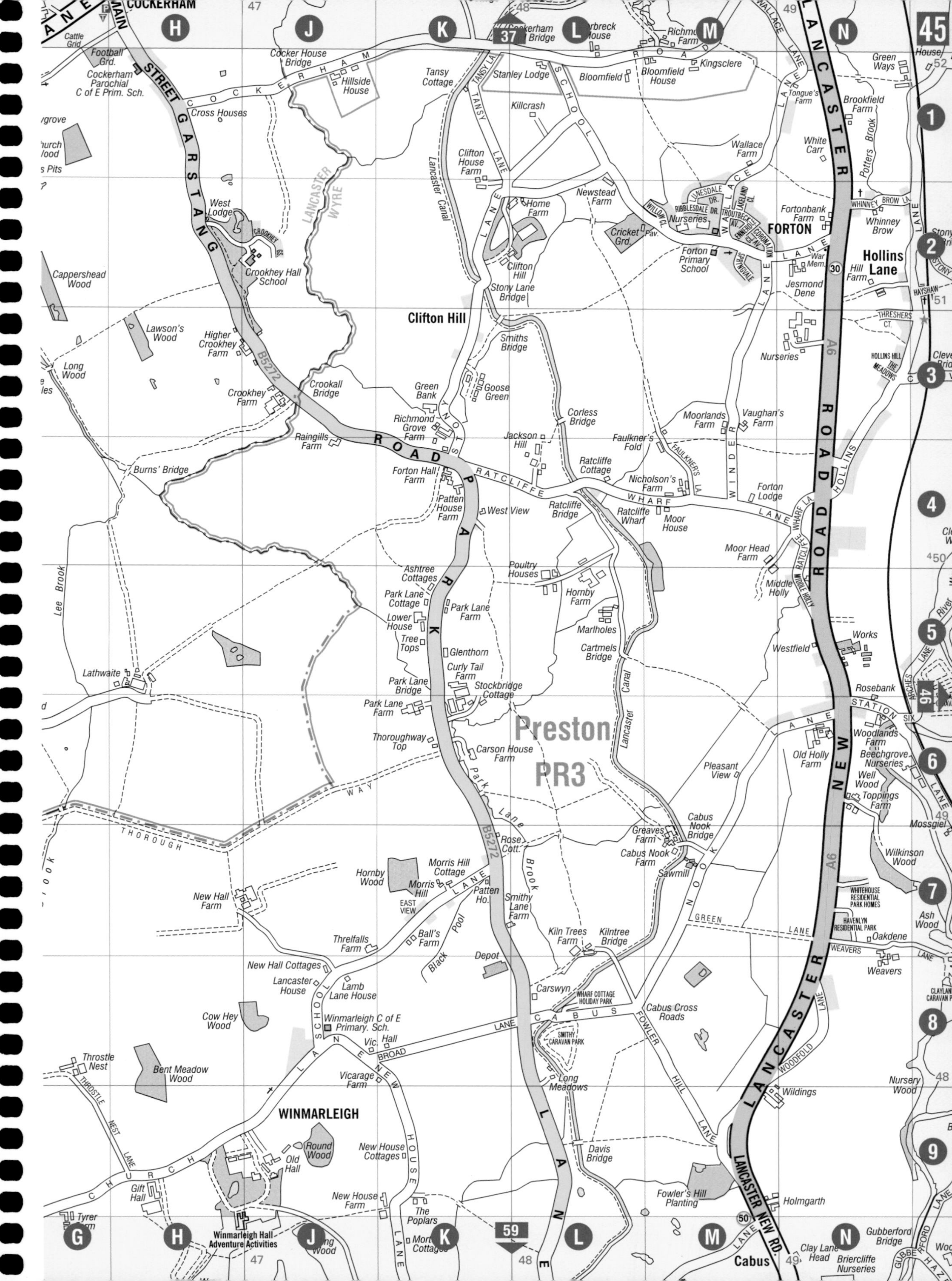
COCKERHAM
Cocker House Bridge
Cockerham Bridge
37
Richmond Farm
Kingsclere
Bloomfield House
Bloomfield
Stanley Lodge
Tansy Cottage
Hillside House
Football Grd.
Cockerham Parochial C of E Prim. Sch.
Cross Houses
Killcrash
Tongue's Farm
Green Ways
Brookfield Farm
Potters Brook
White Carr
Wallace Farm
Clifton House Farm
Lancaster Canal
Lancaster Wyre
West Lodge
Crookhey
Home Farm
Newstead Farm
Cricket Grd.
Pav.
Nurseries
FORTON
Forton Primary School
Fortonbank Farm
Whinney Brow
Hollins Lane
Hill Farm
Jesmond Dene
War Mem.
Clifton Hill
Stony Lane Bridge
Crookhey Hall School
Cappershead Wood
Lawson's Wood
Higher Crookhey Farm
Long Wood
Smiths Bridge
Threshers Ct.
Hollins Hill
The Meadows
Nurseries
Goose Green
Green Bank
Crookall Bridge
Crookhey Farm
Richmond Grove Farm
Raingills Farm
Corless Bridge
Moorlands Farm
Vaughan's Farm
Jackson Hill
Faulkner's Fold
Ratcliffe Cottage
Nicholson's Farm
Forton Lodge
Burns' Bridge
Forton Hall Farm
Patten House Farm
West View
Ratcliffe Bridge
Ratcliffe Wharf
Moor House
Moor Head Farm
Middle Holly
Ashtree Cottages
Poultry Houses
Hornby Farm
Park Lane Cottage
Park Lane Farm
Lower House
Marlholes
Lee Brook
Tree Tops
Glenthorn
Cartmels Bridge
Works
Westfield
Lathwaite
Curly Tail Farm
Park Lane Bridge
Stockbridge Cottage
Rosebank
Park Lane Farm
Preston PR3
Thoroughway Top
Carson House Farm
Woodlands Farm
Old Holly Farm
Beechgrove Nurseries
Pleasant View
Well Wood
Toppings Farm
Thorough Way
Greaves Farm
Cabus Nook Bridge
Cabus Nook Farm
Sawmill
Rose Cott.
Hornby Wood
Morris Hill Cottage
Morris Hill
Patten Ho.
New Hall Farm
East View
Smithy Lane Farm
Wilkinson Wood
Whitehouse Residential Park Homes
Ash Wood
Havenlyn Residential Park
Oakdene
Threlfalls Farm
Ball's Farm
Black Pool
Kiln Trees Farm
Kiltree Bridge
Depot
Weavers
New Hall Cottages
Lancaster House
Lamb Lane House
Carswyn
Wharf Cottage Holiday Park
Cabus Cross Roads
Claylands Caravan Park
Cow Hey Wood
Winmarleigh C of E Primary Sch.
Vic. Hall
Smithy Caravan Park
Throstle Nest
Bent Meadow Wood
Vicarage Farm
Long Meadows
Wildings
Nursery Wood
WINMARLEIGH
Round Wood
New House Cottages
Old Hall
Davis Bridge
Gift Hall
New House Farm
Fowler's Hill Planting
Holmgarth
The Poplars
Winmarleigh Hall Adventure Activities
59
Gubberford Bridge
Clay Lane Head
Cabus
Briercliffe Nurseries
Garstang Road
Park Lane
Lancaster New Road
Cockerham Road
Ratcliffe Wharf Lane
Station Lane
Green Lane
Cabus Lane
Broad Lane
Church Lane
Throstle Nest Lane
New House Lane
Fowler Hill Lane
School Lane
Nook Lane
B5272
A6
H J K L M N
G H J K L M N
1 2 3 4 5 6 7 8 9
47 48 49 50 51 52
46

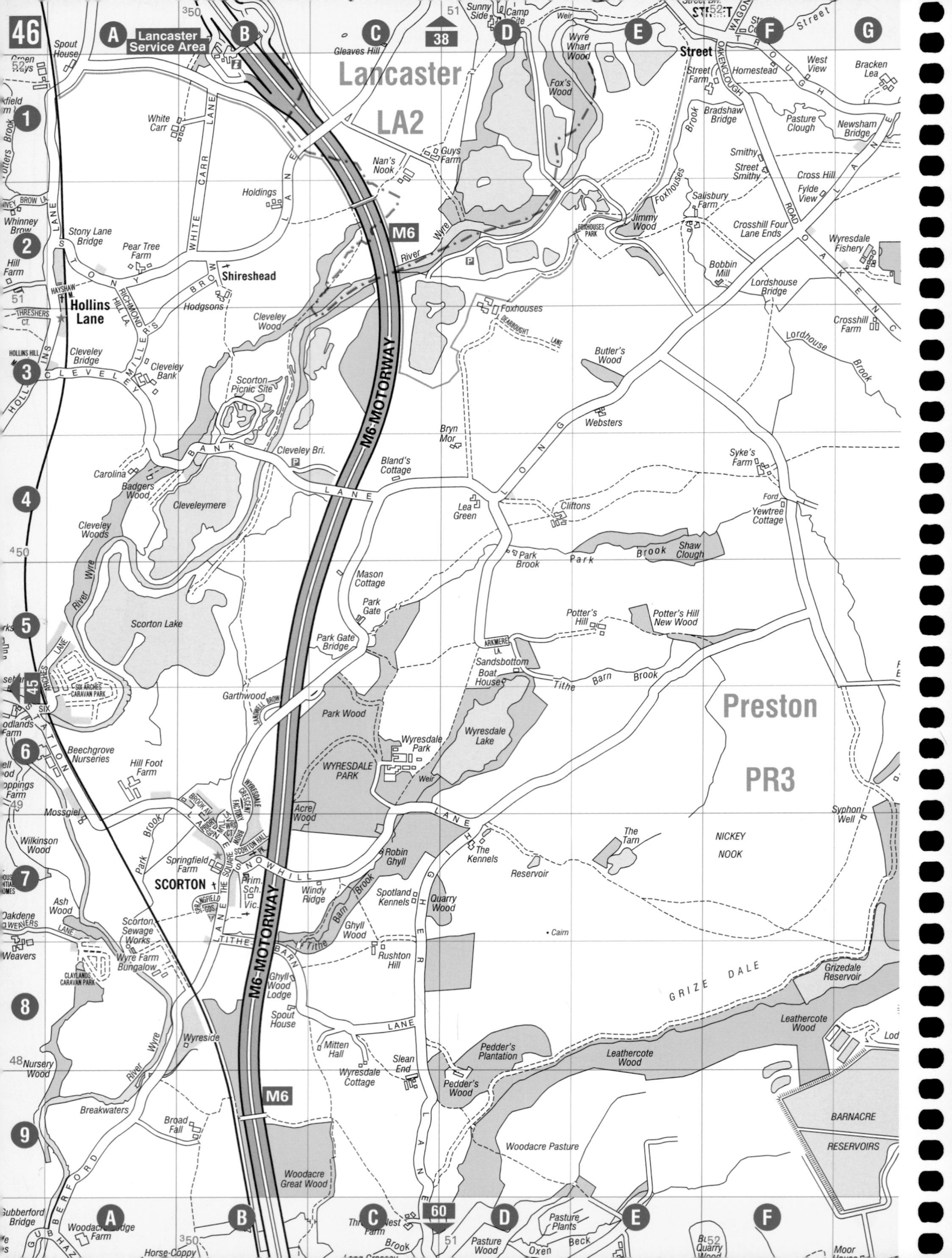
Lancaster Service Area
Lancaster
LA2
Preston
PR3
M6 MOTORWAY
M6
38
60
45
Street
Hollins Lane
Shireshead
SCORTON
Spout House
Gleaves Hill
Sunny Side
Camp Site
Wyre Wharf Wood
Fox's Wood
Street Farm
Homestead
West View
Bracken Lea
White Carr
Guys Farm
Nan's Nook
Holdings
Bradshaw Bridge
Pasture Clough
Newsham Bridge
Smithy
Street Smithy
Cross Hill
Fylde View
Salisbury Farm
Foxhouses
Jimmy Wood
Crosshill Four Lane Ends
Stony Lane Bridge
Pear Tree Farm
Whinney Brow
Hill Farm
Hodgsons
Wyresdale Fishery
Bobbin Mill
Lordshouse Bridge
Crosshill Farm
Cleveley Wood
Cleveley Bridge
Cleveley Bank
Scorton Picnic Site
Butler's Wood
Websters
Bryn Mor
Cleveley Bri.
Bland's Cottage
Syke's Farm
Carolina
Badgers Wood
Cleveleymere
Lea Green
Cliftons
Ford
Yewtree Cottage
Cleveley Woods
Shaw Clough
Park Brook
Mason Cottage
Park Gate
Scorton Lake
Potter's Hill
Potter's Hill New Wood
Park Gate Bridge
Sandsbottom
Boat House
Tithe Barn Brook
Garthwood
Park Wood
Wyresdale Park
Wyresdale Lake
Beechgrove Nurseries
Hill Foot Farm
WYRESDALE PARK
Weir
Mossgiel
Acre Wood
Syphon Well
Wilkinson Wood
The Tarn
NICKEY NOOK
Springfield Farm
Robin Ghyll
The Kennels
Reservoir
Windy Ridge
Spotland Kennels
Quarry Wood
Ash Wood
Scorton Sewage Works
Ghyll Wood
Cairn
Weavers
Wyre Farm Bungalow
Rushton Hill
CLAYLANDS CARAVAN PARK
SIX ARCHES CARAVAN PARK
GRIZE DALE
Grizedale Reservoir
Ghyll Wood Lodge
Spout House
Leathercote Wood
Wyreside
Mitten Hall
Pedder's Plantation
Nursery Wood
Slean End
Wyresdale Cottage
Pedder's Wood
Breakwaters
Broad Fall
BARNACRE
RESERVOIRS
Woodacre Pasture
Woodacre Great Wood
Gubberford Bridge
Woodacre Lodge Farm
Three Nest Farm
Pasture Plants
Pasture Wood
Oxen
Beck
Quarry Wood
Horse Coppy
River Wyre
Lordhouse Brook
A B C D E F G
1 2 3 4 5 6 7 8 9

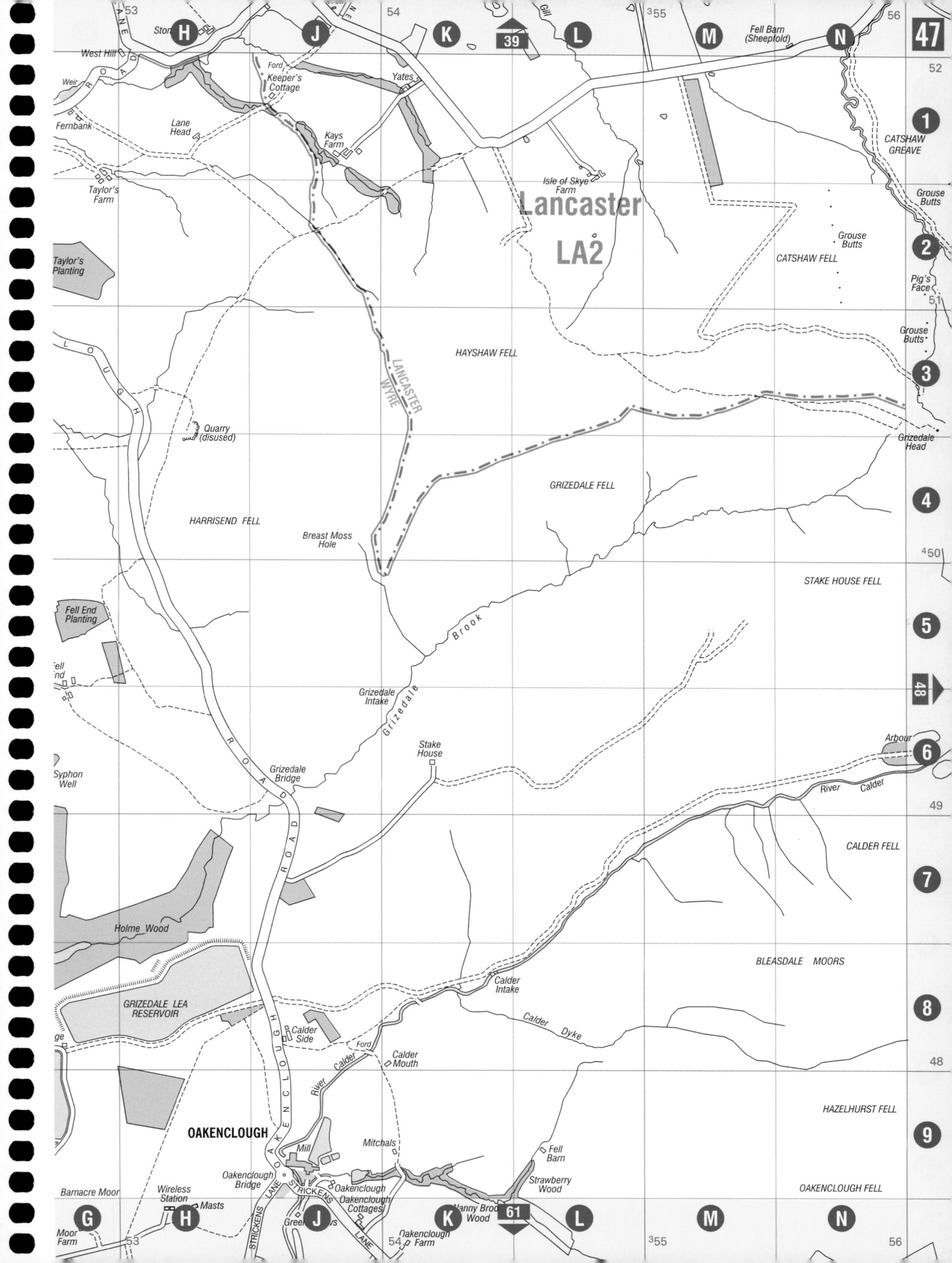

47
Lancaster
LA2
Fell Barn (Sheepfold)
West Hill
Weir
Keeper's Cottage
Ford
Yates
Fernbank
Lane Head
Kays Farm
Taylor's Farm
Isle of Skye Farm
CATSHAW GREAVE
Grouse Butts
CATSHAW FELL
Pig's Face
Taylor's Planting
HAYSHAW FELL
LANCASTER
WYRE
Quarry (disused)
Grizedale Head
GRIZEDALE FELL
HARRISEND FELL
Breast Moss Hole
STAKE HOUSE FELL
Fell End Planting
Brook
Grizedale Intake
Grizedale
Stake House
Arbour
Syphon Well
Grizedale Bridge
River Calder
CALDER FELL
Holme Wood
BLEASDALE MOORS
Calder Intake
GRIZEDALE LEA RESERVOIR
Calder Dyke
Calder Side
Ford
Calder Mouth
River Calder
HAZELHURST FELL
OAKENCLOUGH
Mitchals
Mill
Fell Barn
Oakenclough Bridge
Strawberry Wood
Barnacre Moor
Wireless Station
Masts
Oakenclough
Oakenclough Cottages
OAKENCLOUGH FELL
Moor Farm
Oakenclough Farm
OAKENCLOUGH ROAD
ROAD
LOUGH
STRICKENS LANE
39
48
61

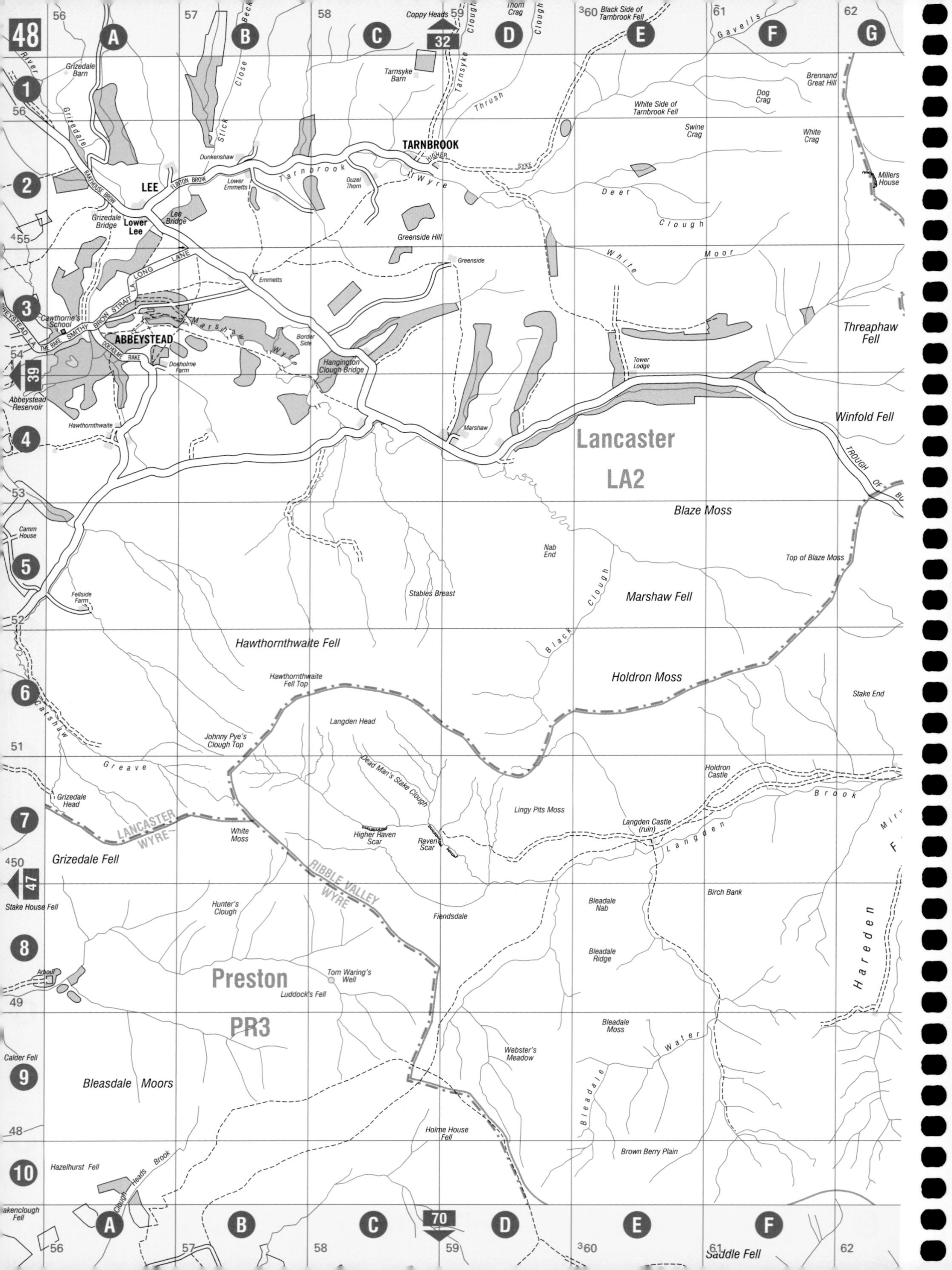

Coppy Heads
32
Thorn Crag
Black Side of Tarnbrook Fell
Gavells
Grizedale Barn
Tarnsyke Barn
Brennand Great Hill
Dog Crag
White Side of Tarnbrook Fell
Swine Crag
White Crag
TARNBROOK
Dunkenshaw
LEE
Lower Emmetts
Ouzel Thorn
Millers House
Deer
Clough
Grizedale Bridge
Lower Lee
Lee Bridge
Greenside Hill
White
Moor
Greenside
Emmetts
Cawthorne's School
ABBEYSTEAD
Border Side
Hangington Clough Bridge
Threaphaw Fell
Tower Lodge
Doeholme Farm
39
Abbeystead Reservoir
Winfold Fell
Hawthornthwaite
Marshaw
Lancaster
LA2
Camm House
Blaze Moss
Nab End
Top of Blaze Moss
Fellside Farm
Stables Breast
Marshaw Fell
Hawthornthwaite Fell
Holdron Moss
Hawthornthwaite Fell Top
Stake End
Langden Head
Johnny Pye's Clough Top
Greave
Holdron Castle
Dead Man's Stake Clough
Grizedale Head
Lingy Pits Moss
LANCASTER
WYRE
White Moss
Higher Raven Scar
Raven Scar
Langden Castle (ruin)
Grizedale Fell
RIBBLE VALLEY
47
Stake House Fell
Hunter's Clough
Fiendsdale
Bleadale Nab
Birch Bank
Bleadale Ridge
Hareden
Preston
Tom Waring's Well
Luddock's Fell
PR3
Bleadale Moss
Calder Fell
Webster's Meadow
Bleasdale Moors
Holme House Fell
Hazelhurst Fell
Brown Berry Plain
Clough Heads Brook
Fairsnape Fell
70
Saddle Fell

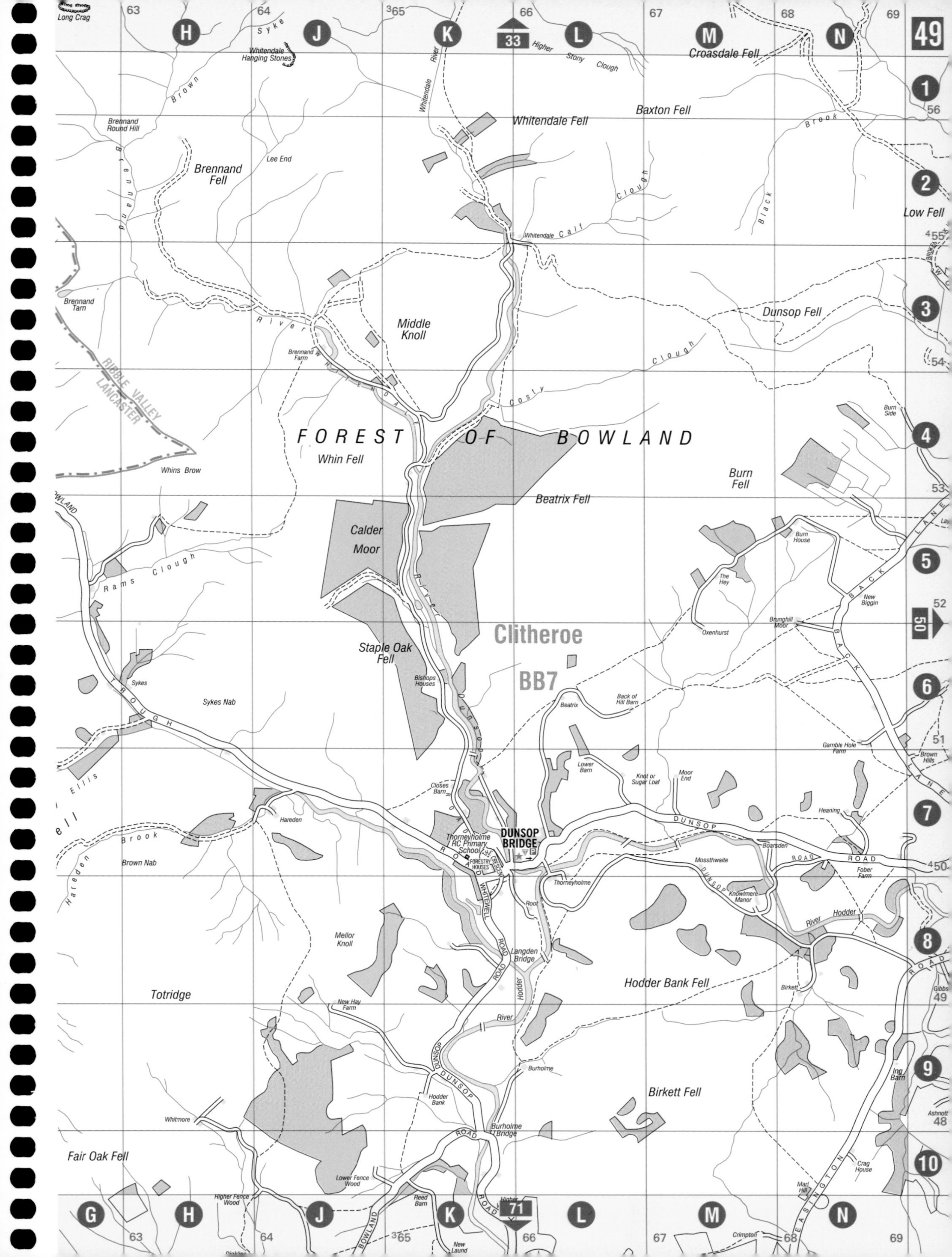

Long Crag
Whitendale Hanging Stones
Higher Stony Clough
Croasdale Fell
Baxton Fell
Whitendale Fell
Brennand Round Hill
Brennand Fell
Lee End
Low Fell
Whitendale
Brennand Tarn
Dunsop Fell
Middle Knoll
Brennand Farm
Costy Clough
RIBBLE VALLEY
LANCASTER
FOREST OF BOWLAND
Whin Fell
Whins Brow
Burn Fell
Beatrix Fell
Calder Moor
Burn House
Rams Clough
The Hey
New Biggin
Brunghill Moor
Oxenhurst
Clitheroe
BB7
Staple Oak Fell
Bishops Houses
Sykes
Sykes Nab
TROUGH
Beatrix
Back of Hill Barn
Gamble Hole Farm
Brown Hills
Lower Barn
Knot or Sugar Loaf
Moor End
Closes Barn
Heaning
Hareden
Hareden Brook
Brown Nab
Thorneyholme RC Primary School
FORESTRY HOUSES
DUNSOP BRIDGE
Boarsden
DUNSOP ROAD
Mossthwaite
Fober Farm
Thorneyholme
Knowlmere Manor
River Hodder
Root
Mellor Knoll
Langden Bridge
WHITEWELL ROAD
Hodder Bank Fell
Birkett
Totridge
New Hay Farm
River Hodder
Burholme
Ing Barn
Birkett Fell
Hodder Bank
Whitmore
Burholme Bridge
Ashnott
Fair Oak Fell
Lower Fence Wood
Crag House
Higher Fence Wood
Reed Barn
Marl Hill
EASINGTON
BOWLAND
Crimpton
New Laund
BACK LANE

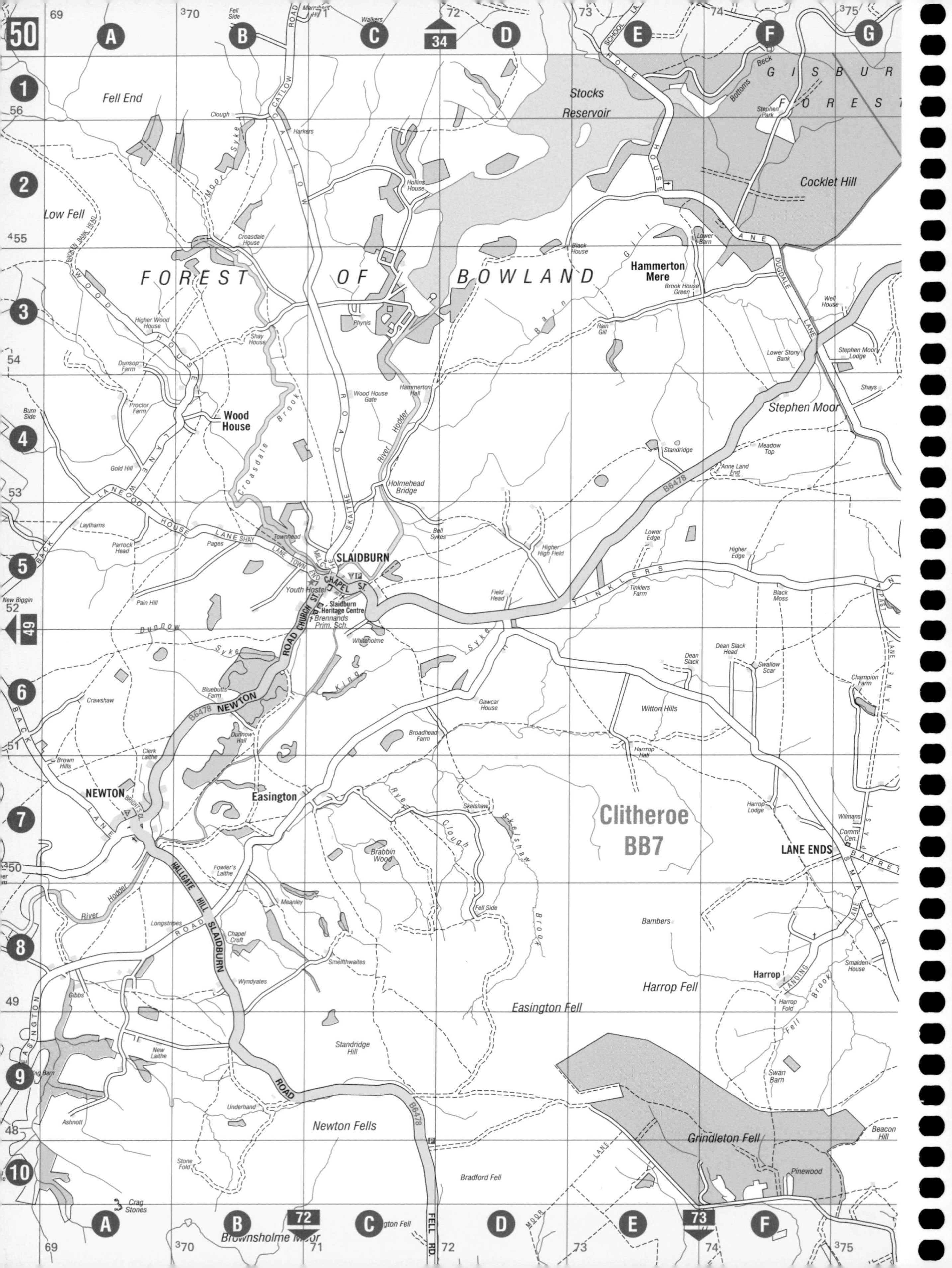

50
FOREST OF BOWLAND
Stocks Reservoir
GISBURN FOREST
Cocklet Hill
Fell End
Low Fell
Hammerton Mere
Wood House
SLAIDBURN
Youth Hostel
Slaidburn Heritage Centre
Brennands Prim. Sch.
Stephen Moor
NEWTON
Easington
Witton Hills
Clitheroe BB7
LANE ENDS
Brabbin Wood
Harrop Fell
Harrop
Easington Fell
Newton Fells
Grindleton Fell
Bradford Fell
Standridge Hill
Pinewood
Beacon Hill
Crag Stones
Brownsholme Moor
B6478
TINKLERS LANE
HALLGATE HILL
SLAIDBURN ROAD
NEWTON ROAD
CHURCH ST.
CHAPEL ST.
FELL RD.
DUGDALE LANE
HOLE HOUSE LANE
SCHOOL LA.
CATLOW ROAD
SKAITHE ROAD
WOOD HOUSE LANE
BACK LANE
34
49
72
73

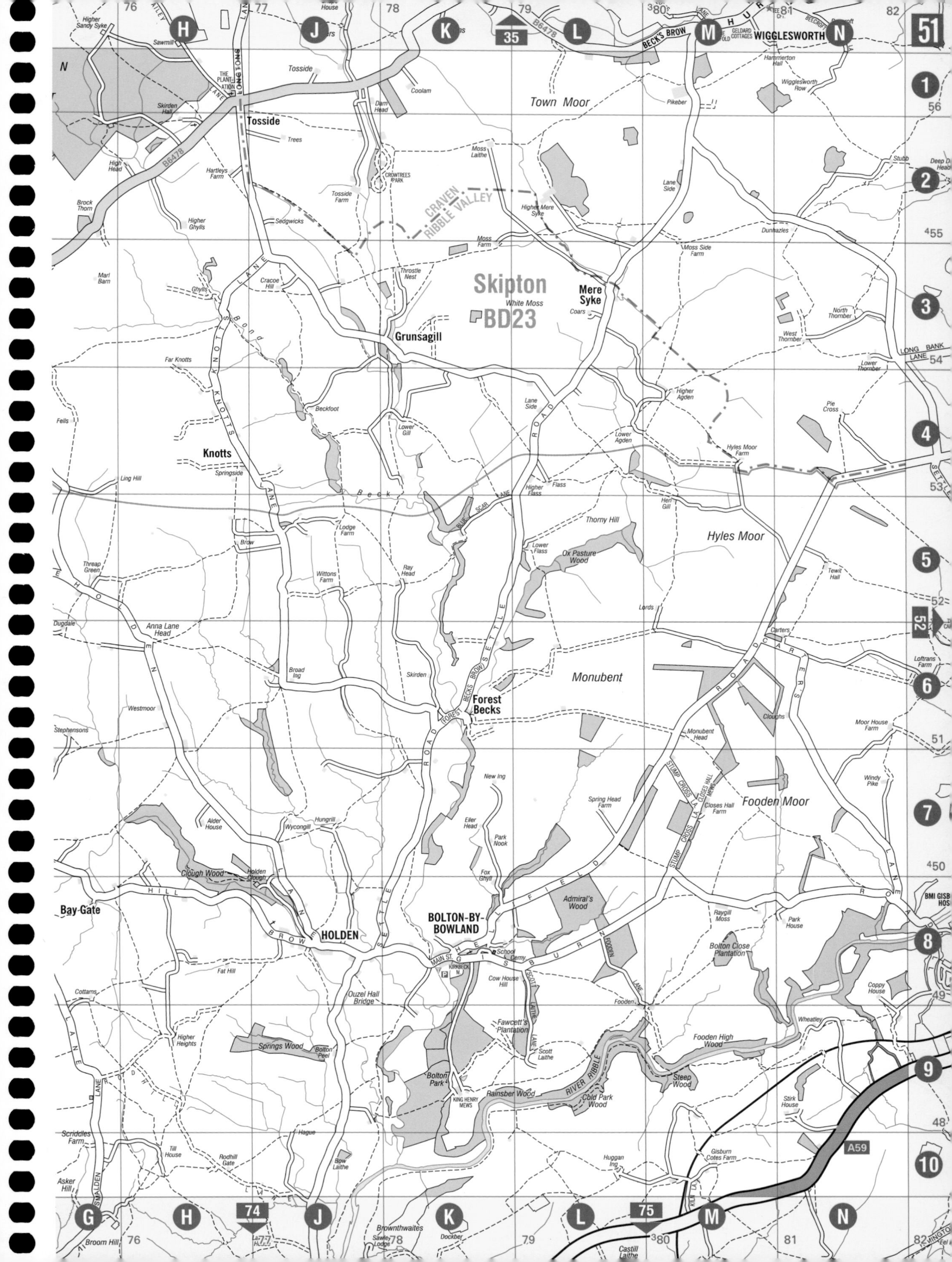
35
B6478
BECK'S BROW
WIGGLESWORTH
Tosside
Coolam
Town Moor
Pikeber
Hammerton Hall
Wigglesworth Row
Sawmill
Higher Sandy Syke
THE PLANTATION
LONGTONS LANE
Skirden Hall
Tosside
Trees
Dam Head
Moss Laithe
High Head
Hartleys Farm
CROWTREES PARK
Tosside Farm
CRAVEN
RIBBLE VALLEY
Higher Mere Syke
Lane Side
Stubb
Brock Thorn
Higher Ghylls
Sedgwicks
Moss Farm
Moss Side Farm
Dunnazles
Marl Barn
Cracoe Hill
Throstle Nest
Skipton
White Moss
BD23
Mere Syke
Coars
North Thornber
West Thornber
Ghylls
Grunsagill
Far Knotts
KNOTTS LANE
Beckfoot
Lower Gill
Lane Side
Higher Agden
LONG BANK LANE
Lower Thornber
Pie Cross
Fells
Knotts
Springside
Lower Agden
Hyles Moor Farm
Ling Hill
Higher Flass
Flass
Hen Gill
Beck
BLUE SCAR LANE
Thorny Hill
Lodge Farm
Brow
Lower Flass
Ox Pasture Wood
Hyles Moor
Threap Green
Wittons Farm
Ray Head
Tewit Hall
HOLDEN
Lords
Dugdale
Anna Lane Head
Carters
SETTLE ROAD
CARTERS ROAD
Loftrans Farm
Broad Ing
Skirden
Monubent
Westmoor
Forest Becks
FOREST BECKS BROW
Stephensons
Monubent Head
Cloughs
Moor House Farm
New Ing
STUMP CROSS LANE
CLOSES HALL MEWS
Fooden Moor
Windy Pike
Spring Head Farm
Closes Hall Farm
Alder House
Hungrill
Wycongill
Eller Head
Park Nook
Clough Wood
Holden Clough
Fox Ghyll
Admiral's Wood
FIELD
Bay Gate
HILL
BROW
HOLDEN
BOLTON-BY-BOWLAND
Raygill Moss
Park House
Bolton Close Plantation
MAIN ST.
School
Cemy
KIRKBECK M.
SAWLEY ROAD
Fat Hill
Cow House Hill
FOODEN LANE
Coppy House
Cottams
Ouzel Hall Bridge
Fooden
Fawcett's Plantation
Wheatley
Higher Heights
Springs Wood
Bolton Peel
Scott Laithe
Fooden High Wood
RIVER RIBBLE
Steep Wood
Bolton Park
KING HENRY MEWS
Rainsber Wood
Cold Park Wood
Stirk House
Scriddles Farm
Hague
A59
Till House
Rodhill Gate
Huggan Ing
Gisburn Cotes Farm
Bow Laithe
Asker Hill
SMALDEN LANE
Broom Hill
74
75
Brownthwaites
Sawley Lodge
Dockber
Castill Laithe
52
BMI GISB HOS

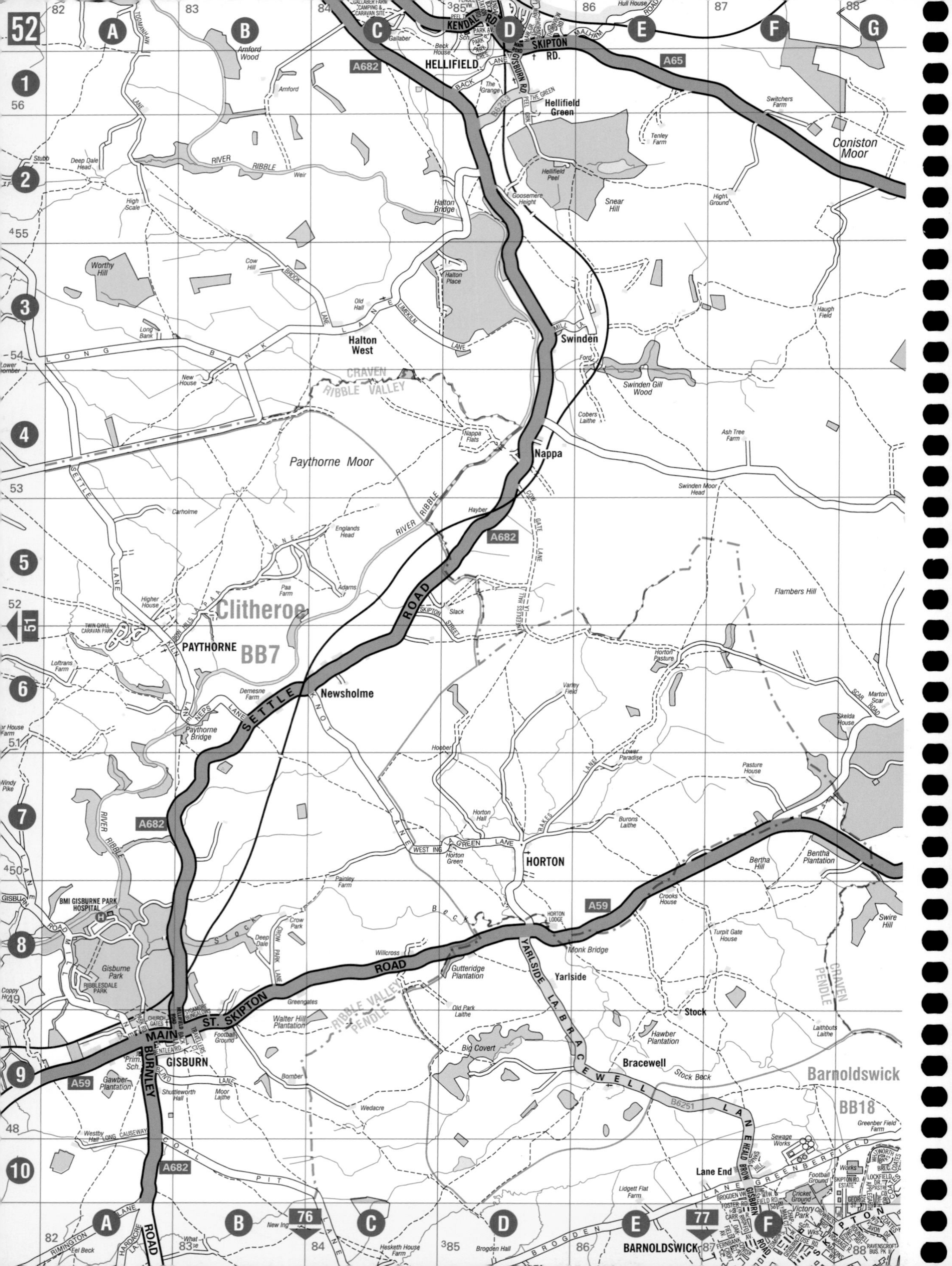
HELLIFIELD
Hellifield Green
SKIPTON RD.
A65
A682
Coniston Moor
RIVER RIBBLE
Halton West
Swinden
CRAVEN
RIBBLE VALLEY
Nappa
Paythorne Moor
Clitheroe
BB7
PAYTHORNE
Newsholme
SETTLE ROAD
HORTON
A59
Yarlside
Stock
Bracewell
Barnoldswick
BB18
GISBURN
ST. SKIPTON ROAD
BMI GISBURNE PARK HOSPITAL
Gisburne Park
BRACEWELL LANE
B6251
Lane End
BARNOLDSWICK
PENDLE
76
77
51

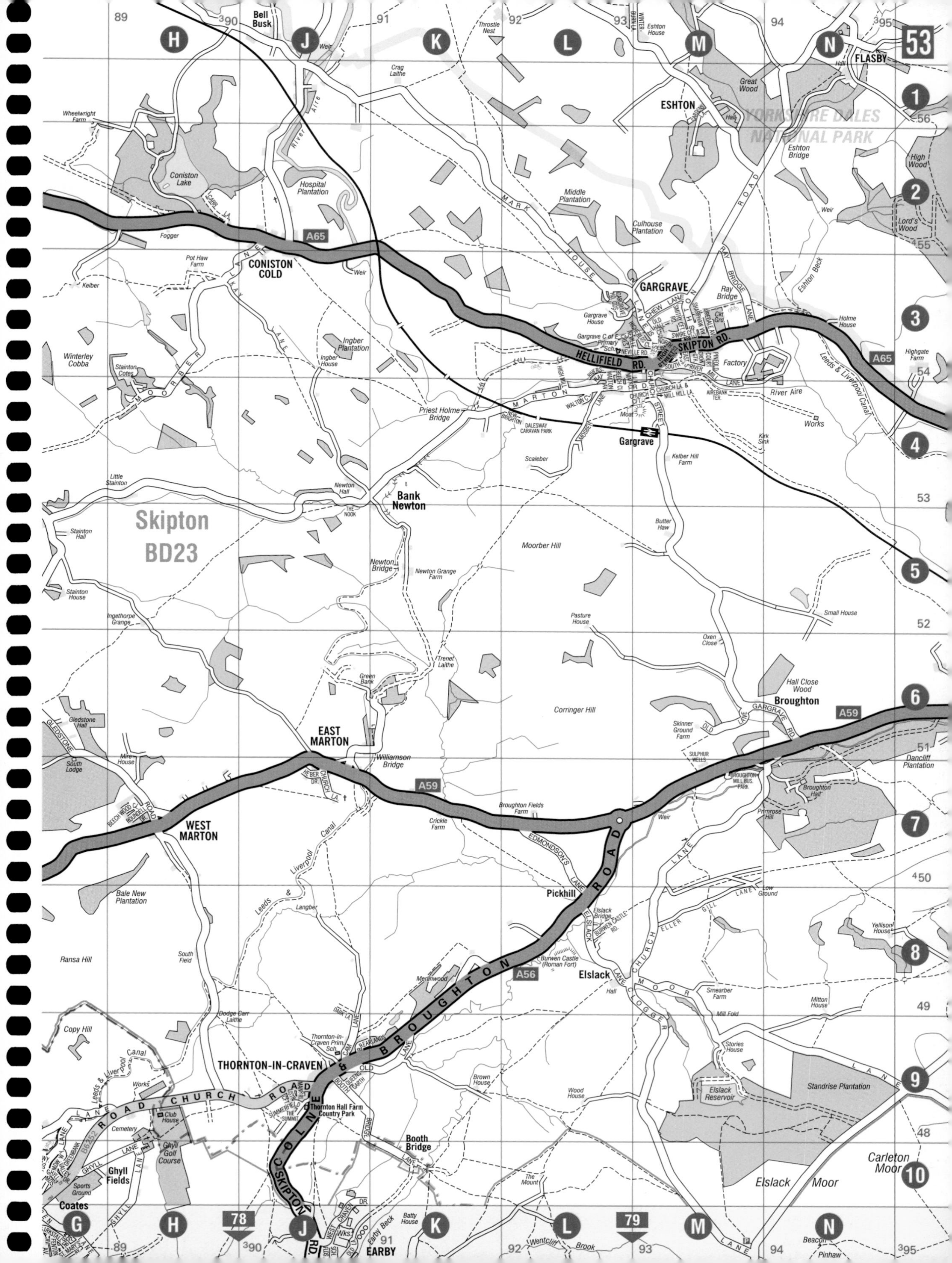
FLASBY
ESHTON
Great Wood
YORKSHIRE DALES NATIONAL PARK
Eshton Bridge
High Wood
Lord's Wood
Bell Busk
Throstle Nest
Crag Laithe
Eshton House
Wheelwright Farm
Coniston Lake
Hospital Plantation
Middle Plantation
Culhouse Plantation
Fogger
A65
CONISTON COLD
Pot Haw Farm
Kelber
GARGRAVE
Ray Bridge
Holme House
Gargrave House
Gargrave C of E Primary Sch.
HELLIFIELD RD.
SKIPTON RD.
Factory
Highgate Farm
Leeds & Liverpool Canal
River Aire
Works
Winterley Cobba
Stainton Cotes
Ingber Plantation
Ingber House
Priest Holme Bridge
DALESWAY CARAVAN PARK
Gargrave
Scaleber
Kelber Hill Farm
Kirk Sink
Little Stainton
Newton Hall
Bank Newton
THE NOOK
Skipton BD23
Stainton Hall
Butter Haw
Moorber Hill
Newton Bridge
Newton Grange Farm
Stainton House
Pasture House
Small House
Ingethorpe Grange
Oxen Close
Trenet Laithe
Hall Close Wood
Broughton
Green Bank
Corringer Hill
Gledstone Hall
EAST MARTON
Skinner Ground Farm
A59
Mire House
South Lodge
Williamson Bridge
SULPHUR WELLS
Dancliff Plantation
Broughton Hall
Broughton Fields Farm
Crickle Farm
Weir
Primrose Hill
WEST MARTON
Bale New Plantation
Pickhill
Low Ground
Langber
Elslack Bridge
Yellison House
Ransa Hill
South Field
Burwen Castle (Roman Fort)
A56
Elslack
Merlinwood
Hall
Smearber Farm
Mitton House
Dodge Carr Laithe
Mill Fold
Copy Hill
Thornton-in-Craven Prim. Sch.
Stories House
THORNTON-IN-CRAVEN
Brown House
Wood House
Standrise Plantation
Works
Elslack Reservoir
Club House
Thornton Hall Farm Country Park
Cemetery
Ghyll Golf Course
Booth Bridge
Carleton Moor
Ghyll Fields
Sports Ground
The Mount
Elslack Moor
Coates
Batty House
78
79
EARBY
Wentcliff Brook
Beacon
Pinhaw
SKIPTON RD.
COLNE RD.
BROUGHTON ROAD
CHURCH ROAD

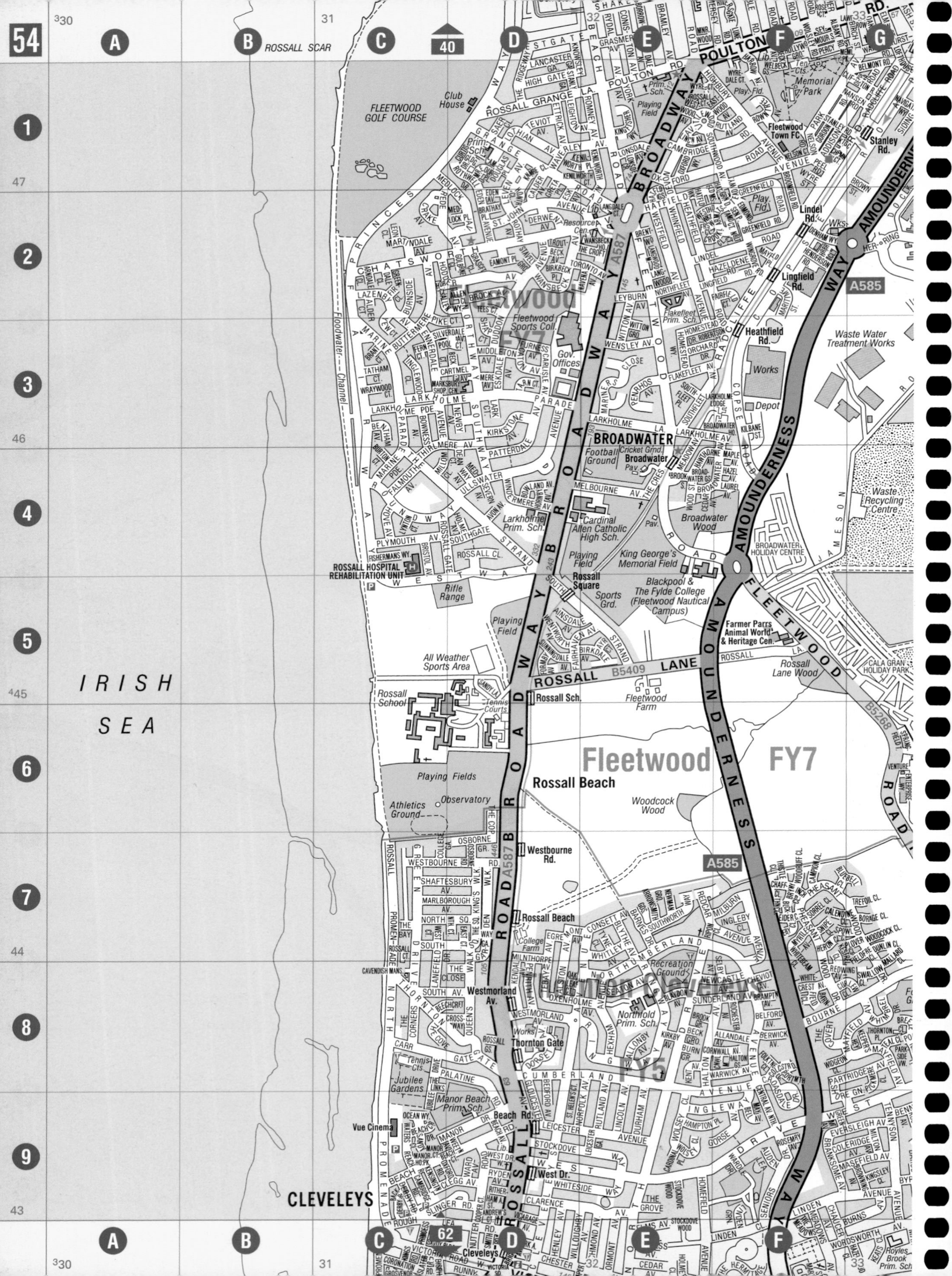
ROSSALL SCAR
40
62
IRISH
SEA
FLEETWOOD
GOLF COURSE
Club
House
Floodwater Channel
PRINCES WAY
MARINE PARADE
ROSSALL GRANGE LA.
POULTON RD.
BROADWAY
A587
Fleetwood Town FC
Memorial
Park
Stanley
Rd.
Lindel
Rd.
Lingfield
Rd.
Heathfield
Rd.
A585
AMOUNDERNESS WAY
Waste Water
Treatment Works
Works
Depot
Fleetwood
FY7
Fleetwood
Sports Coll.
Gov.
Offices
LARKHOLME PARADE
BROADWATER
Football
Ground
Cricket Grnd.
Broadwater
Broadwater
Wood
Waste
Recycling
Centre
BROADWATER
HOLIDAY CENTRE
JAMESON ROAD
Larkholme
Prim. Sch.
Cardinal
Allen Catholic
High Sch.
King George's
Memorial Field
Playing
Field
ROSSALL HOSPITAL
REHABILITATION UNIT
WESTWAY
Rifle
Range
Rossall
Square
Sports
Grd.
Blackpool &
The Fylde College
(Fleetwood Nautical
Campus)
Farmer Parrs
Animal World
& Heritage Cen.
FLEETWOOD ROAD
B5268
CALA GRAN
HOLIDAY PARK
Rossall
Lane Wood
ROSSALL LANE
B5409
All Weather
Sports Area
Rossall
School
Tennis
Courts
Rossall Sch.
Fleetwood
Farm
Fleetwood
FY7
Rossall Beach
Woodcock
Wood
Playing Fields
Athletics
Ground
Observatory
Westbourne
Rd.
Rossall Beach
College
Farm
Recreation
Ground
Thornton Cleveleys
Northfold
Prim. Sch.
Westmorland
Av.
Thornton Gate
FY5
Tennis
Cts.
Jubilee
Gardens
Manor Beach
Prim. Sch.
Beach Rd.
Vue Cinema
West Dr.
CLEVELEYS
Cleveleys
PROMENADE
ROSSALL ROAD
NORTH DRIVE
CUMBERLAND AVENUE
NORTHUMBERLAND AVENUE
INGLEWAY
WEST DRIVE
WHITESIDE WAY
Royles
Brook
Prim. Sch.
330
31
32
33
47
46
445
44
43
A
B
C
D
E
F
G
1
2
3
4
5
6
7
8
9

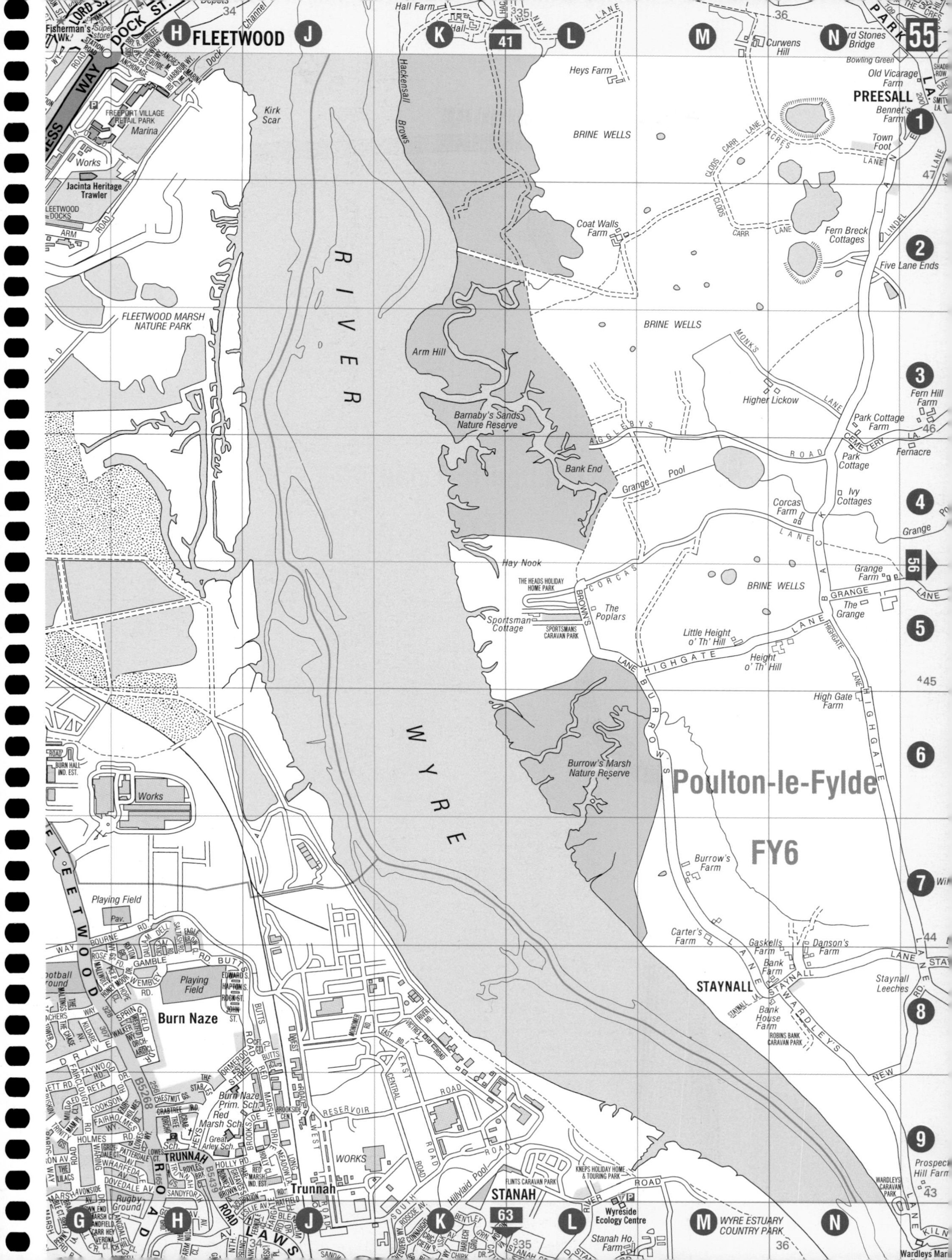
FLEETWOOD
Hall Farm
Heys Farm
PREESALL
Curwens Hill
Bowling Green
Old Vicarage Farm
Bennet's Farm
Town Foot
Kirk Scar
FREEPORT VILLAGE RETAIL PARK
Marina
Works
Jacinta Heritage Trawler
BRINE WELLS
Coat Walls Farm
Fern Breck Cottages
Five Lane Ends
RIVER WYRE
FLEETWOOD MARSH NATURE PARK
Arm Hill
Higher Lickow
Fern Hill Farm
Park Cottage Farm
Fernacre
Park Cottage
Barnaby's Sands Nature Reserve
Bank End
Grange Pool
Corcas Farm
Ivy Cottages
Hay Nook
THE HEADS HOLIDAY HOME PARK
The Poplars
Sportsman Cottage
SPORTSMANS CARAVAN PARK
Grange Farm
The Grange
Little Height o' Th' Hill
Height o' Th' Hill
High Gate Farm
Burrow's Marsh Nature Reserve
Poulton-le-Fylde
FY6
Burrow's Farm
Carter's Farm
Gaskells Farm
Danson's Farm
Bank Farm
STAYNALL
Staynall Leeches
Bank House Farm
ROBINS BANK CARAVAN PARK
Works
BURN HALL IND. EST.
Playing Field
Burn Naze
Burn Naze Prim. Sch.
Red Marsh Sch.
TRUNNAH
Trunnah
WORKS
FLINTS CARAVAN PARK
KNEPS HOLIDAY HOME & TOURING PARK
STANAH
Wyreside Ecology Centre
WYRE ESTUARY COUNTRY PARK
Stanah Ho. Farm
Prospect Hill Farm
WARDLEYS CARAVAN PARK
Wardleys Mar
Rugby Ground
Hillylaid Pool
41
56
63

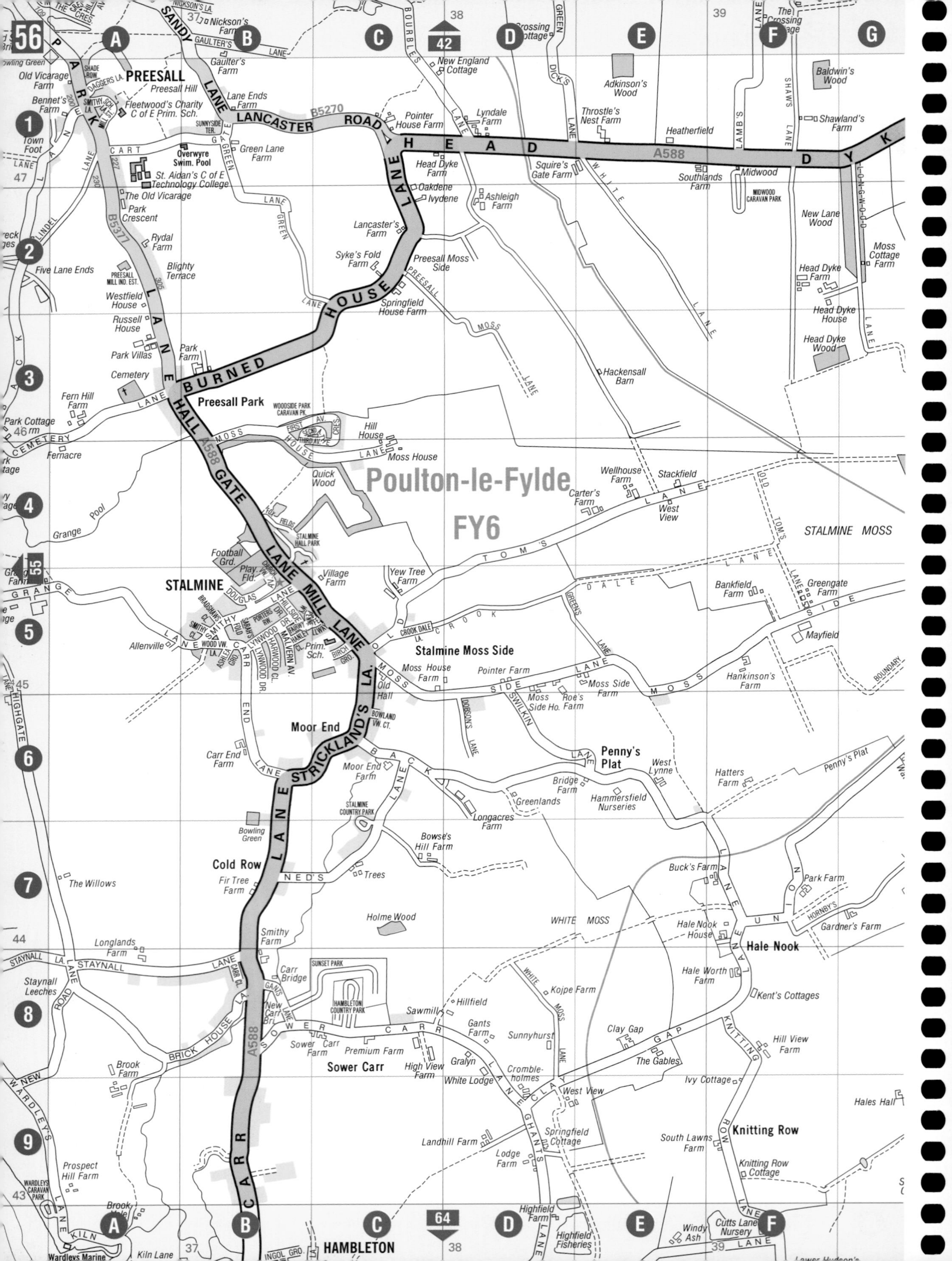

PREESALL
Preesall Hill
Old Vicarage Farm
Bennet's Farm
Town Foot
Fleetwood's Charity C of E Prim. Sch.
Gaulter's Farm
Nickson's Farm
Lane Ends Farm
LANCASTER ROAD
B5270
Overwyre Swim. Pool
St. Aidan's C of E Technology College
Green Lane Farm
The Old Vicarage
Park Crescent
Rydal Farm
Five Lane Ends
Blighty Terrace
PREESALL MILL IND. EST.
Westfield House
Russell House
Park Villas
Park Farm
Cemetery
Fern Hill Farm
Park Cottage
Fernacre
BURNED HOUSE LANE
Preesall Park
WOODSIDE PARK CARAVAN PK.
Hill House
Moss House
Quick Wood
Grange Pool
Football Grd.
Play. Fld.
STALMINE HALL PARK
Village Farm
STALMINE
Allenville
Prim. Sch.
Moor End
Carr End Farm
Moor End Farm
STALMINE COUNTRY PARK
Bowling Green
Cold Row
Fir Tree Farm
The Willows
Longlands Farm
Staynall Leeches
Smithy Farm
Carr Bridge
SUNSET PARK
HAMBLETON COUNTRY PARK
New Carr Bri.
Sower Carr Farm
Premium Farm
Sower Carr
Brook Farm
Prospect Hill Farm
WARDLEYS CARAVAN PARK
Wardleys Marine
Kiln Lane
HAMBLETON
New England Cottage
Pointer House Farm
Lyndale Farm
Crossing Cottage
Adkinson's Wood
Throstle's Nest Farm
Heatherfield
Baldwin's Wood
Shawland's Farm
HEAD DYKE
A588
Head Dyke Farm
Oakdene
Ivydene
Squire's Gate Farm
Ashleigh Farm
Southlands Farm
Midwood
MIDWOOD CARAVAN PARK
New Lane Wood
Moss Cottage Farm
Head Dyke Farm
Head Dyke House
Head Dyke Wood
Lancaster's Farm
Syke's Fold Farm
Preesall Moss Side
Springfield House Farm
Hackensall Barn
Poulton-le-Fylde
FY6
Wellhouse Farm
Stackfield
Carter's Farm
West View
STALMINE MOSS
Yew Tree Farm
Bankfield Farm
Greengate Farm
Mayfield
Stalmine Moss Side
Moss House Farm
Pointer Farm
Moss Side Farm
Moss Side Ho.
Roe's Farm
Hankinson's Farm
Old Hall
Penny's Plat
West Lynne
Hatters Farm
Bridge Farm
Greenlands
Hammersfield Nurseries
Longacres Farm
Bowse's Hill Farm
Trees
Buck's Farm
Park Farm
Holme Wood
WHITE MOSS
Hale Nook House
Hale Nook
Gardner's Farm
Hale Worth Farm
Kent's Cottages
Hillfield
Kojpe Farm
Sawmill
Gants Farm
Sunnyhurst
Clay Gap
Hill View Farm
High View Farm
Gralyn
Cromble-holmes
The Gables
White Lodge
West View
Ivy Cottage
Hales Hall
Springfield Cottage
Landhill Farm
Knitting Row
South Lawns Farm
Lodge Farm
Knitting Row Cottage
Highfield Farm
Highfield Fisheries
Windy Ash
Cutts Lane Nursery

42
55
64

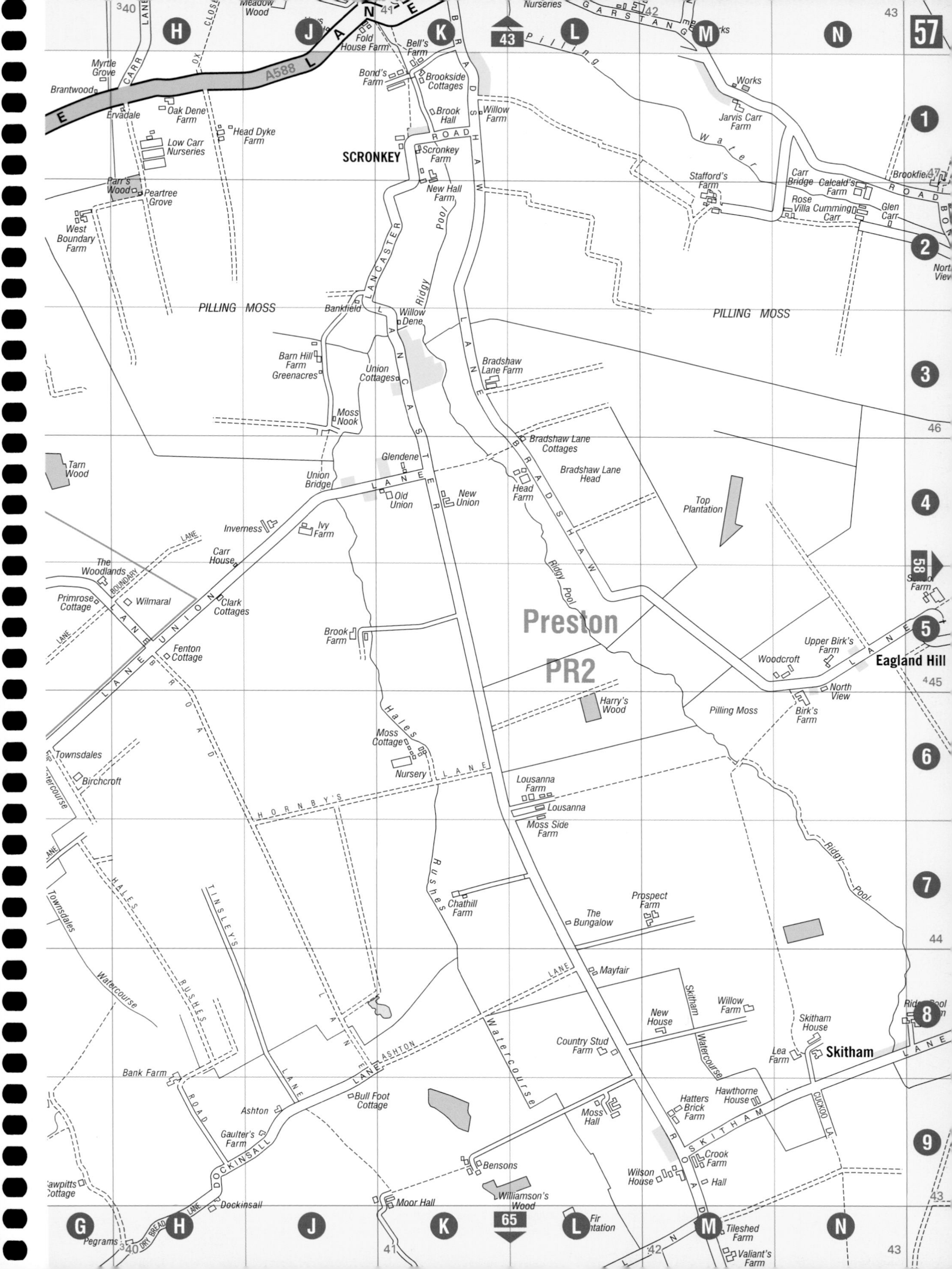
SCRONKEY
PILLING MOSS
Preston
PR2
Eagland Hill
Skitham
Pilling Moss
Myrtle Grove
Brantwood
Ervadale
Oak Dene Farm
Head Dyke Farm
Low Carr Nurseries
Parr's Wood
Peartree Grove
West Boundary Farm
Fold House Farm
Bell's Farm
Bond's Farm
Brookside Cottages
Brook Hall
Willow Farm
Scronkey Farm
New Hall Farm
Works
Jarvis Carr Farm
Stafford's Farm
Carr Bridge
Calcald's Farm
Rose Villa
Cumming Carr
Glen Carr
Brookfield
Bankfield
Willow Dene
Barn Hill Farm
Greenacres
Union Cottages
Bradshaw Lane Farm
Moss Nook
Tarn Wood
Glendene
Union Bridge
Old Union
New Union
Bradshaw Lane Cottages
Bradshaw Lane Head
Head Farm
Top Plantation
Inverness
Ivy Farm
Carr House
The Woodlands
Wilmaral
Primrose Cottage
Clark Cottages
Fenton Cottage
Brook Farm
Upper Birk's Farm
Woodcroft
North View
Birk's Farm
Harry's Wood
Townsdales
Birchcroft
Moss Cottage
Nursery
Lousanna Farm
Lousanna
Moss Side Farm
Chathill Farm
The Bungalow
Prospect Farm
Mayfair
Willow Farm
New House
Country Stud Farm
Skitham House
Lea Farm
Bank Farm
Ashton
Bull Foot Cottage
Moss Hall
Hatters Brick Farm
Hawthorne House
Gaulter's Farm
Bensons
Crook Farm
Wilson House
Hall
Williamson's Wood
Moor Hall
Dockinsall
Pegrams
Tileshed Farm
Valiant's Farm
A588
CARR LANE
OX CLOSE
BRADSHAW LANE
LANCASTER LANE
ROAD
Pilling Water
Ridgy Pool
UNION LANE
BOUNDARY LANE
BROAD ROAD
Hales
Rushes
HORNBY'S LANE
TINSLEY'S LANE
HALES
RUSHES ROAD
Watercourse
Skitham
ASHTON LANE
SKITHAM LANE
CUCKOO LA.
DOCKINSALL LANE
DRY BREAD LANE
GARSTANG ROAD
43
65
58
H J K L M N G
1 2 3 4 5 6 7 8 9
340 41 42 43
46 445 44 43

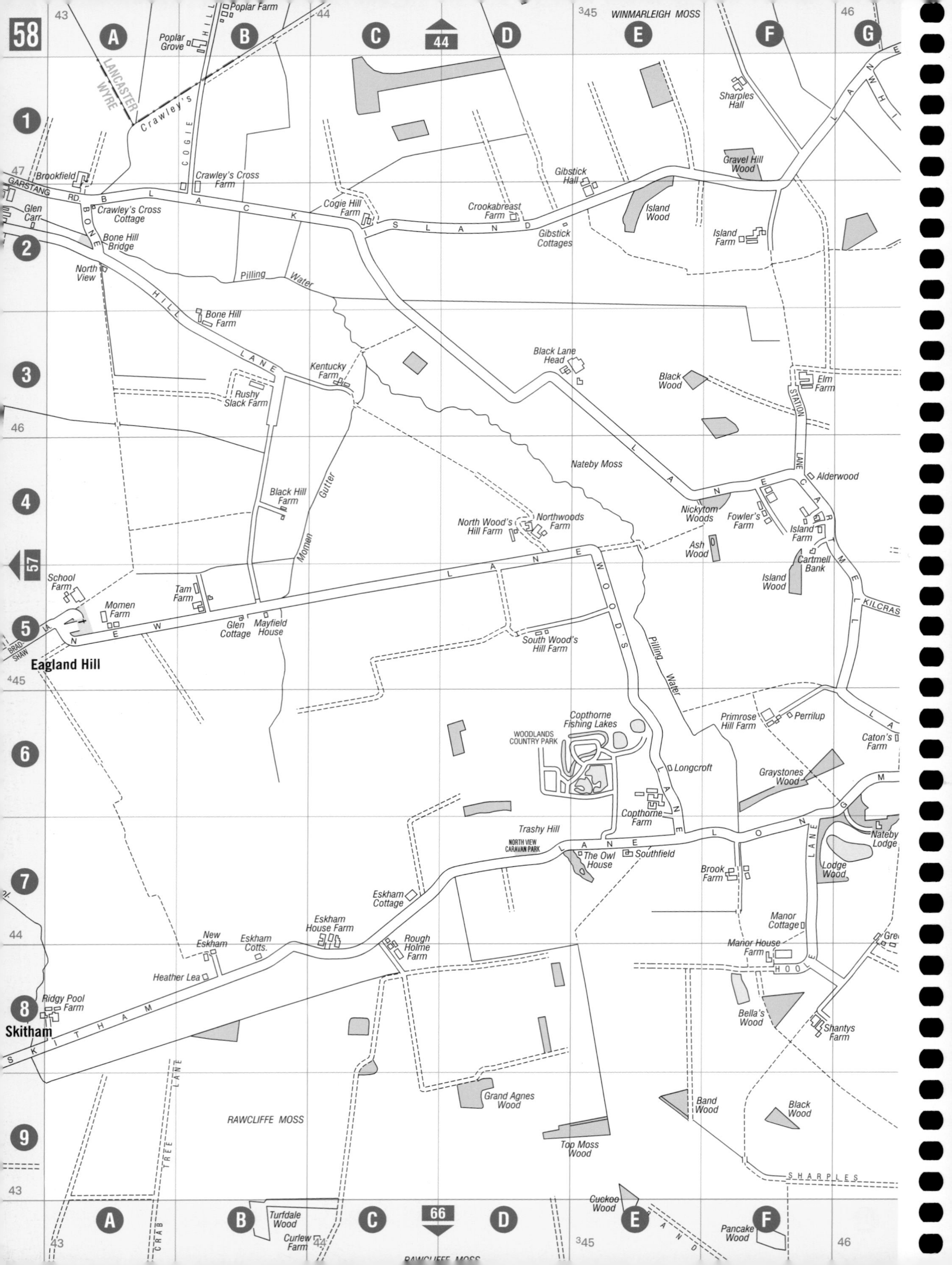

WINMARLEIGH MOSS
44
57
66
Poplar Farm
Poplar Grove
LANCASTER
WYRE
Crawley's
COGIE HILL
Brookfield
GARSTANG RD.
Crawley's Cross Farm
Crawley's Cross Cottage
Glen Carr
BONE
Bone Hill Bridge
North View
BLACK ISLAND
Cogie Hill Farm
Crookabreast Farm
Gibstick Hall
Gibstick Cottages
Island Wood
Sharples Hall
Gravel Hill Wood
Island Farm
Pilling Water
HILL LANE
Bone Hill Farm
Kentucky Farm
Rushy Slack Farm
Black Lane Head
Black Wood
Elm Farm
STATION LANE
Nateby Moss
Alderwood
Black Hill Farm
Gutter
Momen
Nickytom Woods
Fowler's Farm
Island Farm
Ash Wood
Cartmell Bank
Island Wood
CARTMELL
KILCRAS
North Wood's Hill Farm
Northwoods Farm
NEW LANE
WOOD'S LANE
School Farm
Momen Farm
Tarn Farm
Glen Cottage
Mayfield House
South Wood's Hill Farm
BRADSHAW
Eagland Hill
Pilling Water
Primrose Hill Farm
Perrilup
Caton's Farm
Copthorne Fishing Lakes
WOODLANDS COUNTRY PARK
Longcroft
Graystones Wood
Copthorne Farm
Trashy Hill
NORTH VIEW CARAVAN PARK
LONG LANE
The Owl House
Southfield
Nateby Lodge
Lodge Wood
Brook Farm
Eskham Cottage
Manor Cottage
Eskham House Farm
New Eskham
Eskham Cotts.
Rough Holme Farm
Manor House Farm
HOO
Heather Lea
Ridgy Pool Farm
Skitham
SKITHAM
Bella's Wood
Shantys Farm
Grand Agnes Wood
Band Wood
Black Wood
RAWCLIFFE MOSS
Top Moss Wood
CRAB TREE LANE
SHARPLES
Cuckoo Wood
Turfdale Wood
Curlew Farm
Pancake Wood
RAWCLIFFE MOSS

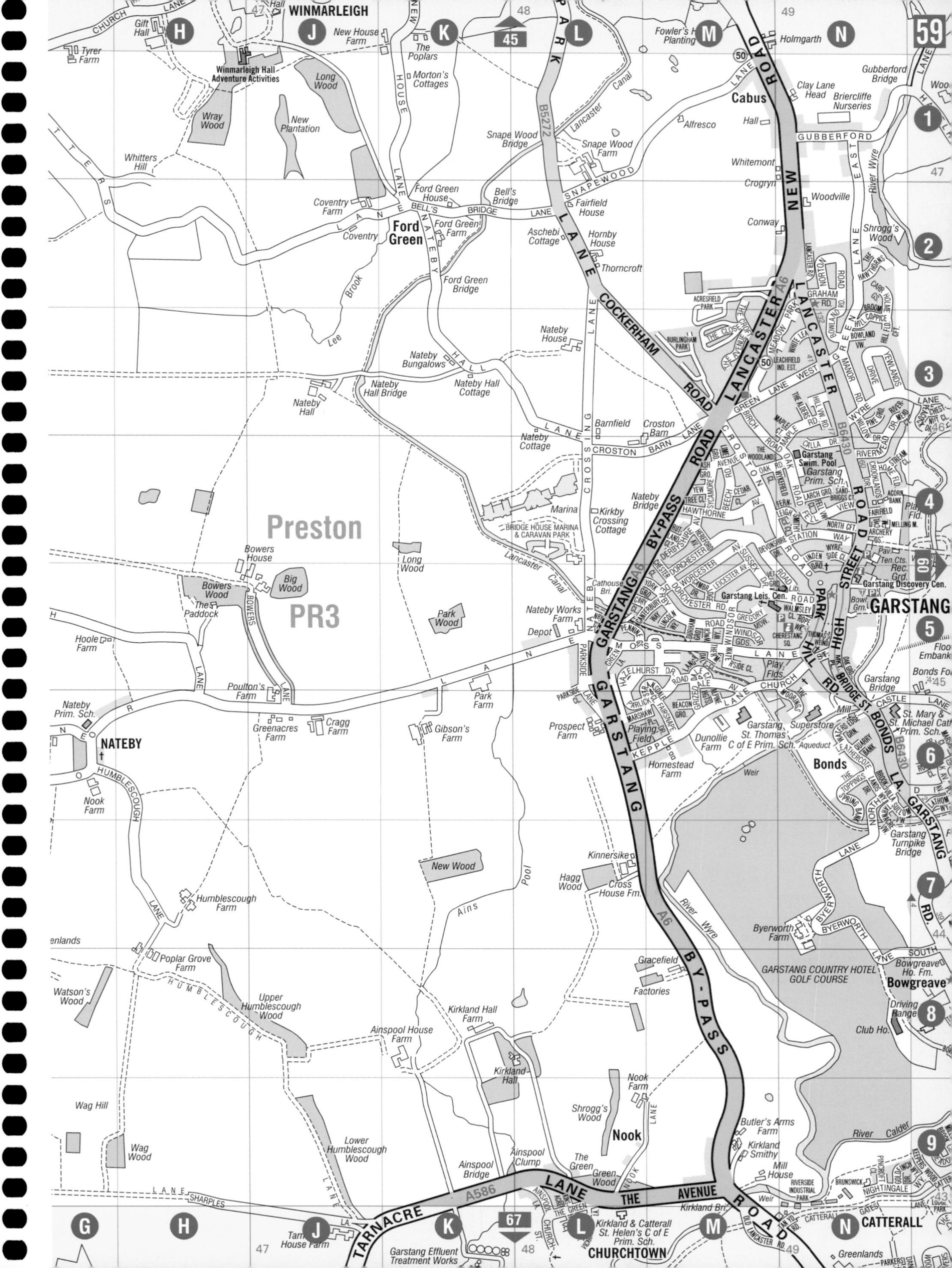
WINMARLEIGH
Winmarleigh Hall Adventure Activities
Gift Hall
Tyrer Farm
Wray Wood
Long Wood
New Plantation
New House Farm
The Poplars
Morton's Cottages
45
Fowler's Hill Planting
Holmgarth
Cabus
Clay Lane Head
Briercliffe Nurseries
Gubberford Bridge
Alfresco
Snape Wood Bridge
Snape Wood Farm
Whitters Hill
Coventry Farm
Ford Green House
Ford Green
Coventry
Ford Green Farm
Bell's Bridge
Fairfield House
Whitemont
Crogryn
Woodville
Conway
Shrogg's Wood
Aschebi Cottage
Hornby House
Thorncroft
Ford Green Bridge
Nateby House
Nateby Bungalows
Nateby Hall Bridge
Nateby Hall Cottage
Nateby Hall
Barnfield
Croston Barn
Nateby Cottage
Garstang Swim. Pool
Garstang Prim. Sch.
Marina
Kirkby Crossing Cottage
Nateby Bridge
BRIDGE HOUSE MARINA & CARAVAN PARK
Preston
PR3
Bowers House
Long Wood
Bowers Wood
Big Wood
The Paddock
Park Wood
Cathouse Bri.
Nateby Works Farm
Depot
Garstang Leis. Cen.
Garstang Discovery Cen.
GARSTANG
Hoole Farm
Poulton's Farm
Park Farm
Nateby Prim. Sch.
NATEBY
Greenacres Farm
Cragg Farm
Gibson's Farm
Prospect Farm
Garstang St. Thomas' C of E Prim. Sch.
Superstore
Dunollie Farm
Homestead Farm
Bonds
Garstang Bridge
St. Mary & St. Michael Cath. Prim. Sch.
Garstang Turnpike Bridge
Nook Farm
Humblescough Farm
Kinnersike
Hagg Wood
Cross House Fm.
New Wood
Byerworth Farm
Poplar Grove Farm
Watson's Wood
Upper Humblescough Wood
Gracefield
Factories
GARSTANG COUNTRY HOTEL GOLF COURSE
Bowgreave Ho. Fm.
Bowgreave
Driving Range
Club Ho.
Kirkland Hall Farm
Ainspool House Farm
Kirkland Hall
Wag Hill
Wag Wood
Lower Humblescough Wood
Shrogg's Wood
Nook
Butler's Arms Farm
Kirkland Smithy
Mill House
Ainspool Bridge
Ainspool Clump
The Green
Green Wood
RIVERSIDE INDUSTRIAL PARK
Tarnacre House Farm
Garstang Effluent Treatment Works
67
Kirkland & Catterall St. Helen's C of E Prim. Sch.
CHURCHTOWN
CATTERALL
Greenlands
A6
A586
B5272
B6430
River Wyre
River Calder
Lancaster Canal
Ains Pool
TARNACRE LANE
THE AVENUE
GARSTANG BY-PASS
GARSTANG ROAD
LANCASTER ROAD
COCKERHAM ROAD
NEW ROAD
PARK LANE
HUMBLESCOUGH LANE
SHARPLES LANE
BOWERS LANE
CROSTON BARN LANE
MOSS LANE
CHURCH LANE
HIGH STREET
BRIDGE ST.
PARK HILL RD.
BONDS LA.
BYERWORTH LANE
G H J K L M N
1 2 3 4 5 6 7 8 9
47 48 49

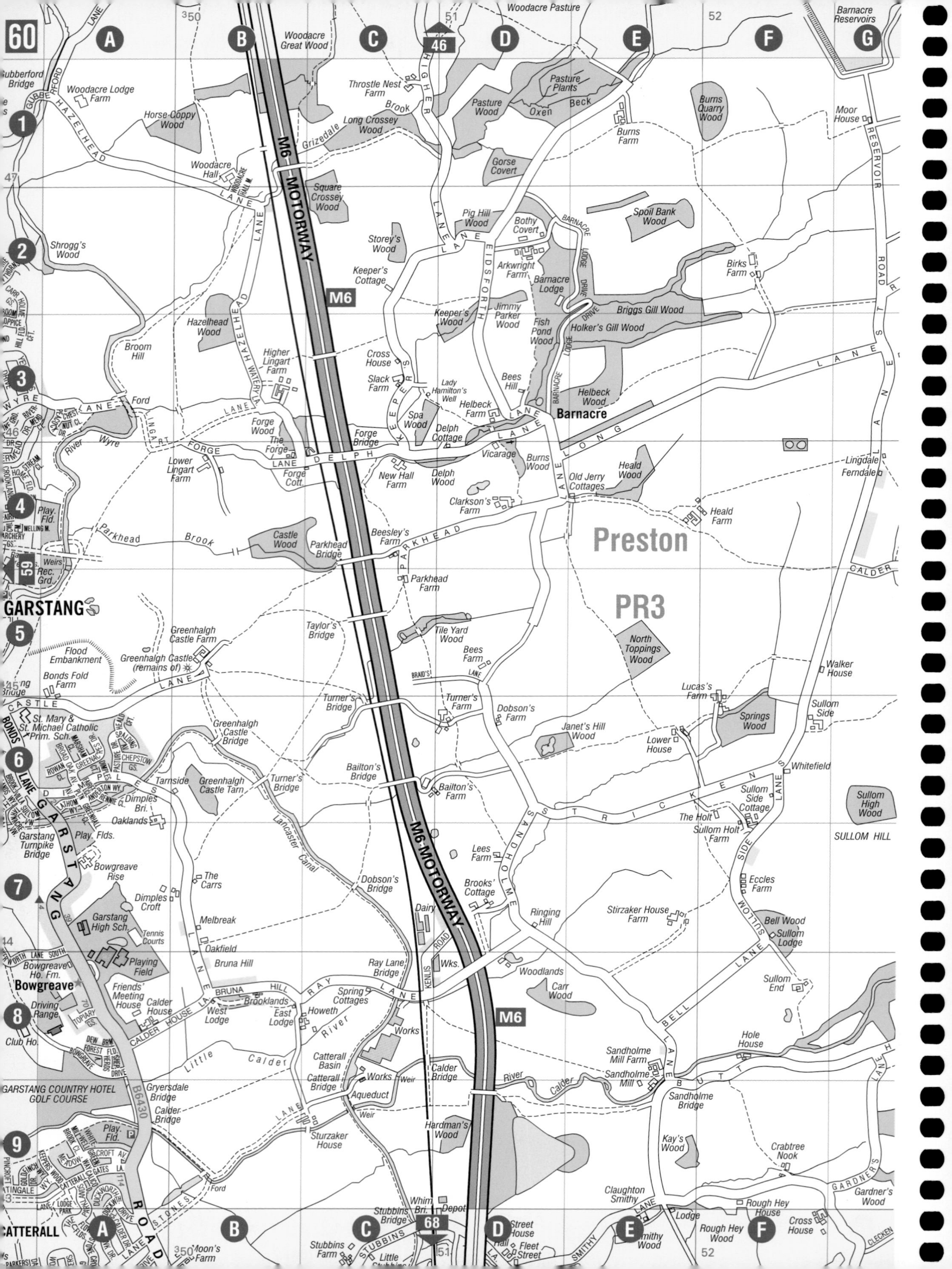

60
A
B
C
D
E
F
G
350
51
52
46
Woodacre Pasture
Barnacre Reservoirs
Woodacre Great Wood
Gubberford Bridge
Woodacre Lodge Farm
Throstle Nest Farm
Pasture Plants
Pasture Wood
Oxen
Beck
Burns Quarry Wood
Moor House
Horse Coppy Wood
Long Crossey Wood
Grizedale
Brook
Burns Farm
Woodacre Hall
Gorse Covert
M6
MOTORWAY
Square Crossey Wood
Pig Hill Wood
Bothy Covert
Spoil Bank Wood
Shrogg's Wood
Storey's Wood
Arkwright Farm
Birks Farm
Keeper's Cottage
Barnacre Lodge
Briggs Gill Wood
Keeper's Wood
Jimmy Parker Wood
Fish Pond Wood
Holker's Gill Wood
Hazelhead Wood
Broom Hill
Higher Lingart Farm
Cross House
Slack Farm
Lady Hamilton's Well
Bees Hill
Helbeck Wood
WYRE LANE
Ford
Spa Wood
Helbeck Farm
Barnacre
Forge Wood
The Forge
Forge Bridge
Delph Cottage
River Wyre
FORGE LANE
DELPH LANE
Vicarage
Burns Wood
LONG LANE
Lingdale
Ferndale
Lower Lingart Farm
Forge Cott.
New Hall Farm
Delph Wood
Old Jerry Cottages
Heald Wood
Clarkson's Farm
Heald Farm
Play. Fld.
Parkhead
Brook
Castle Wood
Parkhead Bridge
Beesley's Farm
PARKHEAD
Preston
59
Weirs
Rec. Grd.
CALDER
GARSTANG
Parkhead Farm
PR3
Flood Embankment
Greenhalgh Castle Farm
Taylor's Bridge
Tile Yard Wood
Greenhalgh Castle (remains of)
Bees Farm
North Toppings Wood
Walker House
Bonds Fold Farm
CASTLE LANE
BRAID'S LANE
Lucas's Farm
Sullom Side
St. Mary & St. Michael Catholic Prim. Sch.
Turner's Bridge
Turner's Farm
Dobson's Farm
Springs Wood
BONDS LANE
Greenhalgh Castle Bridge
Janet's Hill Wood
Lower House
Tarnside
Greenhalgh Castle Tarn
Turner's Bridge
Bailton's Bridge
Bailton's Farm
Whitefield
Dimples Bri.
STRICKENS LANE
Sullom Side Cottage
Sullom High Wood
Oaklands
The Holt
Sullom Holt Farm
SULLOM HILL
Garstang Turnpike Bridge
Play. Flds.
Lancaster Canal
Lees Farm
SANDHOLME
Bowgreave Rise
The Carrs
Dobson's Bridge
Brooks' Cottage
Eccles Farm
Dimples Croft
Ringing Hill
Stirzaker House Farm
Bell Wood
Garstang High Sch.
Tennis Courts
Melbreak
Dairy
SULLOM SIDE
Sullom Lodge
GARSTANG ROAD
Oakfield
Playing Field
Bruna Hill
Ray Lane Bridge
KENLIS ROAD
Wks.
Woodlands
BELL LANE
Bowgreave Ho. Fm.
Bowgreave
Friends' Meeting House
BRUNA HILL
RAY LANE
Spring Cottages
Carr Wood
Sullom End
Calder House
Brooklands
Howeth
Driving Range
CALDER HOUSE LA.
West Lodge
East Lodge
River
Works
Club Ho.
Little Calder
Hole House
Catterall Basin
Works
Calder Bridge
Sandholme Mill Farm
BUTT LANE
GARSTANG COUNTRY HOTEL GOLF COURSE
Gryersdale Bridge
Catterall Bridge
Weir
Aqueduct
River Calder
Sandholme Mill
Sandholme Bridge
B6430
Calder Bridge
Play. Fld.
Sturzaker House
Hardman's Wood
Kay's Wood
Crabtree Nook
GARDNER'S
Gardner's Wood
Ford
Claughton Smithy
STONES LANE
Whim Bri.
Depot
Rough Hey House
Stubbins Bridge
68
Street House
Lodge
Rough Hey Wood
Cross House
CATTERALL
Stubbins Farm
STUBBINS
Fleet Street
SMITHY
Smithy Wood
Moon's Farm
Little Stubbins
ROAD

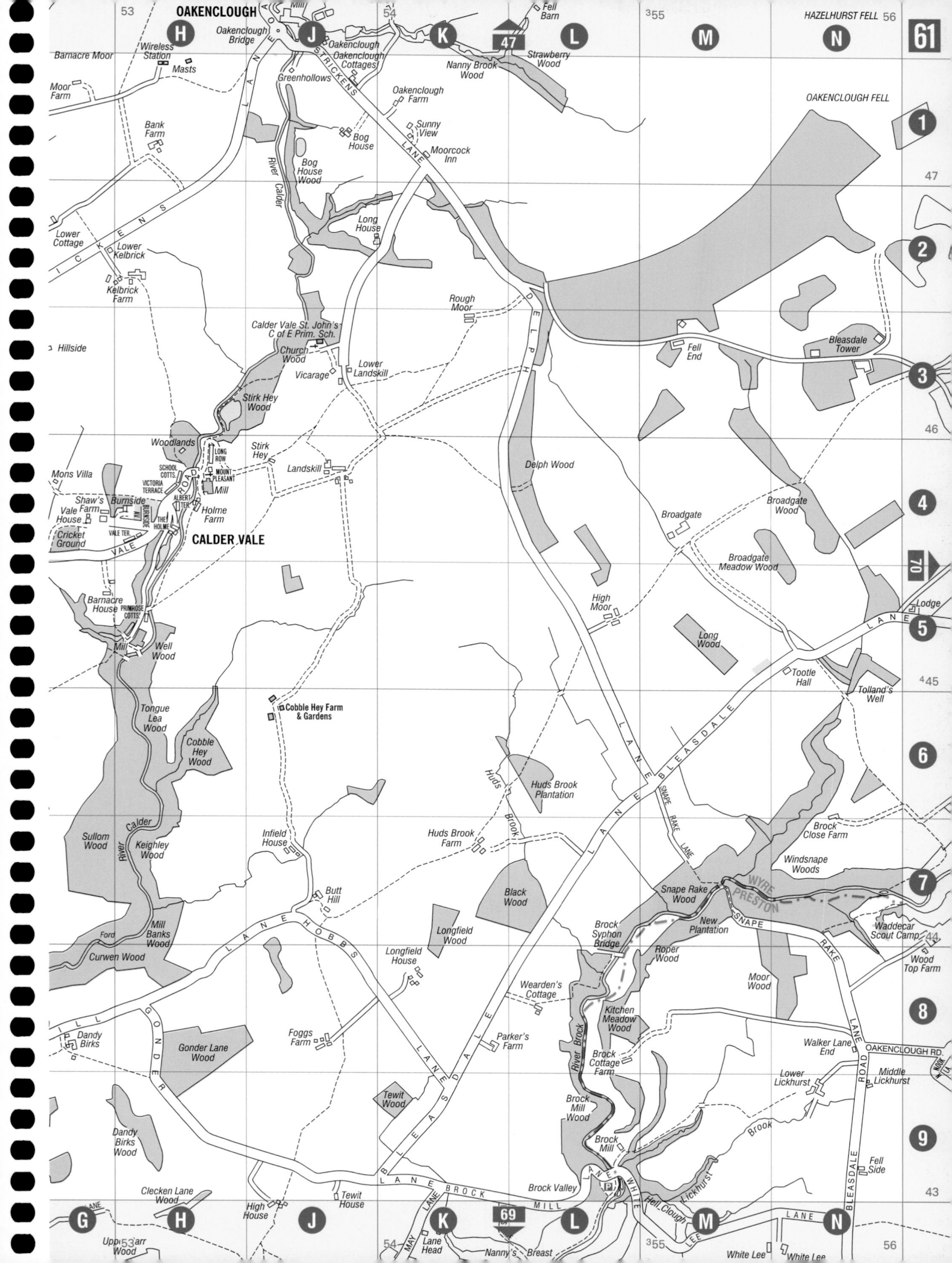
OAKENCLOUGH
Oakenclough Bridge
Oakenclough
Oakenclough Cottages
Greenhollows
Barnacre Moor
Wireless Station
Masts
Moor Farm
Bank Farm
Bog House
Bog House Wood
River Calder
Oakenclough Farm
Sunny View
Moorcock Inn
Nanny Brook Wood
Strawberry Wood
Fell Barn
HAZELHURST FELL
OAKENCLOUGH FELL
Long House
Lower Cottage
Lower Kelbrick
Kelbrick Farm
Hillside
Rough Moor
Calder Vale St. John's C of E Prim. Sch.
Church Wood
Vicarage
Lower Landskill
Fell End
Bleasdale Tower
Stirk Hey Wood
Woodlands
Stirk Hey
Landskill
Mons Villa
Delph Wood
Shaw's Farm
Burnside
Vale House
Cricket Ground
Holme Farm
Mill
CALDER VALE
Broadgate
Broadgate Wood
Broadgate Meadow Wood
Barnacre House
High Moor
Lodge
Long Wood
Well Wood
Tootle Hall
Tolland's Well
Tongue Lea Wood
Cobble Hey Farm & Gardens
Cobble Hey Wood
Huds Brook Plantation
Sullom Wood
Keighley Wood
Infield House
Huds Brook Farm
Brock Close Farm
Windsnape Woods
Butt Hill
Black Wood
Snape Rake Wood
WYRE
PRESTON
Mill Banks Wood
Curwen Wood
Longfield Wood
Longfield House
Brock Syphon Bridge
New Plantation
Roper Wood
Waddecar Scout Camp
Wood Top Farm
Moor Wood
Wearden's Cottage
Kitchen Meadow Wood
Dandy Birks
Foggs Farm
Gonder Lane Wood
Parker's Farm
Walker Lane End
OAKENCLOUGH RD.
Brock Cottage Farm
Lower Lickhurst
Middle Lickhurst
Tewit Wood
Brock Mill Wood
Dandy Birks Wood
Brock Mill
Fell Side
Clecken Lane Wood
High House
Tewit House
Brock Valley
Hell Clough
Lickhurst
White Lee
Upper Sharr Wood
Lane Head
Nanny's Breast
STRICKENS LANE
DELPH LANE
BLEASDALE LANE
HOBBS LANE
GONDER LANE
BROCK MILL LANE
SNAPE RAKE LANE
BLEASDALE ROAD
47
69
70

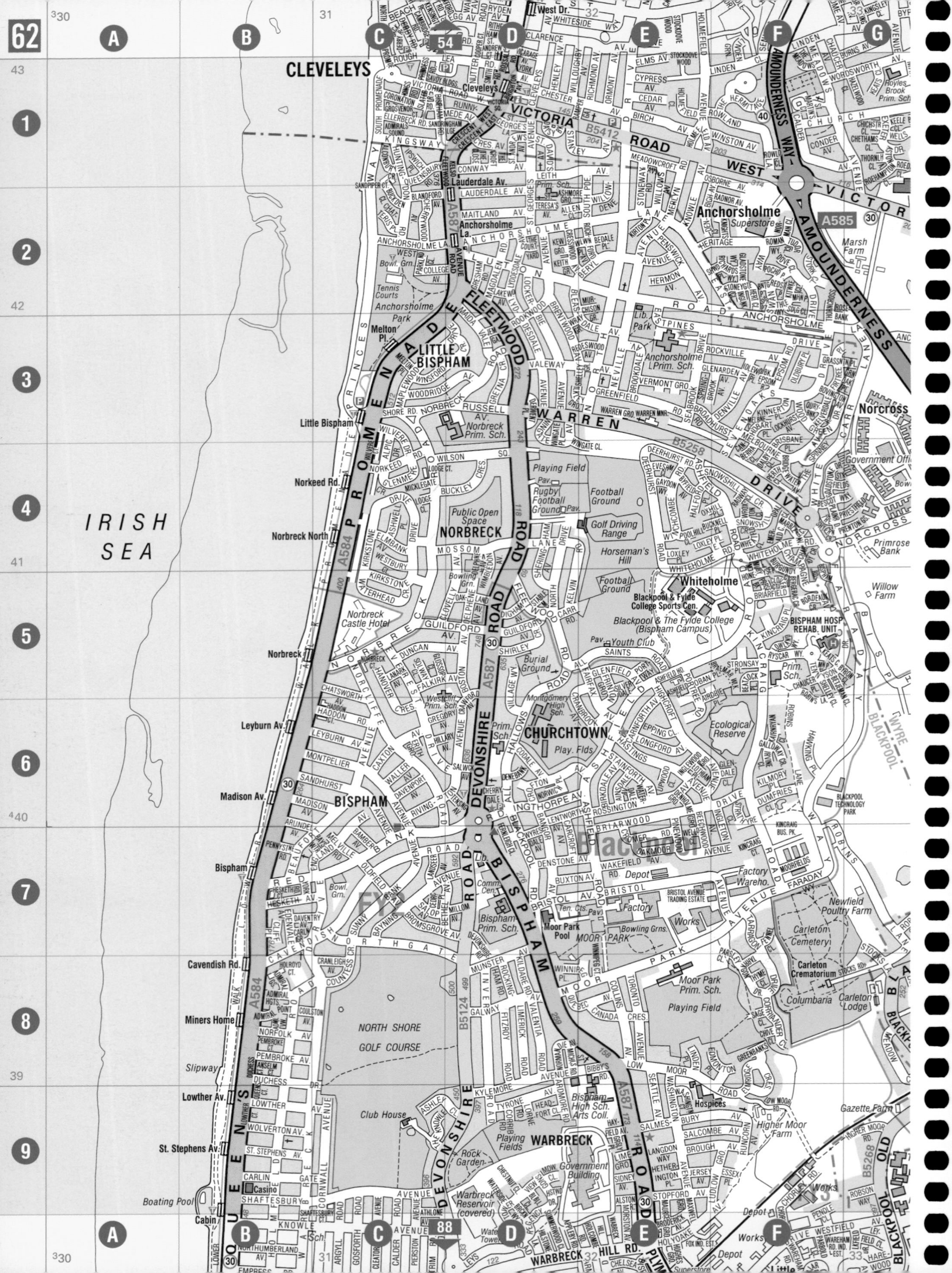

62
A
B
C
D
E
F
G
54
88
CLEVELEYS
IRISH SEA
LITTLE BISPHAM
NORBRECK
BISPHAM
CHURCHTOWN
WARBRECK
Anchorsholme
Norcross
Whiteholme
VICTORIA ROAD WEST
AMOUNDERNESS WAY
PROMENADE
FLEETWOOD ROAD
DEVONSHIRE ROAD
BISPHAM ROAD
QUEENS PROMENADE
WARREN DRIVE
ANCHORSHOLME LANE
NORTH SHORE GOLF COURSE
Club House
Anchorsholme Park
Anchorsholme Prim. Sch.
Norbreck Prim. Sch.
Norbreck Castle Hotel
Public Open Space
Golf Driving Range
Horseman's Hill
Football Ground
Rugby Football Ground
Playing Field
Blackpool & Fylde College Sports Cen.
Blackpool & The Fylde College (Bispham Campus)
Youth Club
Burial Ground
Montgomery High Sch.
Westcliff Prim. Sch.
Ecological Reserve
Bispham Hosp. Rehab. Unit
Moor Park Pool
Moor Park Prim. Sch.
Bispham Prim. Sch.
Bispham High Sch. Arts Coll.
Carleton Cemetery
Carleton Crematorium
Columbaria
Carleton Lodge
Newfield Poultry Farm
Higher Moor Farm
Gazette Farm
Hospices
Marsh Farm
Willow Farm
Primrose Bank
Warbreck Reservoir (covered)
Rock Garden
Government Building
Casino
Boating Pool
Cabin
Slipway
Little Bispham
Norkeed Rd.
Norbreck North
Norbreck
Leyburn Av.
Madison Av.
Bispham
Cavendish Rd.
Miners Home
Lowther Av.
St. Stephens Av.
Melton Pl.
Anchorsholme La.
Lauderdale Av.
Cleveleys
West Dr.
A584
A587
A585
B5412
B5258
B5124
B5268
Blackpool
FY2

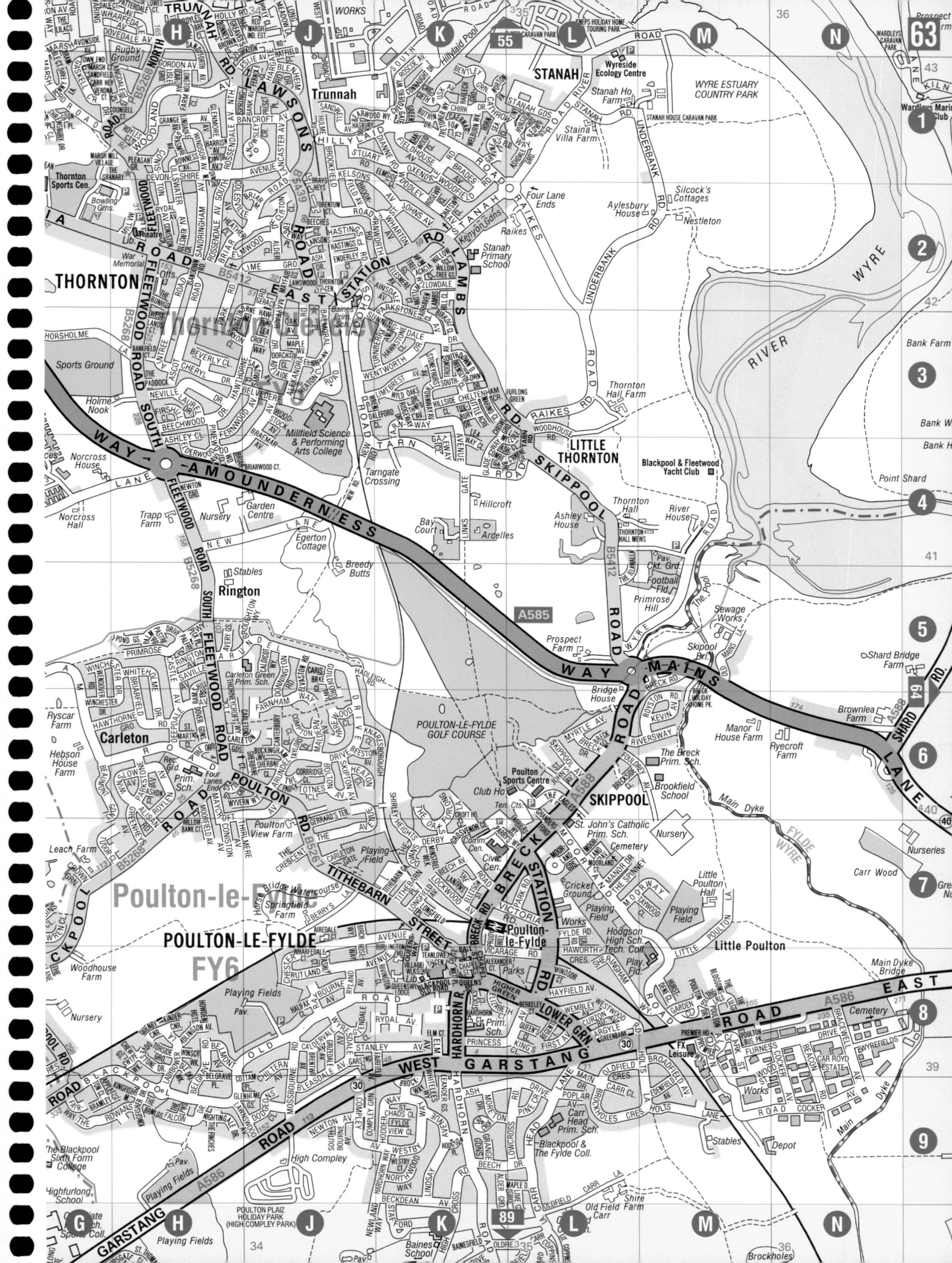
63
THORNTON
Thornton Cleveleys
STANAH
Trunnah
LITTLE THORNTON
Rington
Carleton
SKIPPOOL
Poulton-le-Fylde
POULTON-LE-FYLDE
FY6
Little Poulton
WYRE ESTUARY COUNTRY PARK
RIVER WYRE
POULTON-LE-FYLDE GOLF COURSE
AMOUNDERNESS WAY
MAINS WAY
A585
A586
A588
B5412
B5268
Blackpool & Fleetwood Yacht Club
Millfield Science & Performing Arts College
Blackpool & The Fylde Coll.
The Blackpool Sixth Form College
55
89
64

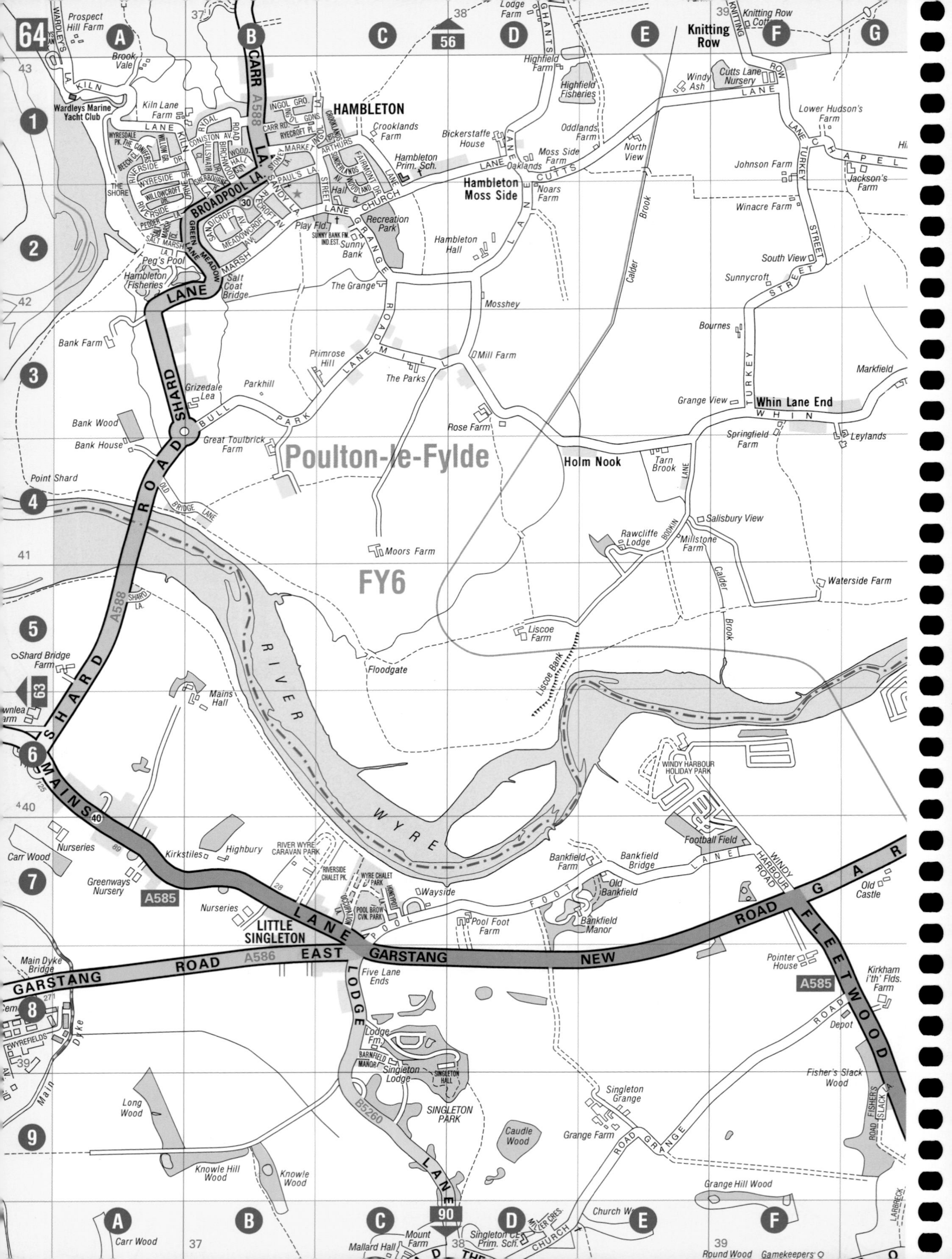
56
63
90
Prospect Hill Farm
Brook Vale
Wardleys Marine Yacht Club
Kiln Lane Farm
HAMBLETON
Crooklands Farm
Lodge Farm
Highfield Farm
Highfield Fisheries
Knitting Row
Knitting Row Cott.
Cutts Lane Nursery
Windy Ash
Lower Hudson's Farm
Bickerstaffe House
Oddlands Farm
North View
Hambleton Prim. Sch.
Moss Side Farm
Oaklands
Hambleton Moss Side
Noars Farm
Johnson Farm
Jackson's Farm
Winacre Farm
THE SHORE
Play Fld.
SUNNY BANK FM. IND.EST.
Sunny Bank
Recreation Park
Hambleton Hall
Peg's Pool
Hambleton Fisheries
Salt Coat Bridge
The Grange
Mosshey
South View
Sunnycroft
Bournes
Bank Farm
Primrose Hill
Mill Farm
The Parks
Grizedale Lea
Parkhill
Markfield
Grange View
Whin Lane End
Bank Wood
Rose Farm
Springfield Farm
Leylands
Bank House
Great Toulbrick Farm
Poulton-le-Fylde
Holm Nook
Tarn Brook
Point Shard
Salisbury View
Rawcliffe Lodge
Millstone Farm
Moors Farm
FY6
Waterside Farm
Liscoe Farm
Shard Bridge Farm
Floodgate
Liscoe Bank
Mains Hall
RIVER WYRE
Calder Brook
WINDY HARBOUR HOLIDAY PARK
Nurseries
Carr Wood
Kirkstiles
Highbury
RIVER WYRE CARAVAN PARK
Football Field
Bankfield Farm
Bankfield Bridge
Greenways Nursery
RIVERSIDE CHALET PK.
WYRE CHALET PARK
Wayside
Old Bankfield
Old Castle
A585
Nurseries
POOL BROW CVN. PARK
Pool Foot Farm
Bankfield Manor
LITTLE SINGLETON
Main Dyke Bridge
GARSTANG ROAD EAST
A586
GARSTANG NEW ROAD
Five Lane Ends
Pointer House
Kirkham i'th' Flds. Farm
WYREFIELDS
Lodge Fm.
Depot
BARNFIELD MANOR
Singleton Lodge
SINGLETON HALL
Fisher's Slack Wood
Long Wood
SINGLETON PARK
Singleton Grange
Caudle Wood
Grange Farm
Knowle Hill Wood
Knowle Wood
Grange Hill Wood
Church Wood
Carr Wood
Mallard Hall
Mount Farm
Singleton CE Prim. Sch.
Round Wood
Gamekeepers
SHARD ROAD
A588
MAINS LANE
LODGE LANE
B5260
FLEETWOOD ROAD
WINDY HARBOUR ROAD
GRANGE ROAD
MILL LANE
BULL PARK LANE
CHURCH LANE
CUTTS LANE
TURKEY STREET
WHIN LANE
BROADPOOL LA.
CARR LA.

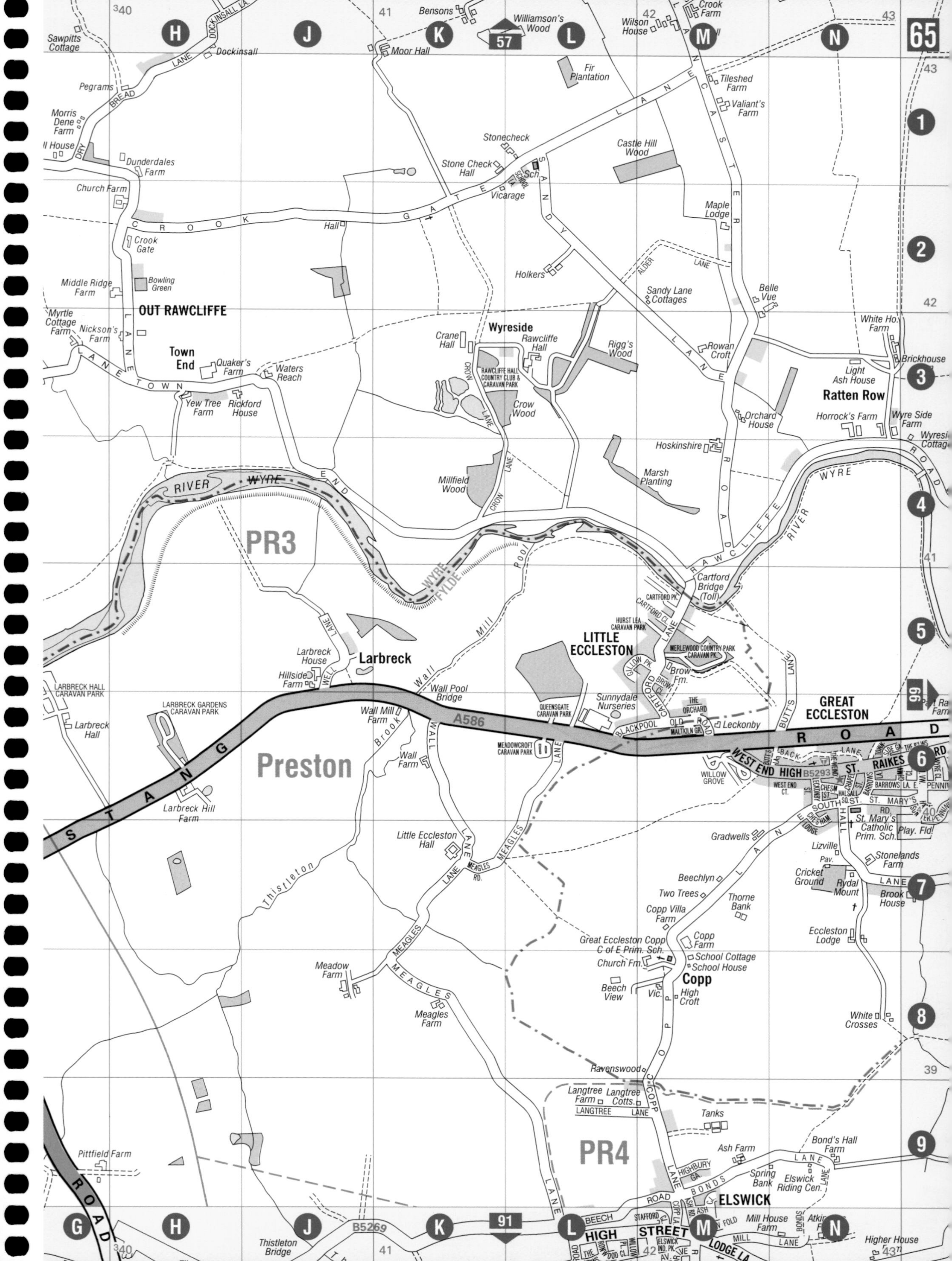
OUT RAWCLIFFE
Town End
Wyreside
Ratten Row
Larbreck
LITTLE ECCLESTON
GREAT ECCLESTON
Copp
ELSWICK
PR3
PR4
Preston
RIVER WYRE
A586
B5269
B5293
STANG ROAD
CROOK GATE LANE
LANCASTER ROAD
SANDY LANE
RAWCLIFFE ROAD
MEAGLES LANE
COPP LANE
HIGH STREET
57
91
66
Crook Farm
Williamson's Wood
Fir Plantation
Castle Hill Wood
Rigg's Wood
Crow Wood
Millfield Wood
Marsh Planting
Cartford Bridge (Toll)
Rawcliffe Hall
Larbreck Hall
Larbreck Hill Farm
Little Eccleston Hall
Meagles Farm
Copp Farm
Great Eccleston Copp C of E Prim. Sch.
St. Mary's Catholic Prim. Sch.
Pittfield Farm
Thistleton Bridge
Higher House

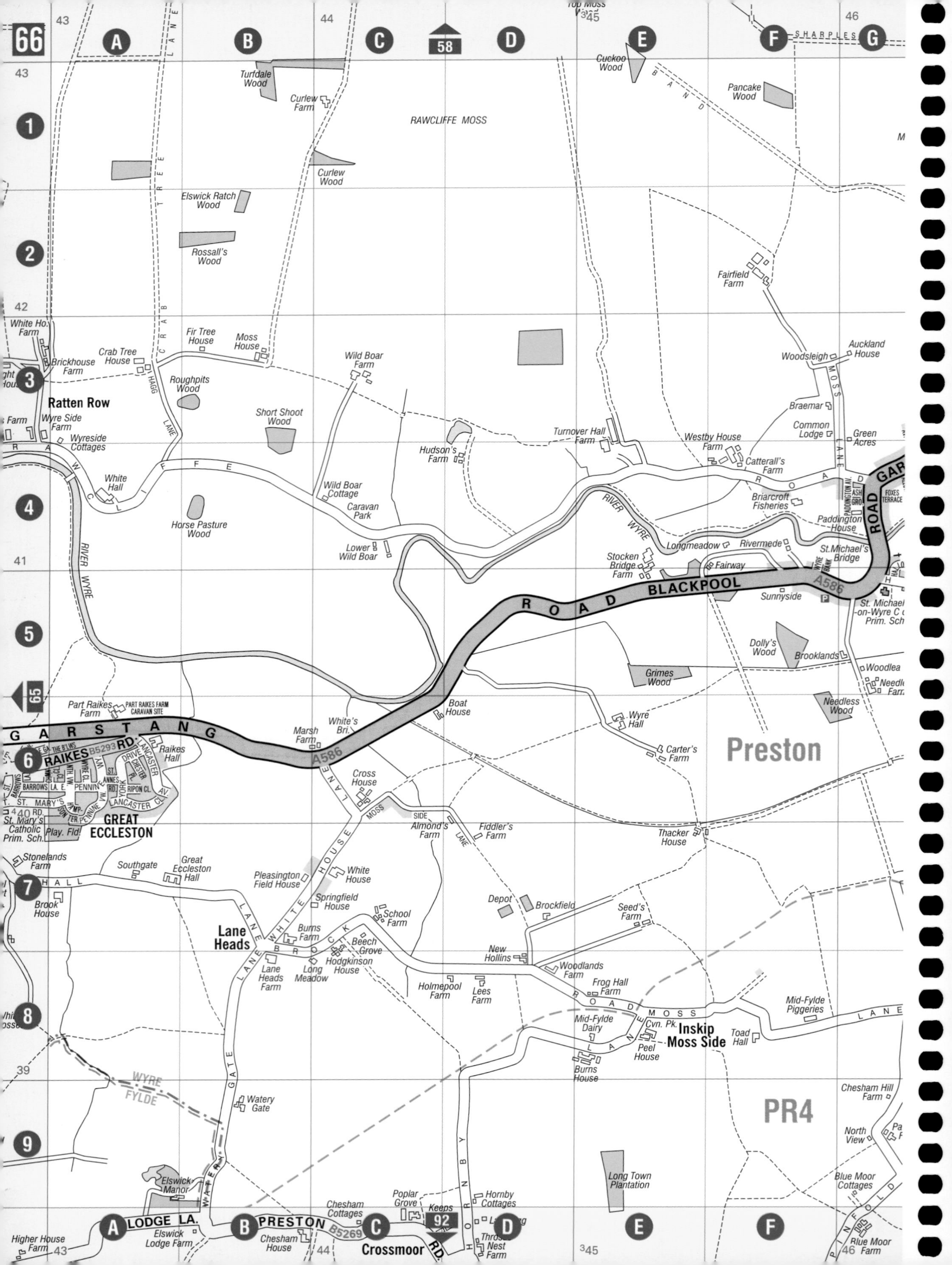
58
65
92
RAWCLIFFE MOSS
Turfdale Wood
Curlew Farm
Curlew Wood
Elswick Ratch Wood
Rossall's Wood
Cuckoo Wood
Pancake Wood
Fairfield Farm
White Ho. Farm
Brickhouse Farm
Crab Tree House
Fir Tree House
Moss House
Wild Boar Farm
Ratten Row
Roughpits Wood
Wyre Side Farm
Wyreside Cottages
Short Shoot Wood
White Hall
Horse Pasture Wood
Wild Boar Cottage
Caravan Park
Lower Wild Boar
Hudson's Farm
Turnover Hall Farm
Westby House Farm
Catterall's Farm
Woodsleigh
Auckland House
Braemar
Common Lodge
Green Acres
Briarcroft Fisheries
Paddington House
Longmeadow
Rivermede
St. Michael's Bridge
Stocken Bridge Farm
Fairway
Sunnyside
St. Michael -on-Wyre C Prim. Sch
RIVER WYRE
CRAB TREE LANE
HAGG LANE
RAWCLIFFE ROAD
BAND
MOSS LANE
BLACKPOOL ROAD
GARSTANG ROAD
A586
B5293
Dolly's Wood
Brooklands
Woodlea
Needless Wood
Grimes Wood
Part Raikes Farm
PART RAIKES FARM CARAVAN SITE
Boat House
Wyre Hall
Carter's Farm
Preston
Marsh Farm
White's Bri.
Raikes Hall
RAIKES RD.
GREAT ECCLESTON
St. Mary's Catholic Prim. Sch.
Play. Fld.
Cross House
MOSS SIDE LANE
Almond's Farm
Fiddler's Farm
Thacker House
Stonelands Farm
Southgate
Great Eccleston Hall
HALL LANE
Brook House
Pleasington Field House
White House
WHITE HOUSE LANE
Springfield House
School Farm
Depot
Brockfield
Seed's Farm
Lane Heads
Burns Farm
Beech Grove
BROCK ROAD
Hodgkinson House
Lane Heads Farm
Long Meadow
New Hollins
Woodlands Farm
Frog Hall Farm
Holmepool Farm
Lees Farm
MOSS LANE
Mid-Fylde Piggeries
Mid-Fylde Dairy
Cvn. Pk.
Inskip Moss Side
Toad Hall
Peel House
Burns House
WYRE
FYLDE
Watery Gate
GATE LANE
PR4
Chesham Hill Farm
North View
Elswick Manor
Long Town Plantation
HORNBY ROAD
Blue Moor Cottages
PINFOLD
Poplar Grove
Hornby Cottages
Keeps
Chesham Cottages
LODGE LA.
PRESTON ROAD
B5269
Higher House Farm
Elswick Lodge Farm
Chesham House
Crossmoor
Throstle Nest Farm
Blue Moor Farm

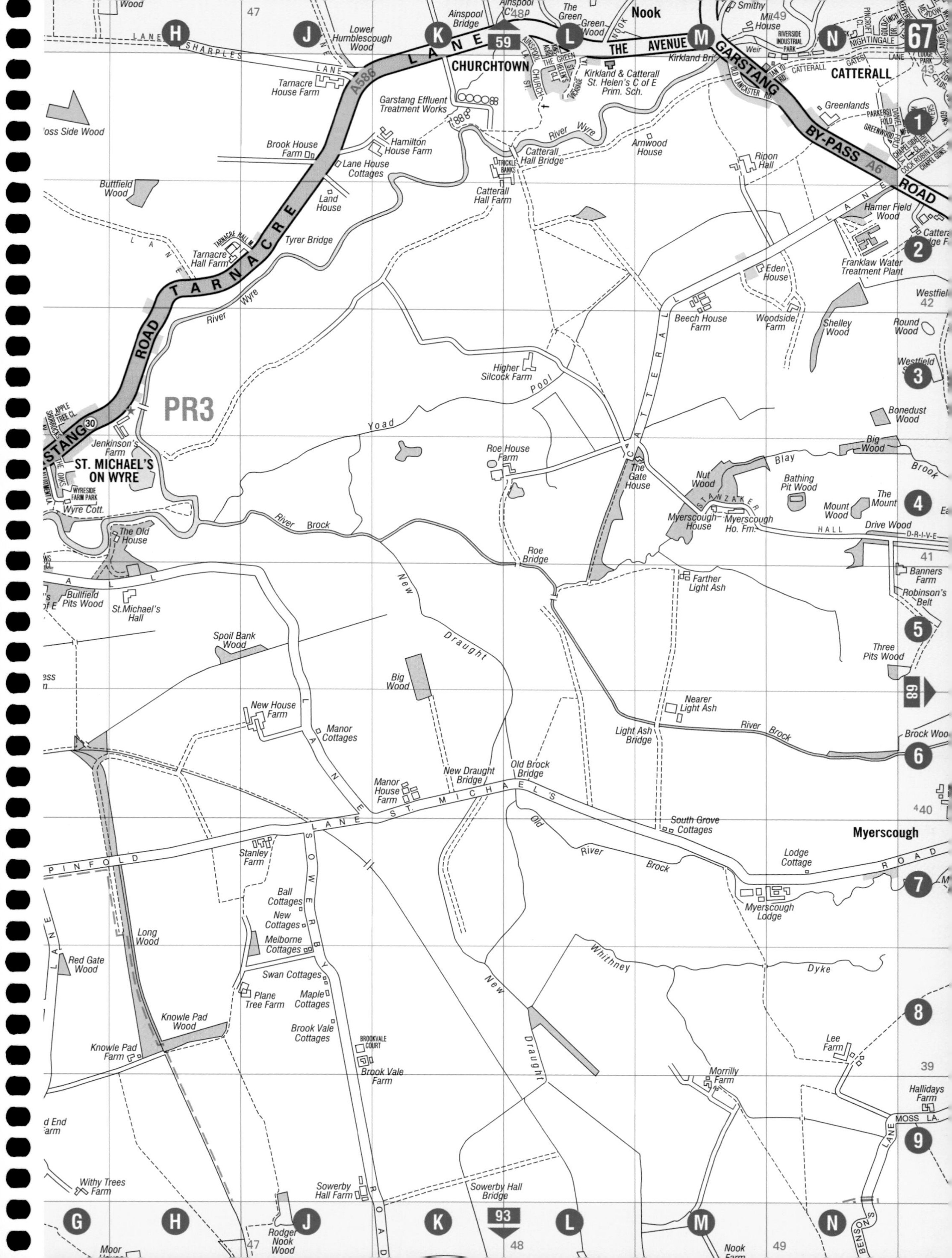

Nook
CHURCHTOWN
CATTERALL
THE AVENUE
GARSTANG BY-PASS ROAD
TARNACRE LANE
GARSTANG ROAD
PR3
ST. MICHAEL'S ON WYRE
River Wyre
River Brock
Myerscough
Lower Humblescough Wood
Ainspool Bridge
Tarnacre House Farm
Garstang Effluent Treatment Works
Kirkland & Catterall St. Helen's C of E Prim. Sch.
Greenlands
Brook House Farm
Hamilton House Farm
Lane House Cottages
Catterall Hall Bridge
Arnwood House
Ripon Hall
Buttfield Wood
Land House
Catterall Hall Farm
Hamer Field Wood
Tarnacre Hall Farm
Tyrer Bridge
Franklaw Water Treatment Plant
Eden House
Beech House Farm
Woodside Farm
Shelley Wood
Round Wood
Higher Silcock Farm
Yoad Pool
Bonedust Wood
Big Wood
Roe House Farm
The Gate House
Nut Wood
Bathing Pit Wood
The Mount
Mount Wood
Myerscough House
Myerscough Ho. Fm.
Drive Wood
Jenkinson's Farm
Wyre Cott.
The Old House
Roe Bridge
Farther Light Ash
Banners Farm
Robinson's Belt
Bullfield Pits Wood
St.Michael's Hall
Spoil Bank Wood
New Draught
Three Pits Wood
Big Wood
New House Farm
Manor Cottages
Nearer Light Ash
Light Ash Bridge
Brock Wood
New Draught Bridge
Old Brock Bridge
Manor House Farm
ST. MICHAEL'S LANE
PINFOLD LANE
South Grove Cottages
Stanley Farm
Old River Brock
Lodge Cottage
Myerscough Lodge
Ball Cottages
New Cottages
Long Wood
Melborne Cottages
Red Gate Wood
Whithney Dyke
Swan Cottages
Plane Tree Farm
Maple Cottages
Knowle Pad Wood
Brook Vale Cottages
Knowle Pad Farm
Lee Farm
Brookvale Court
Brook Vale Farm
Morrilly Farm
Hallidays Farm
MOSS LA.
Withy Trees Farm
Sowerby Hall Farm
Sowerby Hall Bridge
SOWERBY ROAD
Rodger Nook Wood
BENSONS

59
68
93

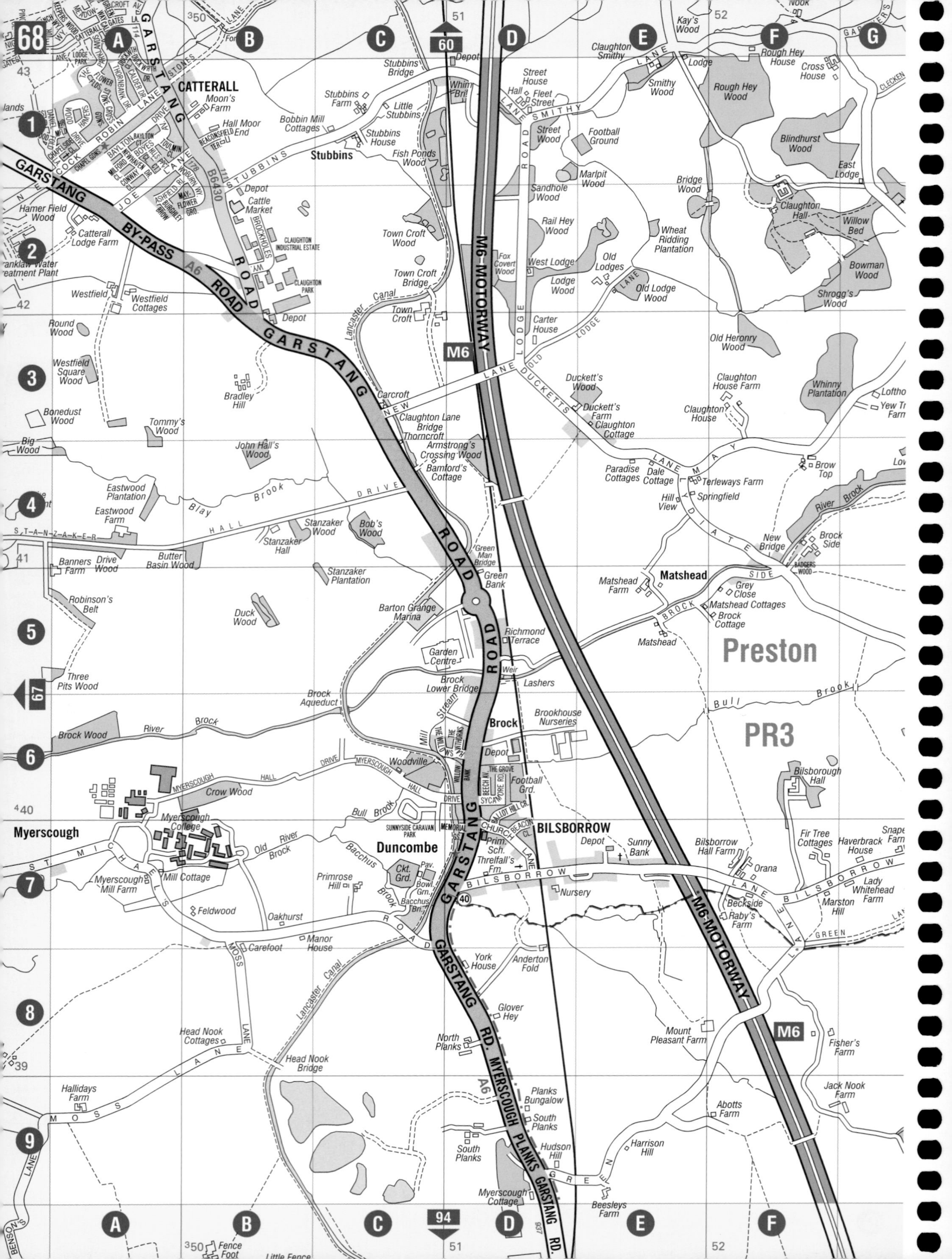
CATTERALL
Stubbins
Catterall Lodge Farm
Westfield
Westfield Cottages
Claughton Industrial Estate
Claughton Park
Garstang By-Pass
A6
Garstang Road
B6430
Stubbins Lane
Stubbins Bridge
Stubbins Farm
Little Stubbins
Bobbin Mill Cottages
Stubbins House
Fish Ponds Wood
Town Croft Wood
Town Croft Bridge
Lancaster Canal
M6 Motorway
M6
Claughton Smithy
Smithy Lane
Smithy Wood
Street House
Fleet Street
Street Wood
Football Ground
Marlpit Wood
Sandhole Wood
Rail Hey Wood
Wheat Ridding Plantation
West Lodge
Lodge Wood
Old Lodges
Old Lodge Wood
Carter House
Lodge Lane
Old Lodge Lane
Rough Hey House
Rough Hey Wood
Cross House
Blindhurst Wood
East Lodge
Bridge Wood
Claughton Hall
Willow Bed
Bowman Wood
Shrogg's Wood
Old Heronry Wood
Whinny Plantation
Claughton House Farm
Claughton House
Duckett's Wood
Duckett's Farm
Claughton Cottage
Ducketts Lane
New Lane
Carcroft
Claughton Lane Bridge
Thorncroft
Armstrong's Crossing Wood
Bamford's Cottage
Paradise Cottages
Dale Cottage
May Lane
Terleways Farm
Springfield
Hill View
Lydiate Lane
Brow Top
River Brock
New Bridge
Brock Side
Round Wood
Westfield Square Wood
Bradley Hill
Bonedust Wood
Tommy's Wood
Big Wood
John Hall's Wood
Eastwood Plantation
Eastwood Farm
Blay Brook
Stanzaker Hall Drive
Stanzaker Wood
Stanzaker Hall
Bob's Wood
Banners Farm
Drive Wood
Butter Basin Wood
Stanzaker Plantation
Green Man Bridge
Green Bank
Matshead
Matshead Farm
Brock Side
Grey Close
Matshead Cottages
Brock Cottage
Robinson's Belt
Duck Wood
Barton Grange Marina
Richmond Terrace
Garden Centre
Weir
Lashers
Preston
PR3
Three Pits Wood
Brock Aqueduct
Brock Lower Bridge
Mill Stream
Brock
Brookhouse Nurseries
Bull Brook
Brock Wood
River Brock
Depot
Woodville
Myerscough Hall Drive
Crow Wood
Football Grd.
Bilsborough Hall
Myerscough
Myerscough College
Old River Brock
Sunnyside Caravan Park
Duncombe
BILSBORROW
Sunny Bank
Bilsborrow Hall Farm
Fir Tree Cottages
Haverbrack House
Orana
Bilsborrow Lane
Myerscough Mill Farm
Mill Cottage
St Michael's Road
Bacchus Brook
Primrose Hill
Ckt. Grd.
Pav.
Bowl Grn.
Bacchus Bri.
Threlfall's Fm.
Nursery
Beckside
Raby's Farm
Marston Hill
Lady Whitehead Farm
Green Lane
Feldwood
Oakhurst
Carefoot
Manor House
Moss Lane
York House
Anderton Fold
Glover Hey
Mount Pleasant Farm
Fisher's Farm
Head Nook Cottages
North Planks
Head Nook Bridge
Myerscough Planks
Garstang Rd.
Hallidays Farm
Moss Lane
Planks Bungalow
South Planks
Hudson Hill
South Planks
Harrison Hill
Abotts Farm
Jack Nook Farm
Myerscough Cottage
Green Lane
Beesleys Farm
Benson's Lane
Fence Foot
Little Fence

60
67
94

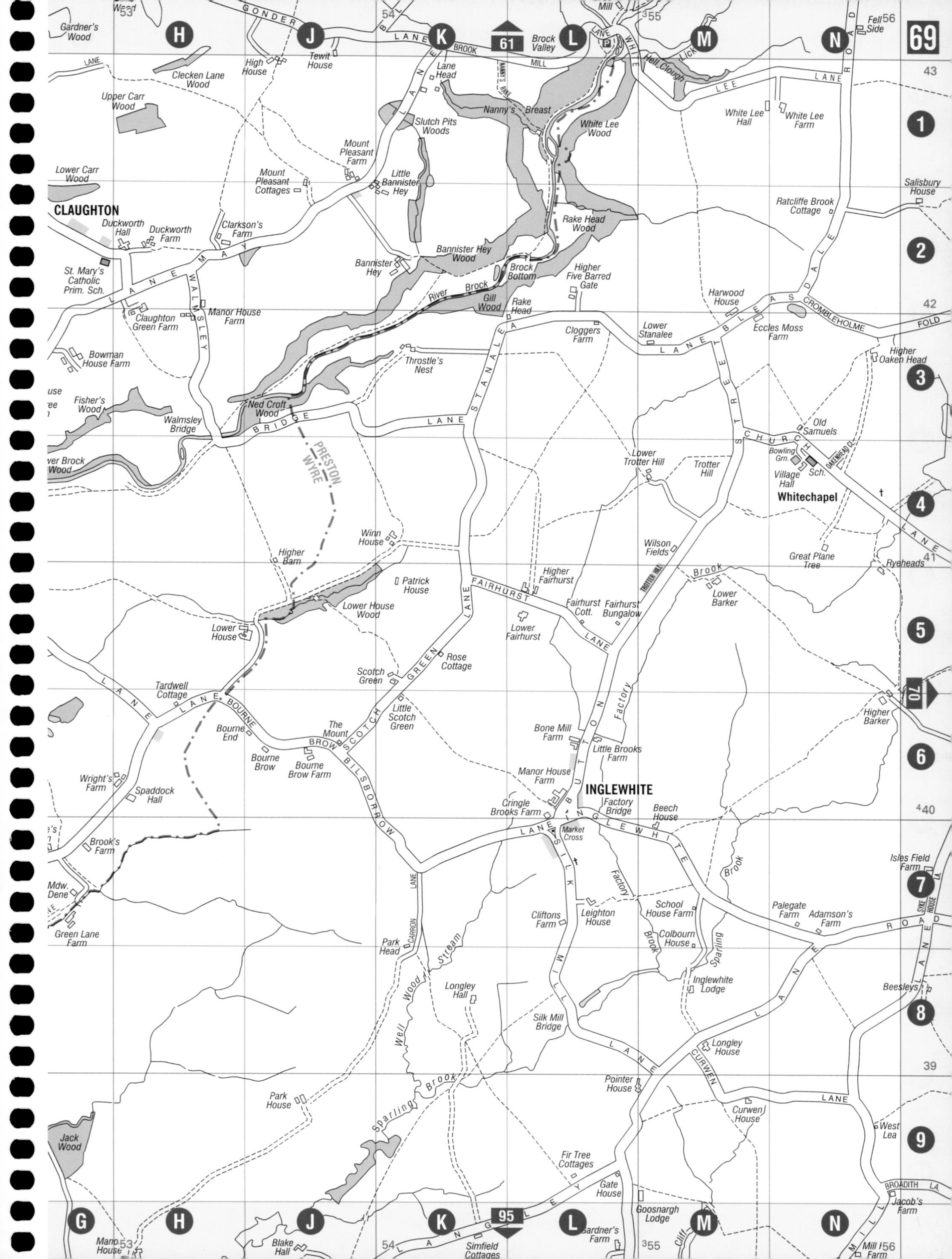

CLAUGHTON
INGLEWHITE
Whitechapel
Gardner's Wood
Clecken Lane Wood
Upper Carr Wood
Lower Carr Wood
High House
Tewit House
Lane Head
Brock Valley
Nanny's Breast
White Lee Wood
White Lee Hall
White Lee Farm
Hell Clough
Slutch Pits Woods
Mount Pleasant Farm
Mount Pleasant Cottages
Little Bannister Hey
Salisbury House
Ratcliffe Brook Cottage
Duckworth Hall
Duckworth Farm
Clarkson's Farm
Rake Head Wood
Bannister Hey Wood
Bannister Hey
St. Mary's Catholic Prim. Sch.
Brock Bottom
Higher Five Barred Gate
River Brock
Gill Wood
Rake Head
Harwood House
Claughton Green Farm
Manor House Farm
Cloggers Farm
Lower Stanalee
Eccles Moss Farm
Higher Oaken Head
Bowman House Farm
Throstle's Nest
Fisher's Wood
Ned Croft Wood
Walmsley Bridge
Old Samuels
Bowling Grn.
Sch.
Village Hall
Lower Trotter Hill
Trotter Hill
PRESTON
WYRE
Winn House
Wilson Fields
Great Plane Tree
Ryeheads
Higher Barn
Patrick House
Higher Fairhurst
Lower Barker
Lower House Wood
Fairhurst Cott.
Fairhurst Bungalow
Lower House
Lower Fairhurst
Rose Cottage
Scotch Green
Tardwell Cottage
Little Scotch Green
Higher Barker
The Mount
Bourne End
Bone Mill Farm
Little Brooks Farm
Bourne Brow
Bourne Brow Farm
Manor House Farm
Wright's Farm
Spaddock Hall
Cringle Brooks Farm
Factory Bridge
Beech House
Market Cross
Brook's Farm
Isles Field Farm
Mdw. Dene
School House Farm
Palegate Farm
Adamson's Farm
Cliftons Farm
Leighton House
Green Lane Farm
Colbourn House
Park Head
Inglewhite Lodge
Longley Hall
Beesleys
Silk Mill Bridge
Longley House
Pointer House
Park House
Curwen House
West Lea
Jack Wood
Fir Tree Cottages
Gate House
Goosnargh Lodge
Jacob's Farm
Mano House
Blake Hall
Simfield Cottages
Gardner's Farm
Mill Farm
Fell Side
GONDER LANE
BROOK MILL
NANNY'S RAKE
LEE LANE
MAY LANE
WALMSLEY
BRIDGE LANE
STANALEE LANE
LANE
CHURCH LANE
CROMBLEHOLME FOLD
STREET
BLEASDALE ROAD
TROTTER HILL
FAIRHURST LANE
SCOTCH GREEN LANE
BUTTON STREET
BOURNE BROW
BILSBORROW LANE
INGLEWHITE ROAD
SILK MILL LANE
CARRON LANE
CURWEN LANE
LANGLEY LANE
SYKE HOUSE LA.
BROADITH LA.
MILL LANE
Factory Brook
Sparling Brook
Well Wood Stream
Lick
Brook
H
J
K
L
M
N
G
61
70
95
1
2
3
4
5
6
7
8
9
43
42
41
440
39
53
54
355
56

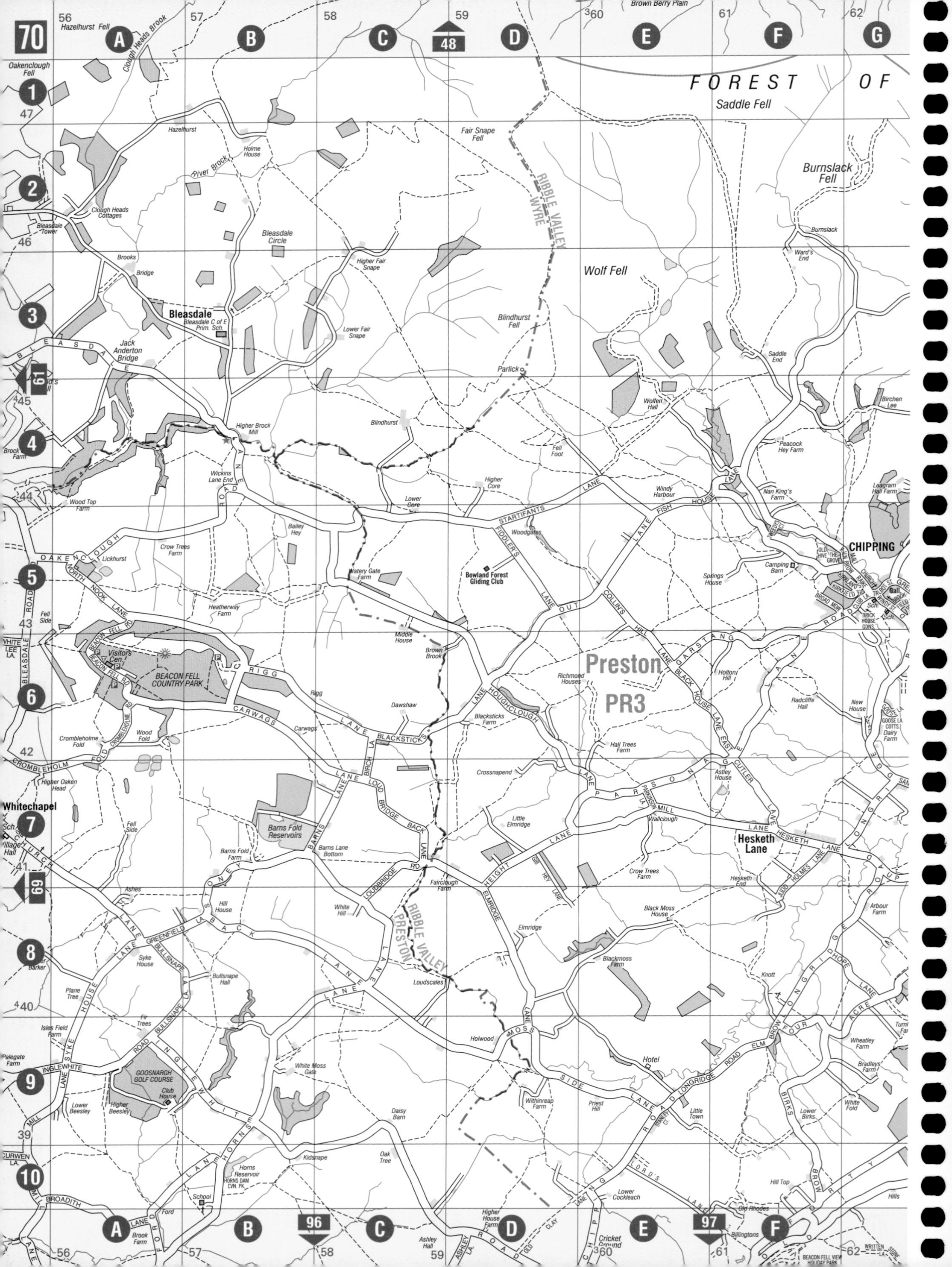
FOREST OF
Saddle Fell
Brown Berry Plain
Hazelhurst Fell
Oakenclough Fell
Clough Heads Brook
Hazelhurst
Holme House
River Brock
Clough Heads Cottages
Bleasdale Tower
Bleasdale Circle
Fair Snape Fell
Burnslack Fell
Burnslack
Ward's End
Higher Fair Snape
Brooks
Bridge
Bleasdale
Bleasdale C of E Prim. Sch.
Jack Anderton Bridge
Lower Fair Snape
Wolf Fell
Blindhurst Fell
Parlick
Saddle End
Wolfen Hall
Birchen Lee
Higher Brock Mill
Blindhurst
Peacock Hey Farm
Brock Farm
Fell Foot
Wickins Lane End
Higher Core
Lower Core
Windy Harbour
Nan King's Farm
Leagram Hall Farm
Wood Top Farm
Bailey Hey
Woodgates
CHIPPING
Crow Trees Farm
Lickhurst
Watery Gate Farm
Bowland Forest Gliding Club
Springs House
Camping Barn
Heatherway Farm
Fell Side
Middle House
Brown Brook
Visitors Cen.
BEACON FELL COUNTRY PARK
Preston
PR3
Richmond Houses
Holton Hill
Radcliffe Hall
New House
Rigg
Dawshaw
Blacksticks Farm
Carwags
Crombleholme Fold
Wood Fold
Hall Trees Farm
Dairy Farm
Crossnapend
Astley House
Higher Oaken Head
Whitechapel
Barns Fold Reservoirs
Little Elmridge
Walclough
Hesketh Lane
Barns Fold Farm
Barns Lane Bottom
Fairclough Farm
Crow Trees Farm
Hesketh End
Ashes
Hill House
White Hill
Arbour Farm
Black Moss House
Elmridge
Syke House
Bullsnape Hall
Blackmoss Farm
Knott
Loudscales
Plane Tree
Fir Trees
Isles Field Farm
Holwood
Wheatley Farm
Hotel
Palegate Farm
White Moss Gate
GOOSNARGH GOLF COURSE
Club House
Bradleys Farm
Lower Beesley
Higher Beesley
Daisy Barn
Withinreap Farm
Priest Hill
Little Town
Lower Birks
White Fold
Kidsnape
Oak Tree
Horns Reservoir
HORNS DAM CVN. PK.
Lower Cockleach
Hill Top
School
Hills
Ford
Old Rhodes
Higher House Farm
Brook Farm
Ashley Hall
Cricket Ground
Billingtons
BEACON FELL VIEW HOLIDAY PARK
RIBBLE VALLEY
WYRE
PRESTON
STARTIFANTS LANE
FISH HOUSE LANE
FIDDLERS LANE
OUT LANE
COLLIN'S HILL LANE
GARSTANG ROAD
BLACK HOUSE LANE EAST
HOUGHCLOUGH LANE
BLACKSTICKS LANE
CARWAGS LANE
RIGG LANE
BIRCH LA.
LOUD BRIDGE BACK LANE
LOUDBRIDGE RD.
HEIGHT LANE
ELMRIDGE LANE
PARSONAGE LANE
MILL LANE
HESKETH LANE
CUTLER LANE
LONGRIDGE ROAD
MOSS SIDE LANE
LORD'S LANE
INGLEWHITE ROAD
BULLSNAPE LANE
SYKE HOUSE LANE
GREENFIELD LANE
BACK LANE
STONEY LANE
HORNS LANE
BROADITH LANE
CHURCH LANE
OAKENCLOUGH ROAD
NORTH NOOK LANE
BLEASDALE LANE
BLEASDALE ROAD
CROMBLEHOLME FOLD
BEACON FELL RD.
WHITE LEE LA.
CURWEN LA.
FORD LANE
ASHLEY LA.
CLAY LANE
CHIPPING LANE
FOUR ACRE LANE
LONGRIDGE ROAD
HOPE LANE
BIRKS BROW
ELM BROW
JUDD HOLMES LANE
SCHOOL
GOOSE LA.
WINDY ST.
CLUB LA.
KIRKLAND
TALBOT ST.
BROAD MDW.
BRICK HOUSE GDNS.
WRITTEN STONE LA.
61
69
48
96
97
56
57
58
59
60
61
62
47
46
45
44
43
42
41
40
39
1
2
3
4
5
6
7
8
9
10
A
B
C
D
E
F
G

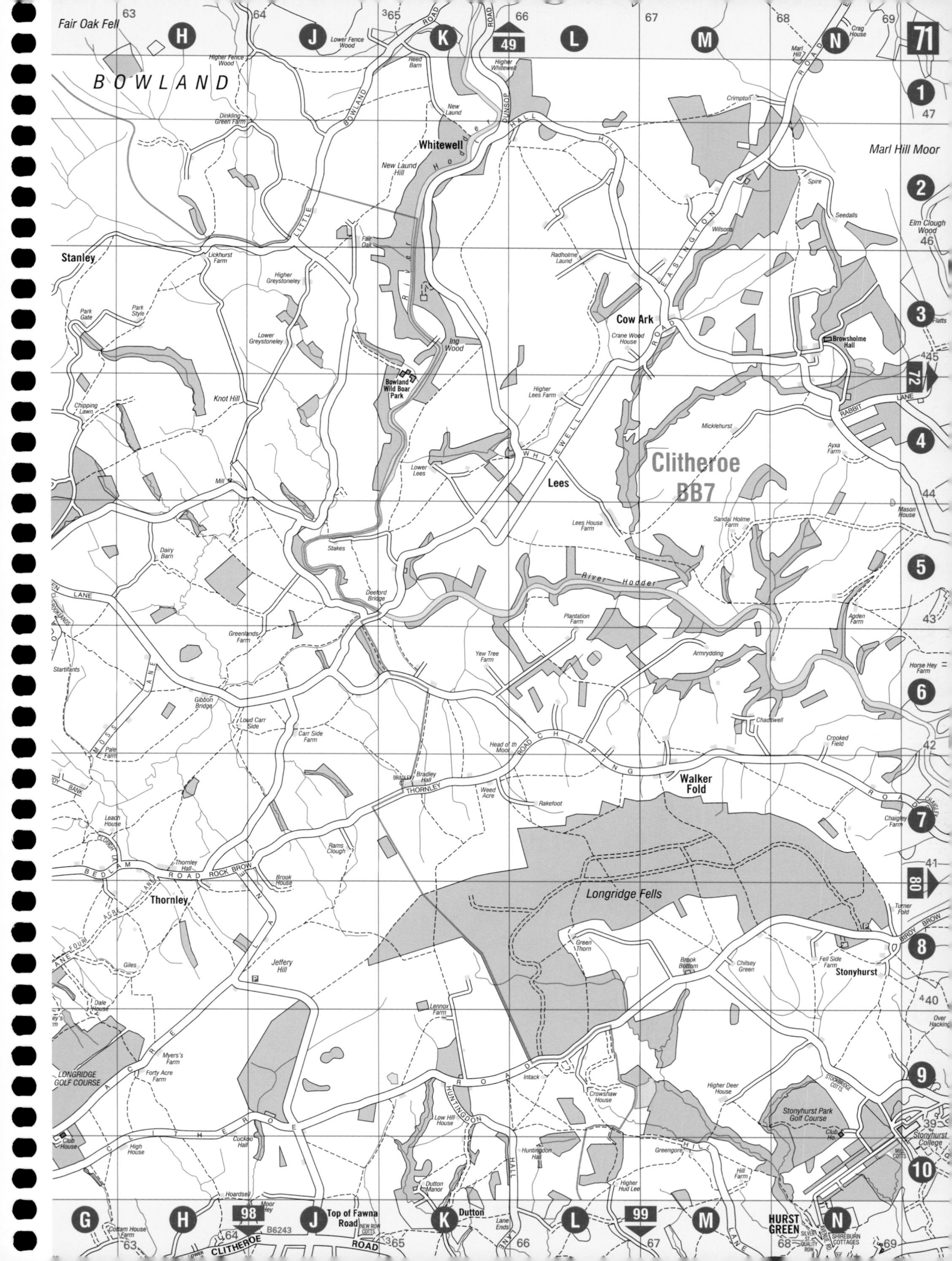

BOWLAND
Fair Oak Fell
Whitewell
Stanley
Cow Ark
Clitheroe
BB7
Lees
Walker Fold
Longridge Fells
Thornley
Stonyhurst
Dutton
Top of Fawna Road
HURST GREEN
Marl Hill Moor
Browsholme Hall
Bowland Wild Boar Park
Knot Hill
Jeffery Hill
LONGRIDGE GOLF COURSE
Stonyhurst Park Golf Course
Stonyhurst College
River Hodder
CHIPPING ROAD
CLITHEROE ROAD
EASINGTON ROAD
WHITEWELL ROAD
RABBIT LANE
49
72
80
98
99

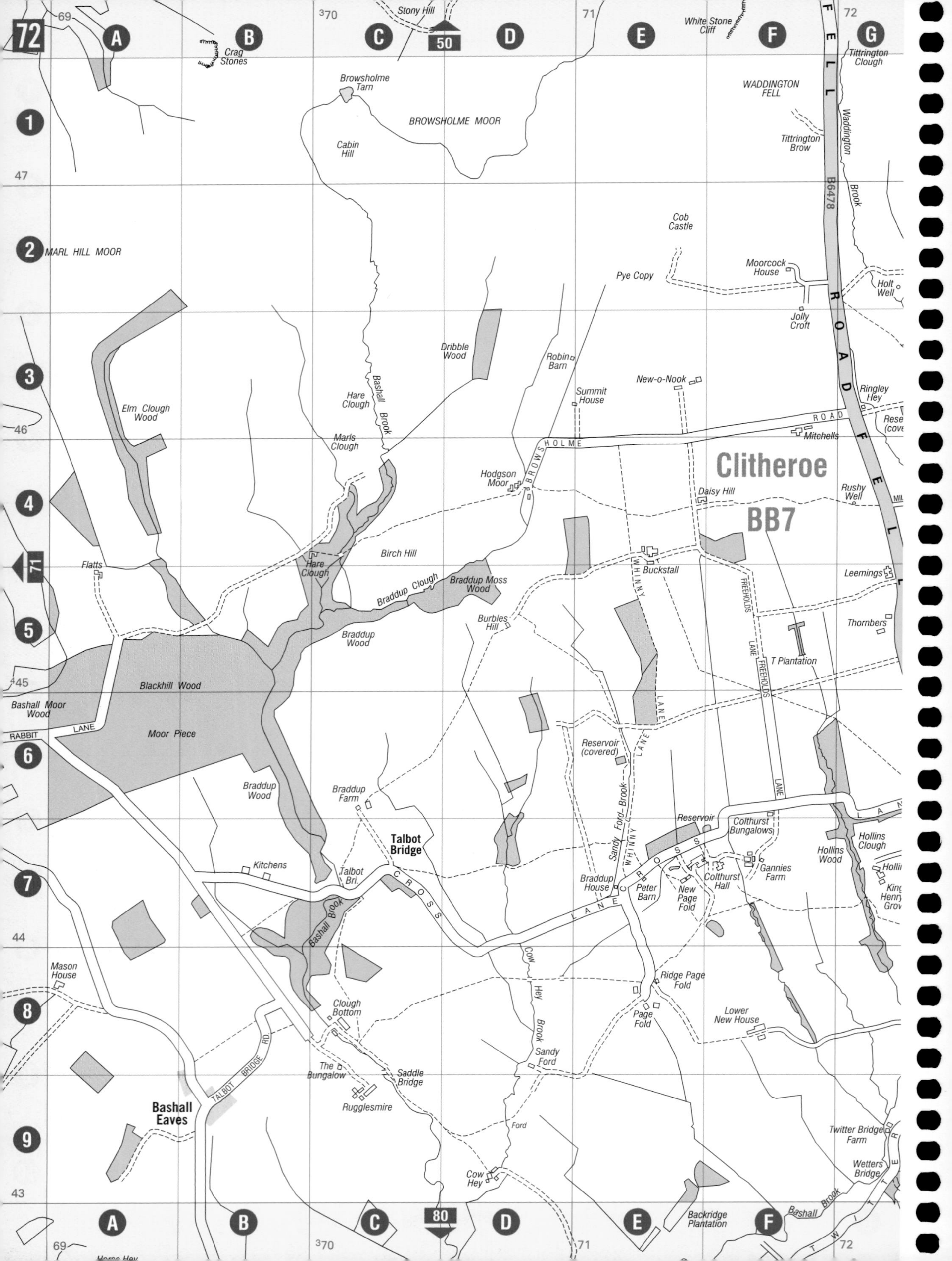

Stony Hill
50
White Stone Cliff
Crag Stones
Browsholme Tarn
BROWSHOLME MOOR
Cabin Hill
WADDINGTON FELL
Tittrington Clough
Tittrington Brow
Waddington Brook
B6478
FELL ROAD
MARL HILL MOOR
Cob Castle
Pye Copy
Moorcock House
Holt Well
Jolly Croft
Dribble Wood
Robin Barn
New-o-Nook
Summit House
Bashall Brook
Hare Clough
Ringley Hey
Elm Clough Wood
Marls Clough
BROWSHOLME ROAD
Mitchells
Clitheroe
BB7
Hodgson Moor
Daisy Hill
Rushy Well
Birch Hill
Buckstall
Leemings
Flatts
71
Braddup Clough
Braddup Moss Wood
WHINNY LANE
FREEHOLDS LANE
Burbles Hill
Thornbers
Braddup Wood
T Plantation
Blackhill Wood
Bashall Moor Wood
RABBIT LANE
Moor Piece
Reservoir (covered)
Braddup Wood
Braddup Farm
Reservoir
Colthurst Bungalows
Hollins Clough
Talbot Bridge
Hollins Wood
Kitchens
Talbot Bri.
Sandy Ford Brook
Braddup House
CROSS LANE
Peter Barn
New Page Fold
Colthurst Hall
Gannies Farm
Bashall Brook
Cow Hey Brook
Mason House
Ridge Page Fold
Clough Bottom
Page Fold
Lower New House
TALBOT BRIDGE RD.
Sandy Ford
The Bungalow
Saddle Bridge
Rugglesmire
Bashall Eaves
Ford
Twitter Bridge Farm
Cow Hey
Wetters Bridge
Backridge Plantation
Bashall Brook
80
Horse Hey

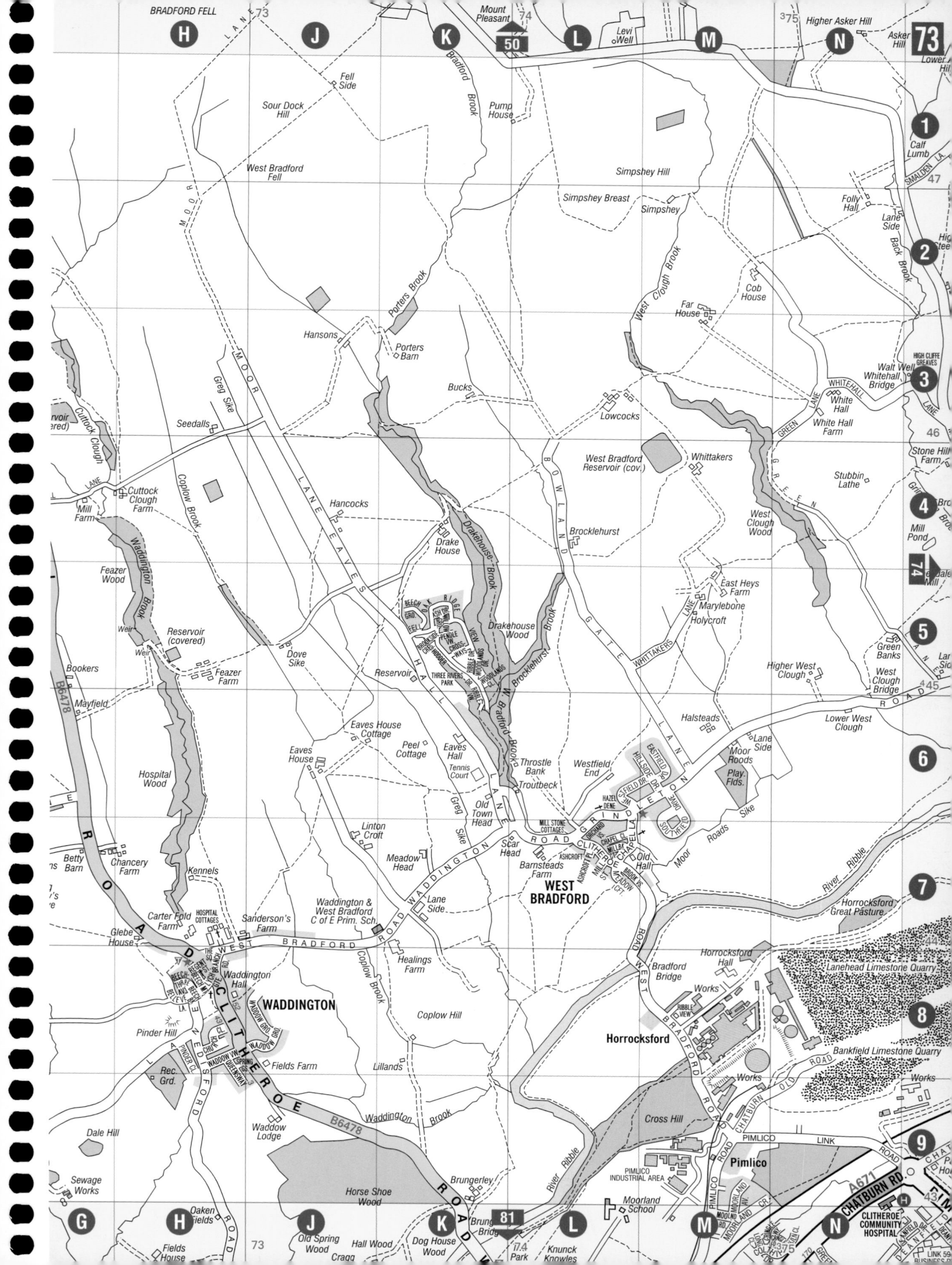
BRADFORD FELL
Mount Pleasant
50
Levi Well
Higher Asker Hill
Asker Hill
Fell Side
Sour Dock Hill
Pump House
West Bradford Fell
Simpshey Hill
Simpshey Breast
Simpshey
Calf Lumb
Folly Hall
Lane Side
Back Brook
West Clough Brook
Cob House
Far House
Porters Brook
Hansons
Porters Barn
Walt Well
Whitehall Bridge
White Hall
White Hall Farm
Bucks
Lowcocks
Seedalls
Greg Sike
Cuttock Clough
Cuttock Clough Farm
Mill Farm
Coplow Brook
West Bradford Reservoir (cov.)
Whittakers
Stubbin Lathe
Stone Hill Farm
Hancocks
West Clough Wood
Brocklehurst
Drake House
Drakehouse Brook
Feazer Wood
Waddington Brook
Mill Pond
East Heys Farm
Marylebone
Holycroft
Drakehouse Wood
Brocklehurst Brook
Reservoir (covered)
Dove Sike
Green Banks
Feazer Farm
Bookers
Reservoir
THREE RIVERS PARK
Higher West Clough
West Clough Bridge
Mayfield
B6478
Eaves House Cottage
Halsteads
Lower West Clough
Eaves House
Peel Cottage
Eaves Hall
Tennis Court
Throstle Bank
Westfield End
Moor Roods
Lane Side
Play. Flds.
Hospital Wood
Troutbeck
Old Town Head
MILL STONE COTTAGES
Linton Croft
Scar Head
Barnsteads Farm
Old Hall
Moor Roads
Sike
Betty Barn
Chancery Farm
Meadow Head
WEST BRADFORD
River Ribble
Kennels
Lane Side
Horrocksford Great Pasture
Carter Fold Farm
HOSPITAL COTTAGES
Sanderson's Farm
Waddington & West Bradford C of E Prim. Sch.
Glebe House
Healings Farm
Horrocksford Hall
Lanehead Limestone Quarry
Bradford Bridge
Works
Waddington Hall
WADDINGTON
Coplow Brook
Coplow Hill
Pinder Hill
Horrocksford
Bankfield Limestone Quarry
Fields Farm
Lillands
Rec. Grd.
Works
Cross Hill
Waddington Brook
Waddow Lodge
Dale Hill
PIMLICO LINK ROAD
Pimlico
PIMLICO INDUSTRIAL AREA
Sewage Works
Horse Shoe Wood
Brungerley
Moorland School
A671
CHATBURN RD.
CLITHEROE COMMUNITY HOSPITAL
Oaken Fields
Old Spring Wood
Hall Wood
Dog House Wood
81
Park
Knunck Knowles
Fields House
Cragg
CLITHEROE ROAD
WADDINGTON ROAD
BRADFORD ROAD
MOOR LANE
EAVES HALL LANE
BOWLAND GATE LANE
WEST BRADFORD ROAD
GRINDLETON ROAD
GREEN LANE
WHITEHALL LANE
WHITTAKERS LANE
SMALDEN LA.
CHATBURN OLD ROAD
74
73
375
47
46
45
44
43

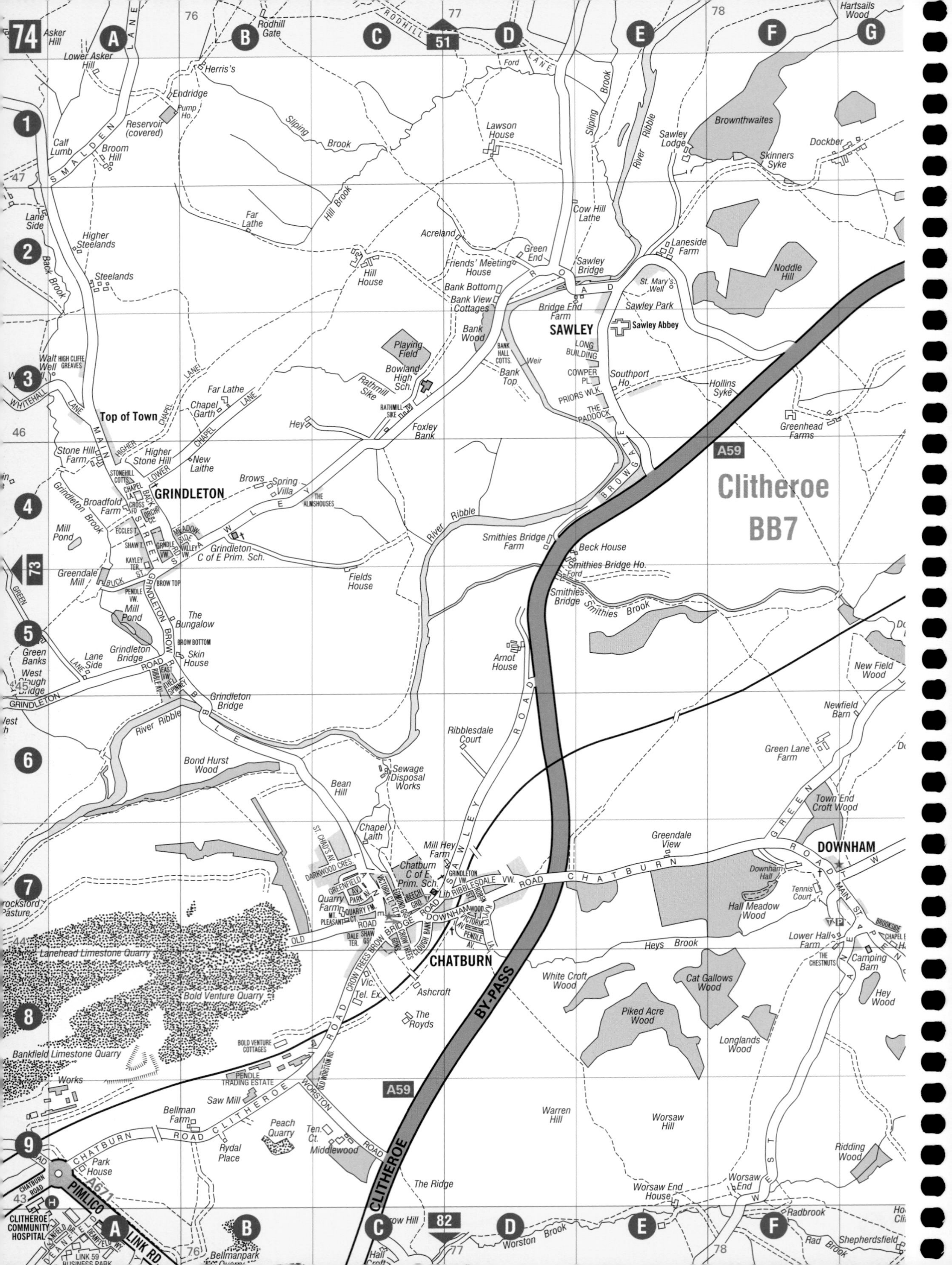
Clitheroe
BB7
GRINDLETON
SAWLEY
CHATBURN
DOWNHAM
Top of Town
Sawley Abbey
Asker Hill
Lower Asker Hill
Rodhill Gate
Herris's
Endridge
Reservoir (covered)
Calf Lumb
Broom Hill
Lane Side
Higher Steelands
Steelands
Back Brook
Sliping Brook
Lawson House
Far Lathe
Hill Brook
Hill House
Acreland
Friends' Meeting House
Green End
Cow Hill Lathe
Sawley Bridge
Bank Bottom
Bank View Cottages
Bridge End Farm
Bank Wood
Playing Field
Bowland High Sch.
Rathmill Sike
Hey
Foxley Bank
Bank Top
Weir
Southport Ho.
Hollins Syke
Sawley Park
St. Mary's Well
Laneside Farm
Sawley Lodge
Browntwaites
Skinners Syke
Dockber
Noddle Hill
Greenhead Farms
Hartsails Wood
River Ribble
Walt Well
Far Lathe
Chapel Garth
Stone Hill Farm
Higher Stone Hill
New Laithe
Brows
Spring Villa
The Almshouses
Grindleton Brook
Broadfold Farm
Mill Pond
Greendale Mill
Grindleton C of E Prim. Sch.
Fields House
Smithies Bridge Farm
Beck House
Smithies Bridge Ho.
Smithies Bridge
Smithies Brook
The Bungalow
Skin House
Green Banks
Lane Side
Grindleton Bridge
West Clough Bridge
Arnot House
New Field Wood
Newfield Barn
Ribblesdale Court
Bond Hurst Wood
Sewage Disposal Works
Bean Hill
Green Lane Farm
Town End Croft Wood
Chapel Laith
Mill Hey Farm
Chatburn C of E Prim. Sch.
Greendale View
Downham Hall
Tennis Court
Hall Meadow Wood
Quarry Farm
Lanehead Limestone Quarry
Bold Venture Quarry
Bankfield Limestone Quarry
Heys Brook
Lower Hall Farm
Camping Barn
Hey Wood
White Croft Wood
Cat Gallows Wood
Piked Acre Wood
Longlands Wood
Ashcroft
The Royds
Vic.
Tel. Ex.
Bold Venture Cottages
Pendle Trading Estate
Works
Saw Mill
Bellman Farm
Peach Quarry
Ten. Ct.
Middlewood
Warren Hill
Worsaw Hill
Ridding Wood
Rydal Place
Park House
The Ridge
Worsaw End House
Worsaw End
Radbrook
Shepherdsfield
Rad Brook
Worston Brook
Clitheroe Community Hospital
Link 59 Business Park
Bellmanpark Quarry
A59
A671
BY-PASS
CLITHEROE
Pimlico Link Rd
Chatburn Road Clitheroe
Old Road
Sawley Road
Chatburn Road
Downham Road
Main St
West Lane
Green Lane
Ribble Lane
Main Street
Grindleton Brow
Grindleton Road
Browgate
Rodhill Lane
Smalden Lane
Worston Road
51
82
73

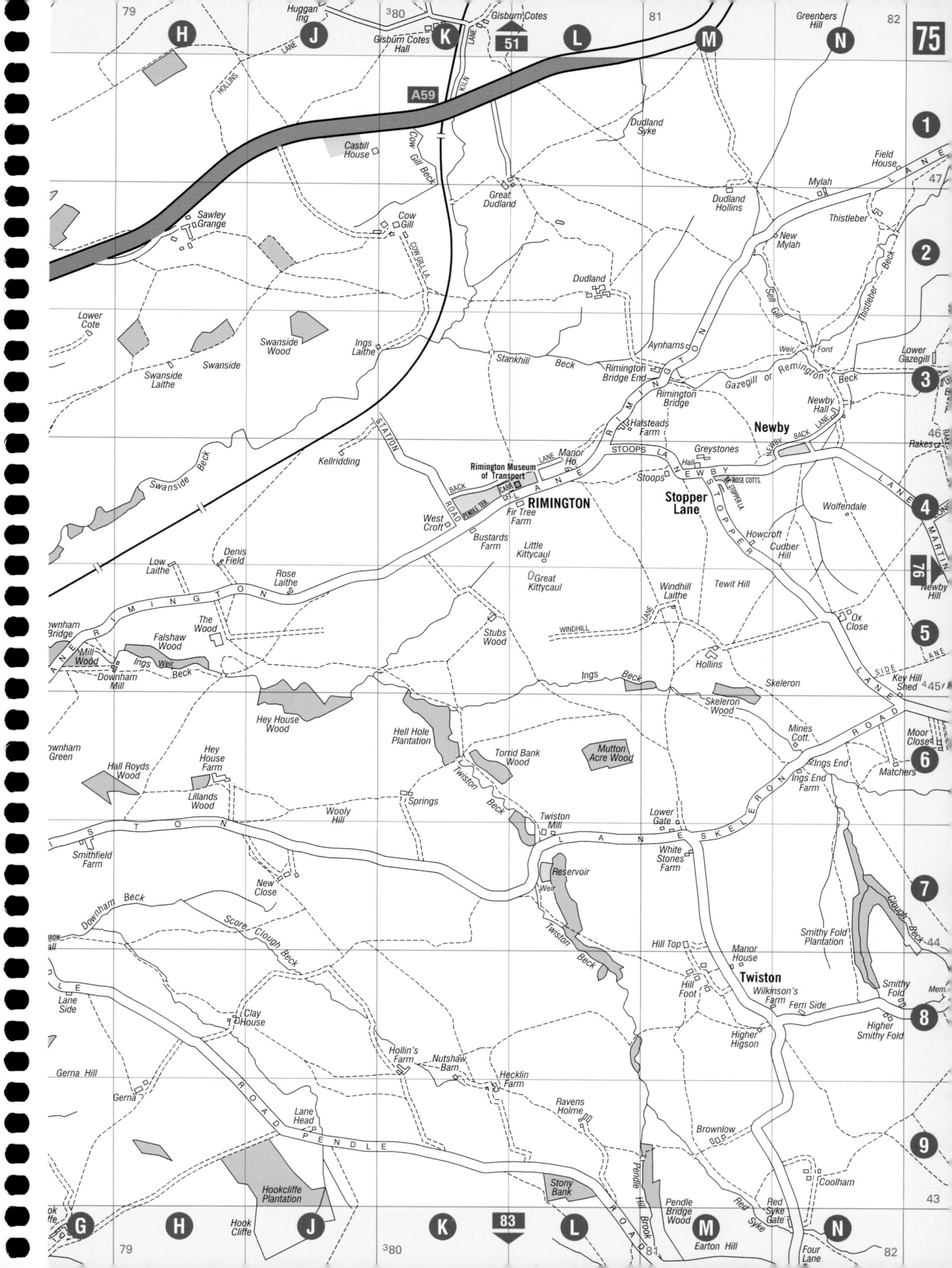
A59
51
83
76
RIMINGTON
Stopper Lane
Newby
Twiston
Rimington Museum of Transport
Gisburn Cotes
Gisburn Cotes Hall
Huggan Ing
Greenbers Hill
Castill House
Cow Gill Beck
Great Dudland
Dudland Syke
Dudland Hollins
Dudland
Field House
Mylah
New Mylah
Thistleber
Thistleber Beck
Sell Gill
Sawley Grange
Cow Gill
Lower Cote
Swanside Wood
Swanside
Swanside Laithe
Ings Laithe
Stankhill Beck
Aynhams
Rimington Bridge End
Rimington Bridge
Gazegill or Remington Beck
Lower Gazegill
Weir
Ford
Newby Hall
Halsteads Farm
Kellridding
Swanside Beck
Manor Ho.
Greystones
Stoops
Rose Cotts.
Rakes
Wolfendale
West Croft
Fir Tree Farm
Bustards Farm
Little Kittycaul
Great Kittycaul
Howcroft
Cudber Hill
Denis Field
Low Laithe
Rose Laithe
Windhill Laithe
Tewit Hill
Newby Hill
Ox Close
Downham Bridge
The Wood
Falshaw Wood
Mill Wood
Downham Mill
Ings Beck
Stubs Wood
Hollins
Skeleron
Skeleron Wood
Key Hill Shed
Hey House Wood
Hell Hole Plantation
Torrid Bank Wood
Mutton Acre Wood
Mines Cott.
Moor Close
Downham Green
Hall Royds Wood
Hey House Farm
Lillands Wood
Springs
Twiston Beck
Ings End
Ings End Farm
Matchers
Wooly Hill
Twiston Mill
Lower Gate
Smithfield Farm
White Stones Farm
Reservoir
New Close
Downham Beck
Score Clough Beck
Clough Beck
Smithy Fold Plantation
Hill Top
Manor House
Hill Foot
Wilkinson's Farm
Fern Side
Smithy Fold
Higher Smithy Fold
Lane Side
Clay House
Higher Higson
Gerna Hill
Gerna
Hollin's Farm
Nutshaw Barn
Hecklin Farm
Ravens Holme
Lane Head
Brownlow
Coolham
Pendle Road
Stony Bank
Pendle Hill Brook
Hookcliffe Plantation
Pendle Bridge Wood
Red Syke
Red Syke Gate
Hook Cliffe
Earton Hill
Four Lane
Rimington Lane
Stoops Lane
Newby Lane
Stopper Lane
Station Road
Back Lane
Windhill Lane
Skeleron Road
Skeleron Lane
Twiston Lane
Martin Lane
Side Lane
Kiln Lane
Hollins Lane
Cow Gill La.
Pendle Ter.
Carr Ct.
Newby Back Lane
79
380
81
82
47
46
45
44
43
H J K L M N G
1 2 3 4 5 6 7 8 9

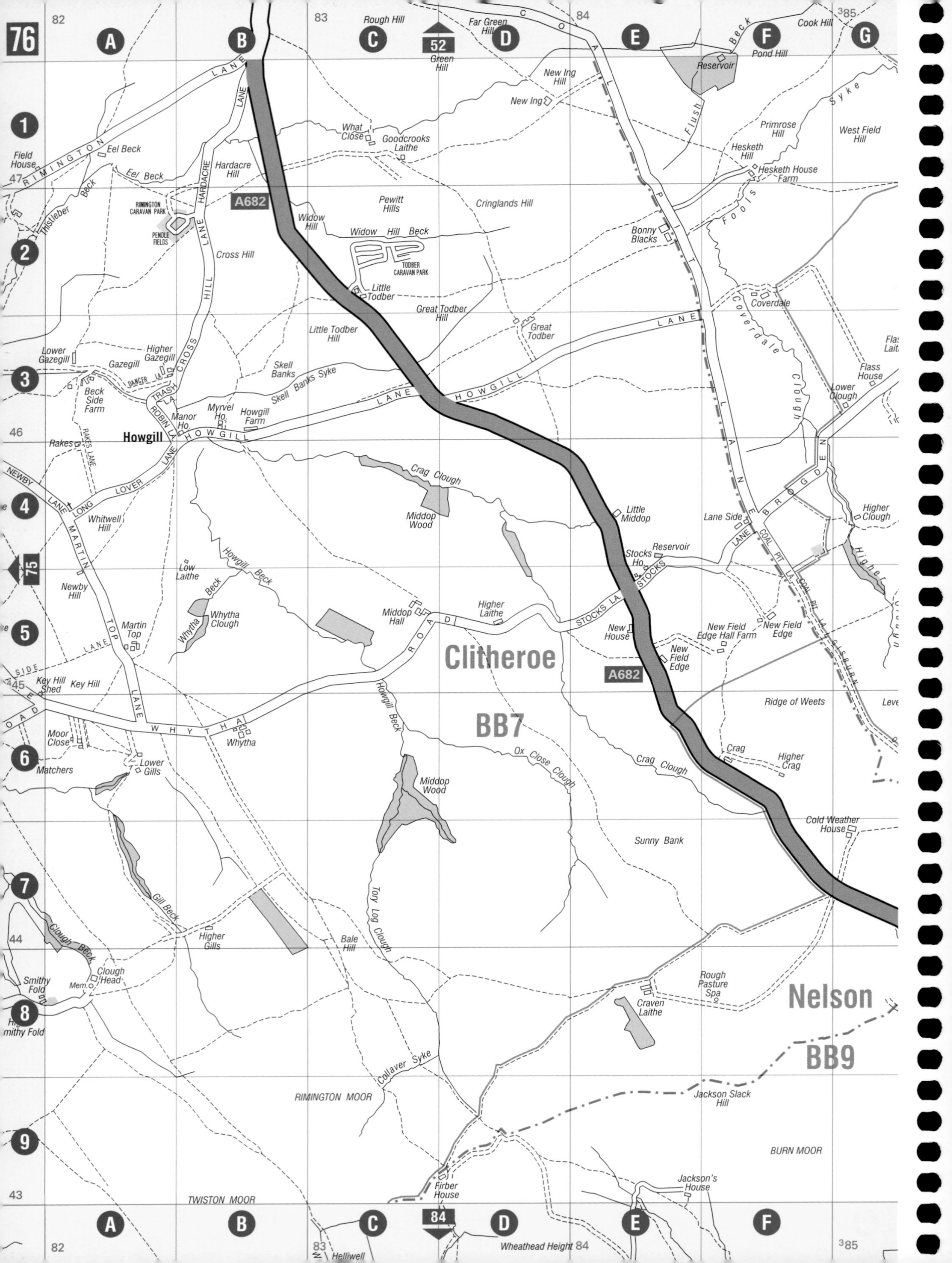

Clitheroe
BB7
Nelson
BB9
Howgill
A682
52
84
75
Rough Hill
Far Green Hill
Green Hill
Cook Hill
Pond Hill
Reservoir
New Ing Hill
New Ing
What Close
Goodcrooks Laithe
Primrose Hill
West Field Hill
Hesketh Hill
Hesketh House Farm
Field House
Eel Beck
Hardacre Hill
RIMINGTON CARAVAN PARK
PENDLE FIELDS
Pewitt Hills
Cringlands Hill
Widow Hill
Widow Hill Beck
Bonny Blacks
Cross Hill
TODBER CARAVAN PARK
Little Todber
Great Todber Hill
Great Todber
Coverdale
Little Todber Hill
Lower Gazegill
Higher Gazegill
Gazegill
Skell Banks
Skell Banks Syke
Beck Side Farm
Manor Ho.
Myrvel Ho.
Howgill Farm
Flass House
Lower Clough
Rakes
Crag Clough
Middop Wood
Little Middop
Higher Clough
Lane Side
Whitwell Hill
Stocks Ho.
Reservoir
Low Laithe
Newby Hill
Whytha Clough
Middop Hall
Higher Laithe
Martin Top
New House
New Field Edge Hall Farm
New Field Edge
Key Hill Shed
Key Hill
Ridge of Weets
Whytha
Moor Close
Matchers
Lower Gills
Ox Close Clough
Crag
Higher Crag
Cold Weather House
Sunny Bank
Gill Beck
Higher Gills
Bale Hill
Tory Log Clough
Clough Beck
Clough Head
Smithy Fold
Rough Pasture Spa
Craven Laithe
Collaver Syke
RIMINGTON MOOR
Jackson Slack Hill
BURN MOOR
Firber House
Jackson's House
TWISTON MOOR
Wheathead Height
Helliwell

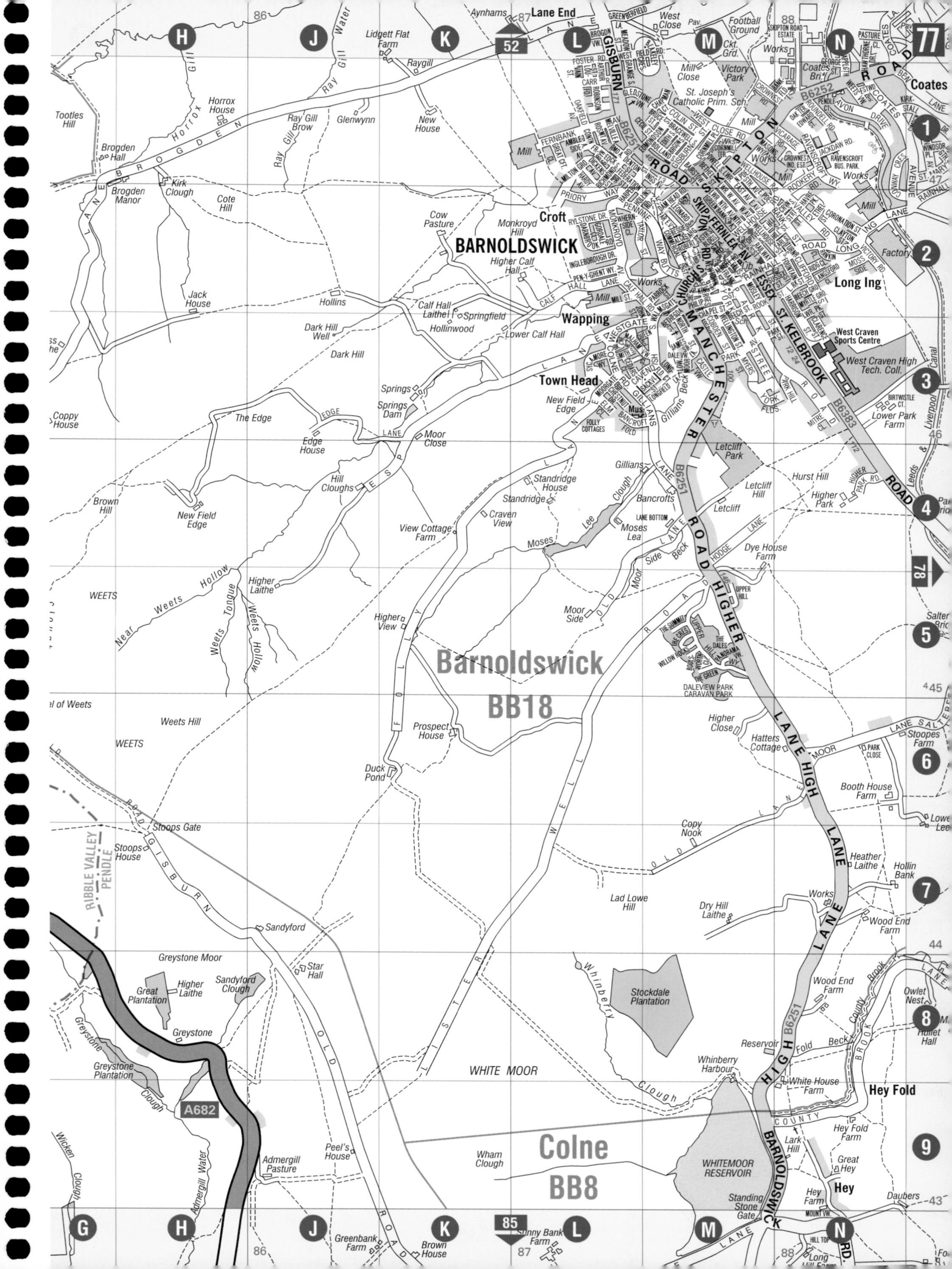
BARNOLDSWICK
Barnoldswick
BB18
Colne
BB8
Croft
Wapping
Town Head
Coates
Long Ing
Hey Fold
Hey
Lane End
West Craven Sports Centre
West Craven High Tech. Coll.
Letcliff Park
Stockdale Plantation
WHITEMOOR RESERVOIR
WHITE MOOR
WEETS
Weets Hill
Brogden Hall
Brogden Manor
Kirk Clough
Cote Hill
Horrox House
Tootles Hill
Ray Gill Brow
Glenwynn
New House
Raygill
Lidgett Flat Farm
Cow Pasture
Monkroyd Hill
Higher Calf Hall
Hollins
Calf Hall Laithe
Springfield
Hollinwood
Lower Calf Hall
Jack House
Dark Hill Well
Dark Hill
Springs
Springs Dam
The Edge
Edge House
Moor Close
Hill Cloughs
Brown Hill
New Field Edge
View Cottage Farm
Higher Laithe
Coppy House
Higher View
Prospect House
Duck Pond
Stoops Gate
Stoops House
Sandyford
Star Hall
Greystone Moor
Great Plantation
Higher Laithe
Sandyford Clough
Greystone
Greystone Plantation
A682
Admergill Pasture
Peel's House
Greenbank Farm
Brown House
Sunny Bank Farm
Wham Clough
Lad Lowe Hill
Dry Hill Laithe
Copy Nook
Higher Close
Hatters Cottage
Stoopes Farm
Booth House Farm
Heather Laithe
Hollin Bank
Works
Wood End Farm
Owlet Nest
Hullet Hall
Reservoir
Whinberry Harbour
White House Farm
Hey Fold Farm
Lark Hill
Great Hey
Hey Farm
Standing Stone Gate
Daubers
Gillians
Standridge House
Standridge
Craven View
Moses
Moses Lea
Bancrofts
Letcliff Hill
Letcliff
Hurst Hill
Higher Park
Dye House Farm
Moor Side
Daleview Park Caravan Park
Lower Park Farm
Mill Close
Victory Park
Football Ground
West Close
St. Joseph's Catholic Prim. Sch.
RIBBLE VALLEY
PENDLE
B6251
B6252
B6383
B625
52
78
85

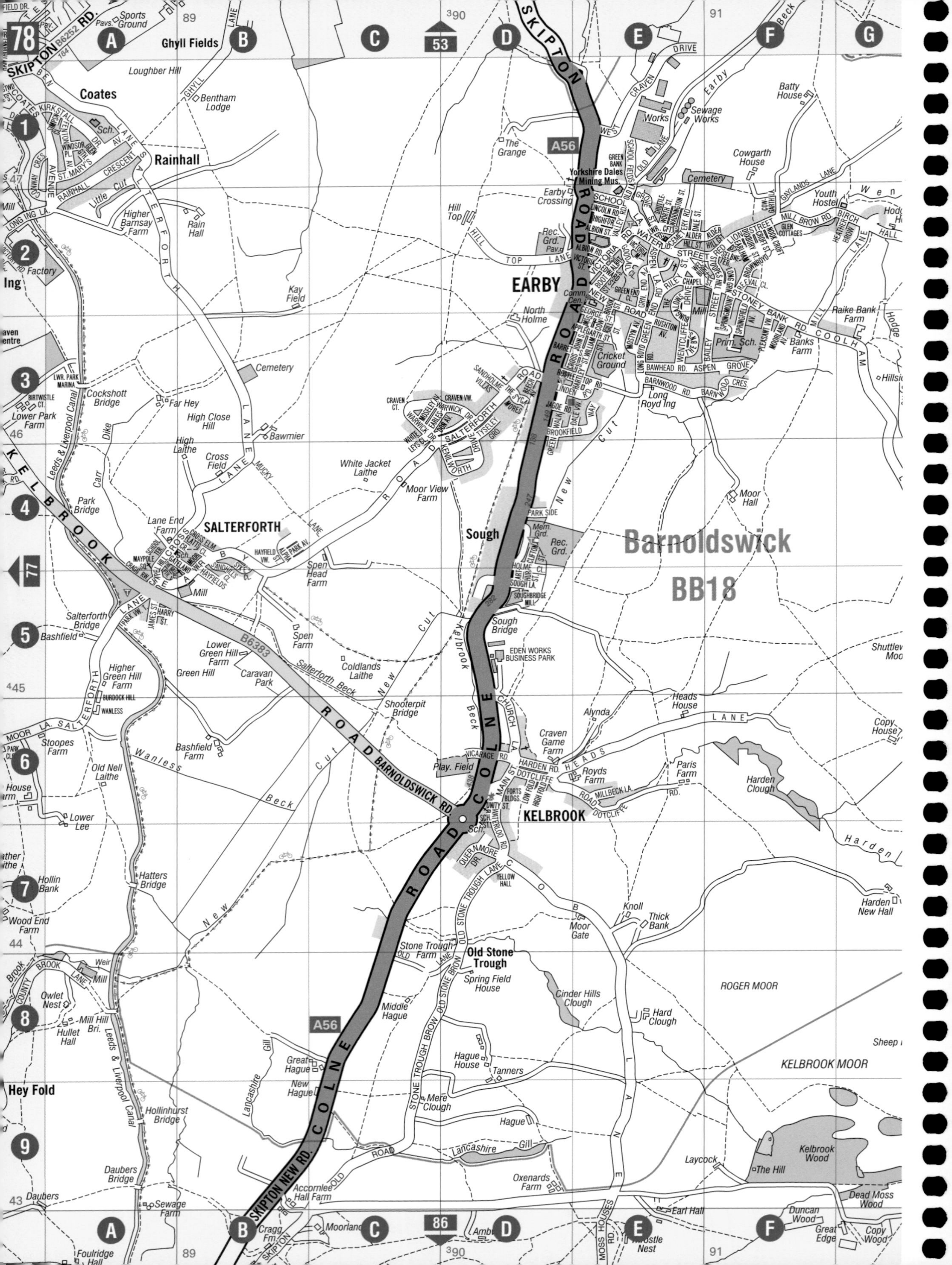
78
53
86
77
A
B
C
D
E
F
G
1
2
3
4
5
6
7
8
9
89
390
91
47
46
445
44
43
SKIPTON RD.
B6252
Sports Ground
Pavs.
Ghyll Fields
Loughber Hill
Coates
Bentham Lodge
KIRKSTALL
Sch.
Rainhall
ST. MARY'S
CRESCENT
RAINHALL
AVENUE
CONWAY CRES.
Little Cut
LONG ING LA.
Higher Barnsay Farm
Rain Hall
Factory
Ing
SALTERFORTH
LANE
Cemetery
Kay Field
The Grange
Hill Top
TOP LANE
HILL
A56
SKIPTON
ROAD
Yorkshire Dales Mining Mus.
Earby Crossing
Rec. Grd.
Pav.
EARBY
SCHOOL
Cemetery
Cowgarth House
Batty House
Sewage Works
Works
CRAVEN
DRIVE
Earby Beck
WEST
Youth Hostel
GAYLANDS LANE
MILL BROW RD.
BIRCH HALL
LANE
Wen
Comm. Cen.
North Holme
NEW ROAD
Mill
STONEY BANK RD.
COOLHAM
Raike Bank Farm
Banks Farm
Prim. Sch.
Cricket Ground
BAWHEAD RD.
ASPEN GROVE
BARNWOOD RD.
BARNWOOD CRES.
Long Royd Ing
Hillside
LWR. PARK MARINA
BIRTWISTLE CT.
Lower Park Farm
Cockshott Bridge
Far Hey
High Close Hill
Bawmier
High Laithe
Cross Field
Dike
Carr
Leeds & Liverpool Canal
KELBROOK ROAD
Park Bridge
Lane End Farm
CRAVEN CT.
CRAVEN VW.
SANDHOLME VILLAS
SALTERFORTH DRIVE
White Jacket Laithe
Moor View Farm
MUCKY LANE
New Cut
Sough
Mem. Grd.
Rec. Grd.
PARK SIDE
Barnoldswick
BB18
Moor Hall
Hodge
Mill
HAYFIELD VW.
PARK AV.
Spen Head Farm
SOUGHBRIDGE MILL
Sough Bridge
EDEN WORKS BUSINESS PARK
Kelbrook Beck
Salterforth Bridge
Bashfield
Lower Green Hill Farm
Spen Farm
Coldlands Laithe
Caravan Park
B6383
Salterforth Beck
Higher Green Hill Farm
BURDOCK HILL
WANLESS
Green Hill
Shooterpit Bridge
Shuttleworth Moor
Heads House
Alynda
HEADS LANE
Copy House
MOOR LA.
Stoopes Farm
Old Nell Laithe
Wanless Beck
Bashfield Farm
BARNOLDSWICK RD.
VICARAGE RD.
Play. Field
CHURCH LA.
COLNE
Craven Game Farm
HARDEN RD.
DOTCLIFFE
Royds Farm
Paris Farm
MILLBECK LA.
Harden Clough
KELBROOK
Sch.
Harden
Lower Lee
Hatters Bridge
Hollin Bank
Wood End Farm
YELLOW HALL
Knoll
Thick Bank
Moor Gate
Harden New Hall
Stone Trough Farm
Old Stone Trough
Spring Field House
Weir
Mill
BROOK LANE
Owlet Nest
Mill Hill Bri.
Hullet Hall
Cinder Hills Clough
ROGER MOOR
Hard Clough
Middle Hague
A56
Sheep
Gill
Great Hague
Hague House
Tanners
KELBROOK MOOR
Hey Fold
New Hague
Mere Clough
STONE TROUGH BROW
Hollinhurst Bridge
Lancashire
Hague
Lancashire Gill
Kelbrook Wood
Laycock
The Hill
Daubers Bridge
SKIPTON NEW RD.
OLD ROAD
Oxenards Farm
Dead Moss Wood
Daubers
Sewage Farm
Accornlee Hall Farm
Earl Hall
Duncan Wood
Cragg Frm.
Moorland
Amb
MOSS HOUSES RD.
Throstle Nest
Great Edge
Copy Wood
Foulridge Hall

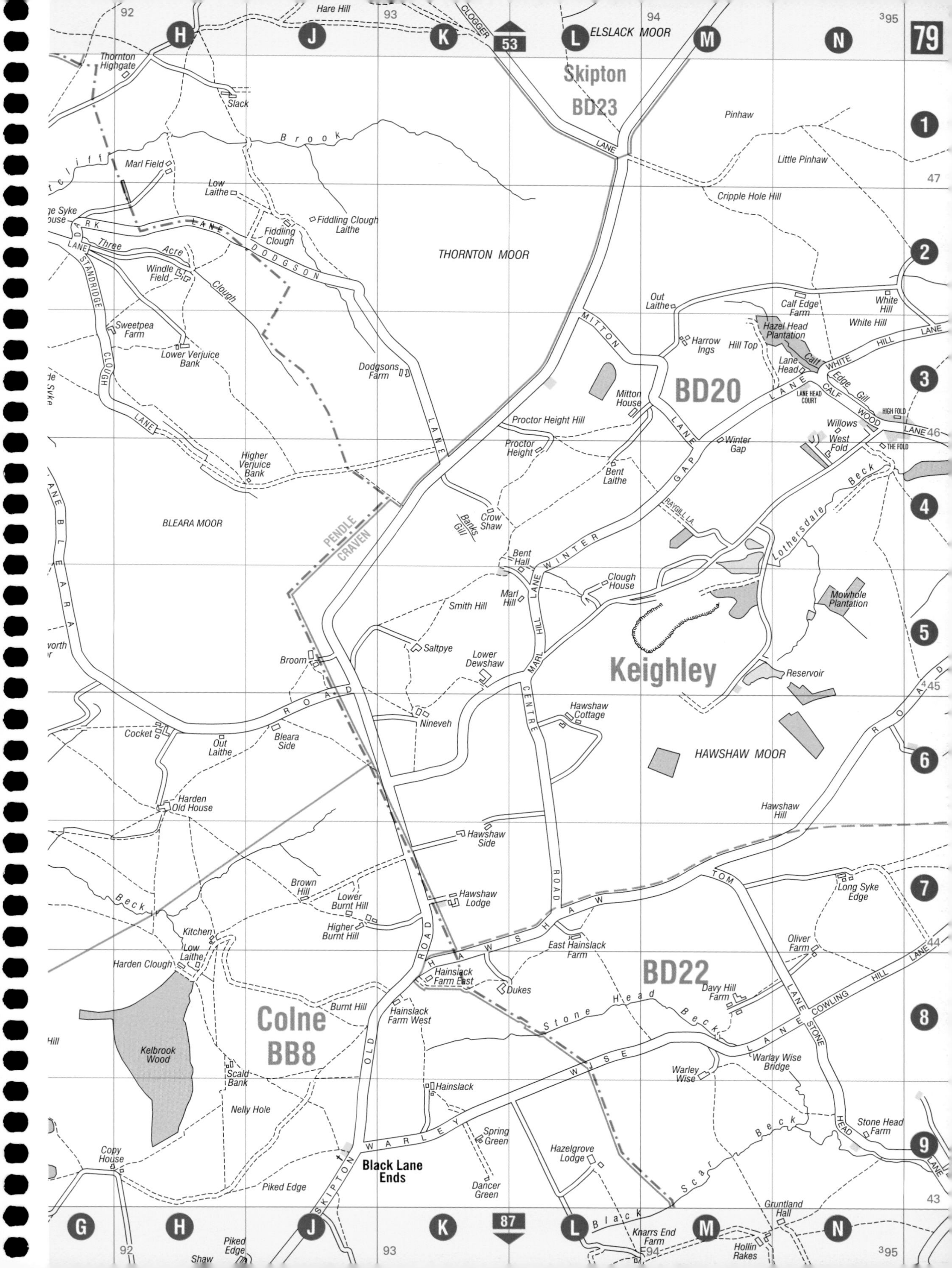

53
87
Skipton
BD23
BD20
Keighley
BD22
Colne
BB8
ELSLACK MOOR
THORNTON MOOR
BLEARA MOOR
HAWSHAW MOOR
Hare Hill
Thornton Highgate
Slack
Pinhaw
Little Pinhaw
Cripple Hole Hill
Marl Field
Low Laithe
Fiddling Clough
Fiddling Clough Laithe
Windle Field
Sweetpea Farm
Lower Verjuice Bank
Higher Verjuice Bank
Dodgsons Farm
Out Laithe
Calf Edge Farm
White Hill
Hazel Head Plantation
Harrow Ings
Hill Top
Lane Head
Lane Head Court
High Fold
Willows
West Fold
The Fold
Mitton House
Proctor Height Hill
Proctor Height
Winter Gap
Bent Laithe
Crow Shaw
Banks Gill
Bent Hall
Clough House
Marl Hill
Smith Hill
Mowhole Plantation
Saltpye
Lower Dewshaw
Broom
Reservoir
Hawshaw Cottage
Nineveh
Cocket
Out Laithe
Bleara Side
Harden Old House
Hawshaw Hill
Hawshaw Side
Brown Hill
Lower Burnt Hill
Higher Burnt Hill
Hawshaw Lodge
Long Syke Edge
Kitchen
Low Laithe
Harden Clough
East Hainslack Farm
Oliver Farm
Hainslack Farm East
Dukes
Davy Hill Farm
Burnt Hill
Hainslack Farm West
Kelbrook Wood
Scald Bank
Warlay Wise Bridge
Warley Wise
Hainslack
Nelly Hole
Spring Green
Stone Head Farm
Copy House
Hazelgrove Lodge
Black Lane Ends
Piked Edge
Dancer Green
Gruntland Hall
Knarrs End Farm
Hollin Rakes
Shaw
CLOGGER
DARK LANE
THREE ACRE CLOUGH
DODGSON LANE
STANDRIDGE CLOUGH LANE
BLEARA LANE
MITTON LANE
GAP LANE
WINTER LANE
RAYGILL LA.
WHITE HILL LANE
CALF WOOD LANE
MARL HILL LANE
CENTRE ROAD
ROAD
OLD ROAD
HAWSHAW
TOM LANE
STONE HEAD LANE
COWLING HILL LANE
WARLEY WISE LANE
SKIPTON
Brook
Lothersdale Beck
Stone Head Beck
Scar Beck
Black
PENDLE
CRAVEN

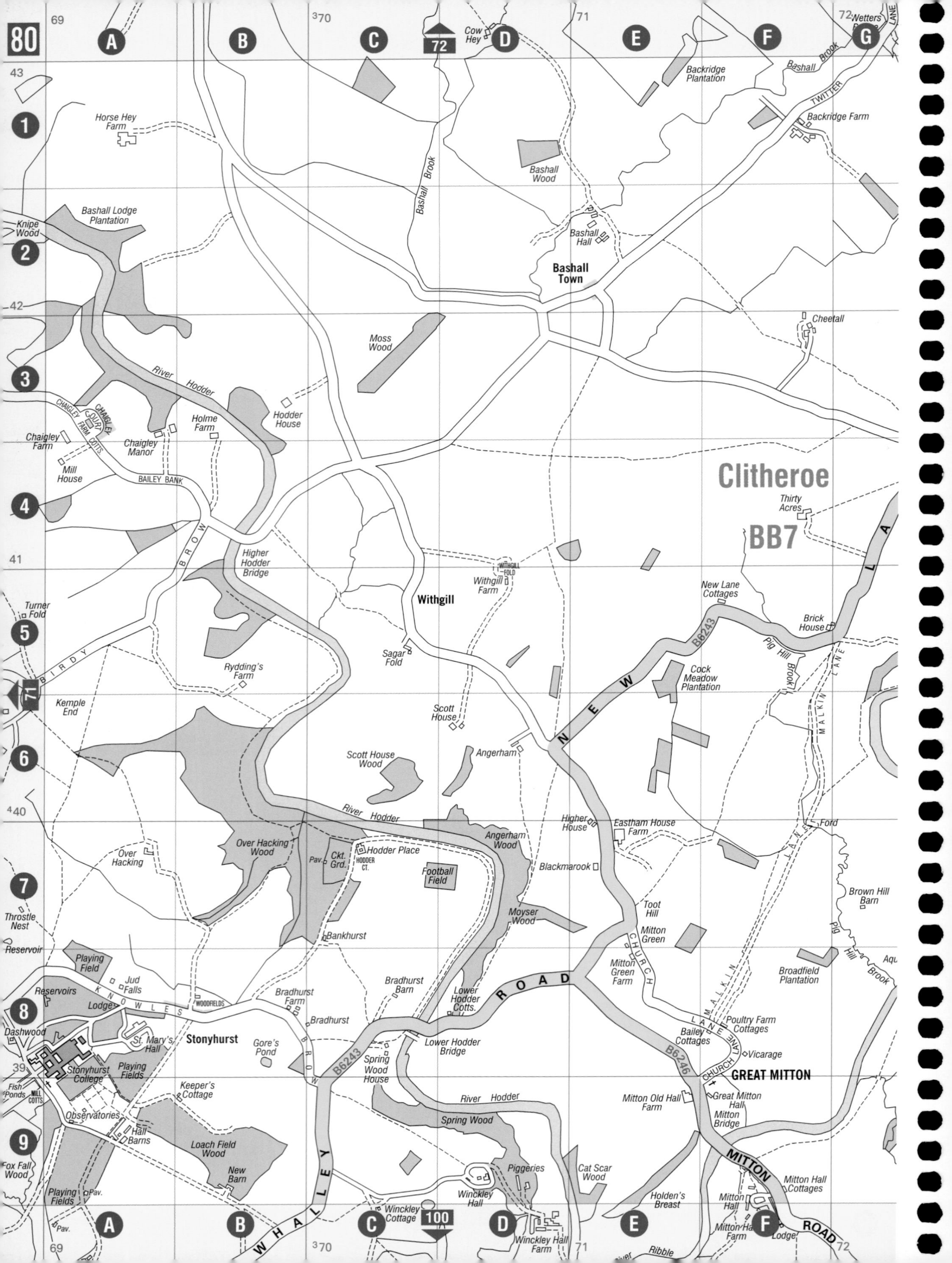
72
Cow Hey
Wetters
Backridge Plantation
Bashall Brook
Horse Hey Farm
TWITTER
Backridge Farm
Bashall Brook
Bashall Wood
Bashall Lodge Plantation
Knipe Wood
Bashall Hall
Bashall Town
Cheetall
Moss Wood
River Hodder
CHAIGLEY COURT
CHAIGLEY FARM COTTS
Hodder House
Holme Farm
Chaigley Farm
Chaigley Manor
Mill House
BAILEY BANK
Clitheroe
Thirty Acres
BB7
BROW
Higher Hodder Bridge
WITHGILL FOLD
Withgill Farm
Withgill
New Lane Cottages
Turner Fold
Brick House
B6243
Pig Hill Brook
BIRDY
Sagar Fold
Rydding's Farm
71
Kemple End
NEW
Cock Meadow Plantation
MALKIN LANE
Scott House
Angerham
Scott House Wood
River Hodder
Higher House
Eastham House Farm
Ford
Over Hacking Wood
Angerham Wood
Hodder Place
Pav.
Ckt. Grd.
HODDER CT.
Over Hacking
Football Field
Blackmarook
Throstle Nest
Moyser Wood
Toot Hill
Mitton Green
Brown Hill Barn
Bankhurst
Reservoir
Playing Field
Pig Hill Brook
Broadfield Plantation
Mitton Green Farm
CHURCH
Jud Falls
Bradhurst Barn
Reservoirs
Bradhurst Farm
ROAD
Lower Hodder Cotts.
KNOWLES
WOODFIELDS
Lodge
Bradhurst
Poultry Farm Cottages
Dashwood
St. Mary's Hall
Stonyhurst
Gore's Pond
Lower Hodder Bridge
Bailey Cottages
Vicarage
Stonyhurst College
Playing Fields
Spring Wood House
B6246
CHURCH LANE
GREAT MITTON
Fish Ponds
MILL COTTS.
Keeper's Cottage
Mitton Old Hall Farm
Great Mitton Hall
Observatories
River Hodder
Mitton Bridge
Spring Wood
Hall Barns
Loach Field Wood
Fox Fall Wood
WHALLEY
New Barn
Piggeries
Cat Scar Wood
MITTON
Mitton Hall Cottages
Playing Fields
Pav.
Winckley Hall
Holden's Breast
Mitton Hall
Winckley Cottage
100
Winckley Hall Farm
Mitton Hall Farm
Lodge
ROAD
Ribble
A
B
C
D
E
F
G
1
2
3
4
5
6
7
8
9
69
370
71
72
43
42
41
440
39

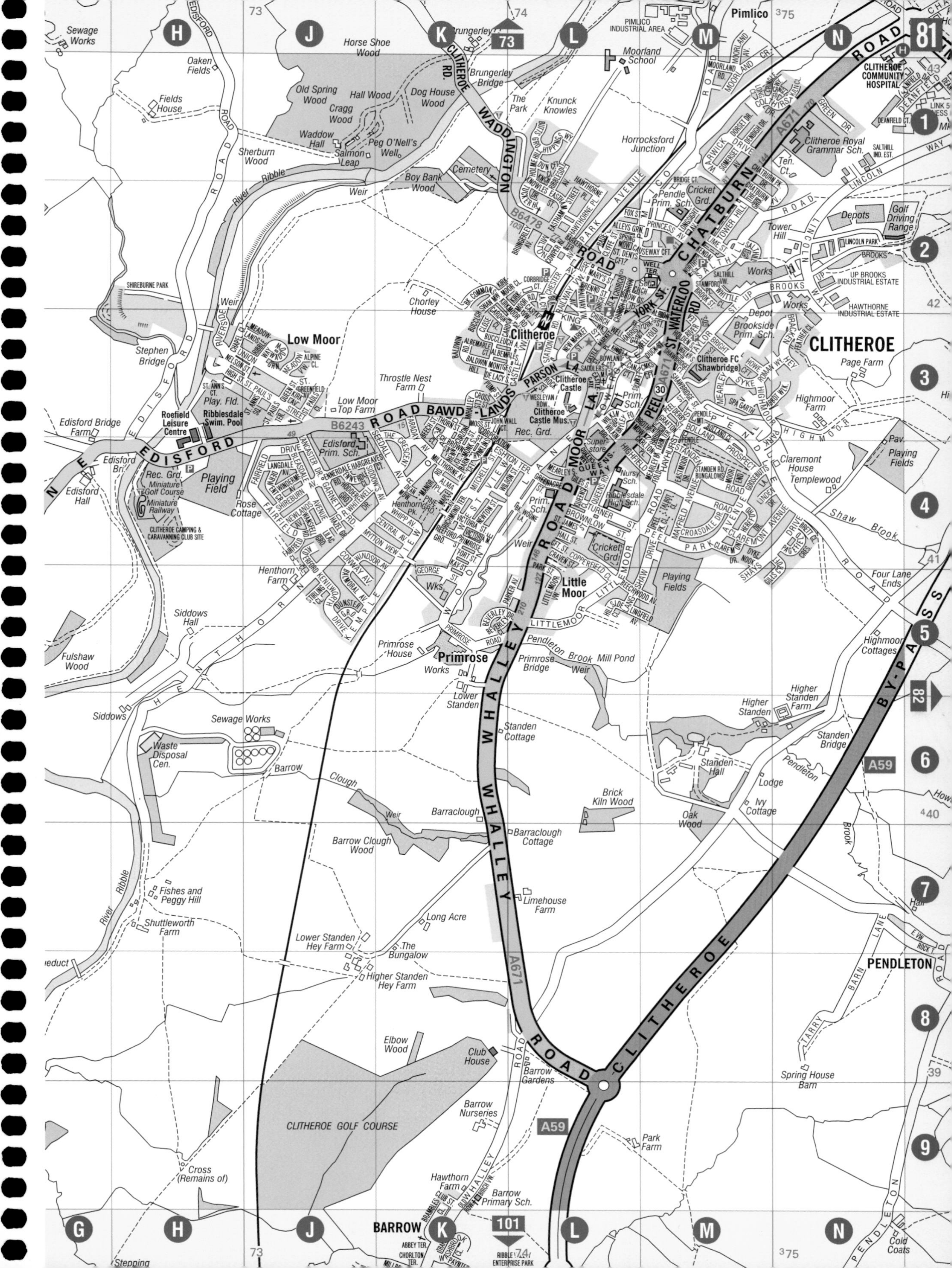

81
CLITHEROE
Clitheroe
Low Moor
Little Moor
Primrose
Pimlico
PENDLETON
BARROW
Clitheroe Castle
Clitheroe Castle Mus.
CLITHEROE COMMUNITY HOSPITAL
Clitheroe Royal Grammar Sch.
Clitheroe FC (Shawbridge)
Roefield Leisure Centre
Ribblesdale Swim. Pool
Edisford Prim. Sch.
Ribblesdale High Sch.
Pendle Prim. Sch.
Brookside Prim. Sch.
Moorland School
Barrow Primary Sch.
CLITHEROE GOLF COURSE
CLITHEROE CAMPING & CARAVANNING CLUB SITE
Miniature Golf Course
Miniature Railway
Playing Field
Playing Fields
Rec. Grd.
Cricket Grd.
Cemetery
Sewage Works
Waste Disposal Cen.
PIMLICO INDUSTRIAL AREA
SALTHILL IND. EST.
UP BROOKS INDUSTRIAL ESTATE
HAWTHORNE INDUSTRIAL ESTATE
Golf Driving Range
Horrocksford Junction
Edisford Bridge Farm
Edisford Hall
Stephen Bridge
Sherburn Wood
Waddow Hall
Salmon Leap
Peg O'Nell's Well
Old Spring Wood
Cragg Wood
Hall Wood
Dog House Wood
Horse Shoe Wood
Boy Bank Wood
Brungerley Bridge
Knunck Knowles
Chorley House
Throstle Nest Farm
Low Moor Top Farm
Henthorn Farm
Siddows Hall
Siddows
Fulshaw Wood
Primrose House
Primrose Bridge
Pendleton Brook Mill Pond
Lower Standen
Standen Cottage
Higher Standen
Higher Standen Farm
Standen Hall
Standen Bridge
Barraclough
Barraclough Cottage
Barrow Clough Wood
Brick Kiln Wood
Oak Wood
Ivy Cottage
Limehouse Farm
Long Acre
Lower Standen Hey Farm
Higher Standen Hey Farm
The Bungalow
Fishes and Peggy Hill
Shuttleworth Farm
Elbow Wood
Club House
Barrow Gardens
Barrow Nurseries
Park Farm
Hawthorn Farm
Cross (Remains of)
Spring House Barn
Cold Coats
Four Lane Ends
Highmoor Cottages
Claremont House
Templewood
Page Farm
Highmoor Farm
Tower Hill
River Ribble
Shaw Brook
WHALLEY ROAD
CLITHEROE BY-PASS
EDISFORD ROAD
BAWDLANDS
CHATBURN ROAD
WADDINGTON ROAD
HENTHORN ROAD
PENDLETON ROAD
A671
A59
B6243
B6478
73
101
82
RIBBLE VALLEY ENTERPRISE PARK

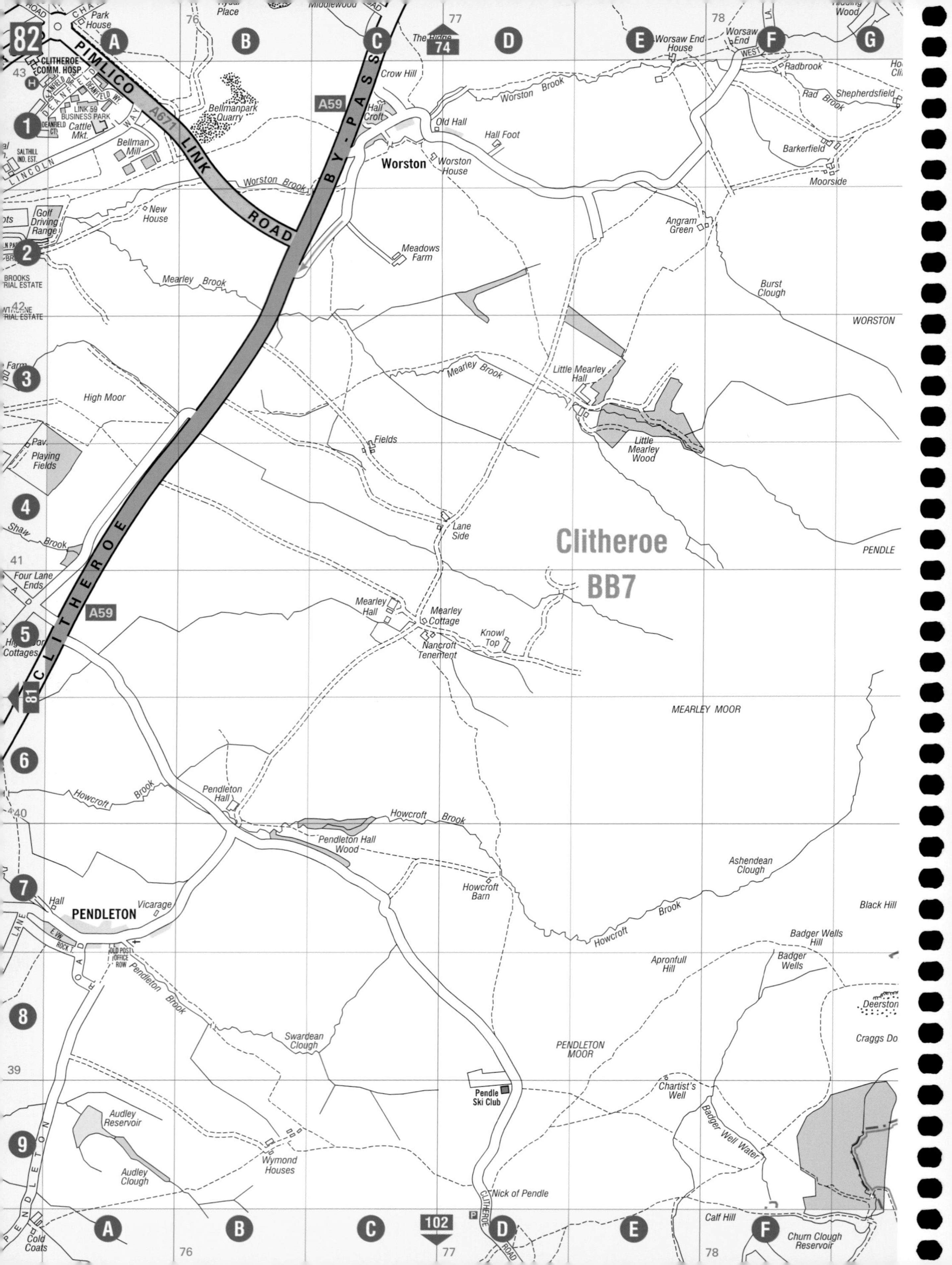
Park House
Place
Middlewood
77
The Ridge
74
Worsaw End House
Worsaw End
78
Wood
CLITHEROE COMM. HOSP.
PIMLICO LINK ROAD
A671
Crow Hill
Radbrook
Worston Brook
Shepherdsfield
Rad Brook
Bellmanpark Quarry
A59
Hall Croft
BY-PASS
Old Hall
Hall Foot
LINK 59 BUSINESS PARK
Cattle Mkt.
SALTHILL IND. EST.
Bellman Mill
Barkerfield
LINCOLN
Worston
Worston House
Moorside
Worston Brook
Golf Driving Range
New House
Angram Green
Meadows Farm
Mearley Brook
BROOKS RIAL ESTATE
Burst Clough
42
WORSTON
Farm
Mearley Brook
Little Mearley Hall
High Moor
Fields
Little Mearley Wood
Pav.
Playing Fields
Lane Side
Shaw Brook
Clitheroe
41
BB7
PENDLE
Four Lane Ends
CLITHEROE
A59
Mearley Hall
Mearley Cottage
Knowl Top
Nancroft Tenement
Cottages
81
MEARLEY MOOR
Pendleton Hall
Howcroft Brook
40
Howcroft Brook
Pendleton Hall Wood
Ashendean Clough
Howcroft Barn
Hall
Vicarage
PENDLETON
Black Hill
Howcroft Brook
Badger Wells Hill
Apronfull Hill
Badger Wells
Pendleton Brook
Deerston
Swardean Clough
Craggs Do
PENDLETON MOOR
39
Chartist's Well
Pendle Ski Club
Badger Well Water
Audley Reservoir
Wymond Houses
Audley Clough
PENDLETON LANE
Nick of Pendle
CLITHEROE ROAD
Calf Hill
102
Churn Clough Reservoir
Cold Coats
76
77
78

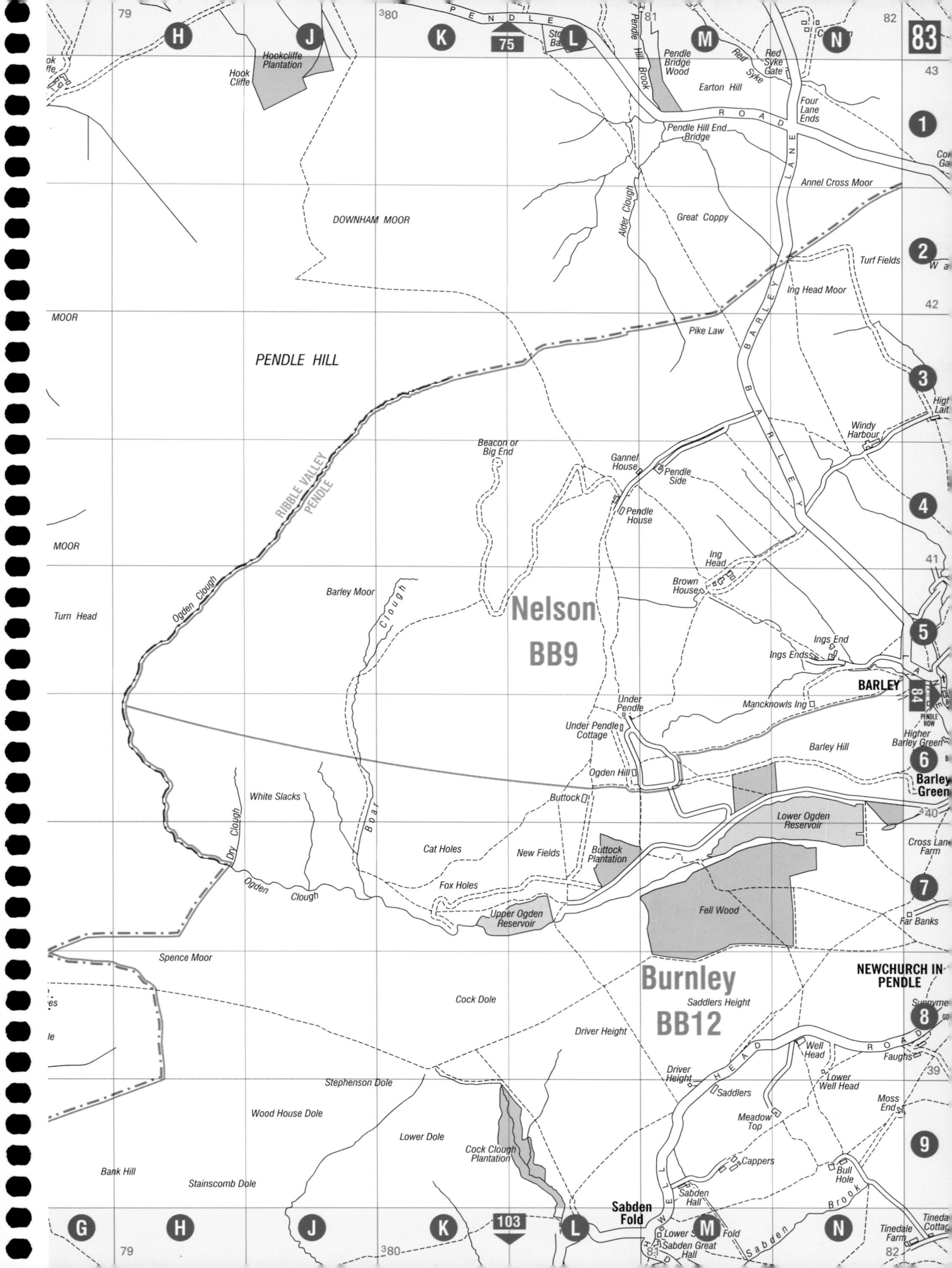
PENDLE ROAD
75
Hook Cliffe
Hookcliffe Plantation
Pendle Hill Brook
Pendle Bridge Wood
Red Syke
Red Syke Gate
Earton Hill
Four Lane Ends
Pendle Hill End Bridge
Annel Cross Moor
DOWNHAM MOOR
Alder Clough
Great Coppy
Turf Fields
Ing Head Moor
MOOR
Pike Law
BARLEY LANE
PENDLE HILL
Windy Harbour
Beacon or Big End
Gannel House
Pendle Side
RIBBLE VALLEY
PENDLE
Pendle House
MOOR
Ing Head
Brown House
Barley Moor
Clough
Nelson
BB9
Ogden Clough
Turn Head
Ings End
Ings Ends
BARLEY
84
Under Pendle
Mancknowls Ing
Under Pendle Cottage
Higher Barley Green
Barley Hill
Ogden Hill
Barley Green
White Slacks
Buttock
Lower Ogden Reservoir
Dry Clough
Boar
Cross Lane Farm
Cat Holes
New Fields
Buttock Plantation
Ogden Clough
Fox Holes
Fell Wood
Upper Ogden Reservoir
Far Banks
Spence Moor
Burnley
NEWCHURCH IN PENDLE
Cock Dole
Saddlers Height
BB12
Driver Height
WELL HEAD ROAD
Well Head
Faughs
Driver Height
Stephenson Dole
Lower Well Head
Saddlers
Moss End
Wood House Dole
Meadow Top
Lower Dole
Cock Clough Plantation
Cappers
Bull Hole
Bank Hill
Stainscomb Dole
Sabden Hall
Sabden Fold
Sabden Brook
103
Fold
Sabden Great Hall
Tinedale Farm
Tineda Cottag
G H J K L M N
79 380 81 82
43 42 41 40 39
1 2 3 4 5 6 7 8 9

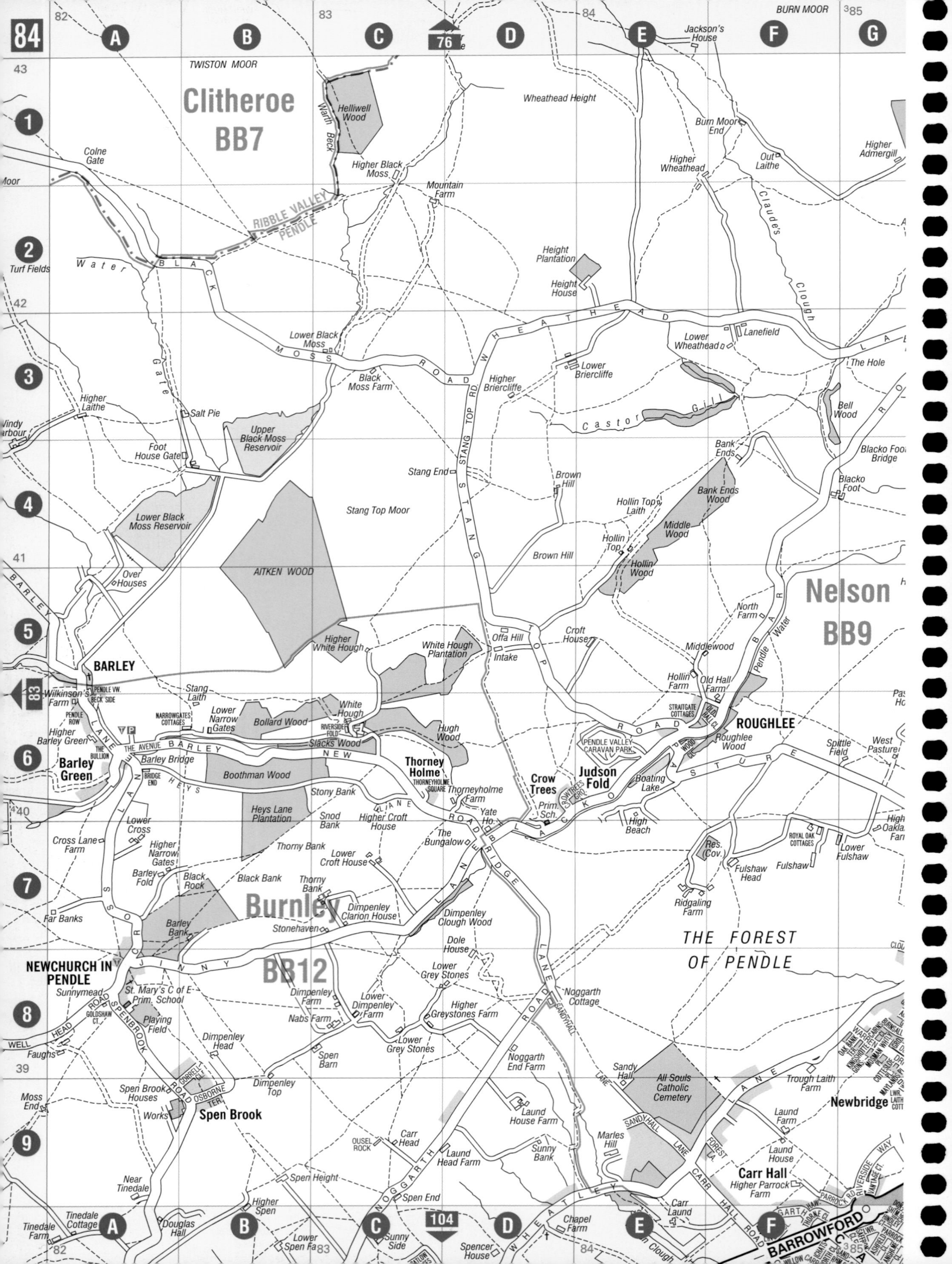
TWISTON MOOR
Clitheroe
BB7
Helliwell Wood
Warth Beck
Wheathead Height
Jackson's House
BURN MOOR
Burn Moor End
Higher Wheathead
Out Laithe
Higher Admergill
Claude's Clough
Colne Gate
Higher Black Moss
Mountain Farm
RIBBLE VALLEY
PENDLE
Turf Fields
Water
BLACK MOSS ROAD
Height Plantation
Height House
WHEATHEAD LANE
Lower Wheathead
Lanefield
The Hole
Lower Black Moss
Black Moss Farm
Higher Briercliffe
Lower Briercliffe
Castor Gill
Bell Wood
Higher Laithe
Salt Pie
Upper Black Moss Reservoir
Gate
Foot House Gate
Stang End
STANG TOP RD
Brown Hill
Bank Ends
Bank Ends Wood
Blacko Foot Bridge
Blacko Foot
Hollin Top Laith
Middle Wood
Hollin Top
Hollin Wood
Lower Black Moss Reservoir
Stang Top Moor
AITKEN WOOD
Over Houses
BARLEY
North Farm
Nelson
BB9
Pendle Water
BAR ROAD
Higher White Hough
White Hough Plantation
Offa Hill
Intake
Croft House
Middlewood
Hollin Farm
Old Hall Farm
BARLEY
PENDLE VW.
BECK SIDE
Wilkinson's Farm
Stang Laith
Lower Narrow Gates
NARROWGATES COTTAGES
Bollard Wood
White Hough
RIVERSIDE FOLD
STRAITGATE COTTAGES
ROUGHLEE
PENDLE ROW
Higher Barley Green
THE BULLION
THE AVENUE
BARLEY NEW ROAD
Slacks Wood
Hugh Wood
Thorney Holme
PENDLE VALLEY CARAVAN PARK
Roughlee Wood
Spittle Field
West Pasture
Barley Green
Barley Bridge
BRIDGE END
HEYS LANE
Boothman Wood
THORNEYHOLME SQUARE
Thorneyholme Farm
Crow Trees
Judson Fold
Boating Lake
PASTURE LANE
Stony Bank
Heys Lane Plantation
Snod Bank
Higher Croft House
Yate Ho.
Prim. Sch.
CROWTREES GRO.
BLACKO BAR ROAD
High Beach
Lower Cross
Cross Lane Farm
Higher Narrow Gates
The Bungalow
Thorny Bank
Lower Croft House
Res. Cov.
ROYAL OAK COTTAGES
Lower Fulshaw
Fulshaw
Fulshaw Head
Barley Fold
Black Rock
Black Bank
Thorny Bank
Ridgaling Farm
Burnley
BB12
Dimpenley Clarion House
Dimpenley Clough Wood
Far Banks
Barley Bank
Stonehaven
THE FOREST OF PENDLE
Dole House
NEWCHURCH IN PENDLE
JINNY LANE
Lower Grey Stones
Sunnymead
St. Mary's C of E Prim. School
Dimpenley Farm
Lower Dimpenley Farm
Higher Greystones Farm
Noggarth Cottage
GOLDSHAW CT.
Playing Field
Nabs Farm
WELL HEAD ROAD
SPENBROOK
Faughs
Dimpenley Head
Lower Grey Stones
Spen Barn
Noggarth End Farm
Sandy Hall
All Souls Catholic Cemetery
Trough Laith Farm
Newbridge
Spen Brook Houses
CORRELL CL.
OSBORNE TER.
ROAD
Dimpenley Top
Moss End
Works
Spen Brook
Laund House Farm
SANDY HALL LANE
Laund Farm
OUSEL ROCK
Carr Head
Laund Head Farm
Sunny Bank
Marles Hill
FOREST LA.
Laund House
Spen Height
Carr Hall
Higher Parrock Farm
Near Tinedale
NOGGARTH ROAD
Spen End
CARR HALL ROAD
Tinedale Cottage
Higher Spen
Douglas Hall
WHEATLEY LANE
Chapel Farm
Carr Laund
Tinedale Farm
Lower Spen Fa
Sunny Side
Spencer House
BARROWFORD
Clough
76
104
83
BURN MOOR

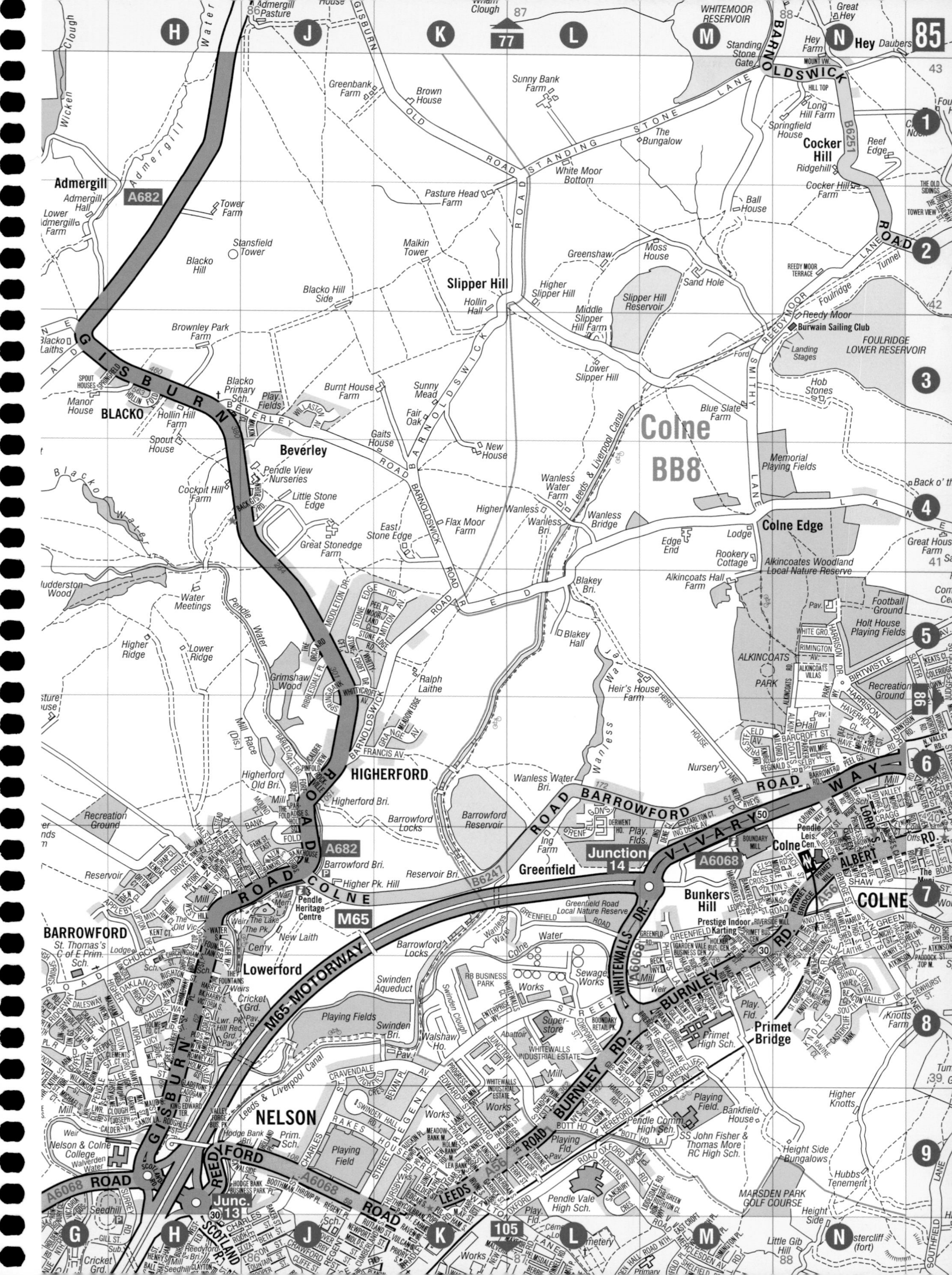

Admergill
A682
Blacko Hill
BLACKO
Beverley
Slipper Hill
Slipper Hill Reservoir
Colne
BB8
FOULRIDGE LOWER RESERVOIR
Burwain Sailing Club
Cocker Hill
Colne Edge
Alkincoats Woodland Local Nature Reserve
ALKINCOATS PARK
HIGHERFORD
Barrowford Reservoir
Greenfield
Junction 14
A6068
COLNE
BARROWFORD
Lowerford
M65
M65 MOTORWAY
Pendle Heritage Centre
Bunkers Hill
Primet Bridge
WHITEWALLS INDUSTRIAL ESTATE
NELSON
Nelson & Colne College
Junc. 13
MARSDEN PARK GOLF COURSE
Pendle Vale High Sch.
SS John Fisher & Thomas More RC High Sch.
Leeds & Liverpool Canal
STANDING STONE LANE
BARNOLDSWICK ROAD
GISBURN ROAD
BARROWFORD ROAD
COLNE ROAD
BURNLEY RD.
VIVARY WAY
WHITEWALLS DR.
REEDYFORD RD.
WHITEMOOR RESERVOIR

77
105
86

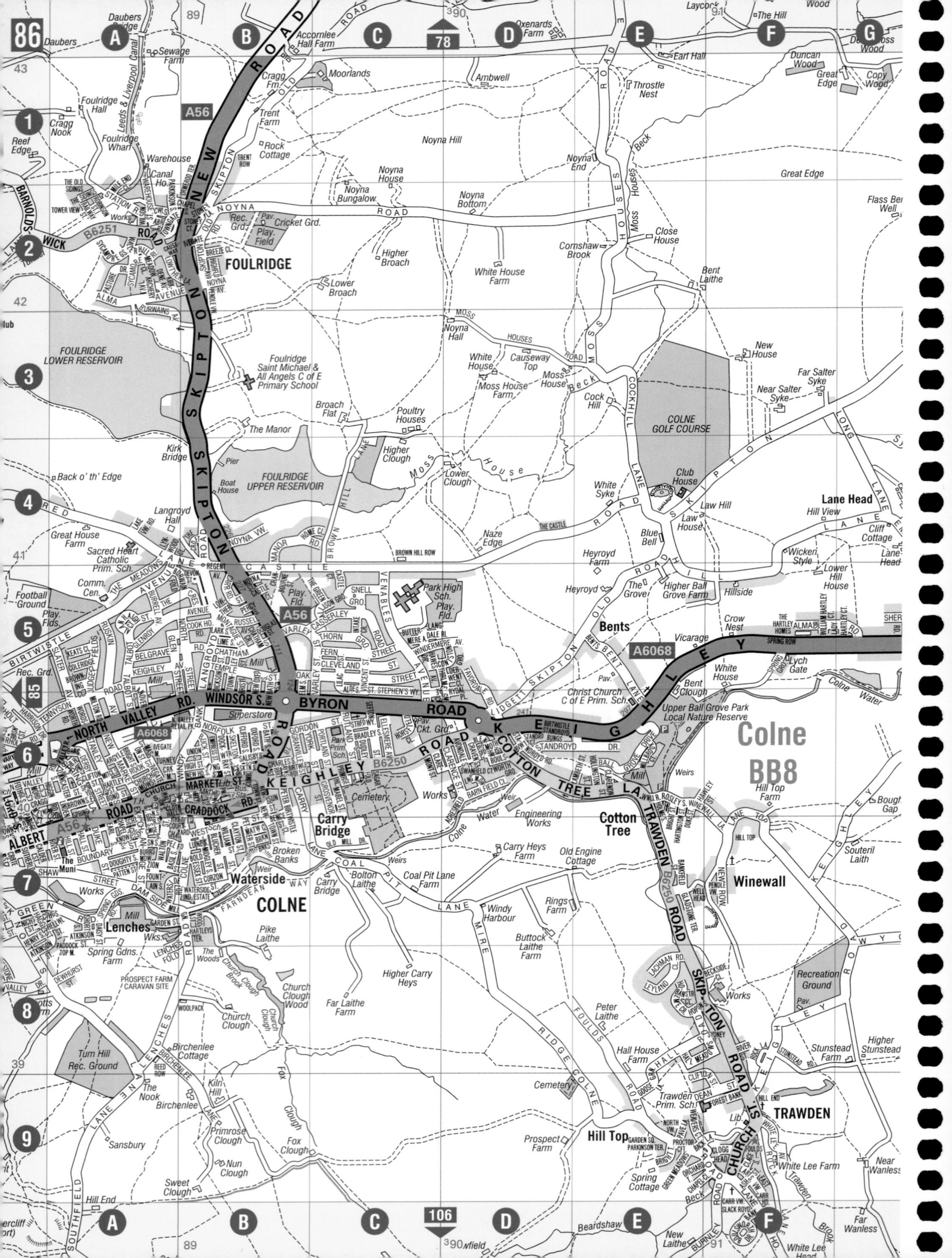

78
85
106
FOULRIDGE
COLNE
Colne
BB8
TRAWDEN
Winewall
Cotton Tree
Waterside
Lenches
Carry Bridge
Bents
Lane Head
Hill Top
FOULRIDGE LOWER RESERVOIR
FOULRIDGE UPPER RESERVOIR
COLNE GOLF COURSE
Foulridge Saint Michael & All Angels C of E Primary School
Christ Church C of E Prim. Sch.
Park High Sch. Play. Fld.
Upper Ball Grove Park Local Nature Reserve
Sacred Heart Catholic Prim. Sch.
Trawden Prim. Sch.
Tum Hill Rec. Ground
Recreation Ground
Noyna Hill
Great Edge
Moorlands
Accornlee Hall Farm
Oxenards Farm
Earl Hall
Throstle Nest
Duncan Wood
Great Edge
Copy Wood
Daubers Bridge
Sewage Farm
Foulridge Hall
Cragg Nook
Reef Edge
Foulridge Wharf
Warehouse
Canal Ho.
Trent Farm
Rock Cottage
Noyna House
Noyna Bungalow
Noyna Bottom
Noyna End
Higher Broach
Lower Broach
White House Farm
Cornshaw Brook
Close House
Bent Laithe
New House
Far Salter Syke
Near Salter Syke
Flass Bent Well
Noyna Hall
White House
Causeway Top
Moss House
Moss House Farm
Cock Hill
Broach Flat
Poultry Houses
The Manor
Higher Clough
Lower Clough
Kirk Bridge
Back o' th' Edge
Boat House
Pier
White Syke
Club House
Law Hill
Law House
Hill View
Cliff Cottage
Langroyd Hall
Great House Farm
Naze Edge
Heyroyd Farm
Blue Bell
Wicken Style
Lower Hill House
Heyroyd
The Grove
Higher Ball Grove Farm
Hillside
Crow Nest
Vicarage
White House
Lych Gate
Bent Clough
Comm. Cen.
Football Ground
Play. Flds.
Superstore
Cemetery
Works
Engineering Works
Weirs
Hill Top Farm
Bough Gap
Souteril Laith
Carry Heys Farm
Old Engine Cottage
Coal Pit Lane Farm
Bolton Laithe
Broken Banks
Windy Harbour
Rings Farm
Buttock Laithe Farm
Pike Laithe
Spring Gdns. Farm
Prospect Farm Caravan Site
The Woods
Church Clough Wood
Church Clough
Higher Carry Heys
Far Laithe Farm
Peter Laithe
Hall House Farm
Stunstead Farm
Higher Stunstead
Birchenlee Cottage
Kiln Hill
The Nook
Birchenlee
Primrose Clough
Nun Clough
Sweet Clough
Sansbury
Hill End
Fox Clough
Prospect Farm
Spring Cottage
White Lee Farm
Near Wanless
Far Wanless
New Laithe
Beardshaw
White Lee Head
A56
A6068
B6251
B6250
SKIPTON NEW ROAD
SKIPTON OLD ROAD
NOYNA ROAD
MOSS HOUSES ROAD
COCKHILL LANE
CASTLE ROAD
BYRON ROAD
KEIGHLEY ROAD
NORTH VALLEY RD.
WINDSOR S.
COTTON TREE LA.
TRAWDEN ROAD
SKIPTON ROAD
CHURCH ST.
COAL PIT LANE
MIRE
RIDGE COLNE
LENCHES
SOUTHFIELD LANE
WICK ROAD
ALBERT

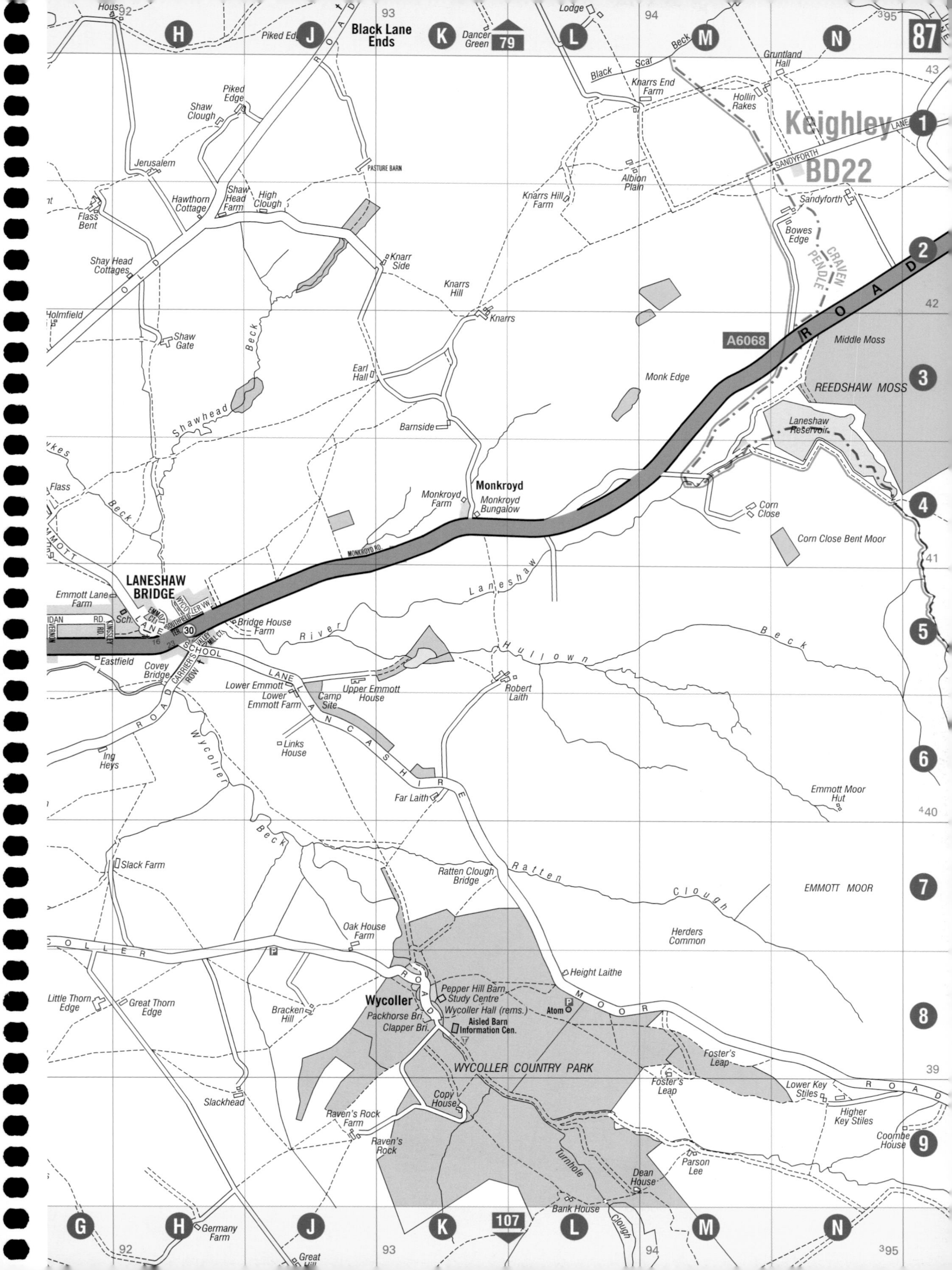
Black Lane Ends
Dancer Green
79
Piked Edge
Shaw Clough
Jerusalem
Hawthorn Cottage
Shaw Head Farm
High Clough
PASTURE BARN
Flass Bent
Shay Head Cottages
Holmfield
Shaw Gate
Knarr Side
Knarrs Hill
Knarrs
Earl Hall
Barnside
Monkroyd
Monkroyd Farm
Monkroyd Bungalow
MONKROYD RD.
Lodge
Black Scar Beck
Knarrs End Farm
Gruntland Hall
Hollin Rakes
Keighley
BD22
SANDYFORTH
Sandyforth
Albion Plain
Knarrs Hill Farm
Bowes Edge
CRAVEN
PENDLE
A6068
ROAD
Middle Moss
Monk Edge
REEDSHAW MOSS
Laneshaw Reservoir
Corn Close
Corn Close Bent Moor
LANESHAW BRIDGE
Emmott Lane Farm
Sch.
Bridge House Farm
River Laneshaw
Hullown Beck
Eastfield
Covey Bridge
SCHOOL LANE
CARRIER'S ROW
Lower Emmott
Lower Emmott Farm
Camp Site
Upper Emmott House
Robert Laith
LANCASHIRE
Links House
Ing Heys
Wycoller Beck
Far Laith
Emmott Moor Hut
Slack Farm
Ratten Clough Bridge
Ratten Clough
EMMOTT MOOR
Herders Common
Oak House Farm
Height Laithe
MOOR ROAD
Wycoller
Pepper Hill Barn Study Centre
Wycoller Hall (rems.)
Packhorse Bri.
Clapper Bri.
Aisled Barn Information Cen.
Atom
Little Thorn Edge
Great Thorn Edge
Bracken Hill
WYCOLLER COUNTRY PARK
Foster's Leap
Lower Key Stiles
Higher Key Stiles
Coombe House
Slackhead
Copy House
Raven's Rock Farm
Raven's Rock
Turnhole Clough
Dean House
Parson Lee
Bank House
107
Germany Farm
Great Hill
G H J K L M N
1 2 3 4 5 6 7 8 9
92 93 94 395
43 42 41 440 39

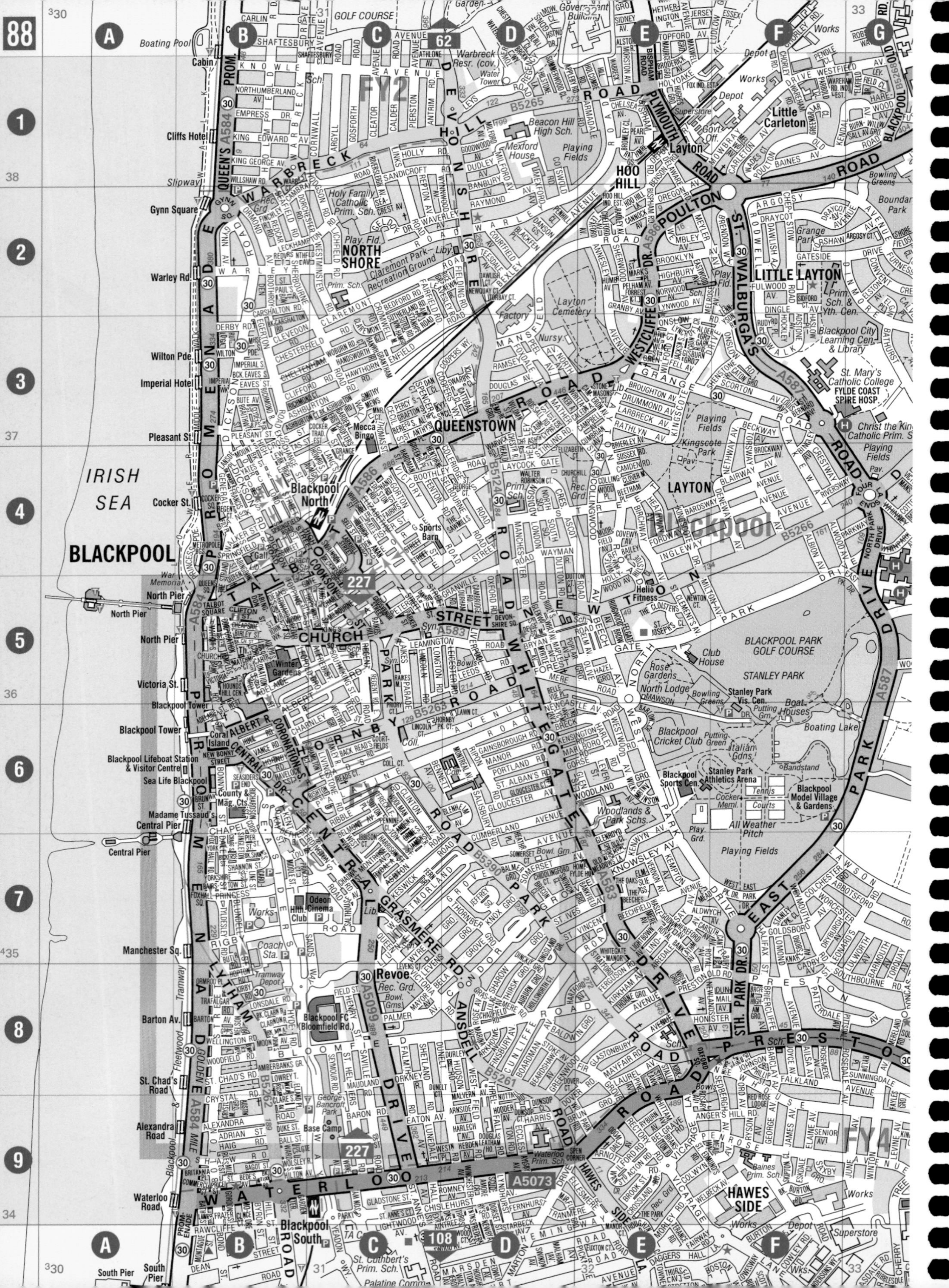

88
IRISH SEA
BLACKPOOL
NORTH SHORE
QUEENSTOWN
LAYTON
LITTLE LAYTON
Little Carleton
Layton
HOO HILL
Revoe
HAWES SIDE
FY2
FY4
Blackpool North
Blackpool South
North Pier
Central Pier
South Pier
Blackpool Tower
Winter Gardens
Coral Island
Blackpool Lifeboat Station & Visitor Centre
Sea Life Blackpool
Madame Tussaud's
Gynn Square
Cliffs Hotel
Imperial Hotel
Boating Pool
Cabin
Layton Cemetery
Beacon Hill High Sch.
Claremont Park Recreation Ground
BLACKPOOL PARK GOLF COURSE
STANLEY PARK
Boating Lake
Blackpool Cricket Club
Italian Gdns
Stanley Park Athletics Arena
Blackpool Model Village & Gardens
Woodlands & Park Schs.
Blackpool Sports Cen.
Kingscote Park
St. Mary's Catholic College
FYLDE COAST SPIRE HOSP.
Blackpool City Learning Cen. & Library
Blackpool FC (Bloomfield Rd.)
Odeon Cinema
Mecca Bingo
Sports Barn
Helio Fitness
County & Mag. Cts
Coach Sta.
Tramway Depot
Base Camp
QUEEN'S PROM.
PROMENADE
WARBRECK HILL
DEVONSHIRE ROAD
POULTON ROAD
ST. WALBURGA'S ROAD
WESTCLIFFE DR.
TALBOT ROAD
CHURCH STREET
WHITEGATE DRIVE
PARK ROAD
HORNBY ROAD
CENTRAL DRIVE
GRASMERE RD.
ANSDELL ROAD
EAST PARK DRIVE
PRESTON OLD ROAD
WATERLOO ROAD
LYTHAM ROAD
GOLDEN MILE
227
62
108

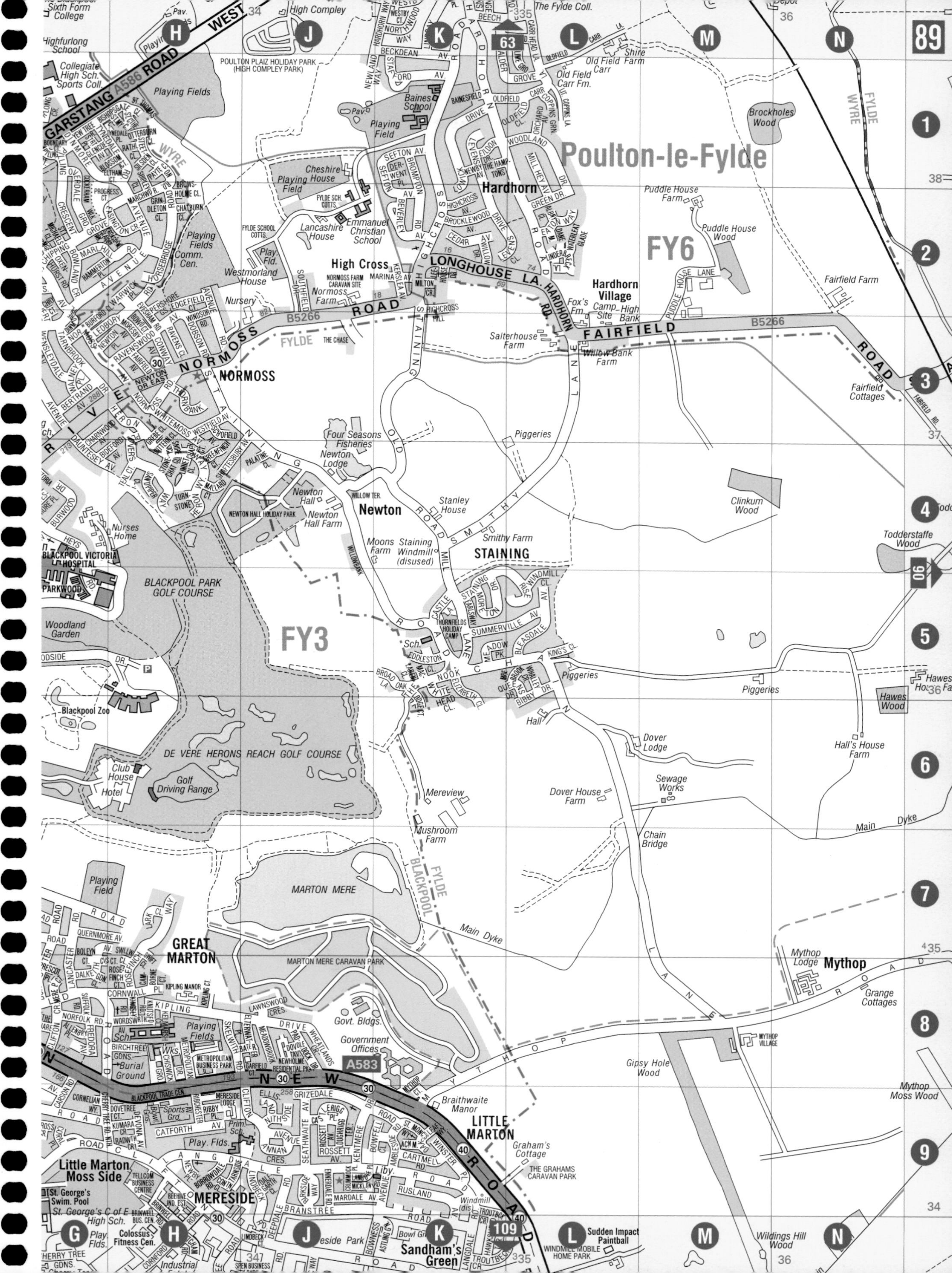
Poulton-le-Fylde
Hardhorn
High Cross
Hardhorn Village
NORMOSS
Newton
STAINING
GREAT MARTON
LITTLE MARTON
Little Marton Moss Side
MERESIDE
Sandham's Green
Mythop
FY6
FY3
GARSTANG A586 ROAD WEST
LONGHOUSE LA.
NORMOSS ROAD
B5266
FAIRFIELD ROAD
A583
NEW ROAD
MYTHOP ROAD
Highfurlong School
Collegiate High Sch. Sports Coll.
High Compley
POULTON PLAIZ HOLIDAY PARK (HIGH COMPLEY PARK)
The Fylde Coll.
Baines School
Playing Field
Playing Fields
Cheshire House
Lancashire House
Emmanuel Christian School
Westmorland House
Nursery
Normoss Farm
NORMOSS FARM CARAVAN SITE
Old Field Farm
Old Field Carr
Shire Carr
Old Field Carr Fm.
Brockholes Wood
Puddle House Farm
Puddle House Wood
Fairfield Farm
Fairfield Cottages
Fox's Fm.
Camp Site
High Bank
Salterhouse Farm
Willow Bank Farm
Piggeries
Four Seasons Fisheries
Newton Lodge
Newton Hall
Newton Hall Farm
NEWTON HALL HOLIDAY PARK
Stanley House
Smithy Farm
Moons Farm
Staining Windmill (disused)
Clinkum Wood
Todderstaffe Wood
Nurses Home
BLACKPOOL VICTORIA HOSPITAL
PARKWOOD
BLACKPOOL PARK GOLF COURSE
Woodland Garden
Blackpool Zoo
DE VERE HERONS REACH GOLF COURSE
Club House
Hotel
Golf Driving Range
THORNFIELDS HOLIDAY CAMP
Hawes Wood
Dover Lodge
Hall's House Farm
Sewage Works
Dover House Farm
Mereview
Mushroom Farm
Chain Bridge
Main Dyke
MARTON MERE
MARTON MERE CARAVAN PARK
Mythop Lodge
Grange Cottages
MYTHOP VILLAGE
Govt. Bldgs.
Government Offices
Burial Ground
METROPOLITAN BUSINESS PARK
Braithwaite Manor
Gipsy Hole Wood
Mythop Moss Wood
Graham's Cottage
THE GRAHAMS CARAVAN PARK
Sports Grd.
Play. Flds.
St. George's Swim. Pool
St. George's C of E High Sch.
Colossus Fitness Cen.
TELLCOM BUSINESS CENTRE
Windmill (dis.)
Wildings Hill Wood
Sudden Impact Paintball
WINDMILL MOBILE HOME PARK
FYLDE
WYRE
BLACKPOOL
63
90
109

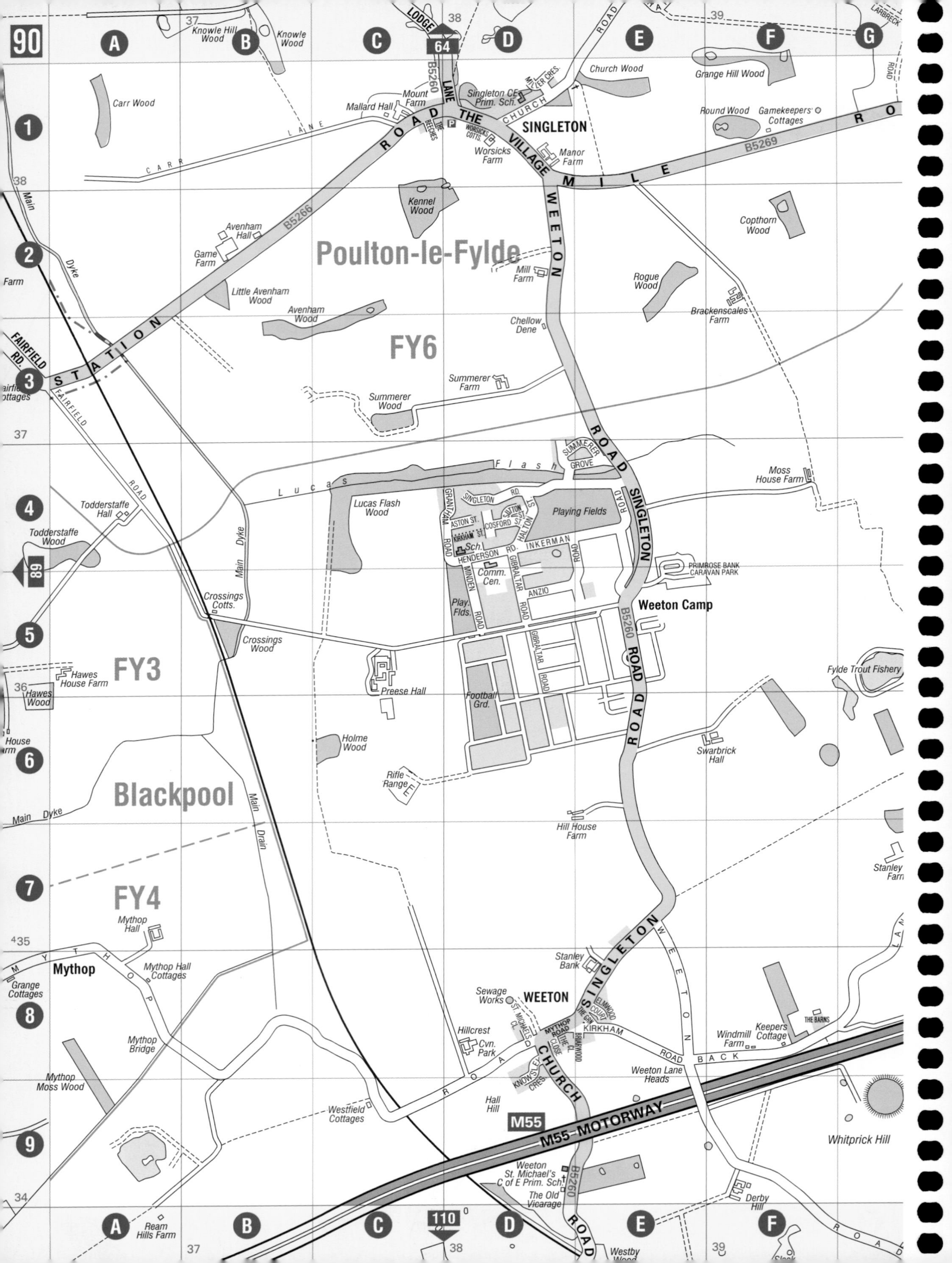
Knowle Hill Wood
Knowle Wood
Carr Wood
Mallard Hall
Mount Farm
Singleton CE Prim. Sch.
SINGLETON
Church Wood
Grange Hill Wood
Round Wood
Gamekeepers' Cottages
Worsicks Farm
Manor Farm
MILE ROAD
B5269
B5260
B5266
LODGE LANE
THE VILLAGE
CHURCH
CARR LANE
STATION ROAD
Kennel Wood
Avenham Hall
Game Farm
Poulton-le-Fylde
Mill Farm
Copthorn Wood
Rogue Wood
Little Avenham Wood
Avenham Wood
Brackenscales Farm
Chellow Dene
FY6
FAIRFIELD RD.
Summerer Farm
Summerer Wood
WEETON ROAD
SUMMERER GROVE
Lucas Flash
Moss House Farm
Todderstaffe Hall
Todderstaffe Wood
Lucas Flash Wood
Playing Fields
SINGLETON ROAD
PRIMROSE BANK CARAVAN PARK
Main Dyke
Crossings Cotts.
Crossings Wood
Comm. Cen.
Play. Flds.
Weeton Camp
Hawes House Farm
FY3
Hawes Wood
Preese Hall
Football Grd.
Fylde Trout Fishery
Holme Wood
Swarbrick Hall
Rifle Range
Blackpool
Main Drain
Hill House Farm
Stanley Farm
FY4
Mythop Hall
Mythop
Mythop Hall Cottages
Grange Cottages
Stanley Bank
Sewage Works
WEETON
Hillcrest Cvn. Park
KIRKHAM ROAD
BACK LANE
Windmill Farm
Keepers Cottage
THE BARNS
Mythop Bridge
Weeton Lane Heads
Mythop Moss Wood
Hall Hill
M55
M55 MOTORWAY
Westfield Cottages
Whitprick Hill
Weeton St. Michael's C of E Prim. Sch.
The Old Vicarage
Derby Hill
CHURCH ROAD
Ream Hills Farm
Westby Wood

64
89
110

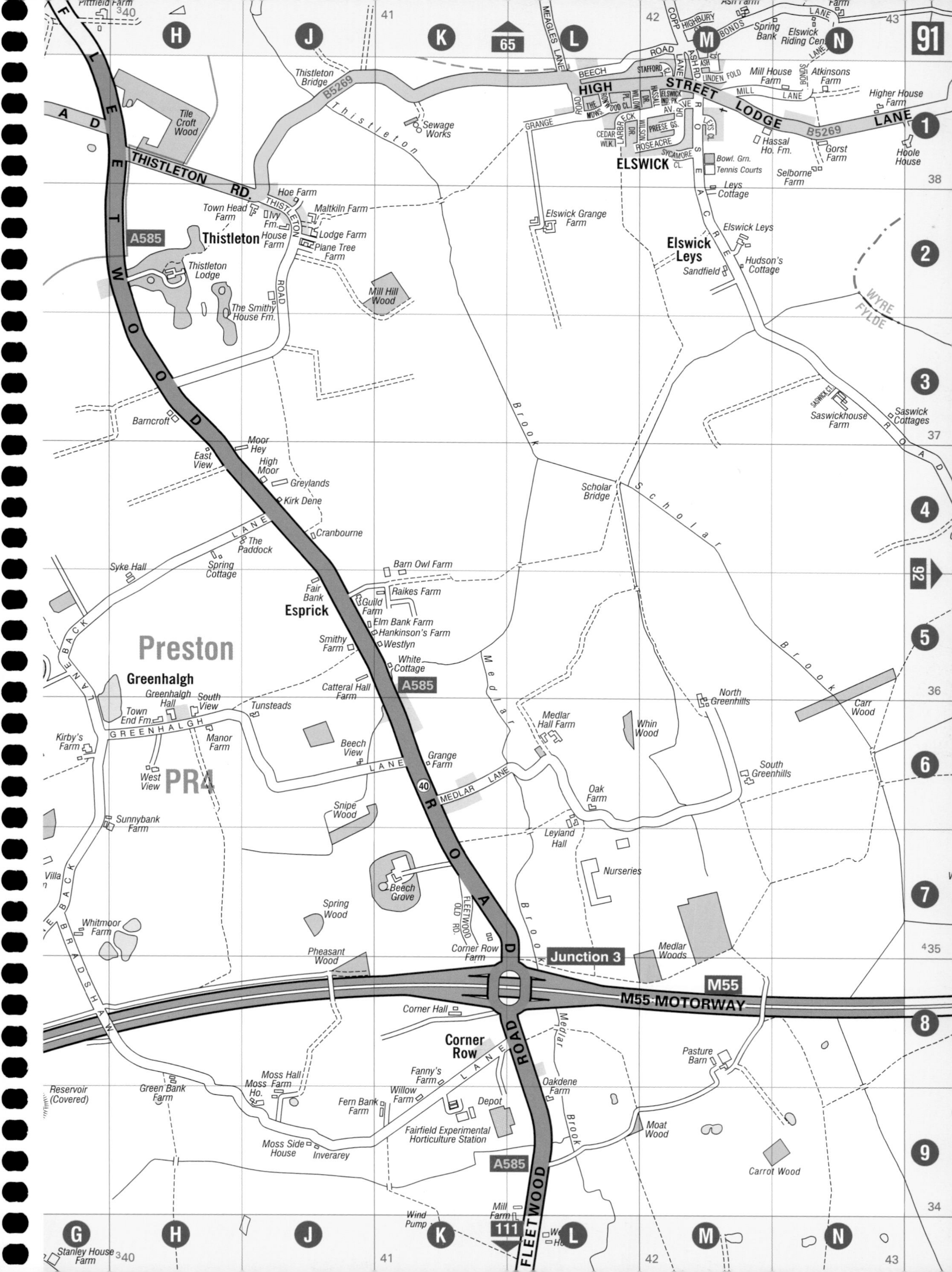

65
FLEETWOOD ROAD
A585
THISTLETON RD.
Tile Croft Wood
Thistleton Bridge
B5269
Thistleton
Sewage Works
HIGH STREET
LODGE LANE
ELSWICK
Elswick Leys
Thistleton
Thistleton Lodge
Town Head Farm
Ivy Fm.
House Farm
Hoe Farm
Maltkiln Farm
Lodge Farm
Plane Tree Farm
The Smithy House Fm.
Mill Hill Wood
Elswick Grange Farm
Sandfield
Hudson's Cottage
Leys Cottage
Hassal Ho. Fm.
Gorst Farm
Hoole House
Higher House Farm
Mill House Farm
Atkinsons Farm
Spring Bank
Elswick Riding Cen.
Selborne Farm
WYRE
FYLDE
Barncroft
Moor Hey
East View
High Moor
Greylands
Kirk Dene
Cranbourne
The Paddock
Syke Hall
Spring Cottage
Barn Owl Farm
Raikes Farm
Fair Bank
Guild Farm
Esprick
Elm Bank Farm
Hankinson's Farm
Westlyn
Smithy Farm
White Cottage
Preston
Greenhalgh
Greenhalgh Hall
South View
Town End Fm.
Tunsteads
Catteral Hall Farm
Kirby's Farm
Manor Farm
West View
PR4
Beech View
Grange Farm
MEDLAR LANE
Snipe Wood
Sunnybank Farm
Beech Grove
Spring Wood
Whitmoor Farm
Pheasant Wood
Corner Row Farm
Junction 3
Medlar Woods
M55
M55 MOTORWAY
Scholar Bridge
Scholar Brook
Saswickhouse Farm
Saswick Cottages
North Greenhills
Carr Wood
Whin Wood
Medlar Hall Farm
South Greenhills
Oak Farm
Leyland Hall
Nurseries
Corner Hall
Corner Row
Moss Hall Farm
Moss Ho.
Green Bank Farm
Reservoir (Covered)
Fanny's Farm
Willow Farm
Fern Bank Farm
Depot
Oakdene Farm
Fairfield Experimental Horticulture Station
Moss Side House
Inverarey
Moat Wood
Pasture Barn
Carrot Wood
Wind Pump
Mill Farm
111
Stanley House Farm
92

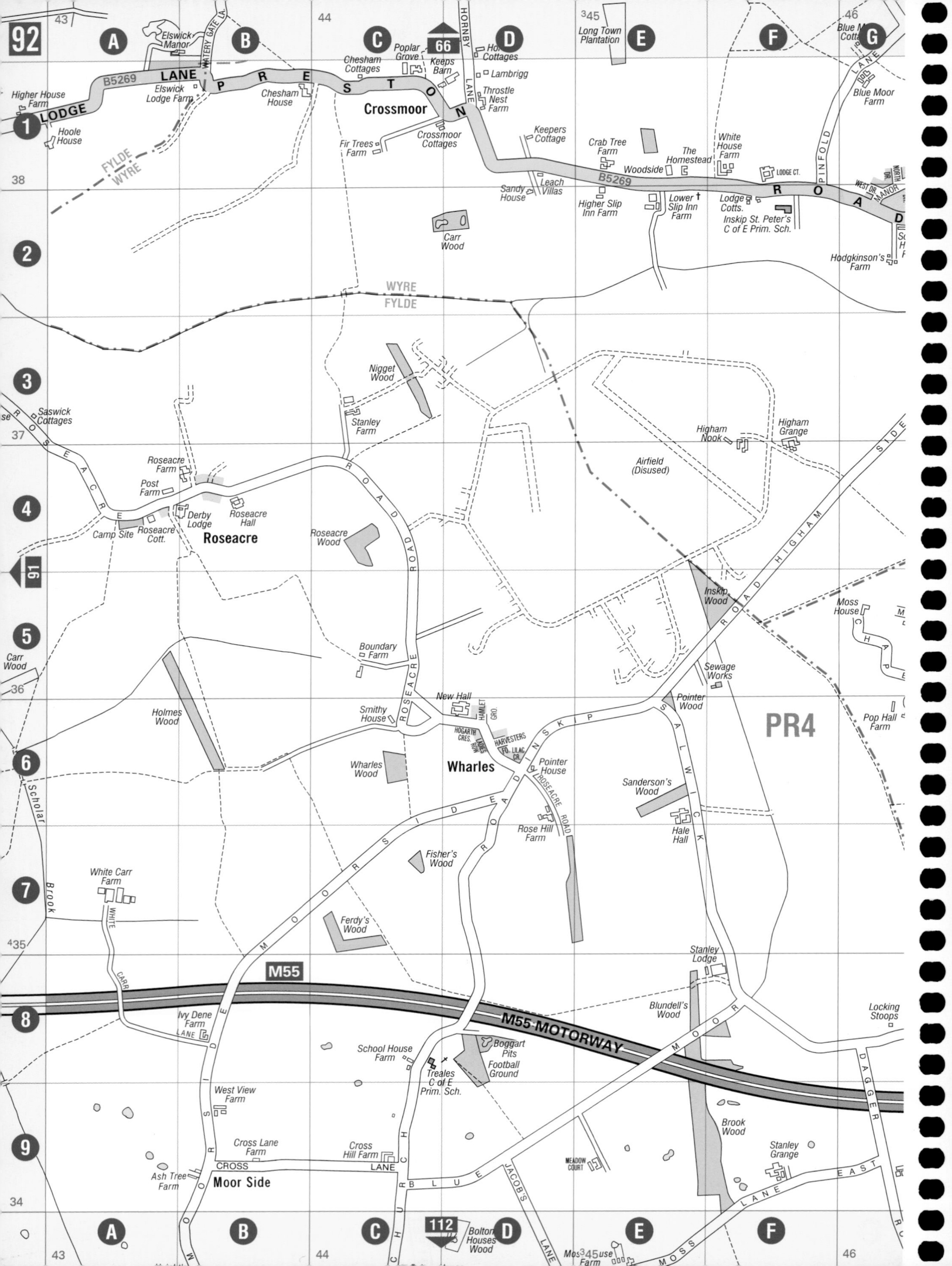
Elswick Manor
WATERY GATE LA.
Poplar Grove
Keeps Barn
66
HORNBY LANE
Cottages
Lambrigg
Throstle Nest Farm
Long Town Plantation
Blue Moor Farm
Higher House Farm
LODGE LANE
B5269
Elswick Lodge Farm
Chesham Cottages
Chesham House
PRESTON ROAD
Crossmoor
Crossmoor Cottages
Fir Trees Farm
Hoole House
FYLDE
WYRE
Keepers Cottage
Crab Tree Farm
The Homestead
White House Farm
Woodside
LODGE CT.
PINFOLD LANE
WEST DR.
MANOR
NORTH DR.
Sandy House
Leach Villas
Higher Slip Inn Farm
Lower Slip Inn Farm
Lodge Cotts.
Inskip St. Peter's C of E Prim. Sch.
Carr Wood
Hodgkinson's Farm
Nigget Wood
Saswick Cottages
Stanley Farm
Higham Nook
Higham Grange
Airfield (Disused)
Roseacre Farm
Post Farm
ROSEACRE
Derby Lodge
Roseacre Hall
Camp Site
Roseacre Cott.
Roseacre
Roseacre Wood
ROAD
HIGHAM SIDE ROAD
91
Inskip Wood
Moss House
Boundary Farm
Carr Wood
Sewage Works
New Hall
HAMLET GRO.
Holmes Wood
Smithy House
ROSEACRE
HOGARTH CRES.
LADIES ROW
HARVESTERS FD.
LILAC CR.
Pointer Wood
INSKIP ROAD
Pop Hall Farm
PR4
Wharles Wood
Wharles
Pointer House
Sanderson's Wood
Scholar Brook
MOOR SIDE
ROSEACRE ROAD
Rose Hill Farm
SALWICK
Hale Hall
Fisher's Wood
White Carr Farm
WHITE CARR LANE
Ferdy's Wood
Stanley Lodge
M55
Blundell's Wood
Locking Stoops
Ivy Dene Farm
M55 MOTORWAY
School House Farm
Boggart Pits
Football Ground
Treales C of E Prim. Sch.
MOOR
DAGGER
West View Farm
Brook Wood
Cross Lane Farm
Cross Hill Farm
Stanley Grange
MEADOW COURT
CROSS LANE
Ash Tree Farm
Moor Side
CHURCH
BLUE MOSS LANE
JACOB'S LANE
EAST
112
Bolton Houses Wood
Moss House Farm
A
B
C
D
E
F
G
1
2
3
4
5
6
7
8
9
43
44
345
46
38
37
36
435
34

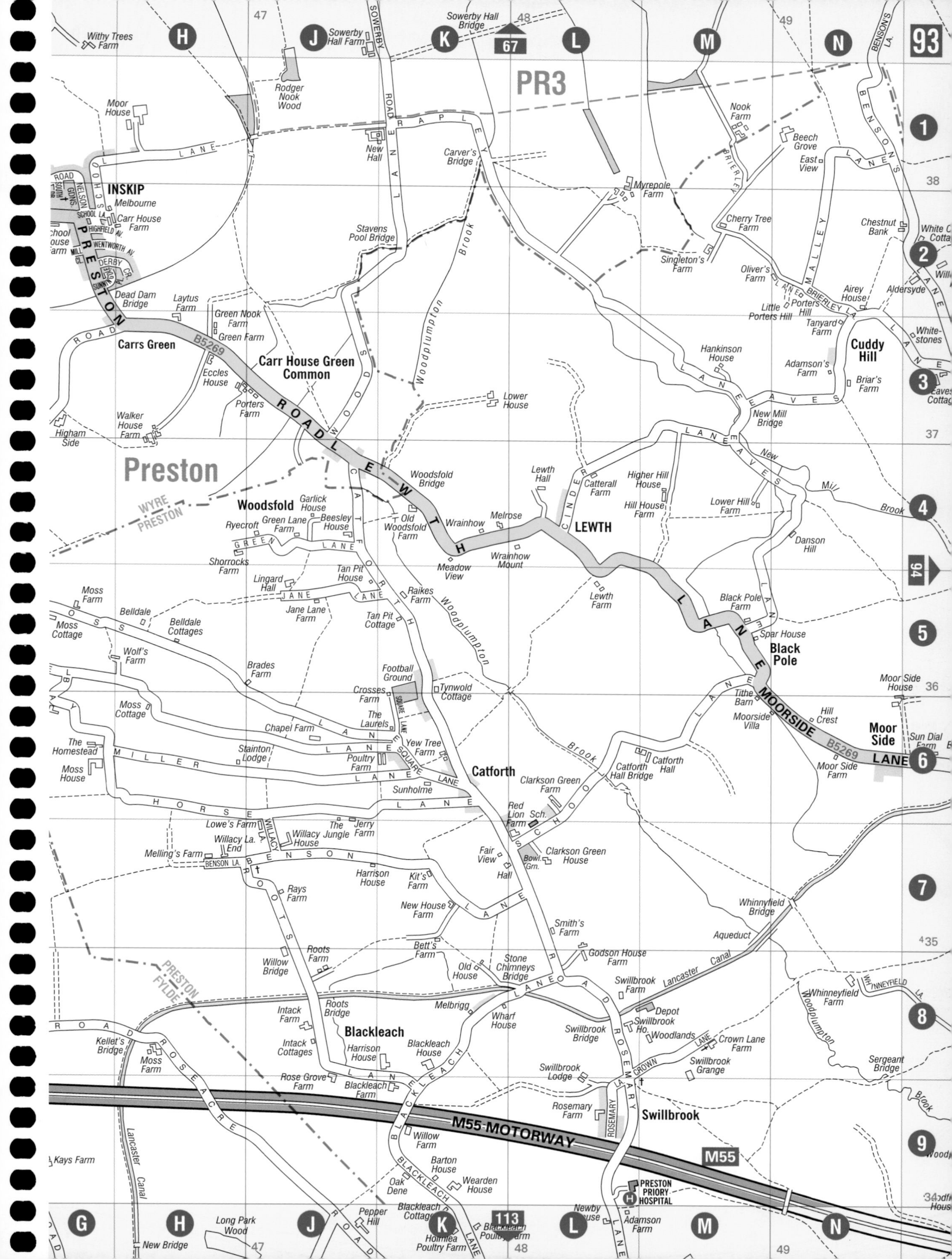
PR3
INSKIP
Carrs Green
Carr House Green Common
Preston
Woodsfold
LEWTH
Cuddy Hill
Black Pole
Moor Side
Catforth
Blackleach
Swillbrook
M55 MOTORWAY
PRESTON PRIORY HOSPITAL
Withy Trees Farm
Sowerby Hall Farm
Sowerby Hall Bridge
Rodger Nook Wood
Moor House
New Hall
Carver's Bridge
Myrepole Farm
Nook Farm
Beech Grove
East View
Cherry Tree Farm
Chestnut Bank
Singleton's Farm
Oliver's Farm
Airey House
Aldersyde
Little Porters Hill
Porters Hill
Tanyard Farm
Whitestones
Hankinson House
Adamson's Farm
Briar's Farm
New Mill Bridge
Stavens Pool Bridge
Dead Dam Bridge
Laytus Farm
Green Nook Farm
Green Farm
Eccles House
Porters Farm
Walker House Farm
Higham Side
Lower House
Woodsfold Bridge
Lewth Hall
Catterall Farm
Higher Hill House
Hill House Farm
Lower Hill Farm
Danson Hill
Garlick House
Ryecroft
Green Lane Farm
Beesley House
Old Woodsfold Farm
Wrainhow
Melrose
Wrainhow Mount
Meadow View
Shorrocks Farm
Tan Pit House
Lingard Hall
Raikes Farm
Lewth Farm
Black Pole Farm
Spar House
Moss Farm
Belldale
Belldale Cottages
Moss Cottage
Jane Lane Farm
Tan Pit Cottage
Wolf's Farm
Brades Farm
Football Ground
Crosses Farm
Tynwold Cottage
Tithe Barn
Moorside Villa
Hill Crest
Moor Side House
Sun Dial Farm
The Laurels
Chapel Farm
The Homestead
Stainton Lodge
Yew Tree Farm
Poultry Farm
Catforth Hall
Catforth Hall Bridge
Moor Side Farm
Moss House
Sunholme
Clarkson Green Farm
Red Lion Farm
Sch.
Lowe's Farm
The Jungle
Jerry Farm
Willacy House
Willacy La. End
Melling's Farm
Fair View
Hall
Clarkson Green House
Bowl. Grn.
Harrison House
Kit's Farm
Rays Farm
New House Farm
Whinnyfield Bridge
Smith's Farm
Aqueduct
Bett's Farm
Godson House Farm
Willow Bridge
Roots Farm
Old House
Stone Chimneys Bridge
Swillbrook Farm
Lancaster Canal
Whinneyfield Farm
Depot
Intack Farm
Roots Bridge
Melbrigg
Wharf House
Swillbrook Ho.
Woodlands
Crown Lane Farm
Kellet's Bridge
Moss Farm
Intack Cottages
Harrison House
Blackleach House
Swillbrook Bridge
Swillbrook Lodge
Swillbrook Grange
Sergeant Bridge
Rose Grove Farm
Blackleach Farm
Rosemary Farm
Willow Farm
Kays Farm
Barton House
Wearden House
Oak Dene
Pepper Hill
Blackleach Cottage
Long Park Wood
New Bridge
Newby House
Adamson Farm
Holmlea Poultry Farm
Blackleach Poultry Farm
B5269
ROAD
LANE
SOWERBY ROAD
RAPLEY LANE
BENSON'S LA.
BENSONS LANE
BRIERLEY
BRIERLEY LA.
MALLEY LANE
EAVES LANE
NEW EAVES LANE
SCHOOL LA.
NELSON GDNS.
HIGHFIELD AV.
WENTWORTH AV.
MILL CL.
DERBY CR.
PRESTON ROAD
LEWTH LANE
MOORSIDE LANE
CINDER LANE
WOODS LANE
CATFORTH ROAD
GREEN LANE
JANE LANE
MOSS LANE
MILLER LANE
SQUARE LANE
HORSE LANE
WILLACY LA.
BENSON LANE
BENSON LA.
ROOTS LANE
SCHOOL LANE
ROSEMARY LANE
CROWN LA.
BLACKLEACH LANE
ROSEACRE ROAD
WHINNYFIELD LA.
Woodplumpton Brook
Brook
New Mill Brook
WYRE PRESTON
PRESTON FYLDE
67
94
113
H J K L M N
G H J K L M N
1 2 3 4 5 6 7 8 9
47 48 49
38 37 36 35 34

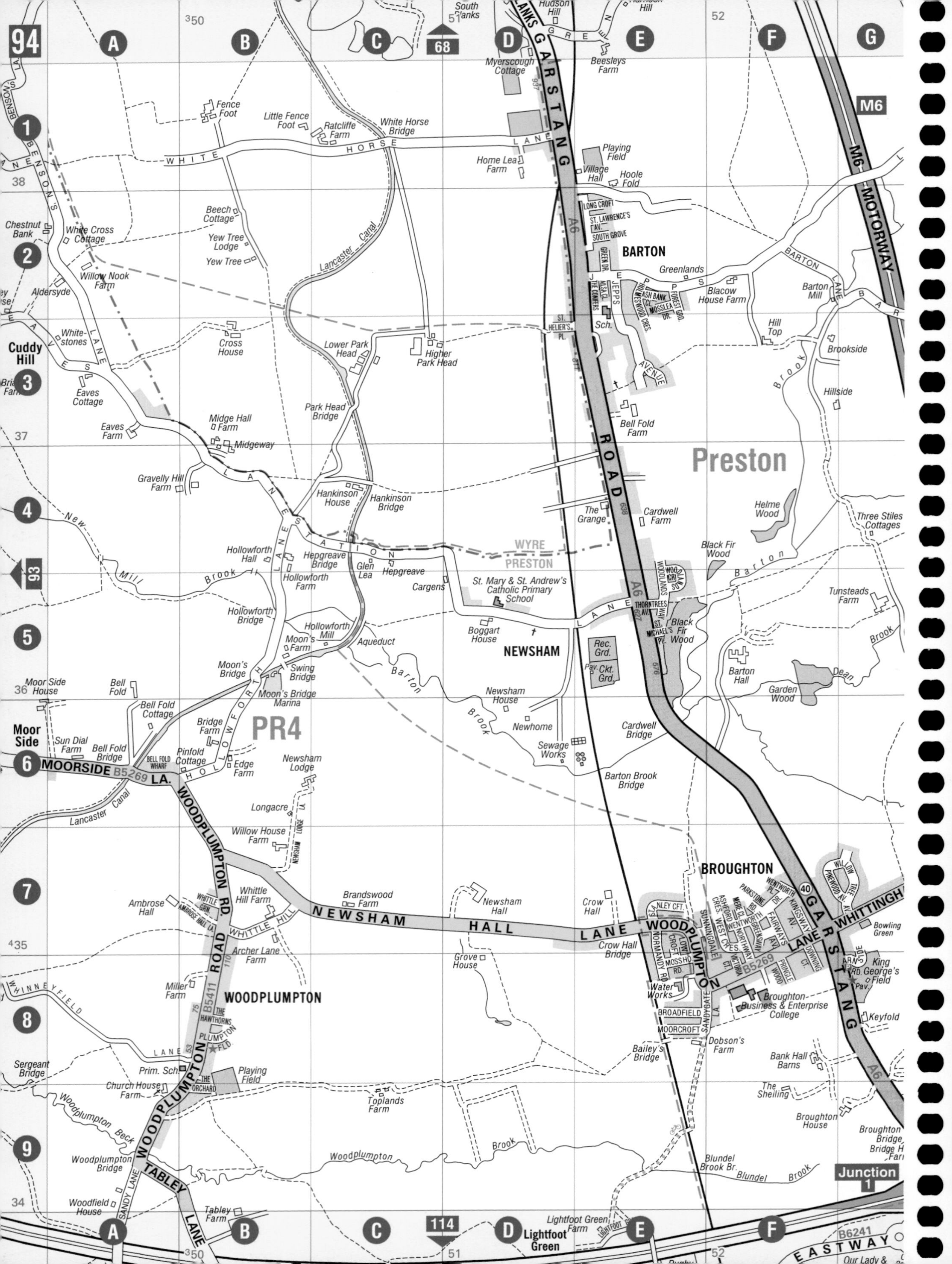

BARTON
Preston
NEWSHAM
PR4
BROUGHTON
WOODPLUMPTON
Cuddy Hill
Moor Side
WYRE
PRESTON
M6
M6 MOTORWAY
GARSTANG ROAD
A6
WHITE HORSE LANE
STATION LANE
HOLLOWFORTH LANE
MOORSIDE B5269 LA.
WOODPLUMPTON RD
WOODPLUMPTON ROAD
NEWSHAM HALL LANE
WHITTLE HILL
TABLEY LANE
SANDY LANE
EAVES LANE
BENSON'S LANE
BARTON LANE
WHITTINGHAM LANE
WOODPLUMPTON LANE
EASTWAY
B6241
Junction 1
Lancaster Canal
Barton Brook
Woodplumpton Brook
Woodplumpton Beck
Blundel Brook
New Mill Brook
Dean Brook
Fence Foot
Little Fence Foot
Ratcliffe Farm
White Horse Bridge
Myerscough Cottage
Beesleys Farm
Home Lea Farm
Playing Field
Village Hall
Hoole Fold
Chestnut Bank
White Cross Cottage
Beech Cottage
Yew Tree Lodge
Yew Tree
Willow Nook Farm
Aldersyde
White-stones
Cross House
Lower Park Head
Higher Park Head
Greenlands
Blacow House Farm
Barton Mill
Hill Top
Brookside
Hillside
Eaves Cottage
Eaves Farm
Midge Hall Farm
Midgeway
Park Head Bridge
Bell Fold Farm
Gravelly Hill Farm
Hankinson House
Hankinson Bridge
The Grange
Cardwell Farm
Helme Wood
Three Stiles Cottages
Black Fir Wood
Hollowforth Hall
Hepgreave Bridge
Glen Lea
Hepgreave
Hollowforth Farm
Cargens
St. Mary & St. Andrew's Catholic Primary School
Tunsteads Farm
Hollowforth Bridge
Hollowforth Mill
Aqueduct
Boggart House
Rec. Grd.
Ckt. Grd.
Moon's Farm
Moon's Bridge
Swing Bridge
Moon's Bridge Marina
Barton Hall
Garden Wood
Moor Side House
Bell Fold
Bell Fold Cottage
Newsham House
Newhome
Cardwell Bridge
Bridge Farm
Sun Dial Farm
Bell Fold Bridge
Pinfold Cottage
Edge Farm
Newsham Lodge
Sewage Works
Barton Brook Bridge
Longacre
Willow House Farm
Whittle Hill Farm
Brandswood Farm
Newsham Hall
Crow Hall
Ambrose Hall
Archer Lane Farm
Crow Hall Bridge
Grove House
Miller Farm
Water Works
Bowling Green
King George's Field
Broughton Business & Enterprise College
Keyfold
Dobson's Farm
Bailey's Bridge
Bank Hall Barns
Sergeant Bridge
Prim. Sch.
Church House Farm
Toplands Farm
The Sheiling
Broughton House
Broughton Bridge
Woodplumpton Bridge
Blundel Brook Br.
Woodfield House
Tabley Farm
Lightfoot Green Farm
Lightfoot Green
Sch.
Pav.
South Planks
Hudson Hill

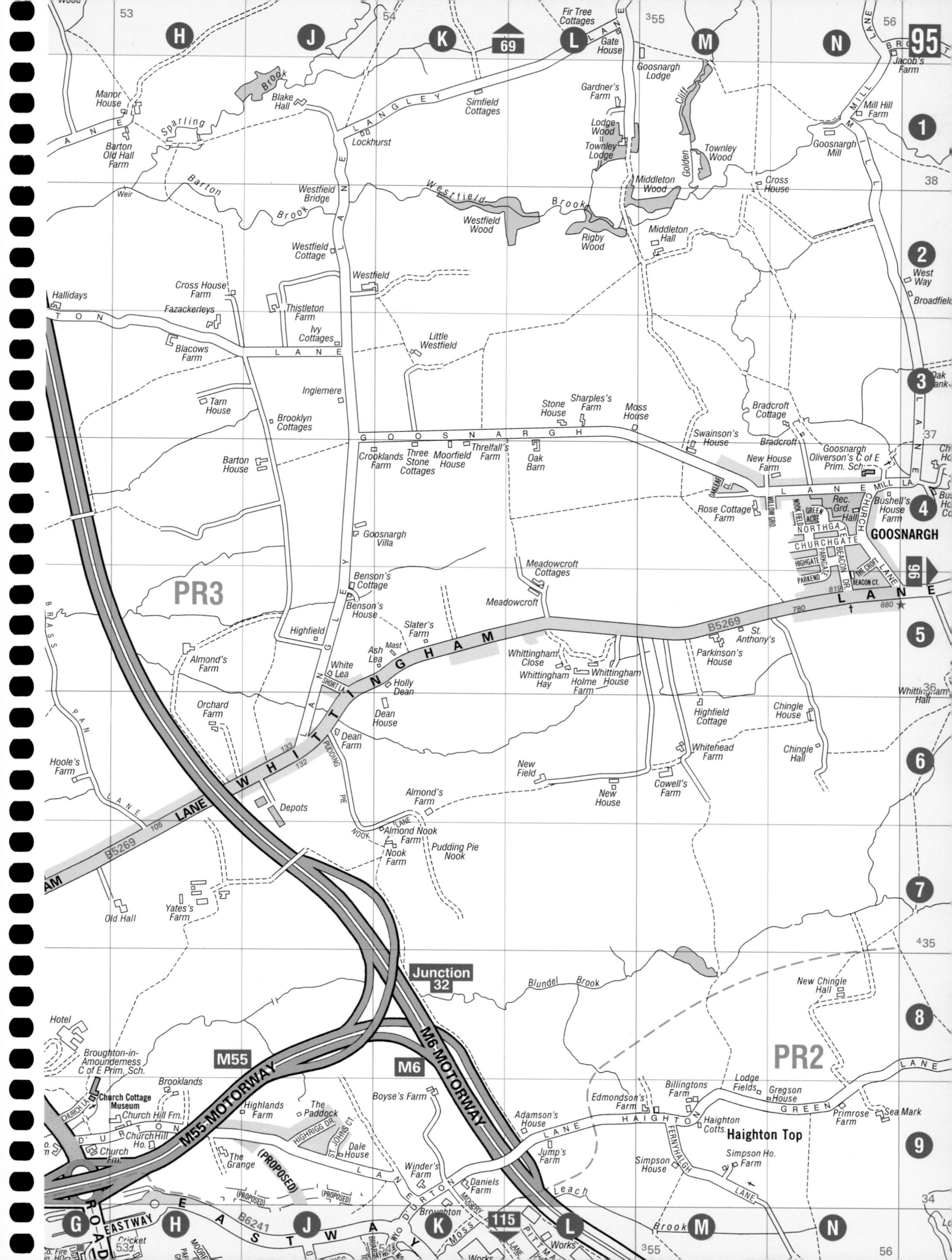
95
69
96
115
H
J
K
L
M
N
G
1
2
3
4
5
6
7
8
9
53
54
355
56
38
37
36
435
34
Fir Tree Cottages
Gate House
Goosnargh Lodge
Jacob's Farm
Mill Hill Farm
Manor House
Blake Hall
Simfield Cottages
Gardner's Farm
Sparling
Brook
Langley
Lockhurst
Barton Old Hall Farm
Lodge Wood
Townley Lodge
Townley Wood
Golden
Cliff
Goosnargh Mill
Mill Lane
Cross House
Weir
Barton Brook
Westfield Bridge
Westfield Brook
Westfield Wood
Rigby Wood
Middleton Wood
Middleton Hall
Westfield Cottage
West Way
Broadfield
Westfield
Cross House Farm
Hallidays
Thistleton Farm
Fazackerleys
Ivy Cottages
Blacows Farm
Little Westfield
Lane
Inglemere
Tarn House
Brooklyn Cottages
Stone House
Sharples's Farm
Moss House
Bradcroft Cottage
Oak Bank
Goosnargh Lane
Swainson's House
Bradcroft
Barton House
Crooklands Farm
Three Stone Cottages
Moorfield House
Threlfall's Farm
Oak Barn
New House Farm
Goosnargh Oliverson's C of E Prim. Sch.
Rose Cottage Farm
Rec. Grd.
Hall
Church Lane
Bushell's House Farm
GOOSNARGH
Northgate
Churchgate
Highgate
Parkend
Beacon Dr.
The Croft
Beacon Ct.
Goosnargh Villa
Meadowcroft Cottages
PR3
Benson's Cottage
Meadowcroft
Benson's House
Slater's Farm
Highfield
B5269
St. Anthony's
Parkinson's House
Ash Lea
Mast
Whittingham Close
Whittingham Hay
Holme Farm
Whittingham House
Almond's Farm
White Lea
Short La.
Holly Dean
Whittingham Hall
Whittingham Lane
Orchard Farm
Dean House
Highfield Cottage
Chingle House
Dean Farm
Whitehead Farm
Chingle Hall
Hoole's Farm
Pudding Pie
New Field
Cowell's Farm
New House
Almond's Farm
Depots
Almond Nook Farm
Nook Lane
Pudding Pie Nook
Nook Farm
Brass Pan Lane
Old Hall
Yates's Farm
Junction 32
Blundel Brook
New Chingle Hall
Hotel
Broughton-in-Amounderness C of E Prim. Sch.
M55
M6
M6 MOTORWAY
M55 MOTORWAY
PR2
Church Cottage Museum
Brooklands
Lodge Fields
Gregson House
Billingtons Farm
Edmondson's Farm
Boyse's Farm
Church Hill Fm.
Highlands Farm
The Paddock
Highrigg Dr.
St. John's Ct.
Church Hill Ho.
Church Fm.
Adamson's House
Haighton Lane
Haighton Cotts.
Haighton Top
Green Lane
Primrose Farm
Sea Mark
Dale House
The Grange
(Proposed)
Jump's Farm
Fernyhalgh Lane
Simpson House
Simpson Ho. Farm
Winder's Farm
Durton Lane
Daniels Farm
Midgery
Leach
Eastway
Road
B6241
Broughton
Moss
Brook
Works
Cricket
Pittman

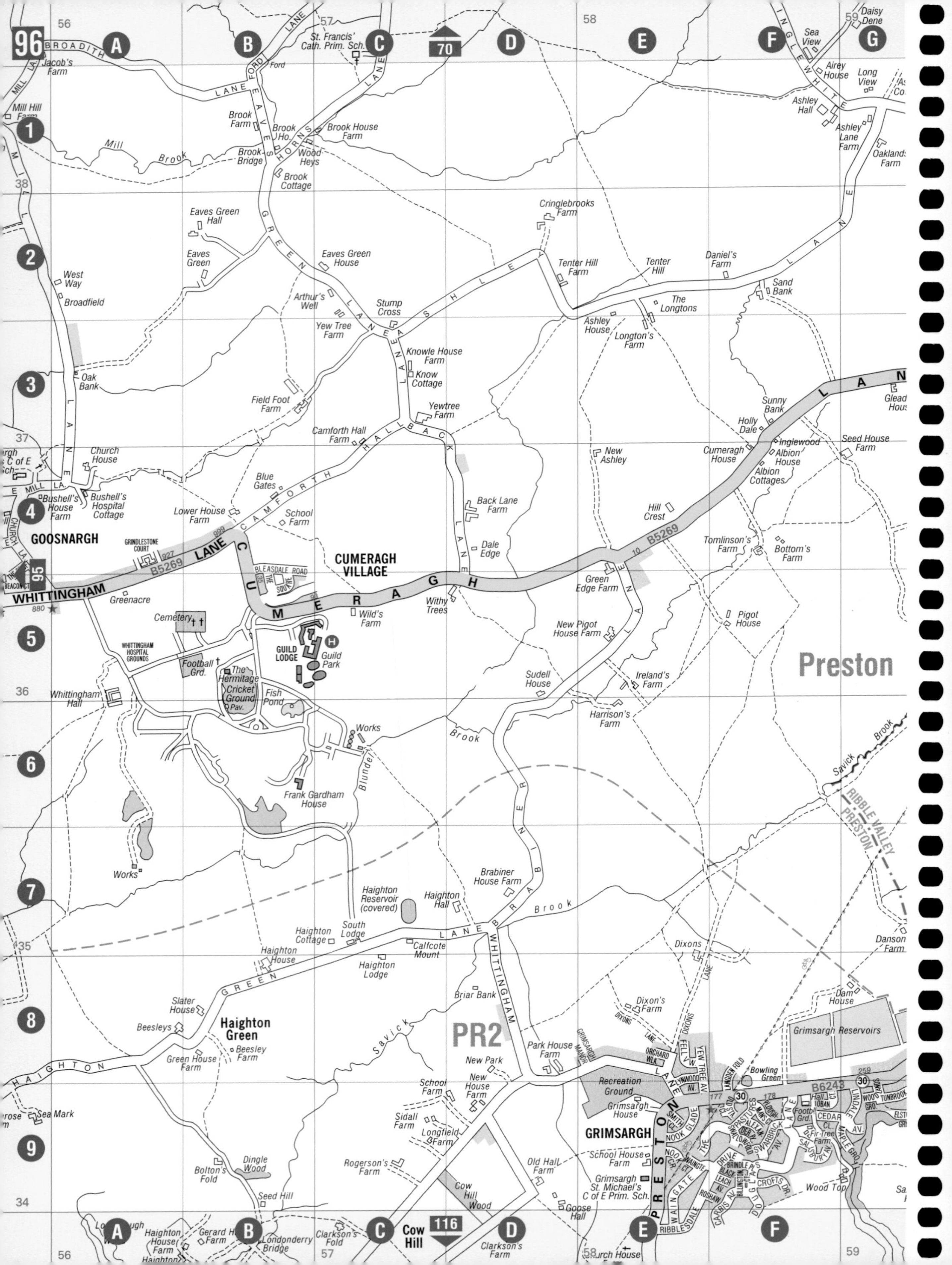

Preston
GOOSNARGH
WHITTINGHAM
CUMERAGH VILLAGE
GRIMSARGH
Haighton Green
PR2
GUILD LODGE
Guild Park
Cemetery
Football Grd.
The Hermitage Cricket Ground
Fish Pond
Works
Frank Gardham House
Whittingham Hall
Greenacre
Haighton Reservoir (covered)
Haighton Hall
Brabiner House Farm
Grimsargh Reservoirs
Recreation Ground
Grimsargh House
School House Farm
Grimsargh St. Michael's C of E Prim. Sch.
Sudell House
Ireland's Farm
Harrison's Farm
New Pigot House Farm
Green Edge Farm
Pigot House
Tomlinson's Farm
Bottom's Farm
Cumeragh House
Albion House
Albion Cottages
Inglewood
Seed House Farm
Sunny Bank
Holly Dale
Hill Crest
New Ashley
Back Lane Farm
Dale Edge
Withy Trees
Wild's Farm
School Farm
Lower House Farm
Blue Gates
Camforth Hall Farm
Yewtree Farm
Knowle House Farm
Know Cottage
Field Foot Farm
Yew Tree Farm
Stump Cross
Arthur's Well
Eaves Green House
Eaves Green Hall
Eaves Green
West Way
Broadfield
Oak Bank
Church House
Bushell's House Farm
Bushell's Hospital Cottage
Jacob's Farm
Mill Hill Farm
Brook Farm
Brook Ho.
Brook House Farm
Brook Bridge
Wood Heys
Brook Cottage
St. Francis' Cath. Prim. Sch.
Cringlebrooks Farm
Tenter Hill Farm
Tenter Hill
Daniel's Farm
Sand Bank
The Longtons
Ashley House
Longton's Farm
Sea View
Airey House
Long View
Ashley Hall
Ashley Lane Farm
Oaklands Farm
Daisy Dene
Haighton Cottage
South Lodge
Calfcote Mount
Haighton Lodge
Haighton House
Slater House
Beesleys
Beesley Farm
Green House Farm
Briar Bank
Dixons
Dixon's Farm
Park House Farm
New Park
New House Farm
School Farm
Sidall Farm
Longfield Farm
Rogerson's Farm
Old Hall Farm
Bolton's Fold
Dingle Wood
Seed Hill
Sea Mark
Cow Hill Wood
Goose Hall
Dam House
Danson Farm
Wood Top
Bowling Green
Haighton House Farm
Gerard H Farm
Londonderry Bridge
Clarkson's Fold
Clarkson's Farm
Cow Hill
WHITTINGHAM LANE
CUMERAGH LANE
B5269
B6243
BROADITH LANE
FORD LANE
EAVES GREEN LANE
HORNS LANE
ASHLEY LANE
INGLEWHITE LANE
CAMFORTH HALL LANE
BACK LANE
MILL LANE
BLEASDALE ROAD
THE SQUARE
GRINDLESTONE COURT
WHITTINGHAM HOSPITAL GROUNDS
BRABINER LANE
GREEN LANE
HAIGHTON GREEN
WHITTINGHAM LANE
PRESTON ROAD
RIBBLESDALE
WAINGATE
Mill Brook
Blundel Brook
Savick Brook
RIBBLE VALLEY
PRESTON

70
95
116

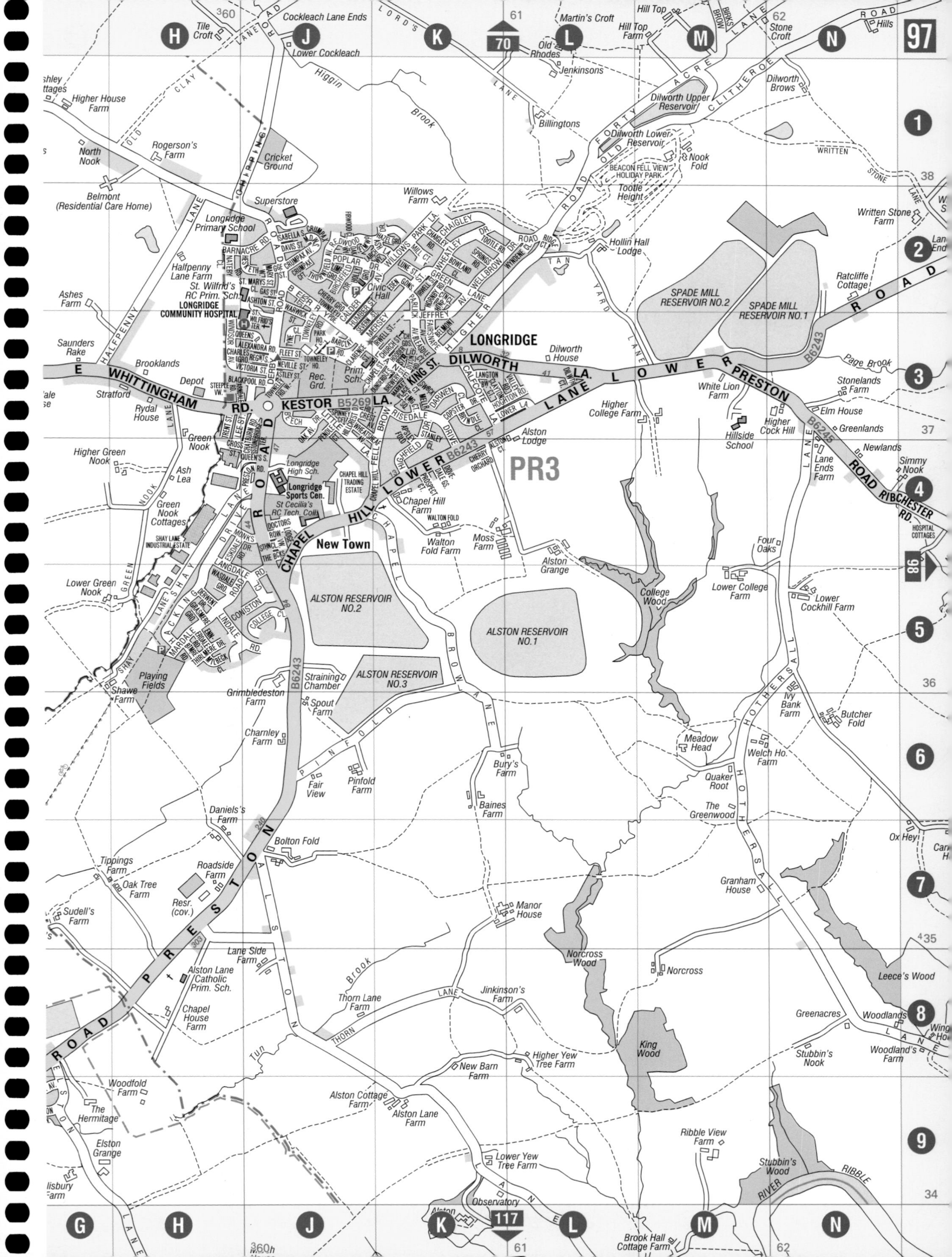

LONGRIDGE
PR3
New Town
Tile Croft
Cockleach Lane Ends
Lower Cockleach
Martin's Croft
Hill Top
Hill Top Farm
Old Rhodes
Jenkinsons
Stone Croft
Hills
Higher House Farm
Higgin Brook
Billingtons
Dilworth Upper Reservoir
Dilworth Lower Reservoir
Dilworth Brows
Nook Fold
BEACON FELL VIEW HOLIDAY PARK
Tootle Height
North Nook
Rogerson's Farm
Cricket Ground
Belmont (Residential Care Home)
Superstore
Willows Farm
Written Stone Farm
Longridge Primary School
Hollin Hall Lodge
Halfpenny Lane Farm
St. Wilfrid's RC Prim. Sch.
LONGRIDGE COMMUNITY HOSPITAL
Civic Hall
Ashes Farm
SPADE MILL RESERVOIR NO.2
SPADE MILL RESERVOIR NO.1
Ratcliffe Cottage
Saunders Rake
Brooklands
Dilworth House
Rec. Grd.
Prim. Sch.
Depot
Stratford
Rydal House
WHITTINGHAM RD.
KESTOR LA.
DILWORTH LA.
KING ST.
LOWER LANE
PRESTON ROAD
RIBCHESTER RD.
Page Brook
Stonelands Farm
White Lion Farm
Higher College Farm
Elm House
Greenlands
Higher Cock Hill
Hillside School
Newlands
Simmy Nook
Lane Ends Farm
Alston Lodge
Green Nook
Higher Green Nook
Ash Lea
Longridge High Sch.
Longridge Sports Cen.
CHAPEL HILL TRADING ESTATE
Chapel Hill Farm
Green Nook Cottages
St Cecilia's RC Tech. Coll.
SHAY LANE INDUSTRIAL ESTATE
Walton Fold Farm
Moss Farm
Alston Grange
Four Oaks
HOSPITAL COTTAGES
Lower College Farm
Lower Cockhill Farm
College Wood
Lower Green Nook
ALSTON RESERVOIR NO.2
ALSTON RESERVOIR NO.1
ALSTON RESERVOIR NO.3
Playing Fields
Shawe Farm
Grimbledeston Farm
Straining Chamber
Spout Farm
Ivy Bank Farm
Butcher Fold
Charnley Farm
Meadow Head
Bury's Farm
Welch Ho. Farm
Pinfold Farm
Fair View
Quaker Root
Daniels's Farm
Baines Farm
The Greenwood
Bolton Fold
Ox Hey
Tippings Farm
Roadside Farm
Oak Tree Farm
Granham House
Resr. (cov.)
Sudell's Farm
Manor House
Norcross Wood
Lane Side Farm
Norcross
Leece's Wood
Alston Lane Catholic Prim. Sch.
Thorn Lane Farm
Jinkinson's Farm
Chapel House Farm
Greenacres
Woodlands
King Wood
Higher Yew Tree Farm
New Barn Farm
Woodland's Farm
Stubbin's Nook
Woodfold Farm
The Hermitage
Alston Cottage Farm
Alston Lane Farm
Ribble View Farm
Elston Grange
Lower Yew Tree Farm
Stubbin's Wood
RIVER RIBBLE
Observatory
Brook Hall Cottage Farm
Alston
70
86
117

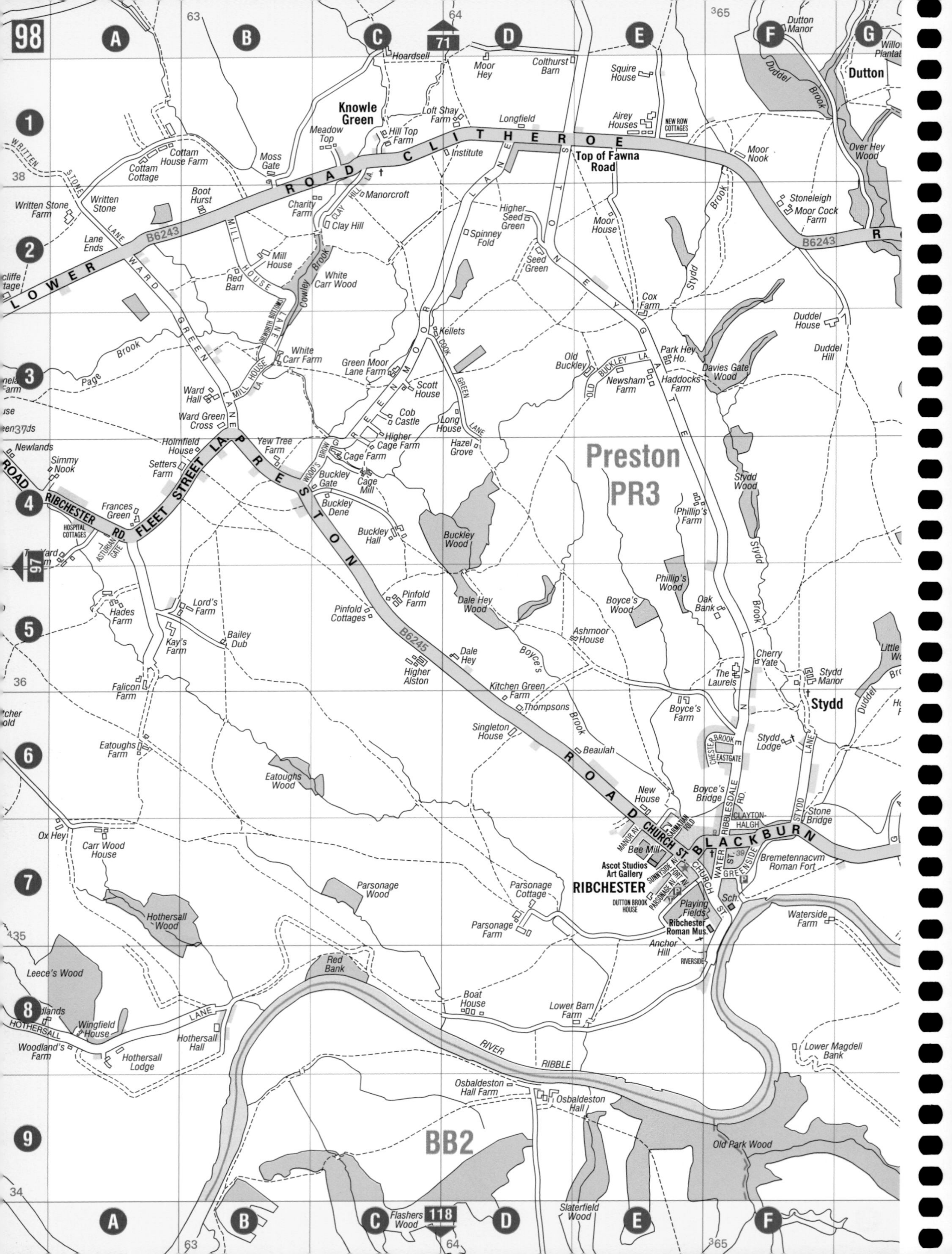
A
B
C
D
E
F
G
63
64
365
71
Hoardsell
Moor Hey
Colthurst Barn
Squire House
Dutton Manor
Willow Plantation
Dutton
Duddel Brook
Knowle Green
Loft Shay Farm
Longfield
Airey Houses
NEW ROW COTTAGES
Meadow Top
Hill Top Farm
Institute
Over Hey Wood
WRITTEN STONE LANE
Cottam House Farm
Cottam Cottage
Moss Gate
CLITHEROE ROAD
Top of Fawna Road
Moor Nook
38
Written Stone Farm
Written Stone
Boot Hurst
Charity Farm
CLAY HILL LA.
Manorcroft
Higher Seed Green
Moor House
Brook
Stoneleigh
Moor Cock Farm
Clay Hill
Spinney Fold
B6243
Lane Ends
Mill House
MILL HOUSE LANE
Seed Green
Stydd
LOWER
Red Barn
Cowley Brook
White Carr Wood
Cox Farm
cliffe tage
WARD GREEN LANE
DUXWORTH BOTTOM LANE
LONGMOOR LANE
Kellets
Duddel House
White Carr Farm
COOK GREEN LANE
Park Hey Ho.
Duddel Hill
Page Brook
Green Moor Lane Farm
Old Buckley
BUCKLEY LA.
Davies Gate Wood
Haddocks Farm
OLD
Newsham Farm
Scott House
MILL HOUSE LA.
Ward Hall
Cob Castle
Ward Green Cross
Long House
37
Newlands
Yew Tree Farm
Higher Cage Farm
Hazel Grove
Preston PR3
Holmfield House
Cage Farm
LONGSIGHT LANE
Simmy Nook
Setters Farm
WOOD'S BROW
Buckley Gate
Cage Mill
Stydd Wood
ROAD
FLEET STREET LA.
PRESTON ROAD
RIBCHESTER RD.
Frances Green
Buckley Dene
Phillip's Farm
HOSPITAL COTTAGES
ASTURIAN GATE
Buckley Hall
Buckley Wood
Stydd Brook
97
Pinfold Farm
Phillip's Wood
Lord's Farm
Pinfold Cottages
Dale Hey Wood
Boyce's Wood
Oak Bank
Hades Farm
Bailey Dub
Ashmoor House
Kay's Farm
B6245
Dale Hey
Boyce's Brook
Cherry Yate
Little Wood
Higher Alston
Stydd Manor
36
Falicon Farm
Kitchen Green Farm
The Laurels
Duddel Brook
Thompsons
Boyce's Farm
Stydd
Singleton House
CHESTER BROOK
EASTGATE
Stydd Lodge
Eatoughs Farm
Beaulah
STYDD LANE
Eatoughs Wood
New House
Boyce's Bridge
RIBBLESDALE RD.
Stone Bridge
CLAYTON-HALGH
CHURCH ST
CARMATHAN FOLD
BLACKBURN
Ox Hey
MANOR AV.
Carr Wood House
Bee Mill
WATER ST.
GREENSIDE
Bremetennacvm Roman Fort
Ascot Studios Art Gallery
SUNNYSIDE AV.
FORT AV.
CHURCH ST.
Parsonage Wood
Parsonage Cottage
RIBCHESTER
PARSONAGE AV.
DUTTON BROOK HOUSE
Playing Fields
Sch.
Hothersall Wood
Waterside Farm
Parsonage Farm
Ribchester Roman Mus.
435
Anchor Hill
Red Bank
RIVERSIDE
Leece's Wood
Boat House
Lower Barn Farm
Woodlands
HOTHERSALL LANE
Wingfield House
Hothersall Hall
RIVER RIBBLE
Lower Magdell Bank
Woodland's Farm
Hothersall Lodge
Osbaldeston Hall Farm
Osbaldeston Hall
BB2
Old Park Wood
34
Flashers Wood
118
Slaterfield Wood
1
2
3
4
5
6
7
8
9

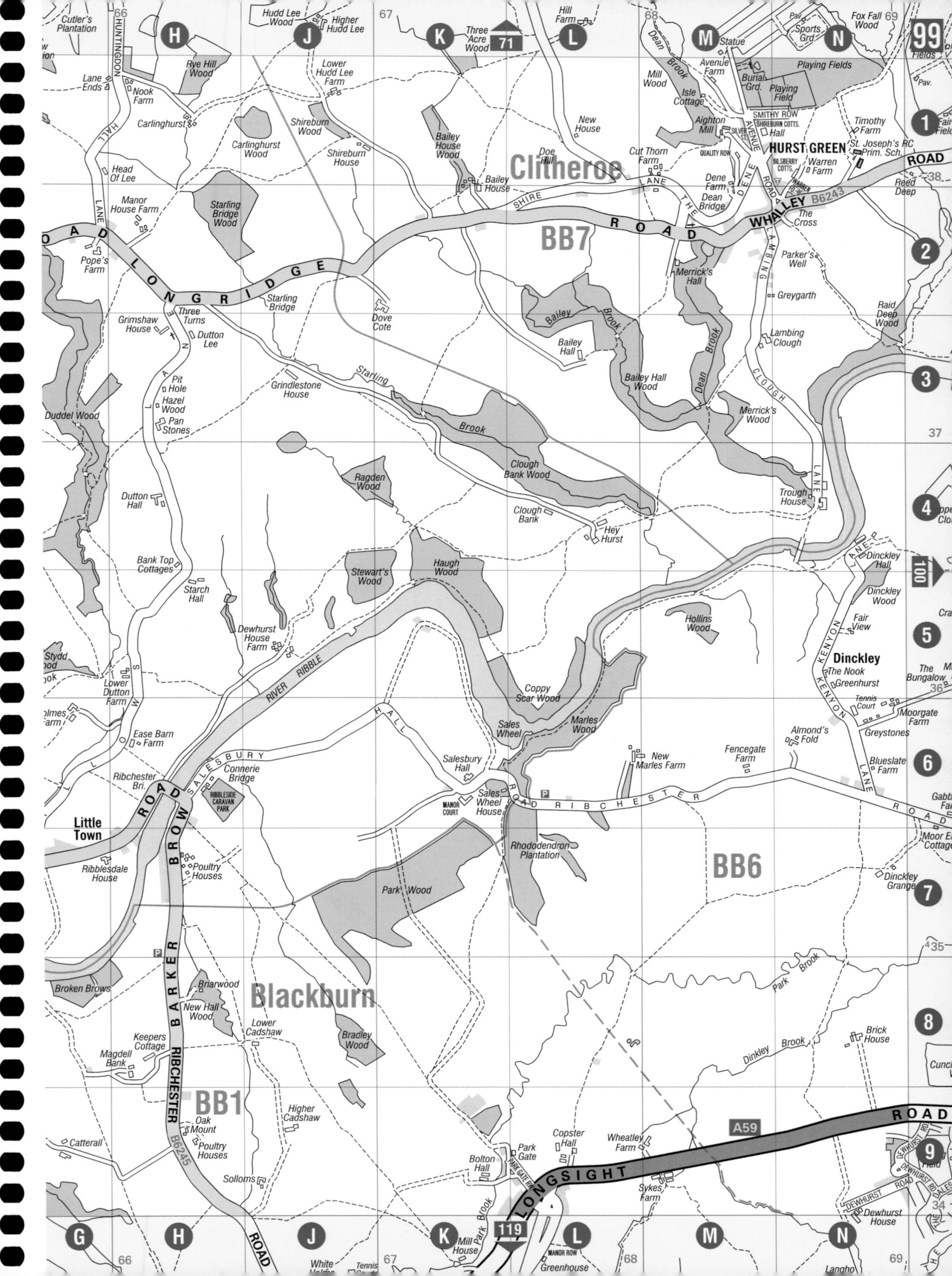
Clitheroe
BB7
HURST GREEN
LONGRIDGE ROAD
WHALLEY ROAD
B6243
RIVER RIBBLE
Dinckley
BB6
Little Town
Blackburn
BB1
RIBCHESTER ROAD
BARKER BROW
B6245
LONGSIGHT ROAD
A59
SALESBURY HALL ROAD
RIBCHESTER ROAD
KENYON LANE
LAMBING CLOUGH LANE
Starling Brook
Bailey Brook
Dean Brook
Park Brook
Dinkley Brook
Cutler's Plantation
Hudd Lee Wood
Higher Hudd Lee
Three Acre Wood
Hill Farm
Fox Fall Wood
Rye Hill Wood
Lane Ends
Nook Farm
Carlinghurst
Lower Hudd Lee Farm
Shireburn Wood
Carlinghurst Wood
Shireburn House
Head Of Lee
Manor House Farm
Starling Bridge Wood
Pope's Farm
Starling Bridge
Three Turns
Grimshaw House
Dutton Lee
Dove Cote
Bailey House Wood
Bailey House
Mill Wood
Isle Cottage
Avenue Farm
Playing Fields
Playing Field
Burial Grd.
Statue
Sports Grd.
New House
Doe Hill
Cut Thorn Farm
Aighton Mill
SMITHY ROW
SHIREBURN COTTS.
Hall
QUALITY ROW
BILSBERRY COTTS.
Timothy Farm
St. Joseph's RC Prim. Sch.
Warren Farm
Dene Farm
Dean Bridge
Reed Deep
The Cross
Parker's Well
Merrick's Hall
Greygarth
Bailey Hall
Bailey Hall Wood
Lambing Clough
Raid Deep Wood
Merrick's Wood
Grindlestone House
Pit Hole
Hazel Wood
Pan Stones
Duddel Wood
Ragden Wood
Clough Bank Wood
Clough Bank
Hey Hurst
Trough House
Dutton Hall
Bank Top Cottages
Starch Hall
Stewart's Wood
Haugh Wood
Dinckley Hall
Dinckley Wood
Hollins Wood
Fair View
Dewhurst House Farm
Lower Dutton Farm
The Nook
Greenhurst
The Bungalow
Coppy Scar Wood
Tennis Court
Moorgate Farm
Greystones
Almond's Fold
Fencegate Farm
New Marles Farm
Marles Wood
Sales Wheel
Ease Barn Farm
Salesbury Hall
Blueslate Farm
Ribchester Bri.
Connerie Bridge
RIBBLESIDE CARAVAN PARK
MANOR COURT
Sales Wheel House
Moor End Cottage
Ribblesdale House
Poultry Houses
Rhododendron Plantation
Dinckley Grange
Park Wood
Broken Brows
Briarwood
New Hall Wood
Lower Cadshaw
Bradley Wood
Keepers Cottage
Magdell Bank
Brick House
Higher Cadshaw
Oak Mount
Catterall
Copster Hall
Wheatley Farm
Park Gate
Bolton Hall
Solloms
Sykes Farm
Dewhurst House
DEWHURST ROAD
Mill House
MANOR ROW
Greenhouse
Langho
71
100
119

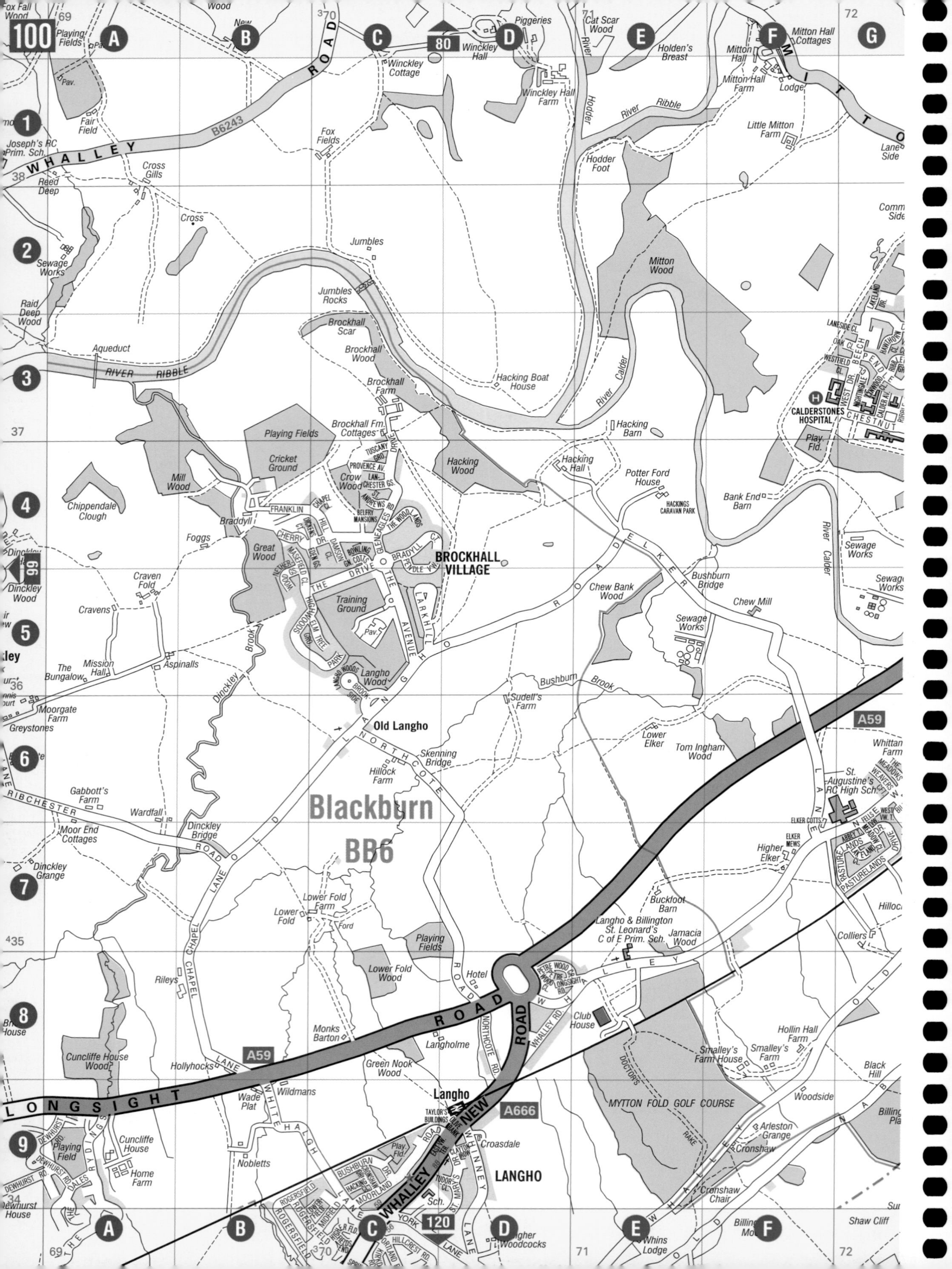
Blackburn
BB6
BROCKHALL VILLAGE
LANGHO
Old Langho
Langho
River Ribble
River Calder
River Hodder
Mitton Wood
Brockhall Wood
Brockhall Scar
Brockhall Farm
Brockhall Fm. Cottages
Jumbles
Jumbles Rocks
Hacking Boat House
Hacking Barn
Hacking Hall
Hacking Wood
Potter Ford House
Hackings Caravan Park
Winckley Hall
Winckley Hall Farm
Winckley Cottage
Piggeries
Cat Scar Wood
Holden's Breast
Mitton Hall
Mitton Hall Farm
Mitton Hall Cottages
Lodge
Little Mitton Farm
Hodder Foot
Fox Fields
Fair Field
Cross Gills
Cross
Reed Deep
Raid Deep Wood
Sewage Works
Aqueduct
Playing Fields
Cricket Ground
Mill Wood
Chippendale Clough
Braddyll
Foggs
Great Wood
Crow Wood
Training Ground
Langho Wood
Craven Fold
Cravens
Dinckley Wood
Mission Hall
The Bungalow
Aspinalls
Moorgate Farm
Greystones
Gabbott's Farm
Wardfall
Moor End Cottages
Dinckley Bridge
Dinckley Grange
Hillock Farm
Skenning Bridge
Sudell's Farm
Bushburn Brook
Lower Elker
Tom Ingham Wood
Chew Bank Wood
Bushburn Bridge
Chew Mill
Bank End Barn
Calderstones Hospital
Play. Fld.
Whittam Farm
St. Augustine's RC High Sch.
Elker Cotts
Higher Elker
Elker Mews
Buckfoot Barn
Langho & Billington St. Leonard's C of E Prim. Sch.
Jamacia Wood
Colliers
Lower Fold Farm
Lower Fold
Ford
Lower Fold Wood
Hotel
Rileys
Monks Barton
Langholme
Green Nook Wood
Hollyhocks
Wildmans
Wade Plat
Cuncliffe House Wood
Cuncliffe House
Home Farm
Playing Field
Nobletts
Club House
Mytton Fold Golf Course
Hollin Hall Farm
Smalley's Farm House
Smalley's Farm
Black Hill
Woodside
Arleston Grange
Cronshaw
Cronshaw Chair
Whins Lodge
Shaw Cliff
Croasdale
Sch.
Higher Woodcocks
WHALLEY ROAD
B6243
MITTON ROAD
LONGSIGHT ROAD
A59
A666
NEW ROAD
WHALLEY RD
NORTHCOTE RD.
NORTHCOTE ROAD
OLD LANGHO ROAD
RIBCHESTER ROAD
CHAPEL LANE
WHITE HALGH LANE
ELKER LANE
DELKER ROAD
THE DRIVE
THE AVENUE
LARKHILL
FRANKLIN
GLENEAGLES
BRADYLL CL.
PENDLE VW.
THE WOODLANDS
TUSCANY GRO.
PROVENCE AV.
LANCHESTER GS.
ST. ANDREWS RD.
BELFRY MANSIONS
CHERRY DR.
MASEFIELD CL.
DAMSON CL.
BOWLING GN. COTTS.
HIGHER ELM TREE PARK
LANGHO WOODS
BROOK SIDE
PETRE WOOD CR.
LONGSIGHT RD.
DEWHURST RD.
RYDINGS
DALES
BUSHBURN DR.
MOORLAND
ROGERSFIELD
YORK LANE
WHINNEY LANE
DOCTOR'S RAKE
PASTURELANDS DR.
ABBEY FIELDS
CHESTNUT
LANESIDE CL.
OAK CL.
BEECH
WESTFIELD CL.
80
120
99
69
370
71
72
38
37
36
435
34

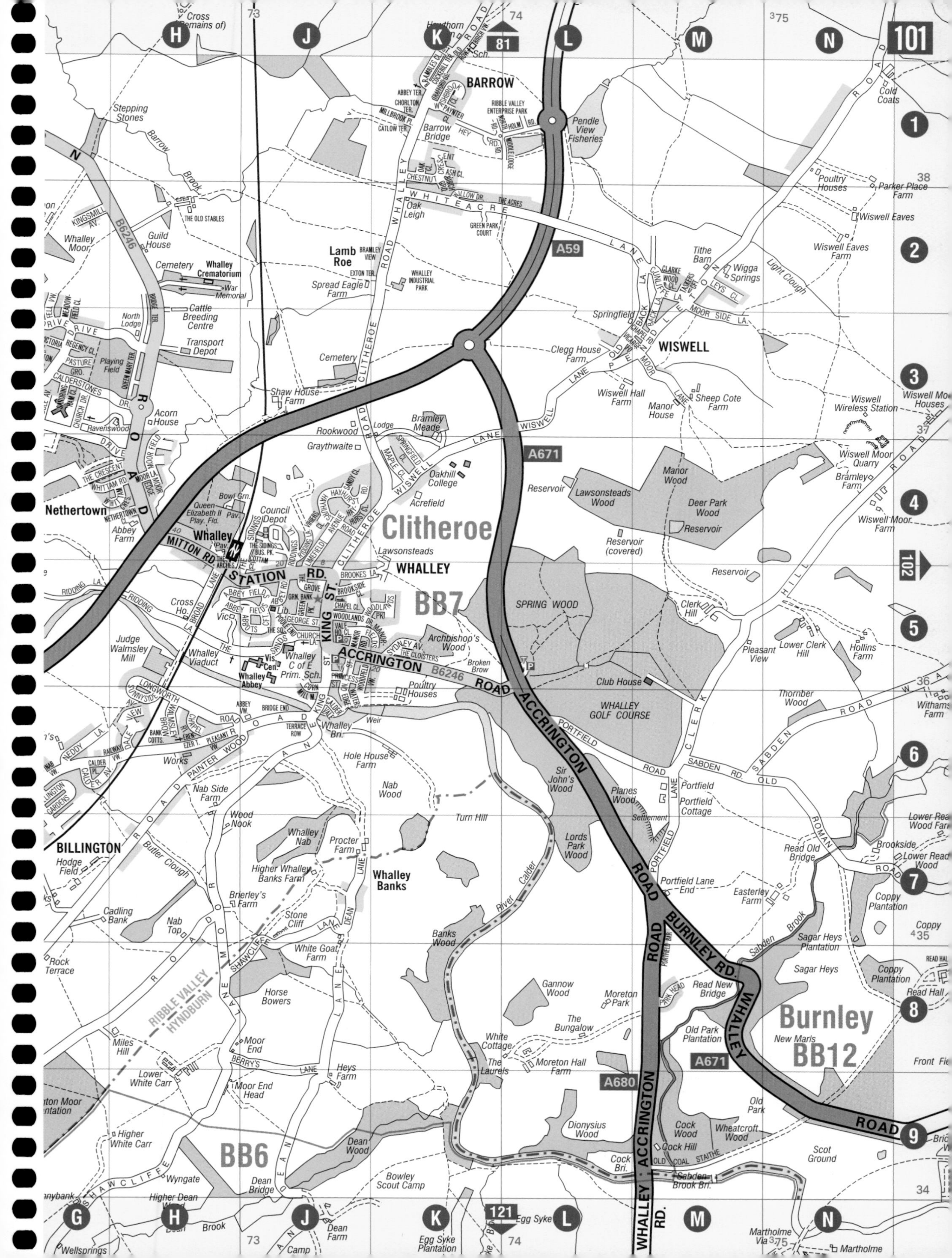
H
J
K
L
M
N
81
121
102
73
74
375
38
37
36
435
34
1
2
3
4
5
6
7
8
9
G
BARROW
Ribble Valley Enterprise Park
Pendle View Fisheries
Cold Coats
Stepping Stones
Barrow Brook
Barrow Bridge
Whiteacre Lane
The Old Stables
Oak Leigh
Green Park Court
A59
Poultry Houses
Parker Place Farm
Wiswell Eaves
Wiswell Eaves Farm
Whalley Moor
Guild House
Lamb Roe
Bramley View
Exton Ter.
Whalley Industrial Park
Spread Eagle Farm
Cemetery
Whalley Crematorium
War Memorial
Cattle Breeding Centre
North Lodge
Transport Depot
Playing Field
Tithe Barn
Wigga Springs
Light Clough
Springfield
Moor Side La.
WISWELL
Clegg House Farm
Wiswell Hall Farm
Manor House
Sheep Cote Farm
Wiswell Wireless Station
Wiswell Moor Houses
Shaw House Farm
Acorn House
Ravenswood
Rookwood
Lodge
Bramley Meade
Graythwaite
Wiswell Lane
A671
Wiswell Moor Quarry
Bramley Farm
Oakhill College
Acrefield
Reservoir
Lawsonsteads Wood
Manor Wood
Deer Park Wood
Reservoir (covered)
Wiswell Moor Farm
Nethertown
Bowl Grn.
Queen Elizabeth II Play. Fld.
Council Depot
Abbey Farm
Clitheroe
Whalley
Lawsonsteads
WHALLEY
Mitton Rd.
Station Rd.
King St.
BB7
Spring Wood
Clerk Hill
Cross Ho.
Judge Walmsley Mill
Whalley Viaduct
Vis. Cen.
Whalley Abbey
Whalley C of E Prim. Sch.
Accrington Road
B6246
Archbishop's Wood
Broken Brow
Poultry Houses
Club House
Whalley Golf Course
Pleasant View
Lower Clerk Hill
Hollins Farm
Thornber Wood
Withams Farm
Whalley Bri.
Weir
Portfield Road
Sabden Rd.
Old Roman Road
Hole House Farm
Nab Wood
Sir John's Wood
Planes Wood
Portfield
Portfield Cottage
Settlement
Nab Side Farm
Wood Nook
Whalley Nab
Procter Farm
Turn Hill
Lords Park Wood
Read Old Bridge
Brookside
Lower Read Wood Farm
BILLINGTON
Hodge Field
Butler Clough
Higher Whalley Banks Farm
Whalley Banks
Portfield Lane End
Easterley Farm
Coppy Plantation
Brierley's Farm
Cadling Bank
Nab Top
Stone Cliff
River Calder
Banks Wood
Sagar Heys Plantation
Sagar Heys
Rock Terrace
White Goat Farm
Shawcliffe
Ribble Valley
Hyndburn
Horse Bowers
Gannow Wood
Moreton Park
Read New Bridge
Read Hall
Burnley
BB12
New Marls
Miles Hill
Moor End
The Bungalow
White Cottage
Old Park Plantation
Whalley Road
Lower White Carr
Berry's Lane
Heys Farm
The Laurels
Moreton Hall Farm
A680
Front Field
Moor End Head
Higher White Carr
Dean Wood
Dionysius Wood
Cock Wood
Wheatcroft Wood
Cock Hill
Old Park
Scot Ground
Burnley Rd.
Accrington Road
BB6
Wyngate
Bowley Scout Camp
Cock Bri.
Old Coal Staithe
Sabden Brook Bri.
Dean Bridge
Higher Dean
Brook
Dean Farm
Egg Syke
Egg Syke Plantation
Whalley Rd.
Martholme Via
Martholme
Wellsprings
Camp

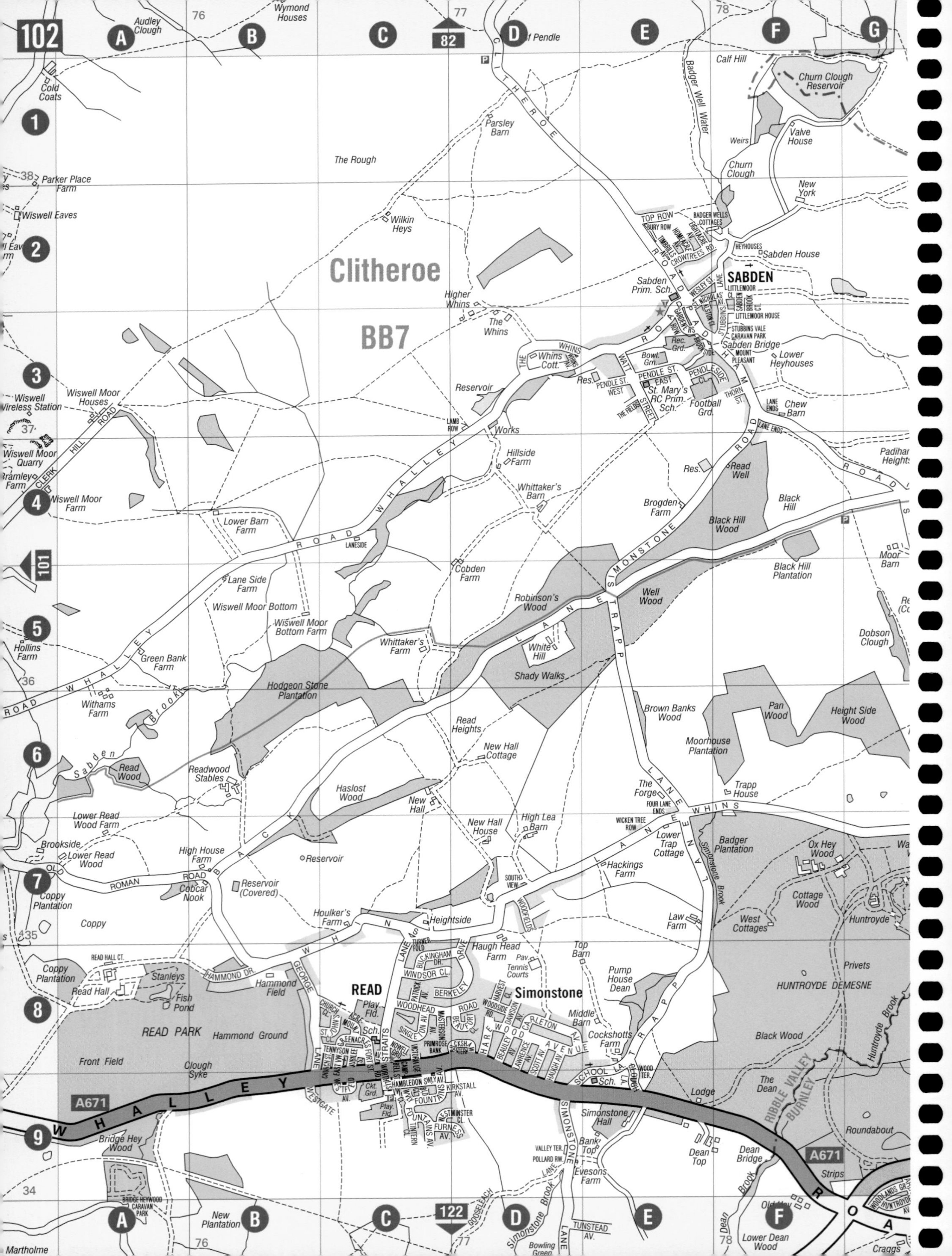

Clitheroe
BB7
SABDEN
READ
Simonstone
Wymond Houses
Audley Clough
Cold Coats
Parker Place Farm
Wiswell Eaves
The Rough
Parsley Barn
Wilkin Heys
Higher Whins
The Whins
Whins Cott.
Calf Hill
Churn Clough Reservoir
Badger Well Water
Weirs
Valve House
Churn Clough
New York
Sabden House
Sabden Prim. Sch.
Sabden Bridge
Lower Heyhouses
St. Mary's RC Prim. Sch.
Football Grd.
Chew Barn
Reservoir
Works
Hillside Farm
Whittaker's Barn
Read Well
Brogden Farm
Black Hill
Black Hill Wood
Padiham Heights
Moor Barn
Black Hill Plantation
Well Wood
Robinson's Wood
Cobden Farm
Wiswell Moor Houses
Wiswell Wireless Station
Wiswell Moor Quarry
Bramley Farm
Wiswell Moor Farm
Lower Barn Farm
Lane Side Farm
Wiswell Moor Bottom
Wiswell Moor Bottom Farm
Whittaker's Farm
White Hill
Shady Walks
Dobson Clough
Hollins Farm
Green Bank Farm
Hodgeon Stone Plantation
Withams Farm
Brown Banks Wood
Pan Wood
Height Side Wood
Moorhouse Plantation
Read Heights
New Hall Cottage
Read Wood
Readwood Stables
Haslost Wood
New Hall
New Hall House
High Lea Barn
The Forge
Trapp House
Lower Read Wood Farm
Brookside
Lower Read Wood
High House Farm
Reservoir
Cobcar Nook
Reservoir (Covered)
Lower Trap Cottage
Hackings Farm
Badger Plantation
Ox Hey Wood
Cottage Wood
Huntroyde
Coppy Plantation
Coppy
Houlker's Farm
Heightside
Law Farm
West Cottages
Haugh Head Farm
Tennis Courts
Top Barn
Pump House Dean
Privets
HUNTROYDE DEMESNE
Coppy Plantation
Read Hall
Stanleys
Fish Pond
Hammond Field
READ PARK
Hammond Ground
Middle Barn
Cockshotts Farm
Black Wood
Front Field
Clough Syke
Lodge
The Dean
RIBBLE VALLEY
BURNLEY
Simonstone Hall
Roundabout
Bridge Hey Wood
Dean Top
Bank Top
Evesons Farm
Dean Bridge
Strips
A671
WHALLEY ROAD
CLITHEROE ROAD
WHALLEY ROAD
SIMONSTONE LANE
TRAPP LANE
WHINS LANE
BACK LANE
ROMAN ROAD
OLD ROMAN ROAD
CLERK HILL ROAD
PADIHAM ROAD
SCHOOL LANE
BRIDGE HEYWOOD CARAVAN PARK
New Plantation
Old Hey
Lower Dean Wood
Craggs
Bowling Green
TUNSTEAD AV.
Simonstone Brook
Martholme
82
101
122

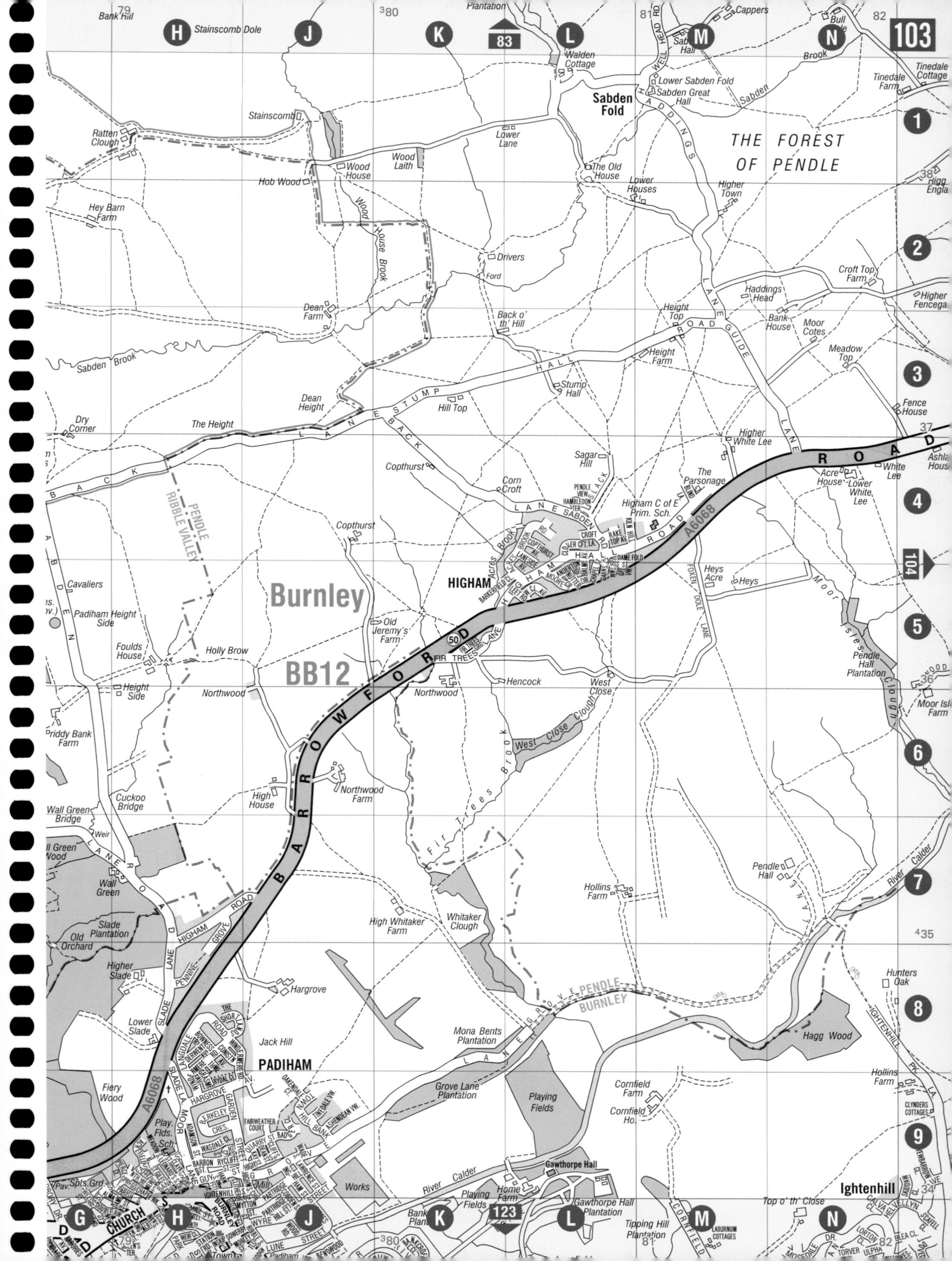

THE FOREST OF PENDLE
Sabden Fold
HIGHAM
Burnley
BB12
PADIHAM
Ightenhill
BARROWFORD ROAD
A6068
STUMP HALL LANE
BACK LANE
HADDINGS LANE
HIGHAM HALL ROAD
GROVE LANE
PENDLE RIBBLE VALLEY
PENDLE BURNLEY
River Calder
Sabden Brook
Gawthorpe Hall
Hagg Wood
Playing Fields
Works

83
104
123

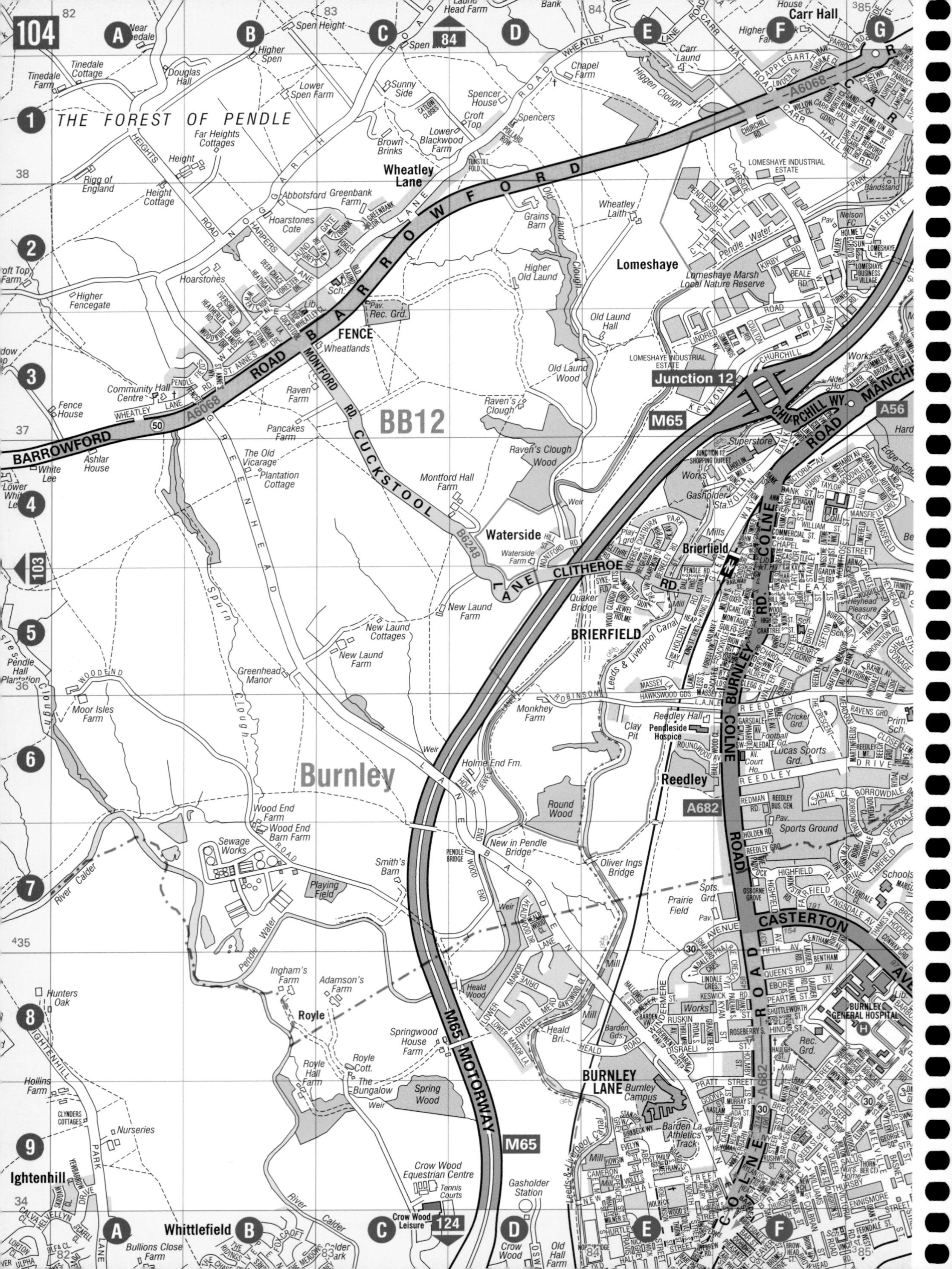

104
THE FOREST OF PENDLE
Tinedale Cottage
Tinedale Farm
Higher Spen
Douglas Hall
Spen Height
Lower Spen Farm
Sunny Side
Spencer House
Chapel Farm
Carr Laund
Carr Hall
Higgen Clough
Far Heights Cottages
Height
Rigg of England
Height Cottage
Brown Brinks
Lower Blackwood Farm
Croft Top
Spencers
Wheatley Lane
Abbotsford
Greenbank Farm
Hoarstones Cote
Hoarstones
Higher Fencegate
BARROWFORD ROAD
FENCE
Wheatlands
Pav. Rec. Grd.
Grains Barn
Higher Old Laund
Wheatley Laith
Lomeshaye
Lomeshaye Marsh Local Nature Reserve
LOMESHAYE INDUSTRIAL ESTATE
Old Laund Hall
Old Laund Wood
Junction 12
Community Hall Centre
Fence House
Raven Farm
Raven's Clough
BB12
M65
A56
A6068
BARROWFORD
Pancakes Farm
Ashlar House
White Lee
The Old Vicarage
Plantation Cottage
CUCKSTOOL RD.
MONTFORD RD.
Montford Hall Farm
Raven's Clough Wood
Superstore
Waterside
Waterside Farm
CLITHEROE RD
Brierfield
BRIERFIELD
Quaker Bridge
Leeds & Liverpool Canal
New Laund Farm
New Laund Cottages
GREENHEAD LANE
Spurn Clough
Greenhead Manor
Moor Isles Farm
Pendle Hall Plantation
Monkhey Farm
Clay Pit
Reedley Hall
Pendleside Hospice
Cricket Grd.
Football Gd.
Lucas Sports Grd.
Burnley
Holme End Fm.
Round Wood
Reedley
A682
Sports Ground
Wood End Farm
Wood End Barn Farm
Sewage Works
Smith's Barn
New in Pendle Bridge
Oliver Ings Bridge
Playing Field
River Calder
Pendle Water
Prairie Field
CASTERTON AVENUE
Schools
Ingham's Farm
Adamson's Farm
Royle
Heald Wood
Hunters Oak
BURNLEY GENERAL HOSPITAL
Springwood House Farm
Royle Cott.
Royle Hall Farm
The Bungalow
Spring Wood
M65 MOTORWAY
Heald Bri.
BURNLEY LANE
Burnley Campus
Barden La Athletics Track
Hollins Farm
Nurseries
Ightenhill
Crow Wood Equestrian Centre
Tennis Courts
Gasholder Station
Crow Wood Leisure
124
Whittlefield
Bullions Close Farm
Crow Wood
Old Hall Farm
103
84

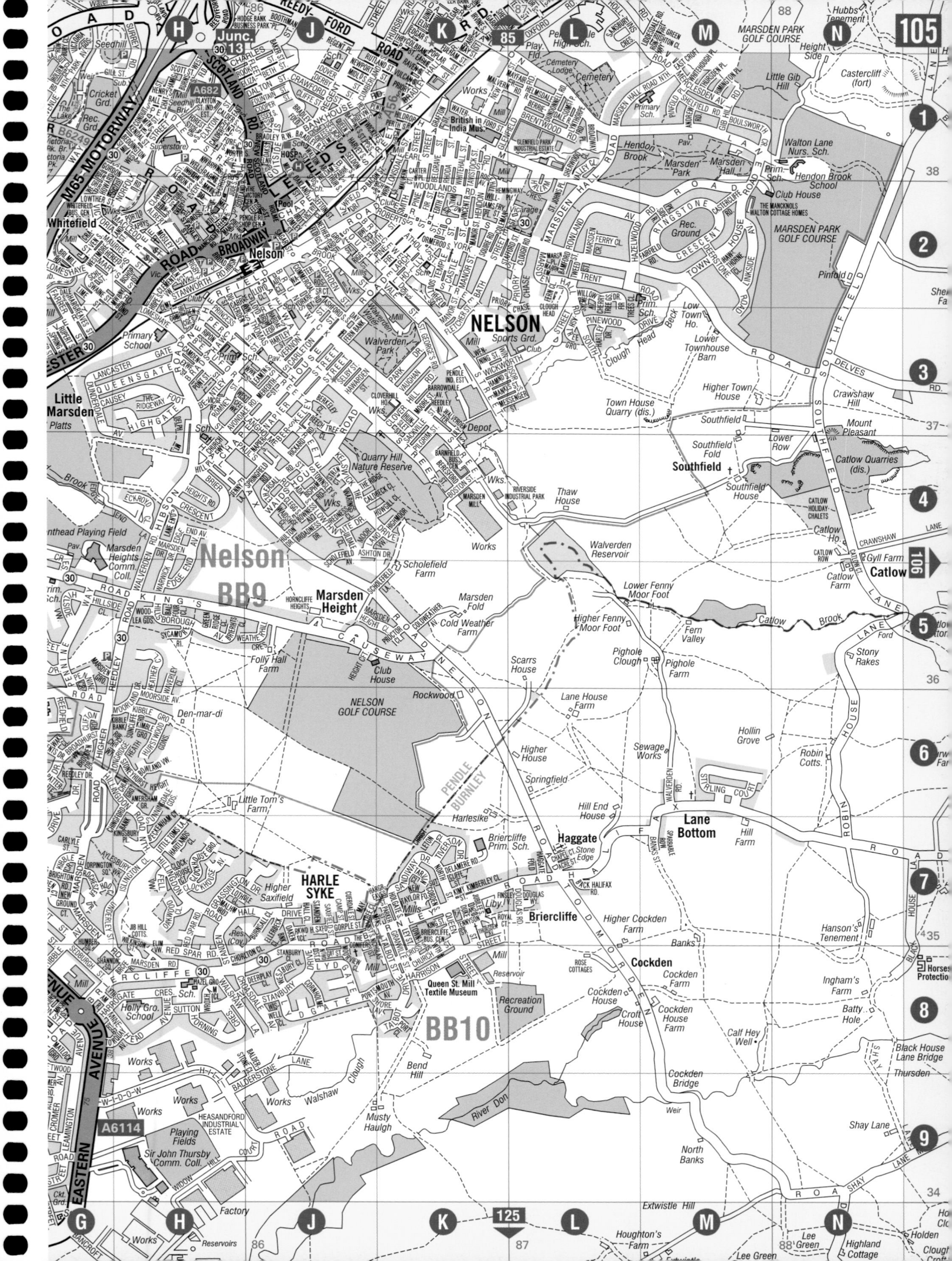

H
J
K
L
M
N
G
86
87
88
85
106
125
1
2
3
4
5
6
7
8
9
38
37
36
35
34
Junc. 13
M65 MOTORWAY
SCOTLAND RD.
LEEDS RD.
A682
A56
A6114
BB9
BB10
NELSON
Nelson
Whitefield
Little Marsden
Marsden Height
HARLE SYKE
Briercliffe
Haggate
Lane Bottom
Cockden
Southfield
Catlow
Seedhill
Cricket Grd.
Rec. Grd.
Superstore
British in India Mus.
GLENFIELD PARK INDUSTRIAL ESTATE
Cemetery
Cemetery Lodge
Primary Sch.
Hendon Brook
Marsden Park
Marsden Hall
Walton Lane Nurs. Sch.
Hendon Brook School
Club House
THE MANCKNOLS WALTON COTTAGE HOMES
MARSDEN PARK GOLF COURSE
Castercliff (fort)
Little Gib Hill
Height Side
Hubbs Tenement
Rec. Ground
Pinfold
Low Town Ho.
Lower Townhouse Barn
Higher Town House
Town House Quarry (dis.)
Crawshaw Hill
Mount Pleasant
Lower Row
Southfield Fold
Southfield House
Catlow Quarries (dis.)
CATLOW HOLIDAY CHALETS
Catlow Ho.
Gyll Farm
Catlow Farm
Thaw House
RIVERSIDE INDUSTRIAL PARK
Walverden Reservoir
Lower Fenny Moor Foot
Higher Fenny Moor Foot
Catlow Brook
Fern Valley
Pighole Clough
Pighole Farm
Stony Rakes
Sports Grd.
Walverden Park
Walverden Water
Quarry Hill Nature Reserve
Depot
Works
Marsden Heights Comm. Coll.
Scholefield Farm
Marsden Fold
Cold Weather Farm
Folly Hall Farm
Club House
NELSON GOLF COURSE
Rockwood
Scarrs House
Lane House Farm
Hollin Grove
Sewage Works
Robin Cotts.
Higher House
Springfield
Den-mar-di
Little Tom's Farm
PENDLE
BURNLEY
Harlesike
Hill End House
Briercliffe Prim. Sch.
Stone Edge
Hill Farm
Higher Saxifield
Higher Cockden Farm
Banks
Hanson's Tenement
Horses Protection
Queen St. Mill Textile Museum
Recreation Ground
Reservoir
Cockden Farm
Cockden House
Croft House
Cockden House Farm
Ingham's Farm
Batty Hole
Calf Hey Well
Black House Lane Bridge
Thursden
Holly Gro. School
Bend Hill
Walshaw Clough
Cockden Bridge
Weir
River Don
Musty Haugh
Shay Lane
North Banks
HEASANDFORD INDUSTRIAL ESTATE
Playing Fields
Sir John Thursby Comm. Coll.
Factory
Reservoirs
Extwistle Hill
Houghton's Farm
Lee Green
Highland Cottage
Holden
EASTERN AVENUE
KING'S CAUSEWAY
NELSON ROAD
HALIFAX ROAD
BURNLEY ROAD
MARSDEN HALL ROAD
SOUTHFIELD LANE
DELVES RD.
CRAWSHAW LANE
WALVERDEN RD.
STIRLING COURT
ROBIN HOUSE LANE
WIDOW HILL ROAD
BALDERSTONE LANE
RINGSTONE CRESCENT
TOWN HOUSE ROAD
BRUNSWICK ST.
HALIFAX

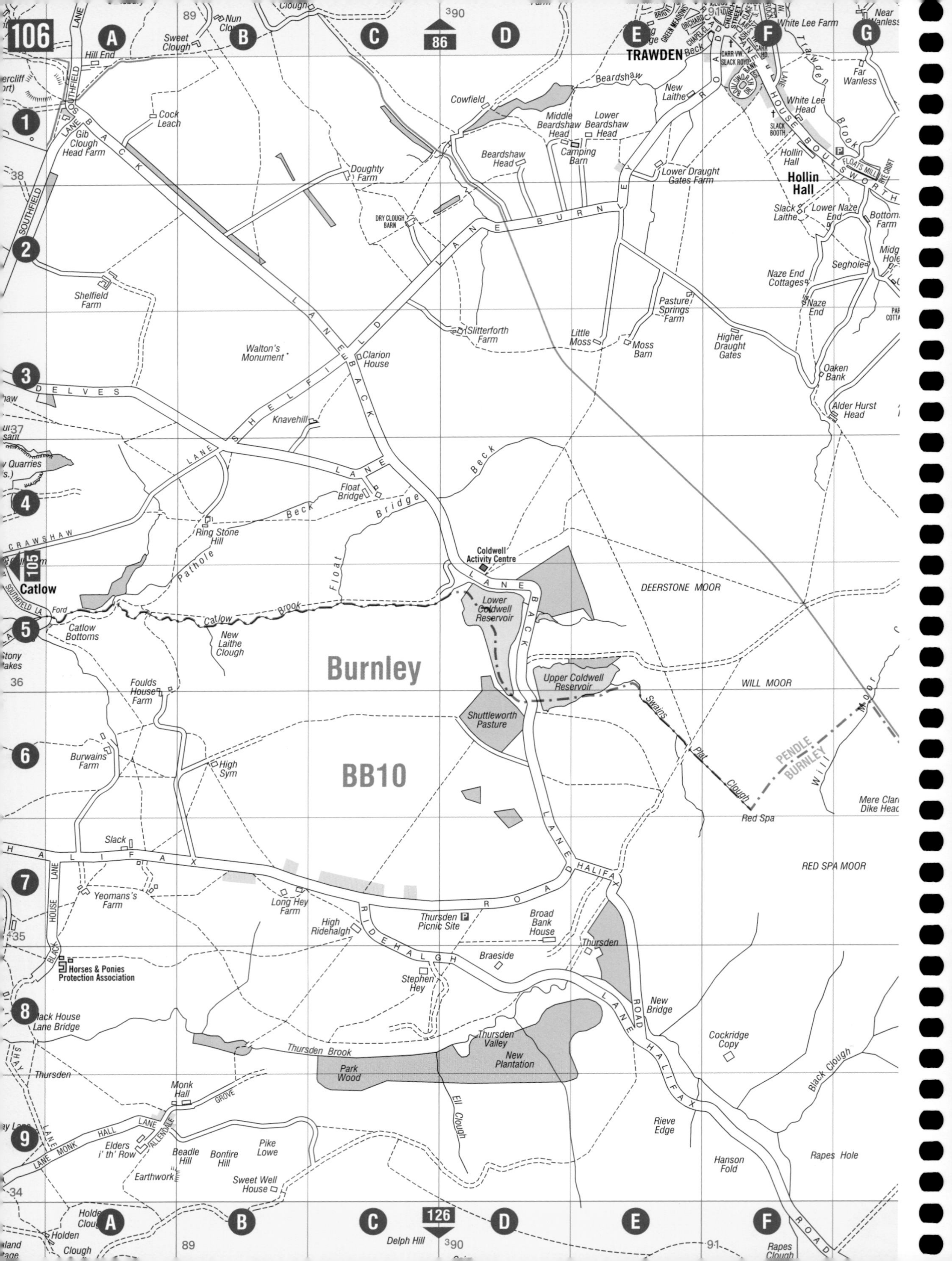

TRAWDEN
Hollin Hall
Catlow
Burnley
BB10
Hill End
Sweet Clough
Cock Leach
Gib Clough Head Farm
Doughty Farm
Cowfield
Beardshaw
Middle Beardshaw Head
Lower Beardshaw Head
Beardshaw Head
Camping Barn
Lower Draught Gates Farm
New Laithe
White Lee Farm
White Lee Head
Far Wanless
Near Wanless
Hollin Hall
Slack Laithe
Lower Naze End
Bottom Farm
Segholes
Naze End Cottages
Naze End
Pasture Springs Farm
Higher Draught Gates
Little Moss
Moss Barn
Slitterforth Farm
Oaken Bank
Alder Hurst Head
DRY CLOUGH BARN
Shelfield Farm
Walton's Monument
Clarion House
Knavehill
Float Bridge
Ring Stone Hill
Coldwell Activity Centre
DEERSTONE MOOR
Lower Coldwell Reservoir
Upper Coldwell Reservoir
WILL MOOR
Shuttleworth Pasture
Catlow Bottoms
New Laithe Clough
Foulds House Farm
Burwains Farm
High Sym
Slack
Yeomans's Farm
Long Hey Farm
High Ridehalgh
Thursden Picnic Site
Broad Bank House
Thursden
Braeside
Stephen Hey
Horses & Ponies Protection Association
Black House Lane Bridge
New Bridge
Cockridge Copy
Thursden Valley
New Plantation
Park Wood
Thursden Brook
Ell Clough
Monk Hall
Elders i' th' Row
Beadle Hill
Bonfire Hill
Pike Lowe
Earthwork
Sweet Well House
Rieve Edge
Hanson Fold
Rapes Hole
Black Clough
Red Spa
RED SPA MOOR
Mere Clough Dike Head
PENDLE
BURNLEY
DELVES
CRAWSHAW
HALIFAX ROAD
RIDEHALGH LANE
SHELFIELD LANE
BACK LANE
BURNLEY LANE
MONK HALL LANE
Catlow Brook
Swains Plat Clough
Holden Clough
Holden
Delph Hill
Rapes Clough
Ford
86
105
126

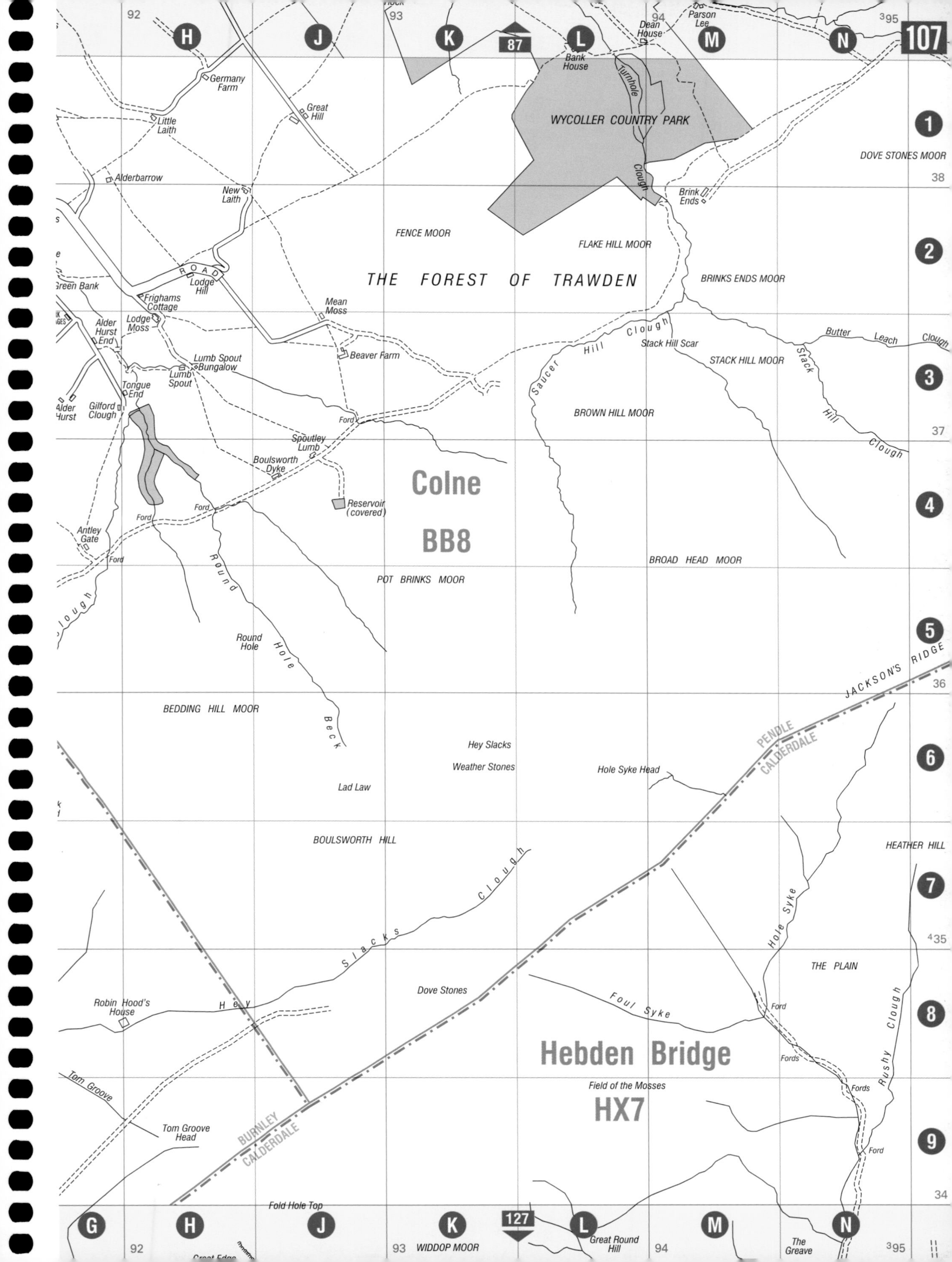

Germany Farm

Little Laith

Great Hill

Alderbarrow

New Laith

Bank House

WYCOLLER COUNTRY PARK

Dean House

Parson Lee

Brink Ends

FENCE MOOR

FLAKE HILL MOOR

Green Bank

ROAD

Lodge Hill

THE FOREST OF TRAWDEN

BRINKS ENDS MOOR

Frighams Cottage

Alder Hurst End

Lodge Moss

Mean Moss

Clough

Stack Hill Scar

Butter   Leach   Clough

Saucer   Hill

STACK HILL MOOR

Stack

Lumb Spout
Bungalow

Beaver Farm

Lumb Spout

Tongue End

Gilford Clough

Alder Hurst

Spoutley Lumb

Boulsworth Dyke

Ford

BROWN HILL MOOR

Hill   Clough

Colne

BB8

Reservoir (covered)

Antley Gate

Ford

Ford

Ford

Round   Hole   Beck

Round Hole

POT BRINKS MOOR

BROAD HEAD MOOR

Clough

BEDDING HILL MOOR

Hey Slacks

Weather Stones

Hole Syke Head

JACKSON'S   RIDGE

PENDLE
CALDERDALE

Lad Law

BOULSWORTH   HILL

HEATHER HILL

Slacks   Clough

Hole Syke

THE PLAIN

Robin Hood's House

Hey

Dove Stones

Foul Syke

Ford

Rushy   Clough

Hebden Bridge

Tom Groove

HX7

Field of the Mosses

Fords

Fords

BURNLEY
CALDERDALE

Tom Groove Head

Ford

Fold Hole Top

Great Edge

Great Round Hill

The Greave

34

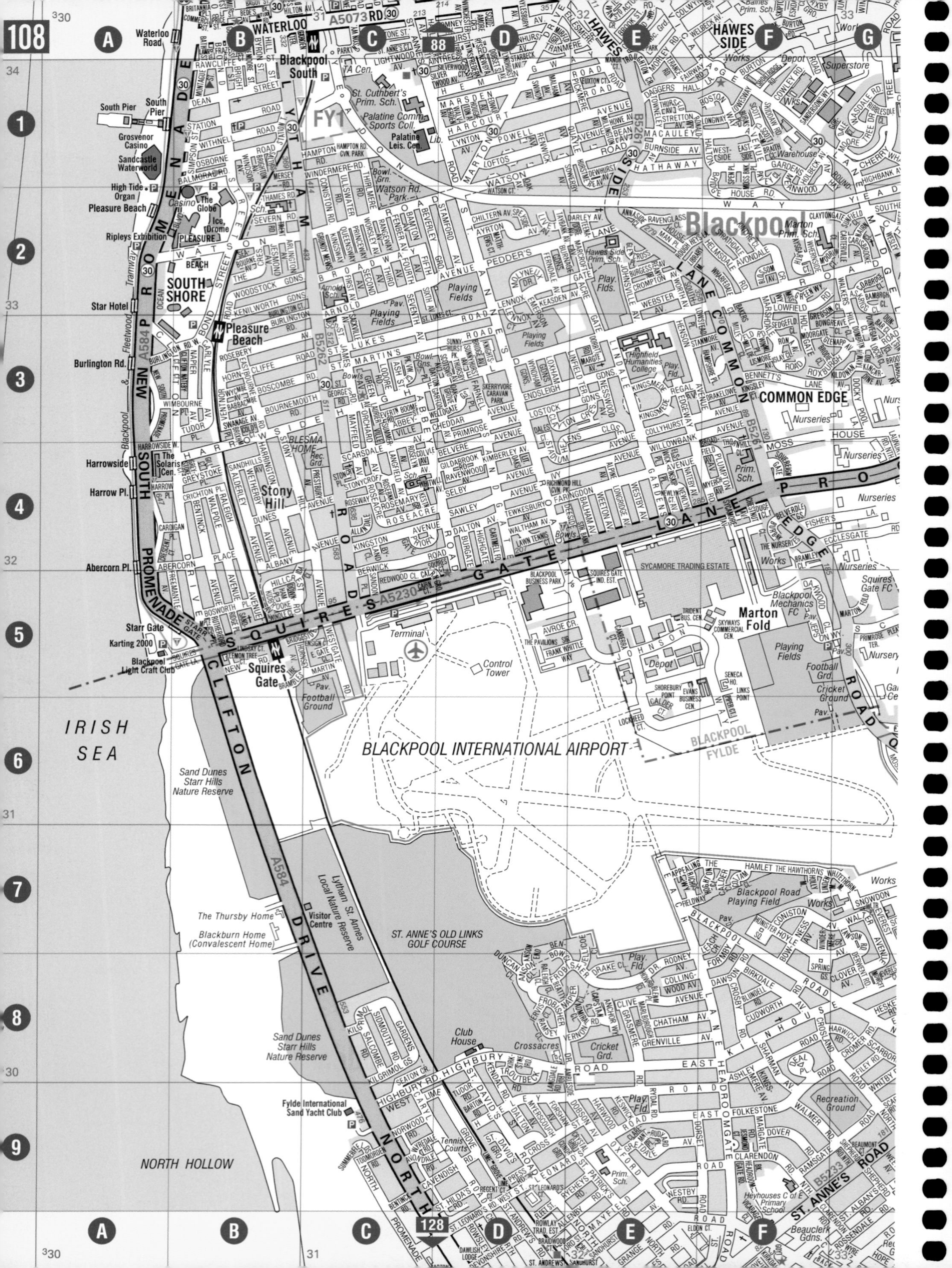

A
B
C
D
E
F
G
1
2
3
4
5
6
7
8
9
WATERLOO
Blackpool South
HAWES SIDE
Blackpool
SOUTH SHORE
Pleasure Beach
COMMON EDGE
Stony Hill
Marton Fold
Squires Gate
IRISH SEA
BLACKPOOL INTERNATIONAL AIRPORT
ST. ANNE'S OLD LINKS GOLF COURSE
NORTH HOLLOW
SQUIRES GATE LANE
NEW SOUTH PROMENADE
CLIFTON DRIVE NORTH
LYTHAM ROAD
South Pier
Pleasure Beach
Star Hotel
Burlington Rd.
Harrowside
Harrow Pl.
Abercorn Pl.
Starr Gate
Blackpool Light Craft Club
Sand Dunes Starr Hills Nature Reserve
Lytham St. Annes Local Nature Reserve
The Thursby Home
Blackburn Home (Convalescent Home)
Fylde International Sand Yacht Club
SYCAMORE TRADING ESTATE
BLACKPOOL BUSINESS PARK
Terminal
Control Tower
Club House
Crossacres
Recreation Ground
Heyhouses C of E Primary School
88
128

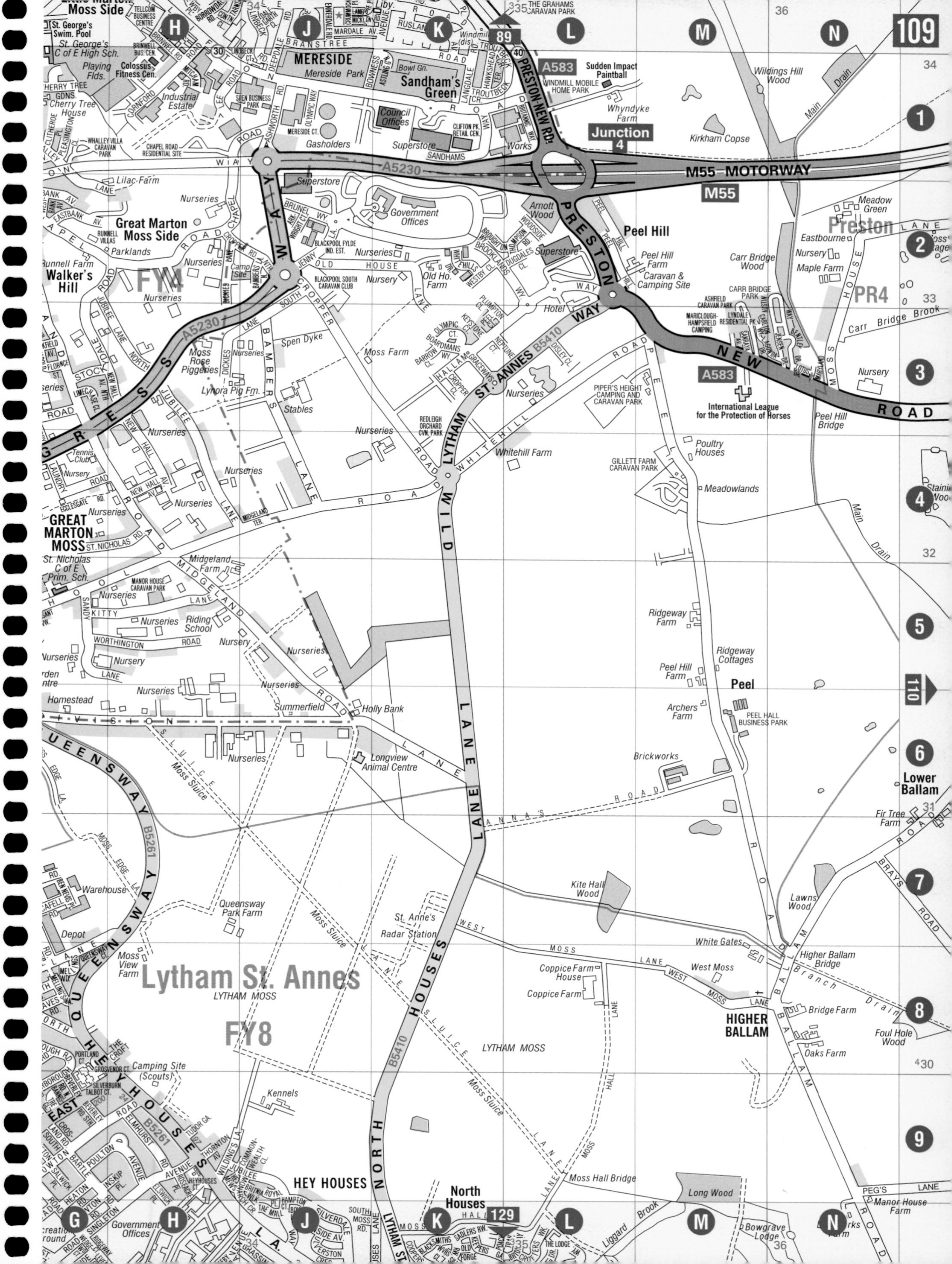

Moss Side
St. George's Swim. Pool
St. George's C of E High Sch.
Playing Flds.
Colossus Fitness Cen.
Cherry Tree House
Industrial Estate
MERESIDE
Mereside Park
Bowl Gn.
Sandham's Green
Council Offices
Gasholders
Superstore
Works
Sudden Impact Paintball
WINDMILL MOBILE HOME PARK
Whyndyke Farm
Junction 4
Wildings Hill Wood
Kirkham Copse
Main Drain
M55 MOTORWAY
M55
A5230
A583
PRESTON NEW RD.
Lilac Farm
Nurseries
Great Marton Moss Side
Parklands
Government Offices
Arnott Wood
Peel Hill
Meadow Green
Preston
Eastbourne
Nursery
Maple Farm
Carr Bridge Wood
Peel Hill Farm
Caravan & Camping Site
CARR BRIDGE PARK
Runnell Farm
Walker's Hill
FY4
Camp Site
BLACKPOOL FYLDE IND. EST.
BLACKPOOL SOUTH CARAVAN CLUB
Old Ho. Farm
Superstore
Hotel
PR4
Carr Bridge Brook
Spen Dyke
Moss Farm
Moss Rose Piggeries
Lynora Pig Fm.
Stables
ST. ANNES
B5410
PIPER'S HEIGHT CAMPING AND CARAVAN PARK
A583
International League for the Protection of Horses
NEW ROAD
Nursery
Peel Hill Bridge
Tennis Club
REDLEIGH ORCHARD CVN. PARK
Whitehill Farm
Poultry Houses
GILLETT FARM CARAVAN PARK
Meadowlands
GREAT MARTON MOSS
St. Nicholas C of E Prim. Sch.
Midgeland Farm
MANOR HOUSE CARAVAN PARK
WILD LANE
Riding School
Ridgeway Farm
Ridgeway Cottages
Peel Hill Farm
Peel
Archers Farm
PEEL HALL BUSINESS PARK
Homestead
Summerfield
Holly Bank
Longview Animal Centre
Brickworks
Lower Ballam
Fir Tree Farm
Moss Sluice
QUEENSWAY
B5261
Warehouse
Depot
Queensway Park Farm
St. Anne's Radar Station
Kite Hall Wood
Lawns Wood
White Gates
Higher Ballam Bridge
Moss View Farm
Lytham St. Annes
LYTHAM MOSS
Coppice Farm House
Coppice Farm
West Moss
FY8
HIGHER BALLAM
Bridge Farm
Branch Drain
Foul Hole Wood
Oaks Farm
LYTHAM MOSS
Camping Site (Scouts)
Kennels
HEYHOUSES
NORTH HOUSES
HEY HOUSES
North Houses
Moss Hall Bridge
Long Wood
Liggard Brook
Bowgrave Lodge
Manor House Farm
PEG'S LANE
Government Offices
THE GRAHAMS CARAVAN PARK
89
129
110

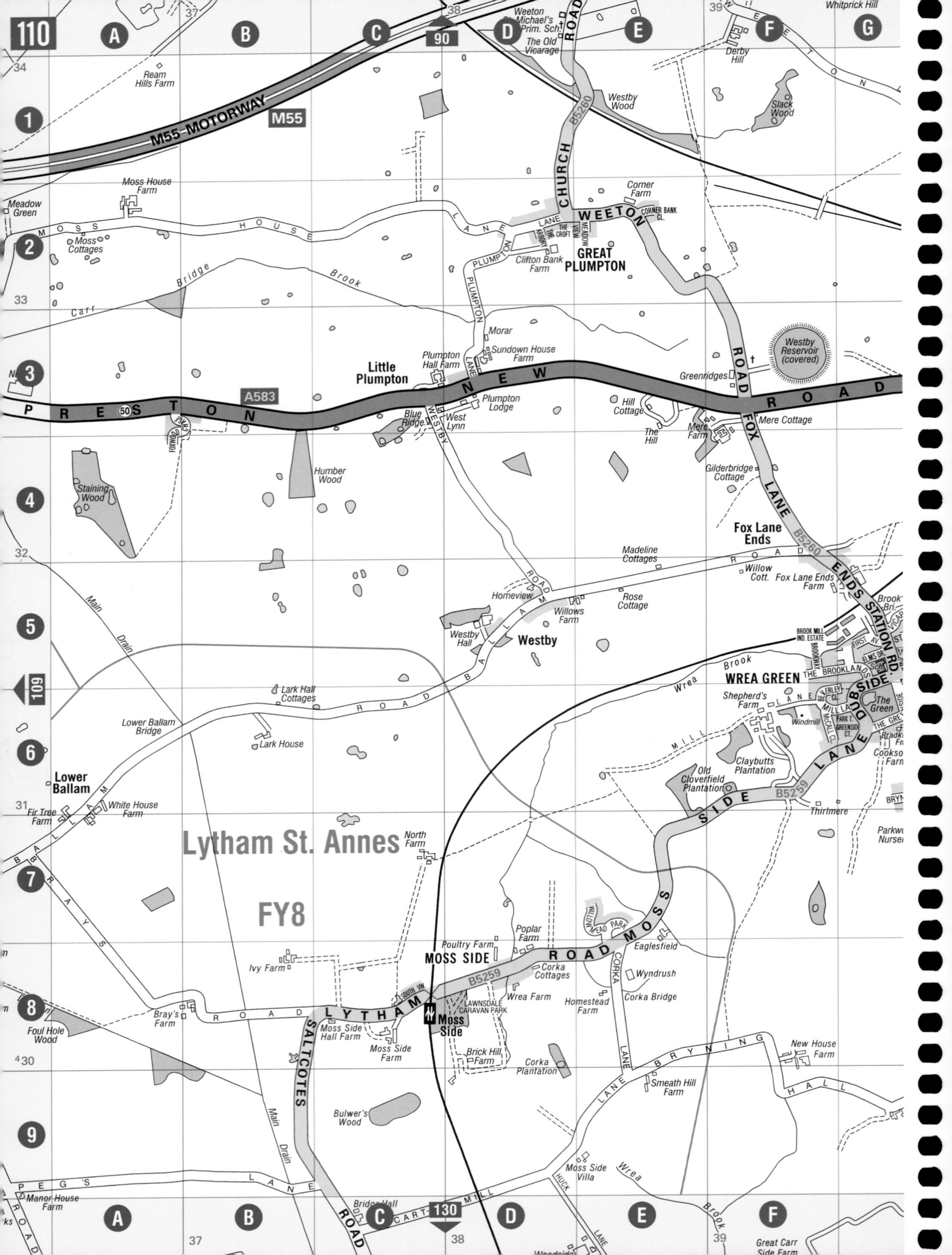

A
B
C
D
E
F
G
1
2
3
4
5
6
7
8
9
90
130
109
M55 MOTORWAY
M55
A583
B5260
B5259
Whitprick Hill
Weeton St. Michael's Prim. Sch.
The Old Vicarage
Derby Hill
Ream Hills Farm
Westby Wood
Slack Wood
Moss House Farm
Meadow Green
Moss Cottages
MOSS HOUSE LANE
CHURCH ROAD
WEETON LANE
WEETON ROAD
Corner Farm
CORNER BANK CL.
THE CROFT
MEADOW VIEW
Clifton Bank Farm
GREAT PLUMPTON
PLUMPTON LANE
Carr Bridge Brook
Morar
Sundown House Farm
Plumpton Hall Farm
Little Plumpton
Westby Reservoir (covered)
Greenridges
PRESTON NEW ROAD
Plumpton Lodge
Blue Ridge
West Lynn
WESTBY ROAD
Hill Cottage
The Hill
Mere Farm
Mere Cottage
FOX LANE
FOXWOOD
Humber Wood
Staining Wood
Gilderbridge Cottage
Fox Lane Ends
Madeline Cottages
Willow Cott.
Fox Lane Ends Farm
Homeview
Rose Cottage
Willows Farm
Westby Hall
Westby
BALLAM ROAD
Main Drain
Lark Hall Cottages
Lower Ballam Bridge
Lark House
Lower Ballam
White House Farm
Fir Tree Farm
BROOK MILL IND. ESTATE
STATION RD.
FIRST AV.
ELMS DR.
THE BROOKLANDS
WREA GREEN
Wrea Brook
Shepherd's Farm
Windmill
MILL LANE
DUBSIDE
The Green
PARK T.
GREENSIDE CT.
McCALL CL.
Claybutts Plantation
Old Cloverfield Plantation
Thirlmere
MOSS SIDE LANE
Parkwood Nurseries
Lytham St. Annes
FY8
North Farm
BRAYS ROAD
Poultry Farm
Poplar Farm
MOSS SIDE
Eaglesfield
MOSS ROAD
Ivy Farm
Corka Cottages
Wyndrush
Wrea Farm
Homestead Farm
Corka Bridge
CORKA LANE
Bray's Farm
LYTHAM ROAD
SOUTH VW.
LAWNSDALE CARAVAN PARK
Moss Side
Foul Hole Wood
Moss Side Hall Farm
Moss Side Farm
Brick Hill Farm
Corka Plantation
New House Farm
BRYNING HALL LANE
Smeath Hill Farm
SALTCOTES ROAD
Bulwer's Wood
Moss Side Villa
Wrea Brook
PEG'S LANE
Manor House Farm
Bridge Hall
CART-MILL
HUCK LANE
Great Carr Side Farm
33
32
31
30
34
37
38
39

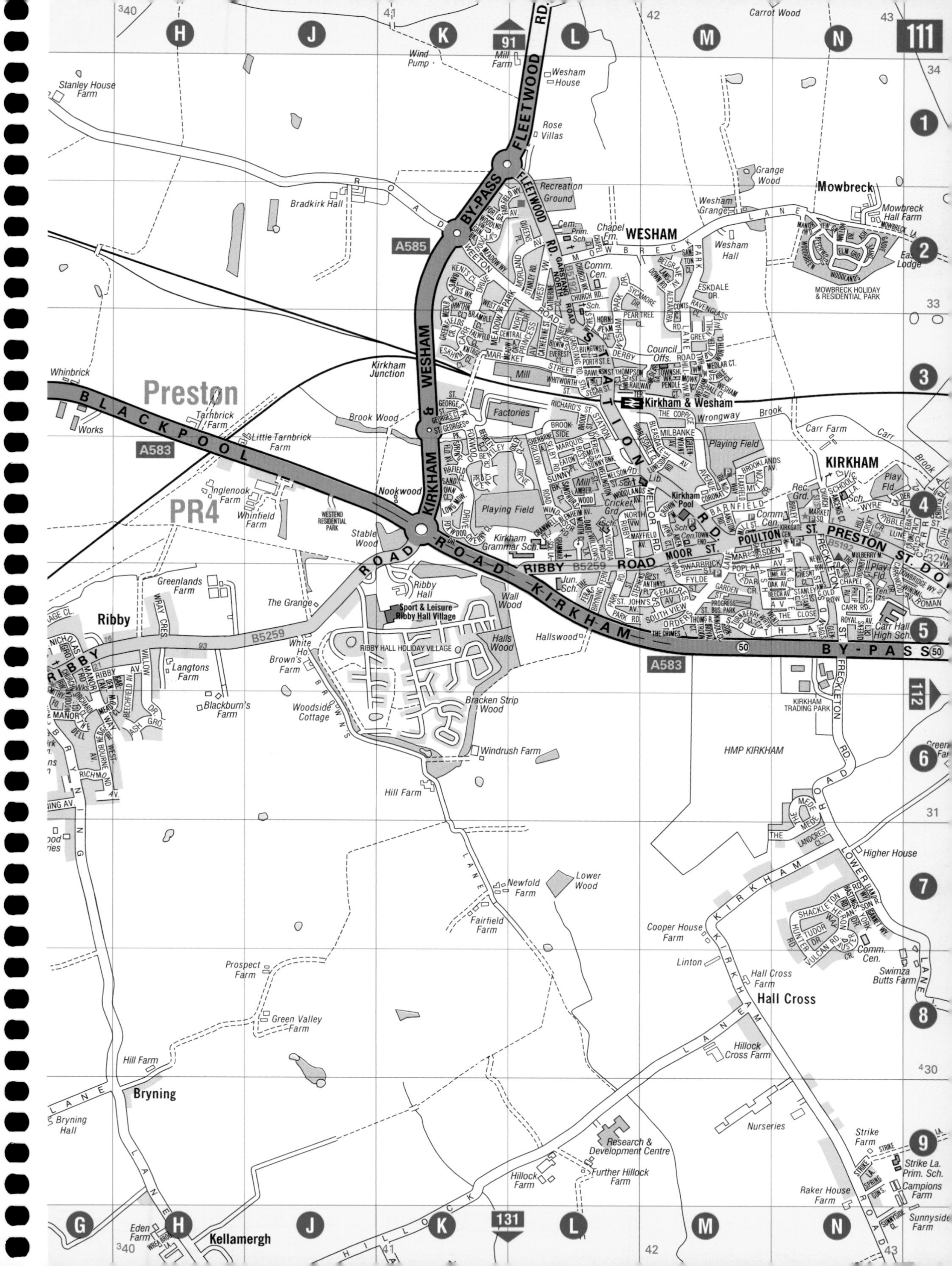

WESHAM
KIRKHAM
Mowbreck
Preston
PR4
Ribby
Bryning
Hall Cross
Kellamergh
Kirkham & Wesham
Kirkham Junction
Stanley House Farm
Wind Pump
Mill Farm
Wesham House
Rose Villas
Recreation Ground
Bradkirk Hall
Grange Wood
Wesham Grange
Wesham Hall
Mowbreck Hall Farm
MOWBRECK HOLIDAY & RESIDENTIAL PARK
East Lodge
Whinbrick
Works
Tarnbrick Farm
Little Tarnbrick Farm
Brook Wood
Factories
Mill
Inglenook Farm
Whinfield Farm
Nookwood
WESTEND RESIDENTIAL PARK
Stable Wood
Playing Field
Kirkham Grammar Sch.
Kirkham Pool
Carr Farm
Greenlands Farm
The Grange
Ribby Hall
Sport & Leisure Ribby Hall Village
Wall Wood
RIBBY HALL HOLIDAY VILLAGE
Halls Wood
Hallswood
White Ho.
Brown's Farm
Langtons Farm
Blackburn's Farm
Woodside Cottage
Bracken Strip Wood
KIRKHAM TRADING PARK
Windrush Farm
HMP KIRKHAM
Hill Farm
Higher House
Lower Wood
Newfold Farm
Fairfield Farm
Cooper House Farm
Linton
Prospect Farm
Hall Cross Farm
Swimza Butts Farm
Green Valley Farm
Hillock Cross Farm
Hill Farm
Bryning Hall
Research & Development Centre
Nurseries
Strike Farm
Strike La. Prim. Sch.
Campions Farm
Hillock Farm
Further Hillock Farm
Raker House Farm
Sunnyside Farm
Eden Farm
Carrot Wood
A585
A583
B5259
B5192
BLACKPOOL ROAD
KIRKHAM BY-PASS
FLEETWOOD RD.
KIRKHAM & WESHAM BY-PASS
STATION RD.
POULTON ST.
PRESTON ST.
RIBBY ROAD
MOOR ST.
KIRKHAM RD.
HILLOCK LANE
BRYNING LANE
91
131
112

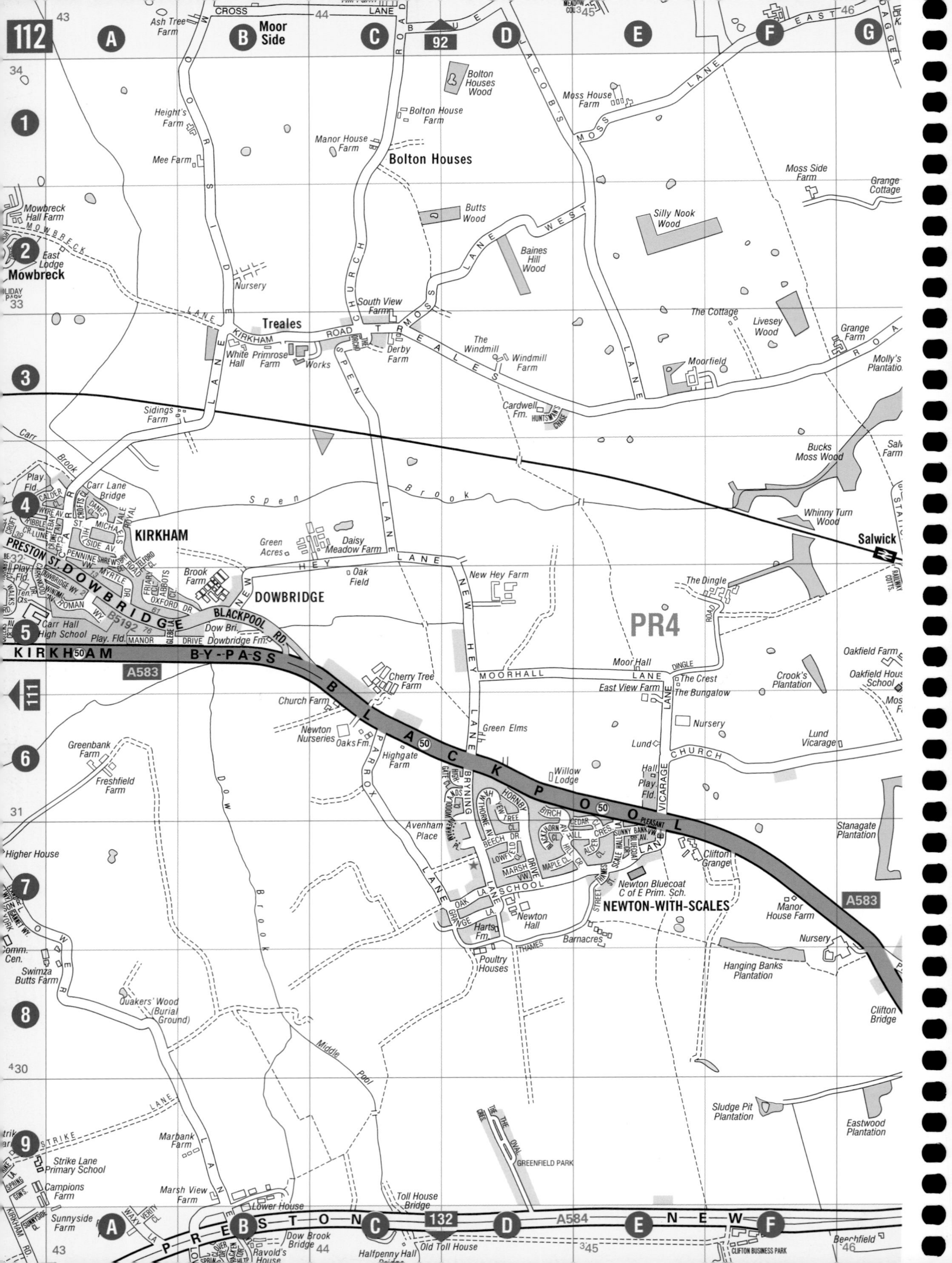
Moor Side
Bolton Houses
Treales
Mowbreck
KIRKHAM
DOWBRIDGE
NEWTON-WITH-SCALES
Salwick
PR4
Bolton Houses Wood
Bolton House Farm
Manor House Farm
Height's Farm
Mee Farm
Ash Tree Farm
Moss House Farm
Moss Side Farm
Grange Cottage
Silly Nook Wood
Butts Wood
Baines Hill Wood
Nursery
South View Farm
White Hall
Primrose Farm
Works
Derby Farm
The Windmill
Windmill Farm
The Cottage
Livesey Wood
Grange Farm
Moorfield
Molly's Plantation
Cardwell Fm.
Sidings Farm
Bucks Moss Wood
Whinny Turn Wood
Carr Lane Bridge
Green Acres
Daisy Meadow Farm
Oak Field
New Hey Farm
Brook Farm
The Dingle
Carr Hall High School
Dow Bri.
Dowbridge Fm.
Moor Hall
The Crest
East View Farm
The Bungalow
Oakfield Farm
Crook's Plantation
Oakfield House School
Cherry Tree Farm
Church Farm
Newton Nurseries
Oaks Fm.
Green Elms
Nursery
Lund
Lund Vicarage
Greenbank Farm
Freshfield Farm
Highgate Farm
Willow Lodge
Hall
Play. Fld.
Avenham Place
Stanagate Plantation
Clifton Grange
Newton Bluecoat C of E Prim. Sch.
Manor House Farm
Higher House
Newton Hall
Harts Fm.
Barnacres
Poultry Houses
Nursery
Hanging Banks Plantation
Comm. Cen.
Swimza Butts Farm
Quakers' Wood (Burial Ground)
Clifton Bridge
Middle Pool
Dow Brook
Spen Brook
Carr Brook
Sludge Pit Plantation
Eastwood Plantation
Marbank Farm
Strike Lane Primary School
Campions Farm
Marsh View Farm
Sunnyside Farm
Lower House
Toll House Bridge
Dow Brook Bridge
Ravold's House
Halfpenny Hall Bridge
Old Toll House
Greenfield Park
Clifton Business Park
Beechfield
KIRKHAM BY-PASS
BLACKPOOL RD.
BLACKPOOL
PRESTON ST.
DOWBRIDGE
PRESTON NEW
A583
A584
B5192
92
111
132
CROSS LANE
MOORSIDE LANE
CHURCH ROAD
JACOB'S LANE
EAST LANE
MOSS LANE
MOSS LANE WEST
KIRKHAM ROAD
TREALES ROAD
SPEN LANE
HEY LANE
NEW HEY LANE
MOORHALL LANE
DINGLE LANE
VICARAGE LANE
CHURCH LANE
SCHOOL LANE
PARROX LANE
BRYNING LANE
WEAR LANE
STRIKE LANE
MARSH LANE
MOWBRECK LANE
MANOR DRIVE

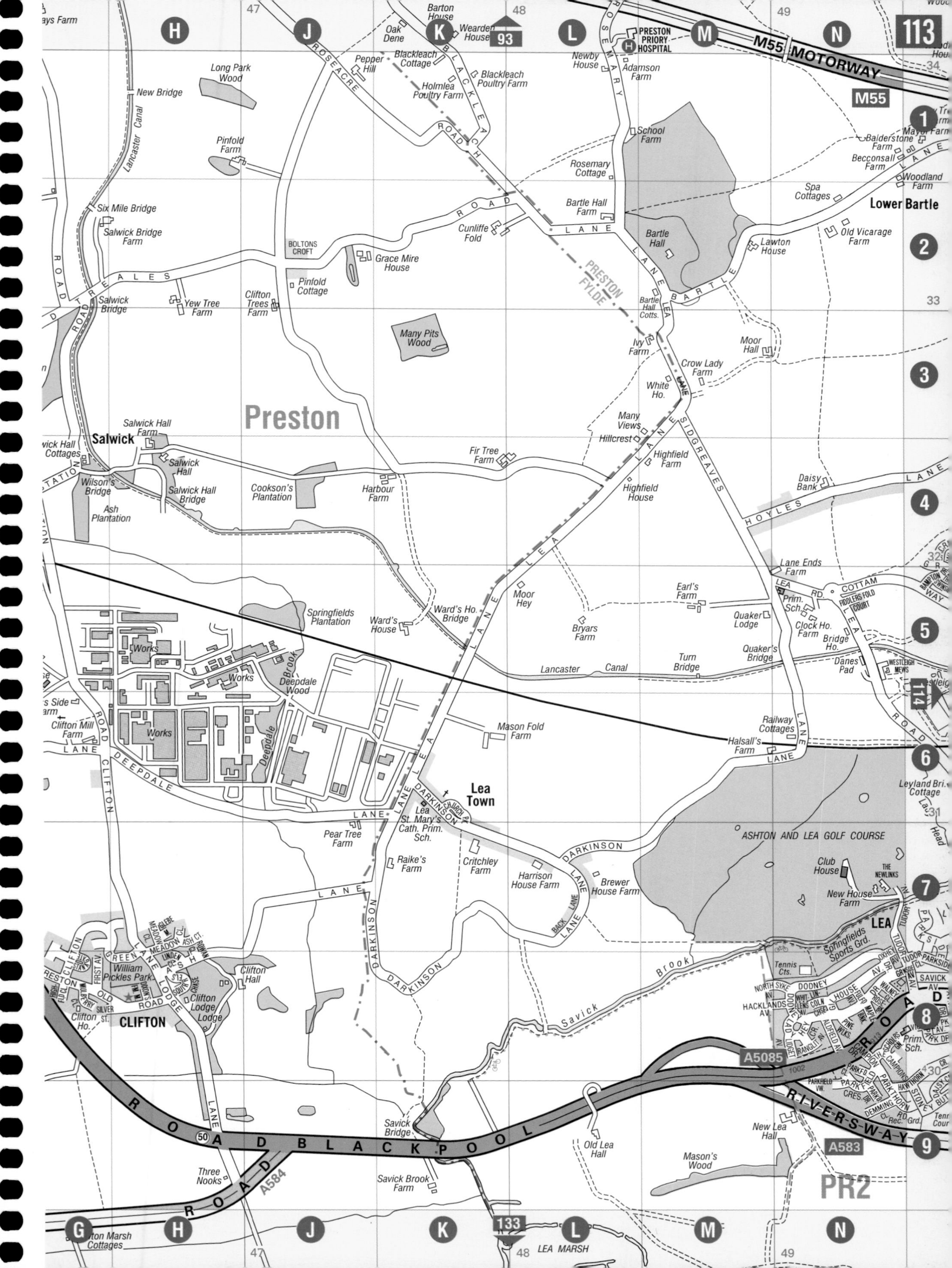
Preston
Salwick
Lea Town
CLIFTON
LEA
Lower Bartle
M55 MOTORWAY
M55
A5085
A583
A584
PR2
PRESTON PRIORY HOSPITAL
ASHTON AND LEA GOLF COURSE
Lancaster Canal
Savick Brook
Long Park Wood
Many Pits Wood
Mason's Wood
Cookson's Plantation
Springfields Plantation
Ash Plantation
Deepdale Wood
William Pickles Park
Springfields Sports Grd.
Barton House
Wearden House
Oak Dene
Pepper Hill
Blackleach Cottage
Blackleach Poultry Farm
Holmlea Poultry Farm
Newby House
Adamson Farm
School Farm
Rosemary Cottage
Bartle Hall Farm
Bartle Hall
Bartle Hall Cotts.
Cunliffe Fold
Grace Mire House
Pinfold Farm
Pinfold Cottage
Bolton's Croft
Clifton Trees Farm
Yew Tree Farm
Salwick Bridge
Salwick Bridge Farm
Six Mile Bridge
New Bridge
Salwick Hall Farm
Salwick Hall
Salwick Hall Bridge
Wilson's Bridge
Fir Tree Farm
Harbour Farm
Ward's House
Ward's Ho. Bridge
Moor Hey
Bryars Farm
Earl's Farm
Quaker Lodge
Quaker's Bridge
Turn Bridge
Mason Fold Farm
Halsall's Farm
Railway Cottages
Ivy Farm
Moor Hall
Crow Lady Farm
White Ho.
Many Views
Hillcrest
Highfield Farm
Highfield House
Daisy Bank
Lane Ends Farm
Prim. Sch.
Clock Ho. Farm
Bridge Ho.
Danes Pad
Lawton House
Old Vicarage Farm
Spa Cottages
Balderstone Farm
Becconsall Farm
Woodland Farm
Mayor Farm
Clifton Mill Farm
Pear Tree Farm
Raike's Farm
Critchley Farm
Harrison House Farm
Brewer House Farm
Lea St. Mary's Cath. Prim. Sch.
Clifton Hall
Clifton Lodge
Lodge
Clifton Ho.
New House Farm
Club House
THE NEWLINKS
Tennis Cts.
Savick Bridge
Savick Brook Farm
Old Lea Hall
New Lea Hall
Three Nooks
Leyland Bri. Cottage
Clifton Marsh Cottages
LEA MARSH
Works
ROSEACRE ROAD
BLACKLEACH ROAD
ROSEMARY LANE
BARTLE LANE
TREALES ROAD
SIDGREAVES LANE
LEA LANE
HOYLES LANE
COTTAM LANE
LEA RD.
DEEPDALE LANE
CLIFTON LANE
DARKINSON LANE
BACK LANE
LODGE LANE
BLACKPOOL ROAD
RIVERSWAY
DODNEY DR.
SAVICK AV.
TUDOR AV.
HACKLANDS AV.
NORTH SYKE AV.
FIDDLERS FOLD COURT
WESTLEIGH MEWS
93
133
114
47
48
49
34
33
32
31
30
G
H
J
K
L
M
N
1
2
3
4
5
6
7
8
9

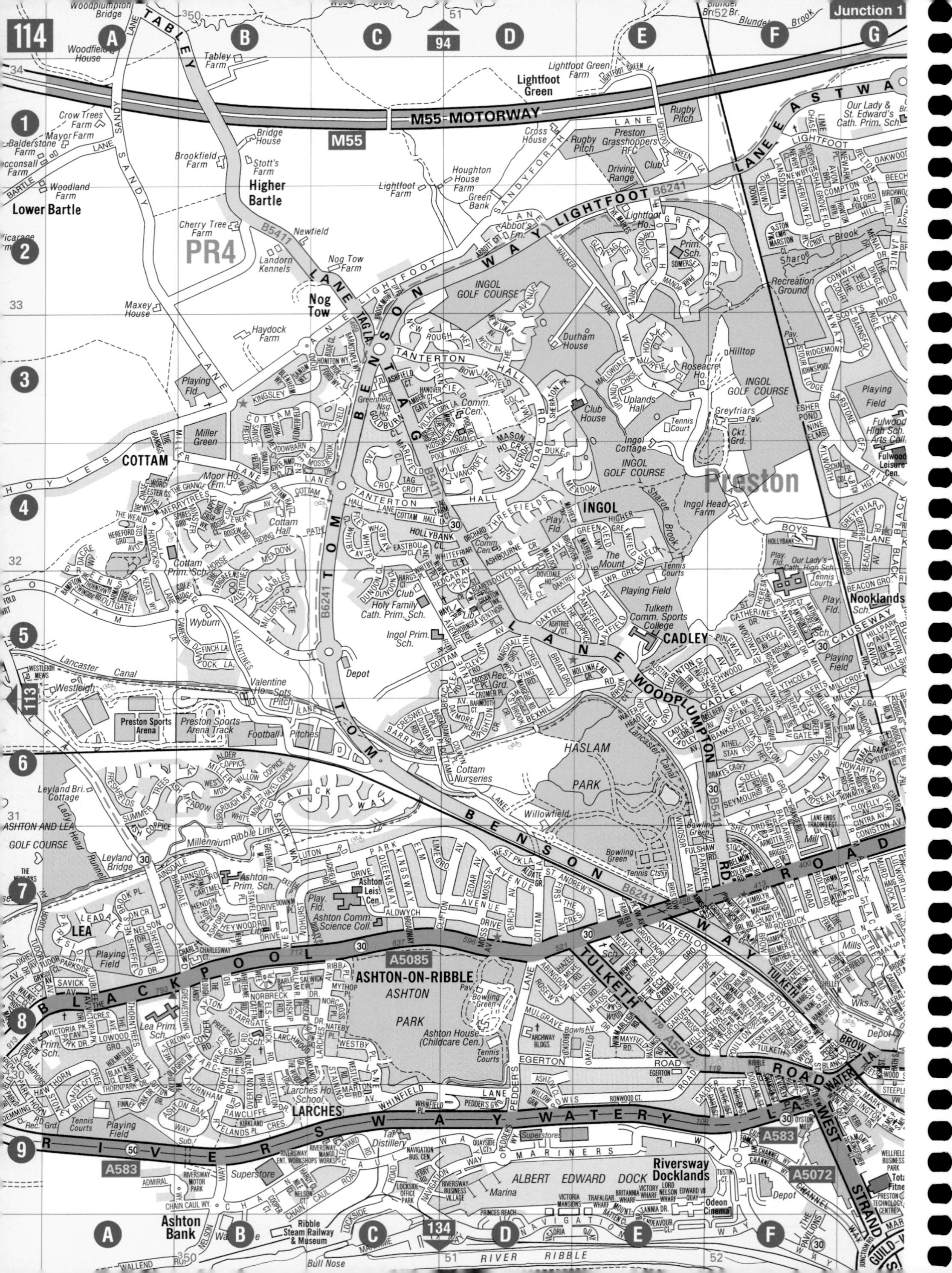

Junction 1
94
M55 MOTORWAY
M55
Lightfoot Green
Lower Bartle
Higher Bartle
PR4
Nog Tow
COTTAM
INGOL
INGOL GOLF COURSE
Preston
CADLEY
Nooklands
HASLAM PARK
ASHTON-ON-RIBBLE
ASHTON PARK
LEA
LARCHES
Ashton Bank
Riversway Docklands
ALBERT EDWARD DOCK
RIVER RIBBLE
BLACKPOOL ROAD
RIVERSWAY
TOM BENSON WAY
LIGHTFOOT LANE
WOODPLUMPTON RD.
TULKETH RD.
WATERY LANE
Lancaster Canal
Preston Sports Arena
Ashton Comm. Science Coll.
Tulketh Comm. Sports College
Ribble Steam Railway & Museum
A5085
A583
A5072
B6241
B5411
113
134

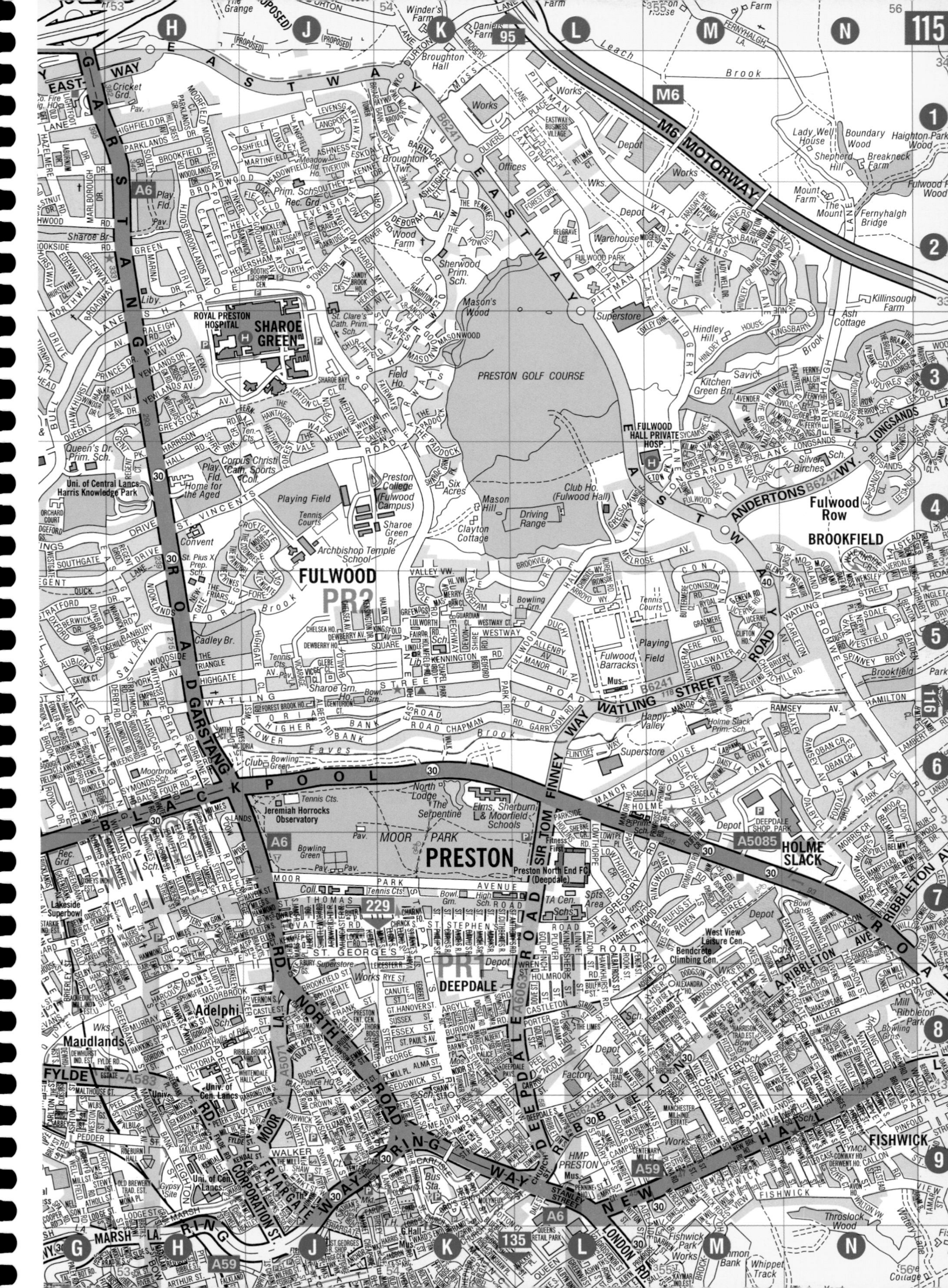

H
J
K
L
M
N
95
M6
M6 MOTORWAY
EASTWAY
Broughton Hall
Works
Depot
Offices
Warehouse
Lady Well House
Boundary Wood
Haighton Park Wood
Shepherd Hill
Breakneck Farm
Fulwood Park Wood
Mount Farm
The Mount
Fernyhalgh Bridge
Killinsough Farm
Ash Cottage
Broughton Twr.
Sherwood Prim. Sch.
Mason's Wood
Superstore
ROYAL PRESTON HOSPITAL
SHAROE GREEN
Hindley Hill
Kitchen Green Br.
Savick Brook
PRESTON GOLF COURSE
FULWOOD HALL PRIVATE HOSP.
LONGSANDS
Silver Birches
ANDERTONS WY.
B6242
Fulwood Row
BROOKFIELD
Field Ho.
Six Acres
Mason Hill
Club Ho. (Fulwood Hall)
Driving Range
Clayton Cottage
Preston College (Fulwood Campus)
Playing Field
Tennis Courts
Sharoe Green Br.
Archbishop Temple School
Corpus Christi Cath. Sports Coll.
Home for the Aged
Uni. of Central Lancs. Harris Knowledge Park
Queen's Dr. Prim. Sch.
Convent
St. Pius X Prep. Sch.
FULWOOD
PR2
Cadley Br.
Fulwood Barracks
Mus.
B6241
WATLING STREET
Happy Valley
Holme Slack Prim. Sch.
GARSTANG ROAD
A6
BLACKPOOL ROAD
North Lodge
The Serpentine
Elms, Sherburn & Moorfield Schools
Jeremiah Horrocks Observatory
MOOR PARK
PRESTON
Preston North End F.C. (Deepdale)
Fitness First
SIR TOM FINNEY WAY
Depot
DEEPDALE SHOP. PARK
A5085
HOLME SLACK
RIBBLETON AV.
Lakeside Superbowl
229
ST. GEORGE'S Superstore
PR1
DEEPDALE
A6063
DEEPDALE ROAD
West View Leisure Cen.
Bendcrete Climbing Cen.
Adelphi
Maudlands
FYLDE
A583
Univ. of Cen. Lancs.
A5071
NORTH ROAD
RING WAY
Police HQ
Bus Sta.
HMP PRESTON
A59
NEW HALL LANE
FISHWICK
Mill Ribbleton Park
Throslock Wood
CORPORATION ST.
FRIARGATE
MARSH LA.
135
G
Fishwick Park
Whipper Track
1
2
3
4
5
6
7
8
9
116

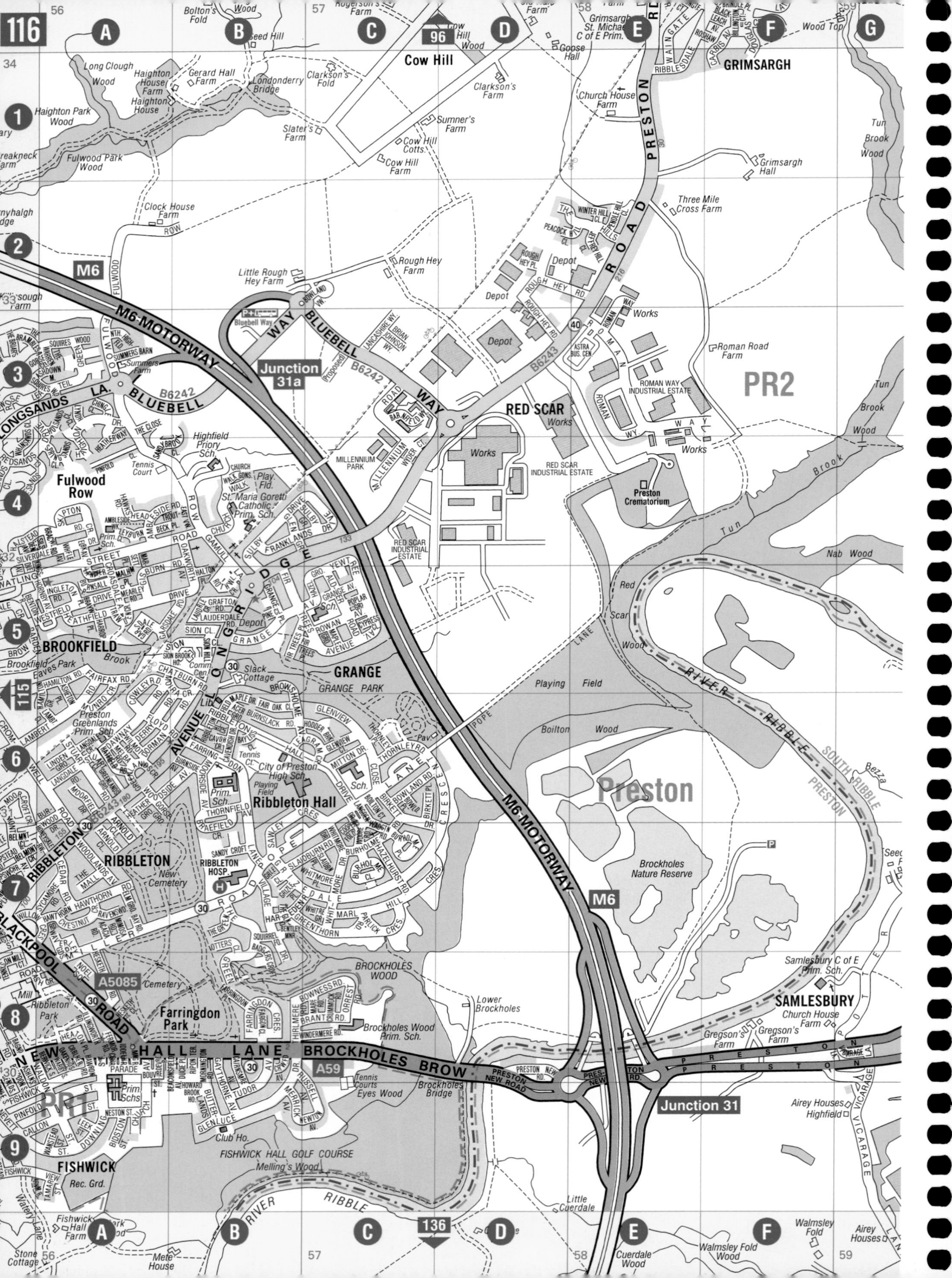

Cow Hill
GRIMSARGH
Haighton Park Wood
Fulwood Park Wood
Long Clough Wood
Haighton House Farm
Gerard Hall Farm
Londonderry Bridge
Clarkson's Fold
Clarkson's Farm
Slater's Farm
Sumner's Farm
Cow Hill Cotts.
Cow Hill Farm
Church House Farm
Grimsargh Hall
Three Mile Cross Farm
Clock House Farm
Little Rough Hey Farm
Rough Hey Farm
M6
M6 MOTORWAY
Junction 31a
BLUEBELL WAY
B6242
B6243
PRESTON ROAD
ROMAN ROAD
Roman Road Farm
ROMAN WAY INDUSTRIAL ESTATE
RED SCAR
RED SCAR INDUSTRIAL ESTATE
MILLENNIUM PARK
Preston Crematorium
PR2
Tun Brook Wood
Nab Wood
Red Scar Wood
Playing Field
Boilton Wood
RIVER RIBBLE
Preston
Brockholes Nature Reserve
Fulwood Row
LONGSANDS LA.
Highfield Priory Sch.
St. Maria Goretti Catholic Prim. Sch.
BROOKFIELD
GRANGE
GRANGE PARK
LONGRIDGE ROAD
City of Preston High Sch.
Ribbleton Hall
RIBBLETON
RIBBLETON HOSP.
New Cemetery
BLACKPOOL ROAD
A5085
Farringdon Park
BROCKHOLES WOOD
Lower Brockholes
Brockholes Wood Prim. Sch.
NEW HALL LANE
BROCKHOLES BROW
A59
PRESTON NEW ROAD
Junction 31
Brockholes Bridge
Eyes Wood
FISHWICK HALL GOLF COURSE
Melling's Wood
FISHWICK
PR1
SAMLESBURY
Samlesbury C of E Prim. Sch.
Gregson's Farm
Airey Houses
Highfield
Little Cuerdale
Cuerdale Wood
Walmsley Fold Wood
Walmsley Fold
Fishwick Hall Farm
Stone Cottage
Mete House

96
115
136

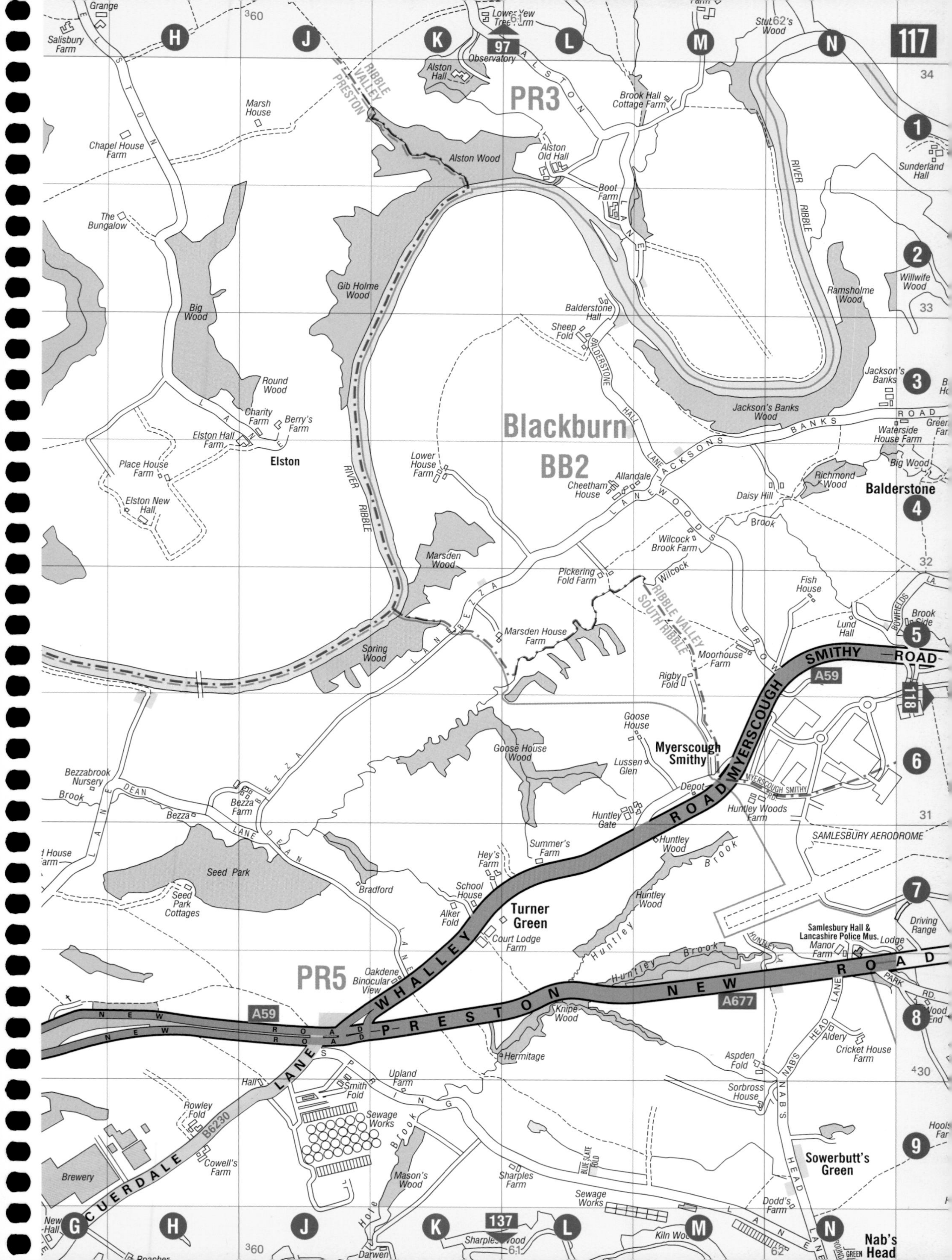
PR3
Blackburn
BB2
PR5
Alston Wood
Alston Hall
Alston Old Hall
Brook Hall Cottage Farm
Boot Farm
Marsh House
Chapel House Farm
The Bungalow
Big Wood
Gib Holme Wood
Round Wood
Charity Farm
Berry's Farm
Elston Hall Farm
Elston
Place House Farm
Elston New Hall
Balderstone Hall
Sheep Fold
Ramsholme Wood
Willwife Wood
Sunderland Hall
Jackson's Banks
Jackson's Banks Wood
Waterside House Farm
Big Wood
Richmond Wood
Balderstone
Daisy Hill
Lower House Farm
Allandale
Cheetham House
Wilcock Brook Farm
Pickering Fold Farm
Marsden Wood
Marsden House Farm
Spring Wood
Fish House
Lund Hall
Moorhouse Farm
Rigby Fold
Goose House
Myerscough Smithy
Goose House Wood
Lussen Glen
Depot
Huntley Gate
Huntley Woods Farm
SAMLESBURY AERODROME
Huntley Wood
Summer's Farm
Hey's Farm
School House
Turner Green
Alker Fold
Court Lodge Farm
Bezzabrook Nursery
Bezza Farm
Seed Park
Seed Park Cottages
Bradford
Samlesbury Hall & Lancashire Police Mus.
Manor Farm
Lodge
Driving Range
Oakdene Binocular View
Knipe Wood
Hermitage
Aspden Fold
Aldery
Cricket House Farm
Sorbross House
Hall
Smith Fold
Upland Farm
Rowley Fold
Sewage Works
Brewery
Cowell's Farm
Mason's Wood
Sharples Farm
Sowerbutt's Green
Dodd's Farm
Sharples Wood
Kiln Wood
Nab's Head
Salisbury Farm
Grange
Lower Yew Tree Farm
Observatory
Stut's Wood
RIVER RIBBLE
RIBBLE VALLEY
PRESTON
SOUTH RIBBLE
SMITHY ROAD
MYERSCOUGH ROAD
WHALLEY NEW ROAD
PRESTON NEW ROAD
CUERDALE LANE
B6230
A59
A677
JACKSONS BANKS ROAD
BALDERSTONE HALL LANE
WOODS BROW
BEZZA LANE
DEAN LANE
ALSTON LANE
ELSTON LANE
NAB'S HEAD LANE
97
118
137
Darwen

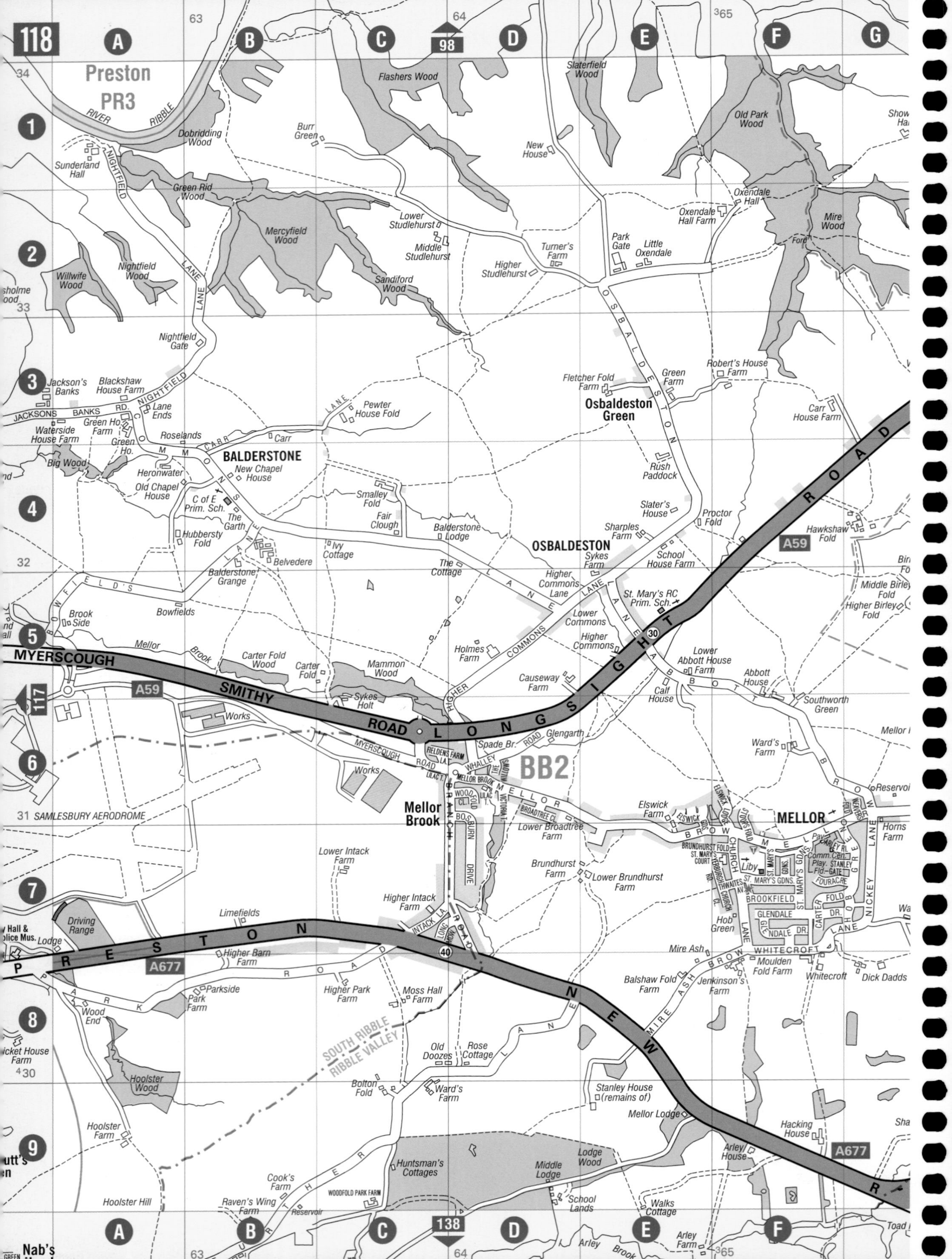
Preston
PR3
River Ribble
Dobridding Wood
Sunderland Hall
Green Rid Wood
Mercyfield Wood
Flashers Wood
Burr Green
Slaterfield Wood
New House
Old Park Wood
Oxendale Hall
Oxendale Hall Farm
Mire Wood
Lower Studlehurst
Middle Studlehurst
Higher Studlehurst
Turner's Farm
Park Gate
Little Oxendale
Willwife Wood
Nightfield Wood
Sandiford Wood
Nightfield Gate
Jackson's Banks
Blackshaw House Farm
Lane Ends
Pewter House Fold
Fletcher Fold Farm
Green Farm
Robert's House Farm
Osbaldeston Green
Carr House Farm
Waterside House Farm
Green Ho. Farm
Green Ho.
Roselands
Carr
BALDERSTONE
Big Wood
Heronwater
New Chapel House
Rush Paddock
Old Chapel House
C of E Prim. Sch.
The Garth
Smalley Fold
Fair Clough
Slater's House
Proctor Fold
Hubbersty Fold
Balderstone Lodge
Sharples Farm
Hawkshaw Fold
Ivy Cottage
Belvedere
OSBALDESTON
Sykes Farm
School House Farm
A59
Balderstone Grange
The Cottage
Higher Commons Lane
St. Mary's RC Prim. Sch.
Middle Birley Fold
Higher Birley Fold
Brook Side
Bowfields
Lower Commons
Higher Commons
Mellor Brook
Carter Fold Wood
Carter Fold
Mammon Wood
Holmes Farm
Lower Abbott House Farm
Abbott House
MYERSCOUGH SMITHY ROAD
LONGSIGHT ROAD
Causeway Farm
Calf House
Southworth Green
117
Sykes Holt
Works
Glengarth
Spade Br.
Ward's Farm
BB2
Fieldens Farm
Whalley Road
Mellor Brook
Myerscough Road
Reservoir
SAMLESBURY AERODROME
Mellor Brook
Elswick Farm
MELLOR
Horns Farm
Lower Broadtree Farm
Lower Intact Farm
Brundhurst Farm
Lower Brundhurst Farm
Higher Intack Farm
Limefields
Driving Range
Hob Green
Mire Ash
Whitecroft
PRESTON NEW ROAD
A677
Higher Barn Farm
Parkside
Park Farm
Higher Park Farm
Moss Hall Farm
Balshaw Fold Farm
Jenkinson's Farm
Moulden Fold Farm
Dick Dadds
Wood End
South Ribble
Ribble Valley
Old Doozes
Rose Cottage
Holster Wood
Bolton Fold
Ward's Farm
Stanley House (remains of)
Mellor Lodge
Hacking House
Hoolster Farm
Huntsman's Cottages
Middle Lodge
Lodge Wood
Arley House
Cook's Farm
School Lands
Walks Cottage
Hoolster Hill
Raven's Wing Farm
Reservoir
Woodfold Park Farm
138
98
Arley Brook
Arley Farm
Nab's

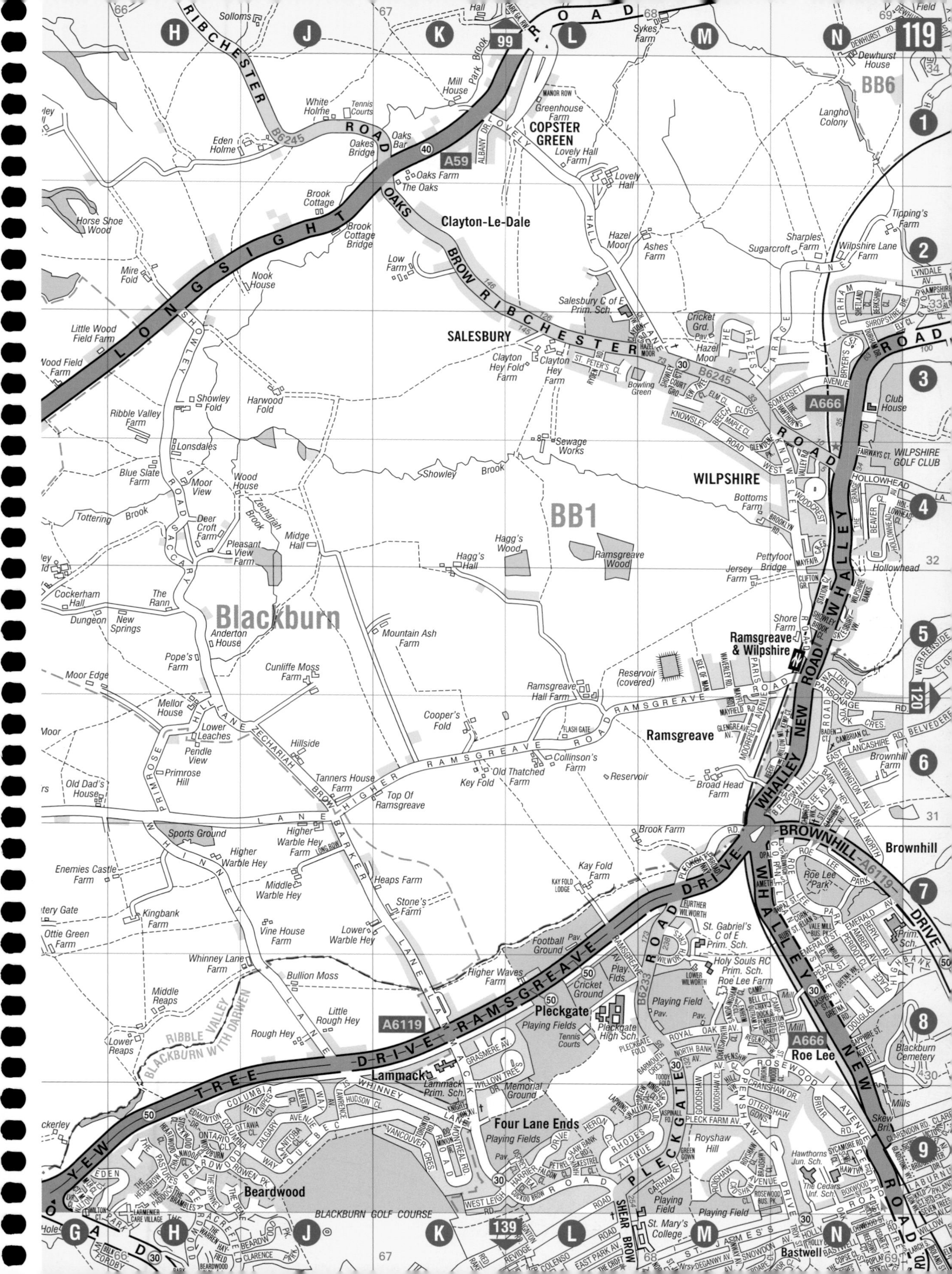
Blackburn
BB1
BB6
Clayton-Le-Dale
COPSTER GREEN
SALESBURY
WILPSHIRE
Ramsgreave
Brownhill
Roe Lee
Pleckgate
Lammack
Four Lane Ends
Beardwood
Bastwell
Ramsgreave & Wilpshire
LONGSIGHT ROAD
RIBCHESTER ROAD
OAKS BROW
WHALLEY NEW ROAD
RAMSGREAVE DRIVE
YEW TREE DRIVE
A59
A666
A6119
B6245
B6233
BLACKBURN GOLF COURSE
RIBBLE VALLEY
BLACKBURN WITH DARWEN
99
139
120

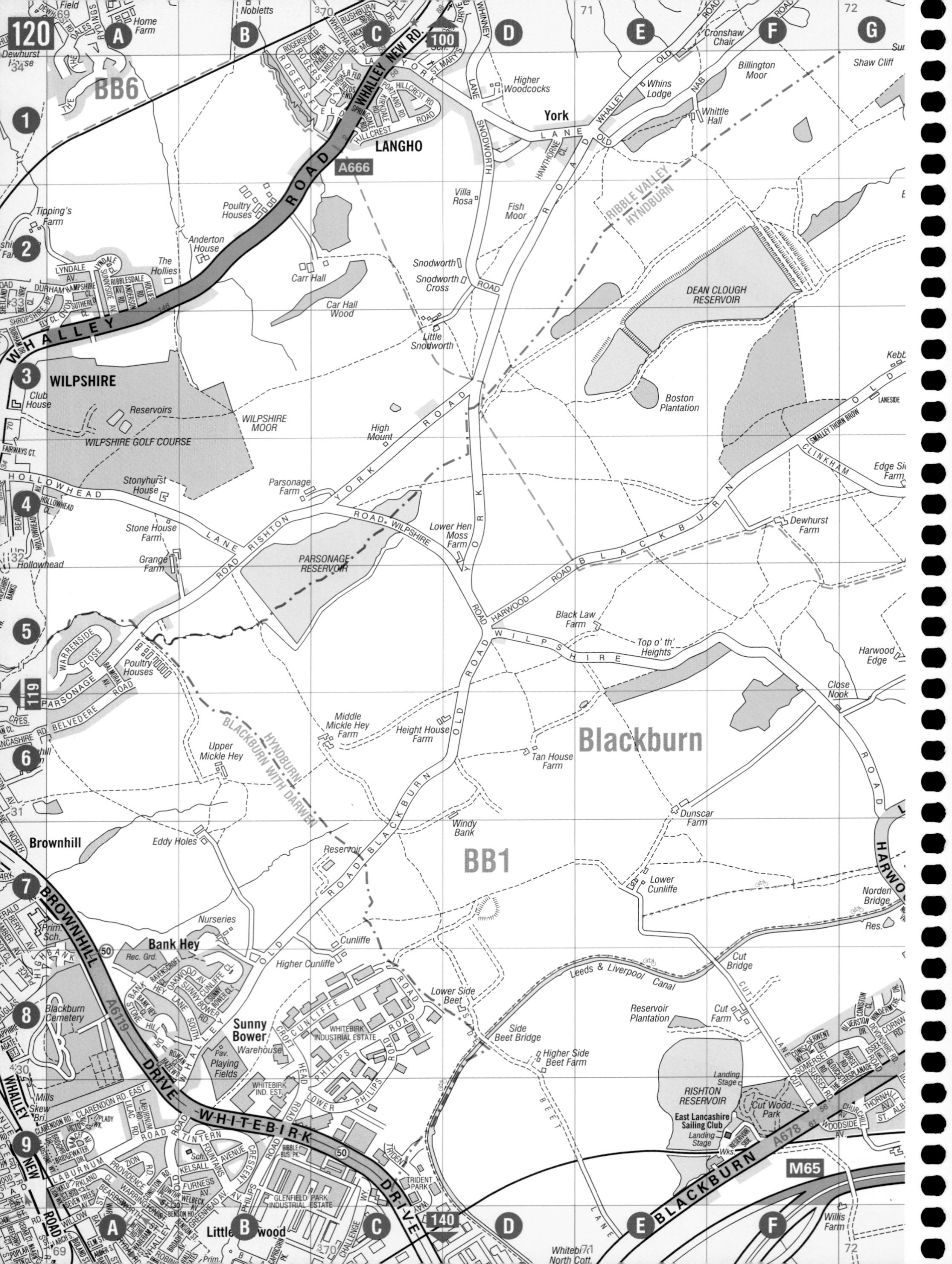

BB6
LANGHO
York
WILPSHIRE
Blackburn
BB1
Brownhill
Bank Hey
Sunny Bower
WHALLEY NEW RD.
WHALLEY ROAD
A666
A6119
A678
M65
WHITEBIRK DRIVE
BLACKBURN ROAD
YORK ROAD
SNODWORTH ROAD
WILPSHIRE ROAD
RISHTON ROAD
HOLLOWHEAD LANE
HARWOOD ROAD
OLD WHALLEY
YORK LANE
Leeds & Liverpool Canal
DEAN CLOUGH RESERVOIR
PARSONAGE RESERVOIR
RISHTON RESERVOIR
WILPSHIRE GOLF COURSE
WILPSHIRE MOOR
RIBBLE VALLEY
HYNDBURN
BLACKBURN WITH DARWEN
WHITEBIRK INDUSTRIAL ESTATE
GLENFIELD PARK INDUSTRIAL ESTATE
Higher Woodcocks
Whins Lodge
Whittle Hall
Billington Moor
Shaw Cliff
Cronshaw Chair
Home Farm
Nobletts
Dewhurst House
Tipping's Farm
Anderton House
The Hollies
Poultry Houses
Carr Hall
Car Hall Wood
Villa Rosa
Fish Moor
Snodworth
Snodworth Cross
Little Snodworth
Boston Plantation
High Mount
Parsonage Farm
Stonyhurst House
Stone House Farm
Grange Farm
Hollowhead
Lower Hen Moss Farm
Dewhurst Farm
Edge Side Farm
Black Law Farm
Top o' th' Heights
Harwood Edge
Close Nook
Middle Mickle Hey Farm
Height House Farm
Tan House Farm
Upper Mickle Hey
Eddy Holes
Windy Bank
Dunscar Farm
Reservoir
Lower Cunliffe
Norden Bridge
Cunliffe
Higher Cunliffe
Nurseries
Lower Side Beet
Side Beet Bridge
Higher Side Beet Farm
Cut Bridge
Cut Farm
Reservoir Plantation
Cut Wood Park
East Lancashire Sailing Club
Blackburn Cemetery
Playing Fields
Warehouse
Mills
Skew Bri.
Trident Park
Willis Farm
Whitebirk North Cott.
Little Harwood

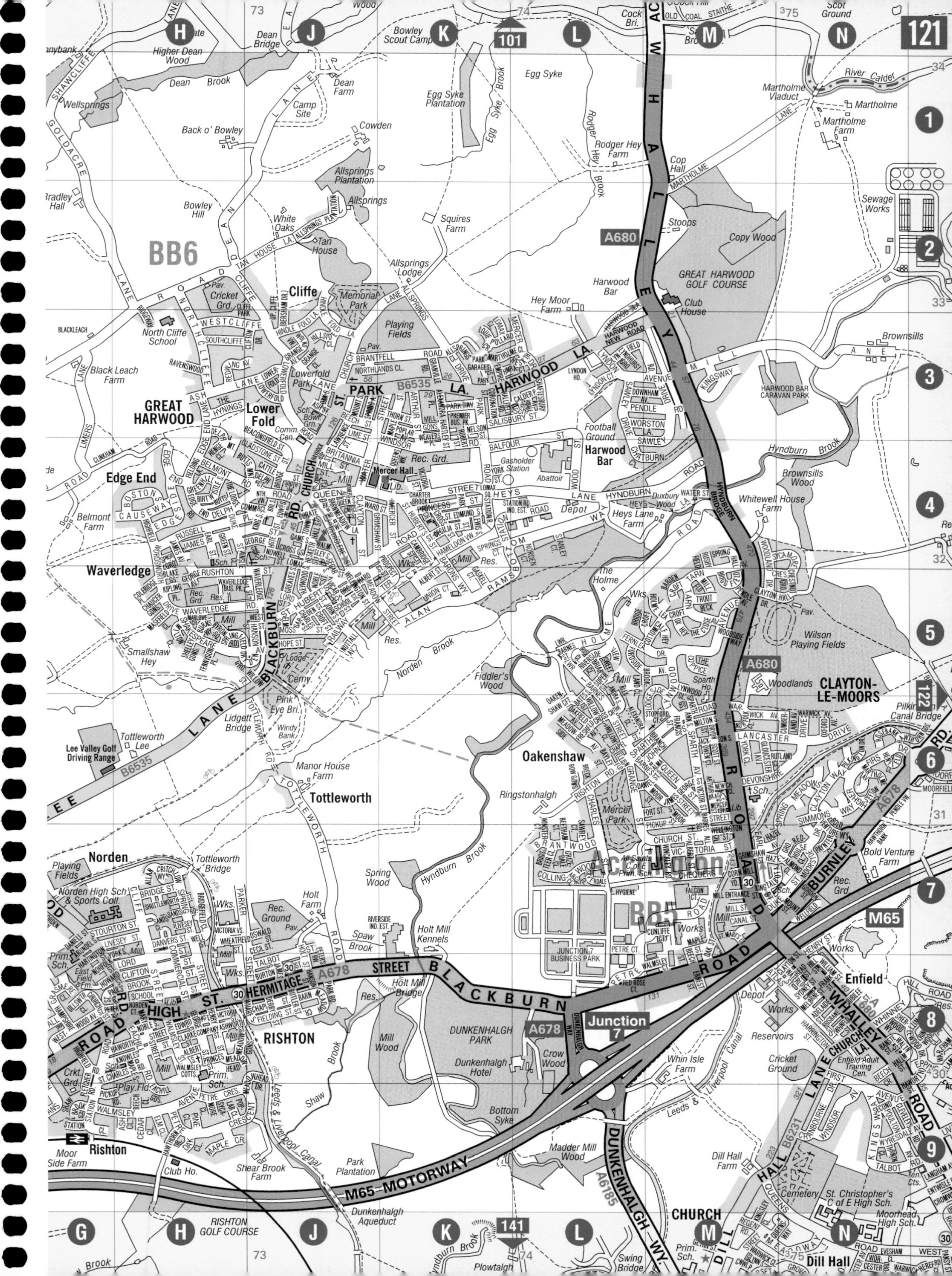

BB6
BB5
Higher Dean Wood
Dean Bridge
Bowley Scout Camp
Dean Brook
Dean Farm
Camp Site
Wellsprings
Back o' Bowley
Cowden
Egg Syke Plantation
Egg Syke
Rodger Hey Farm
Cop Hall
Martholme Viaduct
Martholme
Martholme Farm
River Calder
Bradley Hall
Bowley Hill
Allsprings Plantation
Allsprings
White Oaks
Tan House
Squires Farm
Stoops
A680
Copy Wood
Sewage Works
Allsprings Lodge
GREAT HARWOOD GOLF COURSE
Harwood Bar
Hey Moor Farm
Club House
Cliffe
Cricket Grd.
Memorial Park
Playing Fields
North Cliffe School
Brownsills
Black Leach Farm
Lowerfold Park
HARWOOD BAR CARAVAN PARK
GREAT HARWOOD
Lower Fold
B6535
Football Ground
Harwood Bar
Mercer Hall
Rec. Grd.
Gasholder Station
Abattoir
Hyndburn Brook
Brownsills Wood
Edge End
Whitewell House Farm
Duxbury Wood
Heys Lane Farm
Depot
Belmont Farm
Waverledge
The Holme
Smallshaw Hey
Cemy.
Wilson Playing Fields
Woodlands
CLAYTON-LE-MOORS
Norden Brook
Fiddler's Wood
Pink Eye Bri.
Lidgett Bridge
Windy Bank
Tottleworth Lee
Lee Valley Golf Driving Range
Manor House Farm
Tottleworth
Oakenshaw
Ringstonhalgh
Mercer Park
Pilkington Canal Bridge
Bold Venture Farm
Accrington
Norden
Playing Fields
Tottleworth Bridge
Norden High Sch. & Sports Coll.
Spring Wood
Hyndburn Brook
Holt Farm
Rec. Ground
RIVERSIDE IND. EST.
Spaw Brook
Holt Mill Kennels
JUNCTION 7 BUSINESS PARK
Works
Enfield
M65
Holt Mill Bridge
BLACKBURN ROAD
A678
HIGH ST.
HERMITAGE STREET
RISHTON
Mill Wood
DUNKENHALGH PARK
Dunkenhalgh Hotel
Crow Wood
Junction 7
Reservoirs
Whin Isle Farm
Cricket Ground
Enfield Adult Training Cen.
Leeds & Liverpool Canal
Bottom Syke
Madder Mill Wood
A6185
DUNKENHALGH WAY
Dill Hall Farm
Moor Side Farm
Rishton
Club Ho.
Shear Brook Farm
Park Plantation
M65 MOTORWAY
Cemetery
St. Christopher's C of E High Sch.
Moorhead High Sch.
RISHTON GOLF COURSE
Dunkenhalgh Aqueduct
CHURCH
Swing Bridge
Plowtalgh
Dill Hall
WHALLEY ROAD
BURNLEY ROAD
101
141
122

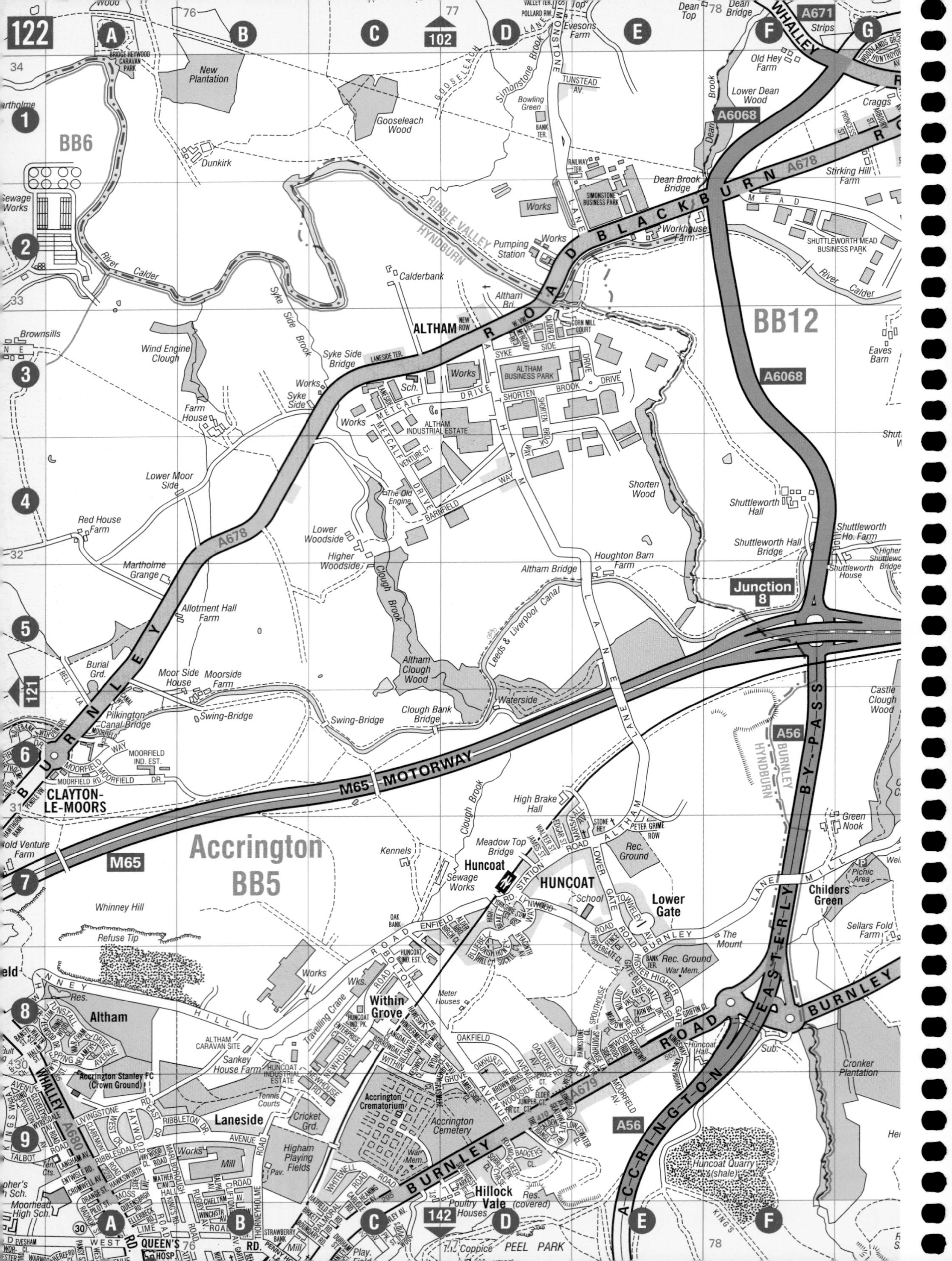

A
B
C
D
E
F
G
102
142
121
1
2
3
4
5
6
7
8
9
New Plantation
Gooseleach Wood
BB6
Dunkirk
Sewage Works
River Calder
RIBBLE VALLEY
HYNDBURN
Evesons Farm
Old Hey Farm
Lower Dean Wood
A671
A6068
A678
BLACKBURN ROAD
Dean Brook Bridge
Simonstone Business Park
Workhouse Farm
Pumping Station
Shuttleworth Mead Business Park
Calderbank
Altham Bri.
ALTHAM
BB12
Brownsills
Wind Engine Clough
Syke Side Bridge
Altham Business Park
Altham Industrial Estate
Eaves Barn
Shorten Wood
Shuttleworth Hall
Shuttleworth Hall Bridge
Lower Moor Side
Red House Farm
Martholme Grange
Lower Woodside
Higher Woodside
Houghton Barn Farm
Altham Bridge
Junction 8
Allotment Hall Farm
Leeds & Liverpool Canal
Altham Clough Wood
Burial Grd.
Moor Side House
Moorside Farm
Waterside
Pilkington Canal Bridge
Swing-Bridge
Clough Bank Bridge
Castle Clough Wood
A56
BURNLEY BY-PASS
M65 MOTORWAY
CLAYTON-LE-MOORS
High Brake Hall
Accrington BB5
M65
Kennels
Meadow Top Bridge
Huncoat
Sewage Works
HUNCOAT
Lower Gate
Green Nook
Childers Green
Sellars Fold Farm
Whinney Hill
Refuse Tip
Works
Within Grove
Altham
Travelling Crane
Altham Caravan Site
Sankey House Farm
Accrington Stanley FC (Crown Ground)
Huncoat Industrial Estate
Accrington Crematorium
Accrington Cemetery
Laneside
Cricket Grd.
Higham Playing Fields
Cronker Plantation
Huncoat Quarry (shale)
Hillock Vale
Poultry Houses
Res. (covered)
Mill
BURNLEY ROAD
A679
A680
ACCRINGTON EASTERLY
QUEEN'S HOSP.
Coppice
PEEL PARK
Moorhead High Sch.

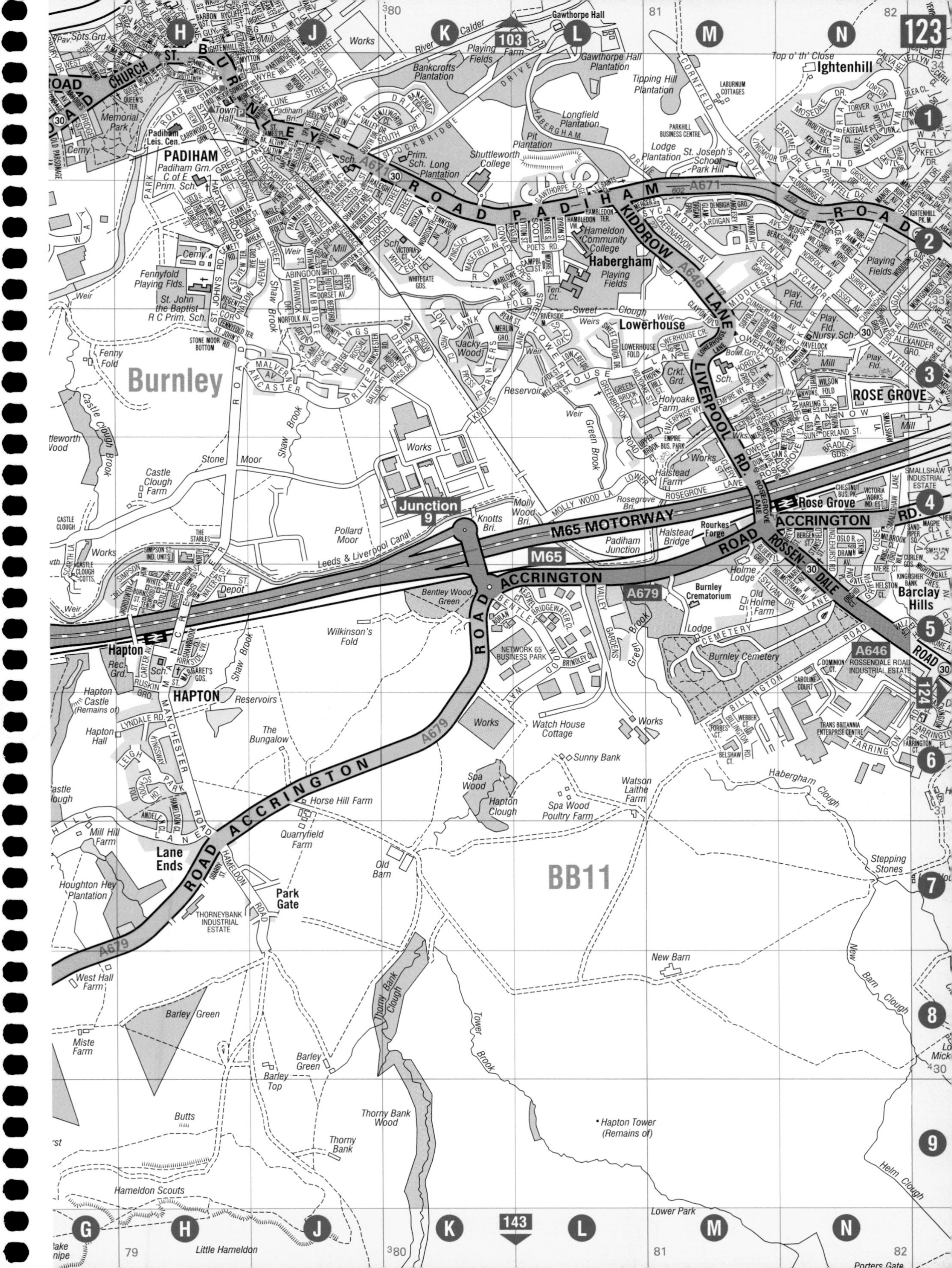

Gawthorpe Hall
103
Works
Playing Fields
Bankcrofts Plantation
Gawthorpe Hall Plantation
Top o' th' Close
Ightenhill
Tipping Hill Plantation
Longfield Plantation
Pit Plantation
Lodge Plantation
St. Joseph's School Park Hill
Shuttleworth College
Prim. Sch. Long Plantation
PADIHAM
Padiham Grn. C of E Prim. Sch.
Padiham Leis. Cen.
Memorial Park
Town Hall
Cemy.
PADIHAM ROAD
A671
KIDDROW LANE
A646
LIVERPOOL RD.
Hameldon Community College
Habergham
Playing Fields
Fennyfold Playing Flds.
St. John the Baptist R C Prim. Sch.
Lowerhouse
Sweet Clough
Burnley
Fenny Fold
Jacky Wood
Reservoir
Holyoake Farm
ROSE GROVE
Castle Clough Brook
Castle Clough Farm
Stone Moor
Shaw Brook
Works
Junction 9
Pollard Moor
Knotts Bri.
Molly Wood Bri.
M65 MOTORWAY
M65
Padiham Junction
Halstead Bridge
Rourkes Forge
Rose Grove
ACCRINGTON RD.
ROSSENDALE ROAD
Leeds & Liverpool Canal
ACCRINGTON ROAD
A679
Bentley Wood Green
Burnley Crematorium
Holme Lodge
Old Holme Farm
Barclay Hills
Wilkinson's Fold
Hapton
HAPTON
Hapton Castle (Remains of)
Hapton Hall
NETWORK 65 BUSINESS PARK
Burnley Cemetery
ROSSENDALE ROAD INDUSTRIAL ESTATE
TRANS BRITANNIA ENTERPRISE CENTRE
Reservoirs
The Bungalow
Watch House Cottage
Sunny Bank
Spa Wood
Hapton Clough
Watson Laithe Farm
Spa Wood Poultry Farm
Habergham Clough
Horse Hill Farm
Quarryfield Farm
Mill Hill Farm
Lane Ends
Old Barn
BB11
Stepping Stones
Houghton Hey Plantation
Park Gate
THORNEYBANK INDUSTRIAL ESTATE
West Hall Farm
New Barn
New Barn Clough
Barley Green
Miste Farm
Thorny Bank Clough
Tower Brook
Barley Green
Barley Top
Thorny Bank Wood
Butts
Hapton Tower (Remains of)
Thorny Bank
Helm Clough
Hameldon Scouts
Lower Park
Little Hameldon
143
124
79
380
81
82

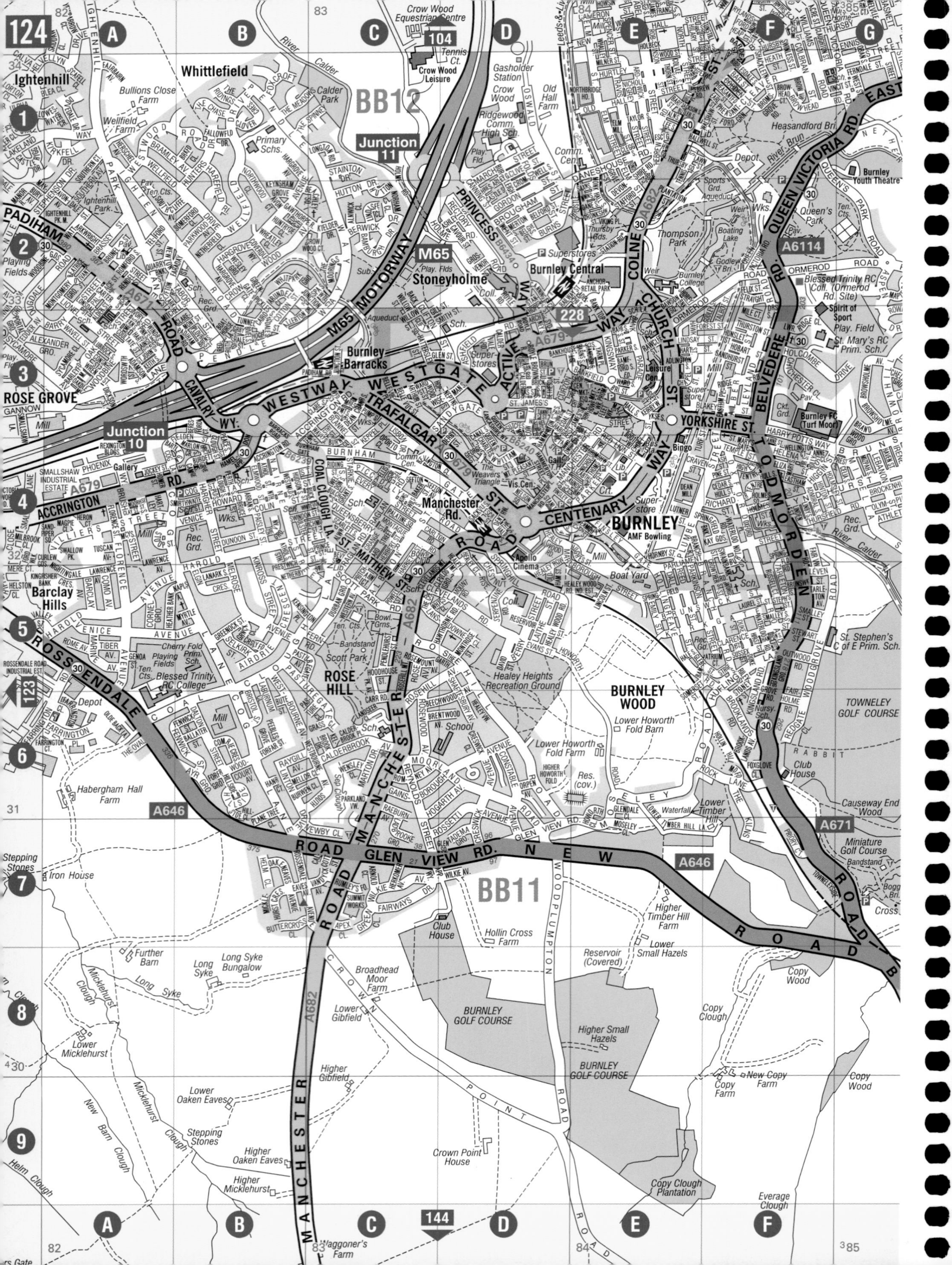
Ightenhill
Whittlefield
BB12
Junction 11
M65
Stoneyholme
Burnley Central
Burnley Barracks
ROSE GROVE
Junction 10
Manchester Rd.
BURNLEY
Barclay Hills
ROSE HILL
Healey Heights Recreation Ground
BURNLEY WOOD
TOWNELEY GOLF COURSE
BB11
BURNLEY GOLF COURSE
Queen's Park
Thompson Park
Scott Park
Burnley FC (Turf Moor)
A646
A682
A671
A679
A6114
104
228
123
144

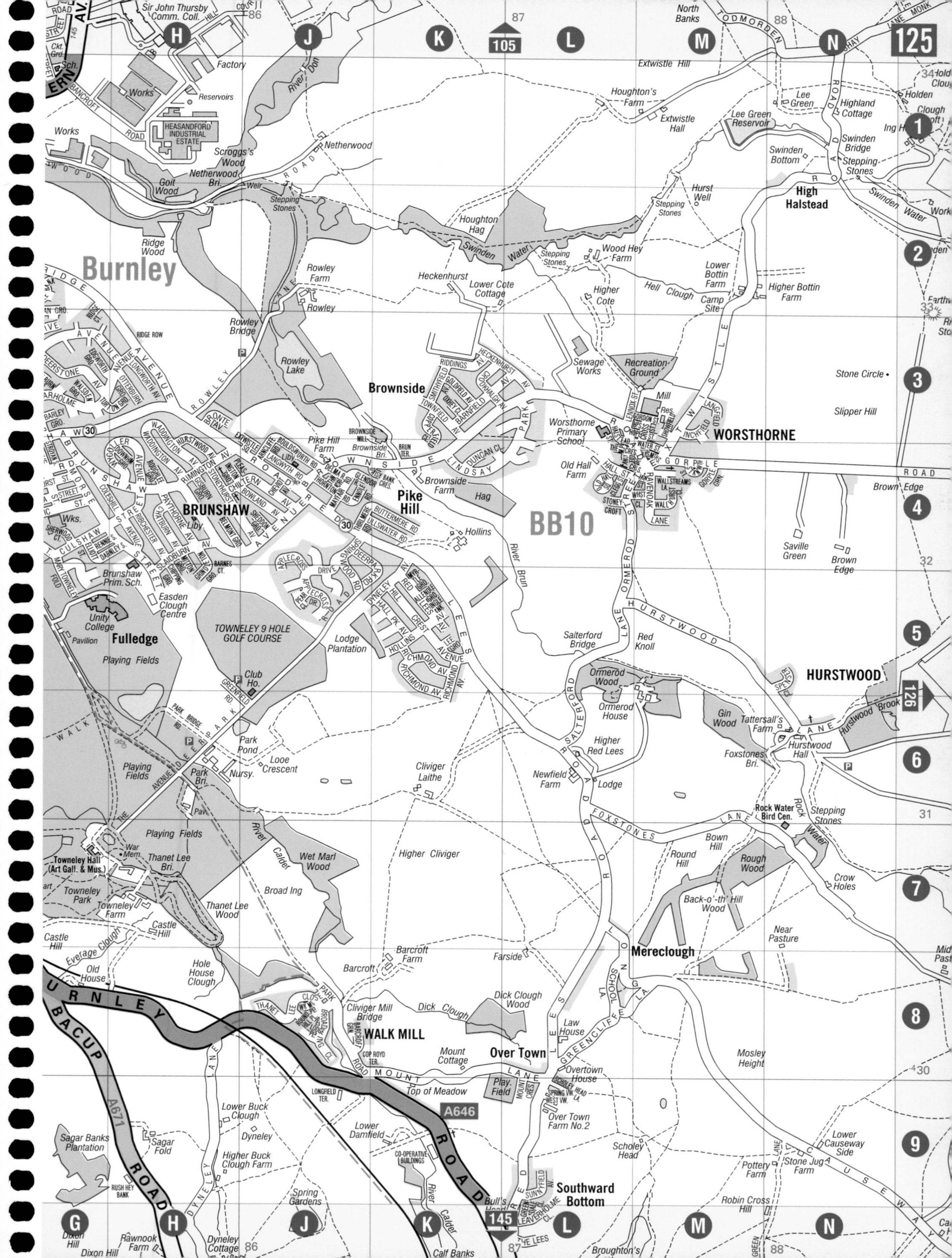
Burnley
BRUNSHAW
Fulledge
Brownside
Pike Hill
WORSTHORNE
BB10
HURSTWOOD
High Halstead
Mereclough
WALK MILL
Over Town
Southward Bottom
TOWNELEY 9 HOLE GOLF COURSE
HEASANDFORD INDUSTRIAL ESTATE
Towneley Hall (Art Gall. & Mus.)
Unity College
Brunshaw Prim. Sch.
Worsthorne Primary School
Rock Water Bird Cen.
Lee Green Reservoir
Rowley Lake
Swinden Water
River Brun
River Calder
Extwistle Hall
Hurstwood Hall
Stone Circle
Slipper Hill
Brown Edge
Saville Green
Salterford Bridge
Red Knoll
Ormerod Wood
Ormerod House
Higher Red Lees
Newfield Farm
Gin Wood
Tattersall's Farm
Foxstones Bri.
Higher Cliviger
Cliviger Laithe
Wet Marl Wood
Broad Ing
Round Hill
Rough Wood
Back-o'-th' Hill Wood
Crow Holes
Near Pasture
Mosley Height
Lower Causeway Side
Stone Jug Farm
Robin Cross Hill
Pottery Farm
Scholey Head
Dick Clough Wood
Barcroft Farm
Farside
Law House
Overtown House
Over Town Farm No.2
Top of Meadow
Mount Cottage
Lower Damfield
Dyneley
Lower Buck Clough
Higher Buck Clough Farm
Sagar Banks Plantation
Sagar Fold
Spring Gardens
Dyneley Cottage
Rawnook Farm
Dixon Hill
Calf Banks
Broughton's
Thanet Lee Wood
Hole House Clough
Old House
Castle Hill
Towneley Farm
Towneley Park
Playing Fields
Park Pond
Looe Crescent
Lodge Plantation
Easden Clough Centre
Hollins
Hag
Brownside Farm
Old Hall Farm
Sewage Works
Recreation Ground
Higher Cote
Lower Cote Cottage
Heckenhurst
Wood Hey Farm
Lower Bottin Farm
Higher Bottin Farm
Hell Clough
Camp Site
Hurst Well
Houghton Hag
Houghton's Farm
Extwistle Hill
North Banks
Lee Green
Highland Cottage
Swinden Bridge
Swinden Bottom
Stepping Stones
Netherwood
Netherwood Bri.
Scroggs's Wood
Goit Wood
Ridge Wood
Rowley Farm
Rowley
Rowley Bridge
Factory
Works
Reservoirs
Sir John Thursby Comm. Coll.
A646
A671
BACUP ROAD
BURNLEY ROAD
TODMORDEN ROAD
GORPLE ROAD
HURSTWOOD LANE
FOXSTONES LANE
CAUSEWAY
MOUNT LANE
SALTERFORD LANE
ORMEROD ROAD
BRUNSHAW ROAD
BRUNSHAW AVENUE
ROWLEY LANE
DEERPARK ROAD
105
126
145
86
87
88
34
33
32
31
30
G H J K L M N
1 2 3 4 5 6 7 8 9

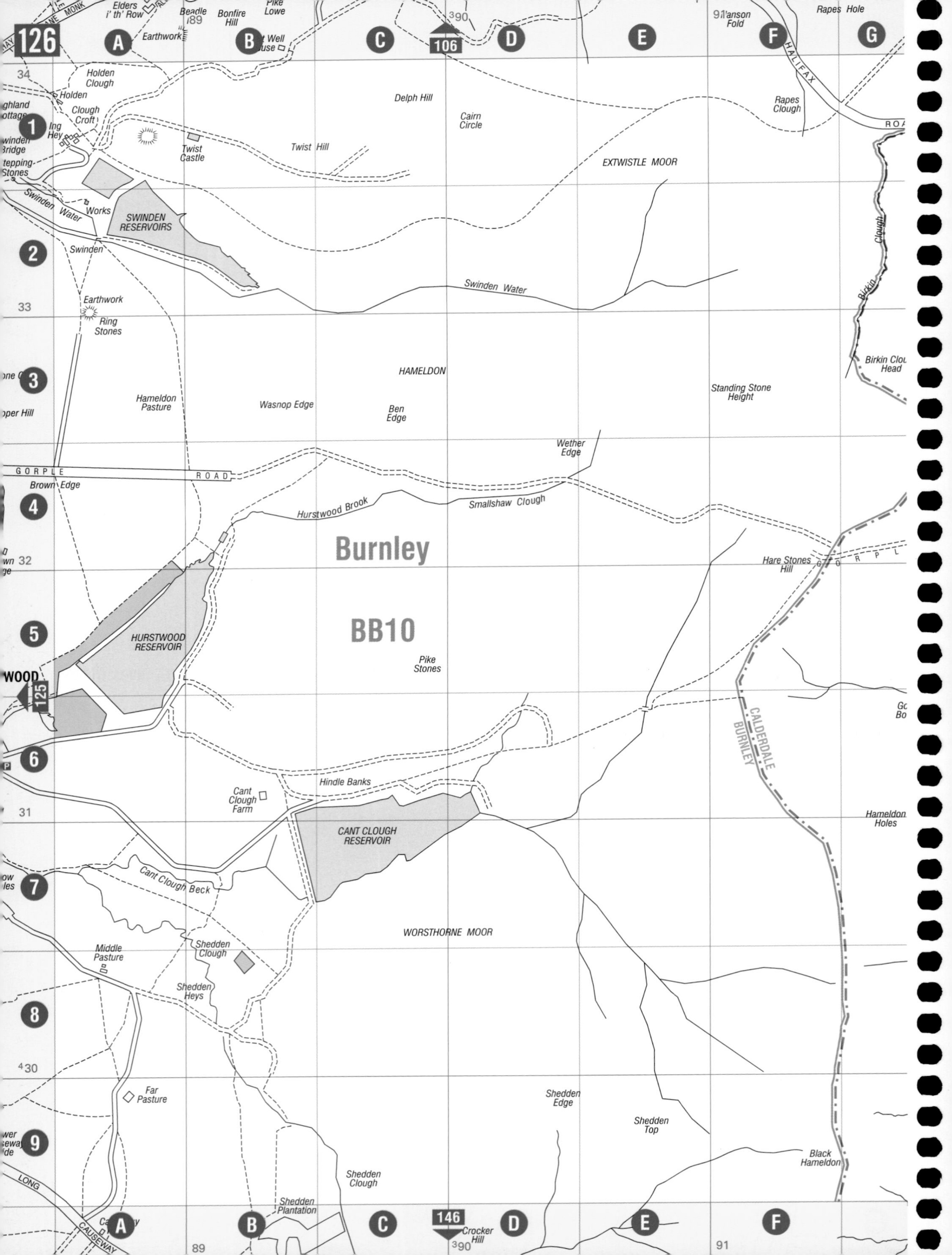
A
B
C
D
E
F
G
106
Elders i' th' Row
Beadle Hill
Bonfire Hill
Pike Lowe
Earthwork
Rapes Hole
Holden Clough
Holden
Clough Croft
Ing Hey
Delph Hill
Cairn Circle
Twist Castle
Twist Hill
Rapes Clough
HALIFAX
ROAD
EXTWISTLE MOOR
Stepping Stones
Swinden Water
Works
SWINDEN RESERVOIRS
Swinden
Swinden Water
Clough
Birkin
Earthwork
Ring Stones
HAMELDON
Birkin Clough Head
Hameldon Pasture
Wasnop Edge
Ben Edge
Standing Stone Height
Wether Edge
GORPLE ROAD
Brown Edge
Hurstwood Brook
Smallshaw Clough
Burnley
Hare Stones Hill
BB10
HURSTWOOD RESERVOIR
Pike Stones
125
CALDERDALE
BURNLEY
Hindle Banks
Cant Clough Farm
CANT CLOUGH RESERVOIR
Hameldon Holes
Cant Clough Beck
WORSTHORNE MOOR
Middle Pasture
Shedden Clough
Shedden Heys
Far Pasture
Shedden Edge
Shedden Top
Black Hameldon
Shedden Clough
Shedden Plantation
LONG CAUSEWAY
146
Crocker Hill
1
2
3
4
5
6
7
8
9
34
33
32
31
430
89
390
91

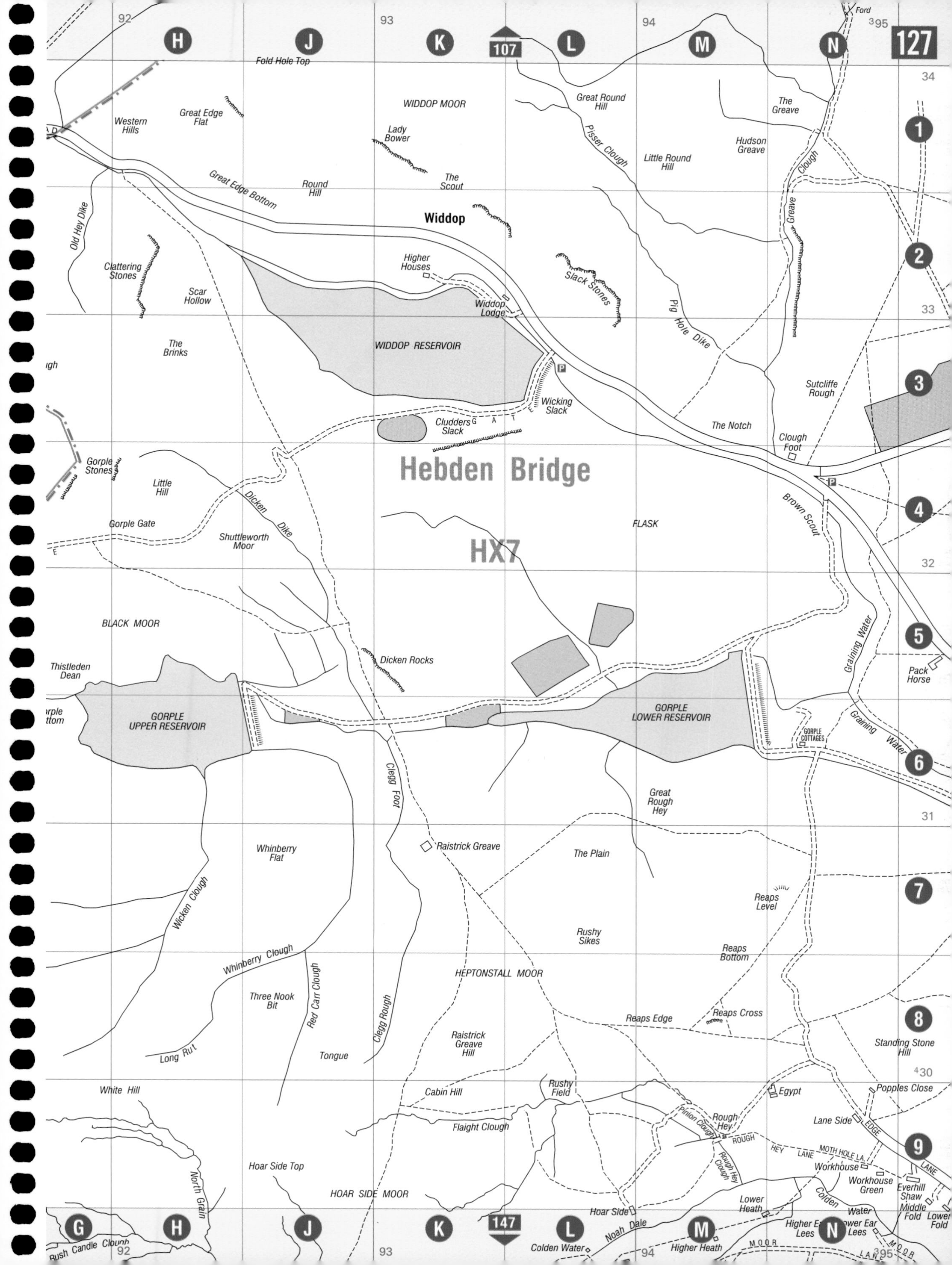

107
147
Hebden Bridge
HX7
Widdop
WIDDOP MOOR
WIDDOP RESERVOIR
GORPLE UPPER RESERVOIR
GORPLE LOWER RESERVOIR
GORPLE COTTAGES
Fold Hole Top
Western Hills
Great Edge Flat
Lady Bower
Great Round Hill
The Greave
Hudson Greave
Little Round Hill
Pisser Clough
Clough
Greave
Great Edge Bottom
Round Hill
The Scout
Old Hey Dike
Clattering Stones
Scar Hollow
Higher Houses
Widdop Lodge
Slack Stones
Pig Hole Dike
The Brinks
Sutcliffe Rough
Wicking Slack
Cludders Slack
GATE
The Notch
Clough Foot
Gorple Stones
Little Hill
Dicken Dike
Brown Scout
Gorple Gate
Shuttleworth Moor
FLASK
BLACK MOOR
Dicken Rocks
Thistleden Dean
Graining Water
Pack Horse
Clegg Foot
Great Rough Hey
Raistrick Greave
The Plain
Whinberry Flat
Wicken Clough
Reaps Level
Rushy Sikes
Reaps Bottom
Whinberry Clough
Red Carr Clough
Three Nook Bit
HEPTONSTALL MOOR
Clegg Rough
Reaps Edge
Reaps Cross
Standing Stone Hill
Raistrick Greave Hill
Long Rut
Tongue
White Hill
Cabin Hill
Rushy Field
Egypt
Popples Close
Pinion Clough
Rough Hey
Lane Side
EDGE
LANE
Flaight Clough
ROUGH HEY LANE
MOTH HOLE LA.
Workhouse
Rough Hey Clough
Hoar Side Top
Workhouse Green
Everhill Shaw
North Grain
HOAR SIDE MOOR
Lower Heath
Colden Water
Middle Fold
Lower Fold
Hoar Side
Noah Dale
Higher Ear Lees
Lower Ear Lees
Rush Candle Clough
Colden Water
Higher Heath
MOOR LANE
MOOR
Ford

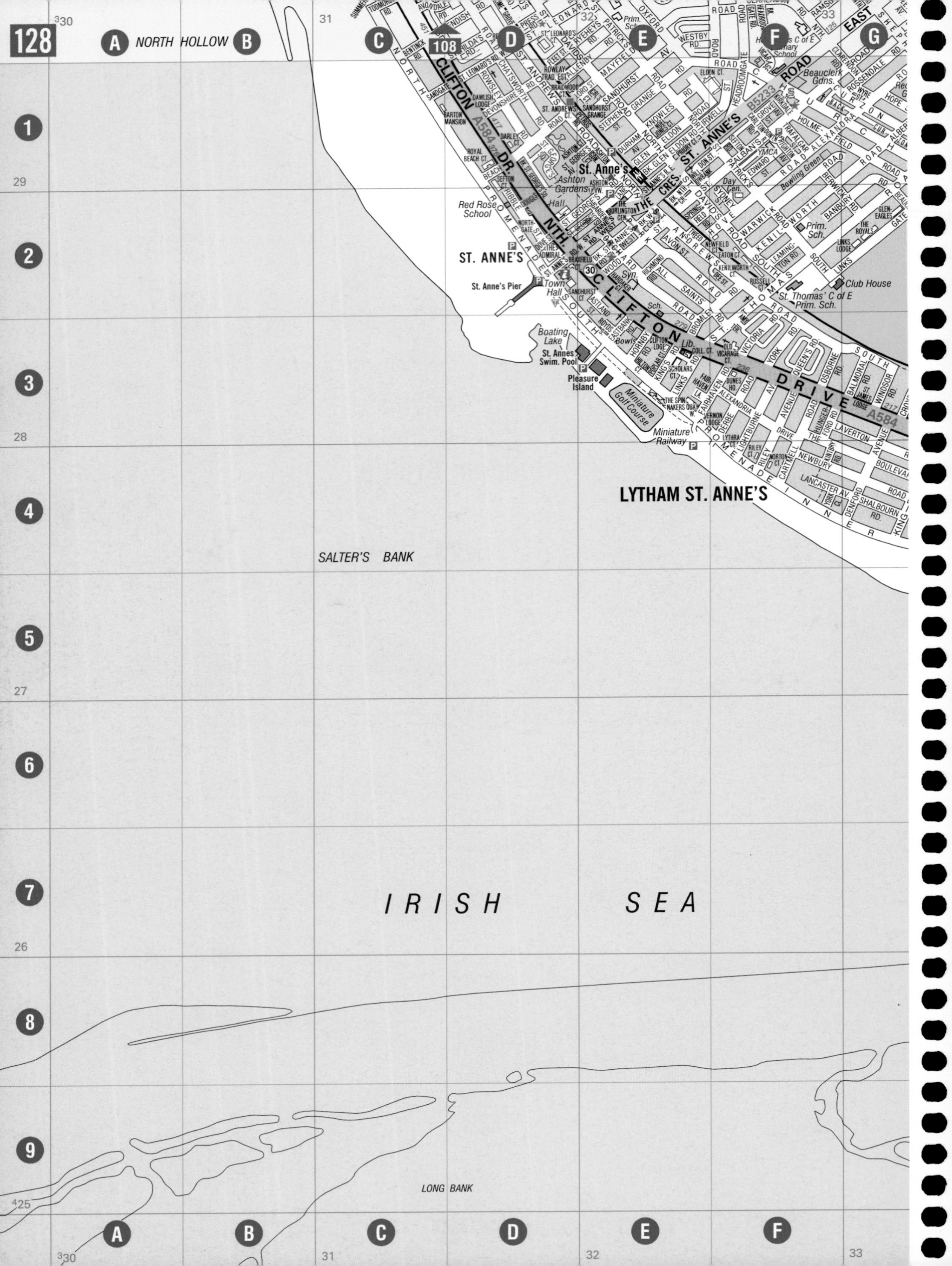

330

A NORTH HOLLOW B

31

C

108

D

E

F

G

29

1

2

ST. ANNE'S

St. Anne's Pier

Red Rose School

Ashton Gardens

3

28

Boating Lake
St. Annes Swim. Pool

Pleasure Island

Miniature Golf Course

Miniature Railway

LYTHAM ST. ANNE'S

4

SALTER'S BANK

5

27

6

7

IRISH   SEA

26

8

9

LONG BANK

425

330

A

B

31

C

D

32

E

F

33

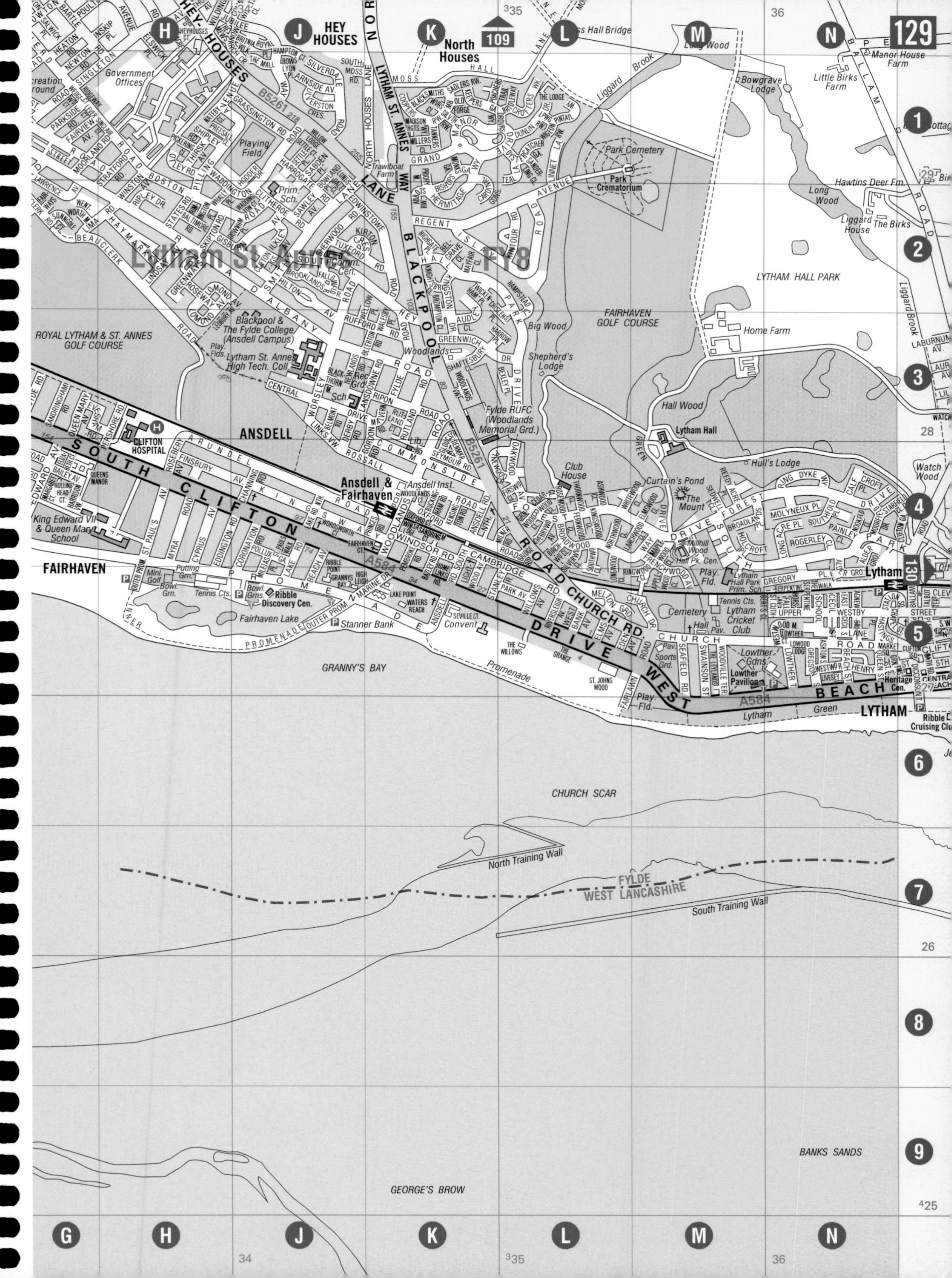
HEY HOUSES
North Houses
Lytham St. Annes
FY8
ROYAL LYTHAM & ST. ANNES GOLF COURSE
FAIRHAVEN GOLF COURSE
LYTHAM HALL PARK
Park Cemetery
Park Crematorium
Lytham Hall
ANSDELL
Ansdell & Fairhaven
FAIRHAVEN
Fairhaven Lake
CLIFTON HOSPITAL
King Edward VII & Queen Mary School
Blackpool & The Fylde College (Ansdell Campus)
Lytham St. Annes High Tech. Coll.
SOUTH CLIFTON DRIVE
WEST BEACH
CHURCH RD.
BLACKPOOL ROAD
LYTHAM ST. ANNES WAY
GRANNY'S BAY
CHURCH SCAR
North Training Wall
South Training Wall
FYLDE
WEST LANCASHIRE
BANKS SANDS
GEORGE'S BROW
LYTHAM
Lytham
Ribble Discovery Cen.
Lowther Pavilion
Heritage Cen.
109
130
G
H
J
K
L
M
N
1
2
3
4
5
6
7
8
9
34
335
36
28
26
425

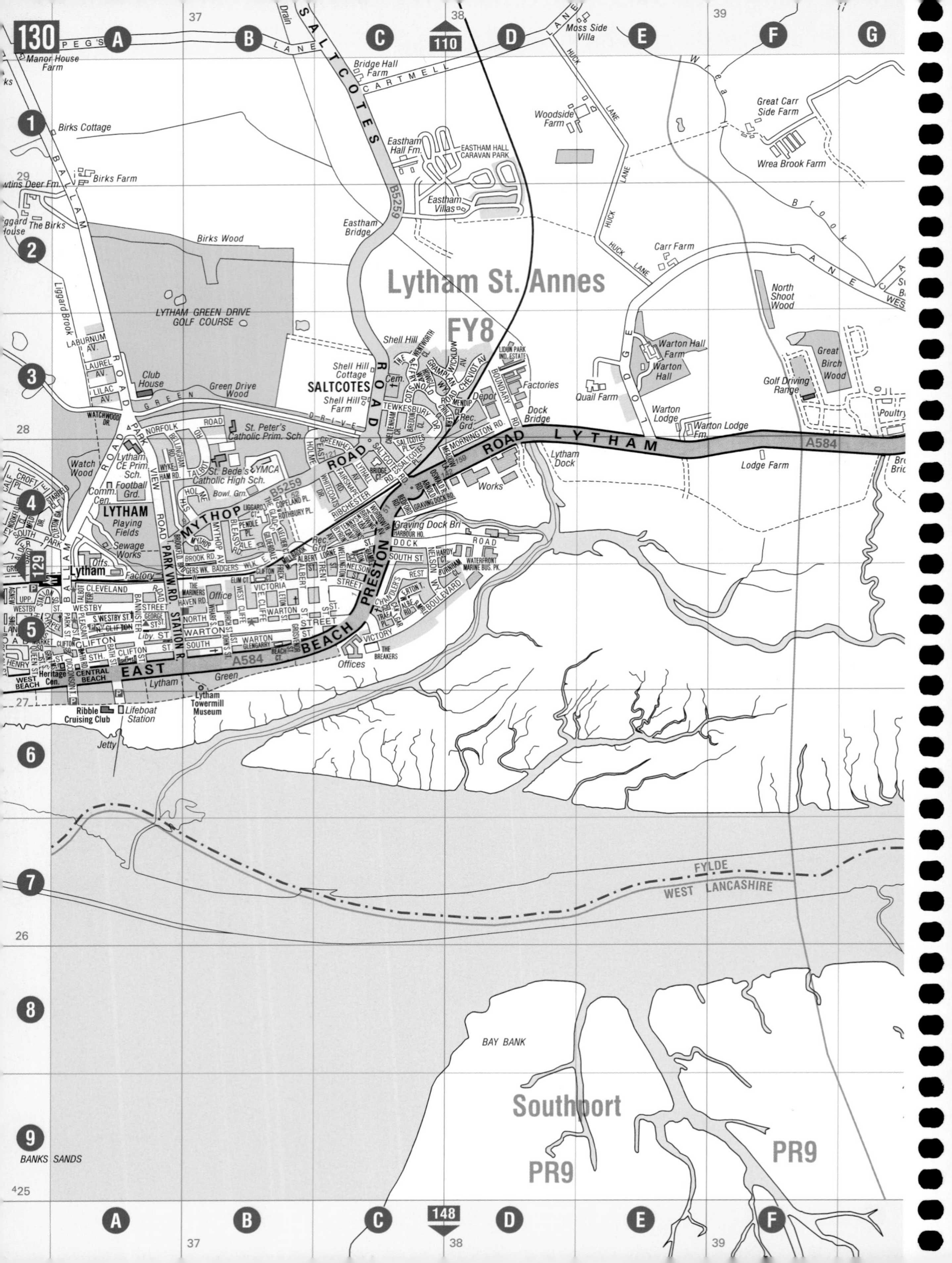
Lytham St. Annes
FY8
LYTHAM
SALTCOTES
Southport
PR9
PR9
Manor House Farm
Birks Cottage
Birks Farm
The Birks
Birks Wood
LYTHAM GREEN DRIVE GOLF COURSE
Club House
Green Drive Wood
Bridge Hall Farm
Eastham Hall Fm.
EASTHAM HALL CARAVAN PARK
Eastham Villas
Eastham Bridge
Moss Side Villa
Woodside Farm
Great Carr Side Farm
Wrea Brook Farm
Carr Farm
North Shoot Wood
Warton Hall Farm
Warton Hall
Great Birch Wood
Golf Driving Range
Quail Farm
Warton Lodge
Warton Lodge Fm.
Lodge Farm
Lytham Dock
Dock Bridge
Factories
Works
Graving Dock Bri
Shell Hill Cottage
Shell Hill Farm
Lytham Playing Fields
Sewage Works
Lifeboat Station
Ribble Cruising Club
Jetty
Lytham Towermill Museum
Offices
BAY BANK
BANKS SANDS
FYLDE
WEST LANCASHIRE
A584
B5259
110
129
148

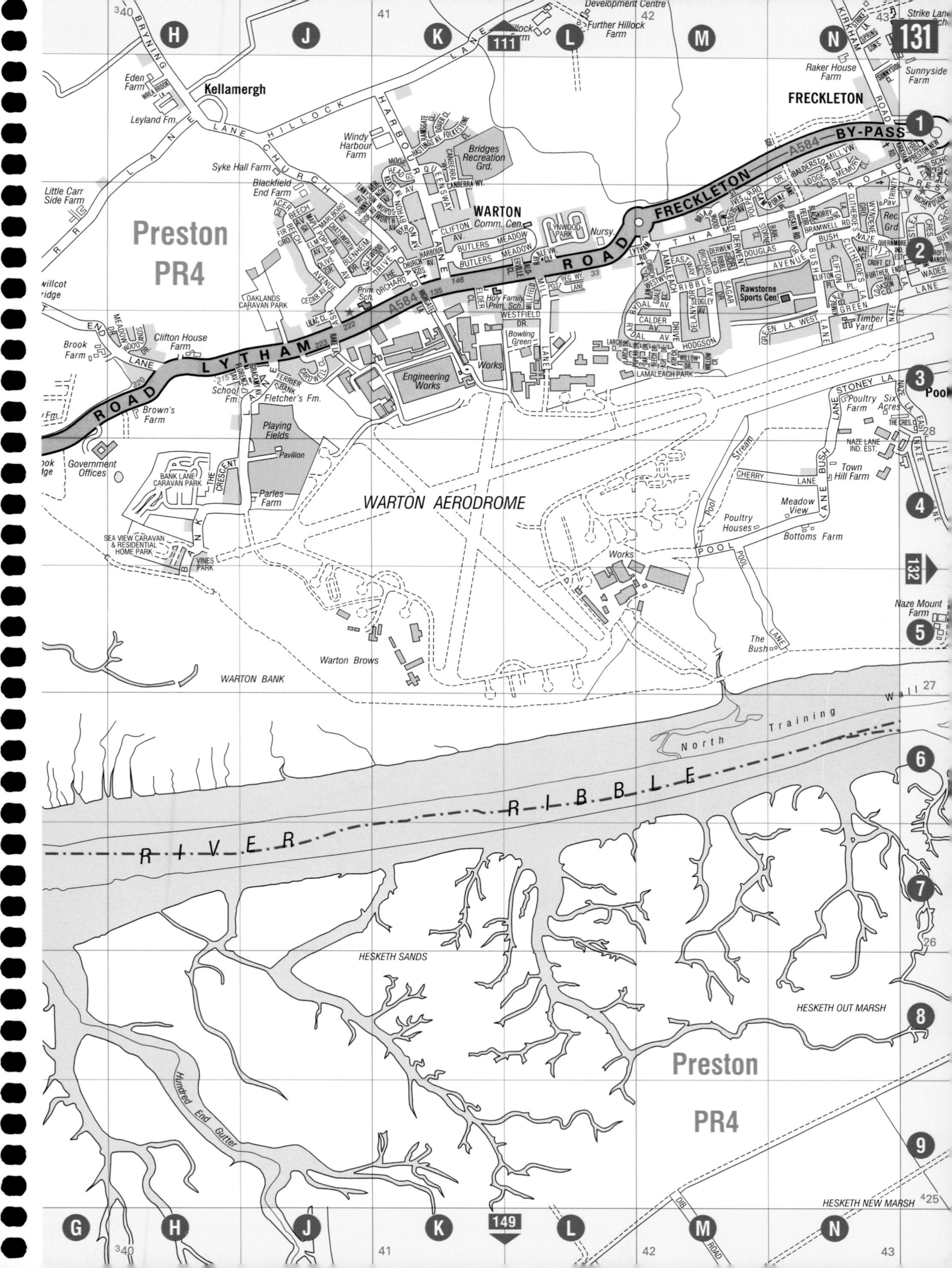
Kellamergh
FRECKLETON
WARTON
Preston
PR4
WARTON AERODROME
RIVER RIBBLE
North Training Wall
HESKETH SANDS
HESKETH OUT MARSH
HESKETH NEW MARSH
Warton Brows
WARTON BANK
Hundred End Gutter
LYTHAM ROAD
FRECKLETON ROAD
A584
BY-PASS
Engineering Works
Playing Fields
Pavilion
Parles Farm
Government Offices
BANK LANE CARAVAN PARK
SEA VIEW CARAVAN & RESIDENTIAL HOME PARK
VINES PARK
Rawstorne Sports Cen.
Bridges Recreation Grd.
Windy Harbour Farm
Syke Hall Farm
Blackfield End Farm
Little Carr Side Farm
Eden Farm
Leyland Fm.
Clifton House Farm
Brook Farm
Brown's Farm
Fletcher's Fm.
Raker House Farm
Sunnyside Farm
Poultry Farm
Six Acres
Town Hill Farm
Meadow View
Bottoms Farm
Poultry Houses
Naze Mount Farm
The Bush
Timber Yard
Further Hillock Farm
Development Centre
OAKLANDS CARAVAN PARK
LAMALEACH PARK
NAZE LANE IND. EST.
Holy Family Prim. Sch.
Bowling Green
Comm. Cen.
Works
Preston
PR4

111
132
149

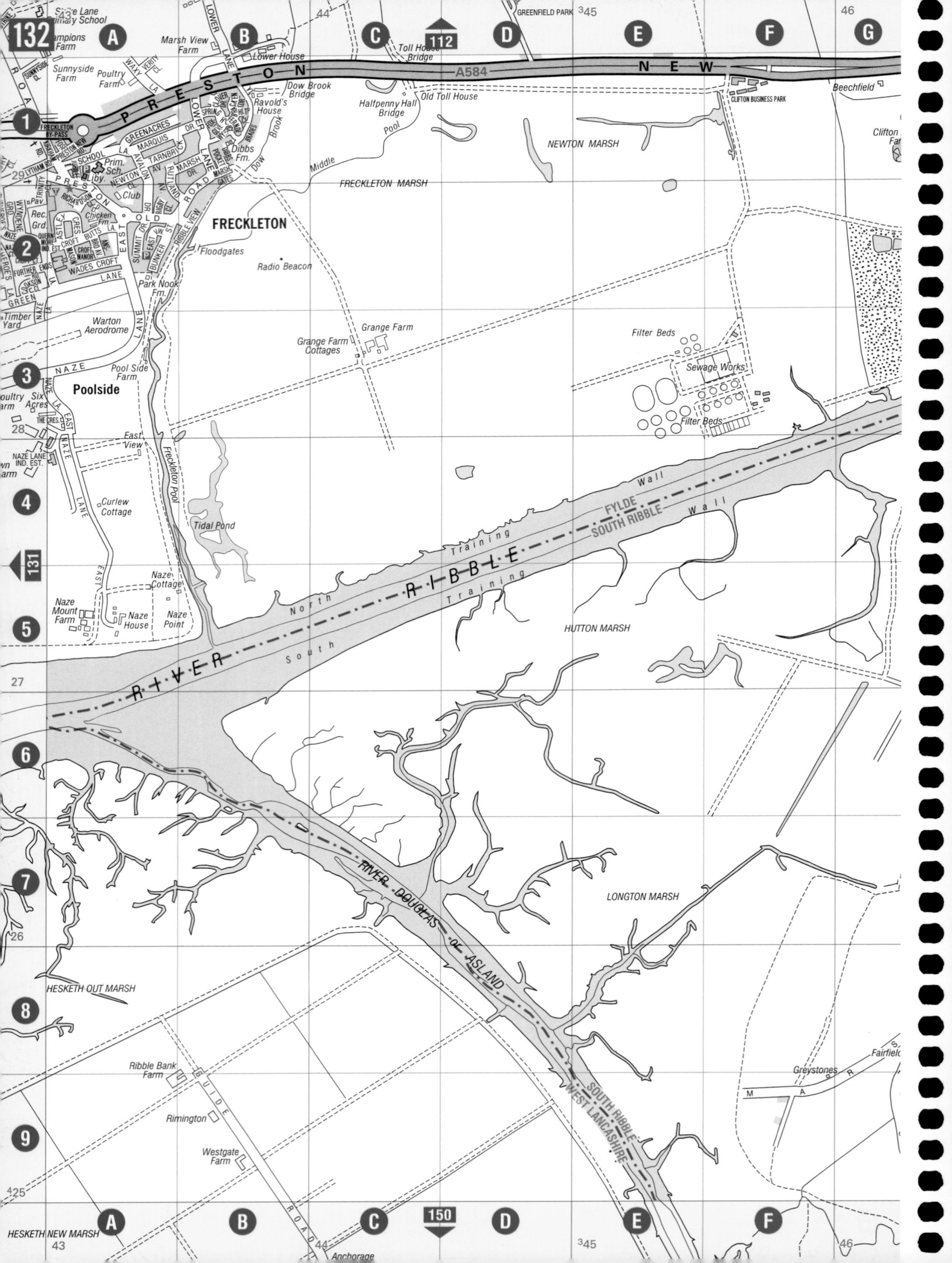

Freckleton Marsh
Newton Marsh
Hutton Marsh
Longton Marsh
Hesketh Out Marsh
Hesketh New Marsh
FRECKLETON
Poolside
RIVER RIBBLE
RIVER DOUGLAS or ASLAND
FYLDE
SOUTH RIBBLE
WEST LANCASHIRE
PRESTON NEW ROAD
A584
Warton Aerodrome
Radio Beacon
Grange Farm
Grange Farm Cottages
Filter Beds
Sewage Works
Clifton Business Park
Beechfield
Tidal Pond
Freckleton Pool
Floodgates
Park Nook Fm.
Pool Side Farm
Curlew Cottage
Naze Cottage
Naze House
Naze Point
Naze Mount Farm
Ribble Bank Farm
Rimington
Westgate Farm
Greystones
Toll House Bridge
Dow Brook Bridge
Halfpenny Hall Bridge
Old Toll House
Ravold's House
Lower House
Marsh View Farm
Sunnyside Farm
Poultry Farm
Dibbs Fm.
North Training Wall
South Training Wall
Greenfield Park
Anchorage
112
131
150

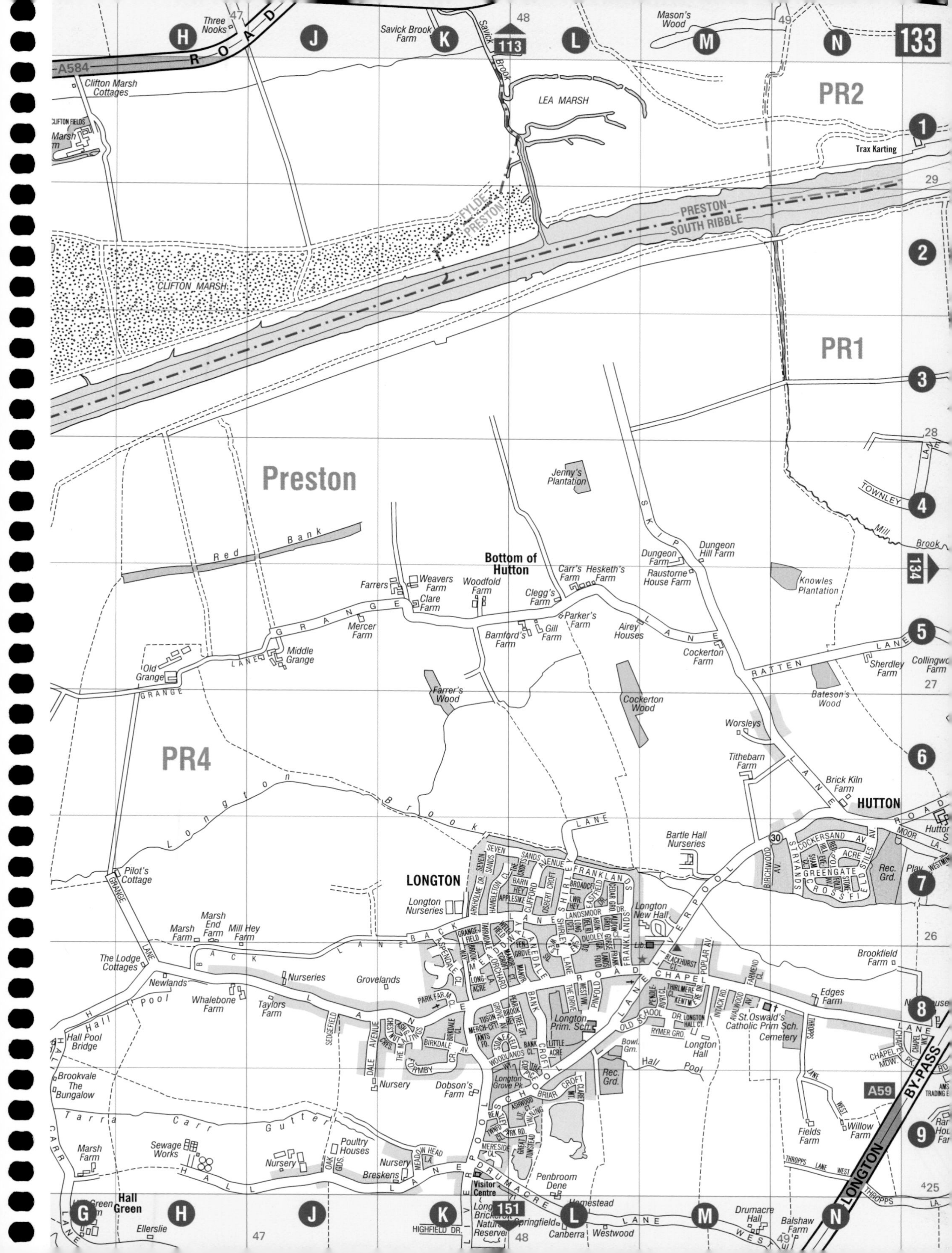

H
J
K
L
M
N
Three Nooks
47
48
49
ROAD
A584
Savick Brook Farm
Savick Brook
113
Mason's Wood
PR2
Clifton Marsh Cottages
LEA MARSH
CLIFTON FIELDS
Marsh
1
Trax Karting
29
FYLDE
PRESTON
PRESTON
SOUTH RIBBLE
2
CLIFTON MARSH
PR1
3
28
Preston
Jenny's Plantation
TOWNLEY
4
Mill Brook
Red Bank
Bottom of Hutton
Dungeon Farm
Dungeon Hill Farm
Carr's Farm
Hesketh's Farm
Raustorne House Farm
134
Knowles Plantation
Farrers
Weavers Farm
Woodfold Farm
Clegg's Farm
Clare Farm
GRANGE
Mercer Farm
Parker's Farm
Bamford's Farm
Gill Farm
Airey Houses
LANE
5
Middle Grange
Cockerton Farm
RATTEN LANE
Sherdley Farm
Old Grange
27
Farrer's Wood
Cockerton Wood
Bateson's Wood
Worsleys
PR4
6
Tithebarn Farm
Longton Brook
Brick Kiln Farm
HUTTON
LANE
ROAD
Bartle Hall Nurseries
30
SEVEN SANDS
FRANKLANDS
COCKERSAND AV.
MOOR LA.
Pilot's Cottage
LONGTON
ACRE
GREENGATE
CROSSFIELD
Rec. Grd.
Play
7
Longton Nurseries
Longton New Hall
LIVERPOOL
BIRCHWOOD AV.
Marsh Farm
Marsh End Farm
Mill Hey Farm
BACK LANE
Lib.
BLACKHURST CT.
POPLAR AV.
26
Brookfield Farm
The Lodge Cottages
Nurseries
Grovelands
CHAPEL
FARMEND CL.
Newlands
Whalebone Farm
Taylors Farm
Hall Pool
ROAD
Longton Prim. Sch.
Edges Farm
8
St.Oswald's Catholic Prim Sch.
Cemetery
THROPPS
Hall Pool Bridge
Longton Hall
Bowl. Grn.
Hall Pool
CHAPEL MDW.
LANE
Brookvale
The Bungalow
Nursery
Dobson's Farm
Longton Grove Pk.
Rec. Grd.
A59
BY-PASS
LONGTON
Tarra Carr Gutter
9
Willow Farm
Fields Farm
Marsh Farm
Sewage Works
Poultry Houses
Nursery
Nursery
Breskens
THROPPS LANE WEST
HALL LANE
Penbroom Dene
DRUMACRE
Visitor Centre
Homestead
425
G
Hall Green
151
Springfield
Drumacre Hall
Ellerslie
HIGHFIELD DR.
Canberra
Westwood
LANE
WEST
Balshaw Farm

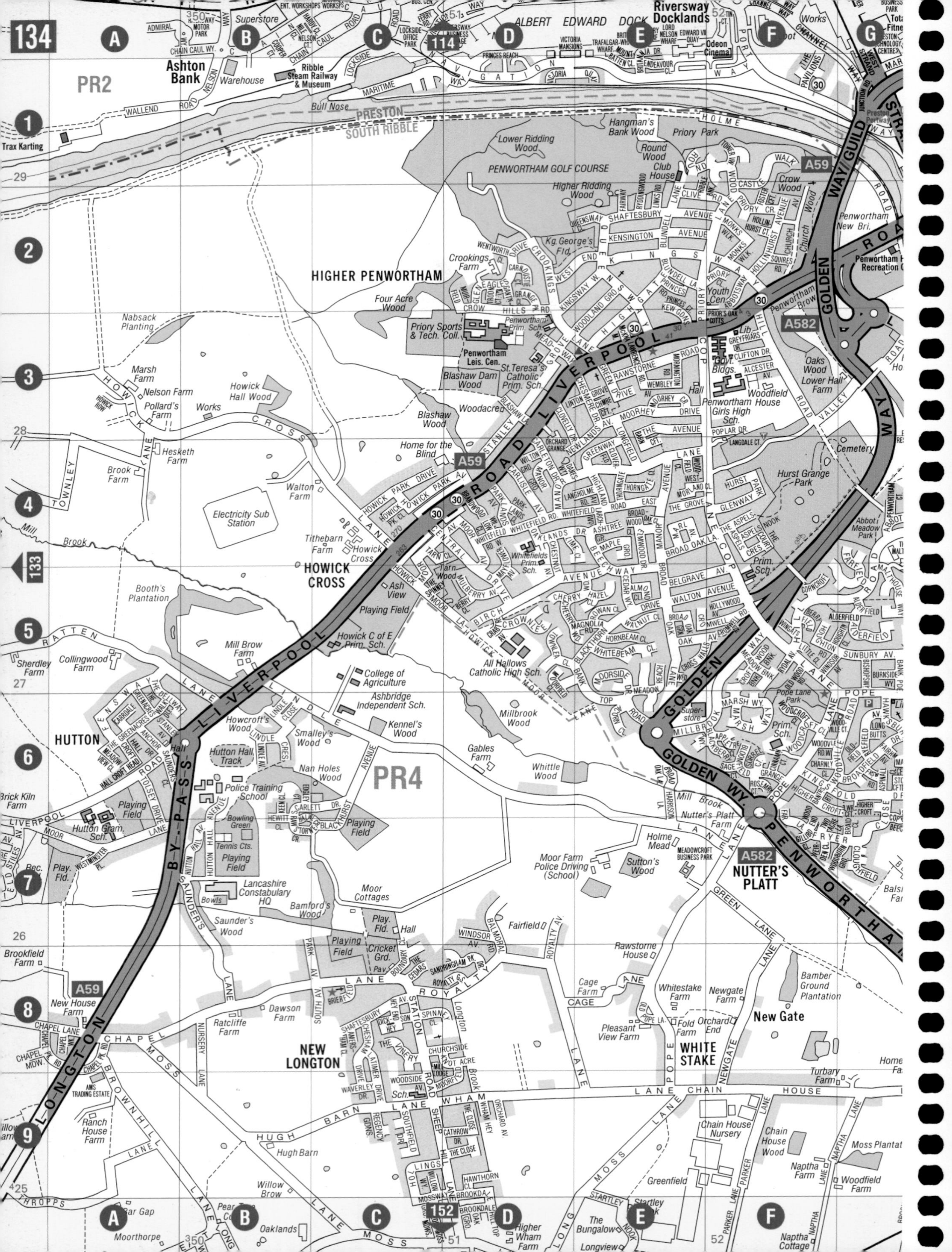

Ashton Bank
PR2
Superstore
Warehouse
Ribble Steam Railway & Museum
Albert Edward Dock
Riversway Docklands
Odeon Cinema
Victoria Mansions
Princes Reach
Navigation Way
Maritime
Bull Nose
Preston
South Ribble
Trax Karting
Wallend Road
Hangman's Bank Wood
Priory Park
Lower Ridding Wood
Penwortham Golf Course
Round Wood
Club House
Higher Ridding Wood
Crow Wood
Penwortham New Bri.
Penwortham Recreation
Higher Penwortham
Crookings Farm
Kg. George's Fld.
Four Acre Wood
Nabsack Planting
Priory Sports & Tech. Coll.
Penwortham Prim. Sch.
Penwortham Leis. Cen.
St.Teresa's Catholic Prim. Sch.
Blashaw Dam Wood
Youth Cen.
Lib.
Govt. Bldgs.
Penwortham House
Penwortham Girls High Sch.
Woodfield Farm
Oaks Wood
Lower Hall Farm
Marsh Farm
Nelson Farm
Pollard's Farm
Works
Howick Hall Wood
Blashaw Wood
Woodacre
Home for the Blind
Hesketh Farm
Brook Farm
Cemetery
Hurst Grange Park
Electricity Sub Station
Walton Farm
Tithebarn Farm
Howick Cross
Whitefields Prim. Sch.
Abbot Meadow Park
Booth's Plantation
Ash View
Playing Field
Howick C of E Prim. Sch.
Mill Brow Farm
Collingwood Farm
Sherdley Farm
All Hallows Catholic High Sch.
College of Agriculture
Ashbridge Independent Sch.
Kennel's Wood
Millbrook Wood
Howcroft's Wood
Smalley's Wood
Hutton
Hutton Hall Track
Nan Holes Wood
PR4
Gables Farm
Whittle Wood
Police Training School
Pope Lane Park
Prim. Sch.
Superstore
Brick Kiln Farm
Hutton Gram. Sch.
Bowling Green
Tennis Cts.
Playing Field
Mill Brook
Nutter's Platt Farm
Holme Mead
Meadowcroft Business Park
Moor Farm Police Driving (School)
Sutton's Wood
Nutter's Platt
Lancashire Constabulary HQ
Moor Cottages
Bamford's Wood
Saunder's Wood
Play. Fld.
Fairfield
Rawstorne House
Brookfield Farm
Cricket Grd.
Pav.
Cage Farm
Whitestake Farm
Newgate Farm
Bamber Ground Plantation
New House Farm
Dawson Farm
Ratcliffe Farm
Pleasant View Farm
Fold Farm
Orchard End
New Gate
New Longton
White Stake
AMS Trading Estate
Turbary Farm
Ranch House Farm
Hugh Barn
Chain House Nursery
Chain House Wood
Moss Plantation
Naptha Farm
Woodfield Farm
Greenfield
Willow Brow
Oaklands
Moorthorpe
The Bungalow
Longview
Higher Wham Farm
Naptha Cottage
Liverpool Road
Golden Way
Penwortham Way
Longton By-Pass
Howick Cross Lane
Chain House Lane
Wham Lane
Hugh Barn Lane
Chapel Lane
Brownhill Lane
Moss Lane
Royalty Lane
Station Road
Green Lane
Pope Lane
A59
A582
30

114
133
152

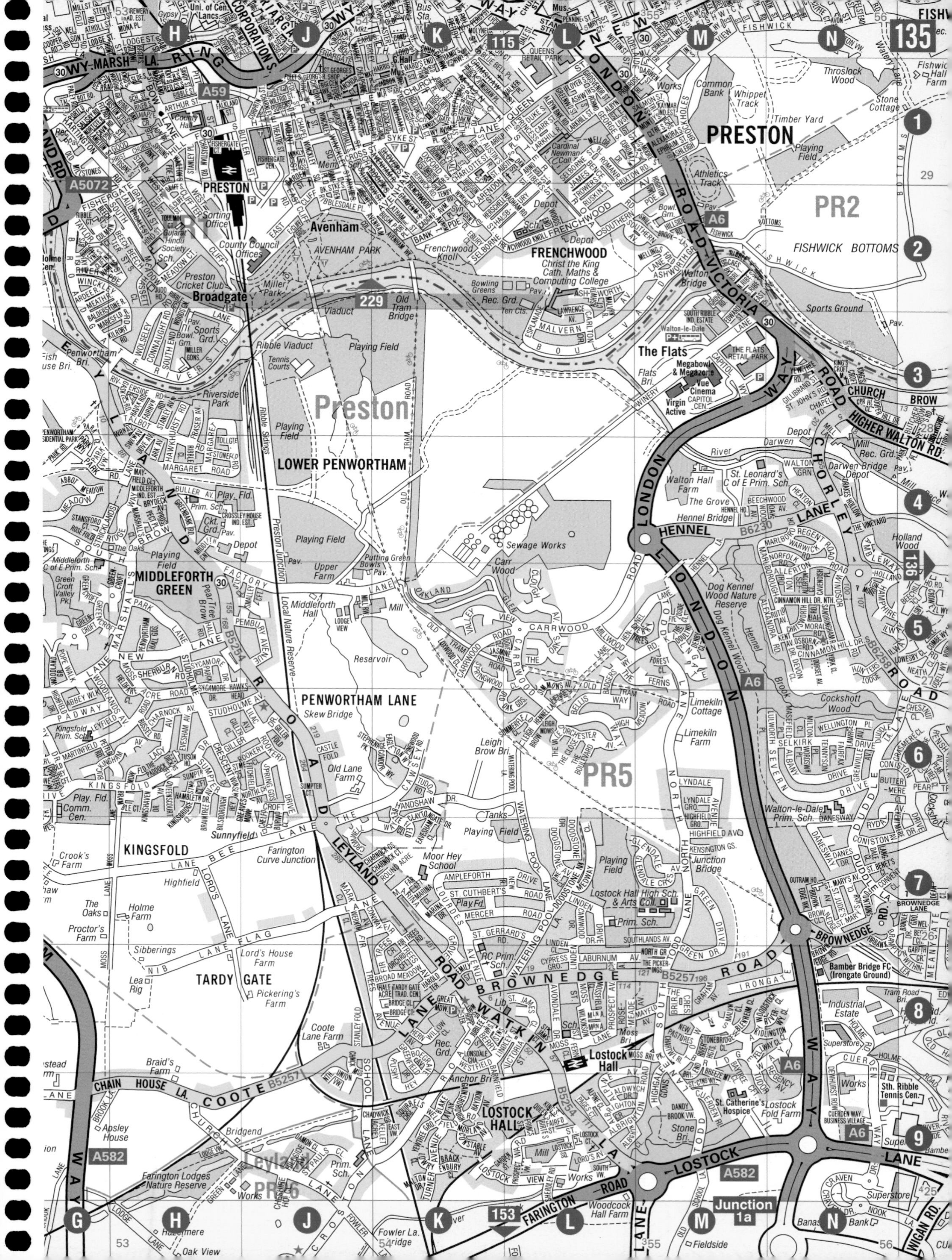
PRESTON
Preston
PR2
PR5
Avenham
AVENHAM PARK
FRENCHWOOD
Christ the King Cath. Maths & Computing College
Broadgate
Preston Cricket Club
County Council Offices
Sorting Office
Miller Park
Frenchwood Knoll
FISHWICK BOTTOMS
Throslock Wood
Fishwick Hall Farm
Stone Cottage
Timber Yard
Playing Field
Athletics Track
Common Bank
Whippet Track
Works
Cardinal Newman Coll.
Walton Bridge
Sports Ground
The Flats
THE FLATS RETAIL PARK
Megabowl & Megazone
Vue Cinema
Virgin Active
Flats Bri.
SOUTH RIBBLE IND. ESTATE
Walton-le-Dale
CHURCH BROW
HIGHER WALTON RD.
Darwen
River
Mill Rec. Grd.
Darwen Bridge Depot
St. Leonard's C of E Prim. Sch.
Walton Hall Farm
The Grove
Hennel Bridge
HENNEL
LONDON ROAD
LONDON WAY
VICTORIA ROAD
CHORLEY LANE
Holland Wood
Dog Kennel Wood Nature Reserve
Dog Kennel Wood
Hennel
Brook
Cockshott Wood
Walton-le-Dale Prim. Sch.
Sewage Works
Carr Wood
Ribble Viaduct
Viaduct
Old Tram Bridge
Tennis Courts
Riverside Park
Penwortham Bri.
LOWER PENWORTHAM
Ribble Sidings
Preston Junction
Local Nature Reserve
Playing Field
Putting Green Bowls
Upper Farm
Middleforth Hall
Mill
Reservoir
MIDDLEFORTH GREEN
Middleforth C of E Prim. Sch.
Green Croft Valley Pk.
PENWORTHAM LANE
Skew Bridge
Leigh Brow Bri.
Old Lane Farm
Limekiln Cottage
Limekiln Farm
Kingsfold Prim. Sch.
Play. Fld.
Comm. Cen.
KINGSFOLD
Sunnyfield
Farington Curve Junction
Crook's Farm
Highfield
The Oaks
Holme Farm
Proctor's Farm
Sibberings
Lord's House Farm
TARDY GATE
Lea Rig
Pickering's Farm
Moor Hey School
Tanks
Playing Field
Lostock Hall High Sch. & Arts Coll.
Prim. Sch.
RC Prim. Sch.
Junction Bridge
BROWNEDGE ROAD
Bamber Bridge FC (Irongate Ground)
Industrial Estate
Superstore
Works
Sth. Ribble Tennis Cen.
CUERDEN WAY BUSINESS VILLAGE
WATKIN LANE
LEYLAND ROAD
Lostock Hall
LOSTOCK HALL
Anchor Bri.
Rec. Grd.
Coote Lane Farm
Braid's Farm
CHAIN HOUSE LA.
COOTE LA.
Bridgend
Apsley House
Farington Lodges Nature Reserve
Leyland PR26
St. Catherine's Hospice
Lostock Fold Farm
Stone Bri.
LOSTOCK LANE
FARINGTON ROAD
Woodcock Hall Farm
Junction 1a
Fowler La. Bridge
Hazelmere
Oak View
Fieldside
A59
A5072
A6
A582
B5254
B5257
B6230
B6258
115
136
153
229
H
J
K
L
M
N
G
1
2
3
4
5
6
7
8
9
53
54
55
56
29
28
27
26
25

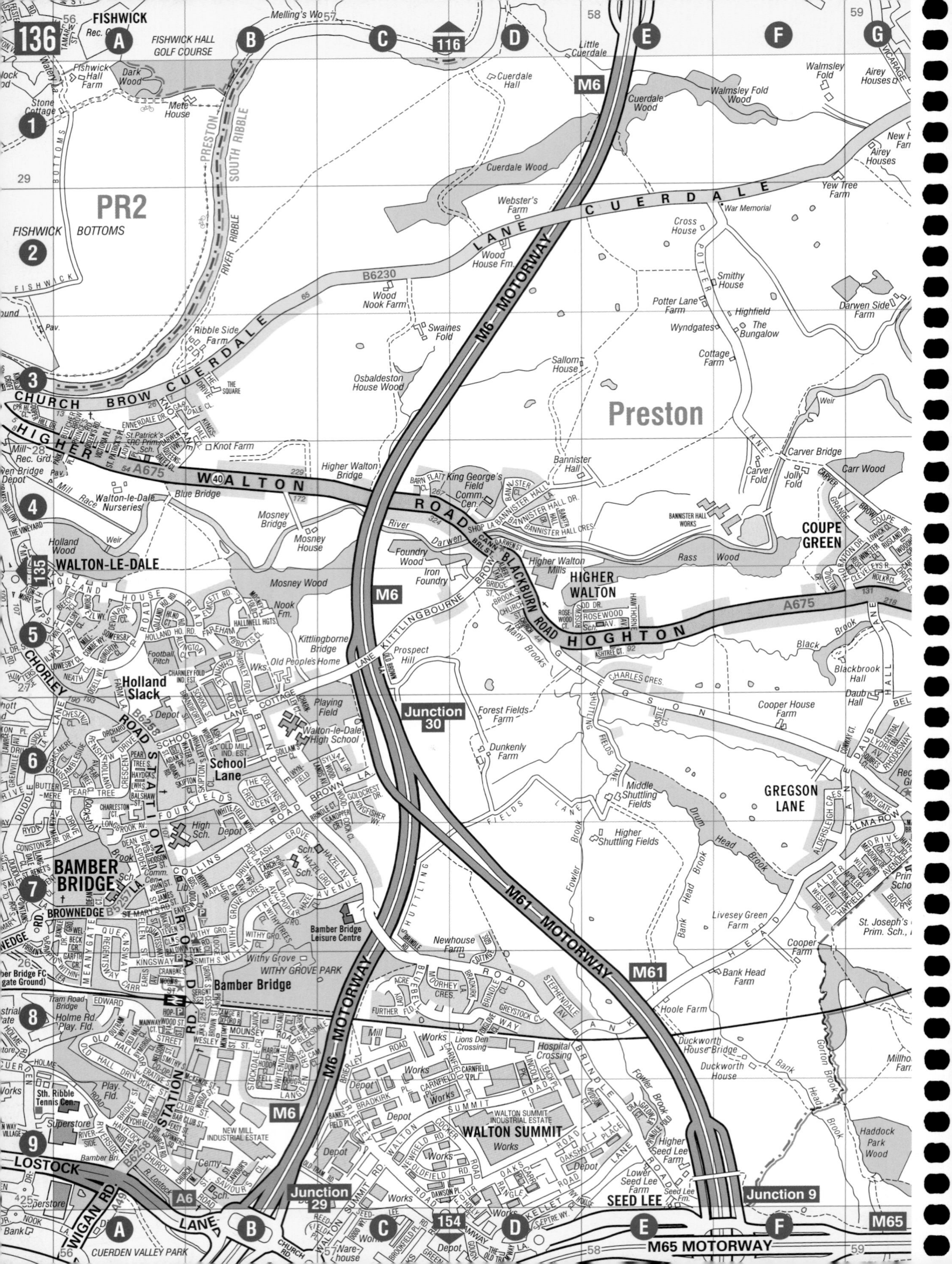
FISHWICK
FISHWICK HALL GOLF COURSE
Melling's Wood
116
Little Cuerdale
Cuerdale Hall
M6
Walmsley Fold
Walmsley Fold Wood
Airey Houses
Fishwick Hall Farm
Dark Wood
Stone Cottage
Mete House
Cuerdale Wood
New Hall Farm
PR2
FISHWICK BOTTOMS
PRESTON
SOUTH RIBBLE
RIVER RIBBLE
Webster's Farm
CUERDALE LANE
War Memorial
Yew Tree Farm
Cross House
Wood House Fm.
B6230
Wood Nook Farm
Smithy House
Potter Lane Farm
Highfield
Darwen Side Farm
Swaines Fold
Wyndgates
The Bungalow
Ribble Side Farm
Cottage Farm
M6 MOTORWAY
CUERDALE BROW
Sallom House
Osbaldeston House Wood
CHURCH BROW
Preston
Weir
HIGHER WALTON ROAD
A675
Knot Farm
Bannister Hall
Higher Walton Bridge
Carver Bridge
Carr Wood
King George's Field
Comm. Cen.
Carver Fold
Jolly Fold
Blue Bridge
Walton-le-Dale Nurseries
Mill Race
Mosney Bridge
Mosney House
River Darwen
BANNISTER HALL WORKS
COUPE GREEN
Holland Wood
Weir
Foundry Wood
Rass Wood
WALTON-LE-DALE
135
Iron Foundry
Higher Walton Mills
Mosney Wood
HIGHER WALTON
Nook Fm.
KITTLINGBOURNE BROW
BLACKBURN ROAD
HOGHTON ROAD
Kittlingborne Bridge
Prospect Hill
Mary Brooks
Black Brook
Football Pitch
Old Peoples Home
Blackbrook Hall
Holland Slack
Playing Field
CHARLES CRES.
Daub Hall
CHORLEY ROAD
B6258
Junction 30
Forest Fields Farm
Cooper House Farm
GREGSON LANE
Walton-le-Dale High School
School Lane
Dunkenly Farm
Middle Shuttling Fields
GREGSON LANE
STATION ROAD
High Sch.
Higher Shuttling Fields
ALMA ROW
Drum Head Brook
BAMBER BRIDGE
BROWNEDGE
Fowler Brook
Bank Head Brook
M61 MOTORWAY
Livesey Green Farm
St. Joseph's Prim. Sch.
Bamber Bridge Leisure Centre
Newhouse Farm
Cooper Farm
Withy Grove
WITHY GROVE PARK
Bamber Bridge
M61
Bank Head Farm
Tram Road Bridge
Holme Rd. Play. Fld.
Mill
Works
Lions Den Crossing
Hospital Crossing
Hoole Farm
Duckworth House Bridge
Duckworth House
Gorton Brook
Play. Fld.
Sth. Ribble Tennis Cen.
M6
WALTON SUMMIT INDUSTRIAL ESTATE
WALTON SUMMIT
Works
Superstore
NEW MILL INDUSTRIAL ESTATE
Higher Seed Lee Farm
Haddock Park Wood
Bamber Bri.
LOSTOCK LANE
A6
Junction 29
Lower Seed Lee Farm
SEED LEE
Junction 9
M65
WIGAN RD.
A49
CUERDEN VALLEY PARK
154
Depot
M65 MOTORWAY
A B C D E F G
1 2 3 4 5 6 7 8 9
56 57 58 59
29 28 27 26 25

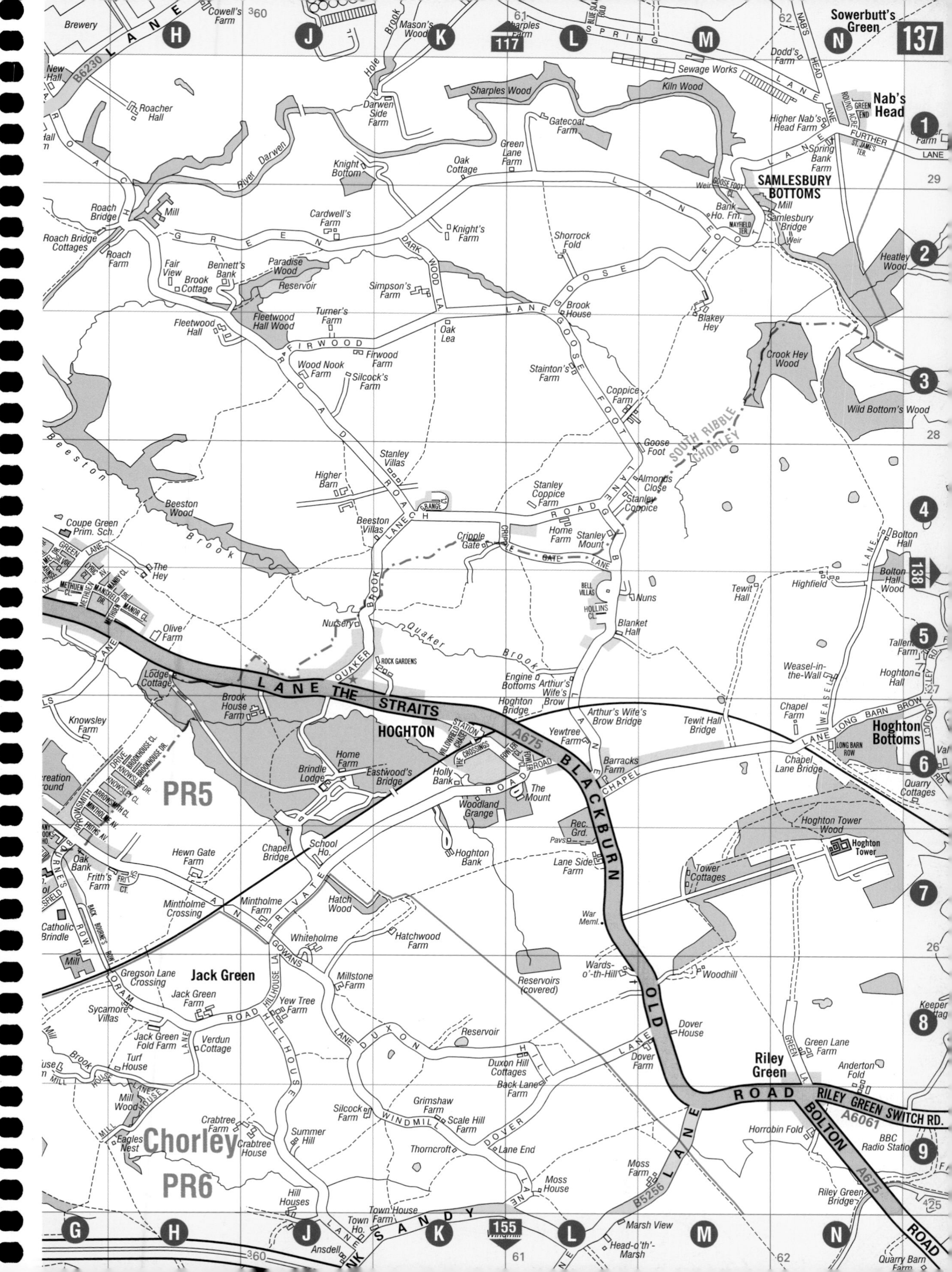
Sowerbutt's Green
Nab's Head
SAMLESBURY BOTTOMS
Sharples Wood
Kiln Wood
Sewage Works
River Darwen
Roach Bridge
Fleetwood Hall Wood
Beeston Wood
Crook Hey Wood
Wild Bottom's Wood
Heatley Wood
SOUTH RIBBLE
CHORLEY
THE STRAITS
HOGHTON
Hoghton Bottoms
Hoghton Tower
Hoghton Tower Wood
BLACKBURN
OLD
ROAD
A675
A6061
B5256
B6230
RILEY GREEN SWITCH RD.
BOLTON
Riley Green
Jack Green
Chorley
PR5
PR6
Coupe Green Prim. Sch.
Reservoirs (covered)
117
138
155

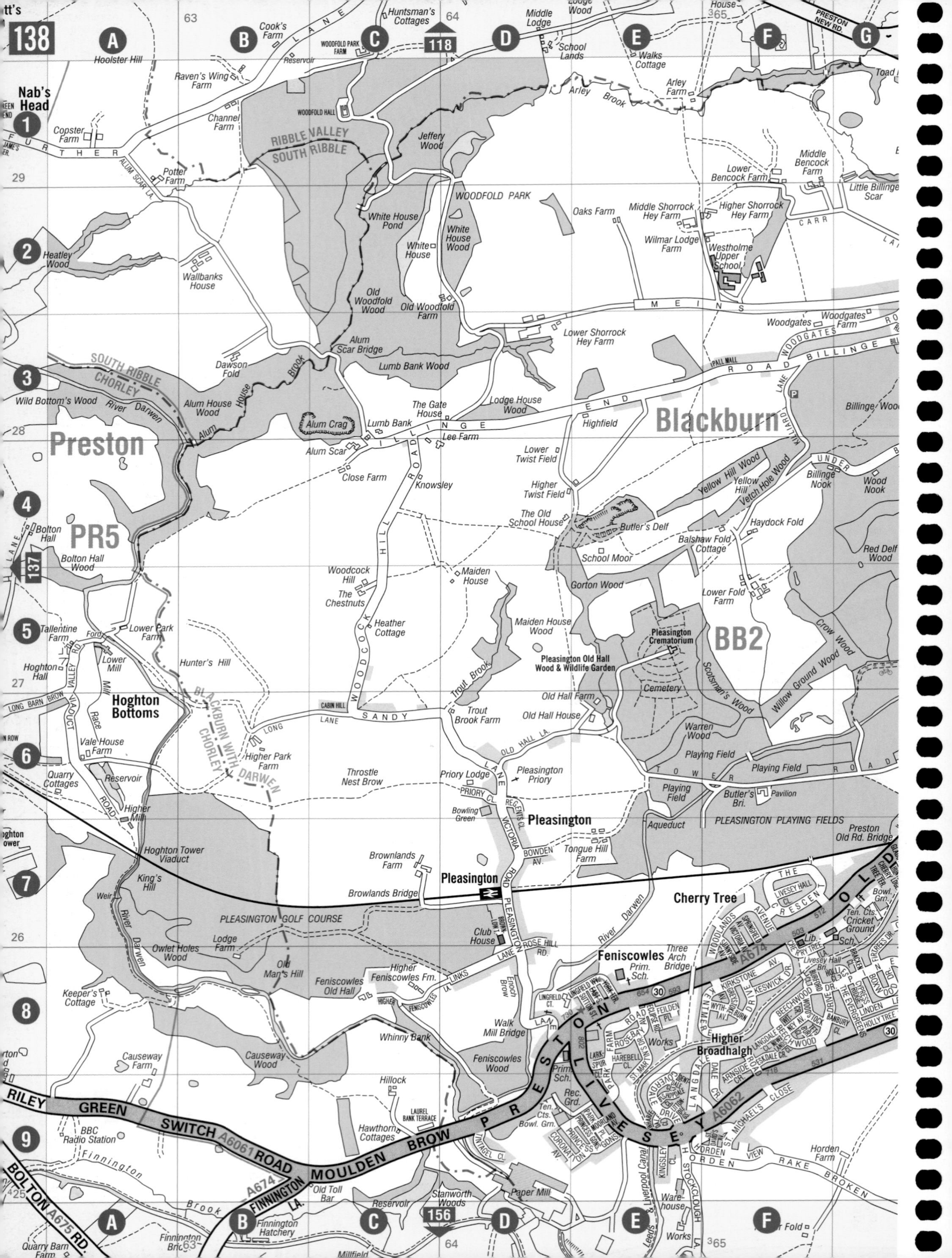
A
B
C
D
E
F
G
63
64
365
118
137
156
1
2
3
4
5
6
7
8
9
29
28
27
26
25
Nab's Head
Hoolster Hill
Cook's Farm
Huntsman's Cottages
Woodfold Park Farm
Reservoir
Middle Lodge
School Lands
Lodge Wood
Walks Cottage
Preston New Rd.
Toad
Raven's Wing Farm
Channel Farm
Copster Farm
Further Lane
Alum Scar La.
Potter Farm
Woodfold Hall
Ribble Valley
South Ribble
Jeffery Wood
Arley Brook
Arley Farm
Middle Bencock Farm
Lower Bencock Farm
Little Billinge Scar
Woodfold Park
Oaks Farm
Middle Shorrock Hey Farm
Higher Shorrock Hey Farm
Carr
Heatley Wood
Wallbanks House
White House Pond
White House
White House Wood
Wilmar Lodge Farm
Westholme Upper School
Old Woodfold Wood
Old Woodfold Farm
Meins
Woodgates
Woodgates Farm
Woodgates Road
Billinge
Alum Scar Bridge
Lower Shorrock Hey Farm
Dawson Fold
Lumb Bank Wood
Pall Mall
Lane
South Ribble
Chorley
Wild Bottom's Wood
River Darwen
Alum House Wood
Alum House Brook
Alum Crag
Lumb Bank
The Gate House
Lodge House Wood
Billinge End Road
Blackburn
Killiard Lane
Billinge Wood
Preston
Alum Scar
Lee Farm
Highfield
Close Farm
Knowsley
Lower Twist Field
Yellow Hill Wood
Yellow Hill
Vetch Hole Wood
Under
Billinge Nook
Wood Nook
Higher Twist Field
PR5
Bolton Hall
Bolton Lane
The Old School House
Butler's Delf
Haydock Fold
Balshaw Fold Cottage
School Moor
Red Delf Wood
Bolton Hall Wood
Woodcock Hill
Maiden House
The Chestnuts
Gorton Wood
Lower Fold Farm
Tallentine Farm
Ford
Lower Park Farm
Heather Cottage
Maiden House Wood
Pleasington Crematorium
BB2
Crow Wood
Woodcock Hill Road
Hoghton Hall
Lower Mill
Hunter's Hill
Pleasington Old Hall Wood & Wildlife Garden
Cemetery
Scotsman's Wood
Willow Ground Wood
Long Barn Brow
Viaduct Road
Valley Road
Mill Race
Hoghton Bottoms
Blackburn with Darwen
Chorley
Cabin Hill
Sandy Lane
Trout Brook
Trout Brook Farm
Old Hall Farm
Old Hall House
Long Lane
Warren Wood
Vale House Farm
Higher Park Farm
Old Hall La.
Playing Field
Tower Road
Quarry Cottages
Reservoir
Throstle Nest Brow
Priory Lodge
Pleasington Priory
Priory Cl.
Playing Field
Butler's Bri.
Pavilion
Higher Mill
Bowling Green
Regents Cl.
Pleasington
Aqueduct
Pleasington Playing Fields
Preston Old Rd. Bridge
Hoghton Tower
Hoghton Tower Viaduct
Brownlands Farm
Victoria Road
Bowden Av.
Tongue Hill Farm
King's Hill
Browlands Bridge
Pleasington
Cherry Tree
The Crescent
Livesey Hall Cl.
Weir
River Darwen
Pleasington Golf Course
Club House
Pleasington Road
River Darwen
Woodlands Avenue
Old Rd.
Bowl. Grn.
Cricket Ground
Ten. Cts.
Lodge Farm
Owlet Holes Wood
Old Man's Hill
Rose Hill Rd.
Feniscowles
Prim. Sch.
Three Arch Bridge
Lib.
Sch.
Cherry Tree La.
Livesey Hall Bri.
Feniscowles Old Hall
Higher Feniscowles Fm.
Links Lane
Enoch Brow
Kirkstone Av.
Keswick Dr.
Keeper's Cottage
Higher
Feniscowles La.
Lingfield Ct.
Walk Mill Bridge
Rosebay Av.
Feilden Pl.
Works
Beechwood
The Evergreens
Holly Tree
Whinny Bank
Lark Spur Cl.
Harebell Cl.
Higher Broadhalgh
Causeway Farm
Causeway Wood
Feniscowles Wood
Prim. Sch.
Hillock
Rec. Grd.
Arnside Cr.
Eskdale Cr.
Riley Green Switch Road
A6061
Laurel Bank Terrace
Ten. Cts.
Bowl. Grn.
Princess Gdns
Coronation Av.
BBC Radio Station
Hawthorn Cottages
Moulden Brow
Preston
Livesey
A6062
A674
St. Michael's Close
Finnington Brook
Tintagel Cl.
Leeds & Liverpool Canal
Horden
Horden View
Horden Farm
Rake
Broken
Kingsley Cl.
Stockclough La.
Bolton Road
A675
A674
Finnington La.
Old Toll Bar
Stanworth Woods
Paper Mill
Ware house
Reservoir
Finnington Hatchery
Finnington Bridge
Quarry Barn Farm
Millfield
Works
Fold
30
512
503
654
593
802
531

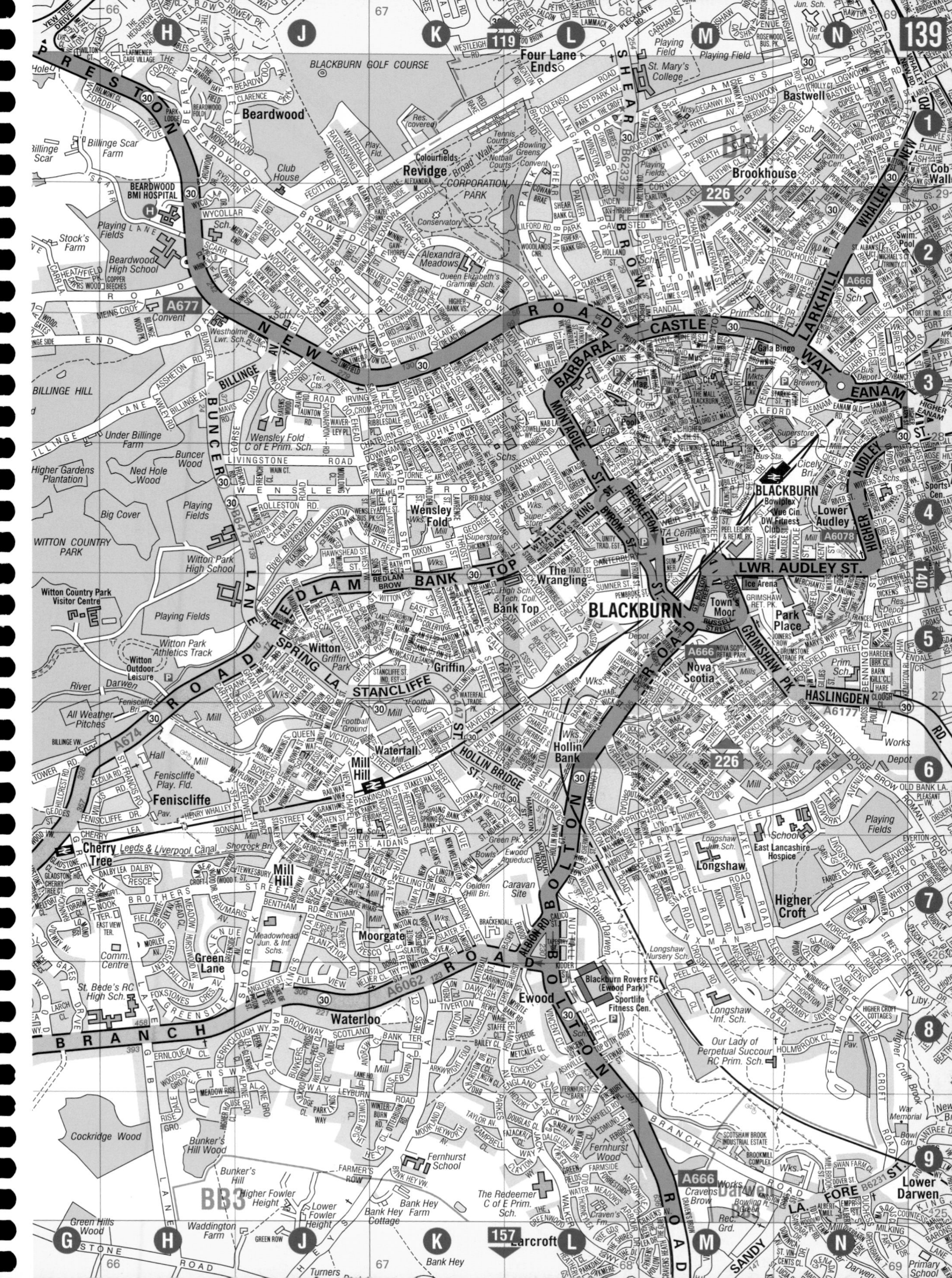

BLACKBURN GOLF COURSE
Four Lane Ends
St. Mary's College
Playing Field
Bastwell
Beardwood
Billinge Scar Farm
Club House
Colourfields
Revidge
CORPORATION PARK
Conservatory
Tennis Courts
Bowling Greens
Netball Courts
BEARDWOOD BMI HOSPITAL
Beardwood High School
Stock's Farm
Alexandra Meadows
Queen Elizabeth's Grammar Sch.
Brookhouse
BB1
PRESTON NEW ROAD
CASTLE WAY
BARBARA CASTLE WAY
Gala Bingo
THE MALL BLACKBURN
Mus.
Mag. Ct.
Cath.
College
Pool
Superstore
Bus Sta.
Brewery
Bus Depot
EANAM
HIGHER EANAM
LARKHILL
WHALLEY NEW RD.
Swim. Pool
Cob Wall
BILLINGE HILL
Under Billinge Farm
Higher Gardens Plantation
Ned Hole Wood
Buncer Wood
Big Cover
WITTON COUNTRY PARK
Witton Country Park Visitor Centre
Witton Park High School
Playing Fields
Witton Park Athletics Track
Witton Outdoor Leisure
River Darwen
All Weather Pitches
Wensley Fold C of E Prim. Sch.
Wensley Fold
LIVINGSTONE ROAD
WENSLEY RD.
REDLAM
BANK TOP
Bank Top
The Wrangling
BLACKBURN
Town's Moor
Ice Arena
LWR. AUDLEY ST.
Lower Audley
Bowlplex
Vue Cin.
DW Fitness Club
Park Place
GRIMSHAW RET. PK.
NOVA SCOTIA RETAIL PARK
Nova Scotia
HASLINGDEN RD.
Witton
Griffin Park
Griffin
SPRING LA.
STANCLIFFE
Football Ground
Waterfall
Mill Hill
Feniscliffe
Feniscliffe Play. Fld.
Cherry Tree
Leeds & Liverpool Canal
HOLLIN BRIDGE ST.
Hollin Bank
Ewood Aqueduct
Caravan Site
BOLTON ROAD
Longshaw
East Lancashire Hospice
Higher Croft
Playing Fields
Mill Hill
Moorgate
Meadowhead Jun. & Inf. Schs.
Green Lane
Comm. Centre
St. Bede's RC High Sch.
Waterloo
BRANCH ROAD
A6062
Ewood
Blackburn Rovers FC (Ewood Park)
Sportlife Fitness Cen.
Longshaw Nursery Sch.
Longshaw Inf. Sch.
Our Lady of Perpetual Succour RC Prim. Sch.
Cockridge Wood
Bunker's Hill Wood
Bunker's Hill
Higher Fowler Height
Lower Fowler Height
Fernhurst School
Fernhurst Wood
Bank Hey Cottage
Bank Hey Farm
Waddington Farm
Green Hills Wood
BB3
The Redeemer C of E Prim. Sch.
Cravens Brow
Darwen
SCOTSHAW BROOK INDUSTRIAL ESTATE
Lower Darwen
War Memorial
Larcroft
Bank Hey
Turners
A677
A674
A666
A6078
A6177
B6447
B6233
B6231
119
226
157
140

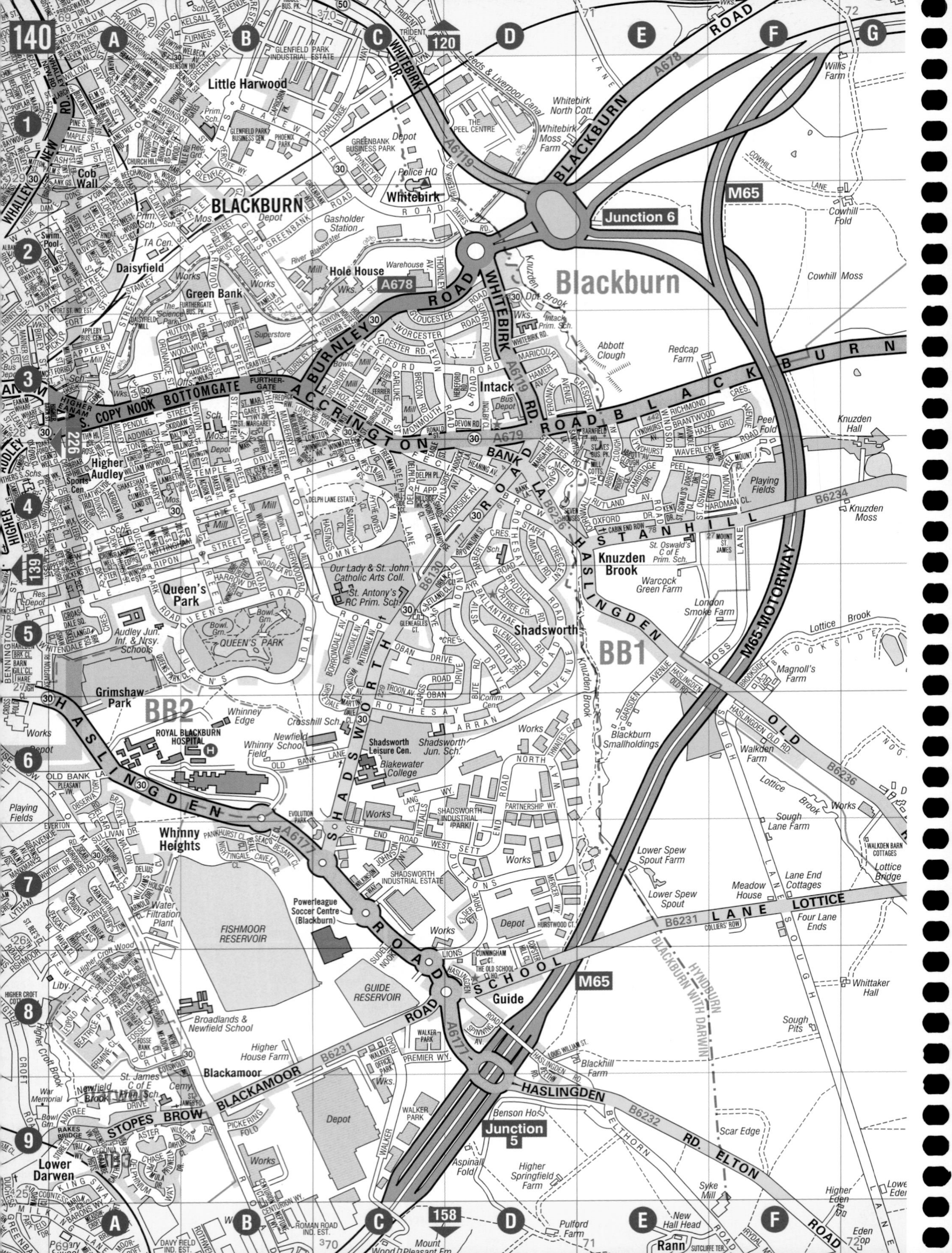

Little Harwood
GLENFIELD PARK INDUSTRIAL ESTATE
Leeds & Liverpool Canal
Whitebirk North Cott.
THE PEEL CENTRE
Whitebirk Moss Farm
GREENBANK BUSINESS PARK
Depot
Police HQ
Whitebirk
Cob Wall
BLACKBURN
Gasholder Station
River Blakewater
Junction 6
M65
Cowhill Fold
Swim. Pool
Daisyfield
Hole House
Warehouse
A678
Blackburn
Cowhill Moss
Green Bank
Superstore
Abbott Clough
Redcap Farm
BURNLEY ROAD
WHITEBIRK RD.
Intack
Bus Depot
COPY NOOK BOTTOMGATE
ACCRINGTON ROAD
BLACKBURN ROAD
A679
Knuzden Hall
Peel Fold
Higher Audley
Sports Cen.
Playing Fields
B6234
Knuzden Moss
DELPH LANE ESTATE
STANHILL
Knuzden Brook
St. Oswald's C of E Prim. Sch.
Warcock Green Farm
Queen's Park
Our Lady & St. John Catholic Arts Coll.
St. Antony's RC Prim. Sch.
London Smoke Farm
M65 MOTORWAY
HASLINGDEN ROAD
Audley Jun. Inf. & Nrsy. Schools
QUEEN'S PARK
Shadsworth
BB1
Magnoll's Farm
Grimshaw Park
BB2
Whinney Edge
Crosshill Sch.
Blackburn Smallholdings
Walkden Farm
ROYAL BLACKBURN HOSPITAL
Whinny Field
Newfield School
Shadsworth Leisure Cen.
Blakewater College
Shadsworth Jun. Sch.
Playing Fields
Lottice Brook
Sough Lane Farm
SHADSWORTH INDUSTRIAL PARK
Whinny Heights
A6177
SHADSWORTH INDUSTRIAL ESTATE
Lower Spew Spout Farm
Lower Spew Spout
Meadow House
Lane End Cottages
Lottice Bridge
Water Filtration Plant
Powerleague Soccer Centre (Blackburn)
FISHMOOR RESERVOIR
Depot
LOTTICE LANE
B6231
Four Lane Ends
BLACKBURN WITH DARWIN
HYNDBURN
GUIDE RESERVOIR
SCHOOL ROAD
Guide
Whittaker Hall
Broadlands & Newfield School
Sough Pits
Higher House Farm
Blackhill Farm
Blackamoor
BLACKAMOOR ROAD
HASLINGDEN ROAD
B6232
St. James C of E Prim. Sch.
Depot
Benson Ho.
Junction 5
Scar Edge
STOPES BROW
ELTON RD.
Lower Darwen
Works
Aspinall Fold
Higher Springfield Farm
Syke Mill
Higher Eden
ROMAN ROAD IND. EST.
Pulford Farm
New Hall Head
Eden Top
Mount Pleasant Fm.
Rann
120
226
139
158

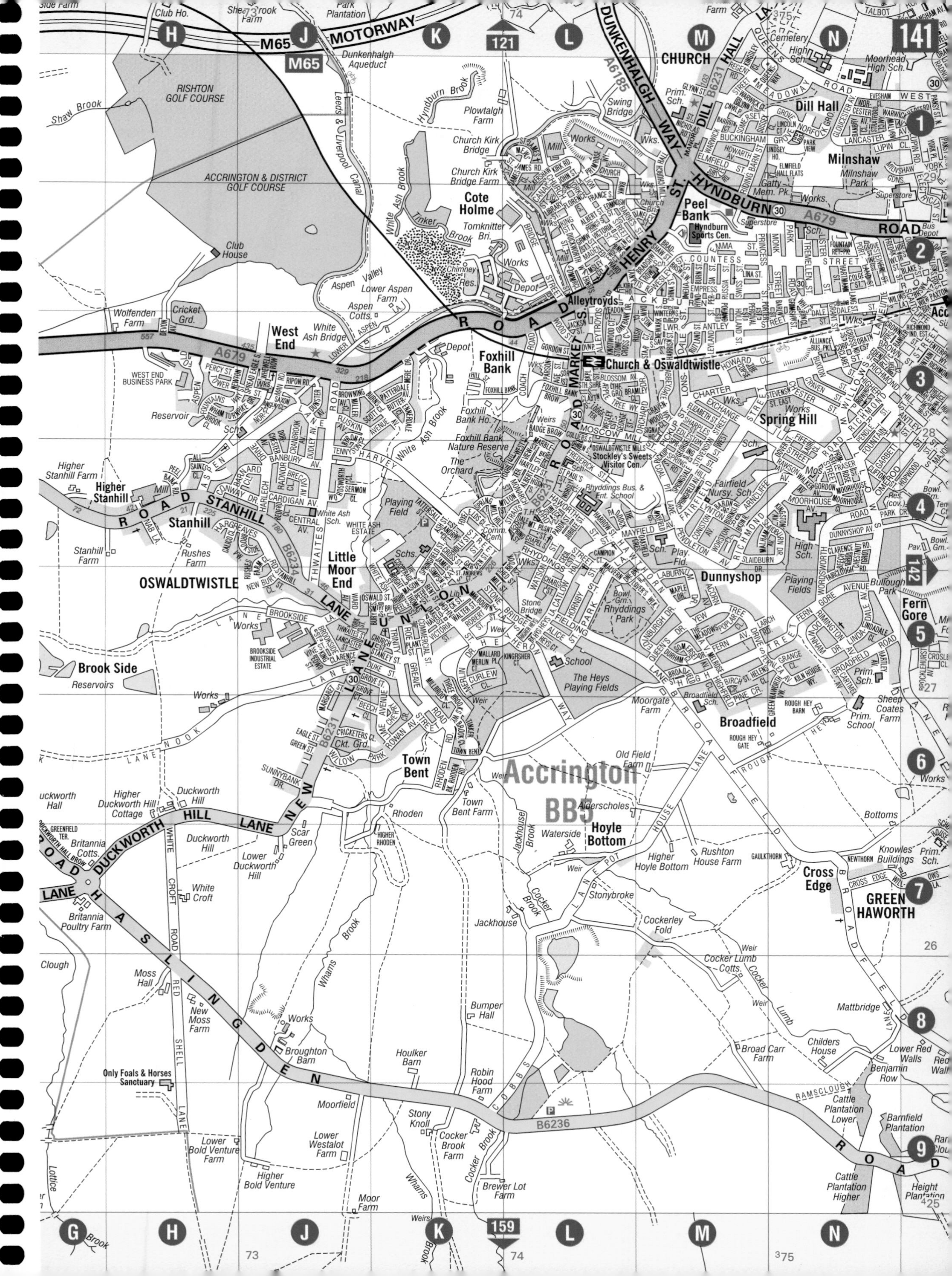

M65 MOTORWAY
RISHTON GOLF COURSE
ACCRINGTON & DISTRICT GOLF COURSE
Dunkenhalgh Aqueduct
Leeds & Liverpool Canal
Hyndburn Brook
Plowtalgh Farm
Church Kirk Bridge
Church Kirk Bridge Farm
Cote Holme
Tomknitter Bri.
Tinker Brook
White Ash Brook
Aspen Valley
Lower Aspen Farm
Aspen Cotts.
Swing Bridge
CHURCH
DUNKENHALGH WAY
A6185
HALL
Dill Hall
Milnshaw
Milnshaw Park
Cemetery
High Sch.
Moorhead High Sch.
Peel Bank
Hyndburn Sports Cen.
Superstore
HYNDBURN ROAD
A679
HENRY ST.
Alleytroyds
Gatty Mem. Pk.
Church & Oswaldtwistle
Foxhill Bank
Foxhill Bank Ho.
Foxhill Bank Nature Reserve
The Orchard
Depot
Chimney Res.
MARKET ST.
Stockley's Sweets Visitor Cen.
Rhyddings Bus. & Ent. School
Spring Hill
Fairfield Nursy. Sch.
Dunnyshop
High Sch.
Playing Fields
Bullough Park
Fern Gore
Wolfenden Farm
Cricket Grd.
West End
White Ash Bridge
WEST END BUSINESS PARK
Reservoir
Club House
Higher Stanhill Farm
Higher Stanhill
Mill
STANHILL ROAD
Stanhill
Stanhill Farm
Rushes Farm
OSWALDTWISTLE
B6234
THWAITES
White Ash Sch.
WHITE ASH ESTATE
Playing Field
Little Moor End
Schs.
UNION LANE
Rhyddings Park
Stone Bridge
Brook Side
Reservoirs
Works
BROOKSIDE INDUSTRIAL ESTATE
School
The Heys Playing Fields
Broadfield
Broadfield Sch.
Moorgate Farm
Prim. Sch.
Sheep Coates Farm
Town Bent
Cricketers Cl.
Ckt. Grd.
B6231
NEW LANE
Accrington
BB5
Old Field Farm
Alderscholes
Waterside
Hoyle Bottom
Higher Hoyle Bottom
Rushton House Farm
Cross Edge
GREEN HAWORTH
Knowles Buildings
Bottoms
Duckworth Hall
Higher Duckworth Hill Cottage
Duckworth Hill
DUCKWORTH HILL LANE
Britannia Cotts.
Britannia Poultry Farm
Lower Duckworth Hill
Scar Green
Rhoden
HIGHER RHODEN
Town Bent Farm
White Croft
WHITE CROFT ROAD
Jackhouse
Cocker Brook
Stonybroke
Cockerley Fold
Cocker Lumb Cotts.
Clough
Moss Hall
New Moss Farm
HASLINGDEN ROAD
Whams Brook
Bumper Hall
Works
Broughton Barn
Houlker Barn
Robin Hood Farm
Broad Carr Farm
Childers House
Mattbridge
Lower Red Walls
Benjamin Row
Only Foals & Horses Sanctuary
SHELL LANE
Moorfield
Stony Knoll
Cocker Brook Farm
COBBS
B6236
RAMSCLOUGH ROAD
Cattle Plantation Lower
Barnfield Plantation
Cattle Plantation Higher
Height Plantation
Lower Bold Venture Farm
Higher Bold Venture
Lower Westalot Farm
Brewer Lot Farm
Moor Farm
Lottice
121
142
159

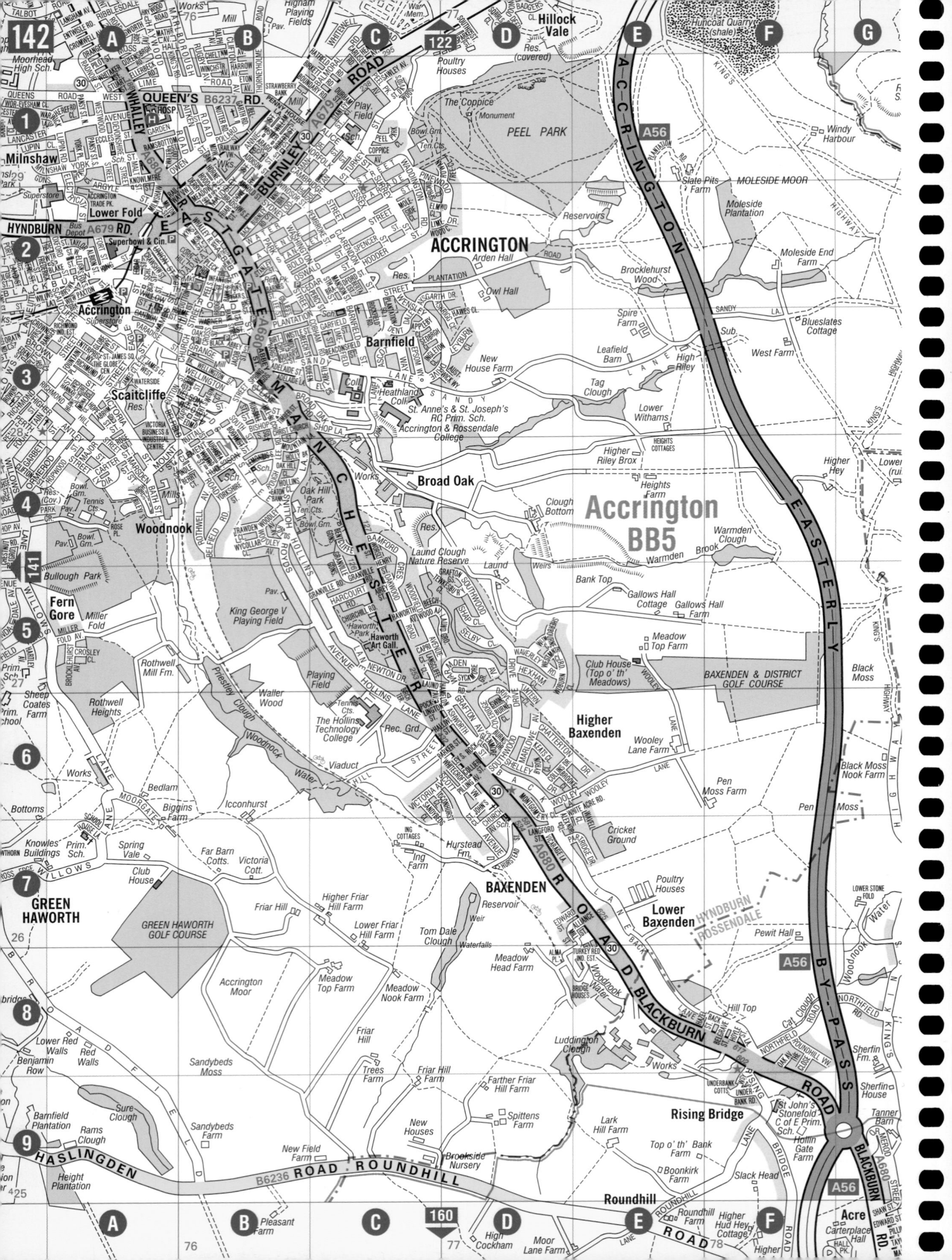

142
ACCRINGTON
Accrington BB5
Milnshaw
Lower Fold
HYNDBURN RD.
Superbowl & Cin.
Accrington
Scaitcliffe
Woodnook
Bullough Park
Fern Gore
Miller Fold
Rothwell Mill Fm.
Rothwell Heights
Sheep Coates Farm
Green Haworth
GREEN HAWORTH GOLF COURSE
Bedlam
Biggins Farm
Icconhurst
Bottoms
Knowles' Buildings
Spring Vale
Club House
Far Barn Cotts.
Victoria Cott.
Friar Hill
Higher Friar Hill Farm
Lower Friar Hill Farm
Accrington Moor
Meadow Top Farm
Meadow Nook Farm
Lower Red Walls
Red Walls
Benjamin Row
Sandybeds Moss
Sure Clough
Barnfield Plantation
Rams Clough
Sandybeds Farm
Height Plantation
New Field Farm
Friar Hill
Trees Farm
Friar Hill Farm
Farther Friar Hill Farm
New Houses
Spittens Farm
Brookside Nursery
Pleasant Farm
High Cockham
Moor Lane Farm
HASLINGDEN ROAD
B6236 ROAD
ROUNDHILL ROAD
Roundhill
Roundhill Farm
Higher Hud Hey Cottage
Slack Head
Boonkirk Farm
Top o' th' Bank Farm
Lark Hill Farm
Rising Bridge
St John's Stonefold C of E Prim. Sch.
Hollin Gate Farm
Acre
Carterplace Hall
Tanner Barn
Sherfin Fm.
Sherfin House
Hill Top
Luddington Clough
Works
BLACKBURN ROAD
A680
Meadow Head Farm
Tom Dale Clough
Waterfalls
Weir
Reservoir
BAXENDEN
Lower Baxenden
HYNDBURN ROSSENDALE
Pewit Hall
Poultry Houses
Cricket Ground
Hurstead Fm.
Ing Farm
Ing Cottages
Viaduct
The Hollins Technology College
Rec. Grd.
Playing Field
Waller Wood
Priestley Clough
Woodnook Water
King George V Playing Field
Haworth Art Gall.
Laund Clough Nature Reserve
Laund
Bank Top
Gallows Hall Cottage
Gallows Hall Farm
Meadow Top Farm
Club House (Top o' th' Meadows)
BAXENDEN & DISTRICT GOLF COURSE
Higher Baxenden
Wooley Lane Farm
Pen Moss Farm
Pen Moss
Black Moss Nook Farm
Black Moss
Warmden Clough
Warmden Brook
Clough Bottom
Heights Farm
Broad Oak
Higher Riley Brox
Heights Cottages
Lower Withams
Tag Clough
High Riley
Leafield Barn
New House Farm
Heathland Coll.
St. Anne's & St. Joseph's RC Prim. Sch.
Accrington & Rossendale College
Barnfield
Owl Hall
Arden Hall
Spire Farm
Brocklehurst Wood
Reservoirs
Slate Pits Farm
MOLESIDE MOOR
Moleside Plantation
Moleside End Farm
SANDY LA.
Bluestates Cottage
West Farm
Higher Hey
Windy Harbour
Huncoat Quarry (shale)
Hillock Vale
Res. (covered)
Poultry Houses
The Coppice
Monument
PEEL PARK
Higham Playing Fields
Moorhead High Sch.
QUEEN'S RD.
B6237
WHALLEY RD.
A679
BURNLEY ROAD
EASTGATE
MANCHESTER ROAD
ACCRINGTON EASTERLY BY-PASS
A56
Lower Stone Fold
Woodnook Water
NORTHFIELD RD.
Cat Clough
122
141
160
A B C D E F G
1 2 3 4 5 6 7 8 9

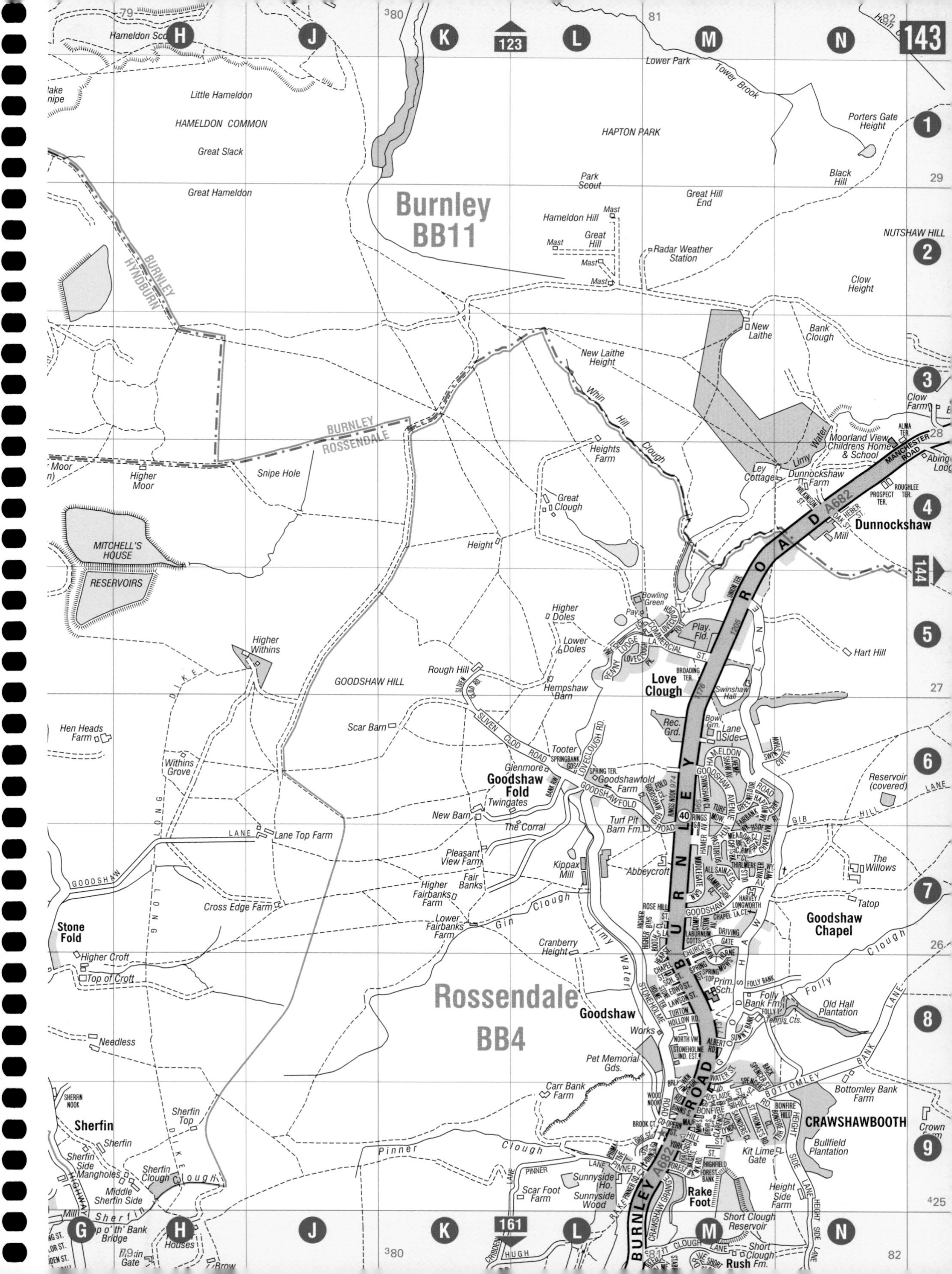
123
161
144
Burnley
BB11
Rossendale
BB4
HAMELDON COMMON
Little Hameldon
Great Slack
Great Hameldon
HAPTON PARK
Lower Park
Tower Brook
Porters Gate Height
Black Hill
NUTSHAW HILL
Clow Height
Park Scout
Hameldon Hill
Great Hill
Great Hill End
Radar Weather Station
Mast
New Laithe
Bank Clough
New Laithe Height
Whin Hill Clough
Heights Farm
Great Clough
Height
MITCHELL'S HOUSE
RESERVOIRS
Higher Moor
Snipe Hole
BURNLEY
HYNDBURN
BURNLEY
ROSSENDALE
Moorland View Childrens Home & School
Limy Water
Dunnockshaw Farm
Ley Cottage
Clow Farm
MANCHESTER ROAD
Dunnockshaw
Mill
A682
ROAD
BURNLEY ROAD
Bowling Green
Play. Fld.
Higher Doles
Lower Doles
Hart Hill
Higher Withins
GOODSHAW HILL
Rough Hill
Hempshaw Barn
Love Clough
Swinshaw Hall
COMMERCIAL ST.
Rec. Grd.
Lane Side
Hen Heads Farm
Scar Barn
SLIVEN CLOUGH ROAD
Tooter
Glenmore
Goodshaw Fold
Goodshawfold Farm
Twingates
Withins Grove
LONG DIKE
Reservoir (covered)
GIB HILL LANE
New Barn
The Corral
Turf Pit Barn Fm.
Lane Top Farm
GOODSHAW LANE
Pleasant View Farm
Fair Banks
Higher Fairbanks Farm
Kippax Mill
Abbeycroft
The Willows
Tatop
Cross Edge Farm
Lower Fairbanks Farm
Gin Clough
Goodshaw Chapel
Stone Fold
Higher Croft
Top of Croft
Cranberry Height
Limy Water
Folly Clough
Goodshaw
Folly Bank Fm.
Old Hall Plantation
Tennis Cts.
Prim. Sch.
Needless
Works
Pet Memorial Gds.
Carr Bank Farm
BOTTOMLEY BANK
Bottomley Bank Farm
CRAWSHAWBOOTH
Crown
Bullfield Plantation
Kit Lime Gate
Sherfin
Sherfin Top
Sherfin Nook
Sherfin Side
Mangholes
Middle Sherfin Side
Sherfin Clough
Pinner Clough
PINNER LANE
Scar Foot Farm
Sunnyside Ho.
Sunnyside Wood
Rake Foot
Height Side Farm
Short Clough Reservoir
Short Clough Fm.
Rush
Top o' th' Bank Bridge
Houses
HUGH
HEIGHT SIDE LANE
CRAWSHAW GRANGE
Sherfin
HIGHWAY
Mill
Gate
Brow

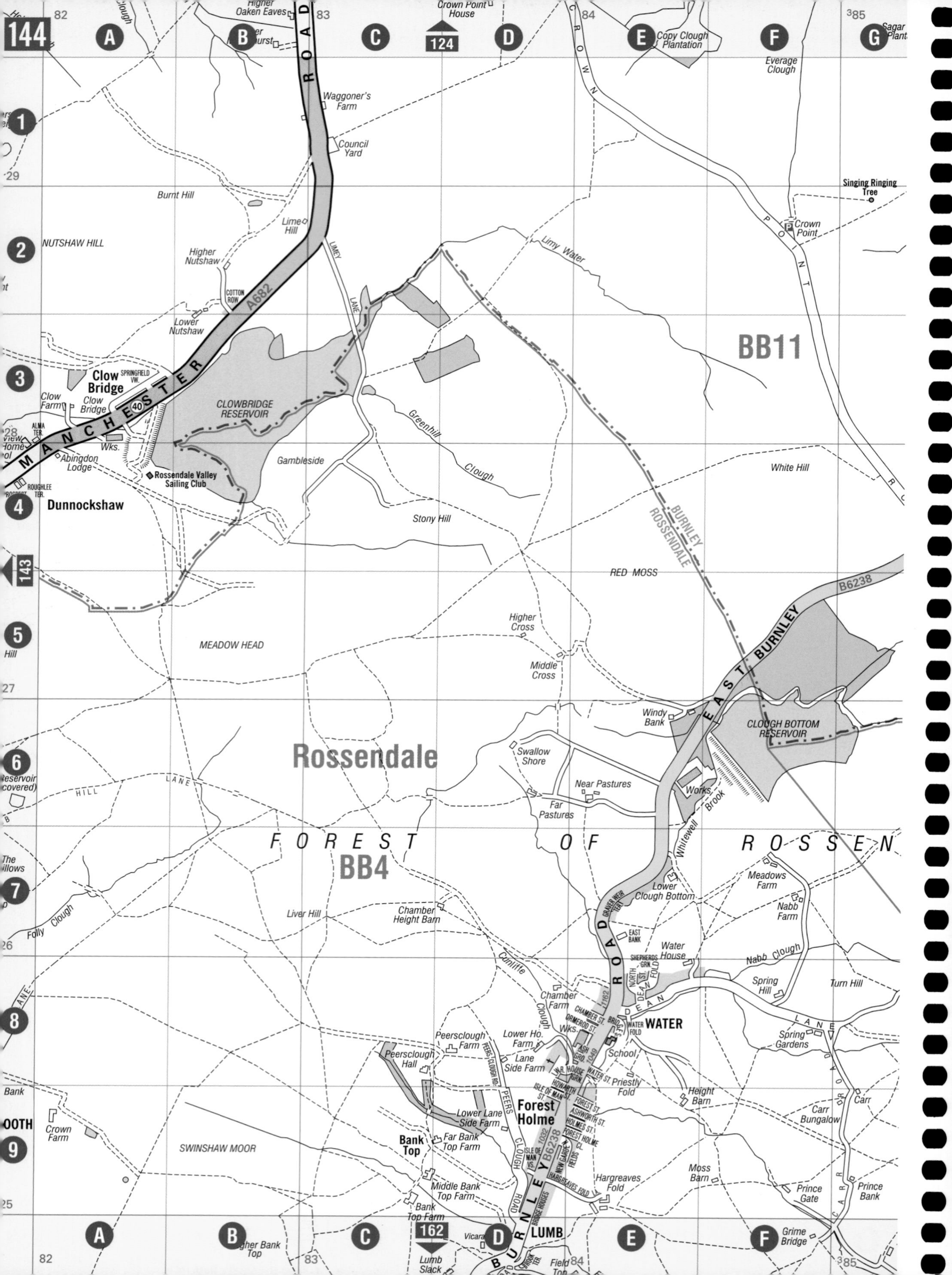

Higher Oaken Eaves
Crown Point House
124
Copy Clough Plantation
Everage Clough
Waggoner's Farm
Council Yard
Burnt Hill
Singing Ringing Tree
Lime Hill
Crown Point
NUTSHAW HILL
Higher Nutshaw
Limy Water
COTTON ROW
A682
Lower Nutshaw
BB11
Clow Bridge
SPRINGFIELD VW.
MANCHESTER
CLOWBRIDGE RESERVOIR
Clow Farm
Clow Bridge
ALMA TER.
Greenhill Clough
Wks.
Abingdon Lodge
Gambleside
White Hill
Rossendale Valley Sailing Club
ROUGHLEE TER.
Dunnockshaw
Stony Hill
BURNLEY ROSSENDALE
143
RED MOSS
B6238
Higher Cross
MEADOW HEAD
EAST BURNLEY
Middle Cross
Windy Bank
CLOUGH BOTTOM RESERVOIR
Rossendale
Swallow Shore
HILL LANE
Near Pastures
Works
Far Pastures
Whitewell Brook
FOREST OF ROSSENDALE
BB4
Meadows Farm
Lower Clough Bottom
Nabb Farm
Liver Hill
Chamber Height Barn
Folly Clough
EAST BANK
Water House
SHEPHERDS GRN.
Nabb Clough
Cunliffe
Spring Hill
Turn Hill
Chamber Farm
DEAN LANE
WATER
WATER FOLD
Spring Gardens
Peersclough Farm
Lower Ho. Farm
Peersclough Hall
Lane Side Farm
School
Priestly Fold
Height Barn
Bank
Carr
Carr Bungalow
Forest Holme
Lower Lane Side Farm
Crown Farm
Bank Top
Far Bank Top Farm
SWINSHAW MOOR
Moss Barn
Middle Bank Top Farm
Hargreaves Fold
Prince Gate
Prince Bank
BURNLEY ROAD
Bank Top Farm
162
LUMB
Grime Bridge
Higher Bank Top
Lumb Slack
Field Top

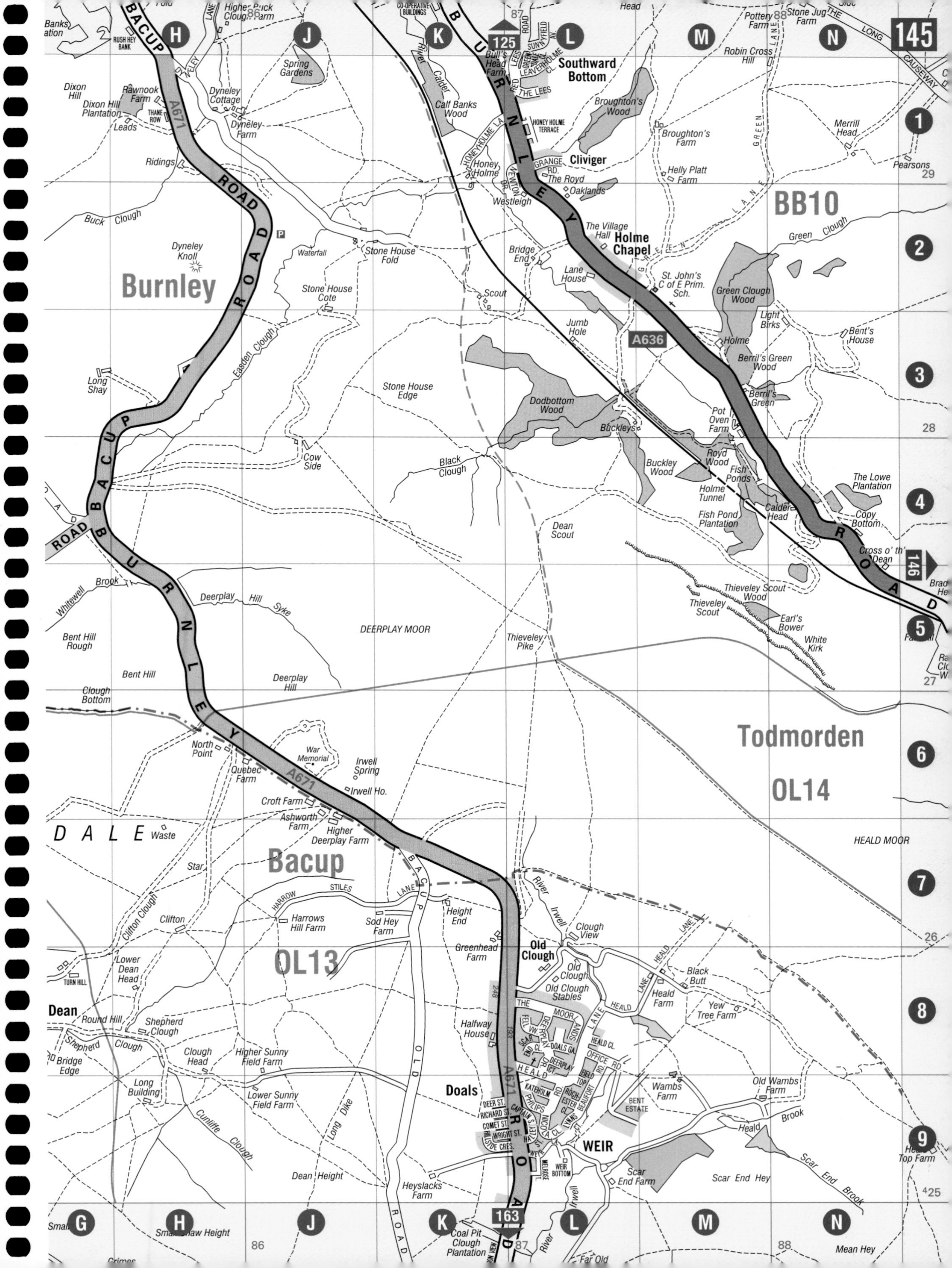

Burnley
BB10
Todmorden
OL14
Bacup
OL13
Southward Bottom
Cliviger
Holme Chapel
Oaklands
The Royd
Westleigh
Dyneley Knoll
Dyneley Cottage
Dyneley Farm
Rawnook Farm
Dixon Hill
Dixon Hill Plantation
Leads
Ridings
Buck Clough
Spring Gardens
Calf Banks Wood
Broughton's Wood
Broughton's Farm
Helly Platt Farm
Merrill Head
Pearsons
Robin Cross Hill
Pottery Farm
Stone Jug Farm
THE LONG CAUSEWAY
Stone House Fold
Stone House Cote
Stone House Edge
Waterfall
Scout
Bridge End
Lane House
Jumb Hole
The Village Hall
St. John's C of E Prim. Sch.
Green Clough
Green Clough Wood
Light Birks
Bent's House
Holme
Berril's Green Wood
Berril's Green
Pot Oven Farm
Dodbottom Wood
Buckleys
Buckley Wood
Royd Wood
Fish Ponds
Holme Tunnel
Fish Pond Plantation
Calder Head
The Lowe Plantation
Copy Bottom
Cross o' th' Dean
Thieveley Scout Wood
Thieveley Scout
Earl's Bower
White Kirk
Thieveley Pike
Dean Scout
Black Clough
Cow Side
Long Shay
Easden Clough
BACUP ROAD
BURNLEY ROAD
A671
A636
Whitewell Brook
Deerplay Hill Syke
DEERPLAY MOOR
Bent Hill Rough
Bent Hill
Deerplay Hill
Clough Bottom
North Point
Quebec Farm
War Memorial
Irwell Spring
Irwell Ho.
Croft Farm
Ashworth Farm
Higher Deerplay Farm
Waste
Star
HEALD MOOR
Harrows Hill Farm
Sod Hey Farm
Height End
Clough View
Old Clough
Old Clough Stables
Greenhead Farm
Clifton
Clifton Clough
Lower Dean Head
Dean
Round Hill
Shepherd Clough
Bridge Edge
Clough Head
Higher Sunny Field Farm
Lower Sunny Field Farm
Long Building
Cunliffe Clough
Long Dike
Halfway House
Doals
WEIR
Heald Farm
Black Butt
Yew Tree Farm
Wambs Farm
Old Wambs Farm
BENT ESTATE
Heald Brook
Scar End Hey
Scar End Brook
Scar End Farm
Dean Height
Heyslacks Farm
Coal Pit Clough Plantation
Smallshaw Height
Mean Hey
River Calder
River Irwell
G H J K L M N
1 2 3 4 5 6 7 8 9
125
146
163
86 87 88
29 28 27 26 25

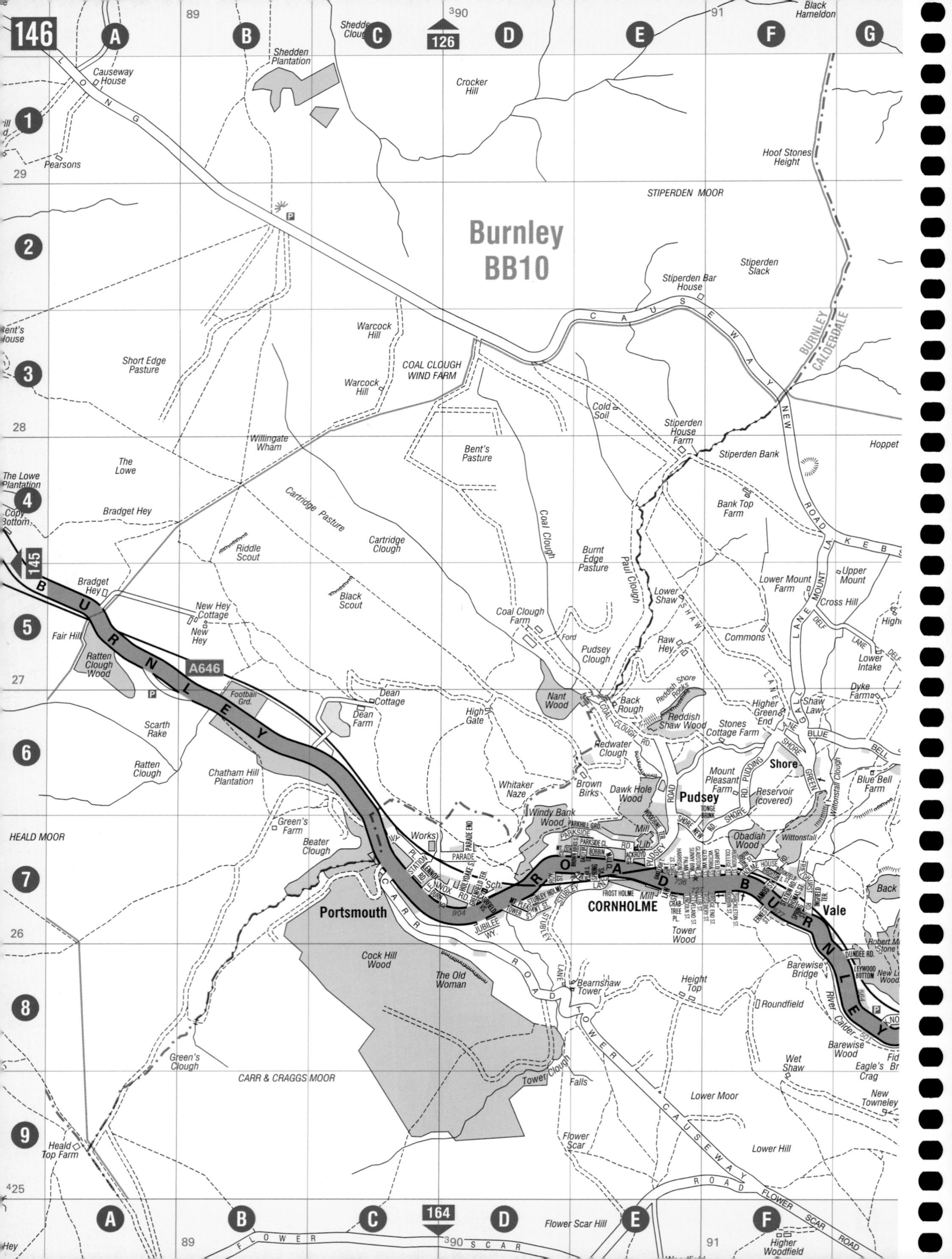
146
A
B
C
D
E
F
G
89
390
91
126
164
425
1
2
3
4
5
6
7
8
9
29
28
27
26
Black Hameldon
Shedden Clough
Shedden Plantation
Causeway House
LONG
Crocker Hill
Pearsons
Hoof Stones Height
STIPERDEN MOOR
Burnley
BB10
Stiperden Slack
Stiperden Bar House
CAUSEWAY
BURNLEY
CALDERDALE
Warcock Hill
Short Edge Pasture
COAL CLOUGH WIND FARM
Cold Soil
Stiperden House Farm
NEW ROAD
Stiperden Bank
Hoppet
Willingate Wham
The Lowe
The Lowe Plantation
Bent's Pasture
Bradget Hey
Copy Bottom
Cartridge Pasture
Bank Top Farm
Coal Clough
Riddle Scout
Cartridge Clough
Burnt Edge Pasture
Paul Clough
145
Bradget Hey
Black Scout
Lower Mount Farm
Upper Mount
MOUNT LANE
Cross Hill
Lower Shaw
New Hey Cottage
New Hey
Coal Clough Farm
Ford
Fair Hill
Ratten Clough Wood
Raw Hey
Commons
SHAW LANE
Lower Intake
A646
Pudsey Clough
Football Grd.
Dean Cottage
Nant Wood
Back Rough
Reddish Shore Rocks
Reddish Shaw Wood
Higher Green End
Shaw Law
Dyke Farm
Scarth Rake
Dean Farm
High Gate
COAL CLOUGH RD.
Stones Cottage Farm
BLUE
BELL
Redwater Clough
Shore
Ratten Clough
Chatham Hill Plantation
Whitaker Naze
Brown Birks
Dawk Hole Wood
Mount Pleasant Farm
Pudsey
Reservoir (covered)
Blue Bell Farm
Windy Bank Wood
TONGE BRINK
Obadiah Wood
Wittonstall
Green's Farm
HEALD MOOR
Beater Clough
Works
PARADE END
PARADE
Mill
Lib.
Sch.
Back
Portsmouth
CORNHOLME
Vale
BURNLEY ROAD
904
736
727
577
JUBILEE WY.
Tower Wood
CARR ROAD
Robert M Stone
DUNDEE RD.
Cock Hill Wood
The Old Woman
Barewise Bridge
LEYWOOD BOTTOM
Beamshaw Tower
Height Top
Roundfield
River Calder
Green's Clough
CARR & CRAGGS MOOR
Tower Clough
Falls
Barewise Wood
Wet Shaw
Eagle's Crag
Lower Moor
New Towneley
Flower Scar
Lower Hill
Heald Top Farm
Hey
Flower Scar Hill
FLOWER SCAR ROAD
TOWER CAUSEWAY
Higher Woodfield

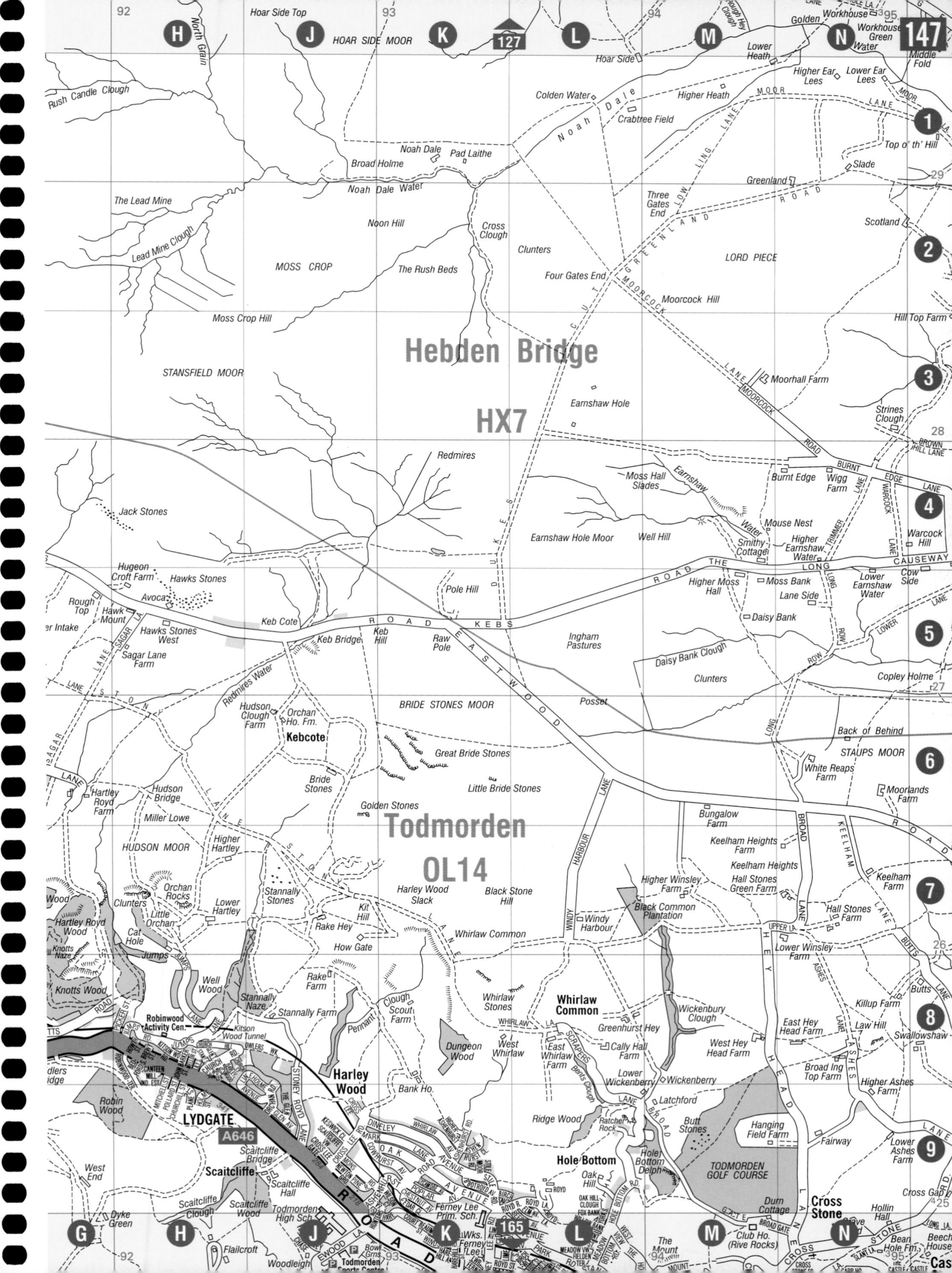
Hebden Bridge
HX7
Todmorden
OL14
Hoar Side Top
HOAR SIDE MOOR
North Grain
Hoar Side
Lower Heath
Golden Water
Workhouse
Workhouse Green Water
Middle Fold
Higher Ear Lees
Lower Ear Lees
Colden Water
Higher Heath
Noah Dale
Crabtree Field
Top o' th' Hill
Slade
Rush Candle Clough
Noah Dale
Pad Laithe
Broad Holme
Noah Dale Water
Greenland
Three Gates End
The Lead Mine
Lead Mine Clough
Noon Hill
Cross Clough
Clunters
Scotland
LORD PIECE
MOSS CROP
The Rush Beds
Four Gates End
Moorcock Hill
Moss Crop Hill
Hill Top Farm
STANSFIELD MOOR
Moorhall Farm
Earnshaw Hole
Strines Clough
Redmires
Moss Hall Slades
Burnt Edge
Wigg Farm
Jack Stones
Mouse Nest
Earnshaw Hole Moor
Well Hill
Smithy Cottage
Higher Earnshaw Water
Warcock Hill
Hugeon Croft Farm
Hawks Stones
Higher Moss Hall
Moss Bank
Lower Earnshaw Water
Cow Side
Rough Top
Hawk Mount
Avoca
Pole Hill
Lane Side
Daisy Bank
Keb Cote
Keb Bridge
Keb Hill
Raw Pole
Ingham Pastures
Hawks Stones West
Sagar Lane Farm
Daisy Bank Clough
Clunters
Copley Holme
Hudson Clough Farm
Orchan Ho. Fm.
BRIDE STONES MOOR
Posset
Kebcote
Back of Behind
STAUPS MOOR
Great Bride Stones
White Reaps Farm
Hartley Royd Farm
Hudson Bridge
Bride Stones
Little Bride Stones
Moorlands Farm
Bungalow Farm
Golden Stones
Miller Lowe
Keelham Heights Farm
Keelham Heights
HUDSON MOOR
Higher Hartley
Higher Winsley Farm
Hall Stones Green Farm
Keelham Farm
Orchan Rocks
Stannally Stones
Harley Wood Slack
Black Stone Hill
Clunters
Little Orchan
Lower Hartley
Kit Hill
Windy Harbour
Black Common Plantation
Hall Stones Farm
Hartley Royd Wood
Rake Hey
Whirlaw Common
Cat Hole
Knotts Naze
Jumps
How Gate
Lower Winsley Farm
Well Wood
Rake Farm
Butts
Knotts Wood
Stannally Naze
Stannally Farm
Clough Scout Farm
Whirlaw Stones
Whirlaw Common
Wickenbury Clough
Killup Farm
Robinwood Activity Cen.
Kitson Wood Tunnel
Pennant
Greenhurst Hey
East Hey Head Farm
Law Hill
Swallowshaw
Dungeon Wood
West Whirlaw
East Whirlaw Farm
Cally Hall Farm
West Hey Head Farm
Harley Wood
Lower Wickenberry
Wickenberry
Broad Ing Top Farm
Higher Ashes Farm
Robin Wood
Bank Ho.
Latchford
LYDGATE
A646
Ridge Wood
Ratcher Rock
Butt Stones
Hanging Field Farm
Fairway
Lower Ashes Farm
Scaitcliffe Bridge
Hole Bottom
Holey Bottom Delph
TODMORDEN GOLF COURSE
West End
Scaitcliffe
Scaitcliffe Hall
Oak Hill
Scaitcliffe Clough
Scaitcliffe Wood
Todmorden High Sch.
Ferney Lee Prim. Sch.
Durn Cottage
Cross Stone
Cross Gap
Hollin Hall
Dyke Green
Club Ho. (Rive Rocks)
Bean Hole Fm.
Beech House
Flailcroft
Woodleigh
Todmorden Sports Centre
Wks. Ferney Lee
The Mount
MOORCOCK ROAD
GREENLAND ROAD
LOW LING LANE
THE LONG CAUSEWAY
KEBS ROAD
EASTWOOD ROAD
DUKES CUT
STONE LANE
SAGAR LANE
WINDY HARBOUR LANE
BROAD LANE
KEELHAM LANE
HEY HEAD LANE
ASHES LANE
BUTTS LANE
WHIRLAW LANE
BURNT EDGE LANE
BROWN HILL LANE
TRIMMER LANE
WARCOCK LANE
LONG ROW
LOWER LANE
STONEY ROYD LANE
CROSS STONE ROAD
HALIFAX ROAD
127
165
92
93
94
95
25
26
27
28
29
H J K L M N G
1 2 3 4 5 6 7 8 9

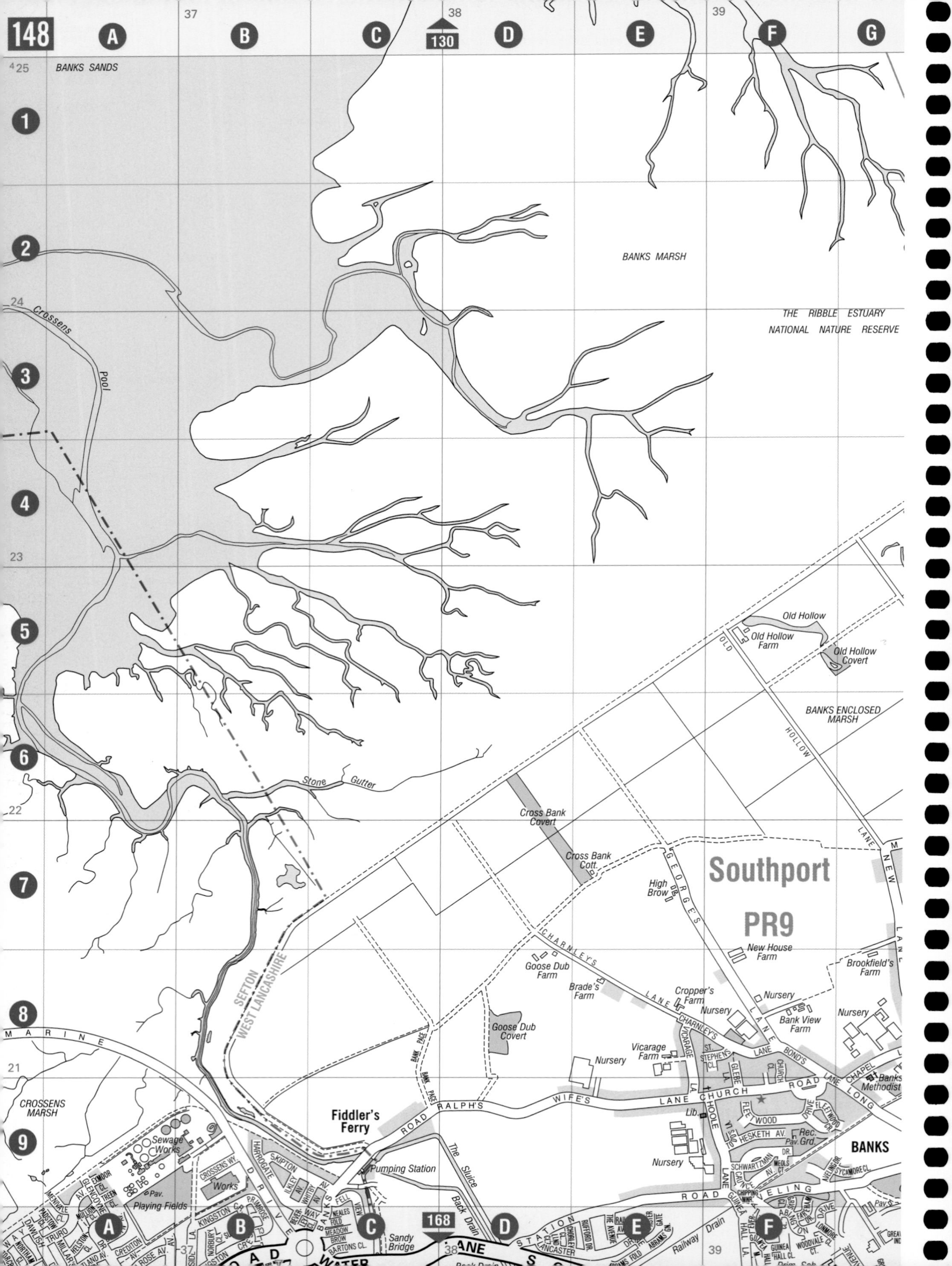
BANKS SANDS
BANKS MARSH
THE RIBBLE ESTUARY NATIONAL NATURE RESERVE
Crossens Pool
Stone Gutter
Old Hollow
Old Hollow Farm
Old Hollow Covert
BANKS ENCLOSED MARSH
Cross Bank Covert
Cross Bank Cott.
High Brow
Southport
PR9
New House Farm
Brookfield's Farm
Goose Dub Farm
Brade's Farm
Cropper's Farm
Nursery
Bank View Farm
Goose Dub Covert
Vicarage Farm
SEFTON
WEST LANCASHIRE
MARINE DRIVE
CROSSENS MARSH
Sewage Works
Works
Playing Fields
Pav.
Fiddler's Ferry
Pumping Station
The Sluice
Back Drain
Sandy Bridge
Railway Drain
RALPH'S WIFE'S LANE
CHURCH ROAD
CHARNLEY'S LANE
GEORGE'S LANE
HOLLOW LANE
NEW LANE
BOND'S LANE
LONG LANE
CHAPEL LANE
BANK PACE
STATION ROAD
GUINEA HALL LANE
HESKETH AV.
FLEETWOOD DRIVE
SCHWARTZMAN DR.
Rec. Grd.
Lib.
Banks Methodist
BANKS
HARROGATE
SKIPTON
ILKLEY AV.
WHITBY AV.
FELL VIEW
NEALES FOLD
MEADOW BROW
BARTONS CL.
KINGSTON CR.
PRIMROSE
CROSSENS WY.
NORBURY
EXMOOR CL.
GLENCOYNE
MENIVALE CL.
PADSTOW
TRURO
DAWLISH
HELSTON
CREDITON
ROSE AV.
THE AVENUE
RUFFORD DR.
LANCASTER
ABRAMS FOLD
ABRAMS GN.
VICARAGE
ST. STEPHENS CL.
GLEBE LA.
HOOLE LA.
CHURCH CT.
SYCAMORE CL.
WOODVALE CT.
GUINEA HALL CL.
130
168

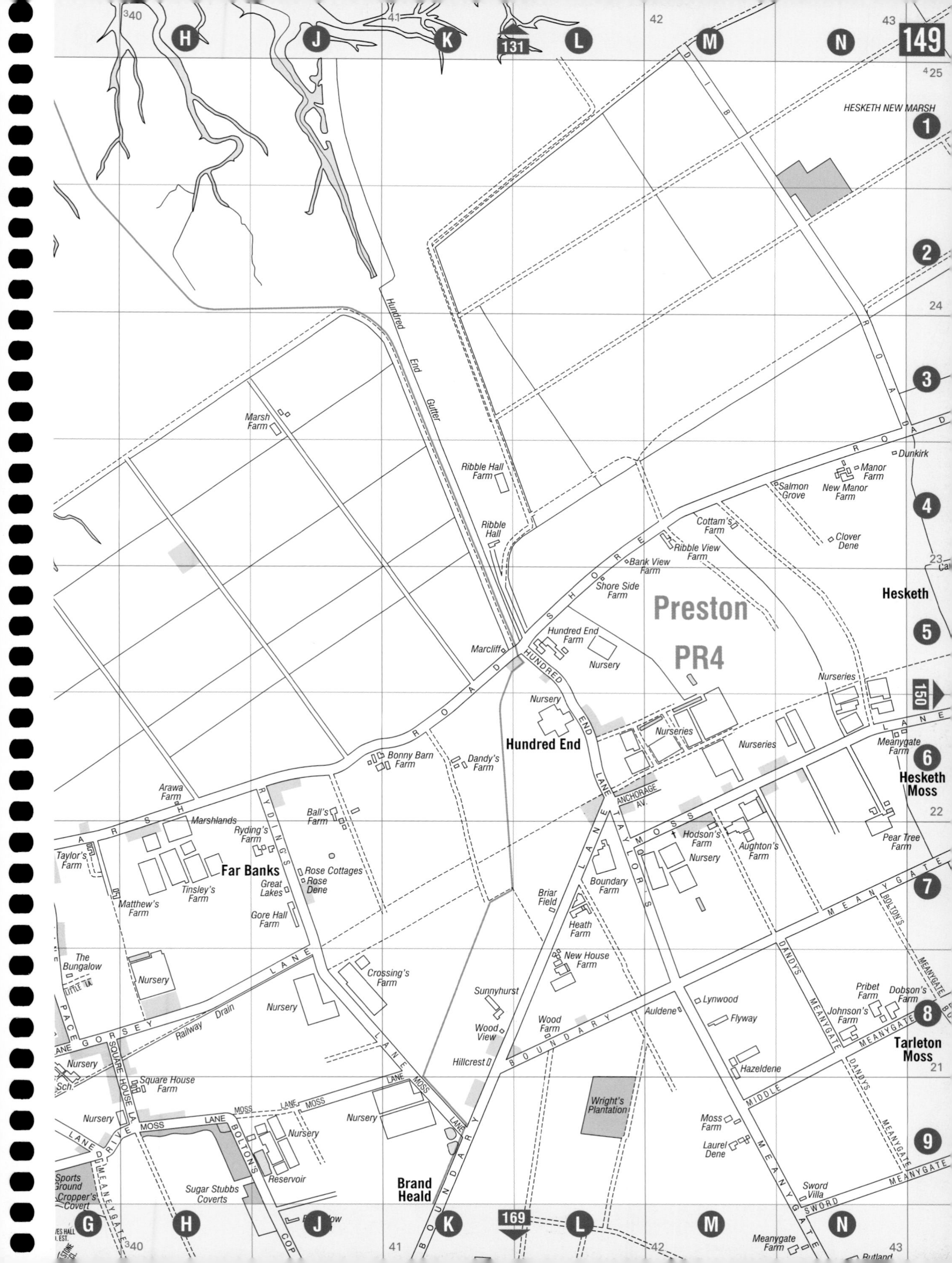
HESKETH NEW MARSH
Hundred End Gutter
DIB ROAD
Marsh Farm
Ribble Hall Farm
Ribble Hall
Dunkirk
Manor Farm
New Manor Farm
Salmon Grove
Cottam's Farm
Clover Dene
Ribble View Farm
Bank View Farm
Shore Side Farm
SHORE ROAD
Preston
PR4
Hesketh
Marcliff
Hundred End Farm
Nursery
HUNDRED END LANE
Nurseries
Hundred End
Bonny Barn Farm
Dandy's Farm
Meanygate Farm
Hesketh Moss
ANCHORAGE AV.
Arawa Farm
MARSH
Marshlands
Ryding's Farm
Ball's Farm
RYDINGS
Taylor's Farm
Far Banks
Rose Cottages
Rose Dene
Great Lakes
Tinsley's Farm
Matthew's Farm
Gore Hall Farm
Hodson's Farm
Aughton's Farm
Pear Tree Farm
MOSS
TAYLOR'S LANE
Boundary Farm
Briar Field
Heath Farm
New House Farm
MEANYGATE
BOLTON'S
The Bungalow
LITTLE LA.
Crossing's Farm
GORSEY LANE
Railway Drain
Sunnyhurst
Wood View
Wood Farm
Hillcrest
BOUNDARY
Auldene
Lynwood
Flyway
Pribet Farm
Dobson's Farm
Johnson's Farm
Tarleton Moss
DANDY'S MEANYGATE
Hazeldene
MIDDLE MEANYGATE
SQUARE HOUSE LA.
Square House Farm
MOSS LANE
Wright's Plantation
Moss Farm
Laurel Dene
Sword Villa
SWORD MEANYGATE
Sports Ground
Cropper's Covert
Sugar Stubbs Coverts
Reservoir
Brand Heald
Meanygate Farm
Rutland
131
169
150

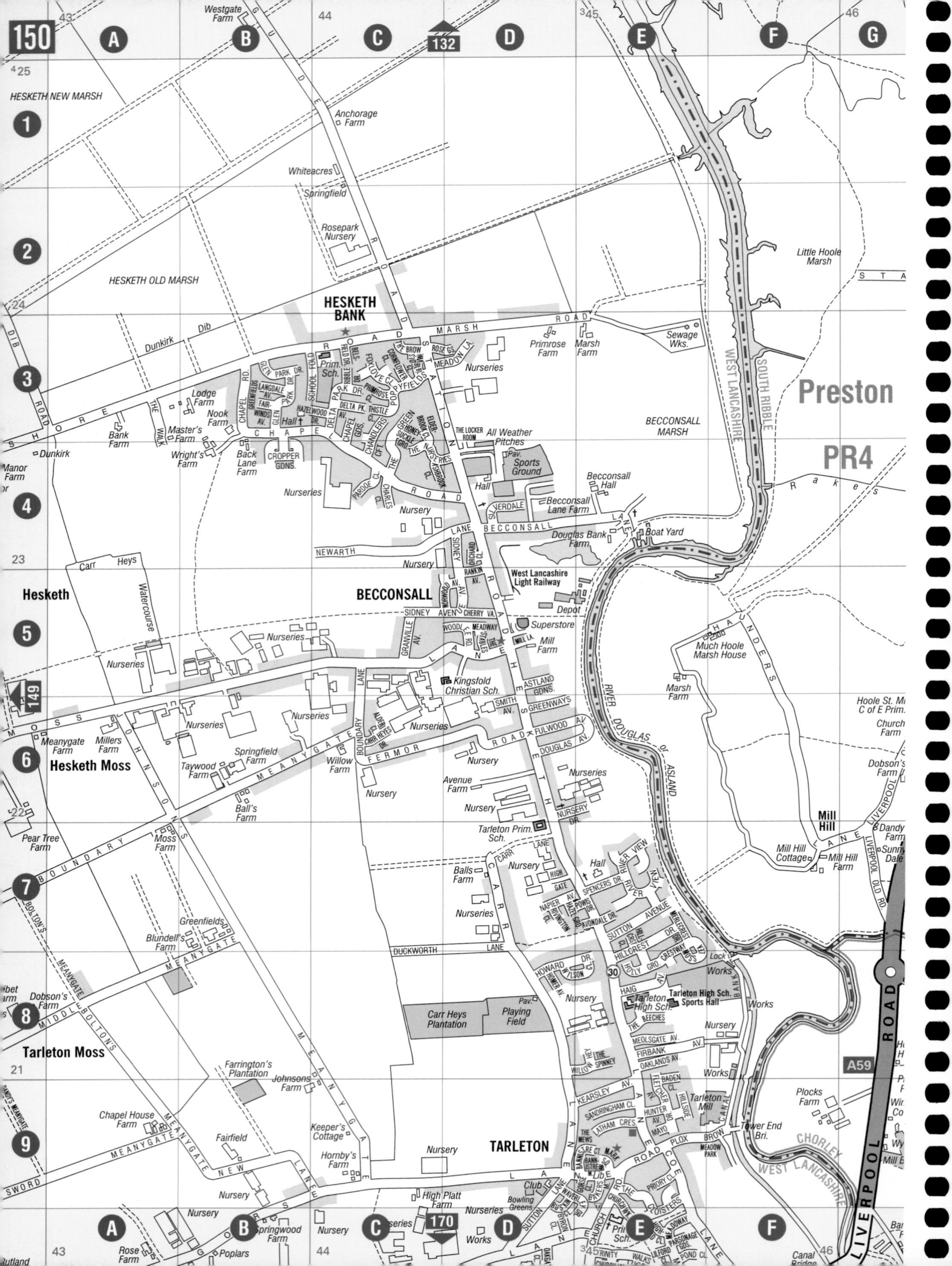
HESKETH NEW MARSH
HESKETH OLD MARSH
HESKETH BANK
BECCONSALL
Hesketh
Hesketh Moss
Tarleton Moss
TARLETON
Preston
PR4
BECCONSALL MARSH
Little Hoole Marsh
Mill Hill
RIVER DOUGLAS or ASLAND
WEST LANCASHIRE
SOUTH RIBBLE
West Lancashire Light Railway
Tarleton High Sch.
Tarleton Prim. Sch.
Kingsfold Christian Sch.
Carr Heys Plantation
Playing Field
Sports Ground
Superstore
Depot
Sewage Wks.
Boat Yard
A59
LIVERPOOL ROAD
CHORLEY
132
170
149

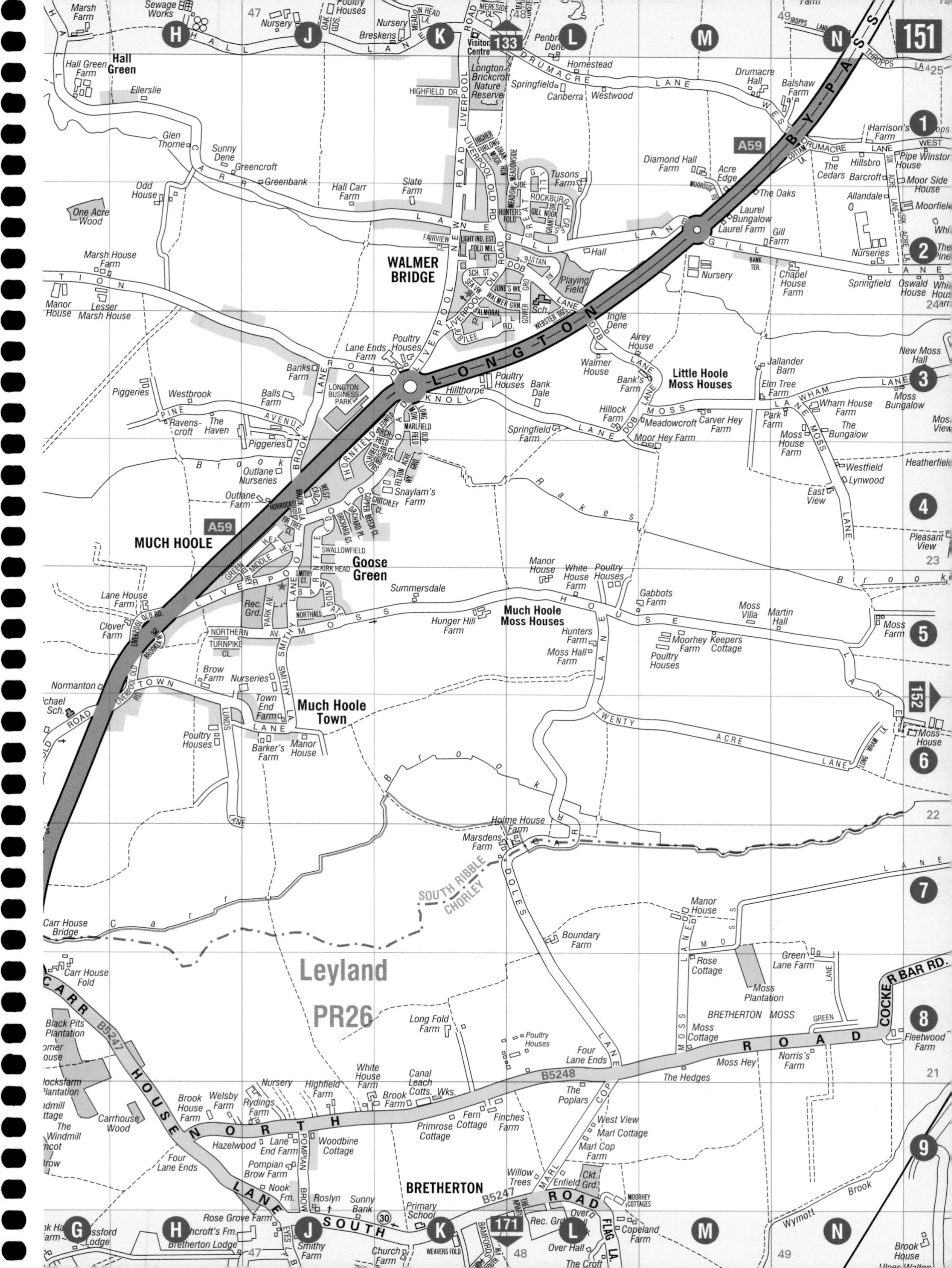

WALMER BRIDGE
MUCH HOOLE
Goose Green
Much Hoole Town
Little Hoole Moss Houses
Much Hoole Moss Houses
BRETHERTON
BRETHERTON MOSS
Leyland
PR26
SOUTH RIBBLE
CHORLEY
LONGTON BY-PASS
A59
B5247
B5248
LONGTON BUSINESS PARK
Longton Brickcroft Nature Reserve
Visitor Centre
Hall Green
Hall Green Farm
Marsh Farm
Sewage Works
Poultry Houses
Nursery
Breskens
Penbro Dene
Homestead
Drumacre Hall
Balshaw Farm
DRUMACRE LANE
Springfield
Canberra
Westwood
Eilerslie
Glen Thorne
Sunny Dene
Greencroft
Greenbank
Odd House
One Acre Wood
Hall Carr Farm
Slate Farm
Tusons Farm
Diamond Hall Farm
Acre Edge
The Oaks
Laurel Bungalow
Laurel Farm
Gill Farm
Harrison's Farm
Pipe Winstor House
Hillsbro
The Cedars
Barcroft
Moor Side House
Allandale
Moorfield
Nurseries
Nursery
Chapel House Farm
Springfield
Oswald House
Marsh House Farm
Manor House
Lesser Marsh House
Ingle Dene
Airey House
Walmer House
Bank's Farm
Jallander Barn
Elm Tree Farm
New Moss Hall
Moss Bungalow
Hillthorpe
Bank Dale
Lane Ends Farm
Banks Farm
Piggeries
Westbrook
Balls Farm
Ravenscroft
The Haven
Outlane Nurseries
Outlane Farm
Snaylam's Farm
Hillock Farm
Meadowcroft
Carver Hey Farm
Moor Hey Farm
Springfield Farm
Park Farm
Moss House Farm
Wham House Farm
The Bungalow
Westfield
Lynwood
East View
Heatherfield
Pleasant View
Manor House
White House Farm
Gabbots Farm
Summersdale
Lane House Farm
Clover Farm
Hunger Hill Farm
Hunters Farm
Moss Hall Farm
Moorhey Farm
Keepers Cottage
Moss Villa
Martin Hall
Moss Farm
Normanton
Brow Farm
Nurseries
Town End Farm
Barker's Farm
Manor House
Moss House
Holme House Farm
Marsdens Farm
Carr House Bridge
Boundary Farm
Manor House
Rose Cottage
Green Lane Farm
Moss Plantation
Carr House Fold
Black Pits Plantation
Carrhouse Wood
Long Fold Farm
Moss Cottage
Moss Hey
Norris's Farm
Fleetwood Farm
Four Lane Ends
The Hedges
The Poplars
Brook House Farm
Welsby Farm
Rydings Farm
Highfield Farm
White House Farm
Canal Leach Cotts.
Wks.
Brook Farm
Fern Cottage
Finches Farm
Primrose Cottage
West View
Marl Cottage
Marl Cop Farm
Hazelwood
Lane End Farm
Woodbine Cottage
Pompian Brow Farm
Four Lane Ends
Nook Fm.
Roslyn
Sunny Bank
Primary School
Willow Trees
Enfield
Ckt. Grd.
Rose Grove Farm
Bretherton Lodge
Smithy Farm
Church Farm
Over Hall
Copeland Farm
The Croft
Wymott
Brook House
COCKER BAR RD.
NORTH ROAD
SOUTH ROAD
CARR HOUSE LANE
DOLES LANE
TWENTY ACRE LANE
FLAG LA.
133
171
152
47
48
49
21
22
23
24
25
G
H
J
K
L
M
N
1
2
3
4
5
6
7
8
9

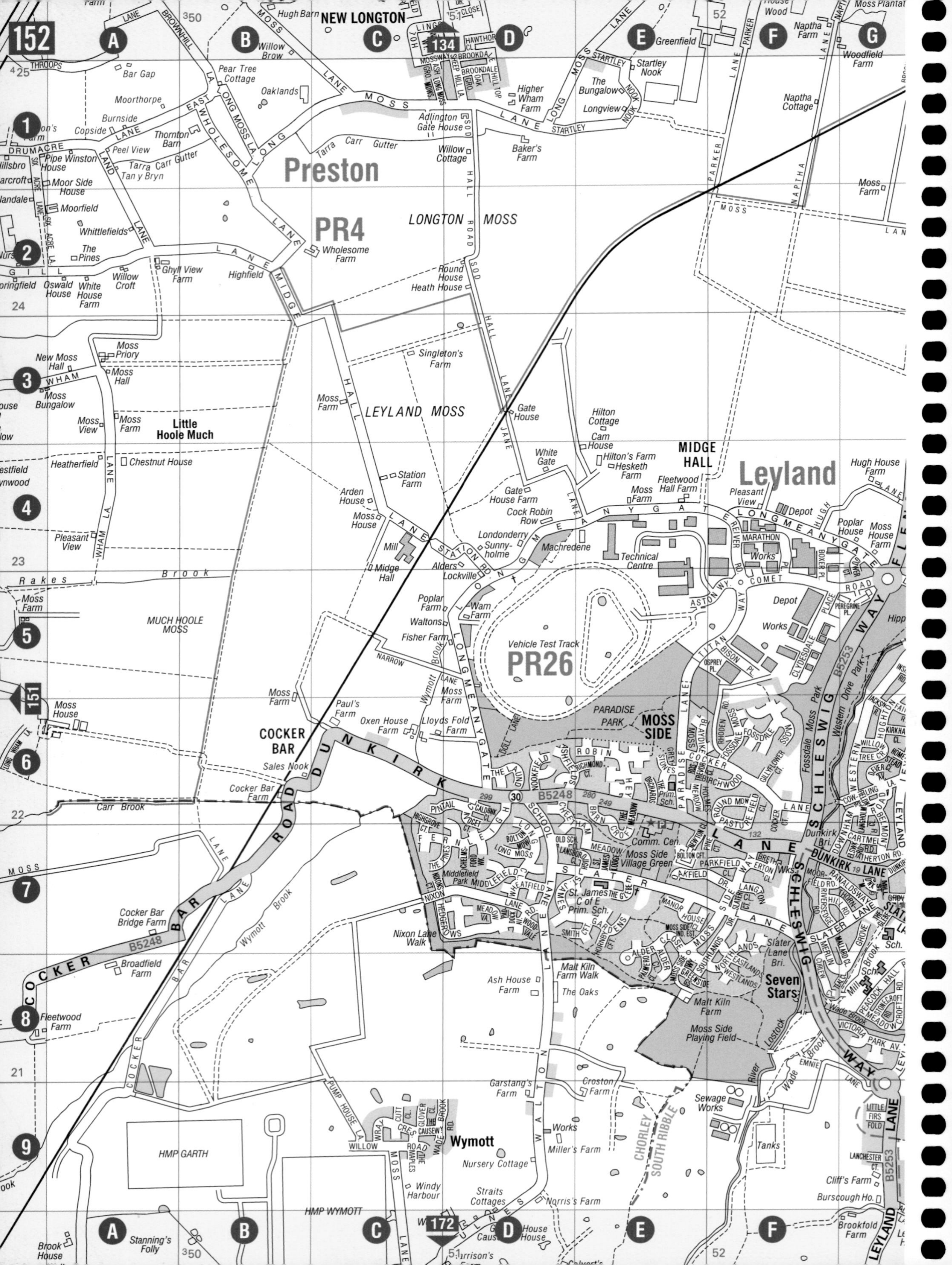
NEW LONGTON
Preston
PR4
LONGTON MOSS
LEYLAND MOSS
Little Hoole Much
MUCH HOOLE MOSS
MIDGE HALL
Leyland
PR26
Vehicle Test Track
MOSS SIDE
PARADISE PARK
COCKER BAR
Wymott
HMP GARTH
HMP WYMOTT
Seven Stars
Moss Side Playing Field
Sewage Works
CHORLEY
SOUTH RIBBLE
DUNKIRK
ROAD
LONGMEANYGATE
SCHLESWIG WAY
B5248
B5253
Hugh Barn
Willow Brow
Pear Tree Cottage
Oaklands
Bar Gap
Moorthorpe
Burnside
Copside
Thornton Barn
Peel View
Pipe Winston House
Moor Side House
Moorfield
Whittlefields
The Pines
Oswald House
White House Farm
Willow Croft
Ghyll View Farm
Highfield
Wholesome Farm
Adlington Gate House
Willow Cottage
Higher Wham Farm
Baker's Farm
Round House
Heath House
The Bungalow
Longview
Startley Nook
Greenfield
Naptha Farm
Naptha Cottage
Woodfield Farm
Moss Farm
Singleton's Farm
Gate House
Hilton Cottage
Cam House
White Gate
Hilton's Farm
Hesketh Farm
Fleetwood Hall Farm
Moss Priory
New Moss Hall
Moss Hall
Moss Bungalow
Moss View
Heatherfield
Chestnut House
Pleasant View
Station Farm
Arden House
Moss House
Mill
Midge Hall
Gate House Farm
Cock Robin Row
Londonderry
Sunnyholme
Machredene
Technical Centre
Alders
Lockville
Poplar Farm
Waltons
Fisher Farm
Wam Farm
Moss House
Paul's Farm
Oxen House Farm
Lloyds Fold Farm
Sales Nook
Cocker Bar Farm
Carr Brook
Rakes Brook
Cocker Bar Bridge Farm
Broadfield Farm
Fleetwood Farm
Nixon Lane Walk
Malt Kiln Farm Walk
The Oaks
Ash House Farm
Malt Kiln Farm
Garstang's Farm
Croston Farm
Works
Miller's Farm
Nursery Cottage
Windy Harbour
Straits Cottages
Norris's Farm
Stanning's Folly
Brook House
Tanks
Cliff's Farm
Burscough Ho.
Brookfold Farm
Hugh House Farm
Pleasant View
Poplar House
Moss House Farm
Depot
Works
Comm. Cen.
Moss Side Village Green
St. James C of E Prim. Sch.
Dunkirk Bri.
Slater Lane Bri.
A B C D E F G
1 2 3 4 5 6 7 8 9
350 51 52
25 24 23 22 21
134 151 172

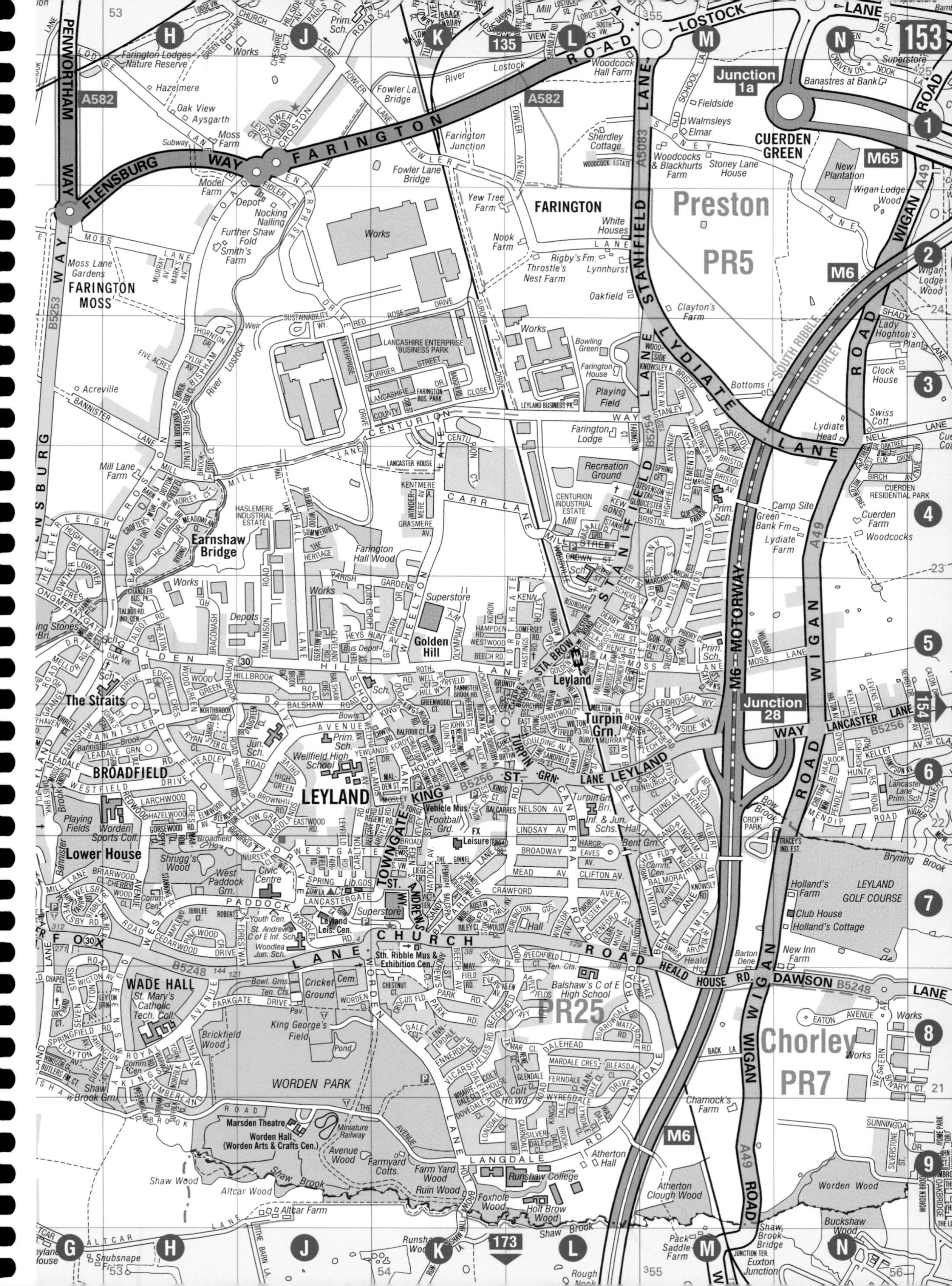

Farington Lodges Nature Reserve
Hazelmere
Oak View
Aysgarth
Moss Farm
Model Farm
FLENSBURG WAY
FARINGTON
PENWORTHAM WAY
A582
LOSTOCK LANE
Woodcock Hall Farm
Junction 1a
Fieldside
Walmsleys
Elmar
Sherdley Cottage
Woodcocks & Blackhurts Farm
Stoney Lane House
CUERDEN GREEN
New Plantation
Wigan Lodge Wood
M65
Superstore
Banastres at Bank
Fowler La. Bridge
Farington Junction
Fowler Lane Bridge
River Lostock
Yew Tree Farm
FARINGTON
White Houses
Nook Farm
Rigby's Fm.
Throstle's Nest Farm
Lynnhurst
Oakfield
Clayton's Farm
Preston
PR5
M6
Wigan Lodge Wood
Lady Hoghton's Plant.
Clock House
Swiss Cott.
Lydiate Head
Bottoms
SOUTH RIBBLE
CHORLEY
STANIFIELD LANE
LYDIATE LANE
WIGAN ROAD
A49
A5083
Works
Nocking Nalling
Further Shaw Fold
Smith's Farm
Moss Lane Gardens
FARINGTON MOSS
B5253
Acreville
LANCASHIRE ENTERPRISE BUSINESS PARK
FARINGTON BUS. PARK
LEYLAND BUSINESS PK.
CENTURION WAY
Bowling Green
Farington House
Playing Field
Farington Lodge
Recreation Ground
CENTURION INDUSTRIAL ESTATE
Mill Lane Farm
HASLEMERE INDUSTRIAL ESTATE
LANCASTER HOUSE
Earnshaw Bridge
Farington Hall Wood
Camp Site
Green Bank Fm.
Lydiate Farm
Cuerden Farm
Woodcocks
CUERDEN RESIDENTIAL PARK
Superstore
Golden Hill
Bus Depot
Depots
Works
Leyland
Turpin Grn.
Junction 28
M6 MOTORWAY
LANCASTER LANE
B5256
The Straits
BROADFIELD
LEYLAND
Wellfield High School
KING ST.
Vehicle Mus.
Football Grd.
Leisure
Croft Park
TRACEY'S IND. EST.
Bryning Brook
Holland's Farm
LEYLAND GOLF COURSE
Club House
Holland's Cottage
Playing Fields
Worden Sports Coll.
Lower House
Shrugg's Wood
West Paddock Grn.
Civic Centre
Lib.
Superstore
Leyland Leis. Cen.
St. Andrew's C of E Inf. Sch.
Woodlea Jun. Sch.
CHURCH ROAD
Sth. Ribble Mus & Exhibition Cen.
FOX LANE
B5248
WADE HALL
St. Mary's Catholic Tech. Coll.
Cricket Ground
Cem.
Balshaw's C of E High School
PR25
HEALD HOUSE RD.
DAWSON LANE
New Inn Farm
Barton Dene
King George's Field
Brickfield Wood
WORDEN PARK
Shaw Brook Grn.
Chorley
PR7
Works
Charnock's Farm
Marsden Theatre
Worden Hall (Worden Arts & Crafts Cen.)
Miniature Railway
Avenue Wood
Farmyard Cotts.
Farm Yard Wood
Ruin Wood
Runshaw College
Atherton Hall
Atherton Clough Wood
Foxhole Wood
Holt Brow Wood
Shaw Wood
Altcar Wood
Altcar Farm
Shaw Brook
Worden Wood
Buckshaw Wood
Pack Saddle Farm
Shaw Brook Bridge
Euxton Junction
Snubsnape
Rough Nook
135
173
154

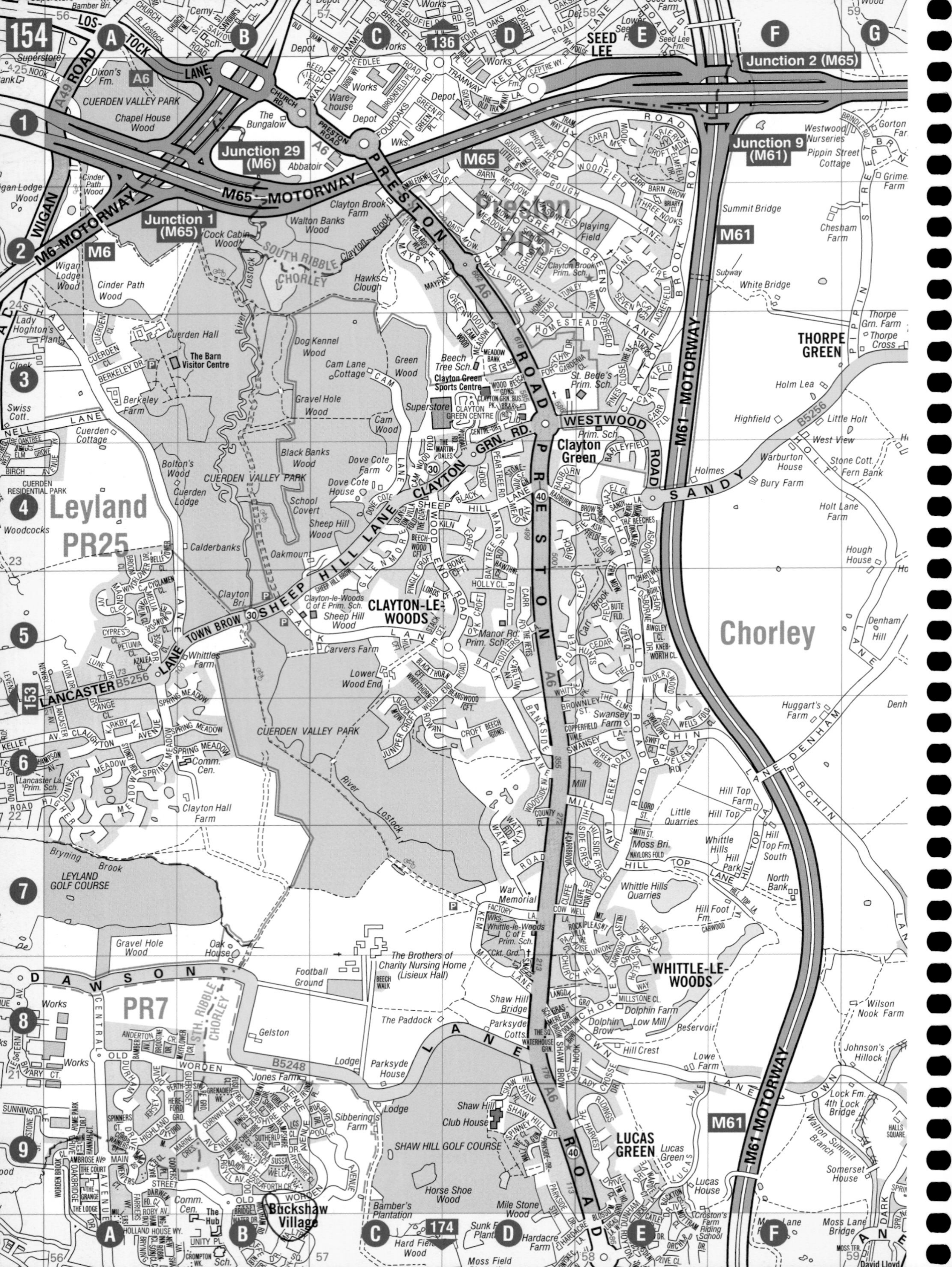
Leyland
PR25
PR7
Chorley
CLAYTON-LE-WOODS
Clayton Green
WHITTLE-LE-WOODS
THORPE GREEN
LUCAS GREEN
SEED LEE
Buckshaw Village
CUERDEN VALLEY PARK
SHAW HILL GOLF COURSE
LEYLAND GOLF COURSE
M65 MOTORWAY
M6 MOTORWAY
M61 MOTORWAY
Junction 29 (M6)
Junction 1 (M65)
Junction 2 (M65)
Junction 9 (M61)
PRESTON ROAD
SHEEP HILL LANE
CLAYTON GRN. RD.
WESTWOOD ROAD
SANDY LANE
DAWSON LANE
WIGAN ROAD
LANCASTER LANE
The Barn Visitor Centre
Clayton Green Sports Centre
Cuerden Hall
The Brothers of Charity Nursing Home (Lisieux Hall)
136
153
174
David Lloyd

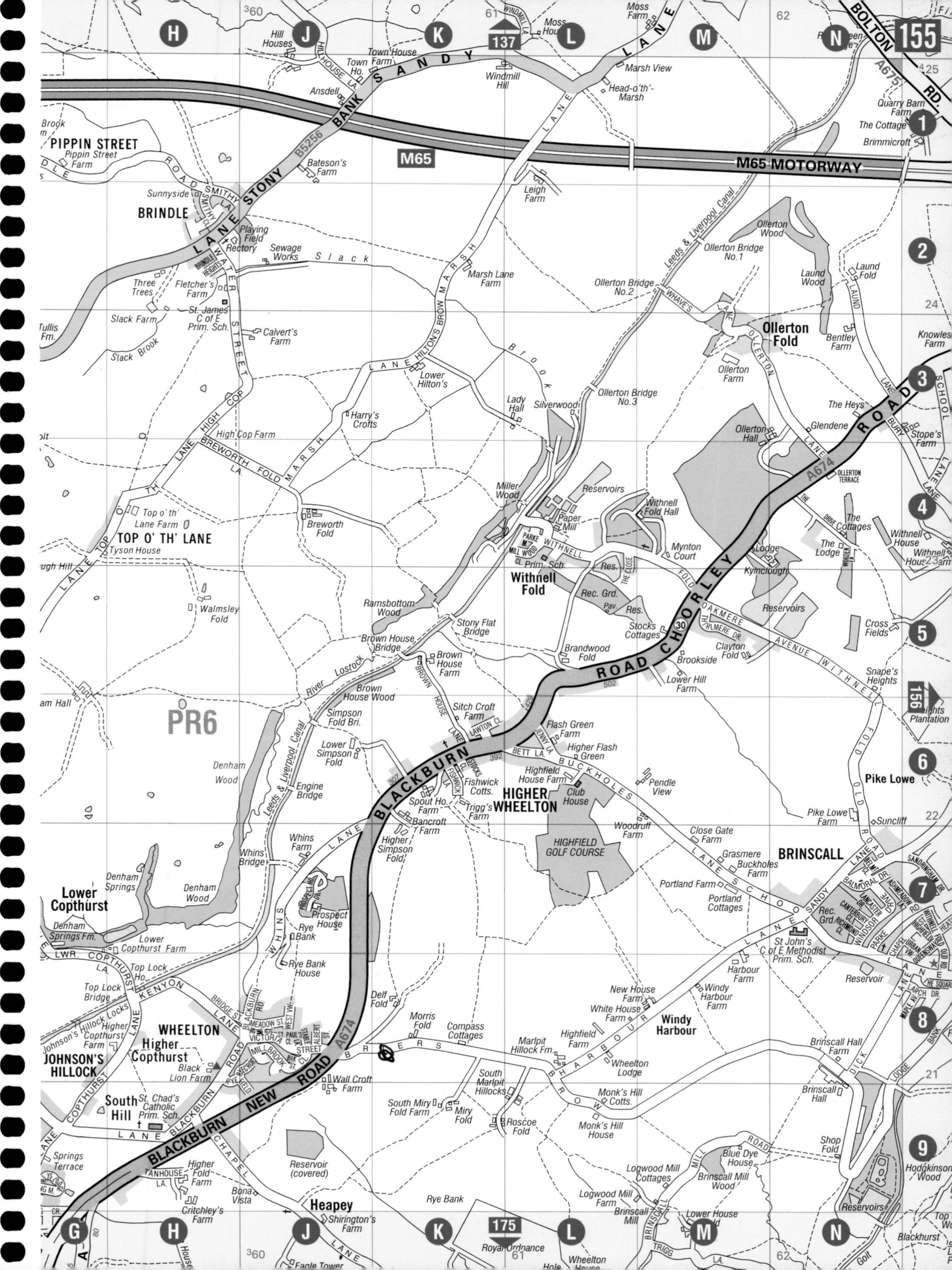

PIPPIN STREET
BRINDLE
TOP O' TH' LANE
Withnell Fold
Ollerton Fold
HIGHER WHEELTON
BRINSCALL
Lower Copthurst
WHEELTON
Higher Copthurst
JOHNSON'S HILLOCK
South Hill
Heapey
Windy Harbour
Pike Lowe
PR6
M65 MOTORWAY
BLACKBURN ROAD
CHORLEY ROAD
BLACKBURN NEW ROAD
STONY LANE
SANDY LANE
BANK
BOLTON RD.
HIGHFIELD GOLF COURSE
Leeds & Liverpool Canal
River Lostock
137
156
175

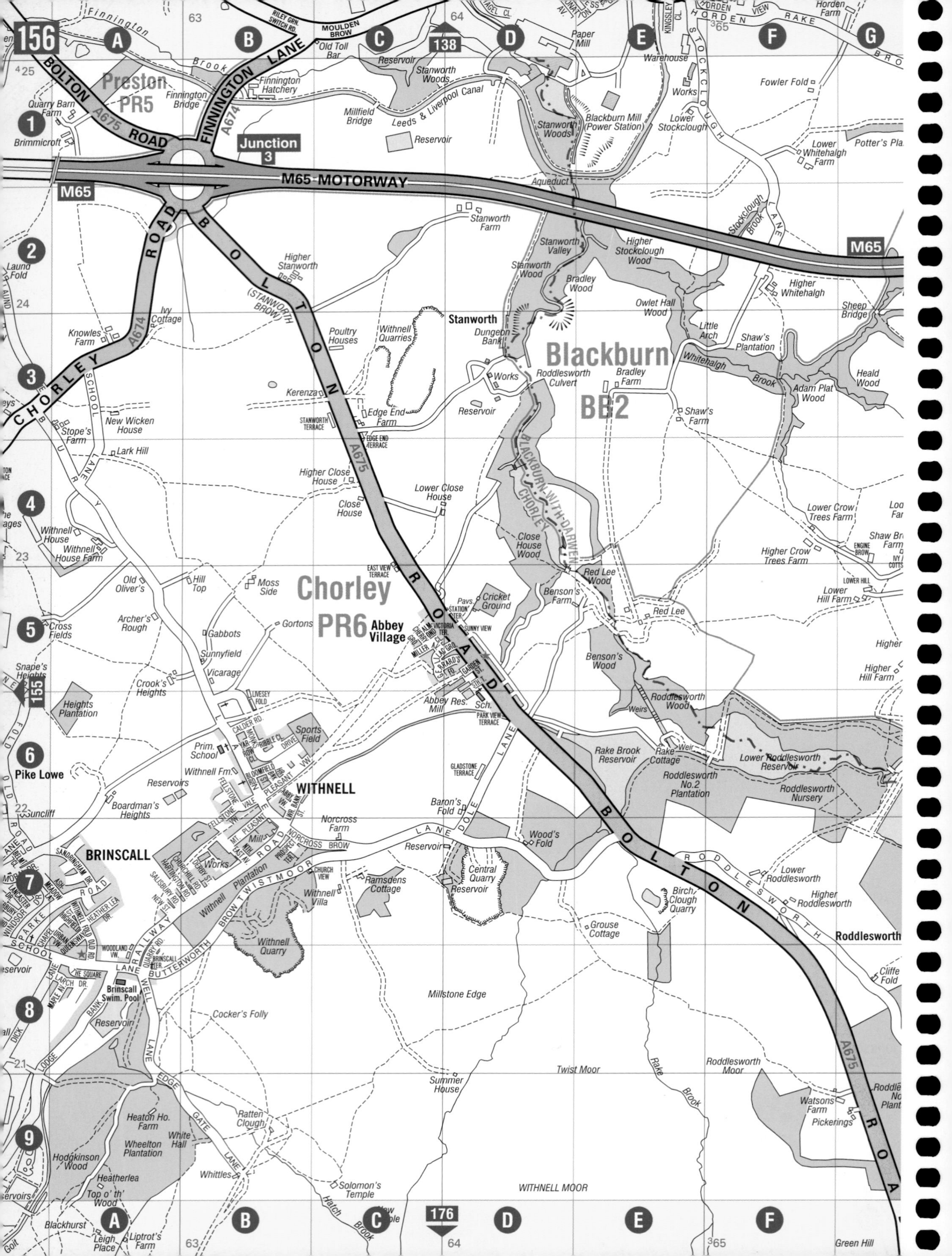

A
B
C
D
E
F
G
1
2
3
4
5
6
7
8
9
63
64
365
25
24
23
22
21
138
176
155
Finnington
Moulden Brow
Riley Grn. Switch Rd.
Old Toll Bar
Reservoir
Stanworth Woods
Paper Mill
Warehouse
Kingsley Cl.
Horden View
Horden Rake
Horden Farm
Bolton Road
A675
Preston PR5
Finnington Bridge
Finnington Hatchery
Finnington Lane
A674
Brook
Quarry Barn Farm
Brimmicroft
Millfield Bridge
Leeds & Liverpool Canal
Junction 3
Stanworth Woods
Blackburn Mill (Power Station)
Works
Lower Stockclough
Stockclough Lane
Fowler Fold
Lower Whitehalgh Farm
Potter's Pla...
M65
M65 Motorway
Aqueduct
Stanworth Farm
Stanworth Valley
Higher Stockclough Wood
Stockclough Brook
Laund Fold
Higher Stanworth
(Stanworth Brow)
Stanworth Wood
Bradley Wood
Owlet Hall Wood
Higher Whitehalgh
Sheep Bridge
Ivy Cottage
Knowles Farm
Chorley Road
Poultry Houses
Withnell Quarries
Stanworth
Dungeon Bank
Little Arch
Shaw's Plantation
Blackburn
Whitehalgh Brook
Works
Roddlesworth Culvert
Bradley Farm
Adam Plat Wood
Heald Wood
BB2
School Lane
Kerenza
New Wicken House
Stope's Farm
Stanworth Terrace
Edge End Farm
Edge End Terrace
Reservoir
Shaw's Farm
Lark Hill
Blackburn with Darwen
Chorley
Higher Close House
Lower Close House
Close House
Withnell House
Withnell House Farm
Close House Wood
Lower Crow Trees Farm
Shaw Br... Farm
Higher Crow Trees Farm
Engine Brow
Old Oliver's
Hill Top
Moss Side
East View Terrace
Chorley
Red Lee Wood
Cricket Ground
Benson's Farm
Lower Hill Farm
Lower Hill
Archer's Rough
Cross Fields
Gortons
PR6
Abbey Village
Station Ter.
Sunny View
Red Lee
Gabbots
Sunnyfield
Benson's Wood
Higher
Higher Hill Farm
Snape's Heights
Vicarage
Crook's Heights
Heights Plantation
Livesey Fold
Abbey Res.
Mill
Sch.
Park View Terrace
Roddlesworth Wood
Weirs
Calder Rd.
Sports Field
Prim. School
Withnell Fm.
Reservoirs
Pike Lowe
Gladstone Terrace
Rake Brook Reservoir
Rake Cottage
Weir
Lower Roddlesworth Reservoir
Roddlesworth No.2 Plantation
Roddlesworth Nursery
WITHNELL
Boardman's Heights
Suncliff
Baron's Fold
Dole Lane
Norcross Farm
Norcross Brow
Wood's Fold
BRINSCALL
Works
Mill
Reservoir
Central Quarry Reservoir
Roddlesworth
Lower Roddlesworth
Higher Roddlesworth
Withnell Plantation
Twistmoor
Church View
Ramsdens Cottage
Withnell Villa
Birch Clough Quarry
Grouse Cottage
Withnell Quarry
School Lane
Woodland Vw.
Butterworth Brow
Railway
Brinscall Swim. Pool
The Square
Reservoir
Roddlesworth
Cliffe Fold
Millstone Edge
Cocker's Folly
Twist Moor
Roddlesworth Moor
Rake Brook
Summer House
Lodge Lane
Edge Gate Lane
Heaton Ho. Farm
White Hall
Wheelton Plantation
Ratten Clough
Watsons Farm
Pickerings
Hodgkinson Wood
Heatherlea
Whittles
Solomon's Temple
Withnell Moor
Top o' th' Wood
Hatch Brook
Blackhurst
Leigh Place
Liptrot's Farm
Green Hill

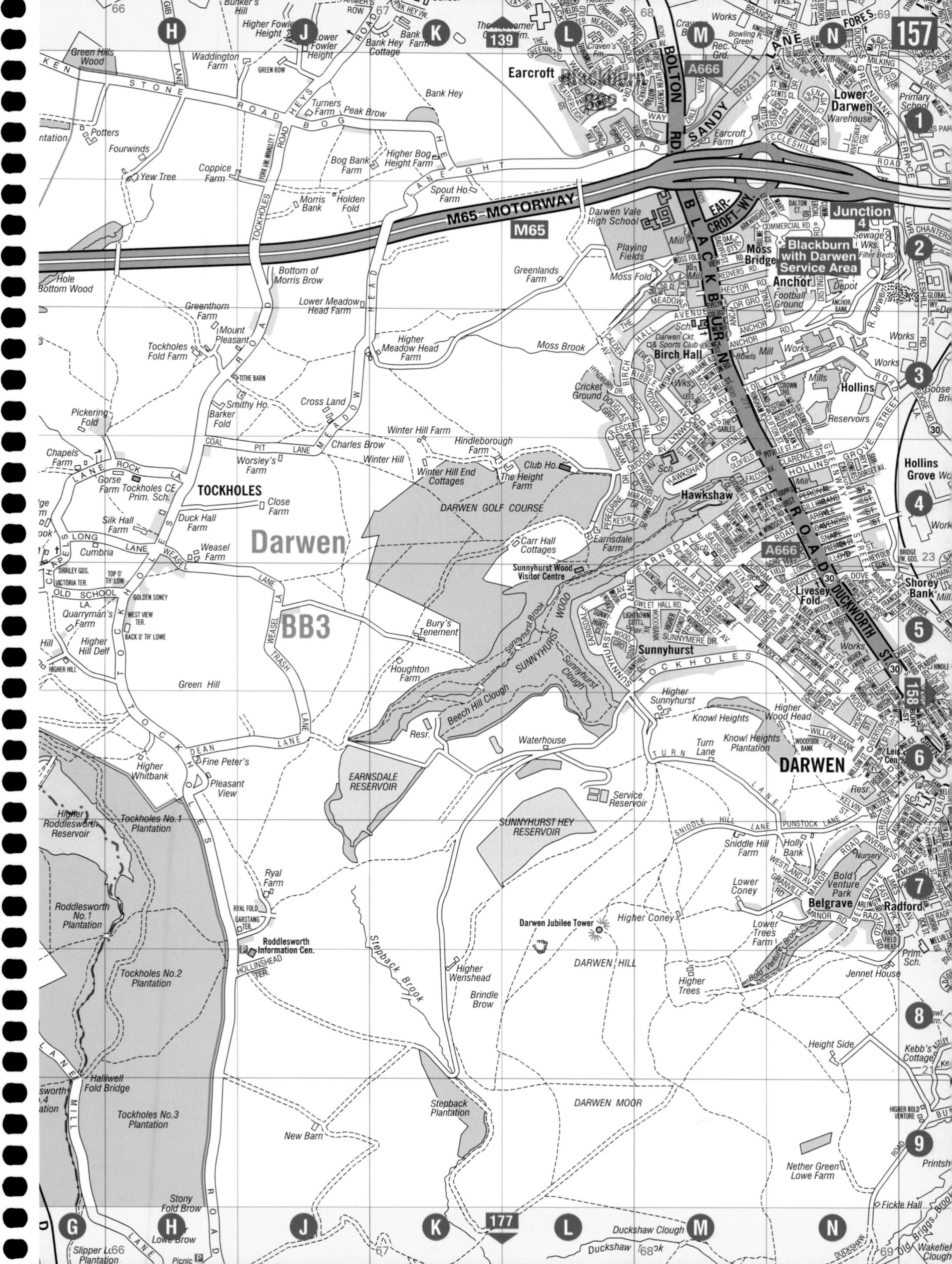
Earcroft
Lower Darwen
M65 MOTORWAY
Junction 4
Blackburn with Darwen Service Area
TOCKHOLES
Darwen
BB3
DARWEN GOLF COURSE
EARNSDALE RESERVOIR
SUNNYHURST HEY RESERVOIR
Darwen Jubilee Tower
DARWEN HILL
DARWEN MOOR
DARWEN
Sunnyhurst
Hawkshaw
Birch Hall
Hollins
Belgrave
Radford
Tockholes No.1 Plantation
Tockholes No.2 Plantation
Tockholes No.3 Plantation
Roddlesworth No.1 Plantation
Higher Roddlesworth Reservoir
Roddlesworth Information Cen.
Sunnyhurst Wood Visitor Centre
Stepback Plantation
Stepback Brook
Bold Venture Park
139
177
158

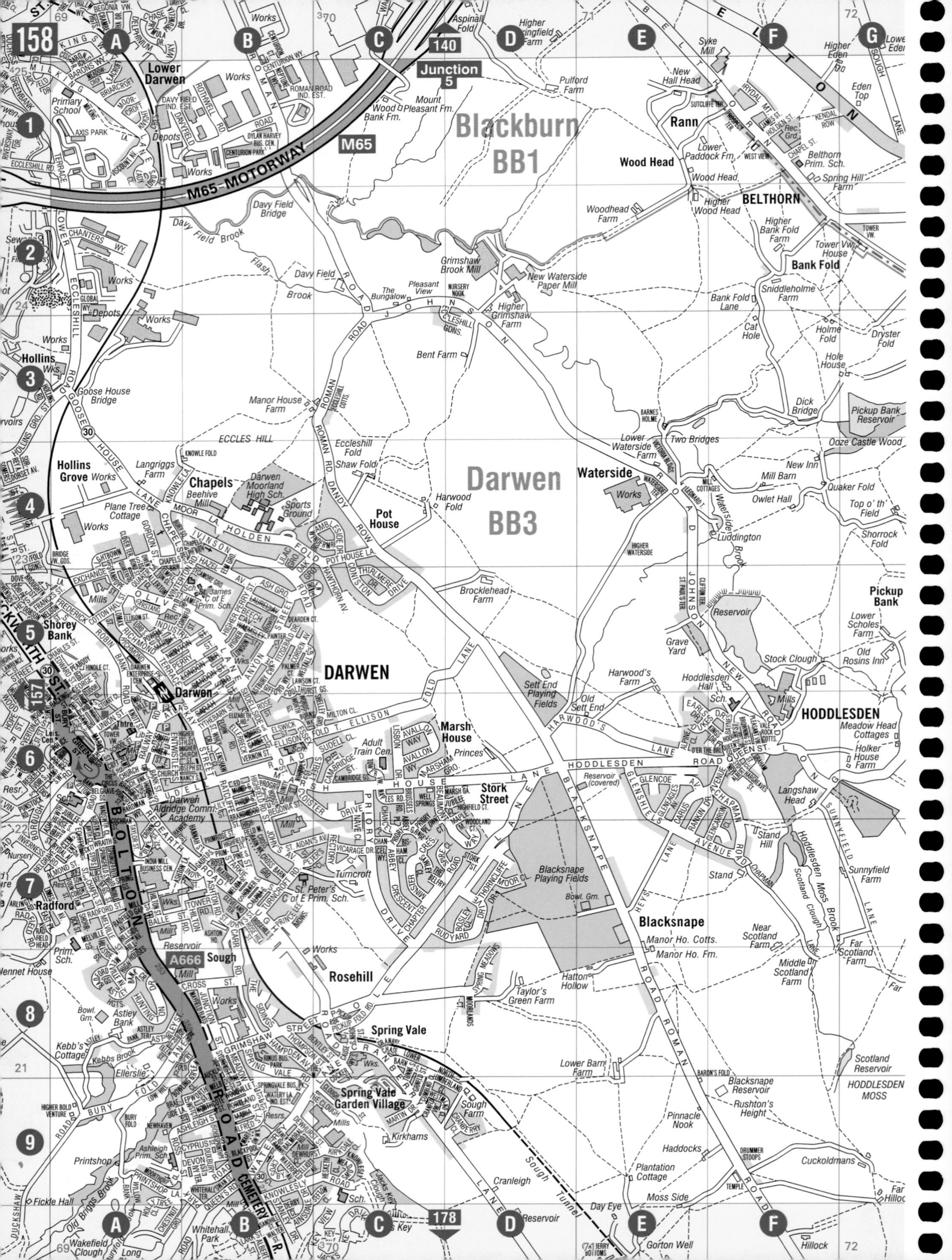
Blackburn
BB1
Darwen
BB3
DARWEN
M65 MOTORWAY
M65
Junction
5
140
157
178
A666
Lower
Darwen
Rann
Wood Head
BELTHORN
Bank Fold
Waterside
HODDLESDEN
Pickup
Bank
Chapels
Hollins
Hollins
Grove
Shorey
Bank
Radford
Sough
Rosehill
Spring Vale
Spring Vale
Garden Village
Marsh
House
Stork
Street
Pot
House
Blacksnape
Langshaw
Head
Higher
Eden
Eden
Top
Pulford
Farm
Aspinall
Fold
Syke
Mill
New
Hall Head
Davy Field
Bridge
Grimshaw
Brook Mill
New Waterside
Paper Mill
Higher
Grimshaw
Farm
Bent Farm
Manor House
Farm
ECCLES HILL
Langriggs
Farm
Eccleshill
Fold
Shaw Fold
Harwood
Fold
Brocklehead
Farm
Sett End
Playing
Fields
Harwood's
Farm
Hoddlesden
Hall
Stock Clough
Reservoir
Grave
Yard
Luddington
Two Bridges
Mill Barn
Owlet Hall
Quaker Fold
Top o' th'
Field
Shorrock
Fold
Pickup Bank
Reservoir
Ooze Castle Wood
Dick
Bridge
Blacksnape
Playing Fields
Manor Ho. Cotts.
Manor Ho. Fm.
Hatton
Hollow
Taylor's
Green Farm
Lower Barn
Farm
Blacksnape
Reservoir
Rushton's
Height
Pinnacle
Nook
Haddocks
Plantation
Cottage
Moss Side
Cuckoldmans
Scotland
Reservoir
HODDLESDEN
MOSS
Near
Scotland
Farm
Middle
Scotland
Farm
Far
Scotland
Farm
Sunnyfield
Farm
Holker
House
Farm
Meadow Head
Cottages
Lower
Scholes
Farm
Old
Rosins Inn
Kirkhams
Cranleigh
Sough
Farm
Sough Tunnel
Day Eye
Gorton Well
Hillock
Printshop
Fickle Hall
Kebb's
Cottage
Ellerslie
Astley
Bank
Whitehall
Park
Wakefield
Clough
Darwen
Aldridge Comm.
Academy
Darwen
Moorland
High Sch.
Sports
Ground
Adult
Train Cen.
St. Peter's
C of E Prim. Sch.
Turncroft
Mount
Pleasant Fm.
Wood
Bank Fm.
Lower
Paddock Fm.
Woodhead
Farm
Higher
Wood Head
Higher
Bank Fold
Farm
Sniddleholme
Farm
Cat
Hole
Holme
Fold
Dryster
Fold
Hole
House
New Inn
Lower
Waterside
Farm
Belthorn
Prim. Sch.
Spring Hill
Farm
Tower Vw.
House
Stand
Hill
Stand
Hoddlesden Moss Brook
Scotland Clough
Old
Sett End
Princes
Goose House
Bridge
Plane Tree
Cottage
Beehive
Mill
Primary
School
Depots
Works

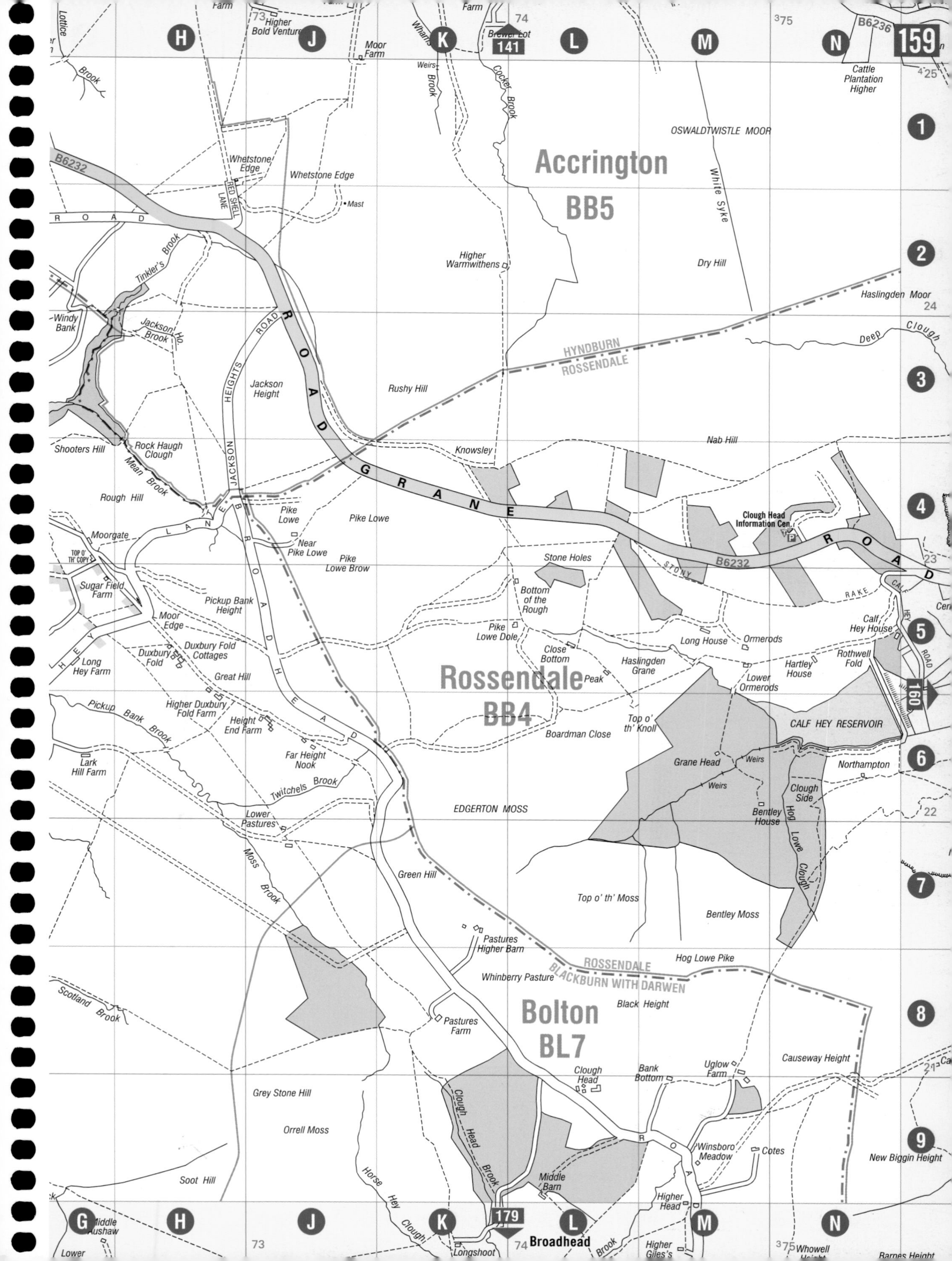
Accrington
BB5
Rossendale
BB4
Bolton
BL7
GRANE ROAD
B6232
B6236
JACKSON HEIGHTS ROAD
HEAD ROAD
RED SHELL LANE
HEY ROAD
CALF HEY ROAD
STONY RAKE
HYNDBURN
ROSSENDALE
BLACKBURN WITH DARWEN
OSWALDTWISTLE MOOR
Whetstone Edge
Higher Bold Venture
Moor Farm
Brewer Lot
Mast
Higher Warmwithens
Dry Hill
White Syke
Haslingden Moor
Deep Clough
Cattle Plantation Higher
Windy Bank
Jackson Ho
Tinkler's Brook
Jackson Height
Rushy Hill
Shooters Hill
Rock Haugh Clough
Mean Brook
Rough Hill
Knowsley
Nab Hill
Moorgate
TOP O' TH' COPY
Sugar Field Farm
Pike Lowe
Near Pike Lowe
Pike Lowe Brow
Stone Holes
Clough Head Information Cen.
Bottom of the Rough
Pickup Bank Height
Moor Edge
Duxbury Fold
Duxbury Fold Cottages
Long Hey Farm
Great Hill
Pike Lowe Dole
Close Bottom
Haslingden Grane
Long House
Ormerods
Lower Ormerods
Hartley House
Calf Hey House
Rothwell Fold
Peak
Higher Duxbury Fold Farm
Pickup Bank Brook
Height End Farm
Boardman Close
Top o' th' Knoll
CALF HEY RESERVOIR
Lark Hill Farm
Far Height Nook
Twitchels Brook
Grane Head
Weirs
Northampton
Clough Side
Bentley House
Hog Lowe Clough
Lower Pastures
EDGERTON MOSS
Moss Brook
Green Hill
Top o' th' Moss
Bentley Moss
Pastures Higher Barn
Hog Lowe Pike
Whinberry Pasture
Black Height
Scotland Brook
Pastures Farm
Causeway Height
Clough Head
Bank Bottom
Uglow Farm
Grey Stone Hill
Clough Head Brook
Orrell Moss
Winsboro Meadow
Cotes
New Biggin Height
Soot Hill
Horse Hey Clough
Middle Barn
Higher Head
Middle Aushaw
Broadhead
Longshoot
Higher Giles's
Whowell
Barnes Height
Lower
Lottice
Wharns Brook
Cocker Brook
141
160
179
73
74
375
425
24
23
22
21
H J K L M N G
1 2 3 4 5 6 7 8 9

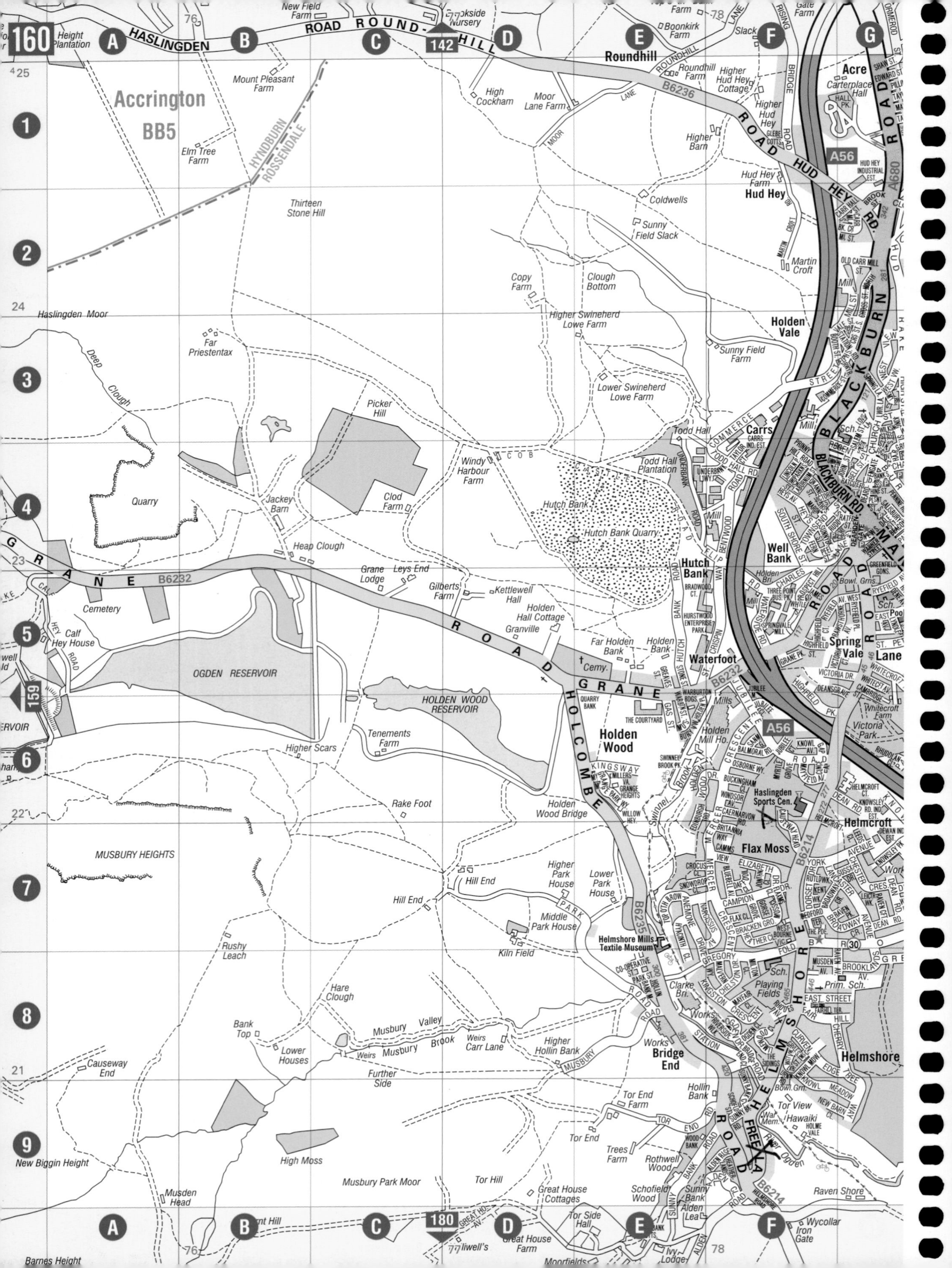
Height Plantation
HASLINGDEN ROAD ROUND-HILL
New Field Farm
Brookside Nursery
142
Boonkirk Farm
Roundhill
Mount Pleasant Farm
Accrington
BB5
HYNDBURN
ROSSENDALE
Elm Tree Farm
High Cockham
Moor Lane Farm
Roundhill Farm
Higher Hud Hey Cottage
Higher Hud Hey
B6236
HUD HEY RD.
Higher Barn
Acre
Carterplace Hall
A56
A680
Hud Hey Farm
Hud Hey
Coldwells
Thirteen Stone Hill
Sunny Field Slack
Martin Croft
Copy Farm
Clough Bottom
Haslingden Moor
Higher Swineherd Lowe Farm
Holden Vale
Far Priestentax
Deep Clough
Sunny Field Farm
BLACKBURN ROAD
Lower Swineherd Lowe Farm
Picker Hill
Todd Hall
Carrs
Todd Hall Plantation
Windy Harbour Farm
Quarry
Jackey Barn
Clod Farm
Hutch Bank
Hutch Bank Quarry
Heap Clough
Well Bank
GRANE ROAD
B6232
Grane Lodge
Leys End
Gilberts Farm
Kettlewell Hall
Hutch Bank
Cemetery
Holden Hall Cottage
Calf Hey House
Granville
Spring Vale
Lane
Far Holden Bank
Holden Bank
Waterfoot
Cemy.
OGDEN RESERVOIR
159
HOLDEN WOOD RESERVOIR
HOLCOMBE
Tenements Farm
Holden Wood
Higher Scars
Holden Mill Ho.
Haslingden Sports Cen.
Helmcroft
Rake Foot
Holden Wood Bridge
Flax Moss
MUSBURY HEIGHTS
B6214
Higher Park House
Lower Park House
Hill End
Hill End
Middle Park House
B6235
Helmshore Mills Textile Museum
Rushy Leach
Kiln Field
Hare Clough
Clarke Bri.
Playing Fields
Bank Top
Musbury Valley
Lower Houses
Musbury Brook
Weirs
Carr Lane
Higher Hollin Bank
Works
Bridge End
Helmshore
Causeway End
Further Side
Hollin Bank
Tor End Farm
Tor View
Hawaiki
Tor End
Trees Farm
New Biggin Height
High Moss
Rothwell Wood
Musbury Park Moor
Tor Hill
Great House Cottages
Schofield Wood
Sunny Bank
Raven Shore
Musden Head
Tor Side Hall
Alden Lea
Wycollar
Iron Gate
180
Great House Farm
Ivy Lodge
Moorfields
Barnes Height
A
B
C
D
E
F
G
1
2
3
4
5
6
7
8
9
76
77
78
25
24
23
22
21

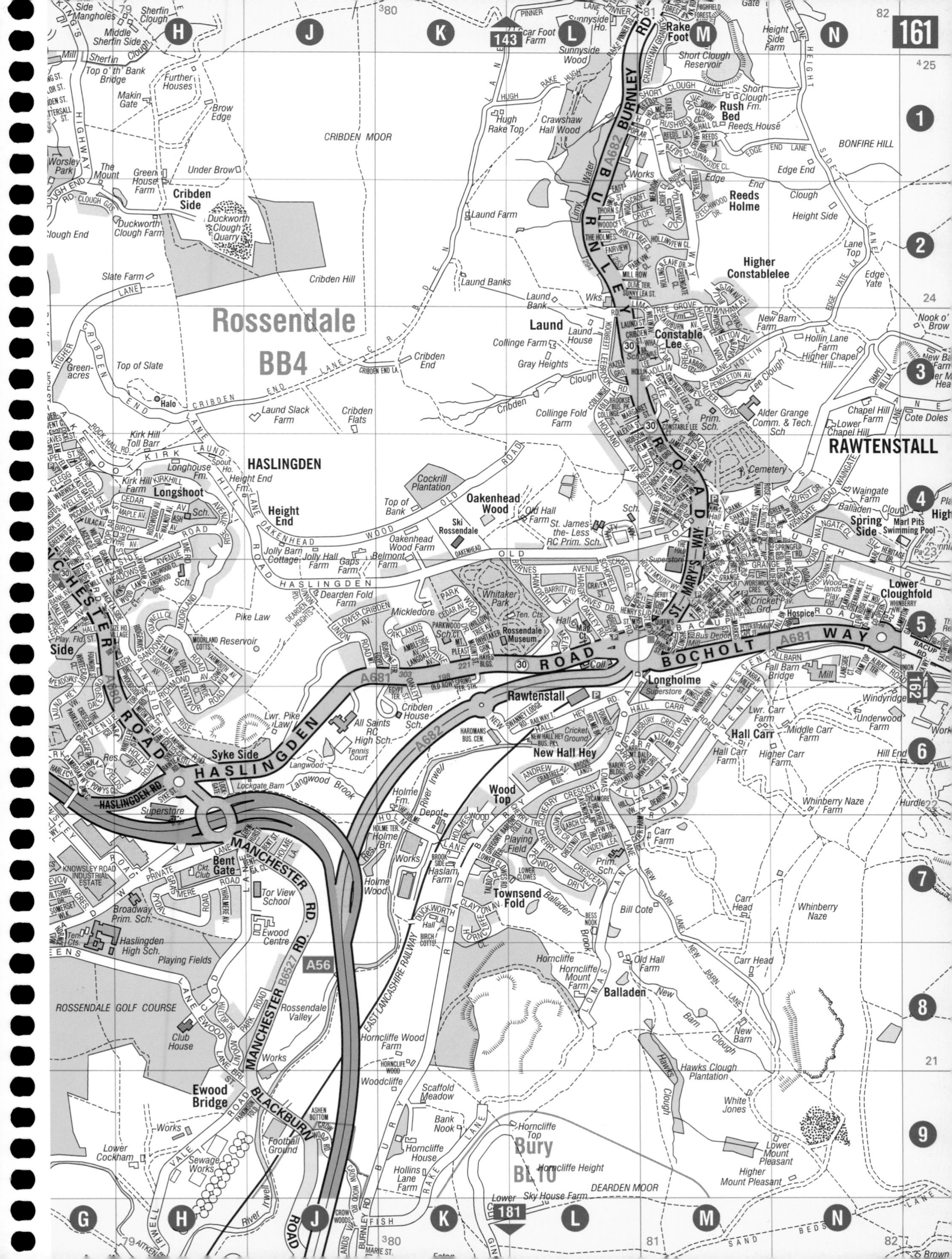
Rossendale
BB4
HASLINGDEN
RAWTENSTALL
Bury
BL10
CRIBDEN MOOR
Cribden Side
Laund
Constable Lee
Higher Constablelee
Reeds Holme
Rush Bed
Rake Foot
Height End
Longshoot
Oakenhead Wood
Ski Rossendale
Whitaker Park
Rossendale Museum
Longholme
Rawtenstall
New Hall Hey
Hall Carr
Wood Top
Townsend Fold
Balladen
Spring Side
Lower Cloughfold
Syke Side
Bent Gate
Ewood Bridge
ROSSENDALE GOLF COURSE
Haslingden High Sch.
Rossendale Valley
Hawks Clough Plantation
DEARDEN MOOR
BOCHOLT WAY
BURNLEY ROAD
HASLINGDEN ROAD
MANCHESTER ROAD
BLACKBURN ROAD
ST. MARY'S WAY
A682
A681
A56
143
162
181

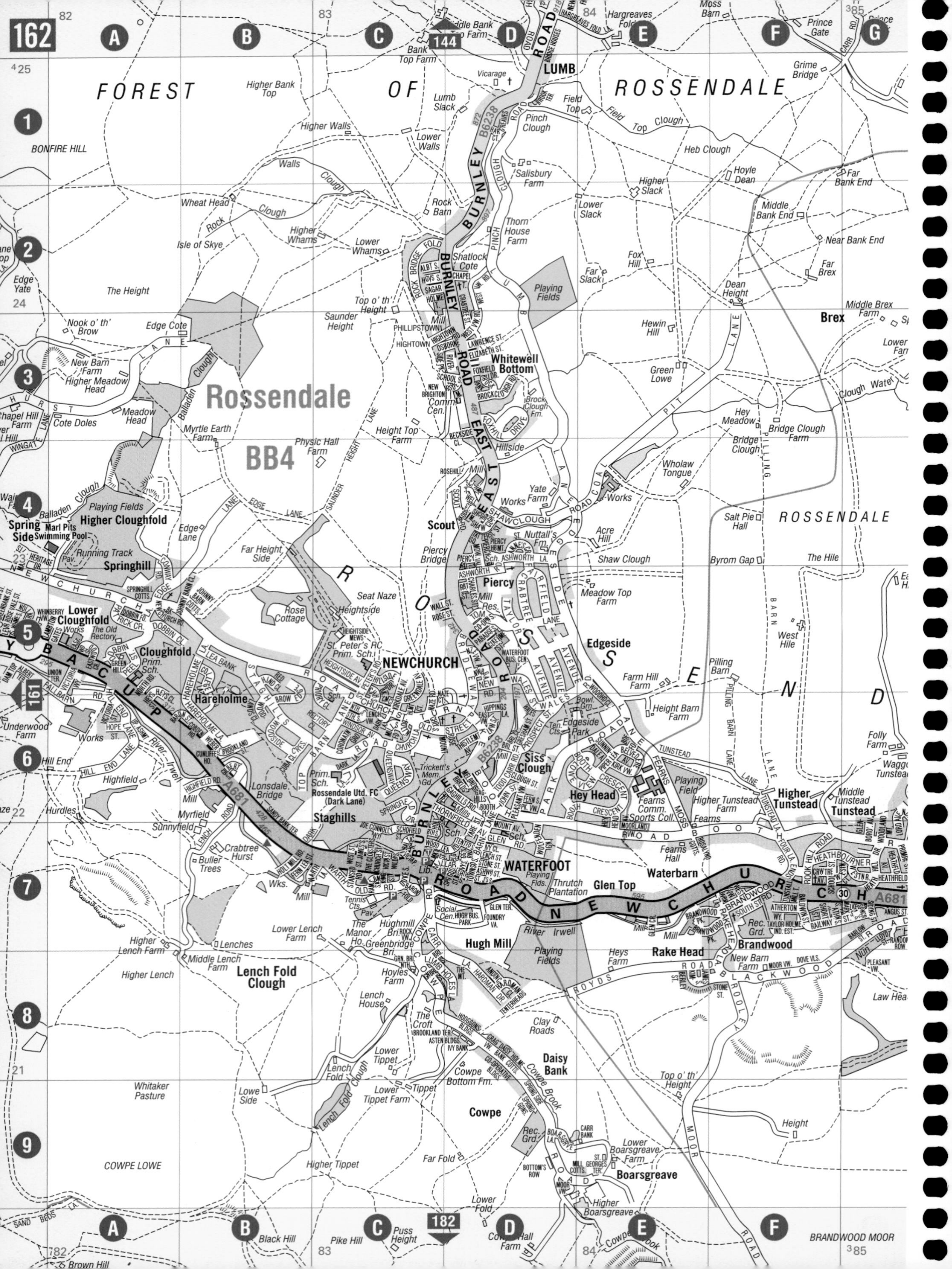
162
A
B
C
D
E
F
G
144
161
182
FOREST
OF
ROSSENDALE
Rossendale
BB4
BONFIRE HILL
Higher Bank Top
Higher Walls
Lower Walls
Lumb Slack
Bank Top Farm
Middle Bank Top Farm
Hargreaves Fold
Moss Barn
Prince Gate
Grime Bridge
LUMB
Vicarage
Field Top
Field Top Clough
Pinch Clough
Heb Clough
Hoyle Dean
Far Bank End
Middle Bank End
Near Bank End
Far Brex
Higher Slack
Salisbury Farm
Walls
Clough
Wheat Head
Rock
Isle of Skye
Higher Whams
Lower Whams
Rock Barn
Thorn House Farm
Lower Slack
Fox Hill
Far Slack
Dean Height
Edge Yate
The Height
Top o' th' Height
Saunder Height
Shatlock Cote
Playing Fields
Middle Brex Farm
Brex
Nook o' th' Brow
Edge Cote
New Barn Farm
Higher Meadow Head
Meadow Head
Cote Doles
Chapel Hill Farm
Myrtle Earth Farm
Physic Hall Farm
Height Top Farm
PHILLIPSTOWN
HIGHTOWN
Whitewell Bottom
Brock Clough Fm.
Hillside
Hewin Hill
Green Lowe
Hey Meadow
Bridge Clough
Bridge Clough Farm
Clough Water
Wholaw Tongue
NEW BRIGHTON
Comm. Cen.
Works
Yate Farm
Salt Pie Hall
ROSSENDALE
Balladen Clough
Playing Fields
Higher Cloughfold
Spring Side
Marl Pits Swimming Pool
Running Track
Springhill
Edge Lane
Far Height Side
Scout
Piercy Bridge
Nuttall's Fm.
Acre Hill
Shaw Clough
Byrom Gap
The Hile
Piercy
Meadow Top Farm
Seat Naze
Rose Cottage
Heightside
West Hile
Lower Cloughfold
The Old Rectory
Cloughfold
Prim. Sch.
St. Peter's RC Prim. Sch.
NEWCHURCH
Edgeside
Pilling Barn
Farm Hill Farm
Hareholme
Underwood Farm
Height Barn Farm
Edgeside Park
Folly Farm
Hill End
Highfield
Trickett's Mem. Gd.
Siss Clough
Hey Head
Fearns Comm. Sports Coll.
Playing Field
Higher Tunstead Farm
Higher Tunstead
Middle Tunstead
Tunstead
Prim. Sch.
Rossendale Utd. FC (Dark Lane)
Lonsdale Bridge
Staghills
Mill
Myrfield
Hurdles
Sunnyfield
Crabtree Hurst
Buller Trees
Wks.
WATERFOOT
Thrutch Plantation
Glen Top
Waterbarn
Fearns Hall
Tennis Cts.
Social Cen.
The Manor Ho.
Hughmill Bri.
Greenbridge Bri.
Lower Lench Farm
Hugh Mill
River Irwell
Playing Fields
Heys Farm
Rake Head
Brandwood
Rec. Grd.
New Barn Farm
Higher Lench Farm
Lenches
Middle Lench Farm
Higher Lench
Lench Fold Clough
Hoyles Farm
Lench House
Clay Roads
The Croft
Law Head
Lower Tippet
Lench Fold
Daisy Bank
Cowpe Bottom Fm.
Top o' th' Height
Whitaker Pasture
Lowe Side
Lower Tippet Farm
Tippet
Cowpe Brook
Cowpe
Height
Rec. Grd.
Lower Boarsgreave Farm
COWPE LOWE
Higher Tippet
Far Fold
Boarsgreave
Higher Boarsgreave
Lower Fold
Black Hill
Pike Hill
Puss Height
Cowpe Hall Farm
BRANDWOOD MOOR
Brown Hill
SAND BEDS
BURNLEY ROAD
BURNLEY ROAD EAST
B6238
A681
BACUP ROAD
NEWCHURCH ROAD
NEWCHURCH ROAD
HURST LANE
EDGE LANE
SAUNDER HEIGHT
HEIGHT LANE
TOP BARN LANE
PINCH CLOUGH ROAD
PIT LANE
COAL ROAD
BOOTH ROAD
ROYDS ROAD
LACKWOOD
ROOLEY MOOR ROAD
MOOR ROAD
PILLING LANE
BARN LANE
TUNSTEAD LANE
ROOK HILL ROAD
HILL END LANE
82
83
84
385
425
24
23
22
21
1
2
3
4
5
6
7
8
9

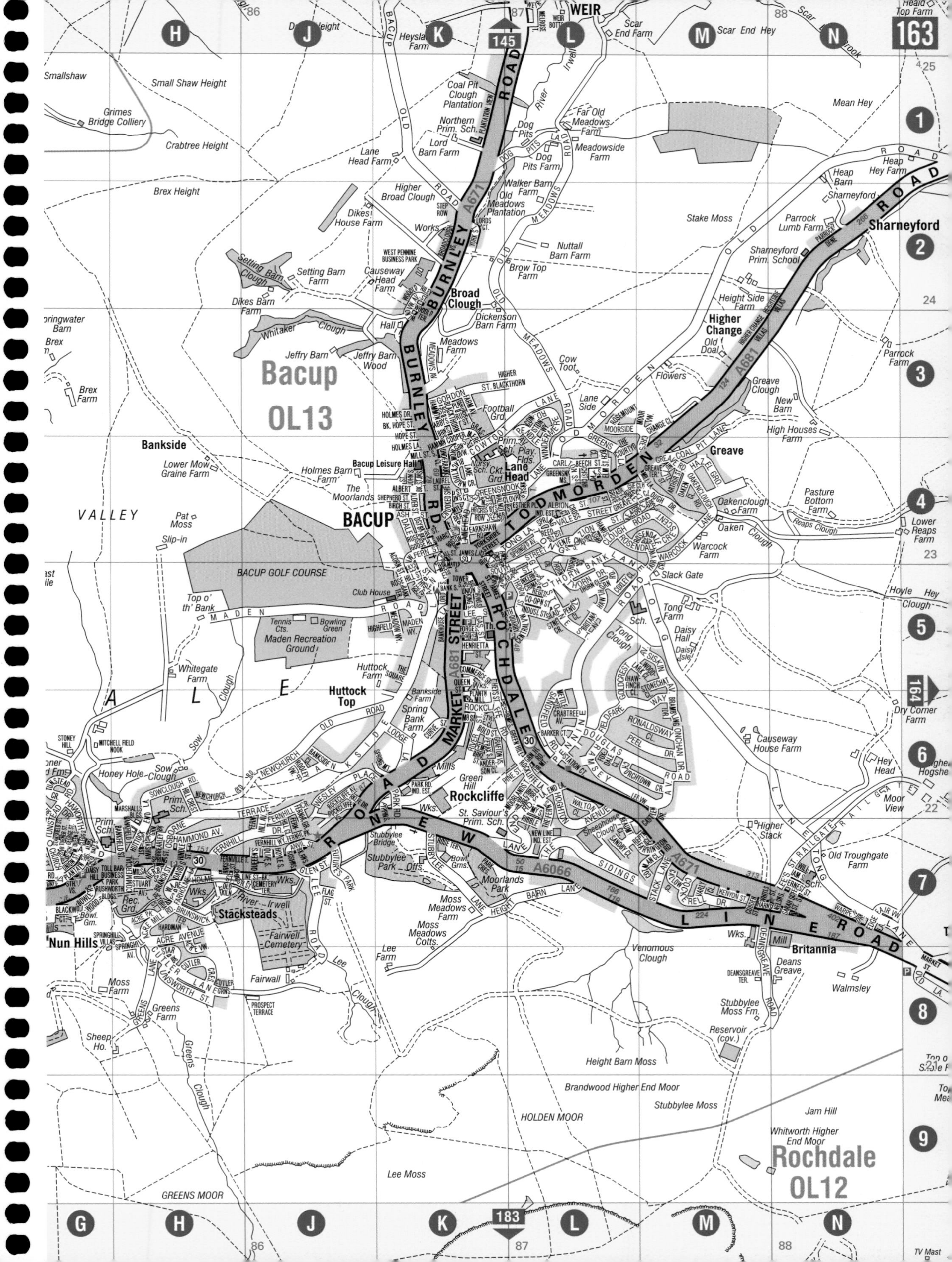

163
145
183
164
H
J
K
L
M
N
G
1
2
3
4
5
6
7
8
9
86
87
88
WEIR
Scar End Farm
Scar End Hey
Heyslack Farm
Smallshaw
Small Shaw Height
Grimes Bridge Colliery
Crabtree Height
Coal Pit Clough Plantation
Northern Prim. Sch.
Lord Barn Farm
Lane Head Farm
Dog Pits
Dog Pits Farm
Far Old Meadows Farm
Meadowside Farm
Mean Hey
Heap Barn
Heap Hey Farm
Sharneyford
Sharneyford Prim. School
Parrock Lump Farm
Stake Moss
Brex Height
Higher Broad Clough
Dikes House Farm
Works
Walker Barn Farm
Old Meadows Plantation
Nuttall Barn Farm
Brow Top Farm
WEST PENNINE BUSINESS PARK
Setting Barn Clough
Setting Barn Farm
Causeway Head Farm
Broad Clough
Dickenson Barn Farm
Dikes Barn Farm
Whitaker Clough
Jeffry Barn
Jeffry Barn Wood
Meadows Farm
Cow Toot
Height Side Farm
Higher Change
Old Doal
Parrock Farm
Bacup
OL13
Brex Farm
Flowers
Greave Clough
New Barn
High Houses Farm
Lane Side
Football Grd.
Bankside
Lower Mow Graine Farm
Holmes Barn Farm
Bacup Leisure Hall
The Moorlands
Lane Head
Greave
Pasture Bottom Farm
Oakenclough Farm
Oaken Clough
Lower Reaps Farm
VALLEY
Pat Moss
Slip-in
BACUP
BACUP GOLF COURSE
Club House
Warcock Farm
Slack Gate
Hoyle Hey Clough
Top o' th' Bank
MADEN ROAD
Tennis Cts.
Bowling Green
Maden Recreation Ground
Tong Farm
Daisy Hall
Tong Clough
Whitegate Farm
Huttock Farm
Huttock Top
Bankside Farm
Spring Bank Farm
Dry Corner Farm
Causeway House Farm
Honey Hole
Sow Clough
Rockcliffe
Green Hill
St. Saviour's Prim. Sch.
Hey Head
Moor View
Higher Stack
Old Troughgate Farm
Stubbylee Bridge
Stubbylee Park
Moorlands Park
Moss Meadows Farm
Moss Meadows Cotts.
Stacksteads
Fairwell Cemetery
Nun Hills
Lee Farm
Fairwall
Venomous Clough
Britannia
Deans Greave
Walmsley
Moss Farm
Greens Farm
Sheep Ho.
Stubbylee Moss Fm.
Reservoir (cov.)
Height Barn Moss
Brandwood Higher End Moor
Stubbylee Moss
HOLDEN MOOR
Jam Hill
Whitworth Higher End Moor
Rochdale
OL12
Lee Moss
GREENS MOOR
BURNLEY ROAD
A671
TODMORDEN ROAD
A681
MARKET STREET
ROCHDALE ROAD
NEWLINE ROAD
A6066
TV Mast

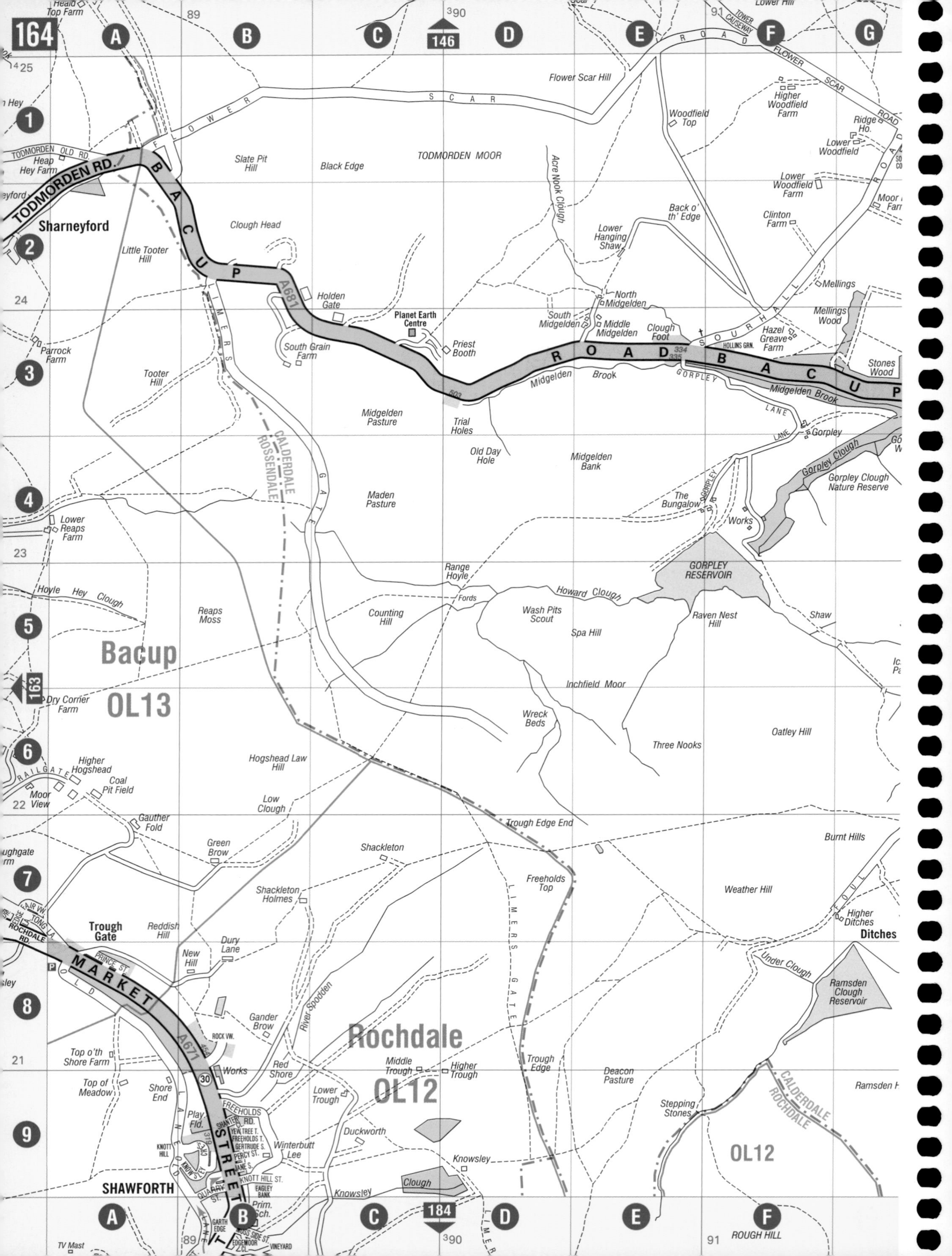
A
B
C
D
E
F
G
146
Heald Top Farm
Flower Scar Hill
TOWER CAUSEWAY
ROAD
FLOWER SCAR ROAD
LOWER SCAR
Woodfield Top
Higher Woodfield Farm
Ridge Ho.
Lower Woodfield
Lower Woodfield Farm
Moor Farm
TODMORDEN OLD RD
Heap Hey Farm
TODMORDEN RD.
Sharneyford
Slate Pit Hill
Black Edge
TODMORDEN MOOR
Acre Nook Clough
Back o' th' Edge
Clinton Farm
Lower Hanging Shaw
Clough Head
Little Tooter Hill
BACUP ROAD
A681
Holden Gate
Planet Earth Centre
Priest Booth
North Midgelden
South Midgelden
Middle Midgelden
Clough Foot
SOUTH HALL ROAD
Mellings
Mellings Wood
Hazel Greave Farm
HOLLINS GRN.
Stones Wood
Parrock Farm
South Grain Farm
Tooter Hill
Midgelden Brook
GORPLEY LANE
Gorpley
Midgelden Pasture
Trial Holes
Old Day Hole
Midgelden Bank
Gorpley Clough
Gorpley Clough Nature Reserve
LIMERS GATE
CALDERDALE
ROSSENDALE
Maden Pasture
The Bungalow
Works
Lower Reaps Farm
GORPLEY RESERVOIR
Range Hoyle
Fords
Howard Clough
Hoyle Hey Clough
Reaps Moss
Counting Hill
Wash Pits Scout
Spa Hill
Raven Nest Hill
Shaw
Bacup
OL13
163
Dry Corner Farm
Inchfield Moor
Wreck Beds
Three Nooks
Oatley Hill
Higher Hogshead
Coal Pit Field
RAILGATE
Moor View
Hogshead Law Hill
Low Clough
Gauther Fold
Trough Edge End
Burnt Hills
Green Brow
Shackleton
Freeholds Top
Weather Hill
Shackleton Holmes
Higher Ditches
Ditches
Trough Gate
Reddish Hill
ROCHDALE RD.
FAIR VW.
TONG LA.
Dury Lane
New Hill
PRINCE ST.
MARKET STREET
A671
Under Clough
Ramsden Clough Reservoir
River Spodden
Gander Brow
Rochdale
ROCK VW.
Top o'th Shore Farm
Works
Red Shore
Middle Trough
Higher Trough
Trough Edge
Deacon Pasture
Top of Meadow
Shore End
OL12
Lower Trough
Ramsden H
FREEHOLDS RD.
Play. Fld.
Stepping Stones
CALDERDALE
ROCHDALE
Duckworth
KNOTT HILL
Winterbutt Lee
YEW TREE T.
FREEHOLDS T.
GERTRUDE S.
PERCY ST.
JANE S.
KNOTT HILL ST.
EAGLEY BANK
OL12
Knowsley
Clough
Knowsley
SHAWFORTH
QUARRY ST.
Prim. Sch.
184
ROUGH HILL
GARTH EDGE
MOSS SIDE ST.
EDGEMOOR CL.
VINEYARD
TV Mast
1
2
3
4
5
6
7
8
9

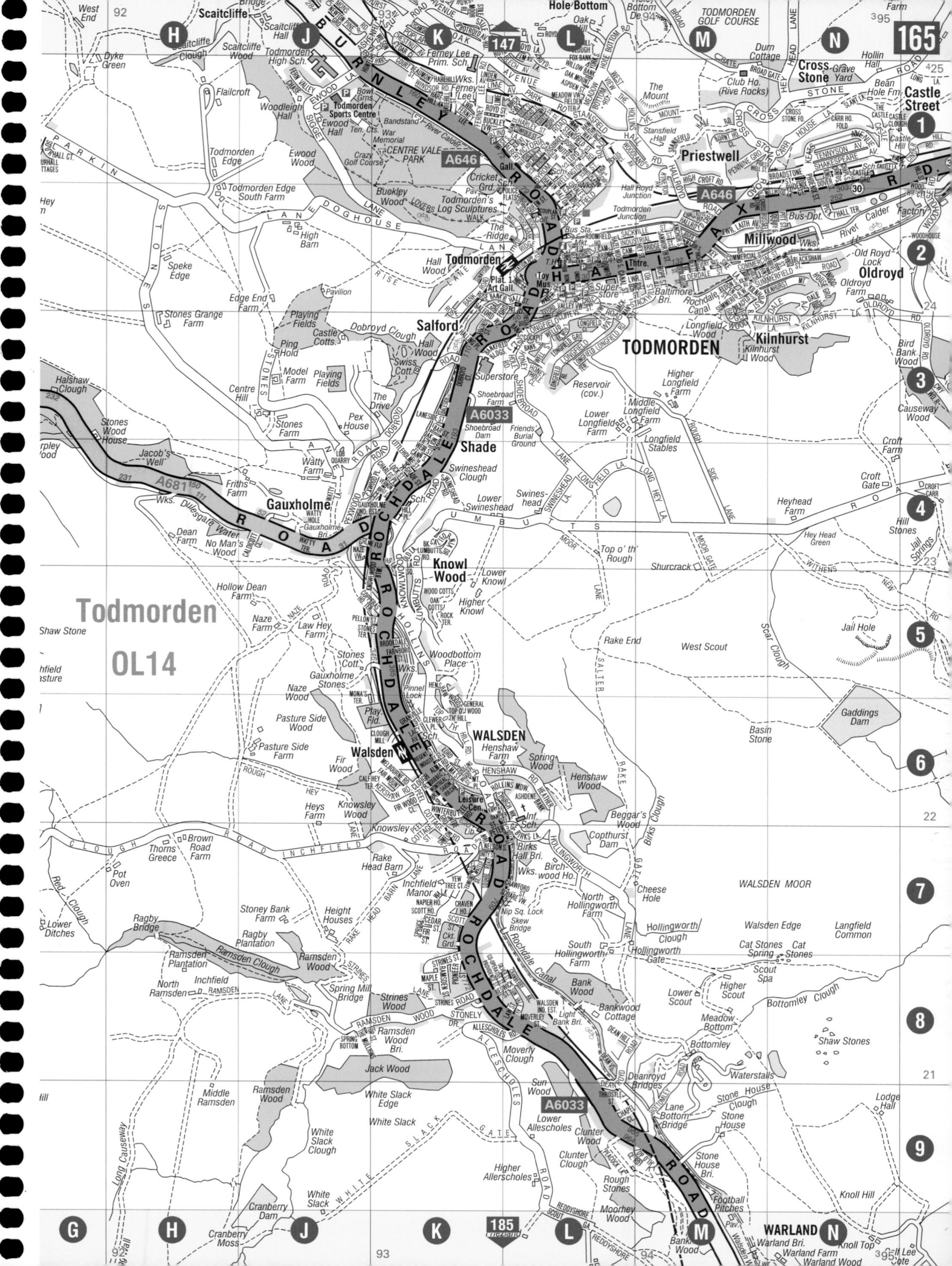

TODMORDEN
Todmorden
OL14
WALSDEN
Walsden
Gauxholme
Salford
Shade
Priestwell
Millwood
Oldroyd
Kilnhurst
Cross Stone
Castle Street
Knowl Wood
WARLAND
Scaitcliffe
Hole Bottom
TODMORDEN GOLF COURSE
Centre Vale Park
Todmorden Sports Centre
Todmorden High Sch.
Todmorden Edge
Dobroyd Clough
Ewood Hall
Woodleigh Hall
Jack Wood
Ramsden Clough
Gaddings Dam
Walsden Moor
West Scout
Shaw Stones
Rochdale Canal
River Calder
A646
A6033
A681
BURNLEY ROAD
HALIFAX RD.
ROCHDALE ROAD
LUMBUTTS ROAD
Superstore
Leisure Cen.
147
185

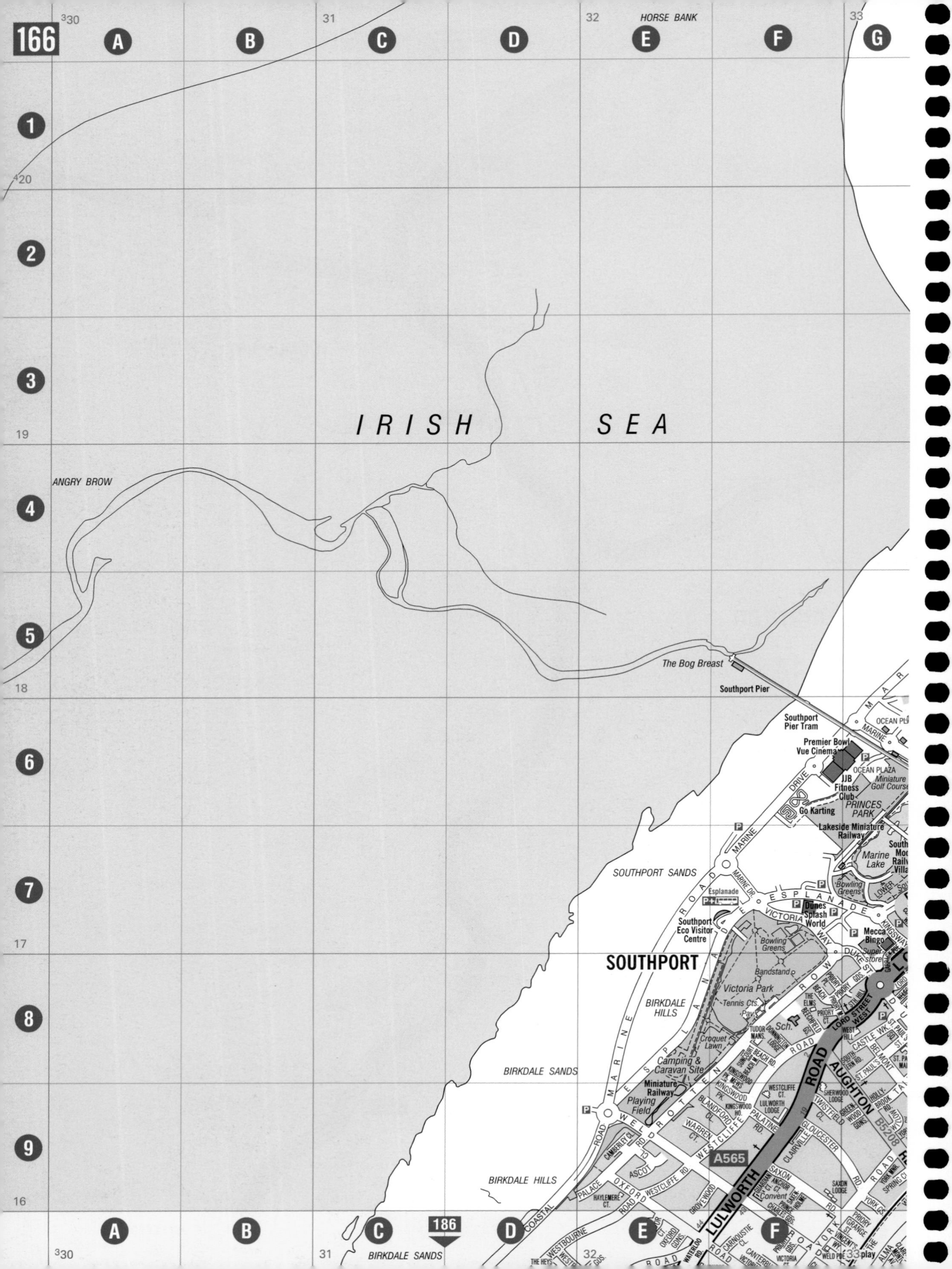

166

A B 31 C D 32 E **HORSE BANK** F 33 G

1

⁴20

2

3

I R I S H   S E A

19

ANGRY BROW

4

5

18

The Bog Breast

Southport Pier

Southport
Pier Tram

Premier Bowl
Vue Cinema

6

OCEAN PLAZA

Miniature
Golf Course

JJB
Fitness
Club

Go Karting

PRINCES PARK

Lakeside Miniature
Railway

Marine
Lake

SOUTHPORT SANDS

7

Esplanade

Dunes
Splash
World

Southport
Eco Visitor
Centre

Bowling
Greens

Mecca
Bingo

SOUTHPORT

Bandstand

Victoria Park

BIRKDALE HILLS

Tennis Cts.

8

Croquet
Lawn

Camping &
Caravan Site

BIRKDALE SANDS

Miniature
Railway

Playing
Field

WESTCLIFFE
CT.

LULWORTH
LODGE

ROAD

AUGHTON

B5208

9

BIRKDALE HILLS

A565

LULWORTH

16

A B C **186** D 32 E F 33

BIRKDALE SANDS

³30 31

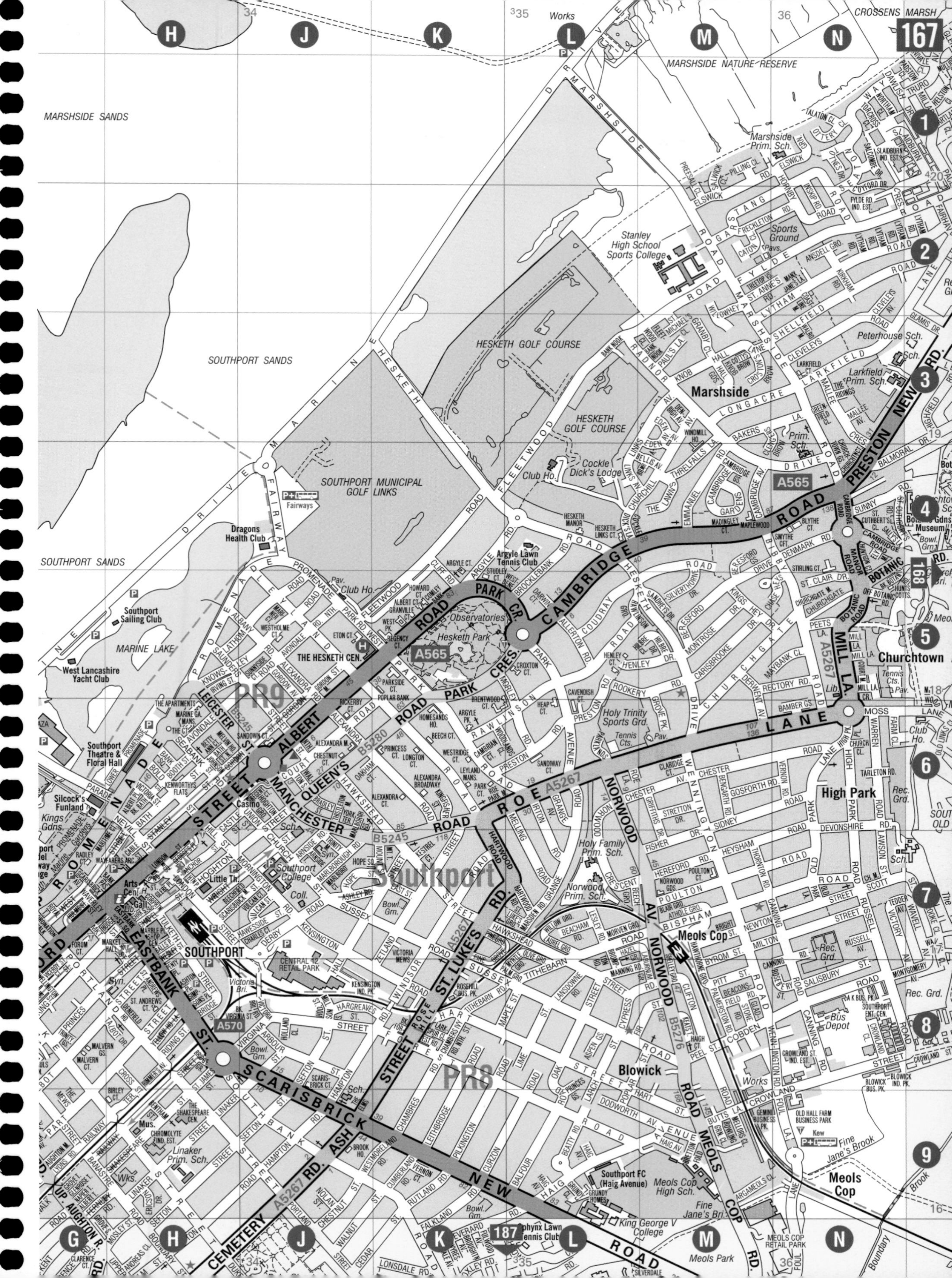
CROSSENS MARSH
MARSHSIDE NATURE RESERVE
MARSHSIDE SANDS
SOUTHPORT SANDS
MARINE DRIVE
MARSHSIDE ROAD
HESKETH DRIVE
HESKETH GOLF COURSE
SOUTHPORT MUNICIPAL GOLF LINKS
Fairways
Dragons Health Club
Southport Sailing Club
MARINE LAKE
West Lancashire Yacht Club
Stanley High School Sports College
Marshside Prim. Sch.
Sports Ground
Marshside
Larkfield Prim. Sch.
Peterhouse Sch.
Cockle Dick's Lodge
Club Ho.
Argyle Lawn Tennis Club
Observatories
Hesketh Park
THE HESKETH CEN.
Botanic Gdns. Museum
Churchtown
Holy Trinity Sports Grd.
High Park
Southport Theatre & Floral Hall
Silcock's Funland
Kings Gdns.
Casino
Arts Cen.
Little Th.
Southport College
SOUTHPORT
CENTRAL 12 RETAIL PARK
Victoria Bri.
Holy Family Prim. Sch.
Norwood Prim. Sch.
Meols Cop
Blowick
Bus Depot
Works
OLD HALL FARM BUSINESS PARK
Fine Jane's Brook
Southport FC (Haig Avenue)
Meols Cop High Sch.
King George V College
MEOLS COP RETAIL PARK
Linaker Prim. Sch.
Mus.
Southport
PR9
PR8
A565
A570
A5267
B5245
B5280
B5276
PRESTON NEW RD.
CAMBRIDGE ROAD
ALBERT ROAD
LORD STREET
PROMENADE
MANCHESTER ROAD
ROE LANE
MILL LA.
SCARISBRICK NEW ROAD
EASTBANK ST.
ST. LUKE'S RD.
NORWOOD AV.
NORWOOD ROAD
MEOLS COP RD.
ASH ST.
CEMETERY RD.
FLEETWOOD ROAD
PARK CRES.
168
187

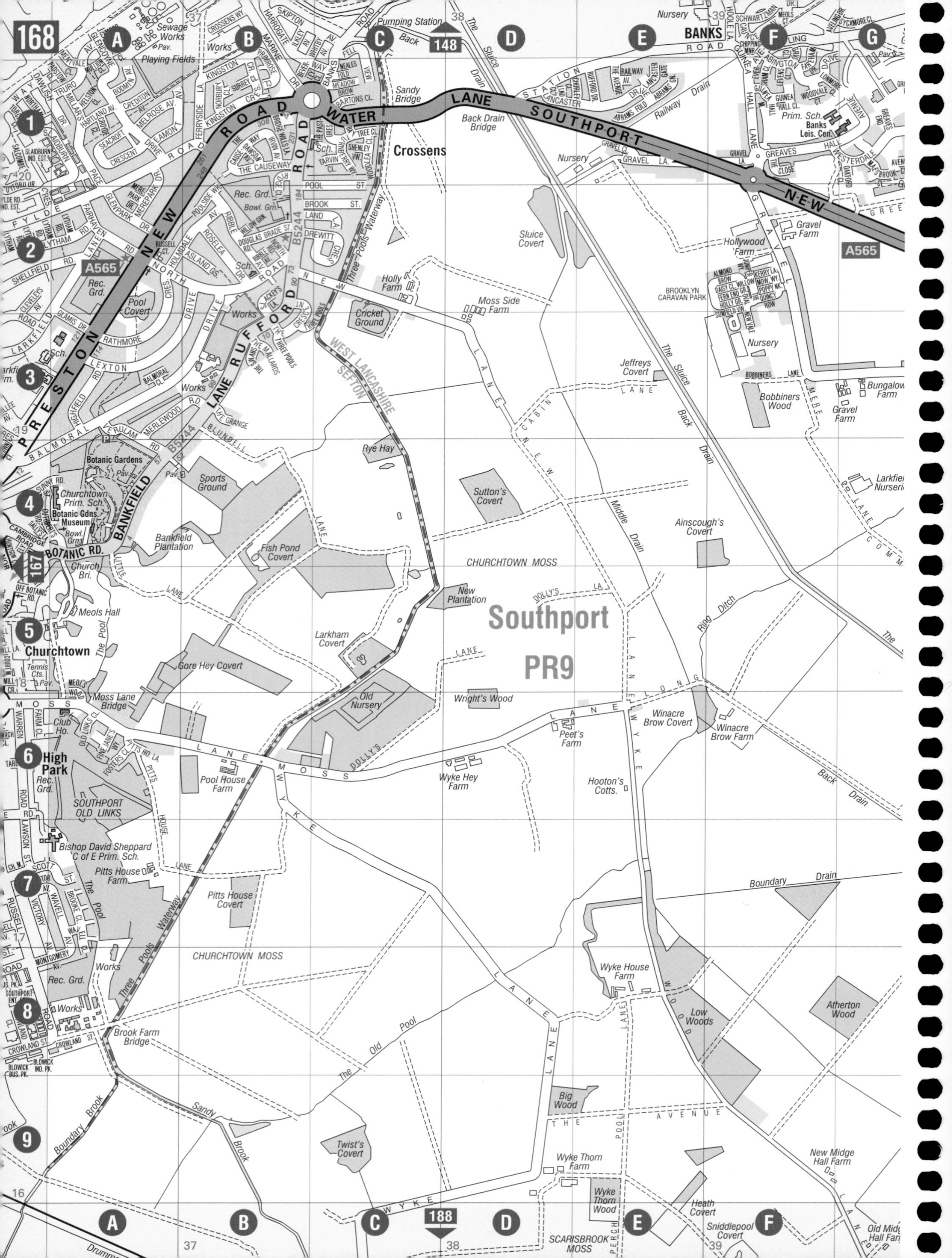

A
B
C
D
E
F
G
1
2
3
4
5
6
7
8
9
148
167
188
37
38
39
Sewage Works
Playing Fields
Works
Pumping Station
Back
The Sluice
Drain
Nursery
BANKS
ROAD
STATION
RAILWAY AV.
Railway Drain
Sandy Bridge
WATER
LANE
SOUTHPORT
NEW
ROAD
PRESTON
Back Drain Bridge
Crossens
Prim. Sch.
Banks Leis. Cen.
GREAVES
GRAVEL LA.
Nursery
Rec. Grd.
Bowl. Grn.
THE CAUSEWAY
POOL ST.
BROOK ST.
DREWITT
A565
B5244
Sluice Covert
Gravel Farm
Hollywood Farm
A565
Holly Farm
Moss Side Farm
BROOKLYN CARAVAN PARK
Three Pools Waterway
Rec. Grd.
Pool Covert
Cricket Ground
Works
RUFFORD
Sch.
LEXTON
RATHMORE
Works
WEST LANCASHIRE
SEFTON
Jeffreys Covert
The Sluice
Nursery
BOBBINERS LANE
Bobbiners Wood
Bungalow Farm
Gravel Farm
MERE
CABIN
LANE
BALMORAL
MERLEWOOD RD
THE GRANGE
BLUNDELL
Botanic Gardens
Pav.
Rye Hay
Sports Ground
Sutton's Covert
Back Drain
Churchtown Prim. Sch.
Botanic Gdns. Museum
BANKFIELD
Bankfield Plantation
Fish Pond Covert
Middle Drain
Ainscough's Covert
Larkfield Nurseries
BOTANIC RD.
Church Bri.
CHURCHTOWN MOSS
New Plantation
DOLLY'S LA.
Meols Hall
Southport
PR9
Ring Ditch
Churchtown
The Pool
Larkham Covert
Gore Hey Covert
Tennis Cts.
Moss Lane Bridge
Old Nursery
Wright's Wood
LONG
Winacre Brow Covert
Winacre Brow Farm
Club Ho.
MOSS
LANE
DOLLY'S
Peet's Farm
High Park
Rec. Grd.
Pool House Farm
Wyke Hey Farm
Hooton's Cotts.
SOUTHPORT OLD LINKS
WYKE
Back Drain
Bishop David Sheppard C of E Prim. Sch.
Pitts House Farm
Pitts House Covert
Boundary Drain
CHURCHTOWN MOSS
Works
Rec. Grd.
Works
Wyke House Farm
Atherton Wood
Low Woods
WOOD
Brook Farm Bridge
The Old Pool
Sandy Brook
Boundary Brook
Big Wood
THE AVENUE
POOL
Twist's Covert
Wyke Thorn Farm
New Midge Hall Farm
Wyke Thorn Wood
Heath Covert
Sniddlepool Covert
Old Midge Hall Farm
WYKE
SCARISBROOK MOSS
PERCH
BLOWICK BUS. PK.
BLOWICK IND. PK.
CROWLAND ST.

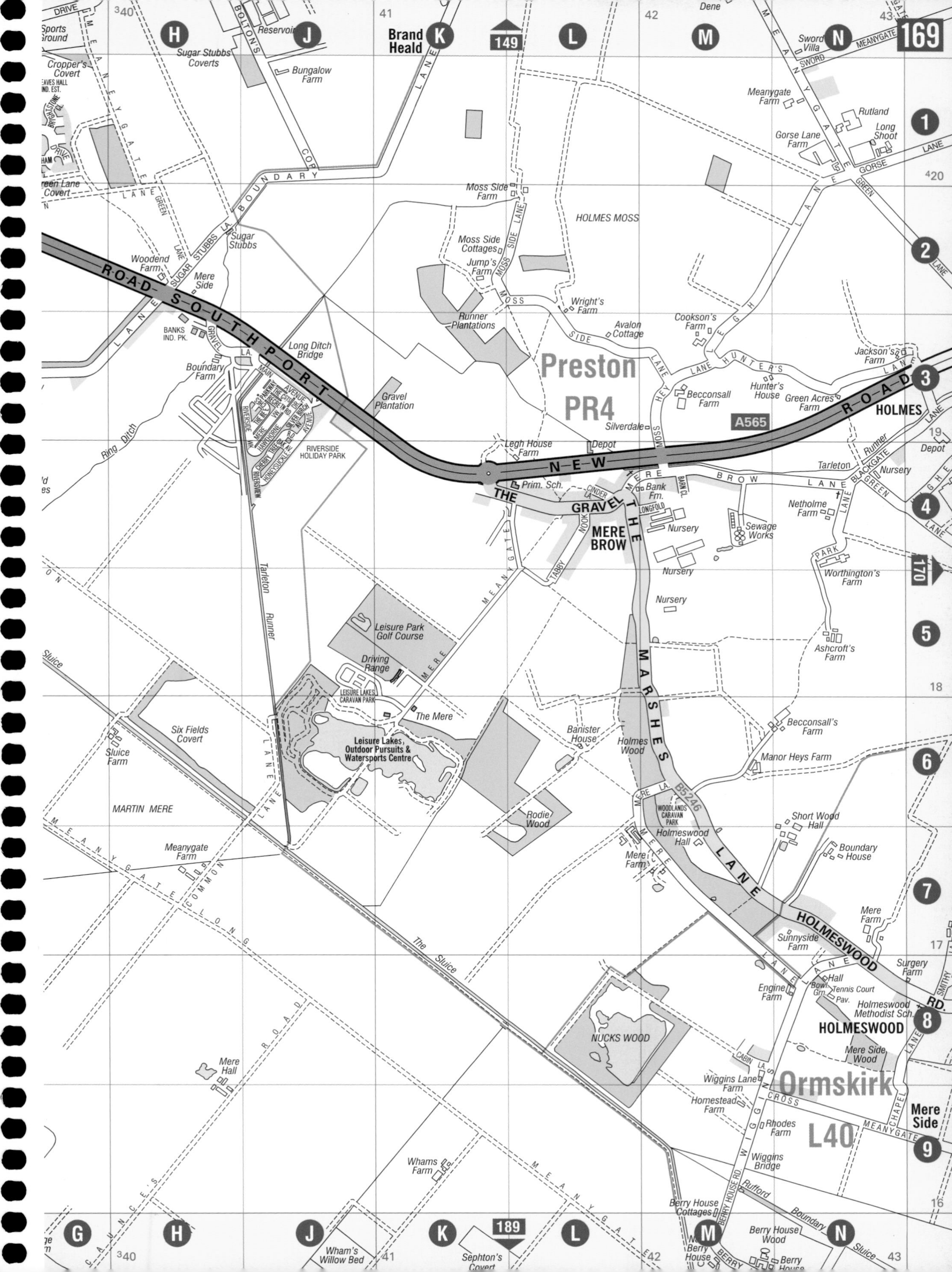
Brand Heald
149
Preston
PR4
Ormskirk
L40
HOLMES
MERE BROW
HOLMESWOOD
Mere Side
A565
B5246
NEW ROAD
SOUTHPORT ROAD
THE GRAVEL
THE MARSHES
HOLMESWOOD RD.
HOLMES MOSS
MARTIN MERE
NUCKS WOOD
Leisure Lakes, Outdoor Pursuits & Watersports Centre
Leisure Park Golf Course
RIVERSIDE HOLIDAY PARK
WOODLANDS CARAVAN PARK
LEISURE LAKES CARAVAN PARK
BANKS IND. PK.
Sugar Stubbs Coverts
Bungalow Farm
Moss Side Farm
Moss Side Cottages
Jump's Farm
Wright's Farm
Avalon Cottage
Cookson's Farm
Runner Plantations
Long Ditch Bridge
Gravel Plantation
Boundary Farm
Woodend Farm
Mere Side
Sugar Stubbs
Legh House Farm
Depot
Silverdale
Becconsall Farm
Hunter's House
Green Acres Farm
Jackson's Farm
Meanygate Farm
Gorse Lane Farm
Rutland
Long Shoot
Sword Villa
Prim. Sch.
Bank Fm.
Nursery
Sewage Works
Netholme Farm
Worthington's Farm
Ashcroft's Farm
Tarleton
Nursery
Driving Range
The Mere
Six Fields Covert
Sluice Farm
Banister House
Holmes Wood
Rodie Wood
Becconsall's Farm
Manor Heys Farm
Short Wood Hall
Boundary House
Holmeswood Hall
Mere Farm
Sunnyside Farm
Mere Farm
Surgery Farm
Engine Farm
Hall
Bowl Grn.
Tennis Court
Pav.
Holmeswood Methodist Sch.
Mere Side Wood
Wiggins Lane Farm
Homestead Farm
Rhodes Farm
Wiggins Bridge
Meanygate Farm
Mere Hall
Whams Farm
Wham's Willow Bed
Sephton's Covert
Berry House Cottages
Berry House Wood
Berry House
Tarleton Runner
The Sluice
Rufford Boundary Sluice
Ring Ditch
MEANYGATE
LONG MEANYGATE
COMMON
GAUNCE'S ROAD
BOUNDARY LANE
MOSS SIDE LANE
HEY LANE
LEGH LANE
HUNTER'S LANE
GORSE LANE
MERE BROW LANE
BLACKGATE LANE
CINDER LA.
NOOK
TABBY
LONGFOLD
BARN CL.
MERE LA.
MERE LANE
CABIN LA.
CROSS
WIGGINS LANE
CHAPEL LANE
SMITHY
BERRY HOUSE RD.
PARK
170
189
H J K L M N G
1 2 3 4 5 6 7 8 9
340 41 42 43
420 19 18 17 16

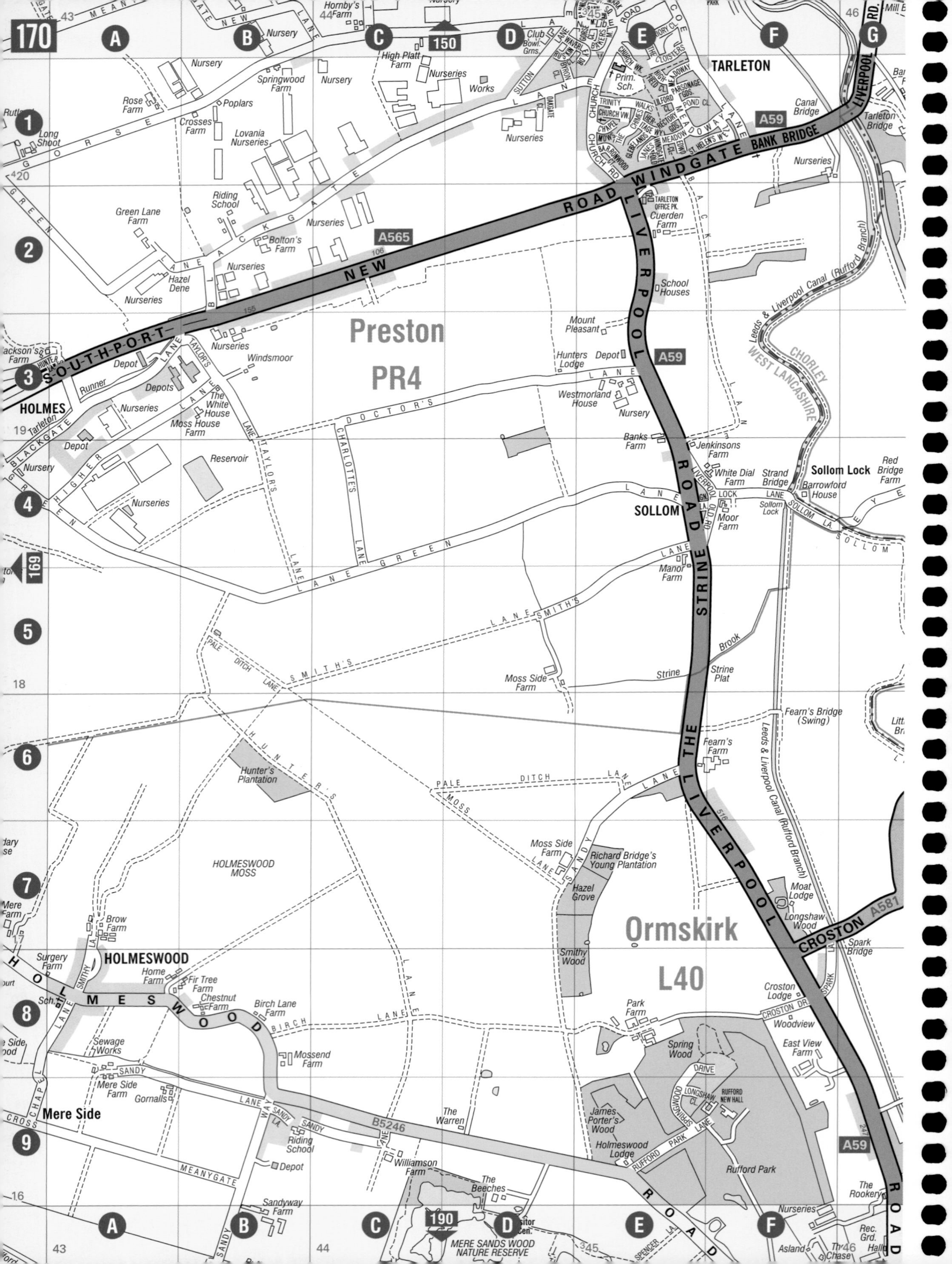
TARLETON
Preston
PR4
Ormskirk
L40
HOLMES
SOLLOM
HOLMESWOOD
Mere Side
Sollom Lock
HOLMESWOOD MOSS
A565
A59
A581
B5246
NEW ROAD
SOUTHPORT
WINDGATE
BANK BRIDGE
LIVERPOOL ROAD
THE LIVERPOOL
STRINE ROAD
CROSTON
Leeds & Liverpool Canal (Rufford Branch)
WEST LANCASHIRE
CHORLEY
Hunter's Plantation
Richard Bridge's Young Plantation
Hazel Grove
Smithy Wood
Spring Wood
James Porter's Wood
Rufford Park
MERE SANDS WOOD NATURE RESERVE
150
169
190

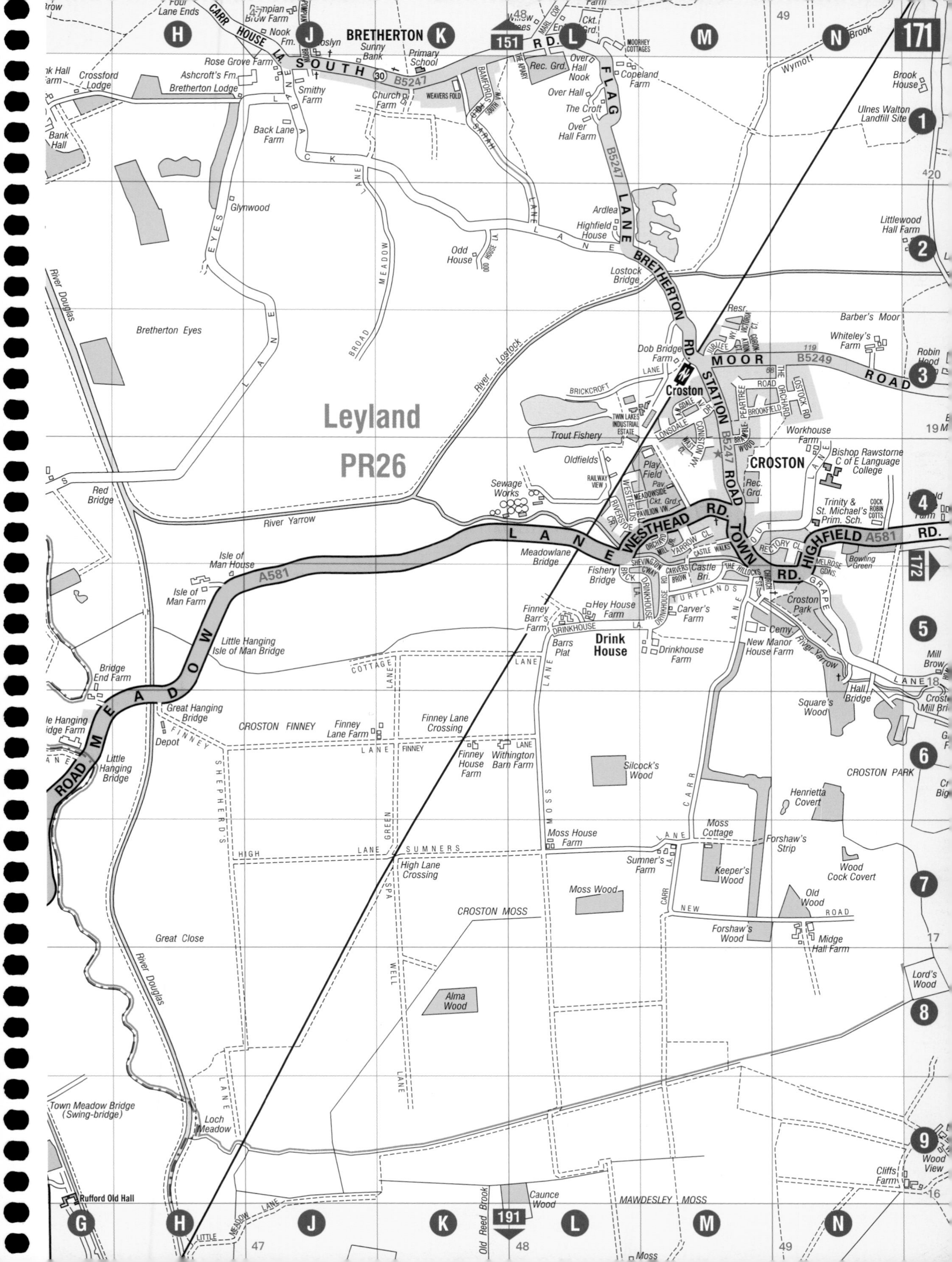
BRETHERTON
Leyland
PR26
CROSTON
Croston
CROSTON FINNEY
CROSTON MOSS
CROSTON PARK
MAWDESLEY MOSS
Drink House
Bretherton Eyes
Great Close
River Douglas
River Lostock
River Yarrow
Ulnes Walton Landfill Site
Barber's Moor
Rufford Old Hall
Town Meadow Bridge (Swing-bridge)
Loch Meadow
Alma Wood
Moss Wood
Silcock's Wood
Keeper's Wood
Forshaw's Wood
Forshaw's Strip
Henrietta Covert
Wood Cock Covert
Old Wood
Square's Wood
Caunce Wood
Lord's Wood
Midge Hall Farm
Sumner's Farm
Moss House Farm
Moss Cottage
High Lane Crossing
Finney Lane Crossing
Finney Lane Farm
Finney House Farm
Withington Barn Farm
Great Hanging Bridge
Little Hanging Bridge
Little Hanging Isle of Man Bridge
Isle of Man House
Isle of Man Farm
Bridge End Farm
Red Bridge
Meadowlane Bridge
Fishery Bridge
Finney Barr's Farm
Barrs Plat
Hey House Farm
Carver's Farm
Drinkhouse Farm
New Manor House Farm
Croston Park
Hall Bridge
Sewage Works
Trout Fishery
Oldfields
Twin Lakes Industrial Estate
Play. Field
Ckt. Grd.
Rec. Grd.
Castle Bri.
Workhouse Farm
Bishop Rawstorne C of E Language College
Trinity & St. Michael's Prim. Sch.
Bowling Green
Whiteley's Farm
Dob Bridge Farm
Lostock Bridge
Highfield House
Ardlea
Odd House
Glynwood
Back Lane Farm
Smithy Farm
Church Farm
Primary School
Sunny Bank
Rose Grove Farm
Ashcroft's Fm.
Bretherton Lodge
Crossford Lodge
Bank Hall
Over Hall Nook
Over Hall
The Croft
Over Hall Farm
Copeland Farm
Moorhey Cottages
Brook House
Littlewood Hall Farm
Cliffs Farm
Wood View
Depot
Carr House La.
South Rd.
Flag Lane
Bretherton Rd.
Station Road
Town Rd.
Westhead Rd.
Highfield Rd.
Moor Road
Meadow Lane
Meadow Road
Back Lane
Eyes Lane
Broad Meadow
Drinkhouse La.
Cottage Lane
Finney Lane
Shepherd's
High Lane
Sumners Lane
Green Lane
Spa Well Lane
Moss Lane
Carr Lane
New Road
Grape Lane
Old Reed Brook
Wymott Brook
B5247
B5249
A581
151
172
191
47
48
49
16
17
18
19
20
G
H
J
K
L
M
N
1
2
3
4
5
6
7
8
9

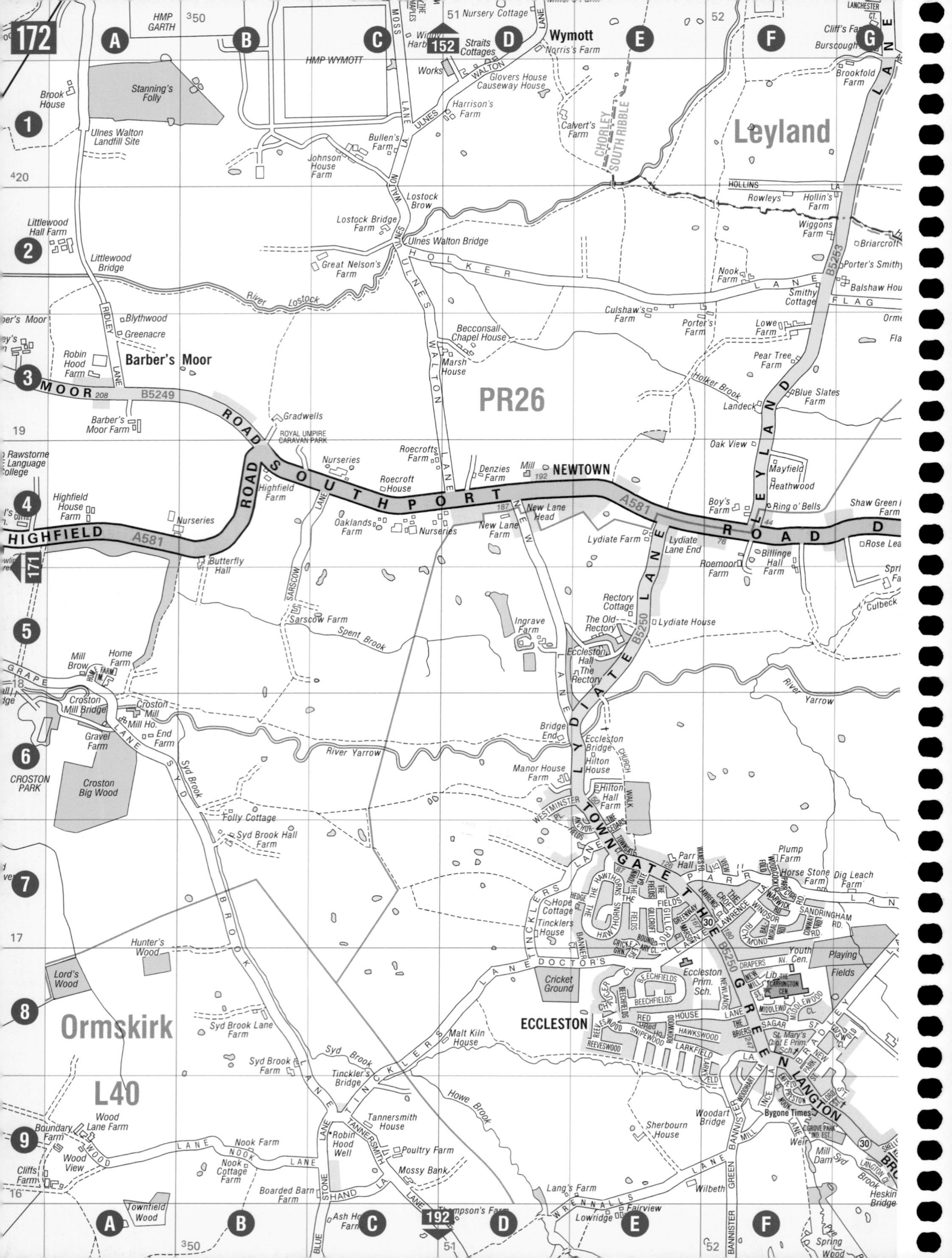
A
B
C
D
E
F
G
1
2
3
4
5
6
7
8
9
HMP GARTH
350
HMP WYMOTT
51
Nursery Cottage
152
Straits Cottages
Wymott
Norris's Farm
52
LANCHESTER CT.
Cliff's Farm
Burscough
Brook House
Stanning's Folly
Works
WALTON
Glovers House
Causeway House
Harrison's Farm
Ulnes Walton Landfill Site
ULNES
Bullen's Farm
Johnson House Farm
Calvert's Farm
CHORLEY
SOUTH RIBBLE
Leyland
Brookfold Farm
420
HOLLINS LA.
Rowleys
Hollin's Farm
Lostock Brow
Littlewood Hall Farm
Lostock Bridge Farm
Wiggons Farm
Ulnes Walton Bridge
Briarcroft
Littlewood Bridge
Great Nelson's Farm
HOLKER LANE
Nook Farm
Porter's Smithy
B5253
Balshaw House
Smithy Cottage
FLAG
River Lostock
Culshaw's Farm
Porter's Farm
Lowe Farm
RIDLEY LANE
Blythwood
Greenacre
Becconsall Chapel House
Pear Tree Farm
Robin Hood Farm
Barber's Moor
Marsh House
Holker Brook
MOOR ROAD
208
B5249
PR26
Blue Slates Farm
Landeck
Gradwells
Barber's Moor Farm
ROYAL UMPIRE CARAVAN PARK
19
Oak View
Rawstorne Language College
Nurseries
Roecrofts Farm
Denzies Farm
Mill
NEWTOWN
192
Mayfield
Heathwood
Roecroft House
Highfield Farm
SOUTHPORT ROAD
Highfield House Farm
187
New Lane Head
A581
Boy's Farm
Ring o' Bells
Shaw Green Farm
Nurseries
Oaklands Farm
Nurseries
New Lane Farm
44
HIGHFIELD
A581
Lydiate Farm
Lydiate Lane End
76
Billinge Hall Farm
Rose Lea
171
Butterfly Hall
Roemoor Farm
SARSCOW
Rectory Cottage
Culbeck
Sarscow Farm
The Old Rectory
Lydiate House
Spent Brook
Ingrave Farm
B5250
Mill Brow
Home Farm
Eccleston Hall
GRAPE
18
The Rectory
River Yarrow
Croston Mill Bridge
Croston Mill
Mill Ho.
End Farm
Gravel Farm
Bridge End
Eccleston Bridge
River Yarrow
Hilton House
CHURCH
Manor House Farm
CROSTON PARK
Croston Big Wood
Syd Brook
Hilton Hall Farm
WALK
WESTMINSTER PL.
Folly Cottage
TOWNGATE
Syd Brook Hall Farm
Plump Farm
Parr Hall
PARR
Horse Stone Farm
Dig Leach Farm
Hope Cottage
Tincklers House
TINCKLERS
THE GREEN
30
BROOK
SANDRINGHAM RD.
17
Hunter's Wood
DOCTOR'S LANE
Playing Fields
Youth Cen.
DRAPERS AV.
Lord's Wood
Cricket Ground
Eccleston Prim. Sch.
BEECHFIELDS
Lib.
CARRINGTON CEN.
Ormskirk
Syd Brook Lane Farm
Malt Kiln House
ECCLESTON
REEVESWOOD
HOUSE
HAWKSWOOD
LARKFIELD
SAGAR ST.
St. Mary's C of E Prim. Sch.
LANGTON
Syd Brook Farm
Tinckler's Bridge
Howe Brook
Bygone Times
L40
Tannersmith House
Woodart Bridge
Sherbourn House
GROVE PARK IND. EST.
Wood Lane Farm
Boundary Farm
Nook Farm
Robin Hood Well
TANNERSMITH
Poultry Farm
NOOK LANE
WOOD
Wood View
Nook Cottage Farm
Mossy Bank
Mill Dam
Cliffs Farm
Boarded Barn Farm
Lang's Farm
Wilbeth
BANNISTER GREEN
Heskin Bridge
16
Townfield Wood
STONE
Ash House Farm
192
Thompson's Farm
WRENNALLS
Fairview
Lowridge
BLUE STONE LANE
350
51
52
Spring Wood

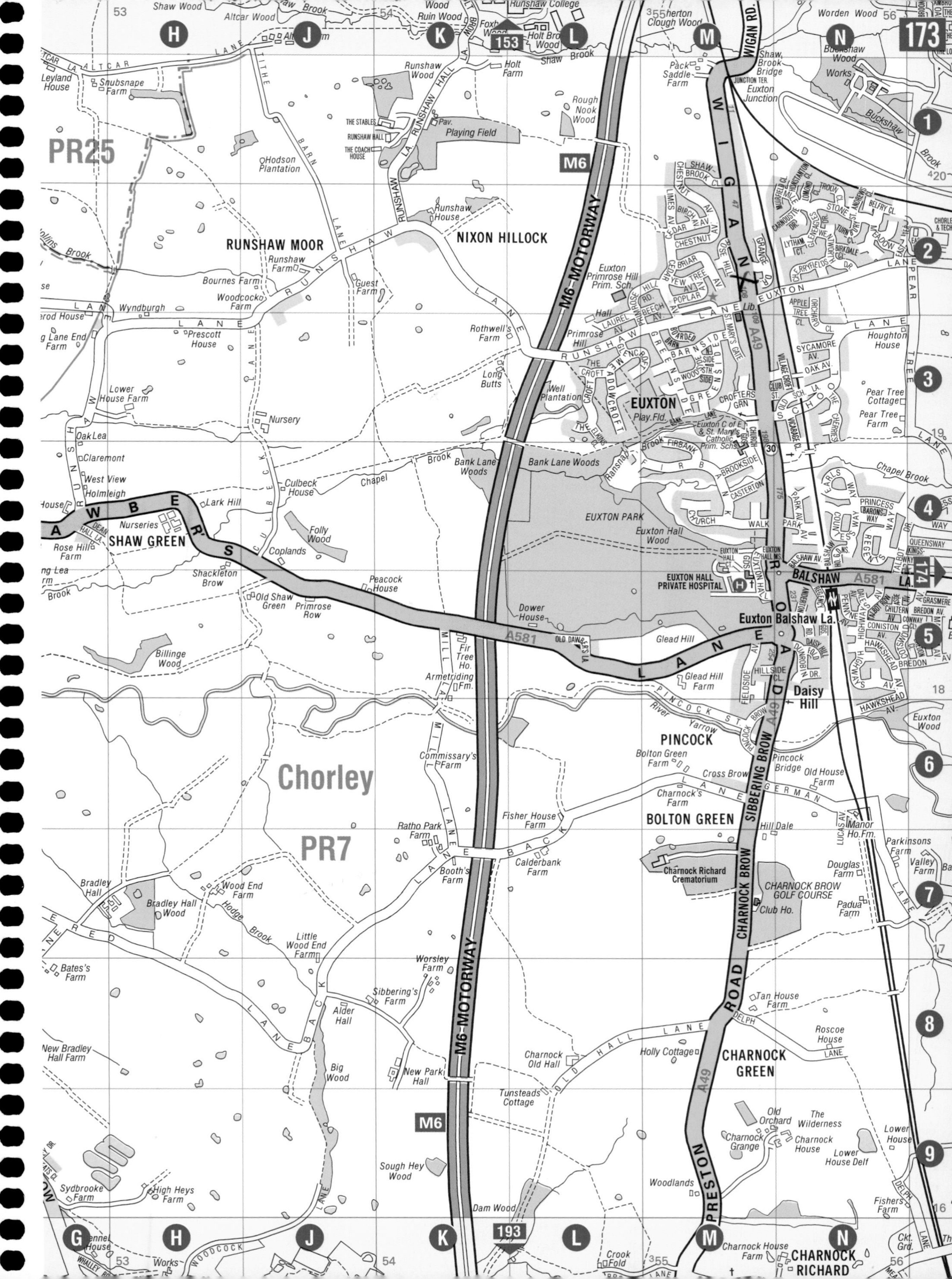

RUNSHAW MOOR
NIXON HILLOCK
EUXTON
SHAW GREEN
PINCOCK
BOLTON GREEN
CHARNOCK GREEN
CHARNOCK RICHARD
Daisy Hill
Chorley
PR7
PR25
M6-MOTORWAY
A581
A49
WIGAN RD.
PRESTON ROAD
SIBBERING BROW
CHARNOCK BROW
Runshaw College
Runshaw Hall
Playing Field
Euxton Park
Euxton Hall Private Hospital
Charnock Richard Crematorium
Charnock Brow Golf Course
Euxton Balshaw La.
153
174
193

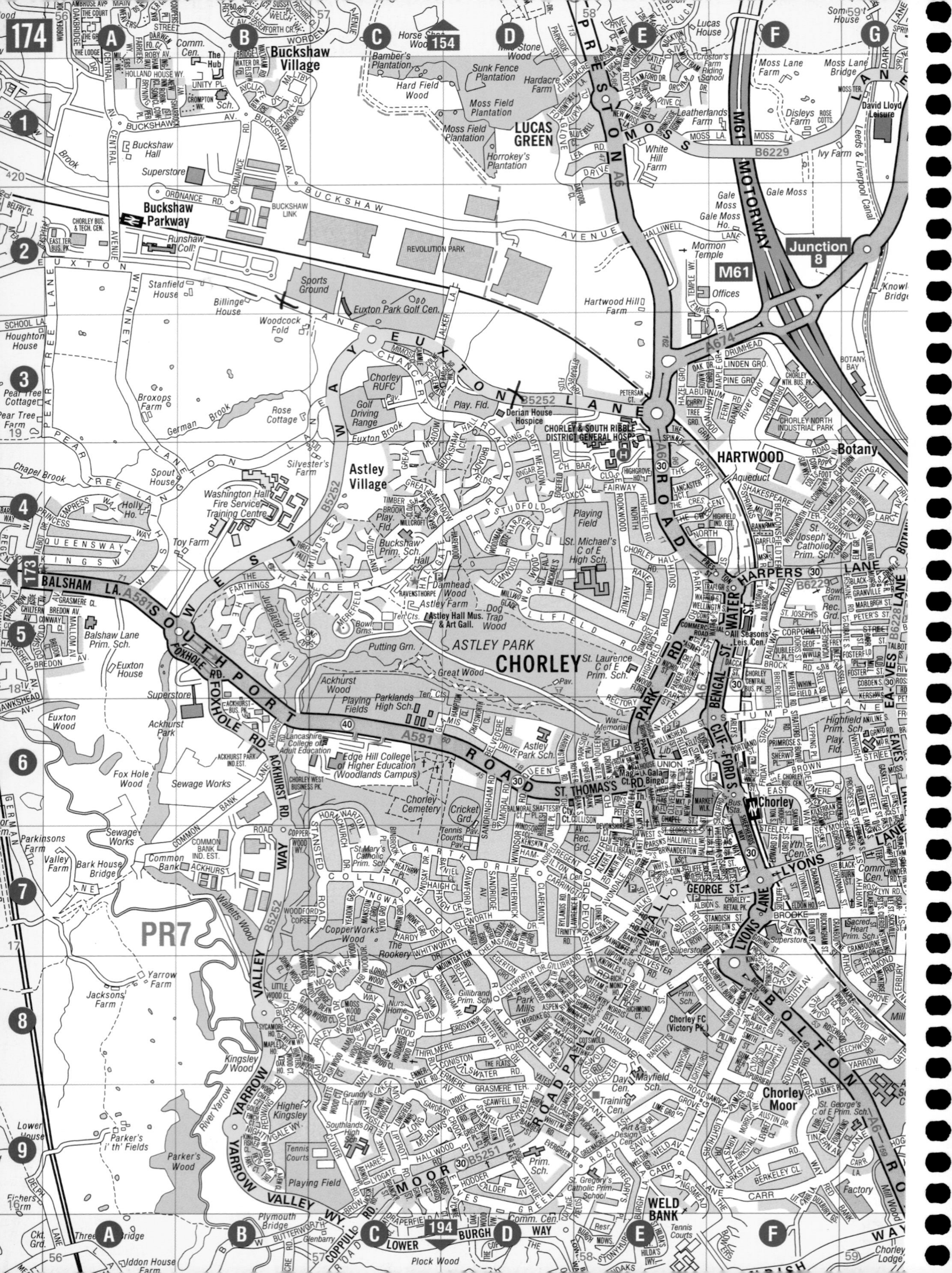
Buckshaw Village
Buckshaw Parkway
Runshaw Coll.
Buckshaw Hall
Superstore
Revolution Park
Sports Ground
Euxton Park Golf Cen.
Lucas Green
Hard Field Wood
Sunk Fence Plantation
Moss Field Plantation
Horrokey's Plantation
Bamber's Plantation
Hardacre Farm
Mormon Temple
Junction 8
M61 Motorway
Leeds & Liverpool Canal
Gale Moss
Moss Lane Farm
Moss Lane Bridge
David Lloyd Leisure
Disleys Farm
Ivy Farm
Leatherlands Farm
White Hill Farm
Hartwood Hill Farm
Offices
Botany
Hartwood
Chorley North Industrial Park
Chorley & South Ribble District General Hosp.
Derian House Hospice
Chorley RUFC
Golf Driving Range
Astley Village
Astley Park
Chorley
Astley Hall Mus. & Art Gall.
Dog Trap Wood
Damhead Wood
Great Wood
Ackhurst Wood
Parklands High Sch.
St. Michael's C of E High Sch.
St. Laurence C of E Prim. Sch.
St. Joseph's Catholic Prim. Sch.
Highfield Prim. Sch.
Washington Hall Fire Service Training Centre
Silvester's Farm
Rose Cottage
Broxops Farm
Stanfield House
Billinge House
Woodcock Fold
Houghton House
Pear Tree Cottage
Spout House
Holly Ho.
Toy Farm
Balshaw Lane Prim. Sch.
Euxton House
Euxton Wood
Ackhurst Park
Fox Hole Wood
Sewage Works
Lancashire College of Adult Education
Edge Hill College of Higher Education (Woodlands Campus)
Chorley Cemetery
Cricket Grd.
Astley Park Sch.
Market Walk
Chorley
Parkinsons Farm
Valley Farm
Bark House Bridge
Common Bank
PR7
Yarrow Farm
Jacksons Farm
Copperworks Wood
The Rookery
Gillibrand Prim. Sch.
Park Mills
Chorley FC (Victory Pk.)
Kingsley Wood
Higher Kingsley
River Yarrow
Parker's Wood
Parker's i' th' Fields
Lower House
Mayfield Sch.
Training Cen.
Day Cen.
Chorley Moor
St. George's C of E Prim. Sch.
St. Gregory's Catholic Prim. School
Weld Bank
Playing Field
Southlands High Sch.
Plymouth Bridge
Three Bridge
Iddon House Farm
Glenbarry
Plock Wood
Chorley Lodge
Factory
Southport Road
Euxton Lane
Preston Road
Bolton Road
Lyons Lane
Harpers Lane
Moor Road
Yarrow Valley Wy.
Valley Way
Balsham La.
Pear Tree Lane
Buckshaw Avenue
A581
A6
A674
B5252
B6229
B5251
154
173
194

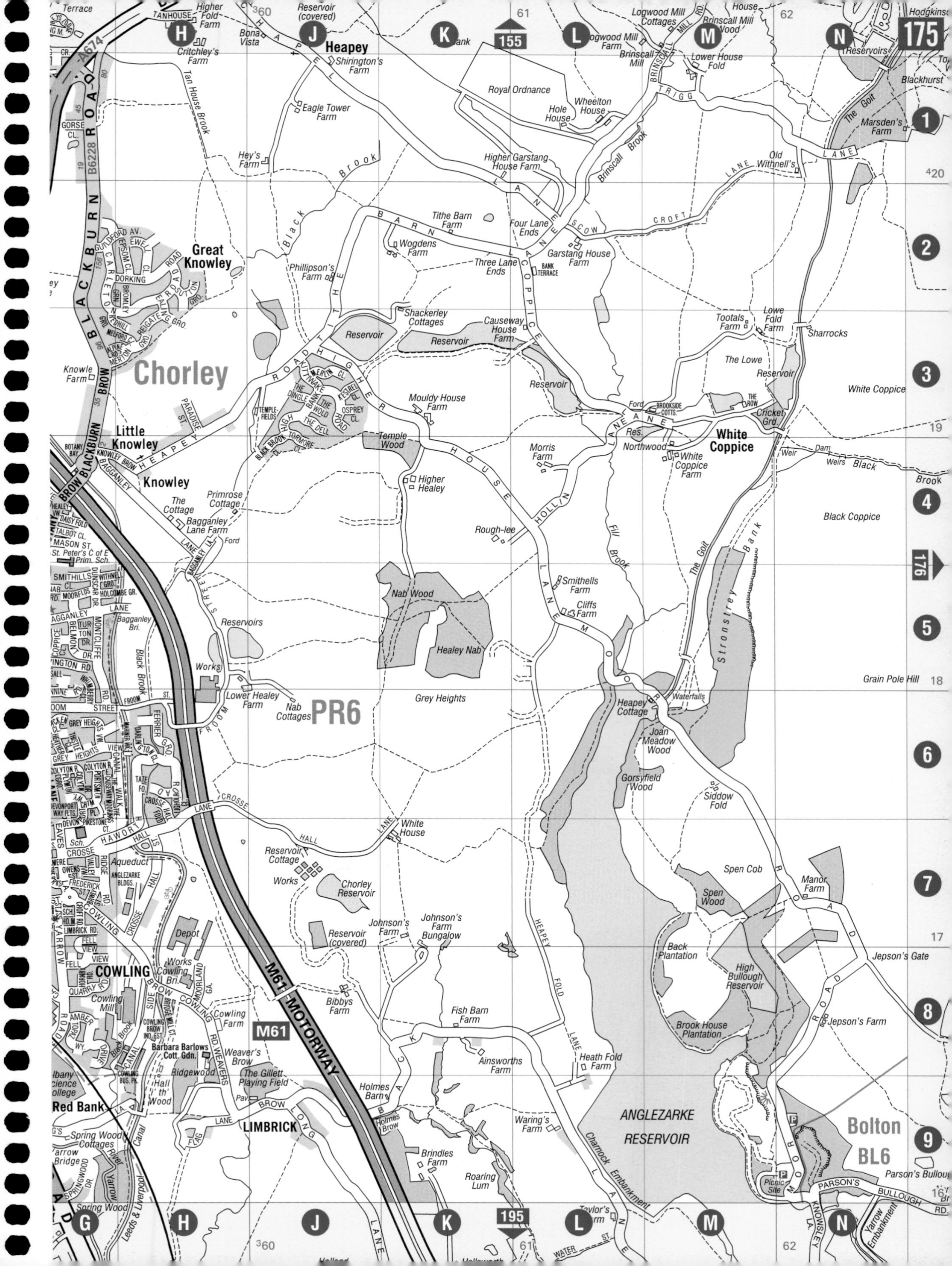
Chorley
Great Knowley
Little Knowley
Knowley
Heapey
White Coppice
COWLING
LIMBRICK
Red Bank
PR6
Bolton
BL6
ANGLEZARKE RESERVOIR
Royal Ordnance
Chorley Reservoir
High Bullough Reservoir
Nab Wood
Healey Nab
Grey Heights
Black Coppice
Grain Pole Hill
M61 MOTORWAY
BLACKBURN ROAD
HIGHER HOUSE LANE
HEAPEY FOLD LANE
MOOR ROAD
155
176
195

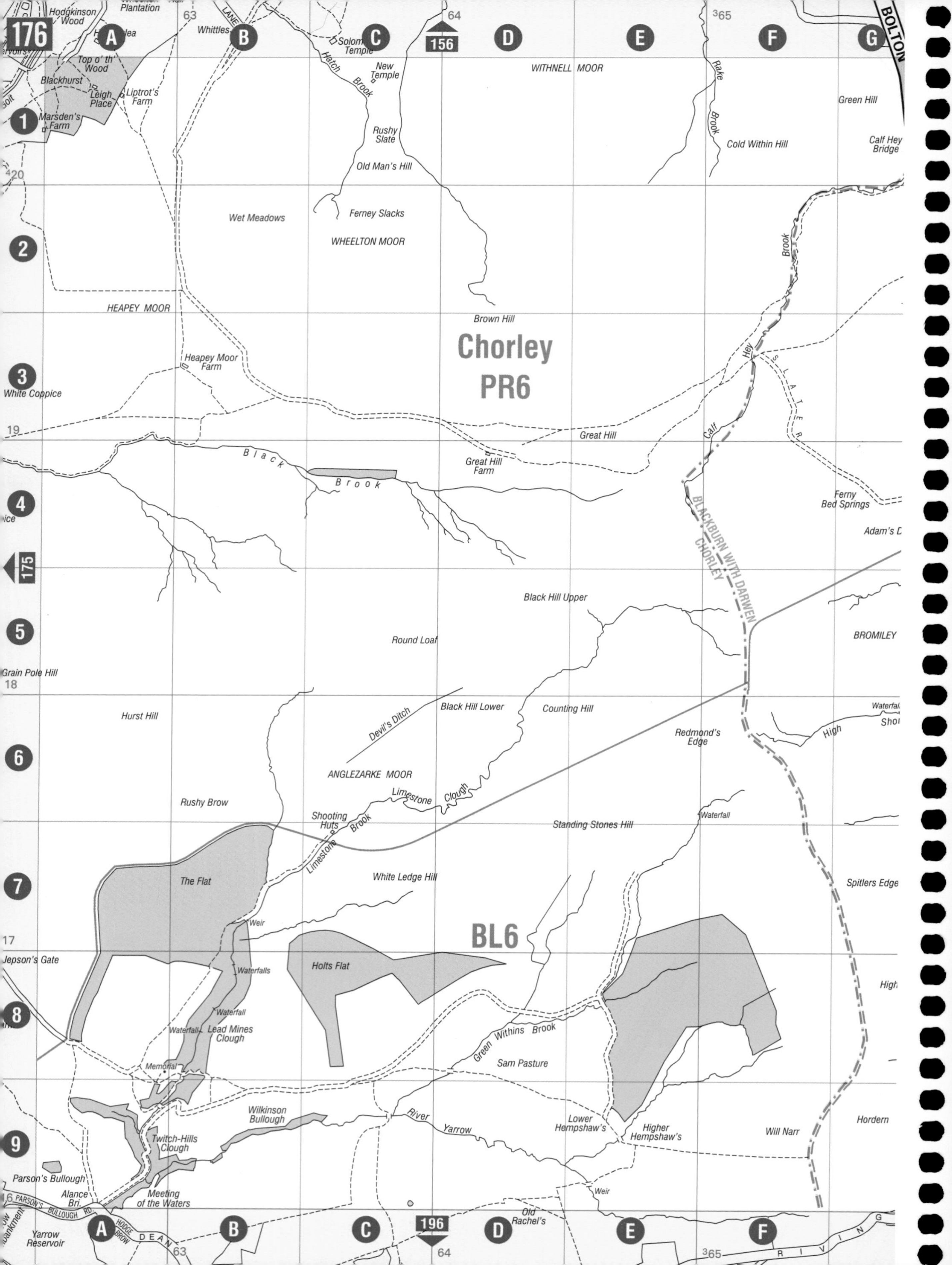
Chorley
PR6
BL6
WITHNELL MOOR
WHEELTON MOOR
HEAPEY MOOR
ANGLEZARKE MOOR
Heapey Moor Farm
White Coppice
Black Brook
Great Hill
Great Hill Farm
Brown Hill
Wet Meadows
Ferney Slacks
Old Man's Hill
Rushy Slate
New Temple
Hatch Brook
Cold Within Hill
Green Hill
Calf Hey Bridge
Rake Brook
Calf Hey
Ferny Bed Springs
BLACKBURN WITH DARWEN
CHORLEY
Black Hill Upper
Round Loaf
BROMILEY
Grain Pole Hill
Hurst Hill
Black Hill Lower
Counting Hill
Devil's Ditch
Redmond's Edge
Rushy Brow
Limestone Clough
Shooting Huts
Limestone Brook
Standing Stones Hill
Waterfall
White Ledge Hill
Spitlers Edge
The Flat
Weir
Waterfalls
Holts Flat
Jepson's Gate
Lead Mines Clough
Memorial
Green Withins Brook
Sam Pasture
Wilkinson Bullough
River Yarrow
Lower Hempshaw's
Higher Hempshaw's
Will Narr
Hordern
Twitch-Hills Clough
Parson's Bullough
Alance Bri.
Meeting of the Waters
Old Rachel's
Yarrow Reservoir
PARSON'S BULLOUGH RD.
HODGE BROW
DEAN
RIVING
Hodgkinson Wood
Plantation
Whittles
LANE
Top o' th' Wood
Blackhurst
Leigh Place
Liptrot's Farm
Marsden's Farm
Solomon Temple
BOLTON
Adam's D
Waterfall
High
Shoi
156
175
196
63
64
365
420
19
18
17

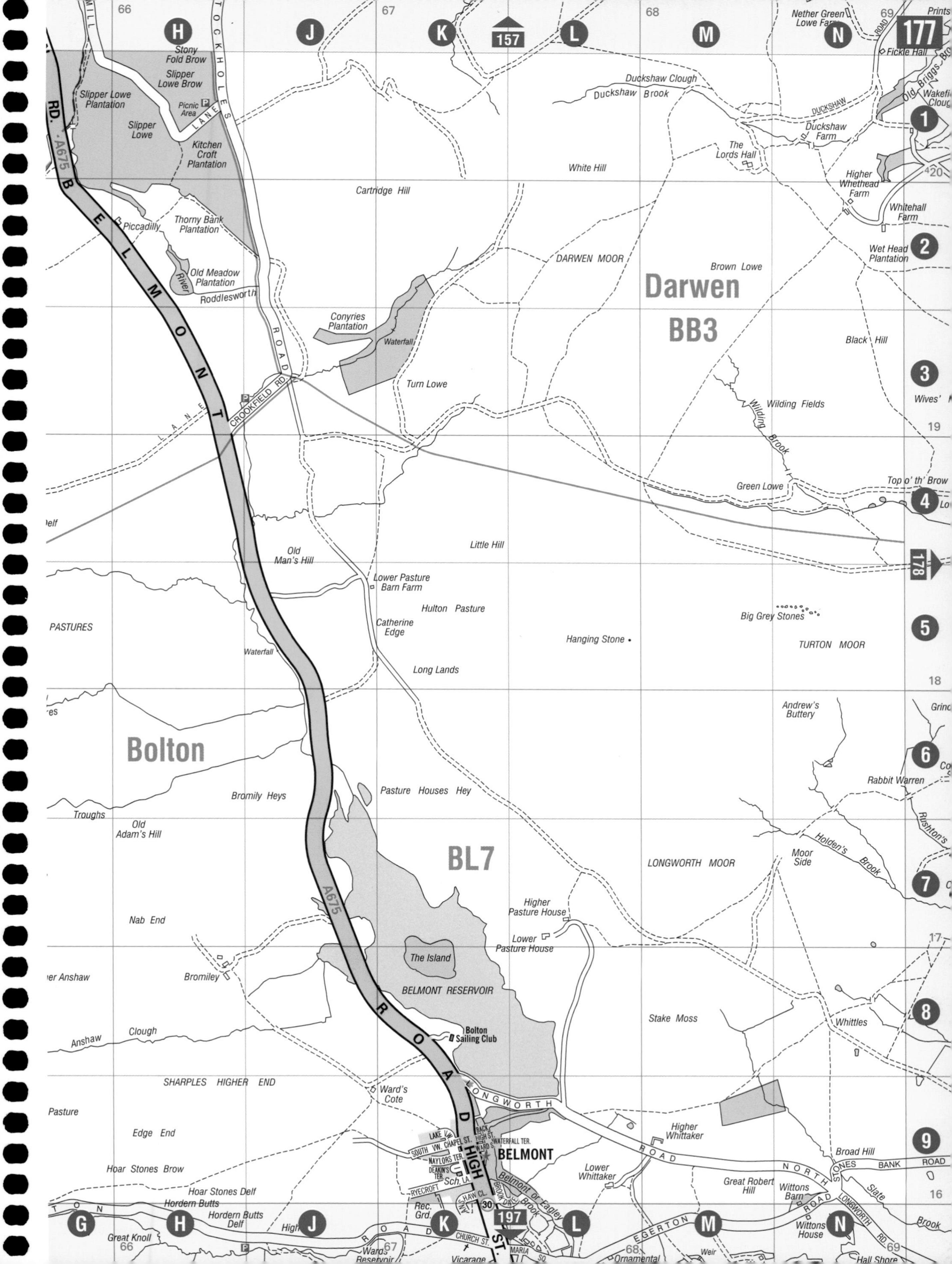
Darwen
BB3
Bolton
BL7
BELMONT
DARWEN MOOR
TURTON MOOR
LONGWORTH MOOR
BELMONT RESERVOIR
The Island
Bolton Sailing Club
BELMONT ROAD
A675
HIGH ST.
LONGWORTH ROAD
NORTH STONES BANK ROAD
EGERTON ROAD
CROOKFIELD RD.
TOCKHOLES ROAD
Slipper Lowe Plantation
Stony Fold Brow
Slipper Lowe Brow
Picnic Area
Slipper Lowe
Kitchen Croft Plantation
Piccadilly
Thorny Bank Plantation
Old Meadow Plantation
River Roddlesworth
Conyries Plantation
Waterfall
Turn Lowe
Cartridge Hill
White Hill
Duckshaw Clough
Duckshaw Brook
Duckshaw Farm
The Lords Hall
Higher Whethead Farm
Whitehall Farm
Wet Head Plantation
Nether Green Lowe Farm
Fickle Hall
Old Briggs Brow
Brown Lowe
Black Hill
Wilding Fields
Wilding Brook
Green Lowe
Top o' th' Brow
Little Hill
Old Man's Hill
Lower Pasture Barn Farm
Hulton Pasture
Catherine Edge
Long Lands
Hanging Stone
Big Grey Stones
PASTURES
Andrew's Buttery
Rabbit Warren
Holden's Brook
Rushton's
Moor Side
Pasture Houses Hey
Bromily Heys
Troughs
Old Adam's Hill
Nab End
Higher Pasture House
Lower Pasture House
Bromiley
Anshaw
Clough
Stake Moss
Whittles
SHARPLES HIGHER END
Ward's Cote
Pasture
Edge End
Higher Whittaker
Lower Whittaker
Hoar Stones Brow
Hoar Stones Delf
Hordern Butts
Hordern Butts Delf
Great Knoll
Great Robert Hill
Wittons Barn
Wittons House
Broad Hill
Slate Brook
Hall Shore
Belmont or Eagley Brook
Rec. Grd.
Sch.
Vicarage
Wards Reservoir
Ornamental
Weir
CHURCH ST.
MARIA SQ.
LAKE VW.
SOUTH VW.
CHAPEL ST.
NAYLORS TER.
DEAKIN'S TER.
RYECROFT
HAW CL.
BACK HIGH ST.
WARD'S
WATERFALL TER.
BROOK
30
157
178
197
66 67 68 69
16 17 18 19 20
G H J K L M N
1 2 3 4 5 6 7 8 9

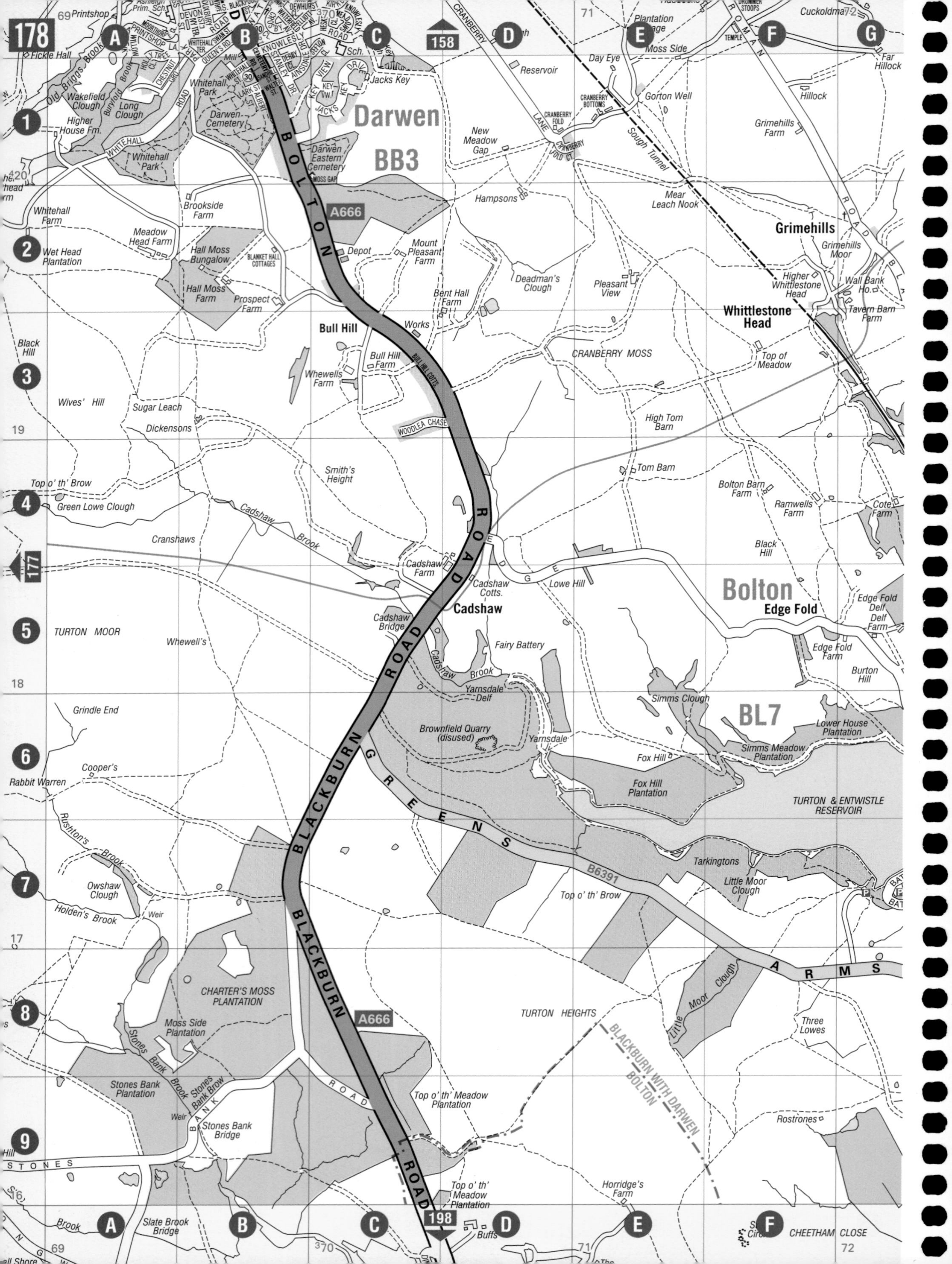

Darwen
BB3
Bolton
BL7
BOLTON ROAD
BLACKBURN ROAD
A666
GREENS
B6391
ARMS
Cadshaw
Edge Fold
Grimehills
Whittlestone Head
Bull Hill
TURTON MOOR
TURTON HEIGHTS
TURTON & ENTWISTLE RESERVOIR
CRANBERRY MOSS
CHARTER'S MOSS PLANTATION
Fox Hill Plantation
Simms Clough
Brownfield Quarry (disused)
Yarnsdale
Yarnsdale Delf
Fairy Battery
Cadshaw Brook
Cadshaw Bridge
Cadshaw Farm
Cadshaw Cotts.
Lowe Hill
Smith's Height
Whewells Farm
Bull Hill Farm
Works
Bent Hall Farm
Mount Pleasant Farm
Depot
Hampsons
New Meadow Gap
Reservoir
Day Eye
Moss Side
Gorton Well
Grimehills Farm
Hillock
Far Hillock
Mear Leach Nook
Sough Tunnel
Pleasant View
Deadman's Clough
Top of Meadow
Tavern Barn Farm
Wall Bank Ho.
Higher Whittlestone Head
Grimehills Moor
High Tom Barn
Tom Barn
Bolton Barn Farm
Ramwells Farm
Cote Farm
Black Hill
Edge Fold Delf
Delf Farm
Edge Fold Farm
Burton Hill
Lower House Plantation
Simms Meadow Plantation
Fox Hill
Tarkingtons
Little Moor Clough
Top o' th' Brow
Three Lowes
Rostrones
Horridge's Farm
Top o' th' Meadow Plantation
Top o' th' Meadow
Buffs
CHEETHAM CLOSE
BLACKBURN WITH DARWEN
BOLTON
Darwen Cemetery
Darwen Eastern Cemetery
Whitehall Park
Jacks Key
Wakefield Clough
Long Clough
Higher House Fm.
Whitehall Farm
Wet Head Plantation
Meadow Head Farm
Brookside Farm
Hall Moss Bungalow
Hall Moss Farm
Prospect Farm
Black Hill
Wives' Hill
Sugar Leach
Dickensons
Top o' th' Brow
Green Lowe Clough
Cranshaws
Cadshaw Brook
Whewell's
Grindle End
Cooper's
Rabbit Warren
Rushton's Brook
Owshaw Clough
Holden's Brook
Weir
Moss Side Plantation
Stones Bank Plantation
Stones Bank Brook
Stones Bank Brow
Stones Bank Bridge
STONES BANK ROAD
Slate Brook Bridge
Printshop
Fickle Hall
Plantation Cottage
Cuckoldmalt
158
177
198

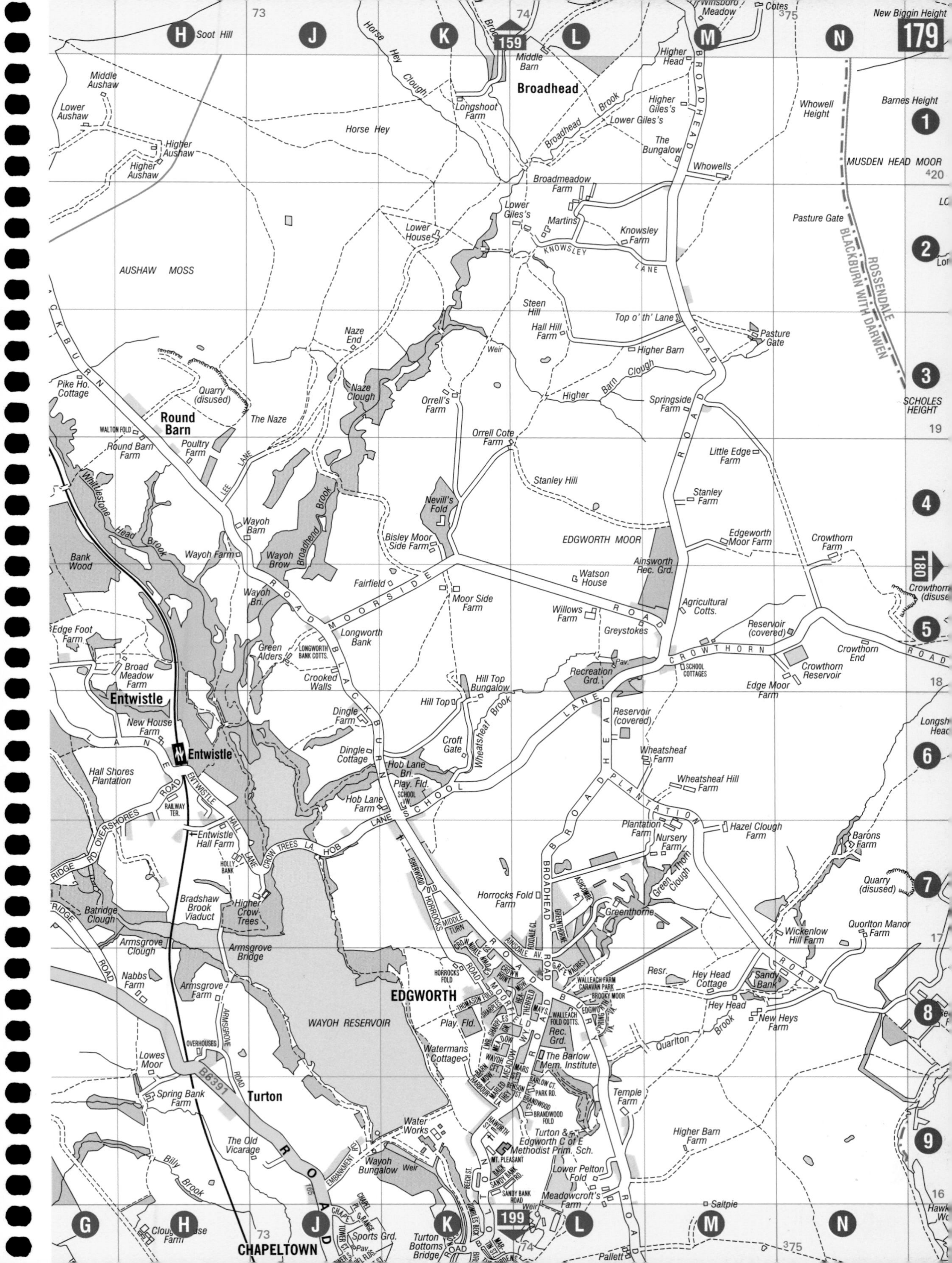

Soot Hill
Middle Aushaw
Lower Aushaw
Higher Aushaw
Higher Aushaw
Horse Hey
Horse Hey Clough
Longshoot Farm
Broadhead
Broadhead Brook
Middle Barn
Higher Head
Higher Giles's
Lower Giles's
The Bungalow
Whowells
Whowell Height
Barnes Height
MUSDEN HEAD MOOR
New Biggin Height
Winsboro Meadow
Cotes
Broadmeadow Farm
Lower Giles's
Martins
Lower House
Knowsley Farm
KNOWSLEY LANE
Pasture Gate
BLACKBURN WITH DARWEN
ROSSENDALE
AUSHAW MOSS
Steen Hill
Top o' th' Lane
Hall Hill Farm
Higher Barn
Pasture Gate
Naze End
Weir
Naze Clough
Higher Barn Clough
Springside Farm
SCHOLES HEIGHT
Pike Ho. Cottage
Quarry (disused)
Round Barn
The Naze
Orrell's Farm
Orrell Cote Farm
WALTON FOLD
Round Barn Farm
Poultry Farm
LEE LANE
Little Edge Farm
Stanley Hill
Stanley Farm
Whittlestone Head Brook
Broadhead Brook
Nevill's Fold
Wayoh Barn
Bisley Moor Side Farm
EDGWORTH MOOR
Edgeworth Moor Farm
Crowthorn Farm
Bank Wood
Wayoh Farm
Wayoh Brow
Ainsworth Rec. Grd.
Fairfield
Watson House
Crowthorn (disused)
Wayoh Bri.
MOORSIDE ROAD
Moor Side Farm
Willows Farm
Agricultural Cotts.
Reservoir (covered)
Edge Foot Farm
Longworth Bank
Greystokes
Crowthorn End
Green Alders
LONGWORTH BANK COTTS.
CROWTHORN ROAD
Broad Meadow Farm
Crooked Walls
Hill Top Bungalow
Recreation Grd.
Pav.
SCHOOL COTTAGES
Crowthorn Reservoir
Edge Moor Farm
Entwistle
BLACKBURN ROAD
Hill Top
Wheatsheaf Brook
Reservoir (covered)
Dingle Farm
New House Farm
Croft Gate
Entwistle
Dingle Cottage
Wheatsheaf Farm
Hall Shores Plantation
Hob Lane Bri.
Play. Fld.
SCHOOL LANE
Wheatsheaf Hill Farm
OVERSHORES ROAD
RAILWAY TER.
ENTWISTLE HALL LANE
SCHOOL VW.
Hob Lane Farm
PLANTATION
Plantation Farm
Hazel Clough Farm
Entwistle Hall Farm
CROW TREES LA
HOB LANE
Nursery Farm
Barons Farm
HOLLY BANK
BROADHEAD ROAD
ASHCOMBE PL.
Green Thorn Clough
Quarry (disused)
Bradshaw Brook Viaduct
Higher Crow Trees
Horrocks Fold Farm
Greenthorne
Batridge Clough
SHERWOOD FOLD
HORROCKS
MIDDLE TURN
Wickenlow Hill Farm
Quorlton Manor Farm
Armsgrove Clough
Armsgrove Bridge
AINSDALE AV.
BURY ROAD
Resr.
Hey Head Cottage
Sandy Bank
Nabbs Farm
HORROCKS FOLD
CROWN POINT
WALLEACH FARM CARAVAN PARK
BROOKY MOOR
Armsgrove Farm
EDGWORTH
THOMASON FOLD
Hey Head
New Heys Farm
WAYOH RESERVOIR
Play. Fld.
WALLEACH FOLD COTTS.
Rec. Grd.
Brook
ARMSGROVE ROAD
OVERHOUSES
Quarlton
Lowes Moor
Watermans Cottage
The Barlow Mem. Institute
B6391
Turton
BARLOW CT.
PARK RD.
Spring Bank Farm
Temple Farm
BRANDWOOD FOLD
Higher Barn Farm
Water Works
Turton & Edgworth C of E Methodist Prim. Sch.
The Old Vicarage
Billy Brook
ROAD
EMBANKMENT
Wayoh Bungalow
Weir
MT. PLEASANT
SANDY BANK ROAD
Lower Pelton Fold
Meadowcroft's Farm
Saltpie
Weir
Clough House Farm
Sports Grd.
Pav.
Turton Bottoms Bridge
CHAPELTOWN
Pallett
Hawk

159
180
199

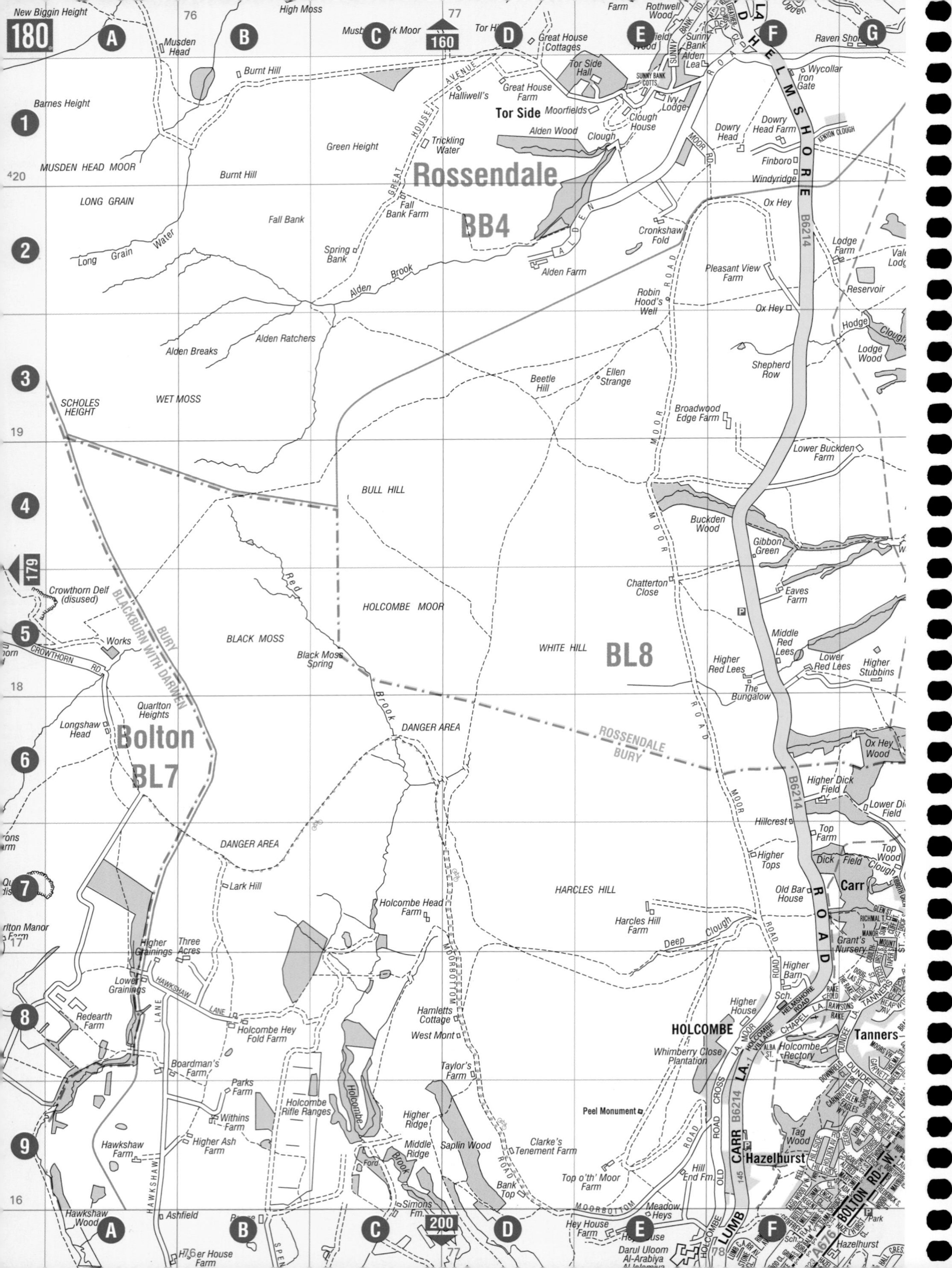
New Biggin Height
High Moss
Musden Head
Burnt Hill
Barnes Height
MUSDEN HEAD MOOR
Burnt Hill
LONG GRAIN
Long Grain Water
Green Height
Trickling Water
Halliwell's
Great House Farm
Tor Side
Great House Cottages
Tor Side Hall
Moorfields
Alden Wood
Clough
Clough House
Ivy Lodge
Rossendale
BB4
Fall Bank Farm
Fall Bank
Spring Bank
Alden Brook
Alden Farm
Cronkshaw Fold
Robin Hood's Well
Alden Ratchers
Alden Breaks
SCHOLES HEIGHT
WET MOSS
Beetle Hill
Ellen Strange
BULL HILL
HOLCOMBE MOOR
BLACK MOSS
Black Moss Spring
WHITE HILL
BL8
Crowthorn Delf (disused)
Works
CROWTHORN RD
BLACKBURN WITH DARWEN
BURY
Quarlton Heights
Longshaw Head
Bolton
BL7
DANGER AREA
ROSSENDALE
BURY
Lark Hill
Holcombe Head Farm
HARCLES HILL
Harcles Hill Farm
Deep Clough
Higher Grainings
Three Acres
Lower Grainings
HAWKSHAW LANE
Redearth Farm
Holcombe Hey Fold Farm
Boardman's Farm
Parks Farm
Withins Farm
Higher Ash Farm
Hawkshaw Farm
Holcombe Rifle Ranges
Hamletts Cottage
West Mont
Taylor's Farm
Higher Ridge
Middle Ridge
Saplin Wood
Clarke's Tenement Farm
Bank Top
Top o'th' Moor Farm
Peel Monument
HOLCOMBE
Whimberry Close Plantation
Higher House
Hill End Fm.
Meadow Heys
Hey House Farm
Darul Uloom Al-Arabiya
Simons Fm.
Hawkshaw Wood
Ashfield
HELMSHORE ROAD
B6214
Wycollar Iron Gate
Dowry Head
Dowry Head Farm
Finboro
Windyridge
Ox Hey
Lodge Farm
Pleasant View Farm
Reservoir
Hodge Clough
Lodge Wood
Shepherd Row
Broadwood Edge Farm
Lower Buckden Farm
Buckden Wood
Gibbon Green
Chatterton Close
Eaves Farm
Middle Red Lees
Higher Red Lees
Lower Red Lees
Higher Stubbins
The Bungalow
Ox Hey Wood
Higher Dick Field
Lower Dick Field
Hillcrest
Top Farm
Top Wood
Dick Field Clough
Higher Tops
Old Bar House
Carr
Grant's Nursery
Higher Barn
Holcombe Rectory
Tanners
Tag Wood
Hazelhurst
Raven Shore
Rothwell Wood
Sunny Bank
Alden Lea
Kenyon Clough
MOOR ROAD
MOORBOTTOM ROAD
CARR LA.
HOLCOMBE OLD ROAD
CROSS LA.
LUMB
BOLTON RD. W.
A676
A
B
C
D
E
F
G
1
2
3
4
5
6
7
8
9
76
77
78
420
19
18
17
16
160
179
200

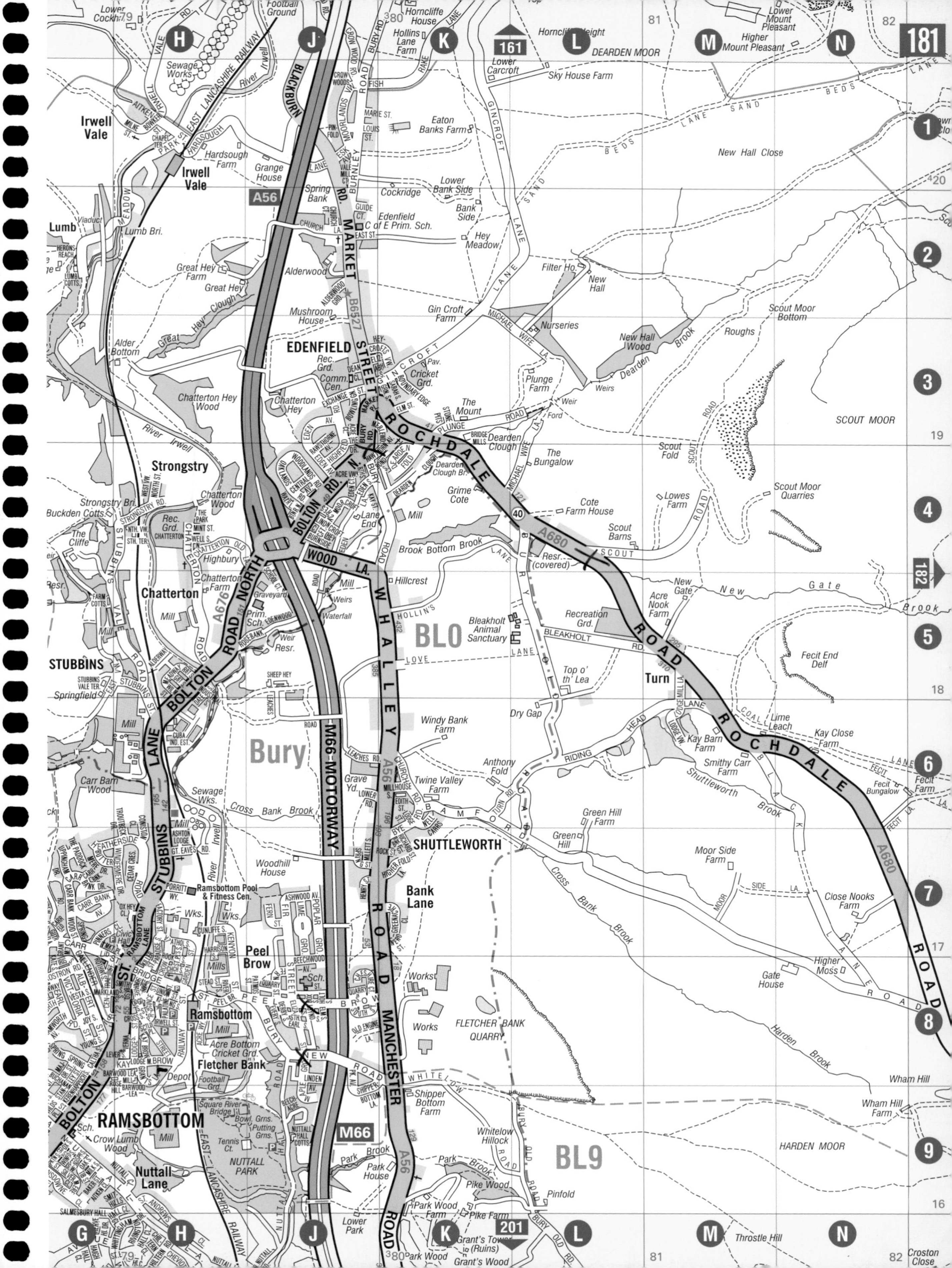

Irwell Vale
Lumb
Strongstry
Chatterton
STUBBINS
EDENFIELD
Bury
BL0
BL9
SHUTTLEWORTH
Turn
Peel Brow
Ramsbottom
Fletcher Bank
RAMSBOTTOM
Nuttall Lane
Bank Lane
SCOUT MOOR
HARDEN MOOR
DEARDEN MOOR
New Hall Close
M66 MOTORWAY
BLACKBURN ROAD
MARKET STREET
ROCHDALE ROAD
BOLTON ROAD NORTH
WHALLEY ROAD
MANCHESTER ROAD
STUBBINS LANE
A56
A680
A676
B6527
M66
161
182
201

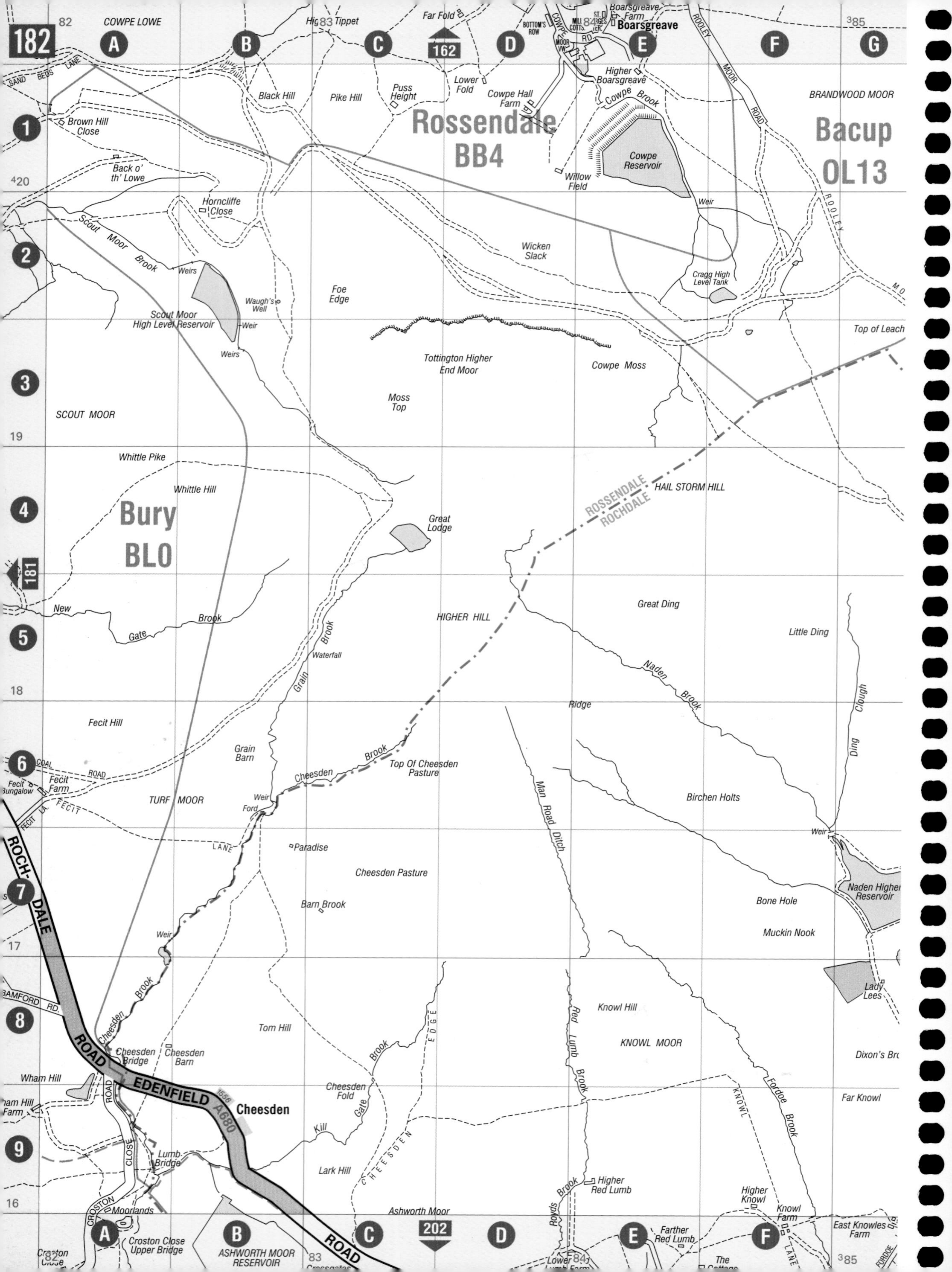

A
B
C
D
E
F
G
1
2
3
4
5
6
7
8
9
162
202
181
COWPE LOWE
Tippet
Far Fold
Boarsgreave
Boarsgreave Farm
Higher Boarsgreave
Cowpe Brook
ROOLEY MOOR ROAD
BRANDWOOD MOOR
Bacup
OL13
Rossendale
BB4
SAND BEDS LANE
Black Hill
Pike Hill
Puss Height
Lower Fold
Cowpe Hall Farm
Brown Hill Close
Back o' th' Lowe
Cowpe Reservoir
Willow Field
Horncliffe Close
Weir
Scout Moor Brook
Weirs
Wicken Slack
Cragg High Level Tank
Waugh's Well
Foe Edge
Scout Moor High Level Reservoir
Top of Leach
Tottington Higher End Moor
Cowpe Moss
Moss Top
SCOUT MOOR
Whittle Pike
Whittle Hill
HAIL STORM HILL
ROSSENDALE
ROCHDALE
Bury
BL0
Great Lodge
New Gate Brook
Great Ding
HIGHER HILL
Little Ding
Grain Brook
Waterfall
Naden Brook
Ridge
Ding Clough
Fecit Hill
Grain Barn
Top Of Cheesden Pasture
COAL ROAD
Fecit Farm
Fecit Bungalow
FECIT LA.
TURF MOOR
Cheesden Brook
Ford
Birchen Holts
Man Road Ditch
Paradise
Cheesden Pasture
ROCHDALE ROAD
Naden Higher Reservoir
Bone Hole
Barn Brook
Muckin Nook
BAMFORD RD.
Lady Lees
Knowl Hill
Tom Hill
KNOWL MOOR
Red Lumb Brook
Dixon's Bro
Cheesden Bridge
Cheesden Barn
Wham Hill
EDENFIELD ROAD
A680
Cheesden
Cheesden Fold
Far Knowl
Fordoe Brook
KNOWL
Kill Gate Brook
CHEESDEN EDGE
Lumb Bridge
Lark Hill
Higher Red Lumb
Royds Brook
Higher Knowl
Knowl Farm
CROSTON CLOSE
Moorlands
Ashworth Moor
East Knowles Farm
Croston Close Upper Bridge
ASHWORTH MOOR RESERVOIR
Farther Red Lumb
The Cottage
Lower Lumb Farm

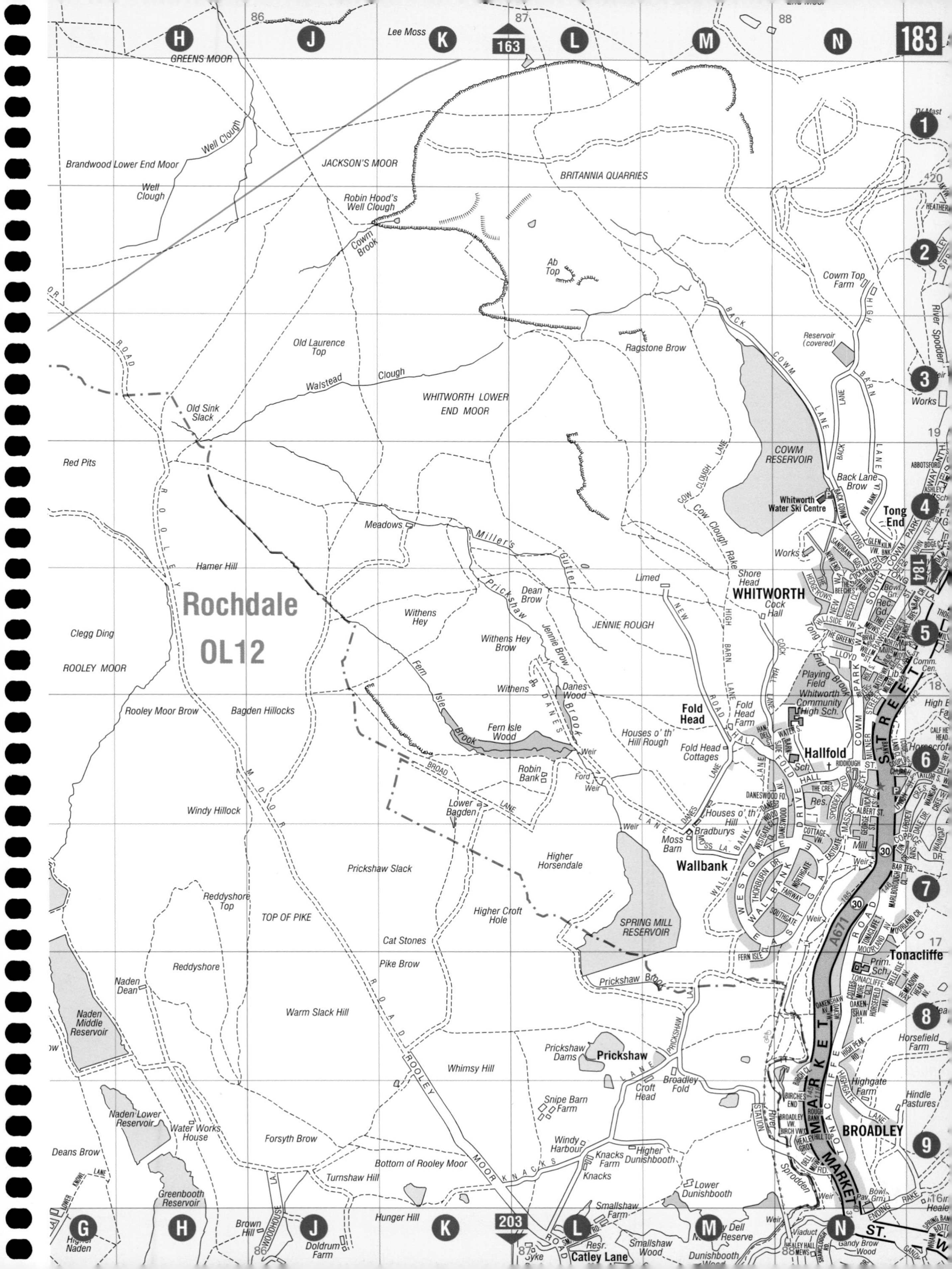

Lee Moss
GREENS MOOR
Well Clough
Brandwood Lower End Moor
Well Clough
JACKSON'S MOOR
BRITANNIA QUARRIES
Robin Hood's Well Clough
Cowm Brook
Ab Top
Cowm Top Farm
Reservoir (covered)
River Spodden
Works
Old Laurence Top
Walstead Clough
Ragstone Brow
Old Sink Slack
WHITWORTH LOWER END MOOR
COWM RESERVOIR
Red Pits
Back Lane Brow
Whitworth Water Ski Centre
Tong End
Meadows
Miller's Gutter
Works
Hamer Hill
Limed
Shore Head
WHITWORTH
Dean Brow
Cock Hall
Rochdale
OL12
Withens Hey
Clegg Ding
JENNIE ROUGH
Withens Hey Brow
ROOLEY MOOR
Jennie Brow
Playing Field
Whitworth Community High Sch.
Withens
Danes Wood
Rooley Moor Brow
Bagden Hillocks
Fold Head
Fold Head Farm
Fern Isle Wood
Houses o' th' Hill Rough
Fold Head Cottages
Hallfold
Robin Bank
Windy Hillock
Lower Bagden
Houses o' th' Hill
Bradburys
Moss Barn
Higher Horsendale
Wallbank
Prickshaw Slack
Reddyshore Top
TOP OF PIKE
Higher Croft Hole
SPRING MILL RESERVOIR
Cat Stones
Tonacliffe
Reddyshore
Pike Brow
Naden Dean
Prickshaw Brook
Naden Middle Reservoir
Warm Slack Hill
Horsefield Farm
Prickshaw Dams
Prickshaw
Whimsy Hill
Highgate Farm
Croft Head
Broadley Fold
Hindle Pastures
Snipe Barn Farm
Naden Lower Reservoir
Water Works House
BROADLEY
Forsyth Brow
Windy Harbour
Deans Brow
Knacks Farm
Higher Dunishbooth
Bottom of Rooley Moor
Knacks
Turnshaw Hill
Lower Dunishbooth
Greenbooth Reservoir
Smallshaw Farm
Hunger Hill
Brown Hill
Doldrum Farm
Higher Naden
Catley Lane
Smallshaw Wood
Dunishbooth
Viaduct
Gandy Brow Wood
A671
MARKET STREET
ROOLEY MOOR ROAD
163
184
203

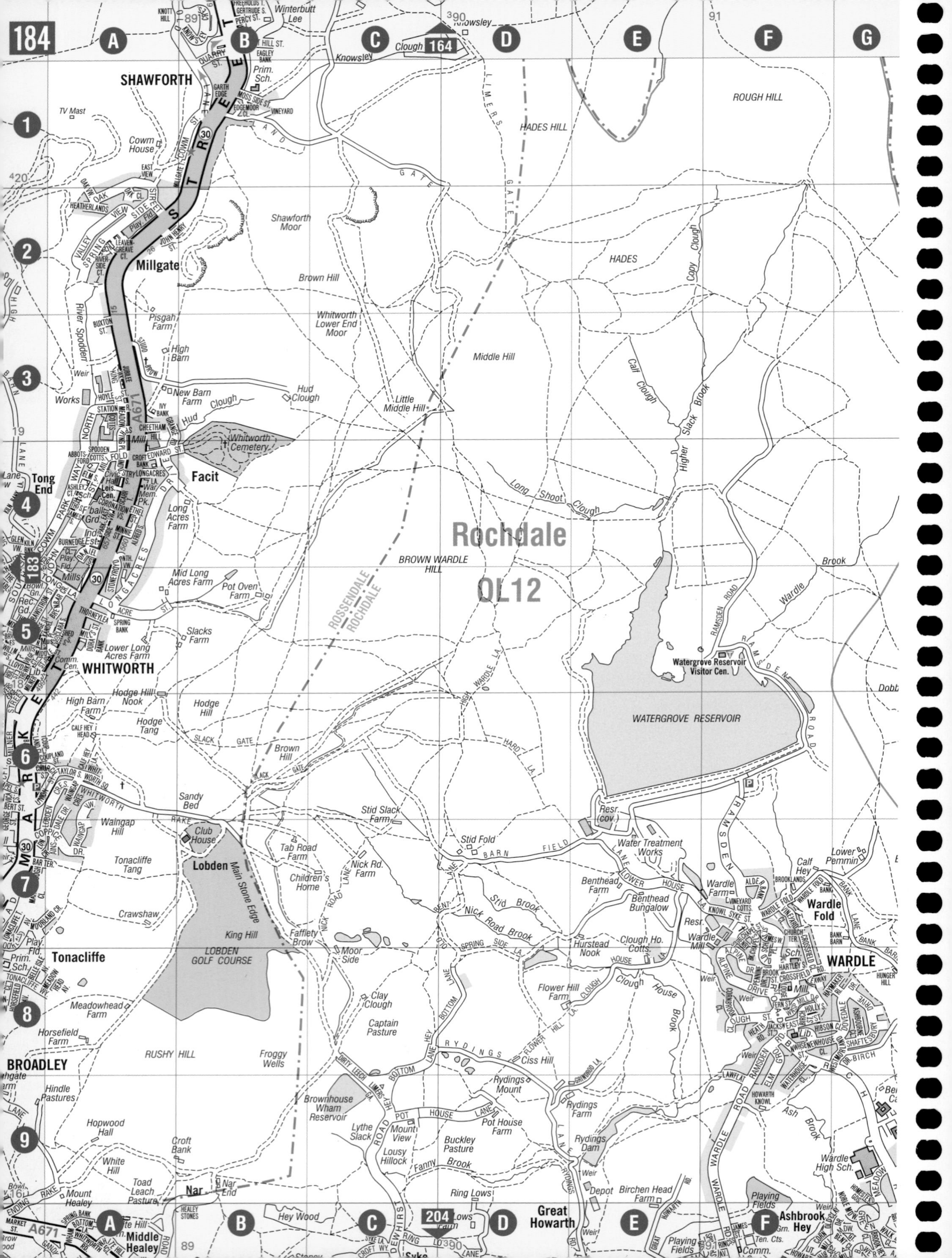
SHAWFORTH
Millgate
Facit
Tong End
WHITWORTH
Lobden
Tonacliffe
BROADLEY
Rochdale
OL12
ROUGH HILL
HADES HILL
HADES
Shawforth Moor
Brown Hill
Whitworth Lower End Moor
Middle Hill
Little Middle Hill
Hud Clough
Whitworth Cemetery
Long Shoot Clough
Higher Slack Brook
Calf Clough
Copy Clough
BROWN WARDLE HILL
ROSSENDALE
ROCHDALE
Watergrove Reservoir Visitor Cen.
WATERGROVE RESERVOIR
Water Treatment Works
Benthead Farm
Benthead Bungalow
Wardle Farm
Wardle Mill
Wardle Fold
WARDLE
Calf Hey
Lower Pemmin
Stid Fold
Stid Slack Farm
Tab Road Farm
Nick Rd. Farm
Children's Home
Club House
Main Stone Edge
King Hill
LOBDEN GOLF COURSE
Fafflety Brow
Moor Side
Clay Clough
Captain Pasture
Hurstead Nook
Clough Ho. Cotts.
Flower Hill Farm
Ciss Hill
Rydings Mount
Rydings Farm
Rydings Dam
Brownhouse Wham Reservoir
Lythe Slack
Mount View
Lousy Hillock
Pot House Farm
Buckley Pasture
Fanny Brook
Ring Lows
Great Howarth
Birchen Head Farm
Playing Fields
Ashbrook Hey
Wardle High Sch.
Depot
RUSHY HILL
Froggy Wells
Meadowhead Farm
Horsefield Farm
Hindle Pastures
Hopwood Hall
Croft Bank
White Hill
Toad Leach Pasture
Nar
Nar End
Mount Healey
Middle Healey
Hey Wood
Crawshaw
Tonacliffe Tang
Waingap Hill
Sandy Bed
Hodge Hill Nook
Hodge Hill
Hodge Tang
High Barn Farm
Slacks Farm
Lower Long Acres Farm
Mid Long Acres Farm
Pot Oven Farm
Long Acres Farm
Pisgah Farm
High Barn
New Barn Farm
Cowm House
TV Mast
Works
Knowsley
Clough
Winterbutt Lee
Prim. Sch.
A671
164
183
204
A B C D E F G
1 2 3 4 5 6 7 8 9

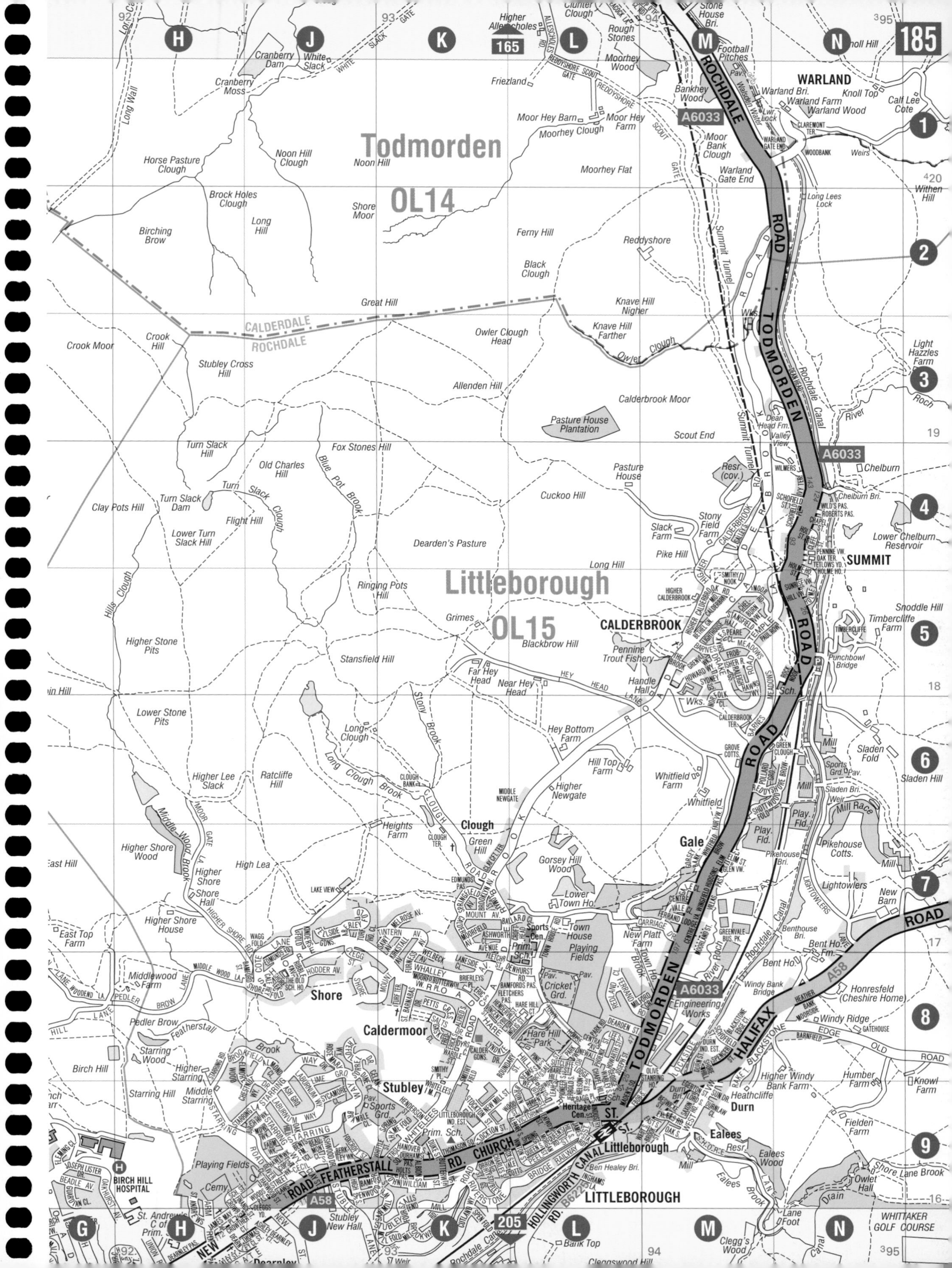
Todmorden
OL14
Littleborough
OL15
WARLAND
SUMMIT
CALDERBROOK
Clough
Gale
Shore
Caldermoor
Stubley
Durn
Ealees
Littleborough
LITTLEBOROUGH
CALDERDALE
ROCHDALE
ROCHDALE ROAD
TODMORDEN ROAD
HALIFAX ROAD
FEATHERSTALL ROAD
CHURCH ST.
HOLLINGWORTH RD.
A6033
A58
165
205
BIRCH HILL HOSPITAL
WHITTAKER GOLF COURSE
Rochdale Canal
Summit Tunnel
Calderbrook Moor
Blackstone Edge Old Road
Higher Allenscholes
Cranberry Dam
Cranberry Moss
White Slack
Long Wall
Horse Pasture Clough
Noon Hill Clough
Noon Hill
Brock Holes Clough
Long Hill
Birching Brow
Shore Moor
Moorhey Flat
Ferny Hill
Reddyshore
Black Clough
Great Hill
Knave Hill Nigher
Knave Hill Farther
Crook Moor
Crook Hill
Stubley Cross Hill
Owler Clough Head
Allenden Hill
Pasture House Plantation
Scout End
Turn Slack Hill
Fox Stones Hill
Old Charles Hill
Turn Slack Dam
Clay Pots Hill
Lower Turn Slack Hill
Flight Hill
Cuckoo Hill
Dearden's Pasture
Long Hill
Pike Hill
Ringing Pots Hill
Grimes
Blackbrow Hill
Higher Stone Pits
Stansfield Hill
Far Hey Head
Near Hey Head
Lower Stone Pits
Hey Bottom Farm
Hill Top Farm
Whitfield Farm
Higher Newgate
Higher Lee Slack
Ratcliffe Hill
Heights Farm
Higher Shore Wood
High Lea
Gorsey Hill Wood
Higher Shore House
East Top Farm
Middlewood Farm
Pedler Brow
Birch Hill
Starring Hill
Starring Wood
Higher Starring
Middle Starring
Chelburn
Lower Chelburn Reservoir
Snoddle Hill
Timbercliffe Farm
Punchbowl Bridge
Sladen Fold
Sladen Hill
Pikehouse Cotts.
Lightowlers
New Barn
Bent Ho.
Honresfeld (Cheshire Home)
Windy Ridge
Higher Windy Bank Farm
Heathcliffe
Humber Farm
Knowl Farm
Fielden Farm
Ealees Wood
Shore Lane Brook
Owlet Hall
Lane Foot
Clegg's Wood
Bank Top
Light Hazzles Farm
Calf Lee Cote
Knoll Top
Warland Farm
Warland Wood
Withen Hill
Pennine Trout Fishery
Handle Hall
Caldermoor
Playing Fields
Cricket Grd.
Hare Hill Park
Heritage Cen.
Sports Grd.
Prim. Sch.
Stubley New Hall
St. Andrew's C of E Prim. Sch.
Deanley
Cleggswood Hill

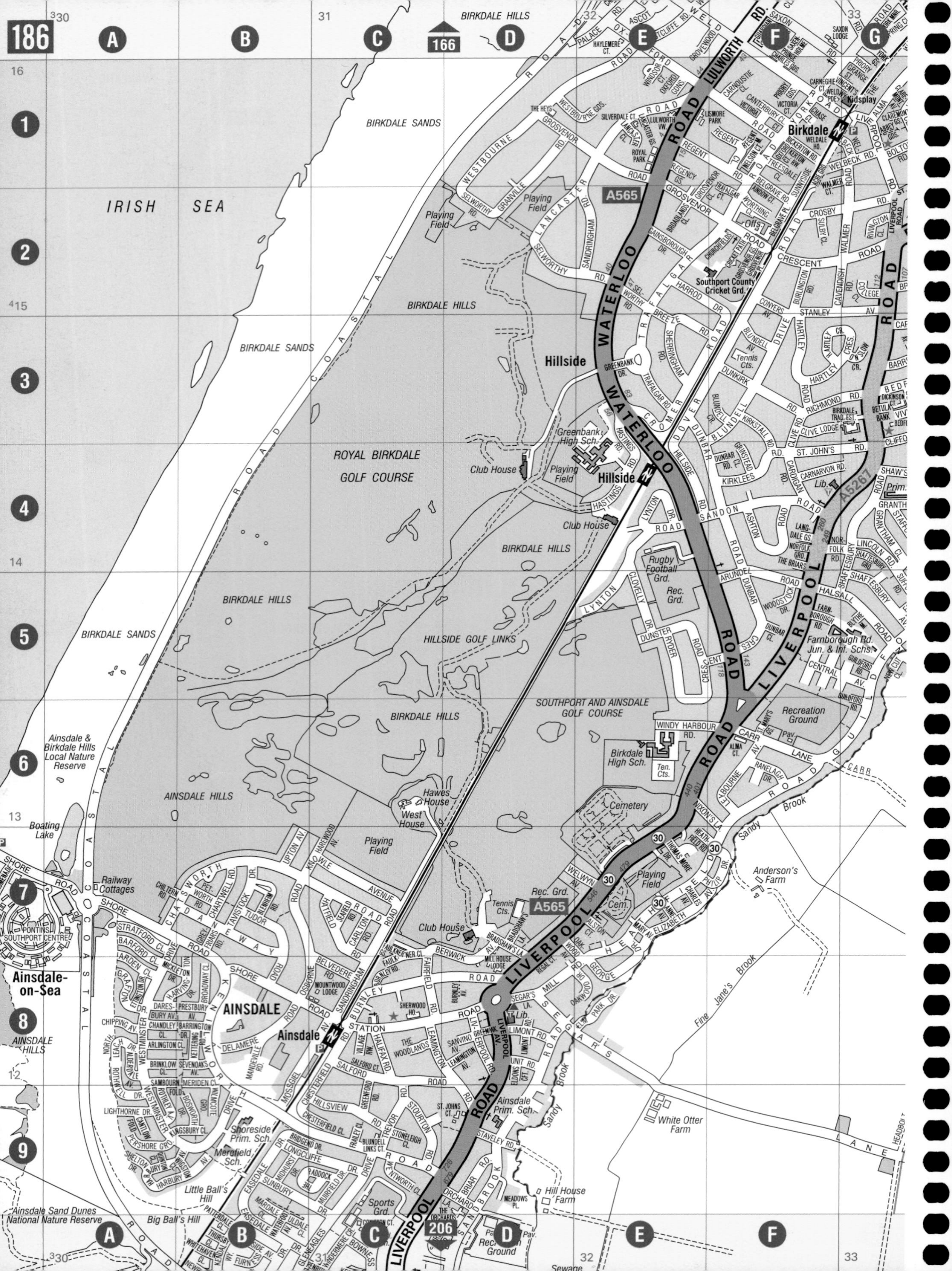
166
206
IRISH SEA
BIRKDALE SANDS
BIRKDALE HILLS
ROYAL BIRKDALE
GOLF COURSE
HILLSIDE GOLF LINKS
SOUTHPORT AND AINSDALE
GOLF COURSE
AINSDALE HILLS
Ainsdale & Birkdale Hills Local Nature Reserve
Ainsdale Sand Dunes National Nature Reserve
Boating Lake
Railway Cottages
PONTINS SOUTHPORT CENTRE
Ainsdale-on-Sea
AINSDALE
Ainsdale
Hillside
Birkdale
Kidsplay
Southport County Cricket Grd.
Greenbank High Sch.
Birkdale High Sch.
Rugby Football Grd.
Rec. Grd.
Recreation Ground
Farnborough Rd. Jun. & Inf. Schs.
Cemetery
Hawes House
West House
Club House
Playing Field
Tennis Cts.
Shoreside Prim. Sch.
Merefield Sch.
Ainsdale Prim. Sch.
Sports Grd.
Anderson's Farm
White Otter Farm
Hill House Farm
Little Ball's Hill
Big Ball's Hill
Fine Jane's Brook
Sandy Brook
A565
A5267
WATERLOO ROAD
LIVERPOOL ROAD
COASTAL ROAD
SHORE ROAD
STATION ROAD
BURNLEY ROAD
SANDON ROAD
WINDY HARBOUR RD.
CARR LANE
GUILDFORD ROAD
SEGAR'S LANE
WENTWORTH ROAD
KENILWORTH ROAD
LULWORTH ROAD
GROSVENOR ROAD
SELWORTHY RD.
WESTBOURNE RD.
TRAFALGAR ROAD
CROMER ROAD
DOVER ROAD
BLUNDELL DRIVE
CRESCENT ROAD
STANLEY AV.
RICHMOND RD.
ST. JOHN'S RD.
ARUNDEL ROAD
HALSALL ROAD
SHAFTESBURY RD.
LYNTON ROAD
HASTINGS RD.
BERWICK AV.

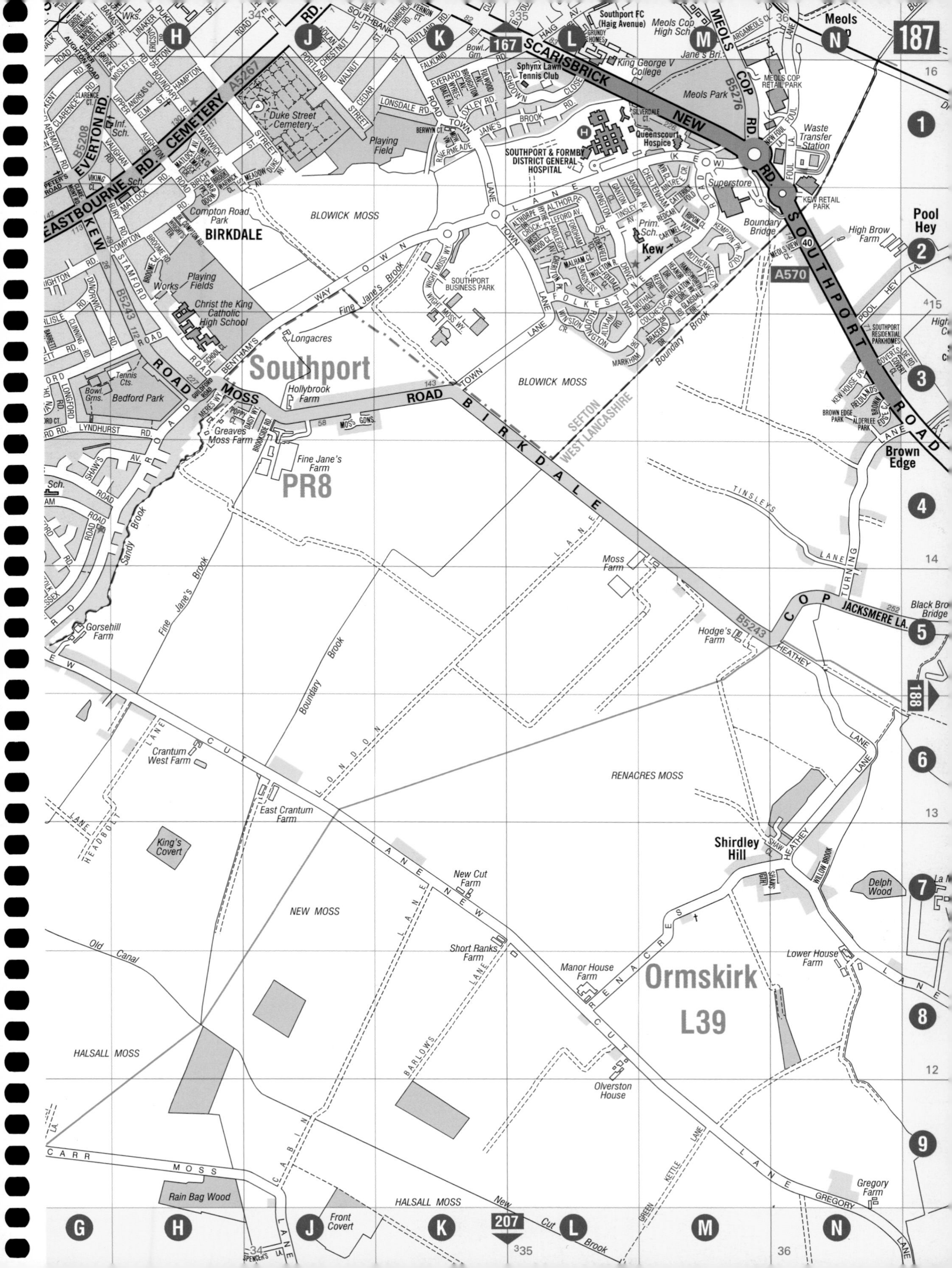
Southport
PR8
Ormskirk
L39
BIRKDALE
Kew
Southport FC (Haig Avenue)
Meols Cop High Sch.
King George V College
Meols Park
Meols Cop Retail Park
Waste Transfer Station
Sphynx Lawn Tennis Club
Duke Street Cemetery
Playing Field
SOUTHPORT & FORMBY DISTRICT GENERAL HOSPITAL
Queenscourt Hospice
Superstore
Kew Retail Park
Boundary Bridge
Pool Hey
High Brow Farm
Brown Edge
BLOWICK MOSS
Compton Road Park
Playing Fields
Christ the King Catholic High School
Southport Business Park
Longacres
Hollybrook Farm
Greaves Moss Farm
Fine Jane's Farm
Bedford Park
SEFTON
WEST LANCASHIRE
Moss Farm
Hodge's Farm
Black Brook Bridge
Gorsehill Farm
Crantum West Farm
East Crantum Farm
King's Covert
RENACRES MOSS
Shirdley Hill
Delph Wood
New Cut Farm
NEW MOSS
Short Ranks Farm
Manor House Farm
Lower House Farm
Old Canal
HALSALL MOSS
Olverston House
Gregory Farm
Rain Bag Wood
Front Covert
SCARISBRICK NEW RD.
SOUTHPORT ROAD
BIRKDALE
MOSS ROAD
TOWN LANE
COP LANE
JACKSMERE LA.
NEW CUT LANE
LONDON LANE
CARR MOSS
RENACRES
HEATHEY LANE
TINSLEYS LANE
TURNING LANE
GREGORY LANE
A570
B5243
B5276
A5267
B5208
167
188
207
G
H
J
K
L
M
N
1
2
3
4
5
6
7
8
9

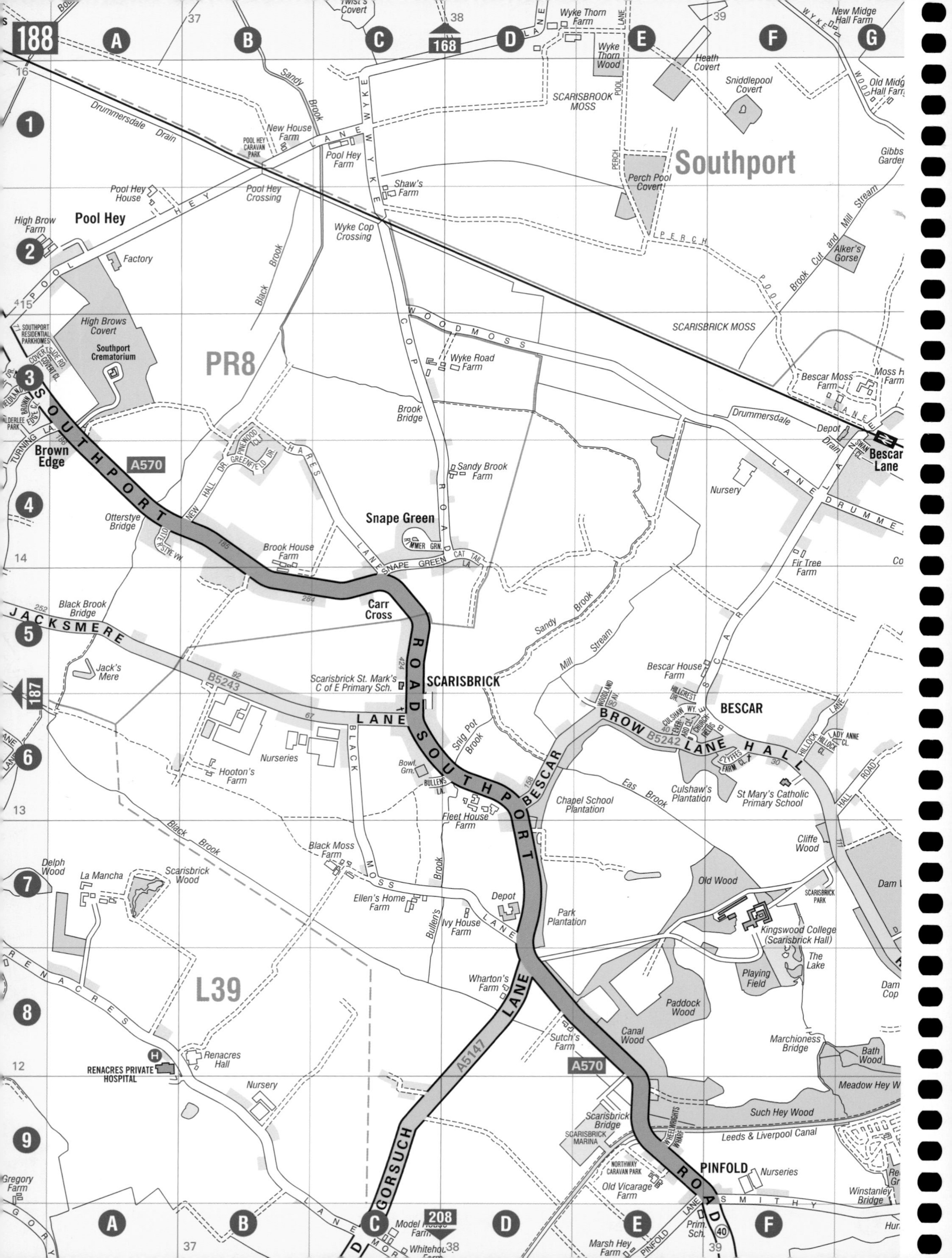
Southport
PR8
L39
Pool Hey
Brown Edge
Snape Green
Carr Cross
SCARISBRICK
BESCAR
PINFOLD
Bescar Lane
Scarisbrick Moss
Scarisbrook Moss
Drummersdale Drain
Southport Crematorium
High Brows Covert
Scarisbrick St. Mark's C of E Primary Sch.
St Mary's Catholic Primary School
Kingswood College (Scarisbrick Hall)
Renacres Private Hospital
Leeds & Liverpool Canal
Such Hey Wood
Scarisbrick Marina
A570
A5147
B5243
B5242
168
187
208

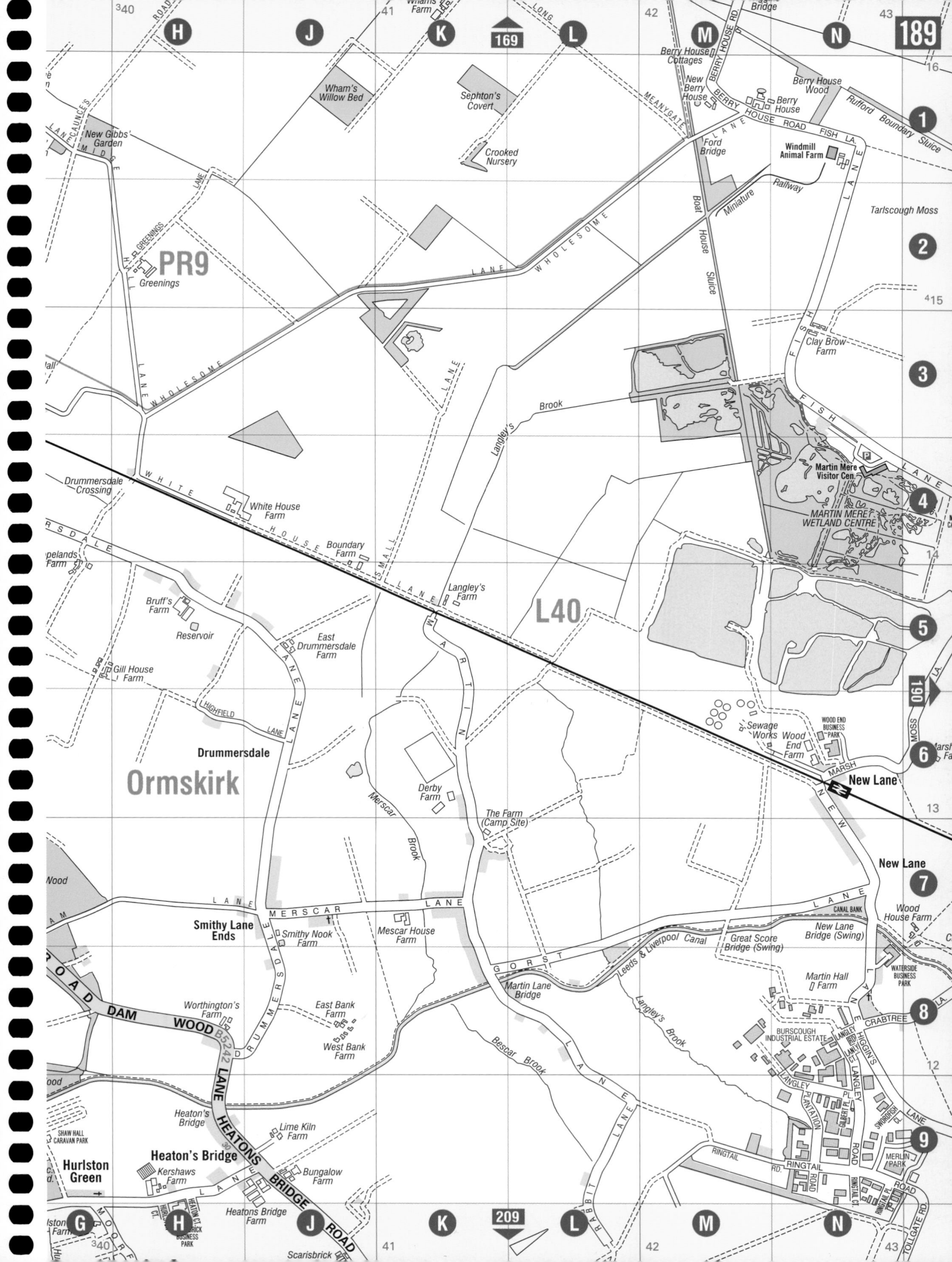

PR9
L40
Ormskirk
Drummersdale
Smithy Lane Ends
Heaton's Bridge
Hurlston Green
New Lane
Wham's Willow Bed
Sephton's Covert
Crooked Nursery
New Gibbs' Garden
Greenings
Berry House Cottages
New Berry House
Berry House Wood
Berry House
Ford Bridge
Windmill Animal Farm
Miniature Railway
Tarlscough Moss
Rufford Boundary Sluice
Boat House Sluice
Clay Brow Farm
Langley's Brook
Martin Mere Visitor Cen.
MARTIN MERE WETLAND CENTRE
Drummersdale Crossing
White House Farm
Boundary Farm
Langley's Farm
Bruff's Farm
Reservoir
East Drummersdale Farm
Gill House Farm
Sewage Works
Wood End Farm
WOOD END BUSINESS PARK
Derby Farm
The Farm (Camp Site)
Merscar Brook
Smithy Nook Farm
Mescar House Farm
Wood House Farm
New Lane Bridge (Swing)
Great Score Bridge (Swing)
Leeds & Liverpool Canal
Martin Hall Farm
WATERSIDE BUSINESS PARK
Martin Lane Bridge
Worthington's Farm
East Bank Farm
West Bank Farm
Bescar Brook
BURSCOUGH INDUSTRIAL ESTATE
Heaton's Bridge
SHAW HALL CARAVAN PARK
Lime Kiln Farm
Kershaws Farm
Bungalow Farm
Heatons Bridge Farm
Scarisbrick
MERLIN PARK
WHOLESOME LANE
WHITE HOUSE LANE
SMALL LANE
MARTIN LANE
MERSCAR LANE
DRUMMERSDALE LANE
HIGHFIELD LANE
GORST LANE
DAM WOOD ROAD
B5242
HEATONS BRIDGE ROAD
FISH LANE
BERRY HOUSE ROAD
MEANYGATE
MARSH
CRABTREE
HIGGIN'S LANE
LANGLEY RD.
LANGLEY PL.
PLANTATION ROAD
RINGTAIL RD.
TOLLGATE RD.
RABBIT LANE
MOSS LA.
CANAL BANK
169
190
209

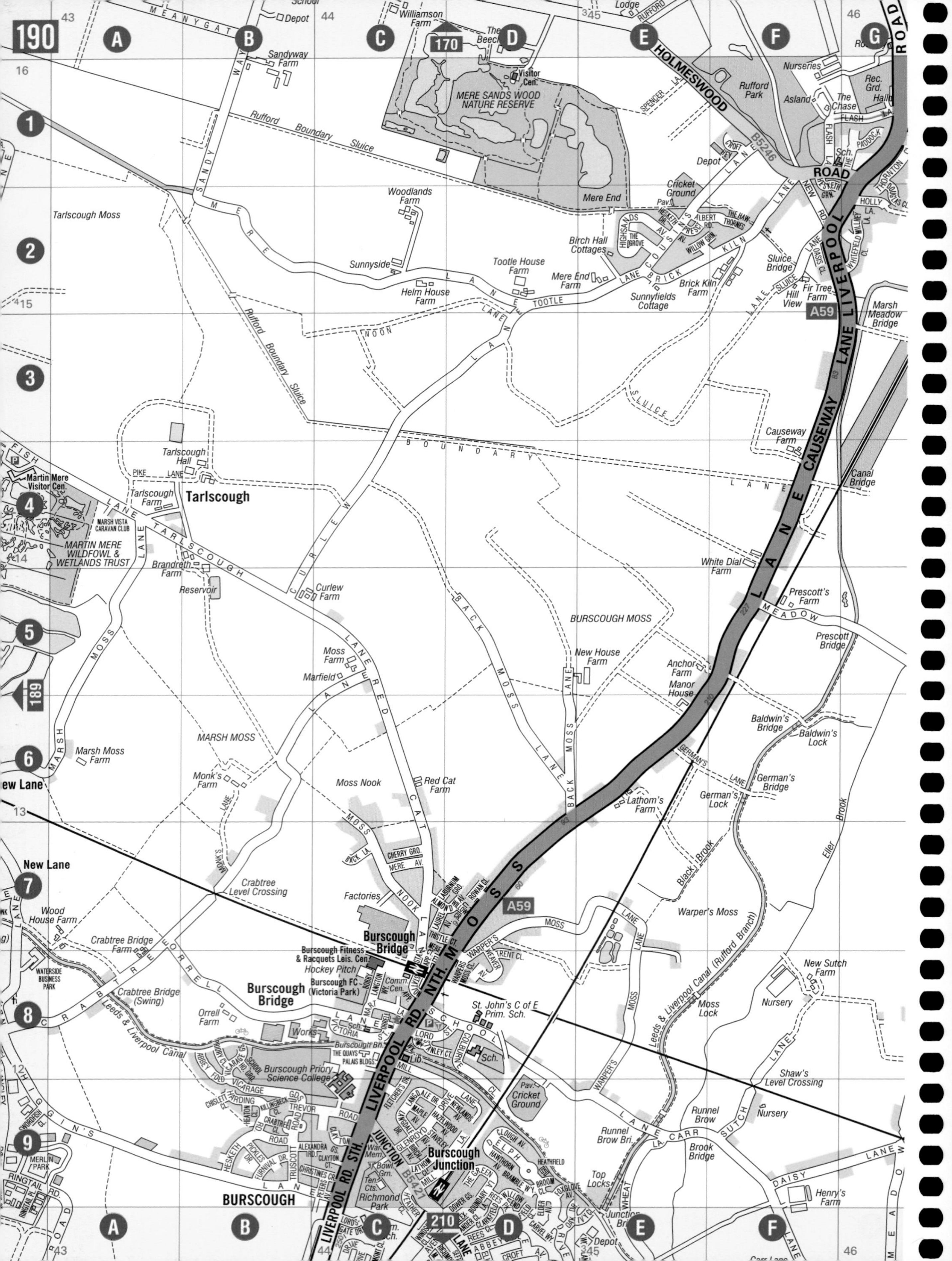

MERE SANDS WOOD NATURE RESERVE
Visitor Cen.
Williamson Farm
Sandyway Farm
Rufford Boundary Sluice
Mere End
Woodlands Farm
Tarlscough Moss
Sunnyside
Helm House Farm
Tootle House Farm
Mere End Farm
Birch Hall Cottages
Cricket Ground
Depot
HOLMESWOOD
Rufford Park
Nurseries
Asland
The Chase
Rec. Grd.
Sluice Bridge
Brick Kiln Farm
Sunnyfields Cottage
Hill View
Fir Tree Farm
A59
Marsh Meadow Bridge
LIVERPOOL ROAD
CAUSEWAY LANE
Causeway Farm
Canal Bridge
Tarlscough Hall
Tarlscough
Tarlscough Farm
Martin Mere Visitor Cen.
MARSH VISTA CARAVAN CLUB
MARTIN MERE WILDFOWL & WETLANDS TRUST
Brandreth Farm
Reservoir
Curlew Farm
White Dial Farm
Prescott's Farm
Prescott Bridge
BURSCOUGH MOSS
Moss Farm
Marfield
New House Farm
Anchor Farm
Manor House
Baldwin's Bridge
Baldwin's Lock
MARSH MOSS
Marsh Moss Farm
Monk's Farm
Moss Nook
Red Cat Farm
German's Bridge
German's Lock
Lathom's Farm
New Lane
Crabtree Level Crossing
Factories
Wood House Farm
Crabtree Bridge Farm
Burscough Bridge
Burscough Fitness & Racquets Leis. Cen.
Hockey Pitch
Burscough FC (Victoria Park)
Warper's Moss
New Sutch Farm
Nursery
Moss Lock
Crabtree Bridge (Swing)
WATERSIDE BUSINESS PARK
Orrell Farm
Works
St. John's C of E Prim. Sch.
Leeds & Liverpool Canal
Leeds & Liverpool Canal (Rufford Branch)
Burscough Priory Science College
Cricket Ground
Shaw's Level Crossing
Runnel Brow
Runnel Brow Bri.
Brook Bridge
Burscough Junction
Top Locks
Junction Bri.
Henry's Farm
Richmond Park
BURSCOUGH
MERLIN PARK
B5246
B5421
Eller Brook
Black Brook

170
189
210

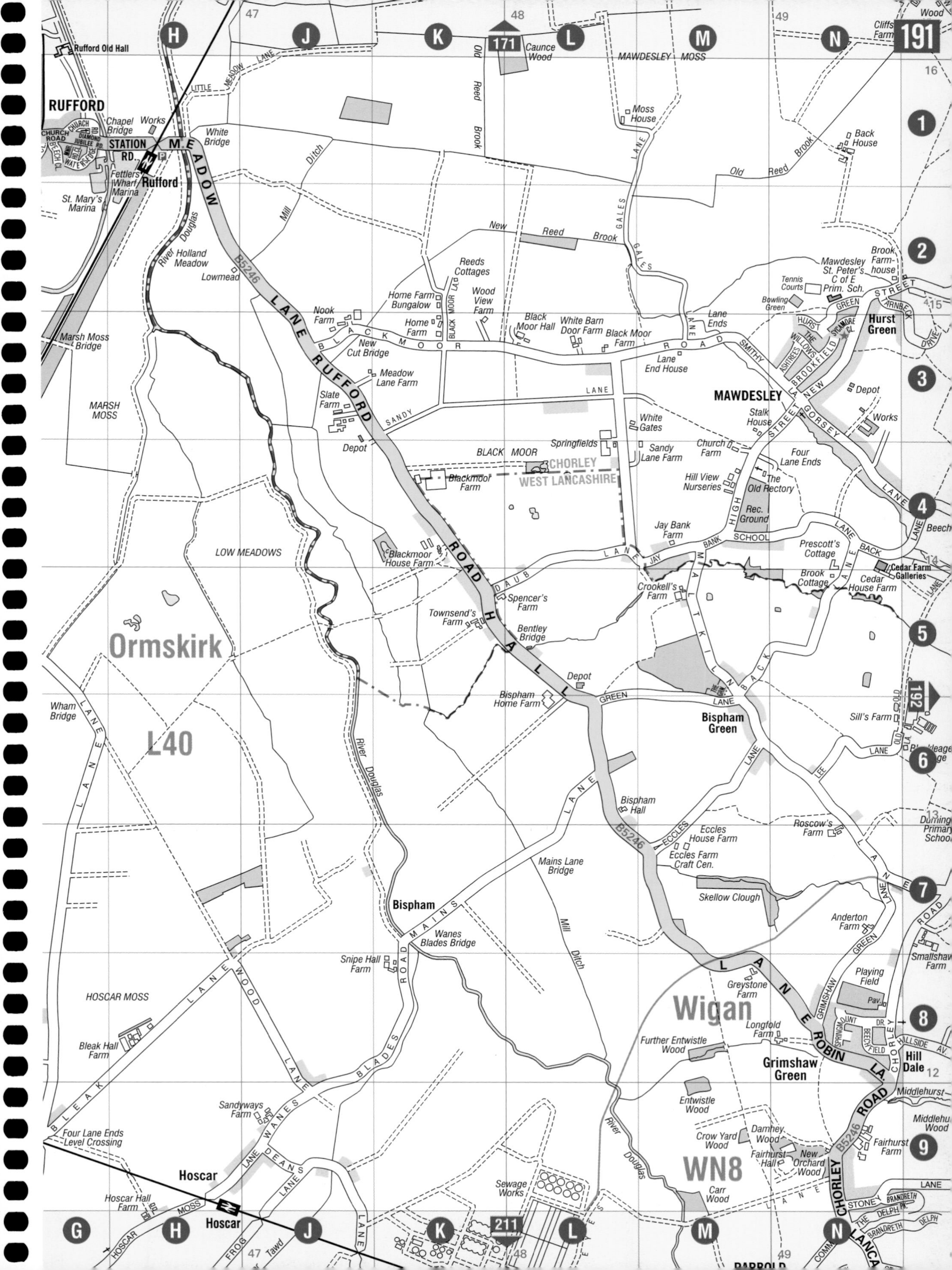

RUFFORD
Rufford Old Hall
Rufford
St. Mary's Marina
Fettlers Wharf Marina
Chapel Bridge
Works
White Bridge
MEADOW LANE
RUFFORD ROAD
HALL ROAD
LANE
B5246
Holland Meadow
Lowmead
Marsh Moss Bridge
MARSH MOSS
LOW MEADOWS
Ormskirk
L40
Wham Bridge
HOSCAR MOSS
Bleak Hall Farm
Four Lane Ends Level Crossing
Hoscar
Hoscar Hall Farm
Sandyways Farm
Snipe Hall Farm
Wanes Blades Bridge
Bispham
Mains Lane Bridge
Sewage Works
Caunce Wood
MAWDESLEY MOSS
Moss House
Old Reed Brook
New Reed Brook
Back House
Reeds Cottages
Wood View Farm
Home Farm Bungalow
Home Farm
Nook Farm
New Cut Bridge
Meadow Lane Farm
Slate Farm
Depot
Black Moor Hall
White Barn Door Farm
Black Moor Farm
BLACKMOOR ROAD
Lane Ends
Lane End House
MAWDESLEY
BLACK MOOR
Springfields
Sandy Lane Farm
White Gates
Blackmoor Farm
CHORLEY
WEST LANCASHIRE
Blackmoor House Farm
Spencer's Farm
Townsend's Farm
Bentley Bridge
Depot
Bispham Home Farm
Bispham Green
Bispham Hall
Eccles House Farm
Eccles Farm Craft Cen.
Skellow Clough
Greystone Farm
Wigan
Longfold Farm
Further Entwistle Wood
Entwistle Wood
Grimshaw Green
Crow Yard Wood
Damhey Wood
Fairhurst Hall
New Orchard Wood
Carr Wood
WN8
Church Farm
Stalk House
Four Lane Ends
Hill View Nurseries
The Old Rectory
Rec. Ground
Jay Bank Farm
Crookell's Farm
Prescott's Cottage
Brook Cottage
Cedar Farm Galleries
Cedar House Farm
Mawdesley St. Peter's C of E Prim. Sch.
Tennis Courts
Bowling Green
Brook Farmhouse
Hurst Green
Depot
Works
Sill's Farm
Roscow's Farm
Anderton Farm
Smallshaw Farm
Playing Field
Hill Dale
Middlehurst
Middlehurst Wood
Fairhurst Farm
ROBIN LANE
CHORLEY ROAD
Cliffs Farm
Wood
171
192
211
47
48
49
G H J K L M N
1 2 3 4 5 6 7 8 9

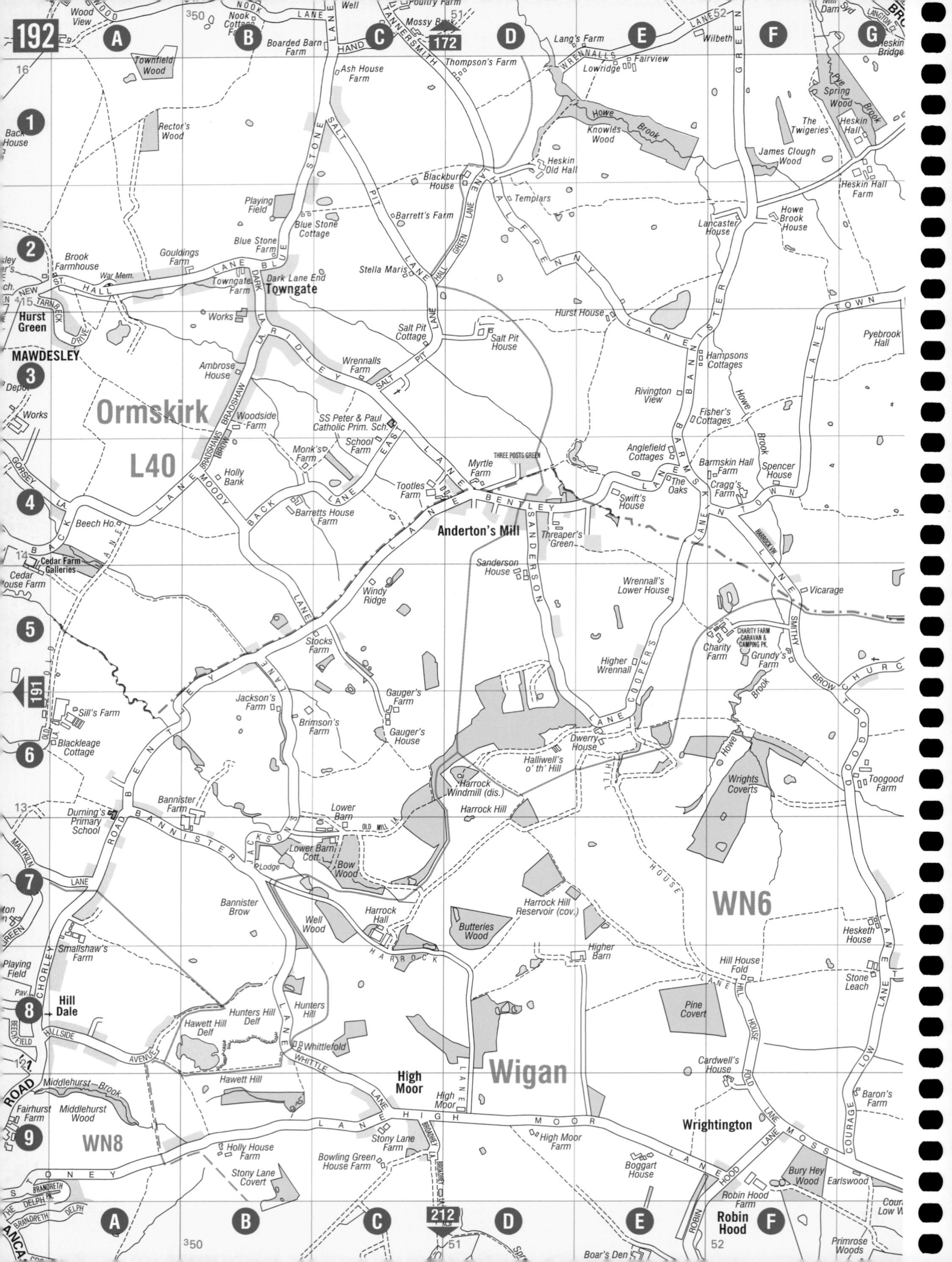
Ormskirk
L40
WN6
WN8
Wigan
Towngate
Anderton's Mill
High Moor
Wrightington
Robin Hood
Hurst Green
MAWDESLEY
Hill Dale
Townfield Wood
Boarded Barn Farm
Ash House Farm
Thompson's Farm
Lang's Farm
Wilbeth
Fairview
Lowridge
Howe Brook
Knowles Wood
Heskin Old Hall
Blackburn House
Templars
Barrett's Farm
Stella Maris
Rector's Wood
Playing Field
Blue Stone Cottage
Blue Stone Farm
Gouldings Farm
Brook Farmhouse
War Mem.
Towngate Farm
Dark Lane End
Works
Salt Pit Cottage
Salt Pit House
Wrennalls Farm
Ambrose House
Woodside Farm
SS Peter & Paul Catholic Prim. Sch.
Monk's Farm
School Farm
Holly Bank
Barretts House Farm
Tootles Farm
Myrtle Farm
THREE POSTS GREEN
Beech Ho.
Cedar Farm Galleries
Cedar House Farm
Windy Ridge
Sanderson House
Threaper's Green
Hurst House
Hampsons Cottages
Rivington View
Fisher's Cottages
Anglefield Cottages
Barmskin Hall Farm
The Oaks
Cragg's Farm
Spencer House
Swift's House
Wrennall's Lower House
Vicarage
Charity Farm
CHARITY FARM CARAVAN & CAMPING PK.
Grundy's Farm
Higher Wrennall
Lancaster House
Howe Brook House
James Clough Wood
Heskin Hall Farm
The Twigeries
Heskin Hall
Pye Spring Wood
Heskin Bridge
Pyebrook Hall
Stocks Farm
Jackson's Farm
Brimson's Farm
Gauger's Farm
Gauger's House
Sill's Farm
Blackleage Cottage
Dwerry House
Halliwell's o' th' Hill
Harrock Windmill (dis.)
Harrock Hill
Wrights Coverts
Toogood Farm
Bannister Farm
Durning's Primary School
Lower Barn
Lower Barn Cott.
Bow Wood
Lodge
Bannister Brow
Well Wood
Harrock Hall
Butteries Wood
Harrock Hill Reservoir (cov.)
Higher Barn
Hesketh House
Hill House Fold
Stone Leach
Pine Covert
Smallshaw's Farm
Hunters Hill
Hunters Hill Delf
Hawett Hill Delf
Whittlefold
Hawett Hill
Middlehurst Brook
Middlehurst Wood
Fairhurst Farm
Cardwell's House
Baron's Farm
Holly House Farm
Stony Lane Covert
Stony Lane Farm
Bowling Green House Farm
High Moor Farm
Boggart House
Bury Hey Wood
Earlswood
Robin Hood Farm
Primrose Woods
Boar's Den
HAND LANE
WRENNALLS LANE
HALL LANE
BLUE STONE LANE
SALT PIT LANE
HALFPENNY LANE
BARMSKIN LANE
TOWN LANE
RIDLEY LANE
BRADSHAW LANE
MOODY LANE
BACK LANE
EAST LANE
BENTLEY LANE
SANDERSON LANE
COOPER'S LANE
SMITHY LANE
CHURCH BROW
TOOGOOD LANE
BANNISTER LANE
JACKSONS LANE
OLD MILL LA.
HARROCK LANE
HILL HOUSE LANE
HOUSE LANE
HIGH MOOR LANE
WHITTLE LANE
LOW COURAGE LANE
MOSS LANE
ROBIN HOOD LANE
STONEY LANE
CHORLEY ROAD
HILLSIDE AVENUE
MALTKILN LANE
GORSEY LA.
TARNBECK DRIVE
NEW ST.
DARK LANE
PIT LANE
BRADSHAWS BROW
HARROCK VW.
BRANDRETH PK.
BRANDRETH DELPH
BROADHEY LA.
172
191
212
350
51
52
16
15
14
13
12

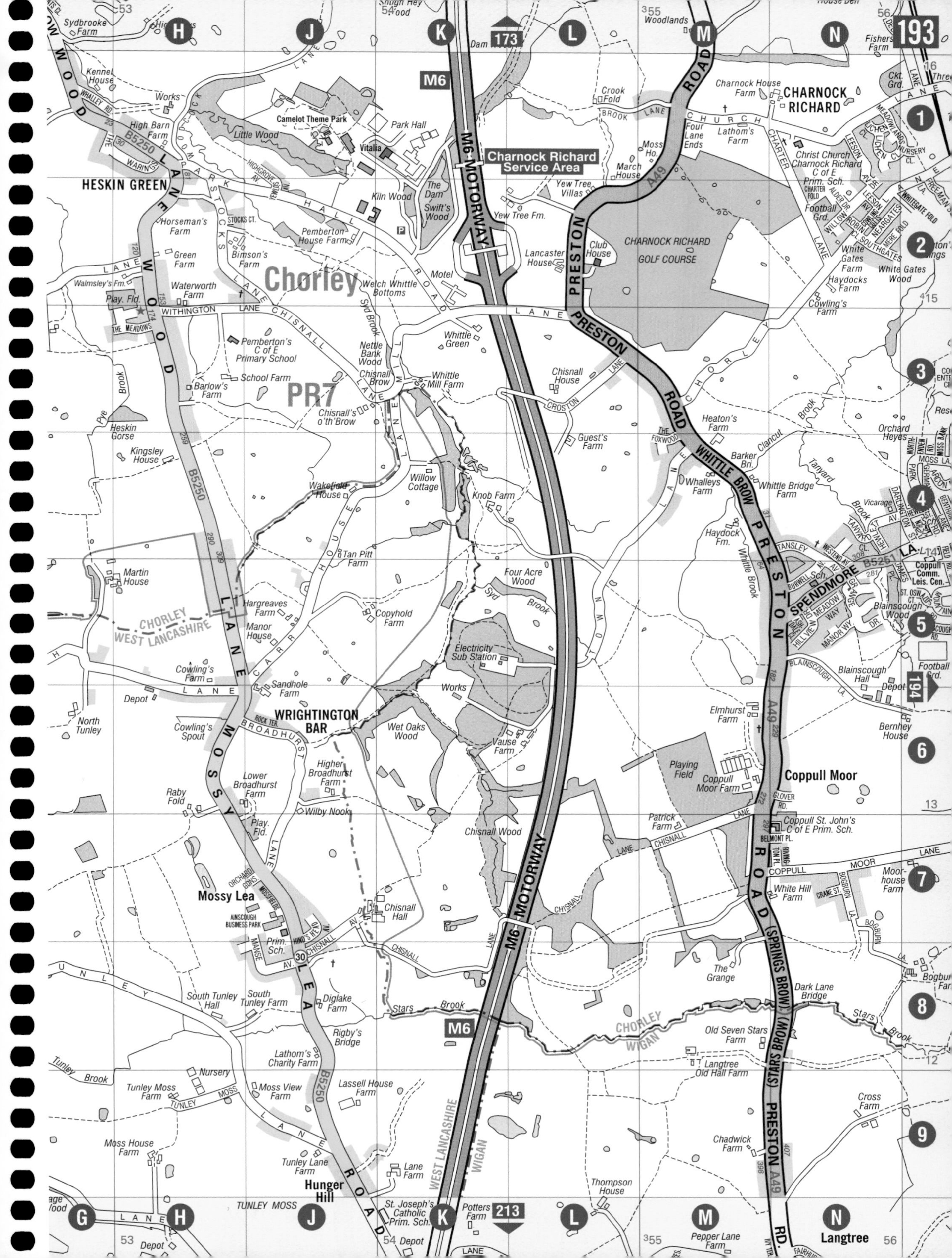
173
M6
CHARNOCK RICHARD
Camelot Theme Park
Park Hall
Little Wood
Vitalia
Charnock Richard Service Area
M6 MOTORWAY
HESKIN GREEN
WOOD LANE
B5250
Horseman's Farm
Green Farm
Waterworth Farm
Chorley
Pemberton's C of E Primary School
School Farm
PR7
Barlow's Farm
Heskin Gorse
Kingsley House
Pemberton House Farm
Bimson's Farm
Kiln Wood
The Dam
Swift's Wood
Yew Tree Fm.
Yew Tree Villas
Crook Fold
Four Lane Ends
Lathom's Farm
Moss Ho.
March House
PRESTON ROAD
A49
CHARNOCK RICHARD GOLF COURSE
Club House
Lancaster House
Charnock House Farm
Christ Church Charnock Richard C of E Prim. Sch.
Football Grd.
White Gates Farm
White Gates Wood
Haydocks Farm
Cowling's Farm
Motel
Welch Whittle Bottoms
Whittle Green
Nettle Bank Wood
Chisnall Brow
Whittle Mill Farm
Chisnall's o'th'Brow
Chisnall House
Heaton's Farm
Guest's Farm
Orchard Heyes
Barker Bri.
Whittle Bridge Farm
Whalleys Farm
WHITTLE BROW
Wakefield House
Willow Cottage
Knob Farm
Haydock Fm.
Tan Pitt Farm
Martin House
Four Acre Wood
SPENDMORE
Copull Comm. Leis. Cen.
Blainscough Wood
Hargreaves Farm
Copyhold Farm
CHORLEY
WEST LANCASHIRE
Manor House
Electricity Sub Station
Blainscough Hall
Depot
Football Grd.
194
Cowling's Farm
Sandhole Farm
Works
Depot
North Tunley
WRIGHTINGTON BAR
Cowling's Spout
Wet Oaks Wood
Vause Farm
Elmhurst Farm
Bernhey House
Higher Broadhurst Farm
Playing Field
Coppull Moor Farm
Coppull Moor
Raby Fold
Lower Broadhurst Farm
Wilby Nook
Patrick Farm
Coppull St. John's C of E Prim. Sch.
Chisnall Wood
MOSSY LANE
Mossy Lea
Chisnall Hall
Moor-house Farm
White Hill Farm
The Grange
South Tunley Hall
South Tunley Farm
Diglake Farm
Stars Brook
Dark Lane Bridge
Rigby's Bridge
CHORLEY
WIGAN
Old Seven Stars Farm
Lathom's Charity Farm
Langtree Old Hall Farm
Nursery
Tunley Brook
Tunley Moss Farm
Moss View Farm
Lassell House Farm
Cross Farm
Moss House Farm
Chadwick Farm
Tunley Lane Farm
Lane Farm
WEST LANCASHIRE
WIGAN
Thompson House
Hunger Hill
TUNLEY MOSS
St. Joseph's Catholic Prim. Sch.
Potters Farm
213
Pepper Lane Farm
Langtree
PRESTON (STARS BROW) (SPRINGS BROW) ROAD
Depot

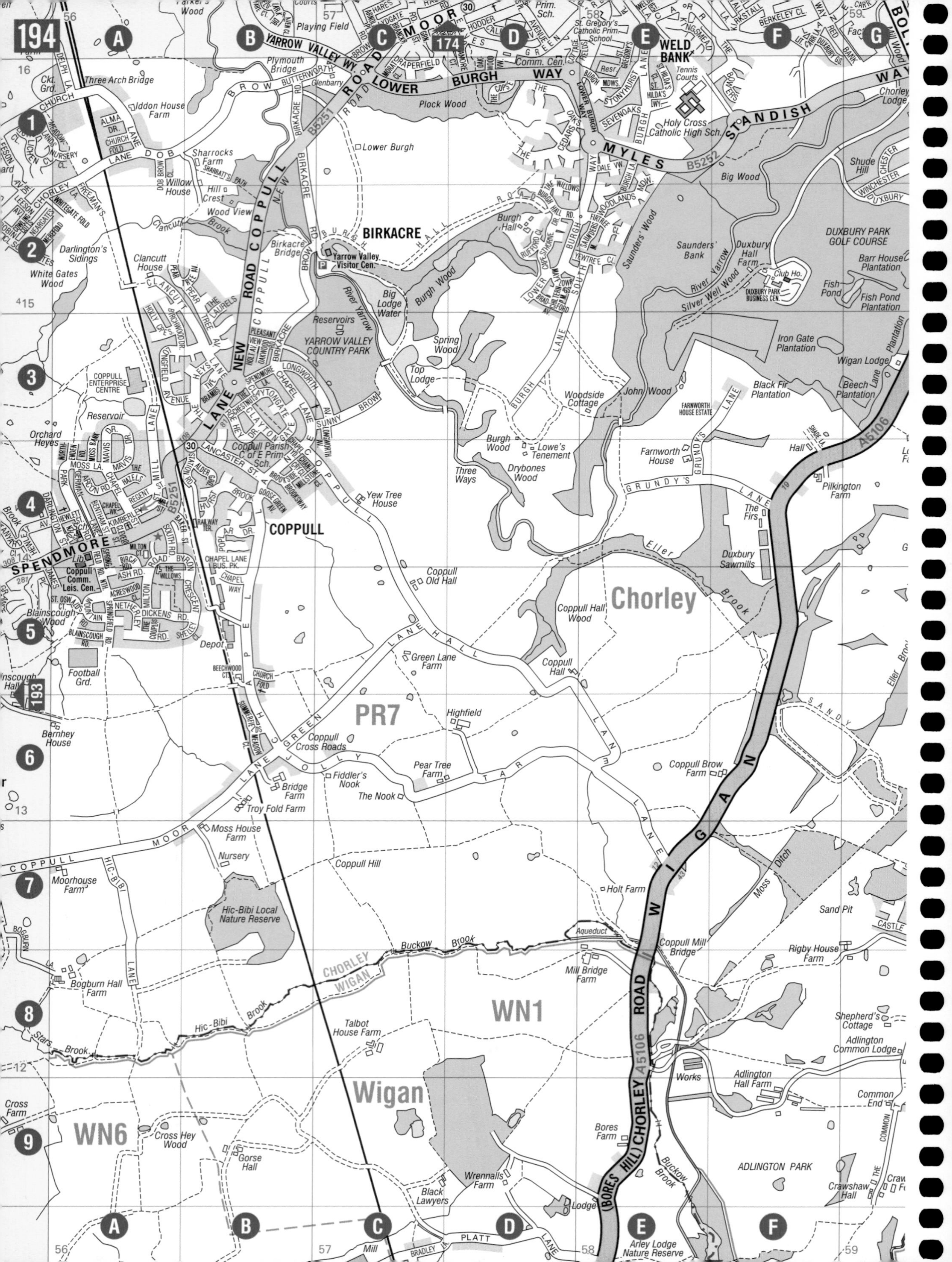
Coppull
Birkacre
Weld Bank
Chorley
Wigan
PR7
WN1
WN6
Yarrow Valley Country Park
Yarrow Valley Visitor Cen.
Duxbury Park Golf Course
Hic-Bibi Local Nature Reserve
Arley Lodge Nature Reserve
Holy Cross Catholic High Sch.
Coppull Parish C of E Prim. Sch.
Coppull Hall
Coppull Old Hall
Coppull Hill
Coppull Cross Roads
Coppull Mill Bridge
Adlington Park
Adlington Hall Farm
Lower Burgh Way
Myles Standish Way
Spendmore Lane
Coppull Moor Lane
Chorley Road (Bores Hill)
Wigan Road
A5106
B5251
B5252
River Yarrow
Buckow Brook
Hic-Bibi Brook
Eller Brook
174
193

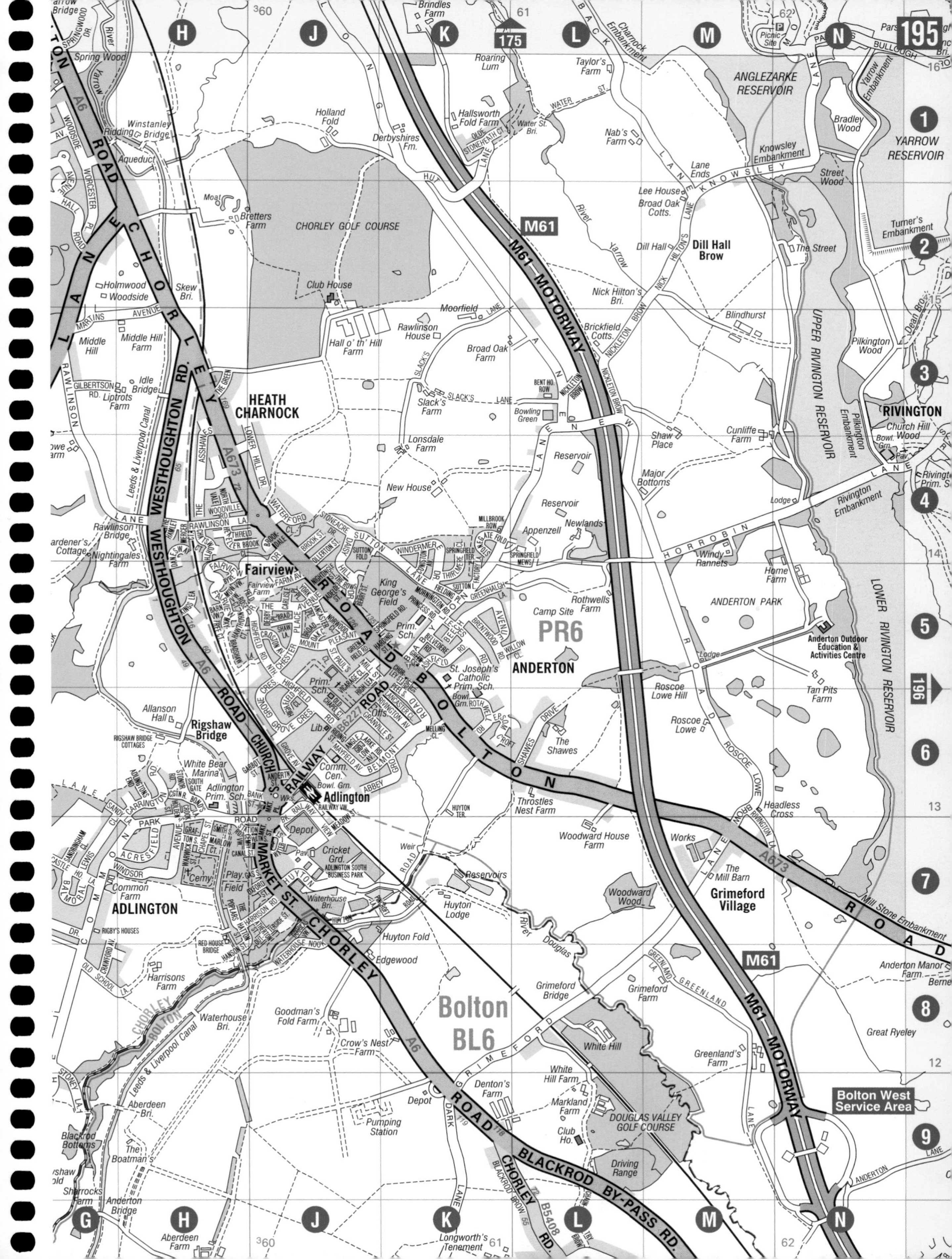
H
J
K
175
L
M
N
360
61
62
1
2
3
4
5
6
7
8
9
196
16
15
14
13
12
ANGLEZARKE RESERVOIR
YARROW RESERVOIR
UPPER RIVINGTON RESERVOIR
LOWER RIVINGTON RESERVOIR
RIVINGTON
Bradley Wood
Street Wood
Pilkington Wood
Turner's Embankment
Knowsley Embankment
Yarrow Embankment
Rivington Embankment
Pilkington Embankment
Charnock Embankment
Mill Stone Embankment
The Street
Church Hill Wood
Rivington Prim. Sch.
Lodge
Dill Hall Brow
Lane Ends
Lee House
Broad Oak Cotts.
Dill Hall
Nick Hilton's Bri.
Brickfield Cotts.
Blindhurst
Cunliffe Farm
Shaw Place
Major Bottoms
Nab's Farm
Taylor's Farm
Roaring Lum
Brindles Farm
Hallsworth Fold Farm
Water St. Bri.
Holland Fold
Derbyshires Fm.
CHORLEY GOLF COURSE
Club House
Moat
Bretters Farm
Hall o' th' Hill Farm
Rawlinson House
Moorfield
Broad Oak Farm
Slack's Farm
Bowling Green
Lonsdale Farm
New House
Reservoir
Appenzell
Newlands
Windy Rannets
Home Farm
ANDERTON PARK
Anderton Outdoor Education & Activities Centre
Tan Pits Farm
Roscoe Lowe Hill
Roscoe Lowe
Headless Cross
Rothwells Farm
Camp Site
PR6
ANDERTON
St. Joseph's Catholic Prim. Sch.
The Shawes
Throstles Nest Farm
Woodward House Farm
Woodward Wood
Works
The Mill Barn
Grimeford Village
Anderton Manor Farm
Great Ryeley
Greenland's Farm
Grimeford Farm
Grimeford Bridge
White Hill
White Hill Farm
Markland Farm
DOUGLAS VALLEY GOLF COURSE
Club Ho.
Driving Range
Denton's Farm
Bolton BL6
Bolton West Service Area
M61
M61 MOTORWAY
A673
A6
B5408
HEATH CHARNOCK
Fairview
Fairview Farm
King George's Field
Prim. Sch.
Lib.
Offs.
Comm. Cen.
Bowl. Grn.
Adlington
Depot
Cricket Grd.
ADLINGTON SOUTH BUSINESS PARK
Pav.
Weir
Reservoirs
Huyton Lodge
Huyton Fold
Edgewood
Waterhouse Bri.
Rigshaw Bridge
RIGSHAW BRIDGE COTTAGES
White Bear Marina
Adlington Prim. Sch.
Allanson Hall
ADLINGTON
Common Farm
Cemy.
Play. Field
RIGBY'S HOUSES
RED HOUSE BRIDGE
Harrisons Farm
Waterhouse Bri.
Leeds & Liverpool Canal
CHORLEY
BOLTON
Goodman's Fold Farm
Crow's Nest Farm
Depot
Pumping Station
Aberdeen Bri.
Blackrod Bottoms
The Boatman's
Sherrocks Farm
Anderton Bridge
Aberdeen Farm
Longworth's Tenement
River Douglas
River Yarrow
Spring Wood
Winstanley Bridge
Ridding
Aqueduct
Holmwood
Woodside
Skew Bri.
Middle Hill
Middle Hill Farm
Idle Bridge
Liptrots Farm
Rawlinson Bridge
Gardener's Cottage
Nightingales Farm
CHORLEY ROAD
WESTHOUGHTON RD.
WESTHOUGHTON ROAD
BOLTON ROAD
CHURCH ST.
RAILWAY RD.
MARKET ST.
CHORLEY ROAD
BLACKROD BY-PASS RD.
CHORLEY RD.
HORROBIN LANE
KNOWSLEY LANE
NICKLETON BROW
NEW LANE
ROSCOE LOWE
GRIMEFORD LANE
GREENLAND LANE
ANDERTON LANE
RAWLINSON LANE
MARTINS AVENUE
PARK ROAD
ACRESFIELD
WINDSOR
BALMORAL
COMMON
LANE
G

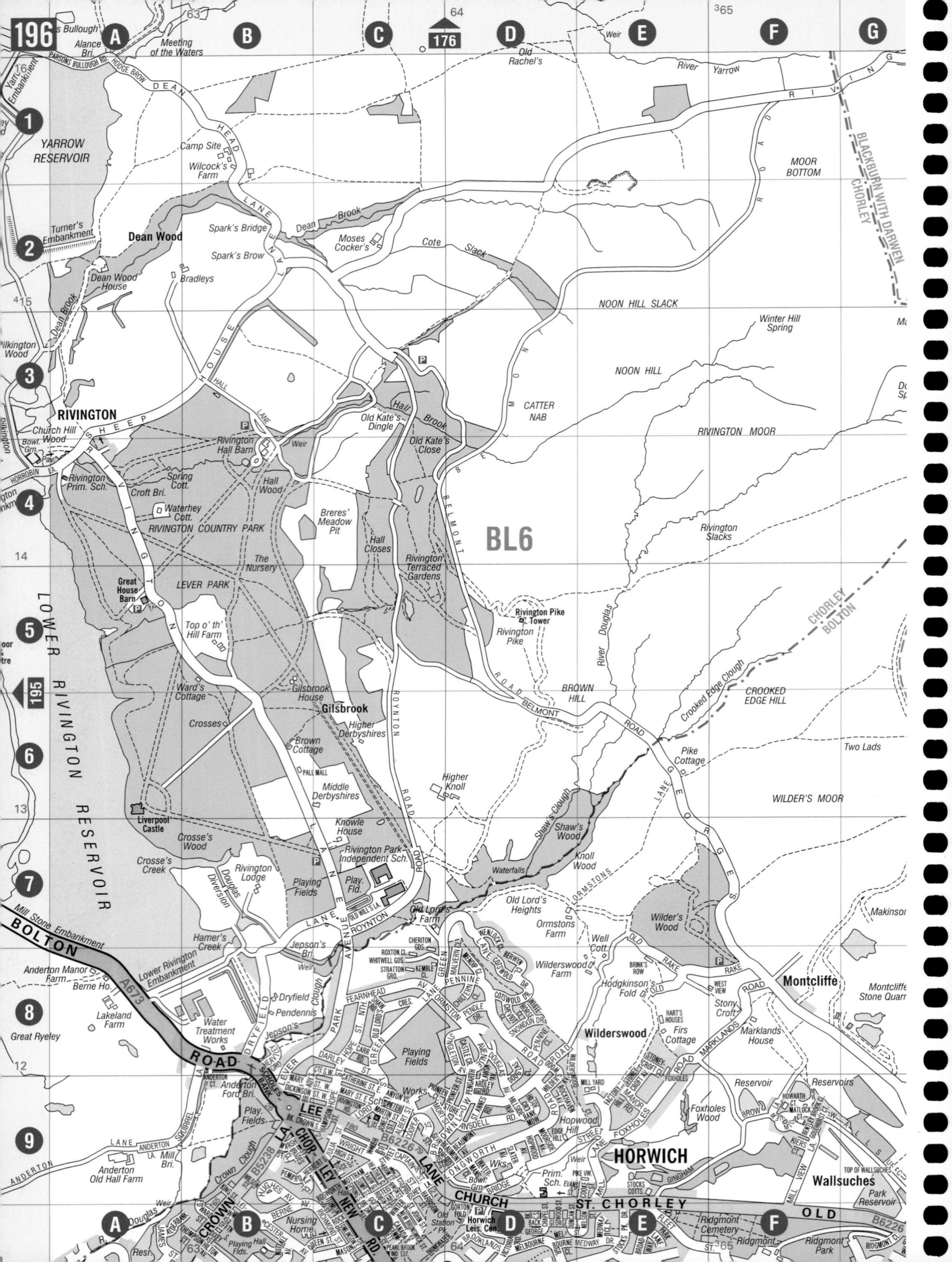
YARROW RESERVOIR
Dean Wood
RIVINGTON
RIVINGTON COUNTRY PARK
LEVER PARK
LOWER RIVINGTON RESERVOIR
BL6
NOON HILL SLACK
NOON HILL
CATTER NAB
RIVINGTON MOOR
MOOR BOTTOM
BLACKBURN WITH DARWEN
CHORLEY
BOLTON
Rivington Pike Tower
Rivington Pike
BROWN HILL
CROOKED EDGE HILL
WILDER'S MOOR
Two Lads
Winter Hill Spring
Rivington Slacks
Montcliffe
Wilderswood
HORWICH
Wallsuches
Old Rachel's
River Yarrow
Meeting of the Waters
Camp Site
Wilcock's Farm
Turner's Embankment
Spark's Bridge
Spark's Brow
Dean Brook
Moses Cocker's
Cote Slack
Bradleys
Dean Wood House
Pilkington Wood
Church Hill Wood
Rivington Hall Barn
Rivington Prim. Sch.
Old Kate's Dingle
Old Kate's Close
Hall Brook
Spring Cott.
Croft Bri.
Hall Wood
Waterhey Cott.
Breres' Meadow Pit
Hall Closes
Rivington Terraced Gardens
The Nursery
Great House Barn
Top o' th' Hill Farm
Ward's Cottage
Gilsbrook House
Gilsbrook
Higher Derbyshires
Crosses
Brown Cottage
Middle Derbyshires
Higher Knoll
Knowle House
Rivington Park Independent Sch.
Liverpool Castle
Crosse's Wood
Crosse's Creek
Rivington Lodge
Douglas Diversion
Playing Fields
Play. Fld.
Shaw's Clough
Shaw's Wood
Knoll Wood
Waterfalls
Old Lord's Farm
Old Lord's Heights
Ormstons Farm
Well Cott.
Wilderswood Farm
Wilder's Wood
Pike Cottage
Crooked Edge Clough
River Douglas
Hamer's Creek
Jepson's Bri.
Mill Stone Embankment
Lower Rivington Embankment
Anderton Manor Farm
Berne Ho.
Lakeland Farm
Great Ryeley
Water Treatment Works
Dryfield
Pendennis
Hodgkinson's Fold
Stony Croft
Firs Cottage
Markland's House
Montcliffe Stone Quarr
Makinson
Reservoir
Reservoirs
Foxholes Wood
Anderton Ford Bri.
Play. Fields
Mill Bri.
Anderton Old Hall Farm
Crown Clough
Nursing Home
Playing Flds.
Horwich Leis. Cen.
Old Station Pk.
Ridgmont Cemetery
Ridgmont Park
Park Reservoir
HODGE BROW
DEAN HEAD LANE
SHEEP HOUSE LANE
HALL LANE
RIVINGTON LANE
BELMONT ROAD
ROYNTON ROAD
GEORGES LANE
RIVINGTON ROAD
BOLTON ROAD
A673
CHORLEY NEW RD.
CHURCH ST.
CHORLEY OLD RD.
B6226
B5238
LEE LA.
CROWN LA.
ANDERTON LA.
MARKLANDS ROAD
OLD RAKE
WEST VIEW
HORROBIN LA.
PARSONS BULLOUGH RD.
176
195

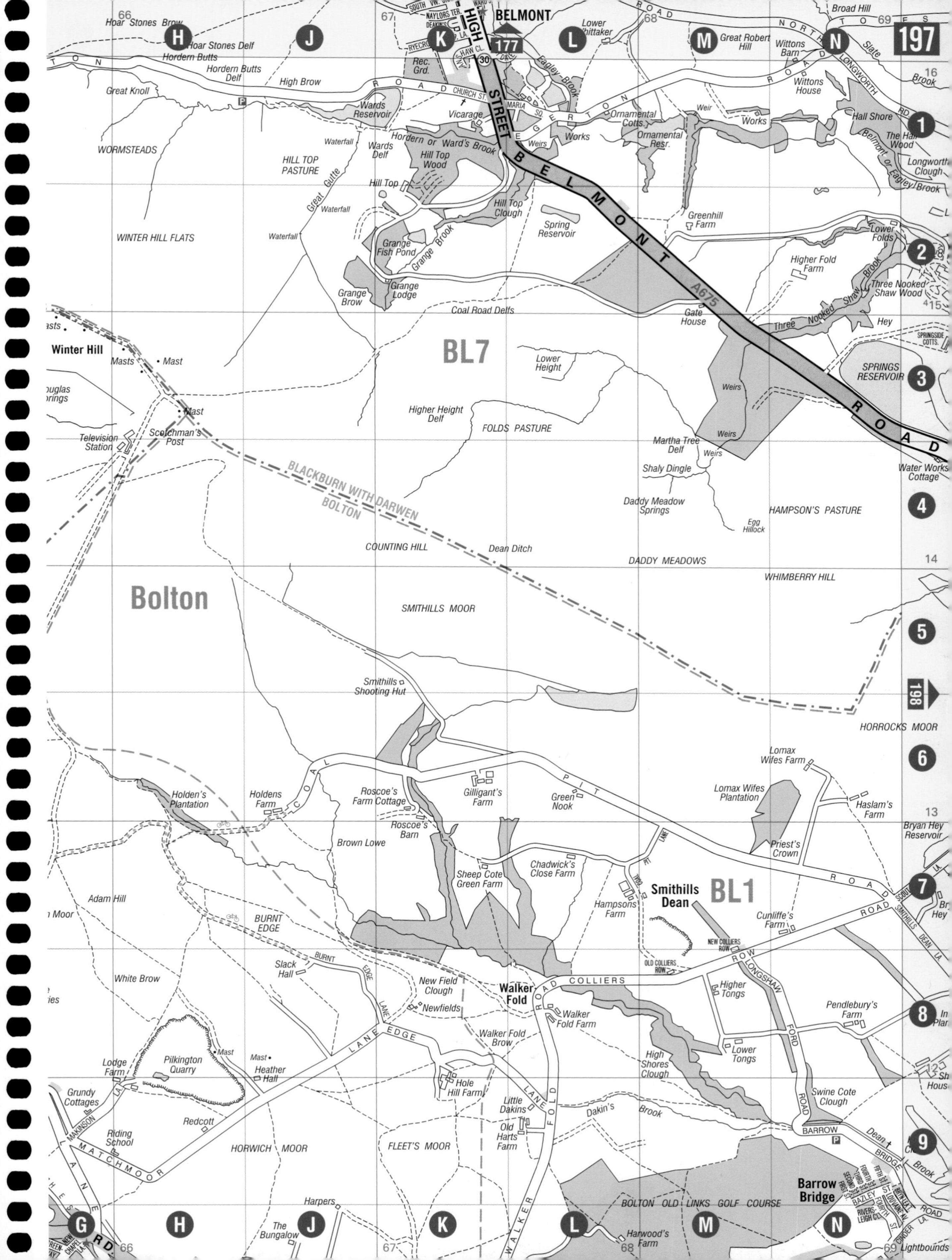
BELMONT
177
HIGH STREET
BELMONT ROAD
A675
Hoar Stones Brow
Hoar Stones Delf
Hordern Butts
Hordern Butts Delf
High Brow
Great Knoll
Wards Reservoir
Vicarage
Rec. Grd.
Lower Whittaker
Great Robert Hill
Wittons Barn
Wittons House
Broad Hill
Hall Shore
The Hall Wood
Longworth Clough
Eagley Brook
Ornamental Cotts.
Ornamental Resr.
Works
Weirs
WORMSTEADS
HILL TOP PASTURE
Hordern or Ward's Brook
Wards Delf
Hill Top Wood
Hill Top
Hill Top Clough
Waterfall
Great Gutter
WINTER HILL FLATS
Grange Fish Pond
Grange Brook
Grange Lodge
Grange Brow
Spring Reservoir
Greenhill Farm
Lower Folds
Higher Fold Farm
Three Nooked Shaw Wood
Three Nooked Shaw Brook
Gate House
Coal Road Delfs
Hey
SPRINGS RESERVOIR
SPRINGSIDE COTTS.
Winter Hill
Masts
Mast
BL7
Lower Height
Higher Height Delf
FOLDS PASTURE
Douglas Springs
Television Station
Scotchman's Post
Martha Tree Delf
Shaly Dingle
Water Works Cottage
BLACKBURN WITH DARWEN
BOLTON
Daddy Meadow Springs
HAMPSON'S PASTURE
Egg Hillock
COUNTING HILL
Dean Ditch
DADDY MEADOWS
WHIMBERRY HILL
Bolton
SMITHILLS MOOR
Smithills Shooting Hut
198
HORROCKS MOOR
Lomax Wifes Farm
Lomax Wifes Plantation
Haslam's Farm
COAL PIT ROAD
Holden's Plantation
Holdens Farm
Roscoe's Farm Cottage
Gilligant's Farm
Green Nook
Roscoe's Barn
Brown Lowe
Priest's Crown
Bryan Hey Reservoir
Sheep Cote Green Farm
Chadwick's Close Farm
PIT LANE
Smithills Dean
BL1
Adam Hill
Hampsons Farm
Cunliffe's Farm
SMITHILLS DEAN LA.
BURNT EDGE
NEW COLLIERS ROW
OLD COLLIERS ROW
COLLIERS ROW
Slack Hall
BURNT EDGE LANE
White Brow
New Field Clough
Newfields
Walker Fold
Walker Fold Farm
Higher Tongs
LONGSHAW FORD ROAD
Pendlebury's Farm
EDGE LANE
Walker Fold Brow
High Shores Clough
Lower Tongs
Lodge Farm
Pilkington Quarry
Mast
Heather Hall
Hole Hill Farm
Grundy Cottages
MAKINSON LA.
Little Dakins
WALKER FOLD LANE
Dakin's Brook
Swine Cote Clough
Redcott
Riding School
HORWICH MOOR
FLEET'S MOOR
Old Harts Farm
BARROW BRIDGE
Dean Brook
MATCHMOOR LANE
Harpers
The Bungalow
BOLTON OLD LINKS GOLF COURSE
Barrow Bridge
Harwood's Farm
Lightbounds
BAZLEY ST.
RIVERSLEIGH CL.
66
67
68
69
16
15
14
13
12
1
2
3
4
5
6
7
8
9
H
J
K
L
M
N
G

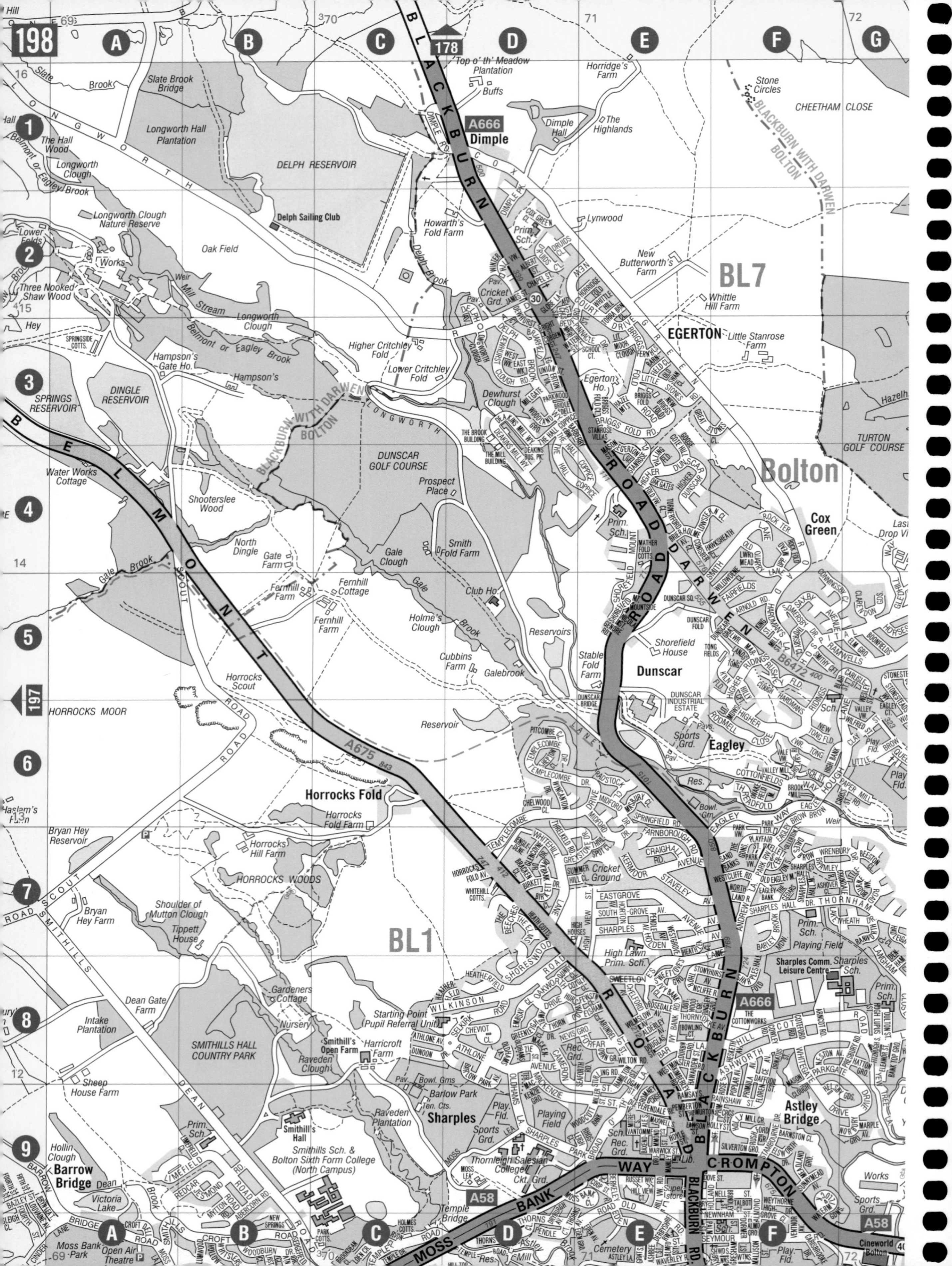
198
178
197
Slate Brook Bridge
Longworth Hall Plantation
DELPH RESERVOIR
Delph Sailing Club
Top o' th' Meadow Plantation
Buffs
A666
Dimple
Dimple Hall
The Highlands
Horridge's Farm
Stone Circles
CHEETHAM CLOSE
BLACKBURN WITH DARWEN
BOLTON
The Hall Wood
Longworth Clough
Belmont or Eagley Brook
Longworth Clough Nature Reserve
Oak Field
Howarth's Fold Farm
Lynwood
New Butterworth's Farm
BL7
Works
Three Nooked Shaw Wood
Mill Stream
Longworth Clough
Whittle Hill Farm
EGERTON
Little Stanrose Farm
Higher Critchley Fold
Lower Critchley Fold
Egerton Ho.
Dewhurst Clough
SPRINGS RESERVOIR
DINGLE RESERVOIR
Hampson's Gate Ho.
DUNSCAR GOLF COURSE
Prospect Place
Bolton
TURTON GOLF COURSE
Water Works Cottage
Shootersslee Wood
North Dingle
Gate Farm
Gale Clough
Smith Fold Farm
Cox Green
Fernhill Farm
Fernhill Cottage
Club Ho.
Holme's Clough
Reservoirs
Shorefield House
Dunscar
Cubbins Farm
Galebrook
Stable Fold Farm
DUNSCAR INDUSTRIAL ESTATE
Horrocks Scout
HORROCKS MOOR
Reservoir
Sports Grd.
Eagley
A675
Horrocks Fold
Horrocks Fold Farm
Bryan Hey Reservoir
Horrocks Hill Farm
HORROCKS WOODS
Cricket Ground
Shoulder of Mutton Clough
Bryan Hey Farm
Tippett House
BL1
High Lawn Prim. Sch.
Sharples Comm. Leisure Centre
Sharples Sch.
Gardeners Cottage
Dean Gate Farm
Intake Plantation
Starting Point (Pupil Referral Unit)
A666
SMITHILLS HALL COUNTRY PARK
Smithill's Open Farm
Harricroft Farm
Raveden Clough
Sheep House Farm
Barlow Park
Sharples
Astley Bridge
Raveden Plantation
Smithills Hall
Smithills Sch. & Bolton Sixth Form College (North Campus)
Thornleigh Salesian College
Hollin Clough
Barrow Bridge
Victoria Lake
A58
CROMPTON WAY
MOSS BANK WAY
Temple Bridge
Moss Bank Park
Open Air Theatre
Cemetery
Cineworld Bolton
BLACKBURN ROAD
DARWEN ROAD
BELMONT ROAD
LONGWORTH ROAD
SMITHILLS DEAN ROAD
SCOUT ROAD

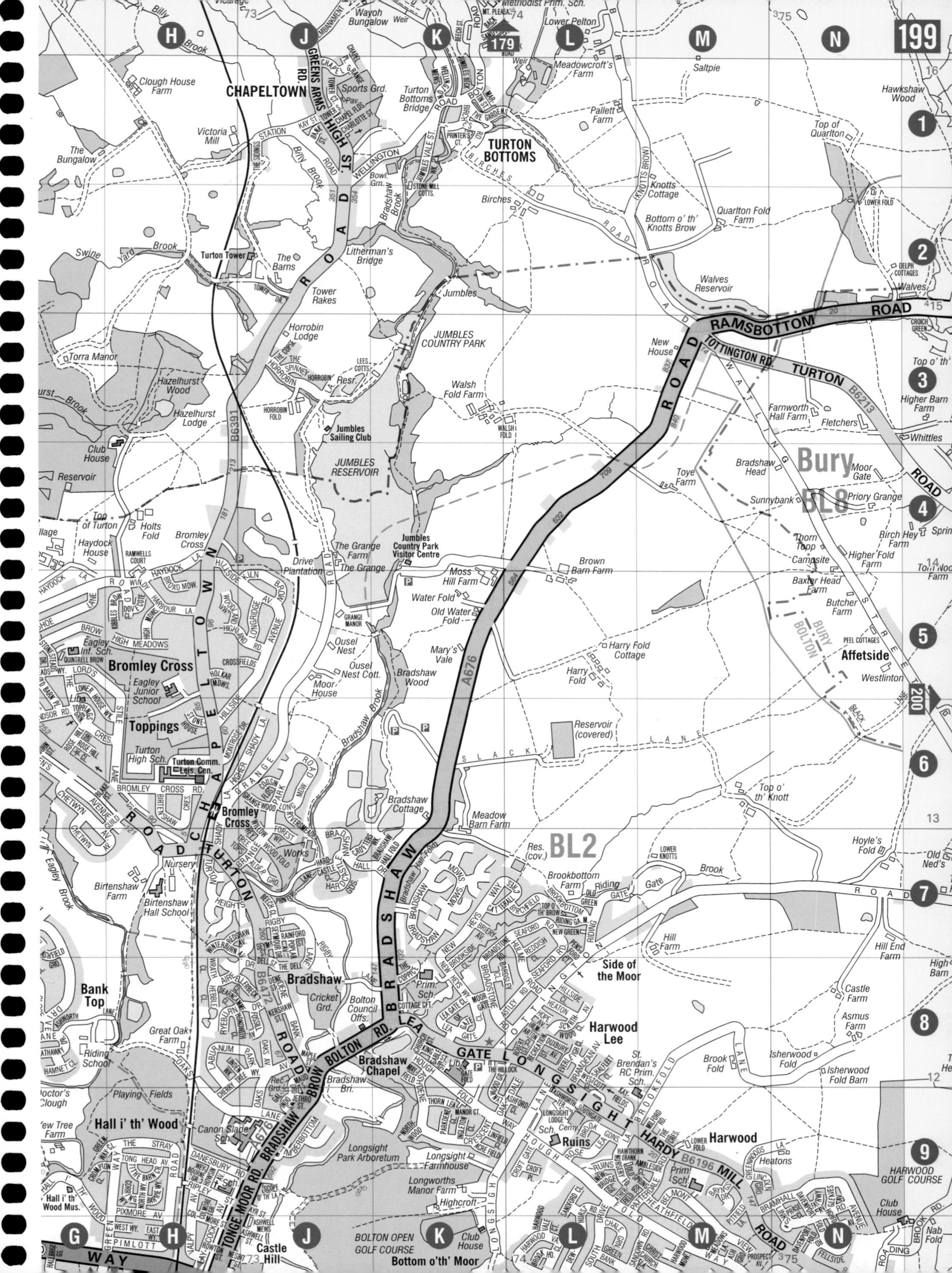
CHAPELTOWN
TURTON BOTTOMS
Turton Tower
JUMBLES COUNTRY PARK
JUMBLES RESERVOIR
Jumbles Sailing Club
Jumbles Country Park Visitor Centre
Walves Reservoir
RAMSBOTTOM ROAD
TOTTINGTON RD.
TURTON ROAD
WATLING STREET
Bury BL8
BURY BOLTON
Affetside
Bromley Cross
Eagley Inf. Sch.
Eagley Junior School
Toppings
Turton High Sch.
Turton Comm. Leis. Cen.
CHAPELTOWN ROAD
TURTON ROAD
BL2
BRADSHAW ROAD
A676
B6391
B6472
B6196
B6213
Bradshaw
Bradshaw Chapel
Bolton Council Offs.
Side of the Moor
Harwood Lee
LEA GATE
LONGSIGHT
HARDY MILL ROAD
Harwood
St. Brendan's RC Prim. Sch.
HARWOOD GOLF COURSE
Hall i' th' Wood
Hall i' th' Wood Mus.
Bank Top
Canon Slade Sch.
Longsight Park Arboretum
BOLTON OPEN GOLF COURSE
Bottom o' th' Moor
Castle Hill
TONGE MOOR RD.
Playing Fields
Birtenshaw Hall School
Great Oak Farm
Riding School
Reservoir (covered)
Top o' th' Knott
Hawkshaw Wood
Top of Quarlton
Knotts Cottage
Quarlton Fold Farm
Walsh Fold Farm
Brown Barn Farm
Harry Fold Cottage
Meadow Barn Farm
Brookbottom Farm
Hill Farm
Hill End Farm
Castle Farm
Asmus Farm
Isherwood Fold
Isherwood Fold Barn
Brook Fold
Heatons
Club House
179
200
H J K L M N G
1 2 3 4 5 6 7 8 9
73 74 375
16 15 14 13 12

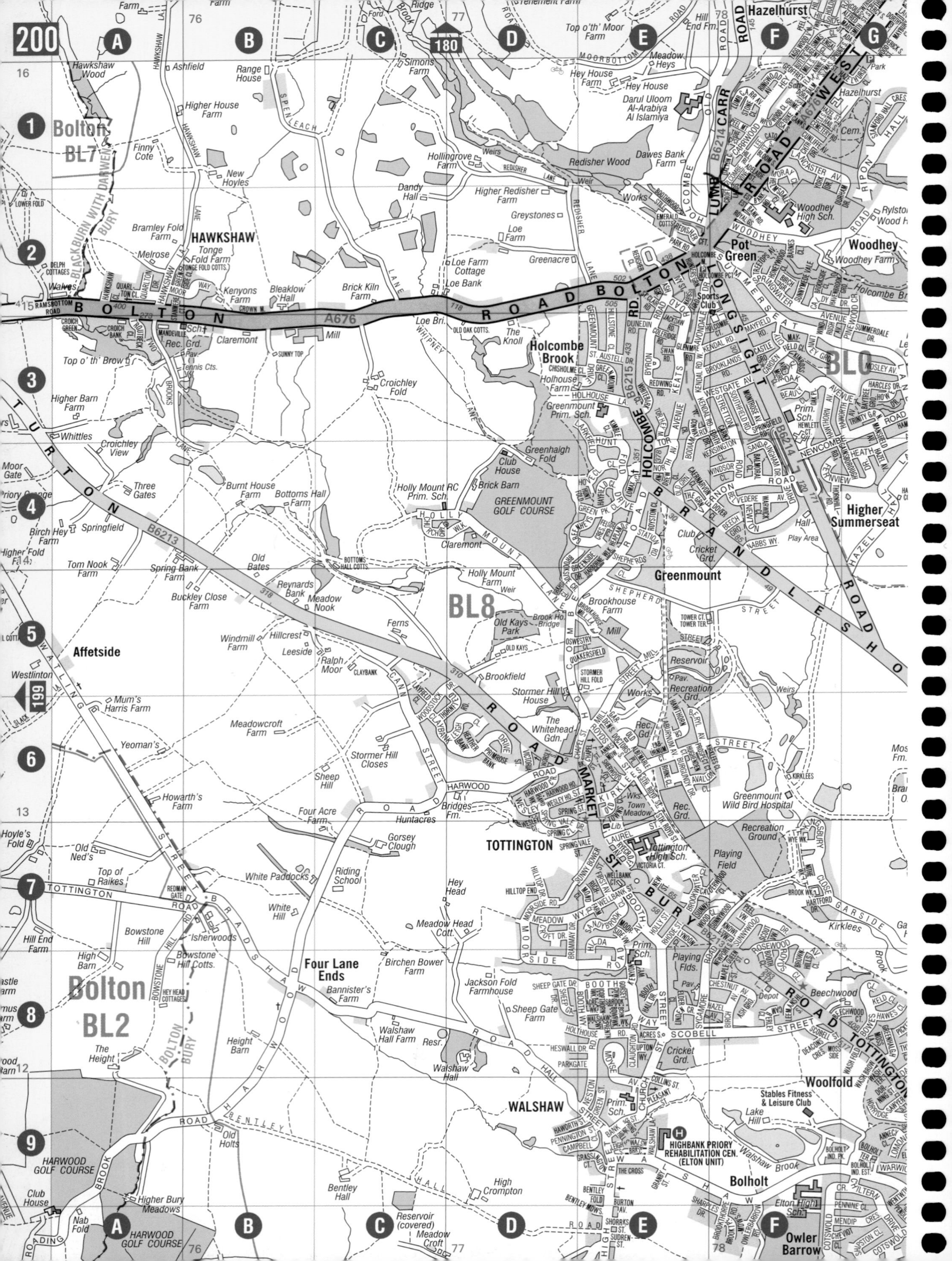
A
B
C
D
E
F
G
76
77
78
180
199
16
13
12
1
2
3
4
5
6
7
8
9
Hazelhurst
Bolton BL7
Bolton BL2
BL8
BL0
HAWKSHAW
Hawkshaw Wood
Ashfield
Range House
Simons Farm
Top o' th' Moor Farm
Meadow Heys
Hey House Farm
Hey House
Darul Uloom Al-Arabiya Al Islamiya
Higher House Farm
Finny Cote
New Hoyles
Hollingrove Farm
Weirs
Redisher Wood
Dawes Bank Farm
Dandy Hall
Higher Redisher Farm
Works
Greystones
Woodhey High Sch.
Rylstone Wood
Bramley Fold Farm
Melrose
Tonge Fold Farm
Loe Farm
Pot Green
Woodhey
Woodhey Farm
Greenacre
Loe Farm Cottage
Loe Bank
Delph Cottages
Walves
Kenyons Farm
Bleaklow Hall
Brick Kiln Farm
Holcombe Brook
BOLTON ROAD
BOLTON ROAD WEST
A676
B6214
B6215
B6213
Sch.
Rec. Grd.
Claremont
Mill
Loe Bri.
The Knoll
Top o' th' Brow
Tennis Cts.
Croichley Fold
Holhouse Farm
Greenmount Prim. Sch.
Higher Barn Farm
Whittles
Croichley View
TURTON ROAD
Greenhalgh Fold
Club House
Brick Barn
GREENMOUNT GOLF COURSE
Holly Mount RC Prim. Sch.
Three Gates
Burnt House Farm
Bottoms Hall Farm
Moor Gate
Priory Grange
Birch Hey Farm
Springfield
Higher Summerseat
Greenmount
Cricket Grd.
Tom Nook Farm
Spring Bank Farm
Old Bates
Holly Mount Farm
Buckley Close Farm
Reynards Bank
Meadow Nook
Brookhouse Farm
Old Kays Park
Affetside
Windmill Farm
Hillcrest
Leeside
Ralph Moor
Ferns
Brookfield
Reservoir
Recreation Grd.
Works
Stormer Hill House
Westlinton
Mum's Harris Farm
The Whitehead Gdn.
Meadowcroft Farm
Yeoman's
Stormer Hill Closes
Sheep Hill
HARWOOD ROAD
Greenmount Wild Bird Hospital
Howarth's Farm
Four Acre Farm
Bridges Fm.
Huntacres
Recreation Ground
Hoyle's Fold
Old Ned's
Gorsey Clough
TOTTINGTON
Tottington High Sch.
Playing Field
Top of Raikes
White Paddocks
Riding School
Hey Head
TOTTINGTON ROAD
WATLING STREET
BRADSHAW ROAD
White Hill
Meadow Head Cott.
Kirklees
Bowstone Hill
Isherwoods
Hill End Farm
High Barn
Bowstone Hill Cotts.
Four Lane Ends
Birchen Bower Farm
Playing Flds.
Bannister's Farm
Jackson Fold Farmhouse
Sheep Gate Farm
Beechwood
Walshaw Hall Farm
Resr.
Cricket Grd.
Height Barn
The Height
Walshaw Hall
Woolfold
Stables Fitness & Leisure Club
WALSHAW
Lake Hill
Old Holts
HIGHBANK PRIORY REHABILITATION CEN. (ELTON UNIT)
HARWOOD GOLF COURSE
Walshaw Brook
Club House
Higher Bury Meadows
Bentley Hall
High Crompton
Bolholt
Elton High Sch.
Nab Fold
Reservoir (covered)
Meadow Croft
Owler Barrow
BLACKBURN WITH DARWEN
BURY
BOLTON

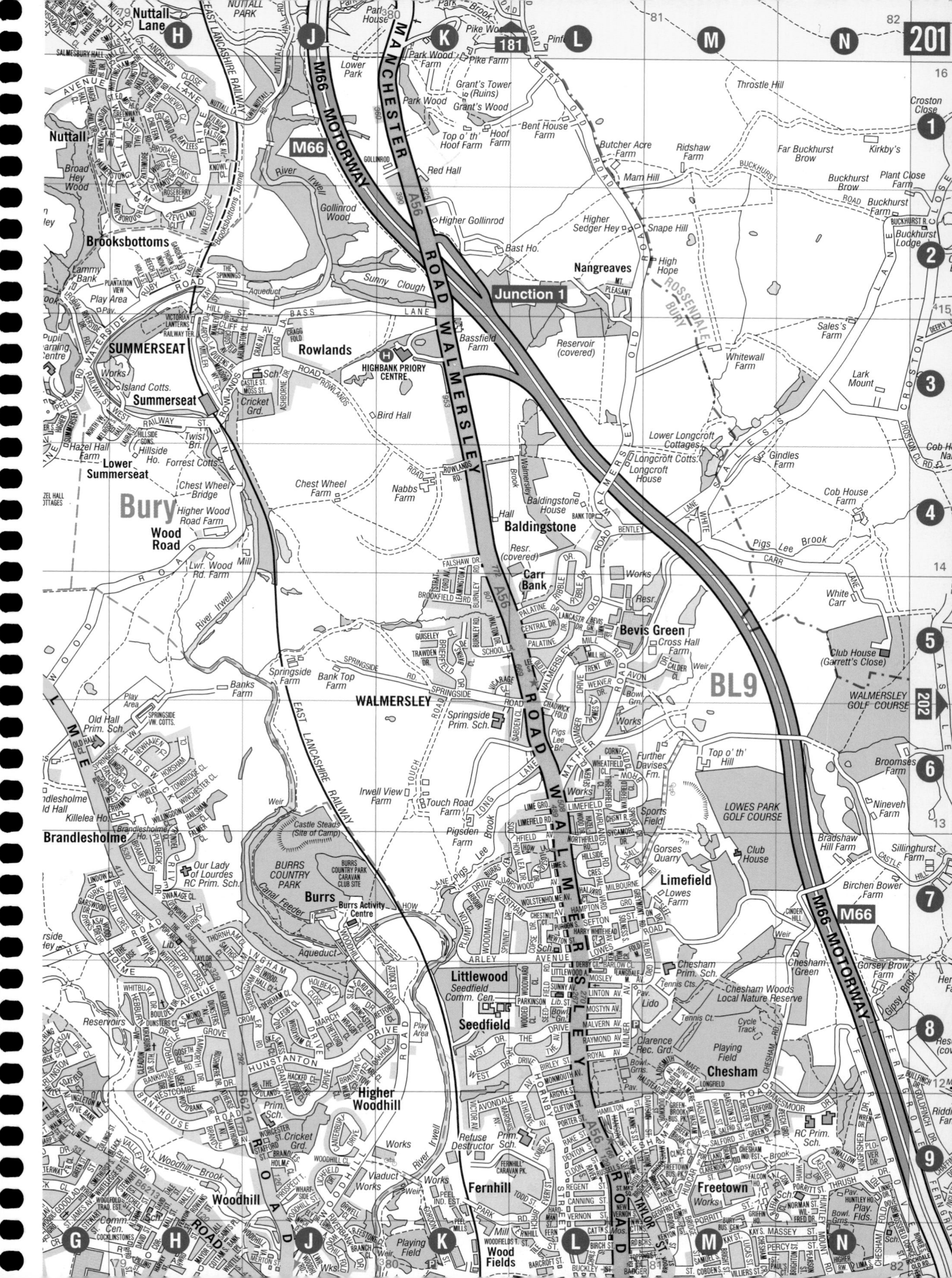
Nuttall Lane
Nuttall
Broad Hey Wood
Brooksbottoms
Lammy Bank
Play Area
SUMMERSEAT
Summerseat
Island Cotts.
Works
Hazel Hall Farm
Lower Summerseat
Bury
Wood Road
Higher Wood Road Farm
Chest Wheel Bridge
Forrest Cotts.
Twist Bri.
Hillside Ho.
Lwr. Wood Rd. Farm
River Irwell
EAST LANCASHIRE RAILWAY
Brooksbottoms Tunnel
NUTTALL PARK
Lower Park
Park House
Park Wood Farm
Pike Farm
Grant's Tower (Ruins)
Park Wood
Grant's Wood
Bent House Farm
Hoof Farm
Top o' th' Hoof Farm
Red Hall
M66
M66 MOTORWAY
MANCHESTER ROAD
WALMERSLEY ROAD
A56
Gollinrod Wood
Higher Gollinrod
Bast Ho.
Sunny Clough
Aqueduct
Junction 1
BASS LANE
Rowlands
Bassfield Farm
HIGHBANK PRIORY CENTRE
Cricket Grd.
Bird Hall
Nabbs Farm
Chest Wheel Farm
Throstle Hill
Croston Close
Butcher Acre Farm
Ridshaw Farm
Far Buckhurst Brow
Kirkby's
Mam Hill
BUCKHURST ROAD
Buckhurst Brow
Plant Close Farm
Buckhurst Farm
Buckhurst Lodge
Higher Sedger Hey
Snape Hill
High Hope
Nangreaves
MT. PLEASANT
ROSSENDALE
BURY
Reservoir (covered)
Whitewall Farm
Sales's Farm
Lark Mount
Lower Longcroft Cottages
Longcroft Cotts.
Longcroft House
Gindles Farm
Cob House Farm
Baldingstone House
Baldingstone
Hall
Resr. (covered)
Carr Bank
Pigs Lee Brook
White Carr
Bevis Green
Cross Hall Farm
BL9
Club House (Garrett's Close)
WALMERSLEY GOLF COURSE
202
Springside Farm
Bank Top Farm
Banks Farm
WALMERSLEY
Springside Prim. Sch.
Play Area
Old Hall Prim. Sch.
Further Davises Fm.
Top o' th' Hill
Broomses Farm
Nineveh Farm
Irwell View Farm
Touch Road Farm
Pigsden Farm
Castle Steads (Site of Camp)
BURRS COUNTRY PARK
Burrs
Burrs Activity Centre
Canal Feeder
Aqueduct
Sports Field
LOWES PARK GOLF COURSE
Gorses Quarry
Club House
Limefield
Lowes Hampton
Bradshaw Hill Farm
Sillinghurst Farm
Birchen Bower Farm
Brandlesholme
Killelea Ho.
Our Lady of Lourdes RC Prim. Sch.
Littlewood
Seedfield Comm. Cen.
Seedfield
Chesham Prim. Sch.
Chesham Woods Local Nature Reserve
Chesham Green
Gorsey Brow Farm
Tennis Cts.
Lido
Cycle Track
Playing Field
Clarence Rec. Grd.
Chesham
Reservoirs
Higher Woodhill
Cricket Grd.
Prim. Sch.
Works
Refuse Destructor
Fernhill
FERNHILL CARAVAN PK.
Freetown
RC Prim. Sch.
Woodhill
Viaduct
Playing Field
Wood Fields
Comm. Cen.
Play. Flds.

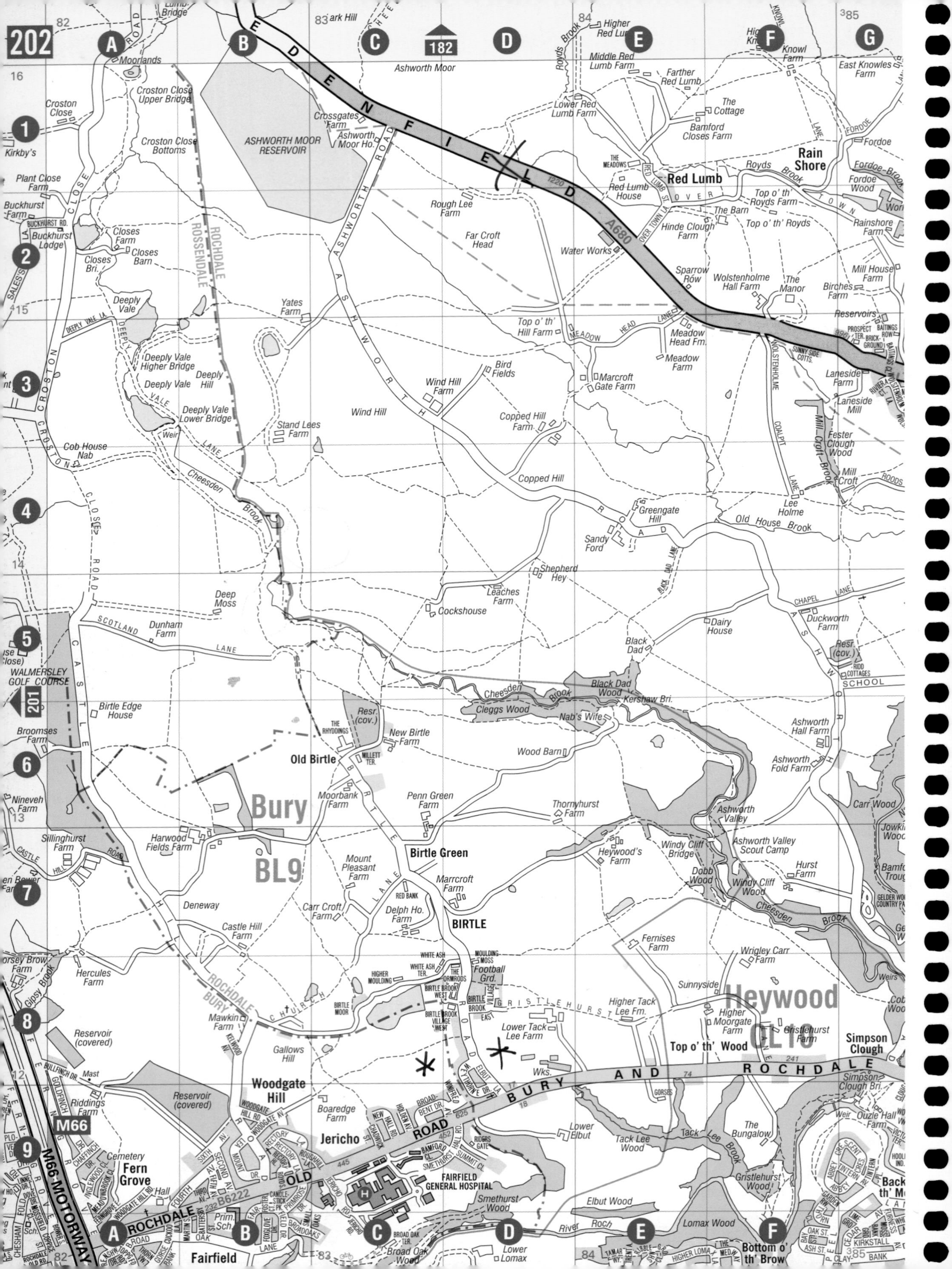
182
201
A
B
C
D
E
F
G
1
2
3
4
5
6
7
8
9
Moorlands
Croston Close Upper Bridge
Croston Close
Kirkby's
Croston Close Bottoms
ASHWORTH MOOR RESERVOIR
Ashworth Moor
Crossgates Farm
Ashworth Moor Ho.
EDENFIELD ROAD
A680
Higher Red Lumb
Middle Red Lumb Farm
Farther Red Lumb
Lower Red Lumb Farm
The Cottage
Bamford Closes Farm
Knowl Farm
East Knowles Farm
Fordoe
Rain Shore
Red Lumb
Red Lumb House
Royds Brook
Fordoe Brook
Fordoe Wood
Top o' th' Royds Farm
The Barn
Top o' th' Royds
Rainshore Farm
Hinde Clough Farm
OVER TOWN LA.
Plant Close Farm
Buckhurst Farm
Buckhurst Lodge
Closes Farm
Closes Barn
Closes Bri.
ROCHDALE
ROSSENDALE
Rough Lee Farm
Far Croft Head
Water Works
Sparrow Row
Wolstenholme Hall Farm
The Manor
Birches Farm
Mill House Farm
Deeply Vale
Yates Farm
Reservoirs
Top o' th' Hill Farm
MEADOW HEAD LANE
Meadow Head Fm.
Meadow Farm
Laneside Farm
Laneside Mill
Deeply Vale Higher Bridge
Deeply Vale
Deeply Hill
Bird Fields
Wind Hill Farm
Marcroft Gate Farm
Wind Hill
Deeply Vale Lower Bridge
Stand Lees Farm
Copped Hill Farm
Fester Clough Wood
Mill Croft Brook
Mill Croft
Cob House Nab
Cheesden Brook
Copped Hill
Greengate Hill
Lee Holme
Old House Brook
Sandy Ford
ASHWORTH ROAD
CROSTON CLOSE ROAD
Shepherd Hey
BLACK DAD LANE
Deep Moss
Leaches Farm
Cockshouse
CHAPEL LANE
Duckworth Farm
SCOTLAND LANE
Dunham Farm
Dairy House
Black Dad
Resr. (cov.)
RIDD COTTAGES
SCHOOL
WALMERSLEY GOLF COURSE
Black Dad Wood
Kershaw Bri.
Cheesden Brook
Cleggs Wood
Nab's Wife
Birtle Edge House
Resr. (cov.)
THE RHYDDINGS
New Birtle Farm
Ashworth Hall Farm
Broomses Farm
Wood Barn
Old Birtle
MILLETT TER.
Ashworth Fold Farm
Bury
Moorbank Farm
Penn Green Farm
Thornyhurst Farm
Carr Wood
Nineveh Farm
Ashworth Valley
BL9
Sillinghurst Farm
Harwood Fields Farm
Heywood's Farm
Windy Cliff Bridge
Ashworth Valley Scout Camp
Birtle Green
Mount Pleasant Farm
Hurst Farm
Dobb Wood
Windy Cliff Wood
Marrcroft Farm
RED BANK
Carr Croft Farm
Delph Ho. Farm
Deneway
BIRTLE
Castle Hill Farm
Fernises Farm
Wrigley Carr Farm
WHITE ASH
MOULDING MOSS
Football Grd.
Hercules Farm
Gipsy Brook
HIGHER MOULDING
Sunnyside
Heywood
BURY ROCHDALE
CHURCH
GRISTLEHURST
Higher Tack Lee Fm.
Higher Moorgate Farm
Gristlehurst Farm
Mawkin Farm
Reservoir (covered)
Lower Tack Lee Farm
Top o' th' Wood
OL10
Simpson Clough
Gallows Hill
Wks.
BURY AND ROCHDALE
Simpson Clough Bri.
Mast
Riddings Farm
Woodgate Hill
Reservoir (covered)
Boaredge Farm
Lower Elbut
M66
Jericho
ROAD
The Bungalow
Ouzle Hall Farm
Tack Lee Wood
Tack Lee Brook
Cemetery
Fern Grove
OLD
FAIRFIELD GENERAL HOSPITAL
Gristlehurst Wood
M66 MOTORWAY
Hall
Smethurst Wood
Elbut Wood
Back o' th' Moss
B6222
ROCHDALE
Prim. Sch.
River Roch
Lomax Wood
Broad Oak Wood
Lower Lomax
Fairfield
Bottom o' th' Brow
HIGHER LOMAX
KIRKSTALL
82
83
84
385
16
15
14
13
12

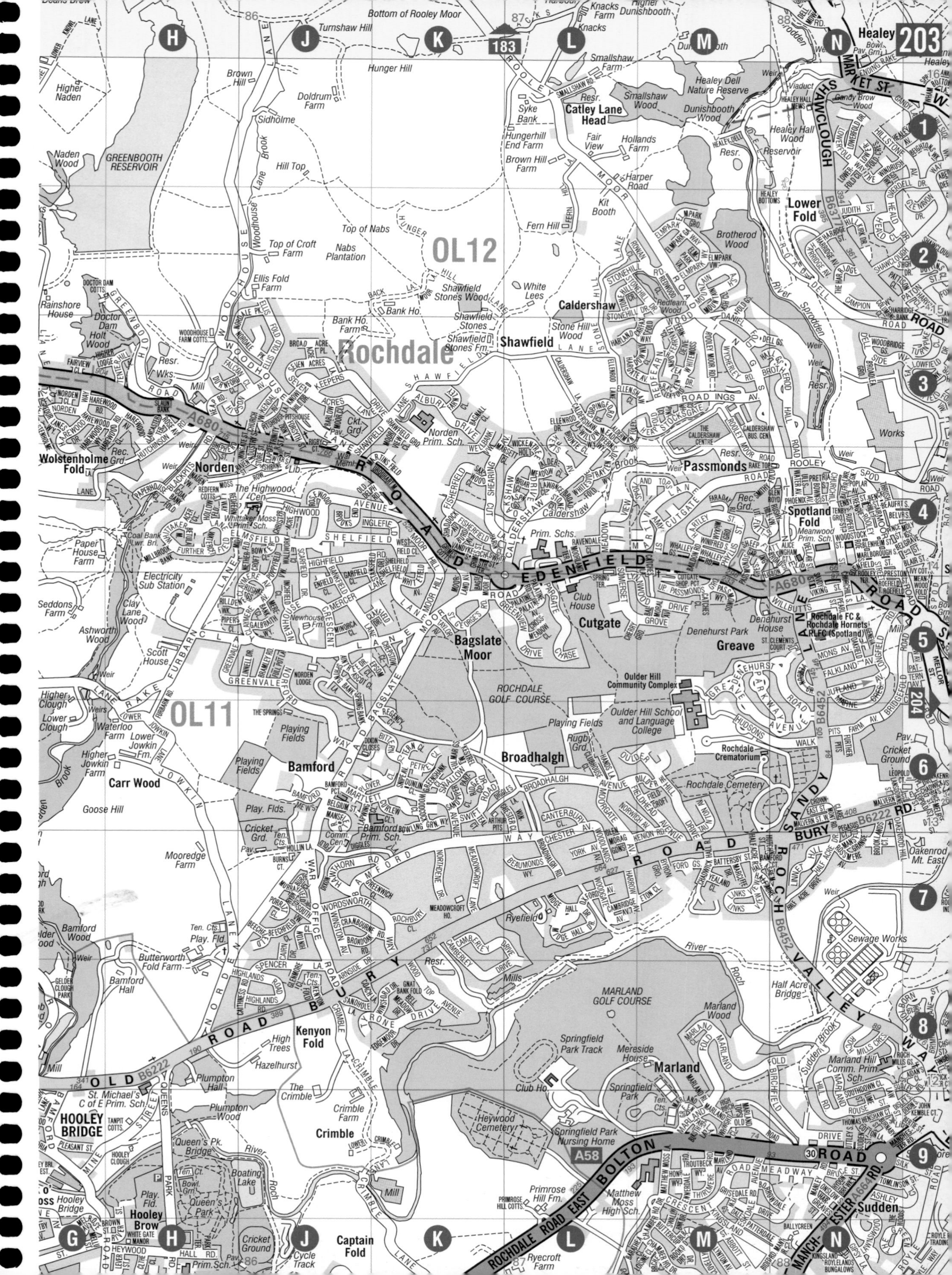
Bottom of Rooley Moor
Turnshaw Hill
183
Knacks Farm
Higher Dunishbooth
Healey
Hunger Hill
Higher Naden
Brown Hill
Doldrum Farm
Smallshaw Farm
Healey Dell Nature Reserve
Smallshaw Wood
Dunishbooth Wood
Catley Lane Head
Syke Bank
Sidholme
Naden Wood
GREENBOOTH RESERVOIR
Hungerhill End Farm
Fair View
Hollands Farm
Healey Hall Wood
Reservoir
Hill Top
Brown Hill Farm
Harper Road
Kit Booth
Lower Fold
Fern Hill
Top of Nabs
Top of Croft Farm
Nabs Plantation
OL12
Brotherod Wood
Ellis Fold Farm
White Lees
Caldershaw
Rainshore House
Doctor Dam Holt Wood
Shawfield Stones Wood
Bank Ho.
Shawfield Stones
Stone Hill Wood
Rochdale
Shawfield
Norden
Wolstenholme Fold
Passmonds
Works
Spotland Fold
Norden Prim. Sch.
The Highwood Cen.
Whittaker Moss Prim. Sch.
Caldershaw
Prim. Schs.
EDENFIELD ROAD
A680
Paper House Farm
Electricity Sub Station
Seddons Farm
Clay Lane Wood
Club House
Cutgate
Denehurst Park
Denehurst House
Rochdale FC & Rochdale Hornets RLFC (Spotland)
Greave
Ashworth Wood
Scott House
Bagslate Moor
ROCHDALE GOLF COURSE
Oulder Hill Community Complex
Oulder Hill School and Language College
Higher Clough
Lower Clough
Waterloo Farm
Lower Jowkin Fm.
OL11
Playing Fields
Rugby Grd.
Rochdale Crematorium
Cricket Ground
Higher Jowkin Farm
Carr Wood
Bamford
Broadhalgh
Rochdale Cemetery
Goose Hill
Play. Flds.
Cricket Grd.
Bamford Prim. Sch.
BURY ROAD
B6222
Oakenrod Mt. East
Mooredge Farm
Ryefield
Sewage Works
Bamford Wood
Butterworth Fold Farm
Bamford Hall
River Roch
Mills
MARLAND GOLF COURSE
Half Acre Bridge
Marland Wood
Kenyon Fold
High Trees
Hazelhurst
Springfield Park Track
Mereside House
Marland Hill Comm. Prim. Sch.
OLD ROAD
Plumpton Hall
St. Michael's C of E Prim. Sch.
HOOLEY BRIDGE
The Crimble
Club Ho.
Marland
Springfield Park
Plumpton Wood
Crimble Farm
Heywood Cemetery
Springfield Park Nursing Home
Crimble
Queen's Pk. Bridge
Boating Lake
Queen's Park
BOLTON ROAD
A58
Mill
ROCHDALE ROAD EAST
Primrose Hill Fm.
Matthew Moss High Sch.
Hooley Bridge
Hooley Brow
Cricket Ground
Cycle Track
Captain Fold
Ryecroft Farm
Sudden
204
H
J
K
L
M
N
G
1
2
3
4
5
6
7
8
9

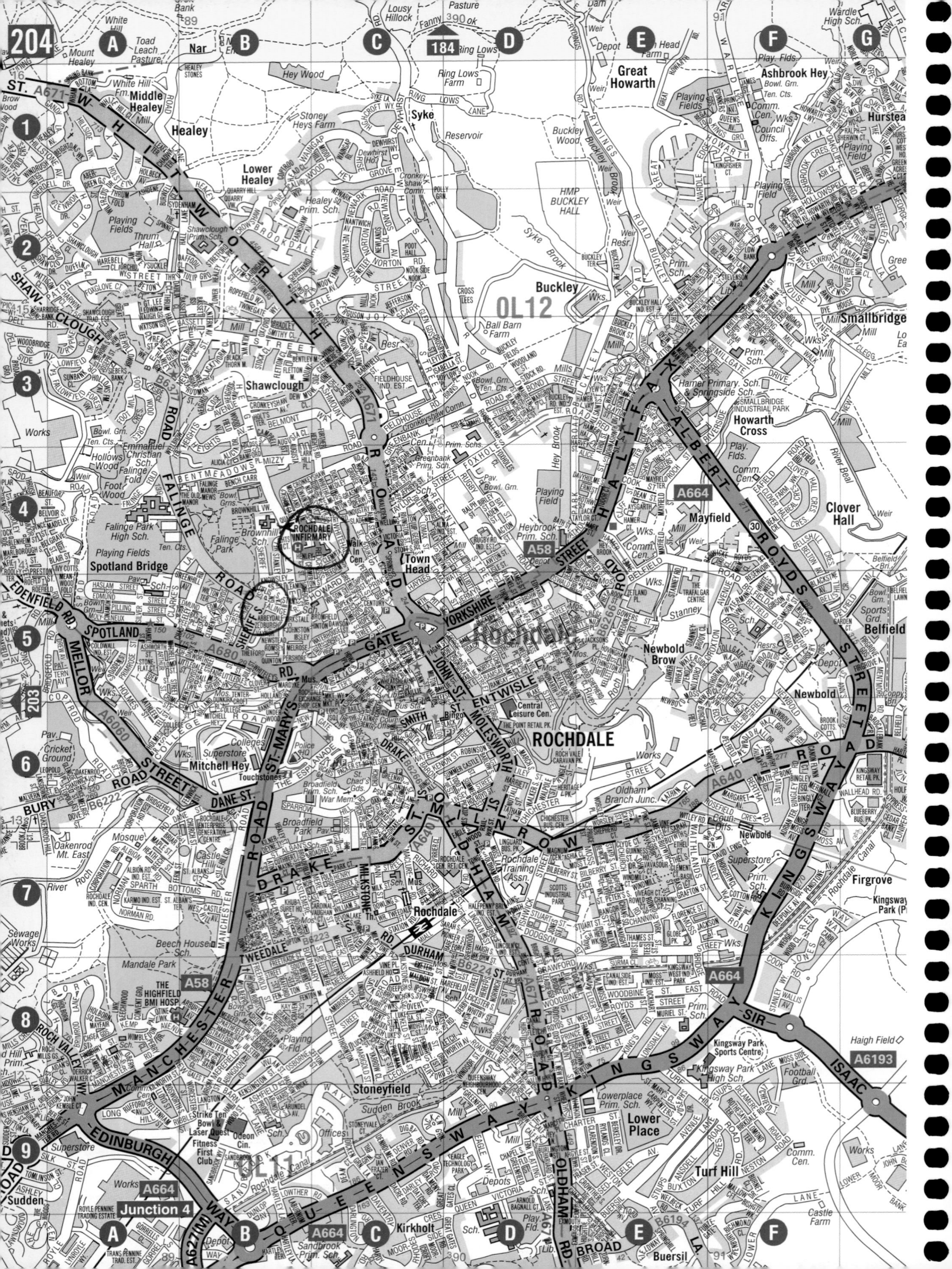

A
B
C
D
E
F
G
184
203
1
2
3
4
5
6
7
8
9
Mount Healey
Toad Leach Pasture
Middle Healey
Healey
Lower Healey
Hey Wood
Stoney Heys Farm
Syke
Reservoir
Ring Lows Farm
Great Howarth
Ashbrook Hey
Buckley Wood
HMP BUCKLEY HALL
Buckley
OL12
Shawclough
Smallbridge
Playing Fields
Thrum Hall
Emmanuel Christian Sch.
Hollows Wood
Falinge Fold
Foot Wood
Falinge Park High Sch.
Falinge Park
Spotland Bridge
ROCHDALE INFIRMARY
Walk In Cen.
Town Head
Howarth Cross
Mayfield
Clover Hall
Newbold Brow
Rochdale
Belfield
Newbold
Central Leisure Cen.
ROCHDALE
Mitchell Hey
Touchstones
Police HQ
Broadfield Park
Oldham Branch Junc.
Oakenrod Mt. East
Castle Hill
Mandale Park
Beech House Sch.
THE HIGHFIELD BMI HOSP.
Rochdale
Stoneyfield
Kingsway Park Sports Centre
Kingsway Park High Sch.
Lower Place
Turf Hill
Firgrove
Sudden
Strike Ten Bowl & Laser Quest
Odeon Cin.
Fitness First Club
OL11
Kirkholt
Buersil
Castle Farm
Haigh Field
Junction 4
A671
A58
A680
A6060
A640
A664
A6193
A627(M)
B6222
B6266
B6223
B6224
B6194
B6377
SPOTLAND
EDENFIELD RD.
MELLOR
BURY ROAD
DANE ST.
MANCHESTER ROAD
ST. MARY'S GATE
YORKSHIRE STREET
HALIFAX ROAD
ALBERT ROYDS STREET
KINGSWAY
QUEENSWAY
EDINBURGH WAY
SIR ISAAC NEWTON WAY
OLDHAM RD
DRAKE ST.
MOLESWORTH ST.
ENTWISLE
MILKSTONE
TWEEDALE
DURHAM
OLDHAM ROAD
WHITWORTH ROAD
FALINGE ROAD
SHAWCLOUGH
ST. MARY'S

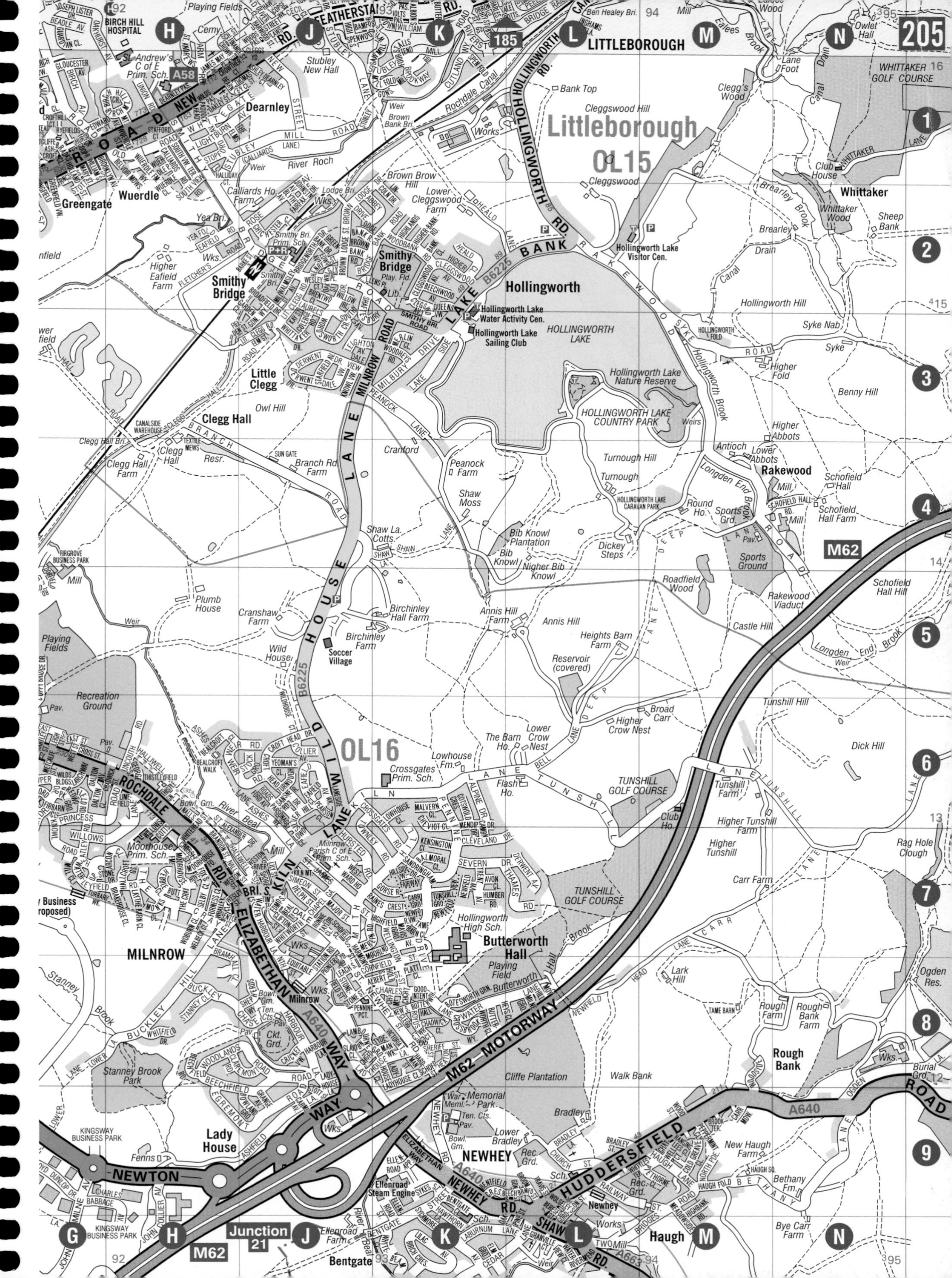
Littleborough
OL15
LITTLEBOROUGH
Birch Hill Hospital
Dearnley
Greengate
Wuerdle
Smithy Bridge
Little Clegg
Clegg Hall
Hollingworth
Hollingworth Lake
Hollingworth Lake Country Park
Hollingworth Lake Nature Reserve
Hollingworth Lake Visitor Cen.
Hollingworth Lake Water Activity Cen.
Hollingworth Lake Sailing Club
Rochdale Canal
River Roch
Whittaker
Whittaker Golf Course
Rakewood
Clegg's Wood
Cleggswood Hill
Brearley
Syke
Benny Hill
Turnough Hill
Bib Knowl Plantation
Annis Hill
Castle Hill
Tunshill Hill
Dick Hill
Tunshill Golf Course
OL16
Crossgates Prim. Sch.
Soccer Village
Recreation Ground
Playing Fields
MILNROW
Milnrow
Butterworth Hall
Hollingworth High Sch.
Cliffe Plantation
Walk Bank
Rough Bank
Ogden Res.
Stanney Brook Park
Lady House
Kingsway Business Park
NEWHEY
Newhey
Ellenroad Steam Engine
Bentgate
Haugh
Junction 21
M62 MOTORWAY
M62
A58
A640
A663
B6225
185
ROCHDALE RD.
ELIZABETHAN WAY
HUDDERSFIELD ROAD
NEWTON
HOLLINGWORTH RD.
LAKE BANK
MILNROW ROAD
HOUSE LANE
WILD HOUSE LANE
KILN LANE
TUNSHILL LANE
NEW ROAD
92
93
94
95
1
2
3
4
5
6
7
8
9
G
H
J
K
L
M
N

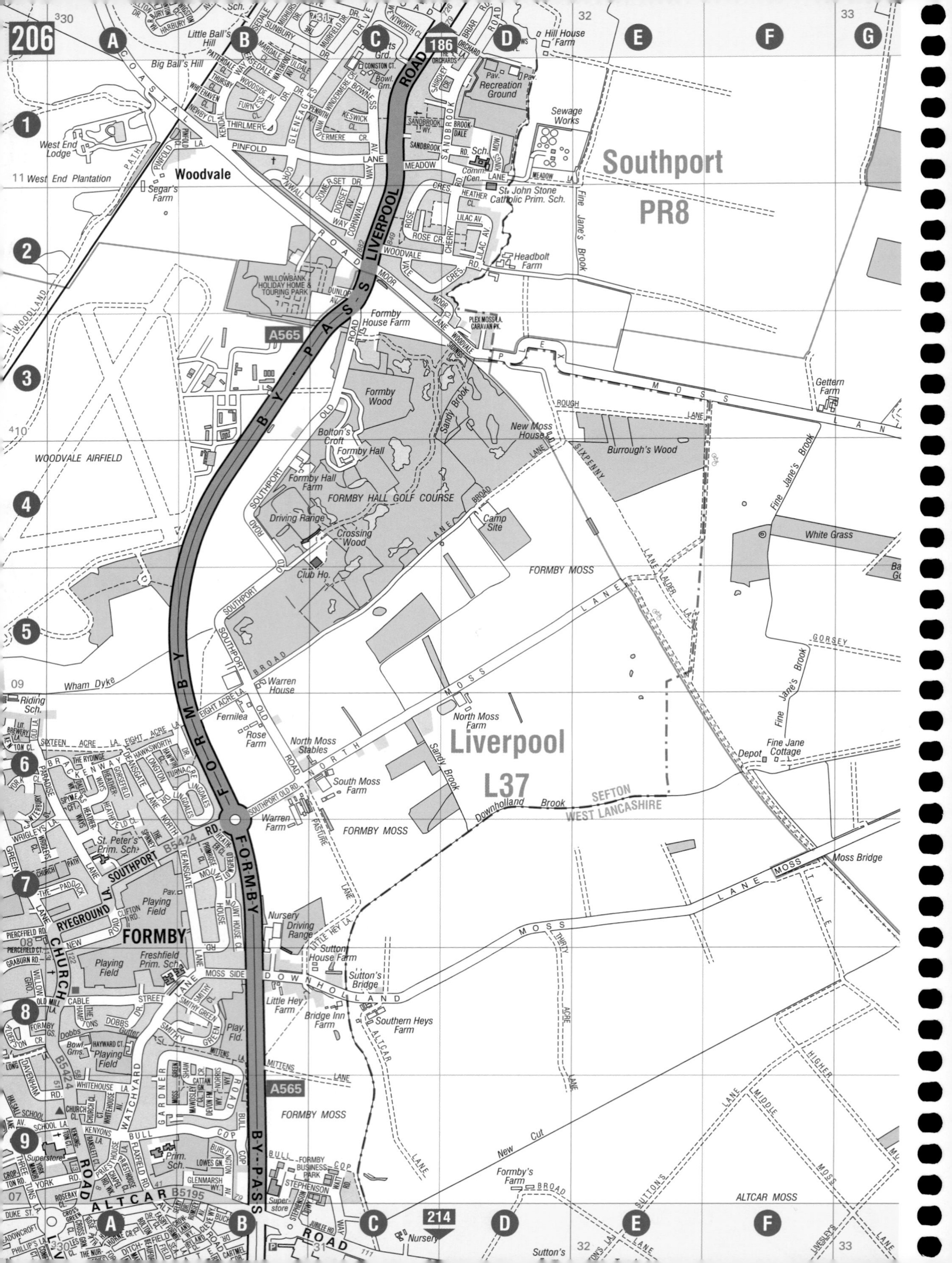

206
186
214
Southport
PR8
Liverpool
L37
Woodvale
FORMBY
Little Ball's Hill
Big Ball's Hill
West End Lodge
West End Plantation
Segar's Farm
Hill House Farm
Recreation Ground
Sewage Works
St. John Stone Catholic Prim. Sch.
Headbolt Farm
WILLOWBANK HOLIDAY HOME & TOURING PARK
Formby House Farm
PLEX MOSS LA. CARAVAN PK.
A565
LIVERPOOL ROAD
FORMBY BY-PASS
WOODVALE AIRFIELD
Formby Wood
Bolton's Croft
Formby Hall
Formby Hall Farm
FORMBY HALL GOLF COURSE
Driving Range
Crossing Wood
Club Ho.
New Moss House
Burrough's Wood
Camp Site
FORMBY MOSS
Gettern Farm
White Grass
Fine Jane's Brook
Sandy Brook
Wham Dyke
Warren House
Fernilea
Rose Farm
North Moss Farm
North Moss Stables
South Moss Farm
Warren Farm
Fine Jane Cottage
Depot
Downholland Brook
SEFTON
WEST LANCASHIRE
Moss Bridge
Riding Sch.
St. Peter's Prim. Sch.
Playing Field
Freshfield Prim. Sch.
Nursery Driving Range
Sutton House Farm
Sutton's Bridge
Little Hey Farm
Bridge Inn Farm
Southern Heys Farm
New Cut
Formby's Farm
ALTCAR MOSS
FORMBY BUSINESS PARK
Superstore
Nursery
B5424
B5195
A B C D E F G
1 2 3 4 5 6 7 8 9

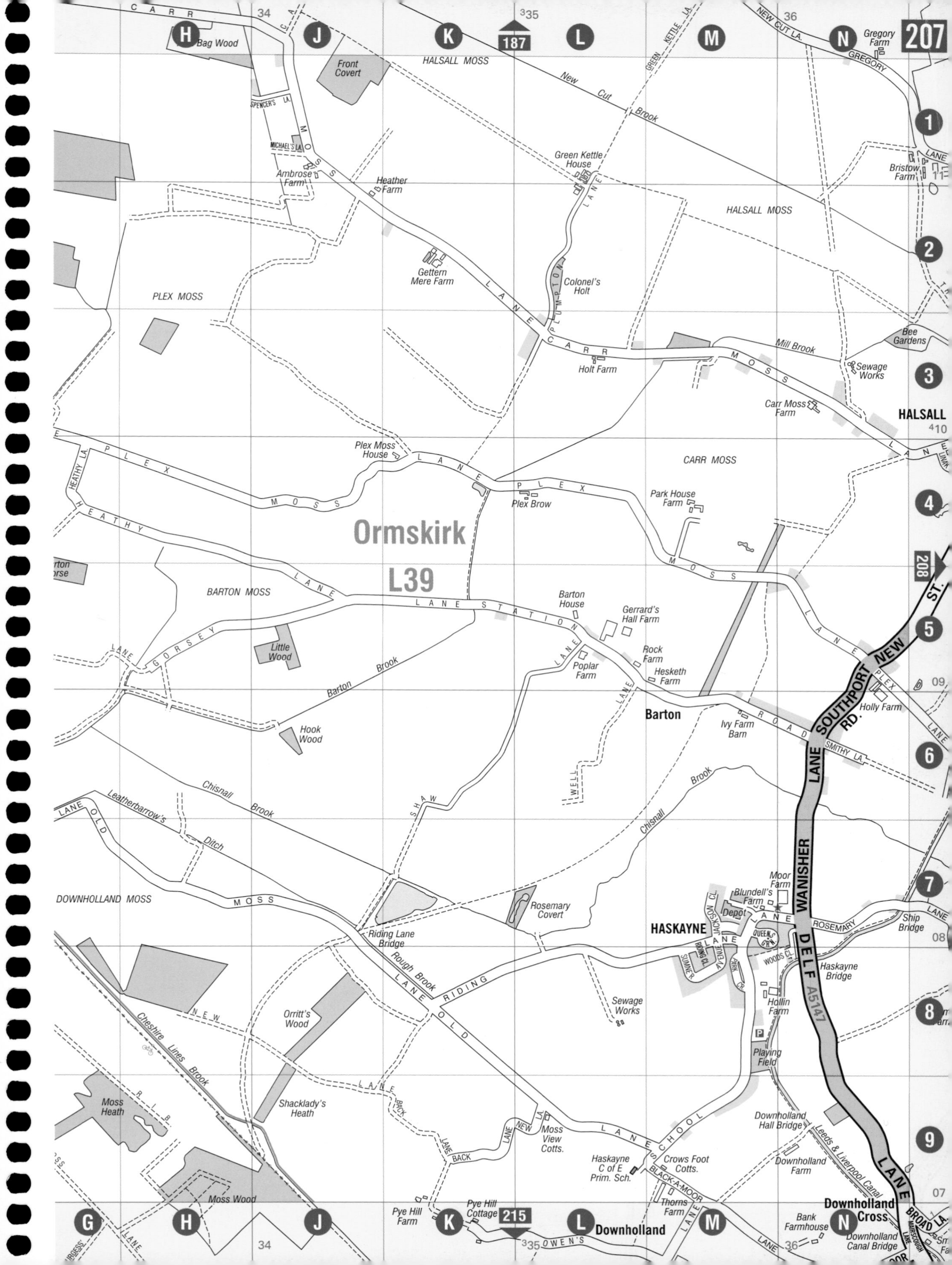

187
HALSALL MOSS
Front Covert
Bag Wood
New Cut Brook
Gregory Farm
Green Kettle House
Heather Farm
Ambrose Farm
Bristow Farm
Gettern Mere Farm
Colonel's Holt
PLEX MOSS
Holt Farm
Mill Brook
Bee Gardens
Sewage Works
Carr Moss Farm
HALSALL
CARR MOSS
Plex Moss House
Plex Brow
Park House Farm
Ormskirk
L39
BARTON MOSS
Barton House
Gerrard's Hall Farm
Little Wood
Rock Farm
Hesketh Farm
Poplar Farm
Barton Brook
Barton
Ivy Farm Barn
Holly Farm
Hook Wood
Chisnall Brook
Leatherbarrow's Ditch
DOWNHOLLAND MOSS
Moor Farm
Blundell's Farm
Depot
HASKAYNE
Rosemary Covert
Riding Lane Bridge
Rough Brook
Ship Bridge
Haskayne Bridge
Hollin Farm
Sewage Works
Orritt's Wood
Playing Field
Cheshire Lines Brook
Moss Heath
Shacklady's Heath
Downholland Hall Bridge
Moss View Cotts.
Haskayne C of E Prim. Sch.
Crows Foot Cotts.
Downholland Farm
Leeds & Liverpool Canal
Moss Wood
Thorns Farm
Pye Hill Farm
Pye Hill Cottage
Downholland Cross
Bank Farmhouse
Downholland Canal Bridge
Downholland
215
208
A5147

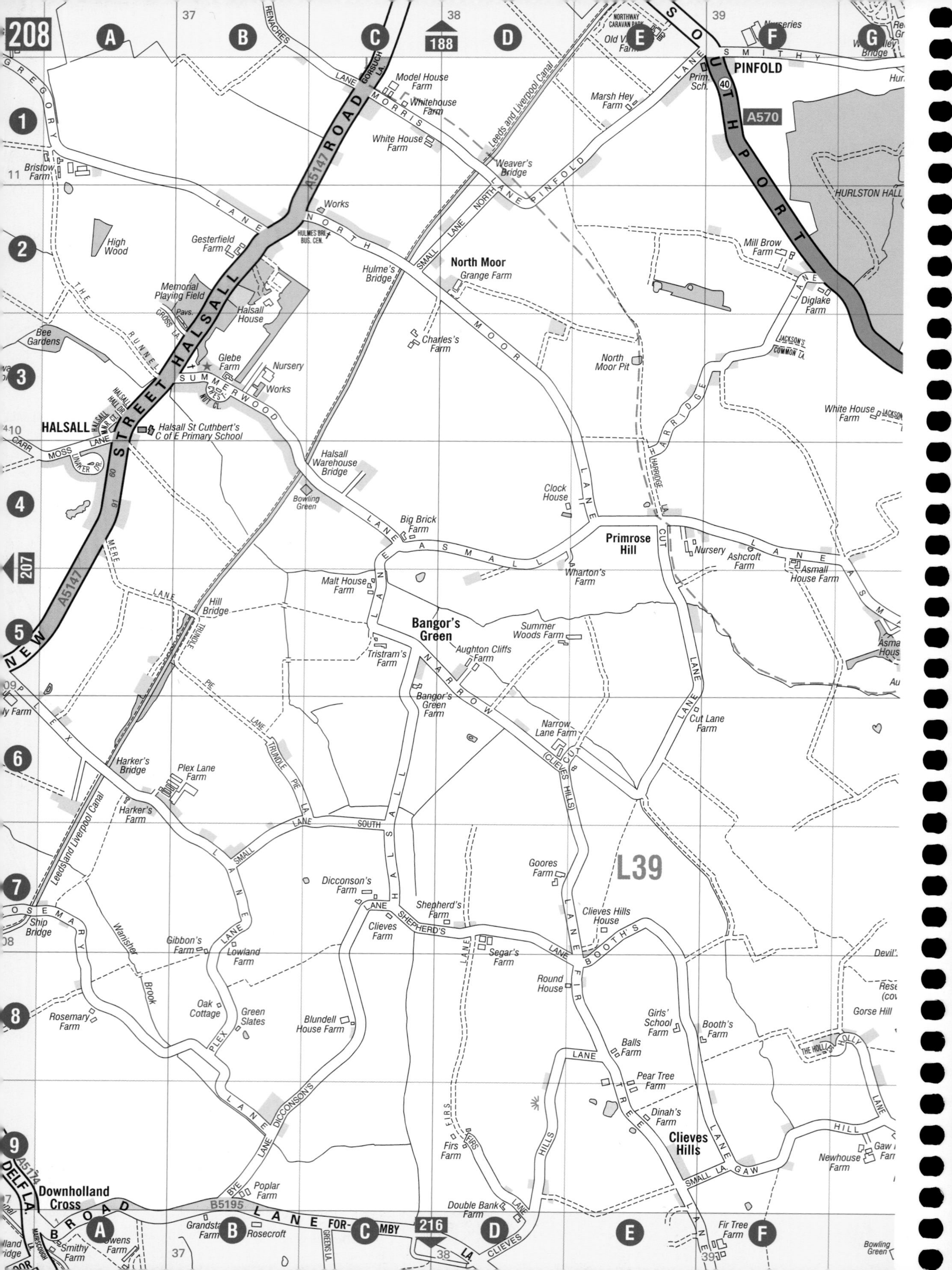

188
207
216
HALSALL
PINFOLD
North Moor
Primrose Hill
Bangor's Green
Clieves Hills
Downholland Cross
L39
A5147
A570
B5195
STREET
ROAD
SOUTHPORT
Model House Farm
Whitehouse Farm
White House Farm
Weaver's Bridge
Leeds and Liverpool Canal
Marsh Hey Farm
Prim. Sch.
Bristow Farm
High Wood
Gesterfield Farm
Works
Hulme's Bridge
Grange Farm
Memorial Playing Field
Halsall House
Bee Gardens
Glebe Farm
Nursery
Charles's Farm
North Moor Pit
Mill Brow Farm
Diglake Farm
HURLSTON HALL
White House Farm
Halsall St Cuthbert's C of E Primary School
Halsall Warehouse Bridge
Bowling Green
Clock House
Big Brick Farm
Wharton's Farm
Ashcroft Farm
Asmall House Farm
Malt House Farm
Hill Bridge
Summer Woods Farm
Aughton Cliffs Farm
Tristram's Farm
Bangor's Green Farm
Narrow Lane Farm
Cut Lane Farm
Harker's Bridge
Plex Lane Farm
Harker's Farm
Goores Farm
Dicconson's Farm
Shepherd's Farm
Clieves Farm
Clieves Hills House
Segar's Farm
Round House
Ship Bridge
Gibbon's Farm
Lowland Farm
Rosemary Farm
Oak Cottage
Green Slates
Blundell House Farm
Girls' School Farm
Booth's Farm
Balls Farm
Pear Tree Farm
Dinah's Farm
Firs Farm
Poplar Farm
Double Bank Farm
Newhouse Farm
Gorse Hill
Rosecroft
Fir Tree Farm
Smithy Farm
Wanisher Brook

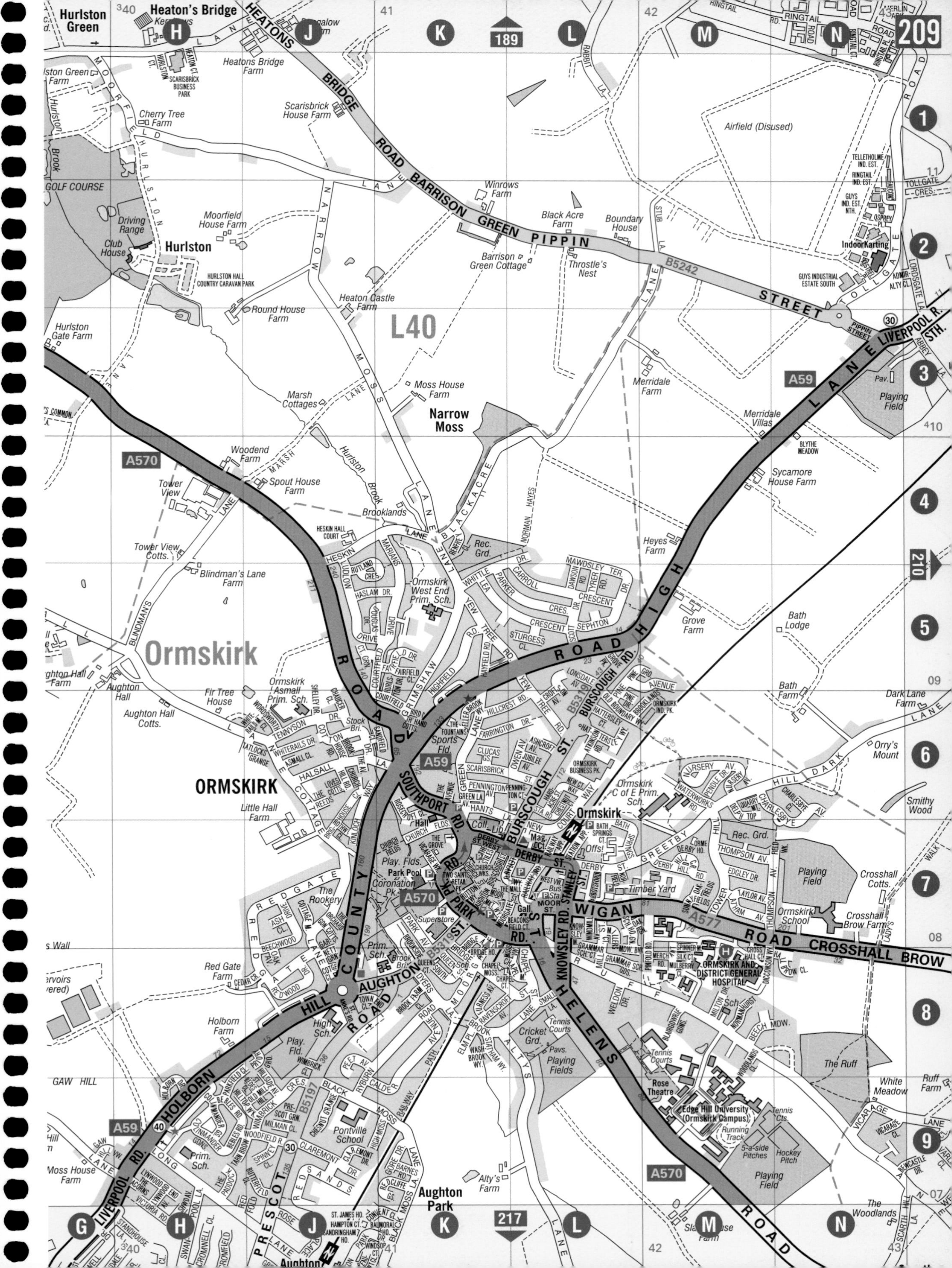
Hurlston Green
Heaton's Bridge
Heatons Bridge Farm
Scarisbrick Business Park
Scarisbrick House Farm
Cherry Tree Farm
Golf Course
Driving Range
Club House
Hurlston
Hurlston Hall Country Caravan Park
Moorfield House Farm
Round House Farm
Heaton Castle Farm
Hurlston Gate Farm
Winrows Farm
Black Acre Farm
Boundary House
Barrison Green Cottage
Throstle's Nest
Airfield (Disused)
Telletholme Ind. Est.
Ringtail Ind. Est.
Guys Ind. Est. Nth.
Indoor Karting
Guys Industrial Estate South
L40
Heatons Bridge Road
Barrison Green Pippin Street
B5242
Moss House Farm
Narrow Moss
Marsh Cottages
Merridale Farm
Merridale Villas
Playing Field
Woodend Farm
Spout House Farm
Tower View
Brooklands
Sycamore House Farm
Blythe Meadow
Heyes Farm
Tower View Cotts.
Blindman's Lane Farm
Heskin Hall Court
Rec. Grd.
Ormskirk West End Prim. Sch.
Grove Farm
Bath Lodge
Ormskirk
Aughton Hall
Aughton Hall Farm
Aughton Hall Cotts.
Fir Tree House
Ormskirk Asmall Prim. Sch.
Bath Farm
Dark Lane Farm
Orry's Mount
Smithy Wood
High Lane
County Road
Southport Rd.
Burscough St.
Burscough Rd.
Wigan Road
Crosshall Brow
A59
A570
A577
B5319
B5197
ORMSKIRK
Little Hall Farm
Ormskirk C of E Prim. Sch.
Ormskirk Business Pk.
Sports Fld.
Park Pool
Coronation Pk.
Play. Flds.
Superstore
Timber Yard
Playing Field
Crosshall Cotts.
Ormskirk School
Crosshall Brow Farm
The Rookery
Red Gate Farm
Reservoirs (covered)
Holborn Farm
Ormskirk & District General Hospital
Knowsley Rd.
St. Helens Road
Cricket Grd.
Tennis Courts
Playing Fields
The Ruff
White Meadow
Ruff Farm
Rose Theatre
Edge Hill University (Ormskirk Campus)
Running Track
5-a-side Pitches
Hockey Pitch
Gaw Hill
Holborn Hill
Liverpool Rd.
Pontville School
High Sch.
Prim. Sch.
Moss House Farm
Alty's Farm
Aughton Park
Slack House Farm
The Woodlands
Vicarage Lane
Prescot Road
Aughton
189
210
217

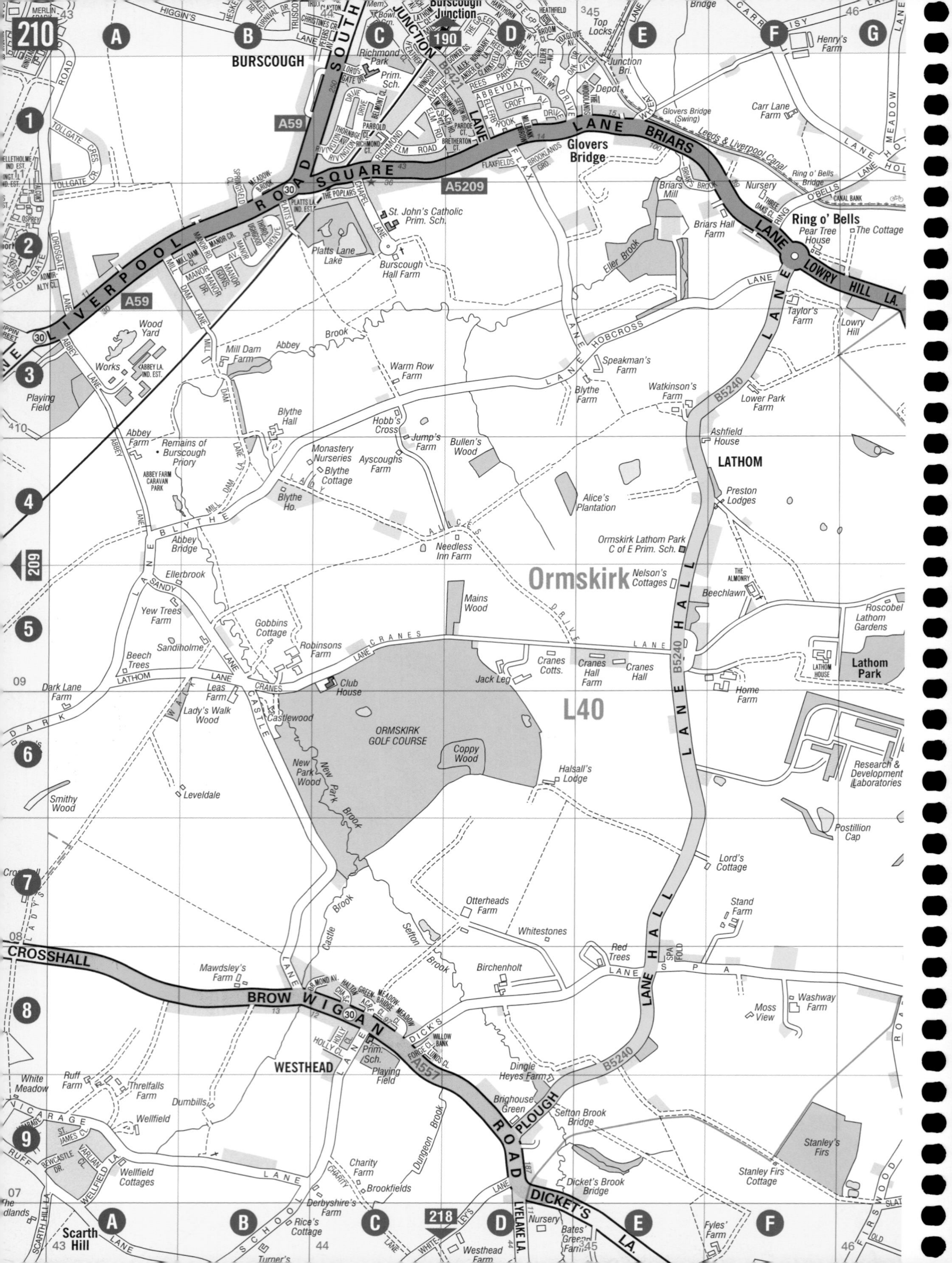
BURSCOUGH
Burscough Junction
190
Top Locks
Junction Bri.
Henry's Farm
Richmond Park
Prim. Sch.
A59
A5209
B5421
LIVERPOOL ROAD
SQUARE
LANE
BRIARS LANE
Glovers Bridge
Glovers Bridge (Swing)
Leeds & Liverpool Canal
Carr Lane Farm
Ring o' Bells Bridge
Ring o' Bells
Pear Tree House
The Cottage
Nursery
Briars Mill
Briars Hall Farm
St. John's Catholic Prim. Sch.
Platts Lane Lake
Burscough Hall Farm
LOWRY HILL LA.
Taylor's Farm
Lowry Hill
Wood Yard
Works
ABBEY LA. IND. EST.
Playing Field
Mill Dam Farm
Abbey Brook
Warm Row Farm
HOBCROSS LANE
Speakman's Farm
Blythe Farm
Watkinson's Farm
B5240
Lower Park Farm
Ashfield House
LATHOM
Blythe Hall
Hobb's Cross
Jump's Farm
Bullen's Wood
Abbey Farm
Remains of Burscough Priory
ABBEY FARM CARAVAN PARK
Monastery Nurseries
Blythe Cottage
Ayscoughs Farm
Blythe Ho.
Alice's Plantation
Preston Lodges
BLYTHE LANE
Abbey Bridge
ALICE'S DRIVE
Needless Inn Farm
Ormskirk Lathom Park C of E Prim. Sch.
Ormskirk
Nelson's Cottages
THE ALMONRY
Beechlawn
Ellerbrook
SANDY LANE
Yew Trees Farm
Mains Wood
Roscobel
Lathom Gardens
Gobbins Cottage
Robinsons Farm
Sandiholme
CRANES LANE
Beech Trees
Cranes Cotts.
Cranes Hall Farm
Cranes Hall
Jack Leg
LATHOM HOUSE
Lathom Park
Home Farm
Dark Lane Farm
LATHOM LANE
Leas Farm
Club House
Lady's Walk Wood
Castlewood
CASTLE LANE
L40
ORMSKIRK GOLF COURSE
Coppy Wood
New Park Wood
New Park Brook
Halsall's Lodge
LANE HALL LANE
Research & Development Laboratories
Leveldale
Smithy Wood
Postillion Cap
Lord's Cottage
Otterheads Farm
Stand Farm
Castle Brook
Sefton Brook
Whitestones
Red Trees
SPA LANE
SPA FOLD
CROSSHALL BROW
WIGAN ROAD
Mawdsley's Farm
Birchenholt
Washway Farm
Moss View
A557
WESTHEAD
Prim. Sch.
Playing Field
DICK'S LANE
WILLOW BANK
Dingle Heyes Farm
Brighouse Green
PLOUGH LANE
Sefton Brook Bridge
White Meadow
Ruff Farm
Threlfalls Farm
Dumbills
Wellfield
VICARAGE LANE
Dungeon Brook
Stanley's Firs
Wellfield Cottages
Charity Farm
Brookfields
Dicket's Brook Bridge
DICKET'S LA.
Stanley Firs Cottage
Derbyshire's Farm
Rice's Cottage
Scarth Hill
SCHOOL LANE
218
LYELAKE LA.
Nursery
Bates' Green Farm
Fyles' Farm
Westhead Farm
Turner's
209
A B C D E F G
1 2 3 4 5 6 7 8 9
43 44 345 46
410 09 08 07

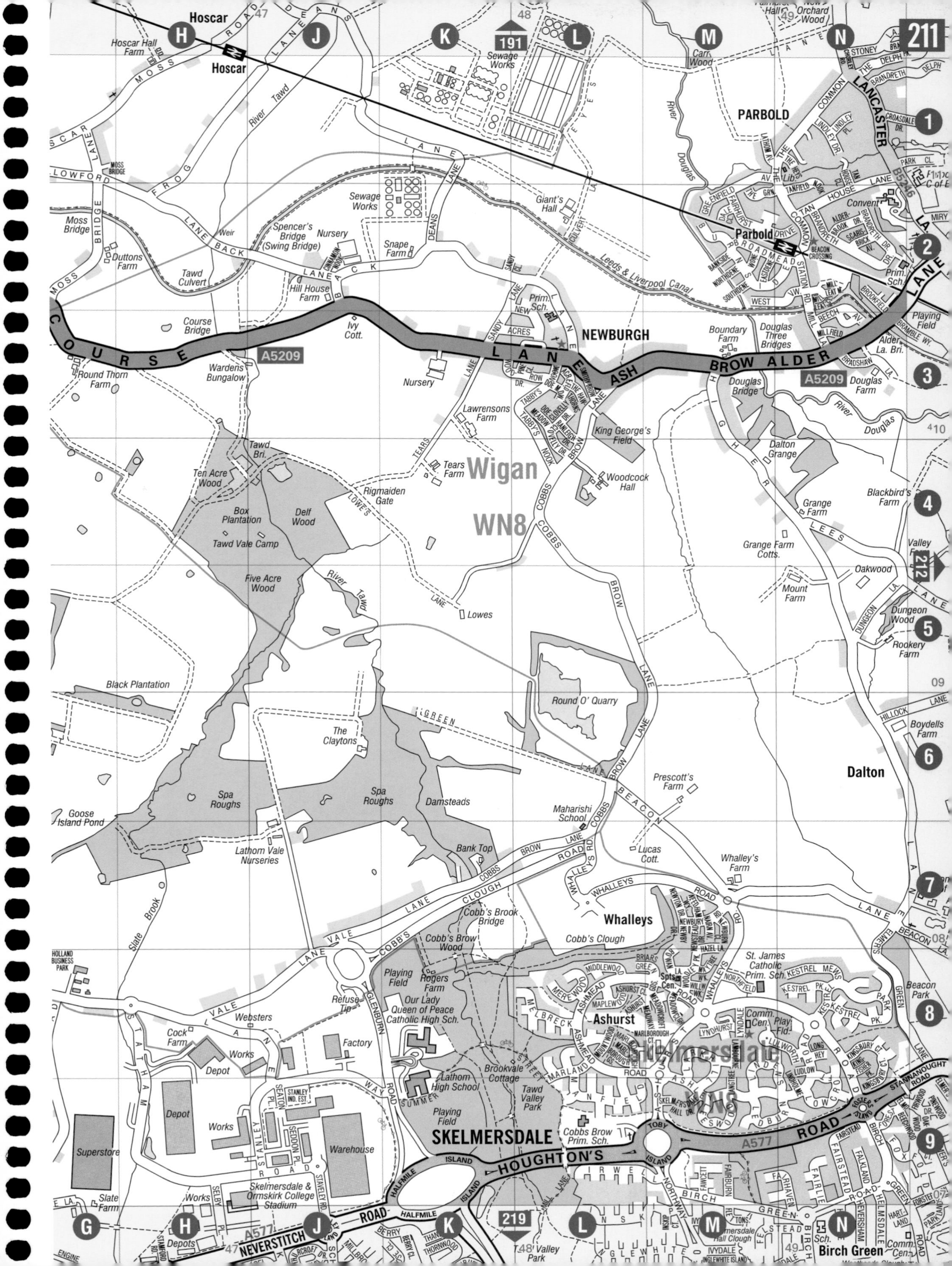
Hoscar
Hoscar Hall Farm
Sewage Works
Parbold
Parbold
Newburgh
Wigan
WN8
Course Lane
A5209
Ash Brow
Alder Lane
Leeds & Liverpool Canal
River Douglas
River Tawd
Spencer's Bridge (Swing Bridge)
Giant's Hall
Moss Bridge
Duttons Farm
Tawd Culvert
Hill House Farm
Course Bridge
Ivy Cott.
Wardens Bungalow
Round Thorn Farm
Nursery
Lawrensons Farm
King George's Field
Tears Farm
Woodcock Hall
Rigmaiden Gate
Ten Acre Wood
Box Plantation
Delf Wood
Tawd Vale Camp
Five Acre Wood
Lowes
Round O' Quarry
Black Plantation
The Claytons
Spa Roughs
Damsteads
Goose Island Pond
Lathom Vale Nurseries
Bank Top
Maharishi School
Prescott's Farm
Lucas Cott.
Whalley's Farm
Douglas Bridge
Douglas Farm
Dalton Grange
Grange Farm
Grange Farm Cotts.
Mount Farm
Oakwood
Dungeon Wood
Rookery Farm
Blackbird's Farm
Boydells Farm
Dalton
Beacon Park
Whalleys
Cobb's Clough
Cobb's Brook Bridge
Cobb's Brow Wood
Playing Field
Rogers Farm
Our Lady Queen of Peace Catholic High Sch.
Refuse Tip
Webster
Cock Farm
Works
Depot
Factory
Lathom High School
Brookvale Cottage
Tawd Valley Park
Skelmersdale
Ashurst
St. James Catholic Prim. Sch.
Cobbs Brow Prim. Sch.
Superstore
Warehouse
Skelmersdale & Ormskirk College Stadium
Slate Farm
Houghton's Road
A577
Neverstitch Road
Birch Green
Holland Business Park
Boundary Farm
Douglas Three Bridges
191
212
219
210
G H J K L M N
1 2 3 4 5 6 7 8 9

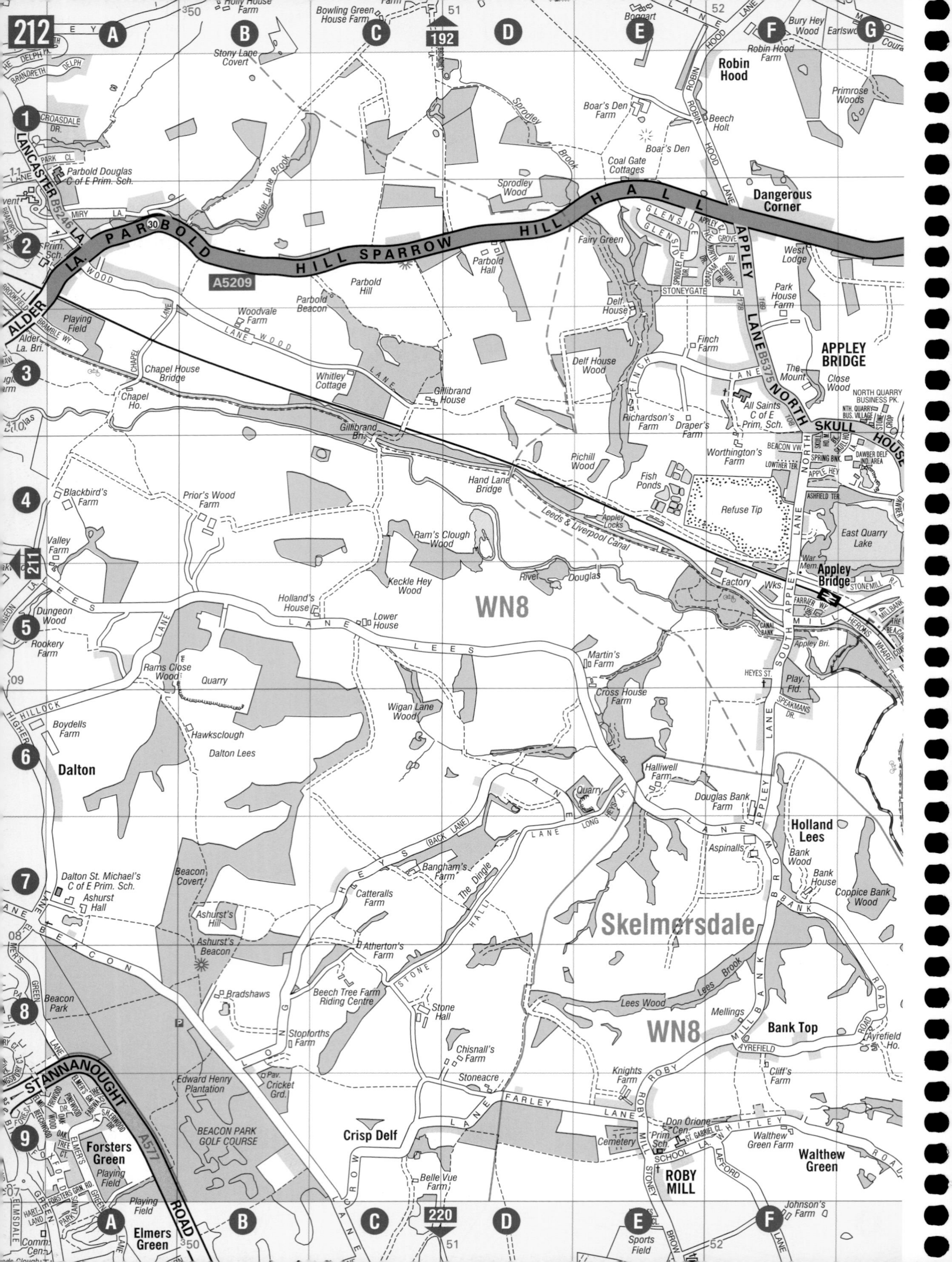
Parbold Douglas C of E Prim. Sch.
PARBOLD HILL
SPARROW HILL
HALL
A5209
Dangerous Corner
Robin Hood
Boar's Den
Appley Bridge
APPLEY BRIDGE
Leeds & Liverpool Canal
Refuse Tip
River Douglas
WN8
Dalton
Holland Lees
Skelmersdale
WN8
Bank Top
Crisp Delf
Forsters Green
Elmers Green
ROBY MILL
Walthew Green
BEACON PARK GOLF COURSE
STANNANOUGHT ROAD
A577
Dalton St. Michael's C of E Prim. Sch.
All Saints C of E Prim. Sch.
East Quarry Lake
Quarry
Hand Lane Bridge
Chapel House Bridge
Beacon Park

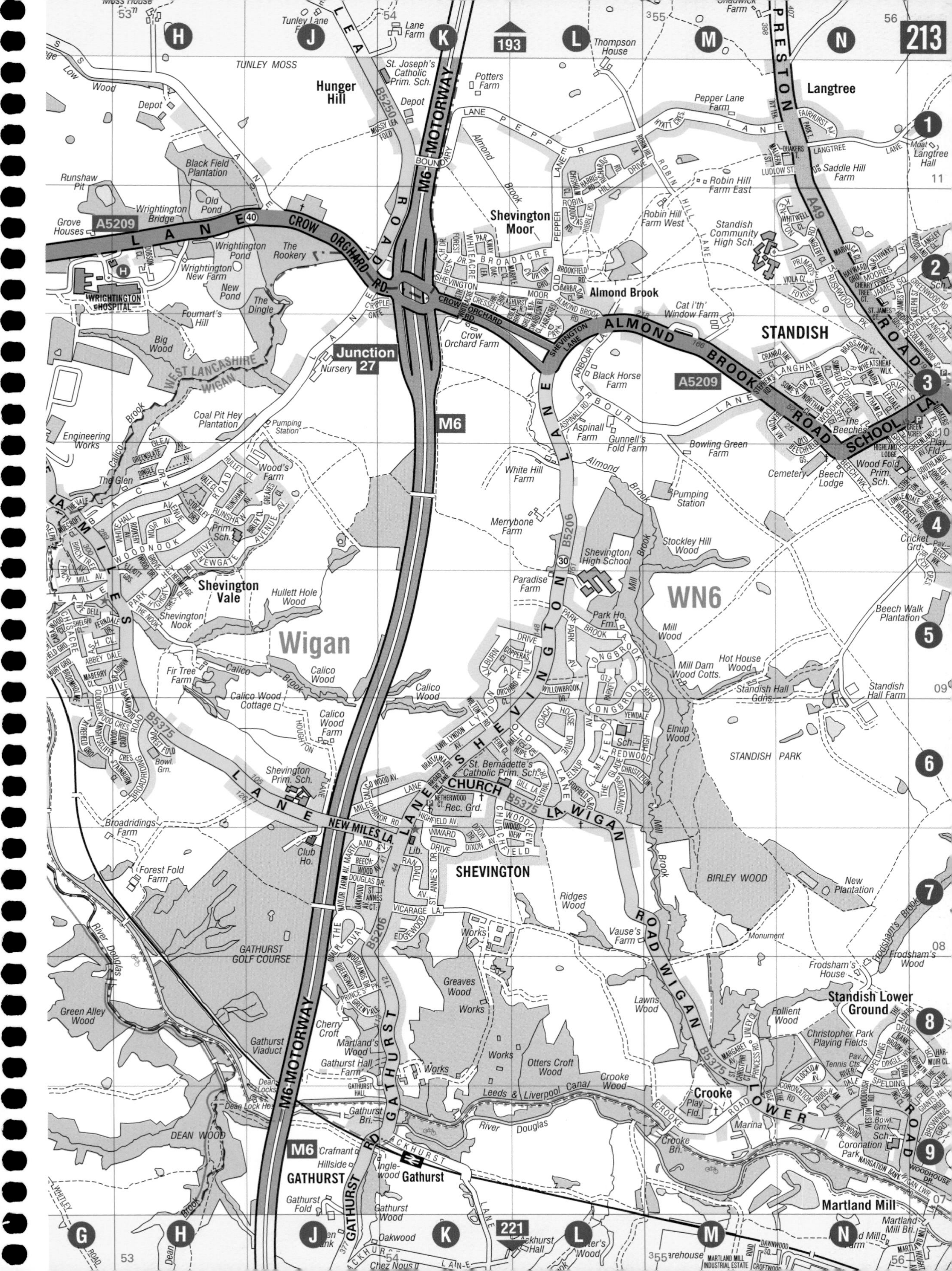
193
221
H
J
K
L
M
N
G
53
54
55
56
1
2
3
4
5
6
7
8
9
11
10
09
08
07
TUNLEY MOSS
Tunley Lane Farm
Lane Farm
St. Joseph's Catholic Prim. Sch.
Hunger Hill
Potters Farm
Thompson House
Langtree
Pepper Lane Farm
PEPPER LANE
PRESTON ROAD
A49
Langtree Hall
Saddle Hill Farm
Robin Hill Farm East
Robin Hill Farm West
Standish Community High Sch.
Depot
Black Field Plantation
Runshaw Pit
Old Pond
Wrightington Bridge
Grove Houses
A5209
CROW ORCHARD ROAD
LANE
Wrightington Pond
Wrightington New Farm
New Pond
The Rookery
The Dingle
WRIGHTINGTON HOSPITAL
Foumart's Hill
Big Wood
WEST LANCASHIRE
WIGAN
M6 MOTORWAY
B5250
Shevington Moor
Almond Brook
Cat i'th' Window Farm
STANDISH
ALMOND BROOK ROAD
SCHOOL LA.
Crow Orchard Farm
Junction 27
Nursery
M6
Black Horse Farm
Aspinall Farm
Gunnell's Fold Farm
Bowling Green Farm
The Beeches
Wood Fold Prim. Sch.
Cemetery
Beech Lodge
Coal Pit Hey Plantation
Pumping Station
Engineering Works
Calico Brook
The Glen
Wood's Farm
White Hill Farm
Merrybone Farm
Shevington High School
Stockley Hill Wood
Cricket Grd.
Paradise Farm
B5206
WN6
Beech Walk Plantation
Shevington Vale
Hullett Hole Wood
Shevington Nook
Wigan
Park Ho. Fm.
Mill Wood
Mill Dam Wood Cotts.
Hot House Wood
Standish Hall Gdns.
Standish Hall Farm
Fir Tree Farm
Calico Wood
Calico Wood Cottage
Calico Wood Farm
Elnup Wood
STANDISH PARK
B5375
St. Bernadette's Catholic Prim. Sch.
Shevington Prim. Sch.
CHURCH LA.
WIGAN
NEW MILES LA.
Rec. Grd.
Broadridings Farm
Club Ho.
Lib.
SHEVINGTON
Forest Fold Farm
BIRLEY WOOD
New Plantation
Ridges Wood
Vause's Farm
Monument
GATHURST GOLF COURSE
River Douglas
Greaves Wood
Works
Frodsham's House
Frodsham's Wood
Standish Lower Ground
Green Alley Wood
Cherry Croft
Lawns Wood
Follient Wood
Christopher Park Playing Fields
Gathurst Viaduct
Martland's Wood
Gathurst Hall Farm
Otters Croft Wood
Crooke Wood
Dean Locks
Leeds & Liverpool Canal
Crooke
Dean Lock Ho.
Gathurst Bri.
WIGAN ROAD
LOWER ROAD
Marina
DEAN WOOD
Crooke Bri.
Coronation Park
Crafnant
Hillside
GATHURST
Gathurst
Gathurst Fold
Gathurst Wood
Oakwood
Martland Mill
Martland Mill Bri.
GATHURST RD
MARTLAND MILL INDUSTRIAL ESTATE

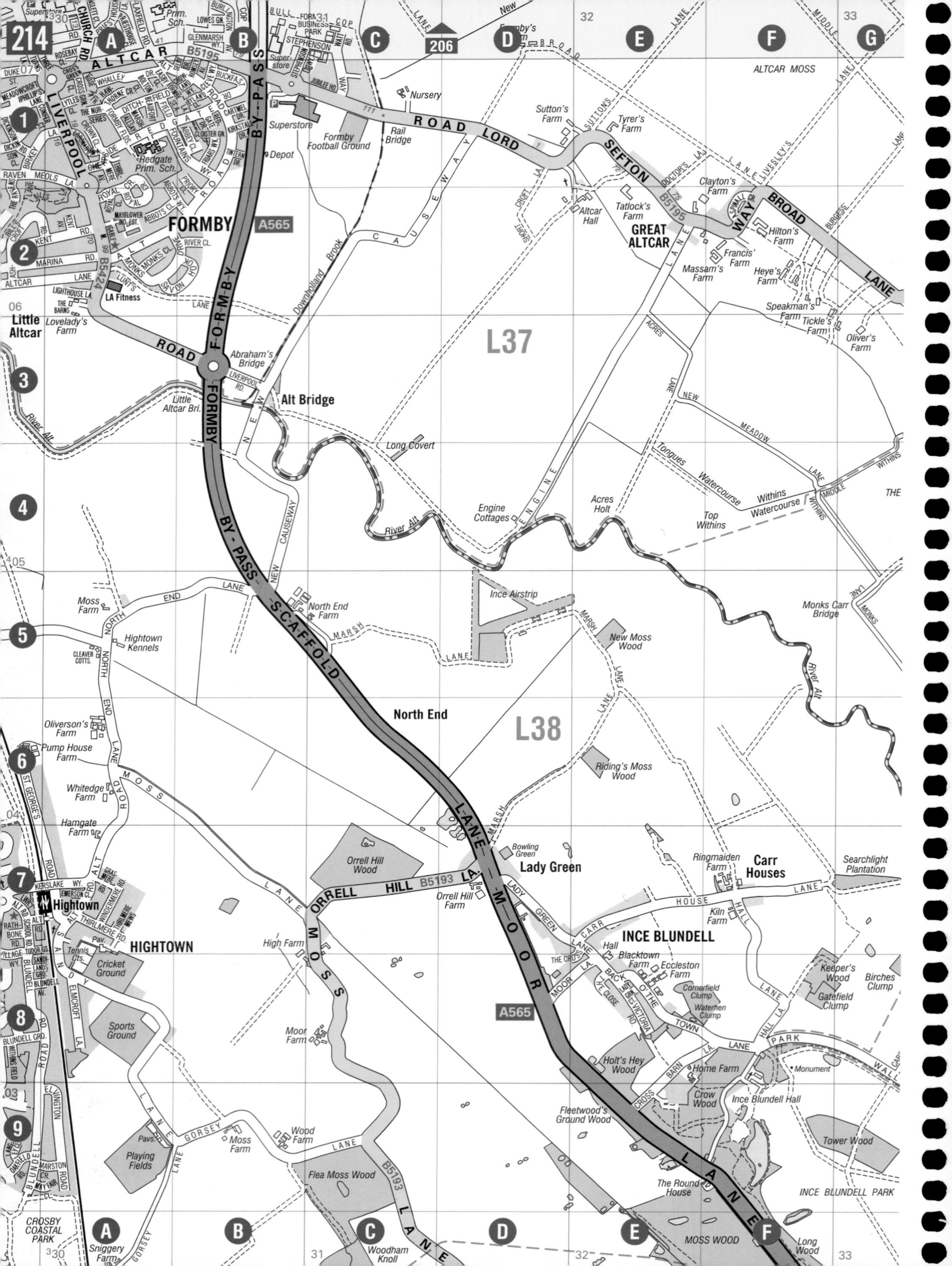
206
FORMBY
GREAT ALTCAR
L37
L38
Little Altcar
Alt Bridge
North End
Lady Green
Carr Houses
INCE BLUNDELL
Hightown
HIGHTOWN
ALTCAR MOSS
FORMBY BY-PASS
A565
B5195
B5193
SEFTON
BROAD LANE
River Alt
Long Covert
Ince Airstrip
North End Farm
New Moss Wood
Riding's Moss Wood
Orrell Hill Wood
Orrell Hill Farm
High Farm
Moor Farm
Moss Farm
Wood Farm
Flea Moss Wood
Woodham Knoll
Sniggery Farm
CROSBY COASTAL PARK
Cricket Ground
Sports Ground
Playing Fields
Holt's Hey Wood
Home Farm
Crow Wood
Ince Blundell Hall
Tower Wood
INCE BLUNDELL PARK
MOSS WOOD
Long Wood
The Round House
Fleetwood's Ground Wood
Keeper's Wood
Birches Clump
Gatefield Clump
Searchlight Plantation
Ringmaiden Farm
Kiln Farm
Blacktown Farm
Eccleston Farm
Monks Carr Bridge
Top Withins
Withins Watercourse
Tongues Watercourse
Engine Cottages
Acres Holt
Altcar Hall
Tatlock's Farm
Clayton's Farm
Hilton's Farm
Francis' Farm
Massam's Farm
Heye's Farm
Speakman's Farm
Tickle's Farm
Oliver's Farm
Sutton's Farm
Tyrer's Farm
Nursery
Rail Bridge
Formby Football Ground
Superstore
Depot
Redgate Prim. Sch.
LA Fitness
Lovelady's Farm
Abraham's Bridge
Little Altcar Bri.
Moss Farm
Hightown Kennels
Oliverson's Farm
Pump House Farm
Whitedge Farm
Hamgate Farm
Bowling Green
A B C D E F G
1 2 3 4 5 6 7 8 9
30 31 32 33

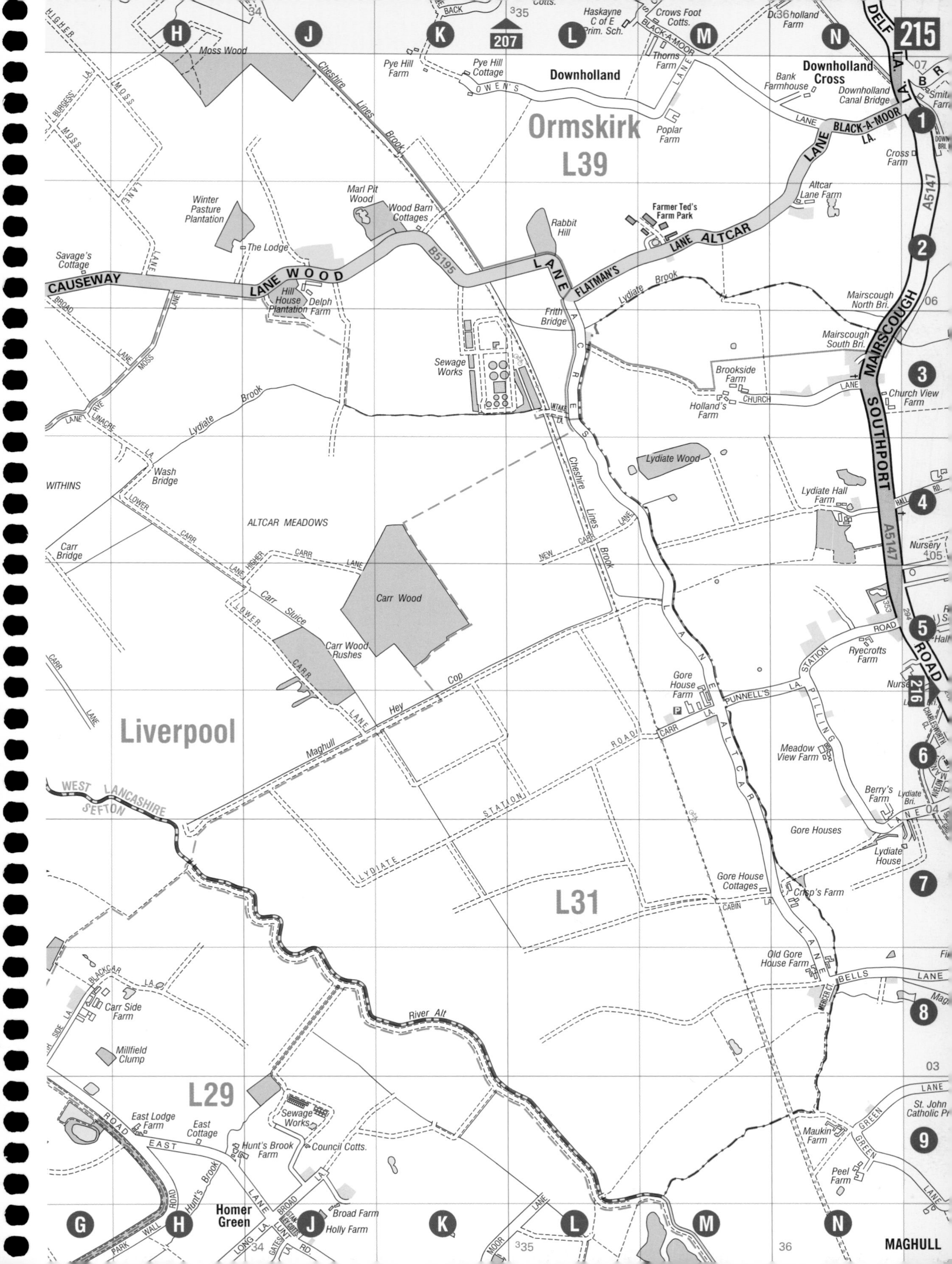
207
216
H
J
K
L
M
N
G
1
2
3
4
5
6
7
8
9
34
35
36
07
06
05
04
03
Moss Wood
Cheshire Lines Brook
Pye Hill Farm
Pye Hill Cottage
OWEN'S
Haskayne C of E Prim. Sch.
Crows Foot Cotts.
BLACK-A-MOOR
Thorns Farm
Downholland
Downholland Cross
Bank Farmhouse
Downholland Canal Bridge
Ormskirk
L39
Poplar Farm
LANE
BLACK-A-MOOR LA.
Cross Farm
A5147
Altcar Lane Farm
Farmer Ted's Farm Park
Rabbit Hill
ALTCAR
FLATMAN'S
Lydiate Brook
HIGHER
BURGESS' LA.
MOSS
Winter Pasture Plantation
Marl Pit Wood
Wood Barn Cottages
The Lodge
B5195
Savage's Cottage
CAUSEWAY
LANE WOOD
Hill House Plantation
Delph Farm
Frith Bridge
Mairscough North Bri.
MAIRSCOUGH
Mairscough South Bri.
BROAD LANE
MOSS
Sewage Works
Brookside Farm
CHURCH
Holland's Farm
Church View Farm
SOUTHPORT
RYE LANE
LINACRE
Lydiate Brook
Lydiate Wood
WITHINS
Wash Bridge
LOWER CARR
Lydiate Hall Farm
HALL RD.
ALTCAR MEADOWS
HIGHER CARR LANE
NEW CARR LANE
Carr Bridge
Nursery
Carr Wood
Carr Sluice
LOWER CARR LANE
Carr Wood Rushes
STATION ROAD
Ryecrofts Farm
Gore House Farm
PUNNELL'S LA.
PILLING
CARR LA.
ROAD
Hey Cop
Maghull
Liverpool
Meadow View Farm
WEST LANCASHIRE
SEFTON
STATION
Berry's Farm
Lydiate Bri.
Gore Houses
Lydiate House
LYDIATE
Gore House Cottages
Crisp's Farm
CABIN LA.
L31
Old Gore House Farm
BELLS LANE
BLACKCAR LA.
Carr Side Farm
River Alt
Millfield Clump
L29
East Lodge Farm
East Cottage
EAST LANE
Sewage Works
Hunt's Brook Farm
Council Cotts.
Hunt's Brook
Maukin Farm
GREEN
St. John Catholic Pr
Peel Farm
Homer Green
Broad Farm
Holly Farm
PARK WALL ROAD
LONG LA.
MOOR LANE
MAGHULL

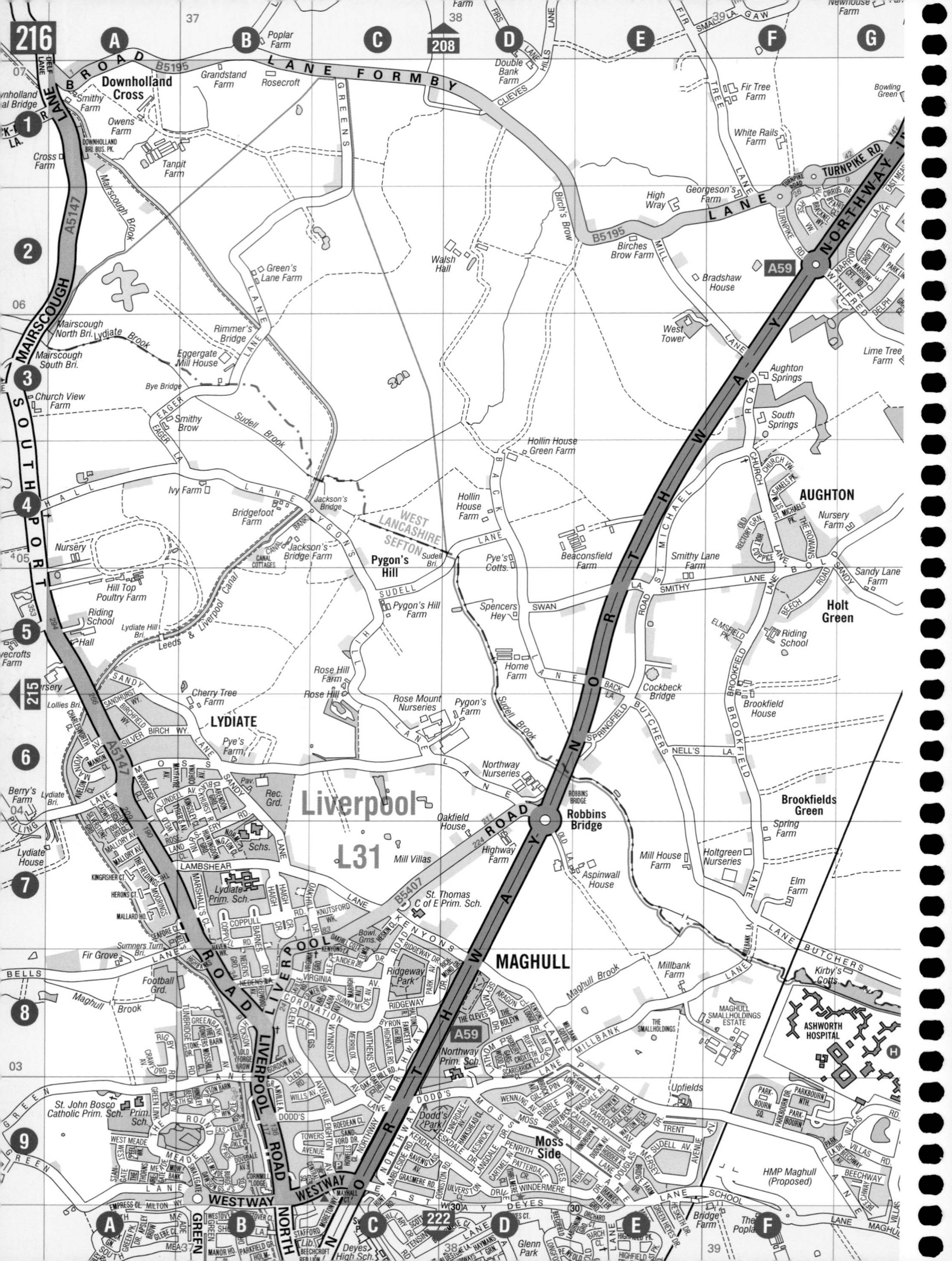

A
B
C
D
E
F
G
1
2
3
4
5
6
7
8
9
37
38
39
07
06
05
04
03
208
215
222
Poplar Farm
Grandstand Farm
Rosecroft
Downholland Cross
Smithy Farm
Owens Farm
Downholland Bri. Bus. Pk.
Cross Farm
Tanpit Farm
Mairscough Brook
BROAD LANE FORMBY
B5195
Double Bank Farm
CLIEVES HILLS
Fir Tree Farm
White Rails Farm
Bowling Green
TURNPIKE RD.
High Wray
Georgeson's Farm
Birch's Brow
Birches Brow Farm
Bradshaw House
Walsh Hall
Green's Lane Farm
GREENS LANE
NORTHWAY
A59
A5147
MAIRSCOUGH LANE
Mairscough North Bri.
Lydiate Brook
Mairscough South Bri.
Rimmer's Bridge
Eggergate Mill House
West Tower
Lime Tree Farm
Aughton Springs
South Springs
Bye Bridge
Church View Farm
Smithy Brow
EAGER LA.
Sudell Brook
Hollin House Green Farm
SOUTHPORT
HALL LANE
Ivy Farm
Bridgefoot Farm
Jackson's Bridge
Jackson's Bridge Farm
Canal Cottages
WEST LANCASHIRE
SEFTON
Hollin House Farm
BACK LANE
Beaconsfield Farm
AUGHTON
Nursery Farm
ST. MICHAEL ROAD
Nursery
Pygon's Hill
Sudell Bri.
Pye's Cotts.
Smithy Lane Farm
SMITHY LANE
BOLD LANE
Sandy Lane Farm
Hill Top Poultry Farm
SUDELL LANE
Pygon's Hill Farm
Spencers Hey
SWAN LA.
Holt Green
Riding School
Lydiate Hill Bri.
Leeds & Liverpool Canal
Hall
Rose Hill Farm
Rose Hill
Home Farm
Cockbeck Bridge
BROOKFIELD LANE
Cherry Tree Farm
Rose Mount Nurseries
Pygon's Farm
Brookfield House
SANDY LANE
LYDIATE
Pye's Farm
BIRCH WY.
SPRINGFIELD
BUTCHERS LANE
NELL'S LA.
Northway Nurseries
Lollies Bri.
MOSS LANE
Rec. Grd.
Liverpool
L31
Robbins Bridge
Brookfields Green
Berry's Farm
Lydiate Bri.
Oakfield House
Spring Farm
PILLING LANE
Lydiate House
Schs.
Mill Villas
Highway Farm
Aspinwall House
Mill House Farm
Holtgreen Nurseries
Elm Farm
LAMBSHEAR LANE
Lydiate Prim. Sch.
B5407
St. Thomas C of E Prim. Sch.
KENYONS LANE
Bowl. Grns.
Sumners Turn Bri.
Fir Grove
MAGHULL
Kirby's Cotts.
BELLS LANE
Football Grd.
Ridgeway Park
Maghull Brook
Millbank Farm
Maghull Smallholdings Estate
The Smallholdings
Ashworth Hospital
Maghull Brook
LIVERPOOL ROAD
CORONATION RD.
Northway Prim. Sch.
MILLBANK LANE
Upfields
PARK LANE
St. John Bosco Catholic Prim. Sch.
Prim. Sch.
GREEN LANE
Dodd's Park
DODD'S LANE
MOSS LANE
Moss Side
TRENT
SUDELL AV.
VILLAS RD.
HMP Maghull (Proposed)
WESTWAY
WINDERMERE
EAST WAY
DEYES LANE
SCHOOL LANE
Bridge Farm
The Poplars
Glenn Park
Deyes High Sch.
NORTH
MAGHULL

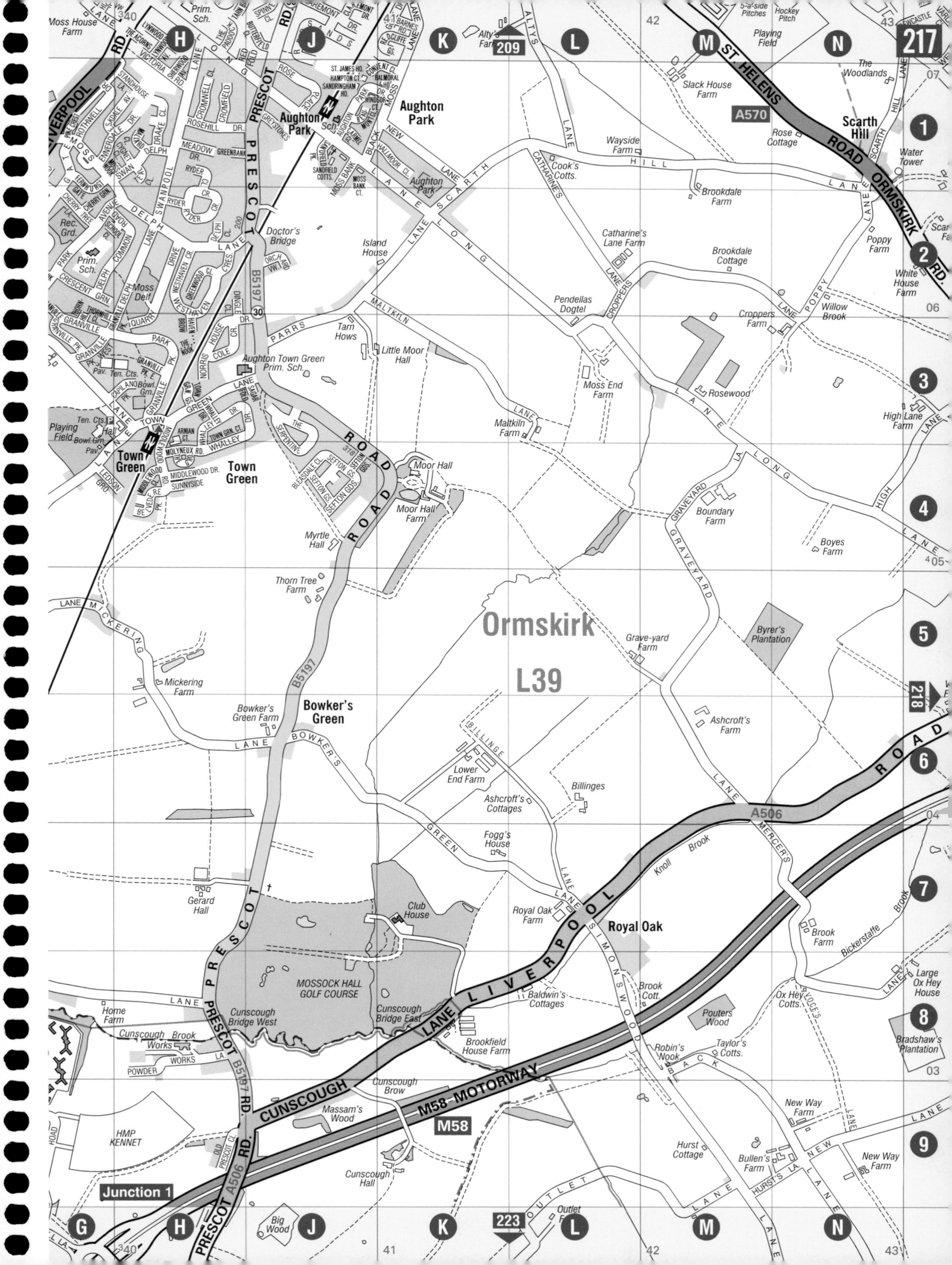

G
H
J
K
L
M
N
1
2
3
4
5
6
7
8
9
209
218
223
340
41
42
43
07
06
05
04
03
Moss House Farm
Prim. Sch.
Aughton Park
Aughton Park
Alty's Farm
ALTYS LANE
5-a-side Pitches
Hockey Pitch
Playing Field
ST. HELENS ROAD
A570
Slack House Farm
The Woodlands
Scarth Hill
Rose Cottage
Water Tower
SCARTH HILL LANE
Wayside Farm
Cook's Cotts.
CATHARINE'S LANE
Brookdale Farm
ORMSKIRK RD.
Poppy Farm
White House Farm
Catharine's Lane Farm
Brookdale Cottage
POPPY LANE
Willow Brook
Croppers Farm
CROPPERS LANE
Pendellas Dogtel
Doctor's Bridge
Island House
LONG LANE
LIVERPOOL RD.
PRESCOT RD.
B5197
MALTKILN LANE
PARRS LANE
Tarn Hows
Little Moor Hall
Aughton Town Green Prim. Sch.
Moss End Farm
Rosewood
High Lane Farm
HIGH LANE
Maltkiln Farm
Moor Hall
Moor Hall Farm
Playing Field
Town Green
Town Green
Rec. Grd.
Prim. Sch.
Moss Delf
Myrtle Hall
Boundary Farm
GRAVEYARD LA.
Boyes Farm
Thorn Tree Farm
Ormskirk
L39
Grave-yard Farm
Byrer's Plantation
MICKERING LANE
Mickering Farm
Bowker's Green Farm
Bowker's Green
BOWKER'S GREEN LANE
BILLINGE
Lower End Farm
Ashcroft's Farm
Ashcroft's Cottages
Billinges
A506
MERCER'S LANE
Fogg's House
Knoll Brook
Gerard Hall
Royal Oak Farm
Royal Oak
Club House
SIMONSWOOD LANE
Brook Farm
Bickerstaffe Brook
MOSSOCK HALL GOLF COURSE
Large Ox Hey House
Home Farm
Cunscough Bridge West
Cunscough Bridge East
Baldwin's Cottages
Brook Cott.
Ox Hey Cotts.
Pouters Wood
Bradshaw's Plantation
Cunscough Brook
Works
POWDER WORKS LA.
Brookfield House Farm
Robin's Nook
Taylor's Cotts.
BACK LANE
CUNSCOUGH LANE
M58 MOTORWAY
M58
Cunscough Brow
Massam's Wood
HMP KENNET
New Way Farm
New Way Farm
NEW LANE
Hurst Cottage
Bullen's Farm
HURST'S LA.
Cunscough Hall
OUTLET LANE
Outlet
Junction 1
Big Wood

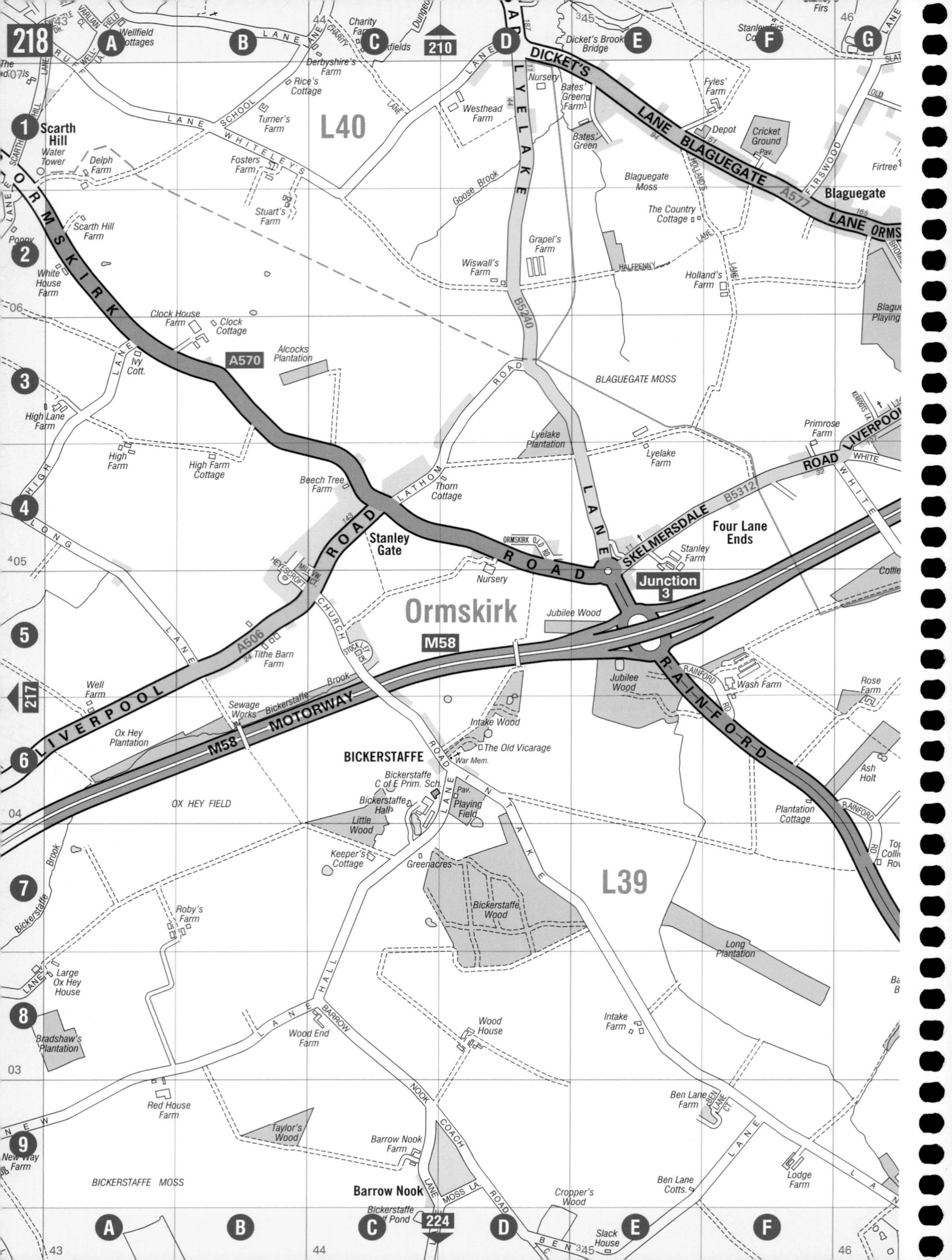

L40
L39
Ormskirk
Scarth Hill
Blaguegate
Four Lane Ends
Stanley Gate
BICKERSTAFFE
Barrow Nook
Junction 3
M58
A570
A506
A577
B5240
B5312
ORMSKIRK ROAD
LIVERPOOL ROAD
MOTORWAY
RAINFORD ROAD
SKELMERSDALE ROAD
LATHOM ROAD
DICKET'S LANE
BLAGUEGATE LANE
LYELAKE LANE
SCHOOL LANE
WHITELEY'S LANE
HIGH LANE
LONG LANE
CHURCH ROAD
INTAKE LANE
HALL LANE
BARROW NOOK LANE
COACH ROAD
MOSS LA
NEW WAY
BEN LANE
Wellfield Cottages
Derbyshire's Farm
Rice's Cottage
Charity Farm
Turner's Farm
Fosters Farm
Stuart's Farm
Delph Farm
Water Tower
Scarth Hill Farm
White House Farm
Clock House Farm
Clock Cottage
Alcocks Plantation
Ivy Cott.
High Lane Farm
High Farm
High Farm Cottage
Beech Tree Farm
Thorn Cottage
Westhead Farm
Nursery
Bates' Green Farm
Bates' Green
Dicket's Brook Bridge
Fyles' Farm
Depot
Cricket Ground
Blaguegate Moss
The Country Cottage
Grapel's Farm
Wiswall's Farm
Holland's Farm
BLAGUEGATE MOSS
Lyelake Plantation
Lyelake Farm
Primrose Farm
Stanley Farm
Jubilee Wood
Tithe Barn Farm
Well Farm
Sewage Works
Bickerstaffe Brook
Ox Hey Plantation
OX HEY FIELD
Intake Wood
The Old Vicarage
War Mem.
Bickerstaffe C of E Prim. Sch.
Bickerstaffe Hall
Little Wood
Playing Field
Keeper's Cottage
Greenacres
Bickerstaffe Wood
Wash Farm
Rose Farm
Ash Holt
Plantation Cottage
Long Plantation
Roby's Farm
Large Ox Hey House
Bradshaw's Plantation
Wood End Farm
Wood House
Intake Farm
Red House Farm
Taylor's Wood
Barrow Nook Farm
Ben Lane Farm
Ben Lane Cotts.
Lodge Farm
Cropper's Wood
Slack House
New Way Farm
BICKERSTAFFE MOSS
Bickerstaffe Pond
Goose Brook
Firtree
210
217
224

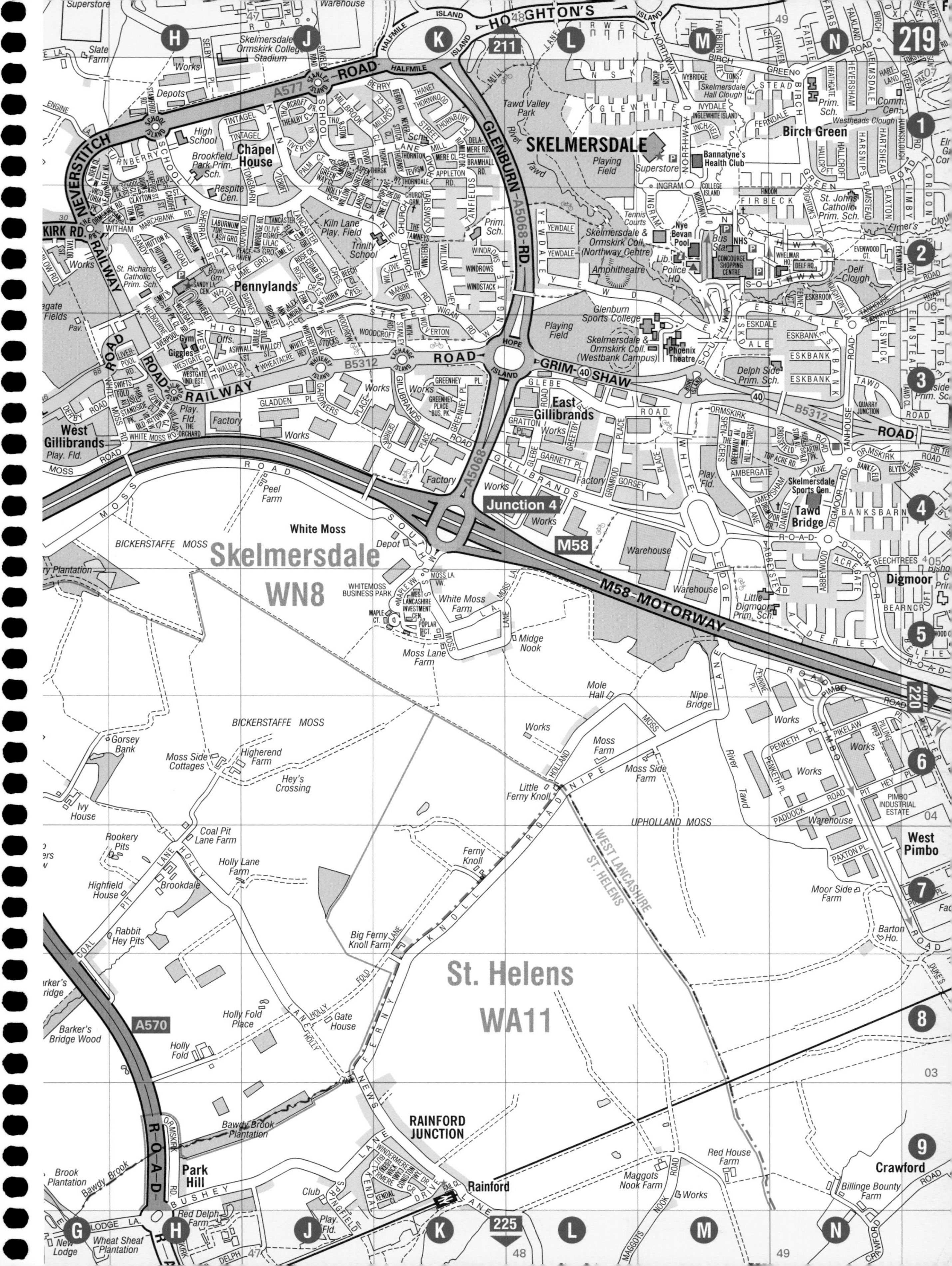
SKELMERSDALE
Skelmersdale
WN8
St. Helens
WA11
Chapel House
Pennylands
East Gillibrands
West Gillibrands
Birch Green
Tawd Bridge
Digmoor
West Pimbo
Crawford
Park Hill
Rainford
RAINFORD JUNCTION
White Moss
BICKERSTAFFE MOSS
UPHOLLAND MOSS
M58 MOTORWAY
Junction 4
GLENBURN A5068 RD.
NEVERSTITCH
HOUGHTON'S
A577
A570
B5312
Skelmersdale & Ormskirk College Stadium
Concourse Shopping Centre
Glenburn Sports College
Tawd Valley Park
WEST LANCASHIRE
ST. HELENS
211
220
225

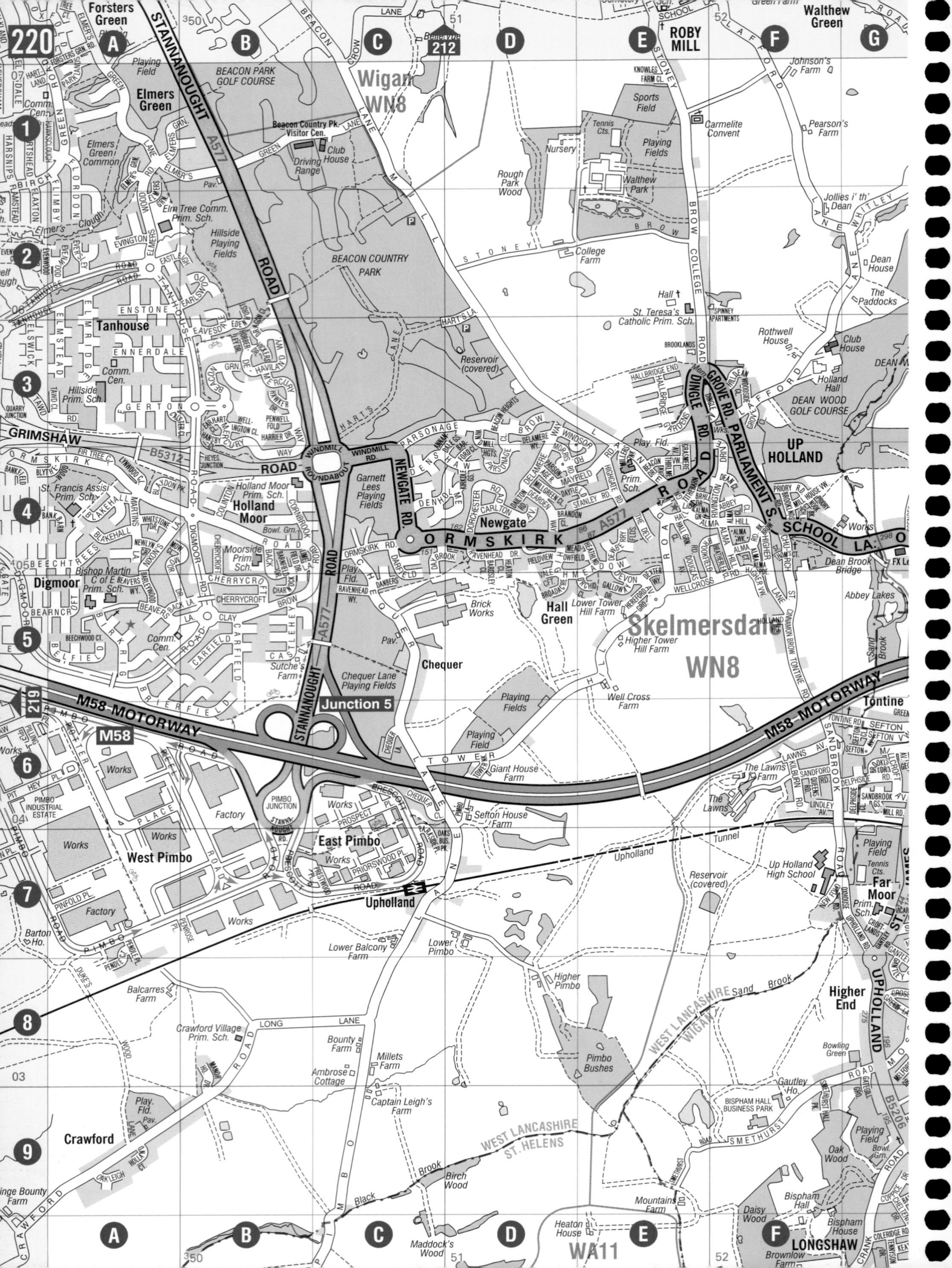

220
Forsters Green
Elmers Green
Elmers Green Common
STANNANOUGHT ROAD
A577
BEACON PARK GOLF COURSE
Wigan WN8
Beacon Country Pk. Visitor Cen.
Club House
Driving Range
BEACON COUNTRY PARK
212
ROBY MILL
Walthew Green
Johnson's Farm
Sports Field
Carmelite Convent
Pearson's Farm
Playing Fields
Nursery
Rough Park Wood
Walthew Park
Jollies i' th' Dean
College Farm
Dean House
The Paddocks
St. Teresa's Catholic Prim. Sch.
Rothwell House
Club House
Holland Hall
DEAN WOOD GOLF COURSE
UP HOLLAND
Reservoir (covered)
Elm Tree Comm. Prim. Sch.
Hillside Playing Fields
Tanhouse
Hillside Prim. Sch.
GRIMSHAW
ORMSKIRK ROAD
B5312
WINDMILL ROUNDABOUT
Holland Moor Prim. Sch.
Holland Moor
St. Francis Assisi Prim. Sch.
Garnett Lees Playing Fields
NEWGATE RD.
Newgate
ORMSKIRK ROAD
DINGLE RD.
GROVE RD.
PARLIAMENT ST.
SCHOOL LA.
Moorside Prim. Sch.
Digmoor
Bishop Martin C of E Prim. Sch.
Comm. Cen.
Brick Works
Hall Green
Lower Tower Hill Farm
Skelmersdale WN8
Higher Tower Hill Farm
Dean Brook Bridge
Abbey Lakes
Chequer
Sutche's Farm
Chequer Lane Playing Fields
Junction 5
Well Cross Farm
Playing Fields
Playing Field
Tontine
M58 MOTORWAY
M58
219
Giant House Farm
The Lawns Farm
The Lawns
PIMBO INDUSTRIAL ESTATE
PIMBO JUNCTION
Factory
Works
West Pimbo
East Pimbo
Sefton House Farm
Tunnel
Upholland
Reservoir (covered)
Up Holland High School
Far Moor
Barton Ho.
Lower Balcony Farm
Lower Pimbo
Higher Pimbo
Balcarres Farm
LONG LANE
Crawford Village Prim. Sch.
Bounty Farm
Millets Farm
Ambrose Cottage
Captain Leigh's Farm
Pimbo Bushes
WEST LANCASHIRE WIGAN
Higher End
UPHOLLAND ROAD
Bowling Green
Gautley Ho.
BISPHAM HALL BUSINESS PARK
SMETHURST
Crawford
WEST LANCASHIRE ST. HELENS
Birch Wood
Black Brook
Sand Brook
Mountains Farm
Heaton House
WA11
Maddock's Wood
Daisy Wood
Bispham Hall
Bispham House
Oak Wood
LONGSHAW
Brownlow Farm
B5206

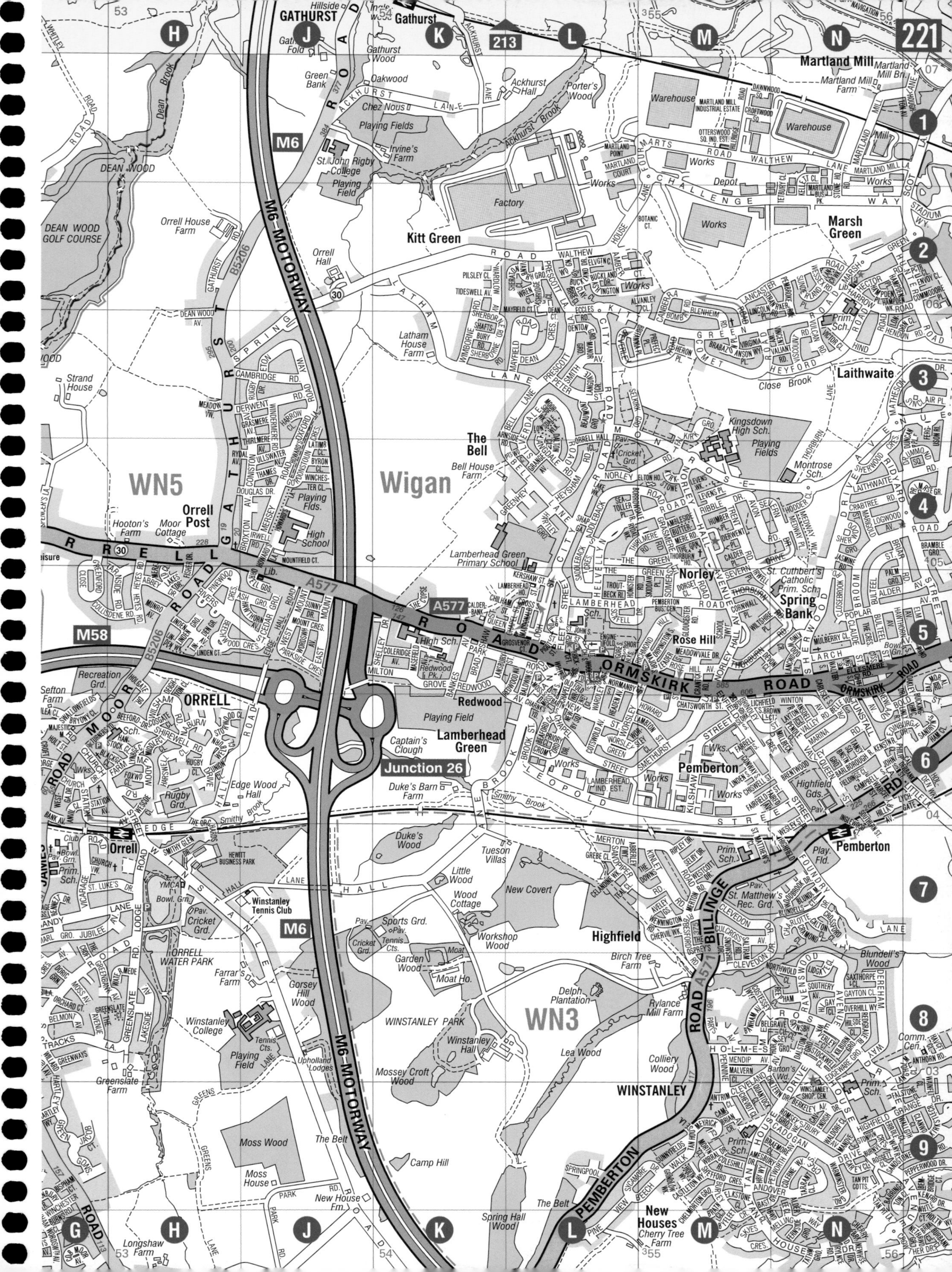

GATHURST
Gathurst
213
Martland Mill
Warehouse
MARTLAND MILL INDUSTRIAL ESTATE
Factory
Kitt Green
Marsh Green
Works
M6
M6 MOTORWAY
Dean Wood
DEAN WOOD
DEAN WOOD GOLF COURSE
Orrell House Farm
Orrell Hall
St. John Rigby College
Playing Fields
Latham House Farm
Laithwaite
Kingsdown High Sch.
Montrose Sch.
The Bell
Bell House Farm
Wigan
WN5
Orrell Post
Hooton's Farm
Moor Cottage
High School
Lamberhead Green Primary School
Norley
St. Cuthbert's Catholic Prim. Sch.
Spring Bank
Rose Hill
A577
M58
B5206
ORMSKIRK ROAD
ORRELL ROAD
Recreation Grd.
Sefton Farm
ORRELL
Redwood
Playing Field
Captain's Clough
Lamberhead Green
Junction 26
Duke's Barn Farm
Edge Wood Hall
Rugby Grd.
Pemberton
Highfield Gds.
Orrell
HEWITT BUSINESS PARK
Duke's Wood
Tueson Villas
Little Wood
Wood Cottage
New Covert
Winstanley Tennis Club
Workshop Wood
Highfield
Birch Tree Farm
ORRELL WATER PARK
Farrar's Farm
Garden Wood
Moat Ho.
Gorsey Hill Wood
WINSTANLEY PARK
Winstanley College
Winstanley Hall
Delph Plantation
WN3
Rylance Mill Farm
Lea Wood
Colliery Wood
WINSTANLEY
Upholland Lodges
Mossey Croft Wood
Greenslate Farm
Moss Wood
The Belt
Camp Hill
Moss House
New House Fm.
Spring Hall Wood
New Houses
Cherry Tree Farm
Longshaw Farm
BILLINGE ROAD
PEMBERTON ROAD
A571
Blundell's Wood
Comm. Cen.
St. Matthew's Rec. Grd.
H J K L M N G
1 2 3 4 5 6 7 8 9
53 54 55 56

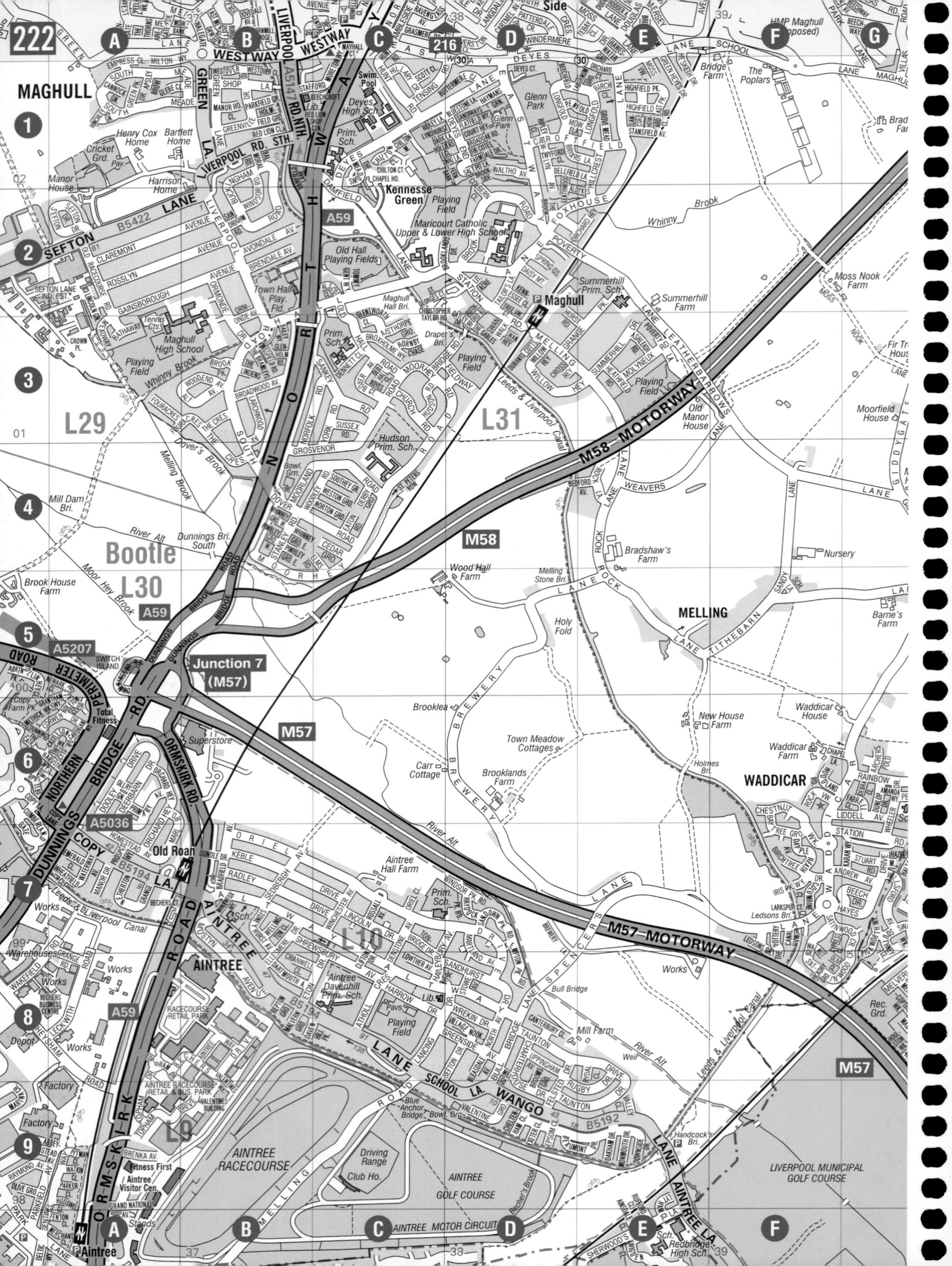

MAGHULL
L29
L30
L31
L10
L9
Bootle
MELLING
WADDICAR
AINTREE
M58 MOTORWAY
M57 MOTORWAY
Junction 7 (M57)
AINTREE RACECOURSE
AINTREE GOLF COURSE
LIVERPOOL MUNICIPAL GOLF COURSE
AINTREE MOTOR CIRCUIT
Leeds & Liverpool Canal
River Alt
WESTWAY
SEFTON LANE
DUNNINGS BRIDGE RD.
ORMSKIRK ROAD
NORTHWAY
Maghull High School
Maricourt Catholic Upper & Lower High School
Deyes High Sch.
Kennesse Green
Old Hall Playing Fields
Hudson Prim. Sch.
Aintree Davenhill Prim. Sch.
Redbridge High Sch.
HMP Maghull (proposed)
Old Roan
Aintree
Maghull
216

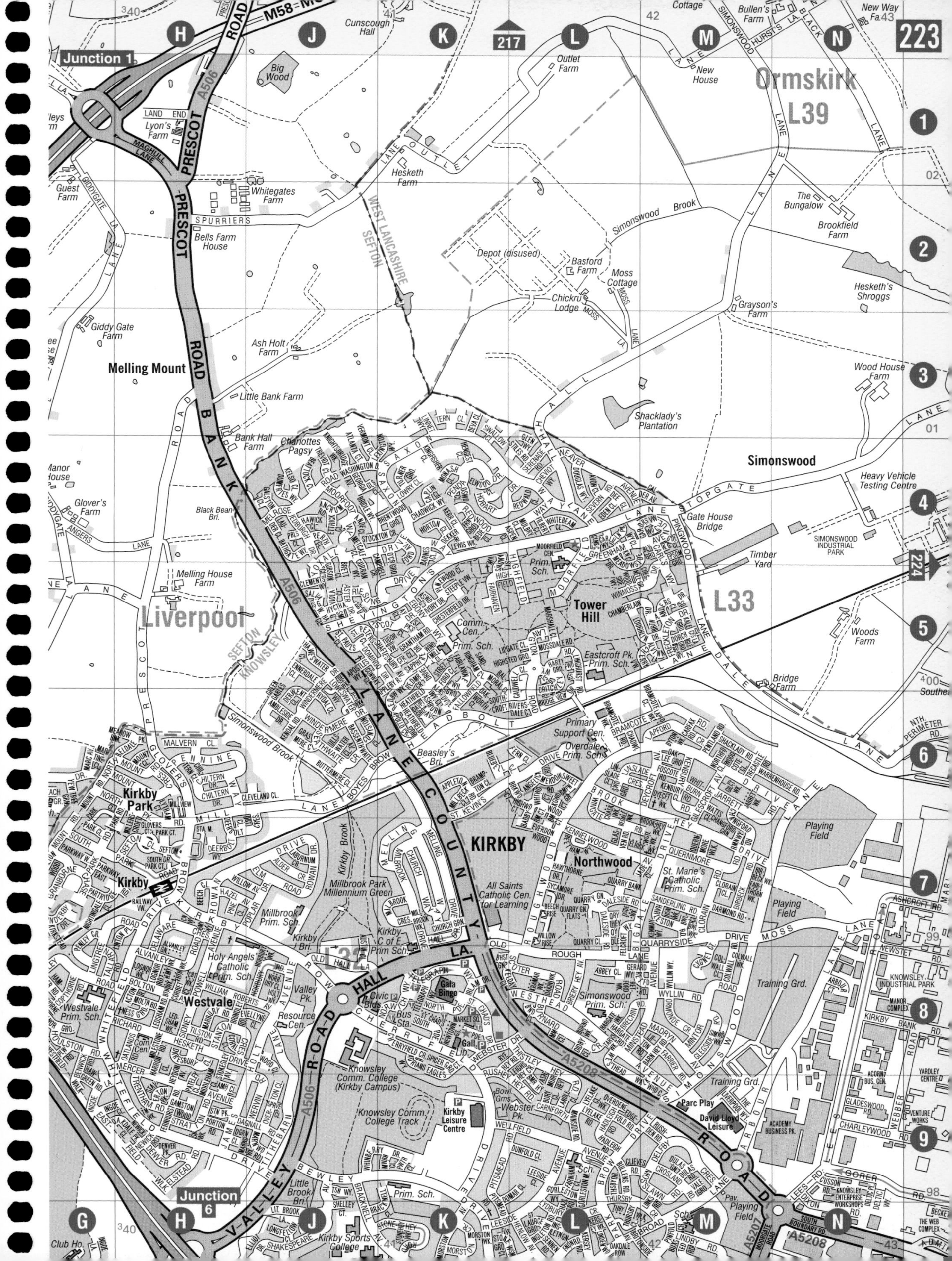
217
224
Junction 1
Junction 6
M58
Ormskirk
L39
L33
L32
Liverpool
KIRKBY
Kirkby
Kirkby Park
Westvale
Northwood
Tower Hill
Simonswood
Melling Mount
PRESCOT ROAD
BANK LANE
COUNTY ROAD
HALL ROAD
VALLEY ROAD
STOPGATE LANE
SPURRIERS LANE
OUTLET LANE
HALL LANE
Cunscough Hall
Big Wood
Outlet Farm
New House
Lyon's Farm
Whitegates Farm
Hesketh Farm
Bells Farm House
Guest Farm
Giddy Gate Farm
Ash Holt Farm
Little Bank Farm
Bank Hall Farm
Charlottes Pagsy
Glover's Farm
Melling House Farm
Depot (disused)
Basford Farm
Moss Cottage
Chickru Lodge
Simonswood Brook
The Bungalow
Brookfield Farm
Hesketh's Shroggs
Grayson's Farm
Wood House Farm
Shacklady's Plantation
Heavy Vehicle Testing Centre
Gate House Bridge
Timber Yard
SIMONSWOOD INDUSTRIAL PARK
Woods Farm
Bridge Farm
Eastcroft Pk. Prim. Sch.
Primary Support Cen.
Overdale Prim. Sch.
Beasley's Bri.
Millbrook Park Millennium Green
Millbrook Prim. Sch.
All Saints Catholic Cen. for Learning
Kirkby C of E Prim Sch.
Holy Angels' Catholic Prim. Sch.
Westvale Prim. Sch.
Valley Pk.
Resource Cen.
Civic Bldgs.
Gala Bingo
Bus Sta.
Knowsley Comm. College (Kirkby Campus)
Knowsley Comm. College Track
Kirkby Leisure Centre
Webster Pk.
Simonswood Prim. Sch.
St. Marie's Catholic Prim. Sch.
Playing Field
Training Grd.
Parc Play
David Lloyd Leisure
ACADEMY BUSINESS PK.
KNOWSLEY INDUSTRIAL PARK
Kirkby Sports College
Little Brook Bri.
Club Ho.
A506
A5208
A5207
WEST LANCASHIRE
SEFTON
KNOWSLEY

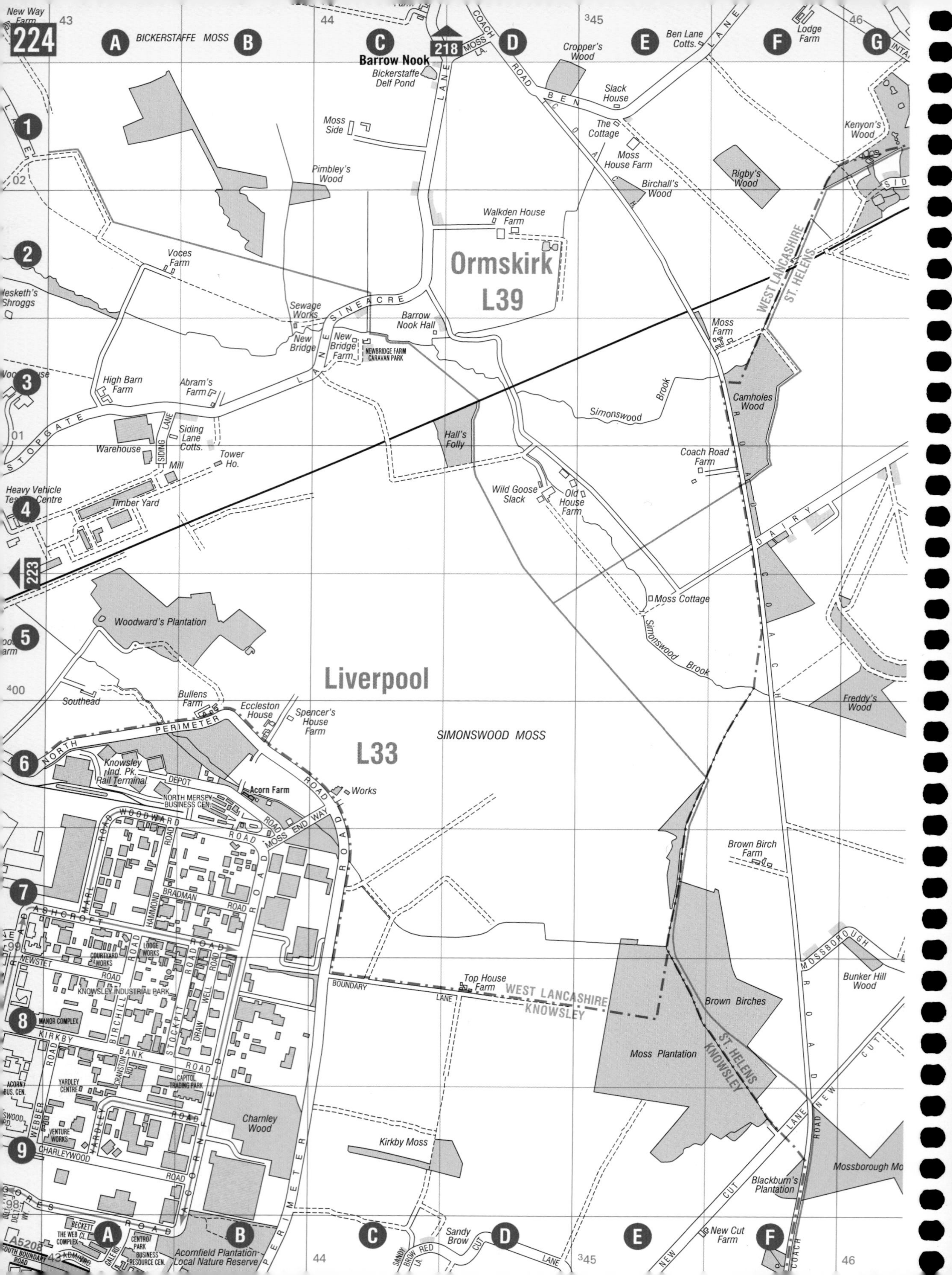

BICKERSTAFFE MOSS
Barrow Nook
Bickerstaffe Delf Pond
New Way Farm
218
Cropper's Wood
Ben Lane Cotts.
Lodge Farm
Slack House
The Cottage
Moss House Farm
Moss Side
Pimbley's Wood
Rigby's Wood
Birchall's Wood
Kenyon's Wood
Walkden House Farm
Ormskirk
L39
Voces Farm
Hesketh's Shroggs
Sewage Works
New Bridge
New Bridge Farm
NEWBRIDGE FARM CARAVAN PARK
Barrow Nook Hall
SINEACRE LANE
STOPGATE
High Barn Farm
Abram's Farm
Siding Lane Cotts.
Warehouse
Mill
Tower Ho.
Heavy Vehicle Testing Centre
Timber Yard
223
Moss Farm
Camholes Wood
Simonswood Brook
Hall's Folly
Coach Road Farm
Wild Goose Slack
Old House Farm
DAIRY
Moss Cottage
WEST LANCASHIRE
ST. HELENS
Woodward's Plantation
Liverpool
Southead
Bullens Farm
Eccleston House
Spencer's House Farm
Freddy's Wood
NORTH PERIMETER
L33
SIMONSWOOD MOSS
Knowsley Ind. Pk. Rail Terminal
DEPOT
Acorn Farm
Works
NORTH MERSEY BUSINESS CEN.
WOODWARD ROAD
MOSS END WAY
Brown Birch Farm
BRADMAN ROAD
HAMMOND
ASHCROFT
COURTYARD WORKS
LODGE WORKS
NEWSTET ROAD
KNOWSLEY INDUSTRIAL PARK
BOUNDARY LANE
Top House Farm
WEST LANCASHIRE
KNOWSLEY
MOSSBOROUGH
Bunker Hill Wood
Brown Birches
MANOR COMPLEX
KIRKBY BANK ROAD
BIRCHILL
STOCKPIT
DRAW WELL
CRANSTON
CAPITOL TRADING PARK
YARDLEY CENTRE
ACORN BUS. CEN.
Moss Plantation
ST. HELENS
KNOWSLEY
Charnley Wood
VENTURE WORKS
WEBBER
YARDLEY
CHARLEYWOOD ROAD
ACORNFIELD
PERIMETER
Kirkby Moss
Mossborough Mo
Blackburn's Plantation
NEW CUT LANE
COACH ROAD
BECKETT CL.
THE WEB COMPLEX
CENTRO PARK
BUSINESS RESOURCE CEN.
Sandy Brow
SANDY BROW LA.
RED CUT LANE
New Cut Farm
Acornfield Plantation Local Nature Reserve
A5208
SOUTH BOUNDARY ROAD

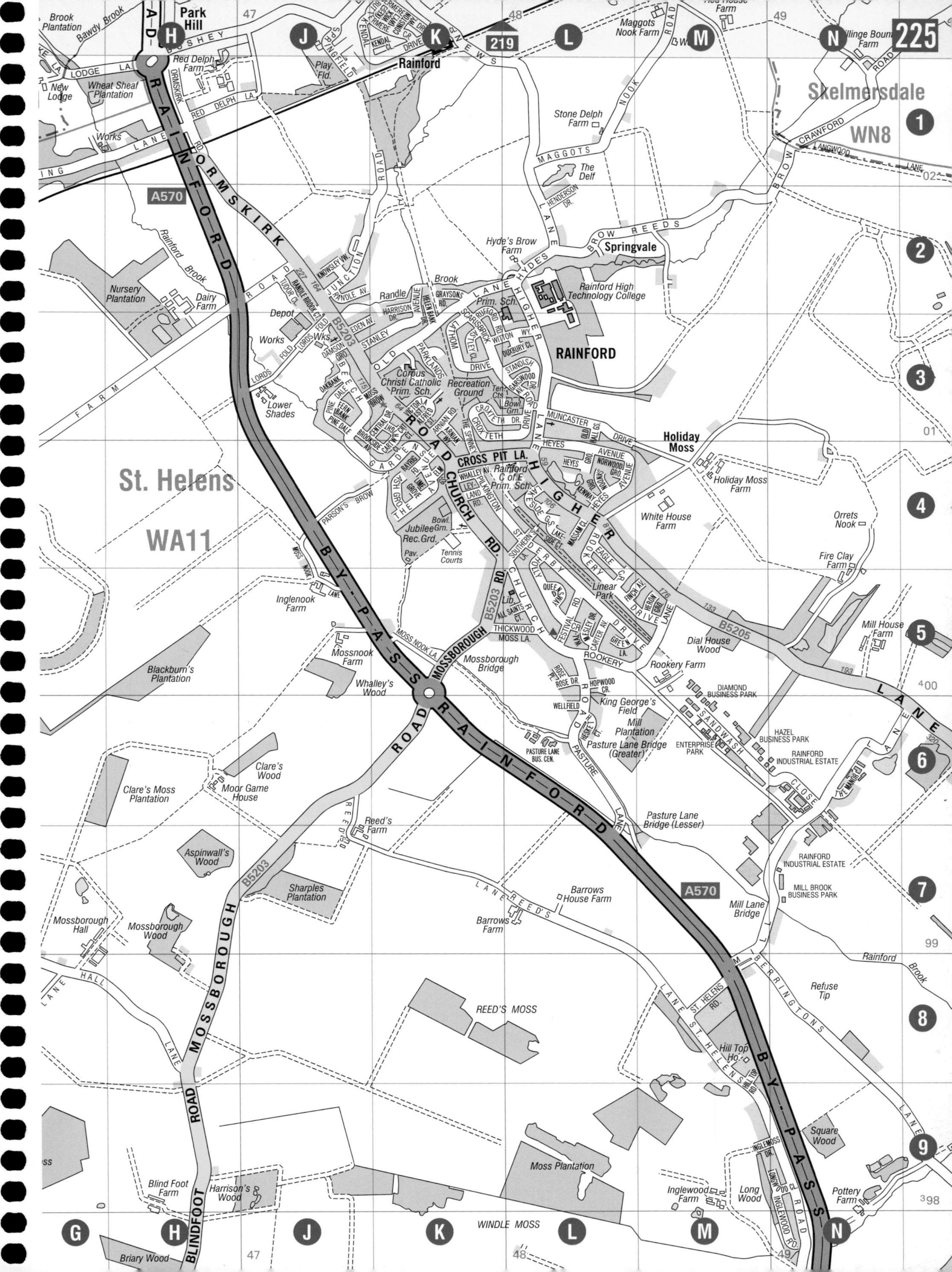
Park Hill
Brook Plantation
Bawdy Brook
Red Delph Farm
Lodge La.
New Lodge
Wheat Sheaf Plantation
Works
Rainford
Play. Fld.
Maggots Nook Farm
Skelmersdale
WN8
Stone Delph Farm
The Delf
Maggots Nook Road
Crawford
Langwood
A570
Rainford Brook
Nursery Plantation
Dairy Farm
Depot
Works
Hyde's Brow Farm
Springvale
Reeds Brow
Rainford High Technology College
Randle Brook
RAINFORD
Corpus Christi Catholic Prim. Sch.
Recreation Ground
Lower Shades
Muncaster Drive
Holiday Moss
Holiday Moss Farm
Cross Pit La.
Rainford C of E Prim. Sch.
St. Helens
WA11
Jubilee Rec. Grd.
Tennis Courts
White House Farm
Orrets Nook
Fire Clay Farm
Linear Park
Inglenook Farm
Mill House Farm
Dial House Wood
B5205
Rainford By-Pass
Church Road
Higher Lane
Mossborough Road
B5203
Mossnook Farm
Mossborough Bridge
Rookery Farm
Rookery Lane
Blackburn's Plantation
Whalley's Wood
Diamond Business Park
King George's Field
Mill Plantation
Hazel Business Park
Pasture Lane Bridge (Greater)
Enterprise Park
Rainford Industrial Estate
Sandwash Close
Clare's Wood
Clare's Moss Plantation
Moor Game House
Reed's Farm
Pasture Lane Bridge (Lesser)
Aspinwall's Wood
Rainford Industrial Estate
Mill Brook Business Park
Sharples Plantation
Barrows House Farm
Reed's Lane
Mill Lane Bridge
Mossborough Hall
Mossborough Wood
Barrows Farm
Hall Lane
Rainford Brook
Refuse Tip
Reed's Moss
Berringtons Lane
St. Helens Rd.
Hill Top Ho.
Square Wood
Moss Plantation
Blind Foot Farm
Harrison's Wood
Inglewood Farm
Long Wood
Pottery Farm
Windle Moss
Blindfoot Road
Briary Wood
219
47
48
49
G
H
J
K
L
M
N
1
2
3
4
5
6
7
8
9

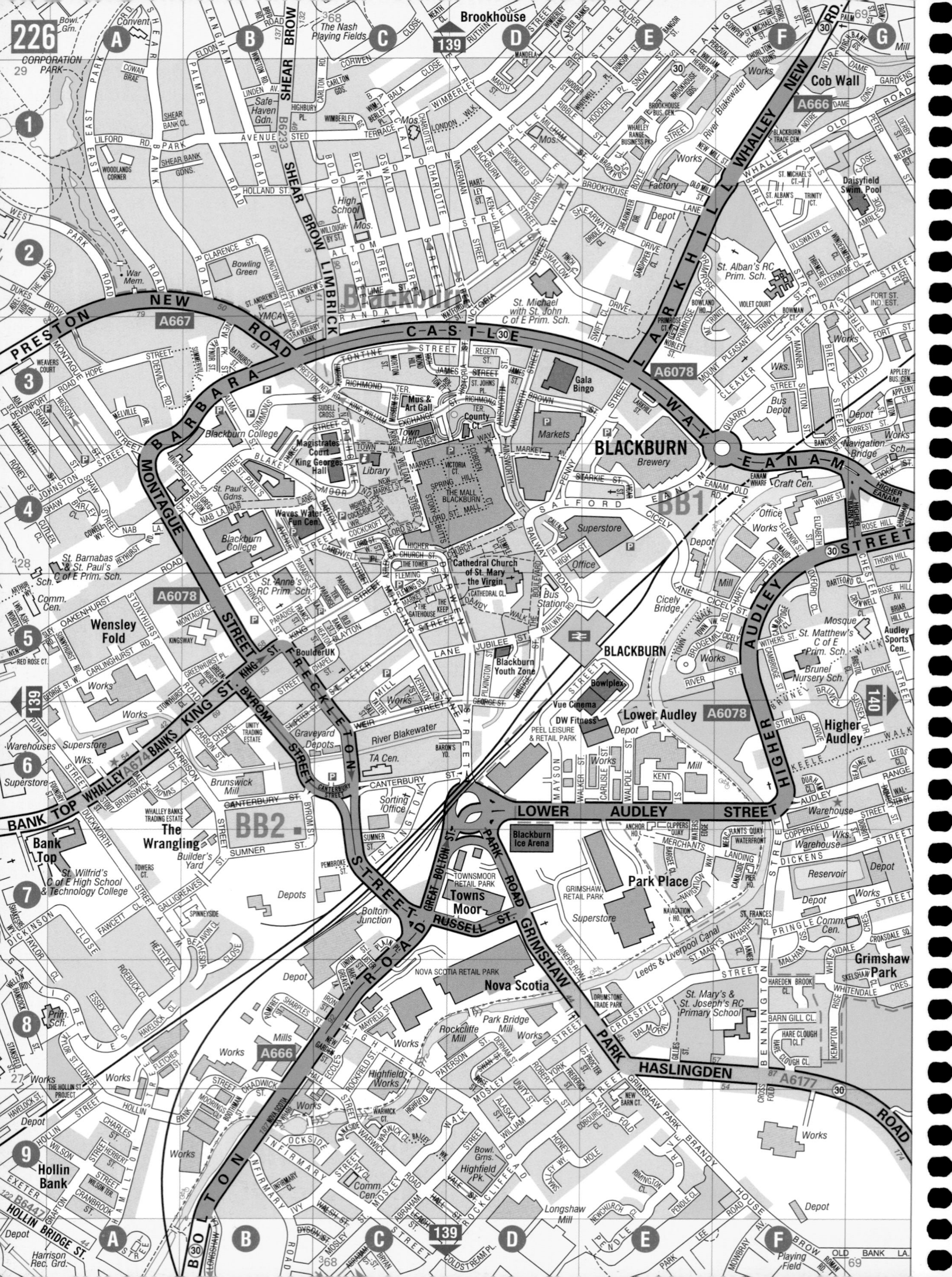

Brookhouse
139
BLACKBURN
Blackburn
BB1
BB2
Corporation Park
Cob Wall
Daisyfield Swim. Pool
Wensley Fold
Lower Audley
Higher Audley
Park Place
Grimshaw Park
Nova Scotia
Towns Moor
The Wrangling
Bank Top
Hollin Bank
Highfield Works
Gala Bingo
Markets
Mus & Art Gall.
Town Hall
County Ct.
Magistrates Court
King Georges Hall
Library
Blackburn College
Waves Water Fun Cen.
Cathedral Church of St. Mary the Virgin
Bus Station
Blackburn Youth Zone
Bowlplex
Vue Cinema
DW Fitness
Peel Leisure & Retail Park
Blackburn Ice Arena
Leeds & Liverpool Canal
River Blakewater
A666
A667
A6078
A674
A6177
B6447
140

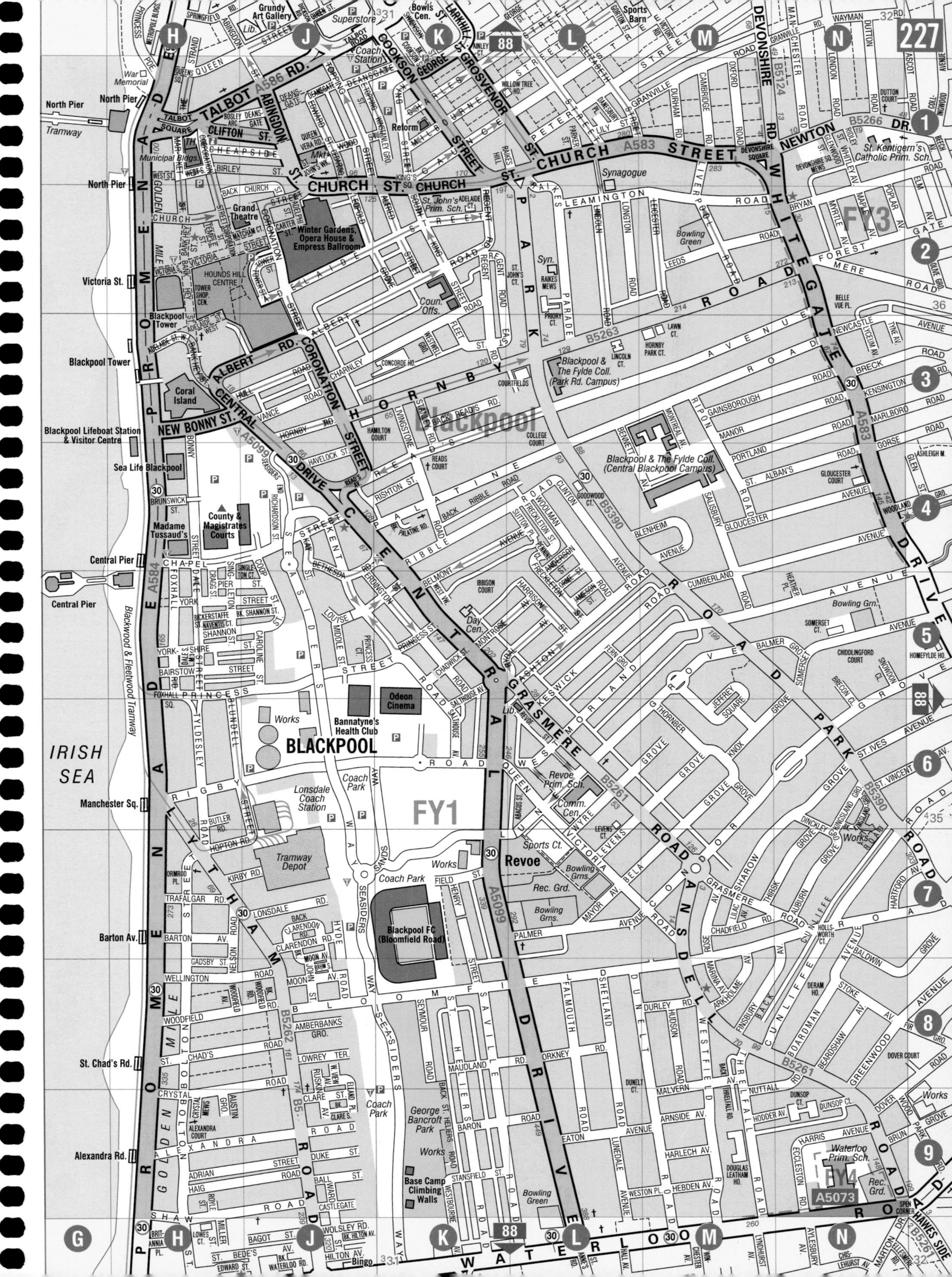

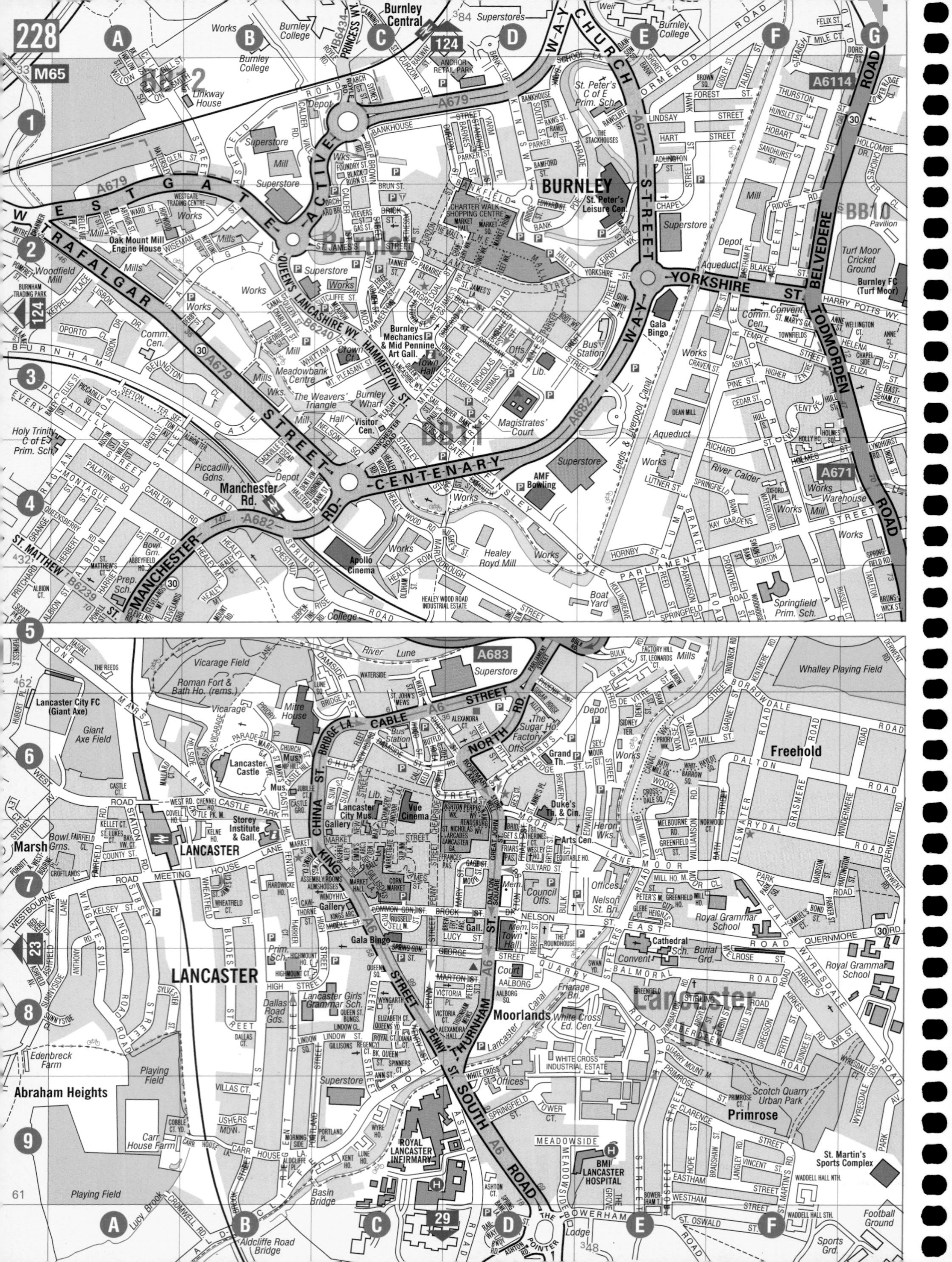

228
A
B
C
D
E
F
G
1
2
3
4
5
6
7
8
9
M65
124
BB12
A679
A682
A671
A6114
BB10
BB11
A6
A683
B6240
B6239
Burnley Central
Burnley College
Superstores
Anchor Retail Park
Linkway House
WESTGATE
TRAFALGAR STREET
MANCHESTER RD.
CENTENARY WAY
CHURCH STREET
YORKSHIRE ST.
BELVEDERE ROAD
TODMORDEN ROAD
ACTIVE WAY
QUEEN'S LANCASHIRE WY.
HAMMERTON ST.
BURNLEY
St. Peter's Leisure Cen.
St. Peter's C of E Prim. Sch.
Charter Walk Shopping Centre
Oak Mount Mill Engine House
Woodfield Mill
Burnham Trading Park
Burnley Mechanics & Mid Pennine Art Gall.
Town Hall
Meadowbank Centre
The Weavers' Triangle
Burnley Wharf
Visitor Cen.
Magistrates' Court
Gala Bingo
Bus Station
Lib.
Turf Moor Cricket Ground
Burnley FC (Turf Moor)
Pavilion
Leeds & Liverpool Canal
Aqueduct
River Calder
Dean Mill
AMF Bowling
Apollo Cinema
Healey Royd Mill
Healey Wood Road Industrial Estate
Boat Yard
Springfield Prim. Sch.
Holy Trinity C of E Prim. Sch.
Piccadilly Gdns.
Manchester Rd.
Prep. Sch.
Comm. Cen.
Convent
River Lune
Lancaster City FC (Giant Axe)
Giant Axe Field
Vicarage Field
Roman Fort & Bath Ho. (rems.)
Mitre House
Lancaster Castle
Lancaster City Mus.
Vue Cinema
Storey Institute & Gall.
LANCASTER
Marsh
Bowl. Grns.
The Sugar Ho. Factory
Grand Th.
Duke's Th. & Cin.
Heron Wks.
Arts Cen.
Freehold
Whalley Playing Field
Royal Grammar School
Cathedral
Convent
Burial Grd.
Council Offs.
Mem. Town Hall
Court
Gala Bingo
Lancaster Girls' Grammar Sch.
Dallas Road Gds.
Moorlands
White Cross Ed. Cen.
White Cross Industrial Estate
Lancaster LA1
Scotch Quarry Urban Park
Primrose
St. Martin's Sports Complex
Royal Lancaster Infirmary
BMI Lancaster Hospital
Abraham Heights
Edenbreck Farm
Playing Field
Carr House Farm
Basin Bridge
Aldcliffe Road Bridge
Lucy Brook
Football Ground
Sports Grd.
Lodge
23
29
KING STREET
CHINA ST.
CABLE STREET
NORTH RD.
THURNHAM ST.
SOUTH ROAD
PENNY ST.
MEETING HOUSE LANE
MOOR LANE
EAST ROAD
QUERNMORE RD.
WYRESDALE ROAD
BOWERHAM

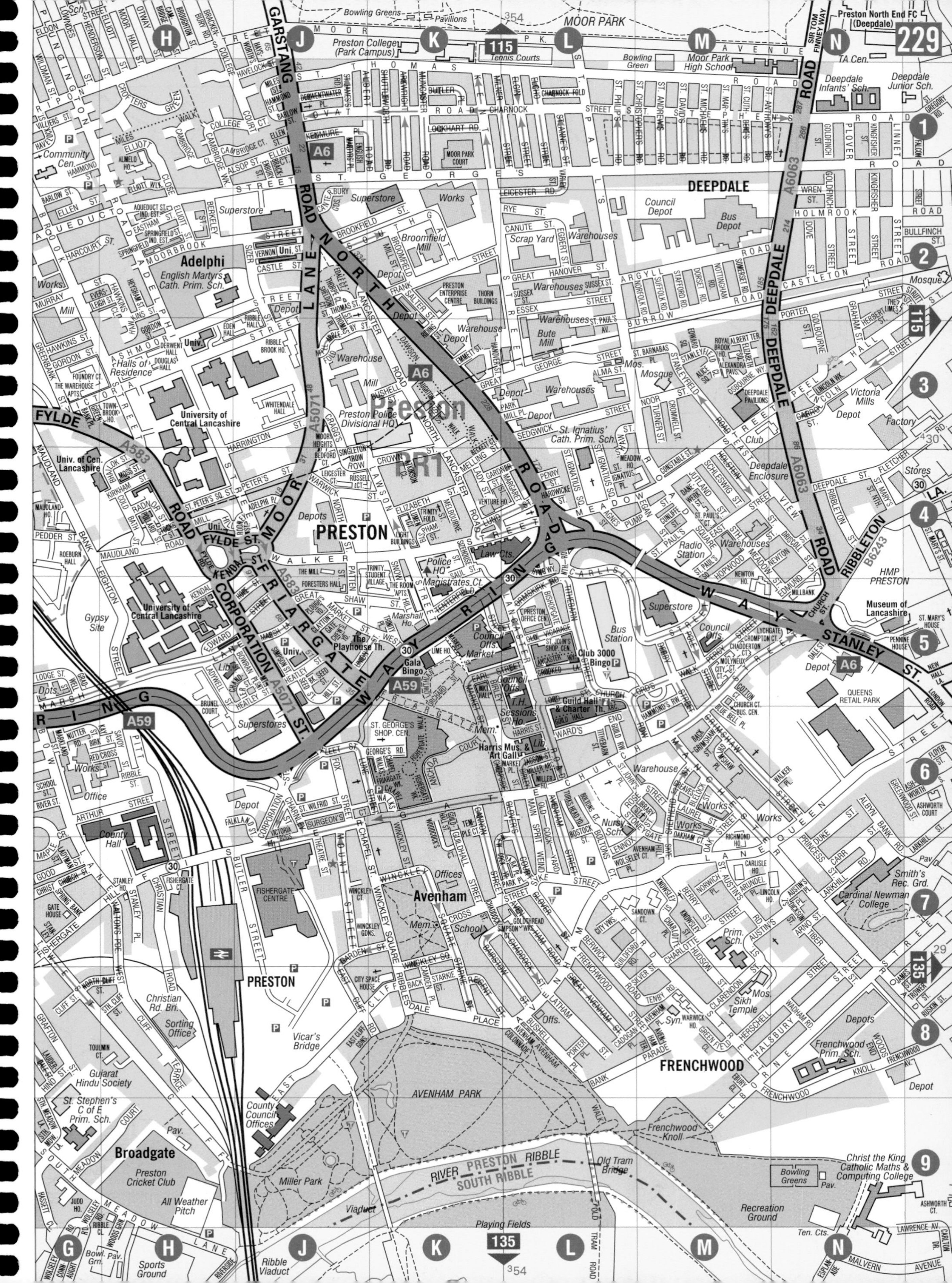
Bowling Greens
Pavilions
MOOR PARK
Preston North End FC (Deepdale)
Preston College (Park Campus)
Tennis Courts
Moor Park High School
Deepdale Infants' Sch.
Deepdale Junior Sch.
TA Cen.
DEEPDALE
Council Depot
Bus Depot
Works
Superstore
Broomfield Mill
Scrap Yard
Warehouses
Adelphi
English Martyrs Cath. Prim. Sch.
Halls of Residence
University of Central Lancashire
Univ. of Cen. Lancashire
Preston Police Divisional HQ
PRESTON
Preston
PR1
Bute Mill
Mosque
Victoria Mills
Deepdale Enclosure
St. Ignatius' Cath. Prim. Sch.
Radio Station
Law Cts.
Police HQ
Magistrates Ct.
Superstore
Bus Station
Council Offs.
Market
Club 3000 Bingo
Gala Bingo
The Playhouse Th.
Guild Hall & Charter Th.
Harris Mus. & Art Gall.
T.H.
Sessions Ho.
St. George's Shop. Cen.
Fishergate Centre
County Hall
Gypsy Site
Superstores
HMP PRESTON
Museum of Lancashire
Queens Retail Park
Avenham
Frenchwood
Frenchwood Prim. Sch.
Cardinal Newman College
Smith's Rec. Grd.
Sikh Temple
Christian Rd. Bri.
Sorting Office
Gujarat Hindu Society
St. Stephen's C of E Prim. Sch.
Broadgate
Preston Cricket Club
All Weather Pitch
County Council Offices
Avenham Park
Miller Park
Vicar's Bridge
River Ribble
Old Tram Bridge
Frenchwood Knoll
Christ the King Catholic Maths & Computing College
Bowling Greens
Recreation Ground
Playing Fields
Sports Ground
Ribble Viaduct
Viaduct
A6
A59
A583
A5071
A6063
B6243
RING WAY
STANLEY ST.
DEEPDALE ROAD
GARSTANG ROAD
NORTH ROAD
MOOR LANE
FRIARGATE
CORPORATION ST.
FYLDE ROAD
115
135
354
H J K L M N G
1 2 3 4 5 6 7 8 9

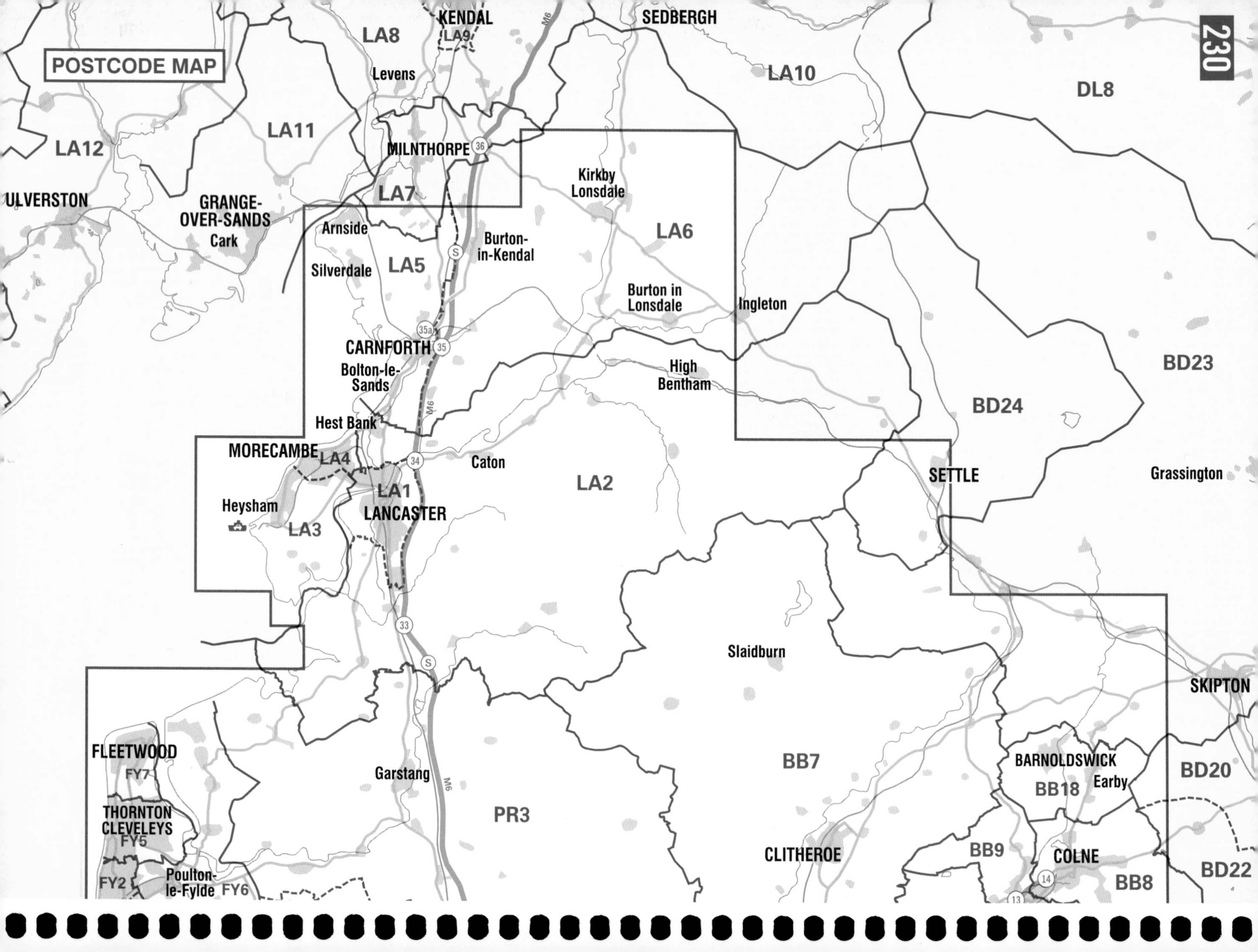

POSTCODE MAP

DL8

BD23

Grassington

SKIPTON

BD20

BD22

BARNOLDSWICK

Earby

BB8

BB18

COLNE

14

BB9

13

BD24

SETTLE

CLITHEROE

BB7

Slaidburn

SEDBERGH

LA10

Ingleton

LA6

Burton in Lonsdale

High Bentham

Kirkby Lonsdale

LA2

PR3

KENDAL

LA9

Burton-in-Kendal

M6

Caton

M6

M6

Levens

LA8

MILNTHORPE

36

Burton-in-Kendal

S

LA7

LA5

35a

35

CARNFORTH

Bolton-le-Sands

34

LANCASTER

LA1

33

S

Garstang

Arnside

Hest Bank

LA4

Silverdale

MORECAMBE

LA3

LA11

GRANGE-OVER-SANDS

Cark

Heysham

FLEETWOOD

FY7

THORNTON CLEVELEYS

FY5

Poulton le-Fylde

FY6

FY2

LA12

ULVERSTON

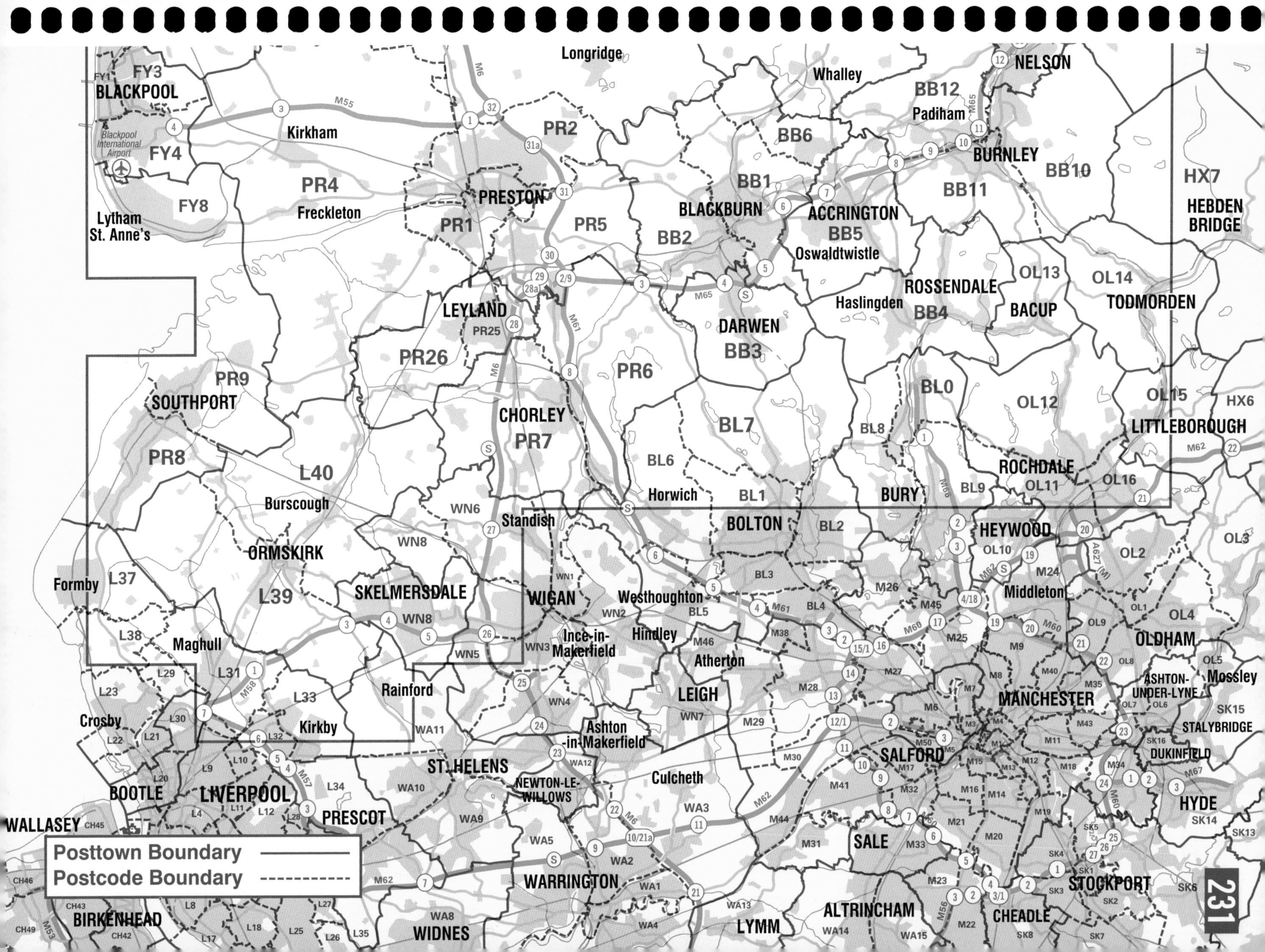
Posttown Boundary
Postcode Boundary
BLACKPOOL
FY1
FY3
FY4
FY8
Blackpool International Airport
Lytham St. Anne's
Kirkham
PR4
Freckleton
M55
M6
Longridge
PRESTON
PR1
PR2
PR5
Whalley
BB6
BB12
Padiham
NELSON
BURNLEY
BB10
BB11
HX7
HEBDEN BRIDGE
BB1
BLACKBURN
BB2
ACCRINGTON
BB5
Oswaldtwistle
M65
LEYLAND
PR25
PR26
M61
PR6
DARWEN
BB3
Haslingden
ROSSENDALE
BB4
OL13
BACUP
OL14
TODMORDEN
SOUTHPORT
PR9
PR8
CHORLEY
PR7
L40
BL6
BL7
BL8
BL0
OL12
OL15
HX6
LITTLEBOROUGH
M62
Burscough
WN6
Horwich
BL1
BURY
BL9
M66
ROCHDALE
OL11
OL16
Standish
BOLTON
BL2
HEYWOOD
OL10
OL2
OL3
A627 (M)
ORMSKIRK
WN8
Formby
L37
L39
SKELMERSDALE
WIGAN
WN1
BL3
M26
M24
Middleton
Westhoughton
WN2
BL5
BL4
M45
M25
OL1
OL4
L38
Maghull
WN3
WN5
Ince-in-Makerfield
Hindley
M46
M38
M60
M9
OL9
OLDHAM
L29
L23
L31
M58
L33
Rainford
Atherton
LEIGH
M28
M27
M8
M40
M35
OL8
OL5
OL6
OL7
ASHTON-UNDER-LYNE
Mossley
Crosby
L30
L22
L21
L32
Kirkby
WN4
WN7
Ashton-in-Makerfield
M29
M7
M6
M4
M3
MANCHESTER
M43
SK15
STALYBRIDGE
WA11
WA12
M50
M1
M11
SK16
DUKINFIELD
L20
L9
L10
ST. HELENS
NEWTON-LE-WILLOWS
Culcheth
M30
SALFORD
M5
M17
M15
M12
M13
M18
M34
M67
BOOTLE
LIVERPOOL
L11
L12
L28
L34
L4
WA10
M57
PRESCOT
WA3
M41
M32
M16
M14
HYDE
SK14
WALLASEY
CH45
WA9
M44
SALE
M33
M21
M20
M19
SK5
SK13
WA5
WA2
M31
SK4
SK1
CH46
M62
WARRINGTON
WA1
M23
STOCKPORT
SK6
SK3
SK2
CH43
L8
L27
WA13
ALTRINCHAM
M56
CHEADLE
CH49
BIRKENHEAD
CH42
M53
L17
L18
L25
L26
L35
WA8
WIDNES
WA4
LYMM
WA14
WA15
M22
SK8
SK7

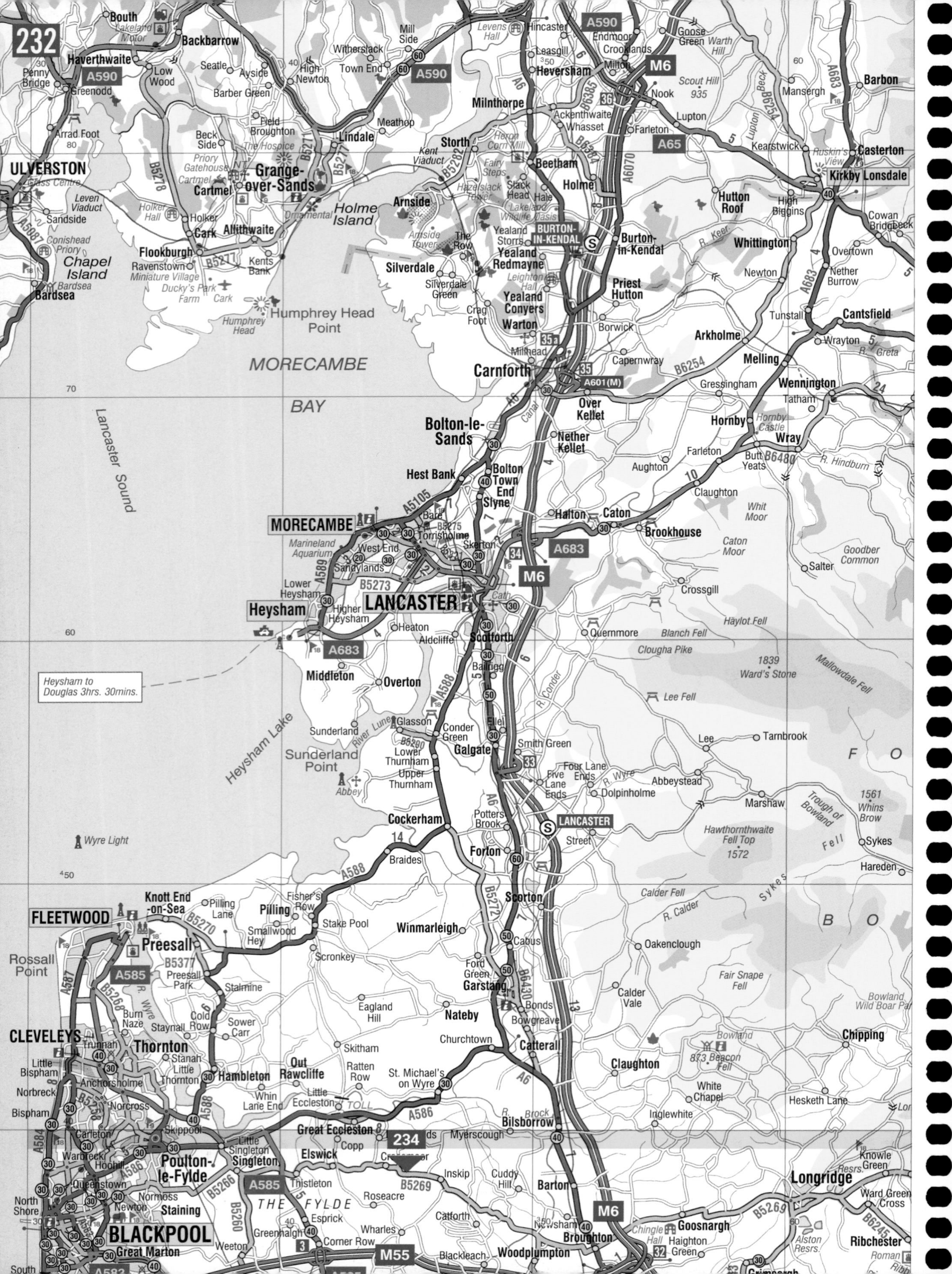

ULVERSTON
Grange-over-Sands
Cartmel
Holme Island
Arnside
Silverdale
Carnforth
MORECAMBE
BAY
Lancaster Sound
Bolton-le-Sands
Hest Bank
MORECAMBE
Heysham
LANCASTER
Heysham to Douglas 3hrs. 30mins.
Heysham Lake
Sunderland Point
Cockerham
Galgate
Wyre Light
FLEETWOOD
Knott End-on-Sea
Preesall
Rossall Point
CLEVELEYS
Thornton
Hambleton
Poulton-le-Fylde
BLACKPOOL
Great Eccleston
Garstang
Longridge
Kirkby Lonsdale
Burton-in-Kendal
Milnthorpe
Heversham
Hornby
Wray
Caton
Scorton
Chipping
Goosnargh
Broughton
Woodplumpton
THE FYLDE
M6
M55
A590
A6
A683
A588
A585
234

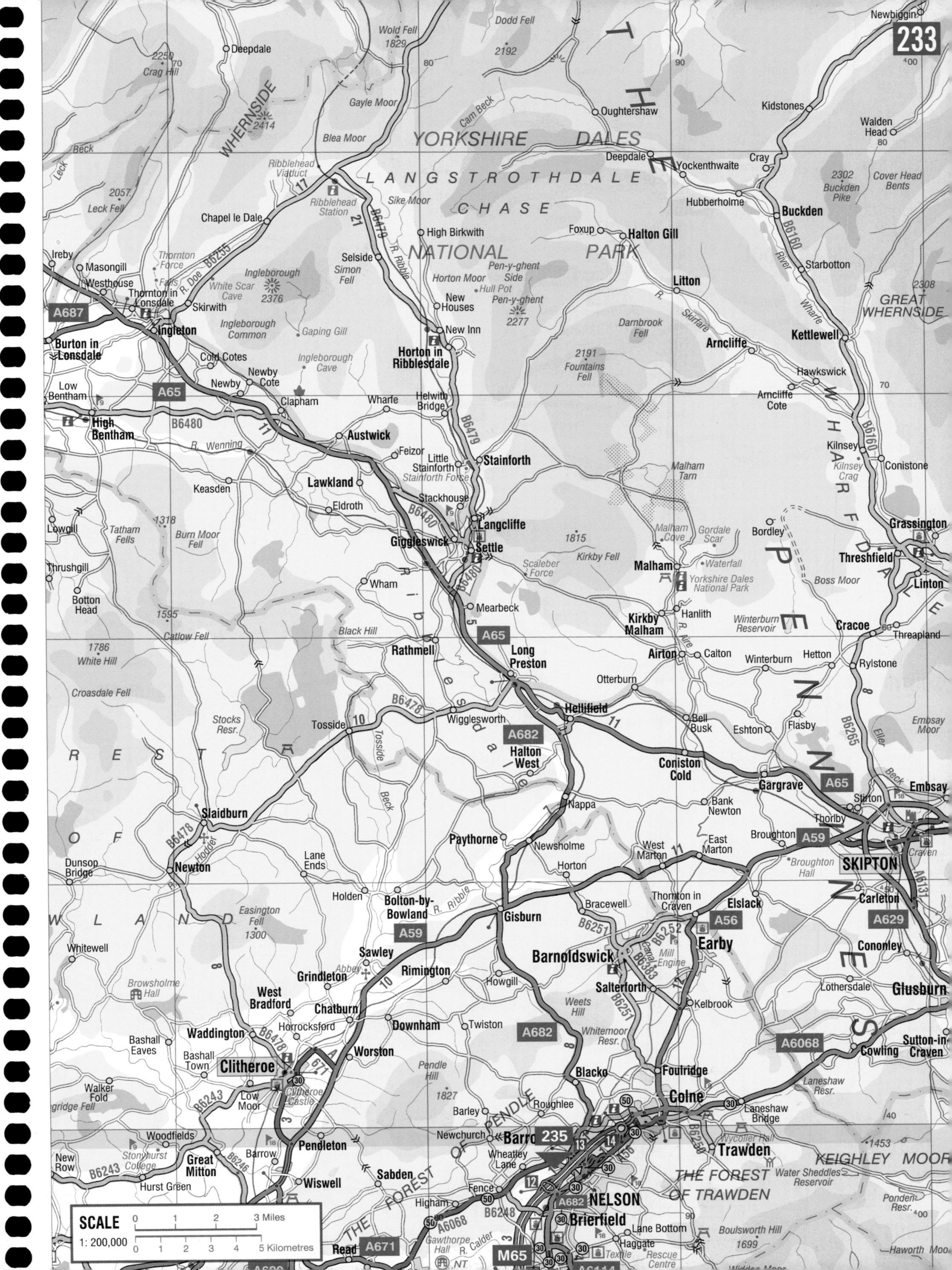

Newbiggin
Dodd Fell
2192
Wold Fell
1829
Deepdale
2250
Crag Hill
WHERNSIDE
2414
Gayle Moor
Blea Moor
Cam Beck
Oughtershaw
Kidstones
Walden Head
YORKSHIRE DALES
THE
Deepdale
Yockenthwaite
Cray
Ribblehead Viaduct
LANGSTROTHDALE
CHASE
Ribblehead Station
Sike Moor
2302
Buckden Pike
Cover Head Bents
Hubberholme
Buckden
Leck
Beck
2057
Leck Fell
Chapel le Dale
High Birkwith
NATIONAL
PARK
Foxup
Halton Gill
B6160
Starbotton
Ireby
Masongill
Westhouse
Thornton Force
Falls
R. Doe
B6255
Thornton in Lonsdale
Skirwith
Ingleborough
2376
White Scar Cave
Selside
Simon Fell
R. Ribble
B6479
Horton Moor
New Houses
Pen-y-ghent Side
Hull Pot
Pen-y-ghent
2277
Litton
R. Skirfare
River Wharfe
2308
GREAT WHERNSIDE
A687
Ingleton
Ingleborough Common
Gaping Gill
New Inn
Horton in Ribblesdale
Darnbrook Fell
Arncliffe
Kettlewell
Burton in Lonsdale
Cold Cotes
Ingleborough Cave
2191
Fountains Fell
Hawkswick
Low Bentham
A65
Newby
Newby Cote
Clapham
Wharfe
Helwith Bridge
Arncliffe Cote
High Bentham
B6480
R. Wenning
Austwick
Feizor
Little Stainforth
Stainforth Force
Stainforth
Kilnsey
Kilnsey Crag
Conistone
Malham Tarn
Keasden
Lawkland
Stackhouse
Eldroth
Langcliffe
Lowgill
Tatham Fells
1318
Burn Moor Fell
Giggleswick
Settle
1815
Malham Cove
Gordale Scar
Bordley
Grassington
Threshfield
Linton
Kirkby Fell
Scaleber Force
Waterfall
Malham
Yorkshire Dales National Park
Thrushgill
Wham
Boss Moor
Botton Head
1595
Mearbeck
Hanlith
Kirkby Malham
R. Aire
Winterburn Reservoir
Cracoe
Threapland
Catlow Fell
Black Hill
1786
White Hill
Rathmell
Ribblesdale
Long Preston
Airton
Calton
Winterburn
Hetton
Rylstone
Otterburn
Croasdale Fell
Hellifield
B6478
Wigglesworth
Bell Busk
Eshton
Flasby
B6265
Stocks Resr.
Tosside
Tosside Beck
A682
Halton West
Coniston Cold
Embsay Moor
Eller Beck
Gargrave
Embsay
FOREST
Nappa
Bank Newton
Skipton
Thorlby
Slaidburn
Paythorne
Newsholme
East Marton
Broughton
A59
R. Hodder
Newton
West Marton
Horton
Broughton Hall
SKIPTON
Craven
Dunsop Bridge
Lane Ends
Holden
Bolton-by-Bowland
R. Ribble
Thornton in Craven
Elslack
Carleton
A6131
BOWLAND
Easington Fell
1300
Gisburn
Bracewell
B6251
A56
A629
Whitewell
Sawley
Abbey
Barnoldswick
B6252
Canal
Mill Engine
B6383
Earby
Cononley
Browsholme Hall
Grindleton
Rimington
Howgill
Salterforth
Lothersdale
Glusburn
West Bradford
Chatburn
Weets Hill
Kelbrook
Horrocksford
Downham
Twiston
Bashall Eaves
Waddington
Whitemoor Resr.
A6068
Sutton-in-Craven
Cowling
Bashall Town
Clitheroe
Worston
Pendle Hill
Blacko
Foulridge
Walker Fold
Clitheroe Castle
Low Moor
B6243
1827
Laneshaw Resr.
Colne
Barley
Roughlee
Laneshaw Bridge
PENDLE
Woodfields
Stonyhurst College
Barrow
Pendleton
Newchurch
Barrowford
235
Wycoller Hall
1453
Trawden
Great Mitton
B6246
Wheatley Lane
KEIGHLEY MOOR
New Row
Sabden
FOREST OF PENDLE
THE FOREST OF TRAWDEN
Water Sheddles Reservoir
Hurst Green
Wiswell
Fence
NELSON
Ponden Resr.
Higham
B6248
Brierfield
SCALE
1: 200,000
0 1 2 3 Miles
0 1 2 3 4 5 Kilometres
Read
A671
Gawthorpe Hall
NT
R. Calder
M65
Lane Bottom
Haggate
Boulsworth Hill
1699
Textile Rescue Centre
Haworth Moor

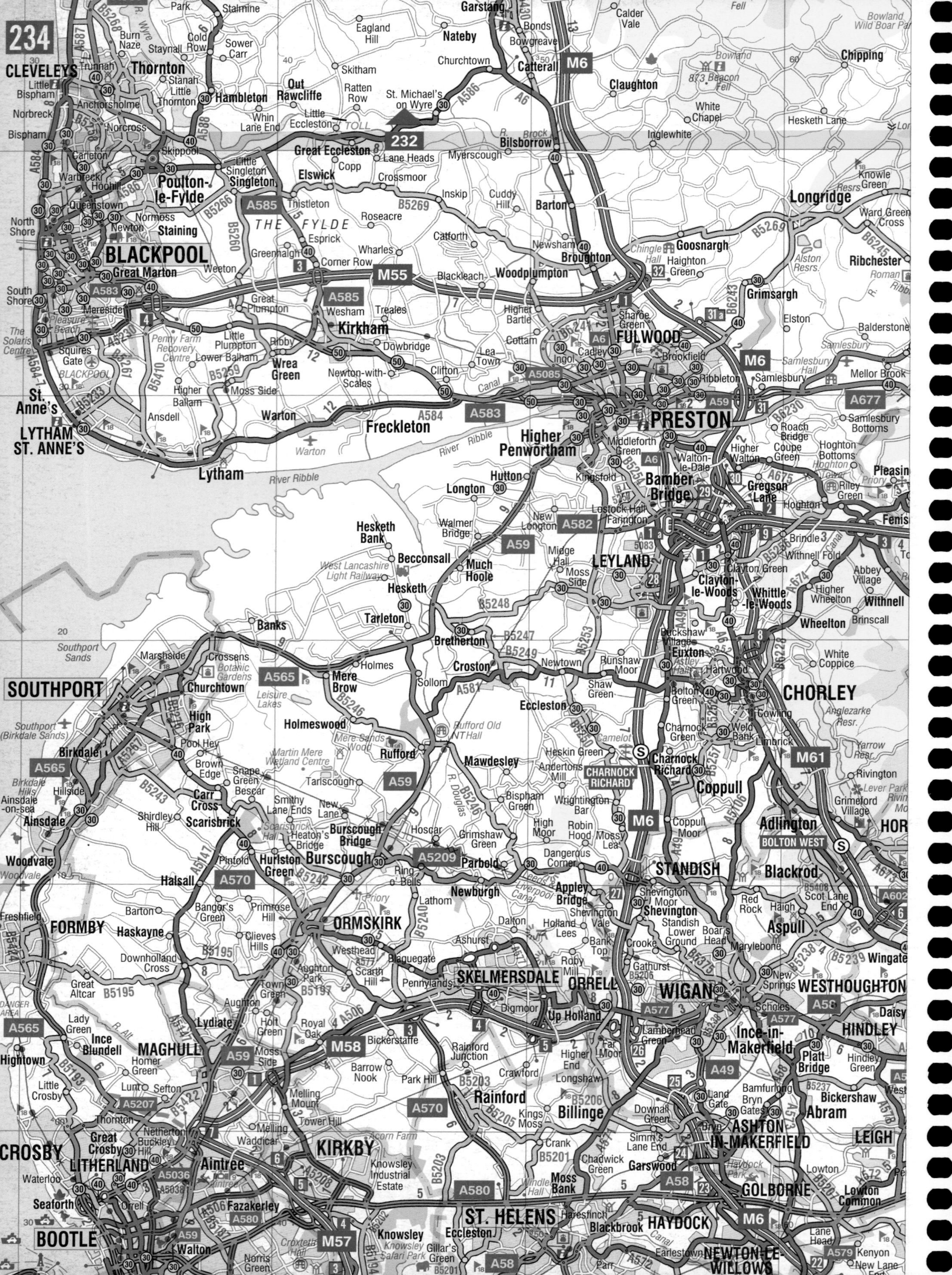
Stalmine
Garstang
Calder Vale
Bowland Wild Boar Park
Burn Naze
Cold Row
Sower Carr
Eagland Hill
Nateby
Bonds
Bowgreave
Staynall
M6
Chipping
CLEVELEYS
Thornton
Skitham
Churchtown
Catterall
Bowland
873 Beacon Fell
Little Bispham
Stanah
Little Thornton
Out Rawcliffe
Ratten Row
St. Michael's on Wyre
Claughton
Anchorsholme
Hambleton
Norbreck
Whin Lane End
Little Eccleston
TOLL
White Chapel
Hesketh Lane
Bispham
Norcross
232
Bilsborrow
Inglewhite
Carleton
Skippool
Great Eccleston
Lane Heads
Myerscough
Little Singleton
Copp
Warbreck
Hoohill
Poulton-le-Fylde
Singleton
Elswick
Crossmoor
Knowle Green
Inskip
Cuddy Hill
Barton
Longridge
Thistleton
Queenstown
A585
B5269
Ward Green Cross
North Shore
Normoss
Newton
Staining
THE FYLDE
Roseacre
Esprick
Catforth
Goosnargh
BLACKPOOL
Greenhalgh
Wharles
Newsham
Chingle Hall
Haighton Green
Alston Resrs.
Ribchester
Weeton
Corner Row
Broughton
Great Marton
M55
Blackleach
Woodplumpton
Grimsargh
A583
South Shore
Great Plumpton
Wesham
Treales
Higher Bartle
Sharoe Green
Elston
Mereside
Pleasure Beach
Kirkham
Balderstone
The Solaris Centre
Penny Farm Recovery Centre
Little Plumpton
Ribby
Dowbridge
Cottam
FULWOOD
Samlesbury
Squires Gate
Lower Balham
Wrea Green
Lea Town
Ingol
Cadley
Brookfield
M6
BLACKPOOL
Newton-with-Scales
Clifton
Ribbleton
Samlesbury
Mellor Brook
St. Anne's
Higher Ballam
Moss Side
Canal
A5085
A59
A677
Ansdell
Warton
A584
A583
PRESTON
Samlesbury Bottoms
LYTHAM ST. ANNE'S
Freckleton
Higher Penwortham
Roach Bridge
Warton
River Ribble
Middleforth Green
Higher Walton
Coupe Green
Hoghton Bottoms
Lytham
River Ribble
Hutton
Kingsfold
Walton-le-Dale
Bamber Bridge
Gregson Lane
Riley Green
Pleasington
Longton
Hoghton
Lostock Hall
Farington
New Longton
A582
Feniscowles
Hesketh Bank
Walmer Bridge
A59
Brindle
Becconsall
Much Hoole
Midge Hall
LEYLAND
Withnell Fold
West Lancashire Light Railway
Moss Side
Clayton Green
Abbey Village
Hesketh
Clayton-le-Woods
Whittle-le-Woods
Higher Wheelton
Withnell
B5248
Tarleton
Wheelton
Brinscall
Banks
Bretherton
B5247
Buckshaw Village
Southport Sands
Marshside
Crossens
Botanic Gardens
Holmes
B5249
Runshaw Moor
Euxton
Astley Hall
White Coppice
Newtown
A565
Mere Brow
Croston
Hartwood
SOUTHPORT
Churchtown
Leisure Lakes
Sollom
A581
Shaw Green
Bolton Green
CHORLEY
Eccleston
Cowling
Southport (Birkdale Sands)
High Park
Holmeswood
B5246
Rufford Old Hall NT
Anglezarke Resr.
Camelot
Charnock Green
Weld Bank
Limbrick
Pool Hey
Mere Sands Wood
Rufford
Mawdesley
Heskin Green
Charnock Richard
M61
Yarrow Resr.
Birkdale
Martin Mere Wetland Centre
Andertons Mill
CHARNOCK RICHARD
Coppull
Rivington
A565
Brown Edge
Snape Green
Tarlscough
A59
Lever Park
Birkdale Hills
Hillside
Bescar
Carr Cross
R. Douglas
Bispham Green
Wrightington Bar
Grimeford Village
Ainsdale-on-sea
B5243
Smithy Lane Ends
New Lane
High Moor
Robin Hood
Mossy Lea
M6
Coppull Moor
Adlington
BOLTON WEST
Ainsdale
Shirdley Hill
Scarisbrick
Scarisbrick Hall
Heaton's Bridge
Burscough Bridge
Hoscar
Grimshaw Green
Dangerous Corner
Woodvale
Pinfold
Hurlston Green
Burscough
A5209
Parbold
STANDISH
Blackrod
Halsall
A570
Ring o' Bells
Appley Bridge
Shevington Moor
Shevington
Red Rock
Haigh
Scot Lane End
Freshfield
Barton
Bangor's Green
Primrose Hill
Priory
Lathom
Newburgh
Liverpool Canal
Shevington Vale
Standish Lower Ground
Boar's Head
Aspull
FORMBY
Haskayne
Clieves Hills
ORMSKIRK
Dalton
Holland Lees
Crooke
Marylebone
Downholland Cross
B5195
Westhead
Ashurst
Bank Top
Gathurst
Wingates
Blaguegate
Roby Mill
New Springs
Great Altcar
B5195
Aughton Park
Scarth Hill
Pennylands
SKELMERSDALE
ORRELL
WIGAN
WESTHOUGHTON
Town Green
B5197
Digmoor
Up Holland
A577
Scholes
A58
DANGER AREA
Aughton
A577
Lady Green
R. Alt
Lydiate
Holt Green
Royal Oak
A506
Lamberhead Green
Daisy
A565
Ince Blundell
MAGHULL
Moss Side
M58
Bickerstaffe
Rainford Junction
Higher End
Far Moor
Ince-in-Makerfield
HINDLEY
Hightown
Homer Green
Barrow Nook
A49
Platt Bridge
Hindley Green
Park Hill
Crawford
Longshaw
Little Crosby
Lunt
Sefton
Melling Mount
B5203
Rainford
B5206
Bamfurlong
Bickershaw
A5207
A570
Billinge
Bryn Gates
Abram
Thornton
Tower Hill
B5205
Kings Moss
Land Gate
Downall Green
Bryn
ASHTON-IN-MAKERFIELD
Netherton
Melling
Acorn Farm
Great Crosby
Buckley Hill
Waddicar
Simm's Lane End
LEIGH
CROSBY
LITHERLAND
Aintree
KIRKBY
Crank
B5201
Chadwick Green
Garswood
Haydock Park
A5036
Aintree
A5208
Knowsley Industrial Estate
B5203
Windle Hall
Moss Bank
A58
Lowton
Waterloo
A580
GOLBORNE
Lowton Common
Seaforth
Orrell
Fazakerley
ST. HELENS
Haresfinch
A580
Blackbrook
HAYDOCK
M6
BOOTLE
A59
Walton
Croxteth Hall
M57
Knowsley
Knowsley Safari Park
Eccleston
Gillar's Green
A58
B5201
Canal
Lane Head
Norris Green
Parr
A572
Earlestown
NEWTON-LE-WILLOWS
A579
Kenyon
New Lane End

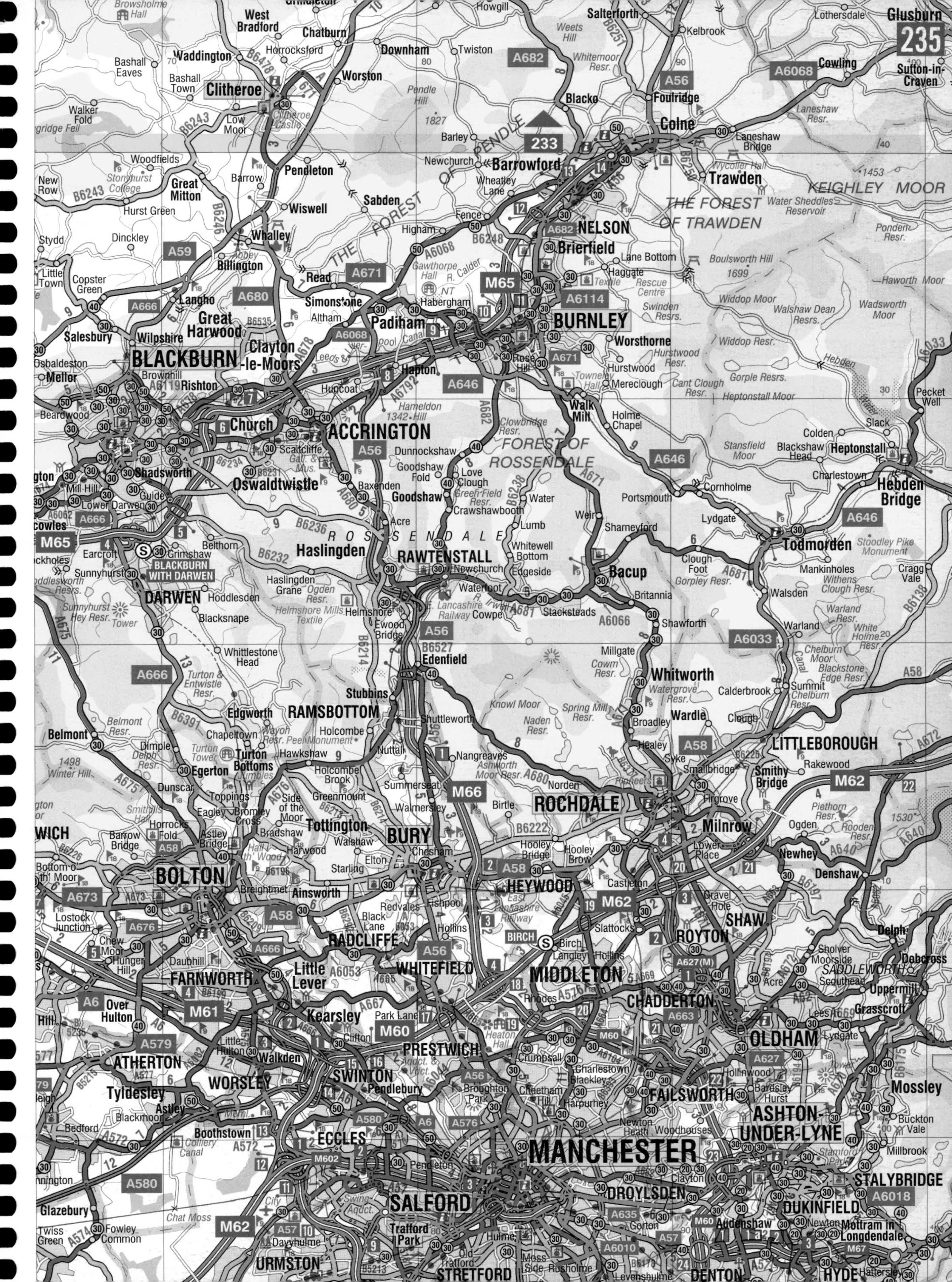
Browsholme Hall
West Bradford
Chatburn
Howgill
Salterforth
Lothersdale
Glusburn
Bashall Eaves
Waddington
Horrocksford
Downham
Twiston
Weets Hill
Kelbrook
Bashall Town
Clitheroe
Worston
A682
Whitemoor Resr.
A6068
Cowling
Sutton-in-Craven
Walker Fold
Clitheroe Castle
Pendle Hill
1827
Blacko
A56
Foulridge
Laneshaw Resr.
Low Moor
Barley
233
Colne
Laneshaw Bridge
Woodfields
Stonyhurst College
Pendleton
Newchurch
Barrowford
Wycoller Hall
New Row
Great Mitton
Barrow
Wheatley Lane
Trawden
KEIGHLEY MOOR
B6243
Hurst Green
Wiswell
Sabden
THE FOREST OF PENDLE
THE FOREST OF TRAWDEN
Water Sheddles Reservoir
Ponden Resr.
Stydd
Dinckley
Whalley
Fence
NELSON
A59
Higham
Brierfield
Lane Bottom
Boulsworth Hill 1699
Little Town
Copster Green
Billington
Read
A671
Gawthorpe Hall
R. Calder
Haggate
Haworth Moor
Langho
A680
M65
Rescue Centre
Widdop Moor
Wadsworth Moor
A666
Great Harwood
Simonstone
Altham
Habergham
A6114
Swinden Resrs.
Walshaw Dean Resrs.
Salesbury
Wilpshire
Padiham
BURNLEY
Clayton-le-Moors
A6068
Worsthorne
Widdop Resr.
BLACKBURN
Hurstwood Resr.
Osbaldeston
Mellor
Brownhill
Rishton
Hapton
Huncoat
A671
Hurstwood
Towneley Hall
Mereclough
Gorple Resrs.
Cant Clough Resr.
Heptonstall Moor
Pecket Well
Beardwood
A646
Hameldon Hill 1342
Walk Mill
Holme Chapel
Clowbridge Resr.
Slack
Church
ACCRINGTON
Colden
Blackshaw Head
Heptonstall
Stansfield Moor
FOREST OF ROSSENDALE
Dunnockshaw
A56
Scaitcliffe
A646
Charlestown
Goodshaw Fold
Love Clough
Shadsworth
Oswaldtwistle
Baxenden
Cornholme
Hebden Bridge
Mill Hill
Goodshaw
Green Field Resr.
Water
Portsmouth
Guide
Lower Darwen
Crawshawbooth
Weir
Lydgate
A646
Acre
Lumb
Sharneyford
M65
Grimshaw
Belthorn
ROSSENDALE
Haslingden
Todmorden
Stoodley Pike Monument
BLACKBURN WITH DARWEN
RAWTENSTALL
Whitewell Bottom
Earcroft
Sunnyhurst
Newchurch
Edgeside
Bacup
Clough Foot
Mankinholes
Cragg Vale
Haslingden Grane
Ogden Resr.
Gorpley Resr.
Withens Clough Resr.
DARWEN
Hoddlesden
Waterfoot
Britannia
Walsden
Sunnyhurst Hey Resr.
Tower
Helmshore Mills Textile
Helmshore
E. Lancashire Railway
Cowpe
Stacksteads
Warland Resr.
Blacksnape
Ewood Bridge
A56
A6066
Shawforth
Warland
White Holme Resr.
A6033
Whittlestone Head
B6527
Edenfield
Millgate
Cowm Resr.
Chelburn Moor
Blackstone Edge Resr.
A666
Turton & Entwistle Resr.
Whitworth
Watergrove Resr.
Calderbrook
Summit
Chelburn Resr.
A58
Stubbins
Knowl Moor
Spring Mill Resr.
Edgworth
RAMSBOTTOM
Naden Resr.
Wardle
Belmont Resr.
Shuttleworth
Broadley
Clough
Belmont
Chapeltown
Holcombe
Wayoh Resr.
Peel Monument
Healey
A58
LITTLEBOROUGH
Dimple
Turton Bottoms
Hawkshaw
Nuttall
Syke
Rakewood
Delph Resr.
Turton Tower
Smallbridge
Smithy Bridge
M62
1498 Winter Hill
Egerton
Holcombe Brook
Nangreaves
Ashworth Moor Resr.
A680
Norden
Dunscar
Toppings
Greenmount
Summerseat
M66
Firgrove
Side of the Moor
Birtle
ROCHDALE
Piethorn Resr.
Eagley
Bromley Cross
Walmersley
Smithills Hall
Milnrow
Ogden
Horrocks Fold
Tottington
B6222
Rooden Resr.
WICH
Barrow Bridge
Astley Bridge
Bradshaw
BURY
Hooley Bridge
Hooley Brow
Lower Place
Newhey
A58
Hall i' th' Wood
Walshaw
Chesham
Bottom o' th' Moor
Harwood
Elton
A58
Denshaw
BOLTON
Starling
HEYWOOD
Castleton
A673
Breightmet
Ainsworth
Gravel Hole
Redvales
Fishpool
M62
Lostock Junction
A58
Black Lane
East Lancashire Railway
SHAW
A676
Hollins
Slattocks
Delph
Chew Moor
RADCLIFFE
BIRCH
ROYTON
Daubhill
A666
Birch
Langley
Hollins
Sholver
Moorside
Dobcross
Hunger Hill
A56
A627(M)
SADDLEWORTH
FARNWORTH
Little Lever
A6053
WHITEFIELD
MIDDLETON
Acre
Scouthead
Uppermill
A6
Over Hulton
Rhodes
CHADDERTON
M61
Kearsley
Park Lane
A663
Lees
Grasscroft
Hill
Little Hulton
Clifton
M60
Heaton Hall
M60
OLDHAM
Lydgate
A579
Walkden
PRESTWICH
ATHERTON
Crumpsall
Charlestown
A627
Hollinwood
Bardsley
Hurst
Mossley
WORSLEY
SWINTON
Pendlebury
Aqdct. & Vict.
Blackley
Harpurhey
Cheetham Hill
A56
Tyldesley
Astley
Broughton Park
FAILSWORTH
Blackmoor
Bedford
A580
A6
A576
Newton Heath
Woodhouses
ASHTON-UNDER-LYNE
Buckton Vale
Boothstown
ECCLES
Colliery Canal
A572
MANCHESTER
Stamford Park
Millbrook
M602
Pendleton
Clayton
STALYBRIDGE
A580
nnington
City
Swing Aqdct.
SALFORD
DROYLSDEN
A6018
Glazebury
Chat Moss
A635
Gorton
DUKINFIELD
Twiss Green
Fowley Common
M62
A57
Trafford Park
Audenshaw
Mottram in Longdendale
Davyhulme
Newton
A6010
A57
M67
URMSTON
Hulme
Old Trafford
Moss Side
Rusholme
Levenshulme
DENTON
HYDE
Hattersley
STRETFORD

INDEX

Including Streets, Places & Areas, Industrial Estates,
Selected Flats & Walkways, Service Areas, Stations and Selected Places of Interest.

HOW TO USE THIS INDEX

1. Each street name is followed by its Postcode District, then by its Locality abbreviation(s) and then by its map reference;
e.g. **Accrington Rd.** BB1: Blackb . . . .3B **140** is in the BB1 Postcode District and the Blackburn Locality and is to be found in square 3B on page **140**. The page number is shown in bold type.

2. A strict alphabetical order is followed in which Av., Rd., St., etc. (though abbreviated) are read in full and as part of the street name; e.g. **Ash Brow** appears after **Ashbrook St.** but before **Ashburn Av.**

3. Streets and a selection of flats and walkways that cannot be shown on the mapping, appear in the index with the thoroughfare to which they are connected shown in brackets;
e.g. **Abbeyfield** BB11: Burnl . . . .5F **124** (off Oxford Rd.)

4. Addresses that are in more than one part are referred to as not continuous.

5. Places and areas are shown in the index in BLUE TYPE and the map reference is to the actual map square in which the town centre or area is located and not to the place name shown on the map;
e.g. ACCRINGTON 2B 142

6. An example of a selected place of interest is Astley Hall Mus. & Art Gallery 5C 174

7. An example of a station is **Accrington Station (Rail)** . . . .2A **142**. Included are Rail (**Rail**), Stop (**Tram**) and Park & Ride.
e.g. **Bluebell Way (Park & Ride)** 3B **116**

8. Service Areas are shown in the index in BOLD CAPITAL TYPE; e.g. BLACKBURN WITH DARWEN SERVICE AREA 2N 157

9. Map references for entries that appear on large scale pages **226-229** are shown first, with small scale map references shown in brackets; e.g. **Aberdeen Rd.** LA1: Lanc 8E **228** (9L **23**)

GENERAL ABBREVIATIONS

All. : Alley	Ct. : Court	Info. : Information	Res. : Residential
App. : Approach	Cres. : Crescent	Junc. : Junction	Ri. : Rise
Arc. : Arcade	Cft. : Croft	La. : Lane	Rd. : Road
Av. : Avenue	Dr. : Drive	Lit. : Little	Rdbt. : Roundabout
Bk. : Back	E. : East	Lwr. : Lower	Shop. : Shopping
Blvd. : Boulevard	Ent. : Enterprise	Mnr. : Manor	Sth. : South
Bri. : Bridge	Est. : Estate	Mans. : Mansions	Sq. : Square
B'way. : Broadway	Fld. : Field	Mkt. : Market	Sta. : Station
Bldg. : Building	Flds. : Fields	Mdw. : Meadow	St. : Street
Bldgs. : Buildings	Gdn. : Garden	Mdws. : Meadows	Ter. : Terrace
Bungs. : Bungalows	Gdns. : Gardens	M. : Mews	Twr. : Tower
Bus. : Business	Gth. : Garth	Mt. : Mount	Trad. : Trading
Cvn. : Caravan	Ga. : Gate	Mus. : Museum	Up. : Upper
C'way. : Causeway	Gt. : Great	Nth. : North	Va. : Vale
Cen. : Centre	Grn. : Green	Pde. : Parade	Vw. : View
Cl. : Close	Gro. : Grove	Pk. : Park	Vs. : Villas
Comn. : Common	Hgts. : Heights	Pas. : Passage	Vis. : Visitors
Cnr. : Corner	Ho. : House	Pl. : Place	Wlk. : Walk
Cott. : Cottage	Ho's. : Houses	Pct. : Precinct	W. : West
Cotts. : Cottages	Ind. : Industrial	Prom. : Promenade	Yd. : Yard

LOCALITY ABBREVIATIONS

Abb : Abbeystead	Carl : Carleton	Foul : Foulridge	Ire : Ireby
Acc : Accrington	Carn : Carnforth	Frec : Freckleton	Kear : Kearstwick
Adl : Adlington	Carr B : Carr Bank	Fulw : Fulwood	Kelb : Kelbrook
Aff : Affetside	Cast : Casterton	Gal : Galgate	Kirk : Kirkby
Ains : Ainsdale	Catf : Catforth	Garg : Gargrave	K Lon : Kirkby Lonsdale
Aint : Aintree	Caton : Caton	Gars : Garstang	K'ham : Kirkham
Ald : Aldcliffe	Catt : Catterall	Gate : Gatebeck	K Sea : Knott End-on-Sea
Alt : Altham	Chaig : Chaigley	Gig : Giggleswick	Know G : Knowle Green
And : Anderton	Char R : Charnock Richard	Gis : Gisburn	Know P : Knowsley Industrial Park
App B : Appley Bridge	Chatb : Chatburn	Glas : Glasson	Lanc : Lancaster
Ark : Arkholme	Chip : Chipping	Goos : Goosnargh	Lane B : Laneshaw Bridge
Arn : Arnside	Chor : Chorley	G Sand : Grange-over-Sands	Langc : Langcliffe
Ash R : Ashton-on-Ribble	Chur : Church	Gt A : Great Altcar	Langh : Langho
Aug : Aughton	C'town : Churchtown	Gt E : Great Eccleston	Larb : Larbreck
Bac : Bacup	Clau : Claughton	Gt H : Great Harwood	Lath : Lathom
Bail : Bailrigg	Claw : Clawthorpe	Gt M : Great Mitton	Lea : Lea
Bald : Balderstone	Clay D : Clayton-le-Dale	Gt P : Great Plumpton	Lea T : Lea Town
Bam B : Bamber Bridge	Clay M : Clayton-le-Moors	Greenh : Greenhalgh	Leck : Leck
Ban N : Bank Newton	Clay W : Clayton-le-Woods	Greenm : Greenmount	Leyl : Leyland
Banks : Banks	Clif : Clifton	Gress : Gressingham	Light G : Lightfoot Green
Barb : Barbon	Clith : Clitheroe	Grim : Grimsargh	Littleb : Littleborough
Barl : Barley	Cliv : Cliviger	Grind : Grindleton	Littled : Littledale
Barn : Barnacre	C'ham : Cockerham	Guide : Guide	Lit C : Little Crosby
Barnw : Barnoldswick	Cold : Colden	Haigh : Haighton	Lit E : Little Eccleston
Barr : Barrow	Colne : Colne	Hale : Hale	Lit H : Little Hoole
Barrf : Barrowford	C Grn : Conder Green	Hals : Halsall	Lit P : Little Plumpton
Bartl : Bartle	Con C : Coniston Cold	Halt : Halton	Lon P : Long Preston
Bart : Barton	Copp : Coppull	Hal W : Halton West	Longr : Longridge
Bas E : Bashall Eaves	Cop G : Copster Green	Ham : Hambleton	Longt : Longton
Bax : Baxenden	Cott : Cottam	Ham G : Hampson Green	Lost H : Lostock Hall
Bay H : Bay Horse	Cow B : Cowan Bridge	Hapt : Hapton	Loth : Lothersdale
Belm : Belmont	Cow A : Cow Ark	Hasl : Haslingden	L Ben : Low Bentham
Belt : Belthorn	Cowl : Cowling	Hawk : Hawkshaw	L Big : Low Biggins
Bick : Bickerstaffe	Crank : Crank	Heap : Heapey	Lwr B : Lower Bartle
Bill : Billinge	Craws : Crawshawbooth	H Charn : Heath Charnock	Lwr D : Lower Darwen
B'ton : Billington	Crossm : Crossmoor	Heat : Heaton	Low : Lowgill
Bils : Bilsborrow	Cros : Croston	Hell : Hellifield	Lumb : Lumb
Birk : Birkdale	Dalt : Dalton	Hept : Heptonstall	Lup : Lupton
Bis G : Bispham Green	Darw : Darwen	Hest B : Hest Bank	Lyd : Lydiate
Blackb : Blackburn	Dinck : Dinckley	Hesk B : Hesketh Bank	L Ann : Lytham St Annes
Blacko : Blacko	Dolp : Dolphinholme	Hesk : Heskin	Magh : Maghull
Blackp : Blackpool	D'ham : Downham	Heys : Heysham	Mans : Mansergh
Blackr : Blackrod	D'holl : Downholland	Heyw : Heywood	Mawd : Mawdesley
Black H : Blackshaw Head	Dunn : Dunnockshaw	High : Higham	Mell : Melling
Bleas : Bleasdale	Dun B : Dunsop Bridge	H Ben : High Bentham	Mellor : Mellor
Bolt : Bolton	Dutt : Dutton	H Big : High Biggins	Mellor B : Mellor Brook
Bolt B : Bolton-by-Bowland	Earl : Earby	H Cas : High Casterton	Mere B : Mere Brow
Bolt S : Bolton-le-Sands	Eas M : East Marton	H Bart : Higher Bartle	Midd : Middleton
Borw : Borwick	E'hill : Eccleshill	H Walt : Higher Walton	Midge H : Midge Hall
Bowg : Bowgreave	E'ton : Eccleston	H Wheel : Higher Wheelton	Milnr : Milnrow
Brac : Bracewell	Eden : Edenfield	Hight : Hightown	Morec : Morecambe
Breth : Bretherton	Edgw : Edgworth	Hodd : Hoddlesden	Moss S : Moss Side
Brierc : Briercliffe	Eger : Egerton	Hogh : Hoghton	Much H : Much Hoole
Brierf : Brierfield	Ell : Ellel	Holc : Holcombe	Nateby : Nateby
Brind : Brindle	Elsl : Elslack	Holme : Holme	Nelson : Nelson
Birns : Brinscall	Elsw : Elswick	Holmesw : Holmeswood	Neth B : Nether Burrow
Brom C : Bromley Cross	Eng H : England Hill	Horn : Hornby	Neth K : Nether Kellet
Brookh : Brookhouse	Esh : Eshton	Hort : Horton	N'ton : Netherton
Bryn : Bryning	Esp : Esprick	Hor : Horwich	N'gin : Newbiggin
Buck V : Buckshaw Village	Eux : Euxton	Hunc : Huncoat	N 'urgh : Newburgh
Burnl : Burnley	Far : Farington	Hurst G : Hurst Green	Newc : Newchurch
Burs : Burscough	Far M : Farington Moss	H'wood : Hurstwood	Newc P : Newchurch in Pendle
Burt K : Burton-in-Kendal	Farl : Farleton	Hutt : Hutton	New L : New Longton
Bur L : Burton in Lonsdale	Faz : Fazakerley	H Roo : Hutton Roof	News : Newsholme
Bury : Bury	Fence : Fence	Ince B : Ince Blundell	Newt : Newton
Cab : Cabus	Fenis : Feniscowles	Ingl : Ingleton	Oaken : Oakenclough
Cald V : Calder Vale	Flee : Fleetwood	Inglew : Inglewhite	Old L : Old Langho
Cap : Capernwray	Form : Formby	Ingol : Ingol	Orms : Ormskirk
	Fort : Forton	Inskip : Inskip	Orr : Orrell

Aalborg Pl.—Alan's Way

Osb : **Osbaldeston**
Osw : **Oswaldtwistle**
Out R : **Out Rawcliffe**
O Bur : **Over Burrow**
Over K : **Over Kellet**
O'ton : **Overton**
Padi : **Padiham**
Parb : **Parbold**
Pay : **Paythorne**
Pend : **Pendleton**
Penw : **Penwortham**
Pick B : **Pickup Bank**
Pill : **Pilling**
Pleas : **Pleasington**
Poul F : **Poulton-le-Fylde**
Pree : **Preesall**
Prest : **Preston**
Prie H : **Priest Hutton**
Quern : **Quernmore**
Rain : **Rainford**
Ramsb : **Ramsbottom**
Ramsg : **Ramsgreave**
Rath : **Rathmell**
Rawt : **Rawtenstall**
Read : **Read**
Reed : **Reedley**
Ribb : **Ribbleton**
Ribc : **Ribchester**
Rim : **Rimington**
Rish : **Rishton**
Ris B : **Rising Bridge**
R'ton : **Rivington**
Roby M : **Roby Mill**
Roch : **Rochdale**
Roeb : **Roeburndale**
Rose : **Roseacre**
Rough : **Roughlee**
Ruff : **Rufford**
Sabd : **Sabden**
St M : **St Michaels**
Sale : **Salesbury**
Salt : **Salterforth**
Salw : **Salwick**
Sam : **Samlesbury**
Saw : **Sawley**
Scar : **Scarisbrick**
Scor : **Scorton**
Seft : **Sefton**
Sett : **Settle**
Shev : **Shevington**
Silv : **Silverdale**
S'stone : **Simonstone**
S'wood : **Simonswood**
Sing : **Singleton**
Skelm : **Skelmersdale**
Slack H : **Slack Head**
Slaid : **Slaidburn**
Slyne : **Slyne**
Sough : **Sough**
S'field : **Southfield**
S'port : **Southport**
Stain : **Staining**
Stal : **Stalmine**
Stand : **Standish**
Stodd : **Stodday**
S Fold : **Stone Fold**
S'hurst : **Stonyhurst**
Storth : **Storth**
Summ : **Summerseat**
S'land : **Sunderland**
Tarl : **Tarleton**
Tat : **Tatham**
Tewit : **Tewitfield**
This : **Thistleton**
T'ley : **Thornley**
T'ton : **Thornton**
T Clev : **Thornton Cleveleys**
T Crav : **Thornton-in-Craven**
Thorn L : **Thornton in Lonsdale**
Thurn : **Thurnham**
Tock : **Tockholes**
Tod : **Todmorden**
Tos : **Tosside**
Tott : **Tottington**
Traw : **Trawden**
Trea : **Treales**
Tuns : **Tunstall**
Turt : **Turton**
Twis : **Twiston**
Uph : **Upholland**
Wadd : **Waddington**
Wal B : **Walmer Bridge**
Wals : **Walsden**
Walt D : **Walton-le-Dale**
Ward : **Wardle**
Wart : **Warton**
Water : **Water**
W'foot : **Waterfoot**
W'side : **Waterside**
Weet : **Weeton**
Weir : **Weir**
Wen : **Wennington**
West B : **West Bradford**
W Mar : **West Marton**
Wesh : **Wesham**
Westby : **Westby**
W'head : **Westhead**
W'ouse : **Westhouse**
Whall : **Whalley**
Wharl : **Wharles**
Wheel : **Wheelton**
Whitec : **Whitechapel**
W Stake : **White Stake**
White : **Whitewell**
W'ham : **Whittingham**
Whit : **Whittington**
Whit W : **Whittle-le-Woods**
Whitw : **Whitworth**
Widd : **Widdop**
Wigan : **Wigan**
Wig : **Wigglesworth**
Wilp : **Wilpshire**
Wind : **Windle**
Wine : **Winewall**
Winm : **Winmarleigh**
Wins : **Winstanley**
Wis : **Wiswell**
Withg : **Withgill**
Withn : **Withnell**
Woodp : **Woodplumpton**
W'thorne : **Worsthorne**
Wors : **Worston**
Wray : **Wray**
W Grn : **Wrea Green**
Wrigh : **Wrightington**
Yea C : **Yealand Coyners**
Yea R : **Yealand Redmayne**

A

Aalborg Pl. LA1: Lanc 8D **228** (9K **23**)
Aalborg Sq. LA1: Lanc 8D **228**
Abacus St. FY1: Blackp 6L **227**
Abberley Way WN3: Wigan 7L **221**
Abberton Pk. L30: N'ton 5A **222**
Abbey Cl. L33: Kirk 8L **223**
L37: Form 1B **214**
WN8: Uph 4F **220**
Abbey Cres. BB3: Darw 7C **158**
OL10: Heyw 9F **202**
Abbey Dale WN6: App B 5G **213**
Abbeydale L40: Burs 1D **210**
LA3: Morec 6B **22**
OL12: Roch 5B **204**
Abbeydale Way BB5: Acc 3M **141**
Abbey Dr. OL15: Littleb 2J **205**
WN5: Orr 5H **221**
Abbey Farm Caravan Pk. L40: Lath 4A **210**
Abbeyfield *BB11: Burnl* *5F* ***124***
(off Oxford Rd.)
Abbeyfield Cl. LA1: Lanc 4L **29**
Abbeyfield Ho. BB11: Burnl 4A **228**
Abbey Flds. BB7: Whall 5H **101**
Abbey Fold L40: Burs 8B **190**
Abbey Gdns. PR8: Birk 1G **186**
Abbey Gro. PR6: Adl 6J **195**
Abbey La. L40: Burs, Lath 3A **210**
Abbey La. Ind. Est. L40: Burs 3A **210**
Abbey Pl. BB3: Darw 7C **158**
Abbey Rd. BB7: Whall 5J **101**
FY4: Blackp 3C **108**
ABBEYSTEAD 3A **48**
Abbeystead WN8: Skelm 4M **219**
Abbeystead Av. L30: N'ton 9A **222**
Abbeystead Dr. LA1: Lanc 4L **29**
Abbeystead Ho. *LA1: Lanc* *4L* ***29***
(off Abbeystead Dr.)
Abbeystead La. LA2: Abb 9L **31**
Abbeystead Rd. LA2: Abb, Dolp 6E **38**
Abbey St. BB5: Acc 2B **142**
OL13: Bac 3K **163**
PR2: Ash R 9G **115**
Abbey Ter. BB7: Barr 1K **101**
BB7: B'ton 7G **100**
Abbey Vw. BB7: B'ton 6J **101**
PR6: Withn 6B **156**
ABBEY VILLAGE 5D **156**
Abbeyville FY4: Blackp 3C **108**
Abbey Wlk. PR1: Penw 6G **135**
Abbeywood WN8: Skelm 5N **219**
Abbot Mdw. PR1: Penw 4G **135**
Abbots Cl. BB4: Rawt 3M **161**
L37: Form 2A **214**
PR4: K'ham 5A **112**
Abbots Cft. BB7: Whall 5J **101**
Abbotsford L39: Orms 7L **209**
OL12: Whitw 4A **184**
Abbotsford Av. BB2: Blackb 7L **139**
Abbotsford M. *L39: Orms* *7L* ***209***
(off Abbotsford)
Abbotsford Rd. FY3: Blackp 7F **88**
Abbotsgate *LA6: K Lon* *6E* ***8***
(off Kendal Rd.)
Abbots Ho. *LA1: Lanc* *7D* ***228***
(off Bridget St)
Abbots Row FY8: L Ann 2K **129**
Abbots Way L37: Form 2A **214**
LA1: Lanc 8G **22**
Abbotsway PR1: Penw 2F **134**
Abbott Brow BB2: Mellor 5E **118**
Abbott Clough Av. BB1: Blackb 4E **140**
Abbott Clough Cl. BB1: Blackb 4E **140**
Abbott Cft. PR4: Light G 2D **114**
Abbotts Cl. PR5: Walt D 5B **136**
Abbott St. BL6: Hor 9C **196**
OL11: Roch 9M **203**
Abbotts Wlk. FY7: Flee 8G **40**
Abbot Wlk. BB7: Clith 3N **81**
Abel St. BB10: Burnl 9E **104**
Abercorn Pl. FY4: Blackp 4A **108**
Abercorn Place Stop (Tram) 4A **108**
Abercorn Rd. BL1: Bolt 9B **198**
Abercrombie Rd. FY7: Flee 8F **40**
Aberdare Cl. BB1: Blackb 1M **139**
Aberdeen Dr. BB1: Blackb 4A **140**
Aberdeen Gdns. OL12: Roch 1A **204**
Aberdeen Rd. LA1: Lanc 8E **228** (9L **23**)
Aberley Fold OL15: Littleb 7J **185**
Abingdon Cl. OL11: Roch 8B **204**
Abingdon Dr. PR2: Ash R 8D **114**
Abingdon Gro. LA3: Heys 9M **21**
Abingdon Rd. BB12: Padi 2J **123**
Abingdon St. FY1: Blackp 1H **227** (4B **88**)
Abinger St. BB10: Burnl 9G **104**
Abington Dr. PR9: Banks 1F **168**
Abner Row BB8: Foul 2A **86**
Aboukir St. OL16: Roch 5E **204**
ABRAHAM HEIGHTS 9A **228** (9H **23**)
Abraham St. BB2: Blackb 9C **226** (6M **139**)
BB5: Acc 3A **142**
BL6: Hor 9C **196**
Abrams Fold PR9: Banks 1E **168**
Abrams Grn. PR9: Banks 1E **168**
Acacia Cl. FY5: T Clev 2K **63**
Acacia Rd. PR2: Ribb 7A **116**
Acacia Wlk. *BB1: Blackb* *3B* ***140***
(off Longton St.)
Academy, The PR9: S'port 6J **167**
Academy Bus. Pk. L33: Know P 9N **223**
ACCRINGTON 2B **142**
Accrington & District Golf Course 2H **141**
Accrington Crematorium BB5: Acc 9C **122**
BB5: Hunc 9C **122**
Accrington Easterly By-Pass
BB5: Acc, Hunc, Ris B 9E **122**
BB11: Hapt 9E **122**
Accrington Rd. BB1: Blackb 3B **140**
BB7: Whall 5J **101**
BB11: Burnl, Hapt 7H **123**
(not continuous)
Accrington Stanley FC 9A **122**
Accrington Station (Rail) 2A **142**
Accrington Trade Pk. BB5: Acc 2A **142**
ACE Centre *2H* ***105***
(off Cross St.)
Acer Cl. OL11: Roch 4H **203**
Acer Gro. PR2: Ribb 6B **116**
Acker St. OL16: Roch 5C **204**
Ackhurst Bus. Pk. PR7: Chor 6B **174**
Ackhurst La. WN5: Orr 9K **213**
Ackhurst Pk. Ind. Est. PR7: Chor 6B **174**
Ackhurst Rd. PR7: Chor 6B **174**
Ackroyd St. OL14: Tod 7E **146**
Acorn Av. BB5: Osw 5M **141**
Acorn Bank PR3: Gars 4N **59**
Acorn Bus. Cen. L33: Know P 8N **223**
Acorn Cl. LA1: Lanc 3K **29**
PR1: Penw 6E **134**
PR1: Prest 8L **115**
PR25: Leyl 7K **153**
Acorn Farm 6B **224**
Acornfield Plantation Local Nature Reserve 9B **224**
Acornfield Rd. L33: Know P 9B **224**
Acorn Gdn. LA3: Morec 6C **22**
Acorn Mdw. LA5: Bolt S 5L **15**
Acorn M. FY4: Blackp 9K **89**
Acorns, The L39: Aug 9H **209**
Acorn St. BB1: Blackb 4B **140**
OL13: Bac 4K **163**
ACRE 1G **160**
Acre Av. OL13: Bac 7H **163**
Acre Cl. BL0: Eden 3J **181**
Acre Ct. *LA1: Lanc* *6K* ***23***
(off Mainway)
Acre Fld. BL2: Bolt 9K **199**
Acrefield BB2: Blackb 1H **139**
BB12: Padi 9H **103**
PR5: Bam B 2E **154**
WN8: N 'urgh 3L **211**
Acrefield Dr. BB4: Rawt 2M **161**
Acre Ga. FY4: Blackp 2E **108**
Acregate WN8: Skelm 4N **219**
Acregate La. PR1: Prest 8N **115**
Acre Gro. PR4: Much H 4K **151**
PR8: Birk 1F **186**
Acre Mill Rd. OL13: Bac 7H **163**
Acre Moss La. LA4: Morec 4A **22**
Acre Mt. BB12: Read 8C **102**
Acre Pk. OL13: Bac 7H **163**
Acres, The BB7: Barr 2L **101**
Acres Brook Rd. BB12: High 5L **103**
Acresbrook Wlk. BL8: Tott 8E **200**
Acresfield BB8: Colne 6D **86**
PR7: Adl 7H **195**
Acresfield Pk. PR3: Gars 2M **59**
Acres La. FY6: Pree 1N **55**
L31: Lyd 3L **215**
L37: Gt A 3E **214**
L39: D'holl 3L **215**
Acres St. BL8: Tott 8E **200**
Acre St. BB10: Brierc 7L **105**
BB10: Burnl 9F **104**
OL12: Whitw 5A **184**
Acreswood Cl. PR7: Copp 5A **194**
Acre Vw. BL0: Ramsb 4J **181**
OL13: Bac 7H **163**
Active Way BB11: Burnl 2C **228** (3D **124**)
BB12: Burnl 2C **228** (3D **124**)
Acton Rd. FY4: Blackp 9E **88**
L32: Kirk 8H **223**
Acton St. OL12: Roch 4D **204**
Adamson St. BB12: Burnl 3A **124**
BB12: Padi 9H **103**
Adam St. OL14: Tod 1L **165**
Ada St. BB2: Blackb 3A **226** (3K **139**)
BB9: Nelson 4J **105**
BB10: Burnl 9F **104**
BL0: Ramsb 9G **180**
OL12: Roch 3D **204**
Addenbrooke Cl. LA1: Lanc 3J **29**
ADDINGTON 4G **17**
Addington Rd. LA2: Halt 4G **17**
LA6: Neth K 4G **17**
Addington St. BB1: Blackb 3A **140**
Addison Cl. BB2: Blackb 3K **139**
L32: Kirk 9J **223**
Addison Ct. *FY6: K Sea* *8K* ***41***
(off Esplanade)
Addison Cres. FY3: Blackp 4D **88**
Addison Rd. FY7: Flee 1F **54**
Addison St. BB2: Blackb 3K **139**
BB5: Acc 1B **142**
Addle St. LA1: Lanc 3L **29**
Adelaide Av. FY5: T Clev 3J **63**
Adelaide Ct. FY1: Blackp 2K **227**
Adelaide La. BB5: Acc 3B **142**
Adelaide St. BB4: Craws 9M **143**
BB5: Acc 3B **142**
BB5: Clay M 8N **121**
BL0: Ramsb 1F **200**
FY1: Blackp 2J **227** (5B **88**)
FY7: Flee 8H **41**
OL14: Tod 1L **165**
PR1: Prest 9L **115**
PR6: Adl 5J **195**
Adelaide St. W. FY1: Blackp 3H **227** (6B **88**)
Adelaide Ter. BB2: Blackb 2A **226** (3K **139**)
ADELPHI 2H **229** (8H **115**)
Adelphi Pl. PR1: Prest 4J **229** (9J **115**)
Adelphi St. BB11: Burnl 2E **124**
FY1: Blackp 2J **227** (5B **88**)
LA1: Lanc 1L **29**
PR1: Prest 2H **229** (8H **115**)
WN6: Stand 2N **213**
Aden St. OL12: Roch 4D **204**
ADLINGTON 6J **195**
Adlington Av. FY6: Poul F 8H **63**
Adlington Sth. Bus. Pk. PR7: Adl 7J **195**
Adlington Station (Rail) 6J **195**
Adlington St. BB11: Burnl 1E **228** (3E **124**)
ADMERGILL 1G **85**
Admin Rd. L33: Know P 9A **224**
Admiral, The FY8: L Ann 2D **128**
Admiral Cl. FY8: L Ann 8E **108**
Admiral Gdns. FY2: Blackp 8B **62**
Admiral Hgts. FY2: Blackp 8B **62**
Admiral Point FY2: Blackp 8B **62**
(not continuous)
Admirals Sound FY5: T Clev 1C **62**
Admiral St. BB10: Burnl 4F **124**
Admiralty Cl. L40: Burs 2N **209**
Admiral Vw. FY2: Blackp 8B **62**
Admiral Way PR2: Ash R 9A **114**
Adrian St. FY1: Blackp 9H **227** (9B **88**)
Adrian's Way L32: Kirk 8K **223**
Adrian Ter. OL16: Roch 7F **204**
Adstone Av. FY3: Blackp 3F **88**
AFFETSIDE 5A **200**
Agate St. BB1: Blackb 8N **119**
Ager St. *OL13: Bac* *7G* ***163***
(off Booth Rd.)
Agglebys Rd. FY6: Pree 4L **55**
Agnes Ing La. LA2: Tat 7E **18**
Agnes St. BB2: Blackb 5K **139**
PR1: Prest 4L **229** (9K **115**)
Agnew Rd. FY7: Flee 8F **40**
Agnew St. FY8: L Ann 5N **129**
Aiken Ct. PR4: K'ham 4M **111**
Aikengill Rd. LA2: Tat 10K **19**
Ailsa Av. FY4: Blackp 8F **88**
Ailsa Cl. PR3: Bart 2E **94**
Ailsa Rd. BB1: Blackb 5D **140**
Ailsa Wlk. LA3: Heys 9K **21**
Aindow Ct. PR8: Birk 2F **186**
Ainley Ct. FY1: Blackp 1K **227**
Ainscough Brook Ho. *PR2: Ribb* *6B* ***116***
(off Ribbleton Hall Cres.)
Ainscough Bus. Pk. WN6: Wrigh 7H **193**
AINSDALE 8C **186**
Ainsdale & Birkdale Hills Local Nature Reserve 6A **186**
Ainsdale Av. BB10: Reed 5G **104**
BL7: Edgw 7K **179**
FY2: Blackp 6E **62**
FY5: T Clev 2K **63**
FY7: Flee 5D **54**
Ainsdale Cl. L10: Faz 9E **222**
LA1: Lanc 5H **23**
Ainsdale Dr. BB3: Darw 1B **178**
OL12: Whitw 7A **184**
PR2: Ash R 7A **114**
AINSDALE-ON-SEA 7A **186**
Ainsdale Sand Dunes National Nature Reserve 9A **186**
Ainsdale Station (Rail) 8C **186**
Ainslie Cl. BB6: Gt H 4H **121**
Ainslie Rd. PR2: Fulw 6G **115**
Ainslie St. BB12: Burnl 3A **124**
Ainspool La. PR3: C'town 9L **59**
Ainsworth Cl. BB3: Darw 7A **158**
Ainsworth Fold *PR4: W Grn* *6G* ***111***
(off The Greenside)
Ainsworth St. BB1: Blackb 4D **226** (3M **139**)
OL16: Roch 7D **204**
AINTREE 8C **222**
Aintree Cotts. *BB2: Mellor B* *6D* ***118***
(off Mellor Brook)
Aintree Ct. *L10: Aint* *7B* ***222***
(off Aintree La.)
Aintree Cres. PR8: S'port 1M **187**
Aintree Dr. BB3: Lwr D 9A **140**
OL11: Roch 5J **203**
Aintree Golf Course 9C **222**
Aintree La. L10: Aint 7B **222**
L10: Faz 9E **222**
Aintree Motor Circuit 9C **222**
Aintree Racecourse 9B **222**
Aintree Racecourse Retail & Bus. Pk.
L9: Aint 9A **222**
Aintree Rd. FY4: Blackp 1C **108**
FY5: T Clev 3H **63**
Aintree Station (Rail) 9A **222**
Aintree Vis. Cen. & Grand National Experience 9A **222**
Aintree Way L9: Aint 8B **222**
Airdrie Cres. BB11: Burnl 5B **124**
Airdrie Pl. FY2: Blackp 6E **62**
Airebank Ter. BD23: Garg 4M **53**
Aire Cl. LA3: Morec 6F **22**
Airedale LA2: Gal 2M **37**
Airedale Av. BD23: Garg 3M **53**
FY3: Blackp 7E **88**
Airedale Ct. FY6: Poul F 7J **63**
Aire Dr. BL2: Bolt 8H **199**
Airegate L31: Magh 9A **216**
Airey St. BB5: Acc 5C **142**
Air Hill Ter. OL12: Roch 4N **203**
Airton Gth. BB9: Barrf 8G **85**
Aisled Barn Info. Cen. 8K **87**
Aisthorpe Gro. L31: Magh 3C **222**
Aitken Cl. BL0: Ramsb 9G **181**
Aitken St. BB5: Acc 1B **142**
BL0: Ramsb 1H **181**
Ajax St. BL0: Ramsb 9G **180**
AK Bus. Pk. PR9: S'port 8N **167**
Akeman Cl. LA3: Morec 5E **22**
Alamein Rd. LA5: Carn 9B **12**
Alandale Cl. PR25: Leyl 8L **153**
Alan Gro. LA3: Heys 1L **27**
Alan Haigh Ct. BB8: Colne 5A **86**
Alan Ramsbottom Way BB6: Gt H 5K **121**
Alan's Way L33: Kirk 5K **223**

Alaska St.—Anchor Bank

Alaska St. BB2: Blackb 9D 226 (6M 139)
Albany, The BB3: Darw 3M 157
(off St Alban's Rd.)
Albany Av. FY4: Blackp 4B 108
Albany Cl. FY6: Poul F 2L 89
Albany Ct. PR6: Chor 6G 175
(off Devonport Way)
Albany Dr. BB1: Sale 1K 119
PR5: Walt D 6N 135
Albany Rd. BB2: Blackb 2J 139
FY7: Flee 9F 40
FY8: L Ann 2J 129
LA4: Morec 4N 21
PR9: S'port 5J 167
Albany St. OL11: Roch 8D 204
Alba St. BL8: Holc 8F 180
Albatross St. PR1: Prest 7L 115
Albemarle Ct. BB7: Clith 3K 81
Albemarle Pl. BL8: Tott 6E 200
Albemarle Rd. FY8: L Ann 5C 130
Albemarle St. BB7: Clith 3K 81
Alberta Cl. BB2: Blackb 9J 119
Albert Ct. PR9: S'port 5K 167
Albert Hill BD24: Sett 3N 35
Albert La. OL14: Tod 1L 165
Albert Mill BB3: Lwr D 9N 139
Albert Pl. BB3: Lwr D 9N 139
PR9: S'port 6H 167
Albert Rd. BB4: Craws 8M 143
BB8: Colne 7N 85
BB18: Barnw 2M 77
FY1: Blackp 3H 227 (6B 88)
FY8: L Ann 1G 128
L40: Ruff 2E 190
LA1: Lanc 7K 23
LA4: Morec 4N 21
PR1: Prest 1J 229 (7J 115)
PR2: Fulw 6J 115
PR9: S'port 6J 167
PR25: Leyl 6M 153
Albert Royds St. OL16: Roch 3E 204
Albert Sq. FY7: Flee 8H 41
Albert St. BB1: Rish 8H 121
BB2: Blackb 6K 139
BB3: Darw 1B 178
BB3: Hodd 6F 158
BB4: Lumb 2C 162
BB5: Acc 3B 142
BB5: Chur 2L 141
BB5: Clay M 7M 121
BB5: Osw 4L 141
BB6: Gt H 5K 121
BB9: Brierf 5F 104
BB9: Nelson 2H 105
BB11: Burnl 2F 228 (3F 124)
BB12: Padi 1H 123
BB18: Earl 2E 78
BL0: Ramsb 8G 181
BL6: Hor 9C 196
BL7: Eger 2D 198
FY7: Flee 9H 41
FY8: L Ann 4B 130
LA5: Carn 9A 12
(Lodge Quarry)
LA5: Carn 7A 12
(Rupert St.)
OL12: Whitw 6N 183
OL14: Tod 1L 165
OL15: Littleb 9L 185
OL16: Milnr 8K 205
PR4: Wesh 3L 111
PR6: Wheel 8J 155
PR7: Chor 7F 174
Albert Ter. BB4: Rawt 5N 161
BB9: Barrf 8H 85
OL13: Bac 4K 163
PR1: Prest 3M 229 (8K 115)
PR3: Cald V 4H 61
PR5: H Walt 5D 136
PR8: Birk 9G 167
Albion Av. FY3: Blackp 4F 88
Albion Ct. BB7: Clith 2M 81
(off Waterloo Rd.)
BB11: Burnl 5A 228 (5C 124)
Albion M. LA1: Lanc 5E 228 (7L 23)
Albion Pl. BB7: Clith 3M 81
(off Albion St.)
Albion Rd. BB2: Blackb 7L 139
BB18: Earl 2E 78
OL11: Roch 7A 204
Albion Rd. Ind. Est. OL11: Roch 7A 204
Albion St. BB2: Blackb 7K 139
BB5: Acc 2A 142
BB7: Clith 3M 81
BB9: Brierf 5F 104
BB9: Nelson 2H 105
BB11: Burnl 5A 228 (5C 124)
BB12: Padi 2J 123
BB18: Earl 2E 78
LA1: Lanc 7L 23
OL13: Bac 7G 163
(Clegg St.)
OL13: Bac 4L 163
(Cross Ct.)
OL15: Littleb 9K 185
PR7: Chor 7E 174
Albion Ter. BB11: Burnl 3B 228
Albion Wlk. PR7: Chor 8F 174
(off Clydesdale Dr.)
Albrighton Cl. PR5: Lost H 9L 135
Albrighton Cres. PR5: Lost H 9L 135
Albrighton Rd. PR5: Lost H 9L 135
Albury Dr. OL12: Roch 3K 203
Albyn Bank Rd. PR1: Prest 6N 229 (1L 135)
Albyn St. E. PR1: Prest 1L 135
Alcester Av. PR1: Penw 3F 134
Alconbury Cres. FY5: T Clev 1C 62
Aldate Gro. PR2: Ash R 7D 114
ALDCLIFFE 2H 29
Aldcliffe Ct. LA4: Morec 5B 22
Aldcliffe Hall Dr. LA1: Ald 2H 29
Aldcliffe M. LA1: Ald 2H 29
Aldcliffe Pl. LA1: Lanc 9B 228
Aldcliffe Rd. LA1: Ald, Lanc 9B 228 (2H 29)
PR2: Ash R 8B 114
Alden Cl. BB4: Hasl 9F 160
Alden Ri. BB4: Hasl 9F 160
Alden Rd. BB4: Hasl 2D 180
Alden Ter. LA1: Lanc 5K 23
(off Clarendon Rd.)
Alder Av. BB4: Rawt 5N 161
WN5: Wigan 5N 221
Alder Bank BB2: Blackb 4J 139
BB4: Rawt 4M 161
BB9: Nelson 3G 104
Alderbank BL6: Hor 9A 196
OL12: Ward 7F 184
Alderbrook Dr.
WN8: Parb 2N 211
Alder Cl. FY5: T Clev 2J 63
PR4: Hesk B 6C 150
PR4: Newt 7E 112
PR26: Leyl 7E 152
Alder Coppice PR2: Lea 6B 114
Alder Ct. FY7: Flee 2C 54
LA1: Lanc 8H 23
(off Alder Gro.)
Alder Cres. L32: Kirk 7J 223
Alderdale Av. PR8: Ains 8A 186
Alder Dr. PR5: Hogh 7F 136
PR7: Char R 2N 193
Alderfield PR1: Penw 5G 134
Alderford Cl. BB7: Clith 4J 81
Alder Gro. BB5: Hunc 7D 122
BL7: Brom C 7J 199
FY3: Blackp 3E 88
FY6: Poul F 9K 63
FY8: L Ann 4N 129
(not continuous)
LA1: Lanc 8H 23
PR2: Ingol 3C 114
PR7: Copp 4B 194
Alder Hill Cft. BB18: Earl 2F 78
Alder Hill St. BB18: Earl 2E 78
Alder La. L39: Bart 5E 206
PR3: Out R 2M 65
WN8: Parb 3N 211
Alder Lee Cl. WN3: Wins 9N 221
Alderlee Pk. PR8: S'port 3N 187
Alderley WN8: Skelm 5N 219
Alderley Av. BL1: Bolt 8E 198
FY4: Blackp 4B 108
Alderley Bank Caravan Pk.
LA3: Midd 8K 27
Alderley Hgts. LA1: Lanc 5K 23
Alderman Foley Dr. OL12: Roch 3L 203
Alderman Rd. LA1: Lanc 3J 29
Aldermeadow Ct. OL12: Roch 4L 203
Alderney Cl. BB2: Blackb 7J 139
Alder Rd. PR2: Ribb 5C 116
Alders, The PR3: Gars 3N 59
WN6: Stand 8N 213
Aldersleigh Cres. PR5: Hogh 7F 136
Alderson Cres. L37: Form 8A 206
Alder St. BB1: Blackb 1A 140
BB4: Rawt 4N 161
BB12: Burnl 3A 124
OL13: Bac 4K 163
Alderville Cl. PR4: Wart 2L 131
Alderway BL0: Ramsb 5H 181
Alderwood BB4: Rawt 5N 161
Alderwood Gro. BL0: Eden 2J 181
Aldfield Av. PR2: Lea 8N 113
Aldford Way WN6: Stand 4N 213
Aldingham Ct. LA4: Morec 5B 22
Aldingham Wlk. LA4: Morec 3A 22
Aldon Gro. PR4: Longt 7L 133
Aldon Rd. FY6: Poul F 8M 63
Aldren's La. LA1: Lanc 6K 23
Aldwych Av. FY3: Blackp 7E 88
Aldwych Dr. PR2: Ash R 7C 114
PR5: Lost H 9L 135
Aldwych Pl. BB1: Blackb 7N 119
Aldykes L31: Magh 2D 222
Alert St. PR2: Ash R 8F 114
Alexander Cl. BB5: Bax 7D 142
L40: Burs 1D 210
Alexander Ct. FY6: Poul F 8K 63
Alexander Dr. L31: Lyd 8C 216
OL16: Milnr 7H 205
Alexander Gro. BB12: Burnl 3N 123
Alexander Pl. PR2: Grim 9F 96
Alexander St. BB9: Nelson 9L 85
Alexander Wharf L31: Magh 1B 222
(off Damfield La.)
Alexandra B'way. PR9: S'port 6K 167
Alexandra Cl. BB5: Clay M 6L 121
WN8: Skelm 2J 219
Alexandra Ct. FY1: Blackp 9H 227
LA1: Lanc 6D 228
PR9: S'port 6K 167
Alexandra Hall LA1: Lanc 8D 228
Alexandra Ho. PR1: Prest 8M 115
Alexandra M. BB2: Blackb 1K 139
L39: Orms 6K 209
(off Courtfield)
PR9: S'port 6J 167
Alexandra Pk. Dr. LA2: Ell 9L 29
Alexandra Pavilions PR1: Prest 3M 229
Alexandra Pl. BB6: Gt H 3K 121
Alexandra Rd. BB2: Blackb 2K 139
BB3: Darw 5N 157
FY1: Blackp 9H 227 (9B 88)
FY5: T Clev 3J 63
FY8: L Ann 1F 128
L40: Burs 9B 190
LA1: Lanc 5K 23
LA3: Morec 4M 21
LA5: Carn 9A 12
PR3: Longr 3J 97
PR4: Wesh 2M 111
PR5: Walt D 5N 135
PR9: S'port 5J 167
Alexandra Road Stop (Tram) 9H 227 (9B 88)
Alexandra Sq. LA1: Bail 8M 29
Alexandra St. BB5: Clay M 5L 121
PR1: Prest 1M 135
Alexandra Vw. BB3: Darw 5N 157
Alexandria Dr. FY8: L Ann 3F 128
Alexandria St. BB4: Rawt 3L 161
Alford Fold PR2: Fulw 2G 114
Alfred's Ct. PR7: Chor 7E 174
Alfred St. BB3: Darw 9B 158
BL0: Ramsb 9G 180
BL7: Eger 2D 198
FY1: Blackp 2K 227 (5C 88)
LA1: Lanc 6E 228 (8L 23)
OL12: Whitw 4A 184
OL15: Littleb 8K 185
WA11: Rain 3K 225
Algar St. BB9: Nelson 9K 85
Alice Av. PR25: Leyl 6K 153
Alice Ingham Ct. OL12: Roch 4N 203
Alice Sq. PR1: Prest 3M 229 (8K 115)
Alice St. BB3: Darw 7A 158
BB5: Acc 1C 142
BB5: Osw 5L 141
BB18: Barnw 2M 77
LA4: Morec 3C 22
OL12: Roch 4E 204
Alicia Ct. OL12: Roch 4B 204
Alicia Dr. OL12: Roch 4B 204
Alisan Rd. FY6: Carl 6H 63
Alker La. PR7: Eux 3D 174
Alker St. PR7: Chor 7E 174
Alkincoates Woodland Local Nature Reserve 4N 85
Alkincoats Rd. BB8: Colne 6N 85
Alkincoats Vs. BB8: Colne 5N 85
Allan Critchlow Way BB1: Rish 7H 121
Allandale FY4: Blackp 4C 108
Allandale Av. FY5: T Clev 8F 54
Allandale Gdns. LA1: Lanc 8H 23
Allandale Gro. BB10: Burnl 5K 125
Allansons Wlk. FY8: L Ann 5A 130
(off Sth. Westby St.)
Allan St. OL13: Bac 6K 163
Allenbury Pl. FY3: Blackp 8G 89
Allenby Av. PR2: Fulw 5L 115
Allenby Rd. FY8: L Ann 1D 128
Allen Cl. FY5: T Clev 2D 62
FY7: Flee 2D 54
Allen Ct. BB10: Burnl 1E 124
(off Allen St.)
Allendale Gro. BB10: Briercl 9A 106
Allendale St. BB8: Colne 5C 86
BB12: Burnl 3N 123
Allengate PR2: Fulw 5J 115
Allen St. BB10: Burnl 1E 124
(not continuous)
OL16: Roch 7D 204
Allen Way FY7: Flee 2C 54
Allerton Cl. BB3: Darw 5A 158
Allerton Ct. PR5: Walt D 5N 135
Allerton Dr. BB12: Burnl 3B 124
Allerton Rd. PR5: Walt D 5N 135
PR9: S'port 5L 167
Allescholes Rd. OL14: Wals 8K 165
Alleys Grn. BB7: Clith 2L 81
ALLEYTROYDS 3L 141
Alleytroyds BB5: Chur 3L 141
All Hallows Rd. FY2: Blackp 6D 62
Alliance Bus. Pk. BB5: Acc 3N 141
Alliance Retail Pk. PR7: Chor 5F 174
(off Water St.)
Alliance St. BB5: Bax 7E 142
Allington OL11: Roch 7B 204
(off Tweedale St.)
Allington Cl. PR5: Walt D 5A 136
Allison Gro. BB8: Colne 5C 86
Allonby Av. FY5: T Clev 8E 54
Allotment La. PR3: St M 4G 67
All Saints Cl. BB4: Craws 7M 143
BB5: Osw 4H 141
BB12: Burnl 2L 123
All Saints Ct. WA11: Rain 5L 225
All Saints Pl. BL8: Bury 9H 201
All Saints Rd. FY5: T Clev 5E 62
FY8: L Ann 2E 128
All Saints Ter. OL12: Roch 3E 204
All Seasons Leisure Cen. 5F 174
Allsprings Cl. BB6: Gt H 3K 121
Allsprings Dr. BB6: Gt H 2K 121
Allsprings Plantation BB6: Gt H 2J 121
Alma Av. BB8: Foul 2A 86
Alma Cl. WN8: Uph 4F 220
Alma Ct. PR8: Ains 6F 186
WN8: Uph 4F 220
Alma Dr. PR7: Char R 1A 194
Alma Grn. WN8: Uph 4E 220
Alma Hill WN8: Uph 4E 220
Alma Ind. Est. OL12: Roch 4C 204
Alma Pde. WN8: Uph 4F 220
Alma Pl. BB5: Bax 8D 142
BB7: Clith 4K 81
Alma Rd. BB8: Colne 5F 86
LA1: Lanc 1K 29
OL14: Wals 6K 165
PR8: Birk 1G 186
WN8: Uph 4F 220
Alma Row PR5: Hogh 7G 136
Alma St. BB2: Blackb 3B 226 (3L 139)
BB5: Clay M 6M 121
BB12: Padi 9G 103
OL12: Roch 4C 204
OL13: Bac 5K 163
OL14: Wals 6K 165
PR1: Prest 3L 229 (8K 115)
Alma Ter. BB11: Dunn 3N 143
Alma Wlk. WN8: Uph 4F 220
Alma Wood Cl. PR7: Chor 8C 174
Almelo Ho. PR1: Prest 1H 229
Almond Av. L40: Burs 7C 190
ALMOND BROOK 2L 213
Almond Brook Rd. WN6: Shev, Stand 2L 213
Almond Brow PR9: Banks 2F 168
Almond Cl. OL15: Littleb 8J 185
PR1: Penw 5E 134
PR2: Fulw 3M 115
PR6: Withn 5C 156
Almond Cres. BB4: Rawt 7L 161
Almond Gro. BL1: Bolt 9F 198
Almond St. BB3: Darw 7A 158
BL1: Bolt 9F 198
Almonry, The L40: Lath 5F 210
Almshouses LA1: Lanc 7C 228
Almshouses, The BB7: Grind 4C 74
Alnwick Cl. BB12: Burnl 2C 124
Alpha St. BB3: Darw 7B 158
BB9: Nelson 9K 85
BB18: Salt 4B 78
Alpic Dr. FY5: T Clev 4C 62
Alpine Av. FY4: Blackp 4E 108
PR5: Lost H 9L 135
Alpine Cl. BB3: Hodd 6E 158
PR5: Lost H 9L 135
Alpine Dr. OL12: Ward 8F 184
OL16: Milnr 6K 205
Alpine Gro. BB2: Blackb 8J 139
Alpine Hgts. PR3: Gars 6M 59
Alpine Rd. PR6: Chor 3G 175
Alpine Vw. LA5: Bolt S 3L 15
Alscot Cl. L31: Magh 2C 222
Alsop St. PR1: Prest 1J 229 (7J 115)
Alston Av. FY5: T Clev 8D 54
Alston Cl. BB7: Sabd 3E 102
Alston Ct. PR3: Longr 4K 97
PR8: Ains 7E 186
Alston Dr. LA4: Morec 3F 22
Alston La. PR3: Longr 7J 97
Alston Rd. FY2: Blackp 9E 62
Alston St. BL8: Bury 9H 201
PR1: Prest 8N 115
Alt Av. L31: Magh 3B 222
ALT BRIDGE 3B 214
Altcar La. L31: Lyd 6M 215
L37: Form 8C 206
(Downholland Moss La.)
L37: Form 2A 214
(Marina Rd.)
L39: D'holl 2M 215
PR25: Leyl 1G 173
Altcar Rd. L37: Form, Gt A 1A 214
ALTHAM
BB5, Clayton-le-Moors 8A 122
BB5, Padiham 3D 122
Altham Bus. Pk. BB5: Alt 3D 122
Altham Caravan Site BB5: Acc 8B 122
Altham Ind. Est. BB5: Alt 3C 122
Altham La. BB5: Alt, Hunc 3D 122
Altham Rd. LA4: Morec 4B 22
PR8: S'port 3L 187
Altham St. BB10: Burnl 1E 124
BB12: Padi 1J 123
Altham Wlk. LA4: Morec 5C 22
Althorp Cl. FY1: Blackp 3C 88
Althorpe Dr. PR8: S'port 2L 187
Altom St. BB1: Blackb 2C 226 (2M 139)
Alt Rd. L37: Form 1A 214
L38: Hight 7A 214
(not continuous)
Altway L10: Aint 7B 222
Altway Ct. L10: Aint 7B 222
(off Altway)
Altys La. L39: Orms 8L 209
Alum Scar La. BB2: Mellor 1A 138
Alvanley Cl. WN5: Wigan 2M 221
Alvanley Grn. L32: Kirk 8H 223
Alvanley Rd. L32: Kirk 8H 223
Alvern Av. PR2: Fulw 5G 114
Alvern Cres. PR2: Fulw 5G 114
Alvina La. L33: Kirk 5M 223
Alwin St. BB11: Burnl 4C 124
Alwood Av. FY3: Blackp 4F 88
Amanda Way L31: Mell 6G 222
Amber Av. BB1: Blackb 7N 119
Amberbanks Gro. FY1: Blackp 8J 227 (8B 88)
Amber Ct. WN5: Wigan 2L 221
Amber Dr. PR6: Chor 8G 175
Ambergate PR2: Ingol 3C 114
WN8: Skelm 4M 219
Amberley St. BB2: Blackb 6K 139
Amberwood PR4: K'ham 4L 111
Amberwood Dr. BB2: Blackb 7H 139
Ambledene PR5: Bam B 1C 154
Ambleside WN5: Wigan 4M 221
Ambleside Av. BB4: Rawt 5K 161
BB18: Barnw 1L 77
FY6: K Sea 7M 41
PR7: Eux 5N 173
Ambleside Cl. BB1: Blackb 2G 226 (2A 140)
BB5: Hunc 9D 122
BL2: Bolt 9M 199
PR5: Walt D 6A 136
Ambleside Dr. BB3: Darw 4C 158
L33: Kirk 6J 223
Ambleside Rd. FY4: Blackp 9K 89
FY8: L Ann 8E 108
L31: Magh 9C 216
LA1: Lanc 7L 23
PR2: Ribb 4A 116
Ambleside Wlk. PR2: Ribb 4A 116
Amblethorn Dr. BL1: Bolt 8D 198
Ambleway PR5: Walt D 4N 135
Ambrose Av. PR7: Buck V 9A 154
Ambrose Hall La. PR4: Woodp 7B 94
Ambrose St. OL11: Roch 8C 204
PR25: Leyl 5L 153
Amelia St. BB1: Blackb 2B 140
Amersham WN8: Skelm 4M 219
Amersham Cl. PR4: New L 8C 134
Amersham Gro. BB10: Burnl 6H 105
Amesbury Dr. WN3: Wins 9M 221
Amethyst St. BB1: Blackb 7M 119
AMF Bowling
Burnley 4D 228 (4E 124)
Amos St. OL14: Tod 7F 146
Amounderness Cl. PR4: K'ham 5N 111
Amounderness Way FY5: T Clev 1F 62
FY7: Flee 4F 54
Ampleforth Cl. L32: Kirk 9H 223
Ampleforth Dr. PR5: Lost H 7K 135
Amsall La. L39: Orms 5G 208
AMS Trad. Est. PR4: Longt 9A 134
Amy Johnson Way FY4: Blackp 4D 108
Amy St. OL12: Roch 4M 203
Amy Ter. FY8: L Ann 3F 128
Ancenis Ct. PR4: K'ham 4N 111
ANCHOR 3M 157
Anchorage Av. PR4: Hesk B 6L 149
Anchorage M. FY7: Flee 1H 55
Anchorage Rd. FY7: Flee 1H 55
Anchor Av. BB3: Darw 3M 157
Anchor Bank BB3: Darw 2N 157

Anchor Ct.—Ashlands Cl.

Anchor Ct. *BB3: Darw* 2N 157
(off Commercial Rd.)
PR1: Prest 6K 229 (1J 135)
PR8: Birk 9F 166
Anchor Dr. PR4: Hutt 6A 134
Anchorfields PR7: E'ton 7E 172
Anchor Gro. BB3: Darw 3M 157
Anchor Ho. BB1: Blackb 6E 226
Anchor La. LA1: Lanc 6C 228
Anchor Retail Pk. BB11: Burnl 1D 228 (2E 124)
Anchor Rd. BB3: Darw 3M 157
ANCHORSHOLME 2F 62
Anchorsholme La. FY5: T Clev 3F 62
Anchorsholme La. E. FY5: T Clev 2D 62
Anchorsholme Lane Stop (Tram) 2D 62
Anchorsholme La. W. FY5: T Clev 2C 62
Anchor St. OL14: Tod 2M 165
PR9: S'port 7H 167
Anchor Way FY8: L Ann 8E 108
Ancliffe La. LA2: Slyne 6M 15
LA5: Bolt S 6M 15
Ancrum Rd. L33: Kirk 4J 223
Andelen Cl. BB11: Hapt 6H 123
Anders Dr. L33: Kirk 5M 223
Anderson Cl. LA1: Lanc 1M 29
OL13: Bac 6K 163
Anderson Rd. BB1: Wilp 2A 120
Anderson St. FY1: Blackp 4L 227 (6C 88)
ANDERTON 5K 195
Anderton Cl. BB4: W'foot 8D 162
Anderton Cl. BL6: Hor 9B 196
Anderton Cres. PR7: Buck V 8A 154
Anderton La. BL6: Hor 9N 195
Anderton M. LA4: Morec 3A 22
Anderton Outdoor Education & Activities Cen. 5N 195
Anderton Rd. BB12: High 5L 103
PR7: Eux 5N 173
ANDERTON'S MILL 4D 192
Anderton St. LA4: Morec 3B 22
PR7: Adl 6J 195
PR7: Chor 7E 174
Andertons Way PR2: Fulw 4M 115
Anderton Way PR3: Gars 6A 60
Andover Cres. WN3: Wins 9M 221
Andreas Cl. PR8: Birk 1H 187
Andrew Av. BB4: Rawt 6L 161
L31: Mell 7G 222
Andrew Cl. BB2: Blackb 8J 139
BL8: Greenm 4E 200
Andrew La. BL1: Bolt 7F 198
Andrew Rd. BB9: Nelson 1M 105
Andrews Ct. FY5: T Clev 9D 54
Andrew St. PR1: Prest 8M 115
Anemone Dr. BB4: Hasl 7E 160
Angela St. BB2: Blackb 7J 139
Angelica Rd. L32: Kirk 6L 223
Angel Way *BB8: Colne* 6B 86
(off Dockray St.)
Anger's Hill Rd. FY4: Blackp 9E 88
Angers La. L31: Mell 4G 223
Anglesey Av. BB12: Burnl 2M 123
Anglesey St. BB2: Blackb 8J 139
Angle St. BB10: Burnl 1E 124
Anglezarke Bldgs. PR6: Chor 7H 175
Anglezarke Rd. PR6: Adl 6J 195
Anglian Cl. BB5: Osw 3J 141
Angus St. OL13: Bac 7G 162
Aniline St. PR6: Chor 6G 174
Annan Cres. FY4: Blackp 9J 89
Annandale Cl. L33: Kirk 4J 223
Annandale Gdns. WN8: Uph 4D 220
Annarly Fold BB10: W'thorne 4L 125
Annaside Cl. FY4: Blackp 2E 108
Anna's Rd. FY4: Blackp 7K 109
Anne Av. PR8: Ains 7E 186
Anne Cl. BB10: Burnl 3G 228 (4F 124)
Annecy Cl. BL8: Bury 9G 200
Anne Line Cl. *OL11: Roch* 8D 204
(off Wellfield St.)
Annesley Av. FY3: Blackp 2E 88
Anne St. BB10: Burnl 3F 228 (4F 124)
Annexe, The *PR9: S'port* 6J 167
(off Hoghton Gro.)
Annie St. BB4: Rawt 5M 161
BB5: Acc 1B 142
BL0: Ramsb 1F 200
Annis St. PR1: Prest 9M 115
Ann St. BB5: Clay M 6M 121
BB9: Barrf 8H 85
BB9: Brierf 4F 104
LA1: Lanc 8C 228 (9K 23)
OL11: Roch 7C 204
OL12: Roch 2G 204
(off Oakcliffe Rd.)
OL16: Roch 7C 204
WN8: Skelm 3J 219
Ansbro Av. PR4: Frec 2A 132
ANSDELL 4K 129
Ansdell & Fairhaven Station (Rail) 4K 129
Ansdell Gro. PR2: Ash R 6F 114
PR9: S'port 2N 167
Ansdell Rd. BL6: Hor 9D 196
FY1: Blackp 7M 227 (8D 88)
OL16: Roch 9E 204
WN5: Wigan 6N 221
Ansdell Rd. Nth. FY8: L Ann 4K 129
Ansdell Rd. Sth. FY8: L Ann 5K 129
Ansdell St. PR1: Prest 8M 115
Ansdell Ter. BB2: Blackb 7M 139
Anselm Ct. FY2: Blackp 8B 62
Anshaw Cl. BL7: Belm 9K 177
Anson Cl. FY8: L Ann 8D 108
Anson Pl. WN5: Wigan 3M 221
Anson Rd. PR4: Frec 7N 111
Anstable Rd. LA4: Morec 3D 22
Anthony Rd. LA1: Lanc 8A 228 (9J 23)
Anthorn Rd. WN3: Wigan 8N 221
Antigua Dr. BB3: Lwr D 1N 157
Antley Ct. BB10: Burnl 9G 104
Antrim Cl. WN3: Wins 9M 221
Antrim Rd. FY2: Blackp 1C 88
Anvil Cl. WN5: Orr 6G 221
Anvil St. OL13: Bac 7J 163
Anyon La. LA2: Bay H 8A 38
Anyon St. BB3: Darw 5B 158
Anyon Vs. BL6: Hor 9C 196
Anzio Rd. PR4: Weet 5D 90
Apartments, The PR9: S'port 6H 167
Apex Cl. BB11: Burnl 7C 124
Apiary, The PR26: Breth 1L 171
Apollo 4 Cinema 3N 21
Apollo Bingo 9J 227
Apollo Cinema
Burnley 4C 228 (4D 124)
Apollo Cres. L33: Kirk 6K 223
Apostles Way L33: Kirk 5J 223
Appealing La. FY8: L Ann 7E 108
Appleby Bus. Cen. BB1: Blackb 3G 226 (3A 140)
Appleby Cl. BB5: Acc 3C 142
PR5: Hogh 7G 136
Appleby Dr. BB9: Barrf 7H 85
Appleby Rd. FY2: Blackp 1D 88
L33: Kirk 6K 223
Appleby St. BB1: Blackb 3G 226 (3A 140)
BB9: Nelson 2H 105
PR1: Prest 3J 229 (8J 115)
Apple Cl. BB2: Blackb 4K 139
Apple Ct. BB2: Blackb 4K 139
Applecross Dr. BB10: Burnl 4J 125
Applefields PR25: Leyl 8L 153
Applegarth BB9: Barrf 1F 104
BB18: Barnw 10G 52
Applegarth Rd. LA3: Heys 8M 21
Applegarth St. BB18: Earl 3E 78
Apple Hey WN6: App B 4F 212
Applesike PR4: Longt 7K 133
Apple St. BB2: Blackb 4K 139
Appleton Cl. FY6: Poul F 9G 63
Appleton Rd. L32: Kirk 6K 223
WN8: Skelm 1K 219
Apple Tree Cl. PR3: St M 3G 67
PR7: Eux 2N 173
Appletree Cl. LA1: Lanc 4L 29
PR1: Penw 6F 134
Appletree Dr. LA1: Lanc 5L 29
Apple Tree Way BB5: Osw 3L 141
Applewood Cl. FY8: L Ann 5M 129
APPLEY BRIDGE 4F 212
Appley Bridge Station (Rail) 5F 212
Appley Cl. WN6: App B 2F 212
Appley La. Nth. WN6: App B 2F 212
Appley La. Sth. WN6: App B 6F 212
WN8: Roby M 6F 212
Approach Way BB11: Burnl 7C 124
Apsley Brow L31: Magh 1A 222
Apsley Fold PR3: Longr 3K 97
Aqueduct Mill Ind. Est. PR1: Prest 8G 115
Aqueduct Rd. BB2: Blackb 6K 139
(not continuous)
Aqueduct St. PR1: Prest 2G 229 (8G 115)
Aqueduct St. Ind. Est. PR1: Prest 2H 229
Aragon Cl. L31: Magh 8D 216
Arago St. BB5: Acc 1B 142
Arbories Av. BB12: Padi 1G 123
Arbory, The PR4: Gt P 2D 110
Arbory Dr. BB12: Padi 9G 102
Arbour Cl. BL9: Bury 7K 201
Arbour Ct. L33: Know P 8N 223
Arbour Dr. BB2: Blackb 9L 139
Arbour La. L33: Know P 9M 223
WN6: Stand 3L 213
Arbour St. OL13: Bac 4L 163
PR8: S'port 8J 167
Arboury St. BB12: Padi 1G 122
Arbury Av. OL11: Roch 8B 204
Arcade *BB5: Acc* 3B 142
(off Church St.)
Arcadia *BB8: Colne* 6B 86
(off Market Pl.)
Arcadia Av. L31: Lyd 8C 216
Archer Hill LA5: Carn 6A 12
Archers Fold L31: Mell 6G 222
Archery Av. BB8: Foul 2A 86
Archery Gdns. PR3: Gars 4N 59
Arches, The BB7: Whall 5H 101
BB8: Colne 7N 85
Arch St. BB3: Darw 6A 158
BB12: Burnl 1C 228 (3D 124)
Archway Bldgs. PR2: Ash R 8D 114
Arcon Cl. OL16: Roch 7H 205
Arcon Rd. PR7: Copp 4A 194
Ardee Rd. PR1: Prest 2G 135
Arden Cl. LA2: Slyne 9J 15
PR8: Ains 8A 186
Ardengate LA1: Lanc 3K 29
Arden Grn. FY7: Flee 9E 40
Ardleigh Av. PR8: S'port 2L 187
Ardley Rd. BL6: Hor 9D 196
Ardmore Rd. FY2: Blackp 9D 62
Ardwick St. BB10: Burnl 1E 124
Argameols Cl. PR8: S'port 9M 167
Argosy Av. FY3: Blackp 2F 88
Argosy Ct. FY3: Blackp 2G 88
Argyle Ct. PR9: S'port 4K 167
Argyle Lawn Tennis Club 4L 167
Argyle Pk. PR9: S'port 6K 167
Argyle Rd. FY6: Poul F 8L 63
PR9: S'port 4K 167
PR25: Leyl 6K 153
Argyle St. BB3: Darw 4N 157
BB5: Acc 2A 142
BB8: Colne 6A 86
BL9: Bury 9L 201
LA1: Lanc 8E 228 (9L 23)
OL16: Roch 9D 204
Argyll Av. PR7: Buck V 9B 154
Argyll Ct. *FY2: Blackp* 1C 88
(off Argyll Rd.)
Argyll Rd. FY2: Blackp 1C 88
PR1: Prest 2M 229 (8K 115)
Ariel Way FY7: Flee 9F 40
ARKHOLME 3C 18
Arkholme Av. FY1: Blackp 8M 227 (8D 88)
Arkholme Cl. LA5: Carn 8B 12
Arkholme Ct. LA4: Morec 5B 22
Arkholme Dr. PR4: Longt 7K 133
Arkmere La. PR3: Scor 5D 46
Arkwright Ct. BB3: Darw 2M 157
FY4: Blackp 2J 109
Arkwright Fold BB2: Blackb 8K 139
Arkwright Rd. PR1: Prest 1K 229 (7J 115)
Arkwright St. BB12: Burnl 2A 124
Arley Av. BL9: Bury 7K 201
Arley Gdns. BB12: Burnl 2D 124
Arley Lodge Nature Reserve 9E 194
Arley Ri. BB2: Mellor 7F 118
Arley St. PR7: Chor 6F 174
Arley Wood Dr. PR7: Chor 8C 174
Arlington Av. FY4: Blackp 2B 108
Arlington Cl. BL9: Summ 3H 201
PR8: Ains 8A 186
Arlington Rd. BB3: Darw 7N 157
Armadale Rd. FY2: Blackp 1E 88
Armaside Rd. PR4: Cott 5A 114
Armitstead Ct. FY7: Flee 2F 54
Armitstead Way FY7: Flee 2F 54
Arm Rd. OL15: Littleb 9H 185
Armsgrove Rd. BL7: Turt 8H 179
Armstrong Hurst Cl. OL12: Roch 2E 204
Armstrong St. PR2: Ash R 7E 114
Arncliffe Av. BB5: Acc 4M 141
Arncliffe Gro. BB9: Barrf 8G 85
Arncliffe Rd. BB10: Burnl 4J 125
LA3: Heys 7L 21
Arncot Rd. BL1: Bolt 8F 198
Arndale Cen. LA4: Morec 3A 22
Arndale Cl. FY7: Flee 2C 54
Arndale Rd. PR3: Longr 3H 97
Arnhem Rd. LA5: Carn 9B 12
PR1: Prest 9N 115
(not continuous)
Arnian Ct. L39: Aug 3H 217
Arnian Rd. WA11: Rain 3K 225
Arnian Way WA11: Rain 3K 225
Arnold Av. FY4: Blackp 2C 108
Arnold Bagnall Ct. OL11: Roch 9D 204
Arnold Cl. BB2: Blackb 7A 140
BB9: Brierf 4G 104
BB11: Burnl 7C 124
PR2: Ribb 7A 116
Arnold Pl. PR7: Chor 9C 174
Arnold Rd. BL7: Eger 5F 198
FY8: L Ann 4C 130
Arnold St. BB5: Acc 2B 142
Arno St. PR1: Prest 7N 229 (1L 135)
Arnott Rd. FY4: Blackp 9E 88
PR2: Ash R 7F 114
ARNSIDE 1F 4
Arnside Av. FY1: Blackp 9M 227 (9D 88)
FY8: L Ann 1J 129
Arnside Cl. BB5: Clay M 7L 121
LA1: Lanc 4M 29
PR5: Hogh 5G 137
Arnside Cres. BB2: Blackb 9F 138
LA4: Morec 3C 22
Arnside Dr. OL11: Roch 8J 203
Arnside Knott 3F 4
Arnside Rd. PR2: Ash R 7B 114
PR3: Brou 8G 94
PR9: S'port 7J 167
WN5: Orr 3L 221
Arnside Sailing Club 1F 4
(off The Promenade)
Arnside Station (Rail) 1G 4
Arnside Ter. PR9: S'port 7J 167
Arnside Tower 5F 4
Arnside Vw. FY6: K Sea 7L 41
Arran Av. BB1: Blackb 6D 140
Arran Cl. LA3: Heys 9K 21
Arran St. BB11: Burnl 4B 124
Arrow La. LA2: Halt 9C 16
Arrowsmith Cl. PR5: Hogh 6G 137
Arrowsmith Dr. PR5: Hogh 6G 137
Arrowsmith Gdns. FY5: T Clev 7E 54
Arroyo Way PR2: Fulw 5L 115
Arthington St. OL16: Roch 5E 204
Arthur Pits OL11: Roch 6K 203
Arthurs La. FY6: Ham 1C 64
Arthur St. BB2: Blackb 4K 139
BB5: Clay M 6M 121
BB6: Gt H 3K 121
BB9: Brierf 5F 104
BB9: Nelson 1J 105
BB11: Burnl 2A 228 (3C 124)
BB18: Barnw 1L 77
BB18: Sough 5D 78
FY7: Flee 8H 41
OL12: Roch 5A 204
OL13: Bac 4M 163
PR1: Prest 6G 229 (1H 135)
Arthur St. Nth. FY7: Flee 8H 41
Arthur Ter. *BB5: Clay M* 6M 121
(off Bk. Arthur St.)
Arthur Way BB2: Blackb 5A 226 (4K 139)
Artlebeck Cl. LA2: Caton 2H 25
Artlebeck Gro. LA2: Caton 2H 25
Artlebeck Rd. LA2: Caton 2H 25
Artle Pl. LA1: Lanc 6J 23
Art School, The *BB3: Darw* 6A 158
(off Union St.)
Arundel Av. FY2: Blackp 6B 62
OL11: Roch 9B 204
Arundel Cl. BB12: Burnl 2B 124
BL8: Bury 7H 201
Arundel Dr. FY6: Carl 5H 63
Arundel Pl. PR1: Prest 7M 229 (1K 135)
Arundel Rd. FY8: L Ann 4H 129
PR4: Longt 7L 133
PR8: Birk 5F 186
Arundel St. BB1: Rish 7G 121
BL1: Bolt 8E 198
OL11: Roch 9B 204
Arundel Way PR25: Leyl 7M 153
Ascot Cl. LA1: Lanc 3M 29
OL11: Roch 5J 203
PR8: Birk 9E 166
Ascot Dr. L33: Kirk 5K 223
Ascot Gdns. LA2: Slyne 9K 15
Ascot Rd. FY3: Blackp 1N 227 (4D 88)
FY5: T Clev 3H 63
Ascot Studios Art Gallery 7E 98
Ascot Way BB5: Acc 3C 142
Ash Av. BB4: Hasl 4H 161
LA2: Gal 2K 37
PR4: K'ham 5M 111
Ash Bank Cl. PR3: Bart 2E 94
Ashbee St. BL1: Bolt 9E 198
Ashborne Dr. BL9: Bury 3J 201
Ashbourne Cl. LA1: Lanc 5K 23
OL12: Ward 8G 184
Ashbourne Cres. PR2: Ingol 4D 114
Ashbourne Dr. LA1: Lanc 5K 23
Ashbourne Gro. LA3: Morec 6C 22
Ashbourne Rd. LA1: Lanc 5K 23
Ashbourne St. OL11: Roch 4J 203
Ashbrook Cl. PR4: Hesk B 4C 150
Ashbrook Cres. OL12: Roch 1F 204
ASHBROOK HEY 1F 204
Ashbrook Hey La. OL12: Roch 1F 204
Ashbrook St. LA1: Lanc 8H 23
Ash Brow WN8: N 'urgh 3L 211
Ashburn Av. L33: Kirk 6K 223
Ashburnham Rd. BB8: Colne 9L 85
Ashburton Ct. FY1: Blackp 3B 88
Ashburton Rd. FY1: Blackp 3B 88
Ashby St. PR7: Chor 8E 174
Ash Cl. BB1: Rish 9H 121
BB7: Barr 1K 101
FY3: Blackp 8J 89
(off Newholme Res. Pk.)
L39: Orms 7J 209
OL12: Roch 1F 204
PR4: Elsw 1M 91
WN6: App B 5G 213
Ashcombe Ga. FY5: T Clev 4K 63
Ashcombe Pl. BL7: Edgw 7L 179
Ash Coppice PR2: Lea 7A 114
Ash Cotts. BL8: Bury 8H 201
Ash Ct. *BB1: Blackb* 1A 140
(off Ash St.)
PR4: Clif 7H 113
Ash Cres. PR4: Frec 3M 131
Ashcroft BB7: West B 7L 73
LA3: Heys 7M 21
OL12: Roch 1G 205
Ashcroft Av. L39: Orms 6L 209
Ashcroft Cl. LA2: Caton 2G 25
Ashcroft Pl. BB7: West B 7L 73
Ashcroft Rd. L33: Know P 7A 224
L37: Form 2A 214
Ashdale Cl. PR7: Copp 5N 193
Ashdale Gro. FY5: T Clev 1L 63
Ashdale Pl. LA1: Lanc 6J 23
Ashdene OL12: Roch 2A 204
OL14: Wals 6L 165
Ashdene Cres. BL2: Bolt 8K 199
Ashdown Cl. FY6: Carl 6H 63
PR8: S'port 1L 187
Ashdown Dr. PR6: Clay W 4E 154
Ashdown M. PR2: Fulw 3A 116
Ash Dr. BB7: West B 5K 73
FY5: T Clev 2J 63
FY6: Poul F 9K 63
LA5: Wart 4B 12
PR4: Frec 3M 131
PR4: Wart 3J 131
Asheldon St. PR1: Prest 8N 115
Ashen Bottom BB4: Hasl 9J 161
Ashendean Vw. BB12: Padi 9J 103
Ashenhurst Cl. OL14: Tod 9K 147
Ashenhurst Rd. OL14: Tod 9J 147
Ashes La. OL14: Tod 8N 147
OL16: Milnr 6H 205
Ash Fld. PR6: Clay W 4E 154
Ashfield PR2: Fulw 1J 115
Ashfield Av. LA1: Lanc 8A 228 (9H 23)
LA4: Morec 2F 22
Ashfield Caravan Pk. FY4: Blackp 2M 109
Ashfield Cl. BB9: Barrf 1G 104
Ashfield Ct. FY2: Blackp 5E 62
PR2: Ingol 3C 114
PR6: And 5K 195
(off Ashfield Rd.)
Ashfield Gro. BL1: Bolt 7G 199
Ashfield Ho. FY2: Blackp 5E 62
OL11: Roch 8C 204
Ashfield La. OL16: Milnr 9J 205
Ashfield Ri. PR3: Catt 2A 68
Ashfield Rd. BB12: Burnl 1B 228 (3D 124)
FY2: Blackp 6E 62
FY5: T Clev 4E 62
OL11: Roch 9B 204
PR6: And 5K 195
PR7: Chor 7D 174
Ashfields PR26: Leyl 6D 152
Ashfield Ter. WN6: App B 4F 212
Ashford Av. LA1: Lanc 4J 29
Ashford Cl. BL2: Bolt 9L 199
LA1: Lanc 4K 29
Ashford Cres. PR3: Brou 7F 94
Ashford Rd. LA1: Lanc 4J 29
PR2: Ash R 7B 114
Ashford St. BB9: Nelson 3J 105
Ash Gro. BB3: Darw 5B 158
BB4: Rawt 4M 161
BB4: Water 8E 144
BB18: Barnw 2M 77
BL0: Ramsb 2E 200
BL2: Bolt 9M 199
BL8: Tott 8F 200
FY6: Pree 9N 41
LA1: Lanc 2K 29
OL15: Littleb 9J 185
PR1: Prest 8A 116
PR3: Gars 4M 59
PR3: St M 4G 66
PR4: Longt 8K 133
PR4: New L 1C 152
PR4: W Grn 6H 111
PR4: Wesh 2N 111
PR5: Bam B 7B 136
PR7: Chor 9E 174
WA11: Rain 4K 225
WN5: Orr 5J 221
WN8: Skelm 2H 219
Ash Holme PR1: Prest 6M 115
Ashia Cl. OL16: Roch 7D 204
Ashiana Lodge *BB9: Nelson* 2J 105
(off Audley Cl.)
Ashington Cl. BL1: Bolt 9B 198
WN5: Wigan 2L 221
Ashlands Cl. *BL0: Ramsb* 4J 181
(off Bolton Rd.)

Ash La.—Bk. Clare St.

Ash La. BB6: Gt H 3H 121
PR3: Longr 2K 97
PR4: Clif 8H 113
Ashlea Gro. FY6: Stal 5B 56
Ashleigh Ct. LA5: Arn 1F 4
PR2: Fulw 2K 115
Ashleigh M. FY3: Blackp 4N 227
Ashleigh Rd. L31: Magh 3E 222
LA5: Arn 1F 4
Ashleigh St. BB3: Darw 9B 158
PR1: Prest 1M 135
Ashley Cl. FY2: Blackp 9C 62
FY5: T Clev 4H 63
L33: Kirk 5K 223
OL11: Roch 9N 203
Ashley Ct. *BB5: Acc* *3M 141*
(off Pickup St.)
FY6: Poul F 8J 63
OL12: Whitw 4A 184
Ashley Dearnley Ct. OL15: Littleb 1J 205
Ashley Gdns. LA2: Gal 3L 37
Ashley La. PR3: Goos, Longr 3C 96
Ashley M. PR2: Ash R 8F 114
Ashley Rd. FY8: L Ann 8F 108
PR9: S'port 7J 167
WN8: Skelm 9M 211
Ashley St. BB12: Burnl 2D 124
Ash Mdw. PR2: Lea 6B 114
Ashmeadow Gro. LA6: Neth K 4C 16
Ashmeadow La. PR6: Birns 7N 155
Ashmeadow Rd. LA5: Arn 1F 4
LA6: Neth K 4C 16
Ashmead Rd. WN8: Skelm 8L 211
Ashmoor St. PR1: Prest 3H 229 (8H 115)
Ashmore Gro. FY5: T Clev 2D 62
Ashmount Dr. OL12: Roch 3C 204
Ashmuir Hey L32: Kirk 9L 223
Ashness Cl. PR2: Fulw 1J 115
Ashover Cl. BL1: Bolt 7F 198
Ashridge Way WN5: Orr 2L 221
Ash Rd. PR4: Elsw 9M 65
PR7: Copp 5A 194
Ash St. BB1: Blackb 1A 140
BB5: Osw 4K 141
BB6: Gt H 3J 121
BB8: Traw 9F 86
BB9: Nelson 2K 105
BB11: Burnl 3F 228 (4F 124)
FY4: Blackp 3C 108
FY7: Flee 9G 40
OL10: Heyw 9F 202
OL13: Bac 4K 163
PR8: S'port 9J 167
Ashton & Lea Golf Course 7N 113
Ashton Av. FY6: K Sea 8K 41
ASHTON BANK 9C 114
Ashton Bank Way PR2: Ash R 9A 114
Ashton Cl. PR2: Ash R 8D 114
Ashton Ct. FY8: L Ann 1D 128
LA1: Lanc 9D 228
Ashton Dr. BB9: Nelson 4J 105
LA1: Lanc 6J 23
Ashton Garden Ct. FY8: L Ann 1E 128
Ashton Gdns. OL11: Roch 8B 204
Ashtongate PR2: Ash R 8B 114
Ashton Ho. BB3: Darw 7B 158
Ashton La. BB3: Darw 7A 158
PR3: Out R 8K 57
Ashton Leisure Cen. 7C 114
Ashton Lodge BL0: Ramsb 7H 181
Ashton Memorial 9M 23
ASHTON-ON-RIBBLE 8B 114
Ashton Pl. PR8: S'port 8H 167
Ashton Rd. BB3: Darw 7B 158
FY1: Blackp 5L 227 (7C 88)
LA1: Lanc 9D 228 (9K 23)
(not continuous)
LA2: Lanc 4J 29
LA4: Morec 3C 22
PR8: Birk 4F 186
Ashton St. FY8: L Ann 5N 129
OL11: Roch 8B 204
PR2: Ash R 9G 115
PR3: Longr 2J 97
Ashton Vw. FY8: L Ann 1E 128
Ashton Wlk. LA1: Lanc 6D 228
Ashtree Ct. PR2: Ingol 5D 114
PR5: H Walt 5E 136
Ash Tree Gro. BB9: Nelson 3L 105
LA5: Bolt S 6K 15
Ashtree Gro. PR1: Penw 4E 134
Ashtrees L40: Mawd 3N 191
Ashtrees Way LA5: Carn 8A 12
Ashtree Wlk. BB9: Barrf 9H 85
ASHURST 8M 211
Ashurst Cl. WN8: Skelm 8L 211
Ashurst Gdns. WN8: Skelm 8L 211
Ashurst Rd. PR25: Leyl 6N 153
WN6: Stand 2L 213
WN8: Skelm 9M 211
Ashville Ter. BB2: Blackb 8L 139
Ashwall St. WN8: Skelm 3H 219
Ashwell M. BL2: Bolt 9J 199
Ashwell Pl. FY5: T Clev 4C 62
Ashwell St. BL2: Bolt 9J 199
Ashwood *WN8: Skelm* *9N 211*
(off Forest Dr.)
Ashwood Av. BB2: Blackb 1L 157
BL0: Ramsb 7J 181
Ashwood Cl. FY8: L Ann 4L 129
L33: Kirk 5K 223
Ash Wood Ct. PR7: Chor 8C 174
Ashwood Ct. LA1: Lanc 2K 29
PR4: Longt 9L 133
Ashwood Dr. BL8: Bury 7G 201
OL15: Littleb 9J 185
Ashwood Rd. PR2: Fulw 2G 115
Ashworth Cl. BB2: Blackb 3K 139
OL15: Littleb 7K 185
Ashworth Ct. FY3: Blackp 3D 88
PR1: Prest 6N 229
(Ashworth St.)
PR1: Prest 9N 229 (2L 135)
(Lawrence Av.)
Ashworth Dr. LA2: Hest B 7J 15
Ashworth Gro. PR1: Prest 2M 135
Ashworth La. BB4: W'foot 4D 162
BL1: Bolt 8F 198
PR1: Prest 2L 135
Ashworth Rd. BB4: W'foot 5D 162
FY4: Blackp 1J 109
OL10: Heyw 5F 202
OL11: Roch 2C 202
Ashworth St. BB1: Rish 8H 121
BB4: Water 9E 144
BB4: W'foot 7D 162
(not continuous)
BB5: Bax 6D 142
OL12: Roch 5A 204
OL13: Bac 7H 163
(Huttock End La.)
OL13: Bac 4L 163
(Zion St.)
PR1: Prest 6N 229 (1L 135)
PR5: Bam B 6B 136
Ashworth Ter. BB3: Darw 7N 157
BL2: Bolt 9L 199
OL13: Bac *7F 162*
(off Newchurch Rd.)
Askew La. LA6: Burt K 8H 7
Askrigg Cl. BB5: Acc 2C 142
FY4: Blackp 2G 108
Asland Cl. PR5: Bam B 8B 136
Asland Gdns. PR9: S'port 2B 168
Asmall Cl. L39: Orms 6J 209
Asmall La. L39: Hals 4D 208
L40: Scar 5G 208
Aspden St. OL14: Tod 1L 165
PR5: Bam B 7A 136
Aspels, The PR1: Penw 4F 134
Aspels Cres. PR1: Penw 4F 134
Aspels Nook PR1: Penw 4F 134
Aspen Cl. L33: Kirk 4L 223
Aspendale Cl. PR4: Longt 8K 133
Aspen Dr. BB10: Burnl 2G 124
Aspen Fold BB5: Osw 3H 141
Aspen Gdns. OL12: Roch 4L 203
PR7: Chor 8D 174
PR8: S'port 8L 167
Aspen Gro. BB18: Earl 3E 78
Aspen La. BB5: Osw 4H 141
BB18: Earl 2E 78
Aspen Way WN8: Skelm 1J 219
Aspinall Cl. PR1: Penw 6G 134
Aspinall Cres. L37: Gt A 2F 214
Aspinall Fold BB1: Blackb 9M 119
Aspinall Rd. WN6: Stand 3L 213
Aspley Gro. *BB8: Traw* *8F 86*
(off Skipton Rd.)
Assembly Rooms LA1: Lanc 7B 228
Asshawes, The PR6: H Charn 4H 195
Assheton Pl. PR2: Ribb 5A 116
Assheton Rd. BB2: Blackb 3H 139
Astbury Chase BB3: Darw 5B 158
Asten Bldgs. BB4: W'foot 8C 162
Aster Chase BB3: Lwr D 9A 140
Aster Dr. L33: Kirk 5J 223
Astland Gdns. PR4: Tarl 5D 150
Astland St. FY8: L Ann 2E 128
Astley Bank BB3: Darw 8A 158
ASTLEY BRIDGE 9F 198
Astley Cl. WA11: Rain 3K 225
Astley Ct. LA1: Lanc 1H 29
Astley Cres. PR4: Frec 2A 132
Astley Gate BB2: Blackb 4C 226 (3M 139)
Astley Hall Dr. BL0: Ramsb 1H 201
Astley Hall Mus. & Art Gallery 5C 174
Astley Hgts. BB3: Darw 8A 158
Astley Rd. BL2: Bolt 8L 199
PR7: Chor 5D 174
Astley St. BB3: Darw 8A 158
PR3: Longr 3J 97
PR7: Chor 5E 174
Astley Ter. BB3: Darw 8A 158
ASTLEY VILLAGE 4C 174
Astling Grn. FY4: Blackp 1K 109
Aston Av. FY5: T Clev 1G 62
Aston St. PR4: Weet 4D 90
Aston Wlk. *BB2: Blackb* *8A 140*
(off Silbury Cl.)
Aston Way PR26: Leyl 5E 152
Astra Bus. Cen. PR2: Ribb 3E 116
Asturian Ga. PR3: Ribc 4A 98
Athelstan Fold PR2: Fulw 6F 114
Athens Vw. *BB10: Burnl* *4G 125*
(off Athletic St.)
Atherfield BL2: Bolt 9L 199
Atherstone *OL12: Roch* *5C 204*
(off Redcross St.)
Atherstone Cl. BL8: Bury 9H 201
Atherton Cl. PR2: Ash R 7F 114
Atherton Rd. LA1: Lanc 7H 23
PR25: Leyl 7G 152
Atherton St. OL13: Bac 7F 162
PR7: Adl 7J 195
Atherton Way OL13: Bac 7F 162
Athletic St. BB10: Burnl 4G 124
Athlone Av. BL1: Bolt 8C 198
BL9: Bury 9L 201
FY2: Blackp 9C 62
Athole Gro. PR9: S'port 7M 167
Athol Gro. PR6: Chor 8G 174
Atholl Cres. L10: Aint 8C 222
Atholl St. PR1: Prest 9G 115
Athol St. BB9: Nelson 2K 105
BL0: Ramsb 7H 181
OL12: Roch 4E 204
(not continuous)
Athol St. Nth. BB11: Burnl 4B 124
Athol St. Sth. BB11: Burnl 4B 124
Atkinson Art Gallery 7H 167
Atkinson Cl. PR1: Prest 4K 229 (9J 115)
Atkinson Rd. L39: Orms 6L 209
Atkinson St. BB8: Colne 8N 85
(not continuous)
BB10: Brierc 7K 105
Atlanta Ct. L33: Kirk 4J 223
Atlas Rd. BB3: Darw 6A 158
Atlas St. BB5: Clay M 8M 121
Atom
Panopticon 8L 87
Atrium Ct. BB11: Burnl 5F 124
Aubigny Dr. PR2: Fulw 5G 115
Aubrey St. OL11: Roch 8C 204
Auburn Gro. FY1: Blackp 7N 227 (8D 88)
Auckland St. BB3: Darw 8B 158
Auden Lea FY5: T Clev 9F 54
Audenshaw Rd. LA4: Morec 4C 22
Audley Cl. BB9: Nelson 2J 105
FY8: L Ann 3K 129
Audley La. BB1: Blackb 3A 140
Audley Range BB1: Blackb 6F 226 (4N 139)
Audley Sports Cen. 5G 226 (4A 140)
Audley St. BB1: Blackb 3A 140
AUGHTON
L39 4F 216
LA2 6M 17
Aughton Brow LA2: Aug 6M 17
Aughton Ct. LA1: Lanc 4K 23
Aughton M. PR8: Birk 9G 167
AUGHTON PARK 1J 217
Aughton Pk. Dr. L39: Aug 1J 217
Aughton Park Station (Rail) 1J 217
Aughton Rd. LA2: Aug, Gress, Halt 6H 17
PR8: Birk 8F 166
Aughton St. FY7: Flee 8H 41
L39: Orms 8J 209
(not continuous)
Aughton Wlk. PR1: Prest 3K 229 (8J 115)
Augusta Cl. OL12: Roch 3B 204
Augusta St. BB5: Acc 4B 142
OL12: Roch 4B 204
Auster Cres. PR4: Frec 7N 111
Austin Cl. L32: Kirk 7J 223
PR25: Leyl 7K 153
Austin Cres. PR2: Fulw 5E 114
Austin Dr. PR7: Chor 9F 174
Austin Gro. FY1: Blackp 9H 227 (9B 88)
Austin St. BB11: Burnl 3A 228 (4C 124)
OL13: Bac *5K 163*
(off Union St.)
Austin Way FY4: Blackp 3M 109
Austwick Rd. LA1: Lanc 6H 23
(not continuous)
Austwick Way BB5: Acc 3D 142
Avallon Cl. BL8: Tott 6E 200
Avallon Way BB3: Darw 6C 158
Avalon Cl. BB12: Burnl 2L 123
Avalon Dr. PR4: Frec 1A 132
Avalwood Av. PR4: Longt 8M 133
Avebury Cl. BB2: Blackb 8A 140
Aveley Gdns. WN3: Wigan 7M 221
Aveling Dr. PR9: Banks 9F 148
Avelon Cl. L31: Lyd 6A 216
AVENHAM 7L 229 (2K 135)
Avenham Cl. PR9: Banks 1G 168
Avenham Colonnade PR1: Prest 8L 229 (2K 135)
Avenham Ct. PR1: Prest 7M 229 (1K 135)
Avenham Gro. FY1: Blackp 4C 88
Avenham La. PR1: Prest 8L 229 (2K 135)
Avenham Pk. 8K 229 (2J 135)
Avenham Pl. PR1: Prest 8M 229 (2K 135)
PR4: Newt 7D 112
Avenham Rd. PR1: Prest 7L 229 (1K 135)
PR7: Chor 7E 174
Avenham St. PR1: Prest 6L 229 (1K 135)
Avenham Ter. PR1: Prest 8M 229 (2K 135)
Avenham Wlk. PR1: Prest 8L 229 (2K 135)
Avenue, The BB6: Old L 5C 100
BB11: Burnl 6H 125
BL2: Barl 6A 84
BL9: Bury 8L 201
FY6: Carl 7J 63
L39: Orms 6J 209
(Church Hill Rd.)
L39: Orms 6K 209
(Southport Rd.)
PR1: Penw 3E 134
PR2: Ingol 3D 114
PR2: Lea 8A 114
PR3: C'town 9L 59
PR3: Gars 3M 59
PR6: Adl 5J 195
PR8: Banks 1E 168
PR9: S'port 9D 168
PR25: Leyl 9J 153
WA11: Rain 4K 225
WN5: Bill 8G 221
WN6: Stand 8N 213
Avenue Pde. BB5: Acc 2B 142
Avenue Rd. BB7: Hurst G 1M 99
FY3: Blackp 2H 89
FY5: T Clev 2D 62
Avery Gdns. FY6: Carl 5H 63
Aviemore Cl. BB1: Blackb 4A 140
BL0: Ramsb 3F 200
Avocet Cl. PR26: Leyl 6D 152
Avon Av. FY7: Flee 4D 54
Avon Bri. PR2: Fulw 1F 114
Avon Cl. BB2: Blackb 7B 226 (5L 139)
L33: Kirk 4L 223
OL16: Milnr 7K 205
Avon Ct. BB12: Burnl 2B 124
Avondale Av. BB1: Blackb 3E 140
BB12: Burnl 2A 124
BL9: Bury 9K 201
L31: Magh 2B 222
Avondale Cl. BB3: Darw 5M 157
Avondale Cres. FY4: Blackp 2F 108
Avondale Dr. BL0: Ramsb 3E 200
PR4: Tarl 7E 150
PR5: Lost H 8L 135
Avondale M. BB3: Darw 4M 157
Avondale Rd. BB3: Darw 5M 157
BB9: Nelson 3H 105
FY8: L Ann 9C 108
LA1: Lanc 1L 29
LA3: Heys 5M 21
PR7: Chor 7E 174
PR9: S'port 6H 167
Avondale Rd. Nth. PR9: S'port 5J 167
Avondale St. BB8: Colne 6D 86
WN6: Stand 3N 213
Avon Dr. BB18: Barnw 1N 77
BL9: Bury 5L 201
Avon Gdns. PR4: Cott 4A 114
Avon Grn. FY7: Flee 9E 40
Avon Ho. PR1: Prest 9N 115
Avon Pl. FY1: Blackp 2C 88
Avon Rd. WN5: Wigan 4M 221
Avonside Av. FY5: T Clev 9G 55
Avon St. FY8: L Ann 2E 128
Avonwood Cl. BB3: Darw 5M 157
Avroe Cres. FY4: Blackp 5D 108
Axis Pk. BB3: Lwr D 1A 158
Aycliffe Dr. PR7: Buck V 1B 174
Aylesbury Av.
FY4: Blackp 9N 227 (9D 88)
Aylesbury Wlk. BB10: Burnl 7G 105
Ayr Cl. PR8: S'port 1M 187
Ayr Ct. FY7: Flee 5E 54
Ayrefield Gro. WN6: Shev 6G 213
Ayrefield Rd. WN8: Roby M 8F 212
Ayr Gro. BB11: Burnl 6B 124
Ayr Rd. BB1: Blackb 5D 140
Ayrshire Cl. PR7: Buck V 9B 154
Ayr St. BL2: Bolt 9J 199
LA1: Lanc 8F 228 (9M 23)
Ayrton Av. FY4: Blackp 2D 108
Ayrton St. BB8: Colne 6B 86
Ayrton Vw. LA1: Lanc 4L 23
Aysgarth OL16: Roch 4E 204
Aysgarth Av. PR2: Fulw 2J 115
Aysgarth Ct. FY4: Blackp 2F 108
Aysgarth Dr. BB3: Darw 5M 157
BB5: Acc 2C 142
LA1: Lanc 4K 23
Aysgarth Rd. LA1: Lanc 8H 23
Azalea Cl. PR2: Fulw 3M 115
PR25: Leyl 5A 154
Azalea Gro. LA4: Morec 3E 22
Azalea Rd. BB2: Blackb 2J 139

B

Babbacombe Av. FY4: Blackp 3B 108
Baber Wlk. *BL1: Bolt* *9E 198*
(off Warwick St.)
Babylon La. PR6: Adl, And 5K 195
Bk. Albert Rd. *BB8: Colne* *7A 86*
(off Albert Rd.)
Bk. Albert St. *BB12: Padi* *1H 123*
(off Albert St.)
FY7: Flee *9H 41*
(off Albert St.)
Bk. Albion Pl. *BL9: Bury* *9L 201*
(off Hanson St.)
Bk. Alfred St. *BL0: Ramsb* *9G 180*
(off Mary St.)
Bk. Altham St. BB12: Padi 1J 123
Bk. Arthur St. BB5: Clay M 6M 121
Bk. Ashburton Rd. FY1: Blackp 3C 88
Bk. Ashby St. PR7: Chor 8F 174
Bk. Atkinson St. *BB8: Colne* *7N 85*
(off Atkinson St.)
Bk. Avondale Rd. E. LA3: Heys 5M 21
Bk. Avondale Rd. W. *LA3: Heys* *5M 21*
(off Avondale Rd.)
Bk. Bath St. PR9: S'port 6H 167
Bk. Beehive Ter. *BB4: Hasl* *2G 160*
(off Blackburn Rd.)
Bk. Birch St. *BL9: Bury* *9L 201*
(off Hornby St.)
Bk. Blackburn Rd. *BL7: Eger* *2D 198*
(off Blackburn Rd.)
Bk. Blackburn Rd. E. *BL7: Eger* *2D 198*
(off Albert St.)
Bk. Bolton Rd. BB3: Darw 8B 158
Bk. Bond St. *BB8: Colne* *6A 86*
(off Bond St.)
Bk. Botanic Rd. PR9: S'port 5N 167
Bk. Boundry St. *BB8: Colne* *7A 86*
(off Boundary St.)
Bk. Bourne's Row PR5: Hogh 7G 137
Bk. Bradshaw Brow *BL2: Bolt* *9J 199*
(off Bradshaw Brow)
Bk. Bradshaw Brow E. *BL2: Bolt* *9J 199*
(off Bradshaw Brow)
Bk. Bradshaw Chapel *BL2: Bolt* *8K 199*
(off Cottage Cft.)
Bk. Bradshaw Rd. *BL2: Bolt* *8K 199*
(off Bradshaw Rd.)
Bk. Bradshaw St. OL16: Roch 5D 204
Bk. Broom St. *OL16: Milnr* *9L 205*
(off Broomfield Ter.)
Back Brow WN8: Uph 4F 220
Bk. Brown St. BB8: Colne 7N 85
Bk. Burnley Rd. BB5: Acc 2B 142
Bk. Burton Rd. FY4: Blackp 9F 88
Bk. Byrom St. OL14: Tod 1L 165
Bk. Calton St. LA4: Morec 2B 22
Bk. Cambridge St. *BB8: Colne* *7A 86*
(off Cambridge St.)
Bk. Canning St. *BL9: Bury* *9L 201*
(off Hornby St.)
Bk. Carr Mill St. BB4: Hasl 2G 160
Bk. Carshalton Rd. FY1: Blackp 3B 88
Bk. Cateaton St. *BL9: Bury* *9L 201*
(off Hornby St., not continuous)
Bk. Cemetery Ter. OL13: Bac 7J 163
Bk. Chapel St. *BB8: Colne* *7A 86*
(off Chapel St.)
BB18: Barnw *3M 77*
(off Cobden St.)
BL6: Hor 9D 196
BL8: Tott 6E 200
OL12: Ward 8F 184
Bk. Chorley New Rd. *BL6: Hor* *9C 196*
(off Chorley New Rd.)
Bk. Church St. BB4: Newc 5C 162
BB6: Gt H 4J 121
BB9: Barrf 8H 85
BB12: Hapt *5H 123*
(off Church St.)
BB18: Barnw *2M 77*
(off Church St.)
FY1: Blackp 2H 227 (5B 88)
Back Claremont *LA4: Morec* *4N 21*
(off Claremont Rd.)
Bk. Clarendon Rd. FY1: Blackp 7J 227 (8B 88)
LA4: Morec *4N 21*
(off Clarendon Rd. E.)
Bk. Clare St. FY1: Blackp 9J 227

Bk. Clayton St.—Banbury Rd.

Bk. Clayton St. BB9: Nelson . . . 1H 105
(off Clayton St.)
Bk. Cobden St. BL9: Bury . . . 9M 201
(off Cobden St.)
Bk. Colne Rd. BB8: Traw . . . 9F 86
(off Colne Rd.)
BB18: Barnw . . . 3L 77
Bk. Commercial St. OL14: Tod . . . 2M 165
Back Commons BB7: Clith . . . 2K 81
Back Commonside FY8: L Ann . . . 4K 129
(off Woodlands Rd.)
Bk. Compton Rd. PR8: Birk . . . 2H 187
Back Constablelee BB4: Rawt . . . 3M 161
Bk. Cookson St. FY1: Blackp . . . 1K 227 (4C 88)
Bk. Cowm La. OL12: Whitw . . . 3M 183
Bk. Crescent St. LA4: Morec . . . 3A 22
Bk. Crown St. BL6: Hor . . . 9B 196
Bk. Cunliffe Rd. FY1: Blackp . . . 8M 227
Bk. Curzon St. FY8: L Ann . . . 1F 128
Bk. Dale St. OL16: Milnr . . . 8J 205
(off Dale St.)
Bk. Darwen Rd. BL7: Brom C . . . 6G 198
(off Darwen Rd.)
Bk. Derby Rd. FY5: T Clev . . . 9C 54
Back Der St. OL14: Tod . . . 2M 165
Bk. Drake St. OL16: Roch . . . 7C 204
Bk. Drinkhouse La. PR26: Cros . . . 5L 171
Bk. Duckworth St. BB3: Darw . . . 6A 158
Bk. Duke St. BB8: Colne . . . 7A 86
(off Duke St.)
Bk. Durham St. OL11: Roch . . . 8D 204
Bk. Earl St. BB8: Colne . . . 7A 86
(off Earl St.)
Bk. East Bank BB9: Barrf . . . 7H 85
Bk. Eaves St. FY1: Blackp . . . 3B 88
Bk. Elizabeth St. BB4: Lumb . . . 3D 162
(off Burnley Rd.)
Bk. Emmett St. BL6: Hor . . . 9C 196
(off Winter Hey La.)
Bk. Epsom Rd. FY5: T Clev . . . 3F 62
Bk. Fazakerley St. PR7: Chor . . . 6E 174
Bk. Forest Rd. PR8: S'port . . . 8K 167
(not continuous)
Bk. George St. BL6: Hor . . . 9D 196
Bk. Gisburn Rd. BB9: Blacko . . . 4J 85
Bk. Glen Eldon Rd. FY8: L Ann . . . 1E 128
Bk. Green St. LA4: Morec . . . 2B 22
Bk. Grimshaw St. PR1: Prest . . . 6M 229 (1K 135)
Bk. Grove Ter. LA4: Morec . . . 4F 22
(off Lancaster Rd.)
Bk. Halifax Rd. BB10: Brierc . . . 7L 105
Bk. Hall St. BB8: Colne . . . 7A 86
(off Hall St.)
Bk. Handsworth Rd. FY1: Blackp . . . 3C 88
(off Handsworth Rd.)
Bk. Harry St. BB9: Barrf . . . 8H 85
Bk. Haslam St. BL9: Bury . . . 9M 201
Bk. Headroomgate Rd. FY8: L Ann . . . 9F 108
Bk. Hesketh St. BB6: Gt H . . . 4J 121
(off Hesketh St.)
Back Heys BB5: Osw . . . 5L 141
Bk. Heysham Rd. LA3: Heys . . . 5M 21
Bk. High St. BL7: Belm . . . 9K 177
FY1: Blackp . . . 4B 88
Bk. Hill St. BB4: Craws . . . 9M 143
(off Clarence St.)
BB9: Brierf . . . 4D 104
(off Hill St.)
Bk. Hilton Av. FY1: Blackp . . . 9J 227
Bk. Hope St. OL13: Bac . . . 3K 163
Bk. Hornby St. E. BL9: Bury . . . 9L 201
(off Rake St.)
Backhouse St. BB5: Osw . . . 4L 141
Bk. Hunter St. LA5: Carn . . . 8A 12
Bk. James St. OL15: Littleb . . . 9J 185
(off James St.)
Bk. Kingsland Gro. FY1: Blackp . . . 6N 227
Bk. Knowlys Rd. LA3: Heys . . . 8L 21
Back La. BB4: Rawt . . . 4M 161
BB5: Bax, Ris B . . . 6D 142
BB7: Gis . . . 9B 52
BB7: Newt, Slaid . . . 5N 49
BB7: Rim . . . 4K 75
BB7: Sabd . . . 4G 103
BB7: Wis . . . 3M 101
(not continuous)
BB8: Traw . . . 9E 86
BB10: S'field . . . 1A 106
BB12: High . . . 3K 103
BB12: Read . . . 7B 102
BD23: Hell . . . 1D 52
BD24: Rath . . . 7M 35
FY6: Pree, Stal . . . 5N 55
FY6: Stal . . . 6C 56
L39: Aug . . . 4D 216
L39: Bick . . . 8M 217
L39: D'holl . . . 9K 207
L40: Bis G, Mawd . . . 5M 191
L40: Burs . . . 7C 190
LA2: Wen . . . 4G 18
LA2: Wray . . . 8D 18
LA5: Arn . . . 1E 4
LA5: Carn . . . 2B 16
LA5: Wart . . . 5A 12
LA6: K Lon . . . 6F 8
(off Lunefield Dr.)
LA6: K Lon . . . 6F 8
(off Salt Pie La.)
LA6: Neth K . . . 2B 16
LA6: Tuns . . . 2E 18
LA7: Hale . . . 1B 6
OL12: Roch . . . 2K 203
OL12: Whitw . . . 4N 183
PR3: Goos . . . 8B 70
PR3: Goos, W'ham . . . 3C 96
PR3: Gt E . . . 6N 65
PR3: Out R . . . 6C 56
PR4: Greenh, Weet . . . 8F 90
PR4: Lea T . . . 7L 113
PR4: Longt . . . 8H 133
PR4: Tarl . . . 2E 170
PR6: Clay W . . . 5B 154
(not continuous)
PR6: H Charn . . . 9K 175
PR7: Char R . . . 8J 173
PR7: Leyl . . . 8M 153
Back La. PR26: Breth . . . 1J 171
WN6: App B, Stand . . . 4G 213
WN8: Dalt . . . 7C 212
WN8: N 'urgh . . . 2H 211
WN8: Skelm . . . 4B 220
(Barnfield Dr.)
WN8: Skelm . . . 5A 220
(Beavers La.)
Back La. E. L40: Mawd . . . 4B 192
Back La. Side BB4: Hasl . . . 5G 161
Bk. Leach St. BB8: Colne . . . 7N 85
(off Leach St.)
Bk. Lee St. BB4: Hasl . . . 5G 161
Bk. Lines St. LA4: Morec . . . 3B 22
Bk. Longfield Rd. OL14: Tod . . . 2L 165
(off Longfield Rd.)
Bk. Longworth Rd. BL6: Hor . . . 9D 196
(off Longworth Rd.)
Bk. Lord St. BB4: Craws . . . 9M 143
(off Lord St.)
FY1: Blackp . . . 4B 88
LA1: Lanc . . . 7K 23
Bk. Louise St. OL12: Roch . . . 2F 204
(off Kitter St.)
Bk. Lumbutts Rd. OL14: Tod . . . 4K 165
Bk. Lune St. BB8: Colne . . . 7B 86
(off Lune St.)
Bk. Main St. LA3: Heys . . . 8K 21
(off Main St.)
Bk. Marine Rd. LA4: Morec . . . 4N 21
Bk. Marine Rd. E. LA4: Morec . . . 2D 22
(off Seaborn Rd.)
Bk. Market St. LA5: Carn . . . 8A 12
(off Market St.)
Bk. Merton St. BL8: Bury . . . 9J 201
(off Merton St.)
Bk. Moon Av. FY1: Blackp . . . 7J 227 (8B 88)
Bk. Morecambe St. LA4: Morec . . . 2B 22
Bk. Moss La. L40: Burs . . . 6D 190
Back Mt. PR7: Chor . . . 6E 174
Bk. Newchurch Rd. BB4: Rawt . . . 5A 162
Bk. New St. LA5: Carn . . . 8A 12
Bk. North Cres. FY8: L Ann . . . 2E 128
Bk. North St. OL14: Tod . . . 2L 165
(off Ridge Rd.)
Bk. Oddfellows Ter. BB4: W'foot . . . 4D 162
Bk. Oldham Rd. OL16: Roch . . . 7D 204
Bk. Olive Bank BL8: Bury . . . 9G 201
(off Elson St.)
Back o' the Town La. L38: Ince B . . . 8E 214
Back o' th' Lowe BB3: Tock . . . 5H 157
Bk. Palatine Rd. FY1: Blackp . . . 4K 227
Bk. Parkinson St. BB2: Blackb . . . 6J 139
Bk. Patience St. OL12: Roch . . . 4N 203
(off Patience St.)
Bk. Peter St. BB9: Barrf . . . 7H 85
(off Park St.)
Bk. Pine St. OL16: Milnr . . . 9L 205
(off Pine St.)
Bk. Pleasant St. FY1: Blackp . . . 3B 88
Bk. Queen St. BB6: Gt H . . . 4J 121
LA1: Lanc . . . 8C 228 (9K 23)
LA4: Morec . . . 3B 22
Bk. Railway Vw. PR7: Adl . . . 7J 195
Bk. Read's Rd. FY1: Blackp . . . 3K 227 (6C 88)
Bk. Regent St. BB4: Hasl . . . 4F 160
(off Blackburn Rd.)
Bk. Rhoden Rd. BB5: Osw . . . 6K 141
Bk. Ribble Rd. FY1: Blackp . . . 4K 227
Bk. Richard Burch St. BL9: Bury . . . 9L 201
(off Richard Burch St.)
Bk. Richard St. BB9: Brierf . . . 5F 104
(off Richard St.)
Bk. Ridge St. OL14: Tod . . . 2L 165
Bk. Rings Row BB4: Craws . . . 7M 143
(off Rings St.)
Back Rd. BB7: Grind . . . 4A 74
Bk. Rosebery Av. Nth. LA4: Morec . . . 3C 22
(off Rosebery Av.)
Bk. Rosebery Av. Sth. LA4: Morec . . . 4C 22
(off Rosebery Av.)
Bk. Rushton St. OL13: Bac . . . 7J 163
Backs, The PR3: Longr . . . 4J 97
Bk. St Anne's Rd. W. FY8: L Ann . . . 2E 128
Bk. St George's Sq. FY8: L Ann . . . 1D 128
Bk. St Heliers Rd. FY1: Blackp . . . 9K 227
Bk. St John St. OL13: Bac . . . 4K 163
Bk. Salford St. BL9: Bury . . . 9M 201
Bk. Sandy Bank Rd. BL7: Edgw . . . 9K 179
Bk. School La. WN8: Skelm . . . 2H 219
WN8: Uph . . . 4F 220
Bk. Scotland Rd. BB9: Nelson . . . 2H 105
(off Scotland Rd.)
Bk. Seed St. PR1: Prest . . . 5J 229 (9J 115)
Bk. Shannon St. FY1: Blackp . . . 5J 227 (7B 88)
Bk. Shed St. OL12: Whitw . . . 5A 184
(off Clara St.)
Bk. Sherbourne Rd. FY1: Blackp . . . 2B 88
(off Sherbourne Rd.)
Bk. Shuttleworth St. BB12: Padi . . . 1H 123
(off Shuttleworth St.)
Bk. Skipton Rd. BB18: Barnw . . . 2M 77
(off Forester's Bldgs.)
Bk. Skull Ho. La. WN6: App B . . . 4G 212
Bk. Smith St. BB18: Barnw . . . 3L 77
(off Smith St.)
Bk. Spencer St. BB4: Craws . . . 8M 143
Bk. Springfield Rd. Nth. FY8: L Ann . . . 2E 128
(off St David's Rd.)
Bk. Square St. BL0: Ramsb . . . 8H 181
Bk. Starkie St. PR1: Prest . . . 8K 229 (2J 135)
Bk. Stopper La. BB7: Rim . . . 4M 75
Back St. LA3: O'ton . . . 7B 28
Bk. Sun St. LA1: Lanc . . . 6C 228
Bk. Threlfall Rd. FY1: Blackp . . . 8M 227
Bk. Tonge Moor Rd. BL2: Bolt . . . 9H 199
(off Tonge Moor Rd.)
Bk. Townley St. LA4: Morec . . . 2B 22
(off Townley St.)
Bk. Vernon St. BL9: Bury . . . 9L 201
(off Hornby St.)
Bk. Virginia St. PR8: S'port . . . 8J 167
Bk. Walmersley Rd. E. BL9: Bury . . . 9L 201
(off Taylor St.)
Bk. Walmersley Rd. W. BL9: Bury . . . 9L 201
(off Eldon St.)
Bk. Warbreck Rd. FY1: Blackp . . . 4B 88
Bk. Waterloo Rd. FY4: Blackp . . . 9J 227 (9B 88)
Bk. Water St. BB5: Acc . . . 2B 142
BB18: Earl . . . 2E 78
(off Lwr. Croft St.)
BL7: Eger . . . 3D 198
(off Water St.)
Bk. Wellfield Ter. OL14: Tod . . . 3L 165
Bk. Wellington St. BB5: Acc . . . 3B 142
Bk. West Cres. FY8: L Ann . . . 2E 128
Bk. Wheatfield St. BB1: Rish . . . 7H 121
(off Wheatfield St.)
Back Whitegate OL15: Littleb . . . 1H 205
(off Whitegate)
Bk. Willow St. BB12: Burnl . . . 1A 228 (2C 124)
Bk. Winterdyne Ter. LA3: Heys . . . 4M 21
Bk. Woodfield Rd. FY1: Blackp . . . 8J 227 (8B 88)
Bk. Woone La. BB7: Clith . . . 4L 81
Bk. Wright St. BL6: Hor . . . 9C 196
(off Walsh St.)
Bk. Yorkshire St. OL13: Bac . . . 4K 163
(off Yorkshire St.)
Bk. York St. BB4: Craws . . . 9M 143
(off Forest Bank Rd.)
BB7: Clith . . . 3L 81
Bk. Zion St. BB8: Colne . . . 7A 86
(off Zion St.)
Bacon St. BB9: Nelson . . . 2J 105
BACUP . . . 4K 163
Bacup Golf Course . . . 5K 163
Bacup Leisure Hall . . . 4J 163
Bacup Natural History Society Mus. . . . 4K 163
(off Yorkshire St.)
Bacup Old Rd. OL13: Bac . . . 7K 145
Bacup Rd. BB4: Rawt, W'foot . . . 5M 161
(not continuous)
BB11: Cliv . . . 8G 125
OL14: Tod . . . 1A 164
Badby Wood L33: Kirk . . . 6L 223
Baden Ct. BB1: Blackb . . . 6N 119
Baden Ter. BB2: Blackb . . . 7L 139
Badge Brow BB5: Osw . . . 3L 141
Badger Cl. BB12: Padi . . . 9J 103
Badger Rd. PR26: Far M . . . 3K 153
Badgers Cl. BB5: Acc . . . 9D 122
Badgers Cft. PR2: Ribb . . . 7B 116
Badgers St. BL9: Bury . . . 9L 201
Badgers Wlk. PR7: Chor . . . 3D 174
Badgers Wlk. E. FY8: L Ann . . . 5B 130
Badgers Wlk. W. FY8: L Ann . . . 5B 130
Badgers Way PR5: Lost H . . . 5L 135
Badgers Wood PR3: Bils . . . 4F 68
Badger Wells Cotts.
BB7: Sabd . . . 2E 102
Badger Wood LA3: Midd . . . 6K 27
OL14: Tod . . . 2M 165
Bagganley La. PR6: Chor . . . 5G 175
(Belmont Dr.)
PR6: Chor . . . 4G 175
(Knowley Brow)
Bagnall Cl. OL12: Roch . . . 3K 203
Bagnold Rd. PR1: Prest . . . 8N 115
Bagot St. FY1: Blackp . . . 9J 227 (9B 88)
BAGSLATE MOOR . . . 5K 203
Bagslate Moor La. OL11: Roch . . . 5K 203
Bagslate Moor Rd.
OL11: Roch . . . 6K 203
Baildon Rd. OL12: Roch . . . 4M 203
Bailey Av. FY8: L Ann . . . 4G 129
Bailey Bank BB7: Chaig . . . 4A 80
Bailey Cl. BB2: Blackb . . . 8K 139
Bailey Ct. FY3: Blackp . . . 4E 88
Bailey La. BD23: Tos . . . 10H 35
LA3: Heys . . . 8K 21
Bailey St. BB11: Burnl . . . 3A 228 (4C 124)
BB18: Earl . . . 3F 78
Bailey Wlk. BB2: Blackb . . . 9C 226
Bailey Way L31: Magh . . . 3B 222
Baillie St. OL16: Roch . . . 5C 204
(Milton St.)
OL16: Roch . . . 6C 204
(Yorkshire St.)
PR2: Fulw . . . 2M 115
Baillie St. E. OL16: Roch . . . 5D 204
BAILRIGG . . . 6L 29
Bailrigg La. LA1: Bail . . . 6K 29
Baines Av. FY3: Blackp . . . 1F 88
Bainesfield FY6: Poul F . . . 1K 89
Bairstow St. BB18: Barnw . . . 1M 77
FY1: Blackp . . . 5H 227 (7B 88)
PR1: Prest . . . 7K 229 (1J 135)
Baitings Cl. OL12: Roch . . . 3G 202
Baitings Row OL12: Roch . . . 3G 202
Baker Cl. PR7: Buck V . . . 9A 154
Bakers Ct. FY4: Blackp . . . 2F 108
Bakers La. PR9: S'port . . . 3M 167
Bakers M. PR4: Tarl . . . 9E 150
Baker St. BB1: Blackb . . . 4B 140
BB9: Nelson . . . 9J 85
BB11: Burnl . . . 4A 228 (4C 124)
BL0: Ramsb . . . 9G 181
LA1: Lanc . . . 5K 23
OL13: Bac . . . 4K 163
PR7: Copp . . . 4A 194
PR25: Leyl . . . 5L 153
Balaclava St.
BB1: Blackb . . . 1C 226 (2M 139)
Bala Cl. BB1: Blackb . . . 1C 226 (2M 139)
Balcarres Cl. PR25: Leyl . . . 6K 153
Balcarres Pl. PR25: Leyl . . . 7K 153
Balcarres Rd. PR2: Ash R . . . 6F 114
PR7: Chor . . . 9D 174
PR25: Leyl . . . 7K 153
Balcombe Cl. BL8: Bury . . . 6G 201
BALDERSTONE . . . 3A 118
Balderstone Cl. BB10: Burnl . . . 8J 105
Balderstone Hall La. BB2: Bald . . . 3L 117
Balderstone La. BB10: Burnl . . . 9H 105
Balderstone Rd. PR1: Prest . . . 3G 135
PR4: Frec . . . 1N 131
BALDINGSTONE . . . 4L 201
Baldwin Gro. FY1: Blackp . . . 7N 227 (8D 88)
Baldwin Hill BB7: Clith . . . 3K 81
Baldwin Rd. BB7: Clith . . . 3K 81
Baldwins Bldgs. BB4: Rawt . . . 4M 161
(off Bank St.)
Baldwin St. BB2: Blackb . . . 5K 139
BB9: Barrf . . . 7H 85
OL13: Bac . . . 7F 162
PR5: Bam B . . . 7A 136
WN5: Orr . . . 5L 221
Bales, The L30: N'ton . . . 6A 222
Balfour Cl. BB9: Brierf . . . 5H 105
FY5: T Clev . . . 4K 63
Balfour Ct. PR25: Leyl . . . 6K 153
Balfour Rd. OL12: Roch . . . 4N 203
PR2: Fulw . . . 6H 115
PR8: S'port . . . 9L 167
Balfour St. BB2: Blackb . . . 4K 139
BB6: Gt H . . . 4K 121
PR25: Leyl . . . 6K 153
Balham Av. FY4: Blackp . . . 4E 108
BALLADEN . . . 8L 161
Ballam Rd. FY8: L Ann . . . 8N 109
PR2: Ash R . . . 8B 114
PR4: Westby . . . 5D 110
Ballam St. BB11: Burnl . . . 5E 124
Ballantrae Rd. BB1: Blackb . . . 5D 140
Ballard Cl. OL15: Littleb . . . 7L 185
Ballater St. BB11: Burnl . . . 6B 124
Balle St. BB3: Darw . . . 7A 158
Ball Gro. Dr. BB8: Colne . . . 6E 86
Balliol Cl. BB12: Padi . . . 9J 103
Ball La. LA2: Caton . . . 2H 25
Ballot Hill Cres. PR3: Bils . . . 6D 68
Balls Pl. PR8: S'port . . . 7H 167
Ball St. BB9: Nelson . . . 1H 105
FY1: Blackp . . . 9J 227 (9B 88)
FY6: Poul F . . . 8K 63
OL16: Roch . . . 5D 204
Ballycreen OL11: Roch . . . 9N 203
Balmer Gro. FY1: Blackp . . . 5M 227 (7D 88)
Balmoral PR7: Adl . . . 7G 195
Balmoral Av. BB1: Blackb . . . 5A 120
BB7: Clith . . . 5J 81
LA3: Heys . . . 5M 21
OL11: Roch . . . 5M 203
PR25: Leyl . . . 7M 153
Balmoral Cl. BB2: Blackb . . . 8E 226 (5N 139)
BL8: Greenm . . . 4F 200
L33: Kirk . . . 5K 223
OL16: Milnr . . . 7K 205
PR4: Wal B . . . 2K 151
PR9: S'port . . . 3A 168
Balmoral Ct. PR7: Chor . . . 6D 174
Balmoral Cres. BB1: Blackb . . . 4F 140
Balmoral Dr. PR6: Birns . . . 7N 155
PR9: S'port . . . 4N 167
Balmoral Ho. L39: Aug . . . 1K 217
Balmoral Pl. FY5: T Clev . . . 3J 63
Balmoral Rd. BB3: Darw . . . 9B 158
BB4: Hasl . . . 6F 160
BB5: Acc . . . 1C 142
FY4: Blackp . . . 1B 108
FY8: L Ann . . . 3G 128
L31: Magh . . . 1B 222
LA1: Lanc . . . 8E 228 (9L 23)
LA3: Heys, Morec . . . 5M 21
LA4: Morec . . . 5M 21
PR4: New L . . . 7D 134
PR5: Walt D . . . 5N 135
PR7: Chor . . . 6D 174
PR7: E'ton . . . 7F 172
WN5: Wigan . . . 5N 221
Balmoral Ter. FY7: Flee . . . 8H 41
Balm St. BL0: Ramsb . . . 1F 200
Balniel Cl. PR7: Chor . . . 7D 174
Balshaw Av. PR7: Eux . . . 4N 173
Balshaw Cres. PR25: Leyl . . . 5J 153
Balshaw Ho. Gdns. PR7: Eux . . . 4N 173
Balshaw La. PR7: Eux . . . 5N 173
Balshaw Rd. LA2: Low . . . 2M 33
PR25: Leyl . . . 6J 153
Balshaw St. PR5: Bam B . . . 6A 136
Balshaw Ter. PR4: K'ham . . . 5N 111
(off Marsden St.)
Baltic Rd. BB4: W'foot . . . 7C 162
Baltimore Rd. FY8: L Ann . . . 2H 129
Bamber Av. FY2: Blackp . . . 7C 62
PR7: Buck V . . . 8A 154
BAMBER BRIDGE . . . 8A 136
Bamber Bridge FC . . . 8N 135
Bamber Bridge Leisure Cen. . . . 7C 136
Bamber Bridge Station (Rail) . . . 8A 136
Bamber Gdns. PR9: S'port . . . 6N 167
Bambers La. FY4: Blackp . . . 3J 109
Bambers La. Nth. FY4: Blackp . . . 2J 109
Bamber St. PR7: Chor . . . 9D 174
Bamber's Wlk. PR4: Wesh . . . 2K 111
Bamburgh Cl. FY4: Blackp . . . 2G 108
Bamburgh Dr. BB12: Burnl . . . 2C 124
BAMFORD . . . 7J 203
Bamford Cl. BL9: Bury . . . 9C 202
Bamford Ct. OL11: Roch . . . 7M 203
Bamford Cres. BB5: Acc . . . 4C 142
Bamford M. OL11: Roch . . . 6J 203
Bamford Pl. OL12: Roch . . . 4B 204
Bamford Pct. OL11: Roch . . . 6J 203
Bamford Rd. BL0: Ramsb . . . 6K 181
OL10: Heyw . . . 9G 203
Bamfords Fold PR26: Breth . . . 1K 171
Bamfords Pas. OL15: Littleb . . . 8L 185
Bamford St. BB9: Nelson . . . 2L 105
BB11: Burnl . . . 1D 228 (3E 124)
OL15: Littleb . . . 8J 185
(Cote La.)
OL15: Littleb . . . 9J 185
(Spenwood Rd.)
Bamford Way OL11: Roch . . . 7J 203
Bampton Dr. PR4: Cott . . . 5A 114
Bamton Av. FY4: Blackp . . . 2C 108
Banastre PR7: Chor . . . 4C 174
Banastre Rd. PR8: S'port . . . 9G 167
Banastre St. BB5: Acc . . . 8N 121
Banbury Av. BB5: Osw . . . 4J 141
FY2: Blackp . . . 2D 88
Banbury Cl. BB2: Blackb . . . 8G 138
BB5: Acc . . . 1N 141
Banbury Dr. PR2: Fulw . . . 5H 115
Banbury Rd. FY8: L Ann . . . 2F 128
LA3: Morec . . . 5C 22
WN5: Bill . . . 9G 220

A-Z Lancashire 241

Bancroft Av.—Baycliffe Cres.

Bancroft Av. BB1: Blackb 9A 120
FY5: T Clev 1J 63
Bancroft Fold BB18: Barnw 3L 77
Bancroft Mill Engine Mus. 3L 77
Bancroft Rd. BB10: Burnl 1G 125
Bancroft St. BB1: Blackb 3F 226 (3N 139)
Band La. PR3: St M 1E 66
Bangor Av. FY2: Blackp 6D 62
BANGOR'S GREEN 5C 208
Bangor St. BB1: Blackb 1E 226 (1N 139)
(not continuous)
OL16: Roch 7E 204
Banham Av. WN3: Wins 8M 221
Bank OL12: Ward 7F 184
Bank, The OL16: Roch 5C 204
Bank Av. WN5: Orr 6G 221
Bank Barn OL12: Ward 7G 184
Bank Barn La. OL12: Ward 7G 184
Bank Bottom BB3: Darw 6A 158
Bank Bri. PR4: Tarl 1F 170
Bankbrook WN6: Stand 8N 213
Bank Brow WN8: Roby M 8F 212
Bank Bldgs. *BB18: Barnw 2M 77*
(off St James' Sq.)
Bank Cl. LA2: Gal 3K 37
OL15: Littleb 2K 205
PR4: Longt 8L 133
Bank Cotts. BB7: B'ton 6H 101
Bank Cft. PR4: Longt 8L 133
Bankcroft Cl. BB12: Padi 1K 123
Bank End Caravan Pk. LA2: C'ham 8B 36
(not continuous)
Bankes Av. WN5: Orr 5K 221
Bankfield BB11: Burnl 1D 228 (3E 124)
WN8: Skelm 4N 219
Bankfield Bldgs. OL14: Tod 3K 165
Bankfield Ct. FY5: T Clev 3H 63
Bankfield Gro. FY1: Blackp 7E 88
Bankfield La. OL11: Roch 5J 203
PR9: S'port 4A 168
Bankfield St. BB8: Colne 7M 85
BB8: Wine 7E 86
OL13: Bac 7H 163
Bankfield Ter. BB18: Barnw 1N 77
OL13: Bac 7H 163
BANK FOLD 2F 158
Bank Fold BB9: Barrf 6J 85
Bank Hall Cotts. BB7: Grind 3D 74
Bank Hall Ter. *BB10: Burnl 2E 124*
(off Stafford St.)
Bank Head La. PR5: Bam B, Hogh 8E 136
BANK HEY 8A 120
Bank Hey Cl. BB1: Blackb 8A 120
Bank Hey La. Nth. BB1: Blackb 6N 119
Bank Hey La. Sth. BB1: Blackb 8A 120
Bank Hey St. FY1: Blackp 2H 227 (5B 88)
Bank Hey Vw. BB2: Blackb 9K 139
Bank Ho. La. LA5: Silv 8G 4
LA6: W'ouse 1M 19
Bankhouse La. OL13: Bac 5K 163
Bankhouse M. BB9: Barrf 7J 85
Bankhouse Rd. BB9: Nelson 1J 105
BL8: Bury 8H 201
BANK HOUSES 7A 36
Bankhouse St. BB9: Barrf 7J 85
BB11: Burnl 1C 228 (3D 124)
(not continuous)
BANK LANE 7K 181
Bank La. BB1: Blackb 4D 140
L31: Mell 3H 223
L33: Kirk 3H 223
OL12: Ward 7G 184
PR4: Wart 4H 131
PR7: Eux 3M 173
Bank La. Caravan Pk. PR4: Wart 4H 131
Bank Mdw. BL6: Hor 9D 196
Bank Mill St. BB4: Hasl 5G 161
BANK NEWTON 4K 53
Bank Nook PR9: S'port 3L 167
(not continuous)
Bank Pace PR9: Banks 8C 148
Bank Pde. BB11: Burnl 1D 228 (3E 124)
PR1: Penw 5G 134
PR1: Prest 8L 229 (2K 135)
Bank Pas. PR8: S'port 7H 167
Bank Pl. BL8: Bury 9H 201
PR2: Ash R 8F 114
Bank Rd. BL1: Bolt 8E 198
LA1: Lanc 5K 23
WN8: Roby M 7F 212
Bank Row BB4: Craws 6L 143
BANKS 9F 148
Banksbarn WN8: Skelm 4N 219
Banks Bri. Cl. BB18: Barnw 10G 52
Banks Cres. LA3: Heys 1L 27
Banksfield Av. PR2: Fulw 6F 114
Banksfield Pl. PR5: Bam B 9C 136
Banks Hill BB18: Barnw 10F 52
BANKSIDE 4H 163
Bankside BB2: Blackb 9C 226 (6M 139)
OL14: Tod 3L 165
PR6: Clay W 6D 154
WN8: Parb 2M 211
Bankside Cl. BB4: Craws 7M 143
OL13: Bac 6J 163
Bankside La. OL13: Bac 6J 163
Banks Ind. Pk. PR9: Banks 3H 169
Banks La. BD24: Sett 3N 35
Banks Leisure Cen. 1F 168
Bank Sq. PR9: S'port 6H 167
Banks Ri. LA2: H Ben 6L 19
Banks Rd. PR2: Fulw 6F 114
PR9: S'port 1C 168
Banks St. BB10: Brierc 7M 105
FY1: Blackp 4B 88
Bank St. BB3: Darw 6A 158
BB4: Hasl 4G 160
BB4: Rawt 5M 161
BB5: Acc 2B 142
BB5: Chur 2L 141
BB8: Traw 1F 106
BB9: Brierf 4F 104
BB9: Nelson 1J 105
BB12: Padi 9H 103
BB18: Barnw 2N 77
BL0: Ramsb 7K 181
Bank St. BL7: Turt 1J 199
BL8: Bury 9E 200
OL11: Roch 9D 204
OL13: Bac 5K 163
OL14: Tod 3L 165
PR7: Adl 6J 195
PR7: Chor 6E 174
Banks Vw. *BD24: Sett 3N 35*
(off Church St.)
Banks Way LA2: H Ben 6L 19
Bank Ter. BB5: Hunc 8E 122
BB12: S'stone 1D 122
OL12: Whitw 6N 183
OL13: Bac 5K 163
PR4: Longt 2M 151
PR6: Heap 2L 175
BANK TOP
BB2 7A 226 (5K 139)
BB4 9C 144
BL1 8G 199
WN8 8F 212
Bank Top BB2: Blackb 6A 226 (5K 139)
BB3: Darw 6A 158
(off Bank Bottom)
BB11: Burnl 1D 228 (2E 124)
BL9: Bury 4L 201
LA6: Ingl 3N 19
OL14: Tod 3L 165
(off Honey Hole Rd.)
Bank Top Gro. BL1: Bolt 8G 198
Bank Top Rd. PR1: Penw 5E 134
Bankwell Cl. BD24: Gig 3N 35
Bankwell Rd. BD24: Gig 3N 35
Bankwood WN6: Shev 6H 213
Bannatyne's Health Club
Blackpool 6J 227 (7B 88)
Skelmersdale 1M 219
Banner Cl. PR7: E'ton 7E 172
Banneriggs Brow LA6: Barb 2H 9
Bannerman Ter. PR6: Chor 4F 174
Bannister Brook Ho. PR25: Leyl 5K 153
Bannister Cl. BB8: Traw 8E 86
PR5: H Walt 4D 136
Bannister Ct. *BB9: Nelson 2J 105*
(off York St.)
FY2: Blackp 7B 62
(off Queen's Prom.)
Bannister Dr. PR25: Leyl 6G 153
Bannister Grn. PR7: E'ton, Hesk 3E 192
Bannister Hall Cres. PR5: H Walt 4D 136
Bannister Hall Dr. PR5: H Walt 4D 136
Bannister Hall La. PR5: H Walt 4D 136
Bannister Hall Works PR5: H Walt 4E 136
Bannister La. L40: Bis G 7A 192
PR7: E'ton 9F 172
PR26: Far M 3G 153
Bannisters Bit PR1: Penw 6F 134
Bannister St. FY8: L Ann 5A 130
PR7: Chor 7E 174
Bannister Way *BB8: Colne 6B 86*
(off King St.)
Bannistre Cl. FY8: L Ann 9G 109
Bannistre Ct. PR4: Tarl 9E 150
Bannistre M. PR4: Tarl 9E 150
Bantry St. OL12: Roch 3D 204
Barathea Cl. OL11: Roch 9L 203
Barbara Barlows Cottage Garden 8H 175
Barbara Castle Way BB1: Blackb 3A 226 (3L 139)
BB2: Blackb 3A 226 (3L 139)
Barberry Bank BL7: Eger 3D 198
BARBER'S MOOR 3A 172
BARBON 2G 9
Barbon Pl. LA1: Lanc 5J 23
Barbon St. BB10: Burnl 8G 104
BB12: Padi 9H 103
Barbrook Cl. WN6: Stand 2L 213
Barclay Av. BB11: Burnl 5A 124
FY4: Blackp 8F 88
BARCLAY HILLS 5A 124
Barclay Rd. PR3: Longr 3J 97
Bar Club St. PR5: Bam B 9A 136
Barclyde St. OL11: Roch 8B 204
Barcroft Grn. BB10: Cliv 8J 125
Barcroft St. BB8: Colne 6N 85
(not continuous)
BL9: Bury 9L 201
Barden Cft. BB5: Clay M 5M 121
Barden La. BB10: Burnl 7D 104
BB12: Burnl 7D 104
Barden Pl. PR2: Ribb 5N 115
Barden Rd. BB5: Acc 4M 141
Barden St. BB10: Burnl 9F 104
Barden Vw. BB10: Burnl 8E 104
Bardsea Pl. PR2: Ingol 6C 114
Bardsley Cl. BL2: Bolt 8K 199
Bardsway FY5: T Clev 9G 55
Bardsway Av. FY3: Blackp 4E 88
BARE 2E 22
Bare Av. LA4: Morec 2E 22
Barehill St. OL15: Littleb 8L 185
Bare La. LA4: Morec 2E 22
Bare Lane Station (Rail) 2F 22
Barford Cl. PR8: Ains 7A 186
WN8: Uph 4D 220
Bargee Cl. BB1: Blackb 7E 226 (5N 139)
Barham St. FY1: Blackp 8J 227
Barker Brow BB1: Clay D 8H 99
PR3: Ribc 8H 99
Barker Cl. LA6: Burt K 5G 7
Barker Ct. *BB9: Brierf 4F 104*
(off Hardy St.)
OL13: Bac 6L 163
Barkerfield Cl. BB12: High 5K 103
Barkerhouse Rd. BB9: Nelson 1J 105
Barker La. BB2: Mellor 7J 119
Barkers Dr. LA2: Ell 9L 29
Barker St. OL14: Tod 1L 165
Barker Ter. BB7: Clith 2L 81
LA6: Burt K 5G 7
(off Neddy Hill)
Barke St. OL15: Littleb 2J 205
Bar La. BL1: Bolt 8E 198
Barlborough Rd. WN5: Wigan 6N 221
BARLEY 5A 84
Barley Bank St. BB3: Darw 5N 157
Barley Brook Mdw. BL1: Bolt 7F 198
Barley Cl. BB2: Blackb 4A 226 (3L 139)
Barley Cop La. LA1: Lanc 4G 22
LA2: Lanc 4G 22
Barleydale Rd. BB9: Barrf 6J 85
Barleyfield *BB9: Nelson 3H 105*
(off High St.)
PR5: Bam B 4E 154
Barleyfield M. BB12: Burnl 3A 124
BARLEY GREEN 6A 84
Barley Gro. BB10: Burnl 3G 125
Barley Holme Rd. BB4: Craws 9M 143
Barley La. BB7: Twis 3M 83
BB9: Barl 3M 83
BB12: Barl 3M 83
Barley New Rd. BB12: Barl, Rough 6B 84
Barley St. BB12: Padi 2H 123
Barlow Cl. BL9: Bury 8L 201
Barlow Ct. BL7: Edgw 9L 179
Barlow Cres. FY3: Blackp 6E 88
Barlow Fold BB4: Rawt 7K 161
Barlow Moor Cl. OL12: Roch 3J 203
Barlow Pk. Av. BL1: Bolt 8D 198
Barlows Bldgs. BB4: Rawt 6L 161
Barlow's La. L39: Hals 8K 187
Barlow St. BB4: Rawt 4M 161
BB5: Acc 2N 141
OL13: Bac 7G 162
OL16: Roch 6D 204
PR1: Prest 2G 229 (8H 115)
(Ellen St., not continuous)
PR1: Prest 1J 229 (7J 115)
(Hammond St.)
Barmouth Av. FY3: Blackp 8G 88
Barmouth Ct. PR2: Ingol 6D 114
Barmouth Cres. BB1: Blackb 8M 119
Barmskin La. PR7: Hesk 4E 192
Barnaby's Sands Nature Reserve 3K 55
BARNACRE 3D 60
Barnacre Cl. LA1: Lanc 5M 29
PR2: Fulw 1K 115
Barnacre Lodge Dr. PR3: Barn 2E 60
Barnacre Rd. PR3: Longr 2H 97
Barnard Cl. BB5: Osw 4J 141
Barn Cl. PR4: Mere B 4M 169
Barn Cft. BB7: Clith 4K 81
PR1: Penw 4E 134
PR26: Leyl 6E 152
Barnes Av. BB4: Rawt 5L 161
Barnes Cl. BL0: Ramsb 2F 200
L33: Kirk 4K 223
Barnes Ct. BB10: Burnl 5H 125
Barnes Dr. FY5: T Clev 7E 54
L31: Lyd 7B 216
Barnes Holme BB3: W'side 3E 158
Barnes Mdws. OL15: Littleb 5M 185
Barnes Rd. L39: Aug 9K 209
LA3: Heys 5M 21
WN8: Skelm 2J 219
Barnes Sq. BB5: Clay M 6M 121
Barnes St. BB4: Hasl 3G 160
BB5: Acc 2B 142
(not continuous)
BB5: Chur 2L 141
BB5: Clay M 6L 121
BB11: Burnl 1D 228 (3E 124)
OL14: Wals 6K 165
BARNFIELD 3B 142
Barnfield OL15: Littleb 8N 185
PR4: K'ham 4M 111
PR4: Much H 5J 151
PR5: Lost H 9K 135
Barnfield Av. BB10: Burnl 3K 125
Barnfield Bus. Cen.
BB9: Nelson 4K 105
Barn Fld. Cl. BB8: Colne 6D 86
Barnfield Cl. BL7: Eger 3E 198
FY5: T Clev 8F 54
Barnfield Dr. WN8: Skelm 4B 220
Barnfield Ho. BB1: Blackb 3E 140
Barn Fld. La. OL12: Ward 7D 184
Barnfield Mnr. FY6: Sing 8C 64
Barnfield St. BB5: Acc 3C 142
OL12: Roch 3C 204
Barnfield Way BB5: Alt 4C 122
PR2: Ribb 3C 116
Barn Flatt Cl. PR5: H Walt 4C 136
Barn Gill Cl. BB2: Blackb 8F 226 (5N 139)
Barn Hey PR4: Longt 7L 133
Barn Hey Dr. PR26: Far M 4H 153
Barn Hey Rd. L33: Kirk 8M 223
Barn Mdw. BL7: Edgw 8K 179
PR5: Bam B 1D 154
Barn Mdw. Cres. BB1: Rish 8J 121
Barnmeadow La. BB6: Gt H 4J 121
BARNOLDSWICK 2M 77
Barnoldswick La. LA6: Bur L 3K 19
Barnoldswick Rd. BB8: Foul 9N 77
BB9: Barrf, Blacko 4K 85
BB18: Kelb 6C 78
Barnrigg LA6: Barb 2G 9
Barns, The L37: Form 2A 214
PR4: Weet 8F 90
Barnsfold PR2: Fulw 3G 114
Barnside OL12: Whitw 6N 183
PR7: Eux 3M 173
Barnside Cl. BL9: Bury 5K 201
Barns La. PR3: Goos 7B 70
Barnstaple Way PR4: Cott 3C 114
Barnston Cl. BL1: Bolt 9F 198
Barn Vw. PR6: H Charn 5H 195
Barn Visitor Centre, The 3B 154
Barnwood Cres. BB18: Earl 3F 78
Barnwood Rd. BB18: Earl 3E 78
Baron Fold BB4: W'foot 7C 162
Baron Rd. FY1: Blackp 9K 227 (9C 88)
Barons Cl. BB3: Lwr D 9A 140
Baron's Fold BB3: Hodd 8E 158
Baron St. BB3: Darw 5M 157
BB4: Rawt 6A 162
OL16: Roch 6C 204
Barons Way BB3: Lwr D 1A 158
BB6: Gt H 4K 121
Baronsway PR7: Eux 4N 173
Baron's Yd. BB2: Blackb 6C 226 (4M 139)
Barracks Rd. BB11: Burnl 3B 124
Barrel Sykes *BD24: Sett 2N 35*
(off Langcliffe Rd.)
Barret Hill Brow BB7: Bolt B 7G 50
Barret St. BB18: Earl 3D 78
Barrett Av. PR8: Birk 3G 187
Barrett Rd. PR8: Birk 3G 186
Barrett St. BB10: Burnl 1E 124
Barrie Way BL1: Bolt 9H 199
Barrington Cl. WN3: Wins 9N 221
Barrington Ct. BB5: Chur 1M 141
Barrington Dr. PR8: Ains 8B 186
Barrison Grn. L40: Scar 2K 209
Barritt Rd. BB4: Rawt 5L 161
Barronwood Ct. PR4: Tarl 1E 170
BARROW 1K 101
BARROW BRIDGE 9N 197
Barrow Bri. Rd. BL1: Bolt 9N 197
Barrow Cl. FY4: Blackp 3K 109
Barrowdale Av. BB9: Nelson 3K 105
Barrowdene Ho. *BL1: Bolt 9N 197*
(off Bazley St.)
BARROWFORD 8H 85
Barrowford Rd. BB8: Colne 6L 85
(not continuous)
BB9: Barrf, Nelson 2C 104
BB12: High, Padi 7J 103
(not continuous)
Barrow La. LA4: Morec 3F 22
BARROW NOOK 9C 218
Barrow Nook La. L39: Bick 8C 218
Barrows La. LA3: Heys 1J 27
PR3: Gt E 6N 65
Barrows La. E. PR3: Gt E 6N 65
Barry Av. PR2: Ingol 6C 114
Barry Gro. LA3: Heys 1L 27
Barry St. BB12: Burnl 3A 124
Bar St. BB10: Burnl 1F 124
OL14: Tod 3K 165
Bar Ter. OL12: Whitw 7N 183
Bartholomew Rd. LA4: Morec 4C 22
Bartle Grn. BB11: Burnl 4A 124
Bartle La. PR4: Lwr B 2M 113
Bartle Pl. PR2: Ash R 8B 114
Bartle Rd. FY8: L Ann 9G 109
BARTON
L39 6M 207
PR3 2E 94
Barton Av. FY1: Blackp 7H 227 (8B 88)
FY6: K Sea 8L 41
Barton Avenue Stop (Tram) 7H 227 (8B 88)
Barton Gdns. LA1: Lanc 2M 29
Barton Grange Marina 5C 68
Barton La. PR3: Bart 2F 94
Barton Mansion FY8: L Ann 1D 128
Barton Mobile Home Pk. LA3: Morec 5D 22
Barton Rd. FY8: L Ann 9D 108
LA1: Lanc 3L 29
Bartons Cl. PR9: S'port 1C 168
Barton Sq. FY6: K Sea 8L 41
Barton St. BB2: Blackb 4C 226 (3M 139)
WN5: Wigan 6L 221
Barwood Lea BL0: Ramsb 9H 181
Barwood Lea Mill BL0: Ramsb 8G 181
Base Camp Climbing Walls 9K 227 (9C 88)
BASHALL EAVES 9A 72
Bashall Gro. PR25: Far 4L 153
BASHALL TOWN 2E 80
Bashful All. LA1: Lanc 7C 228
Basil Ct. OL16: Roch 7E 204
Basil St. BB8: Colne 7A 86
OL16: Roch 7E 204
PR1: Prest 7M 115
Basnett St. BB10: Burnl 9G 104
Bassenthwaite Av. L33: Kirk 6J 223
Bassenthwaite Rd. FY3: Blackp 8J 89
Bassett Cl. OL12: Roch 2B 204
Bassett Gdns. OL12: Roch 2B 204
Bassett Gro. WN3: Wins 9M 221
Bassett Way OL12: Roch 3B 204
Bass La. BL9: Summ 2J 201
BASTWELL 1N 139
Bastwell Rd. BB1: Blackb 1N 139
Bateman Gro. LA4: Morec 3B 22
Bateman Rd. LA4: Morec 3B 22
Bates St. BB5: Clay M 6L 121
Bathgate Way L33: Kirk 4J 223
Bath Mill La. LA1: Lanc 7E 228 (8L 23)
Bath Mill Sq. LA1: Lanc 6E 228
Bath Rd. FY8: L Ann 5A 130
Bath Springs L39: Orms 7L 209
Bath Springs Ct. L39: Orms 7L 209
Bath St. BB2: Blackb 4K 139
BB3: Darw 6A 158
BB5: Acc 4A 142
BB8: Colne 6B 86
BB9: Nelson 2K 105
FY4: Blackp 9B 88
FY8: L Ann 5A 130
LA1: Lanc 7F 228 (8L 23)
LA4: Morec 3A 22
OL12: Roch 4D 204
OL13: Bac 5L 163
OL14: Tod 2L 165
(off Dalton St.)
PR2: Ash R 8G 114
PR9: S'port 6H 167
Bath St. Nth. PR9: S'port 6H 167
Bathurst Av. FY3: Blackp 3G 88
Bathurst St. BB2: Blackb 3B 226 (3L 139)
Batridge Rd. BL7: Turt 7G 178
Battersby St. BL9: Bury 9B 202
OL11: Roch 7M 203
Battismore Rd. LA4: Morec 3A 22
Battle Way *L37: Form 1B 214*
(off Buckfast Dr.)
Baum, The OL16: Roch 5C 204
Bawdlands BB7: Clith 3K 81
Bawhead Rd. BB18: Earl 3E 78
Baxendale Gro. PR5: Bam B 7A 136
Baxendale St. BL1: Bolt 9E 198
BAXENDEN 6D 142
Baxenden & District Golf Course 5E 142
Baxtergate LA4: Morec 2B 22
Bay, The FY5: T Clev 7C 54
Bayard St. BB12: Burnl 3M 123
Baycliffe Cres. LA4: Morec 3A 22

Bay Cl.—Belmont Rd.

Bay Cl. LA3: Heys 1J 27
BAY GATE 8G 51
BAY HORSE 7N 37
Bay Horse Dr. LA1: Lanc 4M 29
Bay Horse La. PR4: Catf 6G 93
Bay Horse Rd. LA2: Bay H, Ell, Quern 5B 38
Bayley Fold BB7: Clith 3L 81
Bayley St. BB5: Clay M 6L 121
Bayliss Cl. PR2: Ribb 6B 116
Baylton Ct. PR3: Catt 1A 68
Baylton Dr. PR3: Catt 1A 68
Baynes St. BB3: Hodd 6F 158
Bay Rd. LA3: Heys 1J 27
PR2: Ribb 7A 116
Bayside FY7: Flee 1H 55
Bay St. BB1: Blackb 1A 140
OL10: Heyw 9F 202
OL12: Roch 4D 204
Bayswater FY2: Blackp 7C 62
Baytree Cl. PR5: Lost H 8M 135
PR9: S'port 1C 168
Bay Tree Farm PR2: Lea 9A 114
Baytree Gro. BL0: Ramsb 3G 200
L31: Mell 7F 222
Bay Tree Rd. PR6: Clay W 4D 154
Baytree Wlk. OL12: Whitw 5N 183
Bay Vw. LA6: Over K 1F 16
Bay Vw. Av. LA2: Slyne 9J 15
Bay Vw. Ct. LA1: Lanc 7A 228
Bay Vw. Cres. LA2: Slyne 9J 15
Bay Vw. Dr. LA3: Heys 8L 21
Baywood St. BB1: Blackb 1N 139
BAZIL 8B 28
Bazil Gro. LA3: O'ton 8B 28
Bazil La. LA3: O'ton 8B 28
Bazley Rd. FY8: L Ann 5K 129
Bazley St. BL1: Bolt 9N 197
Beacham Rd. PR8: S'port 7L 167
Beach Av. FY5: T Clev 9D 54
FY8: L Ann 5J 129
Beachcomber Dr. FY5: T Clev 9C 54
Beach Ct. FY5: T Clev 9D 54
FY8: L Ann 5B 130
Beachley Rd. PR2: Ingol 6D 114
Beachley Sq. BB12: Burnl 2C 124
Beach M. PR8: Birk 8F 166
Beach Priory Gdns. PR8: S'port 8F 166
Beach Rd. FY5: T Clev 9C 54
FY6: Pree 6A 42
FY7: Flee 9E 40
FY8: L Ann 1D 128
PR8: Birk 8F 166
Beach Road Stop (Tram) 9D 54
Beach St. FY8: L Ann 5N 129
LA4: Morec 1E 22
Beach Wood LA5: Arn 2D 4
Beacon Av. PR2: Fulw 4G 114
Beacon Cl. BB8: Colne 8N 85
PR3: Bils 7D 68
Beacon Country Pk. 2C 220
Beacon Country Pk. Vis. Cen. 1B 220
Beacon Ct. PR3: Goos 5N 95
Beacon Crossing WN8: Parb 2N 211
Beacon Dr. PR3: Goos 4N 95
Beacon Fell Rd. PR3: Goos 8K 70
Beacon Fell Vw. Holiday Pk. PR3: Longr 1L 97
Beacon Grn. WN8: Skelm 3B 220
Beacon Gro. PR2: Fulw 5G 114
PR3: Gars 6M 59
Beacon Hgts. WN8: Uph 3D 220
Beacon La. WN8: Dalt 6L 211
Beacon Lodge *PR2: Ribb* *5B 116*
(off Fir Trees Pl.)
Beacon Park Golf Course 1C 220
Beacon Rd. FY6: Poul F 8N 63
WN6: Stand 2L 213
Beacons, The *L37: Form* *9A 206*
(off School La.)
WN6: Shev 5G 212
Beaconsfield Av. PR1: Prest 8B 116
Beaconsfield Ct. L39: Orms 7L 209
Beaconsfield Rd. PR9: S'port 8M 167
Beaconsfield St. BB4: Hasl 4G 160
BB5: Acc 3C 142
BB6: Gt H 3J 121
OL14: Tod 2M 165
Beaconsfield Ter. PR3: Catt 1B 68
PR6: Chor 4F 174
Beacon St. PR7: Chor 7F 174
Beacon Vw. WN6: App B 4F 212
WN6: Stand 3M 213
Beacon Vw. Dr. WN8: Uph 4E 220
Beadle Av. OL12: Roch 9G 185
Beaford Cl. WN5: Wigan 6L 221
Beal Cres. OL16: Roch 4F 204
(not continuous)
Bealcroft Cl. OL16: Milnr 6H 205
Bealcroft Wlk. OL16: Milnr 6H 205
Beale Cl. BB1: Blackb 7B 140
Beale Rd. BB9: Nelson 2F 104
Beal Ter. OL16: Milnr 7J 205
Beamish Av. BB2: Blackb 8L 139
Beamont Dr. PR1: Prest 9G 114
Bean Av. FY4: Blackp 1E 108
Beardshaw Av. FY1: Blackp 8N 227 (8D 88)
Beardsworth St. BB1: Blackb 9A 120
BEARDWOOD 9H 119
Beardwood BB2: Blackb 1H 139
Beardwood Brow BB2: Blackb 1H 139
Beardwood Dr. BB2: Blackb 1H 139
Beardwood Fold BB2: Blackb 1H 139
Beardwood Mdw. BB2: Blackb 1H 139
Beardwood Pk. BB2: Blackb 1J 139
Bearncroft WN8: Skelm 5N 219
Bear St. BB12: Burnl 3K 123
Bearswood Cft. PR6: Clay W 5D 154
Bearwood Way FY5: T Clev 1J 63
Beatie St. BB9: Brierf 4F 104
Beatrice Av. BB12: Burnl 2A 124
Beatrice M. *BL6: Hor* *9C 196*
(off Beatrice St.)
Beatrice Pl. BB2: Blackb 8A 140
Beatrice St. BL6: Hor 9C 196
OL11: Roch 6A 204
Beatrice Ter. BB3: Darw 7B 158
Beattock Cl. L33: Kirk 4J 223
Beattock Pl. FY2: Blackp 5F 62
Beatty Av. PR7: Chor 8D 174
Beatty Cl. FY8: L Ann 8D 108
Beatty Rd. PR8: S'port 9L 167
Beauclerk Rd. FY8: L Ann 2G 128
Beaufort L37: Form 1A 214
Beaufort Av. FY2: Blackp 7B 62
Beaufort Cl. BB12: Read 8D 102
L39: Aug 2F 216
Beaufort Gro. LA4: Morec 3D 22
Beaufort Rd. LA4: Morec 3D 22
OL13: Weir 9L 145
Beaufort St. BB9: Nelson 3H 105
OL12: Roch 4N 203
Beauley Av. BB12: S'stone 8D 102
Beauly Cl. BL0: Ramsb 3F 200
Beaumaris Av. BB2: Blackb 7H 139
Beaumaris Cl. BB4: Hasl 6G 161
Beaumaris Rd. PR25: Leyl 7M 153
Beaumonds Way OL11: Roch 7L 203
BEAUMONT 4K 23
Beaumont Av. BL6: Hor 9D 196
Beaumont Cl. OL13: Bac 7L 163
OL15: Littleb 9J 185
Beaumont Ct. *FY1: Blackp* *4C 88*
(off Elizabeth St.)
FY8: L Ann 9G 108
Beaumont Cres. L39: Aug 1J 217
Beaumont Dr. L10: Aint 9D 222
Beaumont Gdns. FY6: Carl 6G 63
Beaumont Gro. WN5: Orr 3L 221
Beaumont Pl. LA1: Lanc 4K 23
Beaumont Rd. BL6: Hor 9D 196
Beaumont St. LA1: Lanc 4K 23
OL14: Tod 1K 165
Beaumont Way BB3: Darw 6C 158
Beaver Cl. BB1: Wilp 4N 119
Beavers La. WN8: Skelm 5A 220
Beavers Way WN8: Skelm 5A 220
Beaver Ter. OL13: Bac 4L 163
Bebles Rd. L39: Orms 9H 209
BECCONSALL 5D 150
Becconsall La. PR4: Hesk B 4D 150
Bechers Bus. Cen.
L30: N'ton 8A 222
Bechers Ct. L30: N'ton 7A 222
Bechers Dr. L9: Aint 8B 222
Beck Ct. FY7: Flee 3D 54
Beckdean Av. FY6: Poul F 9K 63
Beckenham Ct. BB10: Burnl 7H 105
Beckett Cl. L33: Know P 9A 224
Beckett Ct. *BB3: Darw* *5B 158*
(off Astbury Chase)
PR1: Prest 4K 229 (8J 115)
Beckett St. BB3: Darw 7A 158
Beckgate LA6: Barb 2G 9
Beck Gro. FY5: T Clev 8E 54
Beck Head *LA6: K Lon* *6F 8*
(off Market St.)
Beck La. LA6: Lup 2B 8
Beck's Brow BD23: Wig 10M 35
Beck Side BB12: Barl 6A 84
Beckside LA2: Caton 3H 25
Beckside Cl. BB4: Lumb 3D 162
BB8: Traw 8F 86
Beckside M. LA6: Borw 4G 12
Beck Vw. *LA1: Lanc* *4L 29*
(off Hala Sq.)
Beck Way BB8: Colne 8M 85
Beckway Av. FY3: Blackp 3F 88
Bective Rd. *LA6: K Lon* *6F 8*
(off New Rd.)
Bedale Pl. FY5: T Clev 2E 62
Bedale Wlk. L33: Kirk 7L 223
Beddington St. BB9: Nelson 1H 105
Bede Cl. L33: Kirk 4K 223
Bedford Av. FY5: T Clev 8D 54
L31: Mell 4E 222
Bedford Cl. BB5: Osw 4J 141
Bedford Ct. PR1: Prest 4J 229
PR8: Birk 3G 186
Bedford M. BB3: Darw 3N 157
Bedford Pl. BB12: Padi 2J 123
LA1: Lanc 3L 29
Bedford Rd. FY1: Blackp 2C 88
FY8: L Ann 4C 130
PR2: Fulw 5K 115
PR8: Birk 3G 186
Bedfordshire Av. BB12: Burnl 2N 123
Bedford St. BB2: Blackb 6K 139
BB3: Darw 3N 157
BB9: Barrf 1G 104
BL7: Eger 3D 198
BL9: Bury 9M 201
OL14: Tod 8H 147
PR7: Chor 8E 174
WN5: Wigan 6M 221
Bedford Ter. BB4: Hasl 7F 160
Beechacre BL0: Ramsb 9J 181
Beecham St. LA4: Morec 2B 22
Beech Av. BB3: Darw 5B 158
BB18: Earl 3D 78
FY3: Blackp 1N 227 (5E 88)
FY6: Poul F 7K 63
L31: Mell 7G 222
LA2: Gal 2K 37
OL14: Tod 1L 165
PR3: Bils 6D 68
PR3: K'ham 5N 111
PR4: Wart 2J 131
PR6: And 5K 195
PR7: Eux 2M 173
PR25: Leyl 7K 153
WN8: Parb 3N 211
Beech Bank BB7: Wadd 8H 73
Beech Cl. BB1: Clay D 3M 119
BB1: Rish 9H 121
BB5: Osw 6J 141
BB7: Clith 3K 81
BD23: Garg 3L 53
BL2: Bolt 7J 199
L32: Kirk 7H 223
L40: Ruff 1G 191
OL12: Whitw 5N 183
OL13: Bac 4L 163
WN8: Skelm 2J 219
Beech Ct. LA5: Silv 9G 4
PR9: S'port 6K 167
PR25: Leyl *7J 153*
(off Lancastergate)
Beech Cres. BB5: Acc 8N 121
WN6: Stand 4N 213
Beechcroft FY5: T Clev 8C 54
L31: Magh 1C 222
Beech Dr. BB4: Hasl 5H 161
BB7: Whall 3G 100
FY6: Poul F 9K 63
PR2: Fulw 1G 114
PR3: Longr 3J 97
PR4: Frec 3M 131
PR4: Newt 7D 112
Beeches, The BL1: Bolt 7D 198
FY3: Blackp 7E 88
FY6: Sing 1C 90
OL12: Whitw 5N 183
PR4: Tarl 8E 150
PR6: Clay W 4E 154
PR9: Banks 3J 169
Beeches Ct. FY5: T Clev 2J 63
Beechfield L31: Magh 1D 222
LA1: Lanc 8H 23
OL11: Roch 7J 203
WN8: Parb 8N 191
Beechfield Av. FY3: Blackp 7E 88
FY6: Pree 8N 41
PR4: W Grn 6H 111
Beechfield Cl. OL11: Roch 7J 203
Beechfield Ct. PR25: Leyl 7L 153
Beechfield Gdns. PR8: S'port 8F 166
Beechfield M. PR9: S'port 7H 167
Beechfield Rd. OL16: Milnr 8H 205
PR25: Leyl 8K 153
Beechfields PR7: E'ton 8E 172
Beech Gdns. PR6: Clay W 6D 154
WA11: Rain 3J 225
Beech Gro. BB3: Darw 1L 157
BB5: Acc 4N 141
BB7: Chatb 7C 74
BB7: West B 5K 73
BB10: Reed 6G 104
BB18: Barnw 2N 77
BL8: Greenm 4F 200
FY6: K Sea 7L 41
LA2: Slyne 1J 23
LA4: Morec 3F 22
LA5: Wart 5A 12
PR2: Ash R 8E 114
PR9: S'port 7L 167
Beech Gro. Cl. BL9: Bury 9N 201
Beechill Cl. PR5: Walt D 5A 136
Beech Ind. Est. OL13: Bac 4L 163
Beeching Cl. LA1: Lanc 1K 29
Beech Mdw. L39: Orms 8M 209
Beech Mt. BB1: Blackb 6M 119
BB7: Wadd 8H 73
Beech Ri. L33: Kirk 7L 223
Beech Rd. L39: Aug 5F 216
LA2: Halt 1B 24
PR3: Gars 4M 59
PR4: Elsw 1L 91
PR25: Leyl 5K 153
Beech St. BB1: Blackb 1A 140
BB4: Rawt 4M 161
BB5: Acc 3B 142
BB5: Clay M 8M 121
BB6: Gt H 3J 121
BB7: Clith 3K 81
BB9: Nelson 1J 105
BB12: Padi 2J 123
BB18: Barnw 2M 77
BL7: Edgw 9K 179
BL9: Summ 2H 201
LA1: Lanc 8H 23
OL11: Roch 7A 204
OL13: Bac 4L 163
OL16: Milnr 9L 205
PR1: Prest 2G 135
Beech St. Sth. PR1: Prest 2H 135
Beech Ter. LA6: Ingl 3N 19
PR1: Prest 2H 135
Beechthorpe Av. BB7: Wadd 8H 73
Beech Tree Av. WN6: App B 4G 213
Beech Tree Cl. BB9: Nelson 3J 105
LA5: Bolt S 5L 15
PR25: Leyl 4N 153
Beechtrees WN8: Skelm 4N 219
Beech Wlk. PR6: Whit W 8C 154
WN3: Wins 9M 221
WN6: Stand 4N 213
Beechway L31: Magh 9G 216
PR1: Penw 4E 134
PR2: Fulw 5K 115
Beechway Av. L31: Magh 9G 216
Beechwood PR4: Wesh 2N 111
WN8: Skelm 9N 211
Beechwood Av. BB5: Acc 5C 142
BB7: Clith 5L 81
BB11: Burnl 6C 124
BL0: Ramsb 8J 181
OL15: Littleb 2K 205
PR2: Fulw 5F 114
PR5: Walt D 4M 135
WN6: Shev 7J 213
Beech Wood Cl. BD23: W Mar 7H 53
Beechwood Ct. BB1: Blackb 1N 139
BL8: Tott 8F 200
L31: Magh *1E 222*
(off Deyes La.)
PR7: Copp 5B 194
WN8: Skelm 5A 220
Beechwood Cres. WN5: Orr 5H 221
Beechwood Cft. PR6: Clay W 4C 154
Beechwood Dr. BB2: Blackb 8F 138
BB4: Rawt 2M 161
FY5: T Clev 3H 63
L39: Orms 7J 209
Beechwood Gdns. LA1: Lanc 5L 29
Beechwood Gro. FY2: Blackp 6E 62
Beechwood M. BB1: Blackb 8A 140
Beechwood Rd. BB1: Blackb 1A 140
PR7: Chor 8G 174
Beecroft La. BD23: Wig 10N 35
Beeford Dr. WN5: Orr 6H 221
Beehive Ind. Est. FY4: Blackp 9H 89
Bee La. PR1: Penw 7G 134
Beenland St. PR1: Prest 8N 115
Beeston Av. FY6: Carl 6J 63
Beeston Cl. BL1: Bolt 7G 198
Beeston Dr. L30: N'ton 5A 222
Beetham Caravan Pk. LA7: Slack H 3N 5
Beetham Ct. BB5: Clay M 7L 121
Beetham Pl. FY3: Blackp 4E 88
Beetham Way L33: Kirk 7L 223
Begonia St. BB3: Darw 6B 158
Begonia Vw. BB3: Lwr D 9A 140
Beightons Wlk. OL12: Roch 1A 204
Bela Cl. LA1: Lanc 6G 22
Bela Gro. FY1: Blackp 7L 227 (8C 88)
Beldale Pk. L32: Kirk 6H 223
BELFIELD 5F 204
Belfield WN8: Skelm 5A 220
Belfield Cl. OL16: Roch 5F 204
Belfield La. OL16: Roch 6F 204
(Brocklebank Rd.)
OL16: Roch 6G 204
(East St.)
Belfield Lawn OL16: Roch 5G 204
Belfield Mill La. OL16: Roch 5G 204
Belfield Old Rd. OL16: Roch 5F 204
Belfield Rd. BB5: Acc 3A 142
OL16: Roch 5E 204
Belford Av. FY5: T Clev 8F 54
Belford St. BB12: Burnl 2D 124
Belfry, The BB3: Darw 7C 158
FY8: L Ann 3C 130
Belfry Cl. PR7: Eux 2N 173
Belfry Mans. BB6: Old L 4C 100
Belgarth Rd. BB5: Acc 1B 142
Belgium St. OL11: Roch 6J 203
BELGRAVE 7N 157
Belgrave Av. PR1: Penw 5E 134
PR4: Wesh 2M 111
Belgrave Chapel *BB3: Darw* *6A 158*
(off Belgrave Sq.)
Belgrave Cl. BB2: Blackb 5J 139
FY8: L Ann 2K 129
WN3: Wins 8M 221
Belgrave Ct. *BB12: Burnl* *2D 124*
(off Belgrave St.)
PR2: Fulw 2L 115
PR25: Leyl *6J 153*
(off Belgrave Rd.)
Belgrave Pl. FY6: Poul F 9H 63
PR8: Birk 2F 186
Belgrave Rd. BB3: Darw 7N 157
BB8: Colne 5A 86
FY4: Blackp 9E 88
FY6: Poul F 9H 63
PR8: Birk 1F 186
PR25: Leyl 7J 153
Belgrave Sq. BB3: Darw 6A 158
Belgrave St. BB5: Ris B 8F 142
BB9: Brierf 5E 104
BB9: Nelson 1K 105
BB12: Burnl 2D 124
OL12: Roch 4A 204
BELL, THE 3L 221
Bell-Aire Pk. Homes LA3: Heys 2L 27
Bellamy Av. LA4: Morec 5A 22
BELL BUSK 1J 53
Belle Fld. Cl. PR1: Penw 6K 135
Belle Hill BD24: Gig 2N 35
Belle Isle Av. OL12: Whitw 8N 183
Belle Vue Av. LA1: Lanc 1L 29
Belle Vue Dr. LA1: Lanc 1L 29
Belle Vue La. BB7: Wadd 8H 73
Belle Vue Pl. BB11: Burnl 2A 228 (3C 124)
FY3: Blackp 2N 227 (5D 88)
Belle Vue St. BB2: Blackb 3K 139
BB11: Burnl 2A 228 (3C 124)
WN5: Wigan 6N 221
Belle Vue Ter. LA1: Lanc 1L 29
Bellfield Rd. LA4: Morec 3C 22
Bellflower Cl. PR25: Leyl 4A 154
Bell Fold Wharf PR4: Woodp 6A 94
Bellingham Rd. FY8: L Ann 4A 130
Bellis Av. PR9: S'port 4M 167
Bellis Gro. L33: Kirk 5J 223
Bellis Way PR5: Walt D 6L 135
Bell La. BB5: Clay M 5A 122
OL16: Milnr 6L 205
PR3: Barn 8E 60
WN5: Orr 3L 221
Bell Mdw. Dr. OL11: Roch 8K 203
Bell's Arc. *BB10: Burnl* *1E 124*
(off Ardwick St.)
Bell's Bri. La. PR3: Nateby 2K 59
Bell's Cl. L31: Lyd 7B 216
Bellshill Cres. OL16: Roch 4F 204
(not continuous)
Bells La. L31: Lyd 8N 215
PR5: Hogh 6G 136
Bell St. BB4: Hasl 4G 160
OL16: Roch 5C 204
Bell Vs. PR5: Hogh 5L 137
BELMONT 9K 177
Belmont Av. FY1: Blackp 5K 227 (6C 88)
FY6: Poul F 8H 63
PR2: Ribb 6N 115
WN5: Bill 8G 221
Belmont Cl. BB2: Blackb 1H 139
L40: Burs 1C 210
LA1: Lanc 5H 23
PR2: Ribb 7N 115
PR6: Birns 7N 155
Belmont Ct. PR3: Longr 3K 97
Belmont Cres. PR2: Ribb 7N 115
Belmont Dr. PR6: Chor 5G 175
Belmont Gro. BB10: Burnl 4H 125
Belmont Pl. PR7: Copp 7M 193
Belmont Rd. BB6: Gt H 4H 121
BL1: Bolt 1L 197
BL6: R'ton 4D 196
BL7: Belm 1L 197
BL7: Belm, Withn 2G 177
FY7: Flee 1G 54
FY8: L Ann 3J 129
PR2: Ash R 7F 114

A-Z Lancashire 243

Belmont Rd.—Bison Pl.

Belmont Rd. PR6: Adl 6J **195**
PR6: Withn 2G **177**
PR25: Leyl 6G **152**
Belmont St. PR8: S'port 8G **166**
Belmont Ter. *BB8: Foul 2A 86*
(off Lowther La.)
BB8: Foul 2B 86
(off Skipton Old Rd.)
BB9: Barrf 8H 85
(off Nora St.)
Belmont Vw. BL2: Bolt 9M **199**
Belmont Way OL12: Roch 3B **204**
Belper St. BB1: Blackb 1G **226** (2A **140**)
Belsfield Dr. PR4: Hesk B 3C **150**
Belshaw Ct. BB11: Burnl 6M **123**
BELTHORN 1F **158**
Belthorn Rd. BB1: Belt 9E **140**
BB1: Guide 8D **140**
Belton Av. OL16: Roch 4F **204**
Belton Hill PR2: Fulw 1G **114**
Belvedere Av. BB4: W'foot 6E **162**
BL8: Greenm 4F **200**
Belvedere Dr. PR7: Chor 6D **174**
Belvedere Fold BB4: W'foot 6E **162**
Belvedere Pk. L39: Aug 4H **217**
Belvedere Rd. BB1: Blackb 6A **120**
BB10: Burnl 2F **228** (3F **124**)
FY5: T Clev 3J **63**
PR6: And 5K **195**
PR8: Ains 8C **186**
PR25: Leyl 5L **153**
Belverdale Gdns. FY4: Blackp 4F **108**
Belvere Av. FY4: Blackp 4D **108**
Belvoir Mdws. OL16: Roch 1H **205**
Belvoir St. OL12: Roch 4N **203**
Bember's Cross LA6: Thorn L 2M **19**
Bembridge Ct. WN3: Wins 9N **221**
Benbow Cl. FY8: L Ann 7D **108**
Bence Rd. PR1: Prest 1L **135**
Bence St. BB8: Colne 7B **86**
Bench Carr OL12: Roch 4B **204**
Bendcrete Climbing Cen. 7M **115**
Bendwood Cl. BB12: Padi 1J **123**
Benenden Pl. FY5: T Clev 1G **63**
Bengal St. PR7: Chor 6F **174**
Bengarth Rd. PR9: S'port 6M **167**
Ben La. BB18: Barnw 1A **78**
L39: Bick 1D **224**
Ben La. Ct. L39: Bick 9F **218**
Bennett Av. FY1: Blackp 3L **227** (6C **88**)
Bennett Dr. WN5: Orr 7G **221**
Bennett Rd. FY5: T Clev 9G **54**
Bennett's La. FY4: Blackp 3F **108**
Bennett St. BB9: Nelson 9K **85**
Bennett Wlk. *BB3: Darw 5B 158*
(off Fitzgerald Dr.)
Ben Nevis Pl. FY8: L Ann 7G **109**
Bennington St. BB1: Blackb 8F **226** (5N **139**)
BB2: Blackb 8F **226** (5N **139**)
Benson Av. LA4: Morec 4D **22**
Benson Ho. BB1: Blackb 1A **140**
Benson La. PR4: Catf 7H **93**
Benson Rd. FY3: Blackp 1E **88**
Benson's La. PR3: Woodp 1N **93**
PR4: Woodp 1N **93**
Benson St. BB1: Blackb 1B **140**
BL7: Edgw 9L **179**
Bentcliffe Gdns. BB5: Acc 4C **142**
Bent Est. OL13: Weir 9L **145**
Bentfield Cres. OL16: Milnr 9K **205**
Bent Gap La. BB2: Blackb 4K **139**
BENT GATE 7H **161**
BENTGATE 9K **205**
Bentgate Cl. BB4: Hasl 7J **161**
OL16: Milnr 9K **205**
Bentgate St. OL16: Milnr 9K **205**
Bentham Av. BB10: Burnl 7F **104**
FY7: Flee 3C **54**
Bentham Cl. BB2: Blackb 7J **139**
Bentham Golf Course 6L **19**
Bentham Ind. Est. LA2: H Ben 7L **19**
Bentham Moor Rd. LA6: Bur L 4K **19**
Bentham Rd. BB2: Blackb 7J **139**
LA1: Lanc 5L **29**
LA6: Ingl 4L **19**
Bentham Station (Rail) 6L **19**
Bentham St. PR7: Copp 4A **194**
PR8: S'port 9H **167**
Bentham's Way PR8: S'port 3H **187**
Bent Ho Row PR6: H Charn 3L **195**
Bentinck Av. FY4: Blackp 4B **108**
Bentinck Dr. LA6: K Lon 6F **8**
Bentinck Rd. FY8: L Ann 9C **108**
Bentinck St. OL12: Roch 4N **203**
Bent La. BB8: Colne 5E **86**
PR25: Leyl 6L **153**
Bentlea Rd. BB7: Gis 9A **52**
Bentley Brook Cl. BL6: Hor 9F **196**
Bentley Ct. *BB3: Darw 6A 158*
(off Wadsworth Cl.)
Bentley Dr. FY4: Blackp 3N **109**
PR4: K'ham 4K **111**
Bentley Fold BL8: Bury 9E **200**
Bentley Grn. FY5: T Clev 1K **63**
Bentley Hall Rd. BL8: Bury 9B **200**
Bentley La. BL9: Bury 4L **201**
L40: Bis G 6A **192**
PR7: Hesk 4D **192**
Bentley Mnr. PR2: Ribb 7B **116**
Bentley Mdws. BL8: Bury 9D **200**
Bentley M. OL12: Roch 3B **204**
Bentley Pk. Rd. PR4: Longt 9K **133**
Bentley St. BB1: Blackb 3C **140**
BB3: Darw 8C **158**
BB9: Nelson 3H **105**
OL12: Roch 3A **204**
OL13: Bac 4K **163**
Bentley Wood Way BB11: Hapt 5K **123**
Bentmeadows OL12: Roch 4B **204**
Benton Rd. PR2: Ribb 5N **115**
BENTS 5E **86**
Bents BB8: Colne 5E **86**
Bents Farm Cl. OL15: Littleb 9J **185**
Bents La. LA6: Cast 4G **9**
Bent St. BB4: Hasl 7J **161**
BB5: Osw 5K **141**
Bentwood Rd. BB4: Hasl 4F **160**
Benwick Rd. L32: Kirk 8G **223**
Beresford Ct. BB11: Burnl 3B **124**
Beresford Dr. PR9: S'port 5M **167**
Beresford Gdns. PR9: S'port 4M **167**
Beresford Rd. BB1: Blackb 1B **226** (1L **139**)
Beresford St. BB9: Nelson 4K **105**
FY1: Blackp 3C **88**
OL16: Milnr 9L **205**
Bergen St. BB11: Burnl 4N **123**
Bergerac Cres. FY5: T Clev 5F **62**
Berkeley Av. WN3: Wins 9N **221**
Berkeley Cl. BB9: Nelson 3J **105**
PR7: Chor 9F **174**
Berkeley Ct. FY6: Poul F 8L **63**
Berkeley Cres. BB12: Padi 9H **103**
Berkeley Dr. BB12: Read 8C **102**
OL16: Roch 9E **204**
PR5: Bam B 3A **154**
Berkeley Rd. BL1: Bolt 9E **198**
Berkeley St. BB9: Brierf 5E **104**
BB9: Nelson 3J **105**
PR1: Prest 2H **229** (8H **115**)
Berkley Cl. PR4: K'ham 3K **111**
Berkley Wlk. OL15: Littleb 9J **185**
Berkshire Av. BB12: Burnl 2M **123**
Berkshire Cl. BB1: Wilp 2N **119**
Bernard St. OL12: Roch 2B **204**
Berne Av. BL6: Hor 9B **196**
Berridge Av. BB12: Burnl 3M **123**
Berriedale Rd. BB9: Nelson 1L **105**
Berringtons La. WA11: Rain 8M **225**
Berry Cl. WN8: Skelm 1K **219**
Berry Fld. PR1: Penw 5F **134**
Berry Ho. Rd. L40: Holmesw 1M **189**
Berry La. PR3: Longr 2J **97**
Berry's La. BB7: Whall 8J **101**
FY6: Poul F 7J **63**
Berry St. BB9: Brierf 5F **104**
BB11: Burnl 5D **124**
PR1: Prest 7M **229** (1K **135**)
PR5: Lost H 8K **135**
PR6: Adl 5J **195**
WN8: Skelm 1K **219**
Bersham Dr. BB6: Gt H 3J **121**
Bertha Rd. OL16: Roch 6F **204**
Bertha St. BB5: Acc 2C **142**
Bertie St. OL11: Roch 9A **204**
Bertram Av. LA4: Morec 4A **22**
Bertrand Av. FY3: Blackp 3G **89**
Berwick Av. FY5: T Clev 8F **54**
PR8: Ains 7D **186**
Berwick Dr. BB12: Burnl 2C **124**
PR2: Fulw 5G **115**
Berwick Rd. FY4: Blackp 4C **108**
FY8: L Ann 1F **128**
PR1: Prest 7L **229** (1K **135**)
Berwick St. OL16: Roch 7E **204**
PR1: Prest 8A **116**
Berwick Way LA3: Heys 9K **21**
Berwyn Av. LA4: Morec 2D **22**
Berwyn Cl. BL6: Hor 8D **196**
Berwyn Ct. PR8: S'port 1K **187**
Beryl Av. BB1: Blackb 7N **119**
BL8: Tott 6E **200**
FY5: T Clev 2E **62**
Beryl St. BL1: Bolt 9F **198**
Besant Cl. BB1: Blackb 7B **140**
BESCAR 6F **188**
Bescar Brow La. L40: Scar 6D **188**
Bescar La. L40: Scar 6F **188**
Bescar Lane Station (Rail) 3G **188**
Bescot Way FY5: T Clev 4F **62**
Bessie St. BB18: Barnw 2M **77**
Bess Nook BB4: Rawt 7L **161**
Best St. PR4: K'ham 4L **111**
Beswicke Royds St. OL16: Roch 4F **204**
Beswicke St. OL12: Roch 5B **204**
OL15: Littleb 9M **185**
Beswick St. OL14: Wals 8K **165**
Bethany La. OL16: Milnr 9M **205**
Bethel Av. FY2: Blackp 7C **62**
Bethel Grn. OL15: Littleb 5M **185**
Bethel Rd. BB1: Blackb 1A **140**
Bethel St. BB8: Colne 7M **85**
BB18: Barnw 1M **77**
Bethesda Cl. BB2: Blackb 7B **226** (5L **139**)
Bethesda Rd. FY1: Blackp 4J **227** (6B **88**)
Bethesda St.
BB11: Burnl 2C **228** (3D **124**)
BB18: Barnw 3M **77**
Betjeman Cl. FY2: Blackp 5F **62**
Betony LA4: Morec 2F **22**
Betony La. OL12: Roch 2A **204**
Bett La. PR6: H Wheel 6L **155**
Betty Ann Ct. PR9: S'port 6H **167**
Betula Bank PR8: Birk 3G **186**
Betula M. OL11: Roch 4H **203**
Between Gates La. LA6: Midd 1G **8**
Beulah Av. LA4: Morec 3D **22**
Bevan Pl. BB9: Nelson 9K **85**
BEVERLEY 3J **85**
Beverley Av. FY6: Poul F 2K **89**
Beverley Cl. BB7: Clith 5K **81**
PR2: Ash R 8F **114**
PR4: W Grn 6F **110**
PR9: S'port 1B **168**
Beverley Ct. LA4: Morec 3D **22**
Beverley Dr. BB7: Clith 5K **81**
Beverley Gro. FY4: Blackp 2C **108**
Beverley Pl. OL16: Roch 5D **204**
Beverley Rd. BB9: Blacko 3J **85**
WN5: Wigan 3L **221**
Beverley Rd. Nth. FY8: L Ann 9G **109**
Beverley Rd. Sth. FY8: L Ann 9G **109**
Beverley St. BB2: Blackb 7J **139**
BB11: Burnl 4C **124**
Beverley Ter. *BB2: Blackb 7J 139*
(off Beverley St.)
Beverly Cl. FY5: T Clev 3H **63**
Beverston OL11: Roch 7B **204**
Bevington Cl.
BB11: Burnl 3A **228** (4C **124**)
BEVIS GREEN 5L **201**
Bevis Grn. BL9: Bury 5L **201**
Bewcastle Dr. L40: W'head 9A **210**
Bewley Dr. L32: Kirk 9J **223**
Bexhill Rd. PR2: Ingol 6D **114**
Bexley Av. FY2: Blackp 2D **88**
Bexley Pl. FY8: L Ann 3L **129**
Bezza La. BB2: Bald 5K **117**
PR5: Sam 6J **117**
Bhailok Sq. PR2: Fulw 5J **115**
Bhailok St. PR1: Prest 4H **229** (9H **115**)
Bibby Dr. FY3: Stain 6L **89**
Bibby Rd. PR9: S'port 4N **167**
Bibby's Rd. FY2: Blackp 8E **62**
BICKERSTAFFE 6D **218**
Bickerstaffe St. FY1: Blackp 5H **227** (7B **88**)
Bickerton Rd. PR8: Birk 1F **186**
Bicknell St. BB1: Blackb 1C **226** (2M **139**)
Bideford Av. FY3: Blackp 4G **89**
Bideford Rd. OL11: Roch 9M **203**
Bideford Way PR4: Cott 3C **114**
Bidston St. PR1: Prest 9A **116**
Bigdale Dr. L33: Kirk 7L **223**
Bigforth Dr. LA1: Bail 7L **29**
Biggins La. LA6: H Big 7D **8**
Biggins Rd. LA6: K Lon 6E **8**
Bigholmes La. BD23: Lon P 7N **35**
Bilberry St. OL16: Roch 7D **204**
(not continuous)
Billinge Av. BB2: Blackb 3H **139**
Billinge Cl. BB2: Blackb 3J **139**
Billinge End Rd. BB2: Blackb, Pleas 4C **138**
Billinge La. L39: Bick 6K **217**
Billinge Rd. WN3: Wigan 7M **221**
WN5: Wigan 7M **221**
Billinge Side BB2: Blackb 3G **138**
Billinge St. BB1: Blackb 4A **140**
Billinge Vw. BB2: Blackb 6G **139**
Billinge Wood Pk. BB2: Blackb 3H **139**
BILLINGTON 6G **101**
Billington Av. BB4: Rawt 2M **161**
Billington Ct. PR2: Grim 9F **96**
Billington Gdns. BB7: B'ton 6G **100**
Billington Rd. BB11: Burnl 6M **123**
Billington St. PR4: Wesh 3L **111**
Billington St. E. PR4: Wesh 3L **111**
Billsborrow La. PR3: Inglew 6J **69**
Bill's La. L37: Form 2A **214**
Bilsberry Cotts. BB7: Hurst G 1N **99**
Bilsborough Hey PR1: Penw 7H **135**
Bilsborough Mdw. PR2: Lea 6B **114**
BILSBORROW 7D **68**
Bilsborrow La. PR3: Bils 7D **68**
Bilson Sq. *OL16: Milnr 8K 205*
(off Newhey St.)
Binary Ct. PR7: Buck V 8N **153**
Binbrook Pl. PR7: Chor 7C **174**
Binfold Cft. *LA6: K Lon 6F 8*
(off Lunefield Dr.)
Bingley Av. FY3: Blackp 4F **88**
Bingley Cl. PR6: Clay W 5E **154**
Bingley Rd. OL16: Roch 6F **204**
Bingley Sq. OL16: Roch 6F **204**
Bingley Ter. OL16: Roch 6F **204**
Binns Nook Rd. OL12: Roch 3D **204**
Binns St. BB4: Craws 9M **143**
Binn's Ter. *OL15: Littleb 8L 185*
(off Lodge St.)
Binyon Ct. LA1: Lanc 1K **29**
Binyon Rd. LA1: Lanc 2K **29**
Birbeck Cl. WN3: Wins 9N **221**
Birbeck Rd. L33: Kirk 7M **223**
Birbeck Wlk. L33: Kirk 7M **223**
Birchall Lodge *PR2: Ribb 5B 116*
(off Grange Av.)
Birch Av. BB4: Hasl 4H **161**
BL8: Tott 8F **200**
FY5: T Clev 1E **62**
L40: Burs 9C **190**
LA2: Gal 2K **37**
OL12: Roch 1G **205**
OL14: Tod 9K **147**
PR1: Penw 5D **134**
PR2: Ash R 7D **114**
PR4: Newt 6D **112**
PR7: Eux 2M **173**
PR25: Leyl 4N **153**
Birchbank Gdns.
BB1: Blackb 1F **226** (2N **139**)
Birch Cl. BB5: Hunc 7D **122**
L31: Magh 1E **222**
OL12: Whitw 8N **183**
Birch Cotts. BB4: Rawt 7K **161**
Birch Cres. BB5: Osw 5M **141**
OL16: Milnr 9K **205**
PR5: Hogh 7G **136**
Birch Dr. LA5: Silv 7G **4**
Birchen Bower Wlk. BL8: Tott 8E **200**
Birchenlee La. BB8: Colne 8A **86**
Birches, The PR1: Prest 8M **115**
Birches End OL12: Whitw 9N **183**
Birches Rd. BL7: Turt 1K **199**
Birch Fld. PR6: Clay W 4D **154**
Birchfield BL2: Bolt 7L **199**
PR4: Much H 3K **151**
Birchfield Dr. OL11: Roch 8N **203**
PR3: Longr 2J **97**
Birchfield Way L31: Lyd 6A **216**
BIRCH GREEN 1N **219**
Birch Grn. Rd. WN8: Skelm 9M **211**
Birch Gro. BB7: Barr 1K **101**
BL0: Ramsb 2F **200**
FY6: Stal 5C **56**
LA1: Lanc 8H **23**
LA5: Arn 3D **4**
BIRCH HALL 3M **157**
Birch Hall Av. BB3: Darw 3L **157**
Birch Hall La. BB18: Earl 2G **78**
Birch Hey Cl. OL12: Roch 1F **204**
Birch Hill Cres. OL12: Roch 1H **205**
Birch Hill La. OL12: Ward 8G **184**
Birch Hill Wlk. OL15: Littleb 9J **185**
Birchill Rd. L33: Know P 8A **224**
Birchin La. PR6: Whit W 6E **154**
Birch La. L40: Holmesw 8B **170**
PR3: Goos 7C **70**
Birch Mt. OL12: Roch 1H **205**
Birchmuir Hey L32: Kirk 9L **223**
Birchover Cl. PR2: Ingol 4D **114**
Birch Rd. OL12: Roch, Ward 8F **184**
PR3: Gars 3M **59**
PR6: Chor 4F **174**
PR7: Copp 4A **194**
Birch St. BB5: Acc 2A **142**
BL9: Bury 9L **201**
FY7: Flee 9G **40**
FY8: L Ann 5B **130**
OL12: Ward 8F **184**
OL13: Bac 4K **163**
PR8: S'port 1H **187**
WN8: Skelm 2J **219**
Birch Ter. BB5: Acc 6C **142**
Birchtree Av. LA3: Heys 7M **21**
Birchtree Dr. L31: Mell 7F **222**
Birchtree Gdns. FY3: Blackp 8H **89**
Birch Vw. BB7: Barr 9K **81**
OL12: Roch 1G **205**
Birch Vs. OL12: Whitw 9N **183**
Birch Wlk. BB1: Blackb 4B **140**
OL14: Tod 1L **165**
Birch Way FY6: Poul F 7J **63**
Birchway Av. FY3: Blackp 4E **88**
Birchwood PR26: Leyl 6F **152**
Birchwood Av. PR4: Hutt 7M **133**
Birchwood Cl. BD24: Sett 3N **35**
FY8: L Ann 4L **129**
WN3: Wins 9N **221**
Birchwood Dr. FY6: Ham 1B **64**
PR2: Fulw 2G **114**
PR7: Copp 3A **194**
Birchwood Way L33: Kirk 5M **223**
Bird i' th' Hand Cotts.
L39: Orms 6K **209**
Bird St. BB9: Brierf 5F **104**
PR1: Prest 2G **135**
Birdy Brow BB7: Chaig, S'hurst 5A **80**
BIRKACRE 2C **194**
Birkacre Brow PR7: Copp 3B **194**
Birkacre Rd. PR7: Chor 1B **194**
Birkbeck Pl. FY7: Flee 2D **54**
Birkbeck Way BB10: Burnl 9E **104**
BIRKDALE 1G **186**
Birkdale Av. FY2: Blackp 6E **62**
FY7: Flee 5E **54**
FY8: L Ann 8F **108**
PR4: Longt 8K **133**
Birkdale Cl. FY5: T Clev 3K **63**
LA1: Lanc 5H **23**
PR4: Longt 8K **133**
PR7: Eux 2N **173**
Birkdale Cop PR8: S'port 3K **187**
Birkdale Dr. PR2: Ash R 7B **114**
Birkdale Rd. OL16: Roch 9F **204**
Birkdale Station (Rail) 1F **186**
Birkdale Trad. Est. PR8: Birk 3F **186**
Birkett Cl. BL1: Bolt 7D **198**
Birkett Dr. BL1: Bolt 7D **198**
PR2: Ribb 6C **116**
Birkett Pl. PR2: Ribb 6C **116**
Birkett Rd. BB5: Acc 1B **142**
Birketts Pl. LA4: Morec 2C **22**
Birkey La. L37: Form 1A **214**
Birkland Barrow Rd.
LA6: Neth K, Over K 2F **16**
Birklands Av. LA4: Morec 4C **22**
Birkrig WN8: Skelm 5A **220**
Birks Brow PR3: T'ley 9F **70**
Birks Dr. BL8: Bury 7G **201**
Birkside Way FY4: Blackp 9J **89**
Birks La. OL14: Wals 7L **165**
Birk St. PR1: Prest 6G **229** (1H **135**)
Birkwith La. LA2: L Ben 7K **19**
Birley Cl. WN6: App B 4J **213**
Birley Ct. PR8: S'port 9H **167**
Birley Pl. BB10: Burnl 1E **124**
Birley St. BB1: Blackb 2F **226** (2N **139**)
(not continuous)
BL1: Bolt 9E **198**
BL9: Bury 8L **201**
FY1: Blackp 1H **227** (5B **88**)
OL12: Roch 4D **204**
PR1: Prest 5K **229** (9J **115**)
PR4: K'ham 4N **111**
Birleywood WN8: Skelm 5A **220**
Birnam Grn. FY7: Flee 9E **40**
Birtenshaw Cres. BL7: Brom C 6H **199**
BIRTLE 7D **202**
Birtle Brook Vw. W. *BL9: Bury 8D 202*
(off Birtle Rd.)
Birtle Brook Village E. BL9: Bury 8D **202**
Birtle Brook Village W. BL9: Bury 8C **202**
Birtle Brook W. BL9: Bury 8C **202**
BIRTLE GREEN 7C **202**
Birtle Moor BL9: Bury 8C **202**
Birtle Rd. BL9: Bury 6C **202**
Birtwistle Av. BB8: Colne 5N **85**
Birtwistle Cl. BB9: Brierf 5F **104**
Birtwistle Ct. BB18: Barnw 3N **77**
Birtwistle Fold BB8: Colne 6B **86**
Birtwistle Hyde Pk. BB8: Colne 6A **86**
Birtwistle Standroyd Bungs. BB8: Colne 6D **86**
Birtwistle St. BB5: Acc 3B **142**
BB6: Gt H 4H **121**
PR5: Lost H 9L **135**
Birtwistle Ter. *BB6: Langh 9C 100*
(off Whalley New Rd.)
Bisham Cl. BB3: Darw 7C **158**
Bishopdale Cl. BB2: Blackb 9E **138**
LA3: Morec 5F **22**
Bishopdale Ct. *BD24: Sett 3N 35*
(off Kirkgate)
Bishopdale Rd. LA1: Lanc 9H **23**
Bishopgate PR1: Prest 5L **229** (9K **115**)
Bishops Ga. FY8: L Ann 2K **129**
Bishopsgate FY3: Blackp 1G **89**
LA1: Lanc 3L **29**
Bishopsgate Wlk. OL16: Roch 9F **204**
Bishopstone Cl. BB2: Blackb 8A **140**
Bishop St. BB5: Acc 3B **142**
BB9: Nelson 2H **105**
BB10: Burnl 9F **104**
OL16: Roch 4E **204**
Bishopsway PR1: Penw 5G **134**
Bishopton Cres. PR7: Buck V 1B **174**
Bison Pl. PR26: Leyl 5F **152**

Bispham—Bores Hill

BISPHAM
FY2 7B 62
L40 7K 191
Bispham Av. PR26: Far M 3H 153
Bispham Body Senze 6D 62
(off All Hallows Rd.)
Bispham Ct. WN5: Bill 9G 221
BISPHAM GREEN 6M 191
Bispham Hall Bus. Pk. WN5: Bill 9F 220
Bispham Rd. BB9: Nelson 4J 105
FY2: Blackp 7D 62
(not continuous)
FY3: Blackp 2E 88
FY5: T Clev 5F 62
(Faraday Way, not continuous)
FY5: T Clev 1C 62
(Victoria Rd. W.)
FY6: Carl 5F 62
PR9: S'port 7M 167
Bispham Stop (Tram) 7B 62
Bispham St. PR1: Prest 4K 229 (9J 115)
Bittern Cl. FY3: Blackp 4H 89
OL11: Roch 6K 203
Bivel St. BB12: Burnl 3B 124
Black Abbey St. BB5: Acc 3B 142
Blackacre La. L39: Burs, Orms 4K 209
BLACKAMOOR 9B 140
Black-A-Moor La. L39: D'holl 9M 207
Blackamoor Rd. BB1: Guide 9B 140
Blackberry Hall Cres. LA3: Heys 8M 21
Blackberry Hill LA7: Slack H 1N 5
Blackberry Way PR1: Penw 6F 134
Black Brook Cl. PR6: Heap 4J 175
Black Bull La. PR2: Fulw 4G 114
BLACKBURN 4D 226 (3M 139)
Blackburn Brow PR6: Chor 4G 175
Blackburn Golf Course 2J 139
Blackburn Ice Arena 7D 226 (5M 139)
Blackburn La. PR6: H Wheel 6K 155
Blackburn Mus. & Art Gallery 3C 226 (3M 139)
Blackburn New Rd.
PR6: Heap, Wheel, Whit W 9H 155
Blackburn Old Rd. BB1: Rish 7C 120
BB6: Gt H 4E 120
PR5: Hogh 6L 137
Blackburn Rd. BB1: Blackb 3E 140
BB1: Rish 1D 140
BB3: Darw 2M 157
BB4: Hasl 9G 142
(Commerce St.)
BB4: Hasl 9J 161
(Parkinson Fold)
BB5: Acc, Chur 2L 141
BB5: Chur, Osw 3E 140
BB5: Clay M 8K 121
BB5: Ris B 8E 142
BB6: Gt H 5J 121
BB12: Padi, S'stone 2E 122
BL0: Eden 1J 181
BL1: Bolt 9E 198
BL7: Belm, Eger 7B 178
BL7: Edgw 2G 178
BL7: Eger 9E 198
PR3: Ribc 7F 98
PR5: H Walt 5D 136
PR6: Chor, Whit W 3G 175
PR6: Heap, Wheel 9H 155
Blackburn Rovers FC 8L 139
Blackburn Station (Rail) 5E 226 (4N 139)
Blackburn St.
BB1: Blackb 1D 226 (2M 139)
BB11: Burnl 1C 228 (3D 124)
PR6: Chor 7G 174
Blackburn Trad. Cen.
BB1: Blackb 1F 226
BLACKBURN WITH DARWEN SERVICE AREA
2N 157
Blackburn Youth Zone 5D 226
Blackcar La. L29: T'ton 8G 215
Black Cft. PR6: Clay W 4D 154
Black Dad La. OL11: Roch 5E 202
Blackdown Ho. BB4: Hasl 4G 160
(off Bury Rd.)
Black Dyke Rd. LA5: Arn 1G 4
Blacker St. BB10: Burnl 8E 104
Blackfen Pl. FY2: Blackp 2D 88
Blackfield Rd. PR4: Frec 2N 131
Blackgate La. PR4: Tarl 4N 169
(not continuous)
Black Horse St. PR7: Chor 8D 174
Black Horse Yd. BB8: Colne 6A 86
(off Church St.)
Black Ho. La. BB10: Brierc 8A 106
Black Ho. La. E. PR3: Chip 6E 70
Blackhurst Av. PR4: Hutt 7C 134
Blackhurst Ct. PR4: Longt 8M 133
Blackhurst Rd. L31: Lyd 6B 216
Black Knights Parachute Cen. 9E 36
Black La. BL0: Ramsb 6M 181
PR3: Nateby, Winm 2A 58
Black La. Cft. BB7: Clith 2L 81
BLACK LANE ENDS 9J 79
BLACKLEACH 8J 93
Blackleach BB6: Gt H 3G 121
Blackleach Av. PR2: Grim 9F 96
Blackleach La. PR4: Bartl, Catf 9K 93
Blackledge Cl. WN5: Orr 6H 221
Blackley Gro. L33: Kirk 4M 223
(off Carl's Way)
Black Moor La. L40: Mawd 3K 191
Blackmoor Rd. L40: Mawd 3J 191
Black Moss La. L39: Aug, Orms 9J 209
L40: Scar 6C 188
Black Moss Rd. BB9: Blacko 2A 84
BLACKO 3H 85
Blacko Bar Rd.
BB9: Blacko, Rough 7D 84
Blackpits Rd. OL11: Roch 4H 203
BLACK POLE 5M 93
BLACKPOOL 2H 227 (5B 88)
Blackpool & Fleetwood Yacht Club 4M 63
Blackpool & Fylde College Sports Cen. 5E 62
Blackpool Bus. Pk. FY4: Blackp 5D 108
Blackpool FC 7K 227 (8C 88)
Blackpool Fylde Ind. Est. FY4: Blackp 2J 109
BLACKPOOL INTERNATIONAL AIRPORT 5C 108
Blackpool Lifeboat Station & Visitor Cen.
3G 227 (6A 88)
Blackpool Light Craft Club 5A 108
Blackpool Model Village & Gardens 6F 88
Blackpool North Station (Rail) 4C 88
Blackpool Old Rd. FY3: Blackp 1G 88
FY6: Poul F 9G 63
PR3: Lit E 6L 65
Blackpool Pk. Golf Course 5E 88
Blackpool Rd. FY2: Blackp 7D 62
FY6: Carl 8G 62
FY8: L Ann 2K 129
PR1: Fulw, Ribb 6H 115
PR2: Ash R 8B 114
(off Layton Rd.)
PR2: Ash R, Fulw, Lea 6H 115
PR2: Ash R, Lea 5B 112
PR2: Ribb 6H 115
PR3: Longr 3J 97
PR3: St M 5E 66
PR4: Clif, K'ham, Newt, Prest 5B 112
PR4: K'ham 3G 111
Blackpool Rd. Nth. FY8: L Ann 7F 108
Blackpool Sth. Caravan Club FY4: Blackp 2J 109
Blackpool South Station (Rail) 9C 88
Blackpool Sports Cen. 6E 88
Blackpool St. BB3: Darw 9B 158
BB5: Chur 3L 141
Blackpool Technology Pk. FY2: Blackp 6F 62
Blackpool Tower 3H 227 (6A 88)
Blackpool Tower Stop (Tram) 3H 227 (6B 88)
Blackpool Trade Cen. FY4: Blackp 9H 89
Blackpool Zoo 6G 89
Blackrod Brow BL6: Blackr 9K 195
Blackrod By-Pass Rd. BL6: Blackr 9L 195
Blackshaw St. OL14: Tod 2N 165
Blacksmith La. OL11: Roch 9M 203
Blacksmiths Row FY8: L Ann 1K 129
Blacksmith Wlk. PR7: Buck V 9A 154
(off Main St.)
BLACKSNAPE 7E 158
Blacksnape Rd. BB3: Hodd 6D 158
Blacksticks La. PR3: Chip, Goos 6C 70
Blackstone Av. OL16: Roch 5F 204
Blackstone Edge Ct. OL15: Littleb 8M 185
Blackstone Edge Old Rd. OL15: Littleb 8M 185
Blackstone Rd. PR6: Chor 5G 174
Blackthorn Cl. BB1: Blackb 1N 139
FY5: T Clev 7F 54
OL12: Roch 3B 204
PR2: Lea 8A 114
PR4: Newt 7D 112
Blackthorn Cres. OL13: Bac 4K 163
Blackthorn Cft. PR6: Clay W 5C 154
Blackthorn Dr. PR1: Penw 5E 134
Blackthorn La. OL13: Bac 3K 163
Blackthorn M. FY8: L Ann 3J 129
OL12: Roch 3B 204
Blackthorn Ter. OL13: Bac 3K 163
(off Blackthorn Av.)
Blackwood Ct. OL13: Bac 7G 163
Blackwood M. OL13: Bac 7G 162
(off Blackwood Rd.)
Blackwood Pl. LA1: Lanc 2M 29
Blackwood Rd. OL13: Bac 8F 162
Blades St. LA1: Lanc 7B 228 (9J 23)
BLAGUEGATE 2F 218
Blaguegate La. WN8: Skelm 1E 218
Blainscough La. PR7: Copp 5N 193
Blainscough Rd. PR7: Copp 5A 194
Blairgowrie Gdns. L39: Orms 8M 209
Blair Gro. PR9: S'port 7M 167
Blair St. BL7: Brom C 5F 198
OL12: Roch 4A 204
Blairway Av. FY3: Blackp 4F 88
Blake Av. PR5: Lost H 9K 135
Blake Gdns. BB6: Gt H 5H 121
Blakehall WN8: Skelm 4A 220
(not continuous)
Blake St. BB5: Acc 2A 142
BL7: Brom C 6G 199
OL16: Roch 5D 204
Blakewater Rd. BB1: Blackb 1B 140
Blakey Moor BB2: Blackb 4B 226 (3L 139)
Blakey St. BB11: Burnl 2F 228 (3E 124)
Blakiston St. FY7: Flee 9G 41
Blanche St. OL12: Roch 3D 204
PR2: Ash R 8F 114
Blandford Av. FY5: T Clev 2C 62
Blandford Cl. BL8: Bury 8J 201
PR8: Birk 9E 166
Blanket Hall Cotts. BB3: Darw 2B 178
Blannel St. BB11: Burnl 3A 228 (3C 124)
Blascomay Sq. BB8: Colne 7A 86
(off Boundary St.)
Blashaw La. PR1: Penw 3D 134
Blaydike Moss PR26: Leyl 6E 152
Blaydon Av. FY5: T Clev 8E 54
Blaydon Pk. WN8: Skelm 4A 220
Bleachers Dr. PR25: Leyl 6H 153
Bleackley St. BL8: Bury 9H 201
Blea Cl. BB12: Burnl 1A 124
Bleakholt Rd. BL0: Ramsb 5L 181
Bleak La. L40: Lath 9G 191
Bleara Rd. BB18: Earl 4G 79
BLEASDALE 3B 70
Bleasdale Av. BB7: Clith 4J 81
FY3: Stain 5L 89
FY5: T Clev 2D 62
FY6: Poul F 9J 63
L10: Aint 8D 222
PR4: K'ham 3M 111
Bleasdale Cl. L39: Aug 4J 217
PR5: Bam B 8B 136
PR25: Leyl 8L 153
Bleasdale Ct. PR3: Longr 3K 97
Bleasdale Gro. LA3: Heys 7M 21
Bleasdale La. PR3: Bleas, Clau 9K 61
Bleasdale Rd. FY6: K Sea 8K 41
FY8: L Ann 4B 130
PR3: W'ham 4B 96
PR3: Whitec 3M 69
Bleasdale St. E. PR1: Prest 8L 115
Blea Tarn Pl. LA4: Morec 4D 22
Blea Tarn Rd. LA2: Lanc 4M 29
Blelock St. PR1: Prest 6M 229 (1K 135)
Blenheim Av. FY1: Blackp 4M 227 (6D 88)
PR4: K'ham 4L 111
Blenheim Cl. BB1: Blackb 8M 119
PR5: Lost H 8M 135
Blenheim Dr. FY5: T Clev 1J 63
PR4: Wart 2J 131
Blenheim Pl. FY8: L Ann 8E 108
Blenheim Rd. PR8: Ains 7B 186
WN5: Wigan 2M 221
Blenheim St. BB8: Colne 6D 86
OL12: Roch 4N 203
Blenheim Ter. BB8: Foul 2B 86
(off Skipton Old Rd.)
Blenheim Way PR4: Cott 3B 114
Blesma Ct. FY4: Blackp 3C 108
(off Lytham Rd.)
Blindfoot Rd. WA11: Rain 9H 225
Blind La. BB7: Gis 9A 52
BB12: High 4M 103
LA6: Bur L 3K 19
OL14: Tod 1K 165
Blindman's La. L39: Orms 5H 209
Bloomfield Ct. PR1: Prest 7H 115
Bloomfield Grange PR1: Penw 6F 134
Bloomfield Pk. LA5: Carn 9A 12
Bloomfield Road 7K 227 (8C 88)
Bloomfield Rd. FY1: Blackp 8J 227 (8B 88)
PR6: Withn 6B 156
Bloomfield St. BL1: Bolt 9E 198
Bloom St. BL0: Ramsb 1F 200
Blossom Av. BB5: Osw 3L 141
FY4: Blackp 2F 108
Blossom Ct. FY3: Blackp 1G 89
Blossom Gro. PR6: Whit W 1E 174
Blossom Pl. OL16: Roch 5C 204
Blossoms, The FY6: Poul F 8M 63
PR2: Fulw 3M 115
BLOWICK 8L 167
Blowick Bus. Pk. PR9: S'port 8N 167
Blowick Ind. Pk. PR9: S'port 8N 167
Blucher St. BB8: Colne 7B 86
Bluebell Av. BB4: Hasl 7F 160
Blue Bell Cl. PR3: Pill 8H 43
Bluebell Cl. FY2: Blackp 9D 62
FY5: T Clev 7F 54
L32: Kirk 6K 223
PR4: Hesk B 3C 150
PR6: Whit W 1D 174
Bluebell Cotts. LA6: Neth K 4C 16
Bluebell Dr. OL11: Roch 9M 203
Bluebell Gro. BB11: Burnl 4M 123
Blue Bell La. OL14: Tod 6F 146
Blue Bell Pl. PR1: Prest 6M 229 (1K 135)
Bluebell Way BB5: Hunc 8D 122
PR2: Fulw, Ribb 3A 116
PR5: Bam B 8C 136
Bluebell Way (Park & Ride) 3B 116
Bluebell Wood PR25: Leyl 4J 153
Blueberry Bus. Pk. OL16: Roch 6G 204
Bluecoat Cres. PR4: Newt 7E 112
Blue Moor PR4: Trea, Wharl 9C 92
Blue Scar La. BB7: Bolt B 5K 51
Blue Slate Fold PR5: Sam 9L 117
Blue Stone La. L40: Mawd 2B 192
Bluestone La. L31: Magh 1D 222
Blundell Av. L38: Hight 8A 214
PR8: Birk 3F 186
Blundell Cres. PR8: Birk 3F 186
Blundell Dr. PR8: Birk 3F 186
Blundell Gro. L38: Hight 8A 214
Blundell La. PR1: Penw 2E 134
PR9: S'port 3B 168
Blundell Links Ct. PR8: Ains 9C 186
Blundell M. WN3: Wigan 7N 221
Blundell Rd. FY8: L Ann 8F 108
L38: Hight 8A 214
PR2: Fulw 6H 115
Blundells Ct. WN3: Wigan 7N 221
Blundell St. FY1: Blackp 6H 227 (7B 88)
Blythe Av. OL15: Littleb 2J 205
Blythe Av. FY5: T Clev 7E 54
Blythe Ct. PR9: S'port 4N 167
Blythe La. L40: Lath 4A 210
Blythe Mdw. L40: Burs 4N 209
Blythe M. PR8: Birk 5G 186
Blythewood WN8: Skelm 4N 219
Boarded Barn PR7: Eux 3M 173
Boardman Av. FY1: Blackp 8N 227 (8D 88)
Boardman St. OL14: Tod 1L 165
Boardmans Way FY4: Blackp 3K 109
Board St. BB10: Burnl 9E 104
BOARSGREAVE 9E 162
Boarsgreave La. BB4: W'foot 9D 162
Boathorse La. BB12: Burnl 3B 124
Bobbin Cl. BB5: Acc 3N 141
Bobbiners La. PR9: Banks 3F 168
Bobbin Mill Cl. OL14: Tod 7E 146
Bobbin St. OL14: Tod 7F 146
Bobby Langton Way L40: Burs 8C 190
Bocholt Way BB4: Rawt 5M 161
Bodiam Rd. BL8: Greenm 4E 200
Bodkin La. PR3: Out R 4E 64
Bodmin Av. PR9: S'port 1A 168
Bodmin St. PR1: Prest 8N 115
Bodymasters Fitness Cen. 4D 88
(off Selbourne Rd.)
Boegrave Av. PR5: Lost H 8K 135
Bogburn La. PR7: Copp 7N 193
Bog Height Rd. BB3: Darw 1J 157
Bohuslav Barlow Gallery 1L 165
Boilton Ct. PR2: Ribb 6C 116
Boland St. BB1: Blackb 1A 140
Bold La. L39: Aug 4F 216
Bold St. BB1: Blackb 1C 226 (2M 139)
BB5: Acc 2B 142
BB8: Colne 7B 86
FY7: Flee 8H 41
LA3: Heys 4M 21
OL13: Bac 6K 163
PR1: Prest 7G 115
PR9: S'port 6H 167
WN5: Wigan 6N 221
Bold Venture Cotts. BB7: Chatb 8B 74
Bold Venture Way BB5: Clay M 6N 121
Boleyn, The L31: Magh 8D 216
Boleyn Ct. FY3: Blackp 7G 89
BOLHOLT 9F 200
Bolholt Ind. Est. BL8: Bury 9G 200
Bolholt Ind. Pk. BL8: Bury 9F 200
Bolholt Ter. BL8: Bury 9G 200
Bolland Cl. BB7: Clith 3M 81
Bolland Prospect BB7: Clith 3M 81
Bolland St. BB18: Barnw 1M 77
Bolton Av. BB5: Hunc 8C 122
FY6: Carl 6J 63
L32: Kirk 8H 223
LA1: Lanc 4K 23
BOLTON-BY-BOWLAND 8K 51
Bolton Cl. L37: Form 1A 214
Bolton Ct. BB3: Darw 7A 158
(off Wadsworth Cl.)
Bolton Cft. PR26: Leyl 7E 152
BOLTON GREEN 6M 173
Bolton Gro. BB9: Barrf 8H 85
BOLTON HOUSES 1C 112
Bolton La. LA5: Bolt S 5M 15
BOLTON-LE-SANDS 4L 15
Bolton Mdw. PR26: Leyl 7D 152
Bolton Old Links Golf Course 9L 197
Bolton Open Golf Course 9K 199
Bolton Rd. BB2: Blackb 9B 226 (7L 139)
BB3: Darw 1B 178
(Moss Gap)
BB3: Darw 7A 158
(Taylor St.)
BL2: Bolt 8J 199
BL6: Hor 6K 195
BL7: Edgw, Turt 1K 199
BL8: Hawk 2A 200
OL11: Roch 9L 203
PR5: Hogh 9N 137
PR6: Adl, And 6K 195
PR6: Withn 2B 156
PR7: Chor 8F 174
PR8: Birk 1G 186
Bolton Rd. Nth. BL0: Ramsb 6H 181
Bolton Rd. W. BL0: Ramsb 2E 200
BL8: Hawk 2E 200
Bolton Sailing Club 8K 177
Bolton's Cop PR9: Banks 9H 149
Boltons Ct. BB1: Blackb 3C 226
PR1: Prest 6L 229 (1K 135)
Boltons Cft. PR4: Salw 2J 113
Bolton's Meanygate PR4: Tarl 7N 149
Bolton St. BB4: Newc 6C 162
BB8: Colne 7M 85
BL0: Ramsb 9G 181
FY1: Blackp 9H 227 (9B 88)
PR7: Chor 7E 174
BOLTON TOWN END 6L 15
Bolton Wlk. L32: Kirk 8H 223
BOLTON WEST SERVICE AREA 9N 195
Bombay Rd. WN5: Wigan 3M 221
Bombay St. BB2: Blackb 5K 139
Bonchurch St. BB1: Blackb 4C 140
Bond La. BD24: Sett 3N 35
BONDS 6N 59
Bonds La. PR3: Gars 6N 59
PR4: Elsw 9M 65
PR7: Adl 6H 195
PR9: Banks 8F 148
Bond St. BB3: Darw 4A 158
BB8: Colne 6A 86
BB9: Nelson 3H 105
BB10: Burnl 1E 124
BL0: Eden 4K 181
FY4: Blackp 9B 88
LA1: Lanc 7F 228 (8L 23)
OL12: Roch 3D 204
OL14: Tod 2L 165
Bone Cft. PR6: Clay W 4D 154
Bone Hill La. PR3: Winm 2A 58
Bone Island WN8: Skelm 3M 219
Bonfire Hill BB4: Craws 9N 143
Bonfire Hill Cl. BB4: Craws 9N 143
Bonfire Hill Rd. BB4: Craws 9M 143
Bonney St. FY5: T Clev 9H 55
Bonny Grass Ter. BB7: B'ton 6G 101
(off Whalley New Rd.)
Bonny St. FY1: Blackp 4H 227 (6B 88)
Bonsall St. BB2: Blackb 6H 139
Boome St. FY4: Blackp 3C 108
Boonfields BL7: Brom C 5G 198
Boon Town LA6: Burt K 6H 7
Boon Walks LA6: Burt K 5H 7
BOOTH BRIDGE 9K 53
Booth Bri. La. BD23: T Crav 9J 53
Booth Cl. BL8: Tott 8F 200
Booth Ct. BB10: Burnl 1E 124
(off Old Hall St.)
Booth Cres. BB4: W'foot 6E 162
Boothfield Ho. Caravan Pk. FY6: Pree 7N 41
Booth Hall Dr. BL8: Tott 8E 200
Boothley Rd. FY1: Blackp 4C 88
Boothman Pl. BB9: Nelson 9J 85
Boothman St. BB2: Blackb 9B 226 (6L 139)
Booth Pl. BB4: W'foot 6D 162
Booth Rd. BB4: W'foot 6D 162
OL13: Bac 7F 162
Boothroyden FY1: Blackp 2B 88
Booth's La. L39: Aug 7E 208
Booths Shop. Cen. PR2: Fulw 2J 115
Booth St. BB4: Hasl 3F 160
BB4: W'foot 7C 162
BB5: Acc 3B 142
BB9: Nelson 2H 105
BL8: Tott 7E 200
LA5: Carn 9A 12
OL13: Bac 5K 163
PR9: S'port 6H 167
Booth Way BL8: Tott 8E 200
Boothwood Stile BL8: Holc 2E 200
Bootle St. PR1: Prest 8M 115
(not continuous)
Boot St. BB18: Earl 2E 78
Boot Way BB11: Burnl 3D 228 (4E 124)
Borage Cl. FY5: T Clev 7G 54
Boran Ct. BB11: Hapt 5K 123
Bordeaux Cres. FY5: T Clev 5F 62
Border Ct. LA1: Lanc 7H 23
Border Dr. PR7: Buck V 9B 154
Bores Hill WN1: Stand 9E 194

Borough Rd.—Bretherton Cl.

Borough Rd. BB3: Darw . . . 7N 157
Borrans La. LA3: Midd . . . 3L 27
Borrans La. Caravan Pk. LA3: Midd . . . 3L 27
Borron La. LA6: Cap . . . 6J 13
BORRON LANE END . . . 5K 13
Borrowdale Av. BB1: Blackb . . . 5C 140
FY7: Flee . . . 9E 40
Borrowdale Cl. BB5: Hunc . . . 8C 122
BB10: Reed . . . 7G 104
Borrowdale Dr. BB10: Reed . . . 6G 104
OL11: Roch . . . 9M 203
Borrowdale Gro. LA4: Morec . . . 3D 22
Borrowdale Rd. FY4: Blackp . . . 9H 89
LA1: Lanc . . . 5F 228 (7L 23)
PR25: Leyl . . . 8L 153
WN5: Wigan . . . 4L 221
BORWICK . . . 3G 12
Borwick Av. LA5: Wart . . . 4B 12
Borwick Cl. LA5: Wart . . . 5B 12
Borwick Ct. LA4: Morec . . . 5B 22
LA6: Borw . . . 3F 12
Borwick Dr. LA1: Lanc . . . 6H 23
Borwick Hall . . . 4G 12
Borwick La. LA5: Wart . . . 4B 12
LA6: Carn, Borw, Prie H . . . 4D 12
Borwick M. LA6: Borw . . . 4F 12
Borwick Rd. LA6: Borw, Cap, Ark . . . 3G 12
Bosburn Dr. BB2: Mellor B . . . 6D 118
Boscombe Av. LA3: Heys . . . 6M 21
Boscombe Rd. FY4: Blackp . . . 3B 108
Bosley Arc. FY1: Blackp . . . 1H 227
Bosley Cl. BB3: Darw . . . 7D 158
Bostock St. PR1: Prest . . . 6L 229 (1K 135)
Boston Av. FY2: Blackp . . . 5D 62
Boston Rd. FY8: L Ann . . . 2H 129
OL13: Bac . . . 4K 163
Bostons BB6: Gt H . . . 4H 121
Boston St. BB9: Nelson . . . 4K 105
Boston Way FY4: Blackp . . . 1F 108
Bosworth Dr. PR8: Ains . . . 9B 186
Bosworth Pl. FY4: Blackp . . . 5B 108
Bosworth Sq. *OL11: Roch . . . 9A 204*
(off Bosworth St.)
Bosworth St. BL6: Hor . . . 9C 196
OL11: Roch . . . 9A 204
Botanic Ct. WN5: Wigan . . . 2M 221
Botanic Gdns. . . . 4A 168
Botanic Gdns. Mus. . . . 4A 168
Botanic Rd. PR9: S'port . . . 5N 167
BOTANY . . . 4G 174
Botany Bay PR6: Chor . . . 4G 175
(Blackburn Brow)
PR6: Chor . . . 3G 174
(Chorley Nth. Bus. Pk.)
Botany Brow PR6: Chor . . . 4G 174
Botesworth Grn. OL16: Milnr . . . 8K 205
Bott Ho. La. BB8: Colne . . . 9L 85
Bottomdale Rd. LA2: Slyne . . . 9K 15
Bottomgate BB1: Blackb . . . 3B 140
Bottomley Bank La. BB4: Craws . . . 9M 143
Bottomley Rd. OL14: Wals . . . 9M 165
Bottomley St. BB9: Nelson . . . 2J 105
BOTTOM OF HUTTON . . . 4K 133
BOTTOM O' TH' BROW . . . 9F 202
BOTTOM O' TH' MOOR . . . 9L 199
Bottoms Hall Cotts. BL8: Tott . . . 4C 200
Bottoms La. LA5: Silv . . . 7H 5
Bottom's Row BB4: W'foot . . . 9D 162
Botton Rd. LA2: Wray . . . 3J 33
Boulden Dr. BL8: Bury . . . 8H 201
Boulder St. BB4: Craws . . . 9M 143
BoulderUK
Blackburn . . . 5B 226
Bouldsworth Rd. BB10: Burnl . . . 4J 125
Boulevard PR1: Prest . . . 3L 135
Boulevard, The BB1: Blackb . . . 5D 226 (4M 139)
FY8: L Ann . . . 3F 128
PR5: Walt D . . . 6L 135
Boulsworth Cl. BB18: Salt . . . 5M 77
Boulsworth Cres. BB9: Nelson . . . 1M 105
Boulsworth Dr. BB8: Traw . . . 1F 106
Boulsworth Gro. BB8: Colne . . . 6D 86
Boulsworth Rd. BB8: Traw . . . 1F 106
Boulview Ter. BB8: Colne . . . 6D 86
Boundary Cl. PR4: New L . . . 8C 134
PR7: E'ton . . . 7E 172
Boundary Ct. FY3: Blackp . . . 1G 89
Boundary Edge BL0: Eden . . . 3K 181
Boundary La. FY6: Stal . . . 5G 56
L33: Kirk . . . 8C 224
L40: Burs . . . 9D 190
L40: Burs, Ruff . . . 4C 190
PR3: Pill . . . 5G 56
PR4: Hesk B . . . 6C 150
PR4: Hesk B, Tarl . . . 2J 169
WN6: Wrigh . . . 1K 213
Boundary Meanygate PR4: Hesk B . . . 8L 149
Boundary Mill BB8: Colne . . . 7M 85
Boundary Retail Pk. BB8: Colne . . . 8L 85
Boundary Rd. BB5: Acc . . . 1B 142
FY8: L Ann . . . 3D 130
LA1: Lanc . . . 9D 228 (1K 29)
PR2: Fulw . . . 6G 115
Boundary St. BB8: Colne . . . 7A 86
BB10: Burnl . . . 8G 104
OL11: Roch . . . 7B 204
OL15: Littleb . . . 8K 185
PR8: S'port . . . 1H 187
PR25: Leyl . . . 5L 153
Boundary Wlk. OL11: Roch . . . 8B 204
Bourbles La. FY6: Pree . . . 9C 42
Bourne Brow PR3: Inglew . . . 6H 69
Bourne May Rd. FY6: K Sea . . . 7K 41
Bournemouth Rd. FY4: Blackp . . . 3B 108
Bourne Rd. FY5: T Clev . . . 7G 55
Bournesfield PR5: Hogh . . . 7G 136
Bourne's Row PR5: Hogh . . . 7G 137
Bourne Way FY5: T Clev . . . 8F 54
Bouverie St. PR1: Prest . . . 8A 116
Bovington Av. FY5: T Clev . . . 3F 62
Bow Brook Rd. PR25: Leyl . . . 6L 153
Bowden Av. BB2: Pleas . . . 7D 138
Bowen St. BB2: Blackb . . . 6J 139
Bower Av. OL12: Roch . . . 1G 204
Bower Cl. BB2: Blackb . . . 6J 139
BOWERHAM . . . 1L 29
Bowerham La. LA1: Lanc . . . 4M 29
Bowerham Rd. LA1: Lanc . . . 9E 228 (1L 29)
Bowerham Ter. LA1: Lanc . . . 9E 228
Bowers, The PR7: Chor . . . 9F 174
Bowers La. PR3: Nateby . . . 5J 59
Bower St. BB2: Blackb . . . 6J 139
BL9: Bury . . . 9A 202
Bowes Cl. BL8: Bury . . . 8G 200
Bowes Lyon Pl. FY8: L Ann . . . 1J 129
Bowfell Av. LA4: Morec . . . 3D 22
Bowfell Cl. FY4: Blackp . . . 9K 89
Bowfield's La. BB2: Bald . . . 5A 118
BOWGREAVE . . . 8A 60
Bowgreave Cl. FY4: Blackp . . . 3F 108
Bowgreave Dr. PR3: Bowg . . . 8A 60
Bow Hills La. BB7: Pay . . . 6B 52
Bowker Cl. OL11: Roch . . . 4J 203
BOWKER'S GREEN . . . 6J 217
Bowker's Grn. La.
L39: Aug, Bick . . . 6J 217
Bowker St. BL0: Ramsb . . . 1H 181
Bowland Av. BB10: Burnl . . . 4J 125
FY7: Flee . . . 4D 54
PR6: Chor . . . 6F 174
Bowland Av. E. LA1: Bail . . . 7M 29
Bowland Cl. LA5: Carn . . . 9N 11
PR3: Longr . . . 2K 97
Bowland Ct. BB7: Clith . . . 3L 81
PR9: S'port . . . 6J 167
(off Gordon St.)
Bowland Cres. FY3: Blackp . . . 2G 89
Bowland Dr. LA1: Lanc . . . 6H 23
Bowland Forest Gliding Club . . . 5D 70
Bowland Ga. La. BB7: West B . . . 4L 73
Bowland Gro. OL16: Milnr . . . 9J 205
Bowland Ho. BB1: Blackb . . . 2E 226
Bowland Pl. FY8: L Ann . . . 1J 129
PR2: Ribb . . . 6C 116
Bowland Rd. LA3: Heys . . . 8M 21
PR2: Ribb . . . 6C 116
PR3: Cab . . . 3N 59
Bowlands Av. Sth. LA1: Bail . . . 8L 29
Bowland Vw. BB9: Brierf . . . 6H 105
LA2: Glas . . . 1C 36
PR2: Fulw . . . 2C 116
PR3: Cab . . . 3N 59
Bowland Vw. Cl. FY6: Stal . . . 6C 56
Bowland Vw. Holiday Home Pk. LA3: Midd . . . 6L 27
Bowland Vis. Cen. . . . 6A 70
Bowland Wild Boar Pk. . . . 4K 71
Bow La. PR1: Prest . . . 6G 229 (1H 135)
PR25: Leyl . . . 6L 153
Bowlers Cl. PR2: Fulw . . . 4M 115
Bowlers Wlk. OL12: Roch . . . 3C 204
Bowlers Wood OL13: Bac . . . 7G 163
Bowling Ct. BL1: Bolt . . . 8E 198
Bowlingfield PR2: Ingol . . . 3D 114
Bowling Grn. BL0: Eden . . . 3J 181
Bowling Grn., The *BB3: Darw . . . 4M 157*
(off Oldfield Av.)
Bowling Grn. Cl. BB3: Darw . . . 9A 158
PR8: S'port . . . 9M 167
Bowling Grn. Cotts. BB6: Old L . . . 4C 100
Bowling Grn. Mobile Home Pk. LA5: Carn . . . 9N 11
Bowling Grn. Way OL11: Roch . . . 6K 203
Bowlplex
Blackburn . . . 5E 226 (4N 139)
Bowman Ct. BB1: Blackb . . . 2F 226
Bowness Av. BB9: Nelson . . . 4J 105
FY4: Blackp . . . 1J 109
FY5: T Clev . . . 1H 63
FY7: Flee . . . 3C 54
FY8: L Ann . . . 7F 108
OL12: Roch . . . 4N 203
PR8: Ains . . . 1C 206
Bowness Cl. BB1: Blackb . . . 2A 140
Bowness Rd. BB12: Padi . . . 8H 103
LA1: Lanc . . . 7L 23
PR1: Prest . . . 8C 116
Bowood Ct. FY3: Blackp . . . 3H 89
Bowran St. PR1: Prest . . . 5J 229 (9H 115)
Bowskills Yd. *BD24: Sett . . . 3N 35*
(off Castlebergh La.)
Bowstone Hill Rd. BL2: Bolt . . . 8A 200
Bow St. PR25: Leyl . . . 5L 153
Bow Wood Cl. PR7: Chor . . . 8B 174
Boxer Pl. PR26: Leyl . . . 4F 152
Box St. BL0: Ramsb . . . 8J 181
OL15: Littleb . . . 9K 185
Boxwood Dr. BB2: Blackb . . . 8G 138
Boxwood St. BB1: Blackb . . . 9N 119
Boyer Av. L31: Magh . . . 3C 222
Boyes Av. PR3: Catt . . . 1A 68
Boyes Brow L33: Kirk . . . 6J 223
Boyes Ct. L31: Magh . . . 3C 222
Boyle St. BB1: Blackb . . . 1E 226 (2N 139)
Boys La. PR2: Fulw . . . 4F 114
Brabazon Pl. WN5: Wigan . . . 3M 221
Brabiner La. PR2: Goos, Haigh . . . 7D 96
PR3: W'ham . . . 7D 96
Brabin's Gallery . . . 5G 70
Bracebridge Dr. PR8: S'port . . . 3M 187
BRACEWELL . . . 9E 52
Bracewell Av. FY6: Poul F . . . 8N 63
Bracewell Cl. BB9: Nelson . . . 2J 105
Bracewell La. BB18: Barnw . . . 9D 52
BD23: Brac . . . 9D 52
Bracewell Rd. PR2: Ribb . . . 4A 116
Bracewell St. BB9: Nelson . . . 2J 105
BB10: Burnl . . . 9F 104
BB18: Barnw . . . 1M 77
Brackenber Cl. BD24: Gig . . . 3M 35
Brackenber La. BD24: Gig . . . 4M 35
Brackenbury Cl. PR5: Lost H . . . 9K 135
Brackenbury Rd. PR1: Prest . . . 1H 229 (6H 115)
PR2: Fulw . . . 6H 115
Brackenbury St. PR1: Prest . . . 1J 229 (7J 115)
Bracken Cl. BB2: Blackb . . . 8G 138
BL1: Bolt . . . 7D 198
PR6: Chor . . . 6G 174
Brackendale BB5: Acc . . . 7K 139
Bracken Dr. PR4: Frec . . . 1B 132
Bracken Gro. BB4: Hasl . . . 7F 160
Bracken Hey BB7: Clith . . . 3N 81
Brackenhurst Grn. L33: Kirk . . . 8K 223
Brackenlea Fold OL12: Roch . . . 3M 203
Brackenthwaite Rd. LA5: Yea R . . . 3L 5
LA7: Slack H . . . 3L 5
Bracken Wlk. *L32: Kirk . . . 9J 223*
(off Wervin Rd.)
Bracken Way FY2: Blackp . . . 9D 62
Brackenway L37: Form . . . 6A 206
Bracknell Av. L32: Kirk . . . 9J 223
Bracknell Cl. L32: Kirk . . . 9J 223
Bracknel Way L39: Aug . . . 2F 216
Braconash Rd. PR25: Leyl . . . 5H 153
Bradda Rd. BB2: Blackb . . . 7M 139
Braddocks Cl. OL12: Roch . . . 1G 205
Braddon Cl. LA4: Morec . . . 5C 22
Braddon St. PR1: Prest . . . 8N 115
Brades Av. FY5: T Clev . . . 1K 63
Brades La. PR4: Frec . . . 1B 132
Brade St. PR9: S'port . . . 2B 168
Bradfield Av. L10: Aint . . . 7B 222
Bradford Av. PR7: Chor . . . 2D 194
Bradford Gro. LA3: Heys . . . 1L 27
Bradford St. BB5: Acc . . . 2C 142
Bradkirk La. PR5: Bam B . . . 8D 136
Bradkirk Pl. PR5: Bam B . . . 9C 136
Bradley Ct. PR3: T'ley . . . 7K 71
Bradley Fold BB9: Nelson . . . 1J 105
Bradley Gdns. BB12: Burnl . . . 4N 123
Bradley Hall Rd. BB9: Nelson . . . 1K 105
Bradley La. OL16: Milnr . . . 9L 205
PR7: E'ton . . . 8F 172
WN1: Stand . . . 9C 194
Bradley Pl. *PR8: S'port . . . 7H 167*
(off Eastbank St.)
Bradley Rd. E. BB9: Nelson . . . 1J 105
Bradley Rd. W. BB9: Nelson . . . 1J 105
Bradley Smithy Cl. OL12: Roch . . . 3B 204
Bradley St. BB8: Colne . . . 6C 86
OL16: Milnr . . . 9L 205
PR9: S'port . . . 6J 167
Bradley Vw. BB9: Nelson . . . 1J 105
Bradman Rd. L33: Know P . . . 7A 224
BRADSHAW . . . 8J 199
Bradshaw Brow BL2: Bolt . . . 9J 199
BRADSHAW CHAPEL . . . 8K 199
Bradshaw Cl. BB1: Blackb . . . 9M 119
BB9: Nelson . . . 3J 105
WN6: Stand . . . 3N 213
Bradshawgate Dr. LA5: Silv . . . 7F 4
Bradshaw Hall Dr. BL2: Bolt . . . 7J 199
Bradshaw Hall Fold BL2: Bolt . . . 7K 199
Bradshaw La. L40: Mawd . . . 3B 192
PR3: Pill . . . 9K 43
PR4: Greenh . . . 7G 91
PR6: Adl . . . 5J 195
(Derby Pl.)
PR6: Adl . . . 5H 195
(Maytree Ct.)
WN8: Parb . . . 3N 211
Bradshaw Mdws. BL2: Bolt . . . 7K 199
Bradshaw Mill *BL2: Bolt . . . 8J 199*
(off Maple St.)
Bradshaw Rd. BL2: Bolt . . . 8K 199
BL7: Turt . . . 8K 199
BL8: Tott . . . 7B 200
Bradshaw Row BB5: Chur . . . 2M 141
Bradshaws Brow L40: Mawd . . . 4B 192
Bradshaws Cl. FY6: Stal . . . 5B 56
Bradshaw's La. PR8: Ains . . . 7D 186
Bradshaw St. BB5: Chur . . . 2M 141
BB9: Nelson . . . 3H 105
LA1: Lanc . . . 9F 228 (9L 23)
OL16: Roch . . . 5D 204
WN5: Orr . . . 5K 221
Bradshaw St. E. BB5: Acc . . . 2B 142
Bradshaw St. W. BB5: Acc . . . 2M 141
Bradwood Ct. BB4: Hasl . . . 5E 160
Bradyll Ct. BB6: Old L . . . 4C 100
Brady St. BL6: Hor . . . 9B 196
Braefield Cres. PR2: Ribb . . . 7B 116
Braemar Av. FY5: T Clev . . . 4J 63
PR9: S'port . . . 4M 167
(not continuous)
Braemar Ct. LA4: Morec . . . 4D 22
Braemar Wlk. FY2: Blackp . . . 5F 62
Braemore Ct. WN3: Wins . . . 9N 221
Braeside BB2: Blackb . . . 2K 139
Braeside La. BB3: Darw . . . 9A 158
Braganza Way LA1: Lanc . . . 8G 22
Braid Cl. PR1: Penw . . . 7G 134
Braidhaven WN6: Shev . . . 5H 213
Braid's La. PR3: Barn . . . 5C 60
Braidwood Ct. FY8: L Ann . . . 1D 128
Braintree Av. PR1: Penw . . . 7H 135
Braith Cl. FY4: Blackp . . . 1F 108
Braithwaite WN6: Shev . . . 6K 213
Braithwaite St. FY1: Blackp . . . 3B 88
Brakehouse Cl. OL16: Milnr . . . 7H 205
Bramble Cl. OL15: Littleb . . . 9J 185
PR4: Wesh . . . 3K 111
Bramble Ct. PR1: Penw . . . 6H 135
Bramble Gro. WN5: Wigan . . . 4N 221
Brambles, The BB2: Blackb . . . 9H 119
FY8: L Ann . . . 5B 108
PR2: Fulw . . . 3N 115
PR7: Copp . . . 3B 194
Brambles Cl. BB7: Barr . . . 1K 101
Bramble St. BB10: Burnl . . . 9E 104
Bramble Way L40: Burs . . . 9D 190
WN8: Parb . . . 3N 211
Bramblewood PR26: Cros . . . 4M 171
Brambling Dr. OL13: Bac . . . 6M 163
Bramblings, The FY6: Poul F . . . 9H 63
Bramcote Cl. L33: Kirk . . . 6M 223
Bramcote Rd. L33: Kirk . . . 6L 223
Bramcote Wlk. L33: Kirk . . . 6L 223
Bramdean Av. BL2: Bolt . . . 8L 199
Bramhall Av. BL2: Bolt . . . 9M 199
Bramhall Cl. OL16: Milnr . . . 7H 205
Bramhall Rd. WN8: Skelm . . . 1K 219
Bramley Av. BB12: Burnl . . . 1A 124
FY7: Flee . . . 9E 40
Bramley Cl. BB5: Osw . . . 3M 141
FY4: Blackp . . . 4F 108
Bramley Dr. BL8: Bury . . . 7H 201
Bramley Gdns. FY6: Poul F . . . 9G 63
Bramley Rd. BL1: Bolt . . . 7F 198
OL11: Roch . . . 5J 203
Bramleys, The L31: Magh . . . 3B 222
Bramley Vw. BB7: Barr . . . 2J 101
Bramley Way L32: Kirk . . . 7H 223
Brammay Dr. BL8: Tott . . . 8D 200
Brampton Av. FY5: T Clev . . . 8F 54
Brampton Cl. L32: Kirk . . . 6K 223
Brampton Dr. LA4: Morec . . . 3F 22
PR5: Bam B . . . 7N 135
Brampton St. PR2: Ash R . . . 8F 114
Bramsche Sq. *OL14: Tod . . . 2L 165*
(off Brook St.)
Bramwell Rd. PR4: Frec . . . 2N 131
Bramworth Av. BL0: Ramsb . . . 8G 181
Branch Cl. BL8: Bury . . . 9J 201
Branch Rd. BB2: Blackb . . . 9M 139
BB2: Mellor B . . . 6C 118
BB3: Lwr D . . . 9M 139
BB5: Clay M . . . 6M 121
BB7: Wadd . . . 8H 73
BB11: Burnl . . . 4E 228 (4E 124)
OL15: Littleb . . . 3H 205
Branch St. BB9: Nelson . . . 2K 105
OL13: Bac . . . 7H 163
Brancker St. PR7: Chor . . . 9C 174
BRAND HEALD . . . 9K 149
Brandiforth St. PR5: Bam B . . . 6B 136
Brandle Av. BL8: Bury . . . 9H 201
BRANDLESHOLME . . . 7H 201
Brandlesholme Cl. BL8: Bury . . . 9J 201
Brandlesholme Rd. BL8: Bury, Greenm . . . 4E 200
Brandon Cl. BL8: Bury . . . 8J 201
WN8: Uph . . . 4D 220
Brandon St. OL16: Milnr . . . 7H 205
Brandreth Delph WN8: Parb . . . 1N 211
Brandreth Dr. WN8: Parb . . . 2N 211
Brandreth Pk. WN8: Parb . . . 9N 191
BRANDWOOD . . . 7F 162
Brandwood *BB4: Newc . . . 6C 162*
(off Staghills Rd.)
PR1: Penw . . . 4D 134
Brandwood Ct. BL7: Edgw . . . 9L 179
Brandwood Fold BL7: Edgw . . . 9L 179
Brandwood Gro. BB10: Burnl . . . 3G 124
Brandwood Pk. OL13: Bac . . . 7E 162
(not continuous)
Brandwood Rd. OL13: Bac . . . 7F 162
Brandwood St. BB3: Darw . . . 6B 158
Brandy Ho. Brow BB2: Blackb . . . 9E 226 (6N 139)
Branksome Av. FY5: T Clev . . . 9F 54
Branksome Dr. LA4: Morec . . . 4D 22
Branston Rd. FY4: Blackp . . . 9E 88
Branstree Rd. FY4: Blackp . . . 9J 89
Brant Ct. FY7: Flee . . . 3C 54
Brantfell Dr. BB12: Burnl . . . 1N 123
Brantfell Rd. BB1: Blackb . . . 1L 139
BB6: Gt H . . . 3J 121
Brant Rd. PR1: Prest . . . 8C 116
Brantwood BB5: Clay M . . . 7L 121
Brantwood Av. BB1: Blackb . . . 3E 140
LA4: Morec . . . 2E 22
Brantwood Dr. LA1: Lanc . . . 4L 29
PR25: Leyl . . . 6L 153
Brassey St. BB12: Burnl . . . 2A 124
Brass Pan La. PR3: Brou . . . 5G 95
Brathay Pl. FY7: Flee . . . 2D 54
Bratton Cl. WN3: Wins . . . 9M 221
Braxfield Ct. FY8: L Ann . . . 2D 128
Brayshaw Pl. PR2: Ribb . . . 5A 116
Brays Heys FY5: T Clev . . . 2J 63
Brays Rd. FY8: L Ann, Moss S . . . 7N 109
Bray St. PR2: Ash R . . . 8F 114
Brazil Cl. LA3: Morec . . . 6A 22
Bread St. *BB12: Burnl . . . 3B 124*
(off Redruth St.)
Breakers, The FY8: L Ann . . . 5C 130
Brearlands BD23: T Crav . . . 9J 53
Brearley St. OL13: Bac . . . 7H 163
Brechin Rd. L33: Kirk . . . 8L 223
Breck Cl. FY6: Poul F . . . 6L 63
Breck Dr. FY6: Poul F . . . 6L 63
Breck Holiday Home Pk. FY6: Poul F . . . 6M 63
Breck Rd. FY3: Blackp . . . 3N 227 (6D 88)
FY6: Poul F . . . 7K 63
Breck Row Gdns. BB5: Clay M . . . 6L 121
Breckside Cl. FY6: Poul F . . . 6L 63
Brecon Av. BB5: Osw . . . 4J 141
Brecon Cl. FY1: Blackp . . . 5N 227 (7D 88)
Brecon Rd. BB1: Blackb . . . 3C 140
Bredon Av. PR7: Eux . . . 5A 174
(Grasmere Cl.)
PR7: Eux . . . 5N 173
(Hawkshead Av.)
Bredon Cl. FY8: L Ann . . . 3C 130
PR7: Eux . . . 5A 174
Breeze Cl. BB8: Foul . . . 2B 86
FY5: T Clev . . . 8G 54
Breeze Mt. PR5: Lost H . . . 8M 135
Breeze Rd. PR8: Birk . . . 3E 186
Brenbar Cres. OL12: Whitw . . . 5A 184
Brendale Av. L31: Magh . . . 2B 222
Brendjean Rd. LA4: Morec . . . 4C 22
Brendon Ho. *BB4: Hasl . . . 4G 160*
(off Bury Rd.)
Brendon Wlk. FY3: Blackp . . . 2F 88
Brenka Av. L9: Aint . . . 9A 222
Brennand Cl. LA1: Lanc . . . 6G 22
PR5: Bam B . . . 8B 136
Brennand St. BB7: Clith . . . 2L 81
BB10: Burnl . . . 9F 104
Brennand Ter. *BB7: Grind . . . 4A 74*
(off Main St.)
Brentlea Av. LA3: Heys . . . 9K 21
Brentlea Cres. LA3: Heys . . . 9L 21
Brent St. BB10: Burnl . . . 7G 104
Brentwood FY7: Flee . . . 2E 54
WN5: Wigan . . . 6N 221
Brentwood Av. BB11: Burnl . . . 6C 124
FY5: T Clev . . . 2D 62
FY6: Poul F . . . 8J 63
Brentwood Cl. OL15: Littleb . . . 2J 205
Brentwood Ct. PR9: S'port . . . 5K 167
Brentwood Gro. L33: Kirk . . . 4K 223
Brentwood Rd. BB9: Nelson . . . 1L 105
PR6: And . . . 5K 195
BRETHERTON . . . 1K 171
Bretherton Cl. PR26: Leyl . . . 7F 152

Bretherton Ct.—Bromsgrove Rd.

Bretherton Ct. L40: Burs 1D 210
Bretherton Rd. PR26: Breth, Cros 2M 171
Bretherton Ter. PR25: Leyl 6L 153
Brettargh Cl. LA1: Lanc 1J 29
Brettargh Dr. LA1: Lanc 1J 29
Brett Cl. BB7: Clith 4N 81
L33: Kirk 5J 223
Bretton Fold PR8: S'port 9M 167
Brewery Arc. LA1: Lanc 7D 228
Brewery La. L31: Mell 6D 222
(not continuous)
LA1: Lanc 6D 228 (8K 23)
Brewery St. OL14: Tod 8H 147
PR3: Longr 3K 97
Breworth Fold La. PR6: Brind 4H 155
Brewster St. PR1: Prest 9H 115
BREX 3F 162
Brian Johnson Way PR2: Fulw 3C 116
Briar Av. PR7: Eux 2M 173
Briar Bank Row PR2: Fulw 1K 115
Briar Cl. OL12: Roch 4L 203
Briar Cft. PR4: Longt 9L 133
Briarcroft BB3: Lwr D 1A 158
Briarfield BL7: Eger 3D 198
FY2: Blackp 5F 62
Briarfield Rd. FY6: Carl 5H 63
Briar Gro. PR2: Ingol 5D 114
Briar Hill Cl. BB1: Blackb 5G 226 (4A 140)
Briar Lea Rd. LA6: Neth K 4B 16
Briar M. FY5: T Clev 2J 63
Briar Rd. BB1: Blackb 9N 119
FY5: T Clev 2H 63
PR8: Ains 9D 186
WN5: Wigan 4N 221
Briars, The PR2: Fulw 3N 115
PR8: Birk 4F 186
Briars Brook L40: Lath 1E 210
Briars Grn. WN8: Skelm 8L 211
Briars La. L31: Magh 1D 222
L40: Lath 1E 210
Briar St. OL11: Roch 7A 204
OL13: Bac 6L 163
Briar Ter. OL13: Bac 6L 163
Briarwood PR4: Frec 2M 131
Briarwood Cl. FY5: T Clev 4H 63
PR4: Weet 8E 90
PR25: Leyl 7H 153
Briarwood Ct. FY5: T Clev 4J 63
Briarwood Dr. FY2: Blackp 7E 62
Briary Ct. PR5: Bam B 2E 154
Brickcroft LA2: Glas 2E 36
WN5: Wigan 5L 221
Brickcroft La. PR26: Cros 3L 171
Brickfield St. OL16: Roch 3E 204
Brickground OL12: Roch 3G 202
Brick Ho Gdns. PR3: Chip 5G 70
Brick Ho. La. FY6: Ham 8B 56
Brick Kiln La. L40: Ruff 2E 190
Brickmakers Arms Yd. *L39: Orms 6J 209*
(off Whiterails Dr.)
Brick St. BB11: Burnl 2C 228 (3D 124)
Bride St. OL14: Tod 1L 165
Bridge Av. L39: Orms 7K 209
Bridge Bank PR5: Walt D 2M 135
Bridgebank Ind. Est. *BL6: Hor 9C 196*
(off Emmett St.)
Bridge Bank Rd. OL15: Littleb 2J 205
Bridge Brow LA6: K Lon 6F 8
Bridge Cl. BB4: W'foot 6D 162
PR5: Lost H 8K 135
Bridge Ct. BB7: Clith 1M 81
FY8: L Ann 4C 130
PR5: Lost H 8K 135
Bridge Cft. BB5: Clay M 5L 121
LA5: Bolt S 5L 15
BRIDGE END 8E 160
Bridge End BB7: B'ton 6J 101
BB12: Barl 6A 84
PR5: Lost H 8M 135
Bridge End Cl. BB4: Hasl 8F 160
Bridge End Cotts. *BD24: Sett 2N 35*
(off Langcliffe Rd.)
Bridge End M. *BD24: Sett 2N 35*
(off Church St.)
Bridge End St. OL14: Tod 7F 146
Bridge End Yd. *BD24: Sett 3N 35*
(off Kirkgate)
Bridge Farm Dr. L31: Magh 9E 216
Bridgefield Cl. BB1: Rish 7H 121
Bridgefield St. BB12: Hapt 5H 123
OL11: Roch 6A 204
Bridgefold Rd. OL11: Roch 6N 203
Bridge Gro. PR8: S'port 8H 167
Bridgehall Dr. WN8: Uph 4E 220
Bridge Heywood Caravan Pk. BB12: Read 9A 102
Bridge Ho. L39: Orms 8K 209
LA1: Lanc 6K 23
Bridge Ho. Marina & Caravan Pk.
PR3: Nateby 4L 59
Bridge Ho. Rd. FY4: Blackp 1F 108
Bridge Ho's. BB4: Lumb 1D 162
BB5: Bax 8E 142
Bridge La. LA1: Lanc 6C 228 (8K 23)
(not continuous)
Bridge M. LA6: Ingl 3N 19
Bridge Mill Ct. PR6: Chor 8H 175
Bridge Mill Rd. BB9: Nelson 2G 105
Bridgemill Rd. BB1: Blackb 5E 226 (4N 139)
Bridge Mills BL0: Eden 3K 181
Bridgend LA6: Ingl 2N 19
Bridgend Dr. PR8: Ains 9B 186
Bridgenorth Dr. OL15: Littleb 2J 205
Bridge Rd. BB7: Chatb 7C 74
FY7: Flee 9H 41
FY8: L Ann 4L 129
L31: Magh 3C 222
LA1: Lanc 2K 29
LA4: Morec 3C 22
LA6: Neth K 4B 16
PR2: Ash R 7F 114
PR5: Lost H 8M 135
Bridgeside FY8: L Ann 5B 108
LA5: Carn 9A 12
Bridgeside Ind. Pk. LA5: Carn 8A 12
Bridge St. BB1: Rish 7H 121
BB2: Blackb 5D 226 (4M 139)
Bridge St. BB3: Darw 6A 158
BB4: Hasl 9H 161
BB4: Water 8E 144
BB4: W'foot 8C 162
(Lumb Holes La.)
BB4: W'foot 6D 162
(Prospect St.)
BB5: Acc 2B 142
BB5: Chur 2L 141
BB6: Gt H 4J 121
(not continuous)
BB8: Colne 7N 85
BB9: Brierf 4F 104
BB11: Burnl 2D 228 (3E 124)
BB12: Padi 1G 123
BL0: Ramsb 8H 181
BL6: Hor 9D 196
(not continuous)
BL9: Bury 9M 201
L39: Orms 8K 209
OL12: Roch 2F 204
OL12: Whitw 5N 183
OL14: Tod 2L 165
OL16: Milnr 7J 205
PR3: Gars 5N 59
PR5: Bam B 9A 136
PR5: H Walt 5D 136
PR6: Wheel 8H 155
PR8: S'port 8H 167
Bridge Ter. BB7: Whall 2H 101
PR5: Walt D 2M 135
Bridget St. LA1: Lanc 7D 228 (8K 23)
Bridge Vw. Dr. L33: Kirk 6L 223
Bridge Vw. Gdns. BB3: Darw 4A 158
Bridgewater Av. FY5: T Clev 4F 62
Bridgewater Cl. BB11: Hapt 5L 123
Bridgewater Ct. *BB2: Blackb 4K 139*
(off Bath St.)
Bridgewater Dr. BB1: Blackb 9A 120
PR7: Buck V 9B 154
Bridgeway PR5: Lost H 8M 135
Bridgewills La. PR9: S'port 1B 168
Bridle Dell BL7: Eger 3D 198
Bridle Path, The BB18: Salt 4A 78
Bridle Way L33: Kirk 4J 223
Bridleway BB4: W'foot 5D 162
FY8: L Ann 1L 129
Brief St. BB10: Burnl 1E 124
BRIERCLIFFE 7K 105
Briercliffe Av. BB8: Colne 8M 85
FY3: Blackp 8F 88
Briercliffe Bus. Cen. BB10: Brierc 7K 105
Briercliffe M. FY3: Blackp 8F 88
Briercliffe Rd. BB10: Burnl 9F 104
PR6: Chor 5F 174
Briercliffe St. BB8: Colne 8M 85
Brier Cres. BB9: Nelson 4H 105
Brier Dr. LA3: Heys 9K 21
BRIERFIELD 5F 104
Brierfield PR4: New L 8C 134
WN8: Skelm 5A 220
Brierfield Dr. BL9: Bury 5K 201
Brierfield Station (Rail) 4F 104
Brier Hgts. Cl. BB9: Brierf 5H 105
Brierholme Av. BL7: Eger 4E 198
Brierley Av. FY3: Blackp 4E 88
Brierley Cl. *L30: N'ton 6A 222*
(off Beeston Dr.)
Brierley La. PR4: Woodp 1M 93
Brierley Rd. PR5: Bam B 8C 136
Brierleys Pl. OL15: Littleb 8K 185
Brierley St. PR2: Ash R 8G 115
Briers, The PR7: E'ton 8F 172
Briers Brow PR6: Wheel 8J 155
Briery Av. BL2: Bolt 7K 199
Briery Bank LA5: Arn 2F 4
Briery Cl. PR2: Fulw 5M 115
Brieryfield Rd. PR1: Prest 9G 115
Briery Hey PR5: Bam B 1E 154
Briery Hey Av. L33: Kirk 8L 223
Briery St. LA1: Lanc 7H 23
Brigg Fld. BB5: Clay M 5M 121
Briggs Fold BL7: Eger 3E 198
Briggs Fold Cl. BL7: Eger 3E 198
Briggs Fold Rd. BL7: Eger 3E 198
Briggs Rd. PR2: Ash R 7F 114
Brigholme Pl. BD24: Gig 3N 35
Brighouse Cl. L39: Orms 7J 209
Brighton Av. FY4: Blackp 1B 108
FY5: T Clev 1D 62
FY8: L Ann 1F 128
Brighton Cres. PR2: Ingol 6D 114
Brighton Rd. BB10: Burnl 7G 105
PR8: Birk 2G 187
Brighton St. BL9: Bury 9N 201
OL14: Tod 7F 146
PR6: Chor 6G 174
Brighton Ter. BB2: Blackb 2J 139
BB3: Darw 5M 157
OL14: Tod 7F 146
(off Brighton St.)
Bright's Cl. BB7: Newt 7A 50
Brightstone Cl. PR9: Banks 1G 169
Bright St. BB1: Blackb 2B 140
BB3: Darw 5N 157
BB4: Rawt 4M 161
BB5: Osw 5K 141
BB7: Clith 3M 81
BB8: Colne 6A 86
BB8: Wine 7E 86
BB10: Burnl 9E 104
BB12: Padi 1J 123
BL7: Eger 3D 198
BL9: Bury 9M 201
FY4: Blackp 1B 108
OL13: Bac 5K 163
OL14: Tod 4K 165
OL16: Roch 7D 204
PR9: S'port 7M 167
Bright Ter. BB8: Traw 9E 86
Brigsteer Cl. BB5: Clay M 7L 121
Brimrod La. OL11: Roch 8A 204
BRINDLE 2H 155
Brindle Cl. LA1: Lanc 6G 23
PR3: Longr 3K 97
PR5: Bam B 8D 136
Brindle Ct. PR5: Bam B 6C 136
Brindle Fold PR5: Bam B 9E 136
Brindle Hgts. PR6: Brind 2H 155
Brindle Pl. PR2: Grim 9F 96
Brindle Rd. PR5: Bam B 6B 136
PR6: Brind 1G 154
Brindle St. BB2: Blackb 7K 139
PR1: Prest 9M 115
PR7: Chor 8E 174
Brindley Cl. BB11: Hapt 5L 123
Brindley Rd. L32: Kirk 8H 223
Brindley St. BL1: Bolt 9F 198
WN5: Wigan 6M 221
Brinklow Cl. PR8: Ains 8A 186
Brink's Row BL6: Hor 8E 196
BRINSCALL 8A 156
Brinscall Mill Rd. PR6: Heap 1M 175
Brinscall Swimming Pool 8A 156
Brinscall Ter. PR6: Birns 8A 156
Brinwell Bus. Cen. FY4: Blackp 9H 89
Brinwell Rd. FY4: Blackp 9H 89
Brisbane Pl. FY5: T Clev 4F 62
Brisbane St. BB5: Clay M 8N 121
Bristol Av. FY2: Blackp 7D 62
FY7: Flee 4C 54
PR25: Far 3M 153
Bristol Av. Trad. Est. FY2: Blackp 7E 62
Bristol Cl. BB1: Blackb 5G 226 (4N 139)
Bristol St. BB8: Colne 5B 86
BB11: Burnl 6B 124
LA4: Morec 4C 22
Bristow Av. PR2: Ash R 7E 114
BRITANNIA 7N 163
Britannia Av. OL13: Bac 5L 163
Britannia Dr. PR2: Ash R 1E 134
Britannia Pl. FY1: Blackp 9H 227 (9B 88)
Britannia Rd. WN5: Wigan 3M 221
Britannia St. BB6: Gt H 4J 121
Britannia Wlk. *BB11: Burnl 5F 124*
(off Tarleton St.)
FY8: L Ann 9J 109
Britannia Way BB4: Hasl 7F 160
Britannia Wharf PR2: Ash R 9E 114
Britannic Way FY4: Blackp 1L 109
British Commercial Vehicle Museum, The 6K 153
British in India Mus. 1K 105
British Lawnmower Mus. 9H 167
Britonside Av. L32: Kirk 9L 223
Briton St. OL16: Roch 5D 204
Britten Cl. BB2: Blackb 6A 140
Britten St. BB3: Darw 5N 157
Britwell Cl. BB2: Blackb 8A 140
Brixey St. PR1: Prest 2G 135
Brixham Pl. FY4: Blackp 3B 108
Brixton Rd. PR1: Prest 1L 135
Broad Acre OL12: Roch 3J 203
Broadacre LA2: Caton 3H 25
WN6: Stand 2K 213
WN8: Uph 5D 220
Broadacre Cl. LA2: Caton 3H 25
Broadacre Pl. LA2: Caton 3H 25
Broadacre Vw. LA2: Caton 3H 25
Broadbent Dr. BL9: Bury 9C 202
BROAD CLOUGH 2K 163
Broadclough Vs. OL13: Bac 2K 163
Broadcroft PR4: Longt 7L 133
BROADFIELD
BB5 5M 141
PR25 5H 153
Broadfield BB5: Osw 6M 141
PR3: Brou 8E 94
Broadfield Av. FY4: Blackp 4F 108
FY6: Poul F 8M 63
Broadfield Dr. OL15: Littleb 2J 205
PR1: Penw 6G 134
PR25: Leyl 5H 153
Broadfield Rd. BB5: Acc 5N 141
Broadfields PR7: Chor 4D 174
Broadfields Caravan Pk. LA3: Morec 6A 22
Broadfield Stile OL16: Roch 7B 204
Broadfield St. BB5: Osw 5M 141
OL16: Roch 7C 204
Broadfield Ter. *BB5: Osw 5M 141*
(off Broadfield St.)
Broadfield Wlk. PR25: Leyl 6H 153
Broadfleet Cl. PR3: Pill 7H 43
Broadfold Av. BB1: Blackb 1A 140
BROADGATE 8G 229 (2G 135)
Broad Ga. OL14: Tod 9M 147
(not continuous)
Broadgate PR1: Prest 2G 135
Broadgate Foot Caravan Pk. LA3: Midd 3L 27
Broadgreen Cl. PR25: Leyl 6J 153
BROADHALGH 6L 203
Broadhalgh Av. OL11: Roch 6L 203
Broadhalgh Rd. OL11: Roch 7L 203
BROADHEAD 1L 179
Broadhead Rd. BB3: Pick B 4H 159
BL7: Edgw 4H 159
Broadhey La. WN6: Wrigh 9C 192
Broadhurst La. WN6: Wrigh 6J 193
Broadhurst Rd. FY5: T Clev 3E 62
Broadhurst Way BB9: Brierf 6G 105
Broad Ing OL12: Roch 4N 203
Broad Ing Cl. BB10: Cliv 8J 125
Broading Ter. BB4: Craws 5M 143
Broadith La. PR3: Goos 9N 69
Broadlands PR8: Birk 2E 186
WN6: Shev 6L 213
Broadlands Dr. LA5: Bolt S 6K 15
Broadlands Pl. FY8: L Ann 4M 129
Broad La. BB7: Whall 5H 101
L29: T'ton 9J 215
L32: Kirk 9M 223
L37: Form 5B 206
L37: Gt A 9D 206
L39: D'holl 1A 216
OL12: Whitw 6K 183
OL14: Tod 6N 147
OL16: Roch 9E 204
(not continuous)
PR3: Out R 5H 57
PR3: Winm 8K 45
Broadlea Gro. OL12: Roch 3N 203
BROADLEY 9N 183
Broadley St. BB4: Rawt 4M 161
Broadley Vw. OL12: Whitw 9N 183
Broadmead WN8: Parb 2M 211
Broad Mdw. BL7: Brom C 5H 199
PR3: Chip 5F 70
PR5: Lost H 8K 135
Broad Mdw. La. PR26: Breth 3J 171
Broadness Dr. BB9: Nelson 4J 105
BROAD OAK 4C 142
Broad Oak Av. PR3: Gars 6A 60
Broad Oak Cl. PR6: Adl 5J 195
Broad Oak Grn. PR1: Penw 5E 134
Broad Oak La. BL9: Bury 9A 202
FY3: Stain 5K 89
PR1: Hutt 6E 134
PR1: Penw 4E 134
Broad Oak Rd. BB5: Acc 3B 142
Broadoak Rd. L31: Magh 1D 222
OL11: Roch 7J 203
Broadoaks BL9: Bury 9B 202
Broad Oak Ter. BL9: Bury 9C 202
Broad o' th' La. BL1: Bolt 9E 198
(not continuous)
WN6: Shev 6K 213
Broadpool La. FY6: Ham 2B 64
Broadriding Rd. WN6: Shev 6H 213
Broad Sq. PR25: Leyl 7K 153
Broadstone Cl. OL12: Roch 4L 203
Broadstone Ct. LA1: Lanc 9N 23
Broadstone Dr. PR7: Buck V 8A 154
Broadstone Rd. BL2: Bolt 8K 199
Broadstone St. OL14: Tod 1N 165
Broad St. BB9: Nelson 2H 105
OL14: Tod 1L 165
PR25: Leyl 7K 153
Broadtree Cl. BB2: Mellor 6D 118
BROADWATER 4E 54
Broadwater Av. FY7: Flee 4E 54
Broadwater Gdns. FY7: Flee 4E 54
Broadwater Holiday Cen. FY7: Flee 4F 54
Broadwater Ho. FY7: Flee 3E 54
Broadwater Stop (Tram) 4E 54
Broadway BB1: Blackb 7M 119
BB4: Hasl 7F 160
BB5: Acc 2B 142
BB9: Nelson 2H 105
BL6: Hor 9E 196
FY4: Blackp 2C 108
FY5: T Clev 6D 54
FY7: Flee 4D 54
LA1: Lanc 6K 23
LA4: Morec 2D 22
PR2: Ash R 7C 114
PR2: Fulw 2G 115
PR25: Leyl 7L 153
Broadway Cl. PR8: Ains 8B 186
Broadway Cres. BB4: Hasl 7F 160
Broadway Pl. BB9: Barrf 8H 85
BB9: Nelson 1L 105
Broadway St. BB2: Blackb 7J 139
Broadwood Av. L31: Magh 3B 222
Broadwood Cl. PR1: Penw 4E 134
Broadwood Dr. PR2: Fulw 2H 115
Broadwood Way FY8: L Ann 4L 129
Broche Cl. OL11: Roch 9M 203
BROCK 6D 68
Brock Av. FY7: Flee 2D 54
L31: Magh 9D 216
Brock Bank BB4: Lumb 3D 162
Brockbank Av. LA1: Lanc 8F 22
Brock Cl. LA1: Lanc 5J 23
LA3: Morec 5F 22
Brockclough Rd. BB4: Lumb 3D 162
Brockenhurst St. BB10: Burnl 4G 124
BROCKHALL VILLAGE 4C 100
Brockhole La. BD24: Sett 4N 35
Brockholes Brow PR1: Prest 8C 116
PR2: Prest 8C 116
Brockholes Cres. FY6: Poul F 9L 63
Brockholes Nature Reserve 7E 116
Brockholes Vw. PR1: Prest 1M 135
Brockholes Way PR3: Clau 2B 68
Brockhole Vw. BD24: Sett 3N 35
Brocklebank Rd. OL16: Roch 6G 204
PR9: S'port 5L 167
Brocklehurst Av. BB5: Acc 5A 142
Brocklewood Av. FY6: Poul F 2K 89
Brock Mill La. PR3: Clau 9K 61
Brock Rd. PR3: Gt E 7B 66
PR6: Chor 5F 174
Brock Side PR3: Bils 5E 68
Brock St. LA1: Lanc 7D 228 (8K 23)
Brockway FY6: Poul F 9K 63
Brockway Av. FY3: Blackp 4F 88
Broderick Av. FY2: Blackp 1E 88
Broderick St. BB3: Darw 4N 157
Brodick Rd. BB1: Blackb 5D 140
Brodie Cl. FY4: Blackp 3F 108
Brogden La. BB7: Barnw 4F 76
BB18: Barnw 1H 77
Brogden St. BB18: Barnw 1M 77
Brogden Vw. BB18: Barnw 10F 52
Broken Back La. LA2: Stodd 5J 29
Broken Bank Head BB7: Slaid 3A 50
Broken Banks BB8: Colne 7B 86
Broken Stone Rd. BB2: Fenis 9F 138
BB3: Darw 9F 138
Bromfield OL12: Roch 5C 204
Bromilow Rd. WN8: Skelm 2G 218
Bromley Cl. FY2: Blackp 1E 88
Bromley Ct. *FY2: Blackp 1E 88*
(off Bromley Cl.)
BROMLEY CROSS 6G 199
Bromley Cross Rd. BL7: Brom C 6H 199
Bromley Cross Station (Rail) 6H 199
Bromley Grn. PR6: Chor 2H 175
Bromley Ho. *BB2: Blackb 3K 139*
(off Bromley St.)
Bromley Rd. FY8: L Ann 3E 128
Bromley St. BB2: Blackb 3K 139
PR1: Prest 9G 115
Brompton Av. L33: Kirk 5M 223
Brompton Cl. FY8: L Ann 2K 129
Brompton Rd. FY6: Poul F 1K 89
PR8: S'port 7L 167
Bromsgrove Av. FY2: Blackp 7C 62
Bromsgrove Rd. BB10: Burnl 1F 124

Bronte Av. BB10: Burnl 3H 125
Bronte Cl. OL12: Roch 3L 203
Brooden Dr. BB9: Brierf 6G 105
BB10: Burnl 6G 105
Brook, The L31: Magh 2D 222
OL15: Littleb 5M 185
Brook Av. LA3: Morec 5N 21
PR3: Scor 6B 46
Brookbank *BB9: Barrf 7J 85*
(off Gisburn Rd.)
Brookbottom BL2: Bolt 7L 199
Brook Bldg., The BL7: Eger 3D 198
Brook Cotts. OL16: Roch 6F 204
Brook Ct. BB4: Craws 9L 143
PR2: Ash R 7F 114
(off Blackpool Rd.)
Brook Cft. PR2: Ingol 5E 114
Brookdale BL7: Belm 9K 177
OL12: Roch 2B 204
OL14: Wals 5K 165
PR4: New L 9D 134
PR6: H Charn 4J 195
PR8: Ains 1D 206
Brookdale Av. FY5: T Clev 3E 62
Brookdale Cl. PR25: Leyl 9L 153
Brookdean Cl. BL1: Bolt 9C 198
Brooke Cl. BB5: Bax 6D 142
PR9: S'port 7A 168
Brookes, The PR6: Chor 7G 175
Brookes La. BB7: Whall 5J 101
Brookes St. OL13: Bac 7H 163
Brooke St. PR6: Chor 7F 174
PR7: Chor 7F 174
Brook Farm Cl. L39: Orms 8K 209
BROOKFIELD 4M 115
Brookfield BB2: Mellor 7F 118
L40: Mawd 3N 191
PR26: Cros 3M 171
WN8: Parb 2N 211
Brookfield Av. FY4: Blackp 3G 108
FY5: T Clev 2J 63
PR2: Fulw 5M 115
Brookfield Cl. LA5: Bolt S 4M 15
LA6: Holme 1G 6
Brookfield Ct. PR3: Chip 5G 70
Brookfield Dr. OL15: Littleb 8H 185
PR2: Fulw 1H 115
Brookfield La. L39: Aug 5F 216
Brookfield Pl. PR5: Bam B 1C 154
Brookfield Rd. BL9: Bury 5K 201
FY5: T Clev 1J 63
WN6: Stand 2L 213
WN8: Uph 4E 220
BROOKFIELDS GREEN 6F 216
Brookfield St. BB1: Blackb 1D 226 (2M 139)
OL14: Tod 7F 146
PR1: Prest 2J 229 (8J 115)
Brookfield Ter. FY8: L Ann 4A 130
LA2: Bay H 6B 38
OL14: Tod 7F 146
(off Brighton St.)
Brookfield Vw. LA5: Bolt S 4M 15
Brookfield Way BB18: Earl 3D 78
Brookfold La. BL2: Bolt 9M 199
Brookford Cl. BB12: Burnl 1B 124
Brook Gdns. BL2: Bolt 9L 199
Brook Gro. FY5: T Clev 8E 54
LA3: Morec 5N 21
Brook Hey PR4: Longt 8L 133
Brook Hey Cl. OL12: Roch 1G 204
Brook Hey Dr. L33: Kirk 6L 223
Brook Hey Wlk. L33: Kirk 7M 223
Brookholme Ct. LA1: Lanc 9G 23
BROOKHOUSE
BB1 1D 226 (2N 139)
LA2 2K 25
Brook Ho. PR8: S'port 9J 167
Brookhouse Bus. Cen.
BB1: Blackb 1E 226 (2N 139)
Brook Ho. Cl. BL2: Bolt 9L 199
Brookhouse Cl. BB1: Blackb 1E 226 (2N 139)
BL8: Greenm 5D 200
PR5: Hogh 6H 137
Brookhouse Dr. PR5: Hogh 6H 137
Brookhouse Gdns. BB1: Blackb 1E 226 (2N 139)
Brookhouse La.
BB1: Blackb 2E 226 (2N 139)
Brookhouse Mill La. BL8: Greenm 5E 200
Brookhouse Rd. L39: Orms 6J 209
LA2: Brookh, Caton 2H 25
Brookhouse St. PR2: Ash R 8G 114
Brookland Cl. BB5: Clay M 5M 121
Brooklands BB4: Rawt 6L 161
BB4: W'foot 6D 162
BL6: Hor 9D 196
L39: Orms 6M 209
LA1: Lanc 3L 29
LA6: Bur L 3K 19
OL12: Ward 7F 184
PR2: Ash R 8D 114
PR3: Chip 5G 71
WN8: Uph 3E 220
Brooklands, The PR4: W Grn 5F 110
Brooklands Av. BB4: Hasl 8G 160
BB11: Burnl 6F 124
PR2: Fulw 2H 115
PR4: K'ham 4M 111
Brooklands Ct. OL11: Roch 7N 203
Brooklands Dr. L31: Magh 2C 222
LA3: Heys 1L 27
PR3: Gars 6N 59
WN5: Orr 6G 220
Brooklands Gro. L40: Lath 1D 210
Brooklands Rd. BB11: Burnl 6F 124
BL0: Ramsb 3F 200
FY8: L Ann 2J 129
WN8: Uph 4F 220
Brooklands Ter. BB1: Blackb 1A 140
Brookland St. BB4: Rawt 6B 162
OL16: Roch 9E 204
Brooklands Way FY4: Blackp 2K 109
Brookland Ter. BB4: W'foot 8C 162
Brook La. BD23: Hal W 3B 52
L39: Orms 8K 209
OL16: Roch 9E 204
PR4: Lit H, Much H 4J 151
Brook La. PR4: W Stake 1G 153
(not continuous)
PR7: Char R 1L 193
WN5: Orr 6K 221
Brooklawns PR4: Much H 5H 151
Brooklyn Av. FY3: Blackp 2E 88
OL15: Littleb 7K 185
OL16: Roch 1G 205
Brooklyn Caravan Pk. PR9: Banks 2E 168
Brooklyn Rd. BB1: Clay D 4N 119
Brook Mdw. PR4: H Bart 2C 114
Brook Mill BL7: Bolt 6F 198
Brookmill Complex BB3: Lwr D 9M 139
Brook Mill Ind. Est. PR4: W Grn 5F 110
Brook Pk. L31: Magh 3B 222
Brook Pl. PR2: Lea 7A 114
Brook Rd. FY8: L Ann 4B 130
L31: Magh 2D 222
LA3: Morec 5N 21
BROOKSBOTTOMS 2H 201
Brooksbottoms Cl. BL0: Ramsb 1H 201
Brooks End OL11: Roch 4J 203
Brookshaw St. BL9: Bury 9L 201
(not continuous)
BROOK SIDE 5G 141
Brookside BB4: Rawt 7K 161
BB6: Old L 5C 100
BB7: D'ham 7G 74
BB7: Sabd 3E 102
FY5: T Clev 9J 55
L31: Magh 1D 222
L39: Orms 7K 209
PR4: K'ham 3L 111
PR7: Copp 4B 194
PR7: Eux 4M 173
Brookside Av. WA11: Rain 3J 225
Brookside Bus. Pk. BB4: Rawt 3L 161
Brookside Cen. FY5: T Clev 9J 55
Brookside Cl. BB7: Whall 5J 101
BL0: Ramsb 2F 200
BL2: Bolt 8K 199
PR26: Far M 4H 153
Brookside Cotts. *BB7: Chatb 7C 74*
(off Bridge Rd.)
PR6: Heap 3M 175
Brookside Cres. BB7: West B 5K 73
BL8: Greenm 4D 200
Brookside Dr. LA2: Dolp 6E 38
Brookside Ind. Est. BB5: Osw 5J 141
Brookside La. BB5: Osw 5F 140
Brookside Rd. PR2: Fulw 2G 115
PR8: S'port 4J 187
Brookside St. BB5: Osw 5J 141
Brookside Vw. BB5: Osw 4J 141
Brook's Pl. OL12: Roch 5B 204
Brook St. BB1: Rish 8H 121
BB2: Blackb 6J 139
BB4: Hasl 2G 160
BB5: Osw 5L 141
BB7: Clith 2M 81
BB8: Colne 6A 86
BB9: Nelson 2J 105
BB12: Padi 2J 123
BB18: Barnw 2M 77
BB18: Earl 2E 78
BD23: Hell 1D 52
(off Kendal Rd.)
BL9: Bury 9M 201
(not continuous)
FY4: Blackp 9E 88
FY7: Flee 4E 54
LA1: Lanc 9B 228 (9J 23)
OL12: Ward 8F 184
OL14: Tod 2L 165
OL15: Littleb 9M 185
PR1: Prest 2G 229 (7G 115)
PR2: Fulw 6G 115
PR4: K'ham 3L 111
PR5: H Walt 5D 136
PR6: Adl 4J 195
PR6: Wheel 8J 155
PR9: S'port 2B 168
WN5: Wigan 6L 221
Brook St. Nth. PR2: Fulw 6G 114
Brook Ter. BB4: Lumb 1D 162
OL16: Milnr 9M 205
Brookthorpe Mdws. BL8: Bury 9F 200
Brookthorpe Rd. BL8: Bury 9F 200
Brookvale Ct. PR3: Inskip 8J 67
Brookview PR2: Fulw 4L 115
Brook Vs. BB7: West B 7L 73
Brookville Flats OL12: Whitw 5N 183
Brook Wlk. BL8: Bury 7F 200
Brookward Ct. L32: Kirk 6L 223
Brookwater Cl. BL8: Tott 7E 200
Brookway BB2: Blackb 8J 139
OL15: Littleb 1K 205
PR4: Longt 8K 133
PR4: W Grn 5F 110
Brooky Moor BL7: Edgw 8L 179
Broom Cl. L40: Burs 9D 190
PR25: Leyl 4A 154
Broome Cl. PR8: Birk 2H 187
Broome Rd. PR8: Birk 2H 187
Broom Fld. PR3: Bowg 8A 60
Broomfield Mill St. PR1: Prest 2K 229 (8J 115)
Broomfield Pl. BB2: Blackb 5J 139
Broomfield Rd. FY7: Flee 1F 54
Broomfield Sq. OL11: Roch 8C 204
Broomfield Ter. OL16: Milnr 9L 205
Broom Hill Coppice PR3: Cab 3N 59
Broomholme WN6: Shev 5G 213
Broom Rd. WN5: Wigan 5N 221
Brooms Gro. L10: Aint 8D 222
Broom St. OL16: Milnr 9L 205
Brotherod Hall Rd. OL12: Roch 3N 203
Brothers St. BB2: Blackb 7H 139
Brotherston Dr. BB2: Blackb 8K 139
Brotherton Mdw. BB7: Clith 3M 81
Brougham St. BB12: Burnl 2D 124
Brough Av. FY2: Blackp 9E 62
BROUGHTON
BD23 6N 53
PR3 7F 94
Broughton Av. FY3: Blackp 3E 88
PR8: S'port 1K 187
Broughton Cl. BB2: Blackb 7A 140
Broughton Gro. LA3: Morec 5C 22
Broughton Mill Bus. Pk.
BD23: Brou 7M 53
Broughton St. BB3: Darw 5N 157
BB12: Burnl 3B 124
PR1: Prest 1H 229 (6H 115)
Broughton Tower Way PR2: Fulw 1K 115
Broughton Way FY4: Blackp 2K 109
FY6: Carl 5J 63
Brow, The PR4: Hesk B 3C 150
Brow Bottom BB7: Grind 5B 74
Brow Cl. PR3: Lit E 5M 65
Brow Edge BB4: Newc 6B 162
Browfoot Cl. LA5: Carn 8C 12
Browgate BB7: Saw 4E 74
Browgill Pl. LA1: Lanc 6H 23
Browhead Ct. BB10: Burnl 1F 124
Browhead Rd. BB10: Burnl 1F 124
Brow Hey PR5: Bam B 1D 154
Brow Hill LA2: H Ben 8N 19
Brown Bank Rd. OL15: Littleb 2J 205
Brown Birks Rd. BB5: Hunc 9D 122
Brown Birks St. OL14: Tod 7E 146
Brown Ct. WN5: Wigan 6N 221
BROWN EDGE 3N 187
Brown Edge Cl. PR8: S'port 3N 187
Brownedge Cl. PR5: Walt D 7N 135
Brownedge La. PR5: Bam B 7A 136
Brownedge Rd. PR5: Bam B, Lost H 8K 135
(not continuous)
Brownedge Wlk. PR5: Walt D 7N 135
BROWNHILL 7N 119
Brownhill Av. BB10: Burnl 3G 124
Brownhill Dr. BB1: Blackb 7N 119
Brown Hill La. BB8: Colne 4C 86
HX7: Black H 4N 147
Brownhill La. PR4: Longt 9A 134
Brownhill Rd. BB1: Blackb 6N 119
PR25: Leyl 6J 153
Brown Hill Row BB8: Colne 4C 86
Brownhills Cl. BL8: Tott 8F 200
Brownhill Vw. OL12: Roch 4B 204
Brown Ho. La. PR6: H Wheel 5K 155
Browning Av. BB5: Osw 3J 141
FY5: T Clev 9G 54
FY8: L Ann 4C 130
Browning Cl. BB8: Colne 5A 86
Browning Cres. PR1: Prest 7N 115
Browning Gro. WN6: Stand 9N 213
Browning Rd. PR1: Prest 7N 115
Browning St. BB3: Hodd 6F 158
Brown La. PR5: Bam B 6C 136
Brownley St. PR6: Chor 7G 175
PR6: Clay W 6D 154
Brown Lodge Dr. OL15: Littleb 2J 205
Brown Lodge St. OL15: Littleb 2J 205
Brownlow Rd. BL6: Hor 9C 196
Brownlow St. BB1: Blackb 4D 140
BB7: Clith 4L 81
Brownlow Ter. BB2: Pleas 7D 138
Brownroyd BB18: Earl 2F 78
Browns Hey PR7: Chor 4C 174
BROWNSIDE 3K 125
Brownside Mill BB10: Burnl 3J 125
Brownside Rd. BB10: Burnl, W'thorne 4J 125
Brown's La. FY6: Stal 5L 55
PR4: W Grn 6J 111
Brown Sq. BB11: Burnl 1E 228
Brown St. BB1: Blackb 3D 226 (3M 139)
BB5: Acc 3N 141
BB7: Clith 4K 81
BB8: Colne 7N 85
BB11: Burnl 1C 228 (3D 124)
BL0: Ramsb 9G 180
FY5: T Clev 9H 55
FY7: Flee 1G 54
OL10: Heyw 9H 203
OL13: Bac 3K 163
OL15: Littleb 9L 185
PR5: Bam B 8B 136
PR6: Chor 6F 174
Brown St. E. BB8: Colne 6A 86
Brown St. W. BB8: Colne 7N 85
Browsholme LA1: Lanc 6G 22
Browsholme Av. BB10: Burnl 3G 124
PR2: Ribb 5B 116
Browsholme Cl. FY3: Blackp 2H 89
LA5: Carn 9N 11
Browsholme Hall 3N 71
Browsholme Rd. BB7: Wadd 4D 72
Browside Cl. OL16: Roch 2G 204
Brow St. OL11: Roch 9D 204
Brow Top BB7: Grind 5A 74
Brow Vw. BB10: Burnl 1F 124
Broxholme Way L31: Magh 3C 222
Broxton Av. WN5: Orr 4J 221
Broyd Vw. LA1: Lanc 2K 29
Bruce St. BB1: Blackb 2B 140
BB11: Burnl 4B 124
BB18: Barnw 1M 77
OL11: Roch 9N 203
Bruna Hill PR3: Barn 8B 60
Brundhurst Fold
BB2: Mellor 7E 118
Brunel Ct. PR1: Prest 5H 229
Brunel Dr. BB1: Blackb 5F 226 (4N 139)
Brunel St. BB12: Burnl 2A 124
Brunel Wlk.
BB1: Blackb 6F 226 (4N 139)
Brunel Way FY4: Blackp 2J 109
Brungerley Av. BB7: Clith 2L 81
Brun Gro. FY1: Blackp 9N 227 (9E 88)
BRUNSHAW 4H 125
Brunshaw Av. BB10: Burnl 4G 125
Brunshaw Rd. BB10: Burnl 4G 124
Brun St. BB11: Burnl 2C 228 (3D 124)
Brunswick PR3: Catt 9N 59
Brunswick Dr. BB8: Colne 8L 85
Brunswick Pl. PR2: Ash R 8F 114
Brunswick Rd. LA3: Heys 5M 21
Brunswick St. BB2: Blackb 6A 226 (4L 139)
BB9: Nelson 2J 105
BB11: Burnl 5G 228 (5E 124)
(not continuous)
FY1: Blackp 4H 227 (6B 88)
Brunswick St. *OL14: Wals 8K 165*
(off Beswick St.)
OL16: Roch 5D 204
PR7: Chor 6F 174
Brunswick Ter. BB5: Acc 2A 142
OL13: Bac 7H 163
Brun Ter. BB10: Burnl 4K 125
Brunton Rd. LA1: Lanc 2K 29
Brunton's Warehouse *LA1: Lanc 7J 23*
(off St George's Quay)
Brush St. BB11: Burnl 4A 124
Brussels Rd. BB3: Darw 6C 158
Bryan Rd. FY3: Blackp 2N 227 (5D 88)
Bryan St. BB2: Blackb 9C 226 (6M 139)
Brydeck Av. PR1: Penw 4H 135
Bryer's Cft. BB1: Wilp 3N 119
Bryer St. LA1: Lanc 7D 228 (8K 23)
Bryn Gro. LA2: Hest B 7J 15
Bryngs Dr. BL2: Bolt 9M 199
BRYNING 9H 111
Bryning Av. FY2: Blackp 7C 62
PR4: W Grn 6G 110
Bryning Fern La. PR4: K'ham 5L 111
Bryning Hall La. FY8: L Ann 8E 110
PR4: Bryn 8E 110
Bryning La. PR4: Bryn, Wart, W Grn 6G 111
PR4: Newt 6D 112
Bryning Way PR7: Buck V 1A 174
Bryn Lea Ter. BL1: Bolt 9N 197
Bryony Cl. FY5: T Clev 7F 54
WN5: Orr 6G 221
Bryony Ct. *LA3: Morec 6B 22*
(off Burdock Wlk.)
Buccleuch Av. BB7: Clith 3K 81
Buccleuch Cl. BB7: Clith 3K 81
Buccleuch Rd. BB9: Nelson 1G 105
Buccleuch St. BB11: Burnl 4C 124
Buchanan Ct. PR7: Buck V 9A 154
Buchanan St. BL0: Ramsb 8G 181
FY1: Blackp 4C 88
PR6: Chor 7F 174
Buckden Cl. FY5: T Clev 2C 62
Buckden Ga. BB9: Barrf 8G 85
Buckden Pl. LA3: Heys 8L 21
Buckden Rd. BB5: Acc 4M 141
Buckfast Dr. L37: Form 1B 214
Buckholes La. PR6: H Wheel 6L 155
Buckhurst Rd. BL9: Bury 1M 201
Buckingham Av. PR1: Penw 6G 135
Buckingham Cl. BB4: Hasl 6F 160
WN5: Wigan 6N 221
Buckingham Ct. L33: Kirk 7L 223
Buckingham Dr. BB12: Read 8C 102
Buckingham Gro. BB5: Chur 1M 141
LA3: Morec 5N 21
Buckingham Pl. LA3: Morec 5A 22
Buckingham Rd. FY8: L Ann 4K 129
L31: Magh 2B 222
LA3: Morec 5N 21
LA4: Morec 5N 21
Buckingham St. OL16: Roch 5D 204
PR6: Chor 7F 174
Buckingham Way FY6: Carl 6J 63
Buckland Dr. WN5: Wigan 2L 221
Bucklands Av. PR2: Ash R 7G 115
BUCKLEY 2E 204
Buckley Brook St. OL12: Roch 3E 204
Buckley Chase OL16: Milnr 8H 205
Buckley Cres. FY5: T Clev 4D 62
Buckley Farm La. OL12: Roch 2E 204
Buckley Flds. OL12: Roch 3D 204
Buckley Hall Ind. Est. OL12: Roch 2E 204
Buckley Hill La. OL16: Milnr 8H 205
Buckley La. OL12: Roch 2E 204
Buckley Rd. OL12: Roch 3E 204
Buckley Rd. Ind. Est. OL12: Roch 3D 204
Buckley St. BL9: Bury 9L 201
OL16: Roch 5D 204
Buckley Ter. OL12: Roch 2E 204
Buckley Vw. OL12: Roch 2E 204
OL14: Tod 1K 165
Buckley Wood Bottom *OL14: Tod 2L 165*
(off Doghouse La.)
Bucknell Pl. FY5: T Clev 4E 62
Buckshaw Av. PR6: Chor 2C 174
PR7: Buck V, Chor, Whit W 1A 174
Buckshaw Hall Cl. PR7: Chor 4D 174
Buckshaw Link PR7: Eux 2B 174
Buckshaw Parkway Station (Rail) 2A 174
Buckshaw Ter. BB12: S'stone 8D 102
BUCKSHAW VILLAGE 9B 154
Bucks La. BD24: Gig 3N 35
Buck St. BB7: Grind 5A 74
BB8: Colne 6B 86
BB11: Burnl 4C 124
Buckthorn Pl. FY6: K Sea 7M 41
Buckton Cl. PR6: Whit W 9E 154
Bude Cl. PR4: Cott 3C 114
BUERSIL 9E 204
Buersil Av. OL16: Roch 9E 204
Buersil St. OL16: Roch 9E 204
Buffalo Rd. *PR26: Far M 3K 153*
(off County Cl.)
Buff St. BB3: Darw 7A 158
Bulcock St. BB10: Burnl 9G 104
BULK 7L 23
Bulk Rd. LA1: Lanc 5D 228 (7L 23)
Bulk St. LA1: Lanc 7D 228 (8K 23)
Bull Bri. La. L10: Aint 8D 222
Bull Cop L37: Form 9A 206
(not continuous)
Bullens La. L40: Scar 6C 188
Bullens Rd. L32: Kirk 9L 223
Buller Av. PR1: Penw 4H 135
Buller St. BB4: Rawt 5M 161
LA1: Lanc 5K 23
Bullfinch Dr. BL9: Bury 8A 202
Bullfinch St. PR1: Prest 2N 229 (8L 115)
BULL HILL 3C 178
Bull Hill Cotts. BB3: Darw 3C 178
Bullion, The BB12: Barl 6A 84
Bullough Cl. BB5: Acc 3N 141
Bull Pk. La. FY6: Ham 3B 64
Bullpot Rd. LA6: Cast 5H 9
Bullsnape La. PR3: Goos 8A 70
Bull St. BB11: Burnl 2D 228 (3E 124)

Bulmer St.—Calf Hey Ter.

Bulmer St. PR2: Ash R . . . 7F 114
Bulteel St. WN5: Wigan . . . 5N 221
Bulwer St. OL16: Roch . . . 5D 204
Buncer La. BB2: Blackb . . . 3H 139
Bungalow Camp Site, The
LA3: Morec . . . 6A 22
Bungalows, The BB18: Earl . . . 3E 78
(not continuous)
PR3: Gt E . . . 6A 66
BUNKERS HILL . . . 7M 85
Bunkers Hill Cl. BB2: Blackb . . . 8J 139
Bunker St. PR4: Frec . . . 2A 132
Bunting Pl. FY5: T Clev . . . 2F 62
Bunyan St. OL12: Roch . . . 4C 204
(not continuous)
Buoymasters *LA1: Lanc* . . . *7J 23*
(off St Georges Quay)
Burbank Cl. FY4: Blackp . . . 4F 108
WN3: Wins . . . 9N 221
Burchall Fld. OL16: Roch . . . 6E 204
Burdett Av. OL12: Roch . . . 4K 203
Burdett St. BB11: Burnl . . . 4B 124
Burdock Hill BB18: Salt . . . 5A 78
Burdock Wlk. LA3: Morec . . . 6B 22
Burford Cl. BB2: Blackb . . . 8F 138
FY3: Blackp . . . 3G 89
Burford Dr. LA3: Heys . . . 9M 21
Burgate FY4: Blackp . . . 4D 108
Burgess Av. FY4: Blackp . . . 2E 108
Burgess Gdns. L31: Magh . . . 9B 216
Burgess' La. L37: Gt A . . . 2F 214
Burgess St. BB1: Blackb . . . 3C 140
BB4: Hasl . . . 4G 160
Burghfield Dr. PR7: Buck V . . . 9C 154
Burgh Hall Rd. PR7: Chor . . . 2C 194
Burgh La. PR7: Chor . . . 1E 194
(not continuous)
Burgh La. Sth. PR7: Chor . . . 3D 194
Burghley Brow PR3: Catt . . . 2A 68
Burghley Cl. PR6: Clay W . . . 5E 154
Burghley Ct. PR25: Leyl . . . 6L 153
Burgh Mdws. PR7: Chor . . . 1E 194
Burgh Wood Way PR7: Chor . . . 8B 174
Burgundy Cres. FY5: T Clev . . . 4F 62
Burgundy Dr. BL8: Tott . . . 6E 200
Burholme Cl. PR2: Ribb . . . 7C 116
Burholme Pl. PR2: Ribb . . . 7C 116
Burholme Rd. PR2: Ribb . . . 7C 116
Burleigh Rd. PR1: Prest . . . 1G 135
Burleigh St. BB12: Burnl . . . 1D 124
Burley Cl. L32: Kirk . . . 9L 223
Burley Cres. WN3: Wins . . . 9M 221
Burlingham Pk. PR3: Gars . . . 3M 59
Burlington Av. L37: Form . . . 9B 206
LA4: Morec . . . 3D 22
Burlington Cen., The FY8: L Ann . . . 2E 128
Burlington Ct. FY4: Blackp . . . 2B 108
Burlington Gdns. PR25: Leyl . . . 7L 153
Burlington Gro. LA4: Morec . . . 3D 22
Burlington Ho. FY6: Poul F . . . 8K 63
Burlington Rd. FY4: Blackp . . . 3B 108
PR8: Birk . . . 2F 186
Burlington Road Stop (Tram) . . . 3A 108
Burlington Rd. W. FY4: Blackp . . . 3A 108
Burlington St. BB2: Blackb . . . 3K 139
BB9: Nelson . . . 3G 104
OL11: Roch . . . 9D 204
PR7: Chor . . . 7F 174
Burnaby St. OL11: Roch . . . 9N 203
Burnage Gdns. FY4: Blackp . . . 2D 108
Burnard Cl. L33: Kirk . . . 8L 223
Burnard Cres. L33: Kirk . . . 8L 223
Burnard Wlk. L33: Kirk . . . 8L 223
Burnaston Gro. WN5: Wigan . . . 6N 221
Burnedge Cl. OL12: Whitw . . . 4A 184
Burned Ho. La. FY6: Pree . . . 3B 56
Burneside Cl. LA4: Morec . . . 4C 22
Burnet Cl. OL16: Roch . . . 9F 204
Burnfell Rd. LA1: Lanc . . . 6H 23
Burn Gro. FY5: T Clev . . . 8E 54
Burn Hall Ind. Est. FY7: Flee . . . 6G 55
Burnham Cl. BB11: Burnl . . . 4C 124
FY8: L Ann . . . 5C 130
Burnham Ct. *FY3: Blackp* . . . *5E 88*
(off Hollywood Av.)
LA3: Heys . . . 7M 21
Burnham Ga. BB11: Burnl . . . 3A 228 (4B 124)
Burnham Trad. Pk. BB11: Burnl . . . 2A 228
BURNLEY . . . 2D 228 (3E 124)
Burnley Av. PR8: Ains . . . 8D 186
Burnley Barracks Station (Rail) . . . 3C 124
Burnley Central Station (Rail) . . . 1C 228 (2D 124)
Burnley Cl. BB1: Blackb . . . 3B 140
Burnley Crematorium BB11: Burnl . . . 5M 123
Burnley FC . . . 2G 228 (3F 124)
Burnley Golf Course . . . 7D 124
BURNLEY LANE . . . 9F 104
Burnley La. BB5: Hunc . . . 8E 122
Burnley Mechanics & Mid Pennine Art Gallery . . . 3C 228 (4D 124)
Burnley Rd. BB1: Blackb . . . 3C 140
BB4: Craws, Rawt . . . 1L 161
BB5: Acc, Hunc . . . 1B 142
BB5: Alt, Clay M . . . 7N 121
BB7: Gis, Rim . . . 9A 52
BB7: Whall . . . 7M 101
BB8: Colne . . . 9L 85
BB8: Traw . . . 2D 106
BB9: Brierf . . . 5F 104
BB10: Brierc . . . 7J 105
BB10: Cliv . . . 8G 125
BB11: Cliv . . . 8G 125
(Bacup Rd.)
BB11: Cliv . . . 5F 144
(Burnley Rd. E.)
BB11: Dunn . . . 1L 161
BB11: Hapt . . . 8F 122
BB12: Padi . . . 1H 123
BB12: S'stone . . . 7N 121
BL0: Eden . . . 1J 181
BL9: Bury . . . 5K 201
(not continuous)
OL13: Bac . . . 4G 145
OL13: Bac, Weir . . . 2K 163
OL14: Tod . . . 8G 125
PR8: Ains . . . 8C 186
Burnley Rd. E. BB4: Lumb, Water . . . 2D 162
BB4: W'foot . . . 7C 162
BURNLEY WOOD . . . 5F 124
Burnley Youth Theatre . . . 1G 124
BURN NAZE . . . 8H 55
Burnsall Av. FY3: Blackp . . . 1G 88
LA3: Heys . . . 8L 21
Burnsall Cl. BB10: Burnl . . . 7J 105
Burnsall Pl. BB9: Barrf . . . 8G 84
PR2: Ribb . . . 5A 116
Burnsall Rd. BB5: Acc . . . 4M 141
Burns Av. BB5: Osw . . . 3K 141
FY5: T Clev . . . 9G 54
FY8: L Ann . . . 4C 130
Burns Cl. WN5: Bill . . . 9G 221
Burns Ct. OL11: Roch . . . 7J 203
Burns Dr. BB5: Bax . . . 6D 142
Burnside BL0: Ramsb . . . 4J 181
WN8: Parb . . . 2M 211
Burnside Av. FY4: Blackp . . . 1E 108
FY7: Flee . . . 2C 54
PR2: Ribb . . . 6B 116
PR3: Cald V . . . 4H 61
Burnside Rd. OL16: Roch . . . 7F 204
Burnside Way PR1: Penw . . . 5G 134
Burnslack Rd. PR2: Ribb . . . 6B 116
Burns Pl. FY4: Blackp . . . 1F 108
Burns Rd. FY7: Flee . . . 8G 40
Burns St. BB9: Nelson . . . 1H 105
BB12: Burnl . . . 2D 124
BB12: Hapt . . . 5H 123
BB12: Padi . . . 2J 123
PR1: Prest . . . 7N 115
Burns Wlk. BB3: Darw . . . 6B 158
Burns Way BB6: Gt H . . . 5H 121
Burnt Edge La. BL6: Hor . . . 8J 197
HX7: Black H . . . 4N 147
Burnthorpe Cl. OL11: Roch . . . 7J 203
Burnt Ho. Cl. OL14: Tod . . . 1M 165
Burnvale WN3: Wins . . . 9N 221
Burrans Mdw. BB8: Colne . . . 7A 86
Burrell Av. BB8: Colne . . . 5A 86
Burrington Cl. PR2: Fulw . . . 3N 115
Burrow Hgts. La. LA2: Lanc . . . 7K 29
Burrow Mill La. LA6: Whit . . . 9E 8
Burrow Rd. LA2: Lanc . . . 6K 29
LA6: Neth B, O Bur . . . 9F 8
PR1: Prest . . . 3M 229 (8K 115)
Burrow's La. FY6: Ham, Stal . . . 6M 55
Burrow's Marsh Nature Reserve . . . 6L 55
BURRS . . . 7J 201
Burrs Activity Cen. . . . 7J 201
Burrs Cl. BL8: Bury . . . 7H 201
Burrs Country Pk. . . . 7J 201
Burrs Country Pk. Caravan Club Site
BL8: Bury . . . 7J 201
Burrs Lea Cl. BL9: Bury . . . 7K 201
Burrswood Av. BL9: Bury . . . 7K 201
BURSCOUGH . . . 8C 190
BURSCOUGH BRIDGE . . . 8B 190
Burscough Bridge Station (Rail) . . . 8C 190
Burscough FC . . . 8C 190
Burscough Fitness & Racquets Leisure Cen. . . . 8C 190
Burscough Ind. Est. L40: Burs . . . 8N 189
Burscough Junction Station (Rail) . . . 9C 190
Burscough Rd. L39: Orms . . . 6L 209
Burscough St. L39: Orms . . . 7K 209
Burscough Wharf *L40: Burs* . . . *8C 190*
(off Liverpool Rd. Nth.)
Burton Av. BL8: Bury . . . 9E 200
LA1: Lanc . . . 5G 22
Burton Cl. BB3: Darw . . . 7A 158
Burton Ct. FY7: Flee . . . 4C 54
Burton Gdns. BB9: Brierf . . . 5F 104
Burton Hill LA6: Bur L . . . 3K 19
BURTON-IN-KENDAL . . . 5H 7
BURTON-IN-KENDAL SERVICE AREA . . . 6F 6
BURTON IN LONSDALE . . . 3K 19
Burton Pk. LA6: Burt K . . . 5G 7
Burton Rd. FY4: Blackp . . . 1F 108
LA2: L Ben . . . 6J 19
LA6: Holme . . . 1F 6
LA6: Tewit . . . 3D 12
Burton St. BB1: Rish . . . 8J 121
BB11: Burnl . . . 4F 228 (4F 124)
Burwain Fold BB8: Colne . . . 5A 86
Burwain Sailing Club . . . 3N 85
Burwains Av. BB8: Foul . . . 2A 86
Burwell Av. PR7: Copp . . . 5N 193
Burwell Cl. L33: Kirk . . . 7M 223
OL12: Roch . . . 2A 204
Burwell Wlk. L33: Kirk . . . 7M 223
Burwen Castle Rd. BD23: Elsl . . . 8L 53
Burwen Cl. BB11: Burnl . . . 6B 124
Burwood Cl. PR1: Penw . . . 7J 135
Burwood Dr. FY3: Blackp . . . 4G 89
PR2: Ribb . . . 6A 116
Bury & Rochdale Old Rd. BL9: Bury . . . 9D 202
OL10: Heyw . . . 9D 202
Bury Bus. Cen. BL9: Bury . . . 9M 201
Bury Fold BB3: Darw . . . 9A 158
Bury Fold Cl. BB3: Darw . . . 8A 158
Bury Fold La. BB3: Darw . . . 9A 158
Bury La. PR6: Withn . . . 3N 155
Bury New Rd. BL0: Ramsb . . . 8J 181
Bury Old Rd. BL0: Ramsb . . . 4L 181
BL9: Bury . . . 9L 181
Bury Rd. BB4: Hasl . . . 4G 160
BB4: Rawt . . . 9K 161
BL0: Eden . . . 3J 181
BL7: Edgw . . . 8L 179
BL8: Tott . . . 7E 200
OL11: Roch . . . 8J 203
PR8: Birk . . . 2H 187
Bury Row BB7: Sabd . . . 2E 102
Bury Sq. BB3: Darw . . . 4A 158
Bury St. BB3: Darw . . . 6A 158
BB5: Osw . . . 5K 141
Buseph Barrow LA4: Morec . . . 3F 22
Buseph Ct. LA4: Morec . . . 4F 22
Buseph Dr. LA4: Morec . . . 4F 22
Bushburn Dr. BB6: Langh . . . 9C 100
Bushell Pl. PR1: Prest . . . 8L 229 (2K 135)
Bushell St. PR1: Prest . . . 3K 229 (8J 115)
Bushey La. WA11: Rain . . . 9H 219
Bush La. PR4: Frec . . . 2N 131
(not continuous)
Bush St. BB10: Burnl . . . 9E 104
Business Resource Cen.
L33: Know P . . . 9A 224
Bussel Rd. PR1: Penw . . . 6H 135
Butcher Brow PR5: Walt D . . . 3A 136
Butchers La. L39: Aug . . . 6E 216
Bute Av. FY1: Blackp . . . 3B 88
Bute Rd. BB1: Blackb . . . 5D 140
Bute St. BB11: Burnl . . . 6B 124
Butler Pl. PR1: Prest . . . 1K 229 (7J 115)
Butler Rd. FY1: Blackp . . . 6H 227 (7B 88)
Butlers Farm Ct. PR25: Leyl . . . 8G 153
Butlers Mdw. PR4: Wart . . . 2K 131
Butler St. BB1: Rish . . . 8J 121
BB10: Burnl . . . 1E 124
BL0: Ramsb . . . 1F 200
FY1: Blackp . . . 4C 88
PR1: Prest . . . 7J 229 (1J 135)
Butterbergh LA2: H Ben . . . 6L 19
Buttercross Cl. BB11: Burnl . . . 7B 124
Buttercup Dr. OL11: Roch . . . 9M 203
Butterfield Gdns. L39: Aug . . . 9J 209
Butterfield St. BB9: Barrf . . . 8H 85
LA1: Lanc . . . 6C 228 (8K 23)
Butterlands PR1: Prest . . . 9B 116
Buttermere Av. BB8: Colne . . . 5C 86
FY7: Flee . . . 3C 54
LA4: Morec . . . 4D 22
PR7: Chor . . . 8C 174
Buttermere Cl. BB1: Blackb . . . 2F 226 (2N 139)
L31: Magh . . . 1D 222
L33: Kirk . . . 6J 223
PR2: Fulw . . . 5M 115
PR5: Walt D . . . 6N 135
Buttermere Ct. LA1: Lanc . . . 7M 23
Buttermere Cres. WA11: Rain . . . 9K 219
Buttermere Dr. BB5: Osw . . . 3K 141
BL0: Ramsb . . . 7G 181
FY6: K Sea . . . 8M 41
Buttermere Rd. BB10: Burnl . . . 4K 125
LA1: Lanc . . . 7M 23
PR3: Longr . . . 5H 97
WN5: Wigan . . . 4M 221
Butterworth Brow PR6: Birns . . . 8A 156
PR7: Chor . . . 1B 194
(not continuous)
Butterworth Cl. OL16: Milnr . . . 8K 205
PR4: Wesh . . . 3M 111
BUTTERWORTH HALL . . . 8K 205
Butterworth Hall OL16: Milnr . . . 8K 205
Butterworth Pl. OL15: Littleb . . . 8K 185
Butterworth St. *OL14: Tod* . . . *2L 165*
(off Calder St.)
OL15: Littleb . . . 9K 185
Butt Grn. LA6: Kear . . . 4E 8
Butt Hill La. PR3: Clau . . . 9E 60
Button St. PR3: Inglew, Whitec . . . 6L 69
Butts BB6: Gt H . . . 4H 121
BB18: Barnw . . . 2M 77
Butts, The OL16: Roch . . . 6C 204
Butts Avenue, The *OL16: Roch* . . . *6C 204*
(off Stationers Entry)
Butts Cl. FY5: T Clev . . . 8J 55
Butts Gro. BB7: Clith . . . 1L 81
Butts La. LA2: H Ben . . . 6L 19
OL14: Tod . . . 7N 147
PR3: Gt E . . . 6N 65
PR8: S'port . . . 9M 167
Butts Mt. BB6: Gt H . . . 4H 121
Butts Rd. FY5: T Clev . . . 8H 55
BUTT YEATS . . . 8C 18
Buxted Rd. L32: Kirk . . . 9M 223
Buxton Av. FY2: Blackp . . . 7D 62
Buxton Cres. OL16: Roch . . . 9E 204
Buxton Pk. BD24: Langc . . . 1N 35
Buxton St. BB5: Acc . . . 3N 141
LA4: Morec . . . 4C 22
OL12: Whitw . . . 3A 184
Bye La. L39: D'holl . . . 9B 208
Bye-Pass Rd. LA5: Bolt S . . . 6L 15
Bye Rd. BL0: Ramsb . . . 7K 181
Byerworth La. Nth. PR3: Bowg . . . 7N 59
Byerworth La. Sth. PR3: Bowg . . . 7N 59
Byfield Av. FY5: T Clev . . . 4E 62
Byfleet Cl. WN3: Wins . . . 9M 221
Bygone Times . . . 9F 172
Byland Cl. BB12: S'stone . . . 9C 102
FY4: Blackp . . . 4C 108
L37: Form . . . 1B 214
Bymbrig Cl. PR5: Bam B . . . 8A 136
Byre Vw. PR6: H Charn . . . 5H 195
Byrom St. BB2: Blackb . . . 5B 226 (4L 139)
BL8: Bury . . . 9G 201
OL14: Tod . . . 1L 165
PR9: S'port . . . 7M 167
Byron Av. FY5: T Clev . . . 9G 54
FY8: L Ann . . . 4C 130
LA5: Bolt S . . . 4L 15
PR4: Wart . . . 2K 131
Byron Cl. BB5: Bax . . . 6D 142
BB5: Osw . . . 4J 141
FY2: Blackp . . . 5G 62
PR4: Tarl . . . 1D 170
WN5: Orr . . . 4J 221
Byron Cres. PR7: Copp . . . 4A 194
Byron Gro. BB18: Barnw . . . 1L 77
OL11: Roch . . . 7M 203
Byron Rd. BB8: Colne . . . 6C 86
BL8: Greenm . . . 3E 200
L31: Lyd . . . 8C 216
LA3: Heys . . . 5M 21
Byron Sq. BB6: Gt H . . . 5H 121
Byron St. BB12: Burnl . . . 2L 123
FY4: Blackp . . . 9B 88
FY7: Flee . . . 8G 40
PR7: Chor . . . 6E 174
Byron Ter. BB2: Blackb . . . 5J 139
Byton Wlk. L33: Kirk . . . 6M 223

C

Cabin End Row BB1: Blackb . . . 4E 140
Cabin Hill BB2: Pleas . . . 6C 138
Cabin La. L31: Lyd . . . 7M 215
L39: Hals . . . 9J 187
L40: Holmesw . . . 8M 169
PR9: S'port . . . 3D 168
Cabin Stop (Tram) . . . 1B 88
Cable M. *PR9: S'port* . . . *7H 167*
(off Cable St.)
Cable St. L37: Form . . . 8A 206
LA1: Lanc . . . 6C 228 (8K 23)
PR9: S'port . . . 7H 167
CABUS . . . 1M 59
Cabus Nook La. PR3: Cab . . . 8L 45
Cadby Av. FY3: Blackp . . . 8F 88
CADLEY . . . 5F 114
Cadley Av. PR2: Fulw . . . 6E 114
Cadley C'way. PR2: Fulw . . . 6F 114
Cadley Dr. PR2: Fulw . . . 6E 114
Cadogan Dr. WN3: Wins . . . 9N 221
Cadogan Pl. PR1: Prest . . . 8L 229 (2K 135)
Cadogan St. BB9: Barrf . . . 9H 85
CADSHAW . . . 5D 178
Cadshaw Cl. BB1: Blackb . . . 9M 119
Cadwell Rd. L31: Lyd . . . 6A 216
Caernarfon Cl. FY5: T Clev . . . 1K 63
Caernarvon Av. BB12: Burnl . . . 2M 123
Caernarvon Cl. BL8: Greenm . . . 4E 200
Caernarvon Rd. BB4: Hasl . . . 6F 160
Cage La. PR4: New L . . . 8E 134
Cairn Ct. FY4: Blackp . . . 5C 108
Cairndale Dr. PR25: Leyl . . . 9L 153
Cairn Dr. OL11: Roch . . . 7J 203
Cairn Gro. FY4: Blackp . . . 5C 108
Cairns Cl. BB9: Barrf . . . 8G 84
Cairnsmore Av. PR1: Prest . . . 8B 116
Cairo St. BB12: Burnl . . . 3B 124
Caister Cl. WN8: Skelm . . . 3A 220
Caithness Rd. OL11: Roch . . . 8J 203
Cala Gran Holiday Pk. FY7: Flee . . . 5G 54
Calcott St. BB11: Burnl . . . 7C 124
Caldbeck Cl. BB9: Nelson . . . 4J 105
Caldbeck Rd. LA1: Lanc . . . 7M 23
Calder Av. BB3: Darw . . . 3L 157
BB7: B'ton . . . 6G 101
BB7: Whall . . . 3G 100
FY5: T Clev . . . 1F 62
FY7: Flee . . . 2D 54
L39: Orms . . . 9J 209
OL15: Littleb . . . 7K 185
PR2: Fulw . . . 3J 115
PR3: Longr . . . 3J 97
PR4: Frec . . . 3M 131
PR7: Chor . . . 9D 174
Calderbank WN5: Orr . . . 5K 221
Calderbank Cl. PR26: Leyl . . . 6D 152
Calder Banks BB1: Blackb . . . 1D 226 (1N 139)
(not continuous)
Calderbank St. WN5: Wigan . . . 6N 221
CALDERBROOK . . . 5M 185
Calderbrook Av. BB11: Burnl . . . 6C 124
Calderbrook Pl. BB11: Burnl . . . 6C 124
Calderbrook Rd. OL15: Littleb . . . 8K 185
Calderbrook Ter. OL15: Littleb . . . 6M 185
Calder Cl. BB9: Nelson . . . 1H 105
BL9: Bury . . . 5M 201
FY8: L Ann . . . 7F 108
L33: Kirk . . . 4M 223
LA5: Carn . . . 9M 11
PR4: K'ham . . . 4A 112
Calder Ct. BB5: Alt . . . 3D 122
FY4: Blackp . . . 6E 108
Calder Dr. L31: Magh . . . 9E 216
PR3: Catt . . . 1A 68
Calder Gdns. OL15: Littleb . . . 8K 185
Calder Ho. La. PR3: Bowg . . . 8A 60
CALDERMOOR . . . 8K 185
Calder Pl. BB6: Gt H . . . 3L 121
BB7: B'ton . . . 6G 101
WN5: Wigan . . . 4M 221
Calder Rd. BB4: Rawt . . . 3M 161
FY2: Blackp . . . 1C 88
PR6: Withn . . . 6B 156
CALDERSHAW . . . 3M 203
Caldershaw Bus. Cen. OL12: Roch . . . 3M 203
Caldershaw Cen., The OL12: Roch . . . 3M 203
Caldershaw La. OL12: Roch . . . 3L 203
Caldershaw Rd. OL12: Roch . . . 4L 203
Calderstones Dr. BB7: Whall . . . 3G 101
Calder St. BB1: Blackb . . . 1E 226 (1N 139)
BB8: Colne . . . 7N 85
BB9: Nelson . . . 1H 105
BB11: Burnl . . . 2C 228 (3D 124)
BB12: Padi . . . 1H 123
OL14: Tod . . . 2L 165
OL16: Roch . . . 3E 204
PR2: Ash R . . . 9E 114
Calder Ter. BB9: Nelson . . . 2F 104
CALDER VALE . . . 4H 61
Calder Va. BB7: Whall . . . 6J 101
BB9: Barrf . . . 9H 85
Caldervale Av. FY6: Poul F . . . 8J 63
Calder Va. Rd. BB11: Burnl . . . 1B 228 (3D 124)
PR3: Cald V . . . 5G 60
Calder Vw. BB9: Barrf . . . 6J 85
Calder Way LA3: Morec . . . 6F 22
Calderwood Cl. BL8: Tott . . . 7E 200
Caldew Ct. BB5: Hunc . . . 9D 122
Caldicott Cl. OL14: Tod . . . 4J 165
Caldicot Way FY6: Carl . . . 5J 63
Caldwell Cl. L33: Kirk . . . 6L 223
Caldy Dr. BL0: Ramsb . . . 2F 200
Caleb St. BB9: Nelson . . . 1J 105
Caledonian Av. FY3: Blackp . . . 3E 88
Calendar St. BB1: Blackb . . . 4D 226 (3M 139)
Calendine Cl. FY5: T Clev . . . 7F 54
Calfcote La. PR3: Longr . . . 3K 97
Calf Cft. Pl. FY8: L Ann . . . 4N 129
Calf Hall La. BB18: Barnw . . . 2L 77
Calf Hall Rd. BB18: Barnw . . . 2L 77
Calf Hey BB5: Clay M . . . 5M 121
OL15: Littleb . . . 8J 185
Calf Hey Head OL12: Whitw . . . 6A 184
Calf Hey La. OL12: Whitw . . . 6A 184
Calf Hey Nth. OL11: Roch . . . 9D 204
Calf Hey Rd. BB4: Hasl . . . 5N 159
Calf Hey Sth. OL11: Roch . . . 9D 204
Calf Hey Ter. OL14: Wals . . . 6J 165

Calf Wood La.—Cartwright Ct.

Calf Wood La. BD20: Loth 3N 79
Calgary Av. BB2: Blackb 9J 119
Calico Cl. BB5: Osw 4H 141
Calico Dr. PR3: Catt 9A 60
Calico St. BB2: Blackb 7L 139
Calico Wood Av. WN6: Shev 6J 213
California Dr. OL14: Tod 4K 165
Calkeld La. LA1: Lanc 6C 228 (8K 23)
Calla Dr. PR3: Gars 4N 59
Callander Cl. PR2: Fulw 2M 115
Callender St. BL0: Ramsb 8G 181
Calliards La. OL15: Littleb 1J 205
Calliard's Rd. OL16: Roch 1H 205
Callon St. PR1: Prest 9N 115
Callow Cl. OL13: Bac 7M 163
Caltha Dr. BB3: Lwr D 9A 140
Caltha St. BL0: Ramsb 8G 181
Calton Cl. WN3: Wigan 7N 221
Calva Cl. BB12: Burnl 1N 123
Calverley St. PR1: Prest 8N 115
Calverley Way OL12: Roch 1B 204
Calverley Yd. LA2: H Ben 6L 19
(off Mt. Pleasant)
Calvert Pl. FY3: Blackp 2G 88
Cambell's Ct. FY8: L Ann 1E 128
Camberley Cl. BL8: Tott 8F 200
PR8: Birk 9E 166
Camberley Dr. OL11: Roch 7K 203
Camborne Av. LA5: Carn 1N 15
Camborne Ct. FY3: Blackp 8H 89
Camborne Pl. PR4: Frec 2M 131
Cambray Rd. FY1: Blackp 2B 88
Cambrian Cl. BB1: Blackb 6N 119
Cambrian Ct. PR9: S'port 6K 167
Cambrian Cres. WN3: Wins 9M 221
Cambrian Dr. OL16: Milnr 7K 205
Cambrian Way BB4: Hasl 6G 161
Cambridge Arc. PR8: S'port 7H 167
(off Chapel St.)
Cambridge Av. LA1: Lanc 2M 29
OL11: Roch 7L 203
PR9: S'port 4M 167
Cambridge Cl. BB1: Blackb 5F 226 (4N 139)
BB12: Padi 3J 123
PR1: Prest 1H 229 (7H 115)
Cambridge Ct. PR1: Prest 1H 229 (7H 115)
PR9: S'port 4M 167
(off Cambridge Rd.)
Cambridge Dr. BB1: Blackb 4E 140
BB12: Padi 2J 123
PR3: Gars 5M 59
Cambridge Gdns. BB3: Darw 6C 158
PR9: S'port 4M 167
Cambridge Pl. OL14: Tod 2L 165
Cambridge Rd. FY1: Blackp 1M 227 (5D 88)
FY5: T Clev 9C 54
FY7: Flee 1E 54
FY8: L Ann 4K 129
LA3: Morec 5M 21
PR5: Bam B 8B 136
PR9: S'port 5L 167
WN5: Orr 3J 221
WN8: Skelm 2J 219
Cambridge St. BB1: Blackb 5F 226 (4N 139)
BB3: Darw 6C 158
BB4: Hasl 5G 160
BB5: Acc 1B 142
BB6: Gt H 4K 121
BB8: Colne 7A 86
BB9: Brierf 5F 104
BB9: Nelson 3H 105
BB11: Burnl 4B 124
OL14: Tod 2L 165
PR1: Prest 1H 229 (7H 115)
PR7: Chor 7E 174
Cambridge Wlk. PR1: Prest 1H 229 (7H 115)
Cambridge Walks PR8: S'port 7H 167
(off Cambridge Arc.)
Cam Cl. PR5: Bam B 8B 136
Camden Pl. PR1: Prest 8K 229 (1J 135)
Camden Rd. FY3: Blackp 4E 88
Camden St. BB9: Barrf 8H 85
BB9: Nelson 3H 105
Camellia Dr. PR25: Leyl 5A 154
Camelot Theme Pk. 1J 193
Cameron Av. FY3: Blackp 3E 88
Cameron Cft. PR6: Chor 6F 174
Cameron St. BB10: Burnl 9E 104
BL1: Bolt 8D 198
Camforth Hall La. PR3: Goos 4B 96
Cam La. BD23: T Crav 9J 53
PR6: Clay W 3C 154
Cammock La. BD24: Sett 3N 35
Camms Vw. BB4: Hasl 7F 160
Camomile Cl. PR7: Chor 3C 174
Campbell Av. FY3: Blackp 3E 88
Campbell Cl. BB2: Blackb 9K 139
BL8: Bury 9D 200
Campbell Ct. BB1: Blackb 8M 119
Campbell Cres. L33: Kirk 4J 223
Campbell Pl. BB2: Blackb 5J 139
(off Spring La.)
Campbell St. BB1: Blackb 8N 119
BB12: Burnl 2L 123
BB12: Read 8C 102
OL12: Roch 3B 204
PR1: Prest 9L 115
WN5: Wigan 6N 221
Campion Cl. FY5: T Clev 7F 54
Campion Ct. BB5: Osw 4L 141
Campion Dr. BB4: Hasl 7F 160
PR2: Lea 8N 113
Campion Gro. L32: Kirk 6L 223
Campions, The PR2: Lea 8N 113
Campion Way LA3: Morec 6B 22
OL12: Roch 2N 203
Camp St. BB10: Burnl 7J 105
Cam St. PR1: Prest 7M 115
Camwood PR5: Bam B 3D 154
Camwood Dr. PR5: Lost H 7L 135
Cam Wood Fold PR6: Clay W 4C 154
Canada Cres. FY2: Blackp 8E 62
Canada St. BL6: Hor 9C 196
Canal Bank L31: Lyd 4B 216
L40: Burs 7N 189
L40: Lath 2G 210
Canal Bank PR4: Tarl 9F 150
WN6: App B 5F 212
Canal Cl. LA6: Holme 1G 6
Canal Cotts. L31: Lyd 4B 216
Canal Gdns. LA5: Bolt S 3M 15
Canal M. BB9: Nelson 2H 105
(off Carr Rd.)
Canal Pl. LA5: Carn 9B 12
Canalside BB1: Blackb 7F 226 (5N 139)
BB9: Nelson 9H 85
Canalside Ind. Est. OL16: Roch 8E 204
Canalside Warehouse
OL15: Littleb 3H 205
Canal St. BB2: Blackb 7J 139
BB5: Chur 2L 141
BB5: Clay M 7M 121
BB11: Burnl 2B 228 (3D 124)
OL11: Roch 8D 204
OL14: Tod 2L 165
OL15: Littleb 9L 185
PR7: Adl 7H 195
Canal Vw. L31: Mell 7F 222
Canal Wlk. LA1: Lanc 6E 228 (8L 23)
PR6: Chor 6G 175
Canal Way BB5: Alt 6A 122
Canberra Cl. FY5: T Clev 4F 62
Canberra Ct. FY4: Blackp 5E 108
Canberra La. PR4: Cott 5B 114
Canberra Rd. PR25: Leyl 6L 153
WN5: Wigan 3M 221
Canberra Way PR4: Wart 1K 131
Candlemakers Ct. BB7: Clith 3L 81
Candlemakers Cft. BB7: Clith 3M 81
Candlestick Pk. BL9: Bury 9B 202
Cann Bri. St. PR5: H Walt 4D 136
Canning Rd. PR9: S'port 7N 167
Canning St. BB12: Burnl 2D 124
(Princess Way)
BB12: Burnl 1C 228 (2D 124)
(Stanhope St.)
BB12: Padi 2J 123
BL9: Bury 9L 201
Cannock Av. FY3: Blackp 2E 88
Cannock Grn. L31: Magh 1A 222
Cannon Hill LA1: Lanc 9H 23
PR2: Ash R 8F 114
Cannon St. BB5: Acc 3A 142
BB9: Nelson 1K 105
BL0: Ramsb 1F 200
OL14: Tod 4K 165
PR1: Prest 6K 229 (1J 135)
PR7: Chor 6E 174
(off Cleveland St.)
Cann St. BL8: Tott 5C 200
Canon Flynn Ct. OL16: Roch 6F 204
Canon St. BL9: Bury 9M 201
OL16: Roch 3E 204
Canteen Mill Ind. Est. OL14: Tod 8H 147
Canterbury Av. FY3: Blackp 7F 88
LA1: Lanc 1M 29
Canterbury Cl. FY6: Carl 6J 63
L10: Aint 8D 222
L37: Form 7A 206
LA3: Morec 6B 22
OL11: Roch 6L 203
PR3: Gars 5L 59
PR6: Birns 7N 155
PR8: Birk 1F 186
Canterbury Dr. BL8: Bury 9J 201
Canterbury Gdns. PR1: Prest 2J 229 (8J 115)
Canterbury Rd. PR1: Prest 8N 115
Canterbury St. BB2: Blackb 6B 226 (4L 139)
PR6: Chor 8G 174
Canterbury Way PR3: Gars 5L 59
Cantlow Fold PR8: Ains 9A 186
CANTSFIELD 3G 18
Cantsfield Av. PR2: Ingol 5E 114
Canute St. PR1: Prest 2L 229 (8K 115)
CAPERNWRAY 6H 13
Capernwray Diving Cen. 7G 13
Capernwray Rd. LA6: Cap, Over K 9E 12
Capesthorne Dr. PR7: Chor 2D 194
Cape St. BB4: Rawt 5M 161
Capilano Pk. L39: Aug 3H 217
Capitol Cen. PR5: Walt D 3M 135
Capitol Trad. Pk. L33: Know P 8B 224
Capitol Way PR5: Walt D 3M 135
Caplin Cl. L33: Kirk 4K 223
Capricorn Pk. BB1: Blackb 1B 140
Capstan Cl. FY8: L Ann 8E 108
CAPTAIN FOLD 9K 203
Captain's Row LA1: Lanc 7K 23
Captain St. BL6: Hor 9C 196
OL13: Weir 9L 145
Carawood Cl. WN6: Shev 5G 213
Carbis Av. PR2: Grim 1F 116
Carcroft Av. FY2: Blackp 7D 62
Cardiff St. WN8: Skelm 2H 219
Cardigan Av. BB5: Osw 4J 141
BB7: Clith 3K 81
BB12: Burnl 2M 123
Cardigan Cl. BB7: Clith 3K 81
Cardigan Pl. FY4: Blackp 4A 108
Cardigan Rd. PR8: Birk 4F 186
Cardigan St. OL12: Roch 2B 204
PR2: Ash R 8G 114
Cardigan Way L30: N'ton 6A 222
Cardinal Gdns. FY8: L Ann 2K 129
Cardinal Pl. FY5: T Clev 9E 54
Cardinal St. BB10: Burnl 9F 104
Cardinal Vaughan Ct.
OL11: Roch 7C 204
Cardwell Cl. PR4: Wart 3J 131
Cardwell Pl. BB2: Blackb 4C 226 (3L 139)
Cardwell St. BB12: Padi 2J 123
Carey Cl. WN3: Wins 9N 221
Carfax Fold OL12: Roch 3M 203
Carfax Rd. L33: Kirk 6M 223
Carfield WN8: Skelm 5B 220
Carham Rd. BB1: Blackb 9M 119
Carholme Av. BB10: Burnl 3G 124
Carisbrooke Av. FY4: Blackp 2G 108
Carisbrooke Cl. FY6: Carl 5J 63
Carisbrooke Dr. BL1: Bolt 9F 198
PR9: S'port 5M 167
CARLETON 6H 63
Carleton Av. BB12: S'stone 8D 102
FY3: Blackp 1F 88
PR2: Fulw 5N 115
Carleton Crematorium
FY6: Carl 8F 62
Carleton Dr. PR1: Penw 4D 134
Carleton Gdns. FY6: Carl 6H 63
Carleton Ga. FY6: Carl 7J 63
Carleton Rd. BB8: Colne 8L 85
PR6: Chor 2G 175
Carleton St. BB9: Nelson 3J 105
LA4: Morec 4A 22
Carleton Way FY6: Carl 6J 63
Carley St. BB3: Darw 5M 157
Carlile Way L33: Kirk 4L 223
Carlin Ga. FY2: Blackp 9B 62
Carlinghurst Rd. BB2: Blackb 5A 226 (4L 139)
Carlisle Av. FY7: Flee 3D 54
PR1: Penw 4D 134
Carlisle Gro. FY5: T Clev 1H 63
Carlisle Ho. PR1: Prest 7M 229
Carlisle Pl. PR6: Adl 5J 195
Carlisle Rd. BB5: Acc 9C 122
PR8: Birk 3G 186
Carlisle St. BB1: Blackb 6E 226 (4N 139)
BL7: Brom C 5G 198
OL12: Roch 2C 204
PR1: Prest 4L 229 (9K 115)
WN5: Wigan 5N 221
Carlisle Ter. LA5: Carn 7A 12
Carloway Av. PR2: Fulw 4M 115
Carl's Way L33: Kirk 4M 223
Carlton Av. PR6: Clay W 5D 154
WN8: Uph 4D 220
Carlton Ct. BB8: Colne 6M 85
Carlton Dr. PR1: Prest 9N 229 (3L 135)
Carlton Gdns. BB1: Blackb 1C 226 (2M 139)
Carlton Gro. FY2: Blackp 7B 62
Carlton Pl. BB7: Clith 4M 81
Carlton Rd. BB1: Blackb 1C 226 (2M 139)
BB11: Burnl 4A 228 (4C 124)
FY8: L Ann 1F 128
PR8: Ains 7C 186
PR25: Leyl 7J 153
Carlton St. BB9: Brierf 5F 104
OL13: Bac 4L 163
PR2: Ash R 9G 115
Carlton Way FY4: Blackp 3M 109
Carlton Wharf LA1: Lanc 7J 23
(off St George's Quay)
Carluke St. BB1: Blackb 3C 140
Carlyle Av. FY4: Blackp 3B 108
Carlyle Gro. LA4: Morec 2E 22
Carlyle St. BB10: Burnl 7G 105
Carmel Cl. L39: Aug 1J 217
Carnarvon Rd. BB2: Blackb 3J 139
PR1: Prest 1G 135
PR8: Birk 4F 186
Carneghie Ct. PR8: Birk 1F 186
Carnfield Pl. PR5: Bam B 8D 136
CARNFORTH 8A 12
Carnforth Av. FY2: Blackp 6E 62
L32: Kirk 9L 223
Carnforth Brow LA5: Carn 8C 12
Carnforth Cl. BB2: Blackb 7A 140
Carnforth Community Swimming Pool 9B 12
Carnforth Dr. BL8: Greenm 3F 200
Carnforth Heritage Cen. 8A 12
Carnforth Station (Rail) 8A 12
Carnoustie Cl. PR2: Fulw 2E 114
PR8: Birk 1F 186
Carnoustie Ct. PR1: Penw 2D 134
Carnoustie Dr. BL0: Ramsb 9F 180
PR7: Eux 2N 173
Caroline Cl. LA3: Heys 8L 21
Caroline Ct. BB11: Burnl 5N 123
Caroline St. FY1: Blackp 5J 227 (7B 88)
PR1: Prest 8M 115
Carpenters Way OL16: Roch 9E 204
CARR 7G 181
Carradice Cl. BB9: Nelson 2H 105
CARR BANK
BL9 5L 201
LA7 1J 5
Carr Bank BB4: W'foot 9E 162
BL0: Ramsb 7G 181
Carr Bank Av. BL0: Ramsb 7G 181
Carr Bank Dr. BL0: Ramsb 7G 181
Carr Bank Rd. BL0: Ramsb 7G 181
LA7: Arn, Carr B 2H 5
Carr Barn Brow PR5: Bam B 1E 154
Carr Bridge Pk. FY4: Blackp 2M 109
Carrbrook Cl. PR6: Whit W 7D 154
Carr Cl. FY6: Ham 8N 55
FY6: Poul F 9L 63
OL16: Roch 7F 204
PR3: Pill 8H 43
Carr Cft. BB7: Rim 4K 75
CARR CROSS 5C 188
Carrdale PR4: Hutt 6A 134
Carr Dene Ct. PR4: K'ham 4A 112
Carr Dr. PR4: Wesh 3K 111
Carr End La. FY6: Stal 5B 56
Carr Farm Cl. BB4: Rawt 7L 161
Carr Fld. PR5: Bam B 3E 154
Carrfield Vs. OL14: Tod 7D 146
Carr Fold BL0: Ramsb 7G 181
Carr Gate FY5: T Clev 8C 54
Carr Gro. OL16: Milnr 7K 205
CARR HALL 9F 84
Carr Hall Cl. BB9: Barrf 1G 104
Carr Hall Dr. BB9: Barrf 1F 104
Carr Hall Gdns. BB9: Barrf 1F 104
Carr Hall Rd. BB9: Barrf 9E 84
Carr Hall St. BB4: Hasl 2G 160
Carr Head BB8: Traw 9F 86
Carr Head La. FY6: Poul F 9L 63
Carr Hey FY5: T Clev 1G 63
Carr Heyes Dr. PR4: Hesk B 6C 150
Carr Holme Gdns. PR3: Cab 2N 59
Carr Ho. Fold OL14: Tod 1N 165
CARR HOUSE GREEN COMMON 3J 93
Carr Ho. La. L38: Ince B 7E 214
LA1: Lanc 9B 228 (9J 23)
OL14: Tod 1N 165
PR26: Breth 8G 151
Carr Ho. La. WN6: Hesk 5J 193
WN6: Wrigh 5J 193
CARR HOUSES 7F 214
Carriage Dr. OL15: Littleb 7M 185
Carrick M. FY3: Blackp 8H 89
(off Kingsley Rd.)
Carrier's Row BB8: Lane B 5H 87
Carrington Av. BB2: Blackb 8K 139
Carrington Cen., The PR7: E'ton 8F 172
Carrington Cl. OL16: Roch 2G 204
Carrington Gro. LA4: Morec 3E 22
Carrington Rd. PR7: Adl 6H 195
(not continuous)
PR7: Chor 7D 174
Carr La. BB2: Bald 4B 118
BB2: Blackb 2F 138
BB4: Rawt 6L 161
BB4: W'foot 7C 162
BD23: Con C 2H 53
FY6: Ham, Stal 9B 56
FY6: Sing 1A 90
L31: Lyd 6M 215
L40: Lath 9E 190
LA3: Midd 8K 27
OL16: Milnr 7M 205
PR3: Pill 8H 43
PR4: K'ham, Trea 4A 112
PR4: Much H 7L 151
PR4: Tarl 7D 150
PR4: Wart 2G 130
PR7: Chor 9E 174
PR8: Ains, Birk 6F 186
(not continuous)
PR25: Far 4K 153
PR26: Cros 7M 171
Carr Mdw. OL16: Milnr 9M 205
PR5: Bam B 1E 154
Carr Mill St. BB4: Hasl 2G 160
Carr Moss La. L39: Hals 9G 187
Carr Mt. BB4: Rawt 6L 161
Carroll Cres. L39: Orms 5L 209
Carrol St. PR1: Prest 3N 229 (8L 115)
Carron La. PR3: Inglew 7K 69
Car Royd Est. FY6: Poul F 8N 63
Carr Pl. PR5: Bam B 9D 136
Carr Rd. BB3: Darw 7B 158
BB4: Rawt 6L 161
BB4: Water 9G 144
BB8: Colne 5B 86
BB9: Barrf, Nelson 1G 104
BB11: Burnl 6C 124
BB18: Barnw 1L 77
BL6: Hor 8C 196
FY5: T Clev 5D 62
FY6: Ham 1B 64
FY7: Flee 8F 40
OL14: Tod 7C 146
PR4: K'ham 5N 111
PR6: Clay W 5D 154
CARRS 4F 160
CARRS GREEN 3H 93
Carrside BB9: Nelson 1F 104
Carr Side La. L29: T'ton 8G 214
Carrs Ind. Est. BB4: Hasl 4F 160
Carr St. BB1: Blackb 2D 226 (2M 139)
BL0: Ramsb 7G 181
LA3: Heys 9K 21
PR1: Prest 7N 229 (1L 135)
PR5: Bam B 8A 136
PR6: Chor 5G 174
Carrs Wood BB2: Blackb 2G 139
Carr Vw. BB8: Traw 1F 106
CARR WOOD 6H 203
Carrwood Dr. PR4: K'ham 5N 111
Carrwood Gdns. LA2: Gal 2K 37
Carrwood Grn. BB12: Padi 1H 123
Carrwood Hey BL0: Ramsb 1F 200
Carrwood Pk. PR8: S'port 2H 187
Carrwood Rd. PR5: Walt D 5K 135
Carrwood Way PR5: Walt D 5L 135
CARRY BRIDGE 6B 86
Carry La. BB8: Colne 6B 86
Carshalton Rd. FY1: Blackp 2B 88
Carsluith Av. FY3: Blackp 7E 88
Carson Rd. FY4: Blackp 9G 89
Carter Av. BB11: Hapt 5H 123
WA11: Rain 5L 225
Carter Fold BB2: Mellor 7F 118
Carter Pl. BB9: Nelson 1K 105
Carters, The L30: N'ton 6A 222
Carter's La. BB7: Gis 6N 51
Carter St. BB5: Acc 4A 142
BB12: Burnl 2A 124
FY1: Blackp 2J 227 (5B 88)
PR1: Prest 1G 135
Carterville Cl. FY4: Blackp 2G 108
Cartford Cl. PR3: Lit E 5M 65
Cartford La. PR3: Lit E 6M 65
Cartford Pk. PR3: Lit E 5M 65
Cart Ga. FY6: Pree 1A 56
Cartmel OL12: Roch 5C 204
(off Waterhouse St.)
Cartmel Av. BB5: Acc 5N 141
FY7: Flee 3D 54
L31: Magh 9D 216
OL16: Milnr 9J 205
Cartmel Cen., The LA4: Morec 3B 22
Cartmel Cl. PR8: S'port 2M 187
Cartmel Dr. BB12: Burnl 1N 123
L37: Form 1B 214
PR5: Hogh 4G 136
Cartmell Fold FY4: Blackp 4D 108
Cartmell La. FY8: L Ann 1C 130
PR3: Nateby 4F 58
Cartmell Rd. FY4: Blackp 9K 89
FY8: L Ann 4F 128
Cartmel Pl. LA4: Morec 4C 22
PR2: Ash R 7B 114
Cartmel Rd. BB2: Blackb 5H 139
LA1: Lanc 6M 23
PR25: Leyl 7G 152
Cartmel Sth. Av. LA2: Ell 9L 29
Cartmel West Av. LA2: Ell 9L 29
Cartwright Cl. WA11: Rain 4K 225
Cartwright Ct. LA1: Lanc 2J 29
WA11: Rain 3K 225

Carus Av.—Chapel St.

Carus Av. BB3: Hodd .6E 158
Carus Pk. LA2: Halt .3L 23
LA6: Ark .4C 18
Carvel Way L40: Burs .1D 210
Carver Brow PR5: Hogh .4F 136
Carvers Brow PR26: Cros .5M 171
Carwags La. PR3: Goos .6B 70
Carwood La. PR6: Whit W .8E 154
(not continuous)
Caryl Rd. FY8: L Ann .9C 108
Caspian Way LA1: Lanc .3J 29
Casserley Rd. BB8: Colne .5C 86
Casson Ga. OL12: Roch .4B 204
Castercliff Bank BB8: Colne .8N 85
Castercliffe Rd. BB9: Nelson .2M 105
CASTERTON .5G 8
Casterton PR7: Eux .4M 173
Casterton Av. BB10: Burnl .7F 104
Casterton Golf Course .5G 8
Castle, The BB2: Blackb .5C 226
(off Mincing La.)
BB8: Colne .4D 86
OL14: Tod .1N 165
Castle Av. FY6: Carl .5H 63
OL11: Roch .7B 204
Castle Bank LA5: Silv .7G 4
Castlebergh La. BD24: Sett .3N 35
Castle Casino .9B 62
Castle Cl. BB8: Colne .5B 86
Castle Clough BB12: Hapt .4G 123
OL14: Tod .1N 165
Castle Clough Cotts. BB12: Hapt .5G 123
Castle Ct. BB8: Colne .5C 86
LA1: Lanc .6A 228 (8J 23)
PR5: Hogh .6E 136
Castle Cres. BL6: Hor .8D 196
Castle Dr. PR7: Adl .7J 195
Castle Fold PR1: Penw .6J 135
Castle Gdns. Cres. FY6: Carl .6H 63
Castlegate BB7: Clith .3L 81
FY1: Blackp .9J 227 (9B 88)
Castle Gro. BL0: Ramsb .3F 200
LA1: Lanc .6B 228
OL14: Tod .1N 165
Castlehey WN8: Skelm .5B 220
CASTLE HILL .9H 199
Castle Hill BD24: Sett .3N 35
(off High St.)
LA1: Lanc .6B 228 (8J 23)
Castle Hill Cres. OL11: Roch .7B 204
Castle Hill Rd. BL9: Bury .5A 202
(not continuous)
Castle Ho. La. PR7: Adl .7G 195
Castlekeep Ho. BB7: Clith .3L 81
(off Castle Vw.)
Castlekeep Vw. BB7: Clith .2L 81
Castle La. FY3: Stain .5K 89
L40: Lath, W'head .6B 210
OL14: Tod .1N 165
PR3: Gars .6N 59
Castlemere St. OL11: Roch .7B 204
Castlemere Ter. OL11: Roch .7C 204
Castle Mt. PR2: Fulw .2J 115
Castle Pde. LA1: Lanc .6B 228
Castle Pk. LA1: Lanc .6B 228 (8J 23)
LA2: Horn .7C 18
Castle Pk. M. LA1: Lanc .6B 228 (8J 23)
Castlerigg Dr. BB12: Burnl .1N 123
Castlerigg Pl. FY4: Blackp .9J 89
Castle Rd. BB8: Colne .5B 86
CASTLE STREET .1N 165
Castle St. BB1: Blackb .3B 140
BB7: Clith .3L 81
BB9: Brierf .4F 104
BB9: Nelson .2K 105
BB12: Burnl .2D 124
BB12: Hapt .5H 123
BL9: Summ .3J 201
PR1: Prest .2J 229 (8J 115)
PR7: Chor .7F 174
(off Sutcliffe St.)
PR9: S'port .6H 167
Castleton Dr. L30: N'ton .6A 222
Castleton Rd. PR1: Prest .2N 229 (8L 115)
Castleton Way WN3: Wins .9M 221
Castletown Dr. OL13: Bac .7M 163
Castle Vw. BB7: Clith .3L 81
BB18: Barnw .3M 77
OL14: Tod .3L 165
(off Well St.)
Castle Vw. Caravan Pk. LA6: Cap .6K 13
Castle Wlk. PR1: Penw .2F 134
PR8: S'port .8G 166
Castle Walks PR26: Cros .4M 171
Catches Cl. OL11: Roch .5M 203
Catches La. OL11: Roch .4M 203
Cateaton St. BL9: Bury .9L 201
Cat Fold BB8: Foul .2A 86
(off Barnoldswick Rd.)
CATFORTH .6K 93
Catforth Av. FY4: Blackp .9H 89
Catforth Rd. PR2: Ash R .8B 114
PR4: Catf .4J 93
Catharine's La. L39: Bick .1L 217
Cathedral Church of St Mary the Virgin
.4D 226 (3M 139)
Cathedral Cl. BB1: Blackb .5D 226
Cathedral Dr. LA3: Morec .6B 22
Catherine Cl. PR4: Wesh .2L 111
Catherine St. PR1: Prest .9L 115
PR4: Wesh .3L 111
PR7: Chor .8E 174
Catherine St. E. BL6: Hor .9C 196
Catherine St. W. BL6: Hor .8C 196
Cathrow Dr. PR4: New L .9D 134
Cathrow Way FY5: T Clev .1K 63
Catley Cl. PR6: Whit W .1E 174
CATLEY LANE HEAD .1L 203
CATLOW .4N 105
Catlow Closes BB12: Fence .1C 104
Catlow Ct. BB10: S'field .4N 105
Catlow Hall St. BB5: Osw .5L 141
Catlow Holiday Chalets
BB10: S'field .4N 105
Catlow Rd. BB7: Slaid .8B 34
Catlow Row BB10: S'field .4N 105
Catlow Ter. BB7: Barr .1K 101
CATON .2H 25
Caton Av. FY7: Flee .3D 54
Caton Cl. PR3: Longr .2K 97
PR9: S'port .2M 167
Caton Dr. PR25: Leyl .5A 154
CATON GREEN .1M 25
Caton Grn. Rd. LA2: Brookh .2K 25
Caton Gro. FY3: Blackp .3F 88
Caton Rd. LA1: Lanc .7L 23
(not continuous)
LA2: Caton .2E 24
LA2: Lanc .7L 23
Caton St. OL16: Roch .7C 204
Cato St. BL0: Ramsb .1F 200
Cat Tail La. PR8: S'port .4D 188
Cattan Grn. L37: Form .9B 206
CATTERALL .1A 68
Catterall Cl. FY1: Blackp .3D 88
Catterall Cres. BL2: Bolt .7K 199
Catterall Gates La. PR3: Catt .1N 67
Catterall La. PR3: Catt .3M 67
Catterall St. BB2: Blackb .8K 139
Catterick Fold PR8: S'port .2M 187
Cattle St. BB6: Gt H .4J 121
Caunce Av. PR9: Banks .9F 148
Caunce's Rd. PR9: S'port .1G 189
Caunce St. FY1: Blackp .1K 227 (5C 88)
FY3: Blackp .5C 88
Causeway BB6: Gt H .4H 121
BB8: Foul .2A 86
Causeway, The PR6: Chor .6G 175
PR9: S'port .1B 168
PR26: Leyl .9C 152
Causeway Av. PR2: Fulw .5E 114
Causeway Cft. BB7: Clith .2M 81
Causeway Head BB4: Hasl .6F 160
Causeway La. L37: Gt A .2G 215
L40: Ruff .4F 190
Causeway St. BB3: Darw .8C 158
Causeway Wood Rd.
OL14: Tod .3N 165
Causey Foot BB9: Nelson .3G 105
Cavalry Way BB11: Burnl .3B 124
BB12: Burnl .3B 124
Cavell Cl. BB1: Blackb .7B 140
Cavendish Ct. LA5: Bolt S .4L 15
PR9: S'port .5L 167
Cavendish Cres. PR2: Ribb .6B 116
Cavendish Dr. PR2: Ribb .6B 116
WN3: Wins .9N 221
Cavendish Gdns. LA6: K Lon .6F 8
(off Back La.)
Cavendish Mans. FY5: T Clev .8C 54
Cavendish Pl. BB2: Blackb .5J 139
PR5: Walt D .5N 135
Cavendish Rd. FY2: Blackp .8B 62
FY8: L Ann .9D 108
LA3: Heys .5M 21
PR1: Prest .8A 116
PR8: Birk .2F 186
Cavendish Road Stop (Tram) .8B 62
Cavendish St. BB3: Darw .4N 157
BB18: Barnw .3L 77
LA1: Lanc .8H 23
PR6: Chor .7G 174
Cave St. BB2: Blackb .7J 139
PR1: Prest .9N 115
Cavour St. BB12: Burnl .2D 124
Cawsey, The PR1: Penw .7J 135
Cawthorne St. LA1: Lanc .7B 228 (8J 23)
Caxton Av. FY2: Blackp .6C 62
Caxton Rd. PR2: Fulw .1L 115
Cayley St. OL16: Roch .6E 204
Cecilia Rd. BB2: Blackb .6H 139
Cecilia St. PR1: Prest .8N 115
Cecil St. BB1: Blackb .2G 226 (2A 140)
BB1: Rish .7J 121
BB5: Osw .4L 141
BB18: Barnw .1L 77
FY1: Blackp .3C 88
FY8: L Ann .5N 129
OL11: Roch .8C 204
OL15: Littleb .9J 185
Cedar Av. BB4: Hasl .4H 161
BB4: Rawt .5K 161
FY5: T Clev .1E 62
FY6: Poul F .2K 89
FY6: Pree .8N 41
FY7: Flee .4E 54
PR2: Ash R .7D 114
PR4: Wart .2J 131
PR5: Lost H .8L 135
PR7: Eux .2M 173
Cedar Bank Cl. OL16: Roch .6G 204
Cedar Cl. BB1: Rish .9H 121
OL14: Tod .9K 147
PR2: Grim .9F 96
PR3: Gars .4M 59
PR4: Newt .7E 112
Cedar Ct. BB1: Blackb .1N 139
Cedar Cres. BL0: Ramsb .7H 181
L39: Orms .8H 209
PR4: K'ham .5M 111
Cedar Farm Galleries .4N 191
Cedar Fld. PR6: Clay W .5E 154
Cedar Gro. L31: Magh .4C 222
PR4: Longt .7L 133
WN5: Orr .5J 221
WN8: Skelm .2J 219
Cedar Ho. PR7: Chor .8B 174
(off Hunters Wood Ct.)
Cedar La. OL16: Milnr .9K 205
Cedar Rd. LA1: Lanc .8H 23
PR2: Ribb .7A 116
PR6: Chor .4F 174
Cedars, The BL1: Bolt .7F 198
PR4: New L .8C 134
PR7: Chor .1D 194
PR7: E'ton .7E 172
Cedars Cl. BB18: Barnw .3L 77
Cedar Sq. FY1: Blackp .1J 227 (5B 88)
Cedar St. BB1: Blackb .9N 119
BB5: Acc .2B 142
BB11: Burnl .3F 228 (4F 124)
LA4: Morec .4N 21
Cedar St. OL12: Roch .4C 204
OL14: Wals .7K 165
PR8: S'port .1J 187
Cedar Wlk. PR4: Elsw .1L 91
Cedar Way PR1: Penw .5E 134
Cedarwood Cl. FY8: L Ann .4L 129
Cedarwood Dr. PR25: Leyl .7H 153
Cedarwood Pl. LA1: Lanc .9N 23
Cedric Pl. FY2: Blackp .7C 62
Celandine Cl. OL15: Littleb .8J 185
Celandine Wlk. WN3: Wigan .7L 221
Celia St. BB10: Burnl .4G 124
Cemetery La. BB11: Burnl .5M 123
FY6: Pree .4N 55
Cemetery Rd. BB3: Darw .9B 158
BB12: Padi .2H 123
BB18: Earl .2E 78
BL0: Ramsb .1F 200
PR1: Prest .8M 115
PR8: S'port .1H 187
Cemetery Vw. PR7: Adl .7H 195
Centenary Mill Ct. PR1: Prest .9L 115
Centenary Way BB11: Burnl .4C 228 (4D 124)
Central 12 Retail Pk. PR9: S'port .8J 167
Central Av. BB5: Osw .4J 141
BB7: Clith .4K 81
BL0: Ramsb .4J 181
LA1: Lanc .4K 23
OL15: Littleb .8L 185
PR4: Wesh .3K 111
PR5: Hogh .6G 136
PR7: Buck V .8A 154
PR8: Birk .5F 186
Central Av. Nth. FY5: T Clev .9F 54
Central Beach FY8: L Ann .5A 130
Central Bldgs. BB12: Padi .9H 103
(off Factory La.)
Central Dr. BL9: Bury .5L 201
FY1: Blackp .3H 227 (6B 88)
FY8: L Ann .3J 129
LA4: Morec .3N 21
PR1: Penw .4C 134
WA11: Rain .3K 225
WN6: Shev .6L 213
Central Leisure Cen. .6D 204
Central Pier .5G 227 (7A 88)
Central Pier Stop (Tram) .4H 227 (6B 88)
Central Rd. FY5: T Clev .9K 55
Central Sq. BB4: Hasl .4G 160
(off Bury Rd.)
L31: Magh .9C 216
Central St. BL0: Ramsb .8G 181
Central Vw. OL13: Bac .5L 163
Centre Dr. PR6: Clay W .3D 154
Centre Rd. BD20: Loth .6L 79
Centre Va. OL15: Littleb .7M 185
Centre Va. Cl. OL15: Littleb .7M 185
Centro Pk. L33: Know P .9A 224
Centurion Ct. BB1: Guide .9B 140
PR2: Fulw .6J 115
PR25: Far .3K 153
Centurion Ind. Est. PR25: Far .4L 153
Centurion Pk. BB1: Guide .1B 158
Centurion Way BB1: Guide .1B 158
PR25: Far .3K 153
PR26: Far M .3K 153
Century Gdns. OL12: Roch .5C 204
Ceres Way LA1: Lanc .8G 22
Chadderton Ct. PR1: Prest .5M 229
Chaddock St. PR1: Prest .7K 229 (1J 135)
Chadfield Rd. FY1: Blackp .7M 227 (8D 88)
Chad St. BB8: Colne .9L 85
Chadwell Rd. L33: Kirk .6L 223
Chadwick Cl. OL16: Milnr .8K 205
Chadwick Fold BL9: Bury .6L 201
Chadwick Gdns. PR5: Lost H .9J 135
Chadwick Hall Rd. OL11: Roch .7M 203
Chadwick St. BB2: Blackb .8B 226 (5L 139)
BL9: Bury .9C 202
FY1: Blackp .5K 227 (7C 88)
OL11: Roch .6A 204
OL16: Roch .6H 205
Chadwick Ter. OL12: Roch .1A 204
Chadwick Way L33: Kirk .4K 223
Chaffinch Cl. FY5: T Clev .7F 54
Chaffinch Ct. FY3: Blackp .4H 89
Chaffinch Dr. BL9: Bury .9A 202
Chaigley Ct. BB7: Chaig .3A 80
Chaigley Farm Cotts. BB7: Chaig .3A 80
Chaigley Rd. PR3: Longr .2K 97
Chain Caul Rd. PR2: Ash R .9B 114
Chain Caul Way PR2: Ash R .9B 114
Chain Ho. La. PR4: W Stake .9E 134
Chain La. FY3: Stain .5K 89
Chale Grn. BL2: Bolt .9L 199
Chalfont Fld. PR2: Fulw .4F 114
Challan Hall M. LA5: Silv .5K 5
Challenge Way BB1: Blackb .1C 140
WN5: Wigan .1M 221
Chamber Ho. Dr. OL11: Roch .9M 203
Chamberlain Dr. L33: Kirk .5L 223
Chamber St. BB4: Water .8E 144
Chambres Rd. PR8: S'port .9K 167
Chambres Rd. Nth. PR8: S'port .8K 167
Champagne Av. FY5: T Clev .4F 62
Champness Hall OL16: Roch .6C 204
(off Drake St.)
Chancel Pl. BB3: Darw .6C 158
OL16: Roch .6C 204
Chancel Way BB3: Darw .7C 158
Chancery Cl. PR7: Copp .4B 194
Chancery Ct. LA6: K Lon .6F 8
(off Lunefield Dr.)
Chancery La. LA1: Lanc .6C 228
Chancery Rd. PR7: Chor .3C 174
Chancery Wlk.
BB11: Burnl .2D 228 (3E 124)
Chandler Bus. Pk. PR25: Leyl .5H 153
Chandlers Cft. PR4: Hesk B .4C 150
Chandlers Ford FY6: Poul F .6L 63
Chandlers Rest FY8: L Ann .5C 130
Chandler St. PR1: Prest .5J 229 (9H 115)
Chandley Cl. PR8: Ains .8A 186
Change Cl. OL13: Bac .3M 163
Changford Grn. L33: Kirk .7M 223
Changford Rd. L33: Kirk .6M 223
Channel Way PR1: Prest .9F 114
PR2: Ash R .9F 114
Channing Ct. OL16: Roch .7E 204
Channing Rd. FY8: L Ann .4J 129
Channing Sq. OL16: Roch .7E 204
Channing St. OL16: Roch .7E 204
Chanters Way BB3: Darw .2A 158
Chapel Brow BB7: D'ham .7G 74
PR3: Longr .4K 97
PR25: Leyl .5L 153
Chapel Cl. BB6: Old L .4C 100
BB7: Clith .3H 81
BB7: West B .7L 73
BB7: Whall .5J 101
BB8: Traw .9E 86
LA2: Hest B .8H 15
LA3: O'ton .7A 28
LA6: K Lon .6F 8
(off Main St.)
OL14: Wals .9L 165
PR4: Wesh .2L 111
PR25: Leyl .8G 153
Chapel Ct. BB10: Brierc .7L 105
BD23: Garg .3M 53
(off Skipton Rd.)
L39: Orms .8K 209
Chapel Fld. BB8: Colne .7A 86
Chapel Flds. BL7: Turt .1J 199
Chapel Fold BB7: Wis .3M 101
Chapel Gallery, The .7L 209
Chapel Gdns. BD24: Sett .3N 35
(off High Hill Gro. St.)
BL8: Greenm .4C 200
PR3: Catt .1A 68
PR4: Hesk B .3C 150
Chapel Ga. OL16: Milnr .7J 205
Chapel Grange BL7: Turt .1J 199
Chapel Hill BB18: Salt .5A 78
OL15: Littleb .8L 185
PR3: Longr .4J 97
Chapel Hill La. BB4: Rawt .3N 161
Chapel Hill Trad. Est. PR3: Longr .4J 97
CHAPEL HOUSE .2H 219
Chapel Ho. BB1: Rish .8J 121
(off Chapel St.)
L31: Magh .1C 222
Chapelhouse La. LA6: H Cas .6F 8
Chapel Ho. Rd. BB9: Nelson .4H 105
Chapel Ho's. OL12: Whitw .2A 184
(off Oak St.)
Chapelhouse Wlk. L37: Form .9A 206
Chapel La. BB4: Craws .7M 143
BB6: Langh .7B 100
BB7: Grind .4A 74
BB7: West B .7L 73
BL8: Holc .8F 180
L31: Mell .6F 222
L40: Burs .2C 210
L40: Holmesw .9N 169
LA2: Ell .2M 37
LA2: Gal .2L 37
(not continuous)
LA3: O'ton .6B 28
LA5: Arn .1F 4
LA6: Bur L .3K 19
LA6: K Lon .6F 8
(off Main St.)
OL11: Roch .5F 202
PR3: Out R .1F 64
PR4: Catf .5G 92
PR4: Longt, New L .8M 133
PR5: Hogh .6L 137
PR6: Heap .9H 155
PR7: Copp .3B 194
PR9: Banks .8G 148
WN8: Parb .3A 212
Chapel La. Bus. Pk. PR7: Copp .4B 194
Chapel Mdw. PR4: Longt .8N 133
Chapel Mdws. PR4: Tarl .1E 170
Chapel M. BB18: Earl .3E 78
(off Cowgill St.)
L39: Orms .8L 209
Chapel Moss L39: Orms .8K 209
Chapel Pk. Rd. PR4: Longt .8N 133
Chapel Ri. BB7: B'ton .6H 101
Chapel Rd. FY4: Blackp .2G 108
PR2: Fulw .5K 115
PR4: Hesk B .3B 150
Chapel Rd. Residential Site FY4: Blackp .1H 109
CHAPELS .4A 158
Chapels BB3: Darw .4A 158
Chapels Brow BB3: Darw .4A 158
(not continuous)
Chapelside BB10: Burnl .3G 228
Chapelside Cl. PR3: Catt .1A 68
Chapels La. BB3: Tock .5G 157
Chapel Sq. BB18: Earl .2F 78
(off Earlham St.)
LA2: Brookh .2K 25
Chapel St. BB1: Belt .1F 158
BB1: Rish .8J 121
BB2: Blackb .6B 226 (4L 139)
BB3: Darw .7A 158
BB4: Craws .8M 143
BB4: Hasl .4G 160
BB4: Newc .6C 162
BB5: Acc .3B 142
BB5: Clay M .6L 121
BB5: Osw .4L 141
BB7: Slaid .5C 50
BB8: Colne .7A 86
BB8: Foul .2B 86
BB9: Brierf .4F 104
BB9: Nelson .2J 105
BB10: W'thorne .4L 125
BB11: Burnl .2E 228 (3E 124)
BB12: High .5L 103
BB18: Barnw .2M 77
BB18: Earl .2E 78
BD24: Sett .3N 35
BL6: Hor .9D 196
BL7: Belm .9K 177
BL7: Eger .2D 198
BL8: Tott .6E 200
FY1: Blackp .4H 227 (6B 88)
FY6: Poul F .8K 63

Chapel St.—Chislehurst Av.

Chapel St. FY8: L Ann 5N 129
L39: Orms 8L 209
LA1: Lanc 6C 228 (8K 23)
LA2: Gal 2L 37
LA4: Morec 3A 22
OL11: Roch 9D 204
OL12: Ward 7F 184
OL12: Whitw 6N 183
OL13: Bac 7G 163
OL14: Tod 1N 165
OL15: Littleb 4N 185
PR1: Prest 6J 229 (1J 135)
PR3: Gt E 6N 65
PR3: Longr 3K 97
PR6: Birns 7N 155
PR7: Adl 7H 195
PR7: Chor 6E 174
(not continuous)
PR7: Copp 4A 194
PR8: S'port 7H 167
WN5: Orr 5L 221
WN5: Wigan 6L 221
Chapel St. Ct. FY6: Poul F 8K 63
Chapel St. Sth. *OL14: Wals 6K 165*
(off Barnes St.)
Chapel Ter. BB4: Lumb 2D 162
BL0: Ramsb 1H 181
CHAPELTOWN 1J 199
Chapeltown Rd. BL7: Brom C 6H 199
Chapel Vw. BB4: Craws 7M 143
LA3: O'ton 7B 28
Chapel Wlk. BB12: Padi 9H 103
LA5: Wart 4B 12
PR4: Longt 8A 134
PR7: Copp 4A 194
Chapel Walks PR1: Prest 6K 229 (1J 135)
(not continuous)
PR4: K'ham 5N 111
Chapel Way PR7: Copp 5B 194
Chapel Yd. *BD24: Sett 3N 35*
(off High St.)
PR5: Walt D 3N 135
PR7: Copp 4B 194
Chapman Cl. PR3: Gt E 6A 66
Chapman Ct. BB18: Barnw 1M 77
FY7: Flee 1F 54
Chapman La. BB3: Hodd 7F 158
Chapman Rd. BB3: Hodd 6F 158
PR2: Fulw 6K 115
Chapter Rd. BB3: Darw 7C 158
Chardonnay Cres. FY5: T Clev 4F 62
Charity Farm Caravan & Camping Pk.
WN6: Wrigh 5F 192
Charity La. L40: W'head 9C 210
Charlbury Gro. LA3: Heys 9M 21
Charles Av. PR8: Ains 7E 186
Charles Babbage Av. OL16: Roch 9G 205
Charlesbye Av. L39: Orms 6M 209
Charlesbye Cl. L39: Orms 6N 209
Charles Cl. PR4: Hesk B 4C 150
Charles Ct. FY3: Blackp 3D 88
LA1: Lanc 1K 29
(off Charles St.)
PR9: S'port 7J 167
Charles Cres. PR5: Hogh 5E 136
Charles Gro. PR3: Longr 3H 97
Charles La. BB4: Hasl 5F 160
OL16: Milnr 8K 205
Charles M. OL16: Milnr 8K 205
Charles Pl. OL14: Tod 4K 165
Charles St. BB2: Blackb 9A 226 (6L 139)
BB3: Darw 5A 158
BB4: W'foot 5D 162
BB5: Clay M 6L 121
BB5: Osw 5L 141
BB6: Gt H 5J 121
BB8: Colne 6B 86
BB9: Nelson 1H 105
BL7: Eger 2D 198
BL9: Bury 9L 201
FY1: Blackp 1K 227 (5C 88)
LA1: Lanc 1K 29
LA4: Morec 3C 22
OL15: Littleb 9K 185
Charleston Ct. PR5: Bam B 6A 136
Charles Way PR2: Lea 7B 114
Charlesway Ct. PR2: Lea 7B 114
Charles Whittaker St. OL12: Roch 4K 203
Charlesworth Cl. L31: Lyd 6A 216
Charleywood Rd. L33: Know P 9N 223
Charlotte Dr. WN3: Wigan 7N 221
Charlotte Pl. PR1: Prest 7M 229 (1K 135)
Charlotte's La. PR4: Tarl 4C 170
Charlotte St. BB1: Blackb 1C 226 (2M 139)
BB11: Burnl 3B 228 (4D 124)
BL0: Ramsb 9G 180
BL7: Turt 1J 199
OL16: Roch 9D 204
PR1: Prest 7M 229 (1K 135)
Charnley Cl. PR1: Penw 6F 134
Charnley Ct. PR5: Bam B 6B 136
Charnley Fold PR5: Bam B 5B 136
Charnley Fold Ind. Est.
PR5: Bam B 5A 136
Charnley Fold La. PR5: Bam B 5B 136
Charnley Rd. FY1: Blackp 3J 227 (6B 88)
Charnley's La. PR9: Banks 7D 148
Charnley St. BB2: Blackb 6K 139
LA1: Lanc 7H 23
PR1: Prest 6J 229 (1J 135)
Charnock WN8: Skelm 5B 220
Charnock Av. PR1: Penw 6H 135
Charnock Brow PR7: Char R 7M 173
Charnock Brow Golf Course 7M 173
Charnock Ct. PR1: Penw 7K 135
Charnock Fold PR1: Prest 1L 229 (7K 115)
Charnock Gdns. PR1: Penw 7K 135
CHARNOCK GREEN 8M 173
Charnock Ho. *PR7: Chor 4E 174*
(off Lancaster Ct.)
Charnock Moss PR5: Lost H 8J 135
CHARNOCK RICHARD 1N 193
Charnock Richard Crematorium
PR7: Char R 7M 173
Charnock Richard Golf Course 2L 193
CHARNOCK RICHARD SERVICE AREA 1K 193
Charnock St. PR1: Prest 1K 229 (7K 115)
PR4: Wesh 3L 111
PR6: Chor 7F 174
PR25: Leyl 6K 153
Charnock's Yd. WN5: Wigan 6L 221
Charnwood Av. FY3: Blackp 3G 89
Charnwood Cl. BB2: Blackb 9H 119
Charter Brook BB6: Gt H 4K 121
Charter Fold PR7: Char R 2N 193
Charterhouse Ct. FY7: Flee 9D 40
Charterhouse Dr. L10: Aint 8D 222
Charterhouse Pl. BB2: Blackb 5J 139
Charter La. PR7: Char R 1N 193
Charter St. BB5: Acc 3M 141
OL16: Roch 9D 204
Charter Wlk. Shop. Cen.
BB11: Burnl 2D 228 (3E 124)
Chartwell Cl. PR6: Clay W 5E 154
Chartwell Ri. PR5: Lost H 8M 135
Chartwell Rd. PR8: Ains 7B 186
Chasden Cl. PR6: Whit W 1E 174
Chase, The BB12: Burnl 1B 124
FY3: Blackp 3J 89
FY5: T Clev 8G 55
LA5: Silv 9H 5
PR4: Cott 4A 114
PR25: Leyl 5M 153
Chase Cl. PR8: Birk 1F 186
Chase Heys PR9: S'port 5N 167
Chaseley Rd. OL12: Roch 5B 204
CHATBURN 7C 74
Chatburn Av. BB7: Clith 2M 81
BB10: Burnl 4H 125
Chatburn Cl. BB4: Rawt 3M 161
BB6: Gt H 4L 121
FY3: Blackp 2H 89
Chatburn Old Rd. BB7: Clith 9M 73
Chatburn Pk. Av. BB9: Brierf 4E 104
Chatburn Pk. Dr. BB7: Clith 1M 81
BB9: Brierf 4E 104
Chatburn Rd. BB7: Clith 2M 81
BB7: D'ham 7E 74
PR2: Ribb 5A 116
PR3: Longr 4J 97
Chatburn St. BB2: Blackb 3K 139
Chatham Av. FY8: L Ann 8E 108
Chatham Cres. BB8: Colne 5B 86
Chatham Pl. PR1: Prest 7L 115
PR6: Chor 6G 175
Chatham St. BB8: Colne 5B 86
BB9: Nelson 1H 105
Chatsworth Av. FY2: Blackp 5C 62
FY7: Flee 2C 54
PR4: Wart 2J 131
Chatsworth Cl. BB1: Blackb 8M 119
BB9: Barrf 1F 104
FY5: T Clev 2K 63
PR7: Chor 6D 174
Chatsworth Ct. PR6: H Charn 4H 195
Chatsworth Rd. FY8: L Ann 1D 128
LA1: Lanc 3K 29
LA3: Morec 5N 21
LA4: Morec 5N 21
PR5: Walt D 5N 135
PR8: Ains 7A 186
PR25: Leyl 6K 153
Chatsworth St. OL12: Roch 2B 204
PR1: Prest 9M 115
WN5: Wigan 6M 221
Chatteris Pl. FY5: T Clev 2C 62
CHATTERTON 4H 181
Chatterton BL0: Ramsb 4H 181
Chatterton Dr. BB5: Bax 6D 142
Chatterton Old La.
BL0: Ramsb 4H 181
Chatterton Rd. BL0: Ramsb 4H 181
Chatwell Ct. OL16: Milnr 9M 205
Chaucer Av. FY5: T Clev 9F 54
Chaucer Cl. PR7: E'ton 8E 172
Chaucer Gdns. BB6: Gt H 5H 121
Chaucer Pl. FY2: Blackp 5F 62
Chaucer Rd. FY7: Flee 9G 40
Chaucer St. PR1: Prest 7N 115
Chaucers Wlk. BB1: Blackb 3B 140
Chauntry Brow BL6: Blackr 9L 195
Cheam Av. PR7: Chor 8F 174
Cheapside *BD24: Sett 3N 35*
(off High St.)
FY1: Blackp 1H 227 (5B 88)
L37: Form 1A 214
LA1: Lanc 7C 228 (8K 23)
LA2: L Ben 6J 19
(off Burton Rd.)
PR1: Prest 6K 229 (1J 135)
PR7: Chor 7E 174
Cheddar Av. FY4: Blackp 3D 108
Cheddar Dr. PR2: Fulw 3N 115
Chedworth Av. LA3: Heys 9M 21
CHEESDEN 9B 182
Cheesden Edge OL12: Roch 9C 182
Cheetham Hill OL12: Whitw 3A 184
Cheetham Mdw. PR26: Leyl 6D 152
Cheetham St. BB2: Blackb 3K 139
OL16: Roch 5C 204
Chelburn Gro. BB10: Burnl 3G 124
Chelburn Vw. OL15: Littleb 5M 185
Chelford Av. BL1: Bolt 8E 198
FY3: Blackp 2E 88
Chelford Cl. PR1: Penw 7J 135
Chelmorton Gro. WN3: Wins 9M 221
Chelmsford Cl. LA1: Lanc 2M 29
Chelmsford Gro. PR7: Chor 7D 174
Chelmsford Pl. PR7: Chor 7D 174
Chelmsford Wlk. PR26: Leyl 7D 152
Chelsea Av. FY2: Blackp 1E 88
PR2: Fulw 5J 115
Chelsea Ct. *FY2: Blackp 1E 88*
(off Chelsea Av.)
Chelsea Ho. PR2: Fulw 5J 115
Chelsea M. *FY2: Blackp 1E 88*
(off Bispham Rd.)
LA1: Lanc 6K 23
Chelsea St. OL11: Roch 8A 204
Chelston Dr. BB4: Hasl 8F 160
Cheltenham Av. BB5: Acc 9B 122
Cheltenham Cl. L10: Aint 9D 222
Cheltenham Cres. FY5: T Clev 3K 63
FY8: L Ann 3C 130
Cheltenham Dr. WN5: Bill 9G 220
Cheltenham Rd. BB2: Blackb 3K 139
FY1: Blackp 3B 88
LA1: Lanc 2K 29
Cheltenham St. OL11: Roch 9A 204
Cheltenham Way PR8: S'port 1M 187
Chelwood Cl. BL1: Bolt 6D 198
FY6: Pree 8N 41
Chennell Ho. LA1: Lanc 6B 228
Chepstow Cl. OL11: Roch 5K 203
Chepstow Gdns. PR3: Gars 6A 60
Chepstow Rd. FY3: Blackp 2F 88
CHEQUER 5C 220
Chequer Cl. WN8: Uph 6C 220
Chequer La. WN8: Uph 5C 220
Chequers BB5: Clay M 7M 121
Chequers Av. LA1: Lanc 3M 29
Chequers Way FY5: T Clev 1K 63
Cherestanc Sq. PR3: Gars 5N 59
Cheriton Fld. PR2: Fulw 2F 114
Cheriton Gdns. BL6: Hor 7C 196
Cheriton Pk. PR8: S'port 2L 187
Cherries, The PR7: Eux 3N 173
Cherrybrook Dr. WN3: Wins 9N 221
Cherry Cl. BB1: Blackb 4B 140
PR2: Fulw 3N 115
PR4: K'ham 4K 111
Cherryclough Way BB2: Blackb 8H 139
Cherry Ct. FY3: Blackp 2G 89
Cherry Cres. BB4: Rawt 6L 161
BB5: Osw 6K 141
Cherrycroft WN8: Skelm 4B 220
Cherrydale FY2: Blackp 6D 62
Cherry Dr. BB6: Old L 4B 100
Cherryfield Cres. L32: Kirk 8K 223
Cherryfield Dr. L32: Kirk 8J 223
Cherryfields PR7: Eux 2N 173
Cherry Gdns. BB1: Blackb 9A 120
PR3: Catt 2A 68
(off Ashfield Ri.)
Cherry Grn. L39: Aug 2G 217
Cherry Gro. L40: Burs 7C 190
OL11: Roch 5L 203
PR3: Longr 2J 97
PR6: Withn 5C 156
Cherry La. PR4: Frec 4M 131
Cherry Lea BB2: Blackb 7G 139
Cherry Orchard PR3: Longr 4K 97
Cherry Rd. PR8: Ains 2D 206
Cherry St. BB1: Blackb 3B 140
CHERRY TREE 7F 138
Cherry Tree Cl. FY6: K Sea 7N 41
LA3: Heys 1K 27
LA5: Bolt S 7K 15
PR3: Pill 8K 43
Cherry Tree Ct. BB2: Blackb 7G 139
FY4: Blackp 9H 89
(off Clifton Rd.)
FY7: Flee 8H 41
WN6: Stand 2N 213
Cherry Tree Dr. LA1: Lanc 3K 29
Cherry Tree Gdns. BB9: Nelson 2L 105
FY4: Blackp 1G 109
Cherry Tree Gro. PR6: Chor 3E 174
Cherry Tree La. BB2: Blackb 8F 138
BB4: Rawt 6L 161
L39: Aug 2G 217
Cherry Tree M. *BB11: Burnl 6B 124*
(off Bristol St.)
Cherry Tree Rd. FY4: Blackp 1G 108
PR9: Banks 4J 169
Cherry Tree Rd. Nth. FY4: Blackp 9G 89
Cherry Trees PR5: Lost H 5M 135
Cherry Tree Station (Rail) 7G 139
Cherry Tree Ter. BB2: Blackb 7G 138
Cherry Tree Way BB4: Hasl 8F 160
BL2: Bolt 9H 199
Cherry Va. PR4: Hesk B 5D 150
Cherry Vw. L33: Kirk 5M 223
Cherry Wood PR1: Penw 5D 134
Cherrywood Av. FY5: T Clev 2C 62
FY8: L Ann 4L 129
Cherrywood Cl. PR25: Leyl 7H 153
Chervil Wlk. WN3: Wigan 7M 221
Cheryl Dr. FY5: T Clev 3H 63
CHESHAM 9L 201
Chesham Cres. BL9: Bury 9M 201
Chesham Dr. PR4: New L 8C 134
Chesham Fold Rd. BL9: Bury 9N 201
Chesham Ind. Est. BL9: Bury 9M 201
Chesham Lodge PR3: Gt E 6N 65
Chesham Rd. BL9: Bury 9L 201
Chesham St. PR3: Gt E 6N 65
Chesham Woods Local Nature Reserve 8M 201
Cheshire Ct. BL0: Ramsb 8J 181
PR7: Buck V 9B 154
Cheshire Ho. Cl. PR26: Far M 9J 135
Chesmere Cft. PR1: Penw 3E 134
Chesmere Dr. PR1: Penw 3E 134
Chesnell Gro. L33: Kirk 5M 223
Chessington Grn. *BB10: Burnl 7H 105*
(off Hillingdon Rd. Nth.)
Chester Av. BB7: Clith 2L 81
FY5: T Clev 1D 62
FY6: Poul F 8J 63
OL11: Roch 7L 203
PR7: Chor 1G 194
PR9: S'port 6L 167
Chesterbrook PR3: Ribc 6F 98
Chester Cl. BB1: Blackb 5A 140
LA3: Morec 6B 22
PR3: Gars 5M 59
Chester Cres. BB4: Hasl 7G 160
Chester Dr. BL0: Ramsb 1F 200
Chesterfield Cl. PR8: Ains 9C 186
Chesterfield Dr. L33: Kirk 5K 223
Chesterfield Rd. FY1: Blackp 3B 88
PR8: Ains 9B 186
Chester Pl. LA1: Lanc 2L 29
PR3: Gt E 6A 66
PR6: Adl 5J 195
Chester Rd. FY3: Blackp 3D 88
PR1: Prest 8M 115
PR9: S'port 6M 167
Chester St. BB1: Blackb 4G 226 (4A 140)
BB5: Acc 3N 141
BL9: Bury 9M 201
Chester Ter. LA6: Burt K 6G 7
Chestnut Av. BL8: Tott 8F 200
FY4: Blackp 4F 108
LA2: Brookh 2J 25
LA5: Bolt S 4L 15
OL14: Tod 9K 147
PR1: Penw 4D 134
PR6: Chor 4G 174
PR7: Eux 1M 173
PR9: Banks 3J 169
(off Main Av.)
Chestnut Bus. Pk. BB11: Burnl 4N 123
Chestnut Cl. FY2: Blackp 9D 62
L39: Hals 3B 208
PR3: Gars 3A 60
PR4: K'ham 5N 111
PR5: Walt D 6A 136
Chestnut Ct. BL9: Bury 7L 201
L39: Orms 6L 209
PR9: S'port 6J 167
PR25: Leyl 8K 153
Chestnut Cres. BB7: Barr 1K 101
PR2: Ribb 7A 116
PR4: Longt 8K 133
Chestnut Dr. BB4: Rawt 7L 161
BB7: Whall 3G 100
BB18: Barnw 3L 77
BL9: Bury 6L 201
LA4: Morec 2F 22
PR2: Fulw 2G 115
Chestnut Gdns. BB1: Blackb 1N 139
FY5: T Clev 9H 55
Chestnut Grange L39: Orms 9J 209
Chestnut Gro. BB3: Darw 1A 178
BB5: Acc 4N 141
BB5: Clay M 5N 121
LA1: Lanc 8H 23
Chestnut Pl. OL16: Roch 5E 204
Chestnut Ri. BB11: Burnl 4B 228 (5D 124)
Chestnuts, The BB7: D'ham 8F 74
PR7: Copp 3B 194
Chestnut St. PR8: S'port 1J 187
Chestnut Wlk. *BB1: Blackb 3C 140*
(off Longton St.)
L31: Mell 6F 222
Chestnut Way OL15: Littleb 9H 185
Chethams Cl. FY5: T Clev 1G 62
Chetwyn Av. BL7: Brom C 6G 199
Chevassut Cl. BB9: Barrf 1G 104
Cheviot Av. BB10: Burnl 4J 125
FY5: T Clev 8F 54
FY8: L Ann 3D 130
Cheviot Cl. BL0: Ramsb 1H 201
BL1: Bolt 8D 198
BL6: Hor 8D 196
BL8: Bury 9F 200
OL16: Milnr 6K 205
WN3: Wins 9M 221
Cheviot Ho. *BB4: Hasl 4G 160*
(off Manchester Rd.)
Cheviot St. PR1: Prest 9G 114
Cheviot Way L33: Kirk 4L 223
Chew Gdns. FY6: Poul F 8H 63
Chew La. BD23: Garg 3M 53
Chew's Yd. PR1: Prest 5J 229
Chichester Bus. Cen. OL16: Roch 6D 204
Chichester Cl. BB10: Burnl 1G 228 (3F 124)
FY5: T Clev 1G 62
OL15: Littleb 2J 205
Chichester St. OL16: Roch 6D 204
Chicken St. BB2: Blackb 4K 139
Chiddlingford Ct. FY1: Blackp 5N 227 (7D 88)
CHILDERS GREEN 7F 122
Childrey Wlk. *BB2: Blackb 8A 140*
(off Ridgeway Av.)
Chilham St. WN5: Orr 5K 221
Chiltern Av. BB10: Burnl 4H 125
FY4: Blackp 2D 108
FY6: Poul F 8J 63
PR7: Eux 5N 173
Chiltern Cl. BL0: Ramsb 1H 201
BL6: Hor 8D 196
FY8: L Ann 3C 130
L32: Kirk 6H 223
Chiltern Ct. *LA1: Lanc 2K 29*
(off Cheltenham Rd.)
Chiltern Dr. BL8: Bury 9G 200
L32: Kirk 6H 223
WN3: Wins 9N 221
Chiltern Ho. *BB4: Hasl 4G 160*
(off Salisbury St.)
Chiltern Mdw. PR25: Leyl 6N 153
Chiltern M. PR7: Chor 2D 194
Chiltern Rd. BL0: Ramsb 1H 201
PR8: Ains 7A 186
Chilton Cl. L31: Magh 1C 222
Chilton Ct. L31: Magh 1C 222
Chilton M. L31: Magh 1C 222
Chimes, The PR4: K'ham 5M 111
PR4: Tarl 1E 170
China St. BB5: Acc 2M 141
LA1: Lanc 6C 228 (8K 23)
Chindits Way PR2: Fulw 5L 115
Chines, The PR2: Fulw 5H 115
Chingford Bank BB10: Burnl 7G 105
Chingle Cl. PR2: Fulw 3A 116
Chippendale M. *PR3: Gars 4N 59*
(off Archery Gdns.)
CHIPPING 5G 70
Chipping Av. PR8: Ains 8A 186
Chipping Fold OL16: Milnr 8J 205
Chipping Gro. BB10: Burnl 5H 125
FY3: Blackp 2G 89
Chipping Mnr. PR9: Banks 9F 148
Chipping Rd. BB7: Chaig 6L 71
LA2: Bay H 6B 38
PR3: Longr 1J 97
Chipping St. BB12: Padi 9J 103
Chirk Dr. FY5: T Clev 1K 63
Chisacre Dr. WN6: Shev 5G 213
Chisholm Cl. WN6: Stand 1L 213
Chisholme Cl. BL8: Greenm 3D 200
Chislehurst Av. FY4: Blackp 9N 227 (9C 88)

252 A-Z Lancashire

Clayton Av.—Coldstream Pl.

Clayton Av. BB4: Rawt 7K 161
PR25: Leyl 8G 153
Clayton Brook Rd. PR5: Bam B 2D 154
Clayton Cl. BB9: Nelson 1H 105
Clayton Ct. PR3: Longr 3K 97
Clayton Cres. FY4: Blackp 3D 108
Clayton Fold BB12: Burnl 2M 123
Clayton Gdns. L40: Burs 9C 190
Claytongate FY4: Blackp 2F 108
PR7: Copp 3B 194
Claytongate Dr. PR1: Penw 6K 135
CLAYTON GREEN 4D 154
Clayton Grn. Bus. Pk. PR6: Clay W 3D 154
Clayton Grn. Cen. PR6: Clay W 3D 154
Clayton Grn. Rd. PR6: Clay W 4C 154
Clayton Green Sports Cen. 3D 154
Clayton Gro. BB1: Clay D 3L 119
Claytonhalgh PR3: Ribc 7F 98
Clayton Hall Dr. BB5: Clay M 5M 121
CLAYTON-LE-DALE 2K 119
CLAYTON-LE-MOORS 6M 121
CLAYTON-LE-WOODS 4C 154
Clayton M. WN8: Skelm 2H 219
Clayton Row BB6: Langh 9D 100
Clayton's Ga. PR1: Prest 5J 229 (9J 115)
Clayton St. BB2: Blackb 5C 226 (4M 139)
BB5: Clay M 8N 121
BB5: Osw 3L 141
BB6: Gt H 4J 121
BB8: Colne 7B 86
BB9: Nelson 2H 105
(not continuous)
BB18: Barnw 2N 77
OL12: Roch 3E 204
PR5: Bam B 7A 136
WN8: Skelm 2H 219
Clayton St. Ind. Est. BB9: Nelson 1H 105
Clayton Villa Fold PR6: Clay W 4C 154
Clayton Way BB2: Blackb 9L 139
BB5: Clay M 6N 121
Cleadon Dr. Sth. BL8: Bury 8H 201
Cleator Av. FY2: Blackp 1C 88
Cleaver Cotts. L38: Hight 5A 214
Cleaver St. BB1: Blackb 3F 226 (3N 139)
BB10: Burnl 1F 124
Clecken La. PR3: Clau 1G 68
Clegg Av. FY5: T Clev 9D 54
CLEGG HALL 3H 205
Clegg Hall Rd. OL15: Littleb 3H 205
OL16: Roch 3G 204
Clegg's Av. *OL12: Whitw 4N 183*
(off Tong La.)
Clegg St. BB4: Hasl 4G 161
BB9: Brierf 5F 104
BB9: Nelson 4J 105
BB10: Burnl 1E 124
BB10: W'thorne 4L 125
OL12: Whitw 4N 183
OL13: Bac 7G 163
OL15: Littleb 8J 185
OL16: Milnr 8K 205
PR4: K'ham 4M 111
WN8: Skelm 2H 219
Clegg St. E. *BB10: Burnl 1E 124*
(off Grey St.)
Cleggswood Av. OL15: Littleb 2K 205
Cleggs Yd. OL15: Littleb 9J 185
Clematis Cl. PR7: Chor 3C 174
Clematis St. BB2: Blackb 3J 139
Clement Ct. OL16: Roch 7E 204
Clementina St. OL12: Roch 4C 204
(not continuous)
Clement Pl. *OL12: Roch 5B 204*
(off Clement Royds St.)
OL15: Littleb 9M 185
(off Halifax Rd.)
Clement Rd. PR2: Fulw 2M 115
Clement Royds St. OL12: Roch 5B 204
(not continuous)
Clements Dr. BB9: Brierf 6G 104
Clement St. BB3: Darw 7A 158
BB5: Acc 4B 142
Clements Way L33: Kirk 5J 223
Clement Vw. BB9: Nelson 2H 105
Clengers Brow PR9: S'port 4M 167
Clent Av. L31: Lyd, Magh 8B 216
Clent Gdns. L31: Lyd 8B 216
Clent Rd. L31: Magh 8B 216
Clerk Hill Rd. BB7: Whall, Wis 6M 101
Clerkhill St. BB1: Blackb 3B 140
Clery St. BB12: Burnl 4M 123
Clevedon Dr. WN3: Wigan 7M 221
Clevedon Rd. FY1: Blackp 3B 88
PR2: Ingol 5D 114
Cleveland Av. PR2: Fulw 5M 115
WN3: Wins 9M 221
Cleveland Cl. BL0: Ramsb 2H 201
L32: Kirk 6J 223
Cleveland Dr. LA1: Lanc 1H 29
OL16: Milnr 7K 205
Cleveland Ho. *BB4: Hasl 4G 160*
(off Bury Rd.)
Cleveland Rd. FY8: L Ann 5A 130
PR25: Leyl 5J 153
Clevelands Av. LA3: Morec 5N 21
LA5: Silv 7G 5
Clevelands Gro. BB11: Burnl 5A 228 (5D 124)
LA3: Morec 5N 21
Clevelands Mt. BB11: Burnl 5A 228 (5C 124)
Clevelands Rd. BB11: Burnl 5A 228 (5C 124)
Cleveland St. BB8: Colne 5C 86
OL14: Tod 7E 146
PR7: Chor 6E 174
PR7: Copp 4A 194
Clevelands Wlk. LA3: Morec 5N 21
Cleveland Ter. BB3: Darw 7B 158
Cleveley Bank La. PR3: Fort, Scor 3A 46
CLEVELEYS 1D 62
Cleveleys Av. FY5: T Clev 1D 62
LA1: Lanc 5G 22
PR2: Fulw 5F 114
PR9: S'port 2N 167
Cleveleys Rd. BB2: Blackb 7N 139
BB5: Acc 9N 121
PR5: Hogh 5G 136
PR9: S'port 3N 167
Cleveleys Stop (Tram) 1D 62
Cleves, The L31: Magh 8D 216
Cleves Ct. FY3: Blackp 8G 89
Cleve Way L37: Form 1B 214
Clewer Pl. OL14: Wals 6K 165
CLIEVES HILLS 9E 208
Clieves Hills L39: Hals 6D 208
Clieves Hills La. L39: Aug 1D 216
Clieves Rd. L32: Kirk 9L 223
Cliff Av. BL9: Summ 3H 201
CLIFFE 3J 121
Cliffe Ct. PR1: Prest 9N 115
Cliffe Dr. PR6: Whit W 7D 154
Cliffe La. BB6: Gt H 2H 121
Cliffe Pk. BB6: Gt H 2H 121
Cliffe St. BB9: Nelson 1J 105
OL15: Littleb 4N 185
Cliffe Vs. OL14: Tod 3L 165
Cliff Mt. BL0: Ramsb 7G 180
Clifford Av. LA4: Morec 2D 22
PR4: Longt 7L 133
Clifford Rd. FY1: Blackp 3B 88
PR8: Birk 3G 186
Clifford St. BB8: Colne 6B 86
BB18: Barnw 2N 77
OL11: Roch 8C 204
PR7: Chor 6F 174
Cliff Pl. FY2: Blackp 7B 62
Cliff Rd. PR9: S'port 4K 167
Cliffs, The LA3: Heys 7L 21
Cliffs Hotel Stop (Tram) 1B 88
Cliff St. BB1: Rish 7H 121
BB8: Colne 8M 85
BB12: Padi 9J 103
OL16: Roch 4E 204
PR1: Prest 8G 229 (2H 135)
CLIFTON 8H 113
Clifton Av. BB5: Acc 9B 122
FY4: Blackp 9J 89
PR2: Ash R 7C 114
PR4: Wart 2K 131
PR25: Leyl 7L 153
Clifton Bus. Pk. PR4: Clif 1F 132
Clifton Cl. FY5: T Clev 2J 63
Clifton Ct. FY4: Blackp 3B 108
FY8: L Ann 5B 130
Clifton Cres. FY3: Blackp 8G 89
PR1: Prest 7M 115
Clifton Dr. BB6: Gt H 3J 121
FY4: Blackp 3A 108
FY8: L Ann 4H 129
L10: Aint 8C 222
LA4: Morec 3E 22
PR1: Penw 3F 134
Clifton Dr. Nth. FY8: L Ann 5B 108
Clifton Dr. Sth. FY8: L Ann 2E 128
Clifton Flds. PR4: Clif 1G 133
Clifton Gdns. FY8: L Ann 2J 129
Clifton Ga. FY8: L Ann 4A 130
Clifton Grn. PR4: Clif 8G 113
Clifton Gro. BB1: Wilp 5N 119
PR1: Prest 6M 115
PR7: Chor 7D 174
CLIFTON HILL 3K 45
Clifton Ho. PR2: Fulw 5M 115
Clifton La. PR4: Clif 6G 113
Clifton Lodge FY8: L Ann 3E 128
Clifton Pde. PR25: Far 4M 153
Clifton Pk. Retail Cen.
FY4: Blackp 1K 109
Clifton Pl. PR2: Ash R 7E 114
PR4: Frec 2N 131
Clifton Rd. BB9: Brierf 6G 105
BB12: Burnl 2A 124
FY4: Blackp 9H 89
FY7: Flee 1G 54
L37: Form 7A 206
PR8: S'port 8M 167
Clifton Sq. BB12: Burnl 1A 228 (3C 124)
FY8: L Ann 5A 130
Clifton St. BB1: Rish 8H 121
BB3: Darw 3N 157
BB5: Acc 4N 141
BB8: Colne 6A 86
BB8: Traw 9E 86
BB12: Burnl 1A 228 (3C 124)
BB18: Sough 4D 78
BL9: Bury 9L 201
FY1: Blackp 1H 227 (5B 88)
FY8: L Ann 5A 130
OL11: Roch 8D 204
(off Well St.)
OL16: Milnr 7J 205
PR1: Prest 2G 135
Clifton Ter. BB3: Hodd 5E 158
Climb Rochdale *6C 204*
(off School La.)
Clinkham Rd. BB6: Gt H 4F 120
Clinning Rd. PR8: Birk 3G 187
Clinton Av. FY1: Blackp 4L 227 (6C 88)
Clinton St. BB1: Blackb 2A 140
Clippers Quay BB1: Blackb 6E 226
CLITHEROE 3L 81
Clitheroe By-Pass BB7: Clith, Pend, Wors 8L 81
Clitheroe Camping & Caravanning Club Site
BB7: Clith 4H 81
Clitheroe Castle 3L 81
Clitheroe Castle Mus. 3L 81
Clitheroe Cl. OL10: Heyw 9H 203
Clitheroe FC 3M 81
Clitheroe Golf Course 2K 81
Clitheroe Pl. FY4: Blackp 1G 109
Clitheroe Rd. BB7: Barr, Whall 4J 101
BB7: Chatb 9B 74
BB7: Clith, Wadd 8H 73
BB7: Sabd 9D 82
BB7: West B 7L 73
BB9: Brierf 5D 104
FY8: L Ann 2J 129
PR3: Dutt, Know G 1C 98
Clitheroe's La. PR4: Frec 2N 131
Clitheroe Station (Rail) 3L 81
Clitheroe St. BB12: Padi 9H 103
PR1: Prest 1M 135
Clive Av. FY8: L Ann 8E 108
Clive Lodge PR8: Birk 3F 186
Clive Rd. PR1: Penw 2E 134
PR8: Birk 3F 186
Clive St. BB12: Burnl 1D 124
CLIVIGER 1L 145
Clockhouse Av. BB10: Burnl 7H 105
Clockhouse Ct. BB10: Burnl 7H 105
Clockhouse Gro. BB10: Burnl 7H 105
Clock Twr. Ct. OL16: Milnr 8K 205
Clod La. BB4: Hasl 8H 161
Clods Carr La. FY6: Pree 1M 55
Clogger La. BD23: Elsl 8M 53
Clogg Head BB8: Traw 9F 86
Cloister Dr. BB3: Darw 6B 158
Cloister Grn. L37: Form 1B 214
Cloisters LA3: Morec 6C 22
Cloisters, The BB4: W'foot 7C 162
BB7: Whall 5K 101
FY3: Blackp 5E 88
OL16: Roch 4E 204
PR2: Ash R 8G 115
PR4: Tarl 9E 150
PR9: Banks 3J 169
PR9: S'port 6J 167
(off Hoghton Gro.)
PR25: Leyl 5M 153
Clorain Cl. L33: Kirk 7M 223
Clorain Rd. L33: Kirk 7M 223
Close, The BB5: Clay M 5M 121
BB5: Ris B 8F 142
BL8: Bury 7H 201
FY5: T Clev 1D 62
(Conway Av.)
FY5: T Clev 8D 54
(Lanefield Dr.)
L38: Ince B 8E 214
PR2: Fulw 3A 116
PR3: Gars 3M 59
PR4: K'ham 5N 111
PR4: New L 9D 134
(not continuous)
PR4: Weet 8D 90
PR5: Walt D 6L 135
PR6: Withn 5L 155
PR9: Banks 1F 168
Closebrook Rd. WN5: Wigan 5N 221
Closes Hall M. BB7: Bolt B 7M 51
Cloth Hall St. BB8: Colne 6A 86
CLOUGH 7K 185
Clough, The BB3: Darw 9C 158
PR6: Clay W 4C 154
Clougha Av. LA1: Lanc 1M 29
LA2: Halt 2C 24
Clough Acre PR7: Chor 4C 174
Clough Av. L40: Burs 9D 190
PR5: Walt D 5L 135
Clough Bank BB7: Chatb 7C 74
OL15: Littleb 6K 185
Clough End Rd. BB4: Hasl 2G 161
Cloughfield PR1: Penw 7G 134
CLOUGHFOLD 5A 162
Clough Gdns. BB4: Hasl 2G 161
Clough Head BB9: Nelson 3L 105
OL15: Littleb 4M 185
(off Higher Calderbrook Rd.)
Clough Head Info. Cen. 4M 159
Clough Ho. La. OL12: Ward 8E 184
Clough La. BB12: S'stone 9E 102
OL10: Heyw 9G 202
PR3: T'ley 7G 71
Clough Mill OL14: Wals 6K 165
Clough Rd. BB9: Nelson 2L 105
OL13: Bac 4L 163
OL14: Wals 6K 165
OL15: Littleb 6K 185
Clough Springs BB9: Barrf 7G 84
Clough St. BB3: Darw 9C 158
BB4: W'foot 6D 162
BB11: Burnl 4B 124
(not continuous)
OL12: Ward 8F 184
OL13: Bac 7H 163
Clough Ter. *BB18: Barnw 3M 77*
(off North St.)
OL15: Littleb 7K 185
Cloughwood Cres. WN6: Shev 6G 213
Clovelly Av. FY5: T Clev 5C 62
PR2: Ash R 6G 114
Clovelly Dr. PR1: Penw 3D 134
PR8: Birk 5E 186
WN8: N 'urgh 3L 211
Clovelly St. OL11: Roch 9M 203
Clover Av. FY8: L Ann 8G 108
Clover Ct. FY2: Blackp 5F 62
Clover Cres. BB12: Burnl 1B 124
Clover Cft. BB12: High 4L 103
Clover Dr. PR4: Frec 1B 132
Clover Fld. PR6: Clay W 5D 154
Cloverfield PR1: Penw 4E 134
Cloverfields BB1: Blackb 2A 140
CLOVER HALL 4F 204
Clover Hall Cres. OL16: Roch 4F 204
Cloverhill Ho. BB9: Nelson 3K 105
Clover Hill Rd. BB9: Nelson 3K 105
Clover M. FY3: Blackp 4E 88
Clover Rd. PR7: Chor 9C 174
Clover St. OL12: Roch 5B 204
OL13: Bac 4L 163
Clover Ter. BB3: Darw 4A 158
Clover Vw. OL16: Roch 6F 204
CLOW BRIDGE 3A 144
Club 3000 5L 229
Clubhouse Cl. OL11: Roch 6L 203
Club La. PR3: Chip 5G 70
Club St. BB7: Barr 9K 81
OL14: Tod 7E 146
PR5: Bam B 9A 136
PR7: Eux 3N 173
Clucas Gdns. L39: Orms 6K 209
Clyde Ct. OL16: Roch 7E 204
Clydesdale Dr. PR7: Chor 8F 174
Clydesdale Pl. PR26: Leyl 5F 152
Clyde St. BB2: Blackb 5J 139
FY1: Blackp 3B 88
PR2: Ash R 9F 114
Clyffes Farm Cl. L40: Scar 6F 188
Clynders Cotts. BB12: Burnl 9A 104
Coach Ho., The PR7: Eux 1J 173
Coach Ho. Ct. L40: Burs 1C 210
Coach Ho. Dr. WN6: Shev 6L 213
Coach La. OL11: Roch 8J 203
Coach M. LA4: Morec 4N 21
Coach Rd. BB5: Chur 3L 141
L33: Kirk 9F 224
L39: Bick 9D 218
LA5: Wart 2A 12
WA11: Rain 5F 224
Coal Bank Fold OL11: Roch 4H 203
Coal Clough La. BB11: Burnl 4C 124
Coal Clough Rd. OL14: Tod 6E 146
Coal Hey St. BB4: Hasl 4G 160
Coal Pit La. BB3: Tock 4H 157
BB4: W'foot 4E 162
BB5: Acc 4M 141
BB7: Gis 10B 52
BB8: Colne 7C 86
BL1: Bolt 7L 197
L39: Bick 7G 219
OL13: Bac 4M 163
Coal Pit Rd. BL1: Bolt 6J 197
Coal Rd. BL0: Ramsb 6M 181
Coal St. BB11: Burnl 2C 228 (3D 124)
Coastal Dr. LA2: Hest B 7J 15
Coastal Ri. LA2: Hest B 8H 15
Coastal Rd. LA2: Bolt S, Hest B 7H 15
LA4: Morec 9F 14
LA5: Bolt S 7H 15
PR8: Ains, Birk 7A 186
Coastline M. PR9: S'port 2N 167
COATES 1N 77
Coates Av. BB18: Barnw 1N 77
Coates Flds. BB18: Barnw 10G 52
Coates La. BB18: Barnw 10G 52
Cobble Ct. Yd. LA1: Lanc 9A 228 (9J 23)
Cobble Hey Farm & Gardens 6J 61
Cobbs Brow La. L40: Lath 7K 211
WN8: N 'urgh 4L 211
Cobb's Clough Rd. L40: Lath 7K 211
Cobbs La. BB5: Osw 9K 141
Cob Castle *BD24: Sett 3N 35*
(off Ingfield La.)
Cob Castle Rd. BB4: Hasl 4D 160
Cobden Ct. BB1: Blackb 4D 226 (3M 139)
Cobden Ho. BB4: Rawt 6B 162
Cobden Pl. *BB8: Wine 6E 86*
(off Rosley St.)
Cobden Rd. PR9: S'port 8M 167
Cobden St. BB3: Darw 7A 158
BB9: Nelson 3H 105
BB10: Brierc 7K 105
BB10: Burnl 1F 124
BB12: Hapt 5H 123
BB12: Padi 9J 103
BB18: Barnw 3M 77
BL7: Eger 3D 198
BL9: Bury 9M 201
OL13: Bac 7M 163
OL14: Tod 2L 165
PR6: Chor 5G 174
Cobham Ct. BB4: Newc 6C 162
Cobham Rd. BB5: Acc 3C 142
Cob La. BB18: Kelb 7D 78
Cob Moor Av. WN5: Bill 9G 221
Cobourg Cl. BB2: Blackb 9E 226 (6N 139)
COB WALL 1F 226 (1A 140)
Cob Wall BB1: Blackb 2A 140
Cochran St. BB3: Darw 6A 158
COCKDEN 8L 105
Cocker Av. FY6: Poul F 8N 63
COCKER BAR 6B 152
Cocker Bar Rd. PR26: Breth, Leyl 8N 151
Cocker Ct. PR26: Leyl 6F 152
Cockerell Dr. OL13: Bac 7M 163
COCKERHAM 9G 37
Cockerham Rd. LA2: C'ham, Fort 1H 45
PR3: Nateby 2L 59
Cockerham Sands Caravan Pk. LA2: Thurn 7A 36
Cockerham Wlk. FY3: Blackp 2G 89
COCKER HILL 1N 85
Cockerill St. BB4: Hasl 3G 161
Cockerill Ter. BB7: Barr 1K 101
Cocker La. PR26: Leyl 6E 152
Cocker Rd. PR5: Bam B 9C 136
Cockersand Av. PR4: Hutt 7N 133
Cockersand Dr. LA1: Lanc 4L 29
Cocker Sq. FY1: Blackp 4B 88
Cocker St. BB3: Darw 8C 158
FY1: Blackp 4B 88
Cocker Street Stop (Tram) 4B 88
Cocker Trad. Est. FY1: Blackp 3C 88
Cock Hall La. OL12: Whitw 5N 183
Cockhall La. OL12: Whitw 5N 183
Cockhill La. BB8: Colne 3E 86
Cocking Yd. LA6: Burt K 6H 7
Cockle Dick's La. PR9: S'port 4L 167
Cockle Hill LA6: Over K 9F 12
Cocklinstones BL8: Bury 9G 201
Cockpit OL14: Tod 3L 165
Cockridge Cl. BB2: Blackb 8J 139
Cock Robin Cotts. PR26: Cros 4N 171
Cock Robin La. PR3: Catt 1A 68
Cockwood Ct. *PR1: Prest 9G 115*
(off Marsh La.)
Codale Av. FY2: Blackp 6D 62
Coddington St. BB1: Blackb 3B 140
Coe La. PR4: Tarl 9E 150
Cogie Hill LA2: C'ham 1B 58
PR3: C'ham, Winm 1B 58
Cog La. BB11: Burnl 4A 124
Cog St. BB11: Burnl 4B 124
Colbern Cl. L31: Magh 2D 222
Colbran St. BB9: Nelson 9K 85
BB10: Burnl 1F 124
Colburne Cl. L40: Burs 8D 190
Colchester Av. LA1: Lanc 2M 29
Colchester Dr. FY5: T Clev 8F 54
Colchester Rd. FY3: Blackp 7F 88
PR8: S'port 3M 187
Coldale Ct. FY4: Blackp 3B 108
Cold Bath St. PR1: Prest 4H 229 (9H 115)
Cold Greave Cl. OL16: Milnr 9M 205
COLD ROW 7B 56
Coldstream Pl. BB2: Blackb 9D 226 (6M 139)

Coldwall Ind. Est.—Corporation St.

Coldwall Ind. Est. OL12: Roch 5A 204
Coldweather Av. BB9: Nelson 5K 105
Coldwell Activity Cen. 4D 106
Cold Well La. LA7: Carr B 2K 5
Colebatch PR2: Fulw 4G 114
Cole Cres. L39: Aug 3H 217
Coleman St. BB9: Nelson 2K 105
Colenso Rd. BB1: Blackb 1L 139
PR2: Ash R 7F 114
Coleridge Av. FY5: T Clev 9F 54
WN5: Orr 5K 221
Coleridge Cl. BB8: Colne 5A 86
PR4: Cott 5B 114
Coleridge Dr. BB5: Bax 6D 142
Coleridge Pl. BB6: Gt H 5H 121
Coleridge Rd. BL8: Greenm 3E 200
FY1: Blackp 4D 88
OL15: Littleb 3J 205
WN5: Bill 9G 220
Coleridge St. BB2: Blackb 5K 139
Colerne Way WN3: Wins 9N 221
Colesberg Ct. LA5: Arn 1F 4
Coles Dr. LA5: Arn 2F 4
Coleshill Av. BB10: Burnl 4G 125
Coleshill Ri. WN3: Wins 9M 221
Colesville Av. FY5: T Clev 2H 63
Colinmander Gdns. L39: Orms 9H 209
Colin St. BB11: Burnl 4B 124
BB18: Barnw 1M 77
Colinton WN8: Skelm 4B 220
Colldale Ter. BB4: Hasl 5G 161
College Av. FY5: T Clev 2C 62
College Bank Way OL12: Roch 6B 204
College Cl. BB12: Padi 3J 123
PR3: Longr 5J 97
PR8: Birk 2G 186
College Ct. *BB5: Acc 2N 141*
(off Blackburn Rd.)
FY1: Blackp 3L 227 (6C 88)
FY8: L Ann 3E 128
OL12: Roch 6A 204
PR1: Prest 1H 229 (7H 115)
College Cft. BD24: Rath 6M 35
College Fold BD24: Rath 6M 35
College Ga. FY5: T Clev 7C 54
College Island WN8: Skelm 1M 219
College La. BB4: Rawt 5B 162
College Rd. OL12: Roch 6A 204
WN8: Uph 2E 220
College St. BB5: Acc 2N 141
OL14: Tod 7F 146
Collen Cres. BL8: Bury 7H 201
Colley St. OL16: Roch 4E 204
Collier Av. OL16: Milnr 6J 205
Collier's La. LA6: Cast 5G 8
Colliers' Row BB1: Guide 7F 140
Colliers Row Rd. BL1: Bolt 8L 197
Colliers St. BB5: Osw 3L 141
Collier St. BB5: Bax 6D 142
Collinge Fold La. BB4: Rawt 3L 161
Collinge St. BB4: Rawt 3L 161
BB12: Padi 2H 123
BL8: Bury 9G 201
Collingham Pk. LA1: Lanc 5L 29
Colling St. BL0: Ramsb 9G 180
Collingwood BB5: Clay M 7L 121
Collingwood Av. FY3: Blackp 1N 227 (4E 88)
FY8: L Ann 8E 108
Collingwood Dr. LA2: L Ben 6J 19
Collingwood Pl. FY3: Blackp 4E 88
Collingwood Rd. PR7: Chor 7C 174
Collingwood St. BB8: Colne 7M 85
WN6: Stand 3N 213
Collingwood Ter. *LA2: H Ben 6L 19*
(off Mt. Pleasant)
Collins Av. FY2: Blackp 8E 62
Collins Dr. BB5: Bax 6D 142
Collin's Hill La. PR3: Chip 5E 70
Collinson St. PR1: Prest 8M 115
Collins Rd. PR5: Bam B 7A 136
Collins Rd. Nth. PR5: Bam B 6B 136
Collins St. BL8: Bury 9E 200
Collisdene Rd. WN5: Orr 5G 221
Collison Av. PR7: Chor 6E 174
Colloway Ho. *LA3: Heys 1K 27*
(off Middleton Rd.)
Collyhurst Av. FY4: Blackp 3E 108
Colman Ct. PR1: Prest 2G 135
Colmoor Cl. L33: Kirk 4L 223
Colmore Gro. BL2: Bolt 9H 199
Colmore St. BL2: Bolt 9H 199
Colnbrook WN6: Stand 2L 213
COLNE 6B 86
Colne & Broughton Rd. BD23: Elsl, T Crav 10J 53
COLNE EDGE 4N 85
Colne Golf Course 4E 86
Colne La. BB8: Colne 7B 86
Colne Rd. BB8: Colne 7J 85
BB8: Traw 9E 86
BB9: Barrf 7J 85
BB9: Brierf 4F 104
(not continuous)
BB10: Burnl 2E 124
BB10: Reed 6F 104
BB11: Burnl 2E 124
BB18: Barnw 3L 77
BB18: Earl, Kelb, Sough 9C 78
Colne Station (Rail) 7N 85
Colonnade, The LA1: Lanc 9N 23
Colossus Fitness Cen. 1H 109
Colourfields
Panopticon 1K 139
Colthirst Dr. BB7: Clith 1M 81
Colt Ho. Cl. PR25: Leyl 8K 153
Coltsfoot Dr. PR6: Chor 4F 174
Coltsfoot Wlk. LA3: Morec 6B 22
Columbia Way BB2: Blackb 9H 119
Columbine Cl. L31: Mell 7F 222
OL12: Roch 2N 203
PR7: Chor 3C 174
Colville Av. FY4: Blackp 4C 108
Colville Rd. BB3: Darw 3M 157
Colville St. BB10: Burnl 1E 124
Colwall Cl. L33: Kirk 8M 223
Colwall Rd. L33: Kirk 8M 223
Colwall Wlk. L33: Kirk 8M 223
Colwyn Av. FY4: Blackp 9E 88
LA4: Morec 2D 22
Colwyn Pl. PR2: Ingol 6D 114
Colyton Cl. PR6: Chor 6G 175
Colyton Rd. PR6: Chor 6G 175
Colyton Rd. E. PR6: Chor 6G 175
Combermere Gro. LA3: Heys 2K 27
Combermere Rd. LA3: Heys 1K 27
Comer Gdns. L31: Lyd 8C 216
Comet Rd. PR26: Leyl 5F 152
WN5: Wigan 3M 221
Comet St. OL13: Weir 9K 145
Comley Bank PR9: S'port 5K 167
Commerce St. BB4: Hasl 3F 160
(not continuous)
OL13: Bac 5K 163
Commercial Rd. BB3: Darw 2N 157
BB6: Gt H 4J 121
BB9: Nelson 2J 105
PR7: Chor 5E 174
Commercial St. BB1: Rish 8H 121
BB4: Craws 5M 143
BB5: Chur 2L 141
BB5: Osw 5K 141
BB6: Gt H 4J 121
BB9: Brierf 4F 104
BB18: Barnw 2M 77
BD24: Sett 3N 35
FY1: Blackp 9B 88
OL13: Bac 7H 163
OL14: Tod 2M 165
Commodore Pl. WN5: Wigan 2N 221
Common, The PR7: Adl 9G 194
WN8: Parb 1N 211
Common Bank Ind. Est. PR7: Chor 7B 174
Common Bank La. PR7: Chor 7B 174
COMMON EDGE 3F 108
Common Edge Rd. FY4: Blackp 3F 108
Common Gdn. St. LA1: Lanc 7C 228 (8K 23)
Common La. PR9: Banks, S'port 4G 168
Commonside FY8: L Ann 4K 129
Commons La. BB2: Bald 3A 118
Commonwealth Cl. FY8: L Ann 9J 109
Como Av. BB11: Burnl 5A 124
Company St. BB1: Rish 8H 121
Compley Av. FY6: Poul F 9J 63
Compley Grn. FY6: Poul F 9J 63
Compression Rd. LA3: Midd 5K 27
(not continuous)
Compston Av. BB4: Craws 7M 143
Compton Cl. FY6: Carl 6J 63
Compton Grn. PR2: Fulw 2F 114
Compton Rd. PR8: Birk 2H 187
Comrie Cres. BB11: Burnl 6B 124
Concorde Ho. FY1: Blackp 3K 227
Concourse Shop. Cen. WN8: Skelm 2M 219
Conder Av. FY5: T Clev 1F 62
Conder Brow LA5: Carn 8C 12
CONDER GREEN 1F 36
Conder Grn. Rd. LA2: Gal 3K 37
Conder Pl. LA1: Lanc 6J 23
Conder Rd. PR2: Ash R 8B 114
Condor Gro. FY1: Blackp 7M 227 (8D 88)
FY8: L Ann 9D 108
Condor Way PR1: Penw 6K 135
Conduit St. BB9: Nelson 1H 105
Coneygarth La. LA6: Tuns, Whit 9E 8
(not continuous)
Congleton Cl. FY4: Blackp 9H 89
Congress St. PR7: Chor 5E 174
Conifer Cl. L33: Kirk 5K 223
Conifer Ct. L37: Form 1A 214
Conifers, The BB10: Burnl 7J 105
FY6: Ham 1A 64
L31: Magh 8B 216
PR3: Bart 2E 94
PR4: K'ham 4N 111
Conisber Cl. BL7: Eger 4E 198
Conisborough OL11: Roch 7B 204
Coniston Av. BB5: Acc 4M 141
BB12: Padi 8H 103
BB18: Barnw 1L 77
FY5: T Clev 1H 63
FY6: Carl 7H 63
FY6: Ham 1B 64
FY6: K Sea 7L 41
FY7: Flee 9E 40
FY8: L Ann 7F 108
PR2: Ash R 7G 114
PR6: Adl 5K 195
PR7: Eux 5N 173
WN5: Orr 4J 221
Coniston Cl. BL0: Ramsb 6H 181
L33: Kirk 6J 223
PR3: Longr 5H 97
CONISTON COLD 3J 53
Coniston Ct. *LA4: Morec 2C 22*
(off Thornton Rd.)
PR8: Ains 1C 206
Coniston Cres. FY5: T Clev 2H 63
Coniston Dr. BB3: Darw 5C 158
PR5: Walt D 6N 135
Coniston Gro. BB8: Colne 5D 86
Coniston Ho. LA3: Midd 6K 27
Coniston Rd. BB1: Blackb 1A 140
FY4: Blackp 2C 108
L31: Magh 9D 216
LA1: Lanc 6L 23
LA4: Morec 3C 22
LA5: Bolt S 5L 15
LA5: Carn 1B 16
PR2: Fulw 4M 115
PR7: Chor 8D 174
Coniston St. BB12: Burnl 3A 124
Coniston Way BB1: Rish 8F 120
OL13: Bac 3L 163
PR26: Cros 3M 171
WA11: Rain 9K 219
Connaught Dr. FY5: T Clev 1K 63
Connaught Rd. LA1: Lanc 2M 29
LA3: Heys 2J 27
PR1: Prest 9G 229 (3H 135)
Conningsby Cl. BL7: Brom C 5F 198
Consett Av. FY5: T Clev 7E 54
Constable Av. BB11: Burnl 6D 124
PR5: Lost H 9K 135
CONSTABLE LEE 3M 161
Constable Lee Ct. BB4: Rawt 3M 161
Constable Lee Cres. BB4: Rawt 3M 161
Constable St.
PR1: Prest 4M 229 (9K 115)
Constantine Rd. OL16: Roch 6C 204
Constitution Hill *BD24: Sett 3N 35*
(off Church St.)
Convent Cl. L39: Aug 1J 217
PR5: Bam B 7N 135
PR25: Leyl 5M 153
Convent Cres. FY3: Blackp 2G 88
Convent Gro. OL11: Roch 8A 204
Conway Av. BB1: Blackb 1M 139
BB7: Clith 4J 81
FY3: Blackp 3H 89
FY5: T Clev 1D 62
PR1: Penw 7K 135
PR25: Leyl 7M 153
Conway Cl. BB4: Hasl 6G 161
BL0: Ramsb 8G 180
L33: Kirk 5J 223
PR3: Catt 1A 68
PR7: Eux 5A 174
Conway Ct. PR5: Hogh 6G 136
Conway Cres. BB18: Barnw 1N 77
BL8: Greenm 3E 200
Conway Dr. BB5: Osw 4H 141
PR2: Fulw 2F 114
Conway Gro. BB10: Burnl 7G 104
Conway Ho. PR1: Prest 9N 115
Conway Rd. BB4: Rawt 4A 162
PR7: E'ton 7F 172
Conway St. WN5: Wigan 6M 221
Conyers Av. PR8: Birk 2F 186
Cooke St. BL6: Hor 9E 196
Cook Gdns. BB1: Blackb 4B 140
Cook Grn. La. PR3: Know G 3D 98
Cook Ho. Rd. BB8: Colne 5B 86
Cook Rd. OL16: Roch 8F 204
Cookson Cl. FY8: L Ann 5C 130
PR4: Frec 2N 131
Cookson Rd. FY5: T Clev 9G 55
Cookson St. FY1: Blackp 1K 227 (4C 88)
Cook St. OL16: Roch 4E 204
Cook Ter. OL16: Roch 4E 204
Coolham La. BB18: Earl 3F 78
Coolidge Av. LA1: Lanc 9H 23
Coombes, The PR2: Fulw 4J 115
Cooperage, The BB5: Osw 5K 141
Co-operation St. BB4: Craws 9M 143
BB4: Rawt 5N 161
BB4: W'foot 5D 162
OL13: Bac 5L 163
Co-operative Bldgs. BB4: W'foot 8D 162
BB10: Cliv 9K 125
Co-operative St. BB4: Hasl 8E 160
BB18: Barnw 2M 77
OL14: Wals 8K 165
PR5: Bam B 8A 136
Cooper Ct. FY5: T Clev 9D 54
PR2: Ash R 9B 114
Cooper Hill Cl. PR5: Walt D 3N 135
Cooper Hill Dr. PR5: Walt D 3N 135
Cooper Rd. PR1: Prest 9G 115
Coopers Cl. *BB5: Osw 5K 141*
(off Peel St.)
Coopers Fold PR2: Ribb 7C 116
Cooper's La. PR7: Hesk 6E 192
Coopers Pl. PR7: Buck V 9A 154
Coopers Row FY8: L Ann 1K 129
Cooper St. BB9: Nelson 1J 105
BB11: Burnl 4D 228 (4E 124)
BL6: Hor 9C 196
OL12: Roch 1G 205
OL13: Bac 4K 163
Coopers Wlk. OL16: Roch 3F 204
Coopers Way FY1: Blackp 3D 88
Coop St. BL1: Bolt 9E 198
FY1: Blackp 4J 227 (6B 88)
Coote La. PR4: W Stake 9H 135
PR5: Lost H 9H 135
Cop, The FY5: T Clev 6D 54
Copeland Pl. FY8: L Ann 4B 130
Copenhagen Sq. OL16: Roch 5D 204
Copenhagen St. OL16: Roch 5D 204
(not continuous)
Cop La. PR1: Penw 3E 134
COPP 8M 65
Copperas Cl. WN6: Shev 5L 213
Copperas Ho. Ter. OL14: Wals 5J 165
Copper Beech Cl. PR4: Much H 4J 151
Copper Beeches BB2: Blackb 2H 139
Copperfield PR1: Penw 7G 134
Copperfield Cl. BB7: Clith 4L 81
BB10: Burnl 3K 125
Copperfield St. BB1: Blackb 7F 226 (5N 139)
Copperfield Va. PR6: Clay W 6D 154
Copperwood Way PR7: Chor 7B 174
Coppice, The BB2: Blackb 1H 139
BB5: Clay M 5M 121
BB11: Burnl 5C 124
BL0: Ramsb 1F 200
BL2: Bolt 8K 199
LA4: Morec 3E 22
PR2: Ingol 5D 114
PR4: K'ham 3M 111
PR4: Longt 8L 133
Coppice Av. BB5: Acc 1C 142
Coppice Brow LA5: Carn 8C 12
Coppice Cl. BB9: Nelson 9L 85
PR6: Chor 5G 175
Coppice Dr. OL12: Whitw 7N 183
WN5: Bill 9G 220
Coppice La. PR6: Heap 2L 175
Coppice St. BL9: Bury 9N 201
Coppingford Cl. OL12: Roch 3L 203
Coppins Grn. FY6: Poul F 1L 89
Copp La. PR3: Gt E 8M 65
PR4: Elsw 9M 65
COPPULL 4A 194
Coppull Community Leisure Cen. 5A 194
Coppull Ent. Cen. PR7: Copp 3A 194
Coppull Hall La. PR7: Copp 4C 194
COPPULL MOOR 7N 193
Coppull Moor La. PR7: Copp 7N 193
Coppull Rd. L31: Lyd 7B 216
PR7: Char R, Chor 2B 194
Coppy Bri. Dr. OL16: Roch 5G 205
Cop Royd Ter. BB10: Cliv 8J 125
Copse, The BB5: Acc 3M 141
BL7: Turt 3J 199
PR7: Chor 1D 194
WN5: Orr 5K 221
Copse Cl. BB1: Blackb 1N 139
Copse Dr. BL9: Bury 7L 201
Copse Rd. FY7: Flee 2F 54
Copse Vw. Bus. Pk. *FY7: Flee 2F 54*
(off Henderson Rd.)
Copse Wlk. OL15: Littleb 9J 185
Copster Dr. PR3: Longr 3K 97
COPSTER GREEN 1K 119
Copster Hill Cl. BB1: Guide 8D 140
Copthorne Rd. L32: Kirk 8G 223
Copthorne Wlk. BL8: Tott 8E 200
L32: Kirk 8G 222
Copthurst Av. BB12: High 4L 103
Copthurst La. PR6: Whit W 9G 155
Copthurst St. BB12: Padi 9H 103
Coptrod Head Cl. OL12: Roch 1B 204
Coptrod Rd. OL11: Roch 5A 204
Copy La. L30: N'ton 6A 222
LA2: Caton 3G 25
Copy Nook BB1: Blackb 3A 140
Coral Cl. L32: Kirk 8H 223
Coral Island 3H 227 (6B 88)
Coral Pl. FY4: Blackp 9G 89
Corbet Cl. L32: Kirk 8H 223
Corbett St. OL16: Roch 5E 204
Corbet Wlk. L32: Kirk 8H 223
Corbridge Cl. FY4: Blackp 2G 108
FY6: Carl 6J 63
Corbridge Ct. BB7: Clith 2L 81
Corcas La. FY6: Stal 5L 55
Corden Av. BB3: Darw 5B 158
Cordwainers Ct. PR7: Buck V 9A 154
Corka La. FY8: Moss S 8E 110
Cork Rd. LA1: Lanc 1M 29
Corlass St. BB9: Barrf 8H 85
Corless Cotts. LA2: Dolp 7E 38
Cornall St. BL8: Bury 9H 201
Cornbrook WN8: Skelm 4B 220
Cornbrook Cl. OL12: Ward 8F 184
Corncroft PR1: Penw 5F 134
Cornel Gro. BB11: Burnl 5A 124
Cornelian St. BB1: Blackb 7N 119
Cornelian Way FY4: Blackp 9G 89
Corner Bank Cl. PR4: Gt P 2E 110
CORNER ROW 8K 91
Corners, The FY5: T Clev 8C 54
Cornfield PR4: Cott 3B 114
Cornfield Cl. BL9: Bury 6L 201
Cornfield Gro. BB12: Burnl 1M 123
Cornfield St. BB3: Darw 5B 158
OL14: Tod 1N 165
OL16: Milnr 8J 205
Cornflower Cl. PR4: Hesk B 3C 150
PR6: Chor 4F 174
Cornford Rd. FY4: Blackp 1H 109
Cornhill BB5: Acc 2B 142
Cornhill Arc. *BB5: Acc 2A 142*
(off Cornhill)
CORNHOLME 7E 146
Cornholme BB10: Burnl 8J 105
Cornholme Ter. *OL14: Tod 7E 146*
(off Burnley Rd.)
Corn Mkt. LA1: Lanc 7C 228
Corn Mill Cl. OL12: Roch 1F 204
Corn Mill Ct. BB5: Alt 3E 122
Cornmill Ct. *BB7: Wadd 8H 73*
(off Queensway)
Corn Mill La. *BB4: Rawt 4M 161*
(off Greenfield St.)
FY7: Flee 9H 41
Cornmill Lodge L31: Magh 9B 216
Corn Mill M. BB7: Whall 5J 101
Cornmill Pl. BB18: Barnw 1M 77
Cornmill Ter. BB18: Barnw 1M 77
Corn Mill Yd. BB5: Clay M 7M 121
Cornthwaite Rd. PR2: Fulw 6H 115
Cornwall Av. BB1: Blackb 4E 140
FY2: Blackp 1C 88
FY5: T Clev 8F 54
PR7: Buck V 9B 154
Cornwall M. FY5: T Clev 8F 54
Cornwall Pl. BB5: Chur 1M 141
FY3: Blackp 8H 89
WN5: Wigan 5M 221
Cornwall Rd. BB1: Rish 8G 120
Cornwall Way PR8: Ains 1B 206
Corona Av. L31: Lyd 6B 216
Coronation Av. BB2: Fenis 9D 138
BB12: Padi 3H 123
L37: Form 1A 214
PR3: Fort 2M 45
Coronation Ct. PR26: Cros 3M 171
Coronation Cres. PR1: Prest 1L 135
Coronation Gro. BB4: Newc 6C 162
Coronation Mt. *LA6: Bur L 3K 19*
(off Ireby Rd.)
Coronation Pl. BB9: Barrf 8H 85
Coronation Rd. BB9: Brierf 5G 104
FY5: T Clev 1C 62
FY8: L Ann 4J 129
L31: Lyd 8B 216
PR4: K'ham 4M 111
WN6: Stand 9N 213
Coronation St. BB6: Gt H 3K 121
BB18: Barnw 2N 77
FY1: Blackp 2J 227 (5B 88)
Coronation Ter. *BB6: Langh 9C 100*
(off Whalley New Rd.)
Coronation Vs. OL12: Whitw 4A 184
Coronation Wlk. PR8: S'port 7G 167
Coronation Way LA1: Lanc 4L 23
Coronet Cl. WN6: App B 5F 212
Corporation Rd. OL11: Roch 7A 204
(not continuous)
Corporation St. BB2: Blackb 4C 226 (3M 139)
BB4: Rawt 4M 161
(off Crankshaw St.)
BB5: Acc 3N 141

Corporation St.—Croftland Gdns.

Corporation St. BB7: Clith 3K 81
BB8: Colne 8L 85
FY1: Blackp 1H 227 (5B 88)
PR1: Prest 5H 229 (9H 115)
(not continuous)
PR6: Chor 5F 174
PR8: S'port 7H 167
Corriander Cl. FY2: Blackp 8F 62
Corrib Rd. FY2: Blackp 9D 62
Corricks La. LA2: C Grn 1F 36
Corringham Rd. LA4: Morec 3B 22
Corring Way BL1: Bolt 9H 199
Corwen Cl. BB1: Blackb 1C 226 (2M 139)
Corwen Dr. L30: N'ton 6A 222
Cosford St. PR4: Weet 4D 90
Cosgate Cl. WN5: Orr 6H 221
Costessey Way WN3: Wins 8M 221
COTE HOLME 2L 141
Cote La. OL15: Littleb 8J 185
Cotford Rd. BL1: Bolt 8F 198
Cotman Cl. OL13: Bac 7M 163
Coton Way L32: Kirk 7H 223
Cotswold Av. PR7: Eux 5N 173
WN5: Wigan 6L 221
Cotswold Cl. BL0: Ramsb 1H 201
PR7: E'ton 8G 172
Cotswold Cres. BL8: Bury 9F 200
OL16: Milnr 6K 205
Cotswold Dr. BL6: Hor 8D 196
Cotswold Ho. *BB4: Hasl* *4G 160*
(off Bury Rd.)
PR7: Chor 8E 174
Cotswold M. BB1: Blackb 8A 140
Cotswold Rd. FY2: Blackp 1D 88
FY8: L Ann 3C 130
PR7: Chor 8E 174
Cottage Cl. L39: Orms 8J 209
Cottage Cft. BL2: Bolt 8K 199
Cottage Flds. PR7: Chor 1D 194
Cottage Gdns. PR5: Bam B 8D 136
Cottage La. L39: Orms 6J 209
PR5: Bam B 6B 136
PR26: Cros 5J 171
Cottage M. L39: Orms 7J 209
Cottage Mus. 6B 228
Cottage Row *FY8: L Ann* *5A 130*
(off Bath Rd.)
Cottage Vw. OL12: Whitw 7N 183
Cottage Wlk. OL12: Roch 1N 203
COTTAM 3B 114
Cottam Av. PR2: Ingol 5C 114
Cottam Cl. BB7: Whall 4J 101
FY8: L Ann 7F 108
Cottam Grn. PR4: Cott 3B 114
Cottam Hall La. PR2: Ingol 4C 114
PR4: Cott 4B 114
(not continuous)
Cottam La. PR2: Ash R, Ingol 6D 114
PR4: Longt 1N 151
Cottam Pl. FY6: Poul F 9J 63
Cottam St. BL8: Bury 9H 201
PR7: Chor 8E 174
Cottam Way PR4: Cott 5N 113
Cottesloe Pl. BB9: Barrf 8G 84
Cottesmore Cl. OL12: Whitw 8N 183
Cottesmore Pl. FY3: Blackp 4G 88
Cottingley Cl. BL1: Bolt 8D 198
Cottom Cft. BB5: Clay M 5M 121
Cotton Bldg., The *BL7: Eger* *3D 198*
(off Deakins Mill Way)
Cotton Ct. BB8: Colne 8N 85
PR1: Prest 5M 229 (9K 115)
Cotton Dr. L39: Orms 6J 209
Cottonfields BL7: Bolt 6F 198
Cotton Fold OL16: Roch 7F 204
Cotton Hall St. BB3: Darw 5A 158
Cotton La. OL11: Roch 9N 203
Cotton Mills Works *BB8: Colne* *7N 85*
(off The Arches)
Cotton Row BB11: Dunn 2B 144
Cotton Spinners Ct. *BB3: Darw* *6B 158*
(off Ellenshaw Cl.)
Cotton St. BB5: Acc 3A 142
BB12: Burnl 3B 124
BB12: Padi 2H 123
COTTON TREE 6E 86
Cotton Tree La. BB8: Colne 6D 86
Cottonworks, The BL1: Bolt 8F 198
Cottys Brow PR9: S'port 3M 167
Coudray Rd. PR9: S'port 5L 167
Coulston Av. FY2: Blackp 8B 62
Coulston Rd. LA1: Lanc 1L 29
Coultate St. BB12: Burnl 3A 124
Coulter Beck La. LA6: Leck 8H 9
Coulthurst Gdns. BB3: Darw 5B 158
Coulthurst St. BL0: Ramsb 8G 180
Coulton Rd. BB9: Brierf 3F 104
Counsell Ct. FY5: T Clev 1H 63
Countess Cl. PR4: Wesh 2M 111
Countess Cres. FY2: Blackp 8C 62
Countess Rd. BB3: Lwr D 9N 139
Countess St. BB5: Acc 2M 141
Countess Way PR7: Eux 4N 173
Countessway PR5: Bam B 7A 136
Country M. BB2: Blackb 9G 119
Count St. OL16: Roch 8D 204
County Av. LA1: Bail 7M 29
County Brook La. BB8: Foul 9N 77
County Cl. PR6: Clay W 6D 154
PR26: Far M 3K 153
County Court
Blackburn 3D 226 (3M 139)
Blackpool 4H 227 (6B 88)
Chorley 6D 174
Rawtenstall *5M 161*
(off Grange St.)
County Rd. L32: Kirk 6K 223
L39: Orms 8J 209
County St. LA1: Lanc 7A 228 (8J 23)
COUPE GREEN 4G 136
Coupe Grn. PR5: Hogh 4G 136
Coupland Cl. OL12: Whitw 6N 183
Couplands, The PR7: Copp 5A 194
Coupland St. OL12: Whitw 6N 183
OL14: Tod 2L 165
Courage Low La. WN6: Wrigh 9G 192
Course La. WN8: N 'urgh 3G 211
Court, The PR1: Penw 4F 134
PR2: Fulw 2G 114
PR7: Buck V 9A 154
PR9: S'port 6H 167
Courtfield L39: Orms 5K 209
Courtfield Av. FY2: Blackp 2D 88
Courtfields FY1: Blackp 3L 227 (6C 88)
Court Grn. L39: Orms 5J 209
Court Gro. BB1: Clay D 3M 119
Court Hey L31: Magh 1D 222
Court M. PR9: S'port 5N 167
Court Rd. PR9: S'port 6J 167
Courtyard, The BB4: Hasl 6E 160
BB8: Colne 7A 86
BB11: Burnl *5F 124*
(off Fir Gro. Rd.)
FY5: T Clev 2D 62
OL13: Bac 4L 163
PR4: K'ham *4L 111*
(off Marquis St.)
PR8: S'port *7H 167*
(off Lord St.)
Courtyard Works L33: Know P 7A 224
Cousin Flds. BL7: Brom C 6J 199
Cousin's La. L40: Ruff 2E 190
Cove, The FY5: T Clev 8C 54
LA4: Morec 1E 22
Cove Dr. LA5: Silv 7G 4
Covell Ho. LA1: Lanc 6A 228
Coventry St. PR7: Chor 8E 174
Coverdale Dr. BB2: Blackb 9E 138
Coverdale Rd. LA1: Lanc 8H 23
Coverdale Way BB12: Burnl 2B 124
Cove Rd. LA5: Silv 6E 4
Covert, The FY5: T Clev 8F 54
Covert Cl. PR8: S'port 3N 187
Covertside Rd. PR8: S'port 3N 187
Coveway Av. FY3: Blackp 4E 88
Cowan Brae BB1: Blackb 1A 226 (2L 139)
COWAN BRIDGE 8H 9
COW ARK 3L 71
Cow Clough La. OL12: Whitw 4M 183
Cowdrey M. LA1: Lanc 7H 23
Cowell Way BB2: Blackb 4A 226 (3L 139)
Cowes Av. BB4: Hasl 5H 161
Cowfold St. OL14: Tod 1L 165
Cowgarth La. BB18: Earl 2F 78
Cow Gate La. BD23: Hort 4D 52
Cow Gill La. BB7: Saw 2K 75
Cowgill St. BB18: Earl 3E 78
OL13: Bac 4L 163
COW HILL 1C 116
Cowhill La. BB1: Rish 1F 140
Cowhurst Av. OL14: Tod 9J 147
Cow La. BB11: Burnl 3C 228 (3D 124)
PR25: Leyl 7J 153
(not continuous)
Cowley Cres. BB12: Padi 2K 123
Cowley Rd. BL1: Bolt 8F 198
FY4: Blackp 1F 108
PR2: Ribb 6A 116
COWLING 8G 175
Cowling Brow PR6: Chor 7G 175
Cowling Brow Ind. Est. PR6: Chor 8H 175
Cowling Bus. Pk. PR6: Chor 8H 175
Cowling Cotts. PR7: Char R 2N 193
Cowling Hill La. BD22: Cowl 8N 79
Cowling La. PR25: Leyl 6G 152
Cowling Rd. PR6: Chor 8H 175
Cowm Pk. Way Nth. OL12: Whitw 4N 183
Cowm Pk. Way Sth. OL12: Whitw 6N 183
Cowm St. OL12: Whitw 1B 184
COWPE 9D 162
Cowper Av. BB7: Clith 2L 81
Cowpe Rd. BB4: W'foot 7C 162
Cowper Pl. BB7: Saw 3E 74
PR7: Buck V 1A 174
Cowper St. BB1: Blackb 1F 226 (1N 139)
Cowslip Way PR6: Chor 4F 174
Cowtoot La. OL13: Bac 4K 163
Cow Well La. PR6: Whit W 7D 154
Coxfield Gro. WN6: Shev 5G 212
COX GREEN 4F 198
Cox Grn. Cl. BL7: Eger 2D 198
Cox Grn. Rd. BL7: Eger 1D 198
Coyford Dr. PR9: S'port 2N 167
Crabtree Av. BB4: W'foot 5D 162
OL13: Bac 6L 163
PR1: Penw 5D 134
Crabtree Bldgs. *BB4: Lumb* *3D 162*
(off Crabtree St.)
BB4: Rawt 6L 161
Crabtree Cl. L40: Burs 9B 190
Crab Tree La. PR3: St M 3A 66
Crabtree La. L40: Burs 8N 189
Crabtree Orchard FY5: T Clev 9H 55
Crabtree Pl. OL14: Tod 7E 146
Crabtree Rd. FY5: T Clev 9H 55
WN5: Wigan 4N 221
Crabtree St. BB1: Blackb 3B 140
BB4: Lumb 2D 162
BB8: Colne 7N 85
BB9: Brierf 5F 104
Crabtree Ter. *BB4: Rawt* *6L 161*
(off Andrew Av.)
Cracoe Gill BB9: Barrf 8G 85
Craddock Rd. BB8: Colne 6B 86
Crag Av. BL9: Summ 3J 201
CRAG BANK 1N 15
Crag Bank Cres. LA5: Carn 1N 15
Crag Bank La. LA5: Carn 8M 11
Crag Bank Rd. LA5: Carn 9M 11
Cragdale Gdns. *BD24: Sett* *3N 35*
(off Chapel St.)
CRAG FOOT 2K 11
Cragg Fold BL9: Summ 3J 201
Cragg Pl. OL15: Littleb 9L 185
Cragg Row BB18: Salt 4A 78
Craggs Hill LA6: Over K 1G 16
Craggs La. LA2: Low 2L 33
Cragg's Row PR1: Prest 3J 229 (8J 115)
Cragg St. BB8: Colne 6N 85
FY1: Blackp 5H 227 (7B 88)
Crag La. BL9: Summ 3J 201
LA6: H Roo 6A 8
Crag Rd. LA1: Lanc 7M 23
LA5: Wart 2K 11
Crag Vw. BB4: W'foot 8D 162
Craigflower Ct. PR5: Bam B 9E 136
Craighall Rd. BL1: Bolt 7E 198
Craigholme Ho. Caravan Pk.
LA5: Carn *9N 11*
(off Crag Bank Rd.)
Craiglands Av. LA3: Heys 6L 21
Craiglands Ct. LA1: Ald 2G 29
Craig St. LA3: Heys 5L 21
Crake Av. FY7: Flee 2C 54
Crake Bank LA1: Lanc 6G 22
Crambe Hgts. BB3: Lwr D 9A 140
Cramond Cl. WN3: Wigan 7N 221
Cranberry Av. OL14: Wals 8L 165
Cranberry Bottoms BB3: Darw 1E 178
Cranberry Chase BB3: Darw 8C 158
Cranberry Cl. BB3: Darw 9D 158
Cranberry Fold BB3: Darw 1D 178
Cranberry Fold Ct. BB3: Darw 1D 178
Cranberry La. BB3: Darw 8C 158
Cranberry Ri. BB4: Craws 6M 143
Cranborne Cl. WN6: Stand 3M 213
Cranborne St. PR1: Prest 9M 115
Cranborne Ter. BB2: Blackb 2K 139
Cranbourne Dr. BB5: Chur 9N 121
PR6: Chor 7G 174
Cranbourne Gro. FY5: T Clev 4L 63
Cranbourne Rd. OL11: Roch 7J 203
Cranbourne St. BB8: Colne 5B 86
PR5: Bam B 8A 136
PR6: Chor 7F 174
Cranbrook Av. BB5: Osw 4J 141
FY2: Blackp 6D 62
Cranbrook St. BB2: Blackb 9A 226 (6L 139)
Cranesbill Cl. FY6: K Sea 7M 41
Cranes La. L40: Lath 5B 210
Crane St. PR7: Chor 9E 174
Cranfield Vw. BB3: Darw 9C 158
Crangle Fold BB7: Clith 1N 81
Crank Rd. WN5: Bill 9G 220
Crankshaw St. BB4: Rawt 4M 161
Cranleigh Av. FY2: Blackp 8C 62
Cranmer St. BB11: Burnl 2A 228 (3C 124)
Cranshaw Dr. BB1: Blackb 9M 119
Cranshaw St. BB5: Acc 2A 142
Cranston Rd. L33: Know P 8A 224
Crantock Rd. WN5: Wigan 5M 221
Cranwell Av. LA1: Lanc 2M 29
Cranwell Cl. BB1: Blackb 5G 226 (4N 139)
L10: Aint 8B 222
Cranwell Ct. PR4: K'ham 4L 111
Crask Wlk. L33: Kirk 6L 223
Craven Bank La. BD24: Gig 2L 35
Craven Cl. PR2: Fulw 2J 115
Craven Cnr. FY5: T Clev 4F 62
Craven Cotts. *BD24: Sett* *3N 35*
(off Kirkgate)
Craven Ct. BB18: Earl 3C 78
Cravendale Av. BB9: Nelson 8J 85
Cravendale Ct. *BB8: Colne* *6D 86*
(off Keighley Rd.)
Craven Dr. PR5: Bam B 9N 135
Craven Gdns. OL11: Roch 8B 204
Craven Ho. OL14: Wals 7K 165
Craven's Av. BB2: Blackb 9M 139
Cravens Heath BB2: Blackb 1M 157
Cravens Hollow BB2: Blackb 1M 157
Craven St. BB4: Rawt 5L 161
BB5: Acc 3N 141
BB7: Clith 4L 81
BB8: Colne 6D 86
BB9: Brierf 5F 104
BB9: Nelson 2G 105
BB11: Burnl 3E 228 (4E 124)
BB18: Barnw 2N 77
Craven Ter. *BD23: Hell* *1D 52*
(off Main Rd.)
BD24: Sett *3N 35*
(off Kirkgate)
Craven Vw. BB18: Earl 3D 78
Cravenwood Cl. BB5: Acc 3M 141
CRAWFORD 9A 220
Crawford Av. FY2: Blackp 6D 62
L31: Magh 8A 216
PR1: Prest 8B 116
PR7: Adl 8G 195
PR7: Chor 5D 174
PR25: Leyl 7K 153
Crawford Rd. WN8: Skelm 1N 225
Crawford St. BB9: Nelson 1J 105
OL14: Wals 7L 165
OL16: Roch 8D 204
CRAWSHAWBOOTH 9M 143
Crawshaw Dr. BB4: Rawt 1M 161
Crawshaw Grange BB4: Craws 1M 161
Crawshaw La. BB10: S'field 4N 105
Cray, The OL16: Milnr 7H 205
Crediton Av. PR9: S'port 1A 168
Crediton Cl. BB2: Blackb 8K 139
Crescent, The BB2: Blackb 7F 138
BB4: Hasl 6G 161
BB7: Clith 3K 81
BB7: Dun B 7K 49
BB7: Whall 4G 101
BB8: Colne 5A 86
BB10: Reed 6F 104
BB10: W'thorne 4L 125
BB18: Salt 5M 77
BL2: Bolt 9M 199
BL7: Brom C 5G 199
FY4: Blackp 2B 108
FY6: Carl 7J 63
FY6: Pree 9A 42
FY6: Stal 3C 56
FY7: Flee 4E 54
FY8: L Ann 2E 128
L31: Magh 3B 222
LA2: Hest B 8H 15
LA4: Morec *3A 22*
(off Queen St.)
LA6: Holme 1F 6
OL12: Whitw 6N 183
PR2: Ash R 7D 114
PR2: Lea 8A 114
Crescent, The PR4: Frec 3N 131
(Poolside)
PR4: Frec 9D 112
(Preston New Rd.)
PR4: Wart 4H 131
PR5: Bam B 6B 136
PR5: Lost H 8M 135
PR7: Chor 4E 174
PR9: S'port 3B 168
WN5: Wigan 5N 221
Crescent Av. FY5: T Clev 1D 62
Crescent Ct. FY4: Blackp 4A 108
Crescent E. FY5: T Clev 1D 62
Crescent Grn. L39: Aug 2G 217
Crescent Rd. FY6: Poul F 7L 63
OL11: Roch 9M 203
PR8: Birk 2F 186
Crescent St. OL14: Tod 2L 165
PR1: Prest 8M 115
Crescent West FY5: T Clev 1D 62
Cressell Pk. WN6: Stand 2K 213
Cresswood Av. FY5: T Clev 2D 62
Crestway FY3: Blackp 4F 88
PR4: Tarl 8E 150
Creswell Av. PR2: Ingol 6C 114
Creswick Av. BB11: Burnl 7D 124
Creswick Cl. BB11: Burnl 6D 124
Crewdson St. BB3: Darw 5N 157
Crewgarth Rd. LA3: Morec 6B 22
Cribden End La. BB4: Hasl 3G 161
Cribden La. BB4: Rawt 3K 161
CRIBDEN SIDE 2H 161
Cribden St. BB4: Rawt 3L 161
Criccieth Cl. BB4: Hasl 6G 161
Criccieth Pl. FY5: T Clev 1K 63
Crichton Pl. FY4: Blackp 4B 108
Cricketers Cl. BB5: Osw 6J 141
Cricketers Grn. PR7: E'ton 7E 172
Cricket Path PR8: Birk 2F 186
Cricket Vw. OL16: Milnr 8J 205
CRIMBLE 9J 203
Crimble La.
OL10: Heyw, Roch 8J 203
OL11: Roch 8J 203
Crimbles La. LA2: C'ham 2E 44
Crimble St. OL12: Roch 5A 204
Crimea St. OL13: Bac 5L 163
Crimewell La. LA3: Heys 9K 21
Cringle Way BB7: Clith 1M 81
Cripplegate WN6: Stand 2J 213
Cripple Ga. La. PR5: Hogh 4K 137
CRISP DELF 9C 212
Critchley Cl. PR4: Much H 4K 151
Critchley Way L33: Kirk 6L 223
Croasdale LA1: Lanc 6G 22
Croasdale Av. BB10: Burnl 8H 105
PR2: Ribb 5A 116
Croasdale Cl. LA5: Carn 9N 11
Croasdale Dr. BB7: Clith 4M 81
FY5: T Clev 8F 54
WN8: Parb 1N 211
Croasdale Sq.
BB1: Blackb 7G 226 (5A 140)
Croasdale Wlk. FY3: Blackp 2H 89
Crockleford Av. PR8: S'port 2L 187
Crocus Cl. BB4: Hasl 7E 160
Crocus Fld. PR25: Leyl 8K 153
Crocus St. BL1: Bolt 9F 198
CROFT 1L 77
Croft, The BB1: Blackb 1L 139
BB8: Colne 4B 86
FY5: T Clev 1D 62
FY6: Poul F 9K 63
FY7: Flee 2E 54
FY8: L Ann 8H 109
L31: Lyd 6A 216
LA2: Caton 2G 25
LA6: Bur L 3K 19
PR3: Gars 3M 59
PR3: Goos 4N 95
PR4: Gt P 2D 110
PR4: Longt 7L 133
PR5: Hogh *6K 137*
(off Station Rd.)
PR7: E'ton 7F 172
PR7: Eux 3L 173
WN5: Bill 7G 221
Croft Acres BL0: Ramsb 4J 181
Croft Av. L40: Burs 1D 210
LA2: Slyne 9J 15
WN5: Orr 6G 221
Croft Bank OL12: Whitw 4A 184
PR1: Penw 5F 134
Croft Butts La. PR4: Frec 2A 132
Croft Carr OL14: Tod 4N 165
Croft Cl. BB4: Rawt 2M 161
Croft Ct. FY5: T Clev 8J 55
FY7: Flee *2E 54*
(off The Croft)
PR4: Frec 2N 131
Croft Dell BL1: Bolt 9A 198
Croft Dr. BL8: Tott 7D 200
Crofters Bank BB4: Craws 7M 143
Crofters Fold LA2: Gal 2M 37
LA3: Heys 7M 21
Crofters Grn.
PR1: Prest 1H 229 (7H 115)
PR7: Eux 3M 173
Crofters La. L33: Kirk 5M 223
Crofters Mdw. PR26: Far M 4H 153
Crofters M. FY1: Blackp 3C 88
Crofters Wlk. BL2: Bolt 7J 199
FY8: L Ann 1L 129
PR1: Penw 6G 135
Croftfield L31: Magh 1D 222
Croft Ga. BL2: Bolt 9L 199
Croftgate PR2: Fulw 4J 115
Crofthead OL15: Littleb 7L 185
Croft Head Dr. OL16: Milnr 6J 205
Croft Head Rd. BB1: Blackb 8B 120
Croft Hey BL0: Ramsb 4J 181
L40: Ruff 1F 190
Croft Heys L39: Aug 2G 216
Crofthill Ct. OL12: Roch 1G 205
Croft Ho. FY6: Poul F 6K 63
Croftland Gdns. LA5: Bolt S 3L 15

Croftlands—Daisyfield Mill

Croftlands BL0: Ramsb 2F 200
LA1: Lanc 7A 228
LA5: Wart 4B 12
WN5: Orr 7G 220
Croftlands Caravan Pk. LA2: Slyne 9K 15
Croft La. BB12: High 4L 103
Croft Mnr. PR4: Frec 2A 132
Croft Mdw. PR5: Bam B 1E 154
Crofton Av. FY2: Blackp 6D 62
Croft Pk. PR25: Leyl 6M 153
Croft Rd. LA6: Ingl 3N 19
PR6: Chor 7G 175
Crofts Cl. PR4: K'ham 4A 112
Crofts Dr. PR2: Grim 9F 96
Croftson Av. L39: Orms 6L 209
Croft Sq. OL12: Roch 2F 204
Croft St. BB3: Darw 6A 158
BB6: Gt H 5J 121
BB7: Clith 4L 81
BB11: Burnl 3D 228 (4E 124)
BB18: Earl 2F 78
LA4: Morec 3C 22
OL12: Roch 2F 204
OL13: Bac 4K 163
PR1: Prest 9G 115
(not continuous)
Croftway FY5: T Clev 3J 63
Croftwood Sq. WN5: Wigan 1M 221
Croftwood Ter. BB2: Blackb 7H 139
Croich Bank BL8: Hawk 3A 200
Croich Grn. BL8: Hawk 3A 200
Crombleholme Fold PR3: Goos, Whitec 2N 69
Crombleholme Rd. PR1: Prest 8A 116
PR3: Goos 6A 70
Cromer Av. BB10: Burnl 9G 105
Cromer Gro. BB10: Burnl 9G 104
Cromer Pl. BB1: Blackb 1M 139
PR2: Ingol 5D 114
Cromer Rd. BL8: Bury 8J 201
FY2: Blackp 7E 62
FY8: L Ann 8G 108
PR8: Birk 3E 186
Cromer St. OL12: Roch 4B 204
Cromfield L39: Aug 1H 217
Cromford Dr. WN5: Wigan 6L 221
Cromford Wlk. PR1: Prest 9M 115
Crompton Av. FY4: Blackp 2E 108
Crompton Cl. BL1: Bolt 9G 199
Crompton Ct. PR1: Prest 5M 229
Crompton Fold *BL8: Bury* 9G 200
(off Dorning St.)
Crompton Pl. BB2: Blackb 3J 139
Crompton St. PR1: Prest 8M 115
Crompton Wlk. PR7: Buck V 1B 174
Crompton Way BL1: Bolt 9F 198
BL2: Bolt 9F 198
Cromwell Av. BB5: Acc 9A 122
PR1: Penw 5F 134
Cromwell Cl. L39: Aug 1H 217
Cromwell M. PR3: Gars 4N 59
Cromwell Rd. FY1: Blackp 2C 88
LA1: Lanc 9A 228 (9J 23)
PR1: Penw 5E 134
PR2: Ribb 5N 115
Cromwell St. BB1: Blackb 4A 140
BB8: Foul 2A 86
BB12: Burnl 2D 124
PR1: Prest 3M 229 (8K 115)
Cromwell Ter. *BB9: Barrf* 8H 85
(off Gisburn Rd.)
Cromwell Way PR1: Penw 7J 135
Cronkeyshaw Av. OL12: Roch 3B 204
Cronkeyshaw Rd. OL12: Roch 4B 204
Cronkshaw St. BB10: Burnl 2E 124
Cronshaw Dr. BB6: Langh 9C 100
Cronshaw Ind. Est. *OL11: Roch* 7D 204
(off Durham St.)
Crookall Cl. FY7: Flee 2E 54
Crook Dale La. FY6: Stal 5C 56
CROOKE 9M 213
Crooked La. PR1: Prest 5L 229 (9K 115)
Crooked Shore OL13: Bac 4K 163
Crooke Rd. WN6: Stand 9M 213
Crookfield Rd. PR6: Withn 3H 177
Crook Ga. La. PR3: Out R 2H 65
Crookhalgh Av. BB10: Burnl 3K 125
Crookhey Gdns. LA2: C'ham 2J 45
Crookings La. PR1: Penw 2D 134
Crookland Gdns. FY6: Ham 1C 64
Crooklands Dr. PR3: Gars 4N 59
Crookleigh Pl. LA3: Heys 6L 21
Crook O'Lune Caravan Pk. LA2: Caton 3E 24
Crook St. OL16: Roch 5D 204
PR1: Prest 9L 115
PR7: Adl 6H 195
PR7: Chor 9D 174
Cropper Cl. FY4: Blackp 3K 109
Cropper Gdns. PR4: Hesk B 4B 150
Cropper Rd. FY4: Blackp 2J 109
Cropper Rd. Nth. FY4: Blackp 2H 109
Croppers La. L39: Bick 2L 217
Cropton Rd. L37: Form 9A 206
Crosby Cl. BB3: Darw 9B 158
Crosby Coastal Pk. 9A 214
Crosby Gro. FY3: Blackp 7F 88
Crosby Pl. PR2: Ingol 5D 114
Crosby Rd. BB2: Blackb 7M 139
FY8: L Ann 8F 108
PR8: Birk 2F 186
Crosby St. OL12: Roch 3C 204
Crosfield Av. BL9: Summ 3H 201
Crosier Wlk. PR4: Cott 4B 114
Crosland Rd. L32: Kirk 9M 223
Crosland Rd. Nth. FY8: L Ann 8F 108
Crosland Rd. Sth. FY8: L Ann 9G 109
Crosley Cl. BB5: Acc 5A 142
Cross, The BL8: Bury 9E 200
L38: Ince B 8D 214
Cross Bank *BB12: Padi* 1J 123
(off Hambledon St.)
Cross Barn Gro. BB3: Darw 7B 158
Cross Barn La. L38: Ince B 9E 214
Cross Barn Wlk. BB3: Darw 7B 158
Crossbrook Way OL16: Milnr 8K 205
Cross Bldgs. *BB4: Craws* 9M 143
(off Cross St.)
Cross Ct. OL13: Bac 4L 163
Crossdale Av. LA3: Heys 6L 21
Crossdale Sq. LA1: Lanc 6E 228
CROSS EDGE 7N 141
Cross Edge BB5: Osw 7N 141
Crosse Hall Fold PR6: Chor 6H 175
Crosse Hall La.
PR6: Chor, Heap 7G 175
Crosse Hall St. PR6: Chor 7H 175
CROSSENS 2B 168
Crossens Way PR9: S'port 9B 148
Crossfield PR4: Hutt 7N 133
Crossfield Cl. OL12: Ward 7F 184
Crossfield Ct. LA5: Arn 2E 4
Crossfield Pl. OL11: Roch 8D 204
Crossfield Rd. OL12: Ward 8F 184
WN8: Skelm 3N 219
Crossfields BL7: Brom C 5H 199
Crossfield St. BB2: Blackb 8E 226 (5N 139)
Cross Flatts Cres. BB18: Salt 4B 78
Cross Fold BB2: Blackb 9F 226 (6N 139)
BB7: Grind 4A 74
Crossford Cl. WN3: Wigan 7N 221
Cross Gates BB6: Gt H 4J 121
Crossgates Rd. OL16: Milnr 6J 205
CROSSGILL 7N 25
Crossgill Pl. *LA1: Lanc* 6H 23
(off Austwick Rd.)
Cross Grn. L37: Form 1A 214
Cross Grn. Cl. L37: Form 1A 214
Cross Grn. Rd. PR2: Fulw 3H 115
Cross Hagg St. BB8: Colne 7A 86
Crosshall Brow L39: Orms 7N 209
L40: W'head 7N 209
Cross Hall Ct. L39: Orms 8M 209
Cross Halls PR1: Penw 5E 134
Cross Helliwell St. BB8: Colne 7A 86
Cross Hey L31: Magh 3D 222
Cross Hill Ct. LA5: Bolt S 5L 15
Cross Hill La. BB7: Rim 3B 76
Crosshill Rd. BB2: Blackb 3J 139
Crosshills *BB12: Padi* 9H 103
(off East St.)
Crossings, The PR5: Hogh 6K 137
Cross Keys Dr. PR6: Whit W 8E 154
Crossland Rd. FY4: Blackp 9E 88
Crossland St. BB5: Acc 3N 141
Cross La. BB7: Bas E, Wadd 7C 72
BB12: Barl, Newc P 7A 84
BB18: Salt 4A 78
BL8: Holc 9F 180
L39: Hals 3A 208
LA2: L Ben 6J 19
PR4: Trea 9B 92
WN5: Bill 8G 220
Cross La. Cotts. *BB18: Salt* 4A 78
(off Cross La.)
Cross Lee OL14: Tod 9J 147
Cross Lee Ga. OL14: Tod 9J 147
Cross Lee Rd. OL14: Tod 9J 147
Cross Lees OL12: Roch 2D 204
Crossley Fold BB11: Burnl 5B 124
Crossley Ho. Ind. Est. PR1: Penw 4H 135
Crossley St. OL14: Tod 2L 165
OL16: Milnr 7H 205
Crossmeadow Cl. OL11: Roch 5L 203
Cross Meanygate L40: Holmesw 9N 169
CROSSMOOR 1C 92
Cross Pit La. WA11: Rain 4K 225
Cross Rd. LA2: Tat 7J 19
Cross School St. BB8: Colne 7A 86
Cross Skelton St. BB8: Colne 6B 86
CROSS STONE 1N 165
Cross Stone Fold OL14: Tod 1N 165
Cross Stone Rd. OL14: Tod 1M 165
Cross St. BB3: Darw 8B 158
BB3: Lwr D 9N 139
BB4: Craws 9M 143
BB5: Acc 3B 142
BB5: Clay M 6L 121
BB5: Osw 4K 141
BB6: Gt H 4K 121
BB7: Clith 3K 81
BB9: Barrf 5F 104
BB9: Nelson 2H 105
BB10: Brierc 8K 105
BB10: W'thorne 3M 125
BB12: High 5L 103
BB18: Earl 3D 78
BL0: Ramsb 8H 181
BL7: Brom C 6G 198
FY1: Blackp 3B 88
FY7: Flee 8H 41
FY8: L Ann 9D 108
LA4: Morec 3C 22
OL16: Roch 6G 205
PR1: Prest 7K 229 (1J 135)
PR3: Longr 4H 97
PR7: Chor 5E 174
PR8: S'port 8H 167
PR25: Leyl 5L 153
WN5: Orr 5L 221
WN5: Wigan 5L 221
Cross St. Nth. BB4: Hasl 2G 160
Cross St. Sth. BB4: Hasl 3G 160
Cross St. W. BB8: Colne 7M 85
Cross Swords Cl. PR7: Chor 9D 174
Crossway FY5: T Clev 8D 54
Crossways BB7: West B 5K 73
CROSTON 4M 171
Croston Av. PR6: Adl 5J 195
Croston Barn La. PR3: Nateby 4L 59
Croston Cl. BB1: Blackb 3B 140
Croston Cl. Rd. BL0: Ramsb 3N 201
BL9: Bury 3N 201
Croston Dr. L40: Ruff 8F 170
Croston La. PR7: Char R 3L 193
Croston Rd. L40: Ruff 7F 170
PR3: Gars 3M 59
PR5: Lost H 4H 153
PR26: Far M, Lost H 4H 153
Croston's Brow PR9: S'port 3M 167
Croston Station (Rail) 3M 171
Croston St. BB1: Blackb 3C 140
Crowder Av. FY5: T Clev 1H 63
Crowell Way PR5: Walt D 5A 136
Crowfoot Row *BB18: Barnw* 3M 77
(off Castle Vw.)
Crow Gth. BD23: Garg 3M 53
Crow Hills Rd. PR1: Penw 2D 134
Crowland Cl. PR9: S'port 8N 167
Crowland St. PR9: S'port 9M 167
Crowland St. Ind. Est. PR9: S'port 8N 167
Crowland Way L37: Form 1B 214
Crow La. BL0: Ramsb 8H 181
PR3: Out R 3K 65
WN8: Dalt 9C 212
Crowle St. PR1: Prest 9N 115
Crown Cl. L37: Form 1A 214
Crowndale BL7: Edgw 7K 179
Crowneast St. OL11: Roch 6N 203
Crownest Cotts. *BB18: Barnw* 1N 77
(off Bankfield Ter.)
Crownest Ind. Est. BB18: Barnw 1N 77
Crownest Rd. BB18: Barnw 1M 77
Crown Gdns. BL7: Edgw 8K 179
OL16: Roch 8E 204
Crown Grn. FY6: Carl 7G 63
Crown Ground 9A 122
Crown Ho. BB3: Darw 3N 157
Crown La. BL6: Hor 9B 196
FY7: Flee 9H 41
PR4: Bartl 8M 93
Crownlee PR1: Penw 5D 134
Crown Mdws. *OL13: Bac* 6L 163
(off Lane End La.)
Crown M. BL8: Hawk 2B 200
PR4: K'ham 4M 111
Crown Point BL7: Edgw 8K 179
Crown Point Rd. BB11: Burnl, Cliv 8C 124
Crown St. BB3: Darw 7A 158
BB5: Acc 3N 141
OL16: Roch 8E 204
PR1: Prest 4K 229 (9J 115)
PR7: Chor 6E 174
PR25: Far 4L 153
Crown Way BB8: Colne 6N 85
Crow Orchard Rd. WN6: Wrigh, Stand 2J 213
Crow Pk. La. BB7: Gis 8B 52
Crowshaw Dr. OL12: Roch 2B 204
Crowther Ct. *BB10: W'thorne* 3M 125
(off Showfield)
OL15: Littleb 1H 205
Crowther Dr. WN3: Wins 9N 221
Crowther St. BB5: Clay M 6L 121
BB11: Burnl 4F 228 (5F 124)
OL15: Littleb 9H 185
OL16: Roch 9E 204
Crowthorn Rd. BL7: Edgw 5M 179
Crow Tree Av. OL13: Bac 7F 162
CROW TREES 6D 84
Crowtrees *LA2: L Ben* 6J 19
(off Burton Rd.)
Crow Trees Brow BB7: Chatb 8C 74
Crow Trees Gdns. BB7: Chatb 7C 74
Crowtrees Gro. BB9: Rough 6D 84
Crow Trees La. BL7: Turt 7J 179
Crowtrees Pk. BD23: Tos 2K 51
Crow Trees Rd. BB7: Sabd 2E 102
Crow Wood Av. BB12: Burnl 2B 124
Crow Wood Ct. BB12: Burnl 2C 124
Crow Wood Leisure 1C 124
Crow Wood Rd. BL0: Eden 9J 161
Crow Woods BL0: Eden 1J 181
Croxteth Cl. L31: Magh 8D 216
Croxteth Dr. WA11: Rain 3K 225
Croxton Av. OL16: Roch 5E 204
Croxton Ct. PR9: S'port 5L 167
Croxton Wlk. *BL6: Hor* 9C 196
(off Beatrice St.)
Croyde Cl. PR9: S'port 1A 168
Croyde Rd. FY8: L Ann 3G 128
Croydon Rd. FY3: Blackp 3E 88
Croydon St. BB2: Blackb 3K 139
Crummock Pl. FY4: Blackp 9J 89
Crummock Rd. PR1: Prest 8C 116
Crumpax Av. PR3: Longr 2J 97
Crumpax Cft. PR3: Longr 2J 97
Crumpax Mdw. PR3: Longr 2J 97
Crundale Rd. BL1: Bolt 7G 198
Crystal Gro. FY8: L Ann 9E 108
Crystal M. FY1: Blackp 9H 227 (9B 88)
Crystal Rd. FY1: Blackp 9H 227 (9B 88)
FY5: T Clev 8H 55
Cuba Ind. Est. BL0: Ramsb 6H 181
Cuba St. BB9: Nelson 2H 105
Cub St. PR26: Far M 3K 153
Cuckoo Brow BB1: Blackb 9L 119
Cuckoo La. BL9: Bury 9A 202
PR3: Out R 9N 57
Cuckstool La. BB12: Fence 4C 104
(Montford Rd.)
BB12: Fence 3B 104
(Wheatley Cl.)
CUDDY HILL 3N 93
Cudworth Rd. FY8: L Ann 8F 108
Cuerdale La. PR5: Sam, Walt D 3A 136
Cuerdale St. BB10: Burnl 7J 105
Cuerden Av. PR25: Leyl 8G 153
Cuerden Cl. PR5: Bam B 3A 154
CUERDEN GREEN 1M 153
Cuerden Res. Pk. PR25: Leyl 4N 153
Cuerden Ri. PR5: Lost H 9M 135
Cuerden St. BB8: Colne 8M 85
PR6: Chor 7G 174
Cuerden Valley Pk. 4B 154
Cuerden Way PR5: Bam B 8N 135
Cuerden Way Bus. Village PR5: Bam B 9N 135
Culbeck La. PR7: Eux 4J 173
Culcross Av. WN3: Wigan 7M 221
Culshaw St. BB1: Blackb 4G 226
BB10: Burnl 4G 125
Culshaw Way L40: Scar 6E 188
Culvert La. WN8: N 'urgh 2L 211
Cumberland Av. BB5: Clay M 6N 121
BB12: Burnl 2M 123
FY1: Blackp 5M 227 (7D 88)
FY5: T Clev 8D 54
PR25: Leyl 8H 153
Cumberland Cl. BB3: Darw 9C 158
Cumberland Ga. L30: N'ton 6A 222
Cumberland Rd. PR8: S'port 9K 167
Cumberland St. BB1: Blackb 4A 140
BB8: Colne 6B 86
BB9: Nelson 1J 105
Cumberland Vw. LA1: Lanc 1L 29
Cumberland Vw. Cl. LA3: Heys 5L 21
Cumberland Vw. Rd. LA3: Heys 5L 21
Cumbrian Av. FY3: Blackp 3E 88
Cumbrian Way BB12: Burnl 1N 123
Cumeragh La. PR3: W'ham 4B 96
CUMERAGH VILLAGE 5B 96
Cunliffe Av. BL0: Ramsb 1F 200
Cunliffe Cl. BB1: Blackb 8B 120
Cunliffe Ct. BB5: Clay M 7M 121
Cunliffe Ho. BB4: Rawt 6B 162
Cunliffe La. BB7: Wis 2M 101
Cunliffe Rd. BB1: Blackb 8B 120
FY1: Blackp 8M 227 (8D 88)
Cunliffe St. BL0: Ramsb 7H 181
PR1: Prest 4M 229 (9K 115)
PR7: Chor 7E 174
Cunnery Mdw. PR25: Leyl 6A 154
Cunningham Av. PR7: Chor 8C 174
Cunningham Ct. BB1: Guide 8D 140
Cunningham Gro. BB12: Burnl 3N 123
Cunscough La. L31: Magh 9J 217
Curate St. BB6: Gt H 4J 121
PR6: Chor 5G 174
Curlew Cl. BB1: Blackb 9M 119
BB5: Osw 5K 141
FY5: T Clev 8F 54
OL11: Roch 6K 203
PR25: Leyl 8F 152
Curlew Gdns. BB11: Burnl 4N 123
Curlew Gro. LA3: Heys 2L 27
Curlew La. L40: Burs, Ruff 5B 190
Curran Way L33: Kirk 5J 223
Curtain Theatre 7C 204
Curteis St. BL6: Hor 9C 196
Curtis Dr. FY7: Flee 1D 54
Curtis St. BB4: Rawt 4M 161
WN5: Wigan 5N 221
Curven Edge BB4: Hasl 8F 160
Curve St. OL13: Bac 6K 163
Curwen Av. LA3: Heys 1K 27
Curwen La. PR3: Goos 8M 69
Curwen St. PR1: Prest 8M 115
(not continuous)
Curzon Pl. BB2: Blackb 5K 139
Curzon Rd. FY6: Poul F 8L 63
FY8: L Ann 1G 128
PR8: S'port 9K 167
Curzon St. BB7: Clith 3K 81
BB8: Colne 7B 86
BB11: Burnl 1C 228 (3D 124)
(not continuous)
Cusson Rd. L33: Know P 9N 223
Custom Ho. La. FY7: Flee 8H 41
Customs Way PR2: Ash R 9F 114
CUTGATE 5L 203
Cutgate Rd. OL12: Roch 4M 203
Cutgate Shop. Pct. OL11: Roch 5M 203
Cuthbert Mayne Ct. OL16: Roch 7B 204
Cuthbert St. WN5: Wigan 5N 221
Cutland Way OL15: Littleb 1K 205
Cut La. BB1: Rish 8F 120
L39: Hals 4E 208
OL12: Roch 4K 203
Cutler Cl. BB2: Blackb 4A 226 (3L 139)
Cutler Cres. OL13: Bac 8H 163
Cutler Greens OL13: Bac 8H 163
Cutler La. OL13: Bac 8H 163
PR3: Chip 7F 70
Cutt Cl. PR26: Leyl 9C 152
Cuttle St. PR1: Prest 9N 115
Cutts La. FY6: Ham 1D 64
PR3: Out R 1D 64
Cyclamen Cl. PR25: Leyl 5A 154
Cygnet Cl. L39: Aug 1H 217
Cygnet Ct. L33: Kirk 8M 223
Cyon Cl. PR1: Penw 3H 135
Cypress Av. FY5: T Clev 1E 62
Cypress Cl. L31: Mell 7F 222
LA1: Lanc 8H 23
PR2: Ribb 5C 116
PR25: Leyl 5A 154
Cypress Gdns. OL16: Roch 6G 204
Cypress Gro. FY3: Blackp 3D 88
PR5: Lost H 8L 135
Cypress Ridge BB2: Blackb 8G 138
Cypress Rd. PR8: S'port 8L 167
Cypress St. OL13: Bac 7G 163
Cyprus Av. FY8: L Ann 4H 129
Cyprus Rd. LA3: Heys 1K 27
Cyprus St. BB3: Darw 9B 158

D

Dacca St. PR7: Chor 5F 174
Dacre Rd. OL11: Roch 9C 204
Dacre Way PR4: Cott 4A 114
Daffodil Cl. BB4: Hasl 7F 160
OL12: Roch 2B 204
Daffodil St. BL1: Bolt 8F 198
Dagger Rd. PR4: Trea 8G 92
Daggers Hall La. FY4: Blackp 1E 108
Daggers La. FY6: Pree 1A 56
Dagnall Rd. L32: Kirk 9H 223
Dahlia Cl. BB3: Lwr D 9A 140
OL12: Roch 2A 204
PR25: Leyl 5A 154
Dailton Rd. WN8: Uph 4D 220
Daimler Av. PR7: Chor 9F 174
Dairy Farm Rd. WA11: Rain 4F 224
DAISY BANK 8D 162
Daisy Bank BB4: W'foot 8D 162
FY5: T Clev 1D 62
LA1: Lanc 9A 24
OL13: Bac 4K 163
Daisy Bank Cl. PR25: Leyl 6G 153
Daisy Bank Cres. BB10: Burnl 4K 125
Daisy Bank St. OL14: Tod 7E 146
Daisy Cl. PR9: Banks 2F 168
Daisy Cft. PR2: Lea 9A 114
DAISYFIELD 2A 140
Daisyfield Mill BB1: Blackb 3A 140

Daisyfields PR4: H Bart 2C 114
Daisyfield St. BB3: Darw 2M 157
Daisyfield Swimming Pool 1G 226 (2N 139)
Daisy Fold PR6: Chor 4G 175
DAISY HILL 6N 173
Daisy Hill BB4: Rawt 4M 161
OL13: Bac 7G 163
Daisy Hill Ct. BB5: Hunc 8D 122
Daisy Hill Dr. PR6: Adl 4J 195
Daisy Hill Fold PR7: Eux 5N 173
Daisy La. BB1: Blackb 1F 226 (2N 139)
L40: Lath 9F 190
PR1: Prest 6M 115
Daisy Mdw. PR5: Bam B 1C 154
Daisy Mt. L31: Magh 2D 222
Daisy St. BB1: Blackb 2F 226 (2A 140)
BB8: Colne 7A 86
LA1: Lanc 5K 23
OL12: Roch 5B 204
Daisy Wlk. *PR8: S'port 7L 167*
(off Beacham Rd.)
Daisy Way PR8: S'port 3J 187
Dakin Wlk. L33: Kirk 8L 223
Dalby Cl. FY5: T Clev 4F 62
PR1: Prest 6N 115
Dalby Cres. BB2: Blackb 7H 139
Dalby Lea BB2: Blackb 7H 139
Dale Av. LA2: Slyne 9J 15
OL14: Tod 2N 165
PR4: Longt 8J 133
PR7: Eux 5N 173
Dale Cl. *BB12: Burnl 3B 124*
(off Tunnel St.)
L31: Magh 9B 216
WN8: Parb 2M 211
Dale Cres. BB2: Blackb 8F 138
Dale Dyke Wlk. FY6: Poul F 8H 63
Daleford Cl. FY5: T Clev 3K 63
Dalegarth Cl. FY4: Blackp 9J 89
Dalehead Rd. PR25: Leyl 8K 153
Dale La. L33: Kirk 5M 223
Dales, The BB6: Langh 1A 120
BB18: Salt 5M 77
Dales Brow BL1: Bolt 7F 198
Dales Ct. FY4: Blackp 3D 108
Dalesford BB4: Hasl 6G 161
Daleside OL14: Tod 3K 165
Daleside Rd. L33: Kirk 7L 223
Daleside Wlk. L33: Kirk 7L 223
Dale St. BB2: Blackb 6A 226 (4L 139)
BB4: Hasl 4G 160
BB5: Acc 2N 141
BB5: Osw 4L 141
BB8: Colne 6N 85
BB9: Brierf 5E 104
BB9: Nelson 2G 105
BB12: Burnl 3B 124
BB18: Earl 2E 78
BL0: Ramsb 6H 181
BL8: Bury 9H 201
FY1: Blackp 5H 227 (7B 88)
LA1: Lanc 8E 228 (9L 23)
OL13: Bac 7G 163
(Albion St.)
OL13: Bac 4K 163
(Ash St.)
OL14: Tod 2L 165
OL16: Milnr 7J 205
OL16: Roch 6F 204
PR1: Prest 5N 229 (9L 115)
Dale St. M. FY1: Blackp 5H 227
Dalesview Cres. LA3: Heys 9L 21
Dales Vw. Pk. *BB18: Barnw 1M 77*
(off Powell St.)
Dales Wlk. L37: Form 6A 206
Dalesway BB9: Barrf 8G 85
Dalesway Caravan Pk. BD23: Garg 4L 53
Dale Ter. BB7: Chatb 7C 74
Dale Vw. BB2: Blackb 1M 157
BB4: Rawt 6M 161
BB7: B'ton 6H 101
BB18: Barnw 3M 77
BB18: Earl 3E 78
OL15: Littleb 3J 205
PR7: Chor 1E 194
Daleview Pk. Caravan Pk. BB18: Salt 5M 77
Dalewood Av. FY4: Blackp 9E 88
Dalglish Dr. BB2: Blackb 9L 139
Dalkeith Av. FY3: Blackp 8G 89
Dalkeith Rd. BB9: Nelson 2G 105
Dallam Av. LA4: Morec 2C 22
Dallam Dell FY5: T Clev 8H 55
Dallas Ct. LA4: Morec 4F 22
Dallas Rd. LA1: Lanc 9B 228 (9J 23)
LA4: Morec 4F 22
Dallas St. PR1: Prest 6H 115
Dallicar La. BD24: Gig 3M 35
Dall St. BB11: Burnl 5E 228 (5E 124)
Dalmeny Ter. OL11: Roch 9C 204
Dalmore Rd. PR2: Ingol 6D 114
Dalston Gro. WN3: Wins 8N 221
DALTON
LA6 5K 7
WN8 7A 212
Dalton Av. FY4: Blackp 4D 108
OL16: Roch 6G 205
Dalton Cl. BB1: Blackb 3A 140
BL0: Ramsb 1F 200
OL16: Roch 6G 205
WN5: Orr 4L 221
Dalton Ct. BB3: Darw 2N 157
Dalton Hall Bus. Cen. LA6: Burt K 7J 7
Dalton La. LA6: Burt K 6H 7
Dalton Rd. LA1: Lanc 6F 228 (8L 23)
LA3: Heys 5L 21
Dalton Sq. LA1: Lanc 7D 228 (8K 23)
Dalton St. BB9: Nelson 1J 105
BB11: Burnl 6B 124
FY8: L Ann 9D 108
OL14: Tod 2L 165
Dame Fold BB12: High 4L 103
BB12: Padi 1H 123
Damfield La. L31: Magh 1B 222
Dam Head Rd. BB18: Barnw 2M 77
Dam La. L40: Scar 7G 189
Dampier St. OL14: Wals 6K 165

DAM SIDE 7J 43
Dam Side BB8: Colne 7A 86
BB18: Barnw 1M 77
(off Gisburn St.)
Damside LA2: Ell 1M 37
Damside Cotts. LA2: Ell 1M 37
Damside St. LA1: Lanc 5C 228 (7K 23)
Damson Cl. BB6: Old L 4C 100
Damson Gro. WA11: Rain 3J 225
Dam Top BB4: Rawt 5N 161
Dam Wood Cl. PR7: Chor 8C 174
Dam Wood La. L40: Scar 8H 189
Danbers WN8: Uph 5C 220
Dancer La. BB7: Rim 3A 76
Dandy Brook Vw. PR5: Lost H 9M 135
Dandy Row BB3: Darw 4C 158
Dandy's Meanygate PR4: Tarl 8N 149
Dandy Wlk. BB1: Blackb 5D 226 (4M 139)
Dane M. FY6: Poul F 2L 89
Danesbury Pl. FY1: Blackp 1L 227 (5C 88)
Danesbury Rd. BL2: Bolt 9H 199
Danes Cl. PR4: K'ham 4A 112
Danes Dr. PR5: Walt D 7N 135
Daneshouse Rd. BB10: Burnl 1E 124
Danes La. OL12: Whitw 6L 183
Danesmoor Dr. BL9: Bury 9M 201
Dane St. BB10: Burnl 2E 124
OL11: Roch 6B 204
OL12: Roch 6B 204
Danesway PR1: Penw 4D 134
PR5: Walt D 6N 135
PR7: H Charn 4H 195
Daneswood Av. OL12: Whitw 7N 183
Daneswood Cl. OL12: Whitw 6M 183
Daneswood Fold OL12: Whitw 6M 183
Daneway PR8: Ains 7B 186
Danewerk St. PR1: Prest 4M 229 (9K 115)
DANGEROUS CORNER 2F 212
Daniel Fold OL12: Roch 2M 203
Daniel Fold La. PR3: Catt 1N 67
Daniell St. BB1: Rish 7G 121
Daniels La. WN8: Skelm 4N 219
Daniel St. BB5: Clay M 6L 121
OL12: Whitw 4A 184
Daniel St. Ind. Est. *OL12: Whitw 4A 184*
(off Daniel St.)
Danson Gdns. FY2: Blackp 2D 88
Danvers St. BB1: Rish 7H 121
Danvers Way PR2: Fulw 2M 115
Dapple Heath Av. L31: Mell 7F 222
Darbishire Rd. FY7: Flee 8F 40
Daresbury Av. PR8: Ains 8A 186
Daresbury Cl. L32: Kirk 8H 223
Darfield WN8: Uph 4C 220
Darkinson La. PR4: Lea T 6K 113
Dark Lane 6C 162
Dark La. BB4: Newc 7B 162
BB18: Earl 2G 79
BD23: T Crav 8J 53
BL6: Blackr 9K 195
L31: Magh 1C 222
L40: Lath 6N 209
L40: Mawd 2B 192
PR6: Whit W 1G 174
Darkwood Cres. BB7: Chatb 7C 74
Dark Wood La. PR5: Sam 2K 137
Darley Av. FY4: Blackp 2E 108
Darley Bank *OL13: Bac 7N 163*
(off Tong La.)
Darley Ct. FY8: L Ann 1D 128
Darley Rd. OL11: Roch 9C 204
Darley St. BL6: Hor 8C 196
Darlington Cl. BL8: Bury 8G 201
PR6: Chor 6H 175
Darlington Rd. OL11: Roch 9C 204
Darlington St. PR7: Copp 4N 193
Darmond Rd. L33: Kirk 7M 223
Darnbrook Rd. BB18: Barnw 2L 77
Darnley St. BB10: Burnl 4G 125
Dartford Cl. BB1: Blackb 5F 226 (4N 139)
Dartmouth Av. L10: Aint 8B 222
Dartmouth Cl. PR4: K'ham 4L 111
Dart St. PR2: Ash R 9F 114
DARWEN 6A 158
Darwen Cl. PR3: Longr 3K 97
Darwen Ent. Cen. BB3: Darw 5A 158
Darwen Fold Cl. PR7: Buck V 9A 154
Darwen Golf Course 4L 157
Darwen Jubilee Tower 7L 157
Darwen Leisure Cen. 6N 157
Darwen Library Theatre 6A 158
Darwen Rd. BL7: Brom C, Eger 4E 198
Darwen Station (Rail) 5A 158
Darwen St. BB2: Blackb 5D 226 (4M 139)
BB12: Padi 1H 123
PR1: Prest 1M 135
PR5: H Walt 4D 136
Darwen Vw. PR5: Walt D 3A 136
Darwin Ct. PR9: S'port 5L 167
Darwin St. BB10: Burnl 8E 104
Datchet Ter. OL11: Roch 9C 204
Daub Hall La. PR5: Hogh 6G 136
Daub La. L40: Bis G 5K 191
Dauntesey Av. FY3: Blackp 4G 89
Davenham Rd. BB3: Darw 4M 157
L37: Form 8A 206
Davenhill Pk. L10: Aint 8B 222
Davenport Av. FY2: Blackp 6C 62
Davenport Fold BL2: Bolt 9N 199
Davenport Fold Rd. BL2: Bolt 9N 199
Davenport Gro. L33: Kirk 6K 223
Daventry Av. FY2: Blackp 7B 62
Daventry Rd. OL11: Roch 9C 204
David Lewis Cl. OL16: Roch 7F 204
David Lloyd Leisure
Chorley 1G 174
Liverpool 9M 223
Davidson St. LA1: Lanc 7F 228 (8L 23)
David St. BB9: Barrf 7H 85
BB11: Burnl 5D 124
BL8: Bury 9H 201
(not continuous)
OL12: Roch 4C 204
OL13: Bac 7H 163
David St. Nth. OL12: Roch 4C 204
Davies Rd. BB1: Blackb 2D 140

Davis St. PR3: Longr 2J 97
Davitt Cl. BB4: Hasl 4G 160
Davy Fld. Ind. Est. BB1: Guide 1A 158
Davyfield Rd. BB1: Guide 1A 158
Davyhulme St. OL12: Roch 4E 204
Dawber Delf Ind. Area
WN6: App B 4G 212
Dawber Delph WN6: App B 4G 212
Dawber's La. PR7: Eux 4G 173
Dawlish Av. FY3: Blackp 2F 88
Dawlish Cl. BB2: Blackb 8K 139
Dawlish Ct. FY2: Blackp 2D 88
Dawlish Dr. PR9: S'port 1N 167
Dawlish Lodge FY8: L Ann 1D 128
Dawlish Pl. PR2: Ingol 6D 114
Dawnay Rd. PR2: Ribb 6A 116
Dawnwood Sq. WN5: Wigan 1M 221
Dawson Av. BB12: S'stone 8D 102
PR9: S'port 1B 168
Dawson Cl. BB5: Acc 3M 141
Dawson Gdns. L31: Magh 9B 216
Dawson La. PR6: Whit W 8N 153
PR25: Leyl 8N 153
Dawson Pl. PR5: Bam B 9C 136
Dawson Rd. FY8: L Ann 8F 108
L39: Orms 5L 209
Dawsons Ct. *BD24: Sett 3N 35*
(off Church St.)
Dawson Sq. BB11: Burnl 1E 228 (2E 124)
Dawson St. BL9: Bury 9M 201
OL12: Roch 5C 204
Dawson Wlk. PR1: Prest 3K 229 (8J 115)
Daybrook WN8: Uph 4C 220
Dayfield WN8: Uph 4D 220
Day St. BB9: Nelson 3J 105
Dayton Pl. FY4: Blackp 3C 108
Deacons Cres. BL8: Tott 8F 200
Deacon St. OL16: Roch 4E 204
Deakins Bus. Pk. BL7: Eger 4D 198
Deakins Mill Way BL7: Eger 3D 198
Deakin's Ter. BL7: Belm 9K 177
Deal Pl. FY8: L Ann 8F 108
DEAN 8G 144
Dean Cl. BL0: Eden 3J 181
WN8: Uph 4F 220
Dean Ct. FY7: Flee 4D 54
OL11: Roch 9C 204
PR5: Bam B 7A 136
WN5: Orr 2L 221
Dean Cres. WN5: Orr 3L 221
Deancroft Av. LA3: Heys 6M 21
Deanfield BB7: Clith 1A 82
Deanfield Ct. BB7: Clith 1N 81
Deanfield Dr. BB7: Clith 1A 82
Deanfield Way BB7: Clith 1A 82
Dean Fold BB4: Water 8E 144
Dean Hall La. PR7: Eux 4G 173
Dean Head OL15: Littleb 3N 185
Dean Head La. BL6: R'ton 1A 196
Dean La. BB3: Tock 6H 157
BB4: Water 8E 144
BB6: Gt H, Whall 2H 121
BB7: Whall 7J 101
PR5: Sam 7J 117
Dean Mdw. BB7: Clith 4K 81
Dean Mill BB11: Burnl 3E 228 (4E 124)
Deanpoint LA3: Morec 5C 22
Dean Rd. BB4: Hasl 7G 160
(Chester Cres.)
BB4: Hasl 6G 160
(Knowsley Rd. Ind. Est.)
Deanroyd Rd. OL14: Wals 8L 165
Deansgate FY1: Blackp 1J 227 (5B 88)
LA4: Morec 3B 22
Deansgate La. L37: Form 7B 206
Deansgate La. Nth. L37: Form 6A 206
Deansgrave BB4: Hasl 5F 160
Deansgreave Rd. OL13: Bac 7M 163
Deansgreave Ter. OL13: Bac 8M 163
Deans La. L40: Lath 9J 191
PR5: Sam 6H 117
WN8: N 'urgh 2K 211
Dean St. BB3: Darw 4N 157
BB8: Traw 9E 86
BB11: Burnl 3C 124
BB12: Padi 9J 103
FY4: Blackp 1B 108
OL16: Roch 4E 204
PR5: Bam B 7A 136
Dean Ter. *PR4: K'ham 4M 111*
(off Station Rd.)
Dean Vs. OL14: Wals 8L 165
DEAN WOOD 2A 196
Dean Wood Av. WN5: Orr 3H 221
Dean Wood Cl. PR7: Chor 8C 174
Dean Wood Golf Course 3F 220
Dearbought La. PR3: Scor 3D 46
Dearden Clough BL0: Eden 4K 181
Dearden Ct. BB3: Darw 5B 158
Dearden Fold BL0: Eden 4K 181
Deardengate BB4: Hasl 4G 160
Deardengate Cft. *BB4: Hasl 4G 160*
(off Deardengate)
Dearden Hgts. BB4: Rawt 5J 161
Dearden Nook BB4: Rawt 6M 161
Dearden St. OL15: Littleb 8L 185
Dearden Way WN8: Uph 4D 220
Dearncamme Cl. BL2: Bolt 8H 199
DEARNLEY 1H 205
Dearnley Cl. OL15: Littleb 1H 205
Dearnley Pas. OL15: Littleb 1H 205
Deben Cl. WN6: Stand 3N 213
Deborah Av. PR2: Fulw 2K 115
Debra Cl. L31: Mell 6G 222
Dee Cl. L33: Kirk 4L 223
DEEPDALE 3M 229 (8K 115)
Deepdale 1N 229 (7L 115)
Deepdale Av. FY6: Carl 6H 63
OL16: Roch 7F 204
Deepdale Cl. LA7: Slack H 1N 5
Deepdale Ct. BB9: Barrf 8G 85
Deepdale Dr. BB10: Burnl 7G 104
Deepdale Grn. BB9: Barrf 8G 85
Deepdale La. PR4: Clif, Lea T 6H 113
Deepdale Mill St. PR1: Prest 8L 115
Deepdale Pavilions PR1: Prest 3M 229 (8K 115)

Deepdale Rd. FY4: Blackp 1J 109
FY7: Flee 1G 54
PR1: Prest 2N 229 (9L 115)
Deepdale Shopping Pk. PR1: Prest 6M 115
Deepdale St. PR1: Prest 4N 229 (9L 115)
Deep La. OL15: Littleb 4M 205
OL16: Milnr 6L 205
Deeplish Cotts. *OL11: Roch 8C 204*
(off Clifford St.)
Deeplish Rd. OL11: Roch 8C 204
Deeplish St. OL11: Roch 8C 204
Deeply Va. La. BL9: Bury 3A 202
Deerbarn Dr. L30: N'ton 6A 222
Deerbolt Cl. L32: Kirk 7H 223
Deerbolt Cres. L32: Kirk 7H 223
Deerbolt Way L32: Kirk 7H 223
Deer Chace BB12: Fence 2B 104
Deerfold PR7: Chor 4D 174
Deerhurst Rd. FY5: T Clev 4E 62
Dee Rd. LA1: Lanc 6H 23
Deer Pk. BB5: Acc 9D 122
Deer Pk. La. LA2: Horn 7C 18
Deerpark Rd. BB10: Burnl 4J 125
Deerplay Cl. BB10: Burnl 8J 105
Deerplay Ct. OL13: Weir 8L 145
Deerplay Dr. OL13: Weir 8L 145
Deerstone Av. BB10: Burnl 3G 125
Deerstone Rd. BB9: Nelson 2M 105
Deer St. OL13: Weir 9K 145
Deeside FY4: Blackp 4D 108
Dee St. FY8: L Ann 2F 128
Deganwy Av. BB1: Blackb 1M 139
De-Haviland Way WN8: Skelm 3B 220
Deighton Av. PR25: Leyl 7K 153
Deighton Cl. WN5: Orr 5H 221
Deighton Rd. PR7: Chor 8D 174
Dekker Rd. L33: Kirk 4K 223
De Lacy Ho. BB2: Blackb 3K 139
De Lacy St. BB7: Clith 3K 81
PR2: Ash R 7G 114
Delamere Av. LA3: Heys 1K 27
Delamere Cl. BB2: Blackb 6J 139
BB5: Acc 8A 122
Delamere Pl. PR6: Chor 6F 174
Delamere Rd. BB10: Brierc 7K 105
OL16: Roch 9F 204
PR8: Ains 8B 186
WN8: Skelm 1K 219
Delamere St. BL9: Bury 8M 201
Delamere Way WN8: Uph 4D 220
Delaney Ct. BD24: Sett 3N 35
Delaney Gdns. *BD24: Sett 3N 35*
(off Duke St.)
Delany Dr. PR4: Frec 3M 131
Delaware Cres. L32: Kirk 7H 223
Delaware Rd. FY3: Blackp 1E 88
Delaware St. PR1: Prest 8M 115
Delfby Cres. L32: Kirk 9M 223
Delf Ho. WN8: Skelm 2N 219
Delf La. L39: D'holl 8N 207
OL14: Tod 5F 146
Delius Cl. BB2: Blackb 7A 140
Dell, The BB2: Blackb 1L 157
BL2: Bolt 8J 199
PR2: Fulw 2G 114
PR4: W Grn 6G 111
PR6: Heap 3J 175
WN6: App B 5G 213
WN8: Uph 4E 220
Dellar St. OL12: Roch 4N 203
Dellfield La. L31: Magh 1D 222
Dell Gdns. OL12: Roch 3M 203
Dell La. BB12: Hapt 5H 123
Dell Mdw. OL12: Whitw 9N 183
Dell Rd. OL12: Roch 1M 203
Dell Side Way OL12: Roch 3N 203
Dell St. BL2: Bolt 8J 199
Dellway, The PR4: Hutt 5A 134
Delma Rd. BB10: Burnl 4J 125
Delph, The WN8: Parb 1N 211
Delph App. BB1: Blackb 4C 140
Delph Av. BL7: Eger 2D 198
Delph Brook Way BL7: Eger 3D 198
Delph Cl. BB1: Blackb 4C 140
L39: Aug 2H 217
Delph Comn. Rd. L39: Aug 2G 217
Delph Cotts. BL8: Hawk 2N 199
Delph Ct. BB6: Gt H 4J 121
Delph Dr. L40: Burs 9D 190
Delphene Av. FY5: T Clev 5D 62
(not continuous)
Delphinium Way BB3: Lwr D 9A 140
Delph La. BB1: Blackb 4C 140
L39: Aug 2H 217
PR3: Barn 4C 60
PR3: Bleas, Clau 3L 61
PR7: Char R 8M 173
(not continuous)
Delph La. Est. BB1: Blackb 4C 140
Delph Mt. BB6: Gt H 3H 121
BB9: Nelson 3H 105
Delph Pk. Av. L39: Aug 2G 216
Delph Rd. BB6: Gt H 4H 121
Delph Sailing Club 2B 198
Delphside Cl. WN5: Orr 6G 220
Delphside Rd. WN5: Orr 6G 220
Delph Sq. *BB10: Burnl 8H 105*
(off Marsden Rd.)
Delph St. BB3: Darw 4B 158
BB4: Hasl 3G 160
OL16: Milnr 7J 205
Delph Top L39: Orms 6M 209
Delph Way PR6: Whit W 8E 154
Delta La. FY7: Flee 9G 41
Delta Pk. Av. PR4: Hesk B 3C 150
Delta Pk. Dr. PR4: Hesk B 3C 150
Deltic Pl. L33: Know P 9N 223
Deltic Way L30: N'ton 9A 222
L33: Know P 9N 223
Delves La. BB10: S'field 3N 105
Demming Cl. PR2: Lea 9N 113
Denbigh Av. FY5: T Clev 2E 62
PR9: S'port 3M 167
Denbigh Cl. PR25: Leyl 6L 153
Denbigh Dr. BB7: Clith 1M 81
Denbigh Gro. BB12: Burnl 2M 123

Denby Cl.—Dovedale Gdns.

Denby Cl. PR5: Lost H . . . 5M **135**
Dene, The BB2: Blackb . . . 9H **119**
BB7: Hurst G . . . 2M **99**
Dene Av. BB8: Foul . . . 2A **86**
Dene Bank BL2: Bolt . . . 8J **199**
Denebank FY2: Blackp . . . 6D **62**
Dene Bank Rd. BB5: Osw . . . 5L **141**
Denefield Ho. *PR8: S'port* . . . *8H 167*
(off Portland St.)
Denehurst Rd. OL11: Roch . . . 5M **203**
Dene St. BL2: Bolt . . . 8J **199**
Deneway Av. FY3: Blackp . . . 4F **88**
Denford Av. FY8: L Ann . . . 4G **128**
PR25: Leyl . . . 7L **153**
Denham Cl. BL1: Bolt . . . 8G **198**
Denham La. PR6: Brind . . . 6F **154**
Denham Way FY7: Flee . . . 2F **54**
Denham Wood Cl. PR7: Chor . . . 8B **174**
Denholme WN8: Uph . . . 4C **220**
(not continuous)
Denholme Gro. FY2: Blackp . . . 6E **62**
Denholme Rd. OL11: Roch . . . 9C **204**
Denhurst Rd. OL15: Littleb . . . 8L **185**
Denis St. LA1: Lanc . . . 6E **228** (8L **23**)
Denmark Rd. FY8: L Ann . . . 4K **129**
PR9: S'port . . . 4N **167**
Denmark St. LA1: Lanc . . . 9G **23**
OL16: Roch . . . 5D **204**
Dennett Cl. L31: Magh . . . 3C **222**
Dennis Gro. LA4: Morec . . . 4B **22**
Dennison Ind. Est.
LA3: Morec . . . 6E **22**
Denny Av. LA1: Lanc . . . 6J **23**
Denny Bank LA2: Lanc . . . 3B **24**
Denny Beck La. LA2: Lanc . . . 3B **24**
Denshaw WN8: Uph . . . 4C **220**
Denstone Av. FY2: Blackp . . . 7D **62**
L10: Aint . . . 8C **222**
Dent Dale BB5: Acc . . . 3C **142**
Dentdale Cl. BB2: Blackb . . . 9E **138**
Denton Gro. WN5: Orr . . . 3L **221**
Denton St. BB18: Barnw . . . 1L **77**
BL9: Bury . . . 9L **201**
OL12: Roch . . . 4C **204**
Dent Row BB11: Burnl . . . 4B **228** (4D **124**)
Dent St. BB8: Colne . . . 8M **85**
Denver Pk. L32: Kirk . . . 9H **223**
Denver Rd. L32: Kirk . . . 9H **223**
OL11: Roch . . . 9C **204**
Denville Av. FY5: T Clev . . . 3F **62**
Denville Rd. BB2: Blackb . . . 3A **226** (3L **139**)
PR1: Prest . . . 8M **115**
Depot Rd. FY3: Blackp . . . 1E **88**
L33: Know P . . . 6B **224**
Deram Ho. FY1: Blackp . . . 8N **227**
Derbe Rd. FY8: L Ann . . . 3F **128**
Derby Cl. BB3: Darw . . . 1B **178**
Derby Ct. BL9: Bury . . . 8L **201**
Derby Cres. PR4: Inskip . . . 2G **93**
Derby Dr. WA11: Rain . . . 4L **225**
Derby Gro. L31: Magh . . . 4C **222**
Derby Hill Cres. L39: Orms . . . 7M **209**
Derby Hill Rd. L39: Orms . . . 7M **209**
Derby Ho. *L39: Orms* . . . *7L 209*
(off Derby St.)
LA1: Lanc . . . 7K **23**
Derby Pl. PR6: Adl . . . 5J **195**
Derby Rd. FY1: Blackp . . . 3B **88**
FY5: T Clev . . . 9C **54**
FY6: Poul F . . . 7K **63**
FY8: L Ann . . . 3J **129**
LA1: Lanc . . . 7K **23**
PR2: Fulw . . . 5H **115**
PR3: Gars . . . 5M **59**
PR3: Longr . . . 3J **97**
PR4: Wesh . . . 3L **111**
PR9: S'port . . . 7J **167**
WN8: Skelm . . . 3G **219**
Derbyshire Almshouses *BB2: Blackb* . . . *2J 139*
(off St Silas's Rd.)
Derbyshire Av. PR3: Gars . . . 4M **59**
Derbyshire Row BL1: Bolt . . . 9E **198**
Derby Sq. PR1: Prest . . . 9N **115**
Derby St. BB1: Blackb . . . 1G **226** (2A **140**)
BB1: Rish . . . 8J **121**
BB5: Acc . . . 1B **142**
BB7: Clith . . . 3M **81**
BB8: Colne . . . 6A **86**
BB9: Nelson . . . 1J **105**
BB11: Burnl . . . 3B **228** (4D **124**)
BL0: Ramsb . . . 8J **181**
L39: Orms . . . 7L **209**
LA4: Morec . . . 3A **22**
OL11: Roch . . . 8D **204**
OL14: Tod . . . 2N **165**
PR1: Prest . . . 5M **229** (9K **115**)
PR6: Birns . . . 7B **156**
PR25: Leyl . . . 5L **153**
Derby St. W. L39: Orms . . . 7K **209**
Derby Ter. BB4: Rawt . . . 5M **161**
Derdale St. OL14: Tod . . . 2M **165**
Dereham Cl. BL8: Bury . . . 8J **201**
Dereham Way WN3: Wins . . . 8N **221**
Derek Rd. PR6: Whit W . . . 6E **154**
Derham St.
BB2: Blackb . . . 8D **226** (5M **139**)
Derrick Walker Ct. OL11: Roch . . . 8A **204**
Derry Rd. PR2: Ribb . . . 6A **116**
Der St. OL14: Tod . . . 2M **165**
Dertern La. LA5: Bolt S . . . 2L **15**
Derwent Av. BB10: Burnl . . . 8E **104**
BB12: Padi . . . 8H **103**
FY7: Flee . . . 2D **54**
LA4: Morec . . . 3C **22**
OL16: Milnr . . . 7L **205**
PR9: S'port . . . 5M **167**
Derwent Cl. BB1: Rish . . . 8F **120**
BB4: Hasl . . . 3G **161**
BB8: Colne . . . 5D **86**
FY6: K Sea . . . 7M **41**
L31: Magh . . . 9E **216**
L33: Kirk . . . 6J **223**
PR4: Frec . . . 2M **131**
Derwent Ct. BB3: Darw . . . 7C **158**
LA1: Lanc . . . 6G **23**
Derwent Cres. BB7: Clith . . . 4J **81**
Derwent Dr. OL15: Littleb . . . 3J **205**
PR3: Longr . . . 5H **97**
PR4: Frec . . . 2M **131**
Derwent Hall PR1: Prest . . . 3H **229**
Derwent Ho. BB8: Colne . . . 6L **85**
PR1: Prest . . . 9N **115**
Derwent Pl. FY5: T Clev . . . 3D **62**
FY6: Poul F . . . 1K **89**
WN5: Wigan . . . 4M **221**
Derwent Rd. FY8: L Ann . . . 8G **108**
LA1: Lanc . . . 5G **228** (7M **23**)
PR7: Chor . . . 9D **174**
WN5: Orr . . . 3J **221**
Derwent St. BB3: Darw . . . 5N **157**
OL12: Roch . . . 4C **204**
Derwentwater Pl. PR1: Prest . . . 1J **229** (7J **115**)
Detrongate Caravan Pk. LA5: Bolt S . . . 2L **15**
Deva Cl. L33: Kirk . . . 3K **223**
Dever Av. PR25: Leyl . . . 6G **152**
De Vere Herons Reach Golf Course . . . 6H **89**
De Vitre Cotts. LA1: Lanc . . . 3J **29**
De Vitre St. LA1: Lanc . . . 6E **228** (8L **23**)
Devona Av. FY4: Blackp . . . 9H **89**
Devon Av. BB5: Osw . . . 3H **141**
FY7: Flee . . . 1E **54**
WN8: Uph . . . 5E **220**
Devon Cl. PR5: Walt D . . . 5N **135**
WN5: Wigan . . . 5M **221**
Devon Cres. BB4: Hasl . . . 7G **161**
Devon Farm Way L37: Form . . . 9B **206**
Devon Gro. BB12: Burnl . . . 2M **123**
Devon Pl. BB5: Chur . . . 3L **141**
LA1: Lanc . . . 3L **29**
Devonport Cl. PR5: Walt D . . . 5A **136**
Devonport Ct. *BB2: Blackb* . . . *3K 139*
(off Belle Vue St.)
Devonport Rd. BB2: Blackb . . . 3A **226** (3K **139**)
Devonport Way PR6: Chor . . . 7G **175**
Devonport Way Flats PR6: Chor . . . 6G **175**
Devon Rd. BB1: Blackb . . . 3C **140**
Devonshire Av. FY5: T Clev . . . 1H **63**
Devonshire Cl. L33: Kirk . . . 6K **223**
Devonshire Ct. PR7: Chor . . . 7E **174**
Devonshire Dr. BB5: Clay M . . . 6M **121**
PR3: Gars . . . 4M **59**
Devonshire M. FY5: T Clev . . . 1H **63**
Devonshire Pl. PR1: Prest . . . 8A **116**
Devonshire Rd. BB1: Rish . . . 8G **120**
BB10: Burnl . . . 2E **124**
FY2: Blackp . . . 1M **227** (1D **88**)
FY3: Blackp . . . 1D **88**
FY8: L Ann . . . 1D **128**
LA3: Morec . . . 4M **21**
PR2: Fulw . . . 5K **115**
PR7: Chor . . . 7E **174**
PR9: S'port . . . 6N **167**
Devonshire Sq. FY3: Blackp . . . 1M **227** (5D **88**)
Devonshire Sq. M. FY3: Blackp . . . 1N **227** (5D **88**)
Devonshire St. BB5: Acc . . . 1A **142**
LA1: Lanc . . . 2K **29**
Devonshire Ter. *BB10: Burnl* . . . *2E 124*
(off Devonshire Rd.)
Devon St. BB3: Darw . . . 9B **158**
BB8: Colne . . . 5B **86**
FY4: Blackp . . . 9D **88**
OL11: Roch . . . 7C **204**
Dewan Ind. Est. BB4: Hasl . . . 7G **160**
Dewberry Av. PR2: Fulw . . . 5J **115**
Dewberry Flds. WN8: Uph . . . 4E **220**
Dewberry Ho. PR2: Fulw . . . 5J **115**
Dew Forest PR3: Bowg . . . 8A **60**
Dewhirst Rd. OL12: Roch, Ward . . . 1C **204**
Dewhirst Way OL12: Roch . . . 1C **204**
Dewhurst Av. FY4: Blackp . . . 1E **108**
Dewhurst Cl. BB3: Darw . . . 9B **158**
Dewhurst Clough Rd. BL7: Eger . . . 3D **198**
Dewhurst Ct. BL7: Eger . . . 2D **198**
Dewhurst Ind. Est. PR2: Ash R . . . 8G **115**
Dewhurst Rd. BB6: Langh . . . 9N **99**
BL2: Bolt . . . 9L **199**
Dewhurst Row PR5: Bam B . . . 9N **135**
Dewhurst St. BB1: Blackb . . . 4A **140**
(not continuous)
BB3: Darw . . . 9B **158**
BB8: Colne . . . 8A **86**
PR2: Ash R . . . 8G **115**
Dew Meadow Cl. OL12: Roch . . . 3B **204**
Dexter Way WN8: Uph . . . 5E **220**
Deycroft Av. L33: Kirk . . . 6M **223**
Deycroft Wlk. L33: Kirk . . . 6M **223**
Deyes Ct. L31: Magh . . . 1D **222**
Deyes End L31: Magh . . . 1D **222**
Deyes La. L31: Magh . . . 1C **222**
Deyes Lane Swimming Pool . . . 1C **222**
Diamond Bus. Pk. WA11: Rain . . . 5M **225**
Diamond Jubilee Rd. L40: Ruff . . . 1G **191**
Diamond Vs. *PR6: Whit W* . . . *8D 154*
(off School Brow)
Diana Ct. LA1: Lanc . . . 8C **228**
Dianne Rd. FY5: T Clev . . . 1K **63**
Dibbs Pocket PR4: Frec . . . 1B **132**
Dib Rd. PR4: Hesk B . . . 9M **131**
Dicconson's La. L39: Hals . . . 9B **208**
Dicconson Ter. FY8: L Ann . . . 5A **130**
Dicconson Way L39: Orms . . . 8M **209**
Dicken Grn. OL11: Roch . . . 9C **204**
Dicken Grn. La. OL11: Roch . . . 9C **204**
Dickens Av. BB18: Barnw . . . 1L **77**
Dickens Ct. BB6: Old L . . . 4B **100**
Dickensons Fld. PR1: Penw . . . 6H **135**
Dickens Rd. PR7: Copp . . . 5A **194**
Dickens St. BB1: Blackb . . . 7F **226** (5N **139**)
Dicket's La. WN8: Skelm . . . 9D **210**
Dickies La. FY4: Blackp . . . 2H **109**
Dickies La. Sth. FY4: Blackp . . . 3H **109**
Dickinson Cl. BB2: Blackb . . . 7A **226** (5K **139**)
L37: Form . . . 1A **214**
Dickinson Ct. *BL6: Hor* . . . *9C 196*
(off Hope St.)
PR8: Birk . . . 3G **186**
Dickinson Rd. L37: Form . . . 1A **214**
Dickinson St. W. BL6: Hor . . . 9B **196**
Dick La. PR6: Birns . . . 8N **155**
Dick's La. L40: W'head . . . 8C **210**
Dickson Av. PR1: Prest . . . 7N **115**
Dickson Hey PR4: New L . . . 8C **134**
Dickson Rd. FY1: Blackp . . . 1J **227** (3B **88**)
Dickson St. BB8: Colne . . . 5B **86**
BB12: Burnl . . . 3A **124**
PR1: Prest . . . 7N **229** (1L **135**)
Didsbury Cl. L33: Kirk . . . 8L **223**
Didsbury St. BB1: Blackb . . . 3C **140**
Digby Rd. OL11: Roch . . . 9C **204**
Diggles La. OL11: Roch . . . 7J **203**
(Hawthorn Rd.)
OL11: Roch . . . 6K **203**
(Swift Rd.)
Digham Av. FY2: Blackp . . . 5D **62**
DIGMOOR . . . 5A **220**
Digmoor Dr. WN8: Skelm . . . 4M **219**
Digmoor Rd. WN8: Skelm . . . 4N **219**
DILL HALL . . . 1N **141**
DILL HALL BROW . . . 2M **195**
Dill Hall La. BB5: Chur . . . 1M **141**
Dilworth Bottoms PR3: Longr . . . 3B **98**
Dilworth Ct. PR3: Longr . . . 3L **97**
Dilworth La. PR3: Longr . . . 3K **97**
Dimmock St. BB2: Blackb . . . 6K **139**
DIMPLE . . . 1D **198**
Dimple Pk. BL7: Eger . . . 2D **198**
Dimple Rd. BL7: Eger . . . 1C **198**
Dimples Ct. PR3: Gars . . . 6A **60**
Dimples La. PR3: Barn, Gars . . . 6A **60**
DINCKLEY . . . 5N **99**
Dinckley Gro. FY1: Blackp . . . 6N **227** (7D **88**)
Dinckley Sq. BB2: Blackb . . . 2J **139**
Dineley Av. OL14: Tod . . . 9J **147**
Dineley St. BB5: Chur . . . 2M **141**
Dingle, The PR2: Fulw . . . 2G **114**
PR6: Heap . . . 3J **175**
Dingle Av. FY3: Blackp . . . 2F **88**
WN6: App B . . . 4H **213**
WN8: Uph . . . 3E **220**
Dingle Cl. L39: Aug . . . 2H **217**
Dingle Rd. PR4: Newt . . . 5E **112**
WN8: Uph . . . 3E **220**
Dingle Wlk. WN6: Stand . . . 8N **213**
Dinmore Av. FY3: Blackp . . . 1G **89**
Dinmore Pl. FY3: Blackp . . . 3G **89**
Dinorwic Rd. PR8: Birk . . . 2G **187**
Dirty Leech OL12: Ward . . . 8C **184**
Disley St. OL11: Roch . . . 9N **203**
Disraeli St. BB10: Burnl . . . 8E **104**
Disting Rd. BB3: Darw . . . 2N **157**
DITCHES . . . 7G **164**
Ditchfield L37: Form . . . 1A **214**
Ditton Mead Cl. OL12: Roch . . . 3E **204**
Division La. FY4: Blackp . . . 6G **109**
Division St. OL12: Roch . . . 3E **204**
Dixey St. BL6: Hor . . . 9B **196**
Dixon Av. WN6: Shev . . . 7K **213**
Dixon Closes OL11: Roch . . . 6J **203**
Dixon Dr. WN6: Shev . . . 7K **213**
Dixon Fold OL11: Roch . . . 7J **203**
Dixon Rd. L33: Know P . . . 9N **223**
PR3: Longr . . . 3K **97**
Dixon's Farm M. PR4: Clif . . . 8H **113**
Dixons La. PR2: Grim . . . 8E **96**
Dixon St. BB2: Blackb . . . 4K **139**
BB9: Barrf . . . 8G **85**
BL6: Hor . . . 9C **196**
OL11: Roch . . . 9A **204**
Dixon Ter. LA6: Neth K . . . 5B **16**
DOALS . . . 9K **145**
Doals Ga. OL13: Weir . . . 8L **145**
Dobbin Cl. BB4: Rawt . . . 5A **162**
Dobbin Ct. *BB4: Rawt* . . . *5A 162*
(off Dobbin La.)
Dobbin Fold BB4: Rawt . . . 5A **162**
Dobbin La. BB4: Rawt . . . 5A **162**
Dob Brow PR7: Char R . . . 1A **194**
Dob Brow Cl. PR7: Char R . . . 1A **194**
Dobbs Dr. L37: Form . . . 8A **206**
Dobfield Rd. OL16: Roch . . . 5G **205**
Dob La. PR4: Lit H, Wal B . . . 2L **151**
Dobroyd Ct. OL14: Tod . . . 3K **165**
Dobroyd Rd. OL14: Tod . . . 3K **165**
Dobs La. LA2: Glas . . . 2C **36**
Dobson Av. FY8: L Ann . . . 9E **108**
Dobson Cl. WN6: App B . . . 2H **213**
Dobson Rd. FY3: Blackp . . . 3H **89**
Dobson's La. FY6: Stal . . . 6D **56**
Dobson St. BB3: Darw . . . 5N **157**
DOCKER . . . 10B **8**
Docker La. LA6: Newt . . . 10D **8**
Docker Pk. Farm Vis. Cen. . . . 2A **18**
Dockinsall La. PR3: Out R . . . 9H **57**
Dockray St. BB8: Colne . . . 6B **86**
Dock Rd. FY7: Flee . . . 2G **54**
FY8: L Ann . . . 4C **130**
Dock St. BB1: Blackb . . . 4G **226** (3A **140**)
FY7: Flee . . . 9H **41**
Docky Pool La. FY4: Blackp . . . 3G **108**
Doctor Dam Cotts. OL12: Roch . . . 2G **203**
Dr Robertson Ct. FY7: Flee . . . 3E **54**
Doctor's La. L37: Gt A . . . 1E **214**
PR4: Tarl . . . 3C **170**
PR7: E'ton . . . 8D **172**
Doctor's Rake BB6: Langh . . . 8E **100**
Doctors Row PR3: Longr . . . 4J **97**
Dodd's La. L31: Magh . . . 9B **216**
Dodd Way PR5: Bam B . . . 1C **154**
Dodgeons Cl. FY6: Poul F . . . 9J **63**
Dodgson Ct. *LA6: K Lon* . . . *6F 8*
(off Tram La.)
Dodgson Cft. LA6: K Lon . . . 6E **8**
Dodgson La. BB18: Earl . . . 2J **79**
Dodgson Pl. PR1: Prest . . . 8M **115**
Dodgson Rd. PR1: Prest . . . 8M **115**
Dodgson St. OL16: Roch . . . 7D **204**
Dodney Dr. PR2: Lea . . . 8N **113**
Dodworth Av. PR8: S'port . . . 9L **167**
Doeholme Rake LA2: Abb . . . 3A **48**
Doe Mdw. WN8: N 'urgh . . . 3L **211**
(not continuous)
Doghouse La. OL14: Tod . . . 2J **165**
Dog Kennel Wood Nature Reserve . . . 5M **135**
Dog Pits La. OL13: Bac . . . 1L **163**
Dole La. PR6: Withn . . . 6D **156**
PR7: Chor . . . 6E **174**
Doles La. PR26: Breth . . . 7L **151**
Doll La. PR26: Leyl . . . 6D **152**
Dolly's La. PR9: S'port . . . 6C **168**
(not continuous)
Dollywood La. LA7: Slack H . . . 1K **5**
Dolphin Brow PR6: Whit W . . . 8D **154**
DOLPHINHOLME . . . 6E **38**
Domar Cl. L32: Kirk . . . 9L **223**
Dombey St. BB1: Blackb . . . 6G **226** (4A **140**)
Dome, The . . . 2A **22**
Domingo Dr. L33: Kirk . . . 5J **223**
Dominica Av. BB3: Lwr D . . . 1N **157**
Dominion Ct. BB11: Burnl . . . 5N **123**
Dominion Rd. BB2: Blackb . . . 9K **119**
Doncaster Rd. FY3: Blackp . . . 8G **88**
Donnington OL11: Roch . . . 7B **204**
Donnington Lodge PR8: S'port . . . 8F **166**
Donnington Rd. FY6: Carl . . . 5J **63**
FY8: L Ann . . . 1F **128**
Donshort M. BB9: Barrf . . . 1G **104**
Don St. FY8: L Ann . . . 1E **128**
Doodstone Av. PR5: Lost H . . . 7L **135**
Doodstone Cl. PR5: Lost H . . . 7L **135**
Doodstone Dr. PR5: Lost H . . . 7L **135**
Doodstone Nook PR5: Lost H . . . 7L **135**
Dooley Dr. L30: N'ton . . . 6A **222**
Dora St. BL0: Ramsb . . . 1F **200**
Dorchester Av. BB5: Osw . . . 3J **141**
PR5: Walt D . . . 6L **135**
Dorchester Cl. BB1: Blackb . . . 5B **140**
FY5: T Clev . . . 3J **63**
Dorchester Dr. L33: Kirk . . . 5M **223**
Dorchester Gdns. LA3: Morec . . . 6C **22**
Dorchester Rd. FY1: Blackp . . . 2B **88**
PR3: Gars . . . 5M **59**
WN8: Uph . . . 4D **220**
Doric Grn. WN5: Bill . . . 8G **221**
Doris Henderson Way LA1: Lanc . . . 6F **22**
Doris St. BB11: Burnl . . . 1G **228** (3F **124**)
PR6: Chor . . . 5F **174**
Dorking Rd. PR6: Chor . . . 2H **175**
Dorman Cl. PR2: Ash R . . . 7F **114**
Dorman Rd. PR2: Ribb . . . 6A **116**
Dormer St. BL1: Bolt . . . 9F **198**
Dorning St. BL8: Bury . . . 9G **200**
Dorothy Av. PR25: Leyl . . . 6K **153**
Dorothy St. BB2: Blackb . . . 8K **139**
BL0: Ramsb . . . 9G **180**
Dorrington Rd. LA1: Lanc . . . 2K **29**
Dorritt Rd. FY4: Blackp . . . 3E **108**
Dorritt St. BB1: Blackb . . . 6G **226** (5A **140**)
Dorset Av. BB3: Darw . . . 4N **157**
BB12: Padi . . . 2J **123**
FY5: T Clev . . . 8D **54**
PR5: Walt D . . . 5N **135**
PR8: Ains . . . 2C **206**
Dorset Cl. WN5: Wigan . . . 5M **221**
Dorset Dr. BB1: Blackb . . . 4E **140**
BB4: Hasl . . . 7F **160**
BB7: Clith . . . 1M **81**
PR7: Buck V . . . 9B **154**
Dorset Rd. BB1: Rish . . . 8G **120**
FY8: L Ann . . . 9F **108**
PR1: Prest . . . 2M **229** (8K **115**)
Dorset St. BB12: Burnl . . . 3M **123**
FY4: Blackp . . . 9D **88**
OL11: Roch . . . 7C **204**
Dotcliffe Rd. BB18: Kelb . . . 6D **78**
Double Row BB12: Padi . . . 1G **123**
Doughty St. BB8: Colne . . . 7A **86**
Douglas Av. BL6: Hor . . . 8D **196**
FY3: Blackp . . . 3D **88**
FY6: Stal . . . 5B **56**
LA3: Heys . . . 9L **21**
PR4: Tarl . . . 6D **150**
PR4: Wesh . . . 2K **111**
WN8: Uph . . . 4E **220**
Douglas Cl. BB2: Blackb . . . 9L **139**
BL6: Hor . . . 9D **196**
L40: Ruff . . . 2G **190**
PR5: Bam B . . . 8B **136**
Douglas Ct. PR2: Fulw . . . 6G **115**
Douglas Dr. L31: Magh . . . 9E **216**
L39: Orms . . . 5J **209**
LA3: Heys . . . 9L **21**
PR4: Frec . . . 2M **131**
WN5: Orr . . . 4J **221**
WN6: Shev . . . 7J **213**
Douglas Gro. BB3: Darw . . . 3L **157**
Douglas Hall PR1: Prest . . . 3H **229**
Douglas La. PR2: Grim . . . 9F **96**
Douglas Leatham Ho. FY1: Blackp . . . 9M **227** (9D **88**)
Douglas Pl. BB1: Blackb . . . 8N **119**
FY7: Flee . . . 1D **54**
PR7: Chor . . . 9D **174**
Douglas Rd. BB10: Brierc . . . 7L **105**
OL13: Bac . . . 6L **163**
PR2: Fulw . . . 6G **114**
PR9: S'port . . . 2B **168**
WN6: Stand . . . 2L **213**
Douglas Rd. Nth. PR2: Fulw . . . 6G **114**
Douglas St. BB8: Colne . . . 5B **86**
BL0: Ramsb . . . 8G **180**
BL1: Bolt . . . 8E **198**
FY8: L Ann . . . 2D **128**
PR2: Ash R . . . 8F **114**
Douglas Valley Golf Course . . . 9L **195**
Douglas Vw. BL6: Blackr . . . 7J **195**
PR4: Hesk B . . . 3C **150**
Douglas Way BB10: Brierc . . . 7L **105**
L33: Kirk . . . 4L **223**
Doultons, The PR5: Lost H . . . 5M **135**
Dove Av. PR1: Penw . . . 4H **135**
Dove Cl. FY5: T Clev . . . 2F **62**
Dove Cote PR6: Clay W . . . 4C **154**
Dovecote Cl. BL7: Brom C . . . 5H **199**
Dove Ct. *BB10: Burnl* . . . *8F 104*
(off Shuttleworth St.)
Dovedale Av. FY3: Blackp . . . 8J **89**
FY5: T Clev . . . 9H **55**
L31: Magh . . . 9B **216**
PR2: Ingol . . . 5D **114**
Dovedale Cl. BB10: Reed . . . 6G **104**
PR2: Ingol . . . 5D **114**
PR25: Leyl . . . 9K **153**
Dovedale Dr. BB12: Burnl . . . 1A **124**
OL12: Ward . . . 8G **184**
Dovedale Gdns. PR3: Longr . . . 4K **97**

Dovedale Ho.—Eastern Av.

Dovedale Ho. PR2: Ingol .5D 114
Dove Dr. BL9: Bury .9N 201
Dove La. BB3: Darw .5N 157
Dover Cl. BB1: Blackb .4C 140
BL8: Greenm .4F 200
PR4: Wart .1K 131
Dover Ct. FY1: Blackp .8N 227 (8D 88)
Dover Gdns. FY6: Carl .6H 63
Dover La. PR5: Hogh .9K 137
PR6: Brind .9K 137
Dover Rd. FY1: Blackp .9N 227 (9D 88)
FY8: L Ann .9F 108
L31: Magh .4B 222
PR8: Birk .3E 186
Dover St. BB3: Lwr D .9N 139
BB5: Acc .4N 141
BB9: Nelson .1J 105
OL14: Tod .1N 165
OL16: Roch .3E 204
Dovestone Dr. FY6: Poul F .8H 63
Dove St. BL1: Bolt .9F 198
FY8: L Ann .2D 128
OL11: Roch .6A 204
PR1: Prest .2N 229 (8L 115)
Dovetree Cl. PR5: Walt D .5L 135
Dovetree Ct. FY4: Blackp .9H 89
Dove Vs. OL13: Bac .8F 162
DOWBRIDGE .5B 112
Dowbridge PR4: K'ham .5A 112
Dowbridge Way PR4: K'ham .5A 112
Dowling Cl. WN6: Stand .9N 213
Dowling St. OL11: Roch .7C 204
Downes Gro. LA4: Morec .4D 22
Downeyfield Rd. LA3: Midd .5N 27
Downfield Cl. BL0: Ramsb .8F 180
Downgreen Cl. L32: Kirk .9H 223
DOWNHAM .7G 74
Downham Av. BB4: Rawt .3M 161
BB6: Gt H .3L 121
Downham Dr. BB5: Acc .5N 141
Downham Gro. BB10: Burnl .4H 125
Downham Pl. FY4: Blackp .5B 108
FY8: L Ann .2J 129
PR2: Ash R .7B 114
Downham Rd. BB7: Chatb .7C 74
PR25: Leyl .7F 152
Downham St. BB2: Blackb .4K 139
DOWNHOLLAND .1L 215
Downholland Bri. Bus. Pk.
L39: D'holl .1A 216
DOWNHOLLAND CROSS .1A 216
Downholland Moss La.
L37: Form .8B 206
Downing Ct. PR3: Brou .8F 94
Downing St. PR1: Prest .9A 116
Downley Cl. OL12: Roch .3M 203
Downs, The FY6: Poul F .7K 63
WN3: Wigan .7M 221
Downside Dr. L10: Aint .9E 222
Dowry St. BB5: Acc .2B 142
Dragon Cl. WN8: Skelm .3B 220
Dragons Health Club
Southport .4J 167
Dragon St. BB12: Padi .1H 123
Drake Cl. FY8: L Ann .8E 108
L39: Aug .1H 217
Drakelowe Av. FY4: Blackp .3F 108
Drake Rd. OL15: Littleb .5M 185
Drakes Cft. PR2: Ash R .6F 114
Drakes Hollow PR5: Walt D .4N 135
Drake St. OL11: Roch .7B 204
OL16: Roch .6C 204
Drammen Av. BB11: Burnl .4N 123
Draperfield PR7: Chor .1C 194
Drapers Av. PR7: E'ton .8F 172
Draw Well Rd. L33: Know P .8B 224
Draycombe Ct. LA3: Heys .6L 21
Draycombe Dr. LA3: Heys .6M 21
Draycot Av. FY3: Blackp .2F 88
Drayton Rd. LA3: Heys .9M 21
Drew Av. OL11: Roch .5A 204
Drewitt Cres. PR9: S'port .2B 168
Drew St. BB11: Burnl .4N 123
(not continuous)
Drewton Av. LA3: Heys .6L 21
DRINK HOUSE .5M 171
Drinkhouse La. PR26: Cros .5L 171
Drinkhouse Rd. PR26: Cros .5M 171
Drinkwater La. BL6: Hor .9C 196
Driscoll St. PR1: Prest .4N 229 (9L 115)
Drive, The BB6: Old L .5C 100
BL0: Eden .3J 181
BL9: Bury .8L 201
LA2: Hest B .8H 15
LA3: Heys .9L 21
LA5: Carn .9M 11
OL13: Bac .5K 163
(off Bankside La.)
PR2: Fulw .5K 115
PR4: Longt .8L 133
PR5: Walt D .3B 136
PR6: Withn .4N 155
Driver St. BB4: Craws .9M 143
Driving Ga. BB4: Craws .7M 143
Dronsfield Rd. FY7: Flee .8F 40
Drovers Wlk. LA3: Heys .9L 21
Drovers Way FY8: L Ann .1L 129
LA6: Burt K .5G 6
Druids Cl. BL7: Eger .2D 198
Drumacre La. E. PR4: Longt .1N 151
Drumacre La. W. PR4: Longt .9K 133
Drumhead Rd. PR6: Chor .3F 174
DRUMMERSDALE .6H 189
Drummersdale La. L40: Scar .4G 188
Drummer Stoops BB3: Hodd .9F 158
Drummond Av. FY3: Blackp .3E 88
Drummond Sq. WN5: Wigan .4N 221
Drummond St. BL1: Bolt .9E 198
Drumstone Trade Pk.
BB2: Blackb .8E 226 (5N 139)
Dry Bread La. PR3: Out R .1G 65
Dryburgh Av. BL1: Bolt .9D 198
FY3: Blackp .7F 88
Dry Clough Barn BB10: S'field .2C 106
Dryden Gro. BB6: Gt H .5H 121
Dryden Rd. FY7: Flee .9G 40
Dryden St. BB5: Clay M .6M 121
BB12: Padi .2J 123
(not continuous)
Drydock Mill OL15: Littleb .9J 185
(off James St.)
Dryfield La. BL6: Hor, R'ton .8B 196
Drysdale Vw. BL1: Bolt .9E 198
Dubside PR4: W Grn .6G 110
Duchess Ct. FY2: Blackp .8B 62
Duchess Dr. FY2: Blackp .8B 62
Duchess St. BB3: Lwr D .9N 139
Duchy Av. PR2: Fulw .5L 115
Ducie Pl. PR1: Prest .8B 116
Ducie St. BL0: Ramsb .7G 180
Ducketts La. PR3: Clau .3D 68
Duckett St. BB11: Burnl .3C 124
Duck La. PR2: Fulw .5G 115
Duckshaw Rd. BB3: Darw .1N 177
Duck St. BB7: Clith .3M 81
LA2: Wray .8E 18
PR3: Pill .6F 42
Duckworth Cl. PR3: Catt .9A 60
Duckworth Dr. PR3: Catt .9A 60
Duckworth Hall Brow BB5: Osw .7G 141
Duckworth Hill La. BB5: Osw .7G 141
Duckworth La. BB4: Rawt .7K 161
PR4: Tarl .8C 150
Duckworth St. BB2: Blackb .6A 226 (5L 139)
BB3: Darw .5N 157
BB5: Chur .2L 141
BB9: Barrf .9H 85
BL9: Bury .9M 201
(not continuous)
Duddle La. PR5: Walt D .6N 135
Duddon Av. BB3: Darw .4M 157
FY7: Flee .3D 54
L31: Magh .9E 216
Duddon Cl. LA3: Morec .6F 22
Dudley Av. BB5: Osw .4J 141
FY2: Blackp .1D 88
Dudley Cl. PR4: Longt .7L 133
Dudley Pl. PR2: Ash R .7C 114
Dudley St. BB8: Colne .6C 86
BB9: Brierf .5G 104
LA4: Morec .4C 22
Duerden St. BB9: Nelson .2H 105
Duffins Cl. OL12: Roch .2A 204
Dugdale Cl. FY4: Blackp .4F 108
Dugdale Ct. FY4: Blackp .4F 108
(off Squires Ga. La.)
FY5: T Clev .3D 62
(off Norbreck Rd.)
Dugdale La. BB7: Slaid .3F 50
Dugdale Rd. BB12: Burnl .2N 123
Dugdales Cl. FY4: Blackp .2L 109
Dugdale St. BB11: Burnl .3D 228
Duke Av. PR8: S'port .1J 187
Duke of Sussex St. BB2: Blackb .8J 139
Dukes Brow BB2: Blackb .2A 226 (2J 139)
Dukes Ct. BB2: Blackb .2J 139
Dukes Cut HX7: Black H .4K 147
Dukes Dr. BB3: Hodd .6E 158
Dukes Mdw. PR2: Ingol .4D 114
Dukes Theatre & Cinema .6D 228 (8K 23)
Duke St. BB2: Blackb .4B 226 (3L 139)
BB4: W'foot .7C 162
BB5: Clay M .7M 121
BB5: Osw .5K 141
BB6: Gt H .4H 121
BB8: Colne .7A 86
BB8: Wine .7E 86
BB10: Brierc .7K 105
BB11: Burnl .5F 124
(not continuous)
BD24: Sett .3N 35
BL0: Ramsb .1F 200
FY1: Blackp .9J 227 (9B 88)
L37: Form .1A 214
LA1: Lanc .7J 23
LA2: H Ben .6L 19
LA3: Heys .9K 21
LA6: Bur L .3K 19
LA6: Holme .1F 6
OL12: Roch .4C 204
(not continuous)
OL15: Littleb .9K 185
PR1: Prest .7N 229 (1L 135)
PR5: Bam B .9A 136
PR7: Chor .8E 174
PR8: S'port .7G 166
Duke's Wood La. WN8: Skelm .8A 220
Dulas Grn. L32: Kirk .9M 223
Dulas Rd. L32: Kirk .9M 223
Dumbarton Cl. FY4: Blackp .3G 108
Dumbarton Rd. LA1: Lanc .8E 228 (9L 23)
Dumb Tom's La. LA6: Ingl .4L 19
Dumfries Cl. FY2: Blackp .6F 62
Dumfries Way L33: Kirk .4J 223
Dunald Mill La. LA6: Halt, Neth K .5D 16
Dunbar Cl. FY4: Blackp .3G 108
Dunbar Cres. PR8: Birk .5F 186
Dunbar Dr. LA3: Heys .9K 21
PR2: Fulw .5G 115
Dunbar Rd. PR2: Ingol .6C 114
PR8: Birk .3E 186
Duncan Av. FY2: Blackp .5C 62
Duncan Cl. BB10: Burnl .4K 125
FY8: L Ann .8D 108
Duncan Pl. FY7: Flee .9E 40
WN5: Wigan .3N 221
Duncan Sq. BB5: Osw .3L 141
(off Union Rd.)
Duncan St. BB12: Burnl .4M 123
BL6: Hor .9D 196
DUNCOMBE .7C 68
Duncombe Ter. PR3: Bils .7D 68
(off Garstang Rd.)
Dun Cft. Cl. BB7: Clith .1L 81
Dundas St. BB8: Colne .7N 85
(off John St.)
Dundee Dr. BB1: Blackb .4A 140
Dundee La. BL0: Ramsb .8G 180
Dundee Rd. OL14: Tod .8G 146
Dundee St. LA1: Lanc .8F 228 (9L 23)
Dunderdale Av. BB9: Nelson .3G 105
Dunderdale St. PR3: Longr .3K 97
Dundonald St. PR1: Prest .9N 115
Dundonnell Rd. BB9: Nelson .1L 105
Dunedin Rd. BL8: Greenm .3E 200
Dunelt Ct. FY1: Blackp .8L 227 (8C 88)
Dunelt Rd. FY1: Blackp .8L 227 (8C 88)
Dunes Av. FY4: Blackp .4B 108
Dunes Ho. FY8: L Ann .3F 128
Dunes Splash World .7F 166
Dunfold Cl. L32: Kirk .9L 223
Dungeon La. WN8: Dalt .5N 211
Dunham Dr. PR6: Whit W .1E 174
Dunkeld St. LA1: Lanc .8F 228 (9L 23)
Dunkenhalgh Way BB5: Chur, Clay M .8L 121
Dunkenshaw Cres. LA1: Lanc .5M 29
Dunkirk Av. LA5: Carn .1B 16
PR2: Fulw .5F 114
Dunkirk La. PR25: Leyl .7F 152
PR26: Leyl .6C 152
Dunkirk M. PR25: Leyl .7G 152
Dunkirk Ri. OL12: Roch .5B 204
Dunkirk Rd. PR8: Birk .3F 186
Dunlin Av. LA3: Heys .2L 27
Dunlin Cl. FY5: T Clev .7G 54
OL11: Roch .6K 203
Dunlin Dr. FY8: L Ann .1L 129
Dunlin Ter. BB5: Osw .5L 141
(off Heys)
Dunlop Av. OL11: Roch .9B 204
PR8: Ains .2C 206
Dunlop Dr. L31: Mell .6G 222
Dunmail Av. FY3: Blackp .8F 88
Dunmore St. PR1: Prest .9L 115
Dunnings Bri. Rd. L30: N'ton .7A 222
Dunnings Wlk. L30: N'ton .6A 222
Dunnock La. PR4: Cott .5B 114
DUNNOCKSHAW .4N 143
DUNNYSHOP .5M 141
Dunnyshop Av. BB5: Acc .4N 141
Dunoon Cl. PR2: Ingol .5C 114
Dunoon Dr. BB1: Blackb .5D 140
BL1: Bolt .8C 198
Dunoon St. BB11: Burnl .4B 124
Dunrobin Dr. PR7: Eux .5N 173
DUNSCAR .5E 198
Dunscar Bri. BL7: Eger .5E 198
Dunscar Dr. PR6: Chor .5G 175
Dunscar Fold BL7: Eger .5E 198
Dunscar Golf Course .5D 198
Dunscar Grange BL7: Brom C .5F 198
Dunscar Ind. Est. BL7: Eger .5E 198
Dunscar Sq. BL7: Eger .5E 198
DUNSOP BRIDGE .7K 49
Dunsop Cl. FY1: Blackp .9N 227 (9D 88)
PR5: Bam B .8B 136
Dunsop Ct. FY1: Blackp .9N 227 (9D 88)
Dunsop Gdns. LA3: Morec .6F 22
Dunsop Rd. BB7: Dun B, White .9K 49
BB7: Newt .7M 49
PR2: Ribb .5N 115
Dunsop St. BB1: Blackb .1E 226 (2N 139)
Dunstable OL12: Roch .5C 204
(off Redcross St.)
Dunster Av. BB5: Osw .3J 141
OL11: Roch .8B 204
Dunster Gro. BB7: Clith .5J 81
Dunster Rd. PR8: Birk .5E 186
Dunsters Av. BL8: Bury .8H 201
Dunsters Ct. BL8: Bury .8H 201
Dunsterville Ter. OL11: Roch .8B 204
(off New Barn La.)
Dunvegan Cl. FY4: Blackp .3G 108
Dura Bank OL12: Whitw .5A 184
Durants Cotts. L31: Magh .3D 222
Durban Gro. BB11: Burnl .5C 124
Durban Rd. BL1: Bolt .8E 198
Durham Av. BB12: Burnl .2N 123
FY5: T Clev .9E 54
FY8: L Ann .1E 128
LA1: Lanc .2L 29
Durham Cl. BB1: Blackb .6F 226 (4N 139)
LA3: Morec .6B 22
PR25: Leyl .9H 153
Durham Dr. BB1: Wilp .3N 119
BB5: Osw .5M 141
BL0: Ramsb .2F 200
PR7: Buck V .8A 154
Durham Gro. PR3: Gars .5M 59
Durham Rd. BB1: Wilp .3N 119
BB3: Darw .5M 157
FY1: Blackp .1M 227 (5D 88)
Durhams Pas. OL15: Littleb .9K 185
Durham St. BB5: Acc .1C 142
OL11: Roch .7C 204
WN8: Skelm .1H 219
Durham St. Bri. OL11: Roch .8D 204
Durley Rd. FY1: Blackp .8M 227 (8D 88)
DURN .9M 185
Durnford Cl. OL12: Roch .3H 203
Durn Ind. Est. OL15: Littleb .8M 185
Durnlaw Cl. OL15: Littleb .9M 185
Durn St. OL14: Tod .7C 146
OL15: Littleb .8M 185
D'urton La. PR3: Brou .9G 95
Dutch Barn Cl. PR7: Chor .4D 174
DUTTON .1G 98
Dutton Brook Ho. PR3: Ribc .7E 98
Dutton Ct. FY3: Blackp .1N 227 (5D 88)
Duttonfield Cl. PR26: Far M .4H 153
Dutton Rd. FY3: Blackp .1N 227 (4D 88)
Dutton St. BB5: Acc .2B 142
Duttons Way BB1: Blackb .7D 140
Duxbury Av. BL2: Bolt .8L 199
Duxbury Cl. L31: Magh .8D 216
WA11: Rain .3L 225
Duxbury Gdns. PR7: Chor .9F 174
Duxbury Hall Rd. PR7: Chor .2G 194
Duxbury Pk. Bus. Cen. PR7: Chor .2F 194
Duxbury Pk. Golf Course .2F 194
Duxbury St. BB3: Darw .9B 158
BB18: Earl .2F 78
Duxon Hill PR6: Brind .8K 137
DW Fitness Club
Lower Audley .6D 226 (4M 139)
Dye Ho. La. LA1: Lanc .6C 228 (8K 23)
OL16: Roch .2F 204
Dyers Ct. OL15: Littleb .8K 185
Dyers La. L39: Orms .8K 209
Dyer St. PR4: K'ham .4L 111
Dyke Nook BB7: Clith .4M 81
Dykes La. LA5: Yea C .9B 6
Dylan Harvey Bus. Cen.
BB1: Guide .1B 158
Dymock Rd. PR1: Prest .8N 115
Dyneley Av. BB10: Burnl .5K 125
Dyneley La. BB11: Cliv .1H 145
Dyneley Rd. BB1: Blackb .1C 140
Dyson St. BB2: Blackb .9B 226 (6L 139)

E

Eachill Gdns. BB1: Rish .9H 121
Eachill Rd. BB1: Rish .8H 121
Eafield Av. OL16: Milnr .6J 205
Eafield Cl. OL16: Milnr .6J 205
Eafield Rd. OL15: Littleb .2H 205
OL16: Roch .4F 204
Eager La. L31: Lyd .3A 216
EAGLAND HILL .5N 57
Eagle & Child Weind PR3: Gars .5N 59
(off Park Hill Rd.)
Eagle Brow Cl. FY5: T Clev .7H 55
Eagle Cres. WA11: Rain .4L 225
Eagles, The FY6: Poul F .6L 63
Eagles Ct. L32: Kirk .8K 223
Eagle St. BB1: Blackb .4C 140
BB5: Acc .3A 142
BB5: Osw .6J 141
BB9: Nelson .1K 105
OL14: Tod .1L 165
OL16: Roch .7D 204
Eagle Technology Pk. OL11: Roch .9D 204
Eagleton Way PR1: Penw .6K 135
Eagle Way OL11: Roch .9D 204
EAGLEY .6F 198
Eagley Bank BL1: Bolt .7F 198
OL12: Whitw .9B 164
Eagley Brow BL1: Bolt .7F 198
(not continuous)
Eagley Ct. BL7: Brom C .6G 198
Eagley Rd. BB9: Brierf .6G 104
Eagley Way BL1: Bolt .6F 198
EALEES .9M 185
Ealees Rd. OL15: Littleb .9M 185
Ealing Gro. PR6: Chor .2H 175
Eamont Av. PR9: S'port .1A 168
Eamont Pl. FY7: Flee .2D 54
Eanam BB1: Blackb .4E 226 (3N 139)
Eanam Old Rd. BB1: Blackb .4E 226 (3N 139)
Eanam Wharf BB1: Blackb .4F 226 (3N 139)
EARBY .2E 78
Earby Rd. BB18: Salt .5A 78
EARCROFT .9L 139
Earcroft Way BB3: Darw .2M 157
Eardley Rd. LA3: Heys .8K 21
Earhart Cl. WN8: Skelm .3B 220
Earlesdon Av. BB18: Earl .3C 78
Earlham St. BB18: Earl .2F 78
Earl Rd. BL0: Ramsb .8G 181
Earls Av. PR5: Bam B .8A 136
Earls Dr. BB3: Hodd .6E 158
Earl St. BB1: Blackb .1D 226 (1M 139)
BB5: Clay M .7M 121
BB6: Gt H .4H 121
BB8: Colne .7A 86
BB9: Nelson .1K 105
BB10: Burnl .1F 124
BB18: Barnw .2N 77
BL0: Ramsb .8J 181
LA1: Lanc .7K 23
PR1: Prest .5K 229 (9J 115)
Earls Way PR7: Eux .4N 173
Earlsway FY3: Stain .5K 89
Earlswood WN8: Skelm .2B 220
Earnsdale Av. BB3: Darw .5L 157
Earnsdale Cl. BB3: Darw .5M 157
Earnsdale Rd. BB3: Darw .4M 157
Earnshaw Av. OL12: Roch .2B 204
EARNSHAW BRIDGE .4H 153
Earnshaw Dr. PR25: Leyl .6G 153
Earnshaw Rd. OL13: Bac .4K 163
Easby Cl. L37: Form .1A 214
Easdale Av. LA4: Morec .3E 22
Easedale Cl. BB12: Burnl .1N 123
LA5: Bolt S .7K 15
Easedale Dr. PR8: Ains .9B 186
Easedale Wlk. L33: Kirk .5J 223
EASINGTON .7B 50
Easington LA1: Lanc .6G 22
Easington Cres. FY3: Blackp .2H 89
Easington Rd. BB7: Cow A, Newt .3M 71
East Av. BB18: Barnw .2M 77
East Bank BB4: Water .7E 144
BB9: Barrf .7H 85
E. Bank Av. BB4: Hasl .5G 160
Eastbank Av. FY4: Blackp .2G 109
Eastbank Ho. PR8: S'port .8H 167
(off Eastbank St.)
Eastbank Rd. FY8: L Ann .3E 128
Eastbank St. PR8: S'port .7H 167
Eastbank St. Sq. PR8: S'port .7H 167
East Beach FY8: L Ann .5A 130
East Boothroyden FY1: Blackp .2B 88
Eastbourne Cl. PR2: Ingol .4C 114
Eastbourne Rd. FY4: Blackp .3B 108
PR8: Birk .2G 187
Eastbourne St. OL11: Roch .8C 204
E. Cecil St. FY8: L Ann .5N 129
E. Chorley Bus. Cen. PR6: Chor .6F 174
East Cliff PR1: Prest .8J 229 (2J 135)
East Cliffe FY8: L Ann .5B 130
Eastcliffe LA2: Clau .9A 18
E. Cliff Gdns. PR1: Prest .8J 229 (2J 135)
E. Cliff Rd. PR1: Prest .8J 229 (2J 135)
Eastcott Cl. BB2: Blackb .8A 140
East Ct. FY5: T Clev .7D 54
East Cres. BB5: Acc .9A 122
East Cft. BB9: Nelson .1M 105
Eastdene WN8: Parb .2M 211
East End St. BB8: Colne .7N 85
(off Collingwood St.)
Eastern Av. BB10: Burnl .1G 124

Elletson St.—Extwistle St.

Elletson St. FY6: Poul F 7K 63
Elliot Dr. L32: Kirk 9J 223
Elliott Av. BB3: Darw 9B 158
Elliott Cl. PR1: Prest 1H 229 (7H 115)
Elliott Gdns. WN6: App B 5H 213
Elliott St. BB10: Burnl 4G 125
OL12: Roch 5D 204
PR1: Prest 1H 229 (7H 115)
(Henderson St.)
PR1: Prest 2H 229 (8H 115)
(Moorbrook St.)
Elliott Wlk. PR1: Prest 2H 229 (7H 115)
Ellis Dr. LA4: Morec 2E 22
Ellis Fold OL12: Roch 2J 203
Ellisland FY4: Blackp 9J 89
Ellison Fold BB5: Clay M 6L 121
Ellison Fold La. BB3: Darw 6C 158
Ellison Fold Ter. BB3: Darw 6B 158
Ellison St. BB3: Darw 5A 158
BB5: Acc 2A 142
Ellis St. BB11: Burnl 3A 228 (4C 124)
BB18: Barnw 2M 77
BL0: Ramsb 9G 181
(off Silvermere Cl.)
Ellwood Av. LA1: Lanc 4L 23
LA3: Morec 6C 22
Ellwood Cotts. BD24: Langc 1N 35
Ellwood Ct. LA3: Morec 6C 22
Ellwood Gro. LA3: Morec 6C 22
Elm Av. FY3: Blackp 1N 227 (5E 88)
FY6: Poul F 8K 63
LA2: Gal 2K 37
OL14: Tod 9L 147
PR2: Ash R 7C 114
PR4: Wart 2J 131
WN5: Wigan 5N 221
Elmbank Av. FY5: T Clev 4C 62
Elm Brow PR3: T'ley 9F 70
Elm Cl. BB1: Rish 9H 121
BB4: Hasl 4G 161
BB18: Barnw 3L 77
BB18: Salt 4B 78
Elm Ct. FY6: Poul F 8K 63
WN8: Skelm 2J 219
Elmcroft La. L38: Hight 8A 214
Elm Dr. PR5: Bam B 7B 136
ELMERS GREEN 1A 220
Elmers Grn. WN8: Skelm 1A 220
(not continuous)
Elmer's Grn. La. WN8: Dalt, Skelm 7N 211
(not continuous)
Elmers Wood Rd. WN8: Skelm 2A 220
Elmfield WN6: Shev 6L 213
Elmfield Dr. PR5: Bam B 1E 154
Elmfield Hall Flats BB5: Chur 1N 141
Elmfield St. BB5: Chur 1M 141
Elm Gdns. WA11: Rain 4K 225
Elm Gro. BB3: Darw 4B 158
BL7: Brom C 5G 198
LA4: Morec 1E 22
OL11: Roch 8B 204
OL12: Ward 9F 184
OL16: Milnr 9K 205
PR2: Ribb 7A 116
PR4: Wesh 2N 111
PR6: Chor 4G 174
PR25: Leyl 4N 153
WN8: Skelm 2J 219
Elmhurst Rd. FY8: L Ann 9H 109
Elm Mill BB10: Burnl 1E 124
Elmore Wood OL15: Littleb 8H 185
Elm Pk. Dr. PR8: Ains 8E 186
Elmpark Ga. OL12: Roch 2M 203
Elmpark Gro. OL12: Roch 2M 203
Elmpark Va. OL12: Roch 2M 203
Elmpark Vw. OL12: Roch 2M 203
Elmpark Way OL12: Roch 2M 203
Elm Pl. L39: Orms 8K 209
Elmridge WN8: Skelm 2A 220
Elmridge Cres. FY2: Blackp 9F 62
Elmridge La. PR3: Chip 8D 70
Elm Rd. L32: Kirk 7J 223
L40: Burs 1C 210
PR8: S'port 1H 187
Elms, The FY3: Blackp 7E 88
(off Whitegate Dr.)
L31: Lyd 8C 216
OL15: Littleb 1J 205
PR6: Clay W 6E 154
PR8: S'port 9J 167
(Ash St.)
PR8: S'port 8F 166
(Beach Priory Gdns.)
Elms Av. FY5: T Clev 1E 62
FY8: L Ann 5L 129
Elms Ct. LA4: Morec 1E 22
Elmsdale Cl. LA1: Lanc 6J 23
Elms Dr. LA4: Morec 2E 22
PR4: W Grn 5G 110
Elmsett Rd. PR5: Walt D 5B 136
Elmsfield Av. OL11: Roch 4J 203
Elmsfield Pk. L39: Aug 5F 216
Elmside Cl. FY5: T Clev 1K 63
Elmslack Ct. LA5: Silv 7G 4
Elmslack La. LA5: Silv 7G 4
Elms La. LA4: Morec 1F 22
Elmsley St. PR1: Prest 6H 115
Elmslie Gdns. FY3: Blackp 7E 88
Elms Rd. L31: Magh 4C 222
LA4: Morec 1E 22
Elmstead WN8: Skelm 3A 220
Elm St. BB1: Blackb 1A 140
BB4: Hasl 4G 161
BB4: Rawt 4M 161
BB6: Gt H 5J 121
BB8: Colne 5B 86
BB9: Nelson 1J 105
BB10: Burnl 9E 104
BL0: Eden 3K 181
BL0: Ramsb 8J 181
FY7: Flee 9G 40
LA1: Lanc 7J 23
OL12: Roch 4C 204
OL12: Whitw 4A 184
OL13: Bac 4L 163
OL15: Littleb 3J 205
Elmswood Cl. FY8: L Ann 4M 129
Elm Tree Gro. BB6: Old L 5C 100
Elmwood PR3: Longr 2J 97
PR7: Chor 5D 174
WN8: Skelm 9N 211
Elmwood Av. FY6: Pree 9N 41
PR25: Leyl 6H 153
Elmwood Cl. BB5: Acc 2C 142
Elmwood Ct. PR4: Weet 8E 90
Elmwood Dr. FY5: T Clev 2H 63
PR1: Penw 4E 134
Elmwood Gdns. LA1: Lanc 5L 29
Elmwood St. BB11: Burnl 4B 124
Elnup Av. WN6: Shev 6L 213
Elric Wlk. L33: Kirk 7L 223
Elsby Av. FY5: T Clev 3J 63
Elsham Cl. BL1: Bolt 8E 198
Elsie St. BL0: Ramsb 1F 200
Elsinore Cl. FY7: Flee 8F 40
ELSLACK 8L 53
Elslack La. BD23: Elsl 8L 53
Elson St. BL8: Bury 9G 201
Elstead Rd. L32: Kirk 9H 223
ELSTON 4J 117
Elston Av. FY3: Blackp 2G 88
Elston Grn. PR2: Grim 9G 96
Elston La. PR2: Grim 9G 97
Elston Lodge PR2: Ribb 5B 116
(off Grange Av.)
Elstow Cl. PR7: Buck V 1B 174
ELSWICK 1M 91
Elswick WN8: Skelm 3N 219
Elswick Gdns. BB2: Mellor 6E 118
Elswick Grn. PR9: S'port 1N 167
Elswick Ind. Pk. PR4: Elsw 1M 91
ELSWICK LEYS 2M 91
Elswick Lodge BB2: Mellor 6F 118
Elswick Pl. FY4: Blackp 4E 108
FY8: L Ann 9H 109
Elswick Rd. PR2: Ash R 8B 114
PR9: S'port 2M 167
PR25: Leyl 7G 152
Elswick St. BB3: Darw 6B 158
Elsworth Dr. BL1: Bolt 9F 198
Elterwater FY6: K Sea 7L 41
Elterwater Cl. BL8: Bury 9G 201
Elterwater Pl. FY3: Blackp 8J 89
LA1: Lanc 7L 23
Eltham Ct. FY3: Blackp 1H 89
Elton Ho. WN5: Wigan 4M 221
Elton Rd. BB1: Belt 9F 140
Elton St. PR2: Ash R 8F 114
Elvaston Rd. FY6: Carl 5J 63
Elvington Cl. WN5: Wigan 2L 221
Elvington Rd. L38: Hight 9A 214
Elwood Cl. L33: Kirk 4K 223
Ely Cl. BB1: Wilp 3N 119
BB3: Darw 6C 158
Ely Dr. BL8: Bury 9J 201
Ely M. PR9: S'port 4N 167
Embankment Rd. BL7: Turt 9J 179
Embsay Cl. BL1: Bolt 8D 198
Emerald Av. BB1: Blackb 7N 119
Emerald Cl. BB1: Blackb 7N 119
FY5: T Clev 4F 62
L30: N'ton 7A 222
Emerald Cotts. BL8: Holc 2E 200
Emerald St. BB1: Blackb 7N 119
Emerson Av. FY4: Blackp 2D 108
Emerson Cl. L38: Hight 7A 214
Emerson Rd. PR1: Prest 7N 115
Emerson St. LA1: Lanc 3L 29
Emesgate La. LA5: Silv 8G 4
Emily St. BB1: Blackb 2A 140
BB11: Burnl 5E 124
PR5: Lost H 8K 135
Emmanuel Rd. PR9: S'port 4M 167
Emmanuel St. PR1: Prest 7H 115
(not continuous)
Emma St. BB5: Acc 2M 141
OL12: Roch 5B 204
Emmaus Rd. LA3: Heys 1L 27
Emmett St. BL6: Hor 9C 196
PR1: Prest 3K 229 (8J 115)
Emmott Ct. BB8: Lane B 5H 87
Emmott La. BB8: Lane B 4G 87
Emmie La. PR26: Leyl 8F 152
Empire Bus. Pk. BB12: Burnl 3M 123
Empire Gro. FY3: Blackp 3D 88
Empire Shop. Arc. LA4: Morec 3N 21
Empire St. BB6: Gt H 3K 121
Empire Way BB12: Burnl 3M 123
Empress Av. PR2: Fulw 5H 115
Empress Cl. L31: Magh 1A 222
Empress Dr. FY2: Blackp 1B 88
Empress St. BB3: Lwr D 9N 139
BB5: Acc 2M 141
BB8: Colne 6B 86
Empress Way PR7: Eux 4A 174
Emstrey Wlk. L32: Kirk 8H 223
Endcliffe Rd. LA4: Morec 3C 22
Endeavour Cl. PR2: Ash R 1E 134
Enderley Ct. FY5: T Clev 2J 63
Ending Rake OL12: Whitw 1N 203
Endsleigh Gdns. FY4: Blackp 3D 108
Endsleigh Gro. LA1: Lanc 5G 22
End St. BB8: Colne 7M 85
ENFIELD 8N 121
Enfield Cl. OL11: Roch 5J 203
PR7: E'ton 9F 172
Enfield Rd. BB5: Hunc 7C 122
FY1: Blackp 3C 88
Enfield St. WN5: Wigan 6M 221
Engal Cl. BL0: Ramsb 9F 180
Engine Brow BB3: Tock 4G 156
Engine Fold WN5: Wigan 5L 221
Engine La. L37: Gt A 4D 214
England Av. BB2: Blackb 8L 139
FY2: Blackp 7C 62
Engledene BL1: Bolt 7D 198
English Martyrs Pl. PR1: Prest 1J 229 (7J 115)
Ennerdale WN8: Skelm 3A 220
Ennerdale Av. BB1: Blackb 5C 140
FY7: Flee 3C 54
L31: Magh 9D 216
LA4: Morec 4D 22
Ennerdale Cl. BB5: Osw 3K 141
BB7: Clith 4J 81
FY6: K Sea 7M 41
L33: Kirk 5J 223
LA1: Lanc 6M 23
PR3: Fort 2M 45
PR25: Leyl 8K 153
Ennerdale Dr. L39: Aug 1G 217
PR5: Walt D 3A 136
Ennerdale Rd. BB7: Clith 4J 81
BB10: Burnl 4J 125
FY4: Blackp 9J 89
OL11: Roch 9M 203
PR3: Longr 5H 97
PR7: Chor 8C 174
Ennismore St. BB10: Burnl 9G 104
Ensign Ct. FY8: L Ann 5C 108
Enstone WN8: Skelm 2A 220
Enterprise Ct. BB5: Hunc 8C 122
Enterprise Dr. PR26: Far M 1J 153
Enterprise Pk. WA11: Rain 6M 225
Enterprise Way BB5: Acc 3A 142
BB8: Colne 8K 85
BB12: Burnl 3M 123
FY7: Flee 6G 54
Entwisle Rd. BB5: Acc 9A 122
OL16: Roch 6D 204
Entwisle St. OL16: Milnr 7H 205
ENTWISTLE 6H 179
Entwistle Hall La. BL7: Turt 6H 179
Entwistle Station (Rail) 6H 179
Entwistle St. BB3: Darw 4A 158
Envoy Cl. WN5: Wigan 2N 221
Ephraim St. PR1: Prest 1M 135
Epping Av. BB5: Acc 8A 122
Epping Cl. FY2: Blackp 6E 62
Epping Pl. PR6: Chor 6F 174
Epsom Cl. L10: Aint 9D 222
OL11: Roch 5K 203
PR6: Chor 2H 175
Epsom Cft. PR6: And 6K 195
Epsom Gro. L33: Kirk 4M 223
Epsom Rd. FY5: T Clev 2K 63
Epsom Way BB5: Acc 3C 142
Epworth St. BB3: Darw 9B 158
Equitable Ho. LA1: Lanc 7D 228
Equitable St. OL11: Roch 7D 204
OL16: Milnr 8J 205
Equity St. BB3: Darw 7A 158
Erdington Rd.
FY1: Blackp 5J 227 (7C 88)
Eric Morecambe Statue 2A 22
Ericson Dr. PR8: S'port 9H 167
Eric St. OL15: Littleb 8K 185
Erith Gro. FY2: Blackp 6C 62
Ermine Cl. BB2: Blackb 8A 140
Ermine Pl. LA3: Morec 5E 22
Ernest St. BB5: Chur 2L 141
BB5: Clay M 8M 121
OL13: Bac 7N 163
OL14: Tod 7F 146
Ernest Ter. OL12: Roch 4E 204
Ernlouen Cl. BB2: Blackb 8H 139
Erradale Cres. WN3: Wins 9N 221
Erringden St. OL14: Tod 2M 165
Erskine Rd. PR6: Chor 5G 174
Escar St.
BB11: Burnl 4B 228 (4D 124)
Escott Gdns. BB10: Burnl 1E 124
Esher Pond PR2: Fulw 3F 114
ESHTON 1M 53
Eshton Rd. BD23: Garg 3M 53
Eshton Ter. BB7: Clith 4K 81
Esk Av. BL0: Eden 1J 181
FY7: Flee 2D 54
Eskbank WN8: Skelm 3N 219
Eskbrook WN8: Skelm 2N 219
Eskdale WN8: Skelm 3M 219
Eskdale Av. FY7: Flee 3D 54
L39: Aug 1G 217
OL11: Roch 9M 203
Eskdale Cl. BB10: Reed 6F 104
FY4: Blackp 9F 88
PR2: Fulw 1J 115
Eskdale Cres. BB2: Blackb 8F 138
Eskdale Dr. L31: Magh 9D 216
PR4: Wesh 2M 111
Eskdale Gdns. BB12: Padi 8H 103
(off Windermere Rd.)
Eskdale Gro. FY6: K Sea 7M 41
Eskdale Pl. LA4: Morec 4D 22
Eskdale Rd. PR3: Longr 4H 97
PR25: Leyl 8M 153
Eskew La. LA2: L Ben 7J 19
Eskham Cl. PR4: Wesh 3K 111
ESKRIGGE 6B 18
Eskrigge Ct. LA1: Lanc 4J 23
Eskrigge La. LA2: Gress 6B 18
Esplanade FY6: K Sea 8K 41
PR1: Prest 9N 229 (3L 135)
PR8: S'port 8E 166
Esplanade, The BB1: Rish 9F 120
FY7: Flee 8F 40
OL16: Roch 6B 204
Esplanade (Park & Ride) 7F 166
Esp La. BB18: Barnw 4K 77
ESPRICK 5J 91
Essex Av. BB12: Burnl 2N 123
Essex Cl. BB2: Blackb 8A 226 (5L 139)
Essex Pl. FY2: Blackp 9F 62
Essex Rd. BB1: Rish 8G 120
LA4: Morec 4F 22
PR8: Birk 5G 187
Essex St. BB3: Darw 6B 158
BB5: Acc 2C 142
BB8: Colne 7B 86
BB9: Nelson 1J 105
BB18: Barnw 2L 77
OL11: Roch 7C 204
PR1: Prest 2L 229 (8K 115)
Essie Ter. BB18: Barnw 3M 77
(off Low Moor La.)
Essington Av. LA4: Morec 4A 22
Est Bank Rd. BL0: Ramsb 2F 200
(not continuous)
Esther Pl. OL13: Bac 4L 163
Esther St. BB1: Blackb 3C 140
OL15: Littleb 9J 185
(off Bamford St.)
Esthwaite Gdns. LA1: Lanc 7M 23
Ethel Ct. OL16: Roch 7E 204
Ethel St. BB18: Barnw 2N 77
OL12: Whitw 4A 184
OL16: Roch 7E 204
Ethersall Rd. BB9: Nelson 4J 105
Eton Av. BB5: Acc 1B 142
Eton Cl. BB12: Padi 3K 123
OL11: Roch 7M 203
Eton Ct. PR9: S'port 5J 167
Eton Dr. L10: Aint 8B 222
Eton Pk. PR2: Fulw 4M 115
Eton Way WN5: Orr 3J 221
Ettington Dr. PR8: Ains 8A 186
Ettrick Av. FY7: Flee 1D 54
Ettrick Cl. L33: Kirk 4J 223
Europa Dr. PR26: Far M 2K 153
Europa Ho. BL9: Bury 9L 201
Europa Way LA1: Lanc 9G 22
(not continuous)
Euston Gro. LA4: Morec 3B 22
Euston Rd. LA4: Morec 3A 22
Euston St. PR1: Prest 1H 135
EUXTON 2M 173
Euxton Balshaw Lane Station (Rail) 5N 173
Euxton Cl. FY4: Blackp 1E 108
Euxton Hall Ct. PR7: Eux 4M 173
Euxton Hall Gdns. PR7: Eux 4M 173
Euxton Hall M. PR7: Eux 4M 173
Euxton La. PR7: Chor, Eux 2N 173
Euxton Pk. Golf Cen. 2C 174
Evan Cl. WN6: Stand 8N 213
Evans Bus. Cen. FY4: Blackp 5E 108
OL11: Roch 6B 204
(off Church St.)
Evans St. BB11: Burnl 5D 124
BL6: Hor 9D 196
PR2: Ash R 8G 115
Eva St. OL12: Roch 3D 204
Evellynne Cl. L32: Kirk 8J 223
Evelyn Rd. BB3: Darw 2M 157
Evelyn St. BB10: Burnl 9E 104
Evenwood WN8: Skelm 2A 220
Evenwood Ct. WN8: Skelm 2N 219
Everard Cl. L40: Scar 6E 188
Everard Rd. PR8: S'port 1K 187
Everdon Wood L33: Kirk 7L 223
Everest Cl. FY8: L Ann 8G 108
Everest Ct. PR4: Wesh 3L 111
Everest Dr. FY2: Blackp 5C 62
Everest Rd. FY8: L Ann 7G 108
Evergreen Av. PR25: Leyl 8K 153
Evergreen Cl. PR7: Chor 9D 174
Evergreens, The
BB2: Blackb 8G 138
PR4: Cott 5B 114
Everleigh Cl. BL2: Bolt 8L 199
Eversham Cl. PR9: Banks 1F 168
Eversholt Cl. BB12: Fence 2B 104
Eversleigh Av. FY5: T Clev 9F 54
Eversleigh St.
PR1: Prest 2G 229 (8H 115)
Eversley WN8: Skelm 2A 220
Everton BB2: Blackb 7A 140
Everton Rd. FY4: Blackp 3C 108
PR8: Birk 1G 187
Everton St. BB3: Darw 6N 157
Every St. BB9: Brierf 4F 104
BB9: Nelson 3G 105
BB11: Burnl 3A 228 (4C 124)
BL0: Ramsb 8J 181
BL9: Bury 9L 201
OL14: Tod 2M 165
Evesham Av. PR1: Penw 6H 135
Evesham Cl. BB5: Acc 1N 141
FY5: T Clev 4E 62
LA3: Heys 1L 27
PR4: Hutt 7N 133
Evesham Rd. FY3: Blackp 2H 89
FY8: L Ann 3G 129
Eve St. BB9: Nelson 9L 85
(off Leeds Rd.)
Evington WN8: Skelm 2A 220
Evolution Pk. BB1: Blackb 6B 140
Ewell Cl. PR6: Chor 2H 175
EWOOD 8L 139
Ewood BB2: Blackb 7L 139
EWOOD BRIDGE 9H 161
Ewood La. BB4: Hasl 8H 161
OL14: Tod 1J 165
Ewood Pk. 8L 139
Exbury OL12: Roch 5B 204
(off Falinge Rd.)
Excelsior Ter. OL15: Littleb 2J 205
(off Barke St.)
Exchange Island WN8: Skelm 3K 219
Exchange St. BB1: Blackb 3C 226 (3M 139)
BB3: Darw 5A 158
BB5: Acc 3M 141
BB8: Colne 7A 86
BL0: Eden 3J 181
FY1: Blackp 3B 88
Exe St. PR1: Prest 7L 115
Exeter Av. LA1: Lanc 1M 29
Exeter Cl. L10: Aint 9D 222
Exeter Dr. FY5: T Clev 1G 62
Exeter Gro. OL11: Roch 8C 204
(off Exeter St.)
Exeter Pl. PR2: Ash R 7B 114
Exeter St. BB2: Blackb 9A 226 (6K 139)
FY4: Blackp 9C 88
OL11: Roch 8C 204
Exmoor Cl. PR9: S'port 9A 148
Exmouth Pl. OL16: Roch 9E 204
Exmouth Sq. OL16: Roch 9D 204
Exmouth St. BB11: Burnl 4D 228 (4E 124)
OL16: Roch 9D 204
Exton St. BB9: Brierf 5E 104
Exton Ter. BB7: Barr 2J 101
Extwistle Rd. BB10: W'thorne 4M 125
Extwistle Sq. BB10: Burnl 4J 125
Extwistle St. BB9: Nelson 3H 105
BB10: Burnl 1E 124

Eyes La. PR26: Breth 4G 170
WN8: Parb 1L 211

F

FACIT 4A 184
Factory Brow PR3: Scor 6B 46
Factory Hill BL6: Hor 9E 196
LA1: Lanc 5E 228 (7L 23)
Factory La. BB9: Barrf 7H 85
BB12: Padi 9H 103
PR1: Penw 5H 135
PR6: H Charn 5K 195
PR6: Whit W 7D 154
Factory St. BL0: Ramsb 7H 181
Fairacres WN6: Stand 3L 213
Fairbairn Av. BB12: Burnl 1A 124
Fairbank LA6: K Lon 5E 8
Fairbank Gro. LA4: Morec 5A 22
Fairbank Wlk. BB4: Craws 6M 143
Fairburn WN8: Skelm 9M 211
Fairclough Rd. BB5: Acc 5N 141
FY5: T Clev 9G 55
Fair Elms LA1: Lanc 9H 23
Fairfax Av. FY2: Blackp 5E 62
Fairfax Cl. PR3: Gars 6A 60
Fairfax Dr. OL15: Littleb 2J 205
Fairfax Pl. PR5: Walt D 6N 135
Fairfax Rd. PR2: Ribb 5A 116
FAIRFIELD 9B 202
Fairfield PR3: Gars 4N 59
Fairfield Av. BB4: W'foot 5D 162
FY3: Blackp 3H 89
FY6: Poul F 8K 63
WN5: Wigan 6N 221
Fairfield Cl. BB7: Clith 4J 81
L39: Orms 5K 209
LA1: Lanc 7A 228 (8J 23)
LA5: Carn 9B 12
Fairfield Ct. FY7: Flee 2F 54
Fairfield Dr. BB7: Clith 4J 81
BB10: Burnl 7F 104
BL9: Bury 9B 202
L39: Orms 5K 209
PR2: Ash R 7E 114
Fairfield Gro. LA3: Heys 6M 21
Fairfield Rd. BB9: Nelson 2M 105
FY1: Blackp 2C 88
FY6: Poul F 3L 89
FY6: Sing 3A 90
LA1: Lanc 7A 228 (8J 23)
LA3: Heys 5L 21
PR2: Fulw 5K 115
PR8: Ains 8C 186
PR25: Leyl 7J 153
Fairfields BL7: Eger 5F 198
Fairfield St. BB5: Acc 4M 141
PR5: Lost H 9L 135
WN5: Wigan 6M 221
Fairfield Way PR4: Wesh 2K 111
Fairgarth Dr. LA6: K Lon 5E 8
Fairham Av. PR1: Penw 6G 134
FAIRHAVEN 4H 129
Fairhaven L33: Kirk 5K 223
WN8: Skelm 9N 211
Fairhaven Av. FY7: Flee 5D 54
Fairhaven Cl. FY5: T Clev 3K 63
Fairhaven Ct. FY8: L Ann 4J 129
Fairhaven Golf Course 4L 129
Fairhaven La. FY8: L Ann 3E 128
Fairhaven Rd. BB2: Blackb 7N 139
FY8: L Ann 3E 128
PR1: Penw 3H 135
PR9: S'port 2A 168
PR25: Leyl 6G 152
Fairhaven Way LA4: Morec 3D 22
Fairheath Rd. LA2: Tat 9J 19
Fair Hill BB4: Hasl 8F 160
Fairhill Ter. BB4: Hasl 8F 160
Fairholme Rd. BB11: Burnl 6F 124
Fairholmes Cl. FY5: T Clev 9H 55
Fairholmes Way FY5: T Clev 9G 55
Fairhope Av. LA1: Lanc 5J 23
LA4: Morec 2F 22
Fairhope Ct. BB2: Blackb 2K 139
Fairhurst Av. WN6: Stand 1N 213
Fairhurst Ct. FY5: T Clev 9D 54
(off Rossall Rd.)
Fairhurst Dr. WN8: Parb 2M 211
Fairhurst La. PR3: Inglew 5K 69
Fairhurst St. FY1: Blackp 4C 88
Fairhurst Ter. FY1: Blackp 4C 88
(off Fairhurst St.)
Fairlands Rd. BL9: Bury 6L 201
Fairlawne Cl. L33: Kirk 5K 223
Fairlawn Rd. FY8: L Ann 6L 129
Fairlea Av. LA4: Morec 2F 22
Fairlie WN8: Skelm 9N 211
Fairmont Dr. FY6: Ham 1C 64
Fair Mt. OL14: Wals 6K 165
Fair Oak Cl. PR2: Ribb 6B 116
Fairsnape Av. PR3: Longr 3K 97
Fairsnape Dr. PR3: Gars 6M 59
Fairsnape Rd. FY8: L Ann 4C 130
Fairstead WN8: Skelm 9N 211
Fairthorn Wlk. L33: Kirk 7M 223
FAIRVIEW 5H 195
Fair Vw. OL13: Bac 7N 163
Fairview BB4: Rawt 2L 161
LA6: K Lon 5E 8
(off Fairgarth Dr.)
Fairview Av. FY8: L Ann 1G 129
Fairview Cl. OL12: Roch 3G 203
PR4: Wal B 2K 151
Fair Vw. Cres. OL13: Bac 5M 163
Fairview Dr. PR6: H Charn 5H 195
Fairview Rd. BB11: Burnl 4F 124
Fair Vw. St. OL14: Tod 3L 165
Fair Vw. Ter. OL15: Littleb 6M 185
Fairway FY6: Poul F 9G 63
FY6: Stal 5B 56
FY7: Flee 2C 54
OL12: Whitw 7N 183
OL16: Milnr 7K 205
PR1: Penw 2E 134
Fairway PR7: Chor 4E 174
PR9: S'port 4J 167
Fairway Av. BL2: Bolt 9N 199
Fairway Gdns. FY6: K Sea 8K 41
Fairway Rd. FY4: Blackp 1E 108
Fairways FY8: L Ann 2G 129
PR2: Fulw 3K 115
Fairways, The WN8: Skelm 9A 212
Fairways (Park & Ride) 4J 167
Fairways Av. PR3: Brou 7F 94
Fairways Ct. BB1: Wilp 4N 119
Fairways Dr. BB11: Burnl 7C 124
Fairweather Ct. BB12: Padi 9J 103
Fairwinds Av. PR4: Hesk B 3B 150
Fairy Steps 1M 5
Falcon Av. BB3: Darw 4M 157
Falcon Cl. BB1: Blackb 9L 119
BD24: Sett 3N 35
(off Longdale Av.)
BL9: Bury 9N 201
OL12: Roch 3H 203
Falcon Ct. BB5: Clay M 7M 121
Falcon Dr. FY6: Poul F 9H 63
Falcon Gdns. BD24: Sett 3N 35
Falcon Ho. BL9: Bury 9M 201
Falcon Pl. L40: Burs 2N 209
Falcon St. PR1: Prest 1N 229 (7L 115)
(not continuous)
Falcon Ter. BB5: Osw 5L 141
(off Heys)
Falinge Fold OL12: Roch 4A 204
Falinge Mnr. M. OL12: Roch 4B 204
Falinge M. OL12: Roch 5B 204
Falinge Rd. OL12: Roch 4A 204
Falkirk Av. FY2: Blackp 5C 62
Falkirk Gro. WN5: Wigan 3M 221
Falkland WN8: Skelm 9N 211
Falkland Av. FY4: Blackp 8F 88
OL11: Roch 5N 203
Falkland Rd. PR8: S'port 1K 187
Falkland St. PR1: Prest 6H 229 (1H 135)
Fallbarn Cres. BB4: Rawt 6L 161
Fallbarn Rd. BB4: Rawt 5N 161
(not continuous)
Fall Kirk LA2: Gress 6A 18
Fallowfield L33: Kirk 6K 223
Fallowfield Cl. PR4: Wesh 3K 111
Fallowfield Dr. BB12: Burnl 1B 124
OL12: Roch 3A 204
Fallowfield Rd. FY8: L Ann 2J 129
Falmer Cl. BL8: Bury 7H 201
Falmouth Av. BB4: Hasl 5H 161
FY7: Flee 4C 54
Falmouth Rd. FY1: Blackp 8L 227 (8C 88)
Falmouth St. OL11: Roch 8D 204
Falshaw Dr. BL9: Bury 4K 201
Falstone Av. BL0: Ramsb 1H 201
Falstone Cl. WN3: Wins 9N 221
Faraday Av. BB7: Clith 3K 81
Faraday Ct. PR2: Fulw 2M 115
Faraday Dr. PR2: Fulw 2M 115
Faraday Ri. OL12: Roch 4M 203
Faraday St. BB12: Burnl 2A 124
Faraday Way FY2: Blackp, T Clev 5F 62
Far Arnside Holiday Pk. LA5: Arn 5D 4
FAR BANKS 7H 149
Far Cl. Dr. LA5: Arn 3D 4
Far Cft. PR5: Lost H 7K 135
Far East Vw. BB18: Barnw 2M 77
Fareham Cl. PR2: Fulw 5K 115
PR5: Walt D 5B 136
Fareham Dr. PR9: Banks 1F 168
Farfield PR1: Penw 4G 134
Farfield Dr. BB3: Lwr D 1N 157
Farholme La. OL13: Bac 7H 163
Faringdon OL11: Roch 7B 204
Faringdon Av. FY4: Blackp 4D 108
FARINGTON 2L 153
Farington Av. PR25: Leyl 8G 153
Farington Bus. Pk. PR26: Far M 3K 153
Farington Ct. PR25: Far 3L 153
Farington Ga. PR25: Leyl 5L 153
Farington Lodges Nature Reserve 9H 135
FARINGTON MOSS 2G 153
Farington Rd. PR5: Far, Lost H 1J 153
PR26: Far, Far M 1J 153
Far La. PR1: Penw 7F 134
FARLETON 8B 18
Farleton Cl. LA5: Wart 6N 11
Farleton Ct. LA1: Lanc 4K 23
Farleton Crossing LA2: Farl 8A 18
Farleton Old Rd. LA2: Clau, Farl 9A 18
Farleton Vw. LA6: Holme 2G 7
Farley La. WN8: Roby M 9D 212
Farm Av. OL13: Bac 3K 163
PR6: Adl 5J 195
Farm Cl. BL8: Tott 7E 200
FY5: T Clev 1H 63
PR9: S'port 6N 167
Farm Cotts. BL0: Ramsb 5G 181
Farmdale Dr. L31: Magh 1D 222
Farmdale Rd. LA1: Lanc 2M 29
Farmend Cl. PR4: Longt 8M 133
Farmer Parrs Animal World 5F 54
Farmer's Row BB2: Blackb 9J 139
Farmer Ted's Farm Pk. 2M 215
Farm Ho. Cl. PR6: Whit W 9E 154
Farmhouse Cl. BB1: Blackb 4C 140
Farm La. PR5: Walt D 5A 136
Farm Mdw. Rd. WN5: Orr 6H 221
FAR MOOR 7G 220
Far Moor La. LA1: Lanc 8N 23
Farm Wlk. OL15: Littleb 9J 185
OL16: Roch 4F 204
Farnboro St. OL14: Wals 5K 165
Farnborough Rd. BL1: Bolt 7E 198
PR8: Birk 5F 186
Farndean Way BB8: Colne 7B 86
Farnell Pl. FY4: Blackp 3D 108
Farnham Cl. L32: Kirk 9L 223
Farnham Way FY6: Carl 6J 63
Farnlea Dr. LA4: Morec 3E 22
Farnley Cl. OL12: Roch 3K 203
Far Nook PR6: Whit W 8D 154
Farnworth Gro. L33: Kirk 5K 223
Farnworth Ho. Est. PR7: Chor 3E 194
Farnworth Rd. FY5: T Clev 2K 63
Faroes Cl. BB2: Blackb 7N 139
Farrell Cl. L31: Mell 6G 222
Farrell St. WN5: Wigan 6M 221
Farrer Av. LA1: Bail 8L 29
Farrer St. BB9: Nelson 2G 105
Farrier Rd. L33: Kirk 8M 223
Farriers Fold LA3: Heys 9L 21
Farriers La. OL11: Roch 9M 203
Farriers Way FY6: Poul F 7L 63
PR7: Buck V 9A 154
Farriers Yd. LA2: Caton 2H 25
Farrier Way WN6: App B 5F 212
Farringdon Cl. PR1: Prest 8B 116
Farringdon Cres. PR1: Prest 8B 116
Farringdon La. PR2: Ribb 6B 116
FARRINGDON PARK 8A 116
Farringdon Pl. PR1: Prest 8B 116
Farrington Cl. BB2: Blackb 7K 139
BB11: Burnl 6A 124
Farrington Ct. BB11: Burnl 6A 124
Farrington Dr. L39: Orms 6K 209
Farrington Pl. BB11: Burnl 6A 124
Farrington Rd. BB11: Burnl 6N 123
OL13: Bac 7M 163
Farrington St. PR7: Chor 6E 174
Farthings, The PR7: Chor 5B 174
Faulkner Cl. PR8: Ains 8C 186
Faulkner Gdns. PR8: Ains 7C 186
Faulkner's La. PR3: Fort 4M 45
Faulkner St. OL16: Roch 6C 204
Favordale Rd. BB8: Colne 5D 86
Fawcett WN8: Skelm 9M 211
Fawcett Cl. BB2: Blackb 7A 226 (5L 139)
Fawcett Rd. L31: Lyd 8C 216
Fayles Gro. FY4: Blackp 9G 88
Fazackerley Cl. BB2: Blackb 9L 139
Fazackerley St. PR2: Ash R 8F 114
Fazakerley St. PR7: Chor 6E 174
Fearn Dene OL12: Roch 3M 203
Fearnhead Av. BL6: Hor 8C 196
Fearns Moss OL13: Bac 6E 162
Featherstall Brook Vw. OL15: Littleb 9K 185
(off William St.)
Featherstall Rd. OL15: Littleb 9J 185
Featherstall Sq. OL15: Littleb 9K 185
Fecit La. BL0: Ramsb 6N 181
OL12: Ramsb 6A 182
Fecitt Brow BB1: Blackb 4C 140
Fecitt Rd. BB2: Blackb 2J 139
Federation St. BB18: Barnw 1L 77
Feilden Pl. BB2: Fenis 8E 138
Feilden St. BB2: Blackb 5B 226 (4L 139)
Felcroft Way L33: Kirk 8L 223
Felgate Brow FY3: Blackp 5E 88
Felix St. BB11: Burnl 1F 228 (2F 124)
Fell Brow PR3: Longr 4K 97
Fell Cl. PR5: Bam B 8B 136
Fell End Caravan Pk. LA7: Hale 3B 6
Fellery St. PR7: Chor 6E 174
Fellfoot Rd. LA6: Cast 5H 9
Fellgate LA3: Morec 6E 22
Fell La. LA6: Cast 5J 9
LA6: Mans 1E 8
Fell Rd. BB7: Wadd 1F 72
LA4: Morec 4F 22
Fellside BL2: Bolt 9N 199
Fellside Cl. BL8: Greenm 4E 200
Fellside Gdns. OL15: Littleb 7J 185
Fellside Vw. LA3: Heys 9L 21
Fellstone Va. PR6: Withn 6B 156
Fellstone Vw. PR6: Withn 7B 156
Fells Vw. BB7: B'ton 6G 100
Fell Vw. BB7: West B 5K 73
BB7: Whall 3G 101
BB10: Burnl 7H 105
LA2: Caton 3H 25
OL13: Weir 8L 145
PR2: Grim 8E 96
PR3: Gars 4N 59
PR6: Chor 8G 175
PR9: S'port 9C 148
Fell Vw. Cl. PR3: Gars 4N 59
Fellway FY6: Stal 5C 56
Fellway Cl. PR5: Lost H 8M 135
Felstead WN8: Skelm 1M 219
Felstead St. PR1: Prest 9N 115
Felsted Dr. L10: Aint 9D 222
Feltons WN8: Skelm 1M 219
Felton Way PR4: Much H 4K 151
Fenber Av. FY4: Blackp 2C 108
FENCE 3B 104
Fence End Av. BD23: T Crav 9J 53
(off Colne & Broughton Rd.)
Fencegate BB12: Fence 3B 104
Fengrove PR4: Longt 8L 133
Fenham Carr La. LA1: Lanc 9N 23
FENISCLIFFE 6G 139
Feniscliffe Dr. BB2: Blackb 6G 139
FENISCOWLES 8E 138
Fennel Cl. FY2: Blackp 7F 62
Fenney Ct. WN8: Skelm 2N 219
Fennyfold Ter. BB12: Padi 3H 123
Fensway PR4: Hutt 6A 134
Fenton Av. BB18: Barnw 1A 78
Fenton Cl. L30: N'ton 9A 222
Fenton M. OL11: Roch 8B 204
Fenton Rd. FY1: Blackp 4C 88
PR2: Fulw 5M 115
Fenton St. BL8: Bury 9H 201
LA1: Lanc 7B 228 (8J 23)
OL11: Roch 8B 204
Fenwick St. BB11: Burnl 6B 124
OL12: Roch 6B 204
Ferguson Gdns. OL12: Roch 2C 204
Ferguson Ri. WN5: Wigan 3N 221
Ferguson Rd. FY1: Blackp 8E 88
Ferguson St. BB2: Blackb 9L 139
Fermor Rd. PR1: Prest 8A 116
Fern Av. BB5: Osw 5M 141
Fern Bank BB4: Hasl 8F 160
(off Helmshore Rd.)
BB9: Nelson 3J 105
L31: Magh 1D 222
LA1: Lanc 2L 29
Fern Bank LA5: Carn 9A 12
(off Lancaster Rd.)
WA11: Rain 3J 225
Fernbank PR6: Chor 3F 174
Fernbank Av. BB18: Barnw 1L 77
Fernbank Ct. BB9: Nelson 3J 105
(off Fern Bank)
Ferncliffe Dr. LA3: Heys 6L 21
Fern Cl. BB9: Nelson 2L 105
L32: Kirk 6L 223
PR5: Lost H 8L 135
WN6: Shev 6K 213
WN8: Skelm 2J 219
Fern Ct. FY7: Flee 3C 54
Fern Cft. LA6: Cast 5G 8
Ferndale BB1: Blackb 2A 140
PR2: Fulw 3J 115
WN8: Skelm 1M 219
Ferndale Av. FY4: Blackp 2D 108
Ferndale Cl. FY5: T Clev 1J 63
PR4: Frec 1B 132
PR25: Leyl 8L 153
Ferndale Dr. WN6: App B 5G 213
Ferndale St. BB10: Burnl 1G 124
Fern End PR9: Banks 2F 168
Ferney Lee Rd. OL14: Tod 1K 165
Ferney St. OL14: Tod 1K 165
(off Ferney Lee Rd.)
FERN GORE 5N 141
Fern Gore Av. BB5: Acc 5N 141
FERN GROVE 9A 202
Fern Gro. FY1: Blackp 5L 227 (7C 88)
Ferngrove BL9: Bury 8N 201
Ferngrove East BL9: Bury 9A 202
FERNHILL 9K 201
Fernhill Av. OL13: Bac 7J 163
Fernhill Caravan Pk. BL9: Bury 9K 201
Fernhill Cl. OL13: Bac 7J 163
Fernhill Cres. OL13: Bac 7J 163
Fernhill Dr. OL13: Bac 7H 163
Fernhill Gro. OL13: Bac 6J 163
Fern Hill La. OL12: Roch 2L 203
Fernhill Pk. OL13: Bac 7J 163
Fernhills BL7: Eger 3E 198
Fernhill St. BL9: Bury 9L 201
Fernhill Way OL13: Bac 7J 163
Fernhurst Av. FY4: Blackp 9D 88
Fernhurst Barn BB2: Blackb 8L 139
Fernhurst Ga. L39: Aug 1G 217
Fernhurst Rd. L32: Kirk 9H 223
Fernhurst St. BB2: Blackb 8L 139
Fern Isle Cl. OL12: Whitw 8M 183
Fern Lea LA5: Bolt S 5L 15
(off St Michael's La.)
Fernlea Av. BB5: Osw 5M 141
BB18: Barnw 2M 77
Fernlea Cl. BB2: Blackb 8J 139
OL12: Roch 3M 203
Fernlea Dr. BB5: Clay M 5L 121
Fern Lea St. BB4: W'foot 7B 162
Fernleigh PR26: Leyl 7C 152
Fernleigh Cl. FY2: Blackp 7D 62
PR3: Gars 4N 59
Fernley Rd. PR8: S'port 9G 167
Fern Mdw. PR6: Clay W 4E 154
Fern Rd. BB11: Burnl 5C 124
Ferns, The OL13: Bac 7L 163
PR2: Ash R 7F 114
PR4: K'ham 5L 111
PR5: Lost H 5L 135
Fernside Gro. WN3: Wins 9N 221
Fernside Way OL12: Roch 3L 203
Fern St. BB4: W'foot 6D 162
BB8: Colne 5C 86
BL0: Ramsb 7J 181
(not continuous)
BL9: Bury 9L 201
OL11: Roch 7A 204
OL12: Ward 8F 184
OL13: Bac 4K 163
Fern Ter. BB4: Hasl 4F 160
Fern Valley Chase OL14: Tod 1J 165
Fernview Dr. BL0: Ramsb 4F 200
Fernville Ter. OL13: Bac 7H 163
Fernwood Av. FY5: T Clev 3H 63
Fernwood Cl. FY8: L Ann 4L 129
Fernyhalgh Ct. PR2: Fulw 3N 115
Fernyhalgh Gdns. PR2: Fulw 3N 115
Fernyhalgh Gro. PR2: Fulw 3N 115
Fernyhalgh La. PR2: Fulw 9M 95
(not continuous)
Fernyhalgh Pl. PR2: Fulw 3N 115
Ferny Knoll Rd. WA11: Rain 8J 219
Ferrand Lodge OL15: Littleb 7M 185
Ferrand Rd. OL15: Littleb 8L 185
Ferrier Bank PR4: Wart 3J 131
Ferrier Cl. BB1: Blackb 3C 140
Ferrier Ct. BB1: Blackb 3C 140
Ferrier Gro. PR6: Chor 6H 175
Ferry Rd. PR2: Ash R 9C 114
Ferryside La. PR9: S'port 1B 168
Festival Rd. WA11: Rain 5L 225
Fewston Cl. BL1: Bolt 8E 198
Ffrances Pas. LA1: Lanc 7D 228
FIDDLER'S FERRY 9B 148
Fiddlers Fold Ct. PR4: Lea T 5N 113
Fiddler's La. PR3: Chip 5D 70
Fiddlers La. PR6: Clay W 5D 154
Fidler La. PR26: Far M 2J 153
Field Cl. L40: Burs 1D 210
Fieldcroft OL11: Roch 6M 203
Fieldens Farm La. BB2: Mellor B 6C 118
Fielden Sq. OL14: Tod 3L 165
Fielden St. BB11: Burnl 4A 124
OL15: Littleb 3H 205
(Lit. Clegg Rd.)
OL15: Littleb 5N 185
(off Todmorden Rd.)
PR6: Chor 6G 174
PR25: Leyl 6G 152
Fielden Ter. OL14: Tod 1L 165
Fieldfare Cl. FY5: T Clev 7G 54
PR1: Penw 5H 135
Fieldfare Ct. PR7: Chor 9B 174
Fieldfare Way OL13: Bac 6L 163
Fieldhead Av. OL11: Roch 6L 203

Fieldhouse Av.—Fountain Sq.

Fieldhouse Av. FY5: T Clev . . . 1K 63
Fieldhouse Ind. Est. OL12: Roch . . . 3C 204
Field Ho. La. PR3: Pill . . . 8K 43
Fieldhouse Rd. OL12: Roch . . . 3C 204
Fielding Cres. BB2: Blackb . . . 7H 139
Fielding La. BB5: Osw . . . 5L 141
BB6: Gt H . . . 4H 121
Fielding Pl. PR6: Adl . . . 5K 195
Fielding Rd. FY1: Blackp . . . 2D 88
Fieldings, The L31: Lyd . . . 7A 216
PR2: Fulw . . . 6G 114
Fieldings Bldgs. *BB4: Rawt* . . . *5K 161*
(off Haslingden Rd.)
Fieldings Cl. WN5: Wigan . . . 6N 221
Fielding St. BB1: Rish . . . 8J 121
Fieldlands PR8: S'port . . . 3N 187
Field Maple Dr. PR2: Ribb . . . 6B 116
Field Rd. LA3: Heys . . . 1J 27
OL16: Roch . . . 6G 205
Field Rose Ct. PR6: Adl . . . 5H 195
Fields, The BB7: Sabd . . . 3E 102
PR7: E'ton . . . 7E 172
Fields End BB6: Langh . . . 1C 120
Fieldsend LA3: Heys . . . 9M 21
Fieldside Av. PR7: Eux . . . 5M 173
Fieldside Cl. PR5: Lost H . . . 5M 135
Fields Rd. BB4: Hasl . . . 6G 161
Field St. BB2: Blackb . . . 6J 139
BB12: Padi . . . 2H 123
FY1: Blackp . . . 7K 227 (8C 88)
OL11: Roch . . . 9D 204
WN8: Skelm . . . 1H 219
Field Top OL13: Weir . . . 9L 145
Fieldview WN8: Uph . . . 4D 220
Field Wlk. L39: Orms . . . 7N 209
Field Way FY8: L Ann . . . 7E 108
Fieldway L31: Magh . . . 3D 222
OL16: Roch . . . 9E 204
Fife Cl. PR6: Chor . . . 8G 174
Fife St. BB5: Acc . . . 3N 141
BB9: Barrf . . . 1G 104
Fifth Av. BB10: Burnl . . . 8F 104
BL9: Bury . . . 9B 202
FY4: Blackp . . . 2C 108
Fifth St. BL1: Bolt . . . 9N 197
Filbert Cl. L33: Kirk . . . 4L 223
Filberts, The PR2: Fulw . . . 6F 114
Filberts Cl. PR2: Fulw . . . 6F 114
File St. PR7: Chor . . . 7E 174
Filey Pl. FY1: Blackp . . . 4B 88
PR2: Ingol . . . 5D 114
Filey Rd. FY8: L Ann . . . 8G 108
Filey St. OL16: Roch . . . 2F 204
Filton Gro. LA3: Morec . . . 5E 22
Finance St. OL15: Littleb . . . 9H 185
Finch Av. WA11: Rain . . . 5L 225
Finch Cl. BB1: Blackb . . . 2D 226 (2N 139)
Finches, The FY6: Poul F . . . 9H 63
Finch La. PR4: Cott . . . 5B 114
WN6: App B . . . 3E 212
Finchley Rd. FY1: Blackp . . . 2B 88
Finch Mill Av. WN6: App B . . . 5G 213
Finch's Cotts. *PR1: Penw* . . . *4H 135*
(off Prospect Pl.)
Finch St. BB3: Darw . . . 5N 157
Findon WN8: Skelm . . . 2M 219
Findon Rd. L32: Kirk . . . 9L 223
Fine Jane's Way PR9: S'port . . . 6A 168
Finestra Gallery . . . *6F 8*
(off Main St.)
Finney La. PR26: Cros . . . 6H 171
Finney Pk. Dr. PR2: Lea . . . 9A 114
Finnington La. BB2: Fenis . . . 1B 156
Finsbury Av. FY1: Blackp . . . 8M 227 (8D 88)
FY8: L Ann . . . 4H 129
Finsbury Pl. BB2: Blackb . . . 9L 139
Finsbury St. OL11: Roch . . . 8A 204
Finsley Ga. BB11: Burnl . . . 3C 228 (4D 124)
Finsley St. BB10: Brierc . . . 7J 105
Finsley Vw. BB10: Brierc . . . 7K 105
Firbank PR5: Bam B . . . 7N 135
PR7: Eux . . . 4M 173
Firbank Av. PR4: Tarl . . . 8E 150
Firbank Rd. LA1: Lanc . . . 7L 23
Firbarn Cl. OL16: Roch . . . 6G 205
Firbeck WN8: Skelm . . . 2M 219
Fir Cl. FY7: Flee . . . 2C 54
Fir Cotes L31: Magh . . . 1D 222
Fir Ct. BB5: Hunc . . . 9D 122
Fircroft WN6: Stand . . . 2K 213
Fire Station Yd. OL11: Roch . . . 7C 204
Firfield Cl. PR4: K'ham . . . 4K 111
FIRGROVE . . . 6G 205
Fir Gro. FY1: Blackp . . . 8N 227 (8E 88)
PR4: Wart . . . 2J 131
Firgrove Av. OL16: Roch . . . 5G 204
Firgrove Bus. Pk. OL16: Roch . . . 4G 205
Firgrove Gdns. OL16: Roch . . . 5G 204
Fir Gro. Rd. BB11: Burnl . . . 5F 124
Fir Mt. OL13: Bac . . . 6L 163
Firshill Cl. FY5: T Clev . . . 3H 63
Firs La. L39: Aug, Hals . . . 9D 208
First Av. BB5: Chur . . . 8N 121
BL8: Tott . . . 7E 200
FY4: Blackp . . . 2C 108
FY6: Poul F . . . 8L 63
FY6: Stal . . . 3B 56
PR2: Ash R . . . 7D 114
PR4: Clif . . . 8G 113
PR4: W Grn . . . 5G 110
Firstone Gro. L32: Kirk . . . 9K 223
Fir St. BB4: Hasl . . . 5H 161
BB9: Nelson . . . 2K 105
BB10: Burnl . . . 4F 124
BL0: Ramsb . . . 7J 181
OL14: Wals . . . 7K 165
PR8: S'port . . . 8L 167
First St. BL1: Bolt . . . 9N 197
First Ter. LA3: S'land . . . 6D 26
Firswood Cl. FY8: L Ann . . . 4L 129
Firswood Rd. WN8: Skelm . . . 2F 218
Fir Tree Av. PR2: Fulw . . . 5E 114
Fir Tree Cl. LA5: Bolt S . . . 7K 15
PR4: Much H . . . 4J 151
WN8: Skelm . . . 4A 220
Firtree Cl. PR7: Chor . . . 2E 194
Fir Tree La. L39: Aug, Hals . . . 8E 208
Fir Tree Pl. FY5: T Clev . . . 3F 62
Fir Trees Av. PR2: Ribb . . . 5B 116
PR5: Lost H . . . 7K 135
Fir Trees Cl. BB9: Nelson . . . 2L 105
Fir Trees Cres. PR5: Lost H . . . 8K 135
Firtrees Dr. BB2: Blackb . . . 8G 138
Fir Trees Gro. BB12: High . . . 5K 103
Fir Trees La. BB12: High . . . 5K 103
Fir Trees Pl. PR2: Ribb . . . 5B 116
Fir Trees Rd. PR5: Lost H . . . 7K 135
Firwood WN8: Skelm . . . 9A 212
Fir Wood Cl. OL14: Wals . . . 6K 165
Firwood Cl. PR3: Longr . . . 2J 97
Firwood La. PR5: Sam . . . 3J 137
Fisher Dr. PR9: S'port . . . 7M 167
WN5: Orr . . . 5H 221
Fisherfield OL12: Roch . . . 4K 203
Fishergate PR1: Prest . . . 7H 229 (1H 135)
Fishergate Cen. PR1: Prest . . . 7J 229 (1J 135)
Fishergate Ct. PR1: Prest . . . 7H 229 (1H 135)
Fishergate Hill PR1: Prest . . . 7G 229 (2G 135)
Fishergate Wlk. PR1: Prest . . . 6K 229 (1J 135)
Fishermans Wlk. FY7: Flee . . . 9G 41
Fisherman's Walk Stop (Tram) . . . 9G 41
Fishermans Way FY7: Flee . . . 4C 54
Fishermans Wharf *FY7: Flee* . . . *9G 40*
(off Warrenhurst Rd.)
Fisher's La. FY4: Blackp . . . 4F 108
FISHER'S ROW . . . 8K 43
Fisher's Slack La. FY6: Sing . . . 9G 64
Fisher St. FY1: Blackp . . . 4C 88
Fish Ho. La. PR3: Chip . . . 5E 70
Fish La. L40: Burs, Holmesw . . . 1N 189
Fishmoor Dr. BB2: Blackb . . . 8N 139
Fish Rake La. BB4: Rawt . . . 1J 181
Fish St. PR1: Prest . . . 3K 229 (8J 115)
FISHWICK . . . 9N 115
Fishwick Bottoms PR2: Prest . . . 2M 135
Fishwick Hall Golf Course . . . 9B 116
Fishwick La. PR6: H Wheel . . . 6K 155
Fishwick Pde. PR1: Prest . . . 9M 115
Fishwick Rd. PR1: Prest . . . 9M 115
Fishwick St. OL16: Roch . . . 7D 204
Fishwick Vw. PR1: Prest . . . 9M 115
Fitchfield PR1: Penw . . . 6J 135
Fitness First
Liverpool . . . 9A 222
Preston . . . 7L 115
Rochdale . . . 9B 204
Fitton St. OL16: Roch . . . 5D 204
Fitzgerald Dr. BB3: Darw . . . 5B 158
Fitzgerald St. PR1: Prest . . . 8M 115
Fitzhugh St. BL1: Bolt . . . 8G 198
Fitzroy Rd. FY2: Blackp . . . 8D 62
Fitzroy St. PR1: Prest . . . 1G 135
Five Acres PR26: Far M . . . 3H 153
Five Ashes La. LA2: Lanc . . . 8K 29
Five La. Ends LA2: Bay H . . . 6A 38
Flag La. PR1: Penw . . . 7J 135
PR6: H Charn . . . 9H 175
PR7: Eux . . . 2G 172
PR26: Breth . . . 1L 171
PR26: Leyl . . . 2G 172
Flag St. FY7: Flee . . . 9H 41
OL13: Bac . . . 7J 163
Flakefleet Av. FY7: Flee . . . 3E 54
Flamingo Way FY6: Pree . . . 8N 41
Flamstead WN8: Skelm . . . 2N 219
Flannel St. OL12: Roch . . . 5D 204
Flare Rd. LA3: Heys . . . 1J 27
FLASBY . . . 1N 53
Flash Ga. BB1: Ramsg . . . 6L 119
Flash La. L40: Ruff . . . 1G 190
Flatfield Way L31: Magh . . . 1D 222
Flat La. LA5: Yea C . . . 8B 6
Flatman's La. L39: D'holl . . . 2L 215
FLATS, THE . . . 3M 135
Flats, The PR7: Chor . . . 8D 174
Flats Retail Pk., The
PR5: Walt D . . . 3M 135
Flax Cl. BB4: Hasl . . . 7F 160
Flaxfield Rd. L37: Form . . . 9A 206
Flaxfields L40: Lath . . . 1D 210
Flaxfield Way PR4: K'ham . . . 4M 111
Flax La. L40: Lath . . . 1D 210
FLAX MOSS . . . 7F 160
Flaxmoss Cl. BB4: Hasl . . . 7F 160
Flax St. BL0: Ramsb . . . 1F 200
Flaxton WN8: Skelm . . . 2N 219
Fleece St. OL16: Roch . . . 6C 204
Fleet Grn. LA1: Lanc . . . 5J 23
Fleet La. LA2: Gress . . . 6B 18
Fleet's La. LA6: H Cas . . . 6G 8
Fleet Sq. LA1: Lanc . . . 6C 228
Fleet St. BB9: Nelson . . . 1J 105
BL6: Hor . . . 9E 196
FY1: Blackp . . . 3K 227 (6C 88)
FY8: L Ann . . . 1D 128
PR1: Prest . . . 6J 229 (1J 135)
PR3: Longr . . . 3J 97
PR7: Chor . . . 7E 174
WN5: Wigan . . . 5L 221
Fleet St. La. PR3: Ribc . . . 4A 98
Fleet Wlk.
BB11: Burnl . . . 2D 228 (3E 124)
FLEETWOOD . . . 9G 41
Fleetwood Cl. BB2: Blackb . . . 7N 139
PR9: S'port . . . 3M 167
Fleetwood Ct. *PR9: S'port* . . . *5K 167*
(off Park Rd.)
Fleetwood Cres. PR9: Banks . . . 9F 148
Fleetwood Docks FY7: Flee . . . 2G 55
Fleetwood Dr. PR9: Banks . . . 9F 148
Fleetwood Gdns. L33: Kirk . . . 5L 223
(not continuous)
Fleetwood Golf Course . . . 1D 54
Fleetwood Leisure Cen. . . . 8G 41
Fleetwood Marsh Nature Pk. . . . 3H 55
Fleetwood Mus. . . . 8J 41
Fleetwood Old Rd. PR4: Greenh . . . 7K 91
Fleetwood Rd. BB10: Burnl . . . 8G 104
BB12: Padi . . . 1J 123
FY5: T Clev . . . 1C 62
(not continuous)
FY6: Carl . . . 5H 63
Fleetwood Rd. FY6: Sing . . . 7F 64
FY7: Flee . . . 2E 54
PR4: Esp, Greenh, Wesh . . . 7F 64
PR9: S'port . . . 5J 167
(not continuous)
Fleetwood Rd. Nth. FY5: T Clev . . . 7G 55
FY7: Flee . . . 5F 54
Fleetwood Rd. Sth. FY5: T Clev . . . 2H 63
Fleetwood St. PR2: Ash R . . . 8G 114
PR25: Leyl . . . 5L 153
Fleetwood Town FC
Highbury Stadium . . . 1F 54
Fleming Cl. OL12: Roch . . . 9G 185
Fleming Sq. BB2: Blackb . . . 5C 226 (4M 139)
PR3: Longr . . . 3K 97
Flensburg Way PR26: Far M, Leyl . . . 4G 152
Fletcher Av. PR4: Tarl . . . 9E 150
FLETCHER BANK . . . 8H 181
Fletcher Rd. BB1: Rish . . . 9G 121
PR1: Prest . . . 4N 229 (9L 115)
Fletcher's Dr. L40: Burs . . . 9C 190
Fletchers Pas. OL15: Littleb . . . 8K 185
Fletcher's Rd. OL15: Littleb . . . 2H 205
Fletchers Sq. *OL15: Littleb* . . . *8L 185*
(off Sutcliffe St.)
Fletcher St. BB2: Blackb . . . 8A 226 (5L 139)
BB9: Nelson . . . 3K 105
OL11: Roch . . . 8D 204
OL15: Littleb . . . 8K 185
Fletton Cl. OL12: Roch . . . 3B 204
Fletton M. OL12: Roch . . . 3B 204
Flett St. PR2: Ash R . . . 8F 114
Flimby WN8: Skelm . . . 1A 220
Flimby Cl. BB2: Blackb . . . 8N 139
Flintoff Way PR1: Prest . . . 6L 115
Flinton Brow LA2: Abb . . . 2A 48
Flints Caravan Pk. FY5: T Clev . . . 9L 55
Flip Rd. BB4: Hasl . . . 4F 160
Floats Mill BB8: Traw . . . 1G 106
Flockton Av. WN6: Stand . . . 1N 213
Flockton Ct. *BL6: Hor* . . . *9C 196*
(off High St.)
Flood Dyke *BB5: Hunc* . . . *7E 122*
(off Lwr. Gate Rd.)
Flordon WN8: Skelm . . . 1A 220
Florence Av. BB11: Burnl . . . 4A 124
BL1: Bolt . . . 9F 198
PR4: Wart . . . 3J 131
Florence Pl. BB1: Blackb . . . 2A 140
Florence St. BB1: Blackb . . . 2A 140
BB5: Chur . . . 2L 141
BB11: Burnl . . . 4A 124
FY4: Blackp . . . 3G 109
OL16: Roch . . . 7E 204
Flowerfield PR4: Cott . . . 3B 114
Flower Flds. PR3: Catt . . . 1A 68
Flower Hill La. OL12: Ward . . . 8D 184
Flower Scar Rd. OL14: Tod . . . 1A 164
Flowers Cl. BB2: Blackb . . . 9L 139
Floyd Rd. PR2: Ribb . . . 6A 116
Floyer St. PR1: Prest . . . 6N 229 (1L 135)
Fluke Hall La. PR3: Pill . . . 4E 42
Flush Brow LA6: Cast . . . 4G 9
Fold, The BB4: Rawt . . . 4M 161
BB9: Barrf . . . 6J 85
BD20: Loth . . . 4N 79
Fold Gdns. OL12: Roch . . . 2M 203
FOLD HEAD . . . 6M 183
Fold House Holiday Home Pk. & Lodge Pk.
PR3: Pill . . . 9J 43
Fold M. BL9: Bury . . . 7L 201
Foldside PR4: Frec . . . 1A 132
Folds St. BB12: Burnl . . . 1D 124
Fold Vw. BL7: Eger . . . 4E 198
Folkestone Cl. FY5: T Clev . . . 8F 54
PR4: Wart . . . 1K 131
Folkestone Rd. FY8: L Ann . . . 9F 108
PR8: S'port . . . 2L 187
Folly Bank BB4: Craws . . . 8M 143
Folly Cotts. BB18: Barnw . . . 3L 77
Folly La. BB18: Barnw . . . 6K 77
LA2: Slyne . . . 4H 23
Folly Ter. BB4: Craws . . . 8M 143
Folly Wlk. OL12: Roch . . . 4C 204
Folly Wood Dr. PR7: Chor . . . 8C 174
Fooden La. BB7: Bolt B . . . 8L 51
Footeran La. LA5: Yea C, Yea R . . . 8B 6
Foot Mill Cres. OL12: Roch . . . 3A 204
Foot O' Th' Rake *BL0: Ramsb* . . . *8G 180*
(off Milton St.)
Foot Wood Cres. OL12: Roch . . . 3A 204
Forbes Ct. BB11: Burnl . . . 6M 123
Ford Av. L33: Kirk . . . 4K 223
Ford Gdns. OL11: Roch . . . 7M 203
FORD GREEN . . . 2K 59
Fordham Ct. PR8: S'port . . . 2L 187
Ford La. LA5: Silv . . . 6J 5
PR3: Goos . . . 1B 96
Fordoe La. OL12: Roch . . . 1G 202
Fordside Av. BB5: Clay M . . . 5L 121
Fordstone Av. FY6: Pree . . . 9N 41
Ford St. BB9: Barrf . . . 7J 85
BB10: Burnl . . . 9F 104
LA1: Lanc . . . 7H 23
Fordway Av. FY3: Blackp . . . 4E 88
Foregate PR2: Fulw . . . 5H 115
Foreside BB9: Barrf . . . 6J 85
Forest Av. BB12: Fence . . . 2C 104
Forest Bank BB4: Craws . . . 9M 143
BB8: Traw . . . 9F 86
Forest Bank Ct. BB4: Craws . . . 9M 143
Forest Bank Rd. BB4: Craws . . . 9M 143
FOREST BECKS . . . 6K 51
Forest Becks Brow BB7: Bolt B . . . 6K 51
Forest Brook Ho. PR2: Fulw . . . 6J 115
Forest Cl. PR5: Lost H . . . 5M 135
Forest Dr. FY8: L Ann . . . 4L 129
WN6: Stand . . . 2K 213
WN8: Skelm . . . 9N 211
Forester Dr. BB12: Fence . . . 2B 104
Forester's Bldgs. BB18: Barnw . . . 2M 77
Foresters Hall PR1: Prest . . . 5J 229
Forest Fold WN6: Shev . . . 6H 213
Forest Ga. FY3: Blackp . . . 2N 227 (5D 88)
PR4: Wesh . . . 2K 111
Forestgate LA3: Morec . . . 6E 22
Forest Grn. PR2: Fulw . . . 2L 115
Forest Gro. PR3: Bart . . . 2E 94
FOREST HOLME . . . 8E 144
Forest Holme Cl. BB4: Water . . . 9E 144
Forest La. BB9: Barrf . . . 9F 84
Forest of Bowland . . . 4J 49
FOREST OF MEWITH . . . 8M 19
Forest of Pendle, The . . . 7E 84
Forest of Rossendale . . . 1C 162
Forest of Trawden, The . . . 2K 107
Forest Pk. LA1: Lanc . . . 9G 23
Fore St. BB3: Lwr D . . . 9N 139
Forest Rd. PR8: S'port . . . 8K 167
Forestry Houses BB7: Dun B . . . 7K 49
Forest St. BB4: Water . . . 9E 144
BB9: Nelson . . . 1H 105
(not continuous)
BB11: Burnl . . . 1E 228 (3E 124)
OL13: Bac . . . 5K 163
Forest Vw. *BB9: Barrf* . . . *8H 85*
(off Gisburn Rd.)
BB9: Brierf . . . 5E 104
OL12: Roch . . . 3A 204
Forest Way BL7: Brom C . . . 7J 199
PR2: Fulw . . . 4J 115
Forestway PR25: Leyl . . . 7J 153
Forfar Gro. BB11: Burnl . . . 6B 124
Forfar St. BB11: Burnl . . . 6B 124
BL1: Bolt . . . 8E 198
Forge Cl. L40: W'head . . . 8C 210
Forge La. LA2: Halt . . . 2C 24
PR3: Barn . . . 4B 60
Forge Row L31: Magh . . . 8B 216
Forge St. OL13: Bac . . . 5K 163
PR25: Leyl . . . 6K 153
Forgewood Cl. LA2: Halt . . . 2D 24
Forgewood Dr. LA2: Halt . . . 2C 24
FORMBY . . . 1A 214
Formby Av. FY7: Flee . . . 5D 54
Formby Bus. Pk. L37: Form . . . 9C 206
Formby By-Pass L37: Ains, Form . . . 6B 206
L38: Ince B . . . 3B 214
Formby Cl. BB2: Blackb . . . 8N 139
Formby Cres. PR4: Longt . . . 8K 133
Formby Flds. L37: Form . . . 1A 214
Formby Gdns. L37: Form . . . 8A 206
Formby Hall Golf Course . . . 4C 206
Formby La. L37: Form . . . 1A 214
L39: Aug . . . 1C 216
Formby Pl. PR2: Ash R . . . 7B 114
Formby Rd. FY8: L Ann . . . 8F 108
Forrest Ct. FY3: Blackp . . . 2E 88
Forrester Cl. PR25: Leyl . . . 6H 153
Forrestside BB2: Blackb . . . 9L 139
Forrest St. BB1: Blackb . . . 3G 226 (3A 140)
Forshaw Av. FY3: Blackp . . . 2F 88
FY8: L Ann . . . 9D 108
Forshaw Cl. FY7: Flee . . . 2E 54
Forshaw Rd. PR1: Penw . . . 6G 134
FORSTERS GREEN . . . 9A 212
Forsters Grn. Rd. WN8: Skelm . . . 9A 212
Forsythia Dr. PR6: Clay W . . . 3D 154
Forsyth St. OL12: Roch . . . 3J 203
Fort Av. PR3: Ribc . . . 7E 98
FORTON . . . 2M 45
Forton Rd. PR2: Ash R . . . 9B 114
Forts Bldgs. BB18: Kelb . . . 6D 78
Fort St. BB1: Blackb . . . 3G 226 (3A 140)
BB5: Acc . . . 2A 142
BB5: Clay M . . . 6M 121
BB7: Clith . . . 4K 81
BB12: Read . . . 8C 102
Fort St. Ind. Est. BB1: Blackb . . . 2G 226 (2A 140)
Forty Acre La. PR3: Longr . . . 1L 97
Forum Ct. PR8: S'port . . . 7G 167
Forward Ind. Est. *PR25: Leyl* . . . *5H 153*
(off Talbot Rd.)
Foscote Rd. L33: Kirk . . . 6M 223
Foss Ct. LA3: Morec . . . 5E 22
Fossdale Moss PR26: Leyl . . . 6F 152
Fosse Bank Ct. BB2: Blackb . . . 8A 140
Fosse Cl. BB2: Blackb . . . 8A 140
Fossgill Av. BL2: Bolt . . . 8J 199
Foster Ct. BL9: Bury . . . 9B 202
PR6: Chor . . . *5G 174*
(off Foster St.)
Foster Cft. PR1: Penw . . . 2F 134
Fosterfield Pl. PR6: Chor . . . 5G 174
Foster Rd. BB18: Barnw . . . 1L 77
Fosters Cl. PR9: S'port . . . 6A 168
Fosters Island WN8: Skelm . . . 9N 211
Foster St. BB5: Acc . . . 1B 142
PR6: Chor . . . 5G 174
Fothergill St. BB8: Colne . . . 6N 85
Foul Clough Rd. OL14: Wals . . . 7G 164
Fouldrey Av. FY6: Poul F . . . 7G 63
Foulds Cl. BB8: Colne . . . 8N 85
Foulds Rd. BB8: Traw . . . 8E 86
Foulds Ter. BB8: Traw . . . 9F 86
Foul La. PR8: S'port . . . 1N 187
(not continuous)
PR9: S'port . . . 9N 167
FOULRIDGE . . . 2A 86
Foundary St. PR7: Chor . . . 6E 174
Foundry Ct. PR1: Prest . . . 3G 229
Foundry Gdns. LA5: Carn . . . 7A 12
Foundry La. LA2: Halt, Slyne . . . 1N 23
(not continuous)
WN3: Wigan . . . 7N 221
Foundry St. BB2: Blackb . . . 6A 226 (4K 139)
BB3: Darw . . . 6A 158
BB4: Hasl . . . 5G 161
BB4: Rawt . . . 6L 161
BB11: Burnl . . . 1C 228 (3D 124)
OL13: Bac . . . 5K 163
OL14: Tod . . . 3K 165
Foundry Va. BB4: W'foot . . . 7D 162
Fountain Cl. BB12: Padi . . . 1J 123
Fountain Pl. BB5: Acc . . . 3A 142
Fountain Retail Pk. BB5: Acc . . . 2N 141
Fountains, The BB9: Barrf . . . 8H 85
L39: Orms . . . 6K 209
Fountains Av. BB1: Blackb . . . 9B 120
BB12: S'stone . . . 9C 102
Fountains Cl. PR7: Chor . . . 9F 174
Fountain Sq. BB9: Barrf . . . 7H 85

G

Garstang Rd. PR3: Pill 9K 43
PR3: St M 4G 66
PR9: S'port 2M 167
Garstang Rd. E. FY6: Poul F 8K 63
Garstang Rd. Nth. PR4: Wesh 2L 111
Garstang Rd. Sth. PR4: Wesh 3L 111
Garstang Rd. W. FY3: Blackp 1G 89
FY6: Poul F 1G 89
Garstang St. BB3: Darw 5A 158
Garstang Swimming Pool 4N 59
Garstangs Yd. BD24: Gig 2N 35
(off Church St.)
Garstang Ter. BB3: Tock 7J 157
Garstone Cft. PR2: Fulw 3G 114
Garston St. BL9: Bury 9M 201
Garswood Av. WA11: Rain 3L 225
Garswood Cl. BB12: Burnl 8D 104
L31: Magh 8D 216
Garswood Dr. BL8: Bury 7G 201
Garth, The BB11: Burnl 5D 124
Garth Edge OL12: Whitw 1B 184
Garton Av. FY4: Blackp 3C 108
Gas Fld. Rd. LA3: Midd 5K 27
Gas Ho. La. LA2: H Ben 6L 19
(off Main St.)
Gaskell Cl. LA5: Silv 8G 4
OL15: Littleb 8K 185
Gaskell Ct. BB6: Gt H 5K 121
Gaskell Cres. FY5: T Clev 1G 63
Gaskell Rd. PR1: Penw 3H 135
Gaskell St. PR6: Chor 6G 174
Gas St. BB4: Hasl 6E 160
BB11: Burnl 2C 228 (3D 124)
OL11: Roch 6B 204
OL13: Bac 5K 163
PR3: Longr 2J 97
PR7: Adl 7J 195
Gas Ter. PR25: Leyl 5K 153
Gatefield Ct. BB11: Burnl 5E 124
(off Hollingreave Rd.)
Gate Flats LA6: K Lon 6F 8
(off Lunefield Dr.)
Gate Fold BL2: Bolt 8K 199
Gategill Gro. WN5: Bill 8G 220
Gateheads Brow LA6: Cast 5G 9
Gate Ho. PR1: Prest 7G 229
Gatehouse OL15: Littleb 8N 185
Gatehouse, The BB2: Blackb 5C 226
Gateland BB18: Salt 4A 78
Gatelands Caravan Pk. LA6: Tewit 2F 12
Gatesgarth Av. PR2: Fulw 2J 115
Gateside Ct. FY3: Blackp 2G 88
(off Furness Av.)
Gateside Dr. FY3: Blackp 2F 88
Gates La. L29: T'ton 9J 215
Gate St. BB1: Blackb 3A 140
OL11: Roch 8C 204
Gateway Cl. FY5: T Clev 4K 63
GATHURST 9K 213
Gathurst Golf Course 7J 213
Gathurst Hall WN6: Shev 9J 213
Gathurst La. WN6: Shev 9K 213
Gathurst Rd. PR2: Ash R 7F 114
WN5: Orr 4H 221
WN6: Shev 4H 221
Gathurst Station (Rail) 9K 213
Gatley Dr. L31: Magh 3D 222
Gaulkthorn BB5: Osw 7M 141
Gaulter's La. FY6: Pree 9B 42
GAUXHOLME 4K 165
Gauxholme Fold OL14: Tod 4J 165
Gauxholme Ind. Est. OL14: Tod 4J 165
Gaw Hill La. L39: Aug 9F 208
Gaw Hill Vw. L39: Aug 9G 209
Gawthorpe BB2: Blackb 2K 139
Gawthorpe Edge BB12: Burnl 2L 123
Gawthorpe Hall 9L 103
Gawthorpe Rd. BB12: Burnl 2B 124
Gawthorpe St. BB12: Padi 9H 103
Gawthorpe Vw. BB12: High 5L 103
Gaydon Way FY5: T Clev 4E 62
Gaylands La. BB18: Earl 2F 78
Gayle Way BB5: Acc 4M 141
(off Lynton Rd.)
Gaythorne Av. PR1: Prest 8B 116
Gayton Cl. WN3: Wins 8N 221
Geddes St. BB2: Blackb 6G 139
Gees Ct. LA1: Lanc 6D 228
Geldard Cotts. BD23: Wig 10M 35
Gelder Clough Pk. OL11: Roch 8G 203
Gelder Wood Country Pk. OL11: Roch 7G 202
Geldof Dr. FY1: Blackp 2C 88
Gemini Bus. Pk. PR9: S'port 9M 167
Gendre Rd. BL7: Eger 5E 198
General St. FY1: Blackp 4B 88
General Wood OL14: Wals 6K 165
Geneva Rd. PR2: Fulw 5M 115
Geneva Ter. OL11: Roch 5N 203
Genoa St. BB11: Burnl 5A 124
Geoffrey Lodge PR2: Ribb 5B 116
(off Fir Trees Pl.)
Geoffrey St. BL0: Ramsb 1F 200
BL9: Bury 9M 201
PR1: Prest 8M 115
PR6: Chor 5F 174
George Av. BB6: Gt H 5H 121
FY4: Blackp 9F 88
George Dr. PR8: Ains 8E 186
George Fox Av. LA1: Bail 8M 29
George Ho. FY1: Blackp 4C 88
(off George St.)
George La. BB12: Read 8B 102
George Rd. BL0: Ramsb 9G 180
George's La. BL6: Hor 6E 196
PR9: Banks 7E 148
George's Rd. PR1: Prest 6K 229 (1J 135)
George's Row BB4: W'foot 7D 162
George St. BB1: Rish 8H 121
BB2: Blackb 6D 226 (4M 139)
BB3: Darw 5A 158
BB4: Hasl 3G 160
BB5: Acc 4M 141
BB5: Clay M 6M 121
BB5: Osw 3L 141
BB6: Gt H 4J 121
BB7: Clith 5K 81
George St. BB7: Whall 5J 101
BB9: Nelson 1H 105
BB11: Burnl 3B 228 (4D 124)
BB18: Barnw 10G 52
BB18: Earl 2E 78
BL6: Hor 9D 196
(not continuous)
FY1: Blackp 1K 227 (4C 88)
(not continuous)
FY8: L Ann 5A 130
LA1: Lanc 8D 228 (9K 23)
LA4: Morec 3C 22
OL12: Whitw 7N 183
OL13: Bac 5L 163
(Thorn St.)
OL13: Bac 7G 163
(Turner St.)
OL14: Tod 2L 165
(off Union St. Sth.)
OL15: Littleb 8L 185
OL16: Roch 5D 204
(Ball St.)
OL16: Roch 2G 204
(Greenfield La.)
OL16: Roch 6H 205
(Rochdale Rd.)
PR1: Prest 1L 135
PR3: Longr 2J 97
PR7: Chor 7E 174
PR25: Leyl 5L 153
George St. West BB2: Blackb 5A 226 (4K 139)
George Ter. WN5: Orr 6G 220
George Williams Ho. FY7: Flee 2F 54
(off Broomfield Rd.)
Georgia Av. L33: Kirk 4J 223
Gerard Way L33: Kirk 8L 223
German La. PR7: Char R 6N 173
PR7: Copp 4A 194
German's La. L40: Burs 6E 190
Gerona Ct. FY5: T Clev 2J 63
Gerrard Pl. WN8: Skelm 3K 219
Gerrard's Fold PR6: Withn 5C 156
Gerrard's Ter. FY6: Carl 7J 63
Gerrard St. LA1: Lanc 9G 23
PR1: Prest 1G 135
Gertrude St. BB9: Nelson 9L 85
OL12: Whitw 9B 164
Ghants La. FY6: Ham 9D 56
GHYLL FIELDS 10G 53
Ghyll Golf Course 9H 53
Ghyll La. BB18: Barnw 10G 53
Ghyll Mdws. BB18: Barnw 10G 53
Giant Axe 6A 228 (8J 23)
Giants Hall Rd. WN6: Stand 9N 213
Gibfield Rd. BB8: Colne 8L 85
Gib Hey La. PR3: Chip 7D 70
Gib Hill La. BB4: Craws 6N 143
Gib Hill Rd. BB9: Nelson 1M 105
Gib La. BB2: Blackb 8H 139
PR5: Hogh 4L 137
Gibraltar Rd. PR4: Weet 4D 90
Gibraltar St. BB2: Blackb 2J 139
Gibson Cl. L33: Kirk 5J 223
Gibson St. BB9: Nelson 9K 85
OL14: Tod 2M 165
OL16: Roch 5F 204
Giddygate La. L31: Magh, Mell 2G 223
Gidlow Av. PR6: Adl 6J 195
Gifford Way BB3: Darw 5B 158
Giggles Fun Cen. 3H 219
GIGGLESWICK 3M 35
Giggleswick Station (Rail) 4M 35
Gilbert Pl. L40: Burs 9N 189
Gilbertson Rd. PR7: H Charn 3G 195
Gilbert St. BB4: Rawt 6B 162
BB10: Burnl 8J 105
BL0: Ramsb 5H 181
PR7: Chor 8E 174
Gildabrook Rd. FY4: Blackp 4D 108
Gilderdale Ct. FY8: L Ann 4B 130
Gildersleets BD24: Gig 4M 35
Gildow St. PR1: Prest 9H 115
Gilescroft Av. L33: Kirk 6M 223
Gilescroft Wlk. L33: Kirk 6M 223
Giles St. BB7: Clith 4L 81
BB9: Nelson 1J 105
Gilhouse Av. PR2: Lea 8N 113
Gill Av. WN6: Shev 6L 213
Gill Ct. FY4: Blackp 4B 108
Gillcroft PR7: E'ton 7E 172
Giller Cl. PR1: Penw 6H 135
Giller Dr. PR1: Penw 6H 135
Giller Fold PR1: Penw 6J 135
Gillett Farm Caravan Pk. FY4: Blackp 4L 109
Gillett St. PR1: Prest 8M 115
(not continuous)
Gillhead Brow LA2: H Ben 5L 19
Gillians La. BB18: Barnw 3L 77
Gillibrand Cl. PR1: Penw 7F 134
Gillibrand Ho. PR7: Chor 4E 174
(off Lancaster Ct.)
Gillibrands Rd. WN8: Skelm 3K 219
Gillibrand St. BB3: Darw 4N 157
PR5: Walt D 3N 135
PR7: Chor 7E 174
Gillibrand Walks PR7: Chor 8D 174
Gillies St. BB2: Blackb 8E 226 (5N 139)
BB5: Acc 2B 142
Gillison Cl. LA6: Mell 4D 18
Gillisons LA1: Lanc 8C 228
Gillison's La. LA1: Lanc 7C 228
Gill La. PR4: Longt, Wal B 2L 151
Gill Nook PR4: Wal B 2L 151
Gillow Av. LA1: Bail 8L 29
Gillow Ct. LA1: Lanc 2K 29
Gillow Pk. PR3: Lit E 5L 65
Gillow Rd. PR4: K'ham 4L 111
Gills Cft. BB7: Clith 5M 81
Gill St. BB8: Colne 8M 85
BB9: Nelson 1G 105
BB12: Burnl 1A 228 (3C 124)
Gillyflower Ct. PR26: Leyl 6F 152
Gilpin Av. L31: Magh 9D 216
Gilpin Cl. LA1: Lanc 6G 22
GILSBROOK 6C 196
Gilstead Av. LA3: Heys 8M 21
Gin Bow PR7: Chor 8F 174
Gincroft La. BL0: Eden 1K 181
Gingham Brow BL6: Hor 9E 196
Ginnel, The PR25: Leyl 7K 153
Gipsy La. OL11: Roch 9N 203
(not continuous)
Girvan Gro. BB11: Burnl 4B 124
GISBURN 9A 52
Gisburn Av. FY8: L Ann 2H 129
Gisburn Gro. BB10: Burnl 4H 125
FY3: Blackp 3E 88
Gisburn Old Rd. BB9: Blacko 5G 76
Gisburn Pl. BB2: Blackb 4K 139
Gisburn Rd. BB7: Bolt B 8K 51
BB9: Barrf 9H 85
BB9: Blacko 3G 85
BB18: Barnw 10F 52
BD23: Hell 1D 52
PR2: Ribb 5A 116
Gisburn St. BB18: Barnw 1M 77
Gladden Pl. WN8: Skelm 3J 219
Glade, The BB2: Blackb 1M 157
LA4: Morec 3E 22
WN6: Shev 6L 213
Glades, The FY8: L Ann 4B 130
Gladeswood Rd. L33: Know P 9N 223
Gladeway FY5: T Clev 4K 63
Gladstone Bldgs. BB4: Rawt 4M 161
(off Whittle St.)
Gladstone Cl. BB2: Blackb 7G 139
Gladstone Cres. OL13: Bac 5L 163
Gladstone Hgts. BB5: Acc 2A 142
(off Willow St.)
Gladstone Ho. BB2: Blackb 7G 139
OL12: Ward 8F 184
(off Old School Pl.)
Gladstone Rd. PR9: S'port 8M 167
Gladstone St. BB1: Blackb 2B 140
BB6: Gt H 4J 121
FY4: Blackp 9C 88
OL13: Bac 5L 163
OL14: Tod 7E 146
Gladstone Ter. BB2: Blackb 7G 139
BB8: Wine 7E 86
BB9: Barrf 8H 85
LA1: Lanc 7L 23
(off Bulk Rd.)
PR6: Withn 6D 156
Gladstone Way BB1: Blackb 9N 119
FY5: T Clev 2F 62
Glaisdale Dr. PR8: S'port 2M 187
Glamis Dr. PR7: Chor 6D 174
PR9: S'port 3A 168
Glamis Rd. PR25: Leyl 7M 153
Glamorgan Gro. BB12: Burnl 2M 123
GLASSON 1C 36
Glasson Cl. BB2: Blackb 7N 139
Glasson Sailing Club 1C 36
Glastonbury OL12: Roch 5B 204
(off Redcross St.)
Glastonbury Av. FY1: Blackp 8E 88
Glasven Rd. L33: Kirk 7L 223
Gleaves Av. BL2: Bolt 9N 199
Glebe, The PR25: Leyl 7G 152
PR26: Leyl 7E 152
Glebe Cl. BB5: Acc 3A 142
L31: Magh 1A 222
LA6: Burt K 5H 7
PR2: Fulw 5J 115
Glebe Cotts. BB4: Hasl 1F 160
Glebe Ct. LA1: Lanc 7E 228
LA6: K Lon 5E 8
(off Fairbank)
Glebelands PR4: Tarl 1E 170
Glebe La. PR4: K'ham 5A 112
PR9: Banks 8F 148
Glebe M. PR4: Clif 7H 113
Glebe Pl. PR9: S'port 7H 167
Glebe Rd. WN8: Skelm 3L 219
Glebe St. BB6: Gt H 4J 121
BB11: Burnl 5E 124
Gledhill St. OL14: Tod 1L 165
Gledhill Way BL7: Brom C 5G 198
Gledstone Rd. BD23: W Mar 6G 53
Gledstone Vw. BB18: Barnw 1L 77
Glegside Rd. L33: Kirk 8M 223
Glen, The BB2: Blackb 1M 157
FY6: K Sea 9L 41
LA2: Caton 3H 25
OL14: Tod 9J 147
PR2: Ribb 7B 116
Glenapp Av. FY4: Blackp 3F 108
Glenarden Av. FY5: T Clev 3E 62
Glen Av. OL14: Tod 9J 147
Glenavon Dr. OL12: Roch 2A 204
Glenborough Av. OL13: Bac 7G 162
Glenbrook Cl. BB2: Blackb 8J 139
Glenburn Rd. WN8: Skelm 8J 211
Glen Caravan Pk. LA3: Morec 6B 22
Glencarron Cl. BB3: Hodd 7F 158
Glencoe Av. BB3: Hodd 6E 158
FY3: Blackp 1G 89
Glencoe Pl. OL11: Roch 6A 204
Glen Cotts. BB18: Earl 2F 78
Glencourse Dr. PR2: Fulw 4M 115
Glencoyne Dr. BL1: Bolt 7D 198
PR9: S'port 9A 148
Glen Cres. OL13: Bac 7E 162
Glencroft PR7: Eux 3L 173
Glencross Pl. FY4: Blackp 2E 108
Glendale Av. PR5: Lost H 7M 135
Glendale Cl. BB11: Burnl 6E 124
FY2: Blackp 6F 62
FY6: Poul F 8J 63
PR25: Leyl 8L 153
Glendale Cres. PR5: Lost H 7M 135
Glendale Dr. BB2: Mellor 7F 118
Glendale Gro. L33: Kirk 5M 223
PR2: Ribb 7N 115
Glendene Pk. BB1: Clay D 4M 119
Glenden Foot OL12: Roch 3A 204
Glendor Rd. BB10: Burnl 4J 125
Glen Dr. WN6: App B 4H 213
Gleneagles FY8: L Ann 2G 128
Gleneagles Av. BB3: Hodd 6E 158
Gleneagles Cl. L33: Kirk 4J 223
Gleneagles Ct. BB1: Blackb 5C 140
PR4: K'ham 5N 111
Gleneagles Dr. BB6: Old L 4C 100
LA1: Lanc 9N 23
LA4: Morec 3D 22
PR1: Penw 2D 134
PR2: Fulw 2E 114
PR7: Eux 2N 173
PR8: Ains 1B 206
Gleneagles Way BL0: Ramsb 9G 180
Glen Eldon Rd. FY8: L Ann 1E 128
Glenfield Av. FY2: Blackp 5E 62
Glenfield Caravan Pk. PR3: Pill 8H 43
Glenfield Cl. BB1: Blackb 1B 140
Glenfield Pk. Bus. Cen. BB1: Blackb 1B 140
Glenfield Pk. Ind. Est. BB1: Blackb 9B 120
BB9: Nelson 1L 105
Glenfield Rd. BB9: Nelson 1K 105
Glen Gdns. OL12: Roch 3C 204
Glengarry FY8: L Ann 5B 130
Glen Gth. BB18: Barnw 1A 78
Glengreave Av. BB1: Ramsg 6M 119
Glen Gro. PR2: Ribb 4B 116
Glenholme Gdns. FY6: Poul F 9H 63
Glenholm Rd. L31: Magh 3B 222
Glenluce Cres. BB1: Blackb 5D 140
Glenluce Dr. PR1: Prest 9B 116
Glenmarsh Way L37: Form 9B 206
Glenmere Cres. FY5: T Clev 4C 62
Glen Morag Gdns. OL11: Roch 7L 203
Glenmore PR6: Clay W 4C 154
Glenmore Av. FY5: T Clev 1H 63
Glenmore Cl. BB5: Bax 6D 142
OL11: Roch 8J 203
Glenmore Rd. BL0: Ramsb 3E 200
Glen Pk. Dr. PR4: Hesk B 3B 150
Glenpark Dr. PR9: S'port 2A 168
Glen Rd. BB4: W'foot 7D 162
Glenrose Ter. PR8: Birk 9G 167
Glenroy Av. BB8: Colne 5A 86
Glen Royd OL12: Roch 4N 203
Glenroyd Cl. FY3: Blackp 7E 88
Glenroyd Dr. L40: Burs 9C 190
Glenshiels Av. BB3: Hodd 6E 158
Glenside WN6: App B 2E 212
Glen Sq. BB11: Burnl 7D 124
Glen St. BB8: Colne 5A 86
BB12: Burnl 1A 228 (3C 124)
BL0: Ramsb 7G 180
FY3: Blackp 4N 227 (6E 88)
OL13: Bac 7J 163
Glen Ter. BB4: W'foot 7D 162
OL14: Tod 8H 147
GLEN TOP 7E 162
Glentworth Cl. L31: Magh 3C 222
Glentworth Rd. E. LA4: Morec 5D 22
Glentworth Rd. W. LA4: Morec 5C 22
Glen Vw. OL12: Whitw 4N 183
OL15: Littleb 7M 185
Glen Vw. Av. LA3: Heys 1K 27
Glenview Cl. PR2: Ribb 6C 116
Glenview Ct. PR2: Ribb 6C 116
(not continuous)
Glen Vw. Cres. LA3: Heys 1K 27
Glen Vw. Dr. LA3: Heys 1K 27
Glen Vw. Rd. BB11: Burnl 7C 124
Glen Vw. St. OL14: Tod 7F 146
Glen Way BB9: Brierf 5E 104
L33: Kirk 4L 223
Glenway PR1: Penw 4F 134
Glenwood St. FY3: Blackp 1N 227 (5D 88)
Global Way BB3: Darw 2A 158
Globe, The 2B 108
Globe, The LA6: Burt K 6G 7
Globe Arena 5A 22
Globe Cen., The BB5: Acc 3A 142
Globe La. BL7: Eger 2D 198
Globe Pk. OL16: Roch 7E 204
Globe Way BB5: Acc 3A 142
Glossop Cl. FY2: Blackp 5C 62
Gloucester Av. BB5: Acc 1N 141
BB5: Clay M 6M 121
FY1: Blackp 4M 227 (6D 88)
FY5: T Clev 8D 54
LA1: Lanc 3L 29
OL12: Roch 1G 205
PR25: Far 4M 153
Gloucester Ct. FY1: Blackp 4N 227 (6D 88)
Gloucester Dr. LA3: Heys 5M 21
Gloucester Rd. BB1: Blackb 3C 140
BB1: Rish 8F 120
FY8: L Ann 4K 129
PR7: Chor 7E 174
PR8: Birk 9F 166
WN5: Wigan 5M 221
Glover Cl. PR26: Leyl 9C 152
Glover Rd. PR7: Copp 6N 193
GLOVERS BRIDGE 1D 210
Glover's Brow L32: Kirk 6H 223
Glovers Ct. L32: Kirk 7H 223
PR1: Prest 6L 229 (1J 135)
Glover St. BL6: Hor 9C 196
PR1: Prest 7L 229 (1K 135)
Glynn St. BB5: Chur 1M 141
(not continuous)
Gnat Bank Fold OL11: Roch 8K 203
Godiva St. BB10: Burnl 9E 104
Godley St. BB11: Burnl 1F 228 (3F 124)
Godwin Av. FY3: Blackp 7E 88
Goe La. PR4: Frec 1N 131
Goffa Mill BD23: Garg 4M 53
(off Church La.)
Goit Pl. OL16: Roch 6C 204
Goitside BB9: Nelson 1J 105
Goit St. BB2: Blackb 6K 139
Go Karting 6F 166
Golbourne Cl. FY7: Flee 2D 54
Golbourne St. PR1: Prest 3N 229 (8L 115)
Goldacre La. BB6: Gt H 1G 121
Goldburn Cl. PR2: Ingol 3C 114
Goldcrest Av. OL13: Bac 5L 163
Goldcrest Cl. LA3: Heys 1L 27
Goldcrest Dr. PR5: Bam B 6C 136
Golden Ball La. LA1: Lanc 7C 228
GOLDEN HILL 5K 153
Golden Hill PR25: Leyl 5L 153

Grisedale Av.—Hampstead Rd.

Grisedale Av. BB1: Blackb .5C 140
Grisedale Dr. BB12: Burnl .1N 123
Grisedale Pl. PR7: Chor .9D 174
Grisedale Rd. OL11: Roch .9M 203
Gristlehurst La. BL9: Bury .8D 202
OL10: Heyw .8D 202
Grizedale Av. FY6: Poul F .8J 63
LA1: Bail .8M 29
PR3: Gars .6M 59
Grizedale Cl. BB5: Clay M .7L 121
PR2: Ribb .7B 116
Grizedale Ct. FY3: Blackp .5E 88
(off Forest Ga.)
FY5: T Clev .9G 55
Grizedale Cres. PR2: Ribb .7B 116
Grizedale Pl. LA3: Heys .8M 21
PR2: Ribb .7B 116
Grizedale Rd. FY4: Blackp .9J 89
LA1: Lanc .6L 23
Grosvenor Casino .1A 108
Grosvenor Cl. FY6: Poul F .7K 63
PR8: Birk .2E 186
Grosvenor Ct. FY5: T Clev .1C 62
FY8: L Ann .8G 109
LA5: Carn .9N 11
WN5: Orr .5L 221
Grosvenor Gdns. PR8: Birk .2F 186
Grosvenor Pl. LA5: Carn .9N 11
PR2: Ash R .7E 114
PR8: Birk .2F 186
Grosvenor Rd. L31: Magh .4B 222
LA3: Heys .5L 21
LA5: Carn .9A 12
PR7: Chor .8D 174
PR8: Birk .1D 186
Grosvenor St. BB8: Colne .6C 86
BB12: Burnl .2D 124
FY1: Blackp .1K 227 (5C 88)
FY8: L Ann .5B 130
PR1: Prest .1L 135
Grouse St. OL12: Roch .4C 204
Grove, The BB5: Osw .3L 141
BB7: Clith .2M 81
BB7: Whall .5J 101
BB12: Burnl .3N 123
BB18: Barnw .1N 77
(off Weets Vw.)
FY5: T Clev .9E 54
L39: Aug .4H 217
L39: Orms .7K 209
L40: Ruff .2E 190
LA1: Lanc .9E 228 (9L 23)
LA5: Carn .9M 11
PR1: Penw .4E 134
PR2: Ash R .8E 114
PR3: Bils .6D 68
PR3: Chip .5F 70
PR7: Chor .4E 174
WN6: App B .2F 212
Grove Av. PR4: Longt .8K 133
PR6: Adl .6J 195
Grove Cl. WN8: Uph .3F 220
Grove Cotts. OL15: Littleb .6M 185
Grove Ct. BB5: Osw .5J 141
BD24: Sett .3N 35
(off High Hill Gro. St.)
Grove Cres. PR6: Adl .6J 195
Grove La. BB12: Padi .9J 103
Grove Mead L31: Magh .1E 222
Grove Pk. L39: Orms .5L 209
PR9: S'port .6M 167
Grove Pk. Gdns. BD24: Sett .3N 35
(off High Hill Gro. St.)
Grove Pk. Ind. Est. PR7: E'ton .9F 172
Grove Rd. PR5: Walt D .2M 135
WN8: Uph .3F 220
Groveside Pk. BB12: Burnl .3M 123
Grove St. BB3: Darw .4N 157
BB5: Acc .2N 141
BB5: Osw .5J 141
BB9: Barrf .8H 85
BB9: Nelson .2J 105
BB11: Burnl .4B 124
BB18: Earl .2E 78
FY8: L Ann .1F 128
LA4: Morec .4N 21
OL11: Roch .8B 204
OL13: Bac .4L 163
PR5: Bam B .8B 136
PR8: S'port .1G 187
PR25: Leyl .7G 152
Grove Ter. PR8: Birk .9G 167
Grovewood PR8: Birk .9E 166
Grovewood Dr. WN6: App B .4H 213
Grundy Art Gallery .1J 227 (4B 88)
Grundy Cl. PR8: S'port .9L 167
Grundy Homes PR8: S'port .9L 167
Grundy M. FY4: Blackp .2C 108
Grundy's La. PR7: Chor .4E 194
Grundy St. PR25: Leyl .5K 153
GRUNSAGILL .3K 51
Guardian Cl. OL12: Roch .9G 185
PR2: Fulw .5K 115
Guardian Ct. PR8: Birk .9F 166
Gubberford La. PR3: Gars, Scor .1N 59
Guernsey Av. BB2: Blackb .7N 139
PR7: Buck V .8B 154
GUIDE .8D 140
Guide Ct. BL0: Eden .2J 181
Guide La. BB12: High .3M 103
Guide Rd. PR4: Hesk B .9B 132
Guildford Av. FY2: Blackp .5C 62
PR6: Chor .2G 175
Guildford Rd. PR1: Prest .7L 229 (1K 135)
PR8: Birk .6G 186
Guildford Way FY6: Carl .5J 63
Guild Hall & Charter Theatre .5L 229 (1K 135)
Guild Hall Arc. PR1: Prest .6L 229
Guildhall St. PR1: Prest .6K 229 (1J 135)
Guild Row PR1: Prest .6L 229 (1K 135)
Guild St. BL7: Brom C .6H 199
Guild Trad. Est. PR1: Prest .8L 115
Guild Way PR1: Prest .1G 134
PR2: Prest .1G 134
Guilford St. BB9: Brierf .5F 104
Guinea Hall Cl. PR9: Banks .1F 168
Guinea Hall La. PR9: Banks .9F 148
Guinea Hall M. PR9: Banks .1F 168
Guinness Ho. OL16: Roch .7E 204
Guiseley Cl. BL9: Bury .5K 201
Gulf La. LA2: C'ham .5N 43
PR3: Pill .5N 43
Gummers Howe Wlk. LA5: Carn .1B 16
Gunsmith Pl. BB11: Burnl .2E 228
Gurney St. BB2: Blackb .5J 139
Gutter La. BL0: Ramsb .7G 181
Guys Ind. Est. Nth. L40: Burs .2N 209
Guys Ind. Est. Sth. L40: Burs .2N 209
Guy St. BB12: Padi .9H 103
Guysyke BB8: Colne .7N 85
Gynn Av. FY1: Blackp .2B 88
Gynn Sq. FY1: Blackp .2B 88
Gynn Square Stop (Tram) .2B 88

H

HABERGHAM .2L 123
Habergham Dr. BB12: Burnl .1L 123
Habergham St. BB12: Padi .9H 103
Hackensall Rd. FY6: K Sea .9K 41
Hackford Cl. BL8: Bury .8J 201
Hacking Cl. BB6: Langh .9C 100
Hacking Dr. PR3: Longr .5H 97
Hacking La. OL14: Tod .4K 165
Hackings Caravan Pk. BB7: B'ton .4E 100
Hacking St. BB3: Darw .6A 158
BB9: Nelson .9K 85
Hacklands Av. PR2: Lea .8M 113
Haddings La. BB12: High, Newc P .1M 103
Haddon Ct. FY2: Blackp .6C 62
Haddon Pl. PR2: Fulw .6G 114
Haddon Rd. FY2: Blackp .6C 62
Haddon St. OL11: Roch .8B 204
Hadlee Ter. LA1: Lanc .7H 23
Hadleigh Cl. BL1: Bolt .7G 198
Hadleigh Rd. FY6: Carl .5J 63
L32: Kirk .9L 223
Hadrian Rd. LA3: Morec .5E 22
HAGGATE .7L 105
Haggate Fold BB10: Brierc .7L 105
Hagg La. PR3: St M .3A 66
Hagg St. BB8: Colne .7N 85
Haig Avenue .9L 167
Haig Av. LA1: Lanc .8H 23
PR2: Ash R .7G 114
PR4: Tarl .8E 150
PR8: S'port .9L 167
PR25: Leyl .6J 153
Haigh Cl. PR7: Chor .7C 174
Haigh Ct. PR8: S'port .8M 167
Haigh Cres. L31: Lyd .7B 216
PR7: Chor .7C 174
Haigh Hall Cl. BL0: Ramsb .1G 201
Haigh St. OL11: Roch .7D 204
Haighton Ct. PR2: Fulw .2K 115
Haighton Dr. PR2: Fulw .4A 116
HAIGHTON GREEN .8B 96
Haighton Grn. La. PR2: Haigh .9M 95
HAIGHTON TOP .9M 95
Haig Rd. FY1: Blackp .9H 227 (9B 88)
Haileybury Av. L10: Aint .8C 222
Hailsham Cl. BL8: Bury .6H 201
Hail St. BL0: Ramsb .1F 200
Hailwood St. OL11: Roch .9B 204
Hala Cres. LA1: Lanc .4L 29
Hala Gro. LA1: Lanc .4L 29
Hala Hill LA1: Lanc .4M 29
Hala Rd. LA1: Lanc .4L 29
Hala Sq. LA1: Lanc .4L 29
Halcyon Cl. OL12: Roch .3M 203
Haldane Rd. BB3: Darw .3M 157
Haldane St. BB10: Burnl .8F 104
Halden Rd. LA3: Heys .5M 21
HALE .1B 6
Hale Caravan Pk. LA3: Heys .7M 21
Hale Carr Gro. LA3: Heys .7M 21
Hale Carr La. LA3: Heys .7M 21
HALE NOOK .7F 56
Hales Rushes Rd. PR3: Out R .7H 57
Hale St. BB11: Burnl .5E 124
Half Acre PR5: Lost H .8K 135
Half Acre Dr. OL11: Roch .7N 203
Half Acre La. OL11: Roch .7M 203
Half Acre M. OL11: Roch .7M 203
Half Acre Rd. OL11: Roch .7M 203
Halfmile Island WN8: Skelm .9K 211
Halford Pl. FY5: T Clev .4E 62
Halfpenny Bri. Ind. Est. OL11: Roch .7D 204
Halfpenny La. PR3: Longr .3G 97
PR7: Hesk .2D 192
WN8: Skelm .2E 218
Halifax Rd. BB9: Brierf .5F 104
BB9: Nelson .4H 105
BB10: Brierc .7L 105
OL12: Roch .4E 204
OL14: Tod .2L 165
OL15: Littleb .8M 185
OL16: Roch .4E 204
PR8: Ains .8C 186
Halifax St. FY3: Blackp .7F 88
Halkin Cl. PR2: Fulw .5K 115
Hallam Cres. BB9: Nelson .2L 105
Hallam La. LA3: Midd .5M 27
Hallam Rd. BB9: Nelson .1K 105
Hallam St. BB5: Acc .8N 121
Hallam Way FY4: Blackp .3K 109
Hall Av. FY4: Blackp .9L 227 (9C 88)
Hallbridge Gdns. BL1: Bolt .9G 199
WN8: Uph .3E 220
Hall Brow Cl. L39: Orms .8N 209
HALL CARR .6M 161
Hall Carr La. PR4: Longt, Wal B .8G 133
Hall Carr Rd. BB4: Rawt .6M 161
Hall Cl. BB4: Rawt .1M 161
LA2: Caton .2G 25
WN6: Shev .6L 213
Hall Coppice, The BL7: Eger .3D 198
Hall Cft. PR4: Hutt .6A 134
Hallcroft WN8: Skelm .1N 219
Hallcroft Gdns. OL16: Milnr .7H 205
Hall Cft. Head PR4: Hutt .6A 134
HALL CROSS .8M 111
Hall Dr. L32: Kirk .7K 223
LA2: Caton .2G 25
LA3: Midd .5M 27
LA4: Morec .4E 22
Halley Rd. BB3: Darw .4M 157
Halley St. OL13: Weir .9L 145
Hallfield LA5: Bolt S .3N 15
Hallfield Rd. BB6: Gt H .3K 121
HALLFOLD .6N 183
Hall Fold OL12: Whitw .6M 183
Hall Gdns. OL12: Roch .3M 203
Hall Gth. Gdns. LA6: Over K .9F 12
Hallgate PR7: Chor .5C 174
Hallgate Hill BB7: Newt .7B 50
Hall Ga. La. FY6: Pree, Stal .3B 56
Hall Greaves Cl. LA3: O'ton .7B 28
HALL GREEN
PR4 .1H 151
WN8 .4D 220
Hall Grn. WN8: Uph .4E 220
Hall Grn. Cl. WN8: Uph .4E 220
Hall Grn. La. PR7: Hesk .2C 192
Hall Gro. LA3: Midd .5M 27
Hall Hill BB7: Cow A, White .2L 71
Hall Hill St. BB12: Padi .9H 103
(off St Giles St.)
Halliday Ct. OL15: Littleb .1H 205
Halling Pl. OL14: Tod .3K 165
HALL I' TH' WOOD .9G 199
Hall i' th' Wood BL1: Bolt .9G 199
Hall i' th' Wood Mus. .9G 199
Halliwell Ct. PR7: Chor .7E 174
(off Halliwell St.)
Halliwell Cres. PR4: Hutt .6B 134
Halliwell Hgts. PR5: Walt D .5B 136
Halliwell La. PR6: Chor .2E 174
Halliwell Pl. PR7: Chor .7E 174
Halliwell St. BB5: Bax .6C 142
OL12: Roch .5B 204
(not continuous)
OL16: Milnr, Roch .6H 205
PR7: Chor .7E 174
Hall La. BL6: R'ton .3B 196
L31: Lyd .4A 216
L31: Magh .3B 222
L32: Kirk .8J 223
L33: S'wood .3L 223
L38: Ince B .7F 214
L39: Bick .8C 218
L40: Bis G .5L 191
L40: Lath .7E 210
L40: Mawd .2A 192
PR3: Gt E .7N 65
PR3: St M .5G 67
PR4: Longt .9H 133
PR25: Leyl .4J 153
WN3: Wigan .7J 221
WN5: Bill .7H 221
WN5: Wigan .7J 221
WN6: App B .2E 212
WN8: Parb .5L 191
Hall Mdws. BB8: Traw .8E 86
Hallmoor Cl. L39: Aug .1K 217
Hall More Caravan Pk. LA7: Hale .4A 6
Hallows Cl. PR3: St M .5G 66
Hallows St. BB10: Burnl .8E 104
Hall Pk. BB4: Hasl .1G 160
LA1: Lanc .3K 29
Hall Pk. Av. BB10: Burnl .5K 125
Hall Pk. Dr. FY8: L Ann .2K 129
Hall Rd. BB8: Traw .8E 86
L40: Scar .6F 188
PR1: Penw .5H 135
PR2: Fulw .4H 115
Hallroyd Cres. OL14: Tod .2M 165
Hallroyd Pl. OL14: Tod .2M 165
Hallroyd Rd. OL14: Tod .1M 165
Halls Sq. PR6: Whit W .9G 154
Hall St.
BB2: Blackb .8C 226 (5M 139)
(Eccles St.)
BB2: Blackb .9C 226 (6M 139)
(Vale St.)
BB4: Hasl .5G 161
BB4: Rawt .4M 161
BB7: Clith .4L 81
BB8: Colne .7A 86
BB10: W'thorne .4L 125
BB11: Burnl .2D 228 (3E 124)
BL8: Bury .8D 200
(Parkgate)
BL8: Bury .9H 201
(Rowans St.)
BL9: Summ .3H 201
LA4: Morec .2B 22
OL12: Whitw .6N 183
OL13: Bac .4K 163
OL14: Tod .2L 165
PR2: Ash R .8F 114
PR9: S'port .8J 167
Hallwell St. BB10: Burnl .1E 124
Hallwood Cl. BB10: Reed .6F 104
Hallwood Rd. PR7: Chor .9C 174
Halmot Ct. BB4: Newc .6C 162
Halmote Av. BB12: High .5L 103
Halo
Panopticon .3H 161
HALSALL .3B 208
Halsall Bldgs. PR9: S'port .6K 167
(off Manchester Rd.)
Halsall Cl. BL9: Bury .7L 201
Halsall Ct. L39: Orms .6J 209
(off Halsall La.)
Halsall Dr. LA4: Morec .2F 22
Halsall Hall Dr. L39: Hals .3A 208
Halsall La. L37: Form .9A 206
L39: Hals .7C 208
L39: Orms .6J 209
Halsall Mnr. Ct. L39: Hals .3A 208
Halsall Rd. L39: Hals .3B 208
PR8: Birk .5F 186
Halsall Sq. PR3: Gt E .6N 65
Halsbury St. PR1: Prest .8M 229 (2K 135)
Halstead Cl. BB9: Barrf .7H 85
Halstead La. BB9: Barrf .7H 85
Halstead Rd. PR2: Ribb .4N 115
Halsteads Cotts. BD24: Sett .3N 35
(off High Hill Gro. St.)
Halsteads Ter. BD24: Sett .3N 35
(off Duke St.)
Halstead St. BB10: W'thorne .3L 125
BB11: Burnl .4B 228 (4D 124)
BL9: Bury .8M 201
Halstead Wlk. BL9: Bury .8M 201
L32: Kirk .9H 223
(off Downgreen Cl.)
HALTON .1B 24
Halton Av. FY5: T Clev .8E 54
PR25: Leyl .5N 153
Halton Chase L40: W'head .8C 210
Halton Ct. LA4: Morec .5B 22
Halton Gdns. FY4: Blackp .1F 108
FY5: T Clev .8F 54
HALTON GREEN .1E 24
Halton Pk. LA2: Halt .9G 16
Halton Pl. PR2: Ribb .5B 116
PR3: Longr .2K 97
Halton Rd. L31: Lyd .8C 216
LA1: Lanc .5L 23
LA6: Neth K .4B 16
Halton St. PR4: Weet .4D 90
HALTON WEST .3C 52
Halton Wood L32: Kirk .7G 222
Halvard Av. BL9: Bury .7L 201
Halvard Ct. BL9: Bury .7L 201
Hambledon Ho. BB4: Hasl .4G 160
(off Bury Rd.)
Hambledon St. BB12: Padi .1J 123
Hambledon Ter. BB12: Burnl .2L 123
BB12: High .4L 103
Hambledon Vw. BB12: Burnl .2L 123
BB12: Read .9C 102
HAMBLETON .2B 64
Hambleton Cl. PR4: Longt .7K 133
Hambleton Country Pk. FY6: Ham .8C 56
Hambleton Dr. PR1: Penw .6H 135
Hambleton Fisheries .2A 64
HAMBLETON MOSS SIDE .1D 64
Hameldon App. BB11: Burnl .4B 124
Hameldon Av. BB5: Acc .6D 142
Hameldon Cl. BB11: Hapt .6H 123
Hameldon Rd. BB4: Craws .6M 143
BB11: Hapt .7H 123
Hameldon Vw. BB6: Gt H .4K 121
Hamer Av. BB1: Blackb .3D 140
BB4: Craws .7M 143
Hamer Ct. OL16: Roch .4E 204
Hamer Hall Cres. OL12: Roch .3E 204
Hamer La. OL16: Roch .4E 204
Hamer Rd. PR2: Ash R .6G 114
Hamer St. BB4: Rawt .5M 161
BL0: Ramsb .3G 201
Hamers Wood Dr. PR3: Catt .1A 68
Hamer Ter. BL9: Summ .2H 201
(off Waterside Rd.)
Hamer Va. OL12: Roch .3E 204
Hamilton Cl. FY8: L Ann .4C 130
Hamilton Ct. FY1: Blackp .3K 227 (6C 88)
Hamilton Dr. LA1: Lanc .5G 22
Hamilton Gro. PR2: Ribb .6A 116
Hamilton Rd. BB8: Colne .9L 85
BB9: Barrf .1G 104
LA4: Morec .2G 22
PR2: Ribb .5N 115
PR7: Chor .7D 174
Hamilton St. BB2: Blackb .9A 226 (6L 139)
BL1: Bolt .8E 198
BL9: Bury .9L 201
Hamlet, The FY8: L Ann .7F 108
PR7: H Charn .4H 195
Hamlet Cl. BB2: Blackb .5K 139
Hamlet Gro. PR4: Wharl .6D 92
Hamlet Rd. FY7: Flee .9F 40
Hammerton Grn. OL13: Bac .4K 163
Hammerton Hall Cl. LA1: Lanc .4J 23
Hammerton Hall La. LA1: Lanc .4H 23
LA2: Lanc .4H 23
HAMMERTON MERE .3E 50
Hammerton Pl. FY3: Blackp .2G 89
Hammerton St. BB11: Burnl .3C 228 (4D 124)
OL13: Bac .3K 163
Hammerton Ter. OL14: Tod .1L 165
Hammond Av. OL13: Bac .7H 163
Hammond Ct. PR1: Prest .8H 115
Hammond Dr. BB12: Read .8B 102
Hammond Rd. L33: Know P .7A 224
Hammond's Row PR1: Prest .6M 229 (1K 135)
Hammond St. BB9: Nelson .3K 105
PR1: Prest .1G 229 (7H 115)
(Barlow St.)
PR1: Prest .1J 229 (7J 115)
(Miles St.)
PR1: Prest .8G 115
(Selby St.)
Hamnet Cl. BL1: Bolt .8G 199
Hampden Av. BB3: Darw .8J 158
Hampden Pl. WN5: Wigan .2N 221
(not continuous)
Hampden Rd. PR25: Leyl .5K 153
Hampden St. BB11: Burnl .5F 124
BB12: Hapt .5H 123
OL11: Roch .7C 204
(off Maclure Rd.)
Hampden Wlk. WN5: Wigan .2N 221
Hampsfell Dr. LA4: Morec .5B 22
Hampshire Av. PR7: Buck V .9B 154
Hampshire Cl. BB1: Wilp .2A 120
Hampshire Pl. FY4: Blackp .3F 108
Hampshire Rd. BB1: Rish .8G 121
PR5: Walt D .5N 135
Hampson Av. PR25: Leyl .6N 153
Hampson Cotts. LA2: Ham G .5M 37
HAMPSON GREEN .5N 37
Hampson Gro. FY6: Pree .9N 41
Hampson La. LA2: Ham G .5M 37
Hampson St. BL6: Hor .9C 196
Hampson Ter. PR3: Gt E .6A 66
Hampstead Cl. FY8: L Ann .2L 129
Hampstead M. FY1: Blackp .3C 88
Hampstead Rd. PR2: Ribb .7N 115
WN6: Stand .3N 213

Hampton Cl.—Haverholt Rd.

Hampton Cl. PR7: Chor 6D 174
Hampton Ct. FY8: L Ann 9J 109
L39: Aug 1J 217
Hampton Gro. BL9: Bury 7L 201
Hampton Pl. FY5: T Clev 9E 54
Hampton Rd. FY4: Blackp 1C 108
LA3: Heys 5M 21
PR8: S'port 1H 187
Hampton Rd. Caravan Pk.
FY4: Blackp 1C 108
Hamptons, The FY6: Poul F 1K 89
L37: Form 8A 206
Hampton St. PR2: Ash R 7F 114
Hanbury St. PR2: Ash R 8F 114
Hancock St. BB2: Blackb 8A 226 (5K 139)
(not continuous)
Handbridge, The PR2: Fulw 4H 115
Handel St. OL12: Whitw 6M 183
Hand La. L40: Mawd 9C 172
Handley Rd. FY1: Blackp 4C 88
Handley St. OL12: Roch 5A 204
Handshaw Dr. PR1: Penw 6K 135
Hands La. OL11: Roch 6L 203
Handsworth Ct. FY1: Blackp 3C 88
Handsworth Rd. FY1: Blackp 3C 88
Handsworth Wlk. PR8: S'port 2M 187
Hanging Grn. La. LA2: Hest B 8J 15
Hanging Lees Cl. OL16: Milnr 9M 205
Hanley Cl. FY6: Stal 5B 56
Hanmer Pl. *LA1: Lanc 1L 29*
(off Avondale Rd.)
Hanmer Rd. L32: Kirk 8G 223
Hannah Ct. PR7: Buck V 9A 154
Hannah St. BB3: Darw 7B 158
BB5: Acc 3A 142
OL13: Bac 4L 163
Hanover Ct. BB11: Burnl 6B 124
PR2: Ingol 3C 114
Hanover Cres. FY2: Blackp 5C 62
Hanover St. BB8: Colne 5A 86
LA4: Morec 3B 22
OL15: Littleb 9K 185
PR1: Prest 3K 229 (8J 115)
Hansby Cl. WN8: Skelm 3B 220
Hanson St. BB1: Rish 8J 121
BB6: Gt H 5J 121
BL9: Bury 9L 201
PR7: Adl 8H 195
Hanstock Cl. WN5: Orr 6H 221
Hants La. L39: Orms 6K 209
Happy Mt. Ct. LA4: Morec 1F 22
Happy Mt. Dr. LA4: Morec 1E 22
HAPTON 5H 123
Hapton Rd. BB12: Padi 2H 123
Hapton Station (Rail) 5H 123
Hapton St. BB12: Padi 1J 123
FY5: T Clev 8H 55
Hapton Way BB4: Craws 6M 143
Harborne Wlk. BL8: Greenm 5E 200
Harbour Av. PR4: Wart 2K 131
Harbour Cl. FY7: Flee 2F 54
Harbour Ho. FY8: L Ann 4C 130
Harbour La. BL7: Edgw 9K 179
OL16: Milnr 8J 205
PR4: Wart 1K 131
PR6: Birns, Wheel 8L 155
Harbour La. Nth. OL16: Milnr 7J 205
Harbour Trad. Est. *FY7: Flee 2F 54*
(off Harbour Cl.)
Harbour Way FY7: Flee 1H 55
Harbury Av. PR8: Ains 9A 186
Harcles Dr. BL0: Ramsb 3G 200
Harcourt M. *BL6: Hor 9C 196*
(off Mottram St.)
Harcourt Rd. BB2: Blackb 2K 139
BB5: Acc 5C 142
FY4: Blackp 1D 108
LA1: Lanc 5J 23
Harcourt St. BB11: Burnl 4B 124
OL13: Bac 4K 163
PR1: Prest 2G 229 (8H 115)
Hardacre BB9: Nelson 3J 105
Hardacre La. BB7: Rim 2B 76
PR6: Whit W 1D 174
Hardacre St. L39: Orms 6L 209
Hardaker Ct. FY8: L Ann 2E 128
Hardcastle Cl. BL2: Bolt 7J 199
Hardcastle Gdns. BL2: Bolt 7J 199
Hardcastle Rd. PR2: Fulw 6H 115
Harden Rd. BB18: Kelb 6D 78
HARDHORN 1K 89
Hardhorn Ct. FY6: Poul F 8K 63
Hardhorn Rd. FY6: Poul F 8K 63
HARDHORN VILLAGE 2L 89
Hardhorn Way FY6: Poul F 9K 63
Harding Rd. L40: Burs 9B 190
Harding St. PR6: Adl 5K 195
Hard Knott Ri. LA5: Carn 1B 16
Hardlands Av. LA4: Morec 4F 22
Hard La. OL12: Ward 6D 184
Hardman Av. BB4: Rawt 6M 161
Hardman Cl. BB1: Blackb 4F 140
BB4: W'foot 8D 162
Hardman Dr. BB4: W'foot 8D 162
Hardmans BL7: Brom C 6F 198
Hardmans Bus. Cen.
BB4: Rawt 6K 161
Hardman's La. BL7: Brom C 5F 198
Hardman St. BB2: Blackb 5K 139
BL9: Bury 9L 201
FY1: Blackp 4C 88
OL16: Milnr 8K 205
Hardman Ter. OL13: Bac 7H 163
Hardman Way BB3: Darw 6A 158
Hardsough Fold *BL0: Ramsb 1H 181*
(off Aitken St.)
Hardsough La. BL0: Eden 1H 181
Hardwen Av. *PR2: Lea 8N 113*
(off Greenside Av.)
Hardwicke St. OL11: Roch 9B 204
PR1: Prest 4L 229 (9K 115)
Hardwick Ho. LA1: Lanc 7B 228
Hardy Av. BB9: Brierf 4F 104
BB18: Barnw 1L 77
Hardy Cl. OL11: Roch 9C 204
PR2: Ash R 9B 114
Hardy Ct. *BB9: Nelson 2J 105*
(off Audley Ct.)
FY8: L Ann 4C 130
Hardy Dr. PR7: Chor 7C 174
Hardy Mill Rd. BL2: Bolt 9M 199
Hardy St. BB1: Blackb 8N 119
BB9: Brierf 4F 104
Harebell Cl. BB2: Fenis 8E 138
OL12: Roch 2A 204
Hare Clough Cl. BB2: Blackb 8F 226 (5N 139)
Hare Ct. OL14: Tod 1K 165
Hareden Brook Cl.
BB2: Blackb 8F 226 (5N 139)
Hareden Rd. PR2: Ribb 7B 116
Haredon Cl. PR5: Bam B 8B 136
Harefield Av. OL11: Roch 8D 204
Harefield Ri. BB12: Burnl 1B 124
Harehill OL14: Tod 1K 165
Harehill Av. OL14: Tod 1K 165
Hare Hill Ct. OL15: Littleb 8L 185
Hare Hill Rd. OL15: Littleb 8K 185
Harehill St. OL14: Tod 1K 165
HAREHOLME 6B 162
Hareholme La. BB4: Rawt 5B 162
HARE RUNS 4J 23
Hares La. PR8: S'port 4B 188
Harestone Av. PR7: Chor 9C 174
Hare St. OL11: Roch 8C 204
(not continuous)
Harewood PR7: Chor 4D 174
Harewood Av. BB12: S'stone 8D 102
FY3: Blackp 1G 88
LA1: Lanc 4L 29
LA3: Heys 6M 21
OL11: Roch 3H 203
PR8: Ains 7C 186
Harewood Cl. FY6: Carl 6J 63
OL11: Roch 3H 203
Harewood Dr. OL11: Roch 3G 203
Harewood Rd. OL11: Roch 3G 203
PR1: Prest 7L 115
Harewood Way OL11: Roch 3G 203
Hargate Av. OL12: Roch 3L 203
Hargate Cl. BL9: Summ 3H 201
Hargate Rd. FY5: T Clev 1J 63
L33: Kirk 8L 223
Hargate Wlk. L33: Kirk 8L 223
Hargher St. BB11: Burnl 4B 124
Hargreaves Av. PR25: Leyl 7L 153
Hargreaves Ct. BB4: Lumb 1D 162
BB7: Clith 4J 81
PR2: Ingol 5C 114
Hargreaves Dr. BB4: Rawt 5L 161
Hargreaves Fold La. BB4: Lumb 9D 144
Hargreaves La. BB2: Blackb 8C 226 (5M 139)
Hargreaves Rd. BB5: Osw 4H 141
Hargreaves St. BB3: Hodd 6F 158
BB4: Hasl 4G 160
BB4: Lumb 2C 162
BB5: Acc 3B 142
BB8: Colne 7M 85
BB9: Nelson 2G 105
BB10: Brierc 7K 105
BB11: Burnl 2C 228 (3D 124)
FY5: T Clev 9H 55
OL11: Roch 9N 203
PR8: S'port 8J 167
Hargrove Av. BB12: Burnl 2B 124
BB12: Padi 9H 103
Harland St. PR2: Fulw 6G 115
Harland Way OL12: Roch 3L 203
Harlech Av. FY1: Blackp 9M 227 (9D 88)
Harlech Cl. BB4: Hasl 6G 161
Harlech Dr. BB5: Osw 4J 141
PR25: Leyl 6M 153
Harlech Gro. FY5: T Clev 1K 63
Harleston Rd. L33: Kirk 7M 223
Harleston Wlk. L33: Kirk 7M 223
HARLE SYKE 7K 105
Harley Cl. LA2: L Ben 6K 19
Harley Rd. FY3: Blackp 6E 88
Harley St. BB12: Burnl 3A 124
OL14: Tod 1L 165
Harley Vs. *OL14: Tod 1L 165*
(off Wood St.)
HARLEY WOOD 9K 147
Harley Wood OL14: Tod 8H 147
Harley Wood Vw. *OL14: Tod 8H 147*
(off Church St.)
Harling Bank LA6: K Lon 6E 8
Harling Rd. PR1: Prest 8N 115
Harling St. BB12: Burnl 3N 123
Harmony St. OL16: Milnr 7J 205
Harmuir Cl. WN6: Stand 8N 213
Harold Av. BB11: Burnl 5A 124
FY4: Blackp 3G 108
Harold St. BB8: Colne 7N 85
BB11: Burnl 5B 124
OL16: Roch 3F 204
Harold Ter. PR5: Lost H 8K 135
Harperley PR7: Chor 4D 174
Harpers La. BB12: Fence 2B 104
PR6: Chor 5F 174
Harper St. BB18: Barnw 2L 77
OL11: Roch 8B 204
Harridge, The OL12: Roch 2N 203
Harridge Av. OL12: Roch 2N 203
Harridge Bank OL12: Roch 2N 203
Harridge La. L40: Scar 4E 208
Harridge St. OL12: Roch 2N 203
Harrier Ct. LA1: Lanc 7B 228 (8J 23)
Harrier Dr. BB1: Blackb 9L 119
WN8: Skelm 3B 220
Harriet St. BB11: Burnl 5A 228 (5C 124)
Harriett St. OL16: Roch 6D 204
Harrington Av. FY4: Blackp 4B 108
Harrington Rd. LA3: Heys 5M 21
PR7: Chor 6D 174
Harrington St. BB5: Clay M 8N 121
PR1: Prest 3J 229 (8J 115)
Harris Av. FY1: Blackp 9N 227 (9D 88)
Harris Ct. BB7: Clith 3L 81
Harris Museum & Art Gallery 6K 229 (1K 135)
Harrison Av. FY5: T Clev 1H 63
Harrison Cl. OL12: Roch 4K 203
Harrison Cres. LA3: Heys 7L 21
Harrison Dr. BB8: Colne 5N 85
WA11: Rain 2K 225
Harrison La. PR4: Hutt 6E 134
Harrison Rd. PR2: Fulw 4H 115
PR7: Adl 7J 195
PR7: Chor 8E 174
Harrison St. BB2: Blackb 6A 226 (4L 139)
BB5: Acc 3M 141
BB10: Brierc 8K 105
BB18: Barnw 2N 77
BL0: Ramsb 7H 181
BL6: Hor 9C 196
FY1: Blackp 5L 227 (7C 88)
OL13: Bac 7M 163
OL14: Tod 7E 146
Harrison Ter. *BB7: Grind 4A 74*
(off Cross Fold)
Harrison Trad. Est. PR1: Prest 8M 115
Harrison Vw. FY8: L Ann 4G 129
Harris Rd. WN6: Stand 1L 213
Harris St. FY7: Flee 9G 40
PR1: Prest 6L 229 (1K 135)
Harrock La. WN6: Wrigh 8C 192
Harrock Rd. PR25: Leyl 6N 153
Harrock Vw. PR7: Hesk 4F 192
Harrod Dr. PR8: Birk 2E 186
Harrogate Cres. BB10: Burnl 8G 105
Harrogate Rd. FY8: L Ann 1J 129
Harrogate Way PR9: S'port 9B 148
Harron Cl. L32: Kirk 8H 223
HARROP 8F 50
Harrop Ct. *BB3: Darw 5B 158*
(off Gifford Way)
Harrop Pl. PR2: Ribb 5A 116
Harrow Av. BB5: Acc 1B 142
FY7: Flee 1F 54
OL11: Roch 7L 203
Harrow Cl. BB12: Padi 3K 123
WN5: Orr 3J 221
Harrowdale Pk. LA2: Halt 1C 24
Harrow Dr. BB1: Blackb 5B 140
L10: Aint 8C 222
Harrow Gro. LA4: Morec 4F 22
Harrow Pl. FY4: Blackp 4A 108
FY8: L Ann 3L 129
Harrow Place Stop (Tram) 4A 108
Harrow Rd. WN5: Wigan 2N 221
Harrowside FY4: Blackp 4B 108
Harrowside Stop (Tram) 4A 108
Harrowside W. FY4: Blackp 4A 108
Harrow Stiles La. OL13: Bac 7J 145
Harrow St. BB5: Osw 4L 141
Harry Potts Way BB10: Burnl 2F 228 (3F 124)
Harry St. BB9: Barrf 8H 85
BB18: Salt 5A 78
Harry Whitehead Ct. BL9: Bury 7L 201
Harsnips WN8: Skelm 1N 219
Harswell Cl. WN5: Orr 6H 221
Hartford Av. FY1: Blackp 7N 227 (8D 88)
Hartford Dr. BL8: Bury 7F 200
Hartington Rd. BB3: Darw 3M 157
PR1: Prest 1G 135
PR6: Birns 7A 156
Hartington St. BB1: Rish 8G 121
BB8: Wine 7E 86
BB9: Brierf 5F 104
LA1: Lanc 7G 228 (8M 23)
Hartland WN8: Skelm 1N 219
Hartland Av. PR9: S'port 1A 168
Hartland Ct. *BL1: Bolt 9E 198*
(off Blackburn Rd.)
Hartlands Cl. BB10: Burnl 7H 105
Hartlebury OL11: Roch 7B 204
Hartley Av. BB5: Acc 5N 141
Hartley Cres. PR8: Birk 3F 186
Hartley Dr. BB9: Nelson 3L 105
Hartley Fold *BB7: Grind 4A 74*
(off Main Rd.)
Hartley Grn. Gdns. WN5: Bill 9G 221
Hartley Gro. L33: Kirk 5L 223
WN5: Orr 4L 221
Hartley Homes, The BB8: Colne 5F 86
Hartley La. OL11: Roch 9B 204
Hartley Pl. OL16: Roch 6G 204
Hartley Rd. PR8: Birk 3F 186
Hartleys Ter. BB8: Colne 7B 86
Hartley St. BB1: Blackb 1D 226 (2M 139)
BB4: Hasl 4G 160
BB5: Osw 4L 141
BB6: Gt H 3K 121
BB8: Colne 6A 86
BB9: Nelson 3J 105
BB11: Burnl 4A 124
BB18: Earl 3E 78
OL12: Roch 4M 203
OL12: Ward 8F 184
OL15: Littleb 9K 185
OL16: Roch 6G 205
WN5: Wigan 5L 221
Hartley Ter. OL11: Roch 9B 204
OL15: Littleb 9K 185
(off Featherstall Rd.)
Hartley Way WN5: Bill 9G 221
Hartmann St. BB5: Acc 2N 141
Hartshead WN8: Skelm 1N 219
Hart's Ho's. BL6: Hor 8E 196
Hart's La. WN8: Uph 3C 220
Hart St. BB1: Blackb 5F 226 (4N 139)
BB11: Burnl 1E 228 (3E 124)
PR8: S'port 8K 167
Hart St. Bri. *PR8: S'port 8K 167*
(off Hart St.)
HARTWOOD 4F 174
Hartwood Grn. PR6: Chor 3F 174
Hartwood Rd. PR9: S'port 7K 167
Harvard St. OL11: Roch 9D 204
Harvest Dr. PR6: Whit W 9E 154
Harvesters Fold PR4: Wharl 6D 92
Harvester Way L30: N'ton 6A 222
Harvey Longworth Ct. BB4: Craws 7M 143
Harvey St. BB5: Osw 4K 141
BB9: Nelson 1J 105
BL8: Bury 9H 201
OL12: Roch 3E 204
Harvington Dr. PR8: Ains 8A 186
Harwich Rd. FY8: L Ann 8G 108
Harwin Cl. OL12: Roch 2A 204
HARWOOD 9M 199
Harwood Av. FY8: L Ann 9E 108
HARWOOD BAR 4L 121
Harwood Bar Caravan Pk. BB6: Gt H 3M 121
Harwood Cl. FY6: Stal 5B 56
Harwood Cres. BL8: Tott 6D 200
Harwood Ga. BB1: Blackb 2A 140
Harwood Golf Course 9N 199
Harwood Ho. BL8: Tott 6D 200
Harwood La. BB6: Gt H 3K 121
HARWOOD LEE 8L 199
Harwood Mdw. BL2: Bolt 9M 199
Harwood New Rd. BB6: Gt H 3L 121
Harwood Rd. BB1: Rish 7G 120
(Norden Vw.)
BB1: Rish 5D 120
(Wilpshire Rd.)
BL8: Tott 9B 200
Harwood's La. BB3: Hodd 6D 158
Harwood St. BB1: Blackb 1A 140
(not continuous)
BB3: Darw 5M 157
OL15: Littleb 9J 185
Harwood Va. BL2: Bolt 9L 199
Harwood Va. Ct. BL2: Bolt 9L 199
Harwood Wlk. BL8: Tott 6D 200
Hasbury Dr. FY5: T Clev 1J 63
Hasgill Ct. LA1: Lanc 5A 228 (7J 23)
HASKAYNE 7M 207
Haslam Ct. BB10: Burnl 9F 104
Haslam Dr. L39: Orms 5J 209
Haslam St. BL9: Bury 9M 201
OL12: Roch 5A 204
Haslemere Av. FY3: Blackp 7E 88
Haslemere Ind. Est. PR25: Leyl 4J 153
HASLINGDEN 4G 160
Haslingden Old Rd. BB1: Blackb 4E 140
BB4: Hasl 5J 161
BB5: Osw 6F 140
Haslingden Rd. BB1: Blackb, Guide 8D 140
(not continuous)
BB2: Blackb 8E 226 (5N 139)
BB4: Hasl, Rawt 6G 161
BB5: Osw 7G 141
Haslingden Sports Cen. 6F 160
Haslingden Swimming Pool 5G 160
Haslow Pl. FY3: Blackp 3F 88
Hassall Dr. PR4: Elsw 1M 91
Hassett Cl. PR1: Prest 9G 229 (2H 135)
Hastings, The *LA1: Lanc 2K 29*
(off Cheltenham Rd.)
Hastings Av. FY2: Blackp 6E 62
PR4: Wart 1K 131
Hastings Cl. BB1: Blackb 4C 140
FY5: T Clev 2J 63
Hastings Pl. FY8: L Ann 5N 129
Hastings Rd. FY5: T Clev 2J 63
LA1: Lanc 2K 29
PR2: Ash R 8E 114
PR4: Frec 7N 111
PR8: Birk 3E 186
PR25: Leyl 5L 153
Hastings St. OL11: Roch 8C 204
Haston Lee Av. BB1: Blackb 6N 119
Hasty Brow Rd. LA2: Slyne 2H 23
Hatfield Av. FY7: Flee 2E 54
LA4: Morec 2F 22
Hatfield Cl. FY5: T Clev 1J 63
Hatfield Ct. *LA4: Morec 2G 22*
(off Ranlea Av.)
Hatfield Gdns. FY7: Flee 2E 54
Hatfield M. FY7: Flee 2E 54
Hatfield Rd. BB5: Acc 9C 122
PR2: Ribb 6A 116
PR8: Ains 7C 186
Hatfield Wlk. FY7: Flee 2E 54
Hathaway FY4: Blackp 1E 108
L31: Magh 3A 222
Hathaway Dr. BL1: Bolt 8G 199
Hathaway Fold BB12: Padi 2J 123
Hathaway Rd. FY7: Flee 9E 40
LA1: Lanc 5J 23
Hatlex Dr. LA2: Hest B 7J 15
Hatlex Hill LA2: Hest B 7J 15
Hatlex La. LA2: Hest B 7J 15
Hattersley Ct. L39: Orms 6L 209
Hattersley St. BB12: Burnl 1A 228 (3C 124)
Hattersley Way L39: Orms 6L 209
Hatton Gro. BL1: Bolt 8G 198
Hatton St. PR7: Adl 7H 195
HAUGH 9M 205
Haugh Av. BB12: S'stone 9D 102
Haugh Fold OL16: Milnr 9M 205
Haugh La. OL16: Milnr 9M 205
Haugh Sq. OL16: Milnr 9M 205
Haugh St. BB10: Burnl 8F 104
Haunders La. PR4: Much H 5F 150
Havelock Cl. BB2: Blackb 8A 226 (5L 139)
Havelock Rd. PR1: Penw 3H 135
PR5: Bam B 9A 136
Havelock St. BB2: Blackb 9A 226 (6K 139)
BB5: Osw 5K 141
BB12: Burnl 3N 123
BB12: Padi 9H 103
FY1: Blackp 4J 227 (6B 88)
LA1: Lanc 1L 29
PR1: Prest 7G 115
(Bold St.)
PR1: Prest 1J 229 (7J 115)
(Miles St.)
PR1: Prest 1G 229 (7H 115)
(Villiers St.)
Havenbrook Gro. BL0: Ramsb 2F 200
Haven Brow L39: Aug 3H 217
Havenlyn Residential Pk. PR3: Cab 7N 45
Haven Rd. FY8: L Ann 5B 130
Haven St. BB10: Burnl 4G 124
OL14: Tod 2M 165
Haven Wlk. L31: Lyd 7B 216
HAVERBREAKS 1J 29
Haverbreaks Pl. LA1: Lanc 1J 29
Haverbreaks Rd. LA1: Lanc 1J 29
Havercroft Cl. WN3: Wigan 8N 221
Haverholt Cl. BB8: Colne 6N 85
Haverholt Rd. BB8: Colne 6N 85

Haverthwaite Av.—Helmshore Mills Textile Mus.

Haverthwaite Av. LA3: Heys 9L 21
Havre Pk. BB18: Barnw 2N 77
Hawarden Av. LA4: Morec 3C 22
Hawarden Rd. PR1: Prest 8A 116
Hawarden St. BB9: Nelson 3J 105
BL1: Bolt 8E 198
Hawer St. BB3: Darw 7A 158
Hawes Cl. BL8: Bury 8G 200
Hawes Dr. BB8: Colne 5C 86
HAWES SIDE 9E 88
Hawes Side La. FY4: Blackp 9N 227 (9E 88)
Hawesside St. PR9: S'port 7J 167
Hawes Ter. BB10: Burnl 8F 104
Haweswater Av. PR7: Chor 8D 174
Haweswater Cl. L33: Kirk 5J 223
Haweswater Gro. L31: Magh 9E 216
Haweswater Pl. LA4: Morec 4D 22
Haweswater Rd. BB5: Hunc 8C 122
Hawfinch Cl. OL13: Bac 5L 163
Hawgreen Rd. L32: Kirk 8G 223
Haw Gro. BD23: Hell 1D 52
Haw Gro. Ct. BD23: Hell 1D 52
(off Haw Gro.)
Hawick Cl. L33: Kirk 4J 223
Hawk Cl. BL9: Bury 9N 201
Hawker Dr. WN8: Skelm 3B 220
Hawkeshead Cl. BB2: Blackb 4J 139
Hawkhurst Av. PR2: Fulw 3G 115
Hawkhurst Cres. PR2: Fulw 3G 115
Hawkhurst Rd. PR1: Penw 4H 135
PR1: Prest 7L 115
Hawking Pl. FY2: Blackp 6F 62
Hawkins Cl. PR1: Prest 2H 229 (8H 115)
Hawkins St. BB2: Blackb 6J 139
PR1: Prest 3G 229 (8H 115)
(not continuous)
Hawkins Way OL15: Littleb 5M 185
Hawksbury Dr. PR1: Penw 6G 134
Hawksclough WN8: Skelm 1A 220
Hawks Gro. BB4: Rawt 6M 161
HAWKSHAW
BB3 4M 157
BL8 2A 200
Hawkshaw Av. BB3: Darw 4M 157
Hawkshaw Bank Rd. BB1: Blackb 9L 119
Hawkshaw Cl. BL8: Hawk 2A 200
Hawkshaw Hgts. BB3: Darw 3M 157
(off Hawkshaw Av.)
Hawkshaw La. BL8: Hawk 8A 180
Hawkshead PR1: Penw 5H 135
Hawkshead Av. PR7: Eux 5N 173
Hawkshead Cl. L31: Magh 9D 216
Hawkshead Dr. LA4: Morec 5C 22
Hawkshead Rd. FY6: K Sea 7M 41
PR2: Ribb 4A 116
Hawkshead St. BB2: Blackb 4J 139
PR8: S'port 7K 167
PR9: S'port 6J 167
Hawkshead Ter. FY4: Blackp 1K 109
Hawksheath Cl. BL7: Eger 4F 198
Hawkstone Cl. BB5: Hunc 8E 122
FY5: T Clev 3K 63
Hawkstone Ct. LA4: Morec 2F 22
Hawk St.
BB11: Burnl 1E 228 (3E 124)
LA5: Carn 8B 12
Hawkswood PR7: E'ton 8E 172
Hawkswood Gdns. BB9: Brierf 6E 104
Hawksworth Av. LA3: Heys 6M 21
Hawksworth Cl. L37: Form 6A 206
Hawksworth Dr. L37: Form 6A 206
Hawksworth Gro. LA3: Heys 7L 21
Hawksworth Rd. BB5: Acc 9A 122
Haw La. BD23: Hell 1D 52
Hawley Grn. OL12: Roch 3A 204
Hawley St. BB8: Colne 7N 85
BB8: Wine 6E 86
Haworth Art Gallery 5C 142
Haworth Av. BB4: Rawt 5L 161
BB5: Acc 5C 142
BL0: Ramsb 3G 200
Haworth Cres. FY6: Poul F 8L 63
Haworth Dr. OL13: Bac 6G 163
Haworth Rd. PR6: Chor 7G 175
Haworth St. BB1: Rish 8H 121
BB5: Acc 8A 122
BB5: Osw 4L 141
BL7: Edgw 9K 179
BL8: Bury 9D 200
Haws Av. LA5: Carn 9A 12
Hawshaw Rd. BD20: Loth 8K 79
BD22: Cowl 8K 79
Haws Hill LA5: Carn 9A 12
Hawthorn Av. BB3: Darw 5C 158
BB5: Osw 4L 141
BL0: Eden 4J 181
BL0: Ramsb 3F 200
BL8: Bury 9H 201
L40: Burs 9D 190
LA2: Brookh 3J 25
WN5: Orr 5J 221
WN5: Wigan 5N 221
Hawthorn Bank BB5: Alt 7N 121
BL2: Bolt 9L 199
Hawthorn Cl. BB7: Whall 3G 100
BB9: Nelson 2M 105
LA2: Brookh 3J 25
PR4: New L 9D 134
PR4: Wesh 2K 111
Hawthorn Ct. PR6: Adl 5H 195
Hawthorn Cres. BL8: Tott 6E 200
PR2: Lea 9N 113
WN8: Skelm 2J 219
Hawthorn Dr. BB1: Rish 9H 121
Hawthorne Av. BB10: Reed 5G 104
FY7: Flee 4E 54
PR3: Gars 4M 59
PR4: Newt 6D 112
PR5: H Walt 5E 136
Hawthorne Caravan Pk.
LA3: Midd 8L 27
Hawthorne Cl. BB6: Langh 1D 120
BB9: Barrf 1F 104
PR6: Clay W 4D 154
PR26: Leyl 5G 153
Hawthorne Cres. L37: Form 1A 214
Hawthorne Dr. BB18: Barnw 10G 52
L33: Kirk 7L 223
PR9: Banks 4J 169
Hawthorne Gro. BB9: Barrf 8H 85
FY6: Carl 6G 63
PR9: S'port 7M 167
Hawthorne Ind. Est. BB7: Clith 2N 81
Hawthorne Lea FY5: T Clev 3J 63
Hawthorne Mdws. BB4: Craws 8M 143
Hawthorne Pl. BB7: Clith 2L 81
Hawthorne Rd. BB11: Burnl 5D 124
FY5: T Clev 3H 63
Hawthornes, The L40: Ruff 2F 190
Hawthorne Ter. BB8: Foul 2B 86
(off Skipton Old Rd.)
Hawthorn Gdns. BB5: Clay M 6N 121
Hawthorn La. OL16: Milnr 9K 205
Hawthorn Pl. OL14: Tod 1L 165
Hawthorn Rd. FY1: Blackp 3C 88
LA4: Morec 4F 22
LA5: Bolt S 3L 15
OL11: Roch 7J 203
OL13: Bac 5L 163
PR2: Ribb 7A 116
(not continuous)
Hawthorns, The BB1: Wilp 3N 119
BB4: W'foot 6D 162
(off Melbourne St.)
FY8: L Ann 7F 108
LA1: Lanc 5L 29
PR2: Fulw 3J 115
PR3: Bils 6D 68
PR3: Cab 2N 59
PR4: Woodp 8B 94
PR7: E'ton 7E 172
WN8: N 'urgh 3L 211
Hawthorns Caravan Pk. LA6: Neth K 3D 16
Hawthorn St. BB1: Blackb 9N 119
Hawthorn Wlk. OL15: Littleb 9J 185
Haydock Av. PR25: Leyl 7K 153
Haydock Gro. LA3: Heys 7L 21
Haydock La. BL7: Brom C 5G 199
Haydock Pk. Rd. L10: Aint 7D 222
Haydock Rd. LA1: Lanc 4M 29
Haydocks La. PR4: Cott 4A 114
Haydock Sq. BB6: Gt H 4J 121
Haydock St. BB1: Blackb 8M 119
BB10: Burnl 9G 104
PR5: Bam B 6A 136
Haydon Av. PR5: Lost H 9K 135
Hayes Bldgs. BB4: Rawt 5K 161
Hayes Dr. L31: Mell 7G 222
Hayfell Av. LA4: Morec 5C 22
Hayfell Cres. LA2: Hest B 8H 15
Hayfell Gro. LA2: Hest B 8H 15
Hayfield BB2: Blackb 1H 139
Hayfield Av. FY2: Blackp 9E 62
FY6: Poul F 8L 63
PR5: Hogh 7F 136
Hayfield Cl. BL8: Greenm 4E 200
PR5: Hogh 7G 136
Hayfield Rd. L39: Orms 5K 209
Hayfields BB8: Salt 5B 78
Hayfield Vw. BB18: Salt 4B 78
Hayhurst Cl. BB7: Whall 4J 101
Hayhurst Farm Ter. BB7: Clith 4M 81
Hayhurst Rd. BB7: Whall 4J 101
Hayhurst St. BB7: Clith 4M 81
Haylemere Ct. PR8: Birk 9E 166
Hayling Cl. BL8: Bury 7H 201
Hayling Pl. PR2: Ingol 5D 114
Haylot Dr. LA2: Halt 1C 24
Haylot Sq. LA1: Lanc 6E 228
Haymaker Ri. OL12: Ward 8F 184
Haymans Grn. L31: Magh 1D 222
Haymarket FY8: L Ann 2H 129
Haynes St. OL12: Roch 5C 204
Hayshaw M. PR3: Fort 2A 46
Haysworth St. PR1: Prest 1J 229 (7J 115)
Hayward Ct. L37: Form 8A 206
Hayward Gro. WN6: Stand 2N 213
Hayward St. BL8: Bury 9H 201
Haywood Cl. BB5: Acc 9A 122
PR2: Fulw 1K 115
Haywood Rd. BB5: Acc 9A 122
Hazel Av. BB3: Darw 4B 158
BB5: Clay M 7M 121
BL0: Ramsb 4G 200
BL8: Tott 8F 200
FY7: Flee 4F 54
L32: Kirk 7H 223
PR5: Bam B 7C 136
Hazel Bank BB2: Blackb 2K 139
LA3: Heys 9L 21
Hazelbank LA2: Halt 2B 24
Hazel Bus. Pk. WA11: Rain 6N 225
Hazel Cl. BB2: Blackb 4K 139
FY6: K Sea 7M 41
PR1: Penw 5E 134
PR5: Bam B 7B 136
PR6: Clay W 4E 154
Hazel Coppice PR2: Lea 6B 114
Hazel Dene BB7: West B 6L 73
Hazeldene Av. BB4: Hasl 5G 160
Hazeldene Rd. FY7: Flee 2F 54
Hazel Gro. BB1: Blackb 3E 140
BB4: Rawt 3L 161
BB5: Clay M 7M 121
BB7: Clith 4J 81
BB10: Burnl 8H 105
FY3: Blackp 5E 88
L32: Kirk 9L 223
LA1: Lanc 8H 23
OL13: Bac 4M 163
PR2: Ribb 5C 116
PR3: Longr 2K 97
PR4: Tarl 7D 150
PR5: Bam B 7B 136
PR6: Chor 3E 174
PR8: S'port 7L 167
Hazel Hall Cotts. BL0: Ramsb 4G 200
Hazel Hall La. BL0: Ramsb 4G 200
Hazelhead La. PR3: Barn 3B 60
PR3: Scor 1A 60
HAZELHURST 9G 180
Hazelhurst Cl. BL0: Ramsb 1G 200
Hazelhurst Dr. PR3: Gars 5L 59
Hazelhurst Lodge PR2: Ribb 5B 116
(off Fir Trees Pl.)
Hazelhurst Rd. PR2: Ribb 7C 116
Hazel La. WN8: Skelm 8M 211
Hazelmere Rd. PR2: Ash R 8D 114
PR2: Fulw 1G 115
Hazel M. L31: Mell 7G 222
Hazelmoor BB1: Clay D 3M 119
Hazel Mt. BL7: Eger 3E 198
Hazelmount Av. LA5: Carn 7A 12
Hazelmount Cres. LA5: Carn 7A 12
Hazelmount Dr. LA5: Carn 7A 12
Hazelrigg La. LA1: Ell 1L 37
LA2: Ell 1L 37
Hazels, The BB1: Wilp 3M 119
PR7: Copp 4A 194
HAZELSLACK 1K 5
Hazelslack Caravan Site LA7: Carr B 1J 5
Hazel St. BB5: Ris B 8F 142
BL0: Ramsb 1F 200
Hazelwood LA5: Silv 8G 5
Hazelwood Av. L40: Burs 9C 190
Hazelwood Cl. BB1: Blackb 8A 120
FY5: T Clev 1G 62
PR25: Leyl 6H 153
Hazelwood Dr. BL9: Bury 6L 201
LA4: Morec 2F 22
PR4: Hesk B 3B 150
Hazelwood Gdns. LA1: Lanc 5L 29
Hazelwood Rd. BB9: Nelson 2L 105
Hazelwood St. OL14: Tod 2L 165
Headbolt La. L33: Kirk 6K 223
PR8: Ains 9G 186
PR8: Birk 7G 187
Head Dyke La. FY6: Pree 1D 56
PR3: Pill 1D 56
Headen Av. WN5: Wigan 6L 221
Headfort Cl. FY2: Blackp 9D 62
Headingley Cl. BB5: Hunc 8E 122
Headingly Av. WN8: Skelm 2G 219
Headlands, The LA3: Heys 9J 21
Headlands St. OL12: Roch 4B 204
Headley Rd. PR25: Leyl 6H 153
Headroomgate Rd. FY8: L Ann 8F 108
Heads Holiday Home Pk., The FY6: Stal 5L 55
Heads La. BB18: Kelb 6E 78
Heald Brow BB18: Barnw 10F 52
Heald Cl. OL12: Roch 2N 203
OL13: Weir 8L 145
OL15: Littleb 2K 205
Heald Croft PR3: Gars 6A 60
Heald Dr. OL12: Roch 2N 203
Heald Ho. Rd. PR25: Leyl 8M 153
Heald La. OL13: Weir 8L 145
OL15: Littleb 2K 205
Heald Rd. BB10: Burnl 8E 104
Heald St. FY3: Blackp 4D 88
PR6: Chor 6G 174
Healdwood Cl. BB12: Burnl 7D 104
Healdwood Dr. BB12: Burnl 7D 104
HEALEY 1A 204
Healey Av. OL12: Roch 1N 203
Healey Bottoms OL12: Roch 2M 203
Healey Ct. BB11: Burnl 4B 228 (4D 124)
Healey Dell OL12: Roch 1M 203
Healey Dell Nature Reserve 1M 203
Healey Gro. OL12: Whitw 9N 183
Healey Hall M. OL12: Roch 1N 203
Healey La. OL12: Roch 1B 204
Healey Mt. BB11: Burnl 4B 228 (4D 124)
Healey Row BB11: Burnl 5C 228 (5D 124)
Healey Stones OL12: Roch 1B 204
Healey St. FY3: Blackp 4D 88
OL16: Roch 7B 204
Healey Vw. BB11: Burnl 6D 124
PR6: Chor 4G 175
Healey Wood Rd. BB11: Burnl 4C 228 (4D 124)
(not continuous)
Healey Wood Rd. Ind. Est.
BB11: Burnl 5C 228 (5E 124)
Healing St. OL11: Roch 8D 204
Heaning Av. BB1: Blackb 4D 140
BB5: Acc 9C 122
Heanor Dr. PR8: S'port 2M 187
Heap Ct. PR9: S'port 6L 167
HEAPEY 9J 155
Heapey Fold La. PR6: H Charn 7L 175
Heapey Rd. PR6: Chor, Heap 4H 175
Heapfold OL12: Roch 3M 203
Heaplands BL8: Greenm 4E 200
Heap Rd. OL12: Roch 3H 203
Heap St. BB4: Craws 8M 143
BB9: Brierf 5E 104
BB10: Burnl 9F 104
BB10: W'thorne 3M 125
Heapworth Av. BL0: Ramsb 8G 180
Heartwood Cl. BB2: Blackb 9H 119
Heasandford Ind. Est. BB10: Burnl 9H 105
(not continuous)
Heath Av. BL0: Ramsb 4G 200
Heathbourne Rd. OL13: Bac 7F 162
HEATH CHARNOCK 4H 195
Heathcliffe Ct. LA5: Arn 2E 4
Heath Cotts. BL1: Bolt 7D 198
Heather Bank BB4: Rawt 6L 161
BB11: Burnl 5A 124
BL8: Tott 6D 200
OL14: Wals 6K 165
OL15: Littleb 8N 185
Heather Brow BB18: Earl 2G 78
Heather Cl. BB4: Hasl 7F 160
BB9: Brierf 5H 105
BL6: Hor 9C 196
FY5: T Clev 2H 63
L33: Kirk 6K 223
(off Heathfield Dr.)
L37: Form 7B 206
L40: Burs 9C 190
PR6: Chor 6G 175
PR8: Ains 2D 206
Heatherfield BL1: Bolt 8C 198
(not continuous)
BL7: Edgw 8L 179
Heatherfield Pl. PR2: Ash R 8G 114
Heather Gro. PR2: Ribb 6A 116
Heatherlands BB4: Hasl 9F 160
OL12: Whitw 2A 184
Heatherlea Cl. WN8: Uph 4F 220
Heather Lea Dr. PR6: Birns 7A 156
Heatherlea Rd. BB12: Fence 2B 104
Heatherleigh PR26: Leyl 4G 153
Heatherleigh Gdns. BB2: Blackb 1L 157
Heather Pl. FY1: Blackp 5N 227 (7D 88)
Heathers, The FY6: Pree 8M 41
PR5: Bam B 3E 154
Heatherside Rd. BL0: Ramsb 7G 181
Heatherway PR2: Fulw 4A 116
Heatherways L37: Form 6A 206
Heathey La. L39: Hals, S'port 5N 187
Heathfield BL2: Bolt 9M 199
L40: Burs 9D 190
PR6: H Charn 4H 195
Heathfield Av. OL13: Bac 7G 162
Heathfield Cl. L37: Form 6A 206
Heathfield Dr. L33: Kirk 6K 223
PR2: Ribb 5A 116
Heathfield Pk. BB2: Blackb 2G 139
Heathfield Rd. FY7: Flee 2E 54
L31: Magh 3E 222
OL13: Bac 7G 162
PR8: Ains 7E 186
Heathfield Road Stop (Tram) 3F 54
Heathfoot Av. LA3: Heys 1K 27
Heathfoot Dr. LA3: Heys 1K 27
Heathgate BB12: Fence 2B 104
WN8: Skelm 1N 219
Heath Gro. LA3: Heys 1K 27
Heath Hill Dr. OL13: Bac 7G 162
Heathland WN8: Uph 4E 220
Heathlea Cl. BL1: Bolt 7E 198
Heath Rd. OL12: Ward 8F 184
Heathrow Pl. PR7: Chor 7C 174
Heath St. BB10: Burnl 1F 124
OL11: Roch 7A 204
Heathway PR2: Fulw 3J 115
Heathway Av. FY3: Blackp 4E 88
Heathy La. L39: Bart 4G 207
Heatley Cl. BB2: Blackb 7A 226 (5L 139)
Heatley Rd. OL16: Roch 7G 205
Heatley St. PR1: Prest 5J 229 (1H 135)
HEATON 2C 28
Heaton Av. BL2: Bolt 8L 199
Heaton Bottom Rd. LA3: Heat 3C 28
Heaton Cl. FY5: T Clev 3J 63
FY6: Carl 6J 63
L40: Burs 9B 190
LA3: Morec 5E 22
PR5: Walt D 4N 135
WN8: Uph 4D 220
Heaton Ct. L40: Scar 1H 209
Heaton Ho. LA1: Lanc 2K 29
(off Heaton Rd.)
Heaton Mt. Av. PR2: Fulw 2J 115
Heaton Pl. PR1: Prest 8A 116
Heaton Rd. FY8: L Ann 9G 109
LA1: Lanc 2K 29
HEATON'S BRIDGE 9H 189
Heatons Bri. Rd. L40: Scar 9H 189
Heaton St. BB2: Blackb 5C 226 (4M 139)
OL16: Milnr 8K 205
PR25: Leyl 5H 153
Heaviley Gro. BL6: Hor 8B 196
Hebble Butt Cl. OL16: Milnr 7H 205
Hebble Cl. BL2: Bolt 8H 199
Hebburn Dr. BL8: Bury 8H 201
Hebden Av. FY1: Blackp 9M 227 (9D 88)
Heber Dr. BD23: Eas M 7J 53
Heber St. BB11: Dunn 4N 143
Hebrew Rd. BB10: Burnl 1E 124
(Birley Pl.)
BB10: Burnl 1E 124
(Thursby Sq.)
Hebrew Sq. BB10: Burnl 1E 124
Heckenhurst Av. BB10: Burnl 3K 125
Hector Av. OL16: Roch 5E 204
Hector Rd. BB3: Darw 2M 157
WN5: Wigan 2N 221
Hedge Row PR4: W Grn 6G 111
Hedgerow, The BB2: Blackb 9H 119
Hedgerow Gdns. WN6: Stand 3N 213
Hedgerows, The OL12: Whitw 5N 183
Hedgerows Rd. PR26: Leyl 7C 152
Heeley Rd. FY8: L Ann 9D 108
Height Barn La. OL13: Bac 7K 163
Height Cft. BB9: Brierf 5J 105
HEIGHT END 4J 161
Height La. PR3: Chip 7D 70
Heights Av. OL12: Roch 3B 204
Heights Cl. OL12: Roch 3B 204
Heights Cotts. BB5: Acc 4E 142
Heights Ct. OL12: Roch 4B 204
Heightside Av. BB4: Newc 5C 162
Height Side La. BB4: Craws, Rawt 9N 143
Heightside M. BB4: Newc 5C 162
Heightside Vs. OL13: Bac 2N 163
Heights La. OL12: Roch 3B 204
Heights Rd. BB9: Nelson 4H 105
BB12: Fence 1A 104
Heirs Ho. La. BB8: Colne 6N 85
Helena St. BB10: Burnl 3G 228 (4F 124)
Helen Bank Dr. WA11: Rain 2K 225
Helens Cl. FY4: Blackp 4D 108
Helio Fitness 5E 88
Helks Brow LA2: Wray 3J 33
HELLIFIELD 1D 52
Hellifield PR2: Fulw 2H 115
HELLIFIELD GREEN 1D 52
Hellifield Rd. BB7: Bolt B 8K 51
BB7: Gis 9B 52
BD23: Garg 3L 53
Helm Cl. BB11: Burnl 7B 124
HELMCROFT 6F 160
Helmcroft BB4: Hasl 6F 160
Helmcroft Ct. BB4: Hasl 6G 160
Helmn Way BB9: Nelson 9K 85
Helmsdale WN8: Skelm 1N 219
Helmsdale Cl. BL0: Ramsb 2F 200
Helmsdale Rd. BB9: Nelson 1L 105
FY4: Blackp 2F 108
HELMSHORE 8F 160
Helmshore Mills Textile Mus. 7E 160

Highfield Rd.—Holland Ho.

Highfield Rd. BB7: Clith .4L 81
BB18: Earl .2E 78
BL0: Eden .4J 181
FY4: Blackp .3C 108
L39: Orms .5K 209
LA5: Carn .9B 12
OL11: Roch .4J 203
OL16: Milnr .7K 205
PR6: Adl .5J 195
PR9: S'port .3A 168
PR26: Cros .4N 171
Highfield Rd. Nth. PR6: Adl .5J 195
PR7: Chor .4E 174
Highfield Rd. Sth. PR7: Chor .5E 174
Highfield St. BB3: Darw .7B 158
BB4: Hasl .5F 160
Highfield Ter. LA2: L Ben .6K 19
(off Hillside Rd.)
High Fold BB18: Kelb .6D 78
BD20: Loth .3N 79
Highgale Gdns. PR5: Lost H .9M 135
High Gate FY7: Flee .1D 54
PR4: Tarl .7D 150
Highgate BB9: Nelson .3H 105
FY4: Blackp .4D 108
PR1: Penw .3E 134
PR3: Goos .4N 95
Highgate Av. PR2: Fulw .5H 115
Highgate Cl. PR2: Fulw .5J 115
PR4: Newt .6D 112
Highgate Cres. WN6: App B .5H 213
Highgate La. FY6: Stal .5M 55
OL12: Whitw .8N 183
PR4: Wart .2K 131
Highgate Pl. FY8: L Ann .2K 129
Highgate Rd. L31: Lyd .8C 216
WN8: Uph .4E 220
High Green PR25: Leyl .6J 153
Highgrove Av. PR7: Hesk .1J 193
Highgrove Cl. BL1: Bolt .9F 198
LA4: Morec .4A 22
Highgrove Ct. PR26: Leyl .6C 152
Highgrove Ho. PR7: Chor .4E 174
Highgrove Rd. LA1: Lanc .3K 29
HIGH HALSTEAD .2N 125
High Hill Gro. BD24: Sett .3N 35
(off High Hill Gro. St.)
High Hill Gro. St. BD24: Sett .3N 35
High Houses BL1: Bolt .7D 198
High Knott Rd. LA5: Arn .2F 4
Highland Av. PR1: Penw .4E 134
Highland Brow LA2: Gal .1L 37
Highland Dr. PR7: Buck V .9A 154
Highland Lodge WN6: Stand .4N 213
Highland Rd. BL7: Brom C .5H 199
Highlands OL15: Littleb .2K 205
Highlands Rd. OL11: Roch .8J 203
High La. BB18: Salt .6N 77
L39: Bick .4N 217
L40: Burs .5M 209
PR26: Cros .7J 171
High Lea PR6: Adl .6J 195
High Leigh FY8: L Ann .5J 129
High Level Rd. OL11: Roch .7C 204
High Mdw. PR5: Walt D .6L 135
Highmeadow WN8: Uph .4D 220
High Mdws. BL7: Brom C .5H 199
High Mill BD23: Garg .3L 53
HIGH MOOR .9C 192
Highmoor BB7: Clith .3M 81
BB9: Nelson .4K 105
High Moorgate LA6: Kear .4E 8
High Moor La. WN6: Wrigh .9C 192
Highmoor Pk. BB7: Clith .3M 81
High Moss L39: Orms .9J 209
Highmount Ct. LA1: Lanc .8B 228
Highmount Ho. LA1: Lanc .8B 228
HIGH PARK .6N 167
High Pk. WN6: Shev .6M 213
High Pk. Pl. PR9: S'port .6N 167
High Pk. Rd. PR9: S'port .6N 167
High Peak Rd. OL12: Whitw .8N 183
Highrigg Dr. PR3: Brou .9J 95
High Rd. LA2: Halt .2B 24
LA2: Tat .9J 19
LA6: Midd .1G 9
Highsands Av. L40: Ruff .2E 190
Highsted Gro. L33: Kirk .5K 223
High St. BB1: Blackb .4D 226 (3M 139)
BB1: Rish .8H 121
BB3: Darw .6A 158
BB4: Hasl .3G 161
BB5: Acc .4A 142
BB5: Osw .5M 141
BB7: Clith .3H 81
BB8: Colne .6B 86
BB9: Brierf .5F 104
BB9: Nelson .3H 105
BB12: Padi .9J 103
BD23: Garg .3M 53
BD24: Sett .3N 35
BL6: Hor .9C 196
BL7: Belm .9K 177
BL7: Turt .1J 199
BL8: Bury .9E 200
FY1: Blackp .4B 88
FY7: Flee .9H 41
L40: Mawd .4M 191
LA1: Lanc .7C 228 (9J 23)
LA6: Bur L .3K 19
OL12: Roch .5C 204
OL14: Tod .4K 165
(off Littleholme St.)
OL15: Littleb .9J 185
PR3: Gars .5N 59
PR3: Gt E .6N 65
PR4: Elsw .1L 91
PR7: Chor .6E 174
WN8: Skelm .3H 219
High Tide Organ .2A 108
HIGHTOWN .7A 214
Hightown BB4: Lumb .3C 162
Hightown Rd. BB4: Lumb .3C 162
Hightown Station (Rail) .7A 214
High Vw. St. BL1: Bolt .7E 198
High Wardle La. OL12: Ward .6D 184
Highway BD24: Sett .2N 35
Highways Av. PR7: Eux .5N 173
Highwood OL11: Roch .4J 203
Highwood Ct. L33: Kirk .6L 223
Highwoods Pk. BB6: Old L .5B 100
Higson St. BB2: Blackb .3A 226 (3L 139)
Hilary St. BB10: Burnl .9E 104
Hilbre Cl. PR9: S'port .5M 167
Hilbre Dr. PR9: S'port .5M 167
Hilda Av. BL8: Tott .7E 200
HILDERSTONE .5E 6
Hilderstone La.
LA5: Burt K, Yea R .7E 6
Hildrop Rd. BB9: Nelson .1K 105
Hilgay Cl. WN3: Wins .8N 221
Hillam La. LA2: C'ham .8D 36
Hillary Av. FY2: Blackp .6C 62
WN5: Wigan .6N 221
Hillary Cres. L31: Magh .1C 222
Hillbrook Grn. PR25: Leyl .5J 153
Hillbrook Rd. PR25: Leyl .5J 153
Hill Cl. WN6: App B .5H 213
Hill Cot Rd. BL1: Bolt .8F 198
Hill Cres. PR4: Newt .7E 112
Hill Crest OL13: Bac .6H 163
Hillcrest L31: Magh .1E 222
WN8: Skelm .4M 219
Hill Crest Av. BB10: Burnl .5K 125
Hillcrest Av. LA5: Bolt S .4L 15
PR2: Fulw .1H 115
PR2: Ingol .5D 114
PR3: Longr .3J 97
Hillcrest Cl. PR4: Tarl .7E 150
Hillcrest Dr. L40: Scar .5E 188
LA7: Slack H .1N 5
PR3: Longr .3J 97
PR4: Tarl .8E 150
Hillcrest Rd. BB2: Blackb .6G 139
BB6: Langh .1C 120
FY4: Blackp .5B 108
L39: Orms .6K 209
Hill Cft. PR4: K'ham .4N 111
PR6: Clay W .5C 154
Hillcroft LA2: H Ben .7L 19
(off Wenning Av.)
PR2: Fulw .2F 114
HILL DALE .8A 192
Hilldean WN8: Uph .3F 220
Hill End BB8: Traw .9F 86
Hill End La. BB4: Rawt .6A 162
Hill Fld. Cft. PR3: Cab .3N 59
Hill Ho. Fold La. WN6: Wrigh .8F 192
Hill Ho. La. WN6: Wrigh .6E 192
Hillhouse La. PR6: Brind .8J 137
Hillhouses BB3: Darw .7A 158
Hillingdon Rd. BB10: Burnl .7H 105
Hillingdon Rd. Nth. BB10: Burnl .6G 105
Hillkirk Dr. OL12: Roch .2N 203
Hill La. BB7: Hurst G .10M 71
BB8: Colne .5E 86
LA6: Neth K .5C 16
Hillmount Av. LA3: Heys .8L 21
Hillock, The BL2: Bolt .8K 199
Hillock Cl. L40: Scar .6F 188
Hillock La. L40: Scar .6F 188
PR4: Frec, Wart .1J 131
WN8: Dalt .6N 211
Hillocks, The PR26: Cros .5M 171
HILLOCK VALE .9D 122
Hillpark Av. PR2: Fulw .5G 114
PR5: Hogh .7F 136
Hill Pl. BB9: Nelson .4H 105
OL14: Tod .4K 165
Hillridge Rd. WN5: Wigan .1M 221
Hill Ri. BB4: Hasl .6H 161
BL0: Ramsb .1F 200
Hill Ri. Vw. L39: Aug .2F 216
Hill Rd. LA1: Lanc .5K 23
PR1: Penw .3F 134
PR25: Leyl .6M 153
Hill Rd. Sth. PR1: Penw .5F 134
Hills, The PR2: Ribb .2D 116
Hillsborough Av. BB9: Brierf .5H 105
Hills Ct. BL8: Bury .9G 201
LA1: Lanc .7K 23
Hillsea Av. LA3: Heys .8L 21
HILLSIDE .4E 186
Hillside BB11: Burnl .6B 124
LA1: Lanc .6B 228 (8J 23)
LA6: Holme .1G 6
PR4: Tarl .9E 150
Hillside Av. BB1: Blackb .4C 140
BB3: Darw .7A 158
BB10: Reed .6G 104
BL6: Hor .9D 196
BL7: Brom C .4H 199
FY6: Pree .9A 42
L39: Orms .8J 209
PR2: Fulw .5G 114
PR4: K'ham .4A 112
PR26: Far M .9J 135
WN8: Parb .8A 192
Hillside Cl. BB1: Blackb .4C 140
BB4: Craws .7M 143
BB6: Gt H .3J 121
BB7: Clith .5L 81
BB9: Brierf .5G 105
BB11: Burnl .6B 124
BL2: Bolt .8L 199
FY3: Blackp .4E 88
FY5: T Clev .3K 63
PR7: Eux .5M 173
WN3: Wins .8N 221
Hillside Cres. BL6: Hor .9D 196
BL9: Bury .7L 201
OL13: Weir .9K 145
PR6: Whit W .6E 154
Hillside Dr. BB4: Newc .5C 162
BB7: West B .6L 73
FY6: Stal .5B 56
Hillside Gdns. BB3: Darw .7A 158
BL9: Summ .3H 201
Hillside Golf Links .4E 186
Hillside Rd. BB4: Hasl .5G 161
BL0: Ramsb .9F 180
LA2: L Ben .6K 19
Hillside Rd. PR1: Prest .2M 135
PR8: Birk .4E 186
Hillside Station (Rail) .4E 186
Hillside Vw. BB9: Brierf .5G 105
OL16: Milnr .7K 205
Hillside Wlk. BB1: Blackb .4C 140
OL12: Roch .1A 204
Hillside Way OL12: Whitw .5N 183
Hillstone Av. OL12: Roch .1N 203
Hillstone Cl. BL8: Greenm .3E 200
Hill St. BB1: Blackb .2B 140
BB4: Craws .9M 143
BB5: Acc .3B 142
BB5: Bax .6C 142
BB5: Chur .3K 141
BB5: Clay M .8N 121
BB8: Colne .7A 86
BB9: Brierf .4D 104
(Montford Rd.)
BB9: Brierf .5F 104
(Wood St.)
BB12: Padi .1H 123
BB18: Barnw .2N 77
BL8: Bury .9E 200
BL9: Summ .2H 201
FY4: Blackp .9B 88
LA5: Carn .9A 12
OL14: Tod .1N 165
OL16: Roch .6D 204
PR1: Prest .5J 229 (9J 115)
PR9: S'port .7H 167
Hillsview Rd. PR8: Ains .9C 186
Hillsyde PR6: Whit W .7E 154
HILL TOP .9E 86
Hill Top BB8: Foul .1N 85
BB8: Wine .7F 86
BB9: Barrf .7H 85
OL12: Whitw .9N 183
PR4: New L .1D 152
Hill Top Cl. LA5: Yea R .7B 6
PR4: Frec .1B 132
Hilltop Dr. BB4: Hasl .8H 161
BL8: Tott .7D 200
Hill Top La. BB18: Earl .2D 78
PR6: Whit W .7E 154
Hill Top Rd. WA11: Rain .8M 225
Hilltop Wlk. L39: Orms .9H 209
Hill Vw. BB1: Blackb .8M 119
BB4: Rawt .6L 161
OL15: Littleb .5N 185
Hill Vw. Ct. BL1: Bolt .9E 198
Hill Vw. Dr. PR7: Copp .5N 193
Hill Vw. Rd. BL1: Bolt .9E 198
PR3: Gars .3N 59
Hillview Rd. PR4: Wesh .3M 111
Hill Wlk. PR25: Leyl .5K 153
Hilly Cft. BL7: Brom C .5F 198
Hillylaid Rd. FY5: T Clev .1J 63
Hilmarton Cl. BL2: Bolt .8L 199
Hilmore Way LA4: Morec .3A 22
Hilstone La. FY2: Blackp .1D 88
Hilton Av. BL6: Hor .9B 196
FY1: Blackp .9J 227 (9B 88)
FY8: L Ann .2J 129
Hilton Ct. FY8: L Ann .3E 128
Hilton Rd. BB3: Darw .7B 158
Hilton's Brow PR6: Brind .3K 155
Hilton St. BB3: Darw .7A 158
BL9: Bury .9L 201
Hinchley Grn. L31: Magh .1A 222
Hindburn Av. L31: Magh .9E 216
Hindburn Cl. LA5: Carn .8C 12
Hindburn Pl. LA1: Lanc .6J 23
Hinde St. LA1: Lanc .7L 23
Hindle Ct. BB3: Darw .5A 158
Hindle Fold La. BB6: Gt H .2J 121
Hindle St. BB3: Darw .5M 157
BB4: Hasl .4G 160
BB5: Acc .2A 142
OL13: Bac .7H 163
Hindley Beech L31: Magh .9B 216
Hindley Cl. PR2: Fulw .2M 115
Hindley Ct. BB9: Barrf .1G 104
Hindley Ho. PR2: Fulw .3M 115
Hindley St. PR7: Chor .8D 174
Hind Rd. WN5: Wigan .3N 221
Hind's Head Av. WN6: Wrigh .7J 193
Hind St. BB10: Burnl .8F 104
PR1: Prest .8G 229 (2H 135)
Hinton OL12: Roch .5C 204
Hinton Cl. OL11: Roch .7J 203
Hinton St. BB10: Burnl .4F 124
Hippings La. BB4: W'foot .6D 162
Hippings Va. BB5: Osw .4K 141
(off Kay St.)
Hippings Way BB7: Clith .1L 81
Hippodrome, The
Todmorden .2L 165
Hirst Gdns. BB11: Burnl .5F 124
(not continuous)
Hirst St. BB12: Padi .9H 103
OL14: Tod .7E 146
HMP Buckley Hall OL12: Roch .2D 204
HMP Garth PR26: Leyl .9A 152
HMP Kennet L31: Magh .9H 217
HMP Kirkham PR4: K'ham .6M 111
HMP Preston PR1: Prest .4N 229 (9L 115)
HMP Wymott PR26: Leyl .9C 152
HMYOI Lancaster Farms
LA1: Lanc .7A 24
Hoarstones Av. BB12: Fence .3B 104
Hobart Dr. L33: Kirk .4K 223
Hobart Pl. FY5: T Clev .3F 62
Hobart St. BB11: Burnl .1F 228 (3F 124)
Hobberley Dr. WN8: Skelm .3B 220
Hobbs La. PR3: Clau .7J 61
Hobcross La. L40: Lath .3E 210
Hob Grn. BB2: Mellor .7G 118
Hob La. BL7: Edgw .7J 179
Hobson's La. LA6: Cap .6J 13
Hobson St. BB4: Rawt .4L 161
Hockley Pl. FY3: Blackp .3F 88
Hodder Av. FY1: Blackp .9M 227 (9D 88)
FY7: Flee .2C 54
L31: Magh .9E 216
LA3: Morec .5F 22
Hodder Av. OL15: Littleb .8J 185
PR7: Chor .9D 174
Hodder Brook PR2: Ribb .6C 116
Hodder Cl. FY7: Flee .2C 54
PR5: Bam B .8B 136
WN5: Wigan .4N 221
Hodder Ct. BB7: S'hurst .7C 80
Hodder Dr. BB7: West B .5K 73
FY8: L Ann .1J 129
Hodder Gro. BB3: Darw .3M 157
BB7: Clith .4J 81
Hodder Pl. BB1: Blackb .1E 226 (2N 139)
LA1: Lanc .2M 29
Hodder St. BB1: Blackb .1D 226 (2N 139)
BB5: Acc .2C 142
BB10: Burnl .7G 104
PR3: Longr .3K 97
Hodder Way FY6: Poul F .9K 63
HODDLESDEN .6F 158
Hoddlesden Fold BB3: Hodd .6F 158
Hoddlesden Rd. BB3: Hodd .6E 158
Hodge Bank Bus. Pk. BB9: Nelson .9H 85
Hodge Brow BL6: R'ton .1A 196
Hodge La. BB18: Barnw .4M 77
Hodge St. PR8: S'port .7H 167
Hodgson Av. PR4: Frec .3M 131
Hodgson Pl. FY6: Poul F .9K 63
Hodgson Rd. FY1: Blackp .1C 88
Hodgsons Bldgs. BB4: W'foot .8D 162
Hodgson St. BB3: Darw .6B 158
BB5: Osw .4L 141
Hodson St. PR5: Bam B .7A 136
PR8: S'port .8J 167
Hogarth Av. BB11: Burnl .6C 124
Hogarth Cres. PR4: Wharl .6D 92
Hogg's La. PR7: Chor .9G 174
HOGHTON .6K 137
Hoghton Av. OL13: Bac .6L 163
HOGHTON BOTTOMS .6A 138
Hoghton Cl. FY8: L Ann .7F 108
LA1: Lanc .1H 29
Hoghton Gro. PR9: S'port .6J 167
Hoghton La. PR5: H Walt, Hogh .5E 136
Hoghton Pl. PR9: S'port .7H 167
Hoghton Rd. PR3: Longr .3K 97
PR25: Leyl .6G 152
Hoghton St. PR9: S'port .7H 167
Hoghton Tower .7N 137
Hoghton Vw. PR1: Prest .2M 135
Holbeach Cl. BL8: Bury .8J 201
Holbeck Av. FY4: Blackp .1F 108
LA4: Morec .4F 22
OL12: Roch .1A 204
Holbeck St. BB10: Burnl .9E 104
(not continuous)
Holborn Dr. L39: Orms .9H 209
Holborn Gdns. OL11: Roch .8A 204
Holborn Hill L39: Orms .9H 209
Holborn Sq. OL11: Roch .8A 204
Holborn St. OL11: Roch .8A 204
HOLCOMBE .8F 180
HOLCOMBE BROOK .3F 200
Holcombe Brook BL0: Ramsb .2E 200
(off Redisher Cft.)
Holcombe Brook Sports Club .2E 200
Holcombe Ct. BL0: Ramsb .3F 200
Holcombe Dr. BB10: Burnl .1G 228 (3F 124)
Holcombe Gro. PR6: Chor .5G 175
Holcombe Lee BL0: Ramsb .1F 200
Holcombe M. BL0: Ramsb .2E 200
Holcombe Old Rd. BL8: Holc .2E 200
Holcombe Pct. BL0: Ramsb .2E 200
Holcombe Rd. BB4: Hasl .6D 160
BL8: Ramsb, Tott .6E 200
FY2: Blackp .1E 88
Holcombe Village BL8: Holc .8F 180
Holcroft Pl. FY8: L Ann .4M 129
HOLDEN .8J 51
Holden Av. BL0: Ramsb .9F 180
BL1: Bolt .7E 198
BL9: Bury .9C 202
Holden Cl. BB9: Barrf .1G 105
Holden Fold BB3: Darw .4B 158
Holden La. BB7: Bolt B, Slaid .5G 51
Holden Pl. BB4: Hasl .6E 160
Holden Rd. BB9: Brierf .5E 104
BB10: Reed .7F 104
Holden St. BB1: Belt .1F 158
BB2: Blackb .4K 139
BB5: Acc .3A 142
BB7: Clith .3M 81
BB11: Burnl .2C 228 (3D 124)
OL12: Roch .3D 204
PR7: Adl .6H 195
HOLDEN VALE .3G 160
Holden Wlk. WN5: Wigan .6N 221
Holden Way LA1: Lanc .2K 29
HOLDEN WOOD .6E 160
Holden Wood Dr. BB4: Hasl .6E 160
Holderness St. OL14: Tod .2M 165
HOLE BOTTOM .9L 147
Hole Bottom Rd. OL14: Tod .1L 165
HOLE HOUSE .2C 140
Hole Ho. La. BB7: Slaid .1E 50
Hole Ho. St. BB1: Blackb .3C 140
Holford Wlk. OL16: Roch .6G 205
Holgate FY4: Blackp .3F 108
Holgate Dr. WN5: Orr .5H 221
Holgates Holiday Pk. LA5: Silv .6F 4
Holgate St. BB6: Gt H .4J 121
BB10: Brierc .7K 105
Holhouse La. BL8: Greenm .3E 200
HOLIDAY MOSS .4M 225
Holkar Mdws. BL7: Brom C .5H 199
Holker Bus. Cen. BB8: Colne .7M 85
Holker Cl. LA1: Lanc .1H 29
PR5: Hogh .5G 136
Holker La. PR26: Leyl .2C 172
Holker St. BB3: Darw .7B 158
BB8: Colne .7M 85
Holland Av. BB4: Rawt .3L 161
PR5: Walt D .6A 136
Holland Bus. Pk. L40: Lath .8G 211
Holland Cl. PR8: S'port .8J 167
Holland Ct. WN8: Skelm .9A 220
Holland Ho. WN8: Uph .5F 220

Holland Ho. Ct.—Horwich

Holland Ho. Ct. PR5: Walt D . . . 5A 136
Holland Ho. Rd. PR5: Walt D . . . 5N 135
Holland Ho. Way PR7: Buck V . . . 1A 174
HOLLAND LEES . . . 7F 212
Holland Lodge PR2: Ribb . . . 5B 116
(off Grange Av.)
HOLLAND MOOR . . . 4B 220
Holland Moss WN8: Skelm . . . 6L 219
Holland Pl. BB9: Nelson . . . 9J 85
Holland Ri. OL12: Roch . . . 5B 204
Holland Rd. PR2: Ash R . . . 8F 114
HOLLAND SLACK . . . 5A 136
Holland's La. WN8: Skelm . . . 1E 218
Holland St. BB1: Blackb . . . 2B 226 (2L 139)
BB5: Acc . . . 3M 141
BB12: Padi . . . 1G 123
BL1: Bolt . . . 9F 198
OL12: Roch . . . 6B 204
OL16: Roch . . . 1G 205
Holliers Cl. L31: Magh . . . 1C 222
Hollies, The L39: Aug . . . 8F 208
PR8: S'port . . . 8F 166
(off Beechfield Gdns.)
Hollies Cl. BB2: Blackb . . . 8G 138
PR3: Catt . . . 1A 68
Hollies Rd. BB1: Wilp . . . 2A 120
HOLLIN BANK . . . 9A 226 (6L 139)
Hollin Bank BB9: Brierf . . . 4F 104
Hollin Bank Ct. BB2: Blackb . . . 7L 139
Hollin Bank M. BB4: Hasl . . . 8E 160
Hollin Bri. St. BB2: Blackb . . . 9A 226 (6K 139)
Hollin Cl. BB4: Lumb . . . 3D 162
(off Foxhill Dr.)
Hollin Fold BB9: Blacko . . . 3H 85
Hollinghurst Rd. L33: Kirk . . . 5L 223
Hollingreave Dr. BB4: Rawt . . . 2M 161
Hollingreave Rd. BB11: Burnl . . . 5E 228 (5E 124)
Hollin Gro. BB4: Rawt . . . 3M 161
Hollings PR4: New L . . . 9C 134
Hollington St. BB8: Colne . . . 6E 86
Hollington Way WN3: Wins . . . 9M 221
HOLLINGWORTH . . . 2K 205
Hollingworth Ct. OL15: Littleb . . . 9K 185
(off Stubley Mill Rd.)
Hollingworth Fold OL15: Littleb . . . 3M 205
Hollingworth Lake Caravan Pk.
OL15: Littleb . . . 4L 205
Hollingworth Lake Country Pk. . . . 3L 205
Hollingworth Lake Nature Reserve . . . 3L 205
Hollingworth Lake Sailing Club . . . 3K 205
Hollingworth Lake Vis. Cen. . . . 2L 205
Hollingworth Lake Water Activity Cen. . . . 2K 205
Hollingworth La. OL14: Wals . . . 7L 165
Hollingworth Rd. OL15: Littleb . . . 1L 205
HOLLIN HALL . . . 1F 106
Hollinhead Cres. PR2: Ingol . . . 5E 114
Hollinhey Cl. L30: N'ton . . . 5A 222
Hollin Hill BB11: Burnl . . . 6F 124
Hollinhurst Av. PR1: Penw . . . 2F 134
Hollinhurst Brow LA2: Wray, Low . . . 3J 33
Hollinhurst Ct. PR1: Penw . . . 2F 134
Hollinhurst Vw. BB12: High . . . 5L 103
(off Halmote Av.)
Hollin La. BB4: Rawt . . . 3M 161
OL11: Roch . . . 7J 203
PR6: Heap . . . 4L 175
Hollin Mill St. BB9: Brierf . . . 4F 104
HOLLINS . . . 3N 157
Hollins, The OL14: Tod . . . 1L 165
Hollins Av. BB10: Burnl . . . 5K 125
Hollins Cl. BB5: Acc . . . 4B 142
PR5: Hogh . . . 5L 137
Hollins Ct. BB18: Barnw . . . 1M 77
(off Hollins Rd.)
Hollins Farm Camp Site LA5: Arn . . . 5E 4
Hollins Grn. OL14: Tod . . . 3F 164
HOLLINS GROVE . . . 4N 157
Hollins Gro. PR2: Fulw . . . 6E 114
Hollins Gro. St. BB3: Darw . . . 4N 157
Hollinshead Ct. FY8: L Ann . . . 4G 129
Hollinshead St. PR7: Chor . . . 6E 174
Hollinshead Ter. BB3: Tock . . . 8J 157
Hollins Hill PR3: Fort . . . 3N 45
HOLLINS LANE . . . 2A 46
Hollins La. BB5: Acc . . . 4B 142
BB7: Saw . . . 1H 75
BL0: Ramsb . . . 5K 181
LA5: Arn . . . 2G 4
LA5: Silv . . . 1G 11
PR3: Fort . . . 4N 45
PR26: Leyl . . . 1F 172
Hollins Mdw. OL14: Wals . . . 6K 165
Hollins Pl. OL14: Wals . . . 6K 165
Hollins Rd. BB3: Darw . . . 3M 157
BB9: Nelson . . . 9L 85
BB18: Barnw . . . 2L 77
OL14: Wals . . . 5K 165
PR1: Prest . . . 6L 115
Hollins St. OL14: Wals . . . 7L 165
Hollin St. BB2: Blackb . . . 9A 226 (6K 139)
Hollin Street Project, The
BB2: Blackb . . . 8A 226
Hollinview Cl. BB4: Rawt . . . 2M 161
Hollin Way BB4: Rawt . . . 1M 161
(not continuous)
Hollinwood Dr. BB4: Rawt . . . 2M 161
Hollowbrook Way OL12: Roch . . . 3A 204
Hollow Fld. OL11: Roch . . . 4H 203
Hollowford La. L40: Lath . . . 1G 210
Hollowforth La. PR4: Woodp . . . 6B 94
Hollowhead Av. BB1: Wilp . . . 4N 119
Hollowhead Cl. BB1: Wilp . . . 4A 120
Hollowhead La. BB1: Blackb, Wilp . . . 4N 119
Hollowrayne LA6: Burt K . . . 5H 7
Hollows Farm Av. OL12: Roch . . . 3A 204
Hollowspell OL12: Roch . . . 2F 204
Hollsworth Ct. FY1: Blackp . . . 7N 227 (8D 88)
Holly Av. BB4: Hasl . . . 6H 161
Holly Bank BB5: Acc . . . 4B 142
BL7: Turt . . . 7H 179
LA5: Wart . . . 5A 12
Hollybank PR2: Fulw . . . 4F 114
Hollybank Cl. PR2: Ingol . . . 4C 114
Hollybrook Rd. PR8: S'port . . . 9G 166
Holly Cl. FY5: T Clev . . . 9J 55
L40: W'head . . . 8C 210
Holly Cl. PR6: Clay W . . . 5D 154
WN8: Skelm . . . 2J 219
Holly Ct. BB1: Blackb . . . 1N 139
Holly Cres. PR7: Copp . . . 3A 194
WA11: Rain . . . 4L 225
Holly Fold La. L39: Bick . . . 8J 219
WA11: Bick . . . 8J 219
Holly Gro. PR3: Longr . . . 2J 97
PR4: Tarl . . . 8E 150
PR9: Banks . . . 2F 168
Holly Ho. BB11: Burnl . . . 4F 228
Holly La. L39: Aug . . . 8G 208
L39: Bick . . . 7H 219
L40: Ruff . . . 2G 190
Holly M. FY8: L Ann . . . 7F 108
Holly Mill Cres. BL1: Bolt . . . 9F 198
Holly Mt. BB4: Hasl . . . 8F 160
Holly Mt. La. BL8: Greenm . . . 4C 200
Holly Mt. Way BB4: Rawt . . . 5M 161
Holly Pl. PR5: Bam B . . . 9D 136
Holly Rd. FY1: Blackp . . . 1C 88
FY5: T Clev . . . 9H 55
Holly St. BB1: Blackb . . . 1N 139
BB5: Osw . . . 4K 141
BB9: Nelson . . . 2K 105
BB10: Burnl . . . 4F 124
BL1: Bolt . . . 9F 198
BL8: Tott . . . 7E 200
BL9: Summ . . . 2H 201
OL12: Ward . . . 8F 184
Holly Ter. BB1: Blackb . . . 9N 119
Holly Tree Cl. BB3: Darw . . . 1A 178
BB4: Rawt . . . 2L 161
Holly Tree Way BB2: Blackb . . . 8G 138
Holly Wlk. LA1: Lanc . . . 8H 23
(off Sycamore Gro.)
Hollywood Av. FY3: Blackp . . . 5E 88
PR1: Penw . . . 5F 134
Hollywood Gro. FY7: Flee . . . 9F 40
Holman St. PR1: Prest . . . 8M 115
Holmbrook Cl. BB2: Blackb . . . 8N 139
Holmby St. BB10: Burnl . . . 8F 104
Holmdale Av. PR9: S'port . . . 2A 168
HOLME . . . 1F 6
Holme, The BB4: Rawt . . . 6K 161
PR3: Cald V . . . 4H 61
Holme Av. BL8: Bury . . . 7H 201
FY7: Flee . . . 4D 54
Holme Bank BB4: Rawt . . . 6L 161
Holme Bank M. BB9: Nelson . . . 9K 85
HOLME CHAPEL . . . 2L 145
Holme Cl. BB18: Sough . . . 4D 78
PR3: Pill . . . 8G 42
Holme Cotts. BB4: W'foot . . . 8D 162
Holme Cres. BB8: Traw . . . 8E 86
Holme End BB12: Reed . . . 6D 104
Holmefield BB4: Rawt . . . 4M 161
(off Burnley Rd.)
LA6: Holme . . . 2G 6
Holmefield Av. FY5: T Clev . . . 9E 54
Holmefield Cl. FY5: T Clev . . . 1E 62
Holmefield Ct. BB9: Barrf . . . 8H 85
Holmefield Gdns. BB9: Barrf . . . 8H 85
Holmefield Rd. FY6: K Sea . . . 8L 41
FY8: L Ann . . . 1F 128
Holme Head BD24: Langc . . . 1N 35
Holme Head Caravan Pk. LA6: Ingl . . . 2N 19
Holme Hill BB7: Clith . . . 1L 81
Holme Ho. OL15: Littleb . . . 5N 185
Holmehouse Lodge PR2: Ribb . . . 5B 116
(off Grange Av.)
Holme Ho. Rd. OL14: Tod . . . 7F 146
Holme Ho. St. OL15: Littleb . . . 4N 185
Holme La. BB4: Hasl . . . 7J 161
BB4: Rawt . . . 7K 161
LA2: Brookh, Caton . . . 1J 25
(not continuous)
Holme Lea BB5: Clay M . . . 5M 121
HOLME MILLS . . . 2F 6
Holme Mills Ind. Est.
LA6: Holme . . . 3F 6
Holme Pk. LA2: H Ben . . . 7L 19
(off Wenning Av.)
Holme Rd. BB5: Clay M . . . 5L 121
BB12: Burnl . . . 1C 124
PR1: Penw . . . 1F 134
PR5: Bam B . . . 8N 135
(not continuous)
HOLMES . . . 3N 169
Holmes, The BB4: Rawt . . . 2L 161
Holmes Cotts. BL1: Bolt . . . 9C 198
Holmes Ct. PR1: Prest . . . 6H 115
PR3: Gars . . . 4N 59
(off Oak Rd.)
Holmes Dr. OL13: Bac . . . 3K 163
Holmes Ho. Av. WN3: Wins . . . 8M 221
HOLME SLACK . . . 6M 115
Holme Slack La. PR1: Prest . . . 6L 115
Holmes La. OL13: Bac . . . 4K 163
Holmes Mdw. PR26: Leyl . . . 6E 152
Holmes Rd. FY5: T Clev . . . 9G 55
OL12: Roch . . . 6A 204
Holmes Sq. BB11: Burnl . . . 3F 228 (4F 124)
Holmes St. BB4: Rawt . . . 4N 161
BB4: Water . . . 9E 144
BB11: Burnl . . . 4F 228 (4F 124)
BB12: Padi . . . 1J 123
OL12: Roch . . . 2F 204
(Hollowspell)
OL12: Roch . . . 5A 204
(Primrose St.)
Holmes Ter. BB4: Rawt . . . 2L 161
Holmestrand Av. BB11: Burnl . . . 5N 123
Holme St. BB3: Darw . . . 7A 158
BB5: Acc . . . 2A 142
BB8: Wine . . . 6E 86
BB9: Barrf . . . 9H 85
BB9: Nelson . . . 2J 105
OL13: Bac . . . 7H 163
OL14: Tod . . . 9H 147
HOLMESWOOD . . . 8A 170
Holmeswood PR4: K'ham . . . 4M 111
Holmeswood Cres. PR3: Bart . . . 2E 94
Holmeswood Pk. BB4: Rawt . . . 7K 161
Holmeswood Rd.
L40: Holmesw, Ruff . . . 7N 169
Holme Ter. BB4: Rawt . . . 7K 161
BB9: Nelson . . . 2G 104
OL15: Littleb . . . 5N 185
Holme Va. BB4: Hasl . . . 9F 160
Holmfield Cres. PR2: Lea . . . 8A 114
Holmfield Gro. L31: Magh . . . 1B 222
Holmfield Rd. FY2: Blackp . . . 1B 88
PR2: Fulw . . . 5K 115
HOLM NOOK . . . 4E 64
Holm Rd. BB7: Barr . . . 1L 101
Holmrook Rd. PR1: Prest . . . 2N 229 (8L 115)
Holmsley St. BB10: Burnl . . . 4F 124
Holroyd Ct. FY2: Blackp . . . 8B 62
Holroyd St. OL16: Roch . . . 6D 204
Holsands Cl. PR2: Fulw . . . 3A 116
Holstein Av. OL12: Roch . . . 1A 204
Holstein St. PR1: Prest . . . 4M 229 (9K 115)
Holst Gdns. BB2: Blackb . . . 7A 140
Holt Av. PR7: Copp . . . 3B 194
Holt Brow PR25: Leyl . . . 9K 153
Holt Coppice L39: Aug . . . 4F 216
HOLT GREEN . . . 5F 216
Holthouse Rd. BL8: Tott . . . 8D 200
Holt La. PR6: Brind . . . 4F 154
Holt Mill Rd. BB4: W'foot . . . 7B 162
Holton Way WN3: Wins . . . 9N 221
Holts Bldgs. OL13: Bac . . . 7G 162
(off Siding St.)
Holts La. FY6: Poul F . . . 8M 63
Holts Pas. OL15: Littleb . . . 9K 185
Holt Sq. BB9: Barrf . . . 6J 85
Holts Ter. OL12: Roch . . . 3B 204
Holt St. BB1: Rish . . . 7J 121
BB4: W'foot . . . 7C 162
BL0: Ramsb . . . 8J 181
OL12: Whitw . . . 5N 183
OL15: Littleb . . . 4N 185
OL16: Milnr . . . 8K 205
WN5: Orr . . . 6G 221
Holt St. W. BL0: Ramsb . . . 9G 180
Holt Way L32: Kirk . . . 8J 223
Holyoake Av. FY2: Blackp . . . 1E 88
Holyoake St. BB12: Burnl . . . 3L 123
OL14: Tod . . . 7D 146
Homeacre Av. BB7: Sabd . . . 2E 102
Home Breeze Ho. LA4: Morec . . . 2E 22
(off Beach St.)
Homechase Ho. PR8: Birk . . . 1F 186
(off Chase Cl.)
Home Farm Cl. LA2: Wray . . . 8E 18
Home Farm M. PR26: Cros . . . 5A 172
Home Fld. PR3: Gars . . . 4N 59
Homefylde Ho. FY3: Blackp . . . 5N 227 (7E 88)
Homelinks Ho. FY8: L Ann . . . 5K 129
Home Pk. Dr. PR7: Buck V . . . 9A 154
Homeport Ho. PR9: S'port . . . 6J 167
(off Hoghton St.)
Homer Av. PR4: Tarl . . . 8D 150
HOMER GREEN . . . 9J 215
Homer St. BB11: Burnl . . . 4A 124
Homesands Ho. PR9: S'port . . . 6K 167
Homestead PR5: Bam B . . . 3D 154
Homestead, The FY8: L Ann . . . 5N 129
(off Henry St.)
Homestead Av. L30: N'ton . . . 7A 222
Homestead Cl. PR25: Leyl . . . 6G 152
Homestead Dr. FY7: Flee . . . 3E 54
Homestead Gdns. OL12: Roch . . . 9G 184
Homestead Way FY7: Flee . . . 3E 54
Homewood Av. LA4: Morec . . . 2F 22
Homfray Av. LA3: Morec . . . 5E 22
Homfray Gro. LA3: Morec . . . 5E 22
Hondwith Cl. BL2: Bolt . . . 8H 199
Honey Hole BB2: Blackb . . . 9D 226 (6M 139)
Honey Hole Cl. OL14: Tod . . . 3L 165
Honey Hole Ct. OL14: Tod . . . 3L 165
(off Honey Hole Rd.)
Honey Hole Rd. OL14: Tod . . . 3L 165
Honeyholme La. BB10: Cliv . . . 1K 145
Honey Holme Ter. BB10: Cliv . . . 1L 145
Honey Moor Dr. FY5: T Clev . . . 8G 55
Honeypot La. FY6: Sing . . . 7C 64
Honeysuckle Av. PR9: Banks . . . 4J 169
Honeysuckle Cl. PR6: Whit W . . . 1D 174
Honeysuckle Ct. BB5: Hunc . . . 8D 122
Honeysuckle Gro. PR4: Hesk B . . . 3C 150
Honeysuckle Pl. FY2: Blackp . . . 5F 62
Honeysuckle Row PR2: Ribb . . . 7A 116
Honeysuckle Way OL12: Roch . . . 2A 204
Honeywood Cl. BL0: Ramsb . . . 2F 200
Honister Av. FY3: Blackp . . . 8E 88
Honister Cl. FY7: Flee . . . 2D 54
Honister Rd. BB10: Burnl . . . 7F 104
LA1: Lanc . . . 6M 23
WN5: Wigan . . . 5L 221
Honister Sq. FY8: L Ann . . . 7F 108
Honister Way OL11: Roch . . . 9M 203
Honiton Av. BB2: Blackb . . . 8K 139
Honiton Way PR4: Cott . . . 3C 114
Hoo Cl. BB10: Burnl . . . 7G 105
Hood Ho. St. BB11: Burnl . . . 5C 124
Hood St. BB5: Acc . . . 1B 142
HOO HILL . . . 2E 88
Hoo Hill Ind. Est. FY3: Blackp . . . 2E 88
Hoo Hill La. FY3: Blackp . . . 2E 88
Hoole La. PR3: Nateby . . . 8F 58
PR9: Banks . . . 9F 148
Hooles La. PR3: Pill . . . 8F 42
HOOLEY BRIDGE . . . 9G 203
Hooley Bri. Ind. Est. OL10: Heyw . . . 9G 203
HOOLEY BROW . . . 9H 203
Hooley Clough OL10: Heyw . . . 9H 203
Hope Av. BL2: Bolt . . . 8L 199
Hope Bldgs. OL14: Tod . . . 2M 165
(off Every St.)
Hope Cl. FY5: T Clev . . . 8H 55
Hope Ct. OL12: Roch . . . 5C 204
(off Hope St.)
Hope Cres. WN6: Shev . . . 6L 213
Hope Island WN8: Skelm . . . 3L 219
Hope La. PR3: T'ley . . . 8G 70
Hope Sq. PR9: S'port . . . 7J 167
Hope St. BB2: Blackb . . . 3A 226 (3L 139)
BB3: Darw . . . 6N 157
BB4: Hasl . . . 5G 161
BB4: Rawt . . . 6A 162
Hope St. BB5: Acc . . . 3A 142
BB6: Gt H . . . 5J 121
BB9: Brierf . . . 5F 104
BB9: Nelson . . . 2H 105
BB10: W'thorne . . . 3M 125
BB12: Padi . . . 1J 123
BL0: Ramsb . . . 9G 180
BL6: Hor . . . 9C 196
FY8: L Ann . . . 1G 128
LA1: Lanc . . . 9E 228 (9L 23)
LA4: Morec . . . 4C 22
OL12: Roch . . . 5C 204
OL13: Bac . . . 3K 163
OL14: Tod . . . 2M 165
PR1: Prest . . . 5J 229 (9J 115)
PR6: Adl . . . 5K 195
PR7: Chor . . . 5E 174
PR9: S'port . . . 7J 167
Hope St. Nth. BL6: Hor . . . 8C 196
Hope Ter. BB2: Blackb . . . 2K 139
PR5: Lost H . . . 8K 135
Hophouse La. LA6: K Lon, Mans . . . 5D 8
Hopkinson St. BB8: Traw . . . 8E 86
Hopkinson Ter. BB8: Traw . . . 8E 86
(off Skipton Rd.)
Hopton Rd. FY1: Blackp . . . 7H 227 (8B 88)
Hopwood Av. BL6: Hor . . . 9D 196
Hopwood Cres. WA11: Rain . . . 5L 225
Hopwood St. BB5: Acc . . . 4A 142
BB11: Burnl . . . 2A 228 (3C 124)
PR1: Prest . . . 4M 229 (9K 115)
PR5: Bam B . . . 9B 136
(Club St.)
PR5: Bam B . . . 8A 136
(Mainway Ct.)
Horace St. BB12: Burnl . . . 3B 124
Horden Rake BB2: Fenis . . . 9E 138
Horden Vw. BB2: Blackb . . . 9F 138
Hordley St. BB12: Burnl . . . 3M 123
Horeb Cl. BB12: Padi . . . 2J 123
(off Victoria Rd.)
Horley Cl. BL8: Bury . . . 6H 201
Hornbeam Cl. LA1: Lanc . . . 8G 23
PR1: Penw . . . 5E 134
PR4: Wesh . . . 3L 111
HORNBY . . . 7C 18
Hornby Av. FY7: Flee . . . 4D 54
PR2: Ribb . . . 5A 116
Hornby Bank LA2: Horn . . . 6C 18
LA6: Neth K . . . 4C 16
Hornby Bank Bungs. LA6: Neth K . . . 4C 16
Hornby Chase L31: Magh . . . 3C 222
Hornby Community Swimming Pool . . . 6C 18
Hornby Ct. BB2: Blackb . . . 4K 139
(off Garden St.)
LA1: Lanc . . . 4J 23
PR4: K'ham . . . 5N 111
Hornby Cft. PR26: Leyl . . . 7E 152
Hornby Dr. LA1: Lanc . . . 3L 29
PR4: Newt . . . 6D 112
Hornby Hall Cl. LA2: Horn . . . 7C 18
Hornby La. PR4: Crossm . . . 9D 66
Hornby Pk. Ct. FY1: Blackp . . . 3M 227 (6D 88)
Hornby Rd. FY1: Blackp . . . 3J 227 (6B 88)
FY8: L Ann . . . 3E 128
LA2: Caton . . . 2H 25
LA2: Roeb . . . 3E 32
LA2: Wray . . . 8E 18
PR3: Longr . . . 2K 97
PR6: Chor . . . 8G 175
PR9: S'port . . . 1N 167
Hornby's La. PR3: Out R . . . 7F 56
(not continuous)
Hornby St. BB5: Osw . . . 5L 141
BB11: Burnl . . . 4E 228 (4E 124)
BL9: Bury . . . 8L 201
Hornby Ter. LA4: Morec . . . 2C 22
Horncastle Cl. BL8: Bury . . . 8J 201
Hornchurch Dr. PR7: Chor . . . 6C 174
Horncliffe Cl. BB4: Rawt . . . 7K 161
Horncliffe Hgts. BB9: Brierf . . . 5J 105
Horncliffe Pl. FY4: Blackp . . . 3B 108
Horncliffe Vw. BB4: Hasl . . . 7G 161
Horncliffe Wood BB4: Rawt . . . 8K 161
Horne St. BB5: Acc . . . 1B 142
Horning Cres. BB10: Burnl . . . 8H 105
Horns Dam Caravan Pk. PR3: Goos . . . 10B 70
Hornsea Cl. FY5: T Clev . . . 1K 63
PR2: Ingol . . . 5D 114
Hornsey Av. FY8: L Ann . . . 5B 108
Hornsey Gro. WN3: Wins . . . 8N 221
Horns La. PR3: Goos . . . 1B 96
Horridge Fold BL7: Eger . . . 2E 198
Horridge St. BL8: Bury . . . 9G 200
Horrobin BL7: Turt . . . 3J 199
Horrobin Fold BL7: Turt . . . 3J 199
Horrobin La. BL6: R'ton . . . 4M 195
BL7: Turt . . . 3J 199
PR6: And . . . 4M 195
HORROCKS FOLD . . . 6C 198
Horrocks Fold BL7: Edgw . . . 8K 179
PR4: Much H . . . 4J 151
Horrocks Fold Av. BL1: Bolt . . . 7D 198
HORROCKSFORD . . . 8M 73
Horrocksford Way LA1: Lanc . . . 1H 29
Horrocks Rd. BL7: Edgw . . . 7K 179
Horrocks Woods . . . 7B 198
Horsebridge Rd. FY3: Blackp . . . 2H 89
Horsefield Av. OL12: Whitw . . . 8N 183
Horse Mkt. LA6: K Lon . . . 6F 8
(off Mill Brow)
Horse Pk. La. PR3: Pill . . . 6L 43
Horse Riding Path
PR4: Cott . . . 4B 114
Horses & Ponies Protection Association . . . 8A 106
Horseshoe La. BL7: Brom C . . . 5G 198
Horsfall Av. FY8: L Ann . . . 5N 129
Horsfall Cl. BB5: Acc . . . 1A 142
Horsfield Cl. BB8: Colne . . . 6C 86
Horsham Cl. BL8: Bury . . . 6H 201
HORTON . . . 7D 52
Horton Av. BB10: Burnl . . . 7F 104
BL1: Bolt . . . 7E 198
Horton Cl. L33: Kirk . . . 4K 223
Horton Lodge BD23: Hort . . . 8D 52
HORWICH . . . 9C 196

Horwich Heritage Cen.—Inskip St.

Horwich Heritage Cen. 9D 196
(off Longworth Rd.)
Horwich Leisure Cen. 9D 196
HOSCAR 9H 191
Hoscar Moss Rd. L40: Lath 1G 210
Hoscar Station (Rail) 9H 191
Hospital Cotts. BB7: Wadd 7H 73
PR3: Ribc 4A 98
Hospital Rd. BL7: Brom C 5F 198
Hosta Cl. L33: Kirk 5J 223
Hosticle La. LA6: Whit 8D 8
Hothersall La. PR3: Longr 6M 97
Houghclough La. PR3: Chip 6D 70
Hough Fold Way BL2: Bolt 8K 199
Hough La. BL7: Brom C 6F 198
PR25: Leyl 6K 153
Houghton Av. FY4: Blackp 1D 108
WN5: Wigan 1N 221
Houghton Cl. OL16: Roch 7F 204
PR1: Penw 5G 134
Houghton Ct. FY5: T Clev 9H 55
(off Lowesway)
LA2: Halt 1B 24
Houghton La. WN6: Shev 6J 213
Houghton Rd. PR1: Penw 5F 134
Houghtons Ct. PR4: K'ham 4M 111
(off Poplar Av.)
Houghton's La. WN8: Skelm 2N 219
(not continuous)
Houghtons Rd. WN8: Skelm 9K 211
Houghton St. PR5: Lost H 8K 135
PR6: Chor 6F 174
Houldsworth Rd. PR2: Fulw 6H 115
Houlston Rd. L32: Kirk 8G 223
Houlston Wlk. L32: Kirk 8G 222
Hounds Hill Cen. FY1: Blackp 2H 227 (5B 88)
Houseman Pl. FY4: Blackp 2E 108
Hove Av. FY7: Flee 4C 54
Hove Cl. BL8: Greenm 4E 200
Hove Rd. FY8: L Ann 2F 128
Hovingham St. OL16: Roch 5E 204
Howard Brook Ho. PR1: Prest 8B 116
Howard Cl. BB5: Acc 3M 141
FY8: L Ann 8E 108
L31: Magh 1E 222
Howard Ct. PR9: S'port 5K 167
Howard Dr. PR4: Tarl 8D 150
Howard M. LA5: Carn 9N 11
Howard Pl. OL16: Roch 5C 204
Howard Rd. PR7: Chor 9D 174
Howard's WN5: Orr 4J 221
Howard's La. WN5: Orr 4J 221
(not continuous)
Howard St. BB1: Rish 8G 121
BB9: Nelson 2G 105
BB11: Burnl 4B 124
FY1: Blackp 4C 88
OL12: Roch 5C 204
WN5: Wigan 6M 221
Howard Way OL15: Littleb 5M 185
Howarth Av. BB5: Chur 1M 141
Howarth Ct. BL6: Hor 9F 196
HOWARTH CROSS 3E 204
Howarth Cross St. OL16: Roch 3E 204
Howarth Farm Way OL12: Roch 2F 204
Howarth Grn. OL12: Roch 2G 204
Howarth Knowl OL12: Roch 9F 184
Howarth Rd. PR2: Ash R 6G 114
Howarth Sq. OL16: Roch 5D 204
Howarth St. BB4: Water 8D 144
OL15: Littleb 8L 185
Howden Hgts. FY6: Poul F 8H 63
Howe Av. FY4: Blackp 1E 108
Howe Cft. BB7: Clith 3M 81
Howe Dr. BL0: Ramsb 3G 200
Howe Gro. PR7: Chor 7C 174
Howells Cl. L31: Magh 9C 216
Howe Wlk. BB11: Burnl 2D 228 (3E 124)
HOWGILL 3A 76
Howgill Av. LA1: Lanc 4K 23
Howgill Cl. BB9: Nelson 4K 105
Howgill La. BB7: Gis, Rim 3B 76
(not continuous)
Howgills, The PR2: Fulw 2K 115
Howgill Way FY8: L Ann 3C 130
HOWICK CROSS 4D 134
Howick Cross La.
PR1: Penw 3A 134
Howick Moor La. PR1: Penw 5C 134
Howick Pk. Av. PR1: Penw 4C 134
Howick Pk. Cl. PR1: Penw 4C 134
Howick Pk. Dr. PR1: Penw 4C 134
Howick Row PR1: Penw 3A 134
How La. BL9: Bury 7K 201
How Lea Dr. BL9: Bury 7L 201
Howorth Cl. BB11: Burnl 6E 124
Howorth Rd. BB11: Burnl 5D 124
Howorth St. OL14: Tod 8H 147
Howsin Av. BL2: Bolt 9H 199
Howsin St. BB10: Burnl 9E 104
Howsons La. BD24: Langc 1N 35
Howsons Yd. BD24: Sett 3N 35
(off Market Pl.)
Hoylake Cl. PR2: Fulw 3E 114
Hoyle Av. FY8: L Ann 7F 108
HOYLE BOTTOM 7L 141
Hoyles La. PR4: Cott 4M 113
Hoyle's Ter. OL16: Milnr 7H 205
Hoyle St. BB5: Ris B 8F 142
BL1: Bolt 9E 198
OL12: Whitw 3A 184
OL13: Bac 7J 163
Hozier St. BB1: Blackb 3C 140
Hub, The
Chorley 1B 174
Hubert Pl. LA1: Lanc 6A 228 (8H 23)
Hubie St. BB12: Burnl 2D 124
Huck La. FY8: L Ann 9D 110
Hudcar La. BL9: Bury 9M 201
Huddersfield Rd. OL16: Milnr 9L 205
HUD HEY 1F 160
Hud Hey Ind. Est. BB4: Hasl 1G 160
Hud Hey Rd. BB4: Hasl 1F 160
Hud Rake BB4: Hasl 2G 160
Hudson Cl. BB2: Blackb 9J 119
Hudson Ct. PR5: Bam B 9E 136
Hudson Rd. FY1: Blackp 8M 227 (8D 88)
L31: Magh 3C 222
Hudsons Pas. OL15: Littleb 7M 185
Hudson St. BB5: Acc 4B 142
BB9: Brierf 5F 104
BB11: Burnl 4B 124
OL14: Tod 7F 146
PR1: Prest 7M 229 (2K 135)
Hudsons Wlk. OL11: Roch 6M 203
Hudswell Cl. L30: N'ton 9A 222
Hufling Ct. BB11: Burnl 5F 124
(off Hufling La.)
Hufling La. BB11: Burnl 5F 124
Hugh Barn La. PR4: New L 9B 134
Hugh Bus. Pk. BB4: W'foot 7D 162
Hughenden Ct. BL8: Tott 6E 200
Hughes Av. BL6: Hor 9B 196
Hughes Gro. FY2: Blackp 1E 88
Hughes St. BB11: Burnl 4D 228 (4E 124)
Hugh La. PR26: Leyl 4F 152
(not continuous)
Hugh Lupus St. BL1: Bolt 8G 198
HUGH MILL 7D 162
Hugh Rake BB4: Rawt 1L 161
Hugh St. OL16: Roch 5D 204
Hughtrede St. OL16: Roch 9E 204
Hullet Cl. WN6: App B 4H 213
Hull Rd. FY1: Blackp 3J 227 (6B 88)
Hull St. BB11: Burnl 3F 228 (4F 124)
(not continuous)
PR2: Ash R 9F 114
Hulme Av. FY5: T Clev 1J 63
Hulme Ct. BB3: Darw 2M 157
Hulme Rd. BL2: Bolt 7L 199
Hulmes Bri. Bus. Cen. L39: Hals 2B 208
Hulme St. BL8: Bury 9J 201
PR8: S'port 7G 167
Hulton Dr. BB9: Nelson 4J 105
Humber Av. FY3: Blackp 2E 88
Humber Dr. BL9: Bury 6L 201
Humber Pl. WN5: Wigan 4M 221
Humber Rd. OL16: Milnr 7K 205
Humber Sq. BB10: Burnl 7G 105
Humber St. PR3: Longr 3J 97
Humblescough La. PR3: C'town, Nateby 6G 59
Hume St. OL16: Roch 7D 204
Humphrey St. BB9: Brierf 4F 104
HUNCOAT 7D 122
Huncoat Ind. Est. BB5: Hunc 8C 122
(not continuous)
Huncoat Ind. Pk. BB5: Hunc 8C 122
Huncoat Station (Rail) 7D 122
HUNDRED END 6L 149
Hundred End La. PR4: Hesk B 5L 149
Hungerford Rd. FY8: L Ann 3F 128
HUNGER HILL 1J 213
Hunger Hill OL12: Ward 8G 184
Hunger Hill La. OL12: Roch 2K 203
Hunniball Ct. PR2: Ash R 7F 114
Hunslet St. BB9: Nelson 3K 105
BB11: Burnl 1F 228 (3F 124)
Hunstanton Cl. PR7: Eux 1N 173
Hunstanton Dr. BL8: Bury 8J 201
Hunter Av. PR4: Tarl 9E 150
Hunter Rd. PR4: Frec 7N 111
WN5: Wigan 2N 221
Hunters Dr. BB12: Burnl 1B 124
Hunters Fold PR4: Wal B 2L 151
Hunters Ga. LA1: Lanc 2J 29
Hunters Grn. BL0: Ramsb 2E 200
Hunters La. L40: Holmesw 6B 170
OL14: Tod 1J 165
OL16: Roch 5C 204
PR4: Tarl 3M 169
Hunters Lodge BB2: Blackb 7G 138
PR5: Walt D 5N 135
Hunters Rd. PR25: Leyl 6N 153
Hunter St. BB9: Brierf 5F 104
LA5: Carn 8A 12
Hunters Wood Ct. PR7: Chor 8B 174
Hunt Fold BL8: Greenm 4E 200
Hunt Fold Dr. BL8: Greenm 4E 200
Huntingdon Ct. PR9: S'port 4N 167
Huntingdon Gro. L31: Lyd 7B 216
Huntingdon Hall La. PR3: Dutt 9K 71
Huntingdon Rd. FY5: T Clev 1C 62
Hunting Hill Caravan Pk. LA5: Carn 9N 11
Hunting Hill Rd. LA5: Carn 9M 11
Huntington Dr. BB3: Darw 8A 158
Huntley Av. FY3: Blackp 3E 88
Huntley Cl. LA4: Morec 3E 22
Huntley Ho. BL9: Bury 9N 201
Huntley La. PR5: Sam 7M 117
Huntley Mt. Rd. BL9: Bury 9N 201
Hunt Rd. L31: Magh 9C 216
Huntroyde Av. BB12: Padi 1G 122
Huntroyde Cl. BB12: Burnl 2B 124
Hunts Cotts. PR9: S'port 5N 167
Hunts Fld. PR6: Clay W 5E 154
Huntsman's Chase PR4: Trea 3D 112
Hunt St. PR1: Prest 9G 115
HURLSTON 2H 209
Hurlston Av. WN8: Skelm 3N 219
Hurlston Ct. L40: Scar 1H 209
Hurlston Dr. L39: Orms 5K 209
HURLSTON GREEN 9G 189
Hurlston Hall Country Caravan Pk.
L40: Scar 2H 209
Hurlston Hall Golf Course 2H 209
Hurlston La. L40: Scar 1H 209
Hurn Gro. PR7: Chor 7C 174
Hurstbrook PR7: Copp 4B 194
Hurst Cres. BB4: Rawt 4N 161
Hurstdene Cl. FY6: Poul F 8M 63
HURSTEAD 1G 204
Hurstead Cotts. OL12: Roch 1G 204
Hurstead Grn. OL12: Roch 1G 205
Hurstead M. OL12: Roch 1G 204
(off Braddocks Cl.)
Hurstead St. BB5: Bax 7D 142
Hursted Rd. OL16: Milnr 7J 205
HURST GREEN
BB7 1M 99
L40 2N 191
Hurst Grn. L40: Mawd 3N 191
Hurst La. BB4: Rawt 4M 161
Hurst Lea Caravan Pk. PR3: Lit E 5L 65
Hurstleigh Dr. LA3: Heys 9M 21
Hurstleigh Hgts. FY5: T Clev 1L 63
Hurstmere Av. FY4: Blackp 1E 108
Hurst Pk. PR1: Penw 4F 134
Hurst Platt BB4: Rawt 4N 161
Hurst Rd. L31: Magh 3D 222
Hurst's La. L39: Bick 9M 217
Hurst St. OL11: Roch 8D 204
(not continuous)
Hurstway PR2: Fulw 2G 115
Hurstway Cl. PR2: Fulw 2G 115
HURSTWOOD 5N 125
Hurstwood BL1: Bolt 8D 198
Hurstwood Av. BB2: Blackb 7H 139
BB10: Burnl 4H 125
Hurstwood Ct. BB1: Guide 7D 140
Hurstwood Dr. FY2: Blackp 9D 62
Hurstwood Ent. Pk. BB4: Hasl 5E 160
Hurstwood Gdns. BB9: Brierf 6H 105
Hurstwood La. BB10: H'wood 5M 125
Hurtley St. BB10: Burnl 1E 124
HUTCH BANK 5E 160
Hutch Bank Rd. BB4: Hasl 5E 160
Hutchinson Ct. BB3: Darw 6N 157
Hutchinson Rd. OL11: Roch 4H 203
Hutchinson St. OL11: Roch 7N 203
Hut La. PR6: H Charn 1K 195
Huttock End La. OL13: Bac 7H 163
HUTTOCK TOP 6J 163
HUTTON 6A 134
Hutton Cl. LA6: Burt K 5H 7
Hutton Ct. WN8: Skelm 2H 219
Hutton Cres. LA4: Morec 4A 22
Hutton Dr. BB12: Burnl 2C 124
Hutton Gdns. LA5: Wart 6N 11
Hutton Gro. LA4: Morec 4A 22
Hutton Hall Av. PR4: Hutt 7B 134
Hutton Ho. OL11: Roch 7C 204
(off Henry St.)
Hutton Rd. WN8: Skelm 2H 219
HUTTON ROOF 6B 8
Hutton Roof Crags Nature Reserve 2N 7
Hutton St. BB1: Blackb 3A 140
Hutton Vw. LA6: Prie H 1H 13
Hutton Way L39: Orms 7K 209
LA1: Lanc 7H 23
Huyton Rd. PR7: Adl 7J 195
(not continuous)
Huyton Ter. PR6: Adl 6K 195
Hyacinth Av. BB5: Hunc 7D 122
L33: Kirk 5J 223
Hyacinth Cl. BB4: Hasl 7E 160
Hyatt Cres. WN6: Stand 1M 213
Hydeaway Ct. LA4: Morec 4B 22
Hyde Pk. Pl. OL16: Roch 6F 204
(off Belfield La.)
Hyde Rd. FY1: Blackp 7J 227 (8B 88)
LA4: Morec 4F 22
Hyde's Brow WA11: Rain 2L 225
Hydon Brook Wlk. OL11: Roch 9N 203
Hygiene BB5: Clay M 7L 121
Hynd Brook Ho. BB5: Acc 3N 141
(off Dale St.)
Hyndburn Bri. BB5: Clay M 4M 121
Hyndburn Cl. LA3: Morec 5F 22
Hyndburn Dr. BB3: Darw 3L 157
Hyndburn Rd. BB5: Acc, Chur 2M 141
BB6: Gt H 4L 121
Hyndburn Sports Cen. 2M 141
Hyndburn St. BB5: Acc 2M 141
Hyning Rd. LA5: Wart, Yea C 1B 12
Hynings, The BB6: Gt H 3H 121
Hythe Cl. BB1: Blackb 4C 140
PR8: S'port 2L 187

I

Ian Frazer Ct. OL11: Roch 9C 204
Ibbison Ct. FY1: Blackp 5K 227 (7C 88)
Ibbotroyd Av. OL14: Tod 9K 147
Ibsley OL12: Roch 5B 204
Icconhurst Cl. BB5: Bax 6D 142
Ice Drome 2B 108
Ice St. BB1: Blackb 1D 226 (1M 139)
Iddesleigh Rd. PR1: Prest 8A 116
Iddon Ct. FY1: Blackp 4C 88
(off Elizabeth St.)
Idlewood Pl. FY5: T Clev 3F 62
Idstone Cl. BB2: Blackb 8A 140
IGHTENHILL 1N 123
Ightenhill Pk. La. BB12: Burnl 8N 103
Ightenhill Pk. M. BB12: Burnl 2A 124
Ightenhill St. BB12: Padi 9H 103
Ighten Rd. BB12: Burnl 1A 124
Ilford Rd. FY4: Blackp 9E 88
Ilkley Av. FY8: L Ann 2J 129
PR9: S'port 9B 148
Ilkley Gro. FY5: T Clev 3D 62
Illawalla, The FY5: T Clev 5L 63
Illingworth Rd. PR1: Prest 8A 116
Illston M. BB9: Brierf 5F 104
(off Cambridge St.)
Ilminster OL11: Roch 7B 204
Ilway PR5: Walt D 5N 135
Imperial Ct. BB12: Burnl 3B 124
(off Shale St.)
Imperial Gdns. BB9: Nelson 2H 105
(off Carr Rd.)
Imperial Hotel Stop (Tram) 3B 88
Imperial Rd. LA3: Midd 3M 27
Imperial St. FY1: Blackp 3B 88
Imperial Wlk. FY1: Blackp 3B 88
Imperial Yd. FY1: Blackp 3B 88
(off Bk. Eaves St.)
INCE BLUNDELL 8E 214
Ince La. PR7: E'ton 9F 172
Inchfield BB10: W'thorne 3M 125
WN8: Skelm 1M 219
Inchfield Cl. OL11: Roch 5J 203
Inchfield Rd. OL14: Wals 7J 165
India Mill Bus. Cen. BB3: Darw 7A 158
India St. BB3: Darw 7B 158
BB5: Acc 2M 141
BL9: Summ 2H 201
Indoor Karting
Burscough 2N 209
Industrial Pl. OL13: Bac 5K 163
(off Lee St.)
Industrial St. BL0: Ramsb 5H 181
OL13: Bac 5L 163
OL14: Tod 2L 165
Industry Rd. OL12: Roch 4C 204
Industry St. BB3: Darw 5A 158
OL11: Roch 4J 203
OL12: Whitw 4A 184
OL14: Wals 6K 165
OL15: Littleb 9L 185
Infant St. BB5: Acc 2B 142
Infirmary Cl. BB2: Blackb 9B 226 (6L 139)
Infirmary Rd. BB2: Blackb 9B 226 (6L 139)
Infirmary St. BB2: Blackb 9B 226 (6L 139)
Ing Cotts. BB5: Bax 7C 142
Ing Dene Av. BB8: Colne 7M 85
Ing Dene Cl. BB8: Colne 7M 85
Ingfield Cres. BD24: Sett 3N 35
Ingfield Est. BD24: Sett 3N 35
Ingfield La. BD24: Sett 3N 35
Ingfield Ter. OL14: Tod 7F 146
Ingham Av. PR7: Buck V 1A 174
Inghams La. OL15: Littleb 9L 185
Ingham St. BB9: Barrf 7H 85
BB12: Padi 9J 103
Inglby Cl. BB1: Blackb 3D 140
Ingleborough Dr. BB18: Barnw 2L 77
Ingleborough Rd. LA1: Lanc 5G 23
Ingleborough Vw. LA2: H Ben 6L 19
(off Butts La.)
LA2: Horn 8C 18
LA5: Carn 1B 16
PR6: Withn 7B 156
(off Prospect Ter.)
Ingleborough Way PR25: Leyl 6M 153
Ingleby Cl. FY5: T Clev 7F 54
WN6: Stand 2N 213
Ingle Cl. PR6: Chor 5F 174
Ingledene Mobile Home Pk. FY5: T Clev 2J 63
(off Lawsons Rd.)
Inglefield OL11: Roch 4K 203
Ingle Head PR2: Fulw 3G 114
Inglehurst Rd. BB11: Burnl 4N 123
Inglemere Cl. LA5: Arn 2E 4
Inglemere Dr. LA5: Arn 1F 4
Inglemere Gdns. LA5: Arn 2F 4
Inglemoss Dr. WA11: Rain 9M 225
Ingle Nook BB10: Burnl 5K 125
Inglenook Cl. FY5: T Clev 2F 62
Ingles, The LA6: Ingl 3N 19
(off Main St.)
INGLETON 3N 19
Ingleton Av. FY2: Blackp 6F 62
Ingleton Cl. BB5: Acc 3C 142
BL2: Bolt 9K 199
Ingleton Dr. LA1: Lanc 4L 29
Ingleton Grn. L32: Kirk 9L 223
Ingleton Ho. LA1: Lanc 4L 29
(off Ingleton Dr.)
Ingleton Ind. Est. LA6: Ingl 3N 19
Ingleton M. BL8: Bury 9G 201
Ingleton Rd. L32: Kirk 9L 223
PR2: Ribb 5A 116
PR8: S'port 2L 187
Ingleton Waterfalls 2N 19
Ingleway FY5: T Clev 9E 54
Ingleway Av. FY3: Blackp 4E 88
INGLEWHITE 6L 69
Inglewhite WN8: Skelm 1L 219
Inglewhite Fold BB12: Padi 2J 123
Inglewhite Island WN8: Skelm 1M 219
Inglewhite Rd. PR3: Goos, Inglew 6L 69
PR3: Goos, Longr 9A 70
Inglewood Cl. BL9: Bury 9A 202
FY7: Flee 3C 54
PR4: Wart 2J 131
Inglewood Ct. LA5: Arn 1F 4
(off The Promenade)
WN5: Wigan 6N 221
Inglewood Gro. FY2: Blackp 6E 62
Inglewood Rd. WA11: Rain 9N 225
Inglis St. OL15: Littleb 8L 185
Ingoe Cl. L32: Kirk 9G 223
Ingoe La. L32: Kirk 9G 223
(not continuous)
INGOL 3D 114
Ingol Gdns. FY6: Ham 1B 64
Ingol Golf Course 3E 114
Ingol Gro. FY6: Ham 1B 64
Ingol La. FY6: Ham 1C 64
Ingot St. PR1: Prest 9G 115
Ingram WN8: Skelm 2M 219
Ings, The BD24: Sett 3N 35
(off High Hill Gro. St.)
Ings Av. BB18: Barnw 1M 77
BD24: Sett 4N 35
(off Skipton Rd.)
OL12: Roch 3M 203
Ings La. OL12: Roch 3M 203
Ingthorpe Av. FY2: Blackp 6D 62
Inkerman Rd. PR4: Weet 4D 90
Inkerman St. BB1: Blackb 1D 226 (2M 139)
BB12: Padi 1H 123
OL12: Roch 4C 204
(off Industry Rd.)
OL13: Bac 5L 163
PR2: Ash R 6F 114
Inman's Rd. LA5: Silv 7G 5
Inner Prom. FY8: L Ann 4F 128
(Cartmell Rd.)
FY8: L Ann 5H 129
(Outer Prom.)
INSKIP 2G 93
Inskip WN8: Skelm 1L 219
Inskip Ct. WN8: Skelm 1M 219
INSKIP MOSS SIDE 8E 66
Inskip Pl. FY4: Blackp 4E 108
FY8: L Ann 9H 109
Inskip Rd. PR2: Ash R 8B 114
PR4: Wharl 6D 92
PR9: S'port 2N 167
PR25: Leyl 5G 152
Inskip St. BB12: Padi 1H 123

Institute St.—Keats Av.

Institute St. BB12: Padi 1J 123
INTACK 3D 140
Intack La. BB2: Mellor B 7C 118
Intack Rd. PR4: Longt 8M 133
Intake Cres. BB8: Colne 5C 86
Intake La. L37: D'holl 3L 215
L39: Bick 6D 218
International League for the Protection of Horses 3M 109
Inverness Rd. BB3: Darw 7N 157
Inver Rd. FY2: Blackp 8D 62
Inward Dr. WN6: Shev 7K 213
Ipswich Pl. FY5: T Clev 1C 62
Ipswich Rd. PR2: Ribb 7N 115
Ipswich St. OL11: Roch 8C 204
IREBY 9K 9
Ireby Rd. LA6: Bur L 3K 19
Irene Pl. BB2: Blackb 3J 139
Irene St. BB10: Burnl 4G 124
Iris Cl. BB5: Clay M 5L 121
Iris Gro. L33: Kirk 5J 223
Iris Pk. Wlk. L31: Mell 7F 222
Iris St. BL0: Ramsb 8G 181
Irlam Dr. L32: Kirk 8K 223
Irongate PR5: Lost H 8M 135
Irongate Ground 8N 135
Ironside Cl. PR2: Fulw 5L 115
Iron St. BB2: Blackb 8C 226 (5L 139)
Irton Rd. PR9: S'port 6L 167
Irvin Av. PR9: S'port 1B 168
Irvine Cl. FY2: Blackp 6F 62
Irvine Pl. PR7: Buck V 9B 154
Irvine St. BB9: Nelson 9K 85
Irving Pl. BB2: Blackb 3J 139
Irving St. PR9: S'port 5H 167
Irvin St. PR1: Prest 8L 115
Irwell WN8: Skelm 9L 211
Irwell Ho. *BB4: W'foot* *7C 162*
(off Cowpe Rd.)
Irwell Pl. WN5: Wigan 5M 221
Irwell Rd. WN5: Orr 4J 221
Irwell St. BB12: Burnl 3M 123
BL0: Ramsb 8H 181
FY8: L Ann 1E 128
OL13: Bac 5K 163
PR3: Longr 3K 97
(not continuous)
Irwell Ter. OL13: Bac 4K 163
IRWELL VALE 1H 181
Irwell Va. Rd. BB4: Hasl 1H 181
Irwell Vale Station East Lancashire Railway 1H 181
Isabella St. OL12: Roch 3C 204
PR3: Longr 2J 97
Isa St. BL0: Ramsb 1F 200
Isherwood Fold BL7: Edgw 7K 179
Isherwood St. BB2: Blackb 7L 139
OL11: Roch 7D 204
PR1: Prest 8M 115
Island La. PR3: Winm 2C 58
Islay Cl. FY4: Blackp 3F 108
Islay Rd. FY8: L Ann 2K 129
Isle of Man BB1: Ramsg 5M 119
Isle of Man St. BB4: Water 9D 144
Isle of Man Vs. BB4: Lumb 9D 144
Isleworth Dr. PR7: Chor 7D 174
Islington BB2: Blackb 7C 226 (5M 139)
Islington Cl. BB10: Burnl 7H 105
Ivan St. BB10: Burnl 8F 104
Iveagh Ct. OL16: Roch 7E 204
Ive Ct. BB8: Foul 2B 86
Ivegate BB8: Colne 6A 86
Ivegate M. BB8: Colne 6A 86
Ivinson Rd. BB3: Darw 4B 158
Ivory Dr. L33: Kirk 5K 223
Ivory St. BB12: Burnl 3A 124
Ivy Av. BB4: Hasl 4H 161
FY4: Blackp 4D 108
Ivy Bank BB4: W'foot 8D 162
OL12: Whitw 3A 184
PR2: Fulw 3N 115
Ivy Bank Cl. BL1: Bolt 8E 198
Ivy Bank Rd. BL1: Bolt 8E 198
Ivybridge WN8: Skelm 1M 219
Ivy Cl. BB2: Blackb 9C 226 (6M 139)
BB4: W'foot 7D 162
L40: Burs 1E 210
PR25: Leyl 5A 154
Ivy Cotts. BB3: Tock 4G 156
BB4: W'foot *7D 162*
(off Millar Barn La.)
OL12: Roch 4A 204
Ivydale WN8: Skelm 1M 219
Ivy Dene Cl. *BD24: Sett* *3N 35*
(off Duke St.)
Ivy Fold *BD24: Gig* *2N 35*
(off Church St.)
Ivy Gdns. FY5: T Clev 8H 55
Ivy Gro. BB4: Rawt 4M 161
Ivy Ho. Cl. PR5: Bam B 9D 136
Ivy Ho. Gdns. *BD23: Garg* *3M 53*
(off South St.)
Ivy Pl. OL14: Tod 7C 146
Ivy St. BB2: Blackb 9B 226 (6L 139)
BB4: W'foot 7D 162
BB8: Colne 9L 85
BB10: Burnl 9F 104
BL0: Ramsb 2E 200
PR8: S'port 8K 167
Ivy Ter. BB3: Darw 9B 158
OL15: Littleb 4N 185
WN6: Stand 1M 213
Ivy Vs. *OL14: Tod* *3L 165*
(off Longfield Rd.)

J

Jacinta Heritage Trawler 2G 55
Jackdaw Rd. BB18: Barnw 1N 77
BL8: Greenm 3E 200
JACK GREEN 8H 137
Jack La. BD23: Wig 9M 35
Jack McCann Ct. *OL16: Roch* *5D 204*
(off Trafalgar St.)
Jackman St. OL14: Tod 2L 165
Jacks Key Dr. BB3: Darw 1C 178
Jacksmere La. L40: Scar 5N 187
PR8: S'port 5N 187
Jackson Cl. L39: D'holl 7M 207
LA1: Lanc 9G 23
Jackson Fold *BB12: High* *4L 103*
(off Sabden Rd.)
Jackson Hgts. Rd. BB1: Belt 4H 159
Jackson Rd. PR7: Chor 9C 174
PR25: Leyl 6G 152
Jacksons Banks Rd. BB2: Bald 4M 117
Jackson's Bldgs. *BB4: Rawt* *6L 161*
(off Carr Rd.)
Jackson's Comn. La. L40: Scar 3F 208
(not continuous)
Jackson's La. L40: Bis G 7B 192
Jacksons Pl. OL16: Roch 5E 204
Jackson St. BB5: Chur 3L 141
BB5: Clay M 6M 121
BB10: Burnl 1E 124
FY3: Blackp 3E 88
OL12: Ward 8F 184
OL16: Roch 7E 204
PR5: Bam B 8B 136
PR7: Chor 8F 174
Jackson Ter. LA5: Carn 7A 12
Jack Taylor Ct. OL12: Roch 4E 204
Jack Walker Way BB2: Blackb 9L 139
Jacob Bright M. OL12: Roch 3C 204
Jacob Ct. WN5: Bill 9G 221
Jacob's La. PR4: Trea 9D 92
Jacob St. BB5: Acc 3B 142
Jacson St. PR1: Prest 6L 229 (1K 135)
Jade Cl. L33: Kirk 7M 223
Jagoe M. *BB18: Earl* *3D 78*
(off Jagoe Rd.)
Jagoe Rd. BB18: Earl 3D 78
James Av. BB6: Gt H 4H 121
FY4: Blackp 9F 88
James Butterworth Ct. *OL16: Roch* *7E 204*
(off James Butterworth St.)
James Butterworth St. OL16: Roch 7E 204
James Ct. *BB3: Darw* *6A 158*
(off Foundry St.)
James Hill St. OL15: Littleb 9L 185
James Holt Av. L32: Kirk 9H 223
Jameson Rd. FY7: Flee 4F 54
Jameson St. FY1: Blackp 5L 227 (7C 88)
James Pl. PR7: Copp 5N 193
WN6: Stand 2N 213
James Sq. WN6: Stand 2N 213
James St. BB1: Belt 1F 158
BB1: Blackb 3C 226 (3M 139)
BB1: Rish 8J 121
BB3: Darw 6N 157
BB4: Hasl 5F 160
BB4: Rawt 5M 161
BB5: Clay M 6M 121
BB5: Hunc 7D 122
BB5: Osw 4K 141
BB6: Gt H 4H 121
BB8: Colne *7B 86*
(off West St.)
BB9: Barrf 7H 85
BB10: Burnl 9E 104
BB18: Barnw 3M 77
BB18: Earl 3E 78
BB18: Salt 5A 78
BL6: Hor 9A 196
BL7: Eger 2D 198
LA1: Lanc 7C 228 (8K 23)
LA4: Morec 3C 22
OL12: Roch 5D 204
(Flannel St.)
OL12: Roch 1F 204
(Wardle Rd.)
OL12: Whitw 4A 184
OL13: Bac 8E 162
OL14: Tod *1L 165*
(off Meadow Bottom Rd.)
OL15: Littleb 1H 205
PR1: Prest 8N 229 (1L 135)
PR5: Bam B 7A 136
James St. W. BB3: Darw 6A 158
Jameston Ri. *BL6: Hor* *9C 196*
(off Wright St.)
Jane La. PR4: Catf 5J 93
PR26: Midge H 3D 152
Jane's Brook Rd. PR8: S'port 1K 187
Janes Mdw. PR4: Tarl 1E 170
Jane St. OL12: Roch 5B 204
OL12: Whitw 9B 164
Janice Dr. PR2: Fulw 2G 114
Janine Cl. LA4: Morec 4A 22
Jannat Cl. BB5: Acc 3A 142
Jarrett Rd. L33: Kirk 6M 223
Jarrett Wlk. L33: Kirk 6M 223
Jarvis St. OL12: Roch 4C 204
Jasmine Rd. PR5: Walt D 5K 135
WN5: Wigan 4N 221
Jasper St. BB1: Blackb 8N 119
Jay Bank L40: Mawd 4M 191
Jedburgh Dr. L33: Kirk 4J 223
Jefferson Cl. LA1: Lanc 9H 23
Jefferson Way OL12: Roch 2C 204
Jeffrey Av. PR3: Longr 3K 97
Jeffrey Hill Cl. PR2: Ribb 2E 116
Jeffrey Sq. FY1: Blackp 6M 227 (7D 88)
Jellicoe Cl. FY8: L Ann 8E 108
Jem Ga. FY5: T Clev 3D 62
Jemmett St. PR1: Prest 7H 115
Jennings Wlk. *BB3: Darw* *5B 158*
(off Fitzgerald Dr.)
Jenny La. BB9: Nelson 4H 105
FY4: Blackp 2J 109
PR6: H'Wheel 6L 155
Jenny Nook LA3: Heys 9M 21
Jensen Cl. LA1: Lanc 1J 29
Jensen Dr. FY4: Blackp 3N 109
Jepheys Pl. OL12: Roch 4C 204
Jepheys St. OL12: Roch 4C 204
Jepp Hill BB18: Barnw 2M 77
Jepps Av. PR3: Bart 2E 94
Jepps La. PR3: Bart 2E 94
Jepson St. BB3: Darw 7A 158
Jepson Way FY4: Blackp 5F 108
Jeremiah Horrocks Observatory 6J 115
JERICHO 9C 202
Jericho Rd. BL9: Bury 9C 202
Jermyn St. OL12: Roch 5D 204
Jerrold St. OL15: Littleb 9L 185
Jersey Av. FY2: Blackp 9E 62
Jersey Fold PR7: Buck V 9A 154
Jersey St. BB2: Blackb 7J 139
Jervis Cl. FY8: L Ann 8D 108
Jesmond Av. FY4: Blackp 2B 108
Jesmond Ct. FY8: L Ann 9F 108
Jesmond Dr. BL8: Bury 8H 201
Jesmond Gro. LA4: Morec 5D 22
Jesmond Rd. BL1: Bolt 9B 198
Jessel St. BB2: Blackb 6J 139
Jesson Way LA5: Carn 9N 11
Jethro St. BL2: Bolt 9J 199
Jevington Way LA3: Heys 9M 21
Jewel Holme BB9: Brierf 5E 104
Jewel La. BB12: Reed 6D 104
Jib Hill Cotts. BB10: Burnl 7H 105
Jingling Ct. *LA6: K Lon* *6F 8*
(off Main St.)
Jingling La. *LA6: K Lon* *6F 8*
(off Main St.)
Jinny La. BB12: Newc P, Rough 8A 84
JJB Fitness Club Southport 6G 166
Jobing St. BB8: Colne 8M 85
Jockey St. BB11: Burnl 4A 124
Joe Connolly Way BB4: W'foot 7C 162
Joe La. PR3: Catt 2A 68
John Ashworth St. OL12: Roch 4E 204
John Barker St. OL14: Tod 8H 147
John Boyd Dunlop Dr. OL16: Roch 9G 204
John Collier Av. OL16: Roch 9H 205
John Creed Av. LA1: Bail 7M 29
John Henry St. OL12: Whitw 2A 184
John Hill St. FY4: Blackp 8F 88
John Kay Ct. LA1: Lanc 5H 23
John Kemble Ct. OL11: Roch 9A 204
John Milne Av. OL16: Roch 9G 205
Johnny Barn Cl. BB4: Rawt 5B 162
Johnny Barn Cotts. BB4: Rawt 5B 162
John O'Gaunt St. *BB12: Padi* *9H 103*
(off Guy St.)
John Roberts Cl. OL11: Roch 8B 204
Johnson Cl. LA1: Lanc 9G 23
LA5: Carn 9N 11
Johnson New Rd. BB3: Hodd 5E 158
Johnson Rd. BB3: E'hill, W'side 7C 158
FY4: Blackp 8F 88
JOHNSON'S HILLOCK 9G 155
Johnson's Meanygate
PR4: Hesk B, Tarl 6A 150
Johnson St. *OL11: Roch* *9N 203*
(off Burnaby St.)
PR9: S'port 6H 167
WN5: Wigan 5L 221
Johnson Way BB1: Blackb 7C 140
FY4: Blackp 5E 108
Johnspool PR2: Fulw 3F 114
Johnston OL12: Roch 5B 204
Johnston Av. OL15: Littleb 2J 205
Johnston Cl. BB2: Blackb 3K 139
Johnston St. BB2: Blackb 4A 226 (3K 139)
John St. BB3: Darw 6N 157
BB4: Hasl 4G 160
BB4: W'foot 6D 162
BB5: Chur 1L 141
BB5: Clay M 6M 121
BB5: Osw 5K 141
BB8: Colne 7N 85
BB9: Barrf 7J 85
BB9: Brierf 4F 104
BB18: Barnw 2L 77
BB18: Earl 3E 78
BL7: Brom C 6G 199
FY1: Blackp 8J 227 (8B 88)
FY5: T Clev 8H 55
LA2: Gal 3L 37
LA5: Carn 8A 12
OL12: Whitw 4A 184
OL14: Tod *2L 165*
(off Dalton St.)
OL15: Littleb 9K 185
OL16: Roch 2F 204
(Mitchell St.)
OL16: Roch 5C 204
(Pagan St.)
PR5: Bam B 7A 136
PR7: Copp 4A 194
PR25: Leyl 6K 153
WN5: Wigan 6N 221
Johnsville Av. FY4: Blackp 2E 108
Johns Wood Cl. PR7: Chor 8B 174
John Wall Ct. BB7: Clith 3K 81
John William St. PR1: Prest 9M 115
Joiners All. BB6: Gt H 4J 121
Joiners Row BB2: Blackb 7D 226 (5N 139)
Jolly Tar La. PR7: Copp 6B 194
Jonathan Cl. BB4: Hasl 7F 160
Jones Gro. FY7: Flee 8H 41
Jones St. BL6: Hor 9C 196
OL16: Roch 7D 204
Jones's Yd. LA6: Burt K 6G 7
Jones Way OL16: Roch 8F 204
Joseph Lister Dr. OL12: Roch 9G 185
Joseph St. BB3: Darw 6B 158
BB9: Barrf 9H 85
OL12: Roch 3A 204
OL15: Littleb 8L 185
Joshua St. OL14: Tod 1L 165
Jowkin La. OL11: Roch 6H 203
Joyce Av. FY4: Blackp 8F 88
Joy Pl. OL12: Roch 3C 204
Joy St. BL0: Ramsb 8G 181
OL12: Roch 3C 204
Jubilee Av. FY6: Pree 9N 41
L39: Orms 6L 209
PR2: Lea 8A 114
WN5: Orr 7G 221
Jubilee Cl. BB3: Darw 6D 158
BB4: Hasl 6F 160
Jubilee Ct. BB4: Hasl 6F 160
LA1: Lanc 6B 228
Jubilee Ct. *PR9: S'port* *6N 167*
(off Church Cl.)
PR25: Leyl 7H 153
Jubilee Dr. FY5: T Clev 9C 54
WN8: Skelm 3J 219
Jubilee Ho. L37: Form 1C 214
Jubilee La. FY4: Blackp 3H 109
LA6: Lup, N'gin 5A 8
Jubilee La. Nth. FY4: Blackp 2G 109
Jubilee M. BB4: Hasl 5F 160
Jubilee Pl. PR6: Chor 5F 174
Jubilee Quay FY7: Flee 9H 41
Jubilee Rd. BB4: Hasl 5F 160
BB5: Chur 1M 141
PR4: Wal B 3K 151
PR5: Lost H 8K 135
Jubilee St. BB1: Blackb 5D 226 (4M 139)
BB3: Darw 6A 158
BB5: Clay M 8N 121
BB5: Osw 4L 141
BB10: Brierc 7K 105
BB12: Read 8C 102
Jubilee Ter. *BB6: Langh* *9D 100*
(off Whalley New Rd.)
PR4: Frec 1A 132
Jubilee Wlk. OL12: Whitw 3A 184
Jubilee Way FY8: L Ann 9H 109
OL14: Tod 7D 146
PR26: Cros 3M 171
Judd Holmes La. PR3: Chip 8F 70
Judd Ho. PR1: Prest 9G 229 (2H 135)
Judeland PR7: Chor 4C 174
Jude St. BB9: Nelson 2H 105
Judge Flds. BB8: Colne 5A 86
Judges' Lodgings Mus. 6B 228
Judith St. OL12: Roch 2N 203
JUDSON FOLD 6E 84
Julia M. *BL6: Hor* *9C 196*
(off Wright St.)
Julia St. BL6: Hor 9C 196
OL12: Roch 5B 204
July St. BB1: Blackb 4A 140
Jumbles Beck BL7: Turt 1K 199
Jumbles Country Pk. 3K 199
Jumbles Country Pk. Vis. Cen. 4K 199
Jumbles Sailing Club 3J 199
Jumbles Wlk. BL7: Turt 1K 199
Jumps La. OL14: Tod 8H 147
Jumps Rd. OL14: Tod 8H 147
Junction 7 Bus. Pk. BB5: Clay M 7L 121
Junction 12 Shop. Outlet BB9: Brierf 4E 104
Junction All. OL16: Roch 6C 204
Junction La. L40: Burs 9C 190
Junction Rd. PR1: Prest 1G 134
WA11: Rain 2J 225
Junction St. BB3: Darw 8B 158
BB8: Nelson 8K 85
BB9: Brierf 4F 104
BB12: Burnl 3C 124
(Padiham Rd.)
BB12: Burnl 2C 124
(Spa St.)
Junction Ter. PR7: Eux 1M 173
June Av. FY4: Blackp 9G 88
June St. BB1: Blackb 4A 140
June's Wlk. PR4: Wal B 2K 151
Juniper Cl. FY6: Pree 8N 41
Juniper Ct. BB5: Hunc 9D 122
Juniper Cft. PR6: Clay W 6C 154
Juniper Dr. OL16: Roch 6G 204
Juniper St. BB1: Blackb 1A 140
Juniper Way PR9: Banks 2F 168
Juniper Wood Cl. PR7: Chor 8C 174
Juno St. BB9: Nelson 9K 85
Jutland Av. OL11: Roch 5N 203
Jutland St. PR1: Prest 4M 229 (9K 115)

K

Kairnryan Cl. FY2: Blackp 6F 62
Kale Gro. L33: Kirk 5M 223
Kandel Pl. OL12: Whitw 5A 184
Kane St. PR2: Ash R 8F 114
Karan Way L31: Mell 7G 222
Karmo Ind. Est. OL11: Roch 7A 204
Karting 2000 Blackpool 5A 108
Kateholm OL13: Weir 9L 145
Kate St. BL0: Ramsb 8G 181
Kathan Cl. OL16: Roch 6E 204
Kathleen St. OL12: Roch 6A 204
Kay Brow BL0: Ramsb 8H 181
Kayfields BL2: Bolt 9L 199
Kay Fold Lodge BB1: Blackb 7L 119
Kay Gdns.
BB11: Burnl 4F 228 (4F 124)
Kay La. BD23: Con C 3H 53
Kayley La. BB7: Chatb 7D 74
Kayley Ter. BB7: Grind 4A 74
Kaymar Ind. Est. PR1: Prest 1M 135
Kay St. BB3: Darw 6B 158
BB4: Rawt 5M 161
BB5: Osw 5K 141
BB7: Clith 4K 81
BB9: Brierf 5F 104
BB12: Padi 9J 103
BL0: Eden 4J 181
BL7: Turt 1J 199
BL9: Bury 9M 201
(not continuous)
BL9: Summ 2H 201
FY1: Blackp 4J 227 (6B 88)
OL11: Roch 8B 204
OL15: Littleb 3J 205
PR1: Prest 6H 229 (1H 135)
Kayswell Rd. LA4: Morec 3F 22
Kearsley Av. PR4: Tarl 9E 150
KEARSTWICK 4E 8
Keasden Av. FY4: Blackp 2D 108
Keating Ct. FY7: Flee 1F 54
Keats Av. LA5: Bolt S 4L 15
OL12: Roch 3L 203
OL14: Tod 1N 165
PR4: Wart 2K 131
WN5: Bill 9G 220

276 A-Z Lancashire

Keats Cl.—King St.

Keats Cl. BB5: Bax 6D 142
BB8: Colne 5A 86
FY2: Blackp 5F 62
FY5: T Clev 1G 62
PR7: E'ton 9G 172
Keats Fold BB12: Burnl 2L 123
Keats Rd. BL8: Greenm 3E 200
Keats Ter. PR8: S'port 8M 167
Keats Way PR4: Cott 5A 114
KEBCOTE 6J 147
Keble Dr. L10: Aint 7B 222
Kebs Rd. HX7: Black H 5K 147
OL14: Tod 4G 146
Keele Cl. FY5: T Clev 1G 62
Keele Wlk. BB1: Blackb 6F 226 (4N 139)
Keeley Cl. BB2: Blackb 8K 139
Keelham La. OL14: Tod 7N 147
Keen Cl. PR4: Hutt 6B 134
Keep, The BB2: Blackb 5C 226
Keepers Dr. OL12: Roch 3J 203
Keepers Ga. FY8: L Ann 1K 129
Keeper's Hey FY5: T Clev 8G 54
Keeper's La. PR3: Barn 3C 60
Keepers Wood Way PR3: Catt 9A 60
PR7: Chor 8B 174
Keer Bank LA1: Lanc 6G 22
Keer Bri. Bus. Pk. LA5: Carn 7A 12
Keer Holme La. LA6: Ark, Cap 4J 13
Keer Vs. LA5: Carn 7A 12
Keighley Av. BB8: Colne 5A 86
Keighley Ct. *BB8: Colne 6D 86*
(off Keighley Rd.)
Keighley Rd. BB8: Colne, Lane B 6B 86
BB8: Traw 9F 86
BD22: Cowl 6B 86
Keirby Wlk. BB11: Burnl 2E 228 (3E 124)
Keith Gro. FY5: T Clev 2D 62
Keith St. BB12: Burnl 3A 124
KELBROOK 6D 78
Kelbrook Dr. BB11: Burnl 6C 124
Kelbrook Rd. BB18: Barnw, Salt 3N 77
Kelday Cl. L33: Kirk 8K 223
Keld Cl. BL8: Bury 8G 200
Kelk Beck Cl. L31: Magh 9E 216
KELLAMERGH 1H 131
Kellet Acre PR5: Lost H 9K 135
Kellet Av. PR25: Leyl 6N 153
Kellet Ct. LA1: Lanc 7A 228 (8J 23)
Kellet La. LA2: Lanc, Slyne 3M 23
LA5: Neth K 3M 23
LA6: Borw, Carn, Tewit 2F 12
PR5: Bam B 1D 154
Kellet Rd. LA5: Carn 9B 12
LA6: Over K 9B 12
Kellet Rd. Ind. Est. LA5: Carn 9C 12
Kellett Cl. WN5: Wigan 2N 221
Kellett St. BL1: Bolt 7F 198
OL16: Roch 5E 204
PR7: Chor 6E 174
Kelly St. BB2: Blackb 7K 139
Kelmarsh Cl. FY3: Blackp 8H 89
Kelne Ho. LA1: Lanc 7B 228
Kelsall Av. BB1: Blackb 9B 120
Kelsall St. OL16: Roch 5C 204
Kelsey St. LA1: Lanc 7A 228 (8J 23)
Kelso Av. FY5: T Clev 1D 62
Kelso Cl. L33: Kirk 4J 223
Kelsons Av. FY5: T Clev 1J 63
Kelswick Dr. BB9: Nelson 4J 105
Kelverdale Rd. FY5: T Clev 3F 62
Kelvin Rd. FY5: T Clev 5D 62
Kelvin St. BB3: Darw 6N 157
Kelwood Av. BL9: Bury 8B 202
Kemble Cl. BL6: Hor 8C 196
Kem Mill La. PR6: Whit W 7D 154
Kemp Av. OL11: Roch 8A 204
Kemp Ct. BB1: Blackb 6N 119
Kemple Vw. BB7: Clith 5J 81
Kemp St. FY7: Flee 8H 41
Kempton Av. FY3: Blackp 7E 88
Kempton Pk. Fold PR8: S'port 2M 187
Kempton Pk. Rd. L10: Aint 7D 222
Kempton Ri. BB1: Blackb 8F 226 (5N 139)
Kempton Rd. LA1: Lanc 3M 29
Kenbury Cl. L33: Kirk 6M 223
Kenbury Rd. L33: Kirk 6M 223
Kendal Av. BB9: Barrf 7H 85
FY3: Blackp 1F 88
FY5: T Clev 8D 54
OL12: Roch 3J 203
Kendal Cl. BD23: Hell 1D 52
WA11: Rain 9K 219
Kendal Dr. L31: Magh 9C 216
LA4: Morec 4F 22
WA11: Rain 9J 219
Kendall Cl. BB2: Blackb 8L 139
Kendalmans BD24: Gig 3N 35
Kendal M. *L33: Kirk 6J 223*
(off Windermere Dr.)
Kendal Rd. BD23: Hell 1D 52
BL0: Ramsb 3F 200
FY8: L Ann 8D 108
L33: Kirk 6J 223
LA6: K Lon 6E 8
Kendal Rd. W. BL0: Ramsb 3E 200
Kendal Row BB1: Belt 1F 158
Kendal St. BB1: Blackb 2D 226 (2M 139)
BB7: Clith 2M 81
BB9: Nelson 1H 105
PR1: Prest 5H 229 (9H 115)
(not continuous)
Kendal Way PR8: Ains 1B 206
Kenford Dr. WN3: Wins 9N 221
Kenilworth OL11: Roch 7B 204
Kenilworth Av. FY7: Flee 1E 54
Kenilworth Cl. BB12: Padi 1J 123
Kenilworth Ct. FY7: Flee 1D 54
FY8: L Ann 2F 128
Kenilworth Dr. BB7: Clith 5J 81
BB18: Earl 4D 78
Kenilworth Gdns. FY4: Blackp 2B 108
Kenilworth Pl. FY7: Flee 1D 54
LA1: Lanc 2L 29
Kenilworth Rd. FY8: L Ann 2F 128
LA3: Morec 5B 22
PR8: Ains 8B 186
Kenion Rd. OL11: Roch 7M 203
Kenion St. OL16: Roch 6C 204
Kenlis Rd. PR3: Barn 8C 60
Kenmay Wlk. L33: Kirk 7M 223
Kenmure Pl. PR1: Prest 1J 229 (7J 115)
Kennedy Cl. LA1: Lanc 1H 29
Kennelwood Av. L33: Kirk 7L 223
Kennessee Cl. L31: Magh 2D 222
KENNESSE GREEN 2C 222
Kennet Dr. PR2: Fulw 1J 115
Kennett Dr. PR25: Leyl 5L 153
Kennington Rd. PR2: Fulw 5K 115
Kensington Av. PR1: Penw 2E 134
Kensington Cl. BL8: Greenm 4F 200
OL16: Milnr 7K 205
Kensington Ct. L37: Form 9A 206
LA4: Morec 2E 22
Kensington Dr. PR2: Fulw 5J 115
Kensington Gdns. PR5: Lost H 7M 135
Kensington Ho. *LA1: Lanc 2K 29*
(off Kensington Rd.)
PR2: Fulw 5K 115
(off Kensington Dr.)
Kensington Ind. Est. PR9: S'port 8J 167
Kensington Pl. BB11: Burnl 5B 124
Kensington Rd. FY3: Blackp 3N 227 (6D 88)
FY5: T Clev 9C 54
FY8: L Ann 4K 129
LA1: Lanc 2K 29
LA4: Morec 3B 22
PR7: Chor 7D 174
PR9: S'port 7J 167
WN5: Wigan 6N 221
Kensington St. BB9: Nelson 3G 104
OL11: Roch 9B 204
Kenstone Ct. FY4: Blackp 3K 109
Kent Av. FY5: T Clev 8E 54
L37: Form 2A 214
PR5: Walt D 5N 135
Kent Ct. BB9: Barrf 7H 85
Kent Dr. BB1: Blackb 4E 140
PR25: Leyl 5N 153
Kent Ho. LA1: Lanc 9C 228 (9K 23)
Kentmere Av. OL12: Roch 2E 204
PR5: Walt D 6N 135
PR25: Far 4K 153
Kentmere Cl. BB12: Burnl 1N 123
FY7: Flee 1D 54
Kentmere Dr. BB2: Blackb 8F 138
FY4: Blackp 9J 89
PR4: Longt 8M 133
Kentmere Gro. LA4: Morec 4D 22
Kentmere Rd. LA1: Lanc 5F 228 (7L 23)
Kenton Cl. L37: Form 6A 206
Kent Rd. FY1: Blackp 4J 227 (6B 88)
L37: Form 2A 214
PR8: Birk 1G 187
Kent's Cl. PR4: Wesh 2K 111
Kent St. BB1: Blackb 6E 226 (4N 139)
BB12: Burnl 2D 124
FY7: Flee 8H 41
LA1: Lanc 6K 23
OL11: Roch 7C 204
PR1: Prest 1K 229 (7J 115)
Kent Wlk. BB4: Hasl 7F 160
Kent Way LA3: Morec 5F 22
Kenway WA11: Rain 4L 225
Kenwood Av. LA4: Morec 4A 22
Kenworthys Flats PR9: S'port 6H 167
Kenworthy St. OL16: Roch 6F 204
Kenworthy Ter. OL16: Roch 6F 204
Kenwyn Av. FY3: Blackp 7E 88
Kenyon Cl. L33: Kirk 4L 223
Kenyon Clough BB4: Hasl 1F 180
Kenyon Cres. BL9: Bury 7L 201
KENYON FOLD 8J 203
Kenyon Fold OL11: Roch 8J 203
Kenyon La. BB6: Dinck 5N 99
PR6: Heap 8H 155
Kenyon Rd. BB9: Brierf 3E 104
LA4: Morec 3F 22
WN6: Stand 2N 213
Kenyons La. L31: Lyd, Magh 7C 216
L37: Form 9A 206
Kenyons Lodge L31: Magh 8D 216
Kenyons Pl. L31: Lyd 8C 216
Kenyon St. BB1: Blackb 3C 140
BB4: Rawt 4M 161
BB5: Acc 2B 142
BL0: Ramsb 7H 181
BL9: Bury 9M 201
OL13: Bac 7M 163
Kenyon Way BL8: Tott 8E 200
Keppel Pl.
BB11: Burnl 2A 228 (4C 124)
Kepple La. PR3: Gars 6M 59
Kerenhappuch St. BL0: Ramsb 9G 181
Kerfoots La. WN8: Skelm 3G 218
Kermoor Av. BL1: Bolt 7E 198
Kerr Cl. L33: Kirk 4K 223
Kerr Pl. PR1: Prest 9G 114
Kerry La. PR9: Banks 2F 168
Kersey Rd. L32: Kirk 9L 223
Kersey Wlk. L32: Kirk 9L 223
Kershaw Cl. *BB4: Craws 9M 143*
(off Lord St.)
Kershaw Rd. OL14: Wals 6K 165
Kershaw St. BB5: Chur 1L 141
BL2: Bolt 8J 199
OL12: Roch 5C 204
OL13: Bac 5K 163
(off Union St)
PR6: Chor 5G 174
WN5: Orr 5L 221
Kerslake Way L38: Hight 7A 214
Kerslea Av. FY3: Blackp 2K 89
Kerton Row PR8: Birk 1F 186
Keston Gro. FY4: Blackp 4C 108
Kestor La. PR3: Longr 3J 97
Kestrel Cl. BB1: Blackb 9L 119
FY5: T Clev 7F 54
PR6: Heap 3J 175
Kestrel Ct. BB11: Hapt 5L 123
PR9: S'port 7K 167
Kestrel Dr. BB3: Darw 4L 157
BL9: Bury 9N 201
Kestrel M. OL11: Roch 6K 203
WN8: Skelm 8N 211
Kestrel Pk. WN8: Skelm 8N 211
Kestrel Pl. L40: Burs 2N 209
Kestrel Ter. *BB5: Osw 5L 141*
(off Heys)
Keswick Cl. BB5: Hunc 8C 122
L31: Magh 9D 216
OL14: Tod 9J 147
PR8: Ains 1C 206
Keswick Ct. *LA1: Lanc 7M 23*
(off Keswick Wlk.)
Keswick Dr. BB2: Blackb 8F 138
Keswick Gro. FY6: K Sea 8M 41
LA3: Heys 2K 27
Keswick Rd. BB10: Burnl 8E 104
FY1: Blackp 5L 227 (7C 88)
FY8: L Ann 9E 108
LA1: Lanc 7L 23
Keswick Wlk. LA1: Lanc 7M 23
Keswick Way WA11: Rain 9K 219
Kettering Rd. PR8: Ains 8B 186
Kevin Av. FY6: Poul F 6M 63
Kevin Gro. LA3: O'ton 6B 28
KEW 2L 187
Kew (Park & Ride) 9N 167
Kew Gdns. PR1: Penw 2E 134
PR25: Far 4L 153
Kew Gro. FY5: T Clev 2D 62
Kew Ho. Dr. PR8: S'port 3N 187
Kew Retail Pk. PR8: S'port 2N 187
Kew Rd. BB9: Nelson 9K 85
PR8: Birk 2G 187
Keynsham Gro. BB12: Burnl 2B 124
Key Sike La. OL14: Tod 2M 165
Key Vw. BB3: Darw 1C 178
Khubsuret Ho. OL11: Roch 7B 204
Khyber St. BB8: Colne 7N 85
Kibble Bank BB9: Brierf 6H 105
Kibble Cres. BB10: Burnl 7G 105
Kibble Gro. BB9: Brierf 6H 105
Kibbles Brow BL7: Brom C 5H 199
Kibboth Crew BL0: Ramsb 7G 180
Kidbrooke Av. FY4: Blackp 5B 108
Kidder St. BB2: Blackb 8L 139
Kiddrow La. BB12: Burnl 2L 123
Kidlington Cl. PR5: Lost H 8M 135
Kidsgrove PR2: Ingol 4C 114
Kidsplay 1G 186
Kielder Ct. FY8: L Ann 4B 130
Kielder Dr. BB12: Burnl 2C 124
Kiers Ct. BL6: Hor 9F 196
Kilbane St. FY7: Flee 3F 54
Kilburn Dr. WN6: Shev 5K 213
Kilburn Gro. WN3: Wins 8N 221
Kilburn Rd. WN5: Orr 6F 220
Kilcrash La. PR3: Nateby 5G 58
Kildale Cl. L31: Magh 9B 216
Kildare Av. FY5: T Clev 8G 55
Kildare Rd. FY2: Blackp 8D 62
Kildonan Av. FY4: Blackp 3G 108
Kilgrimol Gdns. FY8: L Ann 8C 108
Kilkerran Cl. PR6: Chor 6F 174
Killer St. BL0: Ramsb 8H 181
Killiard La. BB2: Blackb 3F 138
Killingbeck Cl. L40: Burs 9B 190
Killington St. BB10: Burnl 8G 105
Kilmory Pl. FY2: Blackp 6F 62
Kilmuir Cl. PR2: Fulw 4M 115
Kiln Bank OL12: Whitw 4N 183
Kilnbank Av. LA4: Morec 3A 22
Kiln Bank La. OL12: Whitw 4N 183
Kiln Brow BL7: Brom C 5J 199
Kiln Cl. BB7: Clith 1N 81
Kiln Ct. *LA1: Lanc 6K 23*
(off Mainway)
Kiln Cft. PR6: Clay W 4D 154
Kilnerdeyne Ter. OL16: Roch 7B 204
Kiln Fld. BL7: Brom C 5F 198
Kilngate PR5: Lost H 5M 135
Kiln Hill BB12: High 4L 103
Kilnhouse La. FY8: L Ann 8F 108
Kiln Ho. Way BB5: Osw 5N 141
KILNHURST 2M 165
Kilnhurst Av. OL14: Tod 2M 165
Kilnhurst La. OL14: Tod 3M 165
Kilnhurst Mt. OL14: Tod 2N 165
Kilnhurst Rd. OL14: Tod 2M 165
Kiln La. BB7: Gis 1K 75
BB7: Pay 6A 52
FY6: Ham 1A 64
LA2: Wray 7D 18
OL16: Milnr 7J 205
WN8: Skelm 1J 219
Kiln Mt. OL16: Milnr 7J 205
Kilns, The BB11: Burnl 6F 124
Kiln St. BB9: Nelson 2H 105
BL0: Ramsb 9G 180
Kiln Ter. *OL13: Bac 7H 163*
(off Newchurch Rd.)
Kiln Wlk. OL12: Roch 3B 204
Kilruddery Rd. PR1: Prest 3H 135
Kilsby Cl. PR5: Walt D 5A 136
Kilshaw St. WN5: Wigan 6M 221
Kilworth Height PR2: Fulw 4F 114
Kilworth St. OL11: Roch 9A 204
Kimberley Av. FY4: Blackp 4D 108
Kimberley Cl. BB10: Brierc 7K 105
Kimberley Rd. BL1: Bolt 8E 198
PR2: Ash R 7F 114
Kimberley St. BB10: Brierc 7K 105
OL13: Bac 8E 162
PR7: Copp 4A 194
Kimberly Cl. PR4: Frec 2N 131
Kimble Cl. BL8: Greenm 3E 200
Kimble Gro. BB9: Brierf 6H 105
Kime St. BB12: Burnl 3A 124
Kincardine Av. FY4: Blackp 3G 108
Kincraig Bus. Pk.
FY2: Blackp 7F 62
Kincraig Ct. FY2: Blackp 7F 62
Kincraig Pl. FY2: Blackp 5F 62
Kincraig Rd. FY2: Blackp 5F 62
Kinder Cnr. FY6: Poul F 8H 63
Kinders Fold OL15: Littleb 7J 185
Kineton Av. OL14: Tod 1M 165
King Edward Av. FY2: Blackp 1B 88
FY8: L Ann 4G 128
King Edward St. BB5: Osw 5J 141
King Edward Ter. BB9: Barrf 9H 85
Kingfisher Bank BB11: Burnl 5N 123
Kingfisher Cl. BB1: Blackb 9M 119
L33: Kirk 4K 223
PR7: Chor 9B 174
Kingfisher Ct. BB5: Osw 5L 141
L31: Lyd 7A 216
LA2: Caton 3H 25
OL12: Roch 1F 204
PR1: Prest 9G 114
PR9: S'port 6K 167
Kingfisher Dr. BL9: Bury 9N 201
FY6: Poul F 9H 63
Kingfisher M. FY6: Poul F 9H 63
Kingfisher Pk. WN8: Skelm 8N 211
Kingfisher St. PR1: Prest 1N 229 (7L 115)
(not continuous)
Kingfisher Way FY7: Flee 1E 54
PR5: Bam B 6C 136
King George Av. FY2: Blackp 1B 88
King Georges Hall 4B 226
King Henry M. BB7: Bolt B 9K 51
King La. BB7: Clith 3L 81
Kings Arc. LA1: Lanc 7C 228
Kings Arms Cl. LA1: Lanc 7C 228 (8J 23)
Kings Av. BB4: Rawt 6M 161
Kingsbarn Cl. PR2: Fulw 3N 115
King's Bri. Cl. BB2: Blackb 7J 139
Kingsbridge Cl. PR1: Penw 7H 135
Kingsbridge Ct. *BB2: Blackb 7J 139*
(off Kingsbridge Wharf)
King's Bri. St. BB2: Blackb 7J 139
Kingsbridge Wharf BB2: Blackb 7J 139
Kingsbury Cl. BL8: Bury 7F 200
PR8: Ains 9B 186
Kingsbury Ct. WN8: Skelm 8N 211
Kingsbury Pl. BB10: Burnl 7H 105
King's C'way. BB9: Brierf 5H 105
Kings Cl. FY3: Stain 5L 89
FY6: Poul F 8L 63
LA5: Arn 2F 4
PR7: Buck V 9B 154
Kingscote Dr. FY3: Blackp 3E 88
(not continuous)
Kings Ct. *LA6: K Lon 6F 8*
(off Tram La.)
PR25: Leyl 6K 153
Kings Cres. LA3: Heys 5M 21
PR25: Leyl 6K 153
King's Cft. PR5: Walt D 3N 135
King's Cft. M. PR5: Walt D 3N 135
Kingsdale Av. BB10: Burnl 7F 104
LA3: Heys 7L 21
PR2: Ribb 4N 115
Kingsdale Cl. PR5: Walt D 3B 136
PR25: Leyl 9L 153
Kingsdale Rd. LA1: Lanc 9H 23
Kings Dr. BB3: Hodd 6F 158
BB12: Padi 3J 123
LA5: Carn 9B 12
PR2: Fulw 4G 115
Kingsfield Rd. L31: Magh 3B 222
KINGSFOLD 6G 134
Kingsfold Av. PR2: Fulw 5K 115
Kingsfold Dr. PR1: Penw 6F 134
Kings Gro. OL12: Roch 1F 204
Kingshaven Dr. PR1: Penw 6H 135
Kings Hey Dr. PR9: S'port 5M 167
King's Highway BB4: Hasl 8G 142
BB5: Acc, Hunc, S Fold 1F 142
BB5: Acc, S Fold 3G 142
BB5: Hunc 8E 122
(not continuous)
Kingshotte Gdns. BB9: Barrf 8G 84
Kingsland OL11: Roch 9N 203
Kingsland Gro. BB11: Burnl 5F 124
FY1: Blackp 6N 227 (7D 88)
Kingsland Rd. BB11: Burnl 6F 124
OL11: Roch 9M 203
Kings Lea PR7: Adl 5H 195
Kingsley Av. BB12: Padi 2K 123
Kingsley Cl. BB2: Fenis 9E 138
BB5: Chur 1M 141
FY5: T Clev 9G 54
L31: Lyd 6B 216
Kingsley Ct. FY4: Blackp 3F 108
Kingsley Dr. PR7: Chor 9C 174
Kingsley Rd. BB8: Colne 5G 87
FY3: Blackp 8H 89
PR4: Cott 3B 114
Kingsley St. BB9: Nelson 9K 85
Kingsmead BB1: Blackb 4D 140
PR7: Chor 9E 174
Kings Mdw. PR8: Ains 1D 206
Kingsmede FY4: Blackp 3E 108
Kingsmere Av. FY8: L Ann 8F 108
Kingsmill Av. BB7: Whall 2G 101
Kings Mill La. BD24: Sett 3N 35
Kingsmuir Av. PR2: Fulw 5N 115
Kingsmuir Cl. LA3: Heys 9K 21
Kings Own Royal Regiment Mus. 7C 228
(within Lancaster City Mus.)
Kings Rd. BB2: Blackb 8J 139
BB5: Acc 9A 122
FY5: T Clev 1C 62
FY8: L Ann 3E 128
OL16: Roch 8E 204
King's Sq. FY1: Blackp 1K 227 (5C 88)
Kingston Av. BB5: Acc 4N 141
FY4: Blackp 4C 108
Kingston Cl. FY6: K Sea 7M 41
Kingston Cres. BB4: Hasl 8F 160
PR9: S'port 1B 168
Kingston Dr. FY8: L Ann 2K 129
Kingston M. *FY5: T Clev 9H 55*
(off Crabtree Orchard)
Kingston Pl. BB3: Lwr D 9M 139
King St. BB2: Blackb 6B 226 (4L 139)
BB4: Hasl 3G 160
BB4: W'foot 7C 162
BB5: Acc 2A 142
BB5: Chur 2L 141
BB5: Clay M 7M 121

King St.—Lancaster Dr.

King St. BB6: Gt H 4J 121
BB7: Clith 3L 81
BB7: Whall 6J 101
BB8: Colne 6B 86
BB9: Brierf 5E 104
BB10: Brierc 7K 105
BB12: Padi 1H 123
BB18: Barnw 2M 77
BL0: Ramsb 8H 181
BL2: Bolt 8K 199
BL6: Hor 9B 196
BL7: Brom C 5F 198
FY1: Blackp 1K 227 (5C 88)
FY7: Flee 9G 41
LA1: Lanc 7C 228 (8K 23)
LA2: H Ben 6L 19
(off Main St.)
LA4: Morec 3B 22
LA5: Carn 9A 12
OL12: Whitw 3A 184
OL13: Bac 5K 163
OL14: Tod 1N 165
OL16: Roch 6C 204
PR3: Longr 3K 97
PR5: Lost H 9L 135
PR7: Chor 8F 174
PR8: S'port 8G 167
PR25: Leyl 6K 153
King St. E. OL11: Roch 8C 204
King St. Sth. OL11: Roch 8B 204
(not continuous)
King St. Ter. BB9: Brierf 5E 104
King's Wlk. FY5: T Clev 7D 54
Kingsway BB2: Blackb 5A 226
BB3: Lwr D 9A 140
BB4: Hasl 6E 160
BB5: Chur 9N 121
BB5: Hunc 8E 122
BB6: Gt H 3M 121
BB11: Burnl 1D 228 (3E 124)
BB11: Hapt 6H 123
FY4: Blackp 2C 108
FY5: T Clev 1C 62
FY8: L Ann 4J 129
LA1: Lanc 7L 23
LA3: Heys 9L 21
OL16: Roch 8E 204
PR1: Penw 2E 134
PR2: Ash R 7C 114
PR5: Bam B 8A 136
PR7: Eux 4A 174
PR8: S'port 7G 166
PR25: Leyl 8H 153
Kingsway Av. PR3: Brou 7F 94
Kingsway Bus. Pk. OL16: Roch 9G 205
(not continuous)
Kingsway Ct. LA3: Heys 7M 21
Kingsway Pk. Sports Cen. 8F 204
Kingsway Retail Pk. LA1: Lanc 7L 23
OL16: Roch 6G 204
Kingsway W. PR1: Penw 2D 134
Kingsway W. Ind. Pk. OL16: Roch 8E 204
Kingswood Cl. FY8: L Ann 4L 129
Kingswood Ct. L33: Kirk 6L 223
Kingswood Ho. PR8: Birk 9F 166
Kingswood Pk. PR8: Birk 9F 166
Kingswood Pk. M. PR8: Birk 8F 166
Kingswood Rd. PR25: Leyl 6K 153
Kingswood St. PR1: Prest 1H 135
King William St. BB1: Blackb 3C 226 (3M 139)
(not continuous)
Kingwood Cres. WN5: Wigan 5N 221
Kinlet Rd. WN3: Wigan 7M 221
Kinloch Way L39: Orms 7J 209
Kinnerton Pl. FY5: T Clev 3F 62
Kinnical La. LA7: Hale 1C 6
Kinross Cl. BB1: Blackb 4A 140
BL0: Ramsb 3F 200
Kinross Cres. FY4: Blackp 9G 88
Kinross St. BB11: Burnl 4B 124
Kinross Wlk. BB1: Blackb 4A 140
(off William Hopwood St.)
Kinsacre PR3: C'town 9L 59
Kintbury Rd. FY8: L Ann 4F 128
Kintour Rd. FY8: L Ann 2L 129
Kintyre Cl. FY4: Blackp 2F 108
Kintyre Way LA3: Heys 9K 21
Kipling Ct. FY3: Blackp 8H 89
Kipling Dr. FY3: Blackp 8H 89
Kipling Mnr. FY3: Blackp 8H 89
Kipling Pl. BB6: Gt H 5H 121
Kirby Dr. PR4: Frec 2N 131
Kirby Rd. BB2: Blackb 7L 139
BB9: Nelson 2F 104
FY1: Blackp 7H 227 (8B 88)
Kirk Av. BB7: Clith 3J 81
Kirkbeck Cl. LA2: Brookh 2K 25
Kirkbeck M. BB7: Bolt B 8K 51
Kirkburn Vw. BL8: Bury 8H 201
KIRKBY 8K 223
Kirkby Av. FY5: T Clev 8E 54
PR25: Leyl 6A 154
Kirkby Bank Rd. L33: Know P 8N 223
Kirkby Gallery 8K 223
Kirkby Leisure Cen. 9K 223
KIRKBY LONSDALE 6F 8
Kirkby Lonsdale Golf Course 3F 8
Kirkby Lonsdale Rd.
LA2: Aug, Gress, Halt 1C 24
LA6: Over K 9F 12
KIRKBY PARK 7H 223
Kirkby Row L32: Kirk 7H 223
Kirkby Station (Rail) 7H 223
Kirk Cotts. PR3: Chip 5G 70
(off Church Raike)
Kirkdale Av. BB4: Newc 6C 162
FY8: L Ann 1F 128
Kirkdale Cl. BB3: Darw 9C 158
Kirkdale Gdns. WN8: Uph 4D 220
Kirkdale Rd. BB6: Langh 1C 120
Kirkdene Av. BB8: Foul 2A 86
Kirkdene M. BB8: Foul 2A 86
(off Dene Av.)
Kirkes Rd. LA1: Lanc 8F 228 (9L 23)
Kirkfell Dr. BB12: Burnl 1A 124
Kirkfield PR3: Chip 5F 70
Kirkgate BB11: Burnl 5E 124
(not continuous)
BD24: Sett 3N 35
PR4: K'ham 4N 111
Kirkgate Cen. PR4: K'ham 4N 111
Kirkgate La. LA6: Tewit 3F 12
KIRKHAM 4N 111
Kirkham & Wesham By-Pass
PR4: K'ham, Wesh 4K 111
Kirkham Av. FY1: Blackp 8E 88
Kirkham By-Pass PR4: K'ham 5L 111
Kirkham Cl. PR25: Leyl 6G 152
Kirkham Pool 4M 111
Kirkham Rd. PR4: Frec 7M 111
(not continuous)
PR4: Trea 3B 112
PR4: Weet 8E 90
PR9: S'port 2N 167
Kirkham St. PR1: Prest 4H 229 (9H 115)
PR4: Weet 4D 90
Kirkham Trad. Pk. PR4: K'ham 6N 111
Kirkham & Wesham Station (Rail) 3L 111
Kirk Head PR4: Much H 5J 151
Kirkhill Av. BB4: Hasl 4H 161
Kirk Hill Rd. BB4: Hasl 4H 161
KIRKHOLT 9C 204
Kirk Ho. BB5: Chur 2L 141
Kirkland Cl. BB1: Blackb 9A 120
Kirkland Ct. BB1: Blackb 9A 120
Kirkland Pl. PR2: Ash R 9B 114
Kirklands LA2: Hest B 8J 15
PR3: Chip 5G 70
Kirklands Rd. LA6: Over K 1F 16
Kirklees BL8: Tott 6F 200
Kirklees Cl. BL8: Tott 6F 200
Kirklees Rd. PR8: Birk 4F 186
Kirklees St. BL8: Tott 6E 200
Kirkmoor Cl. BB7: Clith 2K 81
Kirkmoor Rd. BB7: Clith 2K 81
Kirk Rd. BB5: Chur 1L 141
Kirkside Vw. BB11: Hapt 5H 123
Kirkstall OL12: Roch 5B 204
Kirkstall Av. BB12: S'stone 9D 102
FY1: Blackp 8E 88
OL10: Heyw 9G 202
OL15: Littleb 8K 185
Kirkstall Cl. PR7: Chor 9F 174
Kirkstall Dr. BB18: Barnw 1A 78
L37: Form 1B 214
PR7: Chor 9F 174
Kirkstall Rd. PR7: Chor 9F 174
PR8: Birk 3F 186
Kirkstead Wlk. L31: Mell 7G 223
Kirkstile Cres. WN3: Wins 9N 221
Kirkstone WN5: Wigan 4M 221
Kirkstone Av. BB2: Blackb 8F 138
FY7: Flee 3D 54
Kirkstone Dr. FY5: T Clev 4C 62
LA4: Morec 3D 22
Kirkstone Rd. FY8: L Ann 8D 108
Kirk Vw. BB4: W'foot 6E 162
Kirkwood Ct. PR26: Leyl 6D 152
(off Dunkirk La.)
Kirton Cres. FY8: L Ann 2J 129
Kirton Pl. FY5: T Clev 2E 62
Kit Brow La. LA2: Ell 1N 37
Kitchen St. OL16: Roch 5D 204
Kitson Wood Rd. OL14: Tod 8H 147
Kitter St. OL12: Roch 2E 204
KITT GREEN 2L 221
Kitt Grn. Rd. WN5: Wigan 2L 221
Kittiwake Cl. FY5: T Clev 2F 62
Kittiwake Rd. PR6: Heap 3J 175
Kittlingbourne Brow PR5: H Walt 5C 136
Kittygill La. LA6: L Big 6E 8
Kitty La. FY4: Blackp 5G 109
Knacks La. OL12: Roch 9L 183
Knaresboro Av. FY3: Blackp 7F 88
Knaresborough Cl. FY6: Carl 6J 63
Knebworth Cl. PR6: Clay W 5E 154
Kneps Holiday Home & Touring Pk.
FY5: T Clev 9L 55
Knight Cres. BB3: Lwr D 1A 158
Knighton Av. BB2: Blackb 9K 119
Knightsbridge Av. BB8: Colne 6M 85
FY4: Blackp 3D 108
Knightsbridge Cl. FY8: L Ann 2K 129
PR4: Wesh 3K 111
Knightsbridge Wlk. L33: Kirk 4J 223
Knightscliffe Cres. WN6: Shev 6G 213
Knights Cl. FY5: T Clev 2F 62
KNITTING ROW 9F 56
Knitting Row La. PR3: Out R 8F 56
Knob Hall Gdns. PR9: S'port 3M 167
Knob Hall La. PR9: S'port 3M 167
Knoll, The LA2: Hest B 9J 15
Knoll La. PR4: Lit H 3K 151
Knot Acre PR4: New L 8D 134
Knot La. BB7: News 6C 52
PR5: Walt D 3A 136
Knott End Golf Course 8K 41
KNOTT END-ON-SEA 8L 41
Knott End Sailing Club 9K 41
Knott Hill OL12: Whitw 9A 164
Knott Hill St. OL12: Whitw 9B 164
Knott La. LA5: Arn 2E 4
KNOTTS 4H 51
Knotts Brow BL7: Edgw 2M 199
Knotts Dr. BB8: Colne 8N 85
Knotts La. BB8: Colne 7N 85
BB12: Burnl 3K 123
BD23: Tos 3H 51
Knotts Mt. BB8: Colne 8N 85
Knotts Rd. OL14: Tod 8G 146
Knott St. BB3: Darw 6A 158
Knotwood Ct. BB5: Chur 3L 141
Knowe Hill Cres. LA1: Lanc 4M 29
Knowl Cl. BL0: Ramsb 1H 201
Knowle, The FY2: Blackp 9C 62
Knowle Av. FY2: Blackp 1B 88
FY5: T Clev 2E 62
PR8: Ains 7C 186
Knowle Fold BB3: Darw 4B 158
KNOWLE GREEN 1C 98
Knowle La. BB3: Darw 4A 158
Knowles Brow BB7: S'hurst 8A 80
Knowles Farm Cl. WN8: Roby M 1E 220
Knowlesly Mdws. BB3: Darw 9C 158
Knowlesly Rd. BB3: Darw 9B 158
Knowles Rd. FY8: L Ann 1E 128
Knowles St. BB1: Rish 8H 121
PR1: Prest 9N 115
PR7: Chor 8E 174
Knowles Wood Dr. PR7: Chor 8C 174
KNOWLEY 4G 175
Knowley Brow PR6: Chor 4G 175
Knowl Gap Av. BB4: Hasl 6F 160
Knowl Hill Dr. OL12: Roch 3J 203
Knowl La. OL12: Roch 9F 182
Knowl Mdw. BB4: Hasl 8F 160
Knowlmere St. BB5: Acc 1A 142
Knowl Rd. OL16: Roch 7G 205
Knowl Syke St. OL12: Ward 7F 184
Knowl Vw. BL8: Tott 7F 200
OL15: Littleb 3J 205
KNOWL WOOD 5K 165
Knowlwood Bottom OL14: Tod 5J 165
Knowlwood Rd. OL14: Tod 5K 165
Knowlys Av. LA3: Heys 8L 21
Knowlys Cres. LA3: Heys 8L 21
Knowlys Dr. LA3: Heys 8L 21
Knowlys Gro. LA3: Heys 8L 21
Knowlys Rd. LA3: Heys 8K 21
Knowsley Av. FY3: Blackp 7E 88
OL14: Wals 6K 165
PR25: Far 3M 153
Knowsley Cl. LA1: Lanc 1H 29
PR5: Hogh 6H 137
Knowsley Cres. FY5: T Clev 1J 63
OL12: Whitw 9B 164
PR4: Weet 9D 90
Knowsley Dr. PR5: Hogh 6H 137
Knowsley Ent. Workshops
L33: Know P 9N 223
Knowsley Ga. FY7: Flee 9D 40
Knowsley Ind. Pk. L33: Know P 8A 224
Knowsley La. BL6: R'ton 2M 195
BL7: Edgw 2L 179
PR6: H Charn 2M 195
Knowsley M. L39: Orms 7L 209
Knowsley Pk. Way BB4: Hasl 7G 160
Knowsley Rd. BB1: Wilp 4N 119
BB4: Hasl 6G 160
L39: Orms 8L 209
PR9: S'port 5H 167
PR25: Leyl 7M 153
Knowsley Rd. Ind. Est. BB4: Hasl 6G 160
(not continuous)
Knowsley Rd. W. BB1: Clay D 3M 119
Knowsley St. BB8: Colne 7A 86
OL12: Roch 5B 204
PR1: Prest 7M 229 (1K 135)
(not continuous)
Knowsley Vw. WA11: Rain 2J 225
Knox Gro. FY1: Blackp 6M 227 (7D 88)
Knunck Knowles Dr. BB7: Clith 1L 81
Knutsford Rd. FY3: Blackp 8H 89
Knutsford Wlk. L31: Lyd 7C 216
KNUZDEN BROOK 4E 140
Knuzden Cotts. BB1: Blackb 4D 140
(off Haslingden Old Rd.)
Korea Rd. PR2: Fulw 4L 115
Kramar Wlk. L33: Kirk 8L 223
Kumara Cres. FY4: Blackp 9H 89
Kyan St. BB10: Burnl 8F 104
Kylemore Av. FY2: Blackp 9D 62
Kytson Cl. FY1: Blackp 3C 88

L

Laburnum Av. BL8: Tott 6E 200
FY8: L Ann 3A 130
PR5: Lost H 8L 135
Laburnum Cl. BB11: Burnl 5B 124
PR1: Prest 6M 115
Laburnum Cotts. BB4: Craws 7M 143
BB12: Burnl 1M 123
PR3: Pill 8K 43
Laburnum Ct. BL8: Tott 6E 200
Laburnum Cres. L32: Kirk 7J 223
Laburnum Dr. BB5: Osw 5M 141
PR2: Fulw 1G 115
WN8: Skelm 2H 219
Laburnum Gro. L31: Magh 1E 222
L40: Burs 7D 190
LA1: Lanc 8H 23
PR8: S'port 7M 167
Laburnum La. OL16: Milnr 9K 205
Laburnum Pk. BL2: Bolt 8H 199
LA5: Carn 1N 15
Laburnum Rd. BB1: Blackb 9A 120
BB4: Hasl 8F 160
LA1: Lanc 6K 23
PR6: Chor 3E 174
Laburnum St. BB4: Hasl 4F 160
FY3: Blackp 5D 88
Laburnum Ter. OL11: Roch 9B 204
Laburnum Way OL15: Littleb 8J 185
Lacey Ct. BB4: Hasl 4G 161
Lachman Rd. BB8: Traw 8E 86
Lacy Av. OL14: Wals 6K 165
PR1: Penw 6H 135
Ladbrooke Gro. BB11: Burnl 7C 124
Lade End LA3: Heys 8K 21
Ladies Row PR4: Whart 6D 92
Ladies Wlk. LA1: Lanc 6L 23
Ladies Wlk. Trad. Est. LA1: Lanc 6L 23
Lady Acre PR5: Bam B 8C 136
Lady Alice's Dr. L40: Lath 4B 210
Lady Anne Cl. L40: Scar 6G 188
Ladybank Av. PR2: Fulw 2M 115
Ladybower La. FY6: Poul F 9H 63
Lady Cl. BB3: Lwr D 1A 158
Lady Crosse Dr. PR6: Whit W 8E 154
LADY GREEN 7D 214
Lady Grn. Ct. L38: Ince B 8E 214
Lady Grn. La. L38: Ince B 7D 214
Lady Hartley Ct. BB8: Colne 5F 86
Lady Hey Cres. PR2: Lea 8N 113
LADY HOUSE 9H 205
Ladyhouse Cl. OL16: Milnr 8K 205
Ladyhouse La. OL16: Milnr 8J 205
(not continuous)
Ladyman St. PR1: Prest 7G 229 (1H 135)
Lady Pl. PR5: Walt D 4A 136
Ladysmith Av. BL9: Bury 8M 201
Ladysmith Rd. PR2: Ash R 7F 114
Lady St. PR1: Prest 4K 229 (9J 115)
Lady's Wlk. L40: Lath, W'head 7N 209
Lady Well Dr. PR2: Fulw 2M 115
Ladywell St.
PR1: Prest 5H 229 (9H 115)
Lafford La. WN8: Roby M, Uph 9F 212
LA Fitness
Formby 2A 214
Lagonda Dr. FY4: Blackp 3M 109
Laidley's Wlk. FY7: Flee 8E 40
Lairgill LA2: H Ben 6M 19
(off Butts La.)
Laitha La. LA6: H Cas 6F 8
Laithbutts La. LA6: Neth K 4C 16
Laithe St. BB8: Colne 7N 85
BB11: Burnl 5D 124
LAITHWAITE 3N 221
Laithwaite Rd. WN5: Wigan 4N 221
Lake Av. LA4: Morec 4N 21
Lake Bank OL15: Littleb 2K 205
Lakeber Av. LA2: H Ben 6L 19
Lakeber Cl. LA2: H Ben 6L 19
(off Lakeber Av.)
Lakeber Dr. LA2: H Ben 6L 19
Lake District National Pk. 1A 4
Lake Gro. LA4: Morec 4N 21
Lakeland Cl. BB7: B'ton 7G 100
PR3: Fort 2M 45
Lakeland Dr. BB7: Whall 2G 100
Lakeland Gdns. PR7: Chor 9C 174
Lakeland Way BB12: Burnl 1N 123
Lakeland Wildlife Oasis 3C 6
Lakenheath Dr. BL1: Bolt 7F 198
Lake Point FY8: L Ann 5K 129
Lake Rd. FY8: L Ann 5J 129
LA3: Morec 5N 21
Lake Rd. Nth. FY8: L Ann 4J 129
Lakes, The FY4: Blackp 9J 89
(off Mickleden Rd.)
Lakes Dr. WN5: Orr 5H 221
Lake Side OL15: Littleb 3K 205
Lakeside FY6: Pree 8A 42
Lakeside Av. WN5: Bill 8H 221
Lakeside Ct. WA11: Rain 4L 225
Lakeside Gdns. WA11: Rain 4L 225
Lakeside Miniature Railway 7F 166
Lakeside Superbowl
Preston 7G 115
Lake St. OL11: Roch 7C 204
Lake Vw. BL7: Belm 9K 177
OL15: Littleb 7J 185
Lakeview Ct. PR9: S'port 6H 167
Lake Vw. Rd. BB8: Colne 4A 86
Lake Wlk. WN5: Wigan 4L 221
Lakeway FY3: Blackp 4F 88
Lakewood Av. FY5: T Clev 2D 62
Lamaleach Dr. PR4: Frec 2M 131
Lamaleach Pk. PR4: Frec 3M 131
LAMBERHEAD GREEN 5L 221
Lamberhead Ho. WN5: Orr 5L 221
Lamberhead Ind. Est. WN5: Wigan 6L 221
Lamberhead Rd. WN5: Wigan 5L 221
Lambert Cl. PR2: Ribb 6A 116
Lambert Rd. LA1: Lanc 5J 23
PR2: Ribb 6N 115
Lambert St. BB8: Traw 9F 86
Lambeth Cl. BB1: Blackb 4A 140
Lambeth St. BB1: Blackb 3A 140
BB8: Colne 6E 86
Lambeth Ter. OL11: Roch 8A 204
Lambing Clough La. BB7: Hurst G 2M 99
Lambourne WN8: Skelm 8M 211
Lambourne Gro. OL16: Milnr 8J 205
Lambrigg Cl. LA4: Morec 5B 22
LAMB ROE 2J 101
Lamb Row BB7: Sabd 3D 102
Lambshear La. L31: Lyd 7B 216
Lambs Hill Cl. FY5: T Clev 2K 63
Lamb's La. PR3: Pill 1F 56
Lambs Rd. FY5: T Clev 2K 63
Lambton Gates BB4: Rawt 5A 162
Lambton St. WN5: Wigan 6M 221
Lamlash Rd. BB1: Blackb 4D 140
LAMMACK 8K 119
Lammack Rd. BB1: Blackb, Mellor 8K 119
Lamour Pl. FY7: Flee 1D 54
Lanark Av. FY2: Blackp 5C 62
Lanark St. BB11: Burnl 5B 124
Lancambe Ct. LA1: Lanc 6G 22
Lancashire & Yorkshire Ter. BD23: Hell 1D 52
(off Main Rd.)
Lancashire Dr. PR7: Buck V 9B 154
PR26: Far M 3K 153
Lancashire Ent. Bus. Pk. PR26: Far M 3K 153
Lancashire Moor Rd. BB8: Lane B, Traw 6J 87
Lancashire St. LA4: Morec 4M 21
Lancashire Way PR2: Fulw 3C 116
LANCASTER 6B 228 (8J 23)
Lancaster & Morecambe Crematorium
LA2: Lanc 4H 23
Lancaster Av. BB4: Hasl 7F 160
BB5: Acc 1N 141
BL0: Ramsb 1F 200
FY5: T Clev 1J 63
FY8: L Ann 4F 128
PR3: Gt E 6A 66
PR25: Leyl 6A 154
Lancaster Bus. Pk. LA1: Lanc 4N 23
Lancaster Castle 6B 228 (8J 23)
Lancaster City FC 6C 228 (8J 23)
Lancaster City Mus. 6C 228 (8K 23)
Lancaster Cl. FY6: K Sea 8M 41
L31: Magh 1E 222
PR3: Gt E 6A 66
PR6: Adl 6K 195
PR8: Birk 1E 186
Lancaster Ct. PR7: Chor 4E 174
Lancaster Cres. WN8: Skelm 2J 219
Lancaster Dr. BB5: Clay M 6M 121
BB7: Clith 4J 81

278 A-Z Lancashire

Linden Ct.—Long Marsh La.

Linden Ct. BB18: Earl 3D 78
(off Linden Rd.)
WN5: Orr 5H 221
Linden Cres. BB3: Darw 5B 158
BL8: Tott 8E 200
Linden Dr. BB7: Clith 4M 81
PR5: Lost H 8L 135
Linden Fold PR4: Elsw 1M 91
Linden Grn. FY5: T Clev 9F 54
Linden Gro. PR2: Ribb 6A 116
PR3: Gars 4N 59
PR6: Chor 3F 174
WN5: Orr 5H 221
(not continuous)
Linden Lea BB2: Blackb 8G 138
BB4: Rawt 7L 161
Linden M. FY8: L Ann 7F 108
Linden Pl. FY2: Blackp 8E 62
Linden Rd. BB8: Colne 6A 86
BB18: Earl 3D 78
Lindens WN8: Skelm 8M 211
Lindens, The FY6: Pree 9A 42
L31: Magh 3B 222
Linden St. BB10: Burnl 4G 228 (4F 124)
WN5: Wigan 6M 221
Linden Wlk. BL2: Bolt 8H 199
WN5: Orr 5H 221
Lindenwood L32: Kirk 9L 223
Linderbreck La. FY6: Poul F 2L 89
Lindeth Cl. LA5: Silv 9G 4
LA6: Neth K 3C 16
Lindeth Gdns. LA1: Lanc 5K 23
Lindeth Rd. LA5: Silv 9G 4
Lindholme WN8: Skelm 9N 211
Lindisfarne *OL12: Roch* *5B 204*
(off Spotland Rd.)
Lindisfarne Av. BB2: Blackb 7N 139
Lindisfarne Cl. BB12: Burnl 2C 124
Lindle Av. PR4: Hutt 6B 134
Lindle Cl. PR4: Hutt 6B 134
Lindle Cres. PR4: Hutt 6B 134
Lindle La. PR4: Hutt, W Stake 5B 134
Lindley Av. WN5: Orr 6F 220
Lindley Cft. FY5: T Clev 1L 63
Lindley Dr. WN8: Parb 1N 211
Lindley St. BB2: Blackb 6J 139
PR5: Lost H 8K 135
Lindon Pk. Rd. BB4: Hasl 8H 161
Lindow Cl. BL8: Bury 7G 201
LA1: Lanc 8C 228
Lindow Sq. LA1: Lanc 8B 228 (9J 23)
Lindow St. LA1: Lanc 8C 228 (9K 23)
Lindred Rd. BB9: Brierf 3E 104
Lindsay Av. FY3: Blackp 7E 88
FY6: Poul F 9K 63
FY8: L Ann 2H 129
PR25: Leyl 6L 153
Lindsay Ct. FY8: L Ann 5B 108
LA3: Morec 6C 22
Lindsay Dr. PR7: Chor 7C 174
Lindsay Pk. BB10: Burnl 4K 125
Lindsay St. BB11: Burnl 1E 228 (3E 124)
Lindsey Ho. BB5: Chur 1N 141
Linedred La. BB9: Brierf 3F 104
Lineholme Av. OL14: Tod 8H 147
Lines St. LA4: Morec 3B 22
Line St. OL13: Bac 7J 163
Linfield Cl. BL2: Bolt 9K 199
Linfield Ter. FY4: Blackp 3E 108
Lingart La. PR3: Barn 3A 60
Lingdales L37: Form 6B 206
Lingfield Av. BB7: Clith 5L 81
Lingfield Cl. BL8: Bury 6H 201
LA1: Lanc 4M 29
Lingfield Ct. BB2: Fenis 8D 138
Lingfield Rd. FY7: Flee 2E 54
Lingfield Road Stop (Tram) 2F 54
Lingfield Way BB2: Fenis 8E 138
Linghaw La. LA2: H Ben 7N 19
Lingmoor Dr. BB12: Burnl 1M 123
Lingmoor Rd. LA1: Lanc 7M 23
Lingtree Rd. L32: Kirk 8G 223
Linguard Bus. Pk. OL16: Roch 7D 204
Lingwell Cl. PR6: Whit W 1E 174
Link 59 Bus. Pk. BB7: Clith 1A 82
Links, The FY5: T Clev 8C 54
Links Av. PR9: S'port 4L 167
Links Dr. LA2: H Ben 6L 19
Linksfield PR2: Fulw 6F 114
Links Ga. FY5: T Clev 4K 63
FY8: L Ann 2G 128
PR2: Fulw 6F 114
Linkside Av. BB9: Nelson 2M 105
Links La. BB2: Pleas 8D 138
Links Lodge FY8: L Ann 2G 128
Links Point FY4: Blackp 5F 108
Links Rd. BL2: Bolt 9N 199
FY1: Blackp 1C 88
FY6: K Sea 8K 41
FY8: L Ann 3E 128
L32: Kirk 9M 223
PR1: Penw 2E 134
Links Vw. FY8: L Ann 3J 129
OL11: Roch 7M 203
Linley Cl. WN6: Stand 8M 213
Linley Gro. BL0: Ramsb 3F 200
Linley Rd. WN5: Wigan 6N 221
Linnell Dr. OL11: Roch 5J 203
Linnet Cl. FY3: Blackp 4H 89
Linnet Dr. BL9: Bury 9N 201
Linnet Hill OL11: Roch 7N 203
Linnet La. FY8: L Ann 1L 129
Linnet St. PR1: Prest 1N 229 (7L 115)
Linnet Way L33: Kirk 3K 223
Linslade Cl. L33: Kirk 6L 223
Linslade Cres. L33: Kirk 6L 223
Linton Av. BL9: Bury 8L 201
LA3: Heys 7L 21
Linton Dr. BB11: Burnl 6B 124
Linton Gdns. BB9: Barrf 8G 85
Linton Gro. PR1: Penw 3D 134
Linton Pl. L32: Kirk 7H 223
Linton St. PR2: Fulw 6G 115
Lion Ct. BB5: Chur 2L 141
Lionel St. BB12: Burnl 2A 124
Lions Dr. BB1: Blackb, Guide 8D 140
Lion St. BB5: Chur 1L 141
OL14: Tod 4K 165
Lion Wlk. BB1: Blackb 9A 120
Liptrott Rd. PR7: Chor 9C 174
Lisbon Dr. BB3: Darw 6C 158
BB11: Burnl 2A 228 (3C 124)
Lisbon St. OL12: Roch 4N 203
Liskeard Cl. OL16: Roch 4F 204
Lisle St. OL12: Roch 4D 204
Lismore Av. FY4: Blackp 3F 108
Lismore Pk. PR8: Birk 1F 186
Lister Cft. BD23: T Crav 9J 53
Lister Gro. LA3: Heys 8L 21
Lister St. BB2: Blackb 8C 226 (5M 139)
BB5: Acc 2N 141
Lister Well Rd. BB18: Barnw 8K 77
LITTLE ECCLESTON 5M 65
Little Acre FY5: T Clev 3K 63
L31: Magh 2D 222
PR4: Longt 8L 133
LITTLE ALTCAR 2A 214
Lit. Banks Cl. PR5: Bam B 1D 154
LITTLE BISPHAM 3C 62
Little Bispham Stop (Tram) 3C 62
LITTLEBOROUGH 9L 185
Littleborough Coach House & Heritage Cen. 9L 185
Littleborough Ind. Est. OL15: Littleb 9K 185
Littleborough Sports Cen. 7L 185
Littleborough Station (Rail) 9L 185
Littlebourne Wlk. BL1: Bolt 7G 198
Lit. Bowland Rd. BB7: White 2J 71
PR3: Chip 2J 71
Lit. Brewery La. L37: Form 6A 206
Lit. Brook La. L32: Kirk 9J 223
Little Brow BL7: Brom C 6G 198
LITTLE CARLETON 1F 88
Lit. Carr La. PR7: Chor 7F 174
Lit. Church St. WN5: Wigan 5L 221
LITTLE CLEGG 3J 205
Lit. Clegg Rd. OL15: Littleb 3J 205
Little Cl. PR1: Penw 5F 134
PR26: Far M 4H 153
Lit. Coppins La. FY6: Poul F 1L 89
LITTLEDALE 8M 25
Littledale Av. LA3: Heys 8M 21
Littledale M. LA2: Slyne 2M 23
Littledale Rd. LA2: Brookh, Littled, Quern 3K 25
Littledale St. OL12: Roch 5B 204
(not continuous)
Littlefell La. LA2: Lanc, Quern 9C 24
Lit. Firs Fold PR25: Leyl 9G 152
Little Flatt OL12: Roch 4M 203
LITTLE HARWOOD 1A 140
Lit. Hey La. L37: Form 7C 206
Littleholme St. OL14: Tod 4K 165
LITTLE HOOLE MOSS HOUSES 3M 151
LITTLE HOOLE MUCH 3A 152
Lit. Howarth Way OL12: Roch 1F 204
LITTLE KNOWLEY 4H 175
Little La. PR3: Longr 3J 97
PR8: Banks 8G 149
PR9: S'port 4A 168
WN3: Wigan 6N 221
WN5: Wigan 6N 221
LITTLE LAYTON 2F 88
LITTLE MARSDEN 3H 105
LITTLE MARTON 9K 89
LITTLE MARTON MOSS SIDE 9G 89
Lit. Meadow La. L40: Mawd 1H 191
Little Mdws. BL7: Brom C 6F 198
LITTLE MOOR 5L 81
Littlemoor BB7: Clith 5L 81
Littlemoor Cl. BB7: Sabd 2F 102
Lit. Moor Clough BL7: Eger 3E 198
LITTLE MOOR END 5K 141
Littlemoor Ho. BB7: Sabd 3F 102
Littlemoor Rd. BB7: Clith 5L 81
Lit. Moor Vw. BB7: Clith 5L 81
Little Oaks FY4: Blackp 4D 108
LITTLE PLUMPTON 3C 110
LITTLE POULTON 7M 63
Lit. Poulton La. FY6: Poul F 8M 63
Lit. Queen St. BB8: Colne 7N 85
LITTLE SINGLETON 7C 64
Lit. Stones Rd. BL7: Eger 3E 198
Little St. BB5: Acc 2N 141
LITTLE THORNTON 4K 63
Lit. Toms La. BB10: Burnl 7H 105
Lit. Tongues La. FY6: Pree 9A 42
LITTLE TOWN 6G 99
Little Twining PR4: Longt 9L 133
Littlewalk Ct. *BB5: Acc* *3L 141*
(off Stonecross Cl.)
LITTLEWOOD 8L 201
Littlewood FY7: Flee 1E 54
Littlewood Av. BL9: Bury 8L 201
Lit. Wood Cl. PR7: Chor 8B 174
Littondale Gdns. BB2: Blackb 9E 138
Liverpool Av. PR8: Ains 8D 186
Liverpool Castle 7A 196
Liverpool Municipal Golf Course 9G 223
Liverpool New Rd. PR4: Wal B 3K 151
Liverpool Old Rd. PR4: Much H 7G 150
PR4: Tarl 4E 170
PR4: Wal B 1K 151
Liverpool Rd. BB12: Burnl 3M 123
FY1: Blackp 1M 227 (5D 88)
L31: Lyd 8B 216
L37: Form 1A 214
L39: Aug 1G 217
L39: Bick 8K 217
L40: Ruff 6E 170
PR1: Penw 3D 134
PR4: Breth 1G 170
PR4: Hutt, Longt 1K 151
PR4: Tarl 2E 170
PR8: Ains 2C 206
PR8: Birk, Ains 1G 186
PR26: Breth 1G 170
WN8: Skelm 3G 218
(not continuous)
Liverpool Rd. Nth. L31: Magh 8B 216
L40: Burs 9C 190
Liverpool Rd. Sth. L31: Magh 1B 222
L40: Burs 3N 209
Liverpool Wlk. PR7: Buck V 9B 154
Liverpool Way, The L33: Kirk 9M 223
Livesey Branch Rd. BB2: Blackb, Fenis 9E 138
LIVESEY FOLD 5N 157
Livesey Fold BB3: Darw 5N 157
PR6: Withn 6B 156
Livesey Hall Cl. BB2: Blackb 7F 138
Livesey St. BB1: Rish 7G 121
(not continuous)
BB12: Padi 1H 123
FY8: L Ann 5N 129
PR1: Prest 1L 135
Livesley's La. L37: Gt A 1F 214
Livet Av. FY4: Blackp 2D 108
Livingstone Rd. BB2: Blackb 4J 139
BB5: Acc 9A 122
FY1: Blackp 3K 227 (6C 88)
Livingstone St. BB9: Brierf 5F 104
Livingstone Wlk. BB9: Brierf 4F 104
Livsey St. OL16: Roch 6D 204
Lloyd Cl. BB9: Nelson 2J 105
LA1: Lanc 7H 23
Lloyd's Av. LA4: Morec 4A 22
Lloyd St. BB3: Darw 4N 157
OL11: Roch 9A 204
OL12: Whitw 5N 183
OL13: Bac 7G 162
OL14: Tod 1L 165
Lloyd Wlk. BB9: Nelson 3J 105
LOBDEN 7B 184
Lobden Cres. OL12: Whitw 7N 183
Lobden Golf Course 7B 184
Lobley Cl. OL12: Roch 3E 204
Lob Quarry OL14: Tod 4J 165
Lochinch Cl. FY4: Blackp 3G 108
Loch St. WN5: Orr 5L 221
Lock 50 Bus. Cen. *OL16: Roch* *8D 204*
(off League St.)
Locka La. LA1: Lanc 4J 23
LA6: Ark 4N 13
Locke Ind. Est. *BL6: Hor* *9C 196*
(off Winter Hey La.)
Lockerbie Av. FY5: T Clev 2D 62
Locker Room, The PR4: Hesk B 3D 150
Lockfield Dr. BB18: Barnw 10G 52
Lockgate BB4: Rawt 6H 161
Lockhart Rd. PR1: Prest 1K 229 (7J 115)
Lockhart St. OL16: Roch 8E 204
Lockheed Cl. FY4: Blackp 6E 108
Lockhurst Av. FY5: T Clev 3F 62
Lock La. PR4: Tarl 4F 170
Lock Mill Pl. OL16: Roch 8D 204
Lockside BB2: Blackb 9B 226 (6L 139)
OL15: Littleb 8M 185
Lockside Office Pk. PR2: Ash R 9C 114
Lockside Rd. PR2: Ash R 1C 134
Lock St. BB5: Osw 4L 141
OL14: Tod 4K 165
Lockwood Av. FY6: Poul F 7K 63
Lockyer Av. BB12: Burnl 3N 123
Lodge, The BB6: Gt H 4H 121
FY8: L Ann 1L 129
PR7: Buck V 9A 154
Lodge Bank PR6: Birns 8N 155
Lodge Bank Rd. OL15: Littleb 2J 205
Lodge Cl. FY5: T Clev 4C 62
LA6: Holme 1G 6
PR4: Frec 1N 131
PR5: Bam B 7B 136
Lodge Ct. FY3: Stain 6K 89
FY5: T Clev 4C 62
PR4: Inskip 1F 92
Lodge La. FY6: Sing 8C 64
FY8: L Ann 3E 130
L39: Bick 1G 225
LA2: Wen 4E 18
LA6: Mell 4E 18
OL13: Bac 6K 163
PR4: Clif 8H 113
PR4: Elsw 1M 91
PR4: Wart 3E 130
PR26: Far M 1G 153
Lodge M. BL0: Ramsb 8H 181
Lodge Mill La. BL0: Ramsb 6M 181
Lodge Pk. PR3: Catt 9A 60
Lodge Quarry LA5: Carn 9A 12
Lodge Rd. BD24: Sett 4N 35
PR3: Clau 3D 68
WN5: Orr 7H 221
Lodges Gro. LA4: Morec 2E 22
Lodgeside BB5: Clay M 6M 121
Lodge St. BB5: Acc 2B 142
BL0: Ramsb 6K 181
(Edith St.)
BL0: Ramsb 8H 181
(Kay Brow)
LA1: Lanc 6D 228 (8K 23)
OL12: Ward 8F 184
OL15: Littleb 8L 185
PR1: Prest 5G 229 (9G 115)
(not continuous)
Lodge Ter. *BB4: Rawt* *7K 161*
(off Lwr. Clowes Rd.)
BB5: Osw 3L 141
Lodge Vw. *BB5: Acc* *3M 141*
(off Star St.)
BL0: Ramsb 6M 181
PR1: Penw 5J 135
PR3: Longr 4J 97
PR26: Far M 9H 135
Lodge Wood Cl. PR7: Chor 8C 174
Lodge Works L33: Know P 7A 224
Lodgings, The PR2: Fulw 3M 115
Lodore Rd. FY4: Blackp 3C 108
Loen Cres. BL1: Bolt 9C 198
Lofthouse Way FY7: Flee 9G 40
Loftos Av. FY4: Blackp 1D 108
Logan St. BL1: Bolt 8E 198
Lognor Rd. L32: Kirk 8H 223
Lognor Wlk. L32: Kirk 8H 223
Logwood Av. BL8: Bury 9J 201
WN5: Wigan 4N 221
Logwood St. BB1: Blackb 1N 139
Loisine Cl. OL11: Roch 9M 203
Lois Pl. BB2: Blackb 3K 139
Lomas La. BB4: Rawt 6L 161
Lomax Cl. BB6: Gt H 3K 121
Lomax Sq. BB6: Gt H 4K 121
Lomax St. BB3: Darw 5A 158
BB6: Gt H 4J 121
BL8: Greenm 4E 200
OL12: Roch 4C 204
OL15: Littleb 7K 185
Lombard St. OL12: Roch 5A 204
LOMESHAYE 2F 104
Lomeshaye Bus. Village BB9: Nelson 2G 104
Lomeshaye Ind. Est. BB9: Brierf 3E 104
BB9: Nelson 1F 104
Lomeshaye Marsh Local Nature Reserve 2E 104
Lomeshaye Pl. BB9: Nelson 2G 104
Lomeshaye Rd. BB9: Nelson 2G 105
Lomeshaye Way BB9: Nelson 2G 104
Lomond Av. FY3: Blackp 7F 88
FY8: L Ann 2H 129
Lomond Cl. PR7: Eux 2N 173
Lomond Dr. BL8: Bury 9G 200
Lomond Gdns. BB2: Blackb 7G 139
Lomond Ter. OL16: Roch 9F 204
London Cl. WN5: Wigan 3N 221
Londonderry Rd. LA3: Heys 2K 27
London La. PR8: S'port 6J 187
London Rd. BB1: Blackb 1C 226 (2M 139)
FY3: Blackp 1N 227 (4D 88)
PR1: Prest 5N 229 (1L 135)
PR2: Prest 1L 135
London Sq. PR9: S'port 7H 167
London St. FY7: Flee 8G 41
PR9: S'port 7H 167
London Ter. BB3: Darw 5B 158
London Wlk. BB1: Blackb 1C 226 (2M 139)
London Way PR5: Lost H, Walt D 4M 135
Long Acre PR5: Bam B 2E 154
Longacre PR4: Longt 8K 133
PR9: S'port 3M 167
Long Acre Cl. LA5: Carn 1N 15
Long Acre Pl. FY8: L Ann 4N 129
Longacres Dr. OL12: Whitw 5A 184
Longacres La. OL12: Whitw 4A 184
Long Bank La. BD23: Hal W 3A 52
Long Barn Brow PR5: Hogh 6N 137
Long Barn Row PR5: Hogh 6N 137
Longber La. LA6: Bur L 2H 19
Longbrook WN6: Shev 5L 213
Longbrook Av. PR5: Bam B 6A 136
Long Bldg. BB7: Saw 3E 74
Long Butts PR1: Penw 6G 134
Long Causeway BB7: Gis 9A 52
BB10: Cliv 7L 125
Long Causeway, The HX7: Black H 4M 147
Longcliffe Dr. PR8: Ains 9B 186
Long Cl. BB7: Clith 1M 81
PR26: Leyl 7D 152
Long Copse PR7: Chor 5B 174
Long Cft. PR4: Longt 7L 133
Longcroft PR3: Bart 2E 94
Long Cft. Mdw. PR7: Chor 3D 174
Longdale Av. BD24: Sett 3N 35
Long Dales La. LA6: Neth K 6C 16
Long Dike BB5: S Fold 7H 143
Longendale Rd. WN6: Stand 4N 213
Longfellow Cl. L32: Kirk 9J 223
Longfield BL9: Bury 8M 201
L37: Form 7B 206
PR1: Penw 3E 134
PR2: Fulw 1H 115
Longfield Av. FY6: Poul F 7K 63
PR7: Copp 3A 194
Longfield Cl. OL14: Tod 3L 165
Longfield Ct. BB18: Barnw 3M 77
Longfield Dr. LA5: Carn 1N 15
Longfield Gro. OL14: Tod 3L 165
Longfield La. BB18: Barnw 3M 77
OL14: Tod 4L 165
Longfield Mnr. PR7: Chor 9C 174
Longfield Pl. FY6: Poul F 7K 63
Longfield Ri. OL14: Tod 3L 165
Longfield Rd. OL11: Roch 5N 203
OL14: Tod 3L 165
Longfield Ter. BB10: Cliv 9J 125
OL14: Tod 3L 165
Longfield Way OL14: Tod 3L 165
Longfold L31: Magh 1D 222
PR4: Mere B 4M 169
Longford Av. FY2: Blackp 6E 62
Longford Rd. PR8: Birk 3G 187
Long Grn. BB18: Earl 2F 78
Long Hey WN8: Skelm 8N 211
Long Hey La. BB3: Hodd, Pick B 6F 158
OL14: Tod 4M 165
Long Heys La. WN8: Dalt 8B 212
Long Hill OL11: Roch 9A 204
Longhirst Cl. BL1: Bolt 9B 198
LONGHOLME 5M 161
Longholme Rd. BB4: Rawt 5M 161
Longhouse La. FY6: Poul F 2K 89
LONG ING 2N 77
Long Ing La. BB18: Barnw 2N 77
Longlands Av. LA3: Heys 8K 21
Longlands Cres. LA3: Heys 8L 21
Longlands La. LA3: Heys 9K 21
Longlands Rd. LA1: Lanc 5J 23
Long La. BB2: Pleas 6B 138
BB3: Tock 4G 157
BB8: Lane B 3G 86
BL9: Bury 6K 201
L29: T'ton 9H 215
L37: Form 8A 206
L39: Aug, Bick 9H 209
LA2: Abb 3A 48
LA2: Ell, Quern 7C 30
LA2: Tat 7H 19
OL14: Tod 1N 165
PR3: Barn 4D 60
PR3: Scor 4D 46
PR6: H Charn 9J 175
PR9: Banks 9G 148
WN8: Uph 8B 220
Long La. End LA2: Ell 8B 30
Long Level LA6: Cast, K Lon 6G 9
Longley Cl. PR2: Fulw 1J 115
Long Lover La. BB7: Rim 4A 76
Long Marsh La. LA1: Lanc 5A 228 (7H 23)

Long Meadow—Lumb

Long Meadow BB2: Mellor B 7C 118
BB8: Colne 6D 86
BL7: Brom C 6J 199
PR4: K'ham 4K 111
PR4: Lit H 3K 151
Long Mdw. La. FY5: T Clev 9J 55
Longmeadow La. LA3: Heys 9M 21
Long Mdws. PR7: Chor 9C 174
Long Meanygate PR9: S'port 6E 168
Longmeanygate PR26: Leyl, Midge H 5D 152
Longmere Cres. LA5: Carn 1N 15
Longmire Way LA4: Morec 3A 22
Longmoor La. PR3: Gars, Nateby 7F 58
Long Moss PR26: Leyl 7D 152
Long Moss La. PR4: Longt, New L, W Stake 1B 152
Long Moss Mdws. PR4: New L 1C 152
LONGRIDGE 3K 97
Longridge BL7: Brom C 5J 199
Longridge Av. FY4: Blackp 4E 108
Longridge Golf Course 9G 71
Longridge Heath BB9: Brierf 6H 105
Longridge Lodge PR2: Ribb 5B 116
(off Grange Av.)
Longridge Rd. BB7: Hurst G 2H 99
PR2: Ribb 5B 116
PR3: Ribc 2H 99
PR3: T'ley 9E 70
PR3: T'ley, Chip 8F 70
(not continuous)
Longridge Sports Cen. 4J 97
Long Row BB2: Mellor 7J 119
HX7: Black H 5N 147
PR3: Cald V 4H 61
Longroyd Rd. BB18: Earl 3E 78
Longsands La. PR2: Fulw 4M 115
LONGSHAW
BB2 7M 139
WN5 9G 220
Longshaw Cl. L40: Ruff 9E 170
Longshaw Ford Rd. BL1: Bolt 8M 197
Longshaw La. BB2: Blackb 9B 226 (6L 139)
Longshaw St. BB2: Blackb 7L 139
LONGSHOOT 4H 161
Longsight BL2: Bolt 8L 199
Longsight Av. BB5: Hunc 9D 122
BB7: Clith 2M 81
Longsight La. BL2: Bolt 9K 199
(not continuous)
Longsight Lodge BL2: Bolt 9L 199
Longsight Rd. BB1: Clay D, Cop G 6D 118
BB2: Clay D, Osb 6D 118
BB6: Langh 8D 100
BL0: Ramsb 2F 200
BL8: Greenm 2F 200
LONGTON 8K 133
Longton Av. FY5: T Clev 1H 63
Longton Brickcroft Nature Reserve 1K 151
Longton Brickcroft Nature Reserve Vis. Cen. 9K 133
Longton Bus. Pk. PR4: Lit H 3J 151
Longton By-Pass PR4: Hutt, Longt, Wal B 3K 151
Longton Cl. BB1: Blackb 3C 140
Longton Ct. PR9: S'port 6K 167
Longton Dr. L37: Form 6A 206
LA4: Morec 4D 22
Longton Hall Ct. PR4: Longt 8M 133
Longton Rd. BB12: Burnl 1C 124
FY1: Blackp 2L 227 (5C 88)
Longtons La. BD23: Tos 1H 51
Longton St. BB1: Blackb 3B 140
PR6: Chor 6G 174
Longway FY4: Blackp 1F 108
Long Wham La. PR4: Much H 6N 151
Longwood Cl. FY8: L Ann 5L 129
WA11: Rain 9N 225
Longwood La. PR3: Pill 1G 56
Longworth Av. BB10: Burnl 3H 125
PR7: Copp 3B 194
(not continuous)
Longworth Bank Cotts. BL7: Edgw 5J 179
Longworth Clough BL7: Eger 3D 198
Longworth Clough Nature Reserve 2A 198
Longworth La. BL7: Eger 3C 198
Longworth Rd. BB7: B'ton 5H 101
BL6: Hor 9D 196
BL7: Belm, Eger 1N 197
Longworth Rd. Nth. BL7: Belm 9K 177
Longworth St. PR1: Prest 8M 115
PR5: Bam B 6A 136
PR7: Chor 8D 174
Lonmore PR5: Walt D 5N 135
Lonmore Cl. PR9: Banks 1F 168
Lonsdale Av. FY7: Flee 1E 54
L39: Orms 5L 209
LA4: Morec 4E 22
OL16: Roch 8E 204
Lonsdale Chase PR5: Lost H 8K 135
Lonsdale Cl. PR25: Leyl 9K 153
Lonsdale Cres. FY7: Flee 1E 54
Lonsdale Dr. PR26: Cros 3M 171
Lonsdale Gdns. BB9: Barrf 8H 85
Lonsdale Gro. LA4: Morec 4E 22
Lonsdale Pl. LA1: Lanc 1L 29
Lonsdale Ri. LA6: K Lon 6F 8
(off Lunefield Dr.)
Lonsdale Rd. FY1: Blackp 7J 227 (8B 88)
LA2: Hest B 8H 15
LA4: Morec 4E 22
PR1: Prest 8M 115
PR8: S'port 1K 187
Lonsdale Sth. Av. LA2: Ell 9L 29
Lonsdale St. BB5: Acc 3M 141
BB9: Nelson 1K 105
BB12: Burnl 2A 124
Lonsdale Wlk. WN5: Orr 3L 221
Lord Av. OL13: Bac 7G 162
Lord Nelson Wharf PR2: Ash R 9E 114
Lord's Av. PR5: Lost H 9L 135
Lords Cl. BD24: Gig 3N 35
Lord's Cl. Rd. LA2: Low 3M 33
Lords Ct. OL13: Bac 2K 163
Lord's Cres. BB3: Lwr D 1A 158
Lords Cft. PR6: Clay W 5C 154
Lord Sefton Way L37: Gt A 1D 214
Lords Fold WA11: Rain 3J 225
Lordsgate Dr. L40: Burs 1C 210
Lordsgate La. L40: Burs 2A 210
Lord's La. PR1: Penw 7H 135
PR3: Longr 10E 70
Lord's Log Bog Nature Reserve 8L 13
Lord's Lot Rd. LA6: Cap, Over K 1H 17
Lordsome Rd. LA3: Heys 6M 21
Lord Sq. OL16: Roch 6C 204
Lord's Stile La. BL7: Brom C 5G 199
Lord St. BB1: Rish 8H 121
BB2: Blackb 4C 226 (3M 139)
BB3: Darw 5A 158
BB4: Craws 9L 143
BB4: Rawt 5M 161
BB5: Osw 4L 141
BB7: Gt H 5J 121
BB8: Colne 6N 85
BB9: Brierf 5F 104
BL6: Hor 9C 196
FY1: Blackp 4B 88
FY7: Flee 9G 41
FY8: L Ann 1E 128
L40: Burs 8C 190
LA1: Lanc 7K 23
LA4: Morec 2B 22
OL13: Bac 5K 163
OL14: Wals 6K 165
OL15: Littleb 9M 185
PR1: Prest 5L 229 (9K 115)
PR6: Chor 7F 174
PR6: Whit W 6E 154
PR7: E'ton 9F 172
PR8: S'port 8G 166
PR9: S'port 8G 166
Lord St. Mall BB1: Blackb 4C 226 (3M 139)
Lord St. W. BB2: Blackb 4C 226 (3M 139)
PR8: S'port 8G 166
Lord's Wlk. PR1: Prest 5M 229 (9K 115)
Lords Wood Cl. PR7: Chor 8C 174
Lorne Rd. FY2: Blackp 9D 62
Lorne St. BB3: Darw 5N 157
FY8: L Ann 4C 130
OL12: Roch 2E 204
PR7: Chor 7E 174
Lorraine Av. PR2: Fulw 6H 115
Lorton Cl. BB12: Burnl 1N 123
PR2: Fulw 3J 115
Lostock Ct. PR5: Lost H 9L 135
Lostock Dr. BL9: Bury 7L 201
Lostock Gdns. FY4: Blackp 3D 108
LOSTOCK HALL 9L 135
Lostock Hall Station (Rail) 8L 135
Lostock La. PR5: Bam B, Lost H 9M 135
Lostock Mdw. PR6: Clay W 6C 154
Lostock Rd. PR26: Cros 3N 171
Lostock Sq. PR5: Lost H 9L 135
Lostock Vw. PR5: Lost H 9K 135
Lothersdale Cl. BB10: Burnl 7H 105
Lothian Av. FY7: Flee 1D 54
Lothian Ho. PR1: Prest 5K 229
Lothian Pl. FY2: Blackp 6E 62
Lottice La. BB1: Guide 7F 140
BB5: Osw 7F 140
Lotus Dr. FY4: Blackp 3N 109
Lotus St. OL13: Bac 4K 163
(off Laurel St.)
Loud Bri. Back La. PR3: Goos 7C 70
Loudbridge Rd. PR3: Goos 8C 70
Loughlin Dr. L33: Kirk 5L 223
Loughrigg Cl. BB12: Burnl 2N 123
Loughrigg Ter. FY4: Blackp 9J 89
Louie Pollard Cres. BB6: Gt H 3K 121
Louis Av. BL9: Bury 9L 201
Louise Cl. OL12: Roch 2F 204
Louise Gdns. OL12: Roch 2F 204
Louise St. FY1: Blackp 5J 227 (7B 88)
OL12: Roch 2E 204
(not continuous)
Louis St. BL0: Eden 1J 181
Louis William St. BB1: Guide 8D 140
Loupsfell Dr. LA4: Morec 4C 22
Lourdes Av. PR5: Lost H 7K 135
Louvaine Av. BL1: Bolt 9N 197
Louvain St. BB18: Barnw 1L 77
Lovat Rd. PR1: Prest 1J 229 (7J 115)
LOVE CLOUGH 5M 143
Loveclough Fold BB4: Craws 5M 143
Loveclough Pk. BB4: Craws 5L 143
Loveclough Pl. BB4: Craws 5M 143
Loveclough Rd. BB4: Craws 6L 143
Loveclough Vw. BB4: Craws 5L 143
Love La. BL0: Eden, Ramsb 5K 181
Lovely Hall La. BB1: Sale 1K 119
Lovers La. BB4: Hasl 3G 160
Lovers Wlk. BB5: Osw 5M 141
OL14: Tod 2K 165
Loves Cotts. L39: Orms 6J 209
Low Bank BB12: Burnl 3K 123
OL12: Roch 2F 204
LOW BENTHAM 6J 19
Low Bentham Rd. LA2: H Ben 6K 19
LOW BIGGINS 6E 8
Low Cft. PR4: Woodp 7E 94
Lowcroft LA2: H Ben 6L 19
WN8: Skelm 9N 211
Lowcross Rd. FY6: Poul F 9L 63
Lower Abbotsgate LA6: K Lon 6E 8
(off Kendal Rd.)
Lwr. Alt Rd. L38: Hight 7A 214
Lwr. Antley St. BB5: Acc 3M 141
(not continuous)
Lwr. Ashworth Cl. BB2: Blackb 5A 226 (4K 139)
Lwr. Aspen La. BB5: Osw 3J 141
LOWER AUDLEY 6E 226 (4N 139)
Lwr. Audley St. BB1: Blackb 6D 226 (4M 139)
LOWER BALLAM 6A 110
Lwr. Bank Rd. PR2: Fulw 6J 115
Lwr. Bank St. PR6: Withn 6B 156
Lwr. Barnes St. BB5: Clay M 5L 121
Lwr. Barn St. BB3: Darw 8C 158
LOWER BARTLE 2N 113
LOWER BAXENDEN 7E 142
Lower Beechwood OL11: Roch 8A 204
Lwr. Burgh Way PR7: Chor 1C 194
Lower Calderbrook OL15: Littleb 5M 185
(off Calderbrook Rd.)
Lwr. Carr La. L38: Gt A 4H 215
Lwr. Chapel La. BB7: Grind 4A 74
Lower Chesham BL9: Bury 9N 201
(off Chesham Cres.)
LOWER CLOUGHFOLD 5A 162
Lwr. Clough Fold BB9: Barrf 9G 85
Lwr. Clough St. BB9: Barrf 9G 85
Lower Clowes BB4: Rawt 7L 161
Lwr. Clowes Rd. BB4: Rawt 7K 161
Lower Cockcroft
BB2: Blackb 4C 226 (3M 139)
LOWER COPTHURST 7G 155
Lwr. Copthurst La. PR6: Whit W 8G 155
Lwr. Cribden Av. BB4: Rawt 5J 161
Lower Crimble OL11: Roch 9J 203
Lower Cft. PR1: Penw 6G 134
Lwr. Croft St. BB18: Earl 2E 78
BD24: Sett 3N 35
(off Albert Hill)
LOWER DARWEN 9N 139
Lower Dolphinholme LA2: Dolp 7E 38
Lwr. East Av. BB18: Barnw 1M 77
Lwr. Eccleshill Rd. BB3: Darw 2A 158
Lwr. Ferney Lee OL14: Tod 1K 165
Lower Field PR26: Far M 1J 153
Lowerfield BB6: Langh 1C 120
Lowerfields BB12: Burnl 3L 123
LOWER FOLD
BB5 2A 142
BB6 3J 121
OL12 2N 203
Lower Fold BL2: Bolt 9M 199
BL8: Hawk 2N 199
Lowerfold BB6: Gt H 3J 121
Lowerfold Cl. OL12: Roch 1N 203
Lowerfold Cres. OL12: Roch 1N 203
Lowerfold Dr. OL12: Roch 1N 203
Lowerfold Rd. BB6: Gt H 3J 121
Lowerfold Way OL12: Roch 1N 203
LOWERFORD 7H 85
LOWER GATE 7E 122
Lower Gate OL16: Roch 6C 204
(off Newgate)
Lowergate BB7: Clith 3L 81
Lwr. Gate Rd. BB5: Hunc 7E 122
Lwr. George St. OL14: Tod 2L 165
Lower Grn. FY6: Poul F 8L 63
OL12: Roch 4N 203
LOWER GREEN BANK 4G 38
Lower Greenfield PR2: Ingol 5E 114
Lower Greenfoot BD24: Sett 3N 35
Lwr. Hazel Cl. BB2: Blackb 4K 139
LOWER HEALEY 2B 204
Lwr. Healey La. OL12: Roch 2B 204
Lower Hey PR4: Longt 7L 133
LOWER HEYSHAM 9K 21
Lower Hill BB3: Tock 5G 156
Lower Hill Dr. PR6: H Charn 4J 195
Lwr. Hollin Bank St. BB2: Blackb 8A 226 (5L 139)
LOWER HOUSE 7G 153
LOWERHOUSE 3L 123
Lowerhouse Cres. BB12: Burnl 3M 123
Lowerhouse Fold BB12: Burnl 3L 123
Lower Ho. Grn. BB4: Water 8D 144
Lower Ho. La. OL12: Ward 7E 184
Lowerhouse La. BB12: Burnl 3L 123
Lower Ho. Rd. PR25: Leyl 7H 153
Lower Ho. Wlk. BL7: Brom C 5G 199
Lwr. Jowkin La. OL11: Roch 6H 203
Lower Knotts BL2: Bolt 7M 199
Lwr. Knowl La. OL12: Roch 9G 183
Lwr. Laith Av. OL14: Tod 2M 165
Lwr. Laithe Cotts. BB9: Barrf 9G 84
Lwr. Laithe Dr. BB9: Barrf 9G 85
Lower La. BB4: Hasl 3G 160
HX7: Black H 5N 147
OL16: Milnr, Roch 9F 204
PR3: Longr 4K 97
PR4: Frec 7N 111
LOWER LEE 2A 48
Lwr. Lune St. FY7: Flee 8H 41
Lwr. Lyndon Av. WN6: Shev 6K 213
Lwr. Manor La. BB12: Burnl 8D 104
Lower Marlands BL7: Brom C 5F 198
Lower Mead BL7: Eger 4F 198
Lwr. Mead Dr. BB12: Burnl 8D 104
Lower Meadow BL7: Edgw 8K 179
Lwr. North Av. BB18: Barnw 2M 77
Lwr. Nuttall Rd. BL0: Ramsb 1J 201
Lwr. Park Marina BB18: Barnw 3A 78
Lwr. Park St. BB18: Barnw 2N 77
Lwr. Parrock Rd. BB9: Barrf 1G 104
LOWER PENWORTHAM 4H 135
Lwr. Philips Rd. BB1: Blackb 9C 120
LOWER PLACE 9D 204
Lower Promenade PR8: S'port 7G 166
PR9: S'port 6H 167
Lwr. Ridge Cl. BB10: Burnl 1G 228 (3F 124)
Lower Rd. BL0: Ramsb 6J 181
PR3: Longr 3M 97
Lwr. Rook St. BB18: Barnw 2N 77
Lwr. Rosegrove La. BB12: Burnl 4L 123
Lwr. School St. BB8: Colne 7A 86
(off School St.)
Lwr. Sheriff St. OL12: Roch 5B 204
Lower Standrings OL11: Roch 5L 203
(off Bagslate Moor Rd.)
Lwr. Stone Fold BB5: S Fold 7G 142
Lower St. OL16: Roch 9D 204
LOWER SUMMERSEAT 4H 201
Lower Tenterfield OL11: Roch 3H 203
(off Hutchinson Rd.)
Lower Tentre BB11: Burnl 3F 228 (4F 124)
LOWER THURNHAM 3G 36
Lwr. Timber Hill La. BB11: Burnl 6E 124
Lower Tong BL7: Brom C 6F 198
Lwr. Tweedale St. OL11: Roch 7C 204
Lower Wlk. FY1: Blackp 4B 88
FY2: Blackp 1B 88
Lower Waterside BB3: W'side 4E 158
(off Johnson Rd.)
Lwr. West Av. BB18: Barnw 2M 77
LOWER WESTHOUSE 2L 19
Lwr. Wheat End OL16: Roch 5E 204
Lower Wilworth BB1: Blackb 8M 119
Lwr. Wood Bank BB3: Darw 5M 157
(off Higher Avondale Rd.)
Lwr. Woodhill Rd. BL8: Bury 9J 201
(not continuous)
Lowesby Cl. PR5: Walt D 5A 136
Lowes Ct. FY1: Blackp 9H 227
FY5: T Clev 9H 55
Lowes Grn. L37: Form 9B 206
Lowe's La. WN8: N 'urgh 4J 211
Lowes Pk. Golf Course 7M 201
Lowes Rd. BL9: Bury 7L 201
Loweswater Cl. BB5: Hunc 9E 122
Loweswater Cres. BB12: Burnl 1A 124
Loweswater Dr. LA4: Morec 4D 22
Loweswater Way L33: Kirk 5J 223
Lowesway FY4: Blackp 1F 108
FY5: T Clev 9H 55
Lowe Vw. BB4: W'foot 6D 162
Lowfield Cl. PR4: Newt 7D 112
Lowfield Rd. FY4: Blackp 2F 108
Lowfields La. LA6: Cast 3F 8
Low Fold BB18: Kelb 6D 78
BD24: Langc 1N 35
(off Stainforth Rd.)
LOWGILL 2K 33
Lowgill La. LA2: Low 1K 33
Low Green PR25: Leyl 6J 153
Low Hill BB3: Darw 9A 158
OL12: Roch 2F 204
Lowhouse Cl. OL16: Milnr 6K 205
Lowick Cl. PR5: Hogh 4G 136
Lowick Dr. FY6: Poul F 1K 89
Lowlands Rd. LA4: Morec 4C 22
LA5: Bolt S 3L 15
Lowland Way FY2: Blackp 5F 62
Low La. BD23: Wig 10N 35
LA2: Clau 9A 18
LA4: Morec 2F 22
LA6: Leck 8J 9
Low Ling La. HX7: Cold 2M 147
Low Mill LA2: Caton 2G 25
LOW MOOR 3J 81
Low Moorgate LA6: Kear 4E 8
Low Moor La. BB18: Barnw 3M 77
Low Moor Rd. FY2: Blackp 8E 62
Lowndes St. PR1: Prest 1G 229 (7H 115)
Lowood Cl. OL16: Milnr 7J 205
Lowood Gro. PR2: Lea 8A 114
Lowood Lodge FY8: L Ann 5N 129
Lowood Pl. BB2: Blackb 2H 139
Lowrey Ter. FY1: Blackp 8J 227 (8B 88)
Low Rd. LA2: Caton, Halt 2B 24
LA3: Midd 5M 27
Lowry Cl. L33: Kirk 4K 223
PR5: Lost H 9K 135
Lowry Hill La. L40: Lath 2F 210
Lowside La. LA5: Yea R 7C 6
Low's Pl. OL12: Roch 3D 204
Lowstead Pl. FY4: Blackp 3E 108
Lowstern Cl. BL7: Eger 4E 198
Low St. LA6: Bur L 3K 19
Lowther Av. FY2: Blackp 9B 62
L10: Aint 8C 222
L31: Magh 9D 216
LA3: Morec 5E 22
Lowther Avenue Stop (Tram) 9B 62
Lowther Ct. FY2: Blackp 9B 62
FY8: L Ann 5N 129
Lowther Cres. PR26: Leyl 4G 153
Lowther Cft. LA6: H Roo 6A 8
Lowther Dr. PR26: Leyl 5G 153
Lowther La. BB8: Foul 2A 86
Lowther Pavilion 5M 129
Lowther Pl. BB1: Blackb 9A 120
Lowther Rd. FY7: Flee 9F 40
LA1: Lanc 7M 23
OL11: Roch 9B 204
Lowther St. BB8: Colne 5B 86
BB9: Nelson 2G 105
PR2: Ash R 8F 114
Lowther Ter. FY8: L Ann 5N 129
WN6: App B 4F 212
Lowthian St. PR1: Prest 5K 229 (9J 115)
Lowthorpe Cres. PR1: Prest 7L 115
Lowthorpe Pl. PR1: Prest 7L 115
Lowthorpe Rd. PR1: Prest 7L 115
Lowthwaite Dr. BB9: Nelson 4J 105
Lowton Rd. FY8: L Ann 9G 109
Loxham Gdns. FY4: Blackp 3D 108
Loxley Gdns. BB12: Burnl 3L 123
Loxley Grn. PR2: Fulw 3M 115
Loxley Pl. FY5: T Clev 4E 62
Loxley Pl. E. FY5: T Clev 4E 62
Loxley Rd. PR8: S'port 1K 187
Loxwood Cl. PR5: Walt D 5K 135
Loynd St. BB6: Gt H 4J 121
BL0: Ramsb 8J 181
Loyne Pk. LA6: Whit 6H 9
Lubbock St. BB12: Burnl 3A 124
Lucas Av. PR7: Char R 6N 173
LUCAS GREEN 9E 154
Lucas La. PR6: Whit W 9E 154
Lucas La. E. PR6: Whit W 1E 174
Lucas La. W. PR6: Whit W 1E 174
Lucas St. BL9: Bury 9M 201
Lucerne Cl. PR2: Fulw 5M 115
Lucerne Rd. PR2: Fulw 5M 115
Lucknow St. OL11: Roch 8C 204
Lucy St. BB9: Barrf 8H 85
LA1: Lanc 7D 228 (8K 23)
LA4: Morec 2B 22
Ludlow WN8: Skelm 8N 211
Ludlow Dr. L39: Orms 5J 209
Ludlow Gro. FY2: Blackp 9F 62
Ludlow St. WN6: Stand 1M 213
Luke St. OL13: Bac 7G 162
Lulworth WN8: Skelm 8M 211
Lulworth Av. FY3: Blackp 7G 88
PR2: Ash R 7G 114
Lulworth Cl. BL8: Bury 7H 201
Lulworth Lodge PR8: Birk 9F 166
Lulworth Pl. PR5: Walt D 6N 135
Lulworth Rd. PR2: Fulw 5K 115
PR8: Birk 1F 186
Lulworth Vw. PR8: Birk 1E 186
LUMB
BB4 9D 144
BL0 2G 181

Lumb Carr Av.—Manorfields

Lumb Carr Av. BL0: Ramsb 1F 200
Lumb Carr Rd. BL8: Holc 2F 200
Lumb Cotts. BL0: Ramsb 2G 181
Lumb Holes La. BB4: W'foot 8C 162
Lumb La. BB4: Lumb 2D 162
Lumb Scarr OL13: Bac 5K 163
Lumbutts Rd. OL14: Tod 5K 165
(not continuous)
Lumen Ct. PR1: Prest 4K 229
Lumn St. BL9: Bury 5L 201
Lumwood BL1: Bolt 9B 198
Lunds Cl. L40: W'head 8C 210
LUNDSFIELD 9A 12
Lunds La. PR4: Much H 6H 151
Lund St. BB2: Blackb 4K 139
PR1: Prest 4K 229 (9J 115)
Lune Av. L31: Magh 9D 216
Lune Bus. Pk. LA1: Lanc 8G 23
Lunecliffe Rd. LA2: Lanc 4H 29
Lune Cl. LA6: K Lon 6F 8
PR4: K'ham 4N 111
Lunedale Av. FY1: Blackp 9L 227 (9C 88)
Lune Dr. LA3: Morec 5F 22
PR25: Leyl 5A 154
Lunefield Dr. LA6: K Lon 6F 8
Lunefield Gdns. LA6: K Lon 6F 8
(off Ruskin Dr.)
Lune Gro.
FY1: Blackp 6L 227 (7C 88)
Lune Ho. LA1: Lanc 9C 228 (9K 23)
(Kent Ho.)
LA1: Lanc 7K 23
(Owen Rd.)
Lune Ind. Est. LA1: Lanc 8G 22
Lune Rd. FY7: Flee 9F 40
LA1: Lanc 7H 23
Lunesdale Cl. FY8: L Ann 1J 129
Lunesdale Ct. LA1: Lanc 7M 23
(Derwent Rd.)
LA1: Lanc 5H 23
(Meadow Vw.)
LA2: Horn 8C 18
Lunesdale Dr. PR3: Fort 2M 45
Lunesdale Rd. PR4: K'ham 4M 111
Lunesdale Ter. LA2: Clau 9M 17
Lunesdale Vw. LA2: Halt 1C 24
Luneside LA1: Lanc 8G 22
Lune Sq. LA1: Lanc 5C 228 (7J 23)
Lune St. BB8: Colne 7B 86
BB12: Padi 1J 123
LA1: Lanc 7K 23
PR1: Prest 6J 229 (1J 135)
PR3: Longr 2K 97
Lune Ter. LA1: Lanc 7K 23
Lune Valley LA1: Lanc 4M 23
Lune Vw. FY6: K Sea 8L 41
Lune Vw. Park LA2: Halt 2B 24
Lunt Rd. L29: Seft, T'ton 9J 215
Lunt's La. L37: Form 2A 214
Lupin Cl. BB5: Acc 1N 141
PR6: Whit W 1D 174
Lupin Rd. BB5: Acc 1A 142
Lupton Dr. BB9: Barrf 7H 85
Lupton Pl. LA1: Lanc 5H 23
Lupton St. PR7: Chor 7E 174
Lutner St. BB11: Burnl 4E 228 (4E 124)
Luton Rd. FY5: T Clev 2D 62
PR2: Ash R 7B 114
Lutwidge Av. PR1: Prest 8M 115
Lyceum Av. FY3: Blackp 3N 227 (6D 88)
Lyceum Pas. OL16: Roch 6C 204
Lychfield Dr. PR5: Bam B 9A 136
Lych Ga. BB7: Wadd 8H 73
Lychgate PR1: Prest 5M 229 (9K 115)
WN5: Wigan 6N 221
Lydbury Cres. L32: Kirk 9L 223
Lyddesdale Av. FY5: T Clev 2D 62
Lydd Gro. PR7: Chor 7C 174
Lydford OL11: Roch 7B 204
LYDGATE 8H 147
Lydgate BB10: Burnl 8J 105
PR7: Chor 9C 174
Lydia St. BB5: Acc 4A 142
LYDIATE 6A 216
Lydiate La. PR3: Bils, Clau 4E 68
PR7: E'ton 6E 172
PR25: Far, Leyl 3M 153
Lydiate Sta. Rd. L31: Lyd 7J 215
Lydric Av. PR5: Hogh 6G 136
Lyefield Wlk. OL16: Roch 7E 204
Lyelake Cl. L32: Kirk 9L 223
Lyelake Gdns. L32: Kirk 9L 223
(off Lyelake Rd.)
Lyelake La. L39: Bick 1D 218
L40: W'head 1D 218
Lyelake Rd. L32: Kirk 9L 223
Lyme Gro. FY6: K Sea 8L 41
Lymm Av. LA1: Lanc 5G 22
Lynbridge Cl. WN5: Orr 6H 221
Lyncroft Cres. FY3: Blackp 3E 88
Lyndale WN8: Skelm 8M 211
Lyndale Av. BB1: Wilp 2A 120
BB4: Hasl 5G 160
PR5: Lost H 6M 135
Lyndale Cl. BB1: Wilp 2A 120
BB4: Craws 9M 143
PR25: Leyl 9L 153
Lyndale Ct. FY7: Flee 8H 41
(off Bold St.)
Lyndale Dr. OL15: Littleb 8K 185
Lyndale Gro. PR5: Lost H 6M 135
Lyndale Residential Pk. FY4: Blackp 3M 109
Lyndale Rd. BB11: Hapt 6H 123
Lyndale Ter. BB7: Gis 9A 52
(off Main St.)
Lynden Av. LA4: Morec 3E 22
Lyndeth Cl. PR2: Fulw 3A 116
Lyndhurst L31: Magh 1C 222
WN8: Skelm 8M 211
Lyndhurst Av. BB1: Blackb 3E 140
FY4: Blackp 9M 227 (9D 88)
Lyndhurst Dr. PR2: Ash R 7B 114
Lyndhurst Gro. BB6: Gt H 3L 121
Lyndhurst Rd. BB2: Blackb 6M 139
BB3: Darw 4M 157
(not continuous)
Lyndhurst Rd. BB10: Burnl 4G 228 (4F 124)
PR8: Birk 3G 187
Lyndon Av. BB6: Gt H 3L 121
WN6: Shev 6K 213
Lyndon Cl. BL8: Tott 7E 200
Lyndon Ct. BB6: Gt H 3L 121
Lyndon Ho. BB6: Gt H 3L 121
Lynfield Rd. BB6: Gt H 3L 121
Lynn Gro. FY1: Blackp 3B 88
Lynn Pl. PR2: Ribb 7N 115
Lynns Ct. OL13: Weir 9L 145
Lynnwood Dr. OL11: Roch 5L 203
Lynroyle Way OL11: Roch 9A 204
Lynslack Ter. LA5: Arn 3F 4
Lynthorpe Rd. BB2: Blackb 6M 139
BB9: Nelson 1L 105
Lynton Av. FY4: Blackp 1D 108
OL11: Roch 9M 203
PR25: Leyl 7M 153
Lynton Ct. FY7: Flee 4C 54
Lynton Dr. PR8: Birk 4E 186
Lynton Rd. BB5: Acc 4M 141
PR8: Birk 5E 186
Lynwood Av. BB3: Darw 3M 157
BB5: Clay M 6M 121
FY3: Blackp 2E 88
L39: Aug 9H 209
PR2: Grim 8E 96
Lynwood Cl. BB3: Darw 4M 157
BB5: Clay M 5M 121
BB7: Whall 3G 100
BB8: Colne 4A 86
WN8: Skelm 4A 220
Lynwood Dr. FY6: Stal 5B 56
Lynwood End L39: Aug 9H 209
Lynwood Gro. BL2: Bolt 9K 199
Lynwood Pk. PR4: Wart 2L 131
Lynwood Rd. BB2: Blackb 2J 139
BB5: Hunc 7D 122
Lyons La. PR6: Chor 7F 174
PR7: Chor 7F 174
Lyons Rd. PR8: Birk 9G 167
Lythall Av. FY8: L Ann 4C 130
LYTHAM 5A 130
Lytham Cl. L10: Faz 9E 222
LA1: Lanc 9N 23
PR2: Fulw 6G 114
Lytham Ct. L32: Kirk 6H 223
PR7: Eux 2N 173
Lytham Green Drive Golf Course 3A 130
Lytham Hall 3M 129
Lytham Hall Pk. 2N 129
Lytham Heritage Cen. 5N 129
Lytham Rd. BB2: Blackb 8N 139
BB10: Burnl 8G 105
FY1: Blackp 6H 227 (8B 88)
FY4: Blackp 8B 88
FY8: L Ann 3D 130
FY8: Moss S 8C 110
PR2: Ash R, Fulw 6F 114
PR4: Frec, Wart 3H 131
PR9: S'port 2N 167
LYTHAM ST ANNE'S 4F 128
Lytham St Annes Local Nature Reserve 7C 108
Lytham St Annes Vis. Cen. 7C 108
Lytham St Annes Way FY4: Blackp 4K 109
FY8: L Ann 1K 129
Lytham Station (Rail) 5N 129
Lytham St. OL12: Roch 2B 204
PR6: Chor 7G 174
Lytham Towermill Mus. 6B 130
Lythcoe Av. PR2: Fulw 5F 114
Lythe Fell Av. LA2: Halt 1C 24
Lythe Fell La. LA2: Low 3M 33
Lythe La. LA2: Low 3L 33
Lythra Ct. FY8: L Ann 3F 128
Lyth Rd. LA1: Lanc 7M 23
Lytles Cl. L37: Form 1A 214
Lytton St. BB12: Burnl 2L 123

M

Maaruig Caravan Pk. FY6: Pree 7N 41
Mabel Ct. FY4: Blackp 1B 108
(off Lytham Rd.)
Mabel St. BB8: Colne 6C 86
OL12: Roch 3A 204
Maberry Cl. WN6: Shev 5G 213
Macauley Av. FY4: Blackp 1E 108
Macauley St. BB11: Burnl 4A 124
Macbeth Rd. FY7: Flee 9E 40
McCall Cl. PR4: W Grn 6F 110
McDonald Rd. LA3: Heys 2J 27
Macdonald St. WN5: Orr 5L 221
Mackay Cft. PR6: Chor 6F 174
McKenna M. PR1: Penw 3E 134
Mackenzie Cl. PR6: Chor 6F 174
Mackenzie Gro. BL1: Bolt 9D 198
Mackenzie St. BL1: Bolt 8D 198
McKenzie St. PR5: Bam B 8B 136
Maclaren Cl. FY3: Stain 5K 89
Macleod St. BB9: Nelson 2H 105
Maclure Rd. OL11: Roch 7C 204
McNaught St. OL16: Roch 7E 204
Madame Tussaud's
Blackpool 4H 227 (6A 88)
Maddy St. PR1: Prest 9G 114
Madeley Gdns. OL12: Roch 4A 204
Maden Rd. OL13: Bac 5H 163
Maden's Sq. OL15: Littleb 9L 185
Maden St. BB5: Chur 2L 141
Maden Way OL13: Bac 5K 163
Madingley Ct. PR9: S'port 4M 167
Madison Av. FY2: Blackp 6B 62
LA5: Bolt S 7J 15
Madison Avenue Stop (Tram) 6B 62
Madison Hgts. FY8: L Ann 1K 129
Madryn Av. L33: Kirk 8M 223
Maesbrook Cl. PR9: Banks 1G 168
Mafeking Av. BL9: Bury 8M 201
Mafeking Rd. PR2: Ash R 7F 114
Magdalen Rd. FY5: T Clev 2D 62
Maggots Nook Rd. WA11: Rain 1L 225
MAGHULL 9C 216
Maghull La. L31: Magh 1G 222
Maghull Smallholdings Est. L31: Magh 8F 216
Maghull Station (Rail) 3D 222
Magistrates' Court
Blackburn 3C 226 (3M 139)
Blackpool 4H 227 (6B 88)
Chorley 6E 174
Fleetwood 8H 41
Ormskirk 7L 209
Rawtenstall 5L 161
Magnolia Cl. PR2: Fulw 3M 115
Magnolia Dr. PR25: Leyl 5A 154
Magnolia Rd. PR1: Penw 5E 134
Magnolias, The FY8: L Ann 1K 129
(off Silversmiths Row)
Magnum Cen. OL16: Roch 7D 204
Magpie Cl. BB11: Burnl 4A 124
Maida Va. FY5: T Clev 3D 62
Maiden Bridge Art Cen. 9K 19
Maiden Cl. BB4: W'foot 7D 162
(off Millar Barn La.)
WN8: Skelm 1G 219
Maiden St. BB4: Hasl 1G 160
Main Av. LA3: Midd 5L 27
PR9: Banks 3J 169
Main Cl. LA3: O'ton 7B 28
Main Dr. FY6: Poul F 9L 63
Main Rd. BD23: Hell 1D 52
LA2: Gal 2L 37
LA2: Slyne 9K 15
LA2: Thurn 3F 36
LA5: Bolt S 6L 15
LA6: Neth K 4B 16
Mains Dr., The BD24: Gig 2N 35
Mainsfield Cl. BD24: Gig 2N 35
(off Stackhouse La.)
Mainsfield Ri. BD24: Gig 2N 35
(off Stackhouse La.)
Mainside Rd. L32: Kirk 9L 223
Mains La. FY6: Poul F, Sing 5M 63
L40: Bis G 7K 191
Main Sprit Weind PR1: Prest 6L 229 (1K 135)
Main Sq. PR7: Buck V 9A 154
MAINSTONES 9E 30
Main St. BB7: Bolt B 8K 51
BB7: D'ham 7G 74
BB7: Gis 9A 52
BB7: Grind 3A 74
BB18: Kelb 6D 78
BD24: Langc 2N 35
BD24: Rath 7M 35
LA1: Lanc 6K 23
LA2: C'ham 9H 37
LA2: H Ben 6L 19
LA2: Horn 7C 18
LA2: L Ben 6J 19
LA2: Wray 8E 18
LA3: Heys 8K 21
LA3: O'ton 7A 28
LA5: Wart 5N 11
LA6: Burt K 6G 7
LA6: Ingl 3N 19
LA6: K Lon 6F 8
LA6: Whit 8E 8
PR7: Buck V 9A 154
Mains Vw. BD24: Sett 3N 35
(off Church St.)
Mainway LA1: Lanc 6K 23
Mainway Ct. PR5: Bam B 8A 136
Mairscough La. L31: Lyd 3N 215
L39: D'holl 3N 215
Maitland Av. FY5: T Clev 2D 62
Maitland Cl. OL12: Roch 2F 204
OL14: Wals 7K 165
PR1: Prest 9M 115
Maitland Pl. BB4: Rawt 6M 161
Maitland St. OL13: Bac 5K 163
OL14: Wals 7K 165
PR1: Prest 9M 115
(not continuous)
Majestic M. WN5: Orr 6G 221
Major Ind. Est. LA3: Midd 4L 27
Major St. BB4: Craws 9M 143
BB5: Acc 4A 142
BL0: Ramsb 8G 181
OL14: Tod 2M 165
OL16: Milnr 7J 205
WN5: Wigan 5M 221
Makinson La. BL6: Hor 9G 197
Makinsons Row LA2: Gal 2M 37
Malcolm Pl. FY7: Flee 9E 40
Malcolm St. PR1: Prest 8N 115
Malden St. PR25: Leyl 6K 153
Maldern Av. FY6: Carl 6J 63
Maldon Pl. PR2: Ribb 7N 115
Maldon St. OL11: Roch 8C 204
Malham Av. BB5: Acc 4M 141
FY4: Blackp 1D 108
Malham Cl. LA1: Lanc 5H 23
PR8: S'port 2L 187
Malham Gdns. BB1: Blackb 8F 226 (5N 139)
Malham Pl. PR2: Ribb 5A 116
Malham Rd. BB10: Burnl 7H 105
BD23: Hell 1E 52
Malham Vw. Cl. BB18: Barnw 3L 77
Malham Vw. Ct. BB18: Barnw 3M 77
(off Malham Vw. Cl.)
Malham Wend BB9: Barrf 8H 85
Malkin Cl. BB9: Blacko 3J 85
Malkin La. BB7: Gt M, Withg 8F 80
Mall, The BB11: Burnl 2C 228 (3E 124)
FY8: L Ann 1J 129
L39: Orms 7K 209
PR2: Ribb 7A 116
Mallard Cl. FY5: T Clev 7G 54
L39: Aug 1H 217
LA3: Heys 2L 27
PR25: Leyl 7G 152
Mallard Ct. FY3: Blackp 4H 89
LA1: Lanc 6A 228 (8J 23)
Mallard Ho. L31: Lyd 7A 216
Mallard Pl. BB5: Osw 5K 141
Mallards, The PR9: S'port 3B 168
Mallards Wlk. PR5: Bam B 2C 154
Mall Blackburn, The BB1: Blackb 4D 226 (3M 139)
Mallee Av. PR9: S'port 3N 167
Mallee Cres. PR9: S'port 3N 167
Malley La. PR4: Woodp 2N 93
Mallison St. BL1: Bolt 9F 198
Mallom Av. PR7: Eux 5A 174
Mallory Av. L31: Lyd 7A 216
Mallow Cft. OL16: Roch 9F 204
Mallowdale FY5: T Clev 8G 55
PR2: Fulw 3E 114
Mallowdale Av. LA3: Heys 8M 21
Mallowdale Rd. LA1: Lanc 6H 23
Mallow Wlk. LA3: Morec 6B 22
Maltby Pl. FY4: Blackp 8F 88
Maltby Sq. PR7: Buck V 1B 174
Malthouse, The PR2: Ash R 8G 115
(off Malthouse Ct.)
Malthouse Ct. PR2: Ash R 8G 115
Malthouse Way PR1: Penw 5G 134
Maltings, The FY1: Blackp 5J 227
(off Yorkshire St.)
FY5: T Clev 8G 55
LA6: Whit 8E 8
PR1: Penw 4G 134
PR4: Longt 8K 133
Malt Kiln Brow PR3: Chip 5G 70
Maltkiln Gro. PR3: Lit E 6M 65
Maltkiln La. L39: Aug 2J 217
L40: Bis G 4M 191
Malton Dr. PR5: Lost H 9K 135
Malt St. BB5: Acc 1A 142
Malvern Av. BB2: Blackb 7L 139
BB5: Osw 5L 141
BB12: Padi 3J 123
BL9: Bury 8L 201
FY1: Blackp 9M 227 (9D 88)
FY6: Stal 5B 56
LA1: Lanc 1L 29
PR1: Prest 9N 229 (3L 135)
Malvern Cl. BB5: Acc 1N 141
BL6: Hor 8D 196
L32: Kirk 6H 223
OL16: Milnr 6K 205
PR5: Lost H 8M 135
WN3: Wins 8M 221
Malvern Ct. BB9: Nelson 2K 105
PR8: S'port 8G 167
Malvern Gdns. PR8: S'port 8G 167
Malvern Gro. L10: Aint 8B 222
Malvern Rd. BB9: Nelson 1K 105
FY8: L Ann 3K 129
PR1: Prest 2L 135
Malvern St. WN6: Stand 1M 213
Malvern St. E. OL11: Roch 6N 203
Malvern St. W. OL11: Roch 6N 203
Malvern Way BB4: Hasl 8F 160
Manby Cl. PR5: Hogh 5H 137
Manchester Mill Ind. Est. PR1: Prest 9M 115
Manchester Rd. BB4: Hasl 4G 160
(not continuous)
BB5: Acc, Bax 3B 142
BB9: Nelson 3G 104
BB11: Burnl 4C 228 (4D 124)
BB11: Burnl, Dunn 5A 228 (4N 143)
BB11: Hapt 5H 123
BB12: Hapt, Padi 5H 123
BB18: Barnw 3M 77
BL0: Ramsb 8K 181
BL9: Bury 8K 181
FY3: Blackp 1N 227 (4D 88)
OL11: Roch 9N 203
OL16: Roch 8A 204
PR1: Prest 6M 229 (1K 135)
PR9: S'port 6J 167
Manchester Road Station (Rail) 4B 228 (4D 124)
Manchester Square Stop (Tram) 6H 227 (7B 88)
Manchester Wlk. PR7: Buck V 9B 154
(off Dorset Dr.)
Mancknols St. BB9: Nelson 3K 105
Mancknols Walton Cott. Homes, The
BB9: Nelson 2M 105
Mandale Pk. 8A 204
Mandela Ct. BB1: Blackb 1D 226
Manderville Cl. WN3: Wins 9N 221
Mandeville Rd. PR8: Ains 8B 186
Mandeville Ter. BL8: Hawk 3A 200
Manfield WN8: Skelm 9L 211
Manion Av. L31: Lyd 6A 216
Manion Cl. L31: Lyd 6A 216
Manitoba Cl. BB2: Blackb 9J 119
Manley Cl. BL9: Summ 3H 201
Manley Rd. OL11: Roch 9N 203
(not continuous)
Manley Ter. BL1: Bolt 9E 198
Manner Sutton St. BB1: Blackb 3F 226 (3N 139)
Manning Rd. PR1: Prest 8A 116
(not continuous)
PR8: S'port 8L 167
Mannin Way LA1: Lanc 4N 23
Manor, The WA11: Rain 6N 225
Manor Av. L40: Burs 2B 210
LA2: Slyne 9J 15
PR1: Penw 4E 134
PR2: Fulw 5L 115
PR3: Ribc 7E 98
Manor Brook BB5: Acc 2B 142
Manor Cl. LA2: Slyne 9J 15
LA6: Bur L 3K 19
PR5: Hogh 5H 137
Manor Complex L33: Know P 8A 224
Manor Ct. BL2: Bolt 9K 199
FY1: Blackp 3C 88
FY4: Blackp 1E 108
FY5: T Clev 9C 54
PR2: Fulw 2E 114
PR3: Ribc 6K 99
PR4: Longt 8L 133
Manor Courtyard LA3: Heys 8K 21
Manor Cres. L40: Burs 2B 210
LA2: Slyne 9K 15
Manorcroft PR4: Longt 8L 133
Manor Dr. FY5: T Clev 9D 54
FY6: Poul F 7L 63
L30: N'ton 7A 222
L40: Burs 2B 210
LA2: Slyne 9J 15
PR4: K'ham 5A 112
Manor Farm LA6: Whit 8E 8
Manorfields BB7: Whall 5K 101

Manor Gdns.—Marybank Cl.

Manor Gdns. L40: Burs 2B 210
Manor Gro. L32: Kirk 8G 222
LA3: Heys 6N 21
PR1: Penw 4D 134
WN5: Orr 3L 221
WN8: Skelm 2K 219
Manor Ho. Caravan Pk. FY4: Blackp 5H 109
Manor Ho. Cl. L31: Magh 1B 222
L40: Ruff 1G 191
PR26: Leyl 7E 152
Manor Ho. Cres. PR1: Prest 6L 115
Manor Ho. Dr. WN8: Skelm 8B 220
Manor Ho. La. PR1: Prest 6L 115
Manor Ho. Pk. FY5: T Clev 9C 54
Manor La. LA2: Slyne 8J 15
PR1: Penw 4D 134
Mnr. Mill Cl. OL16: Roch 2G 204
Manor Pk. PR2: Fulw 6M 115
Manor Pl. BB5: Chur 1M 141
Manor Ri. BD23: T Crav 9J 53
Manor Rd. BB2: Blackb 3J 139
BB3: Darw 7N 157
BB7: Clith 4K 81
BB7: Whall 5J 101
BB8: Colne 4B 86
BB12: Burnl 2N 123
BL6: Hor 9E 196
FY1: Blackp 3M 227 (6D 88)
FY7: Flee 8E 40
L40: Burs 2B 210
LA2: Slyne 9J 15
PR3: Gars 3N 59
PR4: Inskip 2G 92
PR4: W Grn 5G 111
PR6: Clay W 4D 154
PR9: S'port 4N 167
WN6: Shev 6J 213
Manor Row BB1: Cop G 1L 119
Manor St. BB5: Acc 1B 142
BB9: Nelson 3K 105
BL0: Ramsb 7G 180
OL13: Bac 6K 163
Manor Way PR4: W Grn 6G 111
PR7: Copp 5N 193
Manor Wood FY7: Flee 9E 40
PR4: Wesh 2N 111
Manse Av. WN6: Wrigh 8J 193
MANSERGH 2E 8
Mansergh High La. LA6: Mans 1E 8
Mansergh St. BB10: Burnl 8G 105
Mansfield Av. BL0: Ramsb 3G 200
Mansfield Cres. BB9: Brierf 4G 104
Mansfield Dr. PR5: Hogh 5G 137
Mansfield Grange OL11: Roch 7N 203
Mansfield Gro. BB9: Brierf 4G 104
Mansfield Rd. FY3: Blackp 3D 88
OL11: Roch 6J 203
Mansion, The BB8: Colne 5F 86
(off Alma Rd.)
Mansion Ho. Bldgs. BB4: Craws 9M 143
(off Burnley Rd.)
Mansion St. Sth. BB5: Acc 2C 142
Manston Gro. PR7: Chor 7C 174
Manx Jane's La. PR9: S'port 2N 167
Manxman Rd. BB2: Blackb 7M 139
Many Brooks Ho. PR5: Hogh 7G 137
Maple Av. BB4: Hasl 4H 161
BB7: Clith 4K 81
FY3: Blackp 2N 227 (5D 88)
FY5: T Clev 3J 63
FY7: Flee 4F 54
L40: Burs 9C 190
LA3: Heys 5M 21
PR6: Birns 8A 156
Maple Bank BB10: Burnl 2G 124
Maplebank PR2: Lea 8N 113
Maple Cl. BB1: Clay D 3M 119
BB7: Whall 4K 101
PR4: Newt 7D 112
Maple Ct. PR3: Gars 3N 59
PR25: Leyl 4N 153
(off Elm Gro.)
WN8: Skelm 5K 219
Maple Cres. BB1: Rish 9H 121
PR1: Prest 7G 229 (1H 135)
Maple Dr. BB5: Osw 5M 141
FY6: Poul F 9L 63
PR5: Bam B 7B 136
Maple Gro. BL0: Ramsb 9J 181
BL8: Tott 8F 200
LA1: Lanc 8H 23
(off Sycamore Gro.)
PR1: Penw 4E 134
PR2: Grim 9G 96
PR2: Ribb 5C 116
PR4: Wart 2J 131
PR6: Chor 3F 174
Maple Ho. PR7: Chor 8B 174
Maple Leaf Cl. PR2: Ingol 3C 114
Maple M. BB3: Darw 7D 158
Maple Rd. PR3: Gars 4N 59
Maples, The PR4: Fulw 2E 114
PR26: Leyl 9C 152
Maple St. BB1: Blackb 1A 140
BB1: Rish 8H 121
BB5: Clay M 7M 121
BB6: Gt H 3K 121
BL2: Bolt 8J 199
OL11: Roch 7A 204
OL14: Wals 8K 165
PR8: S'port 8K 167
Maple Vw. WN8: Skelm 5K 219
Maplewood PR9: S'port 4M 167
WN8: Skelm 8L 211
Maplewood Av. FY6: Pree 8N 41
Maplewood Cl. FY8: L Ann 4M 129
PR7: Chor 8G 174
PR25: Leyl 7H 153
Maplewood Dr. FY5: T Clev 3C 62
Maplewood Gdns. LA1: Lanc 5L 29
Marabou Dr. BB3: Darw 4M 157
Marathon Pl. PR26: Leyl 4F 152
Marble Av. FY5: T Clev 4F 62
Marble Pl. Shop. Cen. PR8: S'port 7H 167
Marble St. BB5: Osw 4L 141
Marbury Gro. WN6: Stand 4N 213
Marbury Rd. L32: Kirk 8H 223
Marc Av. L31: Mell 6G 223
Marchbank Rd. WN8: Skelm 2H 219
March Dr. BL8: Bury 8J 201
March St. BB12: Burnl 1D 124
OL16: Roch 6D 204
Marchwood Rd. FY3: Blackp 2H 89
Marcliffe Dr. OL11: Roch 7M 203
Marcroft Av. FY4: Blackp 2E 108
Marcroft Pl. OL11: Roch 9D 204
Mardale Av. FY4: Blackp 9J 89
LA4: Morec 3D 22
Mardale Cl. PR8: Ains 9B 186
Mardale Cres. PR25: Leyl 8L 153
Mardale Rd. LA1: Lanc 7L 23
PR1: Prest 8C 116
PR3: Longr 5H 97
Mardyke OL12: Roch 5B 204
Maresfield Rd. PR1: Prest 3G 135
Margaret Av. OL16: Roch 6F 204
WN6: Stand 8M 213
Margaret Ct. FY8: L Ann 4G 129
Margaret Rd. PR1: Penw 4H 135
Margaret St. BB1: Blackb 4D 140
BB4: Rawt 3L 161
BB5: Osw 6J 141
PR1: Prest 4L 229 (9K 115)
Margaret Ward Ct. OL11: Roch 8D 204
(off Wellfield St.)
Margate Av. FY4: Blackp 3E 108
Margate Rd. FY8: L Ann 9F 108
PR2: Ingol 5D 114
Margroy Cl. OL12: Roch 3D 204
Maria Ct. BB11: Burnl 5E 124
(off Glebe St.)
Marians Dr. L39: Orms 4K 209
Maria Sq. BL7: Belm 1L 197
Maria St. BB3: Darw 9B 158
Mariclough-Hampsfield Camping
FY4: Blackp 3M 109
Maricourt Av. BB1: Blackb 3D 140
Marigold St. OL11: Roch 8C 204
WN5: Wigan 4N 221
Marilyn Av. PR5: Lost H 8L 135
Marina Av. FY1: Blackp 8M 227 (8D 88)
FY3: Blackp 2K 89
Marina Caravan Pk. LA2: Glas 2E 36
Marina Cl. PR5: Lost H 7K 135
Marina Cres. L30: N'ton 9A 222
Marina Dr. PR2: Fulw 2H 115
PR5: Lost H 7K 135
WN5: Wigan 6N 221
Marina Gro. PR1: Lost H 7K 135
PR5: Lost H 7K 135
Marina M. FY7: Flee 1H 55
Marina Rd. L37: Form 2A 214
Marine Av. BB11: Burnl 5A 124
Marine Cres. PR7: Buck V 9B 154
Marine Dr. FY8: L Ann 5K 129
LA2: Hest B 9G 14
PR8: S'port 7F 166
PR9: S'port 3J 167
Marine Ga. Mans. PR9: S'port 6H 167
Marine Hall, The 8G 41
Marine Lake 7G 166
Marine Pde. FY7: Flee 3C 54
PR8: S'port 6G 166
Mariner Ct. PR9: S'port 5J 167
Marine Rd. PR8: S'port 8E 166
Marine Rd. Central LA4: Morec 3N 21
Marine Rd. E. LA4: Morec 2B 22
Marine Rd. W. LA3: Morec 4M 21
LA4: Morec 4M 21
Mariners, The FY8: L Ann 5B 130
Mariners Cl. FY7: Flee 3E 54
Mariners Way PR2: Ash R 9D 114
Mariner Wlk. PR6: Chor 6H 175
Marino Cl. FY5: T Clev 3K 63
Maritime Ct. PR8: S'port 7G 167
Maritime St. FY7: Flee 2F 54
Maritime Way PR2: Ash R 1C 134
Mark Cl. PR1: Penw 7J 135
Market Av. BB1: Blackb 4D 226 (3M 139)
Market Chambers BL0: Ramsb 7H 181
(off Ramsbottom La.)
Marketgate LA1: Lanc 7C 228 (8K 23)
Market Hall BB11: Burnl 2D 228
LA1: Lanc 7C 228
PR1: Prest 5K 229
PR8: S'port 7H 167
Market Pl. BB7: Clith 3L 81
BB8: Colne 6B 86
BD24: Sett 3N 35
BL0: Eden 3J 181
BL0: Ramsb 7G 181
FY6: Poul F 8K 63
FY7: Flee 9J 41
OL16: Roch 6C 204
PR1: Prest 6L 229 (1J 135)
PR3: Gars 5N 59
PR3: Longr 3K 97
PR7: Adl 6J 195
PR7: Chor 6E 174
Market Prom. BB11: Burnl 2D 228 (3E 124)
Market Sq. BB9: Nelson 2H 105
BB11: Burnl 2D 228 (3E 124)
FY8: L Ann 5N 129
L32: Kirk 8K 223
LA1: Lanc 7C 228
LA6: K Lon 6F 8
(off Main St.)
PR4: K'ham 4N 111
Market St. BB3: Darw 6A 158
BB4: W'foot 7C 162
BB5: Chur 3L 141
BB8: Colne 6B 86
BB9: Nelson 2H 105
BB18: Barnw 2M 77
(off Brook St.)
BL0: Eden 2J 181
BL8: Tott 6E 200
FY1: Blackp 1H 227 (5B 88)
FY6: Ham 1B 64
LA1: Lanc 7B 228 (8K 23)
LA4: Morec 3A 22
LA5: Carn 8A 12
Market St. LA6: K Lon 6F 8
OL12: Bac, Whitw 9N 183
OL13: Bac 6K 163
(Curve St.)
OL13: Bac 8A 164
(Old La.)
OL14: Tod 4K 165
(off Rochdale Rd.)
PR1: Prest 5K 229 (9J 115)
PR4: Wesh 3K 111
PR7: Adl 7J 195
PR7: Chor 6E 174
PR8: S'port 7G 167
Market St. La. BB2: Blackb 5C 226 (4M 139)
Market St. W. PR1: Prest 5J 229 (9J 115)
Market Wlk. PR7: Chor 6E 174
Market Way BB1: Blackb 4C 226
BB5: Acc 2B 142
(off Broadway)
L39: Orms 7K 209
OL16: Roch 5C 204
Markham Dr. PR8: S'port 3L 187
Markham Rd. BB2: Blackb 5J 139
Markham St. PR2: Ash R 8F 114
Mark Ho. La. BD23: Garg 2L 53
Marklands Rd. BL6: Hor 8F 196
Markland St. BL0: Ramsb 8G 181
PR1: Prest 6G 229 (1H 135)
Mark La. OL14: Tod 9J 147
Markross St. BB4: Rawt 5M 161
Mark's Av. PR26: Far M 2H 153
Marksbury Shop. Cen.
FY7: Flee 3C 54
Mark Sq. PR4: Tarl 9E 150
Mark St. BB10: Burnl 9F 104
OL12: Roch 4E 204
OL13: Bac 7G 162
MARLAND 9M 203
Marland WN8: Skelm 8L 211
Marland Av. OL11: Roch 9M 203
Marland Cl. OL11: Roch 8M 203
Marland Fold OL11: Roch 9M 203
Marland Golf Course 8L 203
Marland Grn. OL11: Roch 9M 203
Marland Hill Rd. OL11: Roch 8N 203
Marland Old Rd. OL11: Roch 9M 203
Marland Ri. OL11: Roch 8M 203
Marland Tops OL11: Roch 9M 203
Marl Av. PR1: Penw 4E 134
Marlboro Rd. FY3: Blackp 3N 227 (6D 88)
Marlborough WN8: Skelm 8L 211
Marlborough Av. FY5: T Clev 7C 54
L31: Lyd 8C 216
PR4: Wart 2J 131
Marlborough Cl. BL0: Ramsb 2H 201
OL12: Whitw 7N 183
Marlborough Ct. PR9: S'port 7J 167
WN8: Skelm 8L 211
Marlborough Dr. PR2: Fulw 2G 115
PR5: Walt D 4N 135
Marlborough Gdns. PR9: S'port 6J 167
WN8: Skelm 8L 211
Marlborough Rd. BB5: Acc 9A 122
FY8: L Ann 8E 108
LA3: Heys 5M 21
PR9: S'port 7J 167
Marlborough St. BB11: Burnl 4C 228 (4D 124)
OL12: Roch 4N 203
PR6: Chor 5G 174
Marlborough Ter. PR9: S'port 7J 167
(off Marlborough Rd.)
Marl Cop PR26: Breth 9L 151
Marl Cft. PR1: Penw 6G 134
Marled Hey BL7: Edgw 9K 179
Marles Ct. BB10: Burnl 1F 124
(off Pheasantford Grn.)
Marlfield PR4: Lit H 3K 151
Marlfield Cl. PR2: Ingol 4C 114
Marl Gro. WN5: Orr 7G 221
Marl Hill Cres. PR2: Ribb 7C 116
Marl Hill La. BD20: Loth 5L 79
Marlhill Rd. FY3: Blackp 2G 89
Marlin St. BB9: Nelson 9K 85
Marlon Cres. BB11: Burnl 4B 124
Marlow Ct. PR7: Adl 7H 195
Marlowe Av. BB5: Bax 6D 142
BB12: Padi 2K 123
Marlowe Cres. BB6: Gt H 5H 121
Marl Pits BB4: Rawt 4N 161
Marl Pits Swimming Pool 4A 162
Marl Pl. BB5: Hunc 7C 122
(off Whinney Hill Rd.)
Marl Rd. L30: N'ton 7A 222
L33: Know P 7A 224
Marlton Rd. BB2: Blackb 6L 139
Marlton Way LA1: Lanc 1J 29
Marne Cres. OL11: Roch 5N 203
Marnwood Rd. L32: Kirk 9J 223
Marnwood Wlk. L32: Kirk 9H 223
Marple Av. BL1: Bolt 9G 198
Marple Cl. FY4: Blackp 5B 108
WN6: Stand 2L 213
Marquis Av. BL9: Bury 9K 201
Marquis Cl. BB3: Lwr D 9N 139
Marquis Dr. PR4: Frec 1A 132
Marquis St. PR4: K'ham 4L 111
Marron Cl. PR25: Leyl 7H 153
Marsden Cl. PR7: E'ton 7E 172
Marsden Ct. BB10: Burnl 7G 104
Marsden Cres. BB9: Nelson 2L 105
Marsden Dr. BB9: Brierf 4H 105
Marsden Gro. BB9: Brierf 5G 105
Marsden Hall Rd. BB9: Nelson 2L 105
Marsden Hall Rd. Nth. BB9: Nelson 1L 105
Marsden Hall Rd. Sth. BB9: Nelson 2L 105
MARSDEN HEIGHT 5K 105
Marsden Height Cl. BB9: Brierf 5J 105
Marsden M. BB9: Nelson 2L 105
Marsden Mill BB9: Nelson 4K 105
Marsden Pk. Golf Course 2N 105
Marsden Pl. BB9: Nelson 2L 105
Marsden Rd. BB10: Burnl 7G 105
FY4: Blackp 1D 108
PR9: S'port 7L 167
Marsden Sq. BB4: Hasl 4G 161
(off Hargreaves St.)
Marsden's Sq. OL15: Littleb 8L 185
(off Sutcliffe St.)
Marsden St. BB2: Blackb 6J 139
BB4: Hasl 4F 160
BB5: Acc 4A 142
PR4: K'ham 4M 111
Marsden Theatre 9H 153
Marsett Cl. OL12: Roch 4L 203
Marsett Pl. PR2: Ribb 4A 116
MARSH 7A 228 (8H 23)
Marshall Av. BB5: Hunc 7E 122
Marshall Cl. L33: Kirk 5L 223
Marshall Gro. PR2: Ingol 5D 114
Marshallsay L37: Form 1A 214
Marshalls Brow PR1: Penw 5H 135
PR25: Leyl 5L 153
Marshalls Bldgs. OL13: Bac 6H 163
Marshall's Cl. L31: Lyd 7B 216
PR1: Penw 4H 135
Marshall St. OL16: Roch 6F 204
Marsham Cl. PR3: Gars 6A 60
Marsham Gro. BB3: Darw 6C 158
Marshaw Pl. PR3: Gars 6L 59
Marshaw Rd. LA1: Lanc 6H 23
Marsh Cl. LA2: C'ham 1F 44
Marsh Ct. FY5: T Clev 1G 63
Marsh Cres. LA4: Morec 4F 22
Marshdale Rd. FY4: Blackp 2F 108
Marsh Dr. PR4: Frec 1B 132
Marshes La., The PR4: Mere B 4L 169
Marshfield Rd. BD24: Sett 3N 35
Marsh Ga. BB3: Darw 6D 158
Marsh Gates PR4: Frec 1B 132
MARSH GREEN 2N 221
Marsh Grn. WN5: Wigan 2N 221
MARSH HOUSE 6C 158
Marsh Ho. Farm Caravan Pk. LA5: Carn 9L 11
Marsh House Ind. Est. BB3: Darw 6C 158
(off Marsh House La.)
Marsh Ho. La. BB3: Darw 6B 158
MARSH HOUSES 1F 44
Marsh Ho's. LA2: C'ham 1F 44
Marsh La. FY6: Ham 2B 64
L38: Ince B 5C 214
L40: Scar 4J 209
LA2: C'ham 2E 44
LA2: Glas, Thurn 3A 36
PR1: Prest 5G 229 (1G 134)
PR4: Longt 9F 132
PR6: Brind 4J 155
(Breworth Fold La.)
PR6: Brind 2K 155
(Hilton's Brow)
Marsh Mill Village FY5: T Clev 1G 63
Marsh Moss La. L40: Burs 6N 189
Marsh Rd. FY5: T Clev 1G 63
PR4: Hesk B 3D 150
PR9: Banks 7G 149
MARSHSIDE 3N 167
Marshside Nature Reserve 1M 167
Marshside Rd. PR9: S'port 1L 167
Marsh St. BB1: Blackb 1D 226 (2M 139)
BL6: Hor 9B 196
LA1: Lanc 8H 23
Marsh Ter. BB3: Darw 5A 158
Marsh Vw. PR4: Newt 7D 112
Marsh Vista Caravan Club L40: Burs 4A 190
Marsh Way PR1: Penw 6F 134
Mars St. BL7: Edgw 8L 179
Marston Cl. PR2: Fulw 2F 114
Marston Cres. L38: Hight 9A 214
Marston Moor PR2: Fulw 2F 114
Martha's Ter. OL16: Roch 2F 204
Martholme Av. BB5: Clay M 6N 121
Martholme Cl. BB6: Gt H 3K 121
Martholme La. BB6: Gt H 1M 121
Martin Av. FY8: L Ann 5C 108
Martin Cft. Rd. BB4: Hasl 2F 160
Martindale Av. FY7: Flee 2C 54
Martindale Cl. BB1: Blackb 6C 140
Martindales, The PR6: Clay W 4D 154
Martin Dr. BB3: Darw 9C 158
Martine Cl. L31: Mell 6G 223
Martinfield PR2: Fulw 1J 115
Martinfield Rd. PR1: Penw 6G 135
Martinfields BB10: Reed 6G 104
Martinique Dr. BB3: Lwr D 1N 157
Martin La. L40: Burs 5K 189
OL12: Roch 4M 203
Martin Mere Vis. Cen. 4N 189
Martin Mere Wetland Cen. 4N 189
Martins Av. PR7: H Charn 3G 195
Martins Fld. OL12: Roch 4K 203
Martins La. WN8: Skelm 4A 220
Martin St. BB10: Burnl 9F 104
BL7: Turt 1K 199
BL9: Bury 9B 202
Martin Top La. BB7: Rim 4A 76
Martland Av. L10: Aint 7D 222
WN6: Shev 7J 213
Martland Bus. Pk. WN5: Wigan 2N 221
Martland Ct. WN5: Orr 1L 221
MARTLAND MILL 9N 213
Martland Mill Ind. Est. WN5: Wigan 1M 221
Martland Mill La. WN5: Wigan 1N 221
(not continuous)
Martland Point WN5: Orr 1L 221
Mart La. L40: Burs 8C 190
Martlett Av. OL11: Roch 6J 203
Marton Cl. BD23: Garg 3L 53
Marton Dr. BB11: Burnl 6C 124
FY4: Blackp 9N 227 (1D 108)
LA4: Morec 2F 22
MARTON FOLD 5G 108
Marton Fold FY4: Blackp 5G 108
Marton Mere 7J 89
Marton Mere Caravan Pk. FY4: Blackp 8J 89
Marton Pl. LA4: Morec 2F 22
Marton Rd. BD23: Garg 4L 53
PR2: Ash R 9C 114
Marton St. LA1: Lanc 8D 228 (9K 23)
Marton Vw. FY3: Blackp 6E 88
Marton Wlk. BB3: Darw 9B 158
Marwick Cl. WN6: Stand 2N 213
Mary Av. PR8: Ains 7E 186
Marybank Cl. PR2: Fulw 3M 115

Maryland—Melrose Gdns.

Maryland FY4: Blackp 3N 109
Maryland Cl. LA5: Silv 8H 5
Mary Leaver Way BB3: Darw 2N 157
Mary St. BB1: Blackb 4A 140
BB1: Rish 8H 121
BB8: Colne 7N 85
BB10: Burnl 3G 228 (4F 124)
BL0: Ramsb 9G 180
LA1: Lanc 7D 228 (8K 23)
LA5: Carn 7A 12
OL16: Roch 1G 205
Mary St. E. BL6: Hor 9C 196
Mary St. W. BL6: Hor 9B 196
PR3: Longr 2J 97
Mary Towneley Fold BB10: Burnl 5G 125
Masbury Cl. BL1: Bolt 6E 198
Masefield Av. BB12: Padi 2K 123
FY5: T Clev 9G 54
WN5: Orr 5K 221
Masefield Cl. BB6: Gt H 5H 121
BB6: Old L 4B 100
Masefield Pl. PR5: Walt D 6N 135
Mason Cl. PR4: Frec 2A 132
Mason Clough BL1: Bolt 8F 198
Masonfield PR5: Bam B 2D 154
Masonfield Cres. LA1: Lanc 9N 23
MASONGILL 9L 9
Mason Hill Vw. PR2: Fulw 5K 115
Mason Ho. Cres. PR2: Ingol 3D 114
Mason Row BL7: Eger 3D 198
Mason St. BB5: Acc 2B 142
BB5: Osw 5K 141
BB8: Colne 6A 86
BL6: Hor 9C 196
BL7: Eger 4E 198
OL16: Roch 6C 204
PR6: Chor 4G 175
Masons Way BB18: Barnw 1M 77
Masonwood PR2: Fulw 3K 115
Massam Cl. WA11: Rain 4L 225
Massey Cft. OL12: Whitw 6N 183
Massey La. BB9: Brierf 5E 104
Massey St. BB9: Brierf 6E 104
BB11: Burnl 2E 228 (3E 124)
BL9: Bury 9N 201
Masterson Av. BB12: Read 8C 102
Matcham Ct. FY1: Blackp 2J 227 (5B 88)
Matchmoor La. BL6: Hor 9G 197
Mather Av. BB5: Acc 9A 122
Mather Fold Cotts. BL7: Eger 4E 198
Mather Rd. BL9: Bury 6L 201
Mather St. FY3: Blackp 3D 88
Matheson Dr. WN5: Wigan 3N 221
Matlock Av. PR8: Birk 1H 187
Matlock Cl. PR8: Birk 1H 187
Matlock Ct. BL6: Hor 9F 196
Matlock Cres. PR8: Birk 1H 187
Matlock Gro. BB10: Burnl 8G 105
Matlock Pl. PR2: Ingol 4D 114
Matlock Rd. PR8: Birk 2H 187
Matlock St. BB3: Darw 5M 157
MATSHEAD 5E 68
Matterdale Rd. PR25: Leyl 8L 153
Matthew Cl. BB8: Colne 7B 86
Matthew Moss La. OL11: Roch 9M 203
Matthews Ct. FY4: Blackp 2D 108
Matthew St. BB2: Blackb 6J 139
Matthias Ct. *LA4: Morec 2B 22*
(off Matthias St.)
Matthias St. LA4: Morec 2B 22
Mattock Cres. LA4: Morec 3F 22
Maudland Bank PR1: Prest 4G 229 (9H 115)
Maudland Rd. FY1: Blackp 8K 227 (8C 88)
PR1: Prest 4H 229 (9H 115)
MAUDLANDS 8G 115
Maudsley St. BB1: Blackb 4F 226 (3N 139)
BB5: Acc 2B 142
Maud St. BB9: Barrf 9H 85
BL2: Bolt 8J 199
OL12: Roch 3D 204
PR7: Chor 8D 174
Mauldland Ho. PR1: Ash R 4G 229
Maureen Av. PR5: Lost H 8L 135
Maureen St. OL12: Roch 3D 204
Maurice Gro. FY2: Blackp 9E 62
Maurice St. BB9: Nelson 2G 105
Mavis Dr. PR7: Copp 4A 194
Mavis Gro. OL16: Milnr 7K 205
Mavis Rd. BB2: Blackb 3H 139
MAWDESLEY 3N 191
Mawdsley Cl. L37: Form 9B 206
Mawdsley Ter. L39: Orms 4L 209
Mawson Dr. FY3: Blackp 5E 88
Maxwell Gro. FY2: Blackp 9E 62
Maxwell St. BL1: Bolt 9E 198
Maybank Cl. PR9: S'port 5N 167
May Bell Av. FY5: T Clev 9F 54
Maybury Av. BB12: Burnl 2N 123
Maybury Cl. BL0: Ramsb 9G 180
Maycroft Av. FY6: Carl 6H 63
Mayfair Cl. BB4: Hasl 8F 160
FY8: L Ann 2K 129
L38: Hight 9A 214
Mayfair Cres. BB1: Wilp 4N 119
Mayfair Dr. FY5: T Clev 3J 63
Mayfair Gdns. FY5: T Clev 2J 63
OL11: Roch 8A 204
Mayfair Rd. BB9: Nelson 1L 105
BB10: Burnl 4J 125
FY1: Blackp 8E 88
Mayfayre Av. L31: Lyd 6A 216
MAYFIELD 4E 204
Mayfield BL2: Bolt 8K 199
Mayfield Av. BB4: Hasl 6F 160
BB5: Osw 4L 141
BB7: Clith 4M 81
FY4: Blackp 3C 108
FY5: T Clev 8G 54
LA1: Lanc 5J 23
LA6: Holme 1F 6
PR2: Ingol 4D 114
PR4: K'ham 4M 111
PR5: Lost H 8M 135
PR6: Adl 6J 195
Mayfield Cl. BL0: Ramsb 3F 200
PR1: Penw 4H 135
Mayfield Ct. WN5: Orr 2L 221
Mayfield Dr. LA4: Morec 2E 22
Mayfield Flats BB3: Darw 8B 158
Mayfield Fold BB11: Burnl 6F 124
Mayfield Gdns. BB5: Osw 4M 141
Mayfield Pl. FY7: Flee 2F 54
Mayfield Rd. BB1: Ramsg 5M 119
BL0: Ramsb 3F 200
FY8: L Ann 1E 128
LA2: H Ben 7L 19
PR2: Ash R 8E 114
PR6: Chor 5F 174
PR25: Leyl 8K 153
WN5: Orr 3L 221
WN8: Uph 4D 220
(not continuous)
Mayfield St. BB2: Blackb 8C 226 (5M 139)
OL16: Roch 4E 204
(not continuous)
Mayfield Ter. OL16: Roch 4E 204
PR5: Sam 2M 137
Mayflower Av. PR1: Penw 5D 134
Mayflower Cres. PR7: Buck V 8B 154
Mayflower Gdns. PR7: Chor 2D 194
Mayflower Gro. PR3: Catt 2B 68
Mayflower Ind. Est.
L37: Form 2A 214
Mayflower St. BB2: Blackb 6J 139
Mayhall Ct. L31: Magh 9C 216
Maylands Pl. BB9: Barrf 9G 84
Maylands Sq. LA4: Morec 4C 22
May La. PR3: Clau 4E 68
Maynard St. PR1: Prest 8G 114
PR2: Ash R 7G 114
Mayo Dr. PR4: Tarl 9E 150
Mayor Av. FY1: Blackp 7L 227 (8C 88)
Mayor St. BL8: Bury 9H 201
Maypark PR5: Bam B 2C 154
May Pl. *OL11: Roch 9D 204*
(off Burlington St.)
OL15: Littleb 1H 205
Maypole Sq. BB18: Salt 4A 78
Mayson St. BB1: Blackb 6D 226 (4M 139)
May St. BB1: Blackb 4A 140
BB9: Barrf 9H 85
BB9: Nelson 9K 85
BL7: Edgw 8L 179
May Ter. *BB7: B'ton 6G 101*
(off Whalley New Rd.)
May Tree Cl. BB10: Brierc 7J 105
Maytree Ct. PR6: Adl 5H 195
Maytree Wlk. WN8: Skelm 8M 211
Mayville Rd. BB9: Brierf 4F 104
Mayville Ter. *BD24: Sett 3N 35*
(off Church St.)
Mead Av. PR25: Leyl 7L 153
Meadland Gro. BL1: Bolt 9F 198
Meadow, The PR26: Leyl 6E 152
Meadow Av. FY6: Pree 7N 41
FY7: Flee 4E 54
PR8: S'port 1J 187
Meadoway BB5: Chur 1M 141
PR4: Longt 8K 133
PR4: Tarl 1E 170
Meadow Bank BB5: Acc 1B 142
L31: Magh 9A 216
L32: Kirk 6H 223
L39: Orms 8L 209
LA5: Arn 1F 4
PR1: Penw 5F 134
PR5: Bam B 3D 154
Meadow Bank Av. BB10: Reed 5F 104
Meadow Bank M. BB9: Nelson 9K 85
Meadow Bank Rd. BB9: Nelson 2H 105
Meadowbarn Cl. L32: Kirk 9K 223
PR4: Cott 4B 114
Meadow Bottom Rd. OL14: Tod 1L 165
Meadowbridge Cl. L40: W'head 8C 210
Meadowbrook FY3: Blackp 8J 89
L40: Burs 1B 210
Meadowbrook Cl. BL9: Bury 9A 202
Meadow Brow PR9: S'port 1C 168
Meadow Cl. BB1: Blackb 4B 140
BB5: Hunc 8E 122
BB7: B'ton 7G 100
BB8: Foul 2A 86
BB10: Reed 6F 104
FY2: Blackp 9D 62
FY6: Pree 7N 41
L40: W'head 8C 210
PR4: Clif 7H 113
PR4: W Grn 6G 111
PR7: Copp 6B 194
WN8: Skelm 4A 220
Meadowclough WN8: Skelm 8M 211
Meadow Cotts. OL12: Whitw 3A 184
Meadow Ct. *BB5: Osw 4L 141*
(off Haworth St.)
PR1: Prest 9G 229 (2H 135)
PR4: Trea 9E 92
Meadow Ct. Rd. LA4: Morec 4C 22
Meadow Cres. FY6: Carl 8G 62
PR4: Wesh 3K 111
Meadow Cft. BB7: West B 7L 73
BD23: Garg 3M 53
(off Swire Cft. Rd.)
Meadowcroft BB3: Lwr D 1A 158
FY8: L Ann 8G 108
L37: Form 1A 214
LA6: Neth K 5C 16
PR7: Eux 3L 173
WN8: Skelm 8M 211
Meadowcroft Av. FY5: T Clev 1E 62
FY6: Ham 2B 64
PR3: Catt 9A 60
Meadowcroft Bus. Pk. PR4: W Stake 7E 134
Meadowcroft Caravan Pk. PR3: Lit E 6L 65
Meadowcroft Cl. BB4: Rawt 2M 161
Meadowcroft Gro. LA3: Heys 7M 21
Meadowcroft Ho. OL11: Roch 7K 203
Meadowcroft La. OL11: Roch 7K 203
Meadowcroft Rd. PR25: Leyl 8G 152
Meadow Dr. L39: Aug 1H 217
LA5: Bolt S 3L 15
PR4: Wart 3H 131
Meadow Edge BB9: Barrf 6K 85
Meadowfield LA2: Halt 1B 24
PR1: Penw 6H 135
PR2: Fulw 1J 115
WN8: Uph 4D 220
Meadowfield Cl. BB7: Whall 3G 101
LA2: Halt 1B 24
Meadowfields BB2: Blackb 9L 139
Meadow Gdns. BB1: Rish 8H 121
Meadow Head BB1: Rish 8H 121
Meadow Head Av. OL12: Whitw 8A 184
Meadow Head Cl. BB2: Blackb 7H 139
Meadowhead Dr. BB1: Rish 8J 121
Meadow Head La. BB3: Darw 4J 157
OL11: Roch 3E 202
PR4: Longt 9K 133
Meadow Hgts. *BL0: Ramsb 8J 181*
(off Fir St.)
Meadow Ho. PR1: Prest 4L 229
Meadowland Cl. PR26: Far M 4H 153
Meadowlands BB7: Clith 3J 81
PR7: Char R 1N 193
Meadow La. FY8: L Ann 4D 130
L31: Magh 1D 222
L40: Burs, Lath 5F 190
L40: Lath 1G 210
L40: Mawd 1H 191
PR4: Hesk B 3D 150
PR5: Bam B 3D 154
PR8: Ains 1C 206
PR26: Cros 6G 171
Meadow Pk. BL0: Ramsb 2H 181
FY3: Stain 5K 89
LA2: Gal 2K 37
PR3: Cab 3M 59
PR4: Tarl 9F 150
PR4: Wesh 3K 111
Meadow Reach PR1: Penw 5E 134
Meadow Ri. BB2: Blackb 9H 139
BD24: Gig 2N 35
Meadows, The BB3: Darw 3L 157
BB5: Osw 5M 141
BB7: B'ton 6G 100
BB8: Colne 5A 86
BB12: Burnl 1B 124
FY5: T Clev 1F 62
L31: Magh 1C 222
LA5: Arn 3F 4
LA5: Yea R 7B 6
LA6: K Lon 7G 8
OL12: Roch 1E 202
OL12: Whitw 5N 183
PR3: Fort 3N 45
PR4: Elsw 1L 91
PR7: Hesk 3H 193
Meadows Av. BB4: Hasl 5H 161
FY5: T Clev 1F 62
OL13: Bac 3K 163
Meadows Cl. LA5: Yea R 7B 6
Meadows Dr. BB4: Craws 7M 143
Meadowside BB7: Grind 4B 74
LA1: Lanc 9D 228 (9K 23)
LA2: Clau 9A 18
OL16: Milnr 9M 205
PR4: Wal B 2L 151
PR26: Cros 4M 171
Meadowside Av. BB5: Clay M 6L 121
Meadowside Dr. L33: Kirk 4L 223
PR5: Hogh 7G 136
Meadowside Rd. LA4: Morec 5B 22
Meadows La. BL2: Bolt 9M 199
Meadow St. BB3: Darw 8B 158
BB5: Acc 2B 142
BB6: Gt H 5J 121
BB11: Burnl 2C 228 (3D 124)
BB12: Padi 9H 103
BB18: Barnw 10F 52
LA1: Lanc 8H 23
OL14: Tod 1L 165
(off Meadow Bottom Rd.)
PR1: Prest 4L 229 (9K 115)
PR6: Wheel 8J 155
PR7: Adl 7J 195
PR25: Leyl 6K 153
Meadowsweet Rd. L32: Kirk 6L 223
Meadow Ter. *BB3: Darw 2M 157*
(off The Meadows)
Meadow Va. BB2: Blackb 1M 157
PR26: Leyl 7D 152
Meadowvale Dr. WN5: Wigan 5M 221
Meadow Vw. BB7: Clith 3J 81
LA1: Lanc 5H 23
LA2: Farl 9B 18
OL12: Roch 4L 203
OL14: Tod 1L 165
PR4: Gt P 2E 110
PR6: H Charn 5H 195
PR8: S'port 1K 187
WN5: Orr 3H 221
Meadow Vw. Caravan Pk. LA6: Neth K 4E 16
Meadow Vw. Cl. PR4: Hutt 6A 134
Meadow Wlk. OL15: Littleb 9J 185
Meadow Way BB18: Barnw 10G 53
BL7: Edgw 8K 179
BL8: Tott 7D 200
BL9: Summ 3H 201
LA6: Ark 3C 18
OL13: Bac 5K 163
PR3: Cab 2N 59
(off Lancaster Rd.)
PR4: Wesh 2K 111
PR7: Copp 5N 193
PR9: Banks 2F 168
Meads Rd. PR2: Ash R 8E 114
Meadup Ct. LA3: Morec 6A 22
Mead Way BB12: Padi 2F 122
Meadway BL0: Ramsb 5H 181
FY4: Blackp 9F 88
L31: Magh 3A 222
OL11: Roch 9N 203
PR1: Penw 3D 134
PR4: Hesk B 5D 150
PR6: Clay W 4D 154
WN8: Skelm 8M 211
Meagles La. PR3: Lit E 7K 65
(not continuous)
Meagles Rd. PR3: Lit E 7K 65
Mealhouse La. PR7: Chor 6E 174
Mealrigg La. LA6: H Roo 8A 8
Meanwood Av. FY4: Blackp 1F 108
Meanwood Brow *OL12: Roch 5A 204*
(off Rooley Moor Rd.)
Meanwood Fold OL12: Roch 5A 204
Meanygate PR5: Bam B 8A 136
PR9: Banks 9G 149
MEARBECK 6N 35
Mearbeck Pl. *LA1: Lanc 6H 23*
(off Browgill Pl.)
Mearley Brook Fold BB7: Clith 4M 81
Mearley Rd. PR2: Ribb 5A 116
Mearley St. BB7: Clith 4L 81
Mearley Syke BB7: Clith 3M 81
Mears Beck Cl. LA3: Heys 5M 21
Meathop Rd. LA11: G Sand 1A 4
Meath Rd. PR1: Prest 2G 135
Mecca Bingo
Blackpool 3C 88
Rochdale 6D 204
Southport 7G 166
Mede, The PR4: Frec 6N 111
Medina Cl. BB5: Acc 3A 142
Medlar Cl. PR4: Wesh 2K 111
Medlar Ct. PR4: Wesh 3M 111
Medlar Ga. PR4: Wesh 3M 111
Medlar La. PR4: Wesh 6K 91
Medley St. OL12: Roch 4C 204
Medlock Av. FY7: Flee 1C 54
Medlock Pl. FY7: Flee 2D 54
Medway PR2: Fulw 3J 115
Medway, The OL10: Heyw 9F 202
Medway Av. FY7: Flee 4D 54
Medway Cl. BL6: Hor 9E 196
PR5: Lost H 7L 135
Medway Dr. BL6: Hor 9E 196
Medway Ho. *PR1: Prest 9N 115*
(off Samuel St.)
Medway Pl. WN5: Wigan 4N 221
Medway Wlk. WN5: Wigan 4N 221
Meerbrook Gro. *L33: Kirk 5L 223*
(off Langton Rd.)
Meeting Ho. La. LA1: Lanc 7A 228 (8J 23)
Megabowl
Walton-le-Dale 3M 135
Megazone
Morecambe 4N 21
Walton-le-Dale 3M 135
Meins Cft. BB2: Blackb 3H 139
Meins Rd. BB2: Blackb, Pleas 2E 138
Melba Rd. PR2: Ribb 6A 116
Melbert Av. PR2: Fulw 6F 114
Melbourne Av. FY5: T Clev 4F 62
FY7: Flee 4E 54
Melbourne Cl. BL6: Hor 9D 196
Melbourne Ct. FY5: T Clev 3F 62
Melbourne Gro. BL6: Hor 9D 196
Melbourne Rd. LA1: Lanc 7E 228 (8L 23)
OL14: Wals 6K 165
Melbourne St. BB3: Darw 9B 158
BB4: W'foot 6D 162
BB5: Clay M 8N 121
BB5: Osw 5K 141
BB12: Padi 2J 123
PR1: Prest 4K 229 (9J 115)
Melbreak Caravan Site LA3: Midd 6L 27
Melbreck WN8: Skelm 8L 211
Meldon Grange LA3: Heys 8M 21
Meldon Rd. LA3: Heys 8M 21
Melford Cl. PR6: Chor 3G 175
Melford Dr. WN5: Bill 8G 220
Melfort Cl. BB2: Blackb 7G 139
Melia Cl. BB4: Rawt 5L 161
Melita St. BB3: Darw 7B 158
MELLING
L31 5E 222
LA6 4D 18
Melling Brow LA6: Mell 4D 18
Melling Cl. PR6: Adl 6K 195
Melling Ct. BB8: Colne 6N 85
LA4: Morec 5A 22
Melling Dr. L32: Kirk 7K 223
Melling Ho. *LA1: Lanc 4L 29*
(off Hala Rd.)
Melling La. L31: Magh 3D 222
Melling M. PR3: Gars 4N 59
MELLING MOUNT 3H 223
Melling Rd. L9: Aint 9B 222
LA2: Horn 6C 18
PR9: S'port 6L 167
Mellings Fold PR1: Prest 2M 135
Melling's La. FY8: L Ann 8G 109
Melling St. PR1: Prest 4K 229 (9J 115)
Mellings Wood FY8: L Ann 8G 109
Melling Way L32: Kirk 7K 223
WN3: Wins 9N 221
Mellishaw La. LA3: Heat, Morec 6C 22
Mellishaw Pk. LA3: Heat 7E 22
MELLOR 7F 118
MELLOR BROOK 6D 118
Mellor Brook BB2: Mellor B 6D 118
Mellor Brow BB2: Mellor 6D 118
Mellor Cl. BB2: Blackb 9G 119
BB11: Burnl 6B 124
Mellor Ct. PR3: Longr 3K 97
Mellor La. BB2: Mellor 7F 118
Mellor Pl. PR1: Prest 1L 135
Mellor Rd. PR4: K'ham 4M 111
PR25: Leyl 5G 153
Mellors Cl. PR8: S'port 9M 167
Mellor St. OL11: Roch 5A 204
OL12: Roch 5A 204
OL14: Tod 8H 147
Mellwood Av. FY3: Blackp 1F 88
Melrose OL12: Roch 5B 204
Melrose Av. BB5: Osw 5M 141
BB11: Burnl 5B 124
FY3: Blackp 2E 88
LA4: Morec 3C 22
OL10: Heyw 9G 203
OL15: Littleb 7K 185
PR2: Fulw 4L 115
PR9: S'port 1A 168
Melrose Dr. WN3: Wins 8M 221
Melrose Gdns. PR26: Cros 4N 171

Melrose Rd.—Millom Cl.

Melrose Rd. L33: Kirk 4J 223
Melrose St. BB3: Darw 5N 157
BL9: Summ 3G 201
LA1: Lanc 8F 228 (9L 23)
OL11: Roch 6A 204
Melrose Ter. OL13: Weir 9L 145
Melrose Way PR7: Chor 8F 174
Melton Gro. FY8: L Ann 5L 129
Melton Pl. FY5: T Clev 3C 62
PR25: Leyl 6L 153
Melton Place Stop (Tram) 3C 62
Melverley Rd. L32: Kirk 8G 222
Melville Av. BB3: Darw 8A 158
BB18: Barnw 1L 77
Melville Dr. BB2: Blackb 3A 226 (3L 139)
Melville Gdns. BB3: Darw 7A 158
Melville Rd. FY2: Blackp 7C 62
LA3: Heys 2K 27
Melville St. BB3: Darw 7A 158
BB10: Burnl 9G 104
Melvin Ho. PR9: S'port 6H 167
Memorial Gdns. PR3: Bils 7D 68
Memorial Pk. FY7: Flee 9F 40
Memory Cl. PR4: Frec 1N 131
Menai Dr. PR2: Fulw 2G 114
Mendip Av. WN3: Wins 8M 221
Mendip Cl. BL6: Hor 8D 196
FY8: L Ann 3D 130
Mendip Cres. BL8: Bury 9G 200
Mendip Dr. OL16: Milnr 6K 205
Mendip Ho. *BB4: Hasl* *4G 160*
(off Salisbury St.)
Mendip Rd. PR25: Leyl 6N 153
Menivale Cl. PR9: S'port 9A 148
Mentmore Rd. OL16: Roch 5G 204
MEOLS COP 9M 167
Meols Cop Retail Pk. PR8: S'port 1N 187
Meols Cop Rd. PR8: S'port 9M 167
Meols Cop Station (Rail) 7M 167
Meols Ct. PR9: Banks 9F 148
Meolsgate Av. PR4: Tarl 8E 150
Meols Vw. Cl. PR8: S'port 2N 187
Meols Wood PR9: S'port 5A 168
Mercer Av. L32: Kirk 8H 223
Mercer Ct. L31: Lyd 8N 215
PR7: H Charn 4H 195
Mercer Cres. BB4: Hasl 7F 160
Mercer Dr. BB6: Gt H 3L 121
Mercer Hall Leisure Cen. 4K 121
Mercer La. OL11: Roch 5J 203
Mercer Rd. PR5: Lost H 7K 135
Mercer's La. L39: Bick 7M 217
Mercer St. BB5: Clay M 6M 121
BB6: Gt H 4K 121
BB12: Burnl 2L 123
PR1: Prest 9M 115
Mercer Way BB1: Guide 7D 140
Merchant Cl. L30: N'ton 9A 222
Merchant Rd. L39: Orms 8M 209
Merchants Fold PR4: Longt 8K 133
Merchants Ho. *BB1: Blackb* *6F 226*
(off Merchants Quay)
Merchants Landing BB1: Blackb 7E 226 (5N 139)
Merchants Quay BB1: Blackb 7F 226 (5N 139)
Merclesden Av. BB9: Nelson 1M 105
Mercury Ri. BB5: Alt 3D 122
Mercury Way WN8: Skelm 3B 220
Mere Av. FY7: Flee 3D 54
L40: Burs 7C 190
Merebank Cl. OL11: Roch 5J 203
Mere Brook FY3: Stain 5L 89
MERE BROW 4L 169
Mere Brow La. PR4: Mere B 4L 169
Mere Cl. PR3: Brou 7F 94
WN8: Skelm 1K 219
MERECLOUGH 8L 125
Mere Ct. BB11: Burnl 5N 123
L40: Burs 7C 190
Meredith St. BB9: Nelson 3J 105
Merefell Rd. LA5: Bolt S 3L 15
Merefield PR7: Chor 5C 174
Merefield Av. OL11: Roch 8B 204
Merefield St. OL11: Roch 8B 204
Merefield Ter. OL11: Roch 8B 204
Mere Fold PR7: Char R 2N 193
Mereland Cl. WN5: Orr 5H 221
Mereland Rd. FY3: Blackp 8G 88
Mere La. L39: Hals 4A 208
L40: Ruff 2B 190
OL11: Roch 8C 204
PR4: Mere B 6L 169
PR9: Banks 3F 168
Mere Meanygate PR4: Mere B 5K 169
Mere Pk. Ct. FY3: Blackp 8G 89
Merepark Dr. PR9: S'port 2A 168
Mere Rd. FY3: Blackp 2N 227 (5D 88)
Mere Sands Wood Nature Reserve 1D 190
Mere Sands Wood Nature Reserve Vis. Cen. 1D 190
MERE SIDE 9A 170
MERESIDE 9J 89
Mereside Cl. PR4: Longt 9K 133
Mereside Lodge FY4: Blackp 9H 89
Mere St. OL11: Roch 7C 204
Meres Way PR8: S'port 3H 187
MERE SYKE 3L 51
Mere Vw. PR9: Banks 3J 169
Merewood WN8: Skelm 8L 211
Meriden Cl. PR8: Ains 8B 186
Merinall Cl. OL16: Roch 6F 204
Merlecrest Dr. PR4: Tarl 7E 150
Merlewood BL0: Eden 3K 181
Merlewood Av. PR9: S'port 3A 168
Merlewood Country Pk. Caravan Pk.
PR3: Lit E 5M 65
Merlin Cl. OL15: Littleb 3K 205
PR6: Heap 3J 175
Merlin Ct. BB5: Osw 5K 141
Merlin Dr. BB5: Osw 5K 141
Merlin Gro. BB12: Burnl 3K 123
PR25: Leyl 7F 152
Merlin Pk. L40: Burs 9N 189
Merlin Rd. BB2: Blackb 2J 139
OL16: Milnr 7J 205
Merlyn Rd. FY5: T Clev 2E 62
Merrick Av. PR1: Prest 9B 116
Merrilox Av. L31: Lyd 8C 216
Merrybents St. OL14: Tod 2N 165
Merryburn Cl. PR2: Fulw 5K 115
Merryman Hall OL16: Roch 3E 204
Merry Trees *BB4: Rawt* *5N 161*
(off Fallbarn Rd.)
Merrytrees La. PR4: Cott 4A 114
Merscar La. L40: Scar 7J 189
Mersey Av. BB3: Darw 4L 157
L31: Magh 9E 216
Mersey Rd. FY4: Blackp 1B 108
FY7: Flee 9E 40
WN5: Orr 4J 221
Mersey St. BB12: Burnl 3M 123
OL13: Bac 6L 163
PR2: Ash R 9F 114
PR3: Longr 3K 97
Merton Av. PR2: Fulw 3J 115
Merton Gro. PR6: Chor 3H 175
Merton Rd. WN3: Wigan 7L 221
Merton St. BB9: Nelson 1H 105
BB12: Burnl 2D 124
BL8: Bury 9J 201
Merton Ter. FY8: L Ann 5C 130
Messenger St. BB9: Nelson 3L 105
Meta St. BB2: Blackb 6M 139
Metcalf Cl. L33: Kirk 4J 223
Metcalf Dr. BB5: Alt 3C 122
Metcalfe Cl. BB2: Blackb 8L 139
Metcalfe St. BB12: Burnl 4N 123
OL16: Roch 6G 205
Mete St. PR1: Prest 9N 115
Methuen Av. PR2: Fulw 3H 115
PR5: Hogh 5G 137
Methuen Cl. PR5: Hogh 5G 137
Methuen Dr. PR5: Hogh 5H 137
Metropole Bldgs.
FY1: Blackp 1H 227 (4B 88)
Metropolitan Bus. Pk. FY3: Blackp 8H 89
Metropolitan Dr. FY3: Blackp 8H 89
Mettle Cote OL13: Bac 6L 163
MEWITH 8N 19
Mewith La. LA2: Tat, H Ben 8H 19
Mews, The BB3: Darw 8C 158
BB12: Padi 9H 103
FY8: L Ann 9H 109
LA4: Morec 3E 22
PR4: Tarl 9E 150
PR8: S'port 9G 167
Mexford Av. FY2: Blackp 1D 88
Meyler Av. FY3: Blackp 2E 88
Meyrick Cl. WN3: Wins 9M 221
Miall St. OL11: Roch 7C 204
Michael Pl. LA4: Morec 3D 22
Michael's La. L39: Hals 1J 207
Michaelson Av. LA4: Morec 4E 22
Michael Wife La. BL0: Eden, Ramsb 2K 181
(not continuous)
Mickering La. L39: Aug 5G 217
Mickleden Av. PR2: Fulw 2J 115
Mickleden Rd. FY4: Blackp 9J 89
(not continuous)
Micklegate FY5: T Clev 4C 62
Mickle Hill M. *BD23: Garg* *3M 53*
(off Skipton Rd.)
Micklehurst Cres. BB11: Burnl 7B 124
Mickleton Dr. PR8: Ains 8A 186
Middle Calderbrook OL15: Littleb 5M 185
Middlecot Cl. WN5: Orr 6H 221
Middle Fld. OL11: Roch 4H 203
Middlefield PR26: Leyl 7D 152
Middle Fold *BD24: Langc* *1N 35*
(off New St.)
MIDDLEFORTH GREEN 5H 135
Middleforth Grn. PR1: Penw 4H 135
Middleforth Ind. Est. PR1: Penw 4H 135
Middlegate LA3: Morec 6E 22
(not continuous)
Middlegate Grn. BB4: Craws 7M 143
Middleham Cl. L32: Kirk 9H 223
MIDDLE HEALEY 1A 204
Middle Hey PR4: Much H 4J 151
Middle Hill OL12: Roch 1C 204
Middle Holly LA2: Bay H 9K 37
PR3: Fort 5N 45
Middle Lodge Rd. BB7: Barr 1L 101
Middle Meanygate PR4: Tarl 9M 149
Middle Moss La. L37: Gt A 9F 206
Middle Newgate OL15: Littleb 6K 185
Middlesex Av. BB12: Burnl 2M 123
Middle St. BB8: Colne 7N 85
FY1: Blackp 5J 227 (7B 88)
LA1: Lanc 7C 228 (8K 23)
OL12: Whitw 5N 183
MIDDLETON 5M 27
Middleton Av. FY7: Flee 3D 54
Middleton Bus. Pk. LA3: Midd 4M 27
Middleton Dr. BB9: Barrf 5J 85
Middleton Rd. LA3: Heys, Midd, O'ton 2K 27
PR2: Fulw 2M 115
Middleton Towers LA3: Midd 6K 27
Middleton Way LA3: Heys 1K 27
Middle Turn BL7: Edgw 7K 179
Middle Wlk. FY1: Blackp 3B 88
Middle Withins La. L38: Gt A 4F 214
Middlewood WN8: Skelm 8L 211
Middlewood Cl. L39: Aug 4H 217
PR7: E'ton 8F 172
Middlewood Dr. L39: Aug 4H 217
Middle Wood La. OL15: Littleb 8H 185
Middlewood Rd. L39: Aug 3H 217
Midfield BB6: Langh 1C 120
Midford Dr. BL1: Bolt 6E 198
MIDGE HALL 4E 152
Midge Hall Dr. OL11: Roch 7L 203
Midge Hall La. PR9: S'port 1G 189
PR26: Midge H 2B 152
Midgeland Rd. FY4: Blackp 2G 108
Midgeland Ter. FY4: Blackp 4J 109
Midgery Ct. PR2: Fulw 2M 115
Midgery La. PR2: Fulw 1L 115
(not continuous)
PR3: Brou 9K 95
Midgley St. BB8: Colne 7B 86
Midhurst Dr. PR8: Ains 9B 186
Midhurst St. OL11: Roch 8C 204
Midland St. BB5: Acc 3B 142
BB9: Nelson 1J 105
Midland Ter. *BD23: Hell* *1D 52*
(off Station Rd.)
LA5: Carn 7A 12
Midsummer St. BB2: Blackb 3K 139
Midville Pl. BB3: Darw 6A 158
Midwood Caravan Pk. PR3: Pill 2F 56
Milbanke Av. PR4: K'ham 3M 111
Milbeck Cl. PR3: Longr 5H 97
Milbourne Rd. BL9: Bury 7L 201
Milbourne St. FY1: Blackp 1K 227 (5C 88)
Milbrook Cl. BB11: Burnl 4N 123
Milbrook Cres. L32: Kirk 7K 223
Milbrook Dr. L32: Kirk 7K 223
Milbrook Wlk. L32: Kirk 7K 223
Milburn Av. FY5: T Clev 7F 54
Milbury Dr. OL15: Littleb 3K 205
Mildred Cl. FY5: T Clev 9G 55
Mile End Cl. BB8: Foul 2A 86
Mile End Row BB2: Blackb 2J 139
Mile Rd. FY6: Sing 1E 90
Miles Av. OL13: Bac 7H 163
Miles La. WN6: App B, Shev 4G 213
(not continuous)
Miles St. PR1: Prest 1J 229 (7J 115)
Milestone Ho. *LA6: K Lon* *6F 8*
(off Main St.)
Mile Stone Mdw. PR7: Eux 2N 173
Milestone Pl. LA2: Caton 3H 25
Milestone Rd. L32: Kirk 8H 223
Miles Wlk. PR1: Prest 1H 229 (7H 115)
Miletas Pl. FY8: L Ann 5J 129
Milford Av. FY2: Blackp 1D 88
(not continuous)
Milford Cl. PR3: Catt 1A 68
Milford Cres. OL15: Littleb 8L 185
Milford Rd. BL2: Bolt 9M 199
Milford St. BB8: Colne 6N 85
OL12: Roch 4C 204
Milking La. BB3: Lwr D 1N 157
Milking Stile La. LA1: Lanc 8H 23
Milkstone Pl. OL11: Roch 7C 204
Milkstone Rd. OL11: Roch 7C 204
Milk St. BL0: Ramsb 9G 181
OL11: Roch 7C 204
Mill, The PR1: Prest 4J 229 (9J 115)
Mill Acre Ct. LA2: Caton 2G 24
Millar Barn La. BB4: W'foot 7C 162
Millar Ct. LA1: Lanc 2J 29
Millar's Pace PR9: S'port 1A 168
Millbank PR1: Prest 5N 229
PR2: Fulw 6F 114
WN6: App B 5G 212
Millbank Brow L40: Burs 1D 210
Millbank Cotts. L31: Magh 8D 216
Millbank La. L31: Aug, Magh 8E 216
L39: Aug 8F 216
Millbeck Cl. L32: Kirk 6K 223
Millbeck Cres. WN5: Wigan 6N 221
Millbeck La. BB18: Kelb 6E 78
Millbridge Gdns. OL16: Roch 8D 204
Mill Brook PR3: Catt 9A 60
Millbrook BB12: Fence 2C 104
PR8: S'port 1H 187
Millbrook Bank OL11: Roch 4H 203
Mill Brook Bus. Pk. WA11: Rain 7N 225
Millbrook Cl. BB5: Osw 5K 141
PR6: Wheel 8J 155
WN8: Skelm 1J 219
Millbrook Ct. BB7: West B 7L 73
BB8: Colne 6E 86
Millbrook M. FY8: L Ann 4B 130
Millbrook Pl. BB7: Barr 1K 101
Millbrook Row PR6: H Charn 4K 195
Millbrook St. BB3: Lwr D 9N 139
Millbrook Way PR1: Penw 6E 134
Mill Brow LA2: Wray 3J 33
LA6: K Lon 6F 8
Mill Brow Rd. BB18: Earl 2F 78
Mill Bldg., The BL7: Eger 4D 198
Mill Cl. BD24: Sett 3N 35
PR4: Inskip 2G 93
Millcombe Way PR5: Walt D 5A 136
Mill Cotts. BB1: Blackb 4E 140
BB3: W'side 4E 158
BB4: W'foot 9E 162
BB7: S'hurst 10N 71
BB18: Salt *5B 78*
(off Moor Vw.)
Mill Ct. *PR2: Ash R* *7G 114*
(off Atherton Cl.)
PR3: Longr 2K 97
Millcroft PR2: Fulw 5F 114
PR7: Chor 4C 174
Millcroft Av. WN5: Orr 6G 220
Mill Cft. Cl. OL12: Roch 3G 203
MILL DAM 8N 19
Mill Dam Cl. L40: Burs 2B 210
Mill Dam La. L40: Burs, Lath 2A 210
Mill Dyke Cl. FY4: Blackp 3F 108
Millennium Pk. PR2: Ribb 4C 116
Millennium Rd. PR2: Ribb 4C 116
Mill Entrance BB5: Clay M 7M 121
Miller Arc. PR1: Prest 6L 229 (1K 135)
Miller Av. PR6: Withn 5C 156
Miller Cl. BB5: Osw 3J 141
Miller Ct. *LA1: Lanc* *6K 23*
(off Mainway)
Miller Cres. FY6: Sing 1D 90
Miller Fld. PR2: Lea 6B 114
Miller Fold Av. BB5: Acc 5A 142
Miller Gdns. PR1: Prest 3H 135
Miller Ho. PR1: Prest 6L 229
Miller La. PR4: Catf 6H 93
PR4: Cott 3J 114
Miller Rd. PR1: Prest 8N 115
PR2: Ribb 7A 116
Miller's Brow PR3: Fort 3A 46
Millers Cl. FY8: L Ann 1K 129
Millers Ct. L39: Orms 7L 209
Millers Ct., The *LA2: H Ben* *6L 19*
(off Main St.)
Millerscroft L32: Kirk 7H 223
Millersdale Cl. FY5: T Clev 4L 63
Millers Fold LA2: L Ben 6K 19
Millersgate PR4: Cott 5B 114
Millers Nook WN8: Uph 4E 220
Miller St. BL1: Bolt 9E 198
BL9: Summ 3H 201
FY1: Blackp 9H 227 (9B 88)
PR1: Prest 9M 115
Millers Va. BB4: Hasl 6E 160
Millers Wlk. PR7: Buck V 9A 154
Millett St. BL0: Ramsb 7J 181
Millett Ter. BL9: Bury 6C 202
Mill Fld. BB5: Clay M 5M 121
Millfield WN8: Parb 3N 211
Millfield Cl. PR4: Wart 2L 131
Millfield Gro. OL16: Roch 7E 204
Millfield Rd. FY4: Blackp 3F 108
PR7: Chor 5D 174
Mill Fold PR1: Prest 3J 229 (8J 115)
Millfold OL12: Whitw 4A 184
Mill Fold Gdns. OL15: Littleb 1K 205
Mill Gap St. BB3: Darw 7A 158
Mill Gdns. BB6: Gt H 3K 121
LA2: H Ben *6L 19*
(off Banks Ri.)
MILLGATE 1B 184
Mill Ga. BB4: Rawt 4M 161
PR2: Fulw 6G 114
Millgate BL7: Eger 3D 198
OL16: Roch 3F 204
Millgate Rd. BB4: Rawt 4M 161
Millgate Ter. OL12: Whitw 1B 184
Mill Grn. BB8: Colne 7A 86
Millgreen Cl. WN8: Uph 4D 220
Millham St.
BB1: Blackb 1D 226 (2M 139)
Millhaven PR2: Fulw 5G 114
MILLHEAD 7A 12
Mill Hey Av. FY6: Poul F 1L 89
Mill Hey La. L40: Ruff 2G 190
MILL HILL
BB2 6J 139
PR4 7F 150
Mill Hill BB5: Osw 4K 141
BD23: Garg *4M 53*
(off Mill Hill La.)
PR1: Prest 4H 229 (9H 115)
Mill Hill Bri. St. BB2: Blackb 6J 139
Mill Hill Gro. LA3: Midd 5M 27
Mill Hill La. BB11: Hapt 7F 122
BD23: Garg 4M 53
BD24: Gig 2M 35
Mill Hill Station (Rail) 6K 139
Millhill St. BB2: Blackb 6J 139
Millholme Dr. *LA2: H Ben* *7L 19*
(off Wenning Av.)
Mill Ho. BL9: Bury 5L 201
LA1: Lanc 7E 228
Mill Ho. Cl. OL12: Roch 1G 204
Mill Ho. La. PR3: Longr, Ribc 2B 98
(not continuous)
PR6: Brind 8G 137
Mill Ho. Lodge PR8: Ains 8D 186
Mill Ho. M. LA1: Lanc 7E 228
Millhouse St. BL0: Ramsb 6K 181
Mill Ho. Vw. WN8: Uph 4F 220
Millington Av. FY4: Blackp 1E 108
Mill La.
BB2: Blackb 5C 226 (4M 139)
BB6: Gt H 3M 121
BB7: Gis 8A 52
BB7: Wadd 4G 72
BB18: Earl 3F 78
BD23: Garg 3M 53
BD23: Hell 3D 52
BD24: Rath 6K 35
BL6: Hor 9E 196
BL8: Bury 9G 201
FY3: Stain 4K 89
FY6: Ham 3C 64
FY6: Stal 5C 56
FY7: Flee 9H 41
L32: Kirk 6H 223
L39: Aug 2E 216
L40: Burs 9C 190
(not continuous)
LA2: Caton 2G 24
LA2: Halt 2B 24
LA2: L Ben 6J 19
LA5: Bolt S 3L 15
LA5: Carn, Wart 6N 11
LA6: H Roo 6B 8
LA6: L Big 6E 8
LA6: Neth B 9F 8
OL13: Bac 4M 163
PR2: Fulw 5F 114
PR3: Chip 7E 70
PR3: Goos 1N 95
PR3: Scor 7B 46
PR4: Elsw 1M 91
PR4: Hesk B 5D 150
PR4: W Grn 6E 110
PR4: Wart 2L 131
PR5: Walt D 3N 135
PR6: Whit W 6E 154
PR6: Withn 9G 157
PR7: Char R 3K 193
PR7: Char R, Eux 5K 173
(not continuous)
PR7: Copp 4A 194
PR7: E'ton 9F 172
PR9: S'port 5N 167
PR25: Leyl 7G 153
PR26: Far M 4H 153
WA11: Rain 7M 225
WN6: App B 5F 212
WN8: Dalt, Uph 1C 220
WN8: Parb 3N 211
WN8: Skelm 1K 219
(not continuous)
Mill La. Cres. PR9: S'port 5N 167
Mill Leat Cl. WN8: Parb 2N 211
Mill Leat M. WN8: Parb 2N 211
Mill Lodge PR4: New L 8C 134
Mill Nook OL12: Roch 2C 204
Millom Av. FY2: Blackp 7D 62
Millom Cl. FY7: Flee 4C 54
OL16: Roch 4F 204

Millom Ct.—Morecambe Rd.

Millom Ct. LA5: Arn . . . 2F 4
Millrace Ct. LA1: Lanc . . . 6K 23
Mill Rd. BL9: Bury . . . 5L 201
PR8: Ains . . . 8D 186
WN5: Orr . . . 6G 220
Millrose Cl. WN8: Skelm . . . 1K 219
Mill Row BB4: Rawt . . . 2L 161
PR1: Penw . . . 5J 135
Mills Fold BB4: Newc . . . 6C 162
Mill Sq. L10: Aint . . . 8D 222
Mills St. OL12: Whitw . . . 5A 184
Millstone Cl. PR6: Whit W . . . 8E 154
PR7: Copp . . . 4B 194
Mill Stone Cotts. BB7: West B . . . 7L 73
Millstone Ct. LA1: Lanc . . . 5K 23
(off Main St.)
Mill St. BB4: Hasl . . . 2G 160
BB5: Bax . . . 7E 142
BB5: Chur . . . 2M 141
BB5: Clay M . . . 7M 121
BB5: Osw . . . 5K 141
BB6: Gt H . . . 4J 121
BB7: West B . . . 7L 73
BB9: Barrf . . . 7H 85
BB9: Nelson . . . 1J 105
BB12: Padi . . . 1H 123
BB18: Barnw . . . 2L 77
BL0: Ramsb . . . 1F 200
BL7: Brom C . . . 5F 198
BL8: Tott . . . 6E 200
FY6: Pree . . . 1A 56
L39: Orms . . . 8L 209
LA1: Lanc . . . 6E 228 (8L 23)
OL13: Bac . . . 4K 163
OL15: Littleb . . . 2J 205
PR1: Prest . . . 9G 115
PR4: K'ham . . . 4M 111
PR6: Adl . . . 5J 195
PR6: Wheel . . . 8J 155
PR7: Copp . . . 4A 194
PR8: S'port . . . 8J 167
PR25: Far . . . 4L 153
PR25: Leyl . . . 7G 152
Millthorne Av. BB7: Clith . . . 4K 81
Mill Vw. FY5: T Clev . . . 2H 63
PR4: Frec . . . 1N 131
Millview L32: Kirk . . . 6H 223
Mill Vw. Ct. L39: Bick . . . 4B 218
PR26: Leyl . . . 5G 153
Mill Vw. La. BL6: Hor . . . 9F 196
MILLWOOD . . . 2M 165
Mill Wood Cl. PR6: Withn . . . 4L 155
Millwood Cl. BB2: Blackb . . . 7H 139
Millwood Glade PR7: Chor . . . 5D 174
Millwood La. OL14: Tod . . . 2N 165
Millwood Rd. PR5: Lost H . . . 5L 135
Mill Yd. BL6: Hor . . . 9E 196
Milman Cl. L39: Orms . . . 9J 209
Milne Gro. OL16: Milnr . . . 8L 205
Milner Av. BL9: Bury . . . 8L 201
Milner Rd. BB3: Darw . . . 3M 157
FY8: L Ann . . . 4L 129
Milner St. BB10: Burnl . . . 1E 124
OL12: Whitw . . . 6N 183
PR1: Prest . . . 1K 229 (7K 115)
Milne St. BL0: Ramsb . . . 1H 181
Milnes Yd. OL16: Milnr . . . 8J 205
(off Dale St.)
MILNROW . . . 7H 205
Milnrow Rd. OL15: Littleb . . . 3J 205
OL16: Roch . . . 6D 204
Milnrow Stop (Metro) . . . 8J 205
MILNSHAW . . . 1A 142
Milnshaw Gdns. BB5: Acc . . . 1N 141
Milnshaw La. BB5: Acc . . . 2A 142
Milnshaw Ter. BB7: Grind . . . 4A 74
(off Main St.)
Milnthorpe Av. FY5: T Clev . . . 7D 54
Milnthorpe Rd. LA6: Holme . . . 1E 6
Milton Av. BB7: Clith . . . 2L 81
FY3: Blackp . . . 5E 88
FY5: T Clev . . . 9G 54
Milton Cl. BB3: Darw . . . 6C 158
BB4: Hasl . . . 8F 160
BB6: Gt H . . . 5H 121
PR5: Walt D . . . 6N 135
Milton Ct. PR7: Copp . . . 4A 194
Milton Cres. FY6: Poul F . . . 2K 89
Milton Dr. L39: Orms . . . 8M 209
Milton Gro. BB18: Barnw . . . 1L 77
WN5: Orr . . . 5K 221
Milton Pl. FY2: Blackp . . . 5F 62
Milton Rd. BB8: Colne . . . 6A 86
PR7: Copp . . . 5A 194
Milton St. BB1: Blackb . . . 3G 226 (3A 140)
BB5: Acc . . . 2A 142
BB5: Clay M . . . 6M 121
BB5: Osw . . . 4L 141
BB9: Barrf . . . 7H 85
BB9: Brierf . . . 5F 104
BB9: Nelson . . . 1H 105
BB10: Brierc . . . 7J 105
BB12: Padi . . . 2J 123
BL0: Ramsb . . . 8G 180
FY7: Flee . . . 8G 40
OL16: Roch . . . 5C 204
PR9: S'port . . . 7M 167
Milton Ter. PR6: Chor . . . 4F 174
Milton Way L31: Magh . . . 1A 222
Mimosa Cl. PR7: Chor . . . 3C 174
Mimosa Rd. PR2: Ribb . . . 7A 116
Mincing La. BB2: Blackb . . . 5C 226 (4M 139)
Minden Rd. PR4: Weet . . . 5D 90
Minehead Av. BB10: Burnl . . . 8H 105
Miners Home Stop (Tram) . . . 8B 62
Minerva Ter. OL15: Littleb . . . 9K 185
(off William St.)
Mine St. OL10: Heyw . . . 9G 203
Minnie St. OL12: Whitw . . . 4A 184
Minnie Ter. BB2: Blackb . . . 2K 139
Minorca Cl. OL11: Roch . . . 5J 203
Minor St. BB4: Craws . . . 9M 143
Minstead Av. L33: Kirk . . . 8L 223
Minster Cres. BB3: Darw . . . 7C 158
Minster Dr. LA3: Morec . . . 6B 22
Minster Pk. PR4: Cott . . . 4B 114
Minstrel Wlk. FY6: Poul F . . . 7K 63
Mint Av. BB9: Barrf . . . 7H 85
Mintholme Av. PR5: Hogh . . . 6G 137
Mintor Rd. L33: Kirk . . . 8M 223
Mint St. BL0: Ramsb . . . 4H 181
Minverva Rd. LA1: Lanc . . . 8G 22
Mire Ash Brow BB2: Mellor . . . 8E 118
Mire Ridge BB8: Colne, Traw . . . 7D 86
Mirfield Gro. FY4: Blackp . . . 9D 88
Miry La. WN8: Parb . . . 2A 212
Mitcham Rd. FY4: Blackp . . . 1H 109
Mitchelgate LA6: K Lon . . . 6E 8
Mitchell Fld. Nook
OL13: Bac . . . 6G 163
MITCHELL HEY . . . 6B 204
Mitchell Hey OL12: Roch . . . 6B 204
Mitchell St. BB7: Clith . . . 4K 81
BB8: Colne . . . 6A 86
BB12: Burnl . . . 3A 124
BL8: Bury . . . 9H 201
OL12: Roch . . . 5A 204
OL14: Tod . . . 9H 147
OL16: Roch . . . 2F 204
Mitella St. BB10: Burnl . . . 4G 124
Mitre St. BB11: Burnl . . . 2A 228 (3C 124)
BL1: Bolt . . . 9E 198
Mittens La. L37: Form . . . 8B 206
Mitton Av. BB4: Rawt . . . 3M 161
BB9: Barrf . . . 5K 85
Mitton Cl. BB2: Blackb . . . 8K 139
Mitton Cres. PR4: K'ham . . . 4M 111
Mitton Dr. PR2: Ribb . . . 6C 116
Mitton Gro. BB10: Burnl . . . 4H 125
Mitton La. BD20: Loth . . . 3L 79
Mitton Rd.
BB7: Gt M, Whall . . . 9F 80
Mitton St. BB1: Blackb . . . 1N 139
Mizpah St. BB10: Burnl . . . 4G 124
Mizzy Rd. OL12: Roch . . . 4B 204
Moira Cres. PR2: Ribb . . . 5A 116
Moleside Cl. BB5: Acc . . . 2C 142
Molesworth St. OL16: Roch . . . 6D 204
Mollington Rd. BB2: Blackb . . . 1J 139
L32: Kirk . . . 8H 223
Molly Wood La. BB12: Burnl . . . 4L 123
Molyneux Ct. PR1: Prest . . . 5M 229 (9K 115)
Molyneux Dr. FY4: Blackp . . . 2D 108
Molyneux Pl. FY8: L Ann . . . 4N 129
Molyneux Rd. L31: Magh . . . 3E 222
L39: Aug . . . 4H 217
Molyneux St. OL12: Roch . . . 5A 204
Molyneux Way L10: Aint . . . 7B 222
Mona Pl. PR1: Prest . . . 9H 115
Monarch Cres. FY8: L Ann . . . 9J 109
Monarch St. BB5: Osw . . . 4L 141
Mona Rd. BB2: Blackb . . . 7M 139
Monash Cl. L33: Kirk . . . 4K 223
Mona's Ter. OL14: Wals . . . 5J 165
Moneyclose Gro. LA3: Heys . . . 2J 27
Money Cl. La. LA3: Heys . . . 4J 27
Moneyclose La. LA3: Heys . . . 2J 27
Monk Hall La. BB10: Brierc . . . 9A 106
Monk Hall St. BB10: Burnl . . . 2E 124
MONKROYD . . . 4K 87
Monkroyd Av. BB18: Barnw . . . 2L 77
Monkroyd Rd. BB8: Lane B . . . 4J 87
Monks Carr La. L38: Gt A . . . 5G 214
Monks Cl. L37: Form . . . 2A 214
OL16: Milnr . . . 7H 205
Monks Cotts. BB18: Barnw . . . 2M 77
(off Walmsgate)
Monks Dr. L37: Form . . . 2A 214
PR3: Longr . . . 4J 97
PR6: Withn . . . 6B 156
Monks Ga. FY8: L Ann . . . 1K 129
Monk's La. FY6: Pree . . . 3M 55
L40: Burs . . . 7B 190
Monk St. BB5: Acc . . . 2N 141
BB7: Clith . . . 4K 81
Monks Wlk. PR1: Penw . . . 2F 134
Monkswell Av. LA5: Bolt S . . . 4L 15
Monkswell Dr. LA5: Bolt S . . . 4L 15
Monkswood Av. LA4: Morec . . . 3E 22
Monmouth Av. BL9: Bury . . . 8L 201
Monmouth Dr. L10: Aint . . . 9E 222
Monmouth Rd. BB1: Blackb . . . 3C 140
Monmouth St. BB8: Colne . . . 6D 86
BB12: Burnl . . . 3B 124
(off Shale St.)
OL11: Roch . . . 7C 204
Monomer Rd. FY5: T Clev . . . 8J 55
Monroe Dr. FY7: Flee . . . 1D 54
Mons Av. OL11: Roch . . . 5N 203
Mons Rd. OL14: Tod . . . 9J 147
Montague Cl. BB2: Blackb . . . 5B 226 (4L 139)
FY3: Blackp . . . 2G 89
Montague Rd. BB11: Burnl . . . 4A 228 (4C 124)
Montague St. BB2: Blackb . . . 3A 226 (3L 139)
BB7: Clith . . . 3K 81
BB8: Colne . . . 5B 86
BB9: Brierf . . . 5F 104
FY4: Blackp . . . 1B 108
Montbegon LA2: Horn . . . 7C 18
MONTCLIFFE . . . 8F 196
Montcliffe Rd. PR6: Chor . . . 5G 175
Monteagle Dr. LA2: Horn . . . 7C 18
Monteagle Sq. LA2: Horn . . . 7C 18
(off Monteagle Dr.)
Montfieldhey BB9: Brierf . . . 5E 104
Montford Rd. BB9: Brierf . . . 4D 104
BB12: Fence . . . 3B 104
Montgomery OL11: Roch . . . 7B 204
Montgomery Av. PR9: S'port . . . 8N 167
Montgomery Cl. BB5: Bax . . . 6D 142
Montgomery Gro. BB12: Burnl . . . 2A 124
Montgomery St. OL11: Roch . . . 9N 203
(off Manchester Rd.)
PR5: Bam B . . . 8B 136
Monthall Ri. LA1: Lanc . . . 7M 23
(off Patterdale Rd.)
Montjoly St. PR1: Prest . . . 1M 135
Monton Rd. BB3: Darw . . . 3M 157
Montpelier Av. FY2: Blackp . . . 6C 62
Montreal Av. FY1: Blackp . . . 3M 227 (6D 88)
Montreal Rd. BB2: Blackb . . . 9K 119
Montreal St. OL14: Wals . . . 6K 165
Montrose Av. BL0: Ramsb . . . 3F 200
FY1: Blackp . . . 5K 227 (7C 88)
WN5: Wigan . . . 3L 221
Montrose Cl. PR6: Chor . . . 8G 174
Montrose Cres. LA3: Heys . . . 9K 21
Montrose Dr. BL7: Brom C . . . 6H 199
PR9: S'port . . . 5M 167
Montrose St. BB2: Blackb . . . 5K 139
BB9: Brierf . . . 5F 104
BB11: Burnl . . . 5D 124
Montrose Ter. BB18: Barnw . . . 2M 77
(off Skipton Rd.)
Moody La. L40: Mawd . . . 4B 192
Moon Av. FY1: Blackp . . . 8J 227 (8B 88)
Moon Bay Wharf LA3: Heys . . . 1J 27
Moons Acre LA2: H Ben . . . 6L 19
Moon St. BB5: Osw . . . 4L 141
(off Straits)
PR5: Bam B . . . 8A 136
Moor Av. PR1: Penw . . . 5C 134
WN6: App B . . . 4H 213
Moor Bank La. OL16: Roch . . . 9G 204
Moorber La. BD23: Con C . . . 4H 53
Moorbottom Rd. BL8: Holc . . . 8D 180
Moorbrook St. PR1: Prest . . . 2H 229 (8H 115)
Moor Cl. BB3: Darw . . . 7D 158
LA1: Lanc . . . 7E 228 (8L 23)
PR8: Ains . . . 2C 206
Moor Cl. La. LA6: Over K . . . 9F 12
Moorcock La. HX7: Black H . . . 2L 147
Moorcock Rd. HX7: Black H . . . 3M 147
Moorcroft BB3: Lwr D . . . 1A 158
BL0: Ramsb . . . 4J 181
OL11: Roch . . . 9C 204
PR3: Brou . . . 8E 94
Moorcroft Cres. PR2: Ribb . . . 6N 115
Moor Dr. WN8: Skelm . . . 4A 220
Moor Edge BB7: Whall . . . 4H 101
Moore Dr. BB12: High . . . 5L 103
MOOR END . . . 6C 56
Moor End BB7: Clith . . . 4M 81
Moores La. WN6: Stand . . . 2N 213
Moore St. BB8: Colne . . . 6N 85
BB9: Nelson . . . 3K 105
BB12: Burnl . . . 2L 123
(not continuous)
FY4: Blackp . . . 9B 88
OL16: Roch . . . 6C 204
PR1: Prest . . . 1M 135
Moore Tree Dr. FY4: Blackp . . . 1G 108
Moor Fld. BB7: Whall . . . 4H 101
Moorfield BL7: Edgw . . . 8K 179
L33: Kirk . . . 5L 223
PR4: New L . . . 9D 134
Moorfield Av. BB1: Ramsg . . . 6M 119
BB5: Hunc . . . 9E 122
FY3: Blackp . . . 4E 88
FY6: Carl . . . 6H 63
OL15: Littleb . . . 7K 185
Moorfield Cen. L33: Kirk . . . 4L 223
Moorfield Cl. BB5: Alt . . . 6A 122
PR1: Penw . . . 5D 134
PR2: Fulw . . . 1H 115
Moorfield Dr. BB5: Alt . . . 6A 122
FY8: L Ann . . . 4N 129
PR2: Ribb . . . 6A 116
Moorfield Ind. Est. BB5: Alt . . . 6A 122
Moorfield La. L40: Scar . . . 1G 209
Moorfield Pl. OL12: Roch . . . 4C 204
(off Turner St.)
Moorfield Rd. BB5: Alt . . . 6A 122
PR25: Leyl . . . 7F 152
Moorfields FY2: Blackp . . . 7F 62
PR6: Chor . . . 5G 175
Moorfields Av. PR2: Fulw . . . 1H 115
Moorfield Vw. OL15: Littleb . . . 8K 185
Moorfield Way BB5: Alt . . . 6A 122
Moorfoot Ho. BB4: Hasl . . . 4G 160
(off Hindle St.)
Moorfoot Way L33: Kirk . . . 4J 223
MOORGATE . . . 7K 139
Moor Ga. BL2: Bolt . . . 8K 199
LA1: Lanc . . . 7E 228 (8L 23)
OL14: Tod . . . 4M 165
Moorgate BB5: Acc . . . 6A 142
FY4: Blackp . . . 3F 108
L39: Orms . . . 8K 209
PR2: Fulw . . . 4J 115
Moorgate Av. OL11: Roch . . . 6L 203
Moorgate Gdns. BB2: Blackb . . . 7K 139
Moor Ga. La. OL15: Littleb . . . 6H 185
Moorgate Rd. BB18: Barnw . . . 3L 77
L33: Kirk . . . 9M 223
Moorgate St. BB2: Blackb . . . 7K 139
Moorhall La. PR4: Newt . . . 5D 112
Moor Hall St. PR1: Prest . . . 1H 229 (7H 115)
Moorhead Gdns. PR4: Wart . . . 1K 131
Moorhead St. BB8: Colne . . . 6N 85
Moor Hgts. PR1: Prest . . . 3J 229
Moorhen Pl. FY5: T Clev . . . 2F 62
Moorhey Cotts. PR26: Breth . . . 9L 151
Moorhey Cres. PR1: Penw . . . 3E 134
PR5: Bam B . . . 8C 136
Moorhey Dr. PR1: Penw . . . 3E 134
Moorhey Rd. L31: Magh . . . 3C 222
Moor Hill OL11: Roch . . . 5K 203
Moorhouse Av. BB5: Acc . . . 4N 141
Moorhouse Cl. BB5: Acc . . . 4N 141
Moorhouse Farm OL16: Milnr . . . 7H 205
Moorhouse Fold OL16: Milnr . . . 7H 205
Moorhouses Brewery Tour . . . 4A 124
(off Moorhouse St.)
Moorhouse St. BB5: Acc . . . 4N 141
BB11: Burnl . . . 4A 124
FY1: Blackp . . . 3B 88
Moorings, The BB12: Burnl . . . 2C 124
L31: Lyd . . . 7A 216
LA2: Hest B . . . 8H 15
(off Hest Bank La.)
PR3: Gars . . . 6N 59
PR6: Chor . . . 6G 175
Moorings Cl. BB2: Blackb . . . 9B 226 (6L 139)
Moorland Av. BB2: Fenis . . . 9E 138
BB3: Darw . . . 5L 157
BB7: Clith . . . 9M 73
BB18: Earl . . . 3F 78
Moorland Av. FY6: Poul F . . . 7L 63
OL11: Roch . . . 5K 203
OL12: Whitw . . . 7N 183
OL16: Milnr . . . 7K 205
PR2: Ribb . . . 4N 115
Moorland Cl. BB9: Barrf . . . 5K 85
Moorland Cotts. BB4: Hasl . . . 5H 161
Moorland Ct. FY6: Poul F . . . 7L 63
Moorland Cres. BB7: Clith . . . 1M 81
OL12: Whitw . . . 7N 183
PR2: Ribb . . . 4N 115
Moorland Dr. BB9: Brierf . . . 6H 105
Moorland Gdns. FY6: Poul F . . . 7L 63
Moorland Ga. PR6: Chor . . . 8H 175
Moorland Ri. BB4: Hasl . . . 5H 161
Moorland Rd. BB2: Blackb . . . 9K 139
BB6: Langh . . . 9C 100
BB7: Clith . . . 1M 81
BB11: Burnl . . . 6C 124
FY6: Poul F . . . 7L 63
FY8: L Ann . . . 1G 129
L31: Magh . . . 4B 222
MOORLANDS . . . 8D 228 (9L 23)
Moorlands PR1: Prest . . . 6H 115
Moorlands, The OL13: Weir . . . 8L 145
Moorlands Ct. BB3: Darw . . . 8D 158
Moorlands Gro. LA3: Heys . . . 5M 21
Moorlands Ter. OL13: Bac . . . 6L 163
Moorland St. OL12: Roch . . . 4B 204
OL15: Littleb . . . 7M 185
Moorlands Vw. BL0: Eden . . . 1J 181
Moorland Ter. OL12: Roch . . . 4L 203
Moorland Vw. BB4: Bac . . . 7E 162
BB9: Nelson . . . 4J 105
Moor La. BB3: Darw . . . 4B 158
BB4: Hasl . . . 1D 160
BB7: Clith . . . 4L 81
BB7: West B . . . 2H 73
BB7: Whall . . . 4H 101
(Moor Fld.)
BB7: Whall . . . 7H 101
(Shawcliffe La.)
BB7: Wis . . . 3M 101
BB12: Padi . . . 9H 103
BB18: Salt . . . 6N 77
BD23: Elsl . . . 8M 53
HX7: Cold . . . 1M 147
L29: Seft . . . 9K 215
L38: Ince B . . . 7D 214
LA1: Lanc . . . 6A 24
(Ridge La.)
LA1: Lanc . . . 6D 228 (8K 23)
(Stonewell)
LA2: Horn . . . 8C 18
OL12: Roch . . . 2K 203
OL14: Tod . . . 4L 165
PR1: Prest . . . 4J 229 (9J 115)
PR4: Hutt . . . 7A 134
PR8: Ains . . . 2C 206
Moor Pk. . . . 7K 115
Moor Pk. Av. FY2: Blackp . . . 8D 62
PR1: Prest . . . 1J 229 (7J 115)
Moor Pk. Ct. PR1: Prest . . . 1K 229
Moor Pk. Pool . . . 7D 62
Moor Rd. BB4: Hasl . . . 1E 180
BL8: Holc . . . 3E 180
OL15: Littleb . . . 5M 185
PR6: Heap, H Charn . . . 5L 175
PR7: Chor . . . 9C 174
PR26: Cros . . . 3M 171
WN5: Orr . . . 6G 221
MOOR SIDE
PR4, Black Pole . . . 6N 93
PR4, Woodplumpton . . . 9B 92
Moorside LA6: Mell . . . 4E 18
OL11: Roch . . . 9C 204
OL15: Littleb . . . 8N 185
PR4: Trea, Wharl . . . 1B 112
Moorside Av. BB1: Blackb . . . 4D 140
BB9: Brierf . . . 6H 105
BL6: Hor . . . 9D 196
PR2: Ribb . . . 6B 116
Moorside Cl. LA6: Mell . . . 5E 18
Moorside Cres. OL13: Bac . . . 3L 163
Moorside Dr. BB5: Clay M . . . 7N 121
PR1: Penw . . . 5E 134
Moorside Fold PR4: Wal B . . . 1M 151
Moor Side La. BB7: Wis . . . 2M 101
BL0: Ramsb . . . 7M 181
Moorside La. PR4: Woodp . . . 6N 93
Moorside Rd. BL7: Edgw . . . 5J 179
BL8: Tott . . . 7D 200
LA2: Brookh . . . 3K 25
Moorside Vw. BL8: Tott . . . 7E 200
Moorside Wlk. WN5: Orr . . . 3L 221
Moor St. BB5: Clay M . . . 6M 121
(not continuous)
L39: Orms . . . 7K 209
(not continuous)
LA1: Lanc . . . 7D 228
PR4: K'ham . . . 4M 111
Moors Vw. BL0: Ramsb . . . 8G 180
Moorthorpe Cl. BB3: Darw . . . 9A 158
Moorthwaite La. LA6: Barb . . . 2G 9
Moor Vw. BB4: W'foot . . . 9D 162
BB18: Salt . . . 4B 78
OL13: Bac . . . 8F 162
(Blackwood Rd.)
OL13: Bac . . . 3M 163
(Change Cl.)
Moor Vw. Cl. OL12: Roch . . . 3K 203
Moorview Cl. BB10: Burnl . . . 8J 105
Moorview Ct. FY4: Blackp . . . 2F 108
Moor Way BL8: Hawk . . . 2A 200
Moorway FY6: Poul F . . . 7L 63
Moray Cl. BL0: Ramsb . . . 1F 200
MORECAMBE . . . 3A 22
Morecambe & Heysham Yacht Club . . . 2B 22
(off Bk. Calton St.)
Morecambe Bay Nature Reserve . . . 7G 15
Morecambe FC . . . 5A 22
Morecambe Golf Course . . . 1F 22
Morecambe Lodge Caravan Pk. LA5: Bolt S . . . 6J 15
Morecambe Rd. BB2: Blackb . . . 7N 139
LA1: Lanc . . . 7J 23
LA3: Morec . . . 4E 22

Morecambe Station (Rail)—Nateby Cl.

Morecambe Station (Rail) 3A 22
Morecambe St. E. LA4: Morec 2B 22
Morecambe Superbowl 3N 21
Morecambe Townhouse Gallery 2A 22
Morecambe St. W. LA4: Morec 2B 22
Moresby Av. FY3: Blackp 3H 89
Moreton Cl. WN3: Wins 9M 221
Moreton Dr. FY3: Stain 5K 89
FY6: Poul F 9K 63
Moreton Grn. LA3: Heys 9L 21
Morewood Dr. LA6: Burt K 5H 7
Morgan St. OL15: Littleb 9L 185
Morland Av. PR4: Wesh 2L 111
PR5: Lost H 9K 135
Morley Av. BB2: Blackb 7H 139
Morley Cl. LA1: Lanc 5J 23
Morley Cft. PR26: Far M 4H 153
Morley La. PR3: Pill 8M 43
Morley Rd. FY4: Blackp 1E 108
LA1: Lanc 5J 23
PR9: S'port 5L 167
Morley St. BB12: Padi 1H 123
OL16: Roch 4E 204
Morningside LA1: Lanc 9B 228
Morningside Cl. OL16: Roch 7E 204
Mornington Rd. FY8: L Ann 4D 130
PR1: Penw 3E 134
PR1: Prest 8B 116
PR6: Adl 5K 195
PR9: S'port 7J 167
Morris Cl. PR25: Leyl 7K 153
Morris Ct. PR2: Ribb 7N 115
Morris Cres. PR2: Ribb 7N 115
Morris La. L39: Hals 1C 208
Morrison St. PR6: Chor 4F 174
Morris Rd. PR2: Ribb 7N 115
PR6: Chor 5G 174
WN8: Uph 4D 220
Morris Way PR7: Chor 9F 174
Morse St. BB10: Burnl 4G 125
Morston Av. FY2: Blackp 1E 88
L32: Kirk 9K 223
Morston Cres. L32: Kirk 9K 223
Morston Wlk. L32: Kirk 9K 223
Mortimer Gro. LA3: Heys 8M 21
Mortimer Ho. *BL6: Hor* 9C 196
(off Chorley New Rd.)
Morton St. BB1: Blackb 3C 226 (3M 139)
Mort St. BL6: Hor 9C 196
Morven Gro. PR8: S'port 7L 167
Mosber La. BD23: Garg 4L 53
Moscow Mill St. BB5: Acc, Osw 3L 141
Moscow Pl. *BB5: Osw* 4L 141
(off Marble St.)
Mosedale Dr. BB12: Burnl 1N 123
Moseley Av. BB18: Earl 3C 78
Moseley Cl. BB11: Burnl 7E 124
Moseley Rd. BB11: Burnl 6E 124
Mosley Av. BL0: Ramsb 3G 200
BL9: Bury 8L 201
Mosley St. BB2: Blackb 9C 226 (6M 139)
(Abraham St.)
BB2: Blackb 9D 226 (5M 139)
(Rose St.)
BB9: Nelson 2H 105
BB18: Barnw 2M 77
PR1: Prest 9M 115
PR8: S'port 1H 187
PR25: Leyl 6K 153
Mosley Wlk. BB2: Blackb 9C 226 (6M 139)
Mosman Pl. BB9: Barrf 8G 84
Mosney Fold PR5: Walt D 5B 136
Moss Acre Rd. PR1: Penw 5H 135
Moss Av. OL16: Roch 7F 204
PR2: Ash R 7D 114
(not continuous)
WN5: Bill 8G 221
Moss Bank L39: Aug 1J 217
PR7: Copp 4A 194
Mossbank BB1: Blackb 2A 140
Moss Bank Cl. BL1: Bolt 9D 198
Moss Bank Ct. L39: Aug 1J 217
Mossbank Gro. OL10: Heyw 9G 202
Moss Bank Pl. FY4: Blackp 1F 108
Moss Bank Way BL1: Bolt 9C 198
Mossborough Hall La.
WA11: Rain 8F 224
Mossborough Rd. WA11: Rain 8H 225
Mossbourne Rd. FY6: Poul F 9J 63
MOSS BRIDGE 2M 157
Moss Bri. L40: Lath 1H 211
Moss Bri. La. L40: Lath 2G 211
Moss Bri. Pk. PR5: Lost H 8M 135
Moss Bri. Rd. OL16: Roch 7E 204
Mossbrook Dr. PR4: Cott 4C 114
Moss Brow WA11: Rain 3K 225
Moss Cl. BB4: Hasl 7F 160
PR6: Chor 6G 174
Mossdale BB1: Blackb 2A 140
Mossdale Av. PR2: Ribb 5N 115
Mossdale Rd. L33: Kirk 5L 223
Moss Delph La. L39: Aug 1G 217
MOSS EDGE 6A 44
Moss Edge La. FY8: L Ann 6G 108
Moss End Way L33: Know P 7B 224
Mossfield Cl. BL9: Bury 9N 201
PR5: Lost H 8L 135
Mossfield Rd. PR6: Chor 6G 174
Mossfields WN6: Wrigh 7J 193
Moss Fold Rd. BB3: Darw 2M 157
Moss Gap BB3: Darw 1C 178
Moss Gdns. PR8: S'port 3J 187
MOSSGATE 9L 21
Moss Ga. BB1: Blackb 2A 140
Mossgate Pk. LA3: Heys 2L 27
Mossgate Wlk. LA3: Heys 1L 27
Mossgiel Av. PR8: Ains 9B 186
Moss Grn. L37: Form 9A 206
Moss Hall La. FY8: L Ann 1K 129
Moss Hall Rd. BB5: Acc 9A 122
Moss Hey La. PR4: Mere B 3M 169
Mosshill Cl. L31: Magh 8B 216
Moss Ho. La. FY6: Stal 3B 56
PR3: Pill 9L 43
PR4: Gt P, Westby 3N 109
PR4: Much H 5J 151
Moss Ho. Rd. FY4: Blackp 4F 108
(not continuous)
PR4: Woodp 8E 94
Moss Ho's. Rd. BB8: Foul 3D 86
Moss Ind. Est. OL16: Roch 8E 204
Mosslands PR25: Leyl 6G 153
Moss La. BB1: Blackb 5F 140
BB5: Blackb, Osw 5F 140
BL1: Bolt 9A 198
L23: Lit C 6A 214
L31: Lyd 6A 216
L31: Magh 9D 216
L33: Kirk 7N 223
L33: S'wood 2L 223
L38: Hight 6A 214
L39: Bick 9D 218
L39: D'holl 7F 206
L40: Burs 7D 190
L40: Ruff 6D 170
LA2: Thurn 5A 36
LA3: Midd, O'ton 4A 28
LA4: Morec 4A 22
LA5: Burt K 3D 6
LA5: Silv 7K 5
LA5: Yea R 6B 6
LA6: Burt K 3D 6
LA6: Burt K, Holme 1E 6
OL12: Whitw 7M 183
OL16: Roch 7D 204
PR1: Penw 8G 135
PR3: Bils 8B 68
PR3: Chip 6G 71
PR3: Gars 5L 59
PR3: St M 3F 66
PR4: Catf 5G 93
PR4: Hesk B 7M 149
PR4: Inskip 8E 66
PR4: Lit H 3M 151
PR4: New L, W Stake 8A 134
PR5: Lost H 8L 135
PR6: Whit W 1E 174
PR7: Copp 4A 194
PR9: Banks 9H 149
PR9: S'port 6N 167
PR25: Leyl 5L 153
PR26: Breth 8M 151
PR26: Cros 6L 171
PR26: Far M, Leyl 2F 152
(not continuous)
PR26: Leyl 9C 152
WN6: Wrigh 9F 192
WN8: Skelm 5K 219
Moss La. E. PR4: Trea 1E 112
Moss La. Vw. WN8: Skelm 5K 219
Moss La. W. PR4: Trea 3C 112
Mosslawn Rd. L32: Kirk 9M 223
Moss Lea BL1: Bolt 9D 198
(not continuous)
PR4: Tarl 8E 150
Mosslea Dr. PR3: Bart 2E 94
Moss Mill St. OL16: Roch 8E 204
Moss Nook L39: Aug 1G 217
L40: Burs 7C 190
Moss Nook La. L31: Magh, Mell 2F 222
WA11: Rain 4J 225
(not continuous)
Mossock Hall Golf Course 7K 217
Mossom La. FY5: T Clev 4D 62
Moss Pl. LA1: Lanc 4L 23
Moss Rd. LA3: Heat 9A 22
PR8: S'port 3H 187
WN5: Bill 8G 220
Moss Row OL11: Roch 4H 203
MOSS SIDE
FY8 8C 110
L31 9D 216
PR3 8L 43
PR26 6E 152
Moss Side BB18: Barnw 2N 77
BL8: Bury 8F 200
L37: Form 8B 206
Moss Side Ind. Est. PR26: Leyl 7E 152
Moss Side La. FY6: Stal 5C 56
FY8: Moss S 7E 110
OL16: Roch 8F 204
PR3: Gt E 6C 66
PR3: T'ley 9D 70
PR4: Mere B 2K 169
PR4: W Grn 7E 110
Moss Side Station (Rail) 8C 110
Moss Side St. OL12: Whitw 1B 184
Moss Side Way PR26: Leyl 8E 152
Moss St. BB1: Blackb 2A 140
BB6: Gt H 5J 121
BB7: Clith 3K 81
BL9: Summ 3J 201
OL16: Roch 7E 204
PR1: Prest 4H 229 (9H 115)
PR5: Lost H 8L 135
WN5: Wigan 5L 221
Moss Ter. OL16: Roch 7E 204
PR6: Whit W 1G 174
WN5: Wigan 6L 221
Moss Vw. L31: Magh 1E 222
L39: Orms 8L 209
Moss Way FY4: Blackp 2F 108
Mossway PR4: New L 1C 152
Moss Wood Caravan Pk. LA2: C'ham 5F 44
Moss Wood Cl. PR7: Chor 8C 174
MOSSY LEA 7H 193
Mossy Lea Fold WN6: Wrigh 1K 213
Mossy Lea Rd. WN6: Wrigh 6H 193
Mostyn Av. BB18: Earl 3E 78
BL9: Bury 8L 201
L10: Aint 7B 222
Mostyn St. BB3: Darw 3M 157
Motherwell Cres. PR8: S'port 2M 187
Moth Hole La. HX7: Hept 9N 127
Mottram Cl. L33: Kirk 8L 223
PR6: Whit W 1E 174
Mottram M. *BL6: Hor* 9C 196
(off Wright St.)
Mottram St. BL6: Hor 9C 196
Moulden Brow BB2: Fenis 9C 138
Moulding Cl. BB2: Blackb 4J 139
Moulding Moss BL9: Bury 7D 202
Mounsey Rd. PR5: Bam B 8B 136
Mount, The BB2: Blackb 2A 226 (2K 139)
BB4: W'foot 8D 162
OL13: Bac 5K 163
(off Bankside La.)
OL14: Tod 1M 165
WN8: Skelm 3M 219
Mountain Ash OL12: Roch 2M 203
Mountain Ash Cl. OL12: Roch 2M 203
Mountain La. BB5: Acc 4B 142
Mountain Rd. PR7: Copp 5A 194
Mount Apartments FY7: Flee 8G 40
Mount Av. BB4: W'foot 7D 162
LA1: Lanc 5K 23
LA4: Morec 1E 22
OL12: Roch 1H 205
OL15: Littleb 7K 185
Mountbatten Cl. PR2: Ash R 9E 114
Mountbatten Rd. PR7: Chor 8D 174
Mount Cl. L32: Kirk 6H 223
Mount Cres. BB10: Cliv 9L 125
L32: Kirk 6H 223
WN5: Orr 5J 221
Mountfield Ct. WN5: Orr 4J 221
Mount Gdns. LA4: Morec 1E 22
Mount Ho. Cl. L37: Form 7B 206
Mount Ho. Rd. L37: Form 7B 206
Mount La. BB10: Cliv 8K 125
OL14: Tod 5F 146
Mount Pl. *OL12: Roch* 5B 204
(off Clements Royds St.)
OL14: Wals 6K 165
Mt. Pleasant BB1: Blackb 3E 226 (3N 139)
BB4: Rawt 5K 161
BB7: Chatb 7C 74
BB7: Sabd 3F 102
BB10: W'thorne 4L 125
BL7: Edgw 9K 179
BL9: Bury 2L 201
LA2: H Ben 6L 19
LA5: Arn 3G 4
LA6: Holme 1G 6
(off Burton Rd.)
OL13: Bac 7G 163
(off Plantation St.)
OL14: Tod 2L 165
PR1: Prest 5J 229 (9J 115)
PR3: Cald V 4H 61
PR6: Adl 5J 195
PR6: Whit W 7E 154
PR6: Withn 7B 156
PR7: Chor 6E 174
(off St Mary's Wlk.)
Mt. Pleasant La. LA5: Bolt S, Carn 5M 15
Mt. Pleasant St. BB5: Osw 4L 141
BB11: Burnl 3C 228 (4D 124)
OL14: Tod 7D 146
Mount Rd. BB11: Burnl 5B 228 (5D 124)
FY7: Flee 8G 41
L32: Kirk 7G 223
(not continuous)
Mount St James BB1: Blackb 4F 140
Mountside BL7: Eger 5E 198
Mountside Cl. OL12: Roch 3B 204
Mount St. BB4: Rawt 5K 161
BB5: Acc 4A 142
BB5: Clay M 7N 121
BB6: Gt H 3J 121
BB9: Barrf 8H 85
BB9: Brierf 5F 104
BL0: Ramsb 7G 180
FY1: Blackp 4B 88
FY7: Flee 9G 41
OL12: Roch 5B 204
OL14: Tod 1L 165
(off Meadow Bottom Rd.)
PR1: Prest 7J 229 (1J 135)
PR9: S'port 7K 167
Mount Ter. BB4: Rawt 5M 161
PR9: S'port 7K 167
Mt. Trinity BB1: Blackb 3E 226 (3N 139)
Mount Vw. BB8: Foul 1N 85
OL14: Tod 1L 165
Mountwood WN8: Skelm 8L 211
Mountwood Lodge PR8: Ains 8C 186
Mt. Zion Ct. OL14: Tod 7D 146
Moverley St. OL14: Wals 8L 165
Mowbray Av. BB2: Blackb 9F 226 (6N 139)
Mowbray Dr. FY3: Blackp 1F 88
LA6: Burt K 6H 7
Mowbray Pl. FY7: Flee 9E 40
Mowbray Rd. FY7: Flee 9E 40
MOWBRECK 2N 111
Mowbreck Ct. PR4: Wesh 3M 111
Mowbreck Holiday & Residential Pk.
PR4: Wesh 2N 111
Mowbreck La. PR4: Wesh 2L 111
Mowbrick La. LA2: Hest B 8H 15
Mowgrain Vw. OL13: Bac 4K 163
Moy Hill OL16: Milnr 8L 205
Moyse Av. BL8: Bury 8E 200
MUCH HOOLE 5J 151
MUCH HOOLE MOSS HOUSES 5L 151
MUCH HOOLE TOWN 6J 151
Mucky La. BB18: Salt 4B 78
Muirfield PR1: Penw 2D 134
Muirfield Cl. PR2: Fulw 3E 114
PR7: Eux 2N 173
Muirfield Dr. PR8: Ains 9C 186
Mulberry Av. PR1: Penw 5D 134
Mulberry Cl. L33: Kirk 4L 223
L39: Orms 8M 209
OL11: Roch 8B 204
PR4: Clif 8G 113
WN5: Wigan 5N 221
Mulberry Cotts. LA2: Gal 2L 37
Mulberry La. LA1: Lanc 5L 29
Mulberry M. FY2: Blackp 4F 62
PR4: K'ham 4N 111
Mulberry St. BB1: Blackb 3B 140
Mulberry Wlk. BB1: Blackb 3B 140
Mulgrave Av. PR2: Ash R 8D 114
Mullion Cl. PR9: S'port 1A 168
Mullions, The OL14: Wals 8J 165
Muncaster Dr. WA11: Rain 3L 225
Muncaster Rd. PR1: Prest 1K 229 (7J 115)
Muni, The 7A 86
Munro Av. WN5: Orr 5H 221
Munro Cres. PR2: Ribb 6A 116
Munster Av. FY2: Blackp 8D 62
Murchison Gro. FY5: T Clev 2E 62
Murdock Av. PR2: Ash R 7G 114
Murdock St. BB2: Blackb 4J 139
Muriel St. OL16: Roch 8E 204
Murray Av. PR26: Far M 2H 153
Murrayfield OL11: Roch 7J 203
Murray St. BB10: Burnl 9F 104
PR1: Prest 2G 229 (8H 115)
PR25: Leyl 6L 153
Murton Ter. BL1: Bolt 9E 198
Musabbir Sq. *OL12: Roch* 5D 204
(off Jermyn St.)
Musbury Cres. BB4: Rawt 6M 161
Musbury M. BB4: Hasl 6E 160
Musbury Rd. BB4: Hasl 8E 160
Musbury Vw. BB4: Hasl 6E 160
Musden Av. BB4: Hasl 8F 160
Mus. of Lancashire 5N 229 (9L 115)
Museum St. BB1: Blackb 3C 226 (3M 139)
MYERSCOUGH 7N 67
Myerscough Av. FY4: Blackp 4F 108
FY8: L Ann 9D 108
Myerscough Hall Dr. PR3: Bils 6B 68
Myerscough Planks PR3: Bart 9D 68
Myerscough Rd. BB2: Mellor B 6C 118
MYERSCOUGH SMITHY 6M 117
Myerscough Smithy Rd.
BB2: Bald, Mellor B 6M 117
Myers St. BB18: Barnw 3M 77
Myles Standish Way PR7: Chor 1E 194
Myndon St. LA1: Lanc 5K 23
Myra Av. LA4: Morec 4C 22
Myra Rd. FY8: L Ann 4H 129
Myrtle Av. BB11: Burnl 5B 124
FY3: Blackp 2N 227 (5D 88)
FY5: T Clev 7F 54
FY6: Poul F 6L 63
Myrtle Bank Rd. BB2: Blackb 8L 139
OL13: Bac 4K 163
Myrtle Cotts. *OL13: Bac* 5L 163
(off Gladstone St.)
Myrtle Dr. PR4: K'ham 5A 112
Myrtle Gro. BB4: Hasl 6F 160
BB10: Burnl 5K 125
BB18: Barnw 2N 77
LA3: Heys 5N 21
PR8: S'port 8L 167
Myrtle St. OL14: Tod 2L 165
Mystic M. *L39: Orms* 7K 209
(off Burscough St.)
MYTHOP 8N 89
Mythop Av. FY8: L Ann 4B 130
Mythop Cl. FY8: L Ann 4B 130
Mythop Ct. FY4: Blackp 9K 89
Mythop Pl. PR2: Ash R 8C 114
Mythop Rd. FY4: Blackp 9K 89
FY8: L Ann 4B 130
PR4: Weet 9K 89
Mythop Village FY4: Blackp 8M 89
Mytton Fold Golf Course 8E 100
Mytton Rd. BL1: Bolt 9B 198
Mytton St. BB12: Padi 1J 123
Mytton Vw. BB7: Clith 4J 81

N

Naarian Ct. BB1: Blackb 1N 139
Nabbs Fold BL8: Greenm 2E 200
Nabbs Way BL8: Greenm 4F 200
Nab La.
BB2: Blackb 4A 226 (3L 139)
(not continuous)
BB5: Osw 4H 141
Nab Rd. PR6: Chor 5G 175
NAB'S HEAD 1N 137
Nab's Head La. PR5: Sam 8N 117
Naburn Dr. WN5: Orr 6H 221
Nab Vw. BB7: B'ton 6G 101
Nab Wood Dr. PR7: Chor 8C 174
Naden Vw. OL11: Roch 4H 203
Nailers Grn. *BL8: Greenm* 4E 200
(off Brandlesholme Rd.)
Nairn Av. WN8: Skelm 7M 211
Nairn Cl. FY4: Blackp 2G 108
WN6: Stand 3N 213
Nairne St. BB11: Burnl 4B 124
Nall St. OL16: Milnr 6H 205
Nancy St. BB3: Darw 6B 158
NANGREAVES 2L 201
Nanny's Rake PR3: Clau 1K 69
Nansen Rd. BB2: Blackb 5J 139
FY7: Flee 1G 54
Nantwich Av. OL12: Roch 2C 204
Napier Av. FY4: Blackp 3B 108
PR4: Tarl 7D 150
Napier Cl. FY8: L Ann 8E 108
Napier Ho. OL14: Wals 7K 165
Napier St. BB5: Acc 3B 142
BB9: Nelson 4J 105
Napier Ter. PR8: Birk 9G 167
Naples Av. BB11: Burnl 5B 124
Naples Rd. BB3: Darw 6C 158
NAPPA 4D 52
Naptha La. PR4: W Stake 2F 152
NAR 9B 184
Narcissus Av. BB4: Hasl 7E 160
Nares Rd. BB2: Blackb 5J 139
Nares St. PR2: Ash R 8F 114
Narrow Cft. Rd. L39: Aug 2G 216
Narrowgates Cotts.
BB12: Barl 6A 84
Narrow La. L39: Aug 2G 216
L39: Hals 5D 208
PR26: Midge H 5C 152
NARROW MOSS 3K 209
Narrow Moss La. L40: Scar 2J 209
Narvik Av. BB11: Burnl 5N 123
NATEBY 6G 59
Nateby Av. FY4: Blackp 4E 108
Nateby Cl. FY8: L Ann 1H 129
PR3: Longr 2H 97

288 A-Z Lancashire

Nateby Ct.—Nick Hilton's La.

Nateby Ct. FY4: Blackp 3B 108
PR3: Nateby 5L 59
Nateby Crossing La. PR3: Nateby 5L 59
Nateby Hall La. PR3: Nateby 2K 59
Nateby Pl. PR2: Ash R 8C 114
Nathan Gro. L33: Kirk 6L 223
Natterjack La. LA3: Midd 6K 27
Nave Cl. BB3: Darw 7C 158
Navena Av. FY7: Flee 2E 54
Naventis Ct. FY1: Blackp 5H 227
Navigation Bank WN6: Stand 9N 213
Navigation Bus. Cen. PR2: Ash R 9C 114
Navigation Ho. BB1: Blackb 7E 226
Navigation Vw. OL16: Roch 8E 204
Navigation Way BB1: Blackb 7E 226 (5N 139)
FY7: Flee 1G 54
PR2: Ash R 9C 114
Naylor Farm Av. WN6: Shev 7J 213
Naylors Fold PR6: Whit W 7E 154
Naylors Ter. BL7: Belm 9K 177
Naze Ct. BB4: Newc 6C 162
PR4: Frec 2N 131
Naze La. PR4: Frec 2N 131
(not continuous)
Naze La. E. PR4: Frec 3A 132
Naze La. Ind. Est. PR4: Frec 4N 131
Naze Rd. BB4: Newc 6C 162
OL14: Tod 5J 165
Naze Vw. OL14: Tod 4J 165
Naze Vw. Av. BB4: W'foot 5D 162
Neales Fold PR9: S'port 1C 168
Neapsands Cl. PR2: Fulw 4N 115
Neare Mdw. PR6: Clay W 4E 154
Neargates PR7: Char R 2N 193
Near Moss Farm Leisure Limited
LA2: C'ham 6A 44
Neath Cl. BB1: Blackb 1C 226 (1M 139)
PR5: Walt D 5A 136
Neddy Hill LA6: Burt K 5G 7
Neddy La. BB7: B'ton 6G 101
Nedens Gro. L31: Lyd 8B 216
Nedens La. L31: Lyd 8B 216
Ned's La. FY6: Stal 7B 56
PR3: Pill 8E 42
Needham Av. LA4: Morec 5A 22
Needham Ri. LA4: Morec 5A 22
Needham Way WN8: Skelm 7M 211
Needless Hall La. BD23: Hort 5D 52
Nell Carrs BL0: Ramsb 6K 181
Nell La. PR25: Leyl 3N 153
Nell's La. L39: Aug 6E 216
Nell St. BL1: Bolt 9F 198
NELSON 2H 105
Nelson Av. PR25: Leyl 6L 153
Nelson Ct. FY7: Flee 1F 54
LA5: Arn 1F 4
(off Ashleigh Rd.)
PR2: Ash R 9B 114
PR8: Birk 1F 186
Nelson Cres. PR2: Lea 7A 114
Nelson Dr. PR2: Lea 7A 114
Nelson Gdns. PR4: Inskip 2G 93
Nelson Golf Course 5J 105
Nelson Rd. BB10: Brierc 5K 105
FY1: Blackp 8H 227 (8B 88)
FY7: Flee 1F 54
PR7: Chor 7E 174
Nelson Sq. BB11: Burnl 3C 228 (4D 124)
Nelson Station (Rail) 2J 105
Nelson St. BB3: Darw 5N 157
BB5: Acc 3B 142
BB6: Gt H 3K 121
BB7: Clith 3H 81
BB8: Colne 6A 86
BL6: Hor 9E 196
FY8: L Ann 5C 130
LA1: Lanc 7D 228 (8K 23)
LA4: Morec 3A 22
OL13: Bac 7N 163
OL14: Wals 7K 165
OL15: Littleb 9L 185
OL16: Roch 6C 204
PR4: K'ham 4L 111
PR5: Bam B 8A 136
PR8: S'port 8G 166
Nelson Ter. *BB5: Acc 2M 141*
(off India St.)
PR1: Prest 9G 115
Nelson Way FY8: L Ann 4C 130
PR2: Ash R 1B 134
Nene Cl. PR25: Leyl 8L 153
Neps La. BB7: News 6B 52
Neptune Ct. FY4: Blackp 3K 109
Neptune St. BB11: Burnl 2B 228 (3D 124)
Neptune Way BB1: Guide 1B 158
Nero St. BL0: Ramsb 7K 181
Nesbit St. BL2: Bolt 9H 199
Ness Gro. L32: Kirk 8H 223
Nesswood Av. FY4: Blackp 3E 108
Neston Av. BL1: Bolt 8F 198
Neston Rd. BL8: Bury 9E 200
OL16: Roch 9F 204
Neston St. PR1: Prest 9A 116
Netherbeck LA5: Carn 7C 12
LA6: Carn 7C 12
Netherbeck Holiday Home Pk. LA5: Carn 7C 12
NETHER BURROW 9F 8
Netherby St. BB11: Burnl 5B 124
Nethercroft OL11: Roch 4J 203
Netherfield Cl. BB12: Burnl 2B 124
Netherfield Gdns. BB9: Nelson 2J 105
Netherfield Rd. BB9: Nelson 3H 105
Netherheys Cl. BB8: Colne 6M 85
NETHER KELLET 4B 16
Nether Kellet Rd. LA6: Over K 1F 16
Netherlands Rd. LA4: Morec 4C 22
Netherley Rd. PR7: Copp 5A 194
Netherton Grange L30: N'ton 7A 222
NETHERTOWN 4H 101
Nethertown Cl. BB7: Whall 4H 101
Nether Vw. LA2: Wen 5F 18
Netherwood Ct. WN6: Shev 6K 213
Netherwood Gdns. BB6: Old L 5B 100
Netherwood Gro. WN3: Wins 9N 221
Netherwood Rd. BB10: Brierc, Burnl 1G 124
Netherwood St. BB10: Burnl 8J 105
Nethway Av. FY3: Blackp 4F 88
Netley Av. OL12: Roch 2C 204
Network 65 Bus. Pk. BB11: Hapt 5K 123
Neverstitch Cl. WN8: Skelm 1K 219
Neverstitch Rd. WN8: Skelm 2G 219
Nevett St. PR1: Prest 9N 115
Neville Av. FY5: T Clev 3E 62
Neville Ct. *BD23: Garg 3L 53*
(off Neville Rd.)
Neville Cres. BD23: Garg 3L 53
Neville Dr. FY5: T Clev 3H 63
Neville Rd. BD23: Garg 3L 53
Neville St. PR3: Longr 3J 97
Nevill St. PR9: S'port 6H 167
Nevis Gro. BL1: Bolt 8D 198
New Acres LA5: Carn 8C 12
WN8: N 'urgh 2L 211
Newall St. OL14: Wals 7K 165
OL15: Littleb 8L 185
Newark Cl. L30: N'ton 5A 222
Newark Pl. PR2: Ash R 7B 114
PR2: Fulw 1G 114
Newark Rd. OL12: Roch 2C 204
Newark Sq. OL12: Roch 2C 204
Newark St. BB5: Acc 3M 141
Newarth La. PR4: Hesk B 4C 150
New Bank Rd. BB2: Blackb 2J 139
New Barn Cl. BB4: Hasl 9F 160
New Barn Ct. BB2: Blackb 9E 226
New Barn La. BB4: Rawt 7M 161
OL11: Roch 8A 204
New Barns Cl. LA5: Arn 3D 4
New Barns Rd. LA5: Arn 3D 4
New Barn St. OL16: Roch 8D 204
New Bath St. BB8: Colne 6B 86
NEWBIGGIN 5A 8
Newbigging Av. BB4: W'foot 5D 162
Newbiggin La. LA6: N'gin 5A 8
NEWBOLD 6F 204
NEWBOLD BROW 5E 204
Newbold Hall Dr. OL16: Roch 6F 204
Newbold Hall Gdns. OL16: Roch 6F 204
Newbold Moss OL16: Roch 6E 204
Newbold Stop (Metro) 7F 204
Newbold St. OL16: Roch 6F 204
New Bonny St. FY1: Blackp 3H 227 (6B 88)
NEWBRIDGE 8G 85
Newbridge Farm Caravan Pk. L33: S'wood 3C 224
Newbridge Gdns. BL2: Bolt 9L 199
New Briggs Fold BL7: Eger 3E 198
New Brighton BB4: Lumb 3C 162
BD23: Garg 4L 53
New Brighton Cotts. *OL12: Whitw 5A 184*
(off Clara St.)
New Brook Ho. PR1: Prest 9M 115
New Brown St. BB9: Nelson 1H 105
New Brunswick St. BL6: Hor 9C 196
New Bldgs. Pl. *OL16: Roch 5C 204*
(off Bell St.)
NEWBURGH 3L 211
Newburn Cl. WN8: Skelm 7M 211
Newbury Av. FY4: Blackp 1D 108
New Bury Cl. BB5: Osw 5J 141
Newbury Cl. PR2: Fulw 1F 114
Newbury Grn. PR2: Fulw 1F 114
Newbury Rd. FY8: L Ann 4F 128
WN8: Skelm 7M 211
NEWBY 4N 75
Newby Av. FY6: Poul F 1K 89
FY7: Flee 3D 54
Newby Back La. BB7: Rim 4M 75
Newby Cl. BB11: Burnl 7C 124
PR8: Ains 1B 206
Newby Dr. LA1: Lanc 5K 23
PR25: Leyl 5N 153
WN8: Skelm 7M 211
Newby La. BB7: Rim 4M 75
Newby Pl. FY4: Blackp 9H 89
PR2: Ribb 5N 115
(not continuous)
Newby Rd. BB5: Hunc 8D 122
Newby Sq. WN5: Wigan 6L 221
New Carr La. L31: Gt A 4L 215
Newcastle Av. FY3: Blackp 3N 227 (6D 88)
FY5: T Clev 8E 54
Newcastle St. BB2: Blackb 5K 139
New Cateaton St. BL9: Bury 9L 201
New Causeway L37: Gt A 5B 214
L38: Ince B 5B 214
New Chapel La. BL6: Hor 9G 197
New Chapel St. BB2: Blackb 6J 139
NEWCHURCH 6C 162
New Church Cl. BB5: Clay M 6M 121
Newchurch Cl. BB2: Blackb 9E 226 (6N 139)
NEWCHURCH IN PENDLE 8A 84
New Church M. BB10: Burnl 9F 104
Newchurch Old Rd. OL13: Bac 6H 163
Newchurch Rd. BB4: Newc, Rawt 4M 161
OL13: Bac 7E 162
New Cock Yd. PR1: Prest 7K 229 (1J 135)
New Colliers Row BL1: Bolt 7M 197
Newcombe Rd. BL0: Ramsb 4F 200
New Ct. Dr. BL7: Eger 2E 198
New Ct. Way L39: Orms 7L 209
Newcroft LA5: Wart 4B 12
New Cut Cl. PR8: Birk 5G 186
New Cut La. L33: Kirk, Rain 9E 224
L39: Hals 7K 187
PR8: Birk 5G 187
WA11: Rain 9F 224
New England Caravan Pk. LA6: Cap 5G 13
Newe Rd. BD24: Sett 3N 35
New Fid Cl. OL16: Roch 6E 204
Newfield Ct. FY8: L Ann 2F 128
Newfield Dr. BB2: Blackb 8A 140
BB9: Nelson 2J 105
Newfield Head La. OL16: Milnr 8L 205
Newfield Rd. PR5: Bam B 9C 136
Newfield Vw. OL16: Milnr 7K 205
(not continuous)
New Fold WN5: Orr 7F 220
New Foul La. PR8: S'port 1N 187
New Garden Flds. BB4: Water 9D 144
New Garden St. BB2: Blackb 8C 226 (5M 139)
NEW GATE 8F 134
NEWGATE 4D 220
Newgate LA3: Morec 6E 22
OL16: Roch 6B 204
PR2: Fulw 5H 115
Newgate Av. WN6: App B 4H 213
Newgate La. PR4: W Stake 8F 134
Newgate Rd. WN8: Uph 4C 220
New Grn. BL2: Bolt 7L 199
New Ground Ct. BB10: Burnl 7G 105
New Hall Av. FY4: Blackp 3H 109
New Hall Av. Nth. FY4: Blackp 3H 109
New Hall Dr. PR8: S'port 4B 188
NEW HALL HEY 6L 161
New Hall Hey Bus. Pk.
BB4: Rawt 6L 161
New Hall Hey Rd. BB4: Rawt 6K 161
New Hall La. PR1: Prest 5N 229 (9L 115)
New Hall Rd. BL9: Bury 9C 202
New Hall St. BB10: Burnl 9E 104
New Hampshire Ct. *FY8: L Ann 1K 129*
(off Blacksmiths Row)
Newhaven BB3: Darw 9A 158
Newhaven Cl. BL8: Bury 6H 201
Newhaven Dr. PR3: Catt 1A 68
NEWHEY 9L 205
New Hey La. PR4: K'ham, Newt 5B 112
Newhey Rd. OL16: Milnr 8K 205
(not continuous)
Newhey Stop (Metro) 9L 205
New Heys Way BL2: Bolt 7K 199
Newholme Res. Pk. FY3: Blackp 8J 89
New Ho. Caravan Pk.
LA6: K Lon 7G 9
Newhouse Cl. OL12: Ward 8F 184
Newhouse Cres. OL11: Roch 5J 203
Newhouse Dr. WN3: Wins 9N 221
New Ho. La. PR3: Winm 8K 45
Newhouse Rd. BB5: Hunc 9C 122
FY4: Blackp 8F 88
NEW HOUSES 9M 221
New Houses *BB4: Rawt 4N 161*
(off Springfield Rd.)
New Ho. St. BB8: Colne 6B 86
Newhouse St. OL12: Ward 8F 184
Newick Pk. L32: Kirk 9H 223
Newick Rd. L32: Kirk 9H 223
Newington Av. BB1: Blackb 6N 119
New Inn Cl. PR7: Buck V 1A 174
New Inn Yd. *LA4: Morec 2B 22*
(off Poulton Rd.)
Newland Av. WN5: Wigan 6N 221
Newlands PR7: E'ton 8F 172
Newlands Av. BB7: Clith 4J 81
FY3: Blackp 8F 88
L40: Burs 9D 190
LA1: Lanc 2M 29
OL12: Roch 2C 204
PR1: Penw 4D 134
Newlands Cl. BB2: Blackb 8F 138
OL12: Roch 2C 204
Newlands Rd. FY8: L Ann 3J 129
LA1: Lanc 3M 29
LA2: Quern 1A 30
LA4: Morec 4C 22
Newland Way FY6: Poul F 1J 89
NEW LANE 7N 189
New La. BB5: Osw 6J 141
BB7: Clith, Withg 6D 80
FY5: T Clev 4H 63
L39: Aug 1K 217
L39: D'holl 9L 207
(Back La.)
L39: D'holl 8H 207
(Old Moss La.)
L40: Burs 6N 189
LA6: Burt K 6G 7
PR1: Penw 5H 135
PR3: Clau 3C 68
PR3: Eng H 5A 58
PR4: Tarl 9B 150
PR7: E'ton 4D 172
PR9: S'port 2C 168
New La. Pace PR9: Banks 7G 148
New Lane Station (Rail) 6N 189
New Line OL13: Bac 7K 163
New Line Ind. Est. OL13: Bac 7L 163
Newlinks, The PR4: Lea 7N 113
New Links Av. PR2: Ingol 3D 114
NEW LONGTON 8C 134
Newlyn Av. FY4: Blackp 4E 108
L31: Magh 1D 222
Newlyn Ct. FY4: Blackp 4E 108
Newlyn Dr. WN8: Skelm 4A 220
Newlyn Pl. PR2: Ingol 4C 114
Newman Gro. FY5: T Clev 7E 54
Newman Rd. FY1: Blackp 2D 88
Newman St. BB10: Burnl 9F 104
OL16: Roch 2F 204
Newmarket Av. LA1: Lanc 3M 29
New Mkt. St. BB1: Blackb 4C 226 (3M 139)
BB7: Clith 3L 81
BB8: Colne 6A 86
PR7: Chor 6E 174
Newmarket St. LA4: Morec 2D 22
Newmeadow Cl. BB2: Blackb 8A 140
New Meadow La. L37: Gt A 3E 214
New Miles La. WN6: Shev 6J 213
New Mill OL16: Roch 3G 204
New Mill Ind. Est. PR5: Bam B 9B 136
New Mill St. BB1: Blackb 1E 226 (2N 139)
OL15: Littleb 9K 185
PR7: E'ton 8F 172
New Moss La. PR6: Whit W 1E 174
Newnham St. BL1: Bolt 9F 198
New Oxford St. BB8: Colne 5B 86
New Palace Ct. BB12: Burnl 2N 123
New Parkside Farm Caravan Pk.
LA2: Lanc 3D 24
New Pk. St. BB2: Blackb 3B 226 (3L 139)
New Pastures PR5: Lost H 8M 135
New Plough Yd. *BB6: Gt H 4K 121*
(off Victoria St.)
Newport St. BB9: Nelson 1J 105
BL8: Tott 8F 200
Newquay Ct. FY2: Blackp 2D 88
New Quay La. LA1: Lanc 8F 22
New Quay Rd. LA1: Lanc 8F 22
New Rd. BB4: W'foot 5D 162
BB11: Burnl 7D 124
BB18: Earl 2E 78
FY5: T Clev 4J 63
FY6: Ham 9N 55
FY8: L Ann 5B 108
L37: Form 7A 206
L40: Ruff 2F 190
LA1: Lanc 6C 228 (8K 23)
LA5: Silv, Wart 9J 5
LA6: K Lon 6E 8
LA6: W'ouse, Ingl 2M 19
OL12: Whitw 5M 183
OL14: Tod 3F 146
OL15: Littleb 1H 205
PR5: Lost H 7L 135
PR6: And, H Charn 3L 195
PR7: Copp 3B 194
PR26: Cros 7M 171
New Rough Hey PR2: Ingol 3C 114
New Row BB5: Alt 3D 122
BB8: Wine 7F 86
PR4: K'ham 4N 111
New Row Cotts. PR3: Know G 1E 98
New Scotland Rd. BB9: Nelson 1J 105
NEWSHAM 5D 94
Newsham Hall La. PR4: Woodp 7C 94
Newsham Lodge La. PR4: Woodp 7B 94
Newsham Pl. LA1: Lanc 2L 29
Newsham Rd. LA1: Lanc 2L 29
Newsham St. PR2: Ash R 8G 114
NEWSHOLME 6C 52
News La. WA11: Rain 9J 219
Newsome St. PR25: Leyl 6K 153
New South Prom. FY4: Blackp 3A 108
New Springs BL1: Bolt 9B 198
Newstead OL12: Roch 5B 204
Newstead Dr. WN8: Skelm 7M 211
Newstet Rd. L33: Know P 8N 223
New St. BB4: Hasl 4G 160
BB8: Colne 8M 85
BB9: Nelson 1K 105
BB12: Padi 1G 123
BD24: Langc 1N 35
BL8: Tott 7E 200
L39: Hals 5N 207
L40: Mawd 3N 191
LA1: Lanc 7C 228 (8K 23)
LA2: Brookh 2K 25
LA2: Halt 1B 24
LA4: Morec 3A 22
LA5: Carn 8A 12
OL12: Roch 3B 204
OL15: Littleb 1J 205
OL16: Milnr 8K 205
PR6: Birns 7A 156
PR7: E'ton 8F 172
WN5: Wigan 6L 221
New Taylor Fold BB10: Brierc 7K 105
Newthorn BB5: Osw 7N 141
NEWTON
BB7 7A 50
FY3 4J 89
LA1 6L 23
LA6 10D 8
Newton Av. FY6: Poul F 9J 63
PR1: Prest 9C 116
Newton Cl. PR4: Frec 1A 132
PR26: Leyl 7E 152
Newton Ct. FY3: Blackp 5E 88
PR2: Ash R 8E 114
Newton Dr. BB5: Acc 5C 142
BB10: Cliv 1L 145
BL8: Greenm 4F 200
FY3: Blackp 1N 227 (5D 88)
WN8: Skelm 7M 211
Newton Dr. E. FY3: Blackp 3H 89
New Tong Fld. BL7: Brom C 6F 198
Newton Grn. *OL14: Tod 9J 147*
(off Pine Rd.)
Newton Gro. FY5: T Clev 4H 63
OL14: Tod 9J 147
Newton Hall Holiday Pk. FY3: Blackp 4H 89
Newton Ho. PR1: Prest 4M 229
Newton Pl. FY3: Blackp 3G 89
Newton Rd. BB7: Slaid 6B 50
FY8: L Ann 1G 129
PR2: Ash R 7E 114
Newton St. BB1: Blackb 3B 140
BB3: Darw 5A 158
BB5: Osw 3H 141
BB7: Clith 4K 81
BB12: Burnl 2A 124
BL9: Bury 7L 201
OL16: Roch 8E 204
PR1: Prest 4N 229 (9K 115)
(not continuous)
PR9: S'port 7M 167
Newton Ter. LA1: Lanc 5L 23
NEWTON-WITH-SCALES 7D 112
NEW TOWN 4J 97
NEWTOWN 4D 172
Newtown BB18: Barnw 2M 77
Newtown Gdns. L32: Kirk 8K 223
Newtown St. BB8: Colne 6B 86
(not continuous)
New Vale PR9: Banks 3F 168
New Vernon St. BL9: Bury 9L 201
New Way L39: Bick 9N 217
OL12: Whitw 5N 183
New Wellington Cl. BB2: Blackb 7K 139
New Wellington Gdns.
BB2: Blackb 7K 139
New Wellington M. BB2: Blackb 7K 139
New Wellington St. BB2: Blackb 7K 139
Nib La. PR1: Penw 8H 135
Nicholas St. BB3: Darw 6N 157
BB8: Colne 7N 85
BB10: Brierc 7J 105
BB11: Burnl 3D 228 (4E 124)
Nicholl St. BB10: Burnl 1E 124
Nicholson Cres. LA4: Morec 3D 22
Nicholson St. OL11: Roch 8C 204
Nichol St. PR7: Chor 5E 174
Nickey La. BB2: Mellor 7G 118
Nick Hilton's La. PR6: H Charn 2M 195

Nickleton Brow—Oak Grn.

Nickleton Brow PR6: H Charn ... 3L **195**
(not continuous)
Nick Rd. La. OL12: Ward ... 7C **184**
Nickson's La. FY6: Pree ... 9A **42**
Nicola Cl. OL13: Weir ... 9L **145**
Nicola St. BL7: Eger ... 5E **198**
Nigher Moss Av. OL16: Roch ... 6F **204**
Nightfield La. BB2: Bald ... 1A **118**
Nightingale Cl. BB1: Blackb ... 7B **140**
BB7: Whall ... 3G **100**
L32: Kirk ... 7G **223**
Nightingale Cres. BB11: Burnl ... 5A **124**
Nightingale Dr. FY6: Poul F ... 9H **63**
Nightingale St. PR6: Adl ... 5J **195**
Nightingale Way PR3: Catt ... 9N **59**
PR7: Chor ... 9B **174**
Nile Cl. PR2: Ash R ... 9B **114**
Nile St. *BB9: Nelson ... 1H 105*
(off Clayton Cl.)
LA1: Lanc ... 6D **228** (8K **23**)
OL16: Roch ... 5D **204**
Nimes St. PR1: Prest ... 9N **115**
Nine Elms PR2: Fulw ... 3F **114**
Nineteen Acre La. LA5: Yea R ... 7C **6**
Nineveh St. BB8: Colne ... 6B **86**
Nipe La. WN8: Skelm ... 6L **219**
Nip Hill LA1: Lanc ... 6B **228**
Nithe Wlk. BL8: Bury ... 7F **200**
Nithside FY4: Blackp ... 9J **89**
Niton Cl. BB4: Hasl ... 6H **161**
NIXON HILLOCK ... 2K **173**
Nixon La. PR26: Leyl ... 7C **152**
Nixons Ct. PR26: Leyl ... 7C **152**
Nixons La. PR8: Ains ... 6E **186**
WN8: Skelm ... 4A **220**
Noble Mdw. OL12: Roch ... 9G **184**
Noble St. BB1: Rish ... 8H **121**
BB3: Darw ... 7A **158**
BB6: Gt H ... 5J **121**
Noblett Ct. FY7: Flee ... 2F **54**
Noblett St. BB1: Blackb ... 3E **226** (3N **139**)
Noel Ga. L39: Aug ... 2G **216**
Noel Jones Ct. FY8: L Ann ... 1E **128**
Noel Rd. LA1: Lanc ... 5J **23**
Noel Sq. PR2: Ribb ... 8A **116**
Noggarth Rd. BB12: Fence, Rough ... 2B **104**
NOG TOW ... 2C **114**
Nolan St. PR8: S'port ... 9J **167**
NOOK ... 9L **59**
Nook, The BD23: Ban N ... 5J **53**
FY3: Stain ... 5K **89**
L39: Aug ... 3H **217**
LA5: Bolt S ... 5L **15**
WN6: App B ... 5H **213**
Nook Cres. PR2: Grim ... 9E **96**
Nook Cft. BB18: Earl ... 2F **78**
Nook Farm Av. OL12: Roch ... 2C **204**
Nook Fld. PR3: Goos ... 4N **95**
Nookfield PR26: Leyl ... 6D **152**
Nookfield Cl. FY8: L Ann ... 4N **129**
Nook Glade PR2: Grim ... 9E **96**
NOOKLANDS ... 5G **114**
Nooklands PR2: Fulw ... 5H **115**
Nook La. BB2: Blackb ... 7G **139**
BB5: Osw ... 6G **140**
L40: Mawd ... 9B **172**
PR3: C'town ... 9L **59**
PR5: Bam B ... 1N **153**
Nook Side OL12: Roch ... 2C **204**
Nook Ter. BB2: Blackb ... 7H **139**
OL12: Roch ... 2C **204**
Noon La. L40: Ruff ... 3C **190**
Noon Sun St. OL12: Roch ... 4C **204**
Noor St. PR1: Prest ... 3M **229** (8K **115**)
Nora St. BB9: Barrf ... 8H **85**
NORBRECK ... 5C **62**
Norbreck Cl. BB2: Blackb ... 8N **139**
Norbreck Ct. FY2: Blackp ... 5C **62**
Norbreck Dr. PR2: Ash R ... 8B **114**
Norbreck North Stop (Tram) ... 4C **62**
Norbreck Rd. FY5: T Clev ... 5C **62**
Norbreck Stop (Tram) ... 5B **62**
Norbury Cl. L32: Kirk ... 8J **223**
PR9: S'port ... 1B **168**
Norbury Gro. BL1: Bolt ... 9G **198**
Norbury Rd. L32: Kirk ... 8J **223**
Norbury St. OL16: Roch ... 9E **204**
Norbury Wlk. L32: Kirk ... 8J **223**
Norcliffe Rd. FY2: Blackp ... 5C **62**
NORCROSS ... 4F **62**
Norcross Brow PR6: Withn ... 7B **156**
Norcross La. FY5: T Clev ... 4G **62**
Norcross Pl. PR2: Ash R ... 8C **114**
Nordale Pk. OL12: Roch ... 3H **203**
NORDEN
BB1 ... 7H **121**
OL11 ... 4J **203**
Norden Cl. OL11: Roch ... 3G **203**
Norden Ct. BB1: Rish ... 8H **121**
BB6: Gt H ... 4L **121**
Norden Lodge OL11: Roch ... 5J **203**
Norden Rd. OL11: Roch ... 8H **203**
Norden Vw. BB1: Rish ... 7G **121**
Norden Way OL11: Roch ... 3G **203**
Norfield L39: Orms ... 7L **209**
Norfolk Av. BB12: Burnl ... 2N **123**
BB12: Padi ... 3J **123**
FY2: Blackp ... 8B **62**
FY5: T Clev ... 9E **54**
LA3: Heys ... 5M **21**
Norfolk Cl. BB5: Clay M ... 6M **121**
OL15: Littleb ... 6M **185**
PR25: Leyl ... 8H **153**
Norfolk Gro. BB5: Chur ... 1N **141**
PR8: Birk ... 4F **186**
Norfolk Rd. FY3: Blackp ... 8G **89**
FY8: L Ann ... 3A **130**
L31: Magh ... 3B **222**
PR1: Prest ... 2M **229** (8K **115**)
PR5: Walt D ... 4N **135**
PR8: Birk ... 4F **186**
Norfolk St. BB1: Rish ... 8G **121**
BB2: Blackb ... 6K **139**
BB3: Darw ... 6B **158**
BB5: Acc ... 1C **142**
BB8: Colne ... 6B **86**
Norfolk St. BB9: Nelson ... 2H **105**
LA1: Lanc ... 6K **23**
OL11: Roch ... 7B **204**
Norfolk Ter. *BB2: Blackb ... 6K 139*
(off Zebudah St.)
LA2: Glas ... 1C 36
(off West Vw.)
Norford Way OL11: Roch ... 5J **203**
Norham Cl. BB12: Burnl ... 2C **124**
Norkeed Ct. *FY5: T Clev ... 4C 62*
(off Norkeed Rd.)
Norkeed Rd. FY5: T Clev ... 4C **62**
Norkeed Road Stop (Tram) ... 4C **62**
Norland Dr. LA3: Heys ... 8L **21**
NORLEY ... 4M **221**
Norley Hall Av. WN5: Wigan ... 4M **221**
Norley Rd. WN5: Wigan ... 4L **221**
Normanby St. WN5: Wigan ... 5L **221**
Norman Cl. FY5: T Clev ... 2F **62**
Normandie Av. FY2: Blackp ... 8D **62**
Normandy Rd. PR4: Woodp ... 7E **94**
Norman Hayes L39: Orms ... 4L **209**
Normanhurst L39: Orms ... 8M **209**
Norman Rd. BB5: Osw ... 3J **141**
OL11: Roch ... 7A **204**
Norman St. BB2: Blackb ... 5K **139**
BB10: Burnl ... 2E **124**
BL9: Bury ... 9N **201**
Normanton Cl. WN6: Stand ... 8N **213**
Normington Cl. L31: Lyd ... 7B **216**
NORMOSS ... 3H **89**
Normoss Av. FY3: Blackp ... 3G **89**
Normoss Farm Cvn. Site FY3: Blackp ... 2J **89**
Normoss Rd. FY3: Blackp ... 3H **89**
Norreys St. OL16: Roch ... 5D **204**
Norris Ho. Dr. L39: Aug ... 3H **217**
Norris St. BB3: Darw ... 6B **158**
PR1: Prest ... 7G **115**
PR2: Fulw ... 6G **115**
PR7: Chor ... 8E **174**
Norris Way L37: Form ... 9B **206**
Nth. Albert St. FY7: Flee ... 8H **41**
Nth. Albion St. FY7: Flee ... 9G **40**
Northall PR4: Much H ... 5J **151**
Northam Cl. PR9: S'port ... 1N **167**
WN6: Stand ... 3N **213**
North Av. BB18: Barnw ... 2M **77**
BL8: Greenm ... 4E **200**
FY3: Blackp ... 3D **88**
L10: Aint ... 8D **222**
Nth. Bank Av. BB1: Blackb ... 8M **119**
Northbridge Ho. BB10: Burnl ... 1E **124**
Northbrook Gdns. PR25: Leyl ... 6H **153**
Northbrook Rd. PR25: Leyl ... 5H **153**
Nth. Church St. FY7: Flee ... 8H **41**
Northcliffe BB6: Gt H ... 3H **121**
Nth. Cliff St. PR1: Prest ... 8G **229** (2H **135**)
Nth. Clifton St. FY8: L Ann ... 5A **130**
Northcote Rd. BB6: Langh ... 6C **100**
PR1: Prest ... 1G **135**
Northcote St. BB3: Darw ... 9B **158**
BB4: Hasl ... 5G **161**
PR25: Leyl ... 6K **153**
North Ct. FY5: T Clev ... 7D **54**
North Cft. PR3: Gars ... 4N **59**
Northdene WN8: Parb ... 2M **211**
Northdene Dr. OL11: Roch ... 7K **203**
North Dr. FY5: T Clev ... 5D **62**
(Fleetwood Rd.)
FY5: T Clev ... 3E **62**
(Greenfield Rd.)
LA1: Bail ... 7M **29**
PR4: Inskip ... 1G **92**
PR4: Wesh ... 3L **111**
WN6: App B ... 2F **212**
North East Av. PR6: Withn ... 7B **156**
North East Dr. LA1: Bail ... 7M **29**
NORTH END ... 5C **214**
Northenden Rd. PR7: Copp ... 4A **194**
North End La. L38: Hight ... 5A **214**
Northern Av. PR4: Much H ... 5H **151**
Northern Equine Therapy Cen. ... 7M **35**
Northern Perimeter Rd. L30: N'ton ... 6A **222**
Northern Ter. LA5: Silv ... 6K **5**
Northfield WN8: Skelm ... 8M **211**
Northfield Av. FY1: Blackp ... 2B **88**
Northfield Cl. L33: Kirk ... 6M **223**
Northfield Rd. BB1: Blackb ... 1M **139**
BB5: Ris B, S Fold ... 8F **142**
BL9: Bury ... 7L **201**
Northfields Av. BD24: Sett ... 2N **35**
Northfields Cres. BD24: Sett ... 2N **35**
Northfleet Av. FY7: Flee ... 2E **54**
Northgate BB2: Blackb ... 3C **226** (3M **139**)
FY2: Blackp ... 7C **62**
FY8: L Ann ... 2D **128**
LA3: Morec ... 5D **22**
OL12: Whitw ... 7N **183**
PR3: Goos ... 4N **95**
PR25: Leyl ... 5L **153**
Northgate Dr. PR6: Chor ... 4G **174**
North Gro. PR5: Lost H ... 8M **135**
North Highfield PR2: Fulw ... 3A **116**
NORTH HOUSES ... 1K **129**
Nth. Houses La. FY8: L Ann ... 1K **129**
(not continuous)
Northland Rd. BL1: Bolt ... 7F **198**
Northlands PR2: Fulw ... 3H **115**
PR26: Leyl ... 8F **152**
Northlands Cl. BB6: Gt H ... 3J **121**
North La. OL12: Roch ... 5C **204**
Northleach Av. PR1: Penw ... 6J **135**
Northleach Dr. PR8: Ains ... 8A **186**
North Meade L31: Magh ... 9B **216**
North Meadowside PR4: Wal B ... 1K **151**
Nth. Mersey Bus. Cen. L33: Know P ... 6A **224**
NORTH MOOR ... 2D **208**
Nth. Moor La. L39: Hals ... 2C **208**
Nth. Moss La. L37: Form ... 6C **206**
Nth. Mount Rd. L32: Kirk ... 6G **223**
Nth. Nook La. PR3: Goos ... 5A **70**
North Pde. BB18: Barnw ... 1M **77**
L32: Kirk ... 8K **223**
OL16: Milnr ... 9M **205**
North Pk. Av. BB9: Barrf ... 1G **105**
North Pk. Dr. FY3: Blackp ... 5E **88**
North Pk. Rd. L32: Kirk ... 6G **223**
Nth. Perimeter Rd. L33: Know P ... 6A **224**
North Pier ... 1G **227** (5A **88**)
North Pier Stop (Tram) ... 1H **227** (5B **88**)
North Promenade FY5: T Clev ... 8C **54**
FY8: L Ann ... 9C **108**
Nth. Quarry Bus. Pk. WN6: App B ... 3G **212**
Nth. Quarry Bus. Village WN6: App B ... 3G **212**
North Quay LA3: Heys ... 2H **27**
Nth. Ribble St. PR5: Walt D ... 2M **135**
North Rd. BB1: Blackb ... 4B **140**
BB4: Rawt ... 5A **162**
BB7: Barr ... 1K **101**
LA1: Lanc ... 6C **228** (8K **23**)
LA5: Carn ... 9A **12**
LA6: Holme ... 1F **6**
PR1: Prest ... 2J **229** (8J **115**)
PR9: S'port ... 2A **168**
PR26: Breth ... 9H **151**
NORTH SHORE ... 2B **88**
North Shore Golf Course ... 9C **62**
Northside PR7: Eux ... 3M **173**
Northside Caravan Pk. LA6: Carn ... 7D **12**
North Sq. FY3: Blackp ... 4D **88**
FY5: T Clev ... 7C **54**
North St. BB4: Hasl ... 6H **161**
BB4: Newc ... 6C **162**
BB4: Rawt ... 5M **161**
BB4: Water ... 8E **144**
BB7: Clith ... 2M **81**
BB8: Colne ... 5B **86**
BB9: Nelson ... 1H **105**
BB10: Brierc ... 7K **105**
BB10: Burnl ... 9E **104**
BB12: Hapt ... 4H **123**
BB12: Padi ... 9H **103**
BB18: Barnw ... 3M **77**
BD23: Garg ... 3M **53**
BL0: Ramsb ... 4H **181**
FY7: Flee ... 8H **41**
LA4: Morec ... 3B **22**
OL12: Whitw ... 5N **183**
OL15: Littleb ... 9M 185
(off East St.)
OL16: Roch ... 5D **204**
PR1: Prest ... 4J **229** (9J **115**)
PR7: Chor ... 4E **174**
PR9: S'port ... 6J **167**
Nth. Syke Av. PR2: Lea ... 8M **113**
Northumberland Av. FY2: Blackp ... 1B **88**
FY5: T Clev ... 8E **54**
Northumberland Cl. BB3: Darw ... 9C **158**
Northumberland St. LA4: Morec ... 3A **22**
PR7: Chor ... 7F **174**
Nth. Union Vw. PR5: Lost H ... 9J **135**
North Vale PR6: H Charn ... 4H **195**
Nth. Valley Retail Pk. BB8: Colne ... 6A **86**
Nth. Valley Rd. BB8: Colne ... 6N **85**
North Vw. BB4: Craws ... 8M **143**
BB6: Gt H ... 4J **121**
BB8: Traw ... 9E **86**
BL0: Ramsb ... 4H **181**
BL9: Summ ... 3G **201**
OL12: Whitw ... 4A **184**
PR4: K'ham ... 4L **111**
North Vw. Caravan Pk. PR3: Nateby ... 7D **58**
North Vw. Cl. PR3: Gt E ... 6A **66**
Nth. Warton St. FY8: L Ann ... 5B **130**
North Way BL1: Bolt ... 9H **199**
Northway FY7: Flee ... 3D **54**
L31: Aug, Lyd, Magh ... 3B **222**
(not continuous)
L39: Aug ... 6E **216**
PR2: Fulw ... 2G **115**
PR3: Brou ... 7F **94**
WN8: Skelm ... 9M **211**
Northway Caravan Pk. L40: Scar ... 9E **188**
Northways WN6: Stand ... 2N **213**
North West Dr. LA1: Bail ... 8L **29**
Northwold Cl. WN3: Wins ... 8N **221**
NORTHWOOD ... 8L **223**
Northwood BL2: Bolt ... 9K **199**
Northwood Cl. BB12: Burnl ... 1B **124**
FY8: L Ann ... 4L **129**
Northwood Way FY6: Poul F ... 9K **63**
Norton Av. LA3: Heys ... 5L **21**
Norton Ct. FY8: L Ann ... 4F **128**
Norton Dr. LA3: Heys ... 6M **21**
Norton Gro. L31: Magh ... 4C **222**
LA3: Heys ... 6L **21**
Norton Pl. LA3: Heys ... 6L **21**
Norton Rd. LA3: Heys ... 6L **21**
OL12: Roch ... 2C **204**
PR3: Cab ... 2N **59**
Norton St. BB12: Hapt ... 5H **123**
BL1: Bolt ... 9F **198**
Norton Vale FY5: T Clev ... 1K **63**
Norwich Av. OL11: Roch ... 6L **203**
Norwich Dr. BL8: Bury ... 9J **201**
Norwich Pl. FY2: Blackp ... 6D **62**
PR1: Prest ... 7M **229** (1K **135**)
Norwich St. BB1: Blackb ... 1N **139**
OL11: Roch ... 8D **204**
Norwich Way L32: Kirk ... 8K **223**
Norwood Av. BB2: Blackb ... 6M **139**
BB9: Nelson ... 9K **85**
FY3: Blackp ... 2E **88**
PR4: Hesk B ... 5D **150**
PR9: S'port ... 6L **167**
Norwood Cl. PR6: Adl ... 5J **195**
Norwood Ct. LA1: Lanc ... 7F **228**
Norwood Cres. PR9: S'port ... 6L **167**
Norwood Dr. LA4: Morec ... 4E **22**
Norwood Gdns. PR9: S'port ... 7M **167**
Norwood Gro. WA11: Rain ... 4L **225**
Norwood Rd. FY8: L Ann ... 9C **108**
PR8: S'port ... 7M **167**
Notre Dame Gdns. BB1: Blackb ... 1F **226** (2N **139**)
Nottingham Rd. PR1: Prest ... 2M **229** (8K **115**)
Nottingham St. BB1: Blackb ... 4A **140**
Novak Pl. LA4: Morec ... 4F **22**
NOVA SCOTIA ... 8C **226** (5M **139**)
Nova Scotia Retail Pk.
BB2: Blackb ... 8C **226** (5M **139**)
Nova Scotia Wharf BB2: Blackb ... 9B **226**
Nowell Gro. BB12: Read ... 8C **102**
Nowell St. BB6: Gt H ... 4J **121**
Noyna Av. BB8: Foul ... 2B **86**
Noyna Rd. BB8: Foul ... 2B **86**
Noyna St. BB8: Colne ... 5B **86**
Noyna Vw. BB8: Colne ... 4B **86**
Nuffield Theatre ... 7M **29**
NUN HILLS ... 7G **162**
Nun St. LA1: Lanc ... 6E **228** (8L **23**)
Nurseries, The FY4: Blackp ... 4F **108**
L37: Form ... 1A **214**
PR4: Hesk B ... 4C **150**
Nursery Av. L39: Orms ... 6M **209**
Nursery Cl. PR7: Char R ... 1A **194**
PR25: Leyl ... 7J **153**
Nursery Dr. PR4: Tarl ... 6D **150**
Nursery Gdns. OL16: Roch ... 5F **204**
Nursery La. PR4: New L ... 8B **134**
Nursery Nook BB3: E'hill ... 2D **158**
Nursery Rd. L31: Lyd ... 7B **216**
Nutfield St. OL14: Tod ... 1L **165**
Nuthall Rd. PR8: S'port ... 2M **187**
NUTTALL ... 1H **201**
Nuttall Av. BB6: Gt H ... 5J **121**
BL6: Hor ... 9B **196**
Nuttall Cl. BL0: Ramsb ... 9H **181**
Nuttall Hall Cotts.
BL0: Ramsb ... 9J **181**
Nuttall Hall Rd. BL0: Ramsb ... 1J **201**
NUTTALL LANE ... 9H **181**
Nuttall La. BL0: Ramsb ... 9G **181**
Nuttall Rd. FY1: Blackp ... 9M **227** (9D **88**)
Nuttall St. BB2: Blackb ... 7L **139**
(not continuous)
BB4: Rawt ... 4N **161**
BB5: Acc ... 3B **142**
BB11: Burnl ... 5F **124**
OL13: Bac ... 4M **163**
OL16: Roch ... 6D **204**
Nuttall St. M. *BB5: Acc ... 3B 142*
(off Nuttall St.)
Nuttalls Way BB1: Blackb ... 7C **140**
Nutter Cres. BB12: High ... 5L **103**
Nutter Rd. BB5: Acc ... 1B **142**
FY5: T Clev ... 1D **62**
PR1: Prest ... 6G **229** (1H **135**)
NUTTER'S PLATT ... 7F **134**
Nye Bevan Pool ... 2M **219**

O

Oak Av. BB5: Ris B ... 8F **142**
BL0: Ramsb ... 3F **200**
FY4: Blackp ... 1D **108**
FY5: T Clev ... 3J **63**
L39: Orms ... 8J **209**
LA2: Gal ... 2K **37**
LA4: Morec ... 2E **22**
OL14: Tod ... 9K **147**
PR1: Penw ... 5E **134**
PR3: Longr ... 3J **97**
PR4: K'ham ... 5N **111**
PR7: Eux ... 3N **173**
PR9: Banks ... 4J **169**
Oak Bank BB5: Hunc ... 7C **122**
Oakbank Dr. BB5: Acc ... 3L **141**
BL1: Bolt ... 7D **198**
Oak Bank Ter. BB9: Barrf ... 8G **84**
Oakbridge Dr. PR7: Buck V ... 9A **154**
Oakcliffe Rd. OL12: Roch ... 1F **204**
Oak Cl. BB1: Rish ... 9H **121**
BB7: Barr ... 1K **101**
BB7: Whall ... 3G **100**
OL12: Whitw ... 2A **184**
PR1: Penw ... 4E **134**
Oak Cotts. OL14: Tod ... 5K **165**
Oak Cres. WN8: Skelm ... 2H **219**
Oak Cft. PR6: Clay W ... 5D **154**
Oakdale BL2: Bolt ... 9K **199**
Oakdale Cl. L32: Kirk ... 9H **223**
Oakdale M. BB12: Burnl ... 3A **124**
Oakdale Row L32: Kirk ... 9L **223**
Oakdene Av. BB5: Hunc ... 8D **122**
Oak Dr. L40: Burs ... 1D **210**
LA2: Halt ... 1C **24**
PR4: Frec ... 3M **131**
PR6: Chor ... 3E **174**
Oaken Bank BB10: Burnl ... 7J **105**
Oaken Cl. OL13: Bac ... 4M **163**
OAKENCLOUGH ... 9J **47**
Oakenclough Rd. OL13: Bac ... 4M **163**
PR3: Bleas, Goos ... 8N **61**
PR3: Oaken, Scor ... 9J **47**
PR3: Scor ... 9F **38**
Oakeneaves Av. BB11: Burnl ... 7B **124**
Oakengate PR2: Fulw ... 2M **115**
Oakenhead BB4: Rawt ... 4K **161**
Oakenhead Cl. PR3: Whitec ... 4N **69**
Oakenhead St. PR1: Prest ... 8A **116**
OAKENHEAD WOOD ... 4K **161**
Oakenhead Wood Old Rd.
BB4: Rawt ... 4J **161**
Oakenhurst Rd. BB2: Blackb ... 5A **226** (4L **139**)
Oakenrod Hill OL11: Roch ... 6N **203**
Oakenrod Vs. OL11: Roch ... 6A **204**
OAKENSHAW ... 6L **121**
Oakenshaw Av. OL12: Whitw ... 8N **183**
Oakenshaw Ct. OL12: Whitw ... 8N **183**
Oakenshaw Cft. BB5: Clay M ... 6L **121**
Oakenshaw Vw. OL12: Whitw ... 8N **183**
Oakfield PR2: Ash R ... 8E **114**
PR2: Fulw ... 2J **115**
Oakfield Av. BB5: Clay M ... 6L **121**
BB5: Hunc ... 8D **122**
BB18: Barnw ... 1L **77**
Oakfield Cres. BB5: Osw ... 4M **141**
Oakfield Dr. PR26: Leyl ... 7E **152**
Oakfield Rd. BB2: Blackb ... 9L **139**
L38: Hight ... 9A **214**
Oakfields L39: Orms ... 7M **209**
Oakfield Ter. OL11: Roch ... 5N **203**
Oakford Cl. PR9: Banks ... 1G **168**
Oak Gdns. PR4: Longt ... 9J **133**
Oakgate Cl. PR4: Tarl ... 1D **170**
Oak Gates BL7: Eger ... 4E **198**
Oak Grn. L39: Orms ... 7L **209**

Oak Gro.—Orchards, The

Oak Gro. BB3: Darw 5B 158
PR3: Gars 5N 59
PR4: New L 1D 152
Oakgrove FY4: Blackp 3D 108
Oakham Cl. BL8: Bury 8K 181
Oakham Ct. PR1: Prest 6M 229 (1K 135)
PR9: S'port 6J 167
Oakham Dr. L10: Aint 9E 222
Oak Hill OL15: Littleb 9J 185
Oak Hill Cl. BB5: Acc 4B 142
Oakhill Cl. L31: Magh 9C 216
Oak Hill Clough OL14: Tod 9L 147
Oakhill Cott. La. L31: Lyd 7C 216
Oakhill Dr. L31: Lyd 7C 216
Oakhill Rd. L31: Magh 9C 216
Oak Ho. PR7: Chor 8B 174
Oakhurst Av. BB5: Hunc 8D 122
OL12: Roch 9G 185
Oakland Av. FY5: T Clev 5D 62
Oakland Cl. LA1: Lanc 8N 23
Oakland Glen PR5: Walt D 5K 135
Oaklands Av. BB9: Barrf 8H 85
PR4: Tarl 8E 150
Oaklands Caravan Pk. PR4: Wart 2J 131
Oaklands Ct. LA1: Ald 2G 29
Oaklands Dr. BB4: Rawt 5K 161
PR1: Penw 4D 134
Oaklands Gro. PR2: Ash R 8C 114
Oaklands Rd. BL0: Ramsb 4J 181
Oaklands Ter. BB1: Blackb 1N 139
(off Cedar St.)
Oakland St. BB9: Nelson 2J 105
PR5: Bam B 7A 136
Oak La. BB5: Acc 3C 142
PR4: Newt 7D 112
Oaklea WN6: Stand 2K 213
Oakleaf Cl. PR3: Goos 4M 95
Oakleaf Ct. FY5: T Clev 8D 54
Oakleaf Way FY4: Blackp 9K 89
Oaklee Gro. L33: Kirk 6M 223
Oakleigh WN8: Skelm 9A 220
Oakleigh Ter. OL14: Tod 7E 146
Oakley Dr. WN5: Wigan 5N 221
Oakley Rd. BB4: Rawt 5L 161
LA3: Heys 6L 21
Oakley St. BB4: Rawt 6K 161
OL15: Littleb 1H 205
Oakmere PR6: Clay W 4E 154
Oakmere Av. PR6: Withn 5M 155
Oakmere Cl. BB2: Blackb 1L 157
Oakmoor Av. FY2: Blackp 7E 62
Oak Mt. OL14: Tod 1L 165
Oak Mount Mill Engine House 2A 228
Oak Ridge BB7: West B 5K 73
Oakridge Cl. PR2: Fulw 2J 115
Oak Rd. PR3: Gars 4M 59
Oakroyd Cl. LA5: Arn 1F 4
Oaks, The FY3: Blackp 7E 88
FY6: Poul F 6K 63
PR3: St M 4G 67
PR5: Walt D 5L 135
PR7: Chor 1D 194
Oaks Av. BL2: Bolt 8J 199
Oaks Brow BL1: Clay D 2K 119
Oaks Bus. Pk. WN8: Uph 7C 220
Oaksfield BB3: Darw 2M 157
Oakshaw Dr. OL12: Roch 4L 203
Oakshott Pl. PR5: Bam B 9D 136
Oaks La. BL2: Bolt 8H 199
Oak St. BB1: Blackb 1N 139
BB5: Acc 3B 142
BB5: Clay M 7M 121
BB5: Osw 5K 141
BB6: Gt H 3J 121
BB8: Colne 5B 86
BB9: Brierf 4F 104
BB9: Nelson 1J 105
BB11: Dunn 4N 143
BB12: Burnl 3A 124
BL0: Ramsb 9G 181
FY7: Flee 9G 40
OL10: Heyw 9F 202
OL12: Whitw 2A 184
OL13: Bac 4L 163
OL14: Tod 3K 165
OL15: Littleb 2J 205
(Wesley Ct.)
OL15: Littleb 9M 185
(West Vw.)
OL16: Milnr 9K 205
OL16: Roch 6C 204
PR1: Prest 7M 229 (1K 135)
PR8: S'port 8L 167
Oak Ter. BB18: Barnw 1N 77
OL15: Littleb 4N 185
Oaktree Av. PR2: Ingol 5D 114
PR25: Leyl 3N 153
Oaktree Cl. PR2: Ingol 5D 114
Oak Tree Ct. WN8: Skelm 9A 212
Oak Vw. OL12: Whitw 1A 184
PR25: Leyl 5H 153
Oakville Rd. LA3: Heys 2K 27
Oak Way PR3: Longr 2J 97
Oakwood WN8: Skelm 9A 212
Oakwood Av. BB1: Blackb 8A 120
FY8: L Ann 4L 129
PR5: Walt D 4N 135
PR8: Ains 7E 186
WN6: Shev 7J 213
Oakwood Cl. BB3: Darw 2M 157
BB10: Burnl 7H 105
FY4: Blackp 5F 108
FY5: T Clev 1K 63
Oakwood Dr. PR2: Fulw 1G 114
PR8: Ains 8E 186
Oakwood Gdns. LA1: Lanc 5L 29
Oakwood Gro. LA5: Bolt S 7K 15
Oakwood Rd. BB5: Acc 5C 142
PR7: Chor 8D 174
PR7: Copp 3B 194
Oakwood Vw. PR7: Chor 1D 194
Oakworth Av. PR2: Ribb 4B 116
Oakworth Cl. L33: Kirk 6K 223
Oakworth Dr. BL1: Bolt 8D 198
Oasis Cl. L40: Ruff 2F 190
Oatlands Rd. L32: Kirk 8H 223
Oat St. BB12: Padi 2J 123
Oban Ct. PR2: Grim 9F 96
Oban Cres. PR1: Prest 6N 115
Oban Dr. BB1: Blackb 5C 140
Oban Gro. BL1: Bolt 8E 198
Oban Pl. FY2: Blackp 5E 62
Oban St. BB10: Burnl 1G 124
Oberlin St. OL11: Roch 8A 204
Observatory Rd. BB2: Blackb 6A 140
Occupation La. FY6: Sing 7C 64
Occupation Rd. FY5: T Clev 1H 63
LA5: Wart 3L 11
Ocean Blvd. FY4: Blackp 2A 108
Ocean Ct. FY6: K Sea 8K 41
Ocean Edge Caravan Pk. LA3: Heys, Midd 4J 27
(not continuous)
Ocean Plaza PR8: S'port 6G 166
(not continuous)
Ocean Way FY5: T Clev 9C 54
O'Connor Gro. L33: Kirk 4K 223
Odd Ho. La. PR26: Breth 2K 171
Oddies Yd. OL12: Roch 3D 204
(off Isabella St.)
Odell Way PR5: Walt D 5A 136
Odeon Cinema
Blackpool 5K 227 (7C 88)
Preston 9F 114
Rochdale 9B 204
O'er the Bri. BB3: Hodd 6E 158
Off Botanic Rd. PR9: S'port 5N 167
Offerton St. BL6: Hor 9B 196
Office Rd. OL13: Weir 8L 145
Off Mt. Pleasant St. BB5: Osw 4L 141
(off Mt. Pleasant St.)
Ogden Cl. BB4: Hasl 8F 160
Ogden Dr. BB4: Hasl 8F 160
Ogden La. OL16: Milnr 8N 205
O'Hagan Ct. BB9: Brierf 4F 104
Old Auction Mart LA6: K Lon 6F 8
(off Main St.)
Old Back La. BB7: Wis 3L 101
Old Bank La. BB1: Blackb 6B 140
BB2: Blackb 6B 140
(Evolution Pk.)
BB2: Blackb 9F 226 (6A 140)
(Roman Rd.)
Old Bank St. BB2: Blackb 5C 226 (4M 139)
Old Barn Pl. BL7: Brom C 5G 199
Old Beechfield Gdns. WN6: Stand 4N 213
Old Bent La. OL12: Ward 7D 184
OLD BIRTLE 6C 202
Old Boundary Way L39: Orms 6L 209
Old Brewery Trad. Est. PR1: Prest 9H 115
Old Bridge La. FY6: Ham 4A 64
Old Bridge Way PR6: Chor 5F 174
Old Brow La. OL16: Roch 2F 204
(off Wheelwright Dr.)
Old Brown La. PR5: Bam B 5C 136
Old Buckley La. PR3: Know G 3E 98
Oldbury Pl. FY5: T Clev 3F 62
Old Carr Mill St. BB4: Hasl 2G 160
Old Chapel Ct. PR6: Adl 6J 195
Old Clay Dr. OL12: Roch 1F 204
Old Clay La. PR3: Longr 1H 97
Old Clitheroe Rd. PR3: Dutt, Longr 1L 97
OLD CLOUGH 8L 145
Old Coal Staithe BB7: Whall 9M 101
BB12: Read 9M 101
Old Cock Yd. PR1: Prest 6L 229 (1K 135)
Old Colliers Row BL1: Bolt 8M 197
Old Co-op Bldg., The PR3: Longr 3J 97
(off Barclay Rd.)
Old Croft PR2: Fulw 1G 115
Old Cross Stone Rd. OL14: Tod 2M 165
Old Dawber's La. PR7: Eux 5L 173
Old Delph Rd. OL11: Roch 4J 203
Old Doctors St. BL8: Tott 6E 200
Old Eagley M. BL1: Bolt 7F 198
Olde Back La. BB11: Burnl 6A 124
Old Engine La. BL0: Ramsb 8J 181
WN8: Skelm 1G 218
Olde Stoneheath Ct. PR6: H Charn 1K 195
Old Farmside BB2: Blackb 9L 139
Oldfield PR1: Penw 6G 134
PR4: Lit H 3K 151
Oldfield Av. BB3: Darw 4M 157
FY2: Blackp 7C 62
Oldfield Carr La. FY6: Poul F 1K 89
Oldfield Cl. FY6: Poul F 1L 89
Oldfield Cres. FY6: Poul F 8L 63
Oldfield Rd. PR5: Bam B 9C 136
Old Fold WN5: Wigan 5L 221
Old Forge FY8: L Ann 1K 129
Old Gates Dr. BB2: Blackb 7G 139
Old Greaves Town La. PR2: Lea 8A 114
Old Green BL2: Bolt 7L 199
BL8: Greenm 4E 200
Old Ground St. BL0: Ramsb 8H 181
Old Hall Caravan Pk. LA6: Cap 8H 13
Old Hall Cl. BB9: Rough 6F 84
BL8: Bury 6G 201
L31: Magh 3C 222
LA4: Morec 4F 22
PR5: Bam B 8A 136
Old Hall Cft. BD23: Garg 3M 53
Old Hall Dr. BB5: Hunc 8E 122
PR5: Bam B 8A 136
Old Hall Farm Bus. Pk. PR9: S'port 9N 167
Old Hall Fold BD23: Garg 3M 53
(off Old Hall Cft.)
Old Hall Gdns. WA11: Rain 3L 225
Old Hall La. BB2: Pleas 6D 138
L32: Kirk 8J 223
PR7: Char R 8L 173
Old Hall Rd. L31: Magh 2C 222
Old Hall Sq. BB10: W'thorne 4L 125
Old Hall St. BB10: Burnl 1E 124
Oldham Rd. OL11: Roch 9D 204
(not continuous)
OL16: Roch 7D 204
Oldhams La. BL1: Bolt 8D 198
(not continuous)
Oldhams Ter. BL1: Bolt 8D 198
Oldham St. BB11: Burnl 5C 228 (5D 124)
LA4: Morec 2B 22
(off Bk. Morecombe St.)
Old Hey Cft. PR1: Penw 6G 135
Old Hive PR3: Chip 5F 70
Old Hollow La. PR9: Banks 5F 148
Old House La. FY4: Blackp 2J 109
Old Kays BL8: Tott 5D 200
Old Kiln OL13: Bac 7H 163
Old Lancaster La. PR1: Prest 8G 114
Old Lancaster Rd. PR3: Catt 1M 67
Old La. BB18: Barnw 5L 77
(not continuous)
BB18: Earl 2E 78
BB18: Kelb 8C 78
BB18: Salt 7M 77
BD23: Brou 6M 53
BD23: T Crav 9J 53
BL9: Bury 5L 201
L31: Lyd 7D 216
L37: Form 6A 206
L39: D'holl 8K 207
L40: Bis G 6N 191
OL12: Bac, Whitw 9A 164
OL13: Bac 8A 164
OL14: Tod 4K 165
WA11: Rain 3K 225
WN6: Shev 6L 213
OLD LANGHO 6C 100
Old Langho Rd. BB6: B'ton, Old L 7B 100
Old Laund St. BB12: Fence 2C 104
Old Links Cl. PR9: S'port 6A 168
Old Lodge La. PR3: Clau 3D 68
Old Lord's Cres. BL6: Hor 8C 196
Old Mains La. FY6: Poul F 5M 63
Old Manor, The OL12: Roch 4B 204
Old Market Ct. LA4: Morec 2B 22
Old Meadow Ct. FY3: Blackp 7E 88
Old Meadows La. FY3: Blackp 7E 88
Old Meadows Rd. OL13: Bac 2K 163
Old Mill Ct. FY4: Wal B 2K 151
Old Mill Dr. BB8: Colne 7C 86
Old Mill Hill L39: Orms 9J 209
Old Mill Ind. Est. PR5: Bam B 6B 136
Old Mill La. L37: Form 8A 206
L40: Bis G 7C 192
Old Millstones PR1: Prest 1G 135
Old Mill St. BB1: Blackb 2E 226 (2N 139)
Oldmill St. OL12: Roch 5C 204
Old Mill Ter. PR6: Chor 5G 174
Old Moor Rd. LA2: Wen 6F 18
Old Moss La. L39: D'holl 6G 207
Old Nab Rd. BB6: Langh, Whall 1E 120
BB7: Whall 9G 100
Old Nursery Fold BL2: Bolt 9L 199
Old Oak Cotts. BL8: Hawk 3D 200
Old Oak Gdns. PR5: Walt D 6L 135
Old Orchard PR2: Fulw 4G 114
Old Park La. PR9: S'port 7N 167
Old Parsonage La. BB12: Padi 1G 123
Old Penny Gdns. LA4: Morec 4F 22
Old Pepper La. WN6: Stand 2L 213
Old Pope La. PR4: W Stake 8E 134
Old Post Office Row BB7: Pend 7A 82
Old Prescot Cl. L31: Magh 9H 217
Old Quarry La. BL7: Eger 4F 198
Old Racecourse Rd. L31: Magh 2A 222
Old Rake BL6: Hor 7E 196
Old Rectory Grn. L39: Aug 4F 216
Old Riggs Yd. LA6: Burt K 6H 7
(off Main St.)
Old Rd. BB7: Chatb 7B 74
BL1: Bolt 9E 198
OL16: Roch 1H 205
Old Roan Station (Rail) 7B 222
Old Roman Rd. BB7: Whall 6N 101
BB12: Read 6N 101
Old Rough La. L33: Kirk 7K 223
Old Row BB4: Rawt 6K 161
BB7: Barr 9K 81
PR4: K'ham 5N 111
OLDROYD 2N 165
Oldroyd Rd. OL14: Tod 2N 165
Old Sawmill, The BD24: Rath 6L 35
Old School Cl. BD24: Sett 3N 35
(off Castlebergh La.)
PR26: Leyl 7D 152
Old School Dr. PR4: Longt 8L 133
Old School Ho., The BB1: Guide 8D 140
OL15: Littleb 8J 185
Old Schoolhouse, The BB3: Darw 6B 158
(off Edmund St.)
Old School La. BB3: Tock 5G 157
PR5: Lost H 1M 153
PR7: Adl 8G 195
PR7: Eux 3N 173
(not continuous)
Old School M. BB4: Hasl 4G 161
(off Clegg St.)
OL13: Bac 7G 163
PR7: Chor 9E 174
(off Saville St.)
Old School Pl. OL12: Ward 8F 184
Old School Row BB12: Burnl 3N 123
(off Dorset St.)
Old School Sq. PR1: Prest 1H 135
(off Burleigh Rd.)
Old Scotch Rd. LA6: Mans 1D 8
Old Sidings, The BB8: Foul 1A 86
Old Stables, The BB7: Whall 2H 101
Old Station Cl. PR2: Grim 9F 96
Old Station Ct. BB7: Clith 3L 81
(off Station Rd.)
Old Stone Brow BB18: Kelb 8D 78
OLD STONE TROUGH 7D 78
Old Stone Trough La. BB18: Kelb 7D 78
Old St. BB4: Newc 6C 162
Old Swan Cl. BL7: Eger 3E 198
Old Tom's La. FY6: Stal 5C 56
OLD TOWN 1D 8
Old Town Cl. WN8: Skelm 3H 219
Old Towns Cl. BL8: Tott 6E 200
Old Town Way WN8: Skelm 3H 219
Old Trafford Caravan Pk.
LA3: Midd 3L 27
Old Tram Rd. PR1: Penw 9L 229 (4K 135)
(not continuous)
PR5: Bam B 9B 136
PR5: Lost H, Walt D 5L 135
Old Tramway, The PR5: Bam B 1D 154
Old Vicarage PR1: Prest 5L 229 (9K 115)
Old Vicarage Ct. FY8: L Ann 3F 128
Old Will's La. BL6: R'ton 7C 196
Old Wood Cl. PR7: Chor 8C 174
Old Wood Rd. PR1: Penw 5F 134
Old Worden Av. PR7: Buck V 8A 154
Old Worston Rd. BB7: Chatb 9C 74
Olivant St. BB12: Burnl 2A 124
Olive Bank BB6: Langh 9D 100
BL8: Bury 9G 201
Olive Cl. L31: Mell 8F 222
PR6: Whit W 1E 174
Olive Gro. FY3: Blackp 2N 227 (5E 88)
L30: N'ton 9A 222
PR4: Wart 2J 131
PR8: S'port 7L 167
WN8: Skelm 2J 219
Olive La. BB3: Darw 5A 158
Oliver Cl. OL15: Littleb 9J 185
Olive Rd. LA1: Lanc 6K 23
Oliver Pl. LA5: Carn 8B 12
Olivers Pl. PR2: Fulw 1K 115
Oliver St. OL13: Bac 7G 163
Olive Stanring Ho.
OL15: Littleb 8M 185
Olive St. OL13: Bac 7J 163
Olive Ter. BB4: Rawt 2L 161
Ollerton OL12: Roch 5B 204
(off Falinge Rd.)
OLLERTON FOLD 3M 155
Ollerton La. PR6: Withn 3M 155
Ollerton Rd. FY8: L Ann 3K 129
Ollerton St. BL1: Bolt 7F 198
PR6: Adl 4J 195
Ollerton Ter. BL1: Bolt 7F 198
PR6: Withn 4N 155
Ollery Grn. L30: N'ton 6A 222
Olney OL11: Roch 7B 204
Olympian Way PR25: Leyl 5K 153
Olympia St. BB10: Burnl 4G 124
Olympic Ct. FY4: Blackp 3K 109
Olympic Way FY4: Blackp 1J 109
Onchan Dr. OL13: Bac 6M 163
Onchan Rd. BB2: Blackb 7M 139
One Ash Cl. OL12: Roch 3C 204
Only Foals & Horses Sanctuary 8H 141
Onslow Cres. PR8: Birk 3G 186
Onslow Rd. FY3: Blackp 3E 88
Onslow St. OL11: Roch 9N 203
Ontario Cl. BB2: Blackb 9H 119
Oozebooth Ter. BB1: Blackb 1M 139
Oozehead La. BB2: Blackb 3J 139
Opal Cl. FY5: T Clev 4F 62
Opal St. BB1: Blackb 7M 119
Opening, The BB2: Mellor B 6D 118
(off Mellor Brook)
Openshaw Dr. BB1: Blackb 8M 119
Oporto Cl. BB11: Burnl 3A 228 (4C 124)
Oram Rd. PR6: Brind 8H 137
Oram St. BL9: Bury 9M 201
(not continuous)
Orange St. BB5: Acc 9A 122
OL14: Tod 5K 165
(off Lumbutts Rd.)
Orchan Rd. OL14: Tod 9J 147
Orchard, The BB9: Barrf 5J 85
BB11: Burnl 5A 124
(off Heather Bank)
L39: Orms 7J 209
LA2: Wray 8E 18
PR3: Lit E 6M 65
PR4: Trea 3C 112
PR4: Wart 2K 131
PR4: Woodp 9B 94
PR26: Cros 3N 171
WN8: Skelm 3H 219
Orchard Av. FY4: Blackp 3C 108
FY6: Poul F 1L 89
LA5: Bolt S 3L 15
PR4: New L 9D 134
Orchard Bri. BB11: Burnl 2C 228
Orchard Cl. BB2: Blackb 1L 157
BB7: Grind 4A 74
FY5: T Clev 8H 55
LA2: Slyne 9K 15
LA5: Silv 9F 4
LA6: Burt K 5H 7
PR2: Ingol 4D 114
PR4: Frec 2M 131
PR4: Hesk B 4D 150
PR4: W Grn 6G 111
PR5: Walt D 6A 136
PR7: Eux 2N 173
WN6: Shev 5K 213
Orchard Ct. L31: Magh 1E 222
PR2: Fulw 4G 115
PR25: Leyl 8G 153
WN5: Bill 8G 221
Orchard Cres. LA5: Arn 1F 4
Orchard Cft. PR5: Lost H 8K 135
Orchard Dr. BB5: Osw 3M 141
FY7: Flee 3E 54
PR6: Whit W 1E 174
Orchard End PR3: Gt E 6A 66
(off Nth. View Cl.)
Orchard Gdns. PR4: Much H 4J 151
WN6: Wrigh 7H 193
Orchard Grange PR1: Penw 4D 134
Orchard Hey L30: N'ton 6A 222
L31: Magh 2E 222
Orchard La. LA1: Lanc 9H 23
PR4: Longt 8K 133
PR8: Ains 9D 186
Orchard Mill Dr. PR26: Cros 4M 171
Orchard Mill St. BB3: Darw 5N 157
Orchard Pk. BB3: Darw 5N 157
Orchard Pl. PR4: Much H 4J 151
Orchard Rd. FY8: L Ann 2E 128
LA5: Arn 1F 4
Orchards, The BB18: Barnw 1N 77
(off Skipton Rd.)
FY6: Carl 6H 63
LA3: O'ton 7B 28
PR8: Ains 9D 186
PR26: Leyl 6E 152
WN5: Orr 6H 221

Pemberton Bus. Cen.—Pinfold Cl.

Pemberton Bus. Cen.
WN5: Wigan 5M 221
Pemberton Dr. LA4: Morec 3F 22
Pemberton Pl. LA4: Morec 3F 22
Pemberton Rd. WN3: Wins 9L 221
Pemberton Station (Rail) 7N 221
Pemberton St. BB1: Blackb 8M 119
BL1: Bolt 9E 198
Pembroke Av. FY2: Blackp 8B 62
LA4: Morec 2D 22
Pembroke Cl. BL6: Hor 9B 196
Pembroke Ct. BB3: Darw 6A 158
(off William St.)
FY2: Blackp 8B 62
OL12: Roch 4C 204
(off Alma St.)
Pembroke Pl. PR7: Chor 8D 174
PR25: Leyl 7K 153
Pembroke Rd. FY8: L Ann 4K 129
WN5: Wigan 2N 221
Pembroke St. BB2: Blackb 7C 226 (5L 139)
BB5: Acc 2C 142
BB10: Burnl 9F 104
OL13: Bac 6K 163
OL15: Littleb 8L 185
Pembury Av. PR1: Penw 5J 135
Penda Dr. L33: Kirk 4K 223
Pendennis OL11: Roch 7B 204
Pendle Arts Gallery 7J 85
(within Pendle Heritage Cen.)
Pendle Av. BB5: Clay M 5M 121
BB7: Chatb 7D 74
BL1: Bolt 7E 198
LA1: Bail 9M 29
OL13: Bac 3L 163
Pendle Bri. BB12: Reed 7D 104
Pendlebury Cl. PR4: Longt 8M 133
Pendle Cl. BL8: Bury 9G 200
FY3: Blackp 1F 88
OL13: Bac 5L 163
WN5: Wigan 6N 221
Pendle Ct. BB7: Clith 3M 81
BB18: Barnw 1N 77
BL1: Bolt 9D 198
PR3: Longr 3J 97
PR4: Wesh 3M 111
WN8: Skelm 8A 220
Pendle Dr. BB2: Blackb 9E 226 (6N 139)
BB7: Whall 3G 100
BL6: Hor 8D 196
L39: Orms 6M 209
Pendle Flds. BB7: Rim 2A 76
BB12: Fence 3A 104
Pendle Heritage Cen. 7J 85
Pendle Hill Cl. PR2: Ribb 2E 116
Pendle Hippodrome Theatre 6A 86
(off New Market St.)
Pendlehurst St. BB11: Burnl 5C 124
Pendle Ind. Est. BB9: Nelson 3K 105
Pendle Leisure Cen. 6N 85
Pendlemist Vw. BB8: Colne 8N 85
Pendle Mt. BB7: Clith 3M 81
Pendle Pl. FY8: L Ann 4B 130
WN8: Skelm 7A 220
Pendle Ri. Shop. Cen. BB9: Nelson 2J 105
Pendle Rd. BB6: Gt H 3L 121
BB7: Clith 3M 81
BB7: D'ham 7G 74
BB9: Brierf 5E 104
LA1: Lanc 5H 23
PR25: Leyl 6N 153
Pendle Row BB12: Barl 6A 84
Pendleside BB9: Nelson 2E 104
Pendleside Cl. BB7: Sabd 3E 102
Pendle Ski Club 9D 82
Pendle St. BB1: Blackb 3A 140
BB5: Acc 3N 141
BB9: Barrf 9G 85
BB9: Nelson 1H 105
BB12: Padi 2J 123
(not continuous)
Pendle St. E. BB7: Sabd 3E 102
Pendle St. W. BB7: Sabd 3E 102
Pendle Ter. BB7: Rim 4K 75
PENDLETON 7A 82
Pendleton Av. BB4: Rawt 3M 161
BB5: Acc 4M 141
Pendleton Rd. BB7: Wis 3L 101
Pendle Trad. Est. BB7: Chatb 8B 74
Pendle Valley Caravan Pk. BB9: Rough 6E 84
Pendle Vw. BB5: Alt 6N 121
BB6: Old L 4C 100
BB7: Grind 5A 74
BB7: West B 5K 73
BB8: Foul 2B 86
BB8: Wine 7F 86
BB12: Barl 5A 84
BB12: High 4L 103
BD23: Hell 1D 52
BD24: Gig 2N 35
(off Church St.)
Pendle Wavelengths 2J 105
Pendle Way BB9: Nelson 2J 105
(in Arndale Shop. Cen.)
BB12: Burnl 1B 124
Penfold L31: Magh 1D 222
Pengarth Rd. BL6: Hor 9D 196
Penguin St. PR1: Prest 7L 115
Penhale Cl. LA3: Heys 1K 27
Penhale Ct. LA3: Heys 1K 27
Penhale Gdns. LA3: Heys 1K 27
Penhill Cl. FY2: Blackp 2D 88
Penistone Av. OL16: Roch 7F 204
Penistone St. BB12: Burnl 3B 124
(off Shale St.)
Penketh Pl. WN8: Skelm 6N 219
Penley Cres. L32: Kirk 8G 223
Pennine Av. PR7: Eux 5N 173
WN3: Wins 8M 221
Pennine Cl. BL6: Hor 8D 196
BL8: Bury 9G 200
FY1: Blackp 4L 227 (6C 88)
Pennine Cres. BB9: Brierf 5G 105
Pennine Dr. OL12: Ward 8F 184
OL16: Milnr 6K 205
Pennine Gdns. PR3: Gars 5L 59
Pennine Gro. BB12: Padi 8H 103
(not continuous)
OL14: Tod 1M 165
Pennine Ho. BB4: Hasl 4G 160
PR1: Prest 5N 229 (9L 115)
Pennine Pl. WN8: Skelm 5M 219
Pennine Pct. OL16: Milnr 8J 205
Pennine Rd. BL6: Hor 8D 196
OL13: Bac 6L 163
PR6: Chor 6G 174
Pennines, The PR2: Fulw 2K 115
Pennine Vw. FY7: Flee 9H 41
LA2: Dolp 6E 38
LA2: Glas 2C 36
LA4: Morec 4B 22
OL15: Littleb 4N 185
OL16: Roch 5D 204
(off East St.)
PR3: Gt E 6A 66
PR4: K'ham 4A 112
Pennine Way BB9: Brierf 5G 105
BB18: Barnw 2L 77
FY6: Stal 5B 56
L32: Kirk 6H 223
PR3: Gt E 6A 66
Pennington Av. L39: Orms 6K 209
Pennington Ct. L39: Orms 6L 209
LA3: Heys 1K 27
Pennington St. BL8: Bury 9D 200
Penn St. OL16: Roch 5C 204
Penny Farthing La. FY5: T Clev 1G 63
Penny Grn. BD24: Sett 3N 35
Penny Ho. La. BB5: Acc 1B 142
PENNYLANDS 2H 219
Penny Lodge La. BB4: Craws 5L 143
PENNY'S PLAT 6E 56
Penny Stone Rd. LA2: Halt 1B 24
Pennystone Rd. FY2: Blackp 7B 62
Penny St. BB1: Blackb 4D 226 (3M 139)
LA1: Lanc 8C 228 (8K 23)
PR1: Prest 4L 229 (9K 115)
Penrhos Av. FY7: Flee 3E 54
Penrhyn Rd. LA1: Lanc 6G 22
Penrith Av. FY5: T Clev 8D 54
LA3: Heys 8L 21
PR8: Ains 1C 206
Penrith Cres. BB8: Colne 8M 85
L31: Magh 9D 216
Penrith Rd. BB8: Colne 8L 85
Penrith St. OL11: Roch 8C 204
Penrod Way LA3: Heys 2J 27
Penrose Av. FY4: Blackp 9F 88
Penrose Pl. WN8: Skelm 7B 220
Pensford Ct. BL2: Bolt 7L 199
Penshaw Cl. BB1: Blackb 8M 119
Penswick Av. FY5: T Clev 2E 62
Pentland Ho. BB4: Hasl 4G 160
(off Bury Rd.)
Pentland Rd. L33: Kirk 6M 223
Penty Pl. PR8: S'port 8H 167
Penwell Fold WN8: Skelm 3B 220
Penwortham Ct. PR1: Penw 4G 134
Penwortham Golf Course 1E 134
Penwortham Hall Gdns. PR1: Penw 5H 135
Penwortham Holme Recreation Cen. 2G 134
PENWORTHAM LANE 6J 135
Penwortham Leisure Cen. 3D 134
Penwortham Res. Pk. PR1: Penw 3G 135
Penwortham Way PR4: W Stake 7F 134
Penyghent Vw. BD24: Sett 3N 35
(off Church St.)
Pen-y-Ghent Way BB18: Barnw 2L 77
Penzance St. BB2: Blackb 6J 139
Peplow Rd. L32: Kirk 8G 223
LA3: Heys 8M 21
Pepper La. WN6: Shev, Stand 1L 213
Peppermint Cl. OL16: Milnr 9M 205
Pepperwood Dr. WN3: Wins 9N 221
Perch Pool La. L40: Scar 1E 188
PR9: S'port 1E 188
Percival Ct. PR8: S'port 8G 167
(off Lord St.)
Percival St. BB1: Blackb 1F 226 (1N 139)
BB3: Darw 4N 157
BB5: Acc 2M 141
Percliff Way BB1: Blackb 1B 140
Percy Rd. LA1: Lanc 1K 29
Percy St. BB2: Blackb 6J 139
BB5: Acc 2C 142
BB5: Osw 3H 141
BB8: Colne 5B 86
BB9: Nelson 3H 105
BL0: Ramsb 9G 180
BL9: Bury 9M 201
FY1: Blackp 3C 88
FY7: Flee 9F 40
OL12: Whitw 9B 164
OL16: Roch 8E 204
PR1: Prest 5M 229 (9K 115)
PR7: Chor 7F 174
Peregrine Dr. BB3: Darw 4L 157
Peregrine Pl. PR26: Leyl 5G 152
Perendale Ri. BL1: Bolt 9E 198
Peridot Cl. BB1: Blackb 7N 119
Perimeter Rd. L33: Know P 9B 224
Peronne Cres. BB1: Blackb 3D 140
Perpignan Way LA1: Lanc 6D 228
Perry Cl. OL11: Roch 8A 204
Perry St. BB3: Darw 5A 158
Pershore OL12: Roch 5B 204
Pershore Gdns. FY3: Blackp 2H 89
Pershore Gro. PR8: Ains 9A 186
Pershore Rd. FY8: L Ann 4H 129
Persia St. BB5: Acc 2M 141
Perth Cl. FY5: T Clev 4F 62
L33: Kirk 4J 223
Perthshire Gro. PR7: Buck V 9A 154
Perth St. BB2: Blackb 5K 139
BB5: Acc 3N 141
BB9: Nelson 1K 105
BB11: Burnl 4B 124
LA1: Lanc 8F 228 (9L 23)
Peter Birtwistle Cl. BB8: Colne 6B 86
Peterfield Rd. PR1: Penw 6G 135
Peter Grime Row BB5: Hunc 7E 122
Peter La. LA5: Yea C 2A 12
Peter Martin St. BL6: Hor 9C 196
Petersan Ct. PR7: Chor 3E 174
Peters Av. L40: Burs 9C 190
Petersbottom La. LA2: Low 1M 33
Peters Bldgs. FY1: Blackp 4D 88
(off Devonshire Rd.)
Peter Scott Gallery 7M 29
Peter's Row BB1: Rish 8J 121
Peter St. BB1: Blackb 1G 226 (2A 140)
(not continuous)
BB4: Rawt 5M 161
BB5: Acc 3N 141
BB8: Colne 7B 86
BB9: Barrf 7H 85
BL9: Bury 9L 201
FY1: Blackp 1L 227 (5C 88)
LA1: Lanc 8D 228 (9K 23)
PR7: Chor 6E 174
WN5: Orr 3L 221
Petre Ct. BB5: Clay M 7L 121
Petre Cres. BB1: Rish 9H 121
Petrel Cl. BB1: Blackb 9L 119
OL11: Roch 6K 203
Petre Rd. BB5: Clay M 8J 121
Petre Wood Cl. BB6: Langh 8D 100
Petre Wood Cres. BB6: Langh 8D 100
Petrie St. OL12: Roch 4C 204
Petros Ho. FY8: L Ann 1E 128
Petts Cres. OL15: Littleb 8K 185
Petunia Cl. PR25: Leyl 5A 154
Petworth Av. WN3: Wins 9N 221
Petworth Rd. PR8: Ains 7B 186
Pexwood Pl. OL14: Tod 4J 165
Pexwood Rd. OL14: Tod 4J 165
Pharos Ct. FY7: Flee 8H 41
(off Pharos Pl.)
Pharos Gro. FY7: Flee 8H 41
Pharos Pl. FY7: Flee 8H 41
Pharos St. FY7: Flee 8H 41
Pharos Street Stop (Tram) 8H 41
Pheasantford Grn. BB10: Burnl 1F 124
Pheasantford St. BB10: Burnl 1F 124
Pheasant Wood Dr. FY5: T Clev 7F 54
Philip Av. PR4: K'ham 5N 111
Philip Cl. WN5: Wigan 6N 221
Philip Dr. PR8: Ains 7C 186
Philips Rd. BB1: Blackb 1B 140
(Glenfield Cl.)
BB1: Blackb 8C 120
(Whitebirk Ind. Est.)
OL13: Weir 9L 145
Philip St. BB3: Darw 6B 158
BB18: Barnw 2M 77
OL11: Roch 8C 204
Phillips La. BB8: Colne 7M 85
L37: Form 1A 214
Phillipstown BB4: Lumb 3C 162
Phillip St. FY4: Blackp 8F 88
Phoenix Ct. OL14: Tod 1N 165
Phoenix Pk. BB1: Blackb 1B 140
Phoenix St. LA1: Lanc 5D 228 (7K 23)
OL12: Roch 4N 203
OL14: Tod 1N 165
OL15: Littleb 8L 185
Phoenix Theatre
Skelmersdale 3M 219
Phoenix Way BB11: Burnl 4A 124
Phyllis St. OL12: Roch 4M 203
Physics Av. LA1: Bail 7M 29
Piazza, The LA1: Lanc 9N 23
Piccadilly LA1: Lanc 3K 29
Piccadilly Cl. LA1: Lanc 4K 29
Piccadilly Gro. LA1: Lanc 4K 29
(off Piccadilly)
Piccadilly Rd. BB11: Burnl 3A 228 (4C 124)
Piccadilly Sq. BB11: Burnl 3A 228 (4C 124)
Piccadilly St. BB4: Hasl 4G 161
Pickard Cl. BB18: Barnw 10G 53
(off Coates La.)
Pickard St. LA1: Lanc 1K 29
Pickering Cl. BL8: Bury 8G 200
FY8: L Ann 1H 129
Pickering Fold BB1: Guide 9B 140
Pickerings, The PR5: Lost H 8M 135
Pickering St. BB9: Brierf 5F 104
Picker St. OL14: Tod 8H 147
PICKHILL 8L 53
Pickles Ct. OL14: Tod 1L 165
Pickles Dr. L40: Burs 9B 190
Pickles St. BB12: Burnl 2B 124
Pickmere Av. FY4: Blackp 1E 108
Pickmere Cl. FY5: T Clev 8G 54
Pickthall Ter. OL14: Tod 2N 165
Pickthorn Cl. LA1: Lanc 4H 23
PICKUP BANK 5G 159
Pickup Fold BB3: Darw 8C 158
Pickup Fold Rd. BB3: Darw 8C 158
Pickup Rd. BB1: Rish 9G 121
Pickup St. BB1: Blackb 3G 226 (3A 140)
BB5: Acc 4M 141
(not continuous)
BB5: Clay M 6M 121
OL13: Bac 5K 163
OL16: Roch 6D 204
Pickworth Way L31: Mell 8G 222
Picton St. BB2: Blackb 8J 139
Pierce Cl. BB12: Padi 9H 103
LA1: Lanc 9H 23
Piercefield Ct. L37: Form 8A 206
Piercefield Rd. L37: Form 7A 206
PIERCY 5D 162
Piercy Higher Mt. BB4: W'foot 4D 162
Piercy Mdw. BB4: W'foot 4D 162
Piercy Mt. BB4: W'foot 4D 162
(off Piercy Rd.)
Piercy Rd. BB4: W'foot 4D 162
Piercy Ter. BB4: W'foot 4D 162
(off Piercy Rd.)
Pier Ho. BB1: Blackb 7F 226
Pier La. LA5: Arn 1F 4
(off The Promenade)
Pierston Av. FY2: Blackp 1C 88
Pier St. FY1: Blackp 5H 227 (7B 88)
Piethorne Cl. OL16: Milnr 9M 205
Pigot St. WN5: Orr 5L 221
Pike Ct. FY7: Flee 3C 54
PIKE HILL 4J 125
Pike La. BD24: Langc 1N 35
L40: Burs 4A 190
Pikelaw Pl. WN8: Skelm 6N 219
PIKE LOWE 6N 155
Pikestone Ct. PR6: Chor 7G 175
Pike St. OL11: Roch 8C 204
Pike Vw. BL6: Hor 9E 196
Pilgrim St. BB9: Nelson 4K 105
Pilgrims Way LA3: Morec 5E 22
Pilkington Dr. BB5: Clay M 6N 121
Pilkington Rd. PR8: S'port 9K 167
Pilkington St. BB1: Blackb 5D 226 (4M 139)
BB2: Blackb 5D 226 (4M 139)
BL0: Ramsb 9G 181
WA11: Rain 4K 225
PILLING 8H 43
Pilling Av. BB5: Bax 6D 142
FY8: L Ann 2H 129
Pilling Barn La. BB4: W'foot 4F 162
OL13: Bac, W'foot 5F 162
Pilling Cl. PR7: Chor 8F 174
PR9: S'port 1M 167
Pilling Ct. FY3: Blackp 1G 89
Pilling Cres. FY3: Blackp 1G 89
Pilling Fld. BL7: Eger 4E 198
PILLING LANE 7N 41
Pilling La. FY6: Pree 8N 41
L31: Lyd 6N 215
PR7: Chor 9E 174
Pilling Pl. WN8: Skelm 6N 219
Pilling St. BB4: Hasl 1G 160
BB4: W'foot 7D 162
BL8: Bury 9H 201
OL12: Roch 5A 204
Pilmuir Rd. BB2: Blackb 6M 139
Pilot St. BB5: Acc 1A 142
Pilsley Cl. WN5: Orr 2K 221
Pimbley Gro. E. L31: Magh 4B 222
Pimbley Gro. W. L31: Magh 4B 222
Pimbo Ind. Est. WN8: Skelm 6N 219
(not continuous)
Pimbo Junc. WN8: Skelm 6B 220
Pimbo La. WN8: Uph 9C 220
Pimbo Rd. WN8: Skelm 6N 219
PIMLICO 9M 73
Pimlico Ind. Area BB7: Clith 9L 73
Pimlico Link Rd. BB7: Clith 9M 73
Pimlico Rd. BB7: Clith 2M 81
Pimlott Rd. BL1: Bolt 9H 199
Pinch Clough Rd. BB4: Lumb 2D 162
PINCOCK 6M 173
Pincock Brow PR7: Eux 5M 173
Pincock St. PR7: Eux 6M 173
Pincroft Cl. PR3: Catt 9N 59
Pincroft La. PR7: Adl 7J 195
Pinder Cl. BB7: Wadd 8H 73
Pinders La. LA6: Holme 1F 6
Pinder St. BB9: Nelson 9K 85
Pine Av. FY1: Blackp 8E 88
L39: Orms 6L 209
PR4: Lit H 3H 151
Pine Cl. BB1: Rish 9H 121
L32: Kirk 7H 223
LA2: Halt 2B 24
PR2: Ribb 5B 116
WN8: N 'urgh 3L 211
WN8: Skelm 2K 219
Pine Ct. PR26: Leyl 7F 152
Pine Cres. BB5: Osw 6M 141
FY3: Blackp 8J 89
(off Newholme Res. Pk.)
FY6: Poul F 9L 63
Pine Crest L39: Aug 1G 217
Pine Dale WA11: Rain 3J 225
Pine Dr. L39: Orms 6L 209
Pine Gro. BB7: Clith 4K 81
L39: Orms 5L 209
PR3: Gars 3N 59
PR6: Chor 3F 174
PR9: S'port 7K 167
Pine Lake Holiday Cen. LA6: Carn 4D 12
(not continuous)
Pine Rd. OL14: Tod 9J 147
Pines, The PR26: Leyl 7C 152
Pines Cl. PR5: Bam B 3E 154
Pine St. BB1: Blackb 1A 140
BB3: Darw 7B 158
BB4: Hasl 4H 161
BB9: Nelson 2K 105
BB11: Burnl 3F 228 (4F 124)
LA1: Lanc 7J 23
LA4: Morec 4C 22
OL13: Bac 6L 163
OL15: Littleb 8L 185
OL16: Milnr 9L 205
OL16: Roch 6E 204
Pine Vw. WN3: Wins 9L 221
Pine Walks PR2: Lea 8N 113
Pineway PR2: Fulw 5F 114
Pinewood BB2: Blackb 8G 138
WN8: Skelm 9A 212
Pinewood Av. FY2: Blackp 7E 62
FY5: T Clev 3H 63
FY6: Pree 8N 41
LA2: Brookh 3J 25
LA4: Morec 2F 22
LA5: Bolt S 7K 15
PR3: Brou 7F 94
Pinewood Cl. LA2: Lanc 5J 29
PR8: S'port 4B 188
Pinewood Cres. BL0: Ramsb 3G 200
FY8: L Ann 4K 129
PR25: Leyl 7H 153
WN5: Orr 5H 221
Pinewood Dr. BB5: Acc 1C 142
BB9: Nelson 3L 105
Pinewood Gdns. L33: Kirk 5K 223
Pinewood Rd. PR1: Penw 6K 135
PINFOLD 1F 208
Pinfold BB9: Barrf 6J 85
BL0: Eden 1J 181
PR4: Longt 8L 133
Pinfold, The BD23: Wig 10M 35
Pinfold Cl. PR2: Fulw 4A 116
PR8: Ains 1B 206

Pinfold Ct.—Preston Rd.

Pinfold Ct. BD23: Garg 3M 53
LA1: Lanc 6K 23
Pinfold Cres. L32: Kirk 9M 223
Pinfold La. L40: Scar 2D 208
LA1: Lanc 6K 23
PR3: Inskip 7G 67
PR3: Longr 6J 97
PR4: Inskip 1F 92
PR8: Ains 1A 206
(not continuous)
Pinfold Pl. BB9: Nelson 1M 105
PR4: K'ham 4L 111
(off Best St.)
WN8: Skelm 7A 220
Pinfold Rd. L39: Orms 8M 209
Pinfold St. PR1: Prest 9N 115
Pingle Cft. PR6: Clay W 5C 154
Pingwood La. L33: Kirk 4M 223
Pink Pl. BB2: Blackb 5J 139
Pink St. BB12: Burnl 3A 124
Pinnacle Dr. BL7: Eger 3E 198
Pinner La. BB4: Craws 9L 143
Pinners Cl. BL0: Ramsb 7G 181
Pinner Sq. BB4: Craws 9L 143
Pintail Cl. OL12: Roch 3M 203
PR26: Leyl 6C 152
Pintail Way FY8: L Ann 1L 129
Pioneer Cl. BL6: Hor 9C 196
Pioneer St. BL6: Hor 9D 196
OL11: Roch 7D 204
OL14: Wals 8K 165
OL15: Littleb 9L 185
Pioneers Yd. OL16: Milnr 8J 205
Piper Ct. FY4: Blackp 6F 108
Piper Hollin *BB4: Hasl 6H 161*
(off Laneside Rd.)
Piper Lea BB4: W'foot 6E 162
Pipers Cl. OL11: Roch 5H 203
Piper's Height Camping & Caravan Pk.
FY4: Blackp 3L 109
Pipers La. LA6: Claw 2J 7
Pippin Bank *OL13: Bac 6K 163*
(off New Line)
PIPPIN STREET 1G 154
Pippin St. L40: Burs 2L 209
OL13: Bac 6K 163
PR6: Brind 3G 154
Pitcombe Cl. BL1: Bolt 6D 198
Pitfield La. BL2: Bolt 9M 199
Pit Hey Pl. WN8: Skelm 6N 219
Pit La. LA6: H Big, K Lon 6D 8
Pits Farm Av. OL11: Roch 6N 203
Pitshouse OL12: Roch 3J 203
Pitshouse La. OL12: Roch 3J 203
Pitsmead Rd. L32: Kirk 9K 223
Pittman Ct. PR2: Fulw 1L 115
Pittman Way PR2: Fulw 1L 115
(not continuous)
Pittsdale Av. FY3: Blackp 8G 88
Pitts Ho. La. PR9: S'port 6A 168
Pitt St. BB12: Padi 1J 123
LA1: Lanc 6D 228 (8K 23)
OL12: Roch 5C 204
OL14: Tod 2N 165
PR1: Prest 6H 229 (1H 135)
PR9: S'port 8M 167
Pitville St. BB3: Darw 4N 157
Pixmore Av. BL1: Bolt 9H 199
Place De Criel *BB9: Nelson 2H 105*
(off Manchester Rd.)
Plainmoor Dr. FY5: T Clev 4F 62
Plain Pl. BB2: Blackb 7C 226 (5M 139)
Plane St. BB1: Blackb 1A 140
OL13: Bac 3K 163
OL14: Tod 9H 147
Planet Earth Cen. 3C 164
Plane Tree Cl. BB11: Burnl 7B 124
Plane Tree Rd. BB1: Blackb 1A 140
Plantain Wlk. LA3: Morec 6B 22
Plantation, The BD23: Tos 1H 51
Plantation Av. FY6: K Sea 8L 41
LA5: Arn 3G 4
Plantation Gro. LA5: Arn 3G 5
Plantation La. LA2: Abb 4L 39
Plantation Mill OL13: Bac 6K 163
Plantation Rd. BB2: Blackb 7J 139
BB5: Acc, Hunc 2C 142
(not continuous)
BL7: Edgw 6L 179
L40: Burs 9N 189
Plantation Sq. BB5: Acc 2C 142
Plantation St. BB4: Rawt 5N 161
BB5: Acc 3B 142
BB9: Nelson 1K 105
BB10: Burnl 2E 124
OL13: Bac 7G 163
Plantation Vw. BL9: Summ 2H 201
OL13: Weir 1K 163
Planters, The *L30: N'ton 6A 222*
(off Harvester Way)
Plant St. BB5: Osw 5K 141
PR2: Ash R 8F 114
Platform, The 3N 21
Platform 1 Art Gallery 2K 165
Platform Gallery, The *2L 81*
(off Railway Vw.)
Platt Cl. BB5: Acc 3N 141
OL16: Milnr 8K 205
Platting La. OL11: Roch 9D 204
Platt La. WN1: Stand 9D 194
Platton Gro. LA4: Morec 3C 22
Platts La. L40: Burs 2B 210
Platts La. Ind. Est. L40: Burs 2B 210
Platt St. FY1: Blackp 4C 88
Playfair St. BL1: Bolt 7F 198
Playhouse Theatre, The 5J 229 (9J 115)
Plaza Shop. Cen. *LA4: Morec 3B 22*
(off Queen St.)
Pleasant Gro. FY5: T Clev 1H 63
Pleasant Pl. BB11: Burnl 3C 228 (4D 124)
Pleasant St. BB4: Hasl 4G 160
BL8: Bury 9E 200
FY1: Blackp 3B 88
FY8: L Ann 5A 130
OL10: Heyw 9G 203
Pleasant Street Stop (Tram) 3B 88
Pleasant Vw. BB2: Blackb 6A 140
BB3: Hodd 6F 158
BB4: W'foot 6D 162
BB7: B'ton 6H 101
BB8: Foul 2B 86
BB18: Earl 3F 78
FY4: Blackp 5G 108
OL13: Bac 8G 162
OL14: Tod 2L 165
(off Mt. Pleasant)
PR4: Newt 7E 112
PR6: Withn 6B 156
PR7: Copp 3B 194
PLEASINGTON 7D 138
Pleasington Av. PR3: Gars 6A 60
Pleasington Cl. BB2: Blackb 4J 139
FY4: Blackp 1G 109
Pleasington Crematorium
BB2: Pleas 5E 138
Pleasington Golf Course 7D 138
Pleasington Gro. BB10: Burnl 4H 125
Pleasington La. BB2: Fenis, Pleas 7D 138
Pleasington Old Hall Wood & Wildlife Garden
5D 138
Pleasington Station (Rail) 7D 138
Pleasington St. BB2: Blackb 4J 139
Pleasure Beach 2B 108
Pleasure Beach Station (Rail) 3B 108
Pleasure Beach Stop (Tram) 2A 108
Pleasure Island 3D 128
Pleck Farm Av. BB1: Blackb 9M 119
PLECKGATE 8L 119
Pleckgate Fold BB1: Blackb 8L 119
Pleckgate Rd. BB1: Blackb 9M 119
Pleck Pl. FY6: Carl 5H 63
Pleck Rd. BB5: Acc 2B 142
Plessington Ct. *PR3: Longr 3K 97*
(off Brewery St.)
Plevna Rd. PR1: Prest 9M 115
Plex La. L39: Hals 5N 207
Plex Moss La. L39: Hals 3D 206
Plex Moss La. Caravan Pk.
PR8: Ains 3D 206
Plock Grn. PR7: Chor 9E 174
Ploughlands, The PR2: Ash R 8B 114
Plough La. L40: Lath 9D 210
Ploughmans Ct. PR2: Grim 9F 96
Plough's Yd. PR1: Prest 5J 229
Plover Cl. FY5: T Clev 7G 54
OL11: Roch 6J 203
Plover Dr. BL9: Bury 9N 201
LA3: Heys 2L 27
Plover St. BB12: Burnl 3B 124
PR1: Prest 1N 229 (7L 115)
Plovers Way FY3: Blackp 3H 89
Plover Ter. *BB5: Osw 5L 141*
(off Heys)
Plover Vw. *BB12: Burnl 3B 124*
(off Plover St.)
Plox Brow PR4: Tarl 9E 150
Plumbe St. BB11: Burnl 4E 228 (4E 124)
Plumpton Av. FY4: Blackp 4F 108
Plumpton Cl. FY4: Blackp 2K 109
Plumpton Dr. BL9: Bury 7K 201
Plumpton Fld. PR4: Woodp 8B 94
Plumpton La. L39: Hals 3L 207
PR4: Gt P, Lit P 2D 110
Plumpton Rd. PR2: Ash R 7F 114
Plumtree Cl. PR2: Fulw 3M 115
Plunge Rd. BL0: Eden 3K 181
Plungington Rd. PR1: Prest 1G 229 (6G 115)
PR2: Fulw 6G 115
Plymouth Av. FY7: Flee 4C 54
Plymouth Gro. PR6: Chor 6G 175
Plymouth Rd. FY3: Blackp 1E 88
Poachers Trail FY8: L Ann 1K 129
Poachers Way FY5: T Clev 8G 54
Pochard Pl. FY5: T Clev 2F 62
Pockets Leisure Cen. 6K 165
Pocklington St. BB5: Acc 6C 142
Poets Rd. BB12: Burnl 2L 123
Pointer, The LA1: Lanc 9D 228 (1K 29)
Pointer Ct. LA1: Lanc 1K 29
Pointer Gro. LA2: Halt 1C 24
Point Retail Pk., The OL16: Roch 6D 204
Poke St. WN5: Wigan 5L 221
Poland St. BB5: Acc 2M 141
Polefield PR2: Fulw 2H 115
Pole La. BB3: Darw 8C 158
Pole St. PR1: Prest 5M 229 (9K 115)
Police Flats OL14: Tod 2L 165
Police St. BB3: Darw 6A 158
Police Yd. *LA2: H Ben 6L 19*
(off Main St.)
Pollard Gro. OL15: Littleb 6M 185
Pollard Pl. LA1: Lanc 4L 23
Pollard Row BB12: Fence 1D 104
BB12: S'stone 9D 102
Pollards La. BL9: Summ 3H 201
Pollard St. BB5: Acc 1B 142
BB11: Burnl 4B 124
OL14: Tod 9H 147
PR1: Prest 4H 229 (9H 115)
Pollux Ga. FY8: L Ann 4J 129
Polly Grn. OL12: Roch 2C 204
Polperro Dr. PR4: Frec 2M 131
Pomfret St. BB2: Blackb 8B 226 (5L 139)
BB11: Burnl 2A 228 (3C 124)
Pomona St. OL11: Roch 8C 204
Pompian Brow PR26: Breth 9J 151
Pond Cl. PR4: Tarl 1E 170
Pond Gdns. FY6: Carl 5H 63
Pond St. LA5: Carn 8A 12
Pond Ter. LA5: Carn 8A 12
Pondwater Cl. L32: Kirk 9K 223
Pontins Southport Cen. PR8: Ains 7A 186
Pont St. BB9: Nelson 3H 105
Pool Brow Caravan Pk. FY6: Sing 7C 64
Pool Ct. FY7: Flee 3C 54
Poole Av. PR7: Buck V 9C 154
Poole End BB7: Whall 5J 101
Poole Rd. PR2: Fulw 5K 115
Poole St. BB1: Blackb 3C 140
Pool Foot La. FY6: Sing 7C 64
POOL HEY 2A 188
Pool Hey Caravan Pk. PR9: S'port 1B 188
Pool Hey La. PR8: S'port 2N 187
PR9: S'port 2N 187
Poolhill Cl. FY5: T Clev 4E 62
Pool Ho. Ct. PR2: Ingol 3D 114
Pool Ho. La. PR2: Ingol 4C 114
Pool La. PR4: Frec 4M 131
POOLSIDE 3A 132
Poolside Wlk. PR9: S'port 2B 168
Pool St. PR9: S'port 1B 168
Poot Hall OL12: Roch 2C 204
Pope La. PR1: Penw 6F 134
PR2: Ribb 7B 116
PR4: W Stake 9E 134
Pope Wlk. PR1: Penw 5G 135
Poplar Av. BB6: Gt H 3K 121
BL1: Bolt 9F 198
BL2: Bolt 7J 199
FY3: Blackp 2N 227 (5D 88)
FY6: Poul F 9L 63
OL12: Roch 4N 203
OL14: Tod 9K 147
PR4: K'ham 5M 111
PR4: Longt 8M 133
PR4: Wart 2J 131
PR5: Bam B 7B 136
PR7: Eux 2M 173
WN5: Wigan 5N 221
Poplar Bank PR9: S'port 5K 167
Poplar Cl. BB1: Rish 9H 121
BB5: Osw 5M 141
PR5: Bam B 7B 136
Poplar Ct. FY8: L Ann 3E 128
WN8: Skelm 5K 219
Poplar Dr. L32: Kirk 7J 223
PR1: Penw 3F 134
PR3: Longr 2J 97
PR4: Frec 3M 131
PR7: Copp 4B 194
WN8: Skelm 2K 219
Poplar Gdns. *PR3: Catt 2B 68*
(off Woburn Way)
Poplar Gro. BL0: Ramsb 7J 181
PR2: Ribb 5C 116
PR5: Bam B 7B 136
Poplars, The BL8: Bury 7H 201
L40: Burs 2C 210
OL13: Bac 4K 163
(off Burnley Rd.)
PR7: Adl 7H 195
Poplar St. BB1: Blackb 1N 139
BB4: Hasl 4G 161
BB9: Nelson 1K 105
PR7: Chor 8F 174
PR8: S'port 9L 167
Poplar Ter. BB4: Rawt 1L 161
Poppy Av. PR6: Chor 4F 174
Poppy Cl. PR8: S'port 3H 187
Poppyfield PR4: Cott 3C 114
Poppyfields PR4: Hesk B 3C 150
Poppyfield Vw. OL11: Roch 4J 203
Poppy La. L39: Bick 2N 217
Poppy Nook PR9: Banks 2F 168
Porritt Av. LA1: Lanc 7A 228 (8H 23)
Porritt Cl. OL11: Roch 7J 203
Porritt St. BL9: Bury 9M 201
(not continuous)
Porritt Way BL0: Ramsb 7H 181
Portal Gro. BB12: Burnl 3N 123
Porter Pl. PR1: Prest 8L 229 (2K 135)
Porters Row FY6: Stal 5B 56
Porter St. BB5: Acc 2M 141
BL9: Bury 5L 201
PR1: Prest 2N 229 (8L 115)
Porter St. E. PR4: Wesh 3L 111
Porters Wood Cl. WN5: Orr 4L 221
Portfield Bar BB7: Whall 8M 101
Portfield La. BB7: Whall 7M 101
Portfield Rd. BB7: Whall 6L 101
Portland Ct. FY8: L Ann 8G 109
Portland Dr. LA3: Morec 6B 22
Portland Ind. Est. *BL9: Bury 9M 201*
(off Portland St.)
Portland Pl. LA1: Lanc 9C 228 (9K 23)
Portland Rd. BB6: Langh 1C 120
FY1: Blackp 4M 227 (6D 88)
Portland St. BB2: Blackb 5K 139
BB3: Darw 9B 158
BB5: Acc 2N 141
BB8: Colne 6C 86
BB9: Barrf 8H 85
BB9: Nelson 2H 105
BL9: Bury 9M 201
LA1: Lanc 9C 228 (9K 23)
PR1: Prest 1G 135
PR7: Chor 6F 174
PR8: S'port 8G 167
WN5: Wigan 5N 221
Portman St. PR1: Prest 8L 115
Port of Heysham LA3: Heys 2H 27
Port of Heysham Ind. Est. LA3: Heys 1J 27
Porton Rd. L32: Kirk 9H 223
Portree Cl. PR2: Fulw 4M 115
Portree Cres. BB1: Blackb 5D 140
Portree Rd. FY2: Blackp 5E 62
Port Royal Av. LA1: Lanc 9G 22
Portsmouth Av. BB10: Burnl 8J 105
Portsmouth Cl. FY5: T Clev 8F 54
Portsmouth Dr. PR6: Chor 6G 175
Port Way LA3: Heys 1J 27
PR1: Prest 9F 114
PR2: Ash R 9F 114
Portway FY2: Blackp 5E 62
Postern Ga. Rd. LA2: Quern 7D 24
Post Horse La. LA2: Horn 7C 18
Post La. PR4: Wart 2L 131
Post Office Av. *PR9: S'port 7H 167*
(off Anchor St.)
Post Office Bldgs. *BB18: Barnw 2M 77*
(off Station Rd.)
Post Office Row LA6: W'ouse 1M 19
Post Office St. *BB4: Craws 9M 143*
(off Burnley Rd.)
Post Office Yd. *BB8: Colne 6B 86*
(off Market Pl.)
POT GREEN 2F 200
POT HOUSE 4C 158
Pot Ho. La. BB3: Darw 4C 158
BB5: Osw 7L 141
OL12: Ward 9C 184
Potter La. PR5: H Walt 2E 136
PR5: Sam 8G 116
Potter Pl. WN8: Skelm 6A 220
POTTERS BROOK 9M 37
Pottery, The L31: Mell 8F 222
Poulton Av. BB5: Acc 9N 121
FY8: L Ann 9G 109
Poulton Bus. Pk. FY6: Poul F 8M 63
Poulton Ct. PR9: S'port 7M 167
Poulton Cres. PR5: Hogh 5F 136
Poulton Dr. FY6: Poul F 8M 63
Poulton Gdns. FY6: Poul F 8M 63
Poulton Gro. FY7: Flee 9G 41
POULTON-LE-FYLDE 8K 63
Poulton-le-Fylde Golf Course 6K 63
Poulton-le-Fylde Station (Rail) 7K 63
Poulton Old Rd. FY3: Blackp 1F 88
Poulton Plaiz Holiday Pk. (High Compley Pk.)
FY6: Poul F 1H 89
Poulton Rd. FY3: Blackp 2E 88
FY6: Carl 6H 63
FY7: Flee 1E 54
LA4: Morec 3B 22
PR9: S'port 7M 167
Poulton Sports Cen. 6L 63
Poulton Sq. LA4: Morec 2B 22
Poulton St. FY7: Flee 9G 41
PR2: Ash R 8F 114
PR4: K'ham 4M 111
Poverty La. L31: Magh 2D 222
Powderhouse La. LA1: Lanc 5G 23
LA2: Slyne 4G 23
Powder Works La. L31: Magh 8H 217
Powell Av. FY4: Blackp 1D 108
Powell Ho. *BL9: Bury 9L 201*
(off Walmersley Rd.)
Powell St. BB3: Darw 5A 158
BB11: Burnl 5A 228 (5C 124)
BB18: Barnw 1M 77
Powerleague
Blackburn 7B 140
Powis Dr. PR4: Tarl 7E 150
Powis Rd. PR2: Ash R 9D 114
Powys Cl. BB4: Hasl 6G 161
Poynter St. PR1: Prest 8M 115
Prairie Cres. BB10: Burnl 8F 104
Pratt St. BB10: Burnl 9E 104
PREESALL 1A 56
Preesall Cl. FY8: L Ann 1H 129
PR2: Ash R 8B 114
PR9: S'port 1M 167
Preesall Mill Ind. Est. FY6: Pree 2A 56
Preesall Moss La. FY6: Pree 2C 56
PREESALL PARK 3B 56
Preesall Rd. PR2: Ash R 8B 114
Preese Gdns. PR4: Elsw 1M 91
Prefect Pl. WN5: Wigan 3M 221
Premier Bowl 6F 166
Premier Bus. Pk. BB6: Gt H 3K 121
Premier Ho. FY6: Poul F 8M 63
Premier Way BB1: Guide 8C 140
FY6: Poul F 8M 63
Prenton Gdns. FY5: T Clev 4G 62
Prenton Way BL8: Tott 8E 200
Prescot Grn. L39: Orms 9J 209
Prescot Pl. FY3: Blackp 8G 89
FY5: T Clev 1J 63
Prescot Rd. L31: Magh, Mell 6H 223
L39: Aug, Orms 1J 217
Prescott Av. L40: Ruff 2E 190
Prescott La. WN5: Orr 2L 221
Prescott Rd. WN8: Skelm 6C 220
Prescott St. BB10: Burnl 4G 124
OL16: Roch 3F 204
Press Rd. FY8: L Ann 9D 108
Prestbury Av. FY4: Blackp 4C 108
PR8: Ains 8B 186
Prestbury Dr. LA3: Morec 6B 22
Prestbury Rd. BL1: Bolt 8G 198
Prestige Indoor Karting 7M 85
PRESTON 5L 229 (9K 115)
Preston Beck *BB18: Earl 2E 78*
(off Aspen La.)
Preston Crematorium PR2: Ribb 4E 116
Preston Ent. Cen. PR1: Prest 2K 229 (8J 115)
Preston Golf Course 4L 115
Preston Junction Local Nature Reserve 4J 135
Preston Lancaster Rd. LA1: Bail 8L 29
LA2: Fort, Gal, Ham G 4L 37
LA2: Gal 8L 29
Preston New Rd. BB2: Blackb 3A 226 (3L 139)
BB2: Mellor, Mellor B 8K 117
FY3: Blackp 8F 88
FY4: Blackp 8F 88
PR4: Clif, Frec 1A 132
PR4: Gt P, Lit P, Westby 2L 109
PR5: Sam 8D 116
(not continuous)
PR9: S'port 4N 167
Preston Nook PR7: E'ton 9F 172
Preston North End FC 1N 229 (7L 115)
Preston Office Cen. PR1: Prest 5L 229
Preston Old Rd. BB2: Blackb, Fenis 9D 138
FY3: Blackp 8E 88
PR4: Clif 8G 113
PR4: Frec 1A 132
Preston Portway (Park & Ride) 1G 135
Preston Rd. FY8: L Ann 5C 130
PR2: Grim 1E 116
PR3: Longr 8H 97
(Alston La.)
PR3: Longr 3M 97
(Lower Rd.)
PR3: Ribc 4B 98
PR4: Crossm 1B 92
PR5: Bam B 1C 154
PR6: Bam B, Chor, Clay W, Whit W 4D 154
PR7: Char R 2L 193
PR7: Chor 4D 154
PR7: Copp 4M 193
PR9: S'port 6L 167
PR25: Leyl 5L 153
WN6: Stand 9N 193

Preston Sports Arena—Queen St.

Preston Sports Arena 6A 114
Preston Station (Rail) 7H 229 (1H 135)
Preston St. BB3: Darw 4N 157
FY7: Flee 9H 41
LA5: Carn 8A 12
OL12: Roch 4N 203
PR4: K'ham 4N 111
PR7: Chor 4E 174
Preston Street Stop (Tram) 9H 41
Preston Technology Cen.
PR1: Prest 9G 114
Prestwich St. BB11: Burnl 5B 124
Prestwood Pl. WN8: Skelm 7C 220
Pretoria St. OL12: Roch 4N 203
PR5: Bam B 8A 136
Price Cl. LA1: Lanc 5J 23
Price St. FY1: Blackp 9B 88
PRICKSHAW 8M 183
Prickshaw La. OL12: Roch 8M 183
Priestfield FY5: T Clev 4G 62
Priestfield Av. BB8: Colne 6M 85
Priesthouse Cl. L37: Form 9A 206
Priesthouse La. L37: Form 9A 206
PRIEST HUTTON 2H 13
Priestley Nook BB5: Acc 3B 142
(off Royds St.)
Priestly Ter. BB4: Water 8E 144
(off Burnley Rd.)
PRIESTWELL 1M 165
Priestwell St. OL14: Tod 1M 165
Primary Av. L30: N'ton 6A 222
Primative Ter. BB4: Craws 9L 143
PRIMET BRIDGE 8M 85
Primet Bri. BB8: Colne 7N 85
Primet Bus. Cen. BB8: Colne 7M 85
Primet Hgts. BB8: Colne 8M 85
(off Wackersall Rd.)
Primet Hill BB8: Colne 7N 85
Primet St. BB8: Colne 7N 85
PRIMROSE
BB7 5K 81
LA1 9F 228 (9L 23)
Primrose Av. FY4: Blackp 3D 108
Primrose Bank BB1: Blackb 2E 226 (2N 139)
BB12: Read 8C 102
BL8: Tott 6D 200
FY2: Blackp 5F 62
LA6: Holme 1G 7
OL13: Bac 7G 162
(off Tunstead Rd.)
Primrose Bank Caravan Pk. PR4: Weet 4E 90
Primrose Cl. BB2: Blackb 6J 139
BL2: Bolt 9N 199
L37: Form 7B 206
PR4: Hesk B 3C 150
PR9: S'port 9B 148
Primrose Cotts. BB4: Craws 6M 143
(off Goodshaw Fold Cl.)
PR3: Cald V 5H 61
Primrose Ct. BB1: Blackb 3E 226
LA1: Lanc 9F 228
LA4: Morec 3B 22
Primrose Dr. BB1: Blackb 3E 226 (3N 139)
BL9: Bury 9B 202
Primrose Gro. PR1: Prest 6M 115
WN5: Wigan 4N 221
PRIMROSE HILL 4E 208
Primrose Hill BB1: Mellor 6H 119
BB2: Mellor 6H 119
BB8: Colne 6C 86
PR1: Prest 1L 135
Primrose Hill Cotts.
OL10: Heyw 9L 203
Primrose Hill Rd. PR7: Eux 3L 173
Primrose La. PR1: Prest 6M 115
WN6: Stand 2N 213
Primrose Rd. BB7: Clith 5K 81
PR1: Prest 6M 115
Primrose St. BB3: Darw 7B 158
BB5: Acc 4N 141
BB7: Clith 4K 81
BB9: Brierf 5F 104
(off Halifax Rd.)
BB10: Burnl 9G 104
BL1: Bolt 9F 198
LA1: Lanc 8E 228 (9L 23)
LA4: Morec 3B 22
OL12: Roch 5A 204
OL13: Bac 7G 162
PR6: Chor 6F 174
Primrose Ter. BB2: Blackb 6J 139
BB3: Darw 7B 158
BB6: Langh 9C 100
(off Whalley New Rd.)
FY4: Blackp 5G 108
Primrose Way BB5: Chur 1L 141
FY6: Carl 5H 63
Primula Dr. BB3: Lwr D 9A 140
Primula St. BL1: Bolt 9F 198
Prince Av. LA5: Carn 9B 12
Prince Charles Gdns. PR8: Birk 9F 166
Prince Lee Mdws. BB3: Darw 7B 158
Princes Ct. BL0: Ramsb 8H 181
(off Silver St.)
LA4: Morec 2E 22
(off Bare La.)
PR1: Penw 2E 134
Princes Cres. LA4: Morec 1E 22
Princes Dr. PR2: Fulw 3H 115
Princes Gdns. PR8: S'port 8L 167
Prince's Pk. WN6: Shev 8J 213
Princes Reach PR2: Ash R 9D 114
Princes Rd. FY8: L Ann 4K 129
PR1: Penw 2E 134
PR5: Walt D 3A 136
Princess Alexandra Way
LA3: Heys 2J 27
Princess Av. BB7: Clith 2M 81
FY6: Poul F 8K 63
LA1: Lanc 1K 29
OL12: Roch 1F 204
PR4: Wesh 3L 111
Princess Ct. FY1: Blackp 5J 227 (7B 88)
PR9: S'port 6K 167
Princess Gdns. BB2: Fenis 9E 138
Princess Pde. FY1: Blackp 1H 227 (4B 88)
Princess Rd. FY5: T Clev 1C 62
OL16: Roch 6G 205
PR6: And 5K 195
WN6: Stand 8M 213
Princess St. BB2: Blackb 6K 139
BB4: Hasl 5G 161
BB5: Acc 2M 141
BB5: Chur 2L 141
BB6: Gt H 4K 121
BB7: Whall 5J 101
BB8: Colne 6N 85
BB9: Nelson 3H 105
BB12: Padi 1G 122
FY1: Blackp 5H 227 (7B 88)
OL12: Roch 5C 204
OL12: Whitw 6N 183
(off Albert St.)
OL13: Bac 5K 163
PR1: Prest 7N 229 (1L 135)
PR5: Bam B 8B 136
PR5: Lost H 9L 135
PR7: Chor 8F 174
PR25: Leyl 6L 153
Princes St. BB1: Rish 8H 121
BB2: Blackb 5B 226 (4L 139)
PR8: S'port 8G 167
Princess Way BB12: Burnl 1C 228 (2D 124)
PR7: Eux 4N 173
Prince St. BB3: Darw 6N 157
BB11: Burnl 4C 124
BL0: Ramsb 8H 181
OL13: Bac 8A 164
OL16: Roch 8D 204
Princes Way FY5: T Clev 3C 62
FY7: Flee 2C 54
Princeway FY4: Blackp 2C 108
Pringle Bank LA5: Wart 4A 12
Pringle Ct. PR3: Gars 5N 59
(off Park Hill Rd.)
Pringle St. BB1: Blackb 7F 226 (5N 139)
OL16: Roch 6D 204
Pringle Wood PR3: Brou 8F 94
Prinny Hill Rd. BB4: Hasl 4F 160
Printer's Ct. BL7: Turt 1K 199
Printers Fold BB12: Burnl 3K 123
Printers La. BL2: Bolt 7J 199
Printshop La. BB3: Darw 9A 158
Print Works Cotts.
BB5: Clay M 5L 121
(off Riverside Vw.)
Priors Cl. BB2: Blackb 2H 139
Priorsgate LA3: Morec 6C 22
Prior's Oak Cotts. PR1: Penw 3F 134
Priors Wlk. BB7: Saw 3D 74
Priorswood Pl. WN8: Skelm 7C 220
Priory Chase BB9: Nelson 2L 105
Priory Cl. BB1: Blackb 4E 140
BB2: Pleas 6D 138
BB4: Newc 5C 162
L37: Form 1B 214
L40: Burs 8B 190
LA1: Lanc 6B 228
LA3: Morec 6C 22
PR1: Penw 2F 134
PR4: Tarl 9E 150
PR25: Leyl 5M 153
WN5: Wigan 6L 221
Priory Ct. BB11: Burnl 7F 124
FY1: Blackp 3L 227 (6C 88)
FY8: L Ann 1E 128
PR8: S'port 8F 166
Priory Cres. PR1: Penw 2F 134
Priory Dr. BB3: Darw 6C 158
Priory Gdns. PR3: Scor 7B 46
PR8: Birk 1F 186
Priory Ga. FY4: Blackp 4C 108
Priory Grange BB3: Darw 7C 158
PR8: Birk 1G 186
Priory Gro. L39: Orms 8J 209
Priory La. LA2: Horn 7B 18
PR1: Penw 3E 134
Priory M. FY8: L Ann 1K 129
PR8: S'port 8F 166
Priory Nook WN8: Uph 4F 220
Priory Pl. BB3: Darw 7C 158
Priory Rd. WN8: Uph 4F 220
Priory St. BB9: Nelson 1K 105
PR2: Ash R 9G 115
Priory Vw. OL14: Tod 1L 165
(off Garden St.)
Priory Wlk. LA1: Lanc 6E 228
Priory Way BB18: Barnw 2L 77
Pritchard St. BB2: Blackb 6L 139
BB11: Burnl 5A 228 (5C 124)
Private La. BB4: Hasl 7H 161
Private Rd. PR5: Hogh 7J 137
Procter Moss Rd.
LA2: Abb, Ell 6A 30
Procter St. BB2: Blackb 8E 226 (5N 139)
Proctor Cl. BB9: Brierf 5K 105
WN5: Wigan 2N 221
Proctor Cft. BB8: Traw 9E 86
Proctor's Brow LA2: Tat 9J 19
Proctors Row BD24: Sett 3N 35
(off Mill Cl.)
Progress Av. BB1: Blackb 1A 140
Progress Bus. Pk. PR4: K'ham 5M 111
Progress Ct. FY3: Blackp 2G 89
Progress Rd. BB9: Nelson 8K 85
Progress St. BB3: Darw 6B 158
PR6: Chor 6G 174
Progress Way FY4: Blackp 4F 108
Promenade FY1: Blackp 9H 227 (6B 88)
FY4: Blackp 2A 108
FY5: T Clev 5C 62
FY6: K Sea 7L 41
PR8: Ains 7A 186
PR8: S'port 7G 167
PR9: S'port 7G 167
Promenade, The LA5: Arn 1E 4
Promenade Rd. FY7: Flee 8G 40
Prospect Av. BB3: Darw 5M 157
BL2: Bolt 9M 199
LA2: Hest B 8J 15
PR5: Lost H 8L 135
Prospect Cl. BB2: Blackb 8J 139
Prospect Ct. BL8: Tott 6E 200
PR3: Catt 1A 68
PR3: Longr 4K 97
Prospect Dr. LA2: Hest B 8J 15
Prospect Farm Caravan Site BB8: Colne 8A 86
Prospect Gdns. BB3: Darw 5M 157
Prospect Gro. LA4: Morec 4C 22
Prospect Hill BB4: Hasl 5F 160
BB4: Rawt 4M 161
(off Prospect Rd.)
Prospect Ho. Dr. PR6: Wheel 7J 155
Prospect Pl. PR1: Penw 4H 135
PR2: Ash R 8E 114
WN8: Skelm 6C 220
Prospect Rd. BB4: Rawt 4M 161
Prospect St. BB4: W'foot 6D 162
BB6: Gt H 4K 121
LA1: Lanc 9E 228 (9L 23)
OL11: Roch 9B 204
OL15: Littleb 8L 185
Prospect Ter. BB1: Belt 1F 158
BB4: Rawt 2L 161
(off East St.)
BB4: W'foot 6D 162
(off Prospect St.)
BB5: Hunc 7D 122
(off Enfield Rd.)
BB9: Barrf 7H 85
BB11: Dunn 4N 143
BD24: Sett 3N 35
(off Duke St.)
BL8: Bury 9J 201
OL12: Roch 3G 202
OL13: Bac 8J 163
PR6: Withn 7B 156
Prospect Vw. BB4: Rawt 4M 161
PR5: Lost H 9L 135
Prospect Vs. BB4: W'foot 6D 162
(off Prospect St.)
Prospect Way L30: N'ton 7A 222
Provence Av. BB6: Old L 4C 100
Providence St. BB1: Blackb 9A 120
OL14: Wals 8K 165
Prudy Hill FY6: Poul F 7K 63
Prunella Dr. BB3: Lwr D 9A 140
Pudding La. OL14: Tod 6F 146
Pudding Pie Nook La. PR3: Goos 6J 95
Puddle Ho. La. FY6: Poul F 2M 89
PUDSEY 6E 146
Pudsey Rd. OL14: Tod 7F 146
Pulborough Cl. BL8: Bury 6G 201
Pullman St. OL11: Roch 8C 204
Pump Ho. La. PR26: Leyl 9C 152
Pump St. BB2: Blackb 6A 226 (4K 139)
BB7: Clith 3K 81
BB11: Burnl 3C 124
PR1: Prest 4L 229 (9K 115)
Punnell's La. L31: Lyd 6M 215
Punstock La. BB3: Darw 7N 157
Punstock Rd. BB3: Darw 6N 157
Purbeck Dr. BL8: Bury 7H 201
Purdon St. BL9: Bury 7L 201
Pye Busk LA2: H Ben 6M 19
Pye Busk Cl. LA2: H Ben 6M 19
Pye's Bri. La. LA7: Hale 1C 6
PYGON'S HILL 4C 216
Pygon's Hill La. L31: Lyd 4C 216

Q

Quail Holme Rd. FY6: K Sea 8K 41
Quaker Brook La. PR5: Hogh 5J 137
Quakerfields BB3: Darw 5A 158
Quaker La. BB3: Darw 5A 158
Quakersfield BL8: Tott 5D 200
Quakers Pl. WN6: Stand 3N 213
Quakers Ter. WN6: Stand 1N 213
Quakers Vw. BB9: Brierf 5E 104
Quality Row BB7: Hurst G 1M 99
Quantock Cl. WN3: Wins 9M 221
Quantock Ho. BB4: Hasl 4G 160
(off Bury Rd.)
Quarlton Dr. BL8: Hawk 2A 200
Quarry Bank BB4: Hasl 6E 160
L33: Kirk 7L 223
PR3: Gars 6N 59
Quarrybank FY5: T Clev 3F 62
Quarry Bank St. BB12: Burnl 2A 124
Quarry Cl. L33: Kirk 7L 223
Quarry Dale L33: Kirk 7L 223
Quarry Dr. L39: Aug 3H 217
Quarry Farm Ct. BB7: Chatb 7C 74
Quarry Grn. L33: Kirk 7L 223
Quarry Grn. Flats L33: Kirk 7L 223
Quarry Hey L33: Kirk 7L 223
Quarry Hill OL12: Roch 2B 204
Quarry Hill Nature Reserve 4J 105
Quarry Junc. WN8: Skelm 3N 219
Quarry Mt. L39: Orms 6M 209
Quarry Mt. M. LA1: Lanc 8E 228 (9L 23)
Quarry Rd. LA1: Lanc 8D 228 (9K 23)
LA2: Brookh 3L 25
LA2: Halt 2B 24
PR6: Birns 8A 156
PR6: Chor 8G 175
Quarryside Dr. L33: Kirk 7M 223
Quarry St. BB1: Blackb 3F 226 (3N 139)
BB5: Acc 3B 142
BB11: Hapt 7H 123
BB12: Padi 9J 103
BL0: Ramsb 8J 181
(not continuous)
OL12: Roch 4B 204
OL12: Whitw 9B 164
OL13: Bac 5L 163
Quarry Vw. OL12: Roch 2B 204
Quayle Av. FY4: Blackp 1E 108
Quays, The L40: Burs 8C 190
Quayside BB1: Blackb 6F 226
(off Merchants Quay)
FY7: Flee 8J 41
(Queen's Ter.)
FY7: Flee 1H 55
(Seaview Way)
Quayside Ct. PR2: Ash R 9D 114
Quay West FY8: L Ann 3E 128
Quebec Av. FY2: Blackp 8D 62
Quebec Rd. BB2: Blackb 9J 119
Quebec St. OL14: Wals 6K 165
Queen Anne St. BB4: Hasl 4F 160
PR8: S'port 7H 167
(off Market St.)
Queen Charlotte Vs. PR8: Ains 8C 186
(off Station Rd.)
Queen Elizabeth Ct. LA4: Morec 3A 22
(off West End Rd.)
Queen Elizabeth Cres. BB5: Acc 3B 142
Queen Mary Av. FY8: L Ann 3G 129
Queen Mary Ter. BB7: Whall 3H 101
Queens Av. BL7: Brom C 6G 198
OL12: Roch 1F 204
Queensberry Rd. BB11: Burnl 4A 228 (4C 124)
Queensborough Rd. BB5: Acc 1A 142
Queensbury Cl. BL1: Bolt 8D 198
Queensbury Rd. FY5: T Clev 1C 62
Queens Cl. BB7: Clith 4L 81
FY6: Poul F 8L 63
Queens Ct. FY2: Blackp 9B 62
L39: Orms 8K 209
PR2: Fulw 6H 115
(off Queens Rd.)
WN5: Wigan 5L 221
(off Wardley St.)
Queenscourt Av. PR1: Penw 6H 135
Queens Cres. PR4: K'ham 5N 111
Queensdale Cl. PR5: Walt D 4A 136
Queens Dr. BB5: Osw 5M 141
FY3: Stain 5L 89
LA4: Morec 2E 22
LA5: Arn 2F 4
LA5: Carn 9B 12
PR2: Fulw 3G 115
PR3: Longr 3J 97
Queens Gth. BD23: T Crav 9J 53
Queensgate BB9: Nelson 3H 105
PR7: Chor 7D 174
Queensgate Caravan Pk. PR3: Lit E 6L 65
Queens Grn. L39: D'holl 7M 207
Queen's Gro. PR7: Chor 6E 174
Queen's Hotel Ct. PR9: S'port 6H 167
Queens Lancashire Regiment Museum, The 5L 115
Queen's Lancashire Wlk. BB11: Burnl 3C 228
Queen's Lancashire Way
BB11: Burnl 2B 228 (3D 124)
Queens Mnr. FY8: L Ann 4G 129
QUEEN'S PARK 5A 140
Queens Pk. Cl. BB1: Blackb 5A 140
Queen's Pk. Rd. BB1: Blackb 4A 140
BB10: Burnl 1F 124
OL10: Heyw 9H 203
Queens Pl. BL9: Summ 3H 201
PR4: Wesh 2L 111
Queen's Prom. FY2: Blackp 1B 88
FY5: T Clev 1B 88
Queen Sq. LA1: Lanc 8C 228 (9K 23)
Queens Retail Pk. PR1: Prest 5N 229 (9L 115)
Queens Rd. BB1: Blackb 5B 140
BB3: Darw 9B 158
BB5: Acc 1A 142
BB7: Clith 4L 81
BB10: Burnl 8F 104
FY8: L Ann 3F 128
OL15: Littleb 9L 185
PR2: Fulw 6G 115
PR5: Walt D 3A 136
PR7: Chor 6D 174
PR9: S'port 5J 167
WN5: Orr 6F 220
Queen's Rd. Ter. OL15: Littleb 9L 185
(off Queen's Rd.)
Queens Rd. W. BB5: Acc, Chur 9M 121
Queens Sq. BB3: Hodd 6F 158
BB4: Rawt 5M 161
FY1: Blackp 1H 227 (5B 88)
FY6: Poul F 8K 63
Queen's Sq. LA6: K Lon 6F 8
Queen's St. PR3: Longr 4J 97
Queens Ter. BB2: Blackb 7J 139
BB12: Padi 1H 123
FY7: Flee 8J 41
LA6: Holme 1F 6
OL13: Bac 7J 163
QUEENSTOWN 3D 88
Queen St. BB3: Darw 5N 157
BB3: Hodd 6F 158
BB4: Rawt 5M 161
BB5: Acc 2B 142
BB5: Clay M 6M 121
BB5: Osw 4L 141
BB6: Gt H 4J 121
BB7: Clith 3J 81
BB7: Whall 5J 101
BB8: Colne 7N 85
BB9: Barrf 7H 85
BB9: Nelson 1J 105
BB10: Brierc 7K 105
BB11: Burnl 2B 228 (4D 124)
BB12: Padi 1H 123
BB18: Barnw 3M 77
BL0: Ramsb 8G 180
BL6: Hor 9C 196
BL8: Tott 8F 200
FY1: Blackp 1H 227 (5B 88)
FY7: Flee 9G 41
FY8: L Ann 5N 129
L39: Orms 8K 209
LA1: Lanc 8C 228 (9K 23)
LA4: Morec 3B 22
LA5: Carn 9N 11
OL12: Roch 5C 204
OL13: Bac 5K 163
(Commerce St.)
OL13: Bac 7G 163
(George St.)
OL14: Tod 2L 165
OL15: Littleb 9L 185
PR1: Prest 6N 229 (1L 135)
PR5: Lost H 9L 135
WN5: Orr 5K 221
WN5: Wigan 6N 221

296 A-Z Lancashire

Queen St. Bungs.—Red Scar Ind. Est.

Queen St. Bungs. LA1: Lanc 8C 228
Queen St. E. PR7: Chor 8F 174
Queen Street Mill Textile Mus. 8K 105
Queens Vw. OL15: Littleb 2K 205
Queens Wlk. BB6: Gt H 4K 121
FY5: T Clev 8D 54
Queensway BB2: Blackb 9H 139
BB4: Newc 6C 162
BB5: Chur 1M 141
BB7: Clith 4L 81
BB7: Wadd 8H 73
FY4: Blackp 2C 108
FY6: Poul F 8K 63
FY8: L Ann 6G 109
OL11: Roch 9C 204
PR1: Penw 2E 134
PR2: Ash R 7C 114
PR4: Wart 1K 131
PR5: Bam B 7A 136
PR6: Birns 8A 156
PR7: Eux 4A 174
PR25: Leyl 8H 153
WA11: Rain 5L 225
WN6: Shev 8J 213
Queensway Cl. PR1: Penw 2E 134
Queensway Ct. FY8: L Ann 8G 109
Queensway Lodge FY6: Poul F 8K 63
Queensway Neighbourhood Cen.
OL11: Roch 8D 204
Queens Yd. LA1: Lanc 8C 228
Queen Vera Rd. FY1: Blackp 1J 227 (5B 88)
Queen Victoria Rd. BB10: Burnl 9F 104
FY1: Blackp 6L 227 (7C 88)
Queen Victoria St. BB2: Blackb 6J 139
OL11: Roch 9D 204
Quenby Cnr. FY6: Poul F 8H 63
Quermore Rd. LA2: Lanc, Quern 9C 24
QUERNMORE 4F 30
Quernmore Av. FY3: Blackp 7G 89
Quernmore Brow LA2: Quern 4F 30
Quernmore Dr. BB18: Kelb 7D 78
LA2: Glas 2C 36
Quernmore Ind. Est.
PR4: Frec 2N 131
Quernmore Rd. L33: Kirk 7M 223
LA1: Lanc 7F 228 (8M 23)
LA2: Caton, Quern 2G 25
Quernmore Wlk. L33: Kirk 7M 223
Quincey Row PR9: Banks 2F 168
Quins Cft. PR25: Leyl 5J 153
Quin St. PR25: Leyl 6K 153
Quinton OL12: Roch 5B 204
Quinton Cl. PR8: Ains 9A 186
Quintrell Brow BL7: Brom C 5G 199

R

Rabbit La. BB7: Bas E 4N 71
L40: Burs 1L 209
Rabbit Wlk. BB11: Burnl 6F 124
Raby Sq. *LA4: Morec 2B 22*
(off Raby St.)
Raby St. BB4: Rawt 5M 161
LA4: Morec 3B 22
Racecourse Retail Pk. L9: Aint 8A 222
Radburn Brow PR6: Clay W 4D 154
Radburn Cl. PR6: Clay W 4D 154
Radcliffe Ct. BB12: Burnl 3M 123
Radcliffe Rd. FY7: Flee 3F 54
Radeclyffe St. BB7: Clith 2L 81
Radfield Av. BB3: Darw 7A 158
Radfield Head BB3: Darw 7N 157
Radfield Rd. BB3: Darw 7N 157
RADFORD 7A 158
Radford Bank Gdns. BB3: Darw 7A 158
Radford Bank Ho. *BB3: Darw 7A 158*
(off Radford Bank Gdns.)
Radford Gdns. BB3: Darw 8A 158
Radford St. BB3: Darw 7A 158
Radley Av. FY3: Blackp 2E 88
Radley Ct. PR8: S'port 7G 167
Radley Dr. L10: Aint 7B 222
Radnor Av. BB12: Burnl 2M 123
FY5: T Clev 2F 62
Radnor Cl. BB5: Osw 4J 141
Radnor Dr. PR9: S'port 3M 167
Radnor St. BB5: Acc 1A 142
PR1: Prest 4H 229 (9H 115)
Radstock Cl. BL1: Bolt 6E 198
Radway Cl. FY5: T Clev 4F 62
Radworth Cres. FY4: Blackp 9H 89
Raeburn Av. BB11: Burnl 6C 124
Raedale Av. BB10: Reed 6F 104
Raglan Rd. BB11: Burnl 4A 228 (4C 124)
LA3: Heys 5M 21
PR2: Ash R 7G 115
(off Raglan St.)
Raglan St. BB8: Colne 7A 86
BB9: Nelson 1H 105
OL14: Tod 2L 165
PR2: Ash R 7G 114
Raikes Hill FY1: Blackp 1L 227 (5C 88)
Raikes Hill Dr. LA2: Hest B 9H 15
Raikes M. FY1: Blackp 2L 227 (5C 88)
Raikes Pde. FY1: Blackp 2L 227 (5C 88)
Raikes Rd. FY5: T Clev 2L 63
PR1: Prest 8M 115
PR3: Gt E 6N 65
Rail Cl. WA11: Rain 9K 219
Railgate OL13: Bac 7N 163
Railton Av. BB2: Blackb 8H 139
Railway App. L39: Orms 7L 209
Railway Av. PR9: Banks 1E 168
Railway Cotts. PR4: Salw 5G 112
Railway Crossing La. LA1: Ald 2G 28
Railway Gro. BB1: Blackb 1A 140
Railway Island WN8: Skelm 3H 219
Railway Path L39: Orms 9K 209
Railway Pl. LA2: Glas 1D 36
Railway Rd. BB1: Blackb 4D 226 (3M 139)
BB3: Darw 6A 158
BB4: Hasl 3G 160
L39: Orms 7L 209
PR6: Adl 6J 195
PR6: Birns, Withn 8A 156
Railway Rd. PR6: Chor 5F 174
PR7: Adl 6J 195
WN8: Skelm 2G 219
Railway St. BB8: Foul 2A 86
BB9: Brierf 5F 104
BB9: Nelson 2J 105
BB11: Burnl 1C 228 (2D 124)
BB18: Barnw 2M 77
BL0: Ramsb 8H 181
BL9: Summ 3H 201
LA1: Lanc 9D 228 (1K 29)
OL13: Bac 7F 162
OL14: Tod 1L 165
OL15: Littleb 9L 185
OL16: Milnr 9L 205
OL16: Roch 7D 204
PR7: Chor 7F 174
PR8: S'port 9G 167
PR25: Leyl 5L 153
Railway St. W. BL9: Summ 3G 201
Railway Ter. BB4: Rawt 6L 161
BB6: Gt H 5J 121
BB9: Brierf 5E 104
BB12: S'stone 1E 122
BL7: Turt 6H 179
BL9: Summ 3H 201
PR4: Wesh 3L 111
PR7: Copp 4B 194
PR8: S'port 9G 167
Railway Vw. BB2: Blackb 6J 139
BB3: Darw 7B 158
(off Primrose Ter.)
BB5: Acc 2A 142
(Milton St.)
BB5: Acc 1B 142
(Pollard St.)
BB7: B'ton 6H 101
BB9: Brierf 4F 104
(off Wesley St.)
L32: Kirk 7H 223
OL14: Wals 6K 165
(off Winterbutlee Rd.)
PR7: Adl 6J 195
PR26: Cros 4L 171
Railway Vw. Av. BB7: Clith 2L 81
Railway Vw. Rd. BB7: Clith 2L 81
Rainbow Dr. L31: Mell 6G 222
Raines Ct. BD24: Gig 3M 35
Raines Crest OL16: Milnr 7K 205
Raines Rd. BD24: Gig 3N 35
RAINFORD 3L 225
Rainford By-Pass WA11: Rain, Wind 1H 225
Rainford Ind. Est. WA11: Rain 6N 225
(not continuous)
RAINFORD JUNCTION 9K 219
Rainford Rd. L39: Bick 5E 218
Rainford Station (Rail) 9K 219
Rainford St. BL2: Bolt 7J 199
RAINHALL 1A 78
Rainhall Cres. BB18: Barnw 2A 78
Rainhall Rd. BB18: Barnw 2M 77
Rainshaw St. BL1: Bolt 9F 198
RAIN SHORE 1G 202
Rake OL11: Roch 6H 203
Rake, The BL0: Ramsb 8G 180
LA2: Abb 5N 39
Rake Fold BL8: Holc 8F 180
RAKE FOOT 9M 143
Rakefoot BB4: Hasl 3G 161
RAKE HEAD 8E 162
Rake Head Barn La. OL14: Wals 7J 165
Rakehead La. OL13: Bac 7F 162
Rakehouse Brow LA2: Abb 2A 48
Rake La. PR4: Wart 3J 131
Rakes Bri. BB3: Lwr D 9A 140
Rakes Head La. LA2: Hest B 1G 23
Rakes Ho. Rd. BB9: Nelson 9J 85
Rakes La. BB7: Rim 3A 76
BD23: Hort 7D 52
Rakes Rd. LA2: Brookh 1M 25
Rake St. BL9: Bury 9L 201
Rake Ter. OL15: Littleb 8M 185
Rake Top OL12: Roch 4M 203
Rake Top Av. BB12: High 4L 103
RAKEWOOD 4N 205
Rakewood Rd. OL15: Littleb 2L 205
Raleigh Av. FY4: Blackp 4B 108
Raleigh Cl. FY8: L Ann 8D 108
Raleigh Gdns. OL15: Littleb 5M 185
Raleigh Rd. PR2: Fulw 3H 115
Raleigh St. BB12: Padi 2J 123
Ralph Av. BB5: Acc 9B 122
Ralph Sherwin Ct. OL12: Roch 1G 204
Ralph St. OL12: Roch 4D 204
Ralph's Wife's La. PR9: Banks 9D 148
Ramparts, The LA1: Lanc 6L 23
Ramper Ga. FY5: T Clev 1D 62
Ramsay Ct. FY6: K Sea 8K 41
Ramsay Pl. OL16: Roch 5D 204
Ramsay St. BL1: Bolt 9E 198
OL16: Roch 5D 204
Ramsay Ter. OL16: Roch 5D 204
RAMSBOTTOM 8H 181
Ramsbottom Heritage Cen. *7G 181*
(off Carr St.)
Ramsbottom La. BL0: Ramsb 7H 181
Ramsbottom Pool & Fitness Cen. 7H 181
Ramsbottom Rd. BL7: Edgw 3M 199
BL8: Hawk 3M 199
Ramsbottom Station
East Lancashire Railway 8H 181
Ramsbottom St. BB4: W'foot 7C 162
BB5: Acc 1A 142
Ramsclough La. BB5: Osw 9N 141
Ramsden La. OL14: Wals 8H 165
Ramsden Rd. OL12: Ward 5F 184
Ramsden St. LA5: Carn 8A 12
OL14: Wals 8K 165
Ramsden Wood Rd. OL14: Wals 8J 165
Ramsey Av. FY3: Blackp 3D 88
OL13: Bac 6L 163
PR1: Prest 6N 115
Ramsey Cl. FY8: L Ann 8D 108
Ramsey Gro. BB10: Burnl 8G 105
Ramsey Rd. BB2: Blackb 7L 139
Ramsgate Cl. PR4: Wart 1K 131
Ramsgate Rd. FY8: L Ann 9F 108
RAMSGREAVE 6M 119
Ramsgreave Av. BB1: Blackb 7L 119
Ramsgreave Dr. BB1: Blackb 8K 119
Ramsgreave Rd. BB1: Ramsg 6L 119
Ramsgreave & Wilpshire Station (Rail) 5N 119
Ramshill Av. FY6: Carl 6H 63
Ramson Ct. *LA3: Morec 6B 22*
(off Yarrow Wlk.)
Ramwells Brow BL7: Brom C 5F 198
Ramwells Ct. BL7: Brom C 4H 199
Ramwells M. *BL7: Brom C 5H 199*
(off Windy Harbour La.)
Ranaldsway PR25: Leyl 7G 152
Randall Av. WN6: Shev 7K 213
Randall St. BB10: Burnl 9F 104
Randal St. BB1: Blackb 3C 226 (2M 139)
Randle Av. WA11: Rain 2J 225
Randle Brook Ct. WA11: Rain 2J 225
Randolph St. BB1: Blackb 4A 140
Random Row OL13: Bac 7G 162
Ranelagh Dr. PR8: Ains 6F 186
Ranger St. BB5: Acc 3N 141
Rangeway Av. FY4: Blackp 2C 108
Ranglet Rd. PR5: Bam B 9D 136
Rangletts Av. PR7: Chor 8E 174
Ranglit Av. PR2: Lea 8N 113
Rankin Av. PR4: Hesk B 5D 150
Rankin Cl. BB18: Barnw 2N 77
Rankin Dr. BB3: Hodd 7E 158
Ranlea Av. LA4: Morec 2G 22
Ranleigh Dr. WN8: N 'urgh 3L 211
RANN 1E 158
Rannoch Dr. BB2: Blackb 7G 139
Ranslett Ct. L37: Form 9A 206
Rantreefold Rd. LA2: Tat 10K 19
Ranworth Cl. BL1: Bolt 7G 198
Rapley La. PR4: Inskip, Woodp 1K 93
Ratcliffe Fold BB4: Hasl 4G 160
Ratcliffe St. BB3: Darw 6B 158
BB4: Hasl 4G 160
Ratcliffe Wharf La. PR3: Fort 4K 45
Rathbone Rd. L38: Hight 7A 214
Rathbone St. OL16: Roch 6F 204
Rathlyn Av. FY3: Blackp 3E 88
RATHMELL 7M 35
Rathmell Cl. FY3: Blackp 1H 89
Rathmill Sike BB7: Grind 3C 74
Rathmore Cres. PR9: S'port 3A 168
Rathmore Gdns. FY2: Blackp 1E 88
Ratten La. PR4: Hutt 5M 133
RATTEN ROW 3A 66
Raveden Cl. BL1: Bolt 9C 198
Raven Av. BB4: Hasl 8G 160
Raven Cl. PR7: Chor 9B 174
Raven Cft. BB4: Hasl 7G 160
Ravendale Cl. OL12: Roch 4L 203
Ravenglass Av. L31: Magh 9C 216
Ravenglass Cl. BB2: Blackb 7A 140
FY4: Blackp 2E 108
PR4: Wesh 2M 111
Ravenhead Dr. WN8: Uph 4D 220
Ravenhead Way WN8: Uph 5C 220
Ravenhill Dr. PR7: Chor 5E 174
Raven Meols La. L37: Form 1A 214
Ravenoak La. BB10: W'thorne 4M 125
Raven Pk. BB4: Hasl 7G 160
Raven Rd. BB2: Blackb 3J 139
Ravens, The L37: Form 2A 214
Ravens Cl. FY3: Blackp 3H 89
LA1: Lanc 5J 23
Ravens Cl. Brow LA2: Wen 5G 19
Ravenscroft Av. L39: Orms 8K 209
Ravenscroft Bus. Pk. BB18: Barnw 1N 77
Ravenscroft Cl. BB1: Blackb 8A 120
Ravenscroft Way BB18: Barnw 1N 77
Ravens Gro. BB10: Reed 6G 104
Ravensthorpe PR7: Chor 5C 174
Raven St. BB9: Nelson 1K 105
BL9: Bury 9L 201
OL11: Roch 4J 203
PR1: Prest 7M 115
Ravenswing Av. BB2: Blackb 1J 139
Ravens Wood BB2: Blackb 3J 139
Ravenswood BB6: Gt H 3H 121
PR2: Ribb 7A 116
Ravenswood Av. FY3: Blackp 3H 89
WN3: Wins 8N 221
Ravenwood Av. FY4: Blackp 4D 108
Rawcliffe Dr. PR2: Ash R 9B 114
Rawcliffe Hall Country Club & Caravan Pk.
PR3: Out R 3K 65
Rawcliffe Rd. PR3: Out R, St M 4M 65
PR7: Chor 7E 174
Rawcliffe St. BB11: Burnl 1E 228 (3E 124)
FY4: Blackp 1B 108
Rawlinson Ct. *PR9: S'port 6K 167*
(off Rawlinson Rd.)
Rawlinson Gro. PR9: S'port 5L 167
Rawlinson La. PR6: H Charn 4H 195
PR7: H Charn 3G 195
Rawlinson Rd. PR9: S'port 6K 167
Rawlinson St. BB3: Darw 9B 158
BL6: Hor 9C 196
(off Winter Hey La.)
PR4: Wesh 3L 111
Raws Ct. BB11: Burnl 1D 228
Rawson Av. BB5: Acc 4N 141
Rawsons Rake BL0: Ramsb 8F 180
Rawson St. BB10: Burnl 9F 104
Raws St. BB11: Burnl 1D 228
Rawsthorne Av. BB4: Hasl 5G 160
BL0: Eden 4J 181
Rawstorne Cl. PR4: Frec 2M 131
Rawstorne Cres. PR4: Hutt 7B 134
Rawstorne Rd. PR1: Penw 3E 134
Rawstorne Sports Cen. 2M 131
Rawstorne St. BB2: Blackb 4K 139
Rawstron St. OL12: Whitw 5N 183
RAWTENSTALL 5M 161
Rawtenstall Rd. BB4: Hasl 6H 161
Rawtenstall Station
East Lancashire Railway 6L 161
Rawthey Rd. LA1: Lanc 6H 23
Raybourne Av. FY6: Poul F 8J 63
Ray Bridge La. BD23: Garg 3M 53
Raygarth LA6: K Lon 5E 8
Raygarth Gdns. LA6: K Lon 5E 8
Raygarth La. LA6: K Lon 5E 8
Raygill Av. BB11: Burnl 6B 124
Raygill La. BD20: Loth 4M 79
Raygill Pl. LA1: Lanc 6H 23
Ray La. PR3: Barn 8C 60
Raylees BL0: Ramsb 1H 201
Raymond Av. BL9: Bury 8L 201
FY2: Blackp 2D 88
L30: N'ton 9A 222
Raynor St. BB2: Blackb 3B 226 (3L 139)
Rayrig Fold WA11: Rain 4K 225
Rays Dr. LA1: Lanc 4K 29
Ray St. BB9: Brierf 5E 104
RB Bus. Pk. BB8: Colne 8K 85
READ 8C 102
Read Hall Ct. BB12: Read 8A 102
Reading Cl. BB1: Blackb 6G 226 (4A 140)
Read's Av. FY1: Blackp 4J 227 (6C 88)
Reads Ct. FY1: Blackp 4K 227 (6C 88)
Read St. BB5: Clay M 8N 121
Reaney Av. FY4: Blackp 2E 108
Reapers Way L30: N'ton 6A 222
Rebecca Ct. *OL16: Milnr 8J 205*
(off Harbour La.)
Record St. BB18: Barnw 3M 77
Recreation Rd. PR9: Banks 3J 169
Recreation St. BL2: Bolt 8L 199
Rectory Cl. BB3: Darw 7C 158
BB4: Newc 6C 162
PR7: Chor 6E 174
PR26: Cros 4N 171
Rectory Gdns. LA2: C'ham 9G 37
PR4: Tarl 1E 170
Rectory Hill BL9: Bury 9B 202
Rectory La. BL9: Bury 9B 202
Rectory Paddock LA2: Halt 2B 24
Rectory Rd. BB12: Burnl 2D 124
FY4: Blackp 9E 88
PR9: S'port 5M 167
RED BANK 9G 174
Red Bank BL9: Bury 7C 202
PR7: Chor 9F 174
Red Bank Rd. FY2: Blackp 7B 62
Red Bri. La. LA5: Silv 7J 5
Red Brook St. OL11: Roch 6A 204
Redbrow Way L33: Kirk 6K 223
Redcar Av. FY5: T Clev 7E 54
PR2: Ingol 5C 114
Redcar Cl. PR8: S'port 2M 187
Redcar Rd. BL1: Bolt 9B 198
FY1: Blackp 2B 88
LA1: Lanc 4M 29
Redcar St. OL12: Roch 5B 204
Red Cat La. L40: Burs 5C 190
Redcliffe Gdns. L39: Aug 9K 209
Red Cl. Caravan Pk. LA5: Carn 1N 15
Red Cross St. PR1: Prest 6G 229 (1H 135)
Redcross St. OL12: Roch 4C 204
Redcross St. Nth. OL12: Roch 4B 204
Red Cut La. L33: Kirk 9C 224
Red Delph La. WA11: Rain 1H 225
Reddish Cl. BL2: Bolt 7L 199
Reddyshore Brow OL15: Littleb 6M 185
Reddyshore Scout Ga. OL14: Wals 1L 185
Redearth Rd. BB3: Darw 6A 158
Rede Av. FY7: Flee 2C 54
Redeswood Av. FY5: T Clev 3E 62
Redfearn Wood OL12: Roch 3M 203
Redfern Cotts. OL11: Roch 4H 203
Redfern Way OL11: Roch 4H 203
Red Fold L39: Aug 9H 209
Redford St. BL8: Bury 9H 201
Redgate L37: Form 1A 214
L39: Orms 7J 209
Redgate Cl. BB11: Burnl 6F 124
Redgate Dr. L37: Form 1B 214
Redgrave Ct. BB12: Burnl 3M 123
Redgrave Ri. WN3: Wins 8N 221
Redhill PR4: Hutt 7N 133
Redhill Dr. PR8: S'port 2M 187
Redhill Gro. PR6: Chor 3G 175
Red Hills Rd. LA5: Arn 2E 4
Red Hind Cl. BB4: Newc 5B 162
Red Ho. Bri. PR7: Adl 7H 195
Redhouse Cl. BB5: Clay M 7N 121
Red Ho. La. PR7: E'ton 8E 172
Redisher Cl. BL0: Ramsb 2E 200
Redisher Cft. BL0: Ramsb 2E 200
Redisher La. BL8: Hawk 1D 200
Redlam BB2: Blackb 5J 139
Redlam Brow BB2: Blackb 5K 139
Redland Cl. OL15: Littleb 8L 185
Red La. BB8: Colne 5K 85
OL12: Roch 3E 204
PR7: E'ton 7G 173
Red Lees Av. BB10: Burnl 5K 125
Red Lees Rd. BB10: Burnl, Cliv 4J 125
Redleigh Orchard Caravan Pk. FY4: Blackp 3K 109
Red Lion Cl. L31: Magh 1B 222
Red Lion Shop. Cen. L31: Magh 1B 222
Red Lion St. BB11: Burnl 3D 228 (4E 124)
BB18: Earl 2F 78
RED LUMB 1E 202
Red Lumb St. OL12: Roch 1E 202
Redman Gate BL8: Aff 7A 200
Redman Rd. BB10: Reed 6F 104
Red Marsh Dr. FY5: T Clev 9J 55
Red Marsh Ind. Est. FY5: T Clev 9J 55
Redmayne Dr. LA5: Carn 8B 12
Redmayne St. PR1: Prest 9N 115
Redmoor Cres. L33: Kirk 5K 223
Redness Cl. BB9: Nelson 4J 105
Red Rake BB1: Blackb 1K 139
Red Rose Ct. BB2: Blackb 5A 226 (4K 139)
BB5: Clay M 8L 121
Red Rose Dr. PR26: Far M 3J 153
Red Rose Lodge FY4: Blackp 9F 88
Redruth Dr. LA5: Carn 1N 15
Redruth St. BB12: Burnl 3B 124
Redsands L39: Aug 9J 209
Redsands Dr. PR2: Fulw 4N 115
RED SCAR 3E 116
Red Scar Ind. Est. PR2: Ribb 4D 116
(not continuous)

A-Z Lancashire 297

Red Scar St.—Rinus Bus. Pk.

Red Scar St. BB8: Colne 8N 85
Redshank Dr. LA3: Heys 1L 27
Redshaw Av. BL2: Bolt 7H 199
Red Shell La. BB1: Belt 2H 159
BB5: Osw 8H 141
Red Spar Rd. BB10: Burnl 8H 105
Redstart Pl. FY5: T Clev 2F 62
Redvers Rd. BB3: Darw 2M 157
Redvers St. BB10: Burnl 9F 104
LA1: Lanc 7A 228 (9H 23)
Redvers Ter. FY1: Blackp 2B 88
Redwald Cl. L33: Kirk 4L 223
Redwell Fisheries Caravan Pk. LA6: Ark 9L 13
Redwing Av. BB6: Gt H 3H 121
FY5: T Clev 8F 54
Redwing Cl. LA3: Heys 1L 27
Redwing Dr. PR7: Chor 9B 174
Redwing Rd. BL8: Greenm 3E 200
REDWOOD 5K 221
Redwood WN6: Shev 6L 213
Redwood Av. L31: Lyd 8B 216
PR25: Leyl 6H 153
WN5: Orr 5K 221
Redwood Cl. FY4: Blackp 5C 108
OL12: Roch 2M 203
Redwood Dr. BB4: Rawt 7L 161
L39: Orms 8J 209
LA4: Morec 3E 22
PR3: Longr 2J 97
PR7: Chor 8F 174
Redwood Gdns. FY5: T Clev 1L 63
Redwood Hgts. LA1: Lanc 9N 23
Redwood Pk. Gro. OL16: Roch 6G 205
Redwood Way L33: Kirk 4K 223
Reedfield BB10: Reed 6G 105
PR5: Bam B 3E 154
Reedfield Pl. PR5: Bam B 1C 154
Reed Hill OL16: Roch 5C 204
REEDLEY 6F 104
Reedley Av. BB9: Nelson 3K 105
Reedley Bus. Cen. BB10: Reed 6F 104
Reedley Dr. BB10: Burnl 6G 105
BB10: Reed 6F 104
Reedley Farm Cl. BB10: Reed 5F 104
Reedley Gro. BB10: Reed 7F 104
Reedley Mt. BB10: Reed 6G 104
Reedley Rd. BB9: Brierf 6F 104
BB10: Reed 6F 104
Reedmace Wlk. LA3: Morec 6B 22
Reed Row BB8: Colne 8A 86
Reeds, The L39: Orms 6J 209
LA1: Lanc 5A 228
Reeds Brow WA11: Rain 2M 225
Reeds Cl. BB4: Rawt 1M 161
REEDS HOLME 2M 161
Reedsholme Cl. BB4: Rawt 1M 161
Reeds La. BB4: Rawt 1M 161
WA11: Rain 6J 225
Reed St. BB11: Burnl 5E 228 (5E 124)
OL13: Bac 4L 163
Reedy Acre Pl. FY8: L Ann 4M 129
Reedyford Rd. BB9: Nelson 9H 85
Reedymoor La. BB8: Foul 3M 85
Reedy Moor Ter. BB8: Foul 2N 85
Reeford Gro. BB7: Clith 4K 81
Reepham Cl. WN3: Wins 8N 221
Rees Pk. L40: Burs 9D 190
Reeth Way *BB5: Acc 4M 141*
(off Lynton Rd.)
Reeval Cl. BB18: Earl 2F 78
Reeveswood PR7: E'ton 8E 172
Reform Health & Fitness 1K 227
Reform St. OL12: Roch 4C 204
Regal Av. FY4: Blackp 3E 108
Regal Ct. PR8: Ains 8D 186
Regal Fold OL12: Roch 1E 204
Regal Ter. *LA1: Lanc 5K 23*
(off Clarendon Rd.)
Regency Av. PR5: Lost H 9N 135
Regency Cl. BB7: Whall 3G 101
Regency Ct. LA1: Lanc 8C 228
OL11: Roch 6K 203
PR9: S'port 5K 167
Regency Cres. PR4: K'ham 4K 111
Regency Gdns. FY2: Blackp 1D 88
PR4: New L 9C 134
PR7: Eux 5N 173
PR8: Birk 1E 186
Regent Av. BB8: Colne 5B 86
FY8: L Ann 2K 129
Regent Caravan Park, The LA3: Morec 5A 22
Regent Cl. BB12: Padi 2H 123
PR8: Birk 1F 186
Regent Ct. FY1: Blackp 4B 88
FY8: L Ann 9D 108
PR2: Fulw 4H 115
PR9: S'port 6J 167
Regent Dr. PR2: Fulw 5G 115
Regent Gro. PR2: Fulw 4H 115
Regent M. PR8: Birk 1F 186
Regent Pk. PR2: Fulw 3H 115
Regent Pk. Av. LA3: Morec 5N 21
LA4: Morec 5N 21
Regent Pk. Gro. LA4: Morec 4N 21
Regent Pl. BB9: Nelson 9J 85
Regent Rd. BB5: Chur 1M 141
FY1: Blackp 2K 227 (5C 88)
LA3: Morec 4M 21
LA4: Morec 4M 21
PR5: Walt D 4N 135
PR7: Chor 7D 174
PR8: Birk 1E 186
PR25: Leyl 6K 153
Regent Rd. E. FY1: Blackp 2K 227 (5C 88)
Regents Cl. BB2: Pleas 6D 138
Regents Ter. FY6: Poul F 8L 63
Regent St. BB1: Blackb 3D 226 (3M 139)
BB4: Hasl 4F 160
BB7: Wadd 8H 73
BB8: Colne, Nelson 1J 105
BB9: Brierf 5F 104
BB9: Nelson 1J 105
BL0: Ramsb 9F 180
BL9: Bury 9L 201
LA1: Lanc 9B 228 (9J 23)
OL12: Roch 4C 204
Regent St. OL13: Bac 5L 163
OL14: Wals 6K 165
OL15: Littleb 9L 185
PR1: Prest 8K 229 (2J 135)
PR3: Longr 3J 97
PR7: Copp 4A 194
Regents Vw. BB1: Blackb 8M 119
Regents Way PR7: Eux 4N 173
Regentsway PR5: Bam B 7A 136
Regiment Dr. PR7: Buck V 9B 154
Reginald St. BB8: Colne 6M 85
Reigate PR6: Chor 3H 175
Reiver Rd. PR26: Leyl 4F 152
Renacres La. L39: Hals 8L 187
Rendel St. BB12: Burnl 2A 124
Rendsburg Way LA1: Lanc 7D 228
Renfrey Cl. L39: Orms 4K 209
Rennie Cl. PR3: Gars 6A 60
Rennie Ct. LA1: Lanc 2J 29
Rennie St. BB10: Burnl 4G 125
Renshaw Dr. BL9: Bury 9A 202
PR5: Walt D 6A 136
Renshaw St. BB10: Burnl 9F 104
Renwick Av. FY4: Blackp 1D 108
Repton Av. FY1: Blackp 1C 88
LA4: Morec 4F 22
Repton Cl. OL13: Bac 7M 163
Repton Gro. L10: Aint 8B 222
Reservoir Rd. FY5: T Clev 9J 55
PR3: Barn 1G 60
Reservoir Side BB1: Rish 9F 120
Reservoir St. BB3: Darw 6N 157
BB11: Burnl 5D 124
OL16: Roch 5F 204
Reta Dr. FY5: T Clev 9G 55
Retford Av. OL16: Roch 9E 204
Retford Cl. BL8: Bury 8K 201
Retford Rd. L33: Kirk 8L 223
Retford Wlk. L33: Kirk 8L 223
REVIDGE 2J 139
Revidge Rd. BB1: Blackb 2J 139
BB2: Blackb 2J 139
REVOE 7L 227 (8C 88)
Revoe St. FY1: Blackp 6L 227
Revolution Pk. PR7: Chor 2C 174
Rewe Cl. BB2: Blackb 8K 139
Rexington Bldgs. BB11: Burnl 4A 124
Reynolds St. BB11: Burnl 6C 124
LA1: Lanc 7J 23
Rhine Cl. BL8: Tott 6E 200
Rhoda St. BB9: Nelson 1K 105
Rhoden Rd. BB5: Osw 6K 141
PR26: Leyl 6F 152
Rhodes Av. BB1: Blackb 9L 119
BB4: Hasl 8F 160
Rhodes Cres. OL11: Roch 9C 204
Rhodes St. OL12: Roch 2E 204
Rhode St. BL8: Tott 7E 200
Rhodesway PR5: Hogh 6G 136
Rhosleigh Av. BL1: Bolt 9E 198
Rhuddlan Cl. BB4: Hasl 6G 160
Rhuddlan Gdns. *FY5: T Clev 1K 63*
(off Ruthin Dr.)
Rhyddings, The BL9: Bury 6C 202
Rhyddings St. BB5: Osw 4L 141
Rhyl Av. BB1: Blackb 1M 139
Rhyl St. FY7: Flee 8H 41
Rib, The L37: Form, Gt A 7F 206
Ribbesford Rd. WN3: Wigan 7M 221
Ribble Av. BB3: Darw 3M 157
BB6: Gt H 3L 121
BB7: Grind 5A 74
BB7: Whall 3G 100
BB10: Burnl 8G 104
L31: Magh 9D 216
OL15: Littleb 8J 185
PR4: Frec 2M 131
PR9: S'port 2B 168
Ribble Bank PR1: Penw 2E 134
Ribble Bank St. PR1: Prest 1H 135
Ribble Brook Ho. PR1: Prest 3J 229 (8H 115)
Ribble Bus. Pk. BB1: Blackb 9B 120
Ribble Cl. PR1: Penw 4H 135
PR1: Prest 9G 229 (2H 135)
PR4: Frec 2M 131
PR6: Withn 6B 156
Ribble Ct. PR1: Prest 2G 135
PR2: Ash R 8F 114
Ribble Cres. PR4: K'ham 4N 111
PR5: Walt D 2M 135
Ribble Cruising Club 6A 130
Ribble Discovery Cen. 5J 129
Ribble Dr. BB7: West B 5K 73
BL9: Bury 5L 201
PR4: Hesk B 3C 150
WN5: Wigan 4M 221
Ribble Estuary National Nature Reserve, The 3F 148
Ribble Gro. OL10: Heyw 9E 202
Ribble Hall PR1: Prest 3J 229
Ribble Ho. *PR1: Prest 9N 115*
(off Samuel St.)
Ribble La. BB7: Chatb, Grind 5A 74
Ribble Lodge *FY8: L Ann 5N 129*
(off West Beach)
Ribble Point FY8: L Ann 4J 129
Ribble Rd. FY1: Blackp 4K 227 (6C 88)
FY7: Flee 9F 40
PR25: Leyl 7G 153
WN6: Stand 2L 213
Ribblesdale Av. BB1: Wilp 2A 120
BB5: Acc 9A 122
BB7: Clith 2L 81
Ribblesdale Cl. FY4: Blackp 1G 108
PR4: K'ham 3L 111
Ribblesdale Ct. *BB7: Gis 9A 52*
(off Main St.)
LA4: Morec 3B 22
Ribblesdale Dr. PR2: Grim 1E 116
PR3: Fort 2M 45
Ribblesdale Pk. BB7: Gis 8A 52
Ribblesdale Pl. BB2: Blackb 3K 139
BB9: Barrf 6J 85
PR1: Prest 8K 229 (2J 135)
PR7: Chor 7D 174
Ribblesdale Rd. PR3: Ribc 7F 98
Ribblesdale Sq. *BB7: Chatb 7C 74*
(off Bridge Rd.)
Ribblesdale St. BB10: Burnl 1F 124
Ribblesdale Swimming Pool 3H 81
Ribblesdale Vw. *BB6: Langh 9D 100*
(off Whalley New Rd.)
BB7: Chatb 7D 74
Ribbleside Caravan Pk. PR3: Ribc 6H 99
Ribble Steam Railway & Mus. 1B 134
Ribble St. BB1: Blackb 1D 226 (2M 139)
BB12: Padi 1J 123
FY8: L Ann 2D 128
OL11: Roch 9B 204
OL13: Bac 7L 163
PR1: Prest 6H 229 (1H 135)
Ribble Ter. *BD24: Sett 2N 35*
(off Church St.)
RIBBLETON 6A 116
Ribbleton Av. PR1: Prest 8N 115
PR2: Ribb 7N 115
Ribbleton Dr. BB5: Acc 9A 122
Ribbleton Gro. BB7: Whall 3G 100
RIBBLETON HALL 7C 116
Ribbleton Hall Cres. PR2: Ribb 6B 116
Ribbleton Hall Dr. PR2: Ribb 6B 116
Ribbleton La. PR1: Prest 4N 229 (9L 115)
Ribbleton La. Trad. Est. *PR1: Prest 9L 115*
(off Ribbleton La.)
Ribbleton Pl. PR1: Prest 9L 115
Ribbleton St. PR1: Prest 4N 229 (9L 115)
Ribble Valley Ent. Pk. BB7: Barr 1K 101
Ribble Vw. BB7: Clith 8M 73
BB7: West B 6K 73
PR4: Frec 2B 132
Ribble Vw. Cl. PR4: Wart 2L 131
Ribble Way BB7: Clith 3J 81
RIBBY 5G 111
Ribby Av. PR4: K'ham 4L 111
PR4: W Grn 5G 111
Ribby Hall Holiday Village PR4: W Grn 5J 111
Ribby Pl. FY4: Blackp 9H 89
PR2: Ash R 8C 114
Ribby Rd. PR4: K'ham 5L 111
PR4: W Grn 5G 111
RIBCHESTER 7E 98
Ribchester Av. BB10: Burnl 4H 125
FY4: Blackp 9H 89
Ribchester Rd. BB1: Clay D 8H 99
BB1: Clay D, Wilp 2K 119
BB6: Dinck 6L 99
FY8: L Ann 4C 130
PR3: Ribc 4N 97
Ribchester Roman Mus. 7E 98
Ribchester Way BB9: Brierf 6H 105
Rice Gro. FY1: Blackp 2D 88
Richard Burch St. BL9: Bury 9L 201
Richard Hesketh Dr. L32: Kirk 8H 223
Richardson Cl. PR4: Frec 2A 132
Richardson St. FY1: Blackp 4J 227 (6B 88)
Richards Rd. WN6: Stand 1L 213
Richard's St. PR4: K'ham 3L 111
Richard St. BB9: Brierf 5F 104
BB11: Burnl 4F 228 (4F 124)
BL0: Ramsb 7K 181
OL11: Roch 7C 204
OL13: Weir 9K 145
Richards Wlk. LA1: Lanc 7H 23
Richards Way FY5: T Clev 2F 62
FY8: L Ann 7E 108
Richmal Ter. BL0: Ramsb 7G 180
Richmond Av. BB4: Hasl 6H 161
BB5: Acc 3A 142
BB10: Burnl 5K 125
BB18: Barnw 1L 77
FY5: T Clev 1E 62
L40: Burs 1C 210
LA1: Lanc 4K 23
LA4: Morec 3D 22
PR4: W Grn 6G 111
Richmond Cl. BL8: Tott 7E 200
OL16: Roch 9F 204
PR6: Birns 7N 155
Richmond Ct. FY1: Blackp 3B 88
L40: Burs 1C 210
PR7: Chor 8E 174
PR26: Leyl 6E 152
Richmond Cres. BB1: Blackb 3E 140
Richmond Gro. L31: Lyd 8D 216
Richmond Hill BB1: Blackb 3C 226 (3M 139)
WN5: Wigan 5M 221
Richmond Hill Caravan Pk. FY4: Blackp 4D 108
Richmond Hill La. PR3: Fort 2A 46
Richmond Hill St. BB5: Acc 3N 141
Richmond Ho. PR1: Prest 7M 229
PR7: Chor 8E 174
Richmond Ind. Est. BB5: Acc 3A 142
Richmond M. L40: Burs 1D 210
Richmond Pk. BB3: Darw 5A 158
Richmond Rd. BB5: Acc 4M 141
BB9: Barrf 1G 104
BB18: Barnw 1L 77
FY1: Blackp 3B 88
FY8: L Ann 2E 128
PR6: Chor 8G 174
PR7: E'ton 7F 172
PR8: Birk 3F 186
Richmonds Ct. *BB8: Colne 6B 86*
(off New Ho. St.)
Richmond St. BB5: Acc 3N 141
BB11: Burnl 4C 124
BL6: Hor 9C 196
OL14: Tod 2M 165
PR1: Prest 1L 135
Richmond Ter. BB1: Blackb 3C 226 (3M 139)
(not continuous)
BB3: Darw 5A 158
BB7: Clith 4K 81
Rickard Rd. BB9: Nelson 4J 105
Rickerby Ct. PR9: S'port 6J 167
Ridd Cotts. OL11: Roch 5G 202
Ridding La. BB7: Whall 5G 101
Riddings, The BD23: Lon P 6N 35
Riddings Av. BB10: Burnl 3K 125
Riddings La. BB7: Whall 4J 101
Riddiough Ct. OL12: Whitw 6N 183
Ridehalgh La. BB10: Brierc 7C 106
Ridehalgh St. BB8: Colne 8M 85
Riders Ga. BL9: Bury 9D 202
RIDGE 7M 23
Ridge, The BB9: Nelson 4J 105
Ridge Av. BB10: Burnl 2G 125
Ridge Bank OL14: Tod 2L 165
Ridge Cl. PR9: S'port 1B 168
Ridge Ct. BB10: Burnl 3G 125
PR3: Longr 2L 97
Ridgefoot *OL14: Tod 2L 165*
(off Queen St.)
Ridgeford Gdns. PR2: Fulw 4G 115
Ridge Gro. LA3: Heys 8L 21
Ridge La. BB9: Rough 7D 84
LA1: Lanc 6N 23
(Crag Rd.)
LA1: Lanc 7L 23
(Ridge St.)
Ridgemont PR2: Fulw 3F 114
Ridge Rd. BB11: Burnl 2F 228 (3F 124)
OL14: Tod 2L 165
PR6: Chor 7G 175
Ridge Row BB10: Burnl 3H 125
Ridge Sq. LA1: Lanc 7M 23
Ridge Steps *OL14: Tod 2L 165*
(off Ridge Bank)
Ridge St. BB18: Barnw 2M 77
LA1: Lanc 7L 23
Ridge Way PR1: Penw 4H 135
Ridgeway BB6: Gt H 3H 121
BB9: Barrf 8G 85
Ridgeway, The BB9: Nelson 3H 105
FY7: Flee 1D 54
Ridgeway Av. BB2: Blackb 8A 140
Ridgeway Ct. FY8: L Ann 1G 129
Ridgeway Dr. FY5: T Clev 3K 63
L31: Lyd 7C 216
Ridgeways BB4: Hasl 5H 161
Ridgmont Cl. BL6: Hor 9G 196
Ridgwood Av. FY3: Blackp 5E 88
Riding Barn St. BB5: Chur 2M 141
Riding Cl. BB18: Barnw 2N 77
L39: D'holl 8M 207
Riding Ga. BL2: Bolt 7L 199
Riding Ga. M. BL2: Bolt 7L 199
Riding Head La. BL0: Ramsb 6L 181
Riding La. L39: D'holl 8K 207
Ridings, The BB12: Burnl 1B 124
PR6: Whit W 9E 154
PR9: S'port 3N 167
Riding St. BB11: Burnl 4C 124
PR1: Prest 3K 229 (8J 115)
PR6: Adl 6J 195
PR8: S'port 8H 167
Ridley La. L31: Magh 1C 222
L40: Mawd 3B 192
PR26: Cros 3A 172
Ridley Rd. PR2: Ash R 7F 114
Ridley St. FY3: Blackp 1N 227 (5D 88)
Ridyard St. WN5: Wigan 4N 221
Riesling Dr. L33: Kirk 5J 223
Rifle St. BB4: Hasl 5G 161
Rigby Cl. PR4: Frec 2A 132
Rigby Ct. OL12: Roch 3J 203
Rigby La. BL2: Bolt 7J 199
Rigby Rd. FY1: Blackp 6H 227 (7B 88)
L31: Magh 8A 216
Rigby's Ho's. PR7: Adl 7G 195
Rigby St. BB8: Colne 7N 85
BB9: Nelson 2H 105
PR1: Prest 8M 115
Rigby's Yd. WN5: Wigan 5L 221
Rigby Wlk. *PR7: Chor 6E 174*
(off High St.)
Rigg La. LA2: Quern 4F 30
PR3: Goos 6B 70
Rigg St. BB9: Nelson 2J 105
RIGSHAW BRIDGE 6H 195
Rigshaw Bri. Cotts. PR7: Adl 6H 195
Riley Av. FY8: L Ann 4F 128
Riley Cl. PR25: Leyl 7K 153
Riley Ct. FY8: L Ann 4F 128
RILEY GREEN 9N 137
Riley Grn. Switch Rd. BB2: Fenis 9N 137
PR5: Hogh 9N 137
Riley St. BB5: Acc 4A 142
BB9: Brierf 5F 104
BB11: Burnl 5F 124
BB18: Earl 2E 78
OL13: Bac 2K 163
Rilldene Wlk. OL11: Roch 5N 203
RIMINGTON 4L 75
Rimington Av. BB5: Acc 5N 141
BB8: Colne 5N 85
BB10: Burnl 4H 125
Rimington Caravan Pk. BB7: Rim 2A 76
Rimington Cl. BB2: Blackb 9E 226 (6N 139)
Rimington La. BB7: Rim 5G 75
Rimington Mus. of Transport 4K 75
Rimington Pl. BB9: Nelson 1M 105
FY8: L Ann 2H 129
Rimmer Grn. PR8: S'port 4C 188
Rimmer's Av. PR8: S'port 8H 167
Ring Dyke Way FY8: L Ann 4N 129
Ringley Gro. BL1: Bolt 8E 198
Ring Lows La. OL12: Roch 1C 204
RING O' BELLS 2F 210
Ring O'Bells La. L40: Lath 2F 210
Rings Nook BB4: Craws 6M 143
Rings St. BB4: Craws 6M 143
Ringstone Cres. BB9: Nelson 2M 105
Ringstones La. LA2: Low 1L 33
Ringtail Ct. L40: Burs 9N 189
Ringtail Ind. Est. L40: Burs 1N 209
Ringtail Pl. L40: Burs 1N 209
Ringtail Rd. L40: Burs 9M 189
RINGTON 5H 63
Rington Av. FY6: Carl 5H 63
Ring Way PR1: Prest 6G 229 (1H 135)
Ringway FY5: T Clev 8E 54
PR7: Chor 7C 174
Ringwood Av. BL0: Ramsb 1F 200
Ringwood Cl. BB5: Acc 8A 122
FY8: L Ann 5M 129
Ringwood Rd. PR1: Prest 7M 115
Rinus Bus. Pk. BB3: Darw 8B 158

Ripley Cl.—Rose Gro.

Ripley Cl. L31: Magh 1D **222**
Ripley Ct. *LA1: Lanc 1K 29*
(off Princess Av.)
Ripley Dr. FY8: L Ann 2H **129**
WN3: Wigan 7M **221**
Ripleys Believe it or Not! Exhibition 2A **108**
Ripley St. BL2: Bolt 9H **199**
LA1: Lanc 1K 29
(off Railway St.)
Ripon Av. LA1: Lanc 4K **23**
Ripon Brook *PR1: Prest 8B 116*
(off Ripon Ter.)
Ripon Cl. FY5: T Clev 7E **54**
PR3: Gt E 6A **66**
PR8: S'port 2M **187**
Ripon Hall Av. BL0: Ramsb 1G **200**
Ripon Pl. LA3: Heys 1K **27**
Ripon Rd. BB5: Osw 3J **141**
FY1: Blackp 3M **227** (6D **88**)
FY8: L Ann 3K **129**
Ripon St. BB1: Blackb 4A **140**
BB9: Nelson 3H **105**
PR1: Prest 1G **229** (7G **115**)
Ripon Ter. PR1: Prest 8B **116**
Rise, The LA1: Lanc 2J **29**
LA5: Bolt S 3M **15**
WN6: Stand 9M **213**
Risedale Dr. PR3: Longr 3K **97**
Risedale Gro. BB2: Blackb 9H **139**
Rise La. OL14: Tod 2K **165**
(Rose Bank Rd.)
OL14: Tod 2L **165**
(Station App.)
Rise La. Ho. *OL14: Tod 2L 165*
(off Rise La.)
RISHTON 8H **121**
Rishton Golf Course 9H **121**
Rishton Rd. BB1: Blackb, Rish 4B **120**
BB5: Clay M 6L **121**
Rishton Station (Rail) 9G **121**
Rishton St. FY1: Blackp 4K **227** (6C **88**)
RISING BRIDGE 8F **142**
Rising Bri. Rd. BB4: Hasl, Ris B 9F **142**
BB5: Ris B 9F **142**
Ritherham Av. FY5: T Clev 9D **54**
Riverbank Dr. BL8: Bury 9J **201**
Riverbank Garden *BL8: Bury 9J 201*
(off Tottington Rd.)
River Bank Ter. *BB5: Alt 3D 122*
(off Calder Ct.)
River Cl. L37: Form 2B **214**
Riverdale Cl. WN6: Stand 8N **213**
River Dr. BB12: Padi 1J **123**
River Hgts. PR5: Lost H 8M **135**
River Lea Gdns. BB7: Clith 3M **81**
Rivermead OL16: Milnr 9L **205**
Rivermead Ct. PR3: Gars 3N **59**
Rivermead Dr. PR3: Gars 4N **59**
Rivermeade PR8: S'port 1K **187**
River Pde. PR1: Prest 2G **135**
River Pl. BD23: Garg 3M **53**
OL16: Milnr 7J **205**
River Rd. FY5: T Clev 1L **63**
(Stanah Rd.)
FY5: T Clev 8K **55**
(Victrex Rd.)
Riversdale BD24: Gig 3N **35**
Riversdale Cl. L33: Kirk 6L **223**
Riversedge OL12: Whitw 5N **183**
Riversedge Rd. PR25: Leyl 7F **152**
Riversgate FY7: Flee 9F **40**
Riverside BB7: Clith 3H **81**
BD23: Garg 3M 53
(off Church St.)
LA5: Carn 7A 12
(off Mill La.)
PR1: Prest 9H **229** (3H **135**)
PR3: Ribc 8E **98**
PR5: Bam B 9A **136**
Riverside Av. PR26: Far M 3H **153**
Riverside Caravan Pk. LA2: H Ben 7L **19**
LA3: Heat 8D **22**
Riverside Chalet Pk. FY6: Sing 7C **64**
Riverside Cl. LA2: Halt 2B **24**
PR26: Far M 3H **153**
Riverside Ct. OL12: Whitw 2A **184**
Riverside Cres. PR26: Cros 4L **171**
Riverside Dr. BL9: Summ 3G **201**
FY6: Ham 1A **64**
OL16: Roch 3F **204**
Riverside Fold BB12: Barl 6C **84**
Riverside Holiday Pk. PR9: Banks 4J **169**
Riverside Ind. Est. BB1: Rish 7J **121**
Riverside Ind. Pk. BB9: Nelson 4L **105**
PR3: C'town 9N **59**
Riverside Lofts LA1: Lanc 7J **23**
Riverside M. BB4: Lumb 3D **162**
BB12: Burnl 3L **123**
Riverside Mill BB8: Colne 7M **85**
Riverside Pk. BB4: Lumb 3D **162**
Riverside Pk. Ind. Est. LA1: Lanc 4M **23**
Riverside Rd. PR1: Penw 3H **135**
Riverside Ter. *BB18: Earl 3E 78*
(off Cowgill St.)
PR26: Far M 3H **153**
Riverside Vw. BB5: Clay M 5L **121**
Riverside Vw. Apartments *BB5: Clay M 5L 121*
(off Riverside Vw.)
Riverside Wlk. BB4: Hasl 8F **160**
PR9: Banks 3J **169**
Riverside Way BB9: Barrf 9G **84**
Riversleigh Av. FY1: Blackp 1C **88**
FY8: L Ann 5L **129**
Riversleigh Cl. BL1: Bolt 9N **197**
Riversmeade BL7: Brom C 6J **199**
Rivers St. WN5: Orr 5H **221**
Riverstone Bri. OL15: Littleb 9K **185**
River St. BB1: Blackb 5E **226** (4N **139**)
BB3: Darw 5N **157**
BB8: Colne 7A **86**
BB8: Traw 8F **86**
BL0: Ramsb 8H **181**
LA1: Lanc 7J **23**
OL10: Heyw 9H **203**
OL13: Bac 6K **163**
OL14: Tod 2M **165**
River St. OL16: Roch 6C **204**
PR1: Prest 6G **229** (1H **135**)
Riversview PR9: Banks 4J **169**
Rivers Vw. Fold LA2: Dolp 7E **38**
Riversway BD23: Garg 3L **53**
FY3: Blackp 4F **88**
FY6: Poul F 6M **63**
LA1: Lanc 6L **23**
PR2: Ash R, Lea 9N **113**
Riversway Bus. Village PR2: Ash R 9D **114**
RIVERSWAY DOCKLANDS 9E **114**
Riversway Dr. BB3: Lwr D 1N **157**
Riversway Ent. Workshops PR2: Ash R 9B **114**
Riversway Managed Workshops
PR2: Ash R 9C **114**
Riversway Motor Pk. PR2: Ash R 9B **114**
River Vw. *BB9: Barrf 8H 85*
(off River Way)
LA2: Glas 1C **36**
PR4: Tarl 7E **150**
Riverview Ct. LA4: Morec 5B **22**
River Way BB9: Barrf 7H **85**
Riverway Cl. PR5: Lost H 8N **135**
River Wyre Caravan Pk. FY6: Sing 7B **64**
Riviera Ct. OL12: Roch 3G **202**
RIVINGTON 4A **196**
Rivington Av. FY2: Blackp 6C **62**
PR6: Adl 6K **195**
Rivington Cl. *BB1: Blackb 4B 140*
(off Rivington St.)
FY6: Poul F 8K **63**
PR4: Tarl 7D **150**
PR8: Birk 2G **186**
Rivington Country Pk. 4A **196**
Rivington Dr. L40: Burs 1C **210**
WN8: Uph 4F **220**
Rivington Hall Cl. BL0: Ramsb 1H **201**
Rivington Ho. BL6: Hor 9C **196**
Rivington La. BL6: R'ton 4A **196**
PR6: And 7M **195**
Rivington Pike Tower 5D **196**
Rivington Pl. PR7: Copp 7N **193**
Rivington Rd. BL6: R'ton 1F **196**
BL7: Belm, R'ton 1F **196**
PR6: Chor 5G **174**
Rivington St. BB1: Blackb 4B **140**
OL12: Roch 4C **204**
Rivington Terraced Gdns. 4C **196**
Rixton Gro. FY5: T Clev 8H **55**
Roach Pl. OL16: Roch 5D **204**
Roach Rd. PR5: Sam 1G **137**
Roach Va. OL16: Roch 3F **204**
Roading Brook Rd. BL2: Bolt 9N **199**
Road La. OL12: Roch 1A **204**
Roads Ford Av. OL16: Milnr 6J **205**
ROBBINS BRIDGE 6D **216**
Robbins Bri. L31: Lyd 6D **216**
Robert Saville Ct. *OL11: Roch 7N 203*
(off Half Acre M.)
Roberts Ct. LA5: Wart 4A **12**
PR25: Leyl 7H **153**
Roberts Pas. OL15: Littleb 4N **185**
Roberts Pl. *OL15: Littleb 2J 205*
(off Wordsworth Cres.)
Roberts St. BB4: Rawt 4M **161**
BB9: Nelson 2K **105**
PR7: Chor 7E **174**
Robert St. BB2: Blackb 8D **226** (5M **139**)
BB3: Darw 5N **157**
BB4: W'foot 5D **162**
BB5: Acc 1B **142**
BB5: Osw 5K **141**
BB6: Gt H 3K **121**
BB8: Colne 6B **86**
BB18: Barnw 2M **77**
BL0: Ramsb 5H **181**
BL2: Bolt 8L **199**
LA1: Lanc 7D **228** (8K **23**)
OL16: Roch 5D **204**
Robin Bank Rd. BB3: Darw 5A **158**
Robin Cl. PR7: Char R 2N **193**
Robin Cres. LA3: Heys 1L **27**
Robin Cft. LA2: Gress 5B **18**
Robin Hey PR26: Leyl 6E **152**
Robin Hill Dr. WN6: Stand 2L **213**
Robin Hill La. WN6: Stand 1L **213**
ROBIN HOOD 1E **212**
Robin Hood La. WN6: Wrigh 1E **212**
Robin Ho. La. BB10: Brierc 7N **105**
Robin La. BB7: Rim 3A **76**
LA2: H Ben 6L **19**
WN8: Parb 8N **191**
Robin Rd. BL9: Summ 2G **201**
Robins Bank Caravan Pk. FY6: Ham 8N **55**
Robins Cl. FY6: Carl 7G **62**
Robins La. FY2: Blackp 6F **62**
FY6: Carl 7F **62**
Robinson Cl. PR7: Buck V 1A **174**
Robinson Fold BB18: Barnw 1L **77**
Robinson La. BB9: Brierf 6D **104**
Robinson St. BB1: Blackb 1A **140**
BB7: Chatb 7D **74**
BB8: Colne 6N **85**
BB8: Foul 2A **86**
BB10: Burnl 9E **104**
BL6: Hor 9C **196**
OL16: Roch 6D **204**
PR2: Fulw 6G **115**
Robin St. PR1: Prest 8N **115**
Robinwood Activity Cen. 8H **147**
Robinwood Ter. OL14: Tod 8H **147**
Robraine LA6: K Lon 6F **8**
Robson St. BB9: Brierf 4F **104**
Robson Way FY3: Blackp 9G **62**
Roby Av. PR7: Buck V 9A **154**
ROBY MILL 9E **212**
Roby Mill WN8: Roby M 9E **212**
Rochbury Cl. OL11: Roch 7K **203**
ROCHDALE 5C **204**
Rochdale Cen. Retail Cen. OL11: Roch 7D **204**
Rochdale Crematorium OL11: Roch 6M **203**
Rochdale Ent. Generation Cen. OL12: Roch 6B **204**
Rochdale Exchange Shop. Cen.
OL16: Roch 5B **204**
Rochdale FC 5N **203**
Rochdale Golf Course 5L **203**
Rochdale Hornets RLFC 5N **203**
Rochdale Ind. Cen. OL11: Roch 7A **204**
Rochdale Old Rd. BL9: Bury 9A **202**
Rochdale Pioneers Mus. 5C **204**
Rochdale Rd. BL0: Eden, Ramsb 3K **181**
OL13: Bac 5K **163**
OL14: Tod, Wals 4K **165**
OL16: Milnr, Roch 6H **205**
Rochdale Rd. E. OL10: Heyw 9K **203**
Rochdale Station (Rail) 7C **204**
Rochdale Stop (Metro) 7C **204**
Rochester Av. FY5: T Clev 8F **54**
LA4: Morec 5C **22**
Rochester Cl. OL13: Weir 9L **145**
Rochester Dr. BB10: Burnl 7G **105**
Rochford Av. FY5: T Clev 2E **62**
Roch Mills Cres. OL11: Roch 8N **203**
Roch Mills Gdns. OL11: Roch 8N **203**
Roch St. OL16: Roch 4E **204**
Roch Vale Caravan Pk. OL16: Roch 6D **204**
Roch Valley Way OL11: Roch 7N **203**
Rock Bri. Fold BB4: Lumb 2C **162**
Rock Brow PR3: T'ley 7H **71**
Rockburgh Cres. PR4: Wal B 2L **151**
ROCKCLIFFE 6L **163**
Rockcliffe Av. OL13: Bac 6J **163**
Rockcliffe Dr. OL13: Bac 6J **163**
Rockcliffe Rd. OL13: Bac 6K **163**
Rockcliffe St. BB2: Blackb 9D **226** (6M **139**)
Rockcliffe Vs. OL13: Bac 6J **163**
Rockfield Gdns. *L31: Magh 9B 216*
(off East Meade)
Rockfield Rd. BB5: Acc 2C **142**
Rockfield St. BB2: Blackb 8C **226** (5M **139**)
Rock Fold BL7: Eger 4F **198**
Rock Gdns. PR5: Hogh 5K **137**
Rock Hall Rd. BB4: Hasl 3G **161**
Rockhaven Av. BL6: Hor 9D **196**
Rockingham Ct. L33: Kirk 6L **223**
Rockingham Rd. FY2: Blackp 8D **62**
Rock La. BB3: Tock 4H **157**
BB8: Traw 8F **86**
(River St.)
BB8: Traw 9F **86**
(White Lee Av.)
BB11: Burnl 6F **124**
L31: Mell 4E **222**
Rockliffe La. OL13: Bac 6L **163**
Rockliffe St. BB4: Rawt 4M **161**
Rockm'Jock *LA2: Caton 3G 25*
(off Copy La.)
Rock Nook OL15: Littleb 5N **185**
Rock St. BB4: Hasl 4G **161**
BB5: Bax 6D **142**
BB7: Clith 3L **81**
BL0: Ramsb 7K **181**
BL6: Hor 9C **196**
FY5: T Clev 8H **55**
Rock Ter. BB4: Craws 9M **143**
BB7: Pend 7A **82**
BL7: Eger 4F **198**
LA5: Arn 1F **4**
OL14: Tod 5K **165**
WN6: Wrigh 6J **193**
Rock Vw. BB4: W'foot 7C **162**
L31: Mell 6F **222**
OL12: Whitw 8B **164**
Rock Villa Rd. PR6: Whit W 7E **154**
Rockville BB9: Barrf 6J **85**
Rockville Av. FY5: T Clev 3F **62**
Rock Water Bird Cen. 6N **125**
Rockwood Cl. BB10: Burnl 7J **105**
RODDLESWORTH 7F **156**
Roddlesworth Info. Cen. 7J **157**
Roddlesworth La. PR6: Withn 7E **156**
Rodhill La. BB7: Bolt B 9G **51**
Rodmell Cl. BL7: Brom C 6F **198**
Rodney Av. FY8: L Ann 8E **108**
Rodney St. BB2: Blackb 5K **139**
PR1: Prest 4J **229** (9H **115**)
Rodwell Wlk. FY3: Blackp 2F **88**
Roebuck Cl.
BB2: Blackb 8A **226** (5L **139**)
Roebuck St. PR2: Ash R 7F **114**
ROEBURNDALE 4E **32**
Roeburndale Cres. LA3: Heys 8M **21**
Roeburndale Rd. LA2: Littled 5M **25**
Roeburn Dr. LA3: Morec 6F **22**
Roeburn Hall PR2: Ash R 4G **229** (9H **115**)
Roeburn Pl. LA1: Lanc 6J **23**
Roedean Av. LA4: Morec 4F **22**
Roedean Cl. FY5: T Clev 1G **62**
L31: Magh 9C **216**
Roefield OL12: Roch 5N **203**
Roefield Leisure Cen. 3H **81**
Roefield Ter. OL12: Roch 5N **203**
Roe Greave Rd. BB5: Osw 5K **141**
Roehampton Cl. FY5: T Clev 1G **62**
Roe Hey Dr. PR7: Copp 3B **194**
Roe La. PR9: S'port 6L **167**
ROE LEE 8N **119**
Roe Lee Pk. BB1: Blackb 7N **119**
Roe Pk. M. PR9: S'port 6K **167**
Roe St. OL12: Roch 4N **203**
Rogerley Cl. FY8: L Ann 4N **129**
Rogersfield BB6: Langh 9B **100**
Roleton Cl. L30: N'ton 6A **222**
Rollesby Cl. BL8: Bury 3J **201**
Rolleston Rd. BB2: Blackb 4J **139**
Roman Cres. LA2: Caton 3H **25**
Roman Rd. BB1: Guide 6A **140**
BB2: Blackb 9F **226** (6A **140**)
BB3: E'hill 3C **158**
BB3: Hodd 8E **158**
PR1: Prest 1L **135**
Roman Rd. Ind. Est. BB1: Guide 1B **158**
Roman Way BB7: Clith 3M **81**
FY5: T Clev 2F **62**
L33: Kirk 7M **223**
PR2: Ribb 3E **116**
PR4: K'ham 5A **112**
Roman Way Ind. Est. PR2: Ribb 3E **116**
Rome Av. BB11: Burnl 5A **124**
Romford Rd. PR1: Prest 7M **115**
Romford St. BB12: Burnl 2A **124**
Romiley Dr. WN8: Skelm 1K **219**
Romney Av. BB9: Barrf 8H **85**
BB11: Burnl 6C **124**
FY4: Blackp 9D **88**
FY7: Flee 1E **54**
Romney Chase BL1: Bolt 9E **198**
Romney St. BB9: Nelson 3H **105**
Romney Wlk. BB1: Blackb 4C **140**
Romsey OL12: Roch 5B **204**
Romsey Av. L37: Form 1B **214**
Romsey Gro. WN3: Wins 9N **221**
Rona Av. FY4: Blackp 3F **108**
Ronald St. BB1: Blackb 3C **140**
BB12: Burnl 4M **123**
Ronaldsway BB9: Nelson 9M **85**
PR1: Prest 6N **115**
Ronaldsway Cl. OL13: Bac 6L **163**
Ronaldway FY4: Blackp 1E **108**
Ronbury Cl. BB9: Barrf 1G **105**
Roney St. BB2: Blackb 4A **226** (3K **139**)
Ronnie Taylor Ct. OL16: Milnr 7J **205**
Ronwood Cl. PR4: Elsw 1L **91**
Ronwood Ct. PR2: Ash R 9E **114**
Roods, The LA5: Wart 4B **12**
Roods La. OL11: Roch 4G **202**
Rookery Av. WN6: App B 4H **213**
Rookery Cl. PR1: Penw 6J **135**
PR7: Chor 8C **174**
Rookery Dr. PR1: Penw 6J **135**
WA11: Rain 4L **225**
Rookery La. WA11: Rain 5L **225**
Rookery Rd. BB18: Barnw 1N **77**
PR9: S'port 5L **167**
Rook Hill Rd. OL13: Bac 7F **162**
Rook St. BB8: Colne 6A **86**
BB9: Nelson 1J **105**
BB18: Barnw 2M **77**
BL0: Ramsb 8H **181**
PR1: Prest 7L **115**
Rookswood Dr. OL11: Roch 9M **203**
Rookwood PR7: E'ton 8E **172**
Rookwood Av. FY5: T Clev 3D **62**
PR7: Chor 4E **174**
Rooley Moor Rd. OL12: Roch 4H **183**
(not continuous)
OL13: Bac, Roch 8F **162**
Rooley St. OL12: Roch 4N **203**
Rooley Ter. OL12: Roch 4N **203**
Rooley Vw. OL13: Bac 6J **163**
Room Apartments, The PR1: Prest 5K **229**
Roomfield Ct. *OL14: Tod 2L 165*
(off Halifax Rd.)
Roomfield Ho. OL14: Tod 2L **165**
Roomfield St. OL14: Tod 2L **165**
Roosevelt Av. LA1: Lanc 9H **23**
Roots La. PR4: Catf 7J **93**
Ropefield Way OL12: Roch 2B **204**
Rope St. OL12: Roch 5C **204**
Rope Wlk. PR3: Gars 5N **59**
Rosalynd Cotts. OL13: Bac 7E **162**
Rosary Av. FY4: Blackp 9E **88**
Roscoe Av. FY5: T Clev 1K **63**
Roscoe Lowe Brow PR6: And 6M **195**
ROSEACRE 4B **92**
Roseacre FY4: Blackp 4C **108**
Roseacre Cl. *BB4: Lumb 3D 162*
(off Foxhill Dr.)
Roseacre Dr. PR4: Elsw 1M **91**
Roseacre La. LA5: Yea C 9B **6**
Roseacre Pl. FY8: L Ann 9H **109**
PR2: Ash R 8B **114**
Roseacre Rd. PR4: Elsw, Rose, Wharl 1M **91**
PR4: Salw 8H **93**
PR4: Wharl 6D **92**
Rose Av. BB11: Burnl 5C **124**
FY1: Blackp 7M **227** (8D **88**)
OL11: Roch 3H **203**
OL15: Littleb 2J **205**
PR2: Ash R 6F **114**
Rose Bank BB4: Rawt 4M **161**
LA5: Carn 1M **15**
Rosebank BB5: Clay M 6N **121**
BL0: Ramsb 5J **181**
FY5: T Clev 2F **62**
PR2: Lea 8N **113**
Rosebank Av. FY4: Blackp 4C **108**
Rose Bank Rd. OL14: Tod 2K **165**
Rose Bank St. OL13: Bac 4K **163**
Rosebay Av. BB2: Fenis 8E **138**
Rosebay Cl. L37: Form 9A **206**
Roseberry Av. PR4: Cott 4B **114**
Roseberry Cl. BL0: Ramsb 2H **201**
Roseberry St. BB10: Burnl 8F **104**
Rosebery Av. FY4: Blackp 3B **108**
FY8: L Ann 4H **129**
LA1: Lanc 2L **29**
LA4: Morec 4N **21**
Rosebery St. OL14: Tod 7F **146**
PR9: S'port 8N **167**
Rose Cl. PR25: Leyl 5A **154**
Rose Cotts. BB7: Rim 4M **75**
BB10: Brierc 8L **105**
PR6: Whit W 1F **174**
Rose Ct. BB2: Blackb 2J **139**
BB3: Darw 7A 158
(off Wraith St.)
FY7: Flee 9F **40**
Rose Cres. PR8: Ains 2C **206**
WN8: Skelm 2J **219**
Rosecroft Cl. L39: Orms 6K **209**
Rosedale Av. BL1: Bolt 8E **198**
FY4: Blackp 8G **88**
LA3: Heys 8M **21**
Rosedale St. *BB4: Rawt 2L 161*
(off The Holmes)
Rosedene LA2: Slyne 1K **23**
Rosedene Cl. PR4: Cott 4B **114**
Rose Dr. WA11: Rain 5L **225**
Rosefield Cres. OL16: Roch 6F **204**
Rosefinch Ct. FY3: Blackp 8H **89**
Rosefinch Way FY3: Blackp 8H **89**
Rose Fold FY5: T Clev 8G **55**
PR1: Penw 4G **135**
Rose Gdns. PR4: Hesk B 3C **150**
Rosegarth LA2: Slyne 1K **23**
ROSE GROVE 3N **123**
Rose Gro. LA2: Gal 2K **37**

Rosegrove Caravan Pk. FY6: Pree .7N 41
Rosegrove La. BB11: Burnl .4M 123
BB12: Burnl .4M 123
Rose Grove Station (Rail) .4N 123
ROSE HILL
BB11 .6C 124
WN5 .5M 221
ROSEHILL .8C 158
Rose Hill BB1: Blackb .4G 226
BL0: Ramsb .8H 181
PR7: Eux .2M 173
PR9: S'port .8K 167
Rosehill BB4: W'foot .4D 162
Rose Hill Av. BB1: Blackb .5G 226 (4A 140)
WN5: Wigan .5M 221
Rosehill Av. BB9: Nelson .1K 105
BB11: Burnl .6C 124
Rosehill Bus. Pk. PR9: S'port .8K 167
Rose Hill Cl. BL7: Brom C .6G 199
Rose Hill Dr. BL7: Brom C .6G 199
Rosehill Dr. L39: Aug .1H 217
Rosehill Mt. BB11: Burnl .5C 124
Rose Hill Rd. BB2: Pleas .7D 138
Rosehill Rd. BB8: Colne .9L 85
BB11: Burnl .5C 124
Rose Hill St. BB3: Darw .7B 158
BB4: Craws .7M 143
OL13: Bac .5K 163
Rosehill Ter. BB3: Darw .7B 158
Roseland Av. BB9: Brierf .4G 104
Roseland Cl. L31: Lyd .7A 216
Rose La. PR1: Prest .6M 115
Rose Lea BL2: Bolt .9L 199
PR2: Fulw .3N 115
Roselea Dr. PR9: S'port .2B 168
Roselyn Av. FY4: Blackp .4C 108
Rosemary Av. FY4: Blackp .4C 108
FY5: T Clev .9F 54
Rosemary Ct. PR1: Penw .6F 134
Rosemary Dr. OL15: Littleb .8J 185
Rosemary La. L39: D'holl .7N 207
LA1: Lanc .6D 228 (8K 23)
PR4: Bartl .8L 93
Rosemeade Av. PR5: Lost H .8L 135
Rosemede Av. FY4: Blackp .8F 88
Rose Mt. BB4: Newc .6D 162
Rosemount OL13: Bac .3L 163
Rosemount Av. BB11: Burnl .5C 124
BB18: Barnw .1L 77
FY6: Pree .8N 41
Rosendale Cl. OL13: Bac .4M 163
Rosendale Cres. OL13: Bac .4L 163
Rose Path L37: Form .1A 214
Rose Pl. BB5: Acc .4A 142
L39: Aug .1J 217
WA11: Rain .5L 225
Rose St. BB2: Blackb .8D 226 (5M 139)
BB3: Darw .6B 158
BB4: W'foot .5C 162
BB5: Acc .4A 142
LA4: Morec .2B 22
OL13: Bac .5K 163
OL14: Tod .2L 165
PR1: Prest .6L 229 (1K 135)
PR25: Far .4L 153
Rose Ter. OL13: Bac .7K 163
PR2: Ash R .8E 114
Rose Theatre .9M 209
Rose Va. St. BB4: Rawt .5N 161
Roseway FY4: Blackp .4C 108
FY6: Poul F .8J 63
FY8: L Ann .2H 129
PR2: Ash R .8D 114
Rosewood OL11: Roch .4J 203
PR4: Cott .4B 114
PR9: S'port .4M 167
(off Cambridge Rd.)
Rosewood Av. BB1: Blackb .8M 119
BB4: Hasl .4H 161
BB11: Burnl .6C 124
BL8: Tott .7F 200
PR5: H Walt .5E 136
Rosewood Bus. Pk. BB1: Blackb .9M 119
Rosewood Cl. FY5: T Clev .2K 63
FY8: L Ann .4L 129
PR7: Chor .8F 174
Rosewood Ct. PR5: H Walt .5D 136
Rosewood Dr. PR5: H Walt .5D 136
Roshaw PR2: Grim .9F 96
Rosklyn Rd. PR6: Chor .7G 174
Rosley St. BB8: Wine .6E 86
Rossall Av. L10: Aint .7C 222
ROSSALL BEACH .7C 54
Rossall Beach Stop (Tram) .7D 54
Rossall Cl. BB12: Padi .3J 123
FY7: Flee .4D 54
PR5: Hogh .4G 136
Rossall Ct. FY5: T Clev .7C 54
FY7: Flee .1E 54
Rossall Dr. PR2: Fulw .5F 114
Rossall Gdns. FY5: T Clev .8D 54
Rossall Ga. FY7: Flee .4C 54
Rossall Grange La. FY7: Flee .1D 54
Rossall La. FY7: Flee .5D 54
(not continuous)
Rossall Prom. FY5: T Clev .7C 54
Rossall Rd. FY3: Blackp .3D 88
FY5: T Clev .1D 62
FY8: L Ann .4J 129
LA1: Lanc .6G 23
OL12: Roch .3D 204
PR2: Fulw .5F 114
PR6: Chor .5G 174
Rossall School Stop (Tram) .5D 54
Rossall Square Stop (Tram) .5D 54
Rossall St. PR2: Ash R .8F 114
Rossall Ter. BB2: Blackb .7M 139
Ross Cotts. OL13: Bac .6L 163
(off Rockcliffe La.)
Rossendale Av. BB11: Burnl .7B 124
LA1: Bail .7M 29
LA4: Morec .2C 22
Rossendale Av. Nth. FY5: T Clev .1H 63
Rossendale Av. Sth. FY5: T Clev .2H 63
Rossendale Golf Course .8H 161
Rossendale Mus. .5K 161
Rossendale Rd. BB11: Burnl .4N 123
FY8: L Ann .1G 128
Rossendale Rd. Ind. Est. BB11: Burnl .5N 123
Rossendale United FC .6C 162
Rossendale Valley .4F 162
Rossendale Valley Sailing Club .4A 144
Rosser Ct. BB9: Nelson .2J 105
Rosset Cl. WN3: Wins .9N 221
Rossett Av. FY4: Blackp .9J 89
Rossetti Av. BB11: Burnl .7D 124
Rossett M. FY4: Blackp .9J 89
(off Rossett Av.)
Rossington Av. FY2: Blackp .6E 62
Rosslyn Av. FY6: Pree .7N 41
L31: Magh .2A 222
Rosslyn Cres. FY6: Pree .8N 41
Rosslyn Cres. E. FY6: Pree .8A 42
Rossmere Av. OL11: Roch .7N 203
Rossmoyne Rd. LA1: Lanc .3L 29
Ross St. BB3: Darw .9A 158
BB9: Brierf .5F 104
Rostle Top Rd. BB18: Earl .3D 78
Rostrevor Cl. PR26: Leyl .6E 152
Rostron Rd. BL0: Ramsb .8G 181
Rostron's Bldgs. BB4: Rawt .6B 162
(off Bacup Rd.)
Rothay Av. FY7: Flee .2D 54
Rothbury Pl. FY8: L Ann .4B 130
Rotherwick Av. PR7: Chor .7D 174
Rothesay Cres. LA3: Heys .2J 27
Rothesay Rd. BB1: Blackb .4D 140
BB9: Brierf .4G 104
LA3: Heys .2J 27
Rothesay Ter. OL16: Roch .9F 204
Rothley Av. PR8: Ains .9A 186
Rothwell Av. BB5: Acc .4B 142
Rothwell Cl. L39: Orms .7J 209
Rothwell Ct. PR25: Leyl .5K 153
Rothwell Cres. PR2: Ribb .5B 116
Rothwell Dr. FY7: Flee .1D 54
L39: Aug .1G 217
PR8: Ains .8A 186
Rothwell Lodge PR2: Ribb .5B 116
(off Grange Av.)
Rothwell Rd. BB1: Guide .1B 158
PR6: And .6K 195
Rothwell St. BL0: Ramsb .8G 181
OL12: Roch .4E 204
Rotten Row LA2: Brookh .2K 25
PR8: S'port .9E 166
ROUGH BANK .8N 205
Rough Bank OL12: Whitw .9N 183
Rough Hey BB5: Osw .6M 141
Rough Hey Barn BB5: Osw .6N 141
Rough Hey Gate BB5: Osw .6M 141
Rough Hey La. HX7: Hept .9M 127
OL14: Wals .6J 165
Rough Hey Pl. PR2: Ribb .2D 116
Rough Hey Rd. PR2: Ribb .2D 116
Rough Heys La. FY4: Blackp .2E 108
Rough Hey Wlk. OL16: Roch .7E 204
Roughhill La. BL9: Bury .9B 202
Rough La. L39: Bart .3D 206
Rough Lea Rd. FY5: T Clev .1C 62
ROUGHLEE .6F 84
Roughlee Gro. BB10: Burnl .4H 125
Roughlee Gro. BB5: Acc .4B 142
Roughlee St. BB9: Barrf .9H 85
Roughlee Ter. BB11: Dunn .4N 143
Rough Side La. OL14: Tod .3M 165
Roughwood Dr. L33: Kirk .7L 223
Roundabout, The WN8: Skelm .2G 219
Round Acre PR1: Penw .7K 135
PR5: Sam .1N 137
ROUND BARN .3H 179
Roundell Dr. BD23: W Mar .7H 53
Roundell Rd. BB18: Barnw .1N 77
Roundell Ter. BB18: Barnw .1N 77
(off Skipton Rd.)
Roundel St. BB10: Burnl .8F 104
Roundhay FY4: Blackp .1G 108
ROUNDHILL .1E 160
Roundhill La. BB4: Hasl .1E 160
Round Hill Pl. BB10: Cliv .8J 125
Roundhill Rd. BB4: Hasl .9C 142
BB5: Acc .9C 142
Roundhill Vw. BB5: Ris B .8F 142
Roundhouse, The LA1: Lanc .7D 228
Round Meade, The L31: Magh .9A 216
Round Mdw. PR26: Leyl .6F 152
Roundway FY7: Flee .4C 54
Roundway Down PR2: Fulw .2F 114
Round Wood PR1: Penw .1E 134
Roundwood Av. BB10: Reed .6E 104
Rourkes Forge .4M 123
Rouse St. OL11: Roch .9N 203
ROW, THE .7J 5
Row, The LA5: Silv .7J 5
PR6: Heap .3M 175
Rowan Av. BB5: Osw .6K 141
PR2: Ribb .5C 116
Rowan Bank LA2: Halt .1B 24
Rowan Cl. BB1: Blackb .8A 120
L40: Burs .7D 190
OL12: Roch .2L 203
PR1: Penw .5E 134
PR3: Gars .6A 60
PR4: Clif .7H 113
Rowan Cft. PR6: Clay W .6C 154
Rowan Dr. L32: Kirk .7H 223
Rowan Gth. LA6: K Lon .6F 8
(off New Rd.)
Rowangate PR2: Fulw .2M 115
Rowan Gro. BB10: Burnl .3G 124
PR6: Chor .3E 174
Rowan La. WN8: Skelm .8M 211
Rowan Pl. LA1: Lanc .8H 23
Rowans, The FY6: Poul F .9G 63
L39: Aug .4F 216
PR6: Adl .5J 195
Rowans St. BL8: Bury .9H 201
Rowan Tree Cl. BB5: Acc .1D 142
Rowberrow Cl. PR2: Fulw .3N 115
Rowen Pk. BB2: Blackb .9J 119
Rowland Av. BB9: Nelson .2L 105
Rowland Cl. FY5: T Clev .1F 62
Rowland Ct. OL16: Roch .7E 204
Rowland La. FY5: T Clev .1F 62
ROWLANDS .3J 201
Rowlands Rd. BL9: Bury, Summ .3H 201
Rowland St. BB5: Acc .3N 141
OL16: Roch .7E 204
Rowlay Trad. Est. FY8: L Ann .1D 128
Rowley La. BB10: Burnl .3H 125
Rowlings Way L32: Kirk .9L 223
Rowntree Av. FY7: Flee .1F 54
Roworth Cl. PR5: Walt D .5A 136
Rowsley Rd. FY8: L Ann .1D 128
Rowton Heath PR2: Fulw .2F 114
Rowton St. BL2: Bolt .9H 199
Roxburgh Rd. FY4: Blackp .3F 108
Roxton Cl. BL6: Hor .8C 196
Royal Av. BL9: Bury .8L 201
FY3: Blackp .7E 88
PR2: Fulw .3H 115
PR4: K'ham .5N 111
PR25: Leyl .8H 153
Royal Bank Rd. FY3: Blackp .7E 88
Royal Beach Ct. FY8: L Ann .1D 128
Royal Birkdale Golf Course .4D 186
Royal Brook Ho. PR1: Prest .3M 229
Royal Cl. L37: Form .2A 214
Royal Ct. BB10: Brierc .7K 105
LA1: Lanc .8C 228
Royal Court Theatre .5K 163
Royal Cres. L37: Form .2A 214
Royal Dr. PR2: Fulw .6G 115
Royal Fold LA3: Heys .9K 21
Royal Gdns. BL0: Ramsb .2F 200
Royal Lytham St Annes Golf Course .2G 128
ROYAL OAK .7L 217
Royal Oak Av. BB1: Blackb .8M 119
Royal Oak Bldgs. FY4: Blackp .9B 88
(off Waterloo Rd.)
Royal Oak Cotts. BB9: Barrf .7F 84
Royal Oak Mdw. LA2: Horn .6C 18
Royal Pk. PR8: Birk .1E 186
Royal Pl. FY8: L Ann .9J 109
Royal Rd. LA4: Morec .2C 22
Royals, The FY8: L Ann .2G 128
Royal St. OL16: Roch .3F 204
Royal Ter. PR8: S'port .7G 167
Royal Troon Ct. PR4: K'ham .5M 111
Royalty Av. PR4: New L .8D 134
Royalty Gdns. PR4: New L .8D 134
Royalty La. PR4: New L .8C 134
Royalty Mall LA4: Morec .3A 22
(off Arndale Cen.)
Royal Umpire Caravan Pk. PR26: Leyl .3B 172
Royd OL14: Tod .9L 147
Royd La. OL14: Tod .9L 147
Royd Mills Ind. Pk. LA3: Midd .2L 27
Royd Rd. OL14: Tod .9K 147
Royds Av. BB5: Acc .4B 142
LA3: Heys .6L 21
Royds Cl. BL8: Tott .8F 200
Royds Gro. LA3: Heys .7L 21
Royds Pl. OL16: Roch .8D 204
Royds Rd. OL13: Bac .8E 162
Royds St. BB5: Acc .3B 142
BL8: Tott .6E 200
FY8: L Ann .3E 128
OL16: Milnr .8K 205
OL16: Roch .8E 204
Royds St. W. OL16: Roch .8D 204
Royd St. BL9: Bury .9B 202
OL14: Tod .1K 165
ROYLE .8B 104
Roylelands Bungs. OL11: Roch .9N 203
Roylen Av. FY6: Carl .6H 63
Royle Pennine Trad. Est. OL11: Roch .9A 204
Royle Rd. BB12: Burnl .1C 228 (2D 124)
(not continuous)
OL11: Roch .9A 204
PR7: Chor .6D 174
Royles Brook Cl. FY5: T Clev .9H 55
Royles Ct. FY5: T Clev .1H 63
Royle St. FY1: Blackp .9H 227 (9B 88)
Roynton Rd. BL6: R'ton .6C 196
Royshaw Av. BB1: Blackb .9M 119
Royshaw Cl. BB1: Blackb .9M 119
Royston Cl. BL8: Greenm .4E 200
Royston Rd. FY6: Poul F .6M 63
Roy St. OL14: Tod .7D 146
Royton Dr. PR6: Whit W .1E 174
Ruby St. BB1: Blackb .7N 119
BL9: Summ .2H 201
Ruby St. Pas. OL11: Roch .7B 204
(off Manchester Rd.)
Ruddington Rd. PR8: S'port .3L 187
Rudd St. BB4: Hasl .4F 160
Rudgwick Dr. BL8: Bury .6H 201
Rudman St. OL12: Roch .3B 204
Rudyard Dr. BB3: Darw .7D 158
Rudyard Pl. FY3: Blackp .3F 88
FY8: L Ann .9E 108
Ruecroft Cl. WN6: App B .4G 213
Ruff La. L39: Orms .8L 209
L40: W'head .8L 209
RUFFORD .1G 191
Rufford Av. L31: Magh .8D 216
OL11: Roch .9A 204
Rufford Cl. L10: Faz .9E 222
PR7: Chor .2D 194
Rufford Dr. PR9: Banks .1E 168
Rufford New Hall L40: Ruff .9F 170
Rufford Old Hall .9G 171
Rufford Pk. La. L40: Ruff .9E 170
Rufford Rd. FY8: L Ann .3J 129
L40: Bis G .3J 191
PR9: S'port .3B 168
WA11: Rain .3K 225
Rufford Station (Rail) .1H 191
Rufus St. PR1: Prest .7M 115
Rugby Av. BB5: Acc .9B 122
Rugby Cl. WN5: Orr .6H 221
Rugby Dr. L10: Aint .9D 222
WN5: Orr .3J 221
Rugby Rd. OL12: Roch .4D 204
Rugby Rd. Ind. Est. OL12: Roch .4D 204
Rugby St. FY4: Blackp .9D 88
RUINS .9L 199
Ruins La. BL2: Bolt .9L 199
Rumley's Fold BB11: Burnl .7C 124
Runcorn Av. FY2: Blackp .9F 62
Rundle Rd. PR2: Fulw .6G 115
Runley Mill BD24: Sett .4N 35
Runnel, The L39: Hals .2A 208
Runnell Vs. FY4: Blackp .2G 109
Runnymede Av. FY5: T Clev .1D 62
Runriggs, The FY5: T Clev .2H 63
Runshaw Av. WN6: App B .4H 213
Runshaw Hall PR7: Eux .1J 173
Runshaw Hall La. PR7: Eux .1K 173
Runshaw La. PR7: Eux .4G 173
RUNSHAW MOOR .2J 173
Rupert St. BB9: Nelson .3G 105
LA5: Carn .7A 12
OL12: Roch .4N 203
RUSH BED .1M 161
Rushbed Dr. BB4: Rawt .1M 161
Rushden Rd. L32: Kirk .9M 223
Rushes Farm Cl. BB5: Osw .5J 141
Rushey Cl. BB4: Rawt .1M 161
Rushey Fld. BL7: Brom C .5F 198
Rushey Hey Rd. L32: Kirk .8K 223
Rushford Gro. BL1: Bolt .9F 198
Rush Hey Bank BB11: Cliv .9H 125
Rushlake Gdns. OL11: Roch .5J 203
Rushley Dr. LA2: Hest B .8H 15
Rushley Mt. LA2: Hest B .8H 15
Rushmere Dr. BL8: Bury .8H 201
Rushmoor Cl. BB4: Craws .7M 143
Rushton Av. BB18: Earl .3E 78
Rushton Cl. BB9: Nelson .9M 85
Rushton St. BB6: Gt H .5H 121
BB9: Barrf .8H 85
OL13: Bac .7J 163
Rushwood Pk. WN6: Stand .2N 213
Rushworth Bldgs. OL13: Bac .7G 163
Rushworth St. BB10: Burnl .9F 104
Rushworth St. E. BB10: Burnl .9F 104
Rushy Fld. BB5: Clay M .4M 121
Rushy Hey PR5: Lost H .8K 135
Rushy Hill Vw. OL12: Roch .4N 203
Ruskin Av. BB5: Osw .3J 141
BB8: Colne .5A 86
BB12: Padi .2K 123
FY1: Blackp .8J 227 (8B 88)
FY5: T Clev .9G 54
PR25: Leyl .6K 153
Ruskin Cl. PR4: Tarl .9D 150
Ruskin Dr. LA4: Morec .2E 22
LA6: K Lon .6F 8
Ruskin Gro. BB11: Hapt .5H 123
LA5: Bolt S .4L 15
Ruskin Library, The .8L 29
Ruskin Pl. BB9: Nelson .9K 85
Ruskin Rd. LA1: Lanc .5K 23
PR4: Frec .2N 131
Ruskin St. BB10: Burnl .8E 104
PR1: Prest .8N 229 (2L 135)
Ruskin's View .5F 8
Rusland Av. FY4: Blackp .9K 89
Rusland Dr. PR5: Hogh .4G 136
Rusland Gdns. LA4: Morec .4B 22
Russell Av. BB8: Colne .5B 86
FY5: T Clev .3D 62
PR1: Prest .8C 116
PR9: S'port .7N 167
PR25: Leyl .7M 153
Russell Ct. BB11: Burnl .5G 228 (5F 124)
FY8: L Ann .2F 128
PR1: Prest .4J 229
PR9: S'port .2A 168
Russell Dr. LA4: Morec .4F 22
Russell M. LA1: Lanc .7C 228
Russell Pl. BB6: Gt H .4H 121
Russell Rd. LA5: Carn .9B 12
PR9: S'port .7N 167
Russell Sq. PR6: Chor .5F 174
Russell Sq. W. PR6: Chor .5F 174
Russell St. BB2: Blackb .7D 226 (5M 139)
BB5: Acc .3B 142
BB9: Nelson .2H 105
BL9: Bury .9L 201
LA1: Lanc .7C 228 (8K 23)
OL11: Roch .8B 204
(off Grove St.)
OL13: Bac .3K 163
OL14: Tod .2M 165
Russell Ter. BB12: Padi .2J 123
Russet Wlk. BL1: Bolt .9E 198
Russia St. BB5: Acc .2M 141
Rutherford Pl. FY4: Blackp .5B 108
Rutherford Rd. L31: Magh .3D 222
Ruthin Cl.
BB1: Blackb .1D 226 (1M 139)
Ruthin Dr. FY5: T Clev .1K 63
Ruth St. BL0: Eden .4J 181
BL9: Bury .9L 201
Rutland OL11: Roch .7B 204
Rutland Av. BB1: Blackb .4E 140
BB12: Burnl .3M 123
FY5: T Clev .9E 54
FY6: Poul F .8J 63
FY7: Flee .1F 54
LA1: Lanc .3L 29
PR4: Frec .1A 132
PR5: Walt D .5N 135
Rutland Cl. BB5: Clay M .6M 121
PR3: Gars .4M 59
Rutland Ct. FY8: L Ann .3K 129
Rutland Cres. L39: Orms .5J 209
Rutland Ga. FY1: Blackp .3B 88
Rutland Pl. BB12: Padi .2J 123
Rutland Rd. FY8: L Ann .3K 129
PR8: S'port .9K 167
Rutland St. BB2: Blackb .5J 139
BB5: Acc .3M 141
BB8: Colne .6C 86
BB9: Nelson .1J 105
PR1: Prest .9M 115
Rutland Wlk. BB4: Hasl .7F 160
Ryal Fold BB3: Tock .7J 157
Ryan Cl. PR25: Leyl .6H 153
Ryburn Av. BB2: Blackb .1H 139
FY4: Blackp .9E 88

Ryburn Rd.—St Marlowes Av.

Ryburn Rd. L39: Orms 9J 209
Ryburn Sq. OL11: Roch 7J 203
Rycliffe St. BB12: Padi 9H 103
Rydal Av. BB3: Darw 7A 158
FY1: Blackp 5L 227 (7C 88)
FY5: T Clev 2H 63
FY6: Poul F 8K 63
FY7: Flee 9E 40
PR1: Penw 5F 134
PR4: Frec 2L 131
PR5: Walt D 7N 135
WN5: Orr 4J 221
Rydal Cl. BB5: Hunc 8C 122
BB10: Reed 6G 104
BB12: Padi 9H 103
L10: Aint 8E 222
L33: Kirk 6J 223
PR2: Fulw 5M 115
Rydal Ct. LA4: Morec 3B 22
Rydal Gro. FY6: K Sea 7M 41
LA3: Heys 6L 21
Rydal Mt. BB1: Belt 1F 158
Rydal Pl. BB8: Colne 6D 86
PR7: Chor 8D 174
Rydal Rd. BB1: Blackb 1A 140
BB4: Hasl 7H 161
FY6: Ham 1B 64
FY8: L Ann 9E 108
LA1: Lanc 7F 228 (8L 23)
LA3: Heys 6L 21
LA5: Bolt S 5K 15
PR1: Prest 7N 115
Rydal St. BB10: Burnl 8E 104
Rydal Wlk. WN5: Wigan 4L 221
Ryddingwood PR1: Penw 2E 134
Ryde Cl. BB4: Hasl 6H 161
Ryden Av. FY5: T Clev 9D 54
PR25: Leyl 6M 153
Ryden Rd. BB1: Clay D 3L 119
Ryder Cl. L39: Aug 1H 217
Ryder Cres. L39: Aug 2H 217
PR8: Birk 5E 186
Ryding Cl. PR26: Far M 4H 153
Rydinge, The L37: Form 6A 206
Rydings, The BB6: Langh 1A 120
Rydings La. OL12: Ward 8D 184
PR9: Banks 6J 149
Rydings Rd. OL12: Roch 9D 184
Ryeburn Dr. BL2: Bolt 8H 199
Rye Cft. BB8: Traw 1G 106
Ryecroft PR6: Heap 8J 155
Ryecroft Av. BL8: Tott 7E 200
FY6: Ham 2B 64
Ryecroft La. BL7: Belm 9K 177
Ryecroft Pl. FY6: Ham 1B 64
Ryefield PR6: Heap 8H 155
Ryefield Av. BB4: Hasl 5G 160
PR1: Penw 6G 134
Ryefield Av. W. BB4: Hasl 5F 160
Ryefield Pl. BB4: Hasl 5G 160
Ryefields OL12: Roch 1G 205
Rye Gdns. BB2: Blackb 1L 157
Ryeground La. L37: Form 7A 206
Rye Gro. BB12: Padi 2J 123
Rye Hey Rd. L32: Kirk 8K 223
Ryeheys Rd. FY8: L Ann 9E 108
Ryelands Cl. OL16: Roch 9E 204
Ryelands Cres. PR2: Ash R 9B 114
Ryelands Rd. LA1: Lanc 6J 23
Rye Moss La. L37: Gt A 3G 215
Rye St. PR1: Prest 2L 229 (8K 115)
Ryknild Way LA3: Morec 5F 22
Rylance Rd. WN3: Wins 9N 221
Ryland Av. FY6: Poul F 8J 63
Rylands Rd. PR7: Chor 7D 174
Rylands St. BB10: Burnl 9F 104
Ryldon Pl. FY4: Blackp 8G 88
Rylstone Dr. BB18: Barnw 2L 77
LA3: Heys 8L 21
Rymer Gro. PR4: Longt 8M 133
Ryscar Way FY2: Blackp 5F 62
Rysdale Cres. LA4: Morec 4C 22
Ryson Av. FY4: Blackp 9F 88

S

SABDEN 2E 102
Sabden Brook Ct. BB7: Sabd 2F 102
Sabden Cl. BL9: Bury 6L 201
SABDEN FOLD 1M 103
Sabden Pl. FY8: L Ann 1J 129
Sabden Rd. BB7: Whall 6M 101
BB12: High 4L 103
BB12: Padi 4G 103
Saccary La. BB1: Mellor 4H 119
Sackville Av. FY4: Blackp 3C 108
Sackville Gdns. BB9: Brierf 5E 104
Sackville St. BB9: Brierf 5F 104
BB9: Nelson 4K 105
BB11: Burnl 4B 228 (4D 124)
BB18: Barnw 3M 77
OL14: Tod 2L 165
PR6: Chor 7G 174
Saddleback Cres. WN5: Wigan 5L 221
Saddleback Rd. WN5: Wigan 4L 221
Saddle Lodge *PR2: Ribb 5B 116*
(off Fir Trees Pl.)
Saddler Nook La. LA6: H Big 8D 8
Saddlers M. BB7: Clith 3L 81
Sadlers Row FY8: L Ann 1K 129
Sadler St. BB5: Chur 3L 141
Saer Cl. FY7: Flee 1D 54
Saffron Cl. BB9: Barrf 1G 104
Sagar Dr. PR4: Frec 2M 131
Sagar Fold BB8: Colne 6C 86
L39: Aug 3J 217
Sagar Holme Ter. BB4: Lumb 2C 162
Sagar La. OL14: Tod 6G 147
Sagar St. BB9: Nelson 2J 105
PR7: E'ton 8F 172
Sage Cl. FY2: Blackp 8F 62
Sage Ct. PR1: Penw 6F 134
Sage La. PR1: Prest 6L 115
Sahara Fold *BB1: Blackb 1A 140*
(off Warmden Gdns.)
St Aidans Av. BB2: Blackb 7J 139
(not continuous)
BB3: Darw 7B 158
St Aidan's Cl. BB2: Blackb 7K 139
OL11: Roch 8A 204
St Aidan's Pk. PR5: Bam B 6A 136
St Aidans Rd. PR5: Bam B 6A 136
St Albans Ct. BB1: Blackb 2F 226 (2N 139)
OL11: Roch 7B 204
St Albans Ho. *OL16: Roch 7B 204*
(off Latin St.)
St Albans Pl. PR7: Chor 9F 174
St Albans Rd. BB1: Rish 9G 120
BB3: Darw 4M 157
FY1: Blackp 4M 227 (6D 88)
FY8: L Ann 2E 128
LA4: Morec 2F 22
St Albans St. OL16: Roch 7B 204
St Alban's Ter. OL11: Roch 7B 204
St Ambrose Ter. PR25: Leyl 5L 153
St Andrew's Av. FY5: T Clev 1D 62
PR2: Ash R 7D 114
St Andrews Cl. BB5: Osw 4K 141
BB8: Colne 8N 85
BL0: Ramsb 9H 181
LA1: Lanc 8N 23
OL15: Littleb 9H 185
PR7: Eux 2N 173
PR25: Leyl 8K 153
St Andrews Ct. BB5: Osw 5K 141
FY8: L Ann 1D 128
PR8: S'port 8H 167
St Andrews Gro. LA4: Morec 2D 22
St Andrew's Pl. BB1: Blackb 2B 226 (2L 139)
PR8: S'port 8H 167
St Andrews Rd. BB6: Old L 4C 100
PR1: Prest 1M 229 (7K 115)
St Andrew's Rd. Nth. FY8: L Ann 1D 128
St Andrew's Rd. Sth. FY8: L Ann 2E 128
St Andrew's St. BB1: Blackb 2B 226 (2L 139)
BB10: Burnl 9F 104
St Andrews Vw. L33: Kirk 4K 223
St Andrews Way PR25: Leyl 7K 153
ST ANNE'S 2E 128
St Anne's Av. LA4: Morec 2F 22
St Annes Cl. BB2: Blackb 7F 226 (5N 139)
BB5: Chur 3L 141
(off Blackpool St.)
LA2: Brookh 3J 25
St Annes Ct. FY4: Blackp 9C 88
WN6: Shev 7J 213
St Anne's Cres. BB4: W'foot 4D 162
St Anne's Dr. BB12: Fence 3B 104
WN6: Shev 7K 213
St Annes Mdw. BL8: Tott 6E 200
St Anne's Old Links Golf Course 8D 108
St Anne's Pier 2D 128
St Anne's Pl. LA1: Lanc 6D 228
St Annes Rd. BL6: Hor 9D 196
FY4: Blackp 9L 227 (9C 88)
L39: Orms 8J 209
PR3: Gt E 6A 66
PR6: Chor 7G 174
PR9: S'port 2M 167
PR25: Leyl 4M 153
St Anne's Rd. E. FY8: L Ann 1E 128
St Anne's Rd. W. FY8: L Ann 2D 128
St Anne's Station (Rail) 1E 128
St Anne's St. BB12: Padi 2H 123
BL9: Bury 9L 201
(not continuous)
PR1: Prest 1L 229 (7K 115)
St Annes Swimming Pool 3D 128
St Anne's Way BB12: Fence 3B 104
St Ann's Ct. BB7: Clith 3H 81
St Ann's Rd. OL16: Roch 5G 204
St Anns Sq. BB7: Clith 3J 81
St Anthony's Cl. PR2: Fulw 5F 114
St Anthony's Cres. PR2: Fulw 5F 114
St Anthony's Dr. PR2: Fulw 5F 114
St Anthony's Pl. FY1: Blackp 3C 88
PR4: K'ham 5M 111
St Anthony's Rd. PR1: Prest 1M 229 (7K 115)
St Austell Dr. BL8: Greenm 3E 200
St Austell Pl. LA5: Carn 1N 15
St Austin's Pl. PR1: Prest 7M 229 (1K 135)
St Austin's Rd. PR1: Prest 7M 229 (1K 135)
St Barnabas Dr. OL15: Littleb 8K 185
St Barnabas Pl. PR1: Prest 3M 229 (8K 115)
St Barnabas St. BB2: Blackb 3K 139
BB3: Darw 9B 158
St Bede's Av. FY4: Blackp 9H 227 (9B 88)
St Bedes Cl. L39: Orms 9J 209
St Bede's Pk. BB3: Darw 2M 157
St Bee's Cl. BB2: Blackb 7N 139
St Benet's Cl. PR5: Walt D 7N 135
St Bernard Av. FY3: Blackp 3F 88
St Bernard's Rd. FY6: K Sea 8L 41
St Brides Cl. BL6: Hor 9B 196
St Catherine Cl. FY3: Blackp 1H 89
St Catherines Cl. PR25: Leyl 5M 153
St Catherines Ct. *BL6: Hor 9C 196*
(off Richmond St.)
LA1: Lanc 7D 228
St Catherine's Dr. PR2: Fulw 5F 114
St Catherines Way PR5: Lost H 9M 135
St Cecilia St. BB6: Gt H 4K 121
St Celia's Way LA4: Morec 2E 22
St Chad's Av. BB7: Chatb 7C 74
St Chads Cl. FY6: Poul F 9K 63
OL16: Roch 6C 204
St Chad's Ct. *OL16: Roch 6C 204*
(off School La.)
St Chad's Dr. L32: Kirk 8K 223
LA1: Lanc 5H 23
St Chads Pde. L32: Kirk 8K 223
St Chad's Rd. FY1: Blackp 8H 227 (8B 88)
PR1: Prest 8M 115
St Chad's Road Stop (Tram) 8H 227 (8B 88)
St Charles Rd. BB1: Rish 8G 121
St Christine's Av. PR25: Far 3M 153
St Christopher Ct. WN6: Stand 8M 213
St Christopher's Rd. PR1: Prest 1M 229 (7K 115)
St Christopher's Way LA4: Morec 2D 22
St Clair Dr. PR9: S'port 5N 167
St Clair Rd. BL8: Greenm 2E 200
St Clares Av. PR2: Fulw 3K 115
St Clements Av. FY3: Blackp 5E 88
PR25: Far 4M 153
St Clements Cl. BB1: Blackb 4B 140
St Clements Ct. BB9: Barrf 8H 85
OL11: Roch 5M 203
St Clement St. BB1: Blackb 3B 140
(not continuous)
St Crispin Way BB4: Hasl 5F 160
St Cuthbert's Cl. BB3: Darw 4M 157
FY8: L Ann 5N 129
PR2: Fulw 6G 114
PR9: S'port 4N 167
St Cuthberts Rd. PR1: Prest 1M 229 (7K 115)
PR5: Lost H 7K 135
PR9: S'port 4N 167
St Cuthbert St. BB10: Burnl 8F 104
St David's Av. BB2: Blackb 9F 138
FY5: T Clev 1D 62
St David's Gro. FY8: L Ann 9D 108
St David's Rd. PR1: Prest 1M 229 (7K 115)
PR25: Leyl 5M 153
St David's Rd. Nth. FY8: L Ann 8D 108
St David's Rd. Sth. FY8: L Ann 1E 128
St David's Wood BB5: Acc 1C 142
St Denys Cft. BB7: Clith 2L 81
St Edmund Hall Cl. BL0: Ramsb 1H 201
St Edmund's Rd. FY4: Blackp 9E 88
St Edmund St. BB6: Gt H 4K 121
St Frances Cl. BB1: Blackb 7F 226 (5N 139)
St Francis Cl. PR2: Fulw 2K 115
St Francis Rd. BB2: Blackb 6H 139
St Gabriel Cl. WN8: Roby M 9E 212
St Gabriel's Av. BB1: Blackb 6N 119
St George Ct. FY1: Blackp 4D 88
St George's Av. BB2: Blackb 7J 139
FY5: T Clev 2D 62
FY8: L Ann 1D 128
St Georges Cl. BB8: Colne 8N 85
St Georges Ct. L31: Magh 2C 222
PR4: K'ham 3K 111
PR7: Chor 7F 174
(off Halliwell St.)
St George's La. FY5: T Clev 1D 62
FY8: L Ann 2D 128
St Georges Pk. PR4: K'ham 3K 111
St George's Pl. PR9: S'port 7H 167
St George's Quay LA1: Lanc 7H 23
St George's Rd. BB9: Nelson 3K 105
FY4: Blackp 3C 108
FY8: L Ann 2D 128
L38: Hight 6A 214
OL11: Roch 5K 203
PR1: Prest 1J 229 (7J 115)
St George's Shop. Cen.
PR1: Prest 6K 229 (1J 135)
St George's Sq. BB10: Burnl 9G 104
FY8: L Ann 1D 128
St Georges St. PR7: Chor 7E 174
St George's Swimming Pool 9G 89
St Georges Ter. *BB3: Darw 5N 157*
(off Harwood St.)
BB4: W'foot 9E 162
St George's Works LA1: Lanc 7J 23
St Gerrard's Rd. PR5: Lost H 7K 135
St Giles St. BB12: Padi 9H 103
St Giles Ter. *BB12: Padi 9H 103*
(off East St.)
St Gregory Rd. PR1: Prest 1N 229 (7L 115)
St Gregory's Pl. PR7: Chor 9E 174
St Helens Cl. BB5: Osw 5M 141
PR3: C'town 1L 67
St Helen's Ct. FY5: T Clev 9D 54
St Helens Rd. L39: Orms 7L 209
LA3: O'ton 7B 28
PR6: Whit W 6E 154
WA11: Rain 8M 225
St Helens Well PR4: Tarl 1E 170
St Helier Cl. BB2: Blackb 8J 139
St Helier's Pl. PR3: Bart 3D 94
St Heliers Rd. FY1: Blackp 8K 227 (8C 88)
St Hilda's Cl. PR7: Chor 1E 194
St Hilda's Rd. FY8: L Ann 9D 108
St Hilda's Way PR7: Chor 1E 194
St Hubert's Rd. BB6: Gt H 5J 121
St Hubert's St. BB6: Gt H 4K 121
St Ignatius Pl.
PR1: Prest 4L 229 (9K 115)
St Ignatius Sq.
PR1: Prest 4L 229 (9K 115)
(not continuous)
St Ives Av. FY1: Blackp 6N 227 (7D 88)
PR4: Frec 2M 131
St Ives Bus. Pk.
BB1: Blackb 4E 140
St Ives Cres. PR2: Ingol 5D 114
St Ives Rd. BB1: Blackb 4D 140
St James Av. BL8: Bury 9G 201
St James Cl. BB4: Hasl 4G 160
BB5: Chur 1L 141
L40: W'head 9A 210
PR5: Lost H 8L 135
St James Ct. BB1: Blackb 1M 139
BL8: Bury 9G 201
(off St James Av.)
LA1: Lanc 7B 228
LA3: Heys 9K 21
PR5: Lost H 8L 135
WN6: Stand 2N 213
St James Ct. E. BB5: Acc 3A 142
St James Ct. W. BB5: Acc 3A 142
St James Cres. BB3: Darw 5B 158
St James Fold BB3: Lwr D 9B 140
St James Gdns. PR26: Leyl 7D 152
St James Ho. L39: Aug 1J 217
St James Lodge FY8: L Ann 3G 128
PR26: Leyl 7E 152
St James M. BB5: Chur 1L 141
St James Pl. BB12: Padi 1J 123
St James Rd. BB5: Chur 1L 141
BB18: Barnw 2M 77
FY4: Blackp 3C 108
WN5: Orr 7G 220
St James Row BB4: Rawt 4M 161
St James's Dr. LA6: Burt K 5G 7
St James's La. BB11: Burnl 2D 228
St James's Pl. BB1: Blackb 1M 139
PR6: Chor 7G 175
St James Sq. BB5: Acc 3A 142
BB18: Barnw 2M 77
OL13: Bac 4K 163
St James's Rd. BB1: Blackb 1M 139
PR1: Prest 1J 229 (7J 115)
St James's Row BB11: Burnl 3C 228 (3E 124)
St James's St. BB11: Burnl 2C 228 (3D 124)
(not continuous)
PR6: Chor 7G 175
St James St. BB2: Blackb 7K 139
BB4: Rawt 4M 161
BB4: W'foot 7C 162
BB5: Acc 3A 142
BB7: Clith 4L 81
BB9: Brierf 5F 104
OL13: Bac 5K 163
OL16: Milnr 7J 205
PR8: S'port 8H 167
St Jame's Ter. PR5: Sam 1N 137
St James Way OL12: Ward 7F 184
St John Av. FY7: Flee 2D 54
St John's BB1: Blackb 2B 226 (2L 139)
St Johns Av. BB3: Darw 7B 158
FY5: T Clev 2K 63
FY6: Poul F 6L 63
LA3: Heys 6M 21
LA5: Silv 8G 5
PR3: Pill 8H 43
PR4: K'ham 5L 111
St John's Cl. BB3: Darw 8C 158
BB4: Craws 9M 143
BB5: Bax 6D 142
BB12: Read 8C 102
PR6: Whit W 8D 154
St Johns Ct. *BB12: Burnl 3A 124*
(off Gannow La.)
BL0: Ramsb 8H 181
(off Cross St.)
FY1: Blackp 2L 227
FY8: L Ann 5B 130
(off Warton St.)
LA3: Heys 6L 21
(off Norton Rd.)
OL13: Bac 4K 163
OL16: Roch 7E 204
(off St John's Dr.)
PR3: Brou 9J 95
PR8: Ains 9D 186
St John's Dr. OL16: Roch 7E 204
St John's Grn. PR25: Leyl 6H 153
St John's Gro. LA3: Heys 6M 21
LA5: Silv 8G 5
St Johns M. *BL8: Tott 6E 200*
(off Kirklees St.)
LA1: Lanc 6C 228 (7K 23)
St Johns Pl. BB1: Blackb 3D 226
BB9: Nelson 2L 105
PR1: Prest 6L 229 (1K 135)
St John's Rd. BB12: Burnl 3A 124
BB12: Padi 3H 123
LA3: Heys 6L 21
PR5: Walt D 3N 135
PR8: Birk 4F 186
St John's Shop. Cen. PR1: Prest 5L 229
St John's St. BB3: Darw 7B 158
BB4: W'foot 7D 162
BB6: Gt H 5J 121
FY8: L Ann 5B 130
St John's Ter. LA3: Morec 6C 22
St John St. BL6: Hor 9C 196
OL13: Bac 4K 163
WN5: Wigan 5L 221
St John's Wlk. FY1: Blackp 1J 227 (5B 88)
St Johns Wood FY8: L Ann 5L 129
St Joseph's Cl. FY3: Blackp 5E 88
St Joseph's Dr. OL16: Roch 9E 204
St Joseph's Pl. PR6: Chor 5F 174
St Joseph's Ter. PR1: Prest 8M 115
St Jude's Av. PR5: Walt D 7N 135
PR25: Far 3M 153
St Kevin's Dr. L32: Kirk 6K 223
St Kitts Cl. BB3: Lwr D 1M 157
St Laurence Gro. L32: Kirk 9L 223
St Lawrence Av. BB2: Blackb 9J 119
St Lawrence's Av. PR3: Bart 2E 94
St Lawrence St. BB6: Gt H 4J 121
St Leger Ct. *BB5: Acc 3B 142*
(off Midland St.)
St Leonard's Cl. PR2: Ingol 6D 114
St Leonards Ct. FY8: L Ann 9D 108
LA1: Lanc 5E 228
St Leonard's Ga. LA1: Lanc 6D 228 (8K 23)
St Leonard's Rd. FY3: Blackp 8F 88
St Leonard's Rd. E. FY8: L Ann 9D 108
St Leonard's Rd. W. FY8: L Ann 1D 128
St Leonard's St. BB12: Padi 9H 103
St Louis Av. FY3: Blackp 3F 88
St Lucia Cl. BB3: Lwr D 1N 157
St Lukes Ct. FY4: Blackp 3C 108
LA1: Lanc 7A 228
OL11: Roch 8C 204
St Luke's Dr. WN5: Orr 7G 221
St Luke's Gro. PR9: S'port 7L 167
St Luke's Pl. PR1: Prest 8M 115
St Luke's Rd. FY4: Blackp 3C 108
PR9: S'port 8K 167
St Luke St. OL11: Roch 8C 204
St Margarets Cl. PR2: Ingol 5D 114
St Margarets Ct. BB1: Blackb 3B 140
FY7: Flee 9G 41
(off Walmsley St.)
St Margaret's Gdns. BB11: Hapt 5H 123
St Margarets Rd. LA4: Morec 2D 22
LA5: Bolt S 3L 15
PR25: Leyl 5M 153
St Margaret's Way BB1: Blackb 3B 140
St Mark's Pl. BB2: Blackb 4J 139
FY3: Blackp 2E 88
St Mark's Pl. E. PR1: Prest 9G 114
St Mark's Pl. W. PR1: Prest 9G 114
St Mark's Rd. BB2: Blackb 4J 139
PR1: Prest 9G 114
St Marks Sq. BL9: Bury 9L 201
St Marlowes Av. PR25: Far 4M 153

St Martins Cl.—Sankey Rd.

St Martins Cl. FY6: Carl 6H 63
St Martin's Ct. FY5: T Clev 1F 62
St Martin's Dr. BB2: Fenis 8E 138
St Martin's Rd. FY4: Blackp 3C 108
LA1: Lanc 9F 228 (1L 29)
PR1: Prest 1M 229 (7K 115)
St Martin's Sports Complex 9F 228 (9M 23)
St Mary Cl. FY3: Blackp 1H 89
St Mary's Av. BB18: Barnw 1A 78
PR5: Walt D 7N 135
St Marys Cl. BB1: Blackb 3B 140
OL16: Roch 9E 204
PR1: Prest 9M 115
PR3: Longr 2J 97
PR5: Walt D 7N 135
St Mary's Ct. BB2: Mellor 7E 118
BB4: Rawt 5L 161
BB5: Clay M 7M 121
FY7: Flee 9H 41
PR1: Prest 9L 115
St Mary's Dr. BB6: Langh 1C 120
St Marys Gdns. BB2: Mellor 7F 118
PR8: Ains 6F 186
St Mary's Ga. BB11: Burnl 3F 228 (4F 124)
LA1: Lanc 6B 228
OL12: Roch 6B 204
OL16: Roch 6B 204
PR7: Eux 3M 173
St Mary's Ho. PR1: Prest 5N 229
St Mary's Pde. LA1: Lanc 6B 228 (8J 23)
St Mary's Pl. BB4: Rawt 5L 161
St Mary's Rd. LA3: Heys 8K 21
PR3: Gt E 6N 65
PR5: Bam B 7A 136
St Mary's St. BB7: Clith 2L 81
BB9: Nelson 2G 105
PR1: Prest 4N 229 (9L 115)
St Mary's St. Nth. PR1: Prest 4N 229 (9L 115)
St Mary's Ter. BB4: Rawt 5M 161
St Mary's Wlk. PR7: Chor 6E 174
St Mary's Way BB4: Rawt 5M 161
St Mary's Wharfe BB2: Blackb 7E 226 (5N 139)
St Matthew's Cl. WN3: Wigan 7M 221
St Matthew's Ct. BB11: Burnl 4A 228
St Matthew St. BB11: Burnl 4A 228 (4C 124)
St Michael Rd. L39: Aug 5E 216
St Michaels Cl. BB2: Blackb 9F 138
FY3: Blackp 2G 89
LA5: Bolt S 4L 15
PR2: Fulw 6G 114
PR4: Weet 8D 90
PR7: Chor 5D 174
PR9: S'port 3M 167
St Michael's Ct. BB1: Blackb 1F 226 (2N 139)
BB9: Barrf 9G 85
St Michael's Cres. LA5: Bolt S 4L 15
St Michael's Gro. LA4: Morec 4D 22
LA5: Bolt S 5L 15
St Michael's La. LA5: Bolt S 4K 15
(not continuous)
ST MICHAEL'S ON WYRE 4G 66
St Michaels Pk. L39: Aug 4F 216
St Michael's Pl. LA5: Bolt S 5L 15
PR3: Bart 5E 94
St Michael's Rd. FY2: Blackp 8D 62
PR1: Prest 1M 229 (7K 115)
PR3: Bils 6K 67
PR4: K'ham 4A 112
PR25: Leyl 4M 153
St Michael's St. BB1: Blackb 1F 226 (1N 139)
St Mildred's Way LA3: Heys 1K 27
St Monica's Way FY4: Blackp 9K 89
St Nicholas Arcades LA1: Lanc 7D 228 (8K 23)
St Nicholas' Av. BB7: Sabd 2E 102
St Nicholas Cres. LA5: Bolt S 3M 15
St Nicholas Gro. PR4: W Grn 5G 111
St Nicholas La. LA5: Bolt S 3L 15
St Nicholas M. *BB7: Sabd* *2E 102*
(off St Nicholas' Av.)
St Nicholas Rd. BB5: Chur 1M 141
FY4: Blackp 4G 109
St Ogg's Rd. LA4: Morec 5C 22
St Oswald's Cl. BB1: Blackb 4E 140
PR1: Prest 7M 115
St Oswalds Ct. PR7: Copp 5A 194
St Oswald's Rd. BB1: Blackb 4E 140
St Oswald St. LA1: Lanc 9E 228 (1L 29)
St Patrick's Cl. L33: Kirk 5K 223
St Patricks Ct. *FY8: L Ann* *1F 128*
(off St Patricks Rd. Sth.)
St Patrick's Pl. PR5: Walt D 4A 136
St Patrick's Rd. Nth. FY8: L Ann 9E 108
St Patrick's Rd. Sth. FY8: L Ann 1F 128
St Patrick's Wlk. LA3: Heys 9K 21
St Paul's Av. BB2: Blackb 4B 226 (3L 139)
FY8: L Ann 4H 129
PR1: Prest 3L 229 (8K 115)
St Pauls Cl. BB7: Clith 3J 81
L33: Kirk 5J 223
PR6: Adl 5J 195
PR6: Wheel 8J 155
PR26: Far M 9J 135
St Pauls Ct. *BB5: Osw* *4L 141*
(off St Paul's St.)
BB11: Burnl 3C 228 (4D 124)
BL9: Bury 9M 201
PR1: Prest 4M 229
St Paul's Dr. LA1: Lanc 2K 29
LA2: Brookh 3K 25
St Pauls Mansion PR8: S'port 8G 166
St Paul's Pas. *PR8: S'port* *8G 167*
(off St Paul's St.)
St Paul's Rd. BB1: Rish 8G 121
BB9: Nelson 3H 105
FY1: Blackp 2B 88
LA1: Lanc 2K 29
PR1: Prest 1L 229 (7K 115)
St Pauls Sq. PR1: Prest 4M 229 (9K 115)
PR8: S'port 8G 166
St Paul's St. BB2: Blackb 4B 226 (3L 139)
BB5: Osw 4L 141
BB7: Clith 3J 81
BL0: Ramsb 8H 181
PR8: S'port 8G 166
St Pauls Ter. BB3: Hodd 5E 158
BB7: Clith 3J 81
St Pauls Wlk. FY8: L Ann 4J 129
St Peter's Av. BB4: Hasl 5G 160
St Peter's Cathedral
Lancaster 7E 228 (9L 23)
St Peters Cl. BB1: Clay D 3L 119
BB3: Darw 7B 158
L33: Kirk 5J 223
St Peter's Ga. OL14: Wals 7K 165
St Peter's Leisure Cen. 2E 228 (3E 124)
St Peter's M. LA1: Lanc 7E 228 (8L 23)
St Peter's Pl. BB4: Hasl 5G 161
FY7: Flee 9H 41
St Peter's Rd. BB4: Newc 5C 162
LA1: Lanc 8E 228 (9L 23)
PR8: Birk 2G 186
St Peters Row L31: Magh 4C 222
St Peter's Sq. PR1: Prest 4H 229 (9H 115)
St Peter's St. OL16: Roch 7E 204
PR1: Prest 4J 229 (9J 115)
PR6: Chor 5G 174
St Peter St. BB1: Rish 8G 121
BB2: Blackb 6B 226 (4L 139)
St Philip's Ct. *BB2: Blackb* *5K 139*
(off St Philip's St.)
St Philip's Rd. PR1: Prest 1L 229 (7K 115)
St Philips St. BB2: Blackb 5J 139
BB9: Nelson 1J 105
St Philip St. BB10: Burnl 9E 104
St Robert Cl. *BD23: Garg* *3M 53*
(off West St.)
St Robert Ct. *BD23: Garg* *3M 53*
(off West St.)
St Saviour's Cl. PR5: Bam B 9B 136
St Saviours Ct. *OL13: Bac* *6K 163*
(off New Line)
St Silas's Rd. BB2: Blackb 3J 139
St Stephen's Av. BB1: Blackb 1A 140
FY2: Blackp 9B 62
St Stephens Avenue Stop (Tram) 9B 62
St Stephens Cl. PR9: Banks 8F 148
St Stephens Rd. BB1: Blackb 1A 140
PR1: Prest 1M 229 (7K 115)
PR4: K'ham 5L 111
WN6: Stand 3M 213
St Stephen's St. BB11: Burnl 5F 124
St Stephen's Way BB8: Colne 5C 86
St Teresa's Av. FY5: T Clev 2D 62
St Theresa's Ct. *PR4: K'ham* *4M 111*
(off Marsden St.)
St Theresa's Dr. PR2: Fulw 5F 114
St Thomas Cl. BB4: Hasl 8F 160
FY3: Blackp 1H 89
St Thomas More Wlk. LA1: Lanc 8H 23
St Thomas' Pl. PR1: Prest 3J 229 (8J 115)
St Thomas Rd. FY8: L Ann 3F 128
PR1: Prest 1J 229 (7J 115)
PR4: K'ham 5M 111
St Thomas's Ct. WN8: Uph 4F 220
St Thomas's Rd. BB4: Craws 9M 143
PR7: Chor 6D 174
St Thomas St. BB1: Blackb 4B 140
PR1: Prest 2J 229 (8J 115)
St Vincent Av. FY1: Blackp 6N 227 (7D 88)
St Vincents Cl. BB3: Lwr D 1N 157
St Vincents Rd. PR2: Fulw 4H 115
St Vincent's Way PR8: Birk 1G 186
St Walburga's Rd. FY3: Blackp 2F 88
St Walburge Av. PR2: Ash R 9H 115
St Walburge's Gdns. PR2: Ash R 9G 115
St Wilfred's Dr. OL12: Roch 2A 204
St Wilfrid's Pk. LA2: Halt 1B 24
St Wilfrid's Ter. PR3: Longr 3J 97
St Wilfrid St. PR1: Prest 6J 229 (1J 135)
St Wyburn Ct. *PR8: Birk* *9F 166*
(off Westcliffe Rd.)
Salcombe Av. FY2: Blackp 9E 62
Salcombe Dr. PR9: S'port 1N 167
Salcombe Rd. FY8: L Ann 8C 108
Salem M. LA3: Heys 8K 21
Salem St. BB4: Hasl 4G 160
SALESBURY 3M 119
Salesbury Hall Rd. BB6: Dinck 6H 99
PR3: Dinck, Ribc 6H 99
Salesbury Vw. BB1: Wilp 5N 119
Sales's La. BL9: Bury 4M 201
Sale St. OL15: Littleb 8L 185
SALFORD 3L 165
Salford BB1: Blackb 4D 226 (3M 139)
OL14: Tod 2K 165
Salford Cl. PR8: Ains 8C 186
Salford Rd. LA2: Gal 3L 37
PR8: Ains 8C 186
Salford St. BL9: Bury 9M 201
Salford Way OL14: Tod 2K 165
Salik Gdns. OL11: Roch 8C 204
Salisbury Av. FY6: K Sea 8L 41
PR2: Grim 9F 96
Salisbury Cl. LA3: Morec 6B 22
Salisbury Ct. FY6: K Sea 8L 41
LA1: Lanc *8H 23*
(off West Rd.)
Salisbury Rd. BB3: Darw 4M 157
FY1: Blackp 4M 227 (6D 88)
LA1: Lanc 8H 23
PR1: Prest 1G 135
PR6: Birns 7A 156
Salisbury St. BB4: Hasl 4G 160
BB6: Gt H 3K 121
BB8: Colne 6B 86
PR1: Prest 8N 115
PR7: Chor 7F 174
PR9: S'port 8N 167
Salkeld St. OL11: Roch 8C 204
Salley St. OL15: Littleb 4M 185
Sallowfields WN5: Orr 6G 221
Sally Barn Cotts. *BB4: Rawt* *7K 161*
(off Holme La.)
Sally's La. PR9: S'port 4N 167
Salmesbury Av. FY2: Blackp 9E 62
Salmesbury Hall Cl. BL0: Ramsb 9G 181
Salmon St. PR1: Prest 1M 135
Salop Av. FY2: Blackp 7C 62
Saltash Rd. FY5: T Clev 7H 55
Salt Ayre La. LA1: Lanc 7F 22
Saltayre La. LA1: Lanc 7H 23
Salt Ayre Sports Cen. 7G 23
Saltburn St. BB12: Burnl 3N 123
SALTCOTES 4C 130
Saltcotes Pl. FY8: L Ann 4C 130
Saltcotes Rd. FY8: L Ann, Moss S 8B 110
Salter Fell Rd. LA1: Lanc 6H 23
Salterford La. BB10: Burnl, W'thorne 6L 125
SALTERFORTH 4B 78
Salterforth La. BB18: Salt 1A 78
(Ben La.)
BB18: Salt 6A 78
(Moor La.)
Salterforth Rd. BB18: Earl 3D 78
Salter Rake Ga. OL14: Wals 5L 165
Salter St. PR1: Prest 2K 229 (8J 115)
Salthill Gdns. BB7: Clith 2M 81
Salthill Ind. Est. BB7: Clith 1N 81
Salthill Rd. BB7: Clith 2M 81
Salthill Vw. BB7: Clith 2M 81
Salthouse Av. FY1: Blackp 6K 227 (7C 88)
Salthouse Cl. BL8: Bury 7H 201
Salthouses FY4: Blackp 1B 108
Salt Marsh Cl. FY6: Ham 2A 64
Salt Marsh La. FY6: Ham 2A 64
Salt Pie La. LA6: K Lon 6F 8
Salt Pit La. L40: Mawd 1C 192
Saltpit La. L31: Magh 1D 222
Saltram Rd. WN3: Wigan 7M 221
Salts Dr. OL15: Littleb 8K 185
Salus St. BB10: Burnl 9G 104
Salvia Way L33: Kirk 5J 223
SALWICK 4G 113
Salwick Av. FY2: Blackp 6D 62
Salwick Cl. PR9: S'port 1M 167
Salwick Pl. FY8: L Ann 9G 109
PR2: Ash R 8B 114
Salwick Rd. PR4: Salw, Whar 6E 92
Salwick Station (Rail) 4G 112
Sambourn Fold PR8: Ains 8A 186
SAMLESBURY 8G 116
SAMLESBURY BOTTOMS 1M 137
Samlesbury Hall & Lancashire Police Mus.
7N 117
Samson St. OL16: Roch 5F 204
Samuels Ct. LA1: Lanc 7F 228
Samuel St. BL9: Bury 9M 201
PR1: Prest 9N 115
Sandbank Gdns. OL12: Whitw 4N 183
Sand Banks BL1: Bolt 7F 198
Sand Beds La. BL0: Eden, Roch 2L 181
Sandbeds La. LA2: Gress 7B 18
Sandbriggs Ct. PR3: Gars 4N 59
Sandbrook Gdns. WN5: Orr 6G 220
Sandbrook Pk. OL11: Roch 9B 204
Sandbrook Rd. PR8: Ains 1C 206
WN5: Orr 6F 220
Sandbrook Way OL11: Roch 9B 204
(not continuous)
PR8: Ains 1C 206
Sandby Cl. OL13: Bac 7L 163
Sandcastle Waterworld 1A 108
Sand Dunes Starr Hills Nature Reserve 6B 108
Sanderling Cl. FY5: T Clev 2F 62
FY8: L Ann 1L 129
Sanderling Rd. L33: Kirk 7M 223
Sanders Gro. LA4: Morec 4A 22
Sanderson La. PR7: Hesk 4D 192
Sandersons Way FY4: Blackp 1F 108
Sandfield FY5: T Clev 1G 63
Sandfield Cotts. L39: Aug 1J 217
Sandfield Ho. *LA1: Lanc* *4L 29*
(off Hala Rd.)
Sandfield Pk. L39: Aug 1J 217
Sandfield Rd. OL13: Bac 6L 163
OL16: Roch 8E 204
Sandfield St. PR25: Leyl 6L 153
Sandford Cl. BL2: Bolt 9L 199
Sandford Dr. L31: Magh 9C 216
Sandford Rd. WN5: Orr 6F 220
Sandgate FY4: Blackp 4D 108
FY8: L Ann 1C 128
PR7: Chor 9F 174
SANDHAM'S GREEN 1K 109
Sandham St. PR6: Chor 6F 174
Sandhams Way FY4: Blackp 1K 109
Sandheys Dr. PR9: S'port 5M 167
Sandhills Av. FY4: Blackp 4B 108
Sandhills Cl. BB18: Salt 4B 78
Sandhill St. BB3: Darw 1B 178
Sandhole La. OL11: Roch 8J 203
Sandholme Cl. BD24: Gig 3N 35
Sandholme Dr. *BD24: Gig* *3N 35*
(off Station Rd.)
Sandholme La. PR3: Barn 6D 60
Sandholme Vs. BB18: Earl 3D 78
Sandhurst Av. FY2: Blackp 6B 62
FY8: L Ann 1E 128
Sandhurst Cl. PR4: K'ham 4L 111
Sandhurst Ct. FY8: L Ann 2D 128
Sandhurst Dr. L10: Aint 8D 222
Sandhurst Grange FY8: L Ann 1E 128
Sandhurst St.
BB11: Burnl 1F 228 (3F 124)
Sandhurst Way L31: Lyd 6A 216
Sandicroft Av. FY6: Ham 2B 64
Sandicroft Pl. FY6: Pree 9A 42
Sandicroft Rd. FY1: Blackp 1C 88
Sandilands Gro. L38: Hight 8A 214
Sandiway Ct. PR9: S'port 6L 167
Sandiway Dr. BB10: Brierc 7K 105
Sandiways L31: Magh 1D 222
Sandiways Cl. FY5: T Clev 3J 63
Sand La. LA5: Wart 7M 11
Sandlewood Gro. L33: Kirk 6L 223
Sandon Av. PR8: S'port 1L 187
Sandon Gro. WA11: Rain 4L 225
Sandon Pl. FY4: Blackp 5C 108
Sandon Rd. PR8: Birk 4F 186
Sandon St. BB2: Blackb 5K 139
BB3: Darw 5B 158
Sandon Ter. BB2: Blackb 5K 139
Sandown Cl. PR4: K'ham 4K 111
Sandown Ct. PR1: Prest 7M 229 (1K 135)
PR9: S'port 6J 167
Sandown Pk. Rd. L10: Aint 7D 222
Sandown Rd. BB4: Hasl 5H 161
BL2: Bolt 9L 199
Sandown Rd. FY5: T Clev 2H 63
LA1: Lanc 4M 29
Sandpiper Cl. BB1: Blackb 2E 226 (2N 139)
FY3: Blackp 4H 89
OL11: Roch 6K 203
Sandpiper Ct. FY5: T Clev 2C 62
Sandpiper Cres. PR5: Bam B 6C 136
Sandpiper Pl. FY5: T Clev 2F 62
Sandpiper Rd. WN3: Wigan 7L 221
Sandpiper Sq. BB11: Burnl 4A 124
Sandpits La. BB1: Blackb 3D 140
Sandridge Av. PR7: Chor 7D 174
Sandridge Ct. *FY6: K Sea* *7L 41*
(off Arnside Vw.)
Sandridge Pl. FY4: Blackp 5B 108
Sandringham Av. FY5: T Clev 2H 63
PR25: Leyl 6M 153
Sandringham Cl. BB1: Blackb 8M 119
BB7: Whall 3G 101
BB9: Barrf 1G 104
L33: Kirk 5K 223
PR4: Tarl 9E 150
PR7: Adl 7G 195
WN5: Wigan 6N 221
Sandringham Ct. FY8: L Ann 4K 129
LA4: Morec 4A 22
PR9: S'port *6H 167*
(off Gordon St.)
Sandringham Dr. BL8: Greenm 4F 200
OL16: Milnr 7K 205
PR6: Birns 7A 156
Sandringham Gro. BB4: Hasl 6F 160
Sandringham Ho. L39: Aug 1J 217
Sandringham Lodge FY5: T Clev 1C 62
Sandringham Pk. Dr. PR4: New L 8C 134
Sandringham Rd. BB3: Darw 3M 157
FY8: L Ann 3G 129
L31: Magh 2B 222
LA4: Morec 4A 22
PR5: Walt D 5N 135
PR7: Chor 7D 174
PR7: E'ton 7F 172
PR8: Ains 8C 186
PR8: Birk 2E 186
Sandringham Way PR4: Cott 3B 114
Sands, The BB7: Whall 5H 101
FY4: Blackp *5B 108*
(off Marple Cl.)
Sands Cl. BB1: Rish 7H 121
Sandsdale Av. PR2: Fulw 4M 115
SANDSIDE 3B 44
Sandside Caravan Pk. LA5: Bolt S 4K 15
Sandside Dr. LA4: Morec 5C 22
Sandside Rd. LA5: Arn 1G 4
LA7: Carr B 1G 4
Sands La. LA6: Over K 1F 16
Sands Rd. BB1: Rish 7H 121
Sandstone Rd. OL16: Milnr 6J 205
WN3: Wins 9N 221
Sands Way FY1: Blackp 7K 227 (7C 88)
Sandwash Cl. WA11: Rain 6M 225
Sandwell Av. FY5: T Clev 1J 63
Sandwell Brow PR3: Scor 6B 46
Sandwich Cl. BB1: Blackb 4C 140
Sandwick Cl. PR2: Fulw 2J 115
Sandy Bank PR3: Chip 7G 70
Sandy Bank Rd. BL7: Edgw 9K 179
Sandy Bank Ter. BB4: Newc 6B 162
Sandy Bay Caravan Pk. FY6: Pree 7N 41
Sandybeds Cl. BB5: Bax 6C 142
Sandybrook Cl. BL8: Tott 7E 200
PR2: Fulw 4A 116
Sandy Brook Ho. PR2: Fulw 2J 115
Sandy Brow La. L33: Kirk 9C 224
Sandy Cl. FY5: T Clev 9C 54
WN8: N 'urgh 2K 211
Sandy Cft. PR2: Ribb 7B 116
Sandyfields PR4: Cott 3B 114
Sandyforth Av. FY5: T Clev 9H 55
Sandyforth La. BD22: Cowl 1N 87
PR4: Light G 2D 114
Sandygate BB11: Burnl 2B 228 (3D 124)
Sandygate La. PR3: Brou 8F 94
Sandyhall La. BB9: Barrf, Rough 8D 84
Sandyland Arc. LA3: Heys 5L 21
SANDYLANDS 6N 21
Sandylands Prom. LA3: Heys 5L 21
Sandy La. BB2: Pleas 6C 138
BB3: Lwr D 1M 157
BB5: Acc 3B 142
(not continuous)
BB9: Barrf 9H 85
FY4: Blackp 5G 109
FY6: Ham 2B 64
FY6: Pree 8N 41
FY7: Flee 5D 54
L31: Lyd 5A 216
L31: Mell 5F 222
L38: Hight 7A 214
L39: Aug 5G 216
L40: Holmesw 8A 170
(not continuous)
L40: Lath 5A 210
L40: Mawd 3K 191
L40: Ruff 7E 170
OL11: Roch 6N 203
PR3: Out R 1L 65
PR4: Cott, Lwr B 1A 114
PR5: Hogh 1K 155
PR6: Birns 7N 155
PR6: Brind 1K 155
PR6: Brind, Clay W 4E 154
(not continuous)
PR7: Adl 6F 194
PR25: Leyl 7K 153
WN5: Orr 7G 221
WN8: N 'urgh 3K 211
WN8: Skelm 2H 219
(not continuous)
Sandy La. Cen. WN8: Skelm 2H 219
Sandy Pl. PR25: Leyl 7K 153
Sandy Way L40: Holmesw 1B 190
Sanfield Cl. L39: Orms 6K 209
Sangara Dr. BB3: Lwr D 1N 157
Sangness Dr. PR8: S'port 2L 187
Sankey Rd. L31: Magh 3C 222

302 A-Z Lancashire

Seventh Av.—Silverdale Rd.

Seventh Av. FY4: Blackp 2C 108
Seven Trees Av. BB1: Blackb 9A 120
Severn Av. FY7: Flee 4D 54
Severn Cl. BL9: Bury 6L 201
Severn Ct. LA3: Morec 6F 22
Severn Dr. OL16: Milnr 7K 205
PR5: Walt D 6N 135
WN5: Wigan 5M 221
Severn Hill PR2: Fulw 1F 114
Severn Ho. *PR1: Prest* 9N 115
(off Samuel St.)
Severn Rd. FY4: Blackp 2B 108
L33: Kirk 4L 223
Severn St. PR3: Longr 3J 97
Seville Ct. FY8: L Ann 5K 129
Seymour Av. LA3: Heys 9L 21
Seymour Ct. PR1: Prest 7G 115
Seymour Dr. BL2: Bolt 7J 199
L31: Magh 8D 216
Seymour Gro. LA3: Heys 9L 21
Seymour Rd. BL1: Bolt 9F 198
FY1: Blackp 8K 227 (8C 88)
FY8: L Ann 4K 129
PR2: Ash R 6F 114
Seymour St. BL2: Bolt 7J 199
FY7: Flee 9F 40
LA1: Lanc 6E 228 (8L 23)
PR6: Chor 7F 174
Shacklady Rd. L33: Kirk 6M 223
Shackleton Rd. PR4: Frec 7N 111
Shackleton St. BB10: Burnl 1F 124
OL14: Tod 7F 146
Shaddock Av. OL12: Roch 4K 203
SHADE 4K 165
Shade La. PR7: Chor 3F 194
Shade Row FY6: Pree 1A 56
Shade St. OL14: Tod 4K 165
SHADSWORTH 5D 140
Shadsworth Cl. BB1: Blackb 4C 140
Shadsworth Ind. Est. BB1: Blackb 7C 140
Shadsworth Ind. Pk.
BB1: Blackb 6D 140
Shadsworth Leisure Cen. 6C 140
Shadsworth Rd. BB1: Blackb 6C 140
Shady La. BL7: Brom C 7H 199
LA2: Slyne 9J 15
PR5: Bam B 2N 153
PR25: Leyl 2N 153
Shaftesbury Av. BB3: Darw 4M 157
BB6: Gt H 3L 121
BB11: Burnl 5D 124
FY2: Blackp 9B 62
FY3: Stain 4H 89
FY5: T Clev 7C 54
L33: Kirk 5K 223
OL15: Littleb 2J 205
PR1: Penw 2E 134
PR4: New L 8C 134
PR8: Birk 5G 186
Shaftesbury Cl. FY8: L Ann 3K 129
Shaftesbury Ct. FY2: Blackp 9B 62
Shaftesbury Dr. OL12: Ward 8G 184
Shaftesbury Gro. PR8: Birk 4G 186
Shaftesbury Pl. LA1: Lanc 3K 29
PR7: Chor 6D 174
Shaftesbury Rd. PR8: Birk 5G 186
Shaftsbury Rd. WN5: Orr 3K 221
Shakeshaft St. BB1: Blackb 4A 140
Shakespeare Av. BB6: Gt H 5H 121
L32: Kirk 9J 223
OL14: Tod 1N 165
Shakespeare Cen., The PR8: S'port 9H 167
Shakespeare Cl. OL15: Littleb 5M 185
Shakespeare Rd. FY7: Flee 9E 40
LA1: Lanc 4H 23
PR1: Prest 8N 115
(not continuous)
Shakespeare St. BB12: Padi 2J 123
(not continuous)
PR8: S'port 9H 167
Shakespeare Ter. PR6: Chor 4F 174
Shakespeare Way BB2: Blackb 7A 226 (5K 139)
Shalbourn Rd. FY8: L Ann 4G 128
Shale St. BB12: Burnl 3B 124
Shalfleet Cl. BL2: Bolt 8L 199
Shalgrove Fld. PR2: Fulw 2F 114
Shallow Valley Ct. *BB5: Acc* 3L 141
(off Oakbank Dr.)
Shambles, The *BD24: Sett* 3N 35
(off Market Pl.)
Shannon Cl. OL10: Heyw 9E 202
Shannon Sq. BB10: Burnl 8G 105
Shannon St. FY1: Blackp 5H 227 (7B 88)
Shanter Cl. OL12: Whitw 9B 164
Shap Cl. BB5: Bax 5D 142
BB9: Barrf 7H 85
Shap Ct. FY7: Flee 3D 54
Shap Ga. WN5: Wigan 4L 221
Shap Gro. BB10: Burnl 7E 104
Shard La. FY6: Poul F 5A 64
Shard Rd. FY6: Ham, Poul F 6A 64
Shards Ct. LA1: Lanc 6K 23
Sharley Fold *PR3: Longr* 3K 97
(off Dixon Rd.)
Sharman Av. FY8: L Ann 8F 108
SHARNEYFORD 2N 163
Sharoe Bay Ct. PR2: Fulw 3J 115
SHAROE GREEN 2J 115
Sharoe Grn. La. PR2: Fulw 2H 115
Sharoe Grn. Pk. PR2: Fulw 4K 115
Sharoe Mt. Av. PR2: Fulw 2J 115
Sharow Gro. FY1: Blackp 7M 227 (8D 88)
Sharpe's Av. LA1: Lanc 2L 29
Sharphaw Vw. BD23: Garg 3M 53
SHARPLES 9D 198
Sharples Av. BL1: Bolt 7E 198
Sharples Community Leisure Cen. 8F 198
Sharples Ct. *PR3: Longr* 2J 97
(off Berry La.)
Sharples Dr. BL8: Bury 9E 200
Sharples Grn. BL7: Edgw 8K 179
Sharples Hall BL1: Bolt 7F 198
Sharples Hall Dr. BL1: Bolt 7F 198
Sharples Hall Fold BL1: Bolt 8F 198
Sharples Hall M. BL1: Bolt 7F 198
Sharples La. PR3: St M 9F 58
Sharples Mdw. BL7: Edgw 8K 179
(not continuous)
Sharples Pk. BL1: Bolt 9D 198
Sharples St. BB2: Blackb 8B 226 (5L 139)
BB5: Acc 3M 141
Sharp St. BB9: Barrf 8H 85
BB10: Burnl 9F 104
BL8: Bury 9G 201
Sharratt's Path PR7: Char R 1B 194
Sharrock St. PR7: Buck V 1A 174
PR8: S'port 7H 167
Shawbridge 3M 81
Shawbridge Ct. BB7: Clith 3M 81
Shawbridge St. BB7: Clith 3M 81
Shaw Brook Cl. BB1: Rish 9G 121
Shawbrook Cl. BB11: Hapt 5H 123
PR7: Eux 1M 173
Shaw Brook Rd. PR25: Leyl 8G 153
Shaw Brow PR6: Whit W 8D 154
Shawcliffe La. BB6: Gt H 1G 121
BB7: Whall 8H 101
Shaw Cl. BB2: Blackb 4A 226 (3K 139)
L39: Hals 7N 187
SHAWCLOUGH 2B 204
Shawclough Cl. OL12: Roch 2A 204
Shawclough Dr. OL12: Roch 2N 203
Shawclough M. BB4: W'foot 4D 162
Shawclough Ri. *OL12: Roch* 3A 204
(off Shawclough Rd.)
Shawclough Rd. BB4: W'foot 4D 162
OL12: Roch 1N 203
Shawclough St. BB4: W'foot 4D 162
Shawclough Trad. Est. OL12: Roch 2A 204
Shawclough Way OL12: Roch 2N 203
Shaw Cres. L37: Form 8B 206
Shawes Dr. PR6: And 6L 195
SHAWFIELD 3K 203
Shawfield BB4: Rawt 6L 161
Shawfield Gro. OL12: Roch 3K 203
Shawfield La. OL12: Roch 4J 203
SHAWFORTH 9B 164
Shaw Gdns. BB7: Chatb 7C 74
SHAW GREEN 4G 173
Shaw Hall Caravan Pk. L40: Scar 9G 189
Shaw Hill PR6: Whit W 9D 154
Shaw Hill Dr. PR6: Whit W 9D 154
Shaw Hill Golf Course 9D 154
Shaw Hill St. PR7: Chor 7E 174
Shaw La. L39: Bart 6K 207
LA6: Neth K 5B 16
OL14: Tod 5E 146
OL16: Milnr 4K 205
Shaw Lodge *OL12: Ward* 8F 184
(off Lodge St.)
Shaw Rd. BL6: Hor 8C 196
FY1: Blackp 9H 227 (9B 88)
OL16: Milnr 9L 205
Shaw's Av. PR8: Birk 4G 187
Shaws Gth. L39: Hals 7N 187
Shaw's La. PR3: Pill 1F 56
Shaw Sq. *BB18: Earl* 2E 78
(off Water St.)
Shaw's Rd. PR8: Birk 4G 186
Shaw St. BB2: Blackb 3A 226 (3L 139)
BB4: Hasl 1G 160
BB8: Colne 7N 85
LA1: Lanc 6E 228
OL12: Roch 3E 204
PR1: Prest 3L 229 (8K 115)
Shaw Ter. BB7: Grind 4A 74
Shay, The FY5: T Clev 4F 62
Shay La. BB7: Slaid 5B 50
BB10: Brierc 8N 105
PR3: Longr 5H 97
Shay La. Ind. Est. PR3: Longr 4H 97
Shays Dr. BB7: Clith 5M 81
Shear Bank Cl. BB1: Blackb 1A 226 (2L 139)
Shear Bank Gdns. BB1: Blackb 1A 226 (2L 139)
Shear Bank Rd. BB1: Blackb 1A 226 (1L 139)
Shear Brow BB1: Blackb 1B 226 (1L 139)
Shearing Av. OL12: Roch 4K 203
Shearwater Dr. BB1: Blackb 2E 226 (2N 139)
Sheddon Gro. BB10: Burnl 4J 125
Shed St. BB5: Osw 5L 141
BB8: Colne 7N 85
OL12: Whitw 5A 184
Sheep Gap OL12: Roch 4M 203
Sheep Ga. Dr. BL8: Tott 8D 200
Sheep Grn. BB4: Hasl 4G 161
Sheep Hey BL0: Ramsb 5J 181
Sheep Hill Brow PR6: Clay W 5C 154
Sheep Hill La. PR4: New L 9C 134
PR6: Clay W 5B 154
(not continuous)
Sheep Ho. La. BL6: R'ton 3A 196
Sheernest LA6: Holme 2G 6
Sheernest La. LA6: Holme 2F 6
Shefferland's La. LA2: Halt, Slyne 2N 23
Sheffield Dr. PR2: Lea 7A 114
Shefford Cres. WN3: Wins 9M 221
Sheldon Ct. PR1: Prest 2J 229
Shelfield OL11: Roch 4K 203
Shelfield Cl. OL11: Roch 4K 203
Shelfield La. BB10: S'field 3B 106
OL11: Roch 4J 203
Shelfield Rd. BB9: Nelson 1M 105
Shelley Cl. FY2: Blackp 5F 62
LA5: Bolt S 4L 15
PR7: Copp 5B 194
Shelley Ct. L32: Kirk 9J 223
Shelley Dr. BB5: Bax 6D 142
L39: Orms 6J 209
PR7: E'ton 9G 172
WN5: Orr 5K 221
Shelley Gdns. BB6: Gt H 5H 121
Shelley Gro. BB3: Darw 6C 158
FY5: T Clev 3D 62
PR8: S'port 8M 167
Shelley M. PR2: Ash R 8F 114
Shelley Rd. PR2: Ash R 7F 114
Shellfield Rd. PR9: S'port 3N 167
Shellingford Cl. WN6: Shev 5G 213
Shelton Dr. PR8: Ains 9A 186
Shenley Way PR9: S'port 1C 168
Shenstone Rd. FY3: Blackp 3F 88
Shepherd Cl. OL16: Roch 7E 204
Shepherd Rd. FY8: L Ann 9G 108
Shepherd Rd. Nth. FY8: L Ann 9G 108
Shepherd's Av. PR3: Bowg 8A 60
Shepherds Cl. BL8: Greenm 4E 200
Shepherds Grn. BB4: Water 7E 144
Shepherd's La. L39: Hals 7C 208
PR26: Cros 6H 171
Shepherd St. BB3: Darw 8A 158
BL8: Greenm 5E 200
FY8: L Ann 5A 130
OL11: Roch 4H 203
OL12: Roch 5C 204
OL13: Bac 4K 163
PR1: Prest 6M 229 (1K 135)
Shepherds Way OL16: Milnr 8J 205
PR7: Chor 6F 174
Shepton Cl. BL1: Bolt 6D 198
Sheraton Cl. WN5: Orr 2L 221
Sheraton Pk. PR2: Ingol 3D 114
Sherborne Lodge *PR2: Ribb* 5B 116
(off Grange Av.)
Sherborne Rd. WN5: Orr 3K 221
Sherbourne Cl. FY6: Carl 6J 63
Sherbourne Ct. FY6: Carl 6J 63
Sherbourne Cres. PR1: Prest 6L 115
Sherbourne Rd. BB5: Bax 5D 142
FY1: Blackp 2B 88
FY6: Ham 1B 64
Sherbourne St. PR6: Chor 7F 174
Sherburne Av. PR4: K'ham 4L 111
Sherburn Rd. PR1: Penw 5H 135
Sherdley Rd. PR5: Lost H 9L 135
SHERFIN 9G 143
Sherfin Nook BB5: S Fold 9G 143
Sheridan Rd. BB8: Colne 5G 86
Sheridan St. BB9: Nelson 9K 85
BB10: Burnl 8J 105
(off Gilbert St.)
Sheriff St. OL12: Roch 4B 204
(not continuous)
OL16: Milnr 8K 205
Sheringham Av. FY5: T Clev 4D 62
Sheringham Dr. BL8: Bury 8J 201
Sheringham Way FY6: Poul F 8L 63
Sherrat St. WN8: Skelm 2H 219
Sherringham Rd. PR8: Birk 3E 186
Sherwood Av. FY3: Blackp 2E 88
L39: Aug 1H 217
Sherwood Cl. BB9: Nelson 1L 105
BL8: Tott 6E 200
Sherwood Ct. BB10: Burnl 4G 125
FY3: Blackp 2E 88
(off Sherwood Av.)
Sherwood Cres. WN5: Wigan 4N 221
Sherwood Dr. WN5: Wigan 5N 221
WN8: Skelm 9A 212
Sherwood Gro. WN5: Wigan 4N 221
Sherwood Ho. PR8: Ains 8C 186
Sherwood Lodge PR8: Birk 9F 166
Sherwood Pl. FY5: T Clev 2F 62
PR6: Chor 6F 174
Sherwood Rd. BB1: Blackb 4B 140
FY8: L Ann 2J 129
Sherwood's La. L10: Faz 9E 222
Sherwood St. BL1: Bolt 9F 198
Sherwood Way BB5: Acc 8N 121
PR2: Fulw 3K 115
Shetland Cl. BB1: Blackb 5C 140
BB1: Wilp 2N 119
Shetland Rd. FY1: Blackp 8L 227 (8C 88)
SHEVINGTON 6K 213
Shevington C'way. PR26: Cros 4L 171
Shevington La. WN6: Shev, Stand 6K 213
SHEVINGTON MOOR 2K 213
Shevington Moor WN6: Stand 2K 213
Shevington's La. L33: Kirk 5J 223
SHEVINGTON VALE 5G 213
Shilton St. BL0: Ramsb 9G 180
Shipley Cl. FY3: Blackp 1H 89
Shipley Rd. FY8: L Ann 1H 129
Shipperbottom La. BL0: Ramsb 9J 181
Shipston Cl. BL8: Bury 9G 200
Shirburn OL11: Roch 7B 204
Shirdley Cres. PR8: Ains 1C 206
SHIRDLEY HILL 7N 187
Shire Bank Cres. PR2: Fulw 4H 115
Shireburn Av. BB7: Clith 4J 81
Shireburn Cotts. BB7: Hurst G 1M 99
Shireburne Pk. BB7: Clith 2H 81
Shire Gro. PR7: Buck V 9B 154
Shire La. BB7: Hurst G 2L 99
Shires, The BB2: Blackb 1L 157
SHIRESHEAD 2B 46
Shireshead Cres. LA1: Lanc 5L 29
Shirewell Rd. WN5: Orr 6H 221
Shirley Cres. FY2: Blackp 5D 62
Shirley Gdns. BB3: Tock 5G 157
Shirley Hgts. FY6: Poul F 6K 63
Shirley La. PR4: Longt 7L 133
Shoebroad La. OL14: Tod 3L 165
Shop La. BB5: Acc 3C 142
L31: Magh 1B 222
PR5: H Walt 4D 136
Shoppers Wlk. *FY8: L Ann* 5A 130
(off Clifton St.)
SHORE
OL14 6F 146
OL15 8J 185
Shore, The FY6: Ham 2A 64
LA2: Hest B 8G 15
LA5: Bolt S 4J 15
Shore Av. BB10: Burnl 8K 105
Shorebury Point FY4: Blackp 5E 108
Shore Cl. LA5: Silv 9F 4
Shorefield Caravan Pk.
LA2: Hest B 7H 15
Shorefield Cl. *OL16: Milnr* 6J 205
(off Silver Hill)
Shorefield Mt. BL7: Eger 5E 198
Shore Flds. FY3: Blackp 2G 88
Shorefields Caravan Pk. LA3: Midd 7K 27
Shore Fold OL15: Littleb 8J 185
Shore Grn. FY5: T Clev 9F 54
LA5: Silv 9F 4
OL14: Tod 6F 146
Shore Hill OL15: Littleb 8M 185
Shore La. LA5: Bolt S 6J 15
OL15: Littleb 9M 185
Shore Lea OL15: Littleb 8J 185
Shore Mt. OL15: Littleb 8J 185
Shore New Rd. OL14: Tod 7E 146
Shore Rd. FY5: T Clev 3C 62
LA3: Heys 1H 27
LA5: Carn 7M 11
LA5: Silv 9F 4
OL14: Tod 7F 146
OL15: Littleb 8J 185
PR4: Hesk B 5L 149
PR8: Ains 7A 186
Shore St. OL16: Milnr 7J 205
Shoreswood BL1: Bolt 8D 198
SHOREY BANK 5N 157
Shorey Bank BB11: Burnl 1E 228 (2E 124)
Shorrock La. BB2: Blackb 8J 139
Shorrocks Av. PR3: St M 3G 67
Shorrocks St. BL8: Bury 9E 200
Shorrock St. BB3: Darw 7A 158
Shortbutts La. LA6: H Roo 6B 8
Short Clough Cl. BB4: Rawt 1M 161
Short Clough La. BB4: Rawt 1M 161
Short Cft. La. L37: Gt A 2D 214
Shorten Brook Dr. BB5: Alt 3D 122
Shorten Brook Way BB5: Alt 3D 122
Shortlands, The BB12: Padi 8H 103
Shortlands Dr. LA3: Heys 9K 21
Short La. PR3: Goos 5J 95
Shortridge Rd. FY4: Blackp 1F 108
Short St. BB8: Colne 7A 86
OL13: Bac 7F 162
OL14: Tod 2L 165
(off Dalton St.)
WN5: Wigan 5L 221
Shottwood Fold OL15: Littleb 6M 185
Showfield BB10: W'thorne 3M 125
Showley Brook Cl. BB1: Wilp 5N 119
Showley Ct. BB1: Clay D 3M 119
Showley Rd. BB1: Clay D, Mellor 3H 119
Shrewsbury Av. L10: Aint 7B 222
Shrewsbury Cl. PR4: K'ham 4A 112
Shrewsbury Dr. FY5: T Clev 1G 63
LA1: Lanc 2M 29
Shropshire Dr. BB1: Wilp 3N 119
Shuttle Cl. *BB5: Acc* 2N 141
(off Dale St.)
SHUTTLEWORTH 6K 181
Shuttleworth Mead Bus. Pk. BB12: Padi 2F 122
Shuttleworth Rd. PR1: Prest 1K 229 (7J 115)
Shuttleworth St. BB1: Rish 7H 121
BB10: Burnl 8F 104
BB12: Padi 1H 123
BB18: Earl 2E 78
Shuttling Flds. La. PR5: Bam B, Hogh 6E 136
(not continuous)
Sibbering Brow PR7: Char R, Eux 6M 173
Sibsey St. LA1: Lanc 7A 228 (8J 23)
Siddow's Av. BB7: Clith 4J 81
Side Beet La. BB1: Rish 8D 120
Sidegarth La. LA2: Halt 3K 17
Side La. BB7: Rim 5N 75
SIDE OF THE MOOR 8L 199
Sidford Ct. FY3: Blackp 2F 88
Sidgreaves La. PR4: Lea T 3M 113
Siding La. L33: S'wood 4A 224
WA11: Rain 1G 224
Siding Rd. FY7: Flee 1G 54
Sidings, The BB3: Darw 8B 158
BB4: Hasl 8F 160
BB7: Whall 4J 101
BB8: Colne 7N 85
BB8: Foul 2A 86
BD24: Sett 3N 35
BL7: Turt 1J 199
LA2: L Ben 6K 19
OL13: Bac 7L 163
Sidings Bus. Pk., The BB7: Whall 4J 101
Sidings Ind. Est., The *BD24: Sett* 3N 35
(off The Sidings)
Sidings Rd. LA3: Midd 5L 27
Siding St. OL13: Bac 7G 162
Sidmouth Av. BB4: Hasl 5H 161
Sidmouth Rd. FY8: L Ann 8C 108
Sidney Av. FY2: Blackp 9E 62
PR4: Hesk B 4D 150
Sidney Powell Av. L32: Kirk 8H 223
Sidney Rd. PR9: S'port 6M 167
Sidney Ter. LA1: Lanc 6E 228
Siebers Bank OL12: Roch 3A 204
Sigget La. OL14: Tod 1J 165
Signal Ho. BB5: Acc 3M 141
Silbury Cl. BB2: Blackb 8A 140
Silcock's Funland 6G 167
Silk Ct. L39: Orms 8M 209
Silk Mill La. PR3: Inglew 7L 69
Silk St. OL11: Roch 9N 203
Silloth Cl. BB2: Blackb 7N 139
Silly La. LA2: Low 2L 33
Silsden Av. PR2: Ribb 4N 115
Silsden Cl. FY3: Blackp 1H 89
Silver Birch Av. PR9: Banks 3J 169
Silver Birch Way L31: Lyd 6A 216
Silverburn FY8: L Ann 9G 109
SILVERDALE 9G 4
Silverdale FY2: Blackp 5E 62
PR4: Hesk B 4D 150
Silverdale Av. FY7: Flee 3C 54
LA3: Heys 9L 21
Silverdale Cl. BB2: Blackb 8N 139
BB5: Clay M 7L 121
BB10: Burnl 7G 104
PR5: Hogh 4G 137
PR25: Leyl 9L 153
Silverdale Ct. PR8: Birk 1E 186
PR8: S'port 1M 187
Silverdale Dr. PR2: Ribb 4N 115
Silverdale Golf Course 8K 5
SILVERDALE GREEN 9H 5
Silverdale Moss Rd. LA5: Silv 4H 5
Silverdale Rd. FY8: L Ann 1J 129
LA5: Arn 1F 4
LA5: Yea R 6N 5
PR6: Chor 7G 174
WN5: Orr 4L 221

Silverdale Station (Rail)—South Pk. Dr.

Silverdale Station (Rail) . . . 8K 5
Silver Hill OL16: Milnr . . . 6J 205
Silvermere Cl. BL0: Ramsb . . . 9G 181
Silver Ridge Caravan Pk. LA7: Hale . . . 2B 6
Silversmith Row FY8: L Ann . . . 1K 129
Silverstone Gro. L31: Lyd . . . 6A 216
Silverstone St. PR7: Buck V . . . 9N 153
Silver St. BB7: Hurst G . . . 1M 99
BL0: Ramsb . . . 8H 181
OL14: Wals . . . 8K 165
PR1: Prest . . . 8M 229 (2K 135)
PR4: Clif . . . 8G 113
Silverthorne Dr. PR9: S'port . . . 5M 167
Silverton Gro. BL1: Bolt . . . 9F 198
Silverwell St. BL6: Hor . . . 9C 196
Silverwood Av. FY4: Blackp . . . 1C 108
Silverwood Cl. FY8: L Ann . . . 4L 129
Silverwood Ct. FY4: Blackp . . . 1D 108
Silvester Rd. PR7: Chor . . . 8E 174
Silvia Way FY7: Flee . . . 9E 40
Simeon St. OL14: Wals . . . 7K 165
OL16: Milnr . . . 7J 205
Simfield Cl. WN6: Stand . . . 3N 213
Simmonds Way BB9: Brierf . . . 3F 104
Simmons Av. PR5: Walt D . . . 5L 135
Simmons St. BB2: Blackb . . . 3B 226 (3L 139)
Simmons Way BB5: Clay M . . . 6N 121
Simms Cl. BL0: Ramsb . . . 9F 180
Simon's Ter. FY6: K Sea . . . 7L 41
SIMONSTONE . . . 8D 102
Simonstone Bus. Pk. BB12: S'stone . . . 2E 122
Simonstone La. BB12: S'stone . . . 9D 102
Simonstone Rd. BB7: Sabd . . . 5E 102
SIMONSWOOD . . . 4M 223
Simonswood Ind. Pk. L33: S'wood . . . 4N 223
Simonswood La. L33: Kirk . . . 9M 223
L39: Bick . . . 7L 217
Simonswood Wlk. L33: Kirk . . . 8M 223
Simpson Cl. BB18: Barnw . . . 1A 78
SIMPSON CLOUGH . . . 8G 202
Simpson Ct. PR1: Prest . . . 7L 229
Simpsons Pl. OL12: Roch . . . 4C 204
(off Victoria St.)
PR8: S'port . . . 8H 167
Simpson St. BB5: Osw . . . 5K 141
BB12: Hapt . . . 5H 123
FY4: Blackp . . . 1B 108
PR1: Prest . . . 5J 229 (9J 115)
Simpson St. Ind. Units BB12: Hapt . . . 4H 123
Sinclair Ct. FY8: L Ann . . . 1H 129
Sinclair Pl. WN5: Wigan . . . 3N 221
Sineacre La. L33: S'wood . . . 2C 224
L39: Bick . . . 2C 224
Singing Ringing Tree
Panopticon . . . 1G 144
SINGLETON . . . 1D 90
Singleton Av. BB12: Read . . . 8C 102
BL6: Hor . . . 8D 196
FY8: L Ann . . . 1G 129
Singleton Cl. PR2: Fulw . . . 2J 115
Singleton Ct. FY1: Blackp . . . 4J 227
Singleton Hall FY6: Sing . . . 9C 64
Singleton Rd. PR4: Weet . . . 4D 90
(not continuous)
Singleton Row PR1: Prest . . . 4J 229 (8J 115)
Singleton St. FY1: Blackp . . . 4H 227 (7B 88)
Singleton Way PR2: Fulw . . . 2J 115
Sion Brook Ho. PR2: Ribb . . . 5B 116
Sion Cl. PR2: Ribb . . . 5B 116
Sion Hill PR2: Ribb . . . 5B 116
Sir Frank Whittle Way FY4: Blackp . . . 5D 108
Sir Isaac Newton Way OL16: Milnr, Roch . . . 8F 204
Sir Simon's Arc. LA1: Lanc . . . 7C 228 (8K 23)
Sir Tom Finney Way PR1: Prest . . . 1N 229 (7L 115)
PR2: Prest . . . 7L 115
Sir William Hartley Ct. BB8: Colne . . . 5F 86
Siskin Av. OL13: Bac . . . 5M 163
SISS CLOUGH . . . 6D 162
Six Acre La. PR4: Longt . . . 1N 151
Six Arches Caravan Pk. PR3: Scor . . . 6A 46
Six Arches La. PR3: Scor . . . 6A 46
Sixfields FY5: T Clev . . . 4F 62
Sixpenny La. L39: Bart . . . 4E 206
Sixteen Acre La. L37: Form . . . 6A 206
Sixth Av. BL9: Bury . . . 9B 202
FY4: Blackp . . . 2C 108
Size Ho. Rd. BB4: Hasl . . . 5G 161
Sizehouse St. PR1: Prest . . . 4K 229 (9J 115)
Size Ho. Village BB4: Hasl . . . 5H 161
Sizergh Ct. LA1: Lanc . . . 9H 23
Sizergh Rd. LA4: Morec . . . 3E 22
Sizer St. PR1: Prest . . . 2J 229 (8J 115)
Size St. OL12: Whitw . . . 5A 184
Skaithe, The BB7: Slaid . . . 5C 50
Skeffington Rd. PR1: Prest . . . 7L 115
Skegness Cl. BL8: Bury . . . 8J 201
Skeleron Rd. BB7: Rim . . . 7M 75
SKELMERSDALE . . . 2M 219
Skelmersdale Hall Dr. WN8: Skelm . . . 9M 211
(not continuous)
Skelmersdale Rd. L39: Bick, Skelm . . . 4E 218
WN8: Skelm . . . 4E 218
Skelmersdale Sports Cen. . . . 4N 219
Skelshaw Cl.
BB1: Blackb . . . 8G 226 (5A 140)
Skelton St. BB8: Colne . . . 6B 86
Skelwith Rd. FY3: Blackp . . . 8H 89
Skerryvore Caravan Pk. FY4: Blackp . . . 3D 108
SKERTON . . . 5K 23
Skerton Ho. LA1: Lanc . . . 6L 23
Skiddaw Cl. BB12: Burnl . . . 9A 104
Skiddaw Pl. WN5: Wigan . . . 5M 221
Skiddaw Rd. FY4: Blackp . . . 1F 108
LA1: Lanc . . . 6L 23
Skiddaw St. BB1: Blackb . . . 3A 140
Skip La. PR4: Hutt . . . 4M 133
SKIPPOOL . . . 6L 63
Skippool Av. FY6: Poul F . . . 6L 63
Skippool Rd. FY5: T Clev . . . 4L 63
Skipton Av. FY6: Carl . . . 6J 63
PR9: S'port . . . 9B 148
Skipton Cl. FY4: Blackp . . . 9F 88
PR5: Bam B . . . 6A 136
Skipton Cres. PR2: Ribb . . . 4A 116
Skipton Ga. LA6: Bur L . . . 4K 19
Skipton New Rd. BB8: Foul . . . 3B 86
Skipton Old Rd. BB8: Colne . . . 5D 86
BB8: Foul . . . 2B 86
Skipton Rd. BB7: Gis . . . 9B 52
BB8: Colne . . . 4B 86
BB8: Traw . . . 8E 86
BB18: Barnw . . . 1M 77
BB18: Earl . . . 10J 53
BD23: Garg . . . 3M 53
BD23: Hell . . . 1D 52
BD23: T Crav . . . 10J 53
BD24: Sett . . . 4N 35
FY8: L Ann . . . 2H 129
Skipton St. BB7: News . . . 5C 52
LA4: Morec . . . 3A 22
Ski Rossendale . . . 4K 161
SKITHAM . . . 8N 57
Skitham La. PR3: Nateby, Out R . . . 9M 57
Skull Ho. La. WN6: App B . . . 3F 212
Skull Ho. M. WN6: App B . . . 4F 212
Skye Cres. BB1: Blackb . . . 5C 140
Skyes Cres. WN3: Wins . . . 9M 221
Skyways Commercial Cen. FY4: Blackp . . . 5F 108
Slack BB12: High . . . 4L 103
Slack Booth BB8: Traw . . . 1F 106
Slackey's La. PR9: S'port . . . 2B 168
Slack Ga. OL12: Ward . . . 6B 184
OL12: Whitw . . . 6B 184
SLACK HEAD . . . 1N 5
Slack La. BL2: Bolt . . . 6K 199
BL8: Aff . . . 6N 199
LA2: Thurn . . . 5A 36
Slack Royd BB8: Traw . . . 1F 106
Slack's La. PR6: H Charn . . . 3K 195
Slack St. OL16: Roch . . . 6D 204
Slackwood La. LA5: Silv . . . 9J 5
Slade La. BB12: Padi . . . 8H 103
(not continuous)
Sladen St. OL12: Roch . . . 4C 204
Slade St. PR1: Prest . . . 1H 135
SLAIDBURN . . . 5C 50
Slaidburn Av. BB4: Rawt . . . 3M 161
BB10: Burnl . . . 4H 125
Slaidburn Cl. OL16: Milnr . . . 8J 205
Slaidburn Cres. PR9: S'port . . . 1N 167
Slaidburn Dr. BB5: Acc . . . 4N 141
LA1: Lanc . . . 4L 29
Slaidburn Heritage Cen. . . . 5C 50
Slaidburn Ind. Est. PR9: S'port . . . 1N 167
Slaidburn Pl. PR2: Ribb . . . 7C 116
Slaidburn Rd. BB7: Newt . . . 8B 50
LA2: Low . . . 9M 19
PR2: Ribb . . . 7B 116
Slaidburn Wlk. FY3: Blackp . . . 2G 89
Slant La. OL14: Tod . . . 1N 165
Slape La. LA6: Burt K . . . 5H 7
Slate La. WN8: Skelm . . . 9G 210
Slater Av. BB8: Colne . . . 5A 86
BL6: Hor . . . 9D 196
Slater Ct. PR26: Leyl . . . 7F 152
Slater La. PR6: Withn . . . 3F 176
PR25: Leyl . . . 7F 152
PR26: Leyl . . . 7E 152
Slater Rd. FY5: T Clev . . . 1C 62
Slater St. BB2: Blackb . . . 7K 139
(not continuous)
Slaunt Bank OL12: Roch . . . 3H 203
Sleaford Cl. BL8: Bury . . . 8J 201
Sledbrook St. WN5: Wigan . . . 6M 221
Slinger Rd. FY5: T Clev . . . 9C 54
Slip Inn La. LA1: Lanc . . . 7C 228 (8K 23)
SLIPPER HILL . . . 2K 85
Sliven Clod Rd. BB4: Craws . . . 5K 143
Sluice La. FY4: Blackp . . . 6H 109
FY8: L Ann . . . 8K 109
L40: Ruff . . . 3E 190
SLYNE . . . 9K 15
Slyne Hall Hgts. LA2: Slyne . . . 8L 15
Slyne Holiday Pk. LA2: Slyne . . . 9K 15
Slyne Rd. LA1: Lanc . . . 5K 23
LA2: Slyne . . . 8K 15
LA4: Morec . . . 4F 22
LA5: Bolt S . . . 6L 15
Slynewoods LA2: Slyne . . . 1M 23
Smalden La. BB7: Bolt B, Grind . . . 7G 50
SMALLBRIDGE . . . 2F 204
Smallbridge Ind. Pk. OL16: Roch . . . 3F 204
Smalley Cft. PR1: Penw . . . 5J 135
Smalley St. BB11: Burnl . . . 5F 124
(not continuous)
Smalley Thorn Brow BB6: Gt H . . . 4F 120
Smalley Way BB2: Blackb . . . 9D 226 (6M 139)
Smallholdings, The L31: Magh . . . 8E 216
Small La. L39: Aug . . . 9F 208
L39: Orms . . . 8L 209
L40: Scar . . . 4K 189
Small La. Nth. L39: Hals . . . 2C 208
Small La. Sth. L39: Hals . . . 7B 208
Smallshaw Ind. Est. BB11: Burnl . . . 4A 124
Smallshaw La. BB11: Burnl . . . 4N 123
BB12: Burnl . . . 3N 123
Smallshaw Rd. OL12: Roch . . . 1L 203
SMALLWOOD HEY . . . 8F 42
Smallwood Hey Rd. PR3: Pill . . . 8F 42
Smethick Wlk. L30: N'ton . . . 6A 222
Smethurst Hall Pk. WN5: Bill . . . 9F 220
Smethurst Hall Rd. BL9: Bury . . . 9C 202
Smethurst La. WN5: Wigan . . . 6M 221
Smethurst Rd. WN5: Bill . . . 9E 220
Smethurst St. BL8: Bury . . . 9G 201
Smirthwaite St. BB11: Burnl . . . 4B 124
Smith Av. PR4: Tarl . . . 6D 150
WN5: Orr . . . 3L 221
Smith Cl. PR2: Grim . . . 9E 96
Smith Cft. PR26: Leyl . . . 7D 152
SMITH GREEN . . . 3N 37
Smith Hill OL16: Milnr . . . 7J 205
Smithills Cl. PR6: Chor . . . 5G 175
Smithills Cft. Rd. BL1: Bolt . . . 9A 198
SMITHILLS DEAN . . . 7M 197
Smithills Dean Rd. BL1: Bolt . . . 7A 198
Smithill's Hall . . . 9B 198
Smithills Hall Cl. BL0: Ramsb . . . 9G 181
Smithills Hall Country Pk. . . . 8B 198
Smithill's Open Farm . . . 8C 198
Smith La. BL7: Eger . . . 4F 198
Smith Rd. FY5: T Clev . . . 1D 62
Smith's La. PR4: Tarl . . . 5B 170
Smith St. BB8: Colne . . . 7N 85
BB9: Nelson . . . 2J 105
(not continuous)
BB10: W'thorne . . . 4M 125
BB12: Burnl . . . 1A 228 (3D 124)
BB18: Barnw . . . 3L 77
BL0: Ramsb . . . 9G 180
BL9: Bury . . . 9M 201
OL15: Littleb . . . 9L 185
(off Barehill St.)
OL16: Roch . . . 6C 204
PR4: K'ham . . . 4L 111
PR5: Bam B . . . 8B 136
PR6: Whit W . . . 7E 154
PR7: Adl . . . 7H 195
PR7: Chor . . . 8F 174
WN8: Skelm . . . 2H 219
SMITHY BRIDGE . . . 2J 205
Smithy Bridge (Park & Ride) . . . 2J 205
Smithy Bri. Rd. OL15: Littleb . . . 1H 205
OL16: Littleb . . . 1H 205
Smithy Bridge Station (Rail) . . . 2J 205
Smithy Bri. St. BB5: Osw . . . 5K 141
Smithy Brow BB4: Hasl . . . 3G 160
(off West Vw.)
LA2: Abb . . . 3A 48
WN6: Wrigh . . . 5F 192
WN8: N 'urgh . . . 3L 211
Smithy Brow Ct. BB4: Hasl . . . 3G 160
Smithy Caravan Pk. PR3: Cab . . . 8L 45
Smithy Cl. FY6: Stal . . . 5B 56
L37: Form . . . 8B 206
PR3: Gars . . . 4N 59
PR6: Brind . . . 2H 155
Smithy Ct. PR4: Much H . . . 5J 151
Smithy Cft. BL7: Brom C . . . 5F 198
Smithy Cft. Rd. BD23: Garg . . . 3M 53
Smithy Fld. OL15: Littleb . . . 8K 185
Smithyfield Av. BB10: Burnl . . . 3K 125
Smithy Fold OL12: Roch . . . 4M 203
PR4: W Grn . . . 6G 111
Smithy Glen Dr. WN5: Bill . . . 7H 221
Smithy Grn. L37: Form . . . 8B 206
Smithy How LA6: Cast . . . 5G 8
Smithy La. BB8: Colne . . . 3M 85
FY3: Stain . . . 4K 89
FY6: Pree . . . 1A 56
FY6: Stal . . . 5B 56
FY8: L Ann . . . 2J 129
L39: Aug . . . 5E 216
L39: Bart . . . 6N 207
L40: Holmesw . . . 8A 170
L40: Mawd . . . 3M 191
L40: Scar . . . 9F 188
LA3: Heys . . . 1J 27
LA6: W'ouse . . . 2M 19
PR3: Clau . . . 1D 68
PR4: Much H . . . 5J 151
PR6: Brind . . . 2H 155
SMITHY LANE ENDS . . . 7H 189
Smithy M. FY1: Blackp . . . 3C 88
Smithy Nook OL15: Littleb . . . 5M 185
Smithy Row BB7: Hurst G . . . 1M 99
Smithy's Ct. BB12: Padi . . . 1H 123
Smithy St. BB4: Hasl . . . 4G 160
(off Ratcliffe St.)
BL0: Ramsb . . . 8H 181
PR5: Bam B . . . 8A 136
Smithy Wlk. L40: Burs . . . 8C 190
Smythe Cft. PR9: S'port . . . 4N 167
Snaefell Rd. BB2: Blackb . . . 7M 139
SNAPE GREEN . . . 4C 188
Snape Grn. PR8: S'port . . . 5C 188
Snape La. LA5: Yea C . . . 1B 12
Snape Rake La. PR3: Clau, Goos . . . 6M 61
(not continuous)
Snape St. BB3: Darw . . . 4N 157
Snapewood La. PR3: Cab . . . 2L 59
Snell Gro. BB8: Colne . . . 5C 86
Sniddle Hill La. BB3: Darw . . . 7M 157
Snipe Av. OL11: Roch . . . 6K 203
Snipe Cl. FY3: Blackp . . . 4H 89
FY5: T Clev . . . 7F 54
Snipewood PR7: E'ton . . . 8E 172
Snodworth Rd. BB6: Langh . . . 1D 120
Snowden Av. LA3: Heys . . . 5L 21
Snowden St. BB12: Burnl . . . 3N 123
Snowdon Av. BB1: Blackb . . . 1M 139
Snowdon Cl. FY1: Blackp . . . 5N 227 (7D 88)
Snowdon Dr. BL6: Hor . . . 8D 196
Snowdon Rd. FY8: L Ann . . . 7G 108
Snowdrop Cl. BB4: Hasl . . . 7E 160
PR25: Leyl . . . 5A 154
Snowdrop Dell FY6: Poul F . . . 2L 89
(off Linderbreck La.)
Snow Hill PR1: Prest . . . 4K 229 (9J 115)
Snowhill La. PR3: Scor . . . 7B 46
Snowshill Cres. FY5: T Clev . . . 4F 62
Snowshill Dr. WN3: Wigan . . . 7M 221
Snow St. BB1: Blackb . . . 1E 226 (2N 139)
Soccer Village . . . 5J 205
Sod Hall La. PR4: New L . . . 2D 152
Sod Hall Rd. PR4: New L . . . 1D 152
Solaris Centre, The . . . 4A 108
Solomon's Cl. PR5: Bam B . . . 6B 136
SOLLOM . . . 4E 170
Sollom La. L40: Breth . . . 4G 170
PR4: Breth . . . 4F 170
SOLLOM LOCK . . . 4F 170
Solness St. BL9: Bury . . . 7L 201
Solway Av. BB2: Blackb . . . 7G 139
Solway Cl. FY2: Blackp . . . 5C 62
PR1: Penw . . . 5H 135
Somerby Rd. LA4: Morec . . . 4C 22
Somerford Cl. BB12: Burnl . . . 2B 124
Somersby Cl. PR5: Walt D . . . 5A 136
Somersby Dr. BL7: Brom C . . . 5F 198
Somerset Av. BB1: Wilp . . . 3N 119
BB3: Darw . . . 4N 157
BB7: Clith . . . 1M 81
FY1: Blackp . . . 5N 227 (7D 88)
LA1: Lanc . . . 1L 29
PR7: Chor . . . 5E 174
Somerset Cl. BB5: Osw . . . 5M 141
Somerset Ct. FY1: Blackp . . . 5N 227 (7D 88)
Somerset Dr. PR8: Ains . . . 2C 206
Somerset Gro. BB5: Chur . . . 1M 141
OL11: Roch . . . 5L 203
Somerset Pk. PR2: Fulw . . . 2E 114
Somerset Pl. BB9: Nelson . . . 1L 105
Somerset Rd. BB1: Rish . . . 8F 120
PR1: Prest . . . 2M 229 (8K 115)
PR25: Leyl . . . 5L 153
WN5: Wigan . . . 5M 221
Somerset St. BB11: Burnl . . . 6E 124
Somerset Wlk. BB4: Hasl . . . 7G 161
Somerton Cl. WN6: Stand . . . 3N 213
Sorrel Cl. FY5: T Clev . . . 7F 54
FY6: K Sea . . . 7N 41
Sorrel Ct. PR1: Penw . . . 6F 134
Sorrel Dr. OL15: Littleb . . . 8J 185
Soudan St. BB10: Burnl . . . 8F 104
SOUGH
BB3 . . . 8B 158
BB18 . . . 5D 78
Soughbridge Mill BB18: Sough . . . 5D 78
Sough La. BB1: Belt, Guide . . . 6F 140
BB18: Sough . . . 5D 78
Sough Rd. BB3: Darw . . . 7B 158
Soulby Cl. BB2: Blackb . . . 7K 139
Sourhall Cotts. OL14: Tod . . . 1G 164
Sourhall Ct. OL14: Tod . . . 1G 165
Sourhall Rd. OL14: Tod . . . 3F 164
South Av. BB18: Barnw . . . 1M 77
FY5: T Clev . . . 8C 54
LA4: Morec . . . 3C 22
PR4: New L . . . 8C 134
PR7: Chor . . . 8F 174
South Bank FY4: Blackp . . . 4E 108
Southbank Av. FY4: Blackp . . . 2G 108
Southbank Rd. PR8: S'port . . . 8H 167
Sth. Boundary Rd. L33: Know P . . . 9N 223
Southbourne Av. FY6: Poul F . . . 9J 63
Southbourne Rd. FY3: Blackp . . . 8G 88
Southbrook Rd. PR25: Leyl . . . 6J 153
Southcliffe BB6: Gt H . . . 3H 121
Southcliffe Av. BB12: Burnl . . . 2A 124
Sth. Cliff St. PR1: Prest . . . 8H 229 (2H 135)
Sth. Clifton St. FY8: L Ann . . . 5A 130
South Ct. OL16: Roch . . . 5D 204
Southcroft L33: Kirk . . . 6K 223
Southdene WN8: Parb . . . 2M 211
Southdown Cl. OL11: Roch . . . 9N 203
Southdown Dr. FY5: T Clev . . . 3K 63
Southdowns Rd. PR7: Chor . . . 8F 174
South Dr. BB12: Padi . . . 1J 123
BL2: Bolt . . . 9L 199
LA1: Bail . . . 9M 29
PR2: Fulw . . . 2H 115
PR4: Inskip . . . 2G 93
WN6: App B . . . 2F 212
South East Dr. LA1: Bail . . . 9M 29
South End PR1: Prest . . . 3H 135
Southend BD24: Gig . . . 3N 35
(off Raines Rd.)
Southern Av. BB12: Burnl . . . 2A 124
PR1: Prest . . . 2M 135
Southern Cl. PR3: Longr . . . 4J 97
Southern Ct. BB12: Burnl . . . 1A 124
Southern Pde. PR1: Prest . . . 2L 135
Southern Rd. PR8: S'port . . . 8G 166
Southern's La. WA11: Rain . . . 4L 225
Southern St. WN5: Wigan . . . 6N 221
Southery Av. WN3: Wins . . . 8N 221
Southey Cl. OL15: Littleb . . . 3J 205
PR2: Fulw . . . 2J 115
Southey Gro. L31: Magh . . . 4C 222
Southey St. BB11: Burnl . . . 3C 124
SOUTHFIELD . . . 4M 105
Southfield PR4: Much H . . . 4J 151
Southfield Av. BL9: Bury . . . 6L 201
Southfield Dr. BB7: West B . . . 7M 73
FY3: Blackp . . . 2J 89
PR4: New L . . . 9C 134
Southfield Gdns. PR4: Much H . . . 4K 151
Southfield La. BB8: Colne . . . 1A 106
BB10: S'field . . . 3N 105
Southfield Rd. BL0: Ramsb . . . 3F 200
Southfield Sq. BB9: Nelson . . . 2K 105
Southfield St. BB9: Nelson . . . 2J 105
Southfield Ter. BB8: Lane B . . . 5H 87
Southfleet Av. FY7: Flee . . . 3E 54
Southfleet Pl. FY7: Flee . . . 3E 54
Southfold Pl. FY8: L Ann . . . 4N 129
South Gate PR7: Adl . . . 6H 195
Southgate BL2: Bolt . . . 9L 199
FY7: Flee . . . 4D 54
LA3: Morec . . . 6D 22
OL12: Whitw . . . 7N 183
PR1: Prest . . . 2K 229 (8J 115)
PR2: Fulw . . . 4G 115
Southgates PR7: Char R . . . 2N 193
South Gro. LA4: Morec . . . 3C 22
PR2: Fulw . . . 1H 115
PR3: Bart . . . 2E 94
Southgrove Av. BL1: Bolt . . . 7E 198
South Hey FY8: L Ann . . . 2J 129
SOUTH HILL . . . 9H 155
South Hill PR8: S'port . . . 8G 166
South Holme FY8: L Ann . . . 4B 130
Sth. King St. FY1: Blackp . . . 2K 227 (5C 88)
Southlands PR4: K'ham . . . 5M 111
Southlands Av. PR5: Lost H . . . 7L 135
WN6: Stand . . . 4N 213
Southlands Dr. PR26: Leyl . . . 8E 152
South Lawn FY4: Blackp . . . 8E 88
South Meade L31: Magh . . . 1A 222
South Mdw. La. PR1: Prest . . . 9G 229 (2H 135)
South Mdw. St. PR1: Prest . . . 4M 229 (9K 115)
Sth. Moss Rd. FY8: L Ann . . . 1J 129
Southney Cl. L31: Mell . . . 7G 222
South Pde. BB18: Barnw . . . 1M 77
(off South Av.)
BD24: Sett . . . 3N 35
(off Duke St.)
FY5: T Clev . . . 2E 62
L32: Kirk . . . 8K 223
OL16: Roch . . . 6C 204
South Pk. FY8: L Ann . . . 4M 129
South Pk. Ct. L32: Kirk . . . 7H 223
South Pk. Dr. FY3: Blackp . . . 8F 88

South Pk. Rd.—Squires Rd.

South Pk. Rd. L32: Kirk 7G 223
South Pier 1A 108
South Pier Stop (Tram) 1A 108
South Pl. OL16: Roch 5D 204
SOUTHPORT 7H 167
Southport & Ainsdale Golf Course 7D 186
Southport Arts Cen. 7H 167
Southport Bus. Cen. PR9: S'port 7H 167
(off Lord St.)
Southport Bus. Pk. PR8: S'port 2K 187
Southport County Cricket Ground 2E 186
Southport Crematorium PR8: S'port 3A 188
Southport Eco Vis. Cen. 7E 166
Southport Ent. Cen. PR9: S'port 8N 167
Southport FC 9L 167
Southport Little Theatre 7H 167
Southport Model Railway Village 7G 166
Southport Municipal Golf Links 5J 167
Southport New Rd. PR4: Mere B, Tarl 2H 169
PR9: Banks 1D 168
Southport Old Links 6A 168
Southport Old Rd. L37: Form 5B 206
Southport Pier 5F 166
Southport Pier Tram 6F 166
Southport Res. Parkhomes PR8: S'port 3N 187
Southport Rd. L31: Lyd 3N 215
L37: Form 7A 206
L39: Bart 6N 207
L39: Orms 6K 209
L40: Scar 6C 188
PR7: Chor, Eux 5A 174
PR7: E'ton 4B 172
PR8: S'port 2N 187
PR26: Leyl 4B 172
Southport Sailing Club 5H 167
Southport Station (Rail) 7H 167
Southport Ter. PR6: Chor 7G 174
Southport Theatre & Floral Hall 6G 167
South Prom. FY5: T Clev 1C 62
FY8: L Ann 2D 128
South Quay LA3: Heys 2H 27
Sth. Ribble Ind. Est. PR5: Walt D 3M 135
South Ribble Mus. & Exhibition Cen. 7K 153
Sth. Ribble St. PR5: Walt D 2M 135
South Ribble Tennis Cen. 9N 135
South Rd. FY5: T Clev 1K 63
LA1: Lanc 9D 228 (9K 23)
LA4: Morec 3C 22
PR7: Copp 4A 194
PR26: Breth 1J 171
Sth. Royd St. BL8: Tott 6E 200
SOUTH SHORE 2B 108
Sth. Shore St. BB4: Hasl 4F 160
BB5: Chur 3L 141
Southside PR7: Eux 3M 173
South Sq. FY3: Blackp 4D 88
FY5: T Clev 7C 54
South Strand FY7: Flee 5D 54
South St. BB3: Darw 6A 158
BB4: Hasl 6H 161
BB4: Newc 6C 162
BB4: Rawt 4M 161
BB5: Acc 3B 142
(Bishop St.)
BB5: Acc 9D 122
(Parker St.)
BB11: Burnl 1D 228 (3E 124)
BD23: Garg 3M 53
BL0: Ramsb 8J 181
(Earl St.)
BL0: Ramsb 8J 181
(Old Engine La.)
FY8: L Ann 4C 130
OL13: Bac 7F 162
(Brandwood Rd.)
OL13: Bac 5K 163
(St James St.)
OL16: Roch 5D 204
PR3: Gt E 6N 65
South Ter. BL0: Ramsb 4H 181
L39: Orms 8K 209
OL12: Roch 4K 203
PR6: Withn 5D 156
South Ter. Ct. OL16: Roch 8D 204
Sth. Valley Dr. BB8: Colne 8N 85
South Vw. BB4: Hasl 4G 161
BB6: Gt H 4J 121
BB9: Nelson 3H 105
(off High St.)
BB12: S'stone 7D 102
BD23: Hell 1D 52
(off Skipton Rd.)
BD24: Rath 6M 35
BL7: Belm 9K 177
FY8: Moss S 8C 110
OL11: Roch 7J 203
PR4: K'ham 5M 111
PR5: Lost H 9L 135
(Lord's Av.)
PR5: Lost H 9K 135
(off School La.)
PR26: Breth 1K 171
South Vw. Rd. OL16: Roch 2H 205
South Vw. St. OL14: Tod 7F 146
South Vw. Ter. OL16: Roch 1H 205
PR25: Leyl 7K 153
South Vs. OL13: Bac 7G 163
SOUTHWARD BOTTOM 9L 125
Southwark BB12: Burnl 3A 124
(off Woodbine Rd.)
Sth. Warton St. FY8: L Ann 5B 130
Southway FY7: Flee 3D 54
WN8: Skelm 2M 219
Sth. Westby St. FY8: L Ann 5A 130
South West Dr. LA1: Bail 8L 29
South Whiteacre WN6: Stand 2K 213
Southwood Av. FY7: Flee 1E 54
Southwood Cl. FY8: L Ann 4L 129
Southwood Dr. BB5: Bax 5D 142
Southworth Av. FY4: Blackp 2E 108
Southworth St. BB2: Blackb 6L 139
Southworth Way FY5: T Clev 7E 54
Sovereign Ct. FY5: T Clev 2D 62
(off Anchorsholme La. E.)
Sovereign Ga. FY4: Blackp 4F 108
Sowarth Fld. BD24: Sett 3N 35
Sowarth Light Ind. Est. BD24: Gig 3N 35
Sowclough Rd. OL13: Bac 6H 163
SOWERBUTT'S GREEN 9N 117
Sowerby Av. FY4: Blackp 1D 108
Sowerby Rd. PR3: Inskip 7J 67
Sowerby St. BB12: Padi 1H 123
SOWER CARR 8C 56
Sower Carr La. FY6: Ham 8B 56
Spa Fold L40: Lath 8E 210
Spa Gth. BB7: Clith 3M 81
Spa La. L40: Lath 8E 210
Spalding Av. PR3: Gars 6A 60
Spark La. L40: Ruff 8F 170
Spa Rd. PR1: Prest 9G 115
Sparrable Row BB10: Brierc 7M 105
Sparrow Hill OL16: Roch 6B 204
WN8: Parb 2C 212
Sparth Av. BB5: Clay M 6M 121
Sparth Bottoms Rd. OL11: Roch 7A 204
Sparthfield Av. OL11: Roch 8B 204
Sparth Gdns. BB5: Clay M 6M 121
Sparth Rd. BB5: Clay M 6L 121
Spa St. BB12: Burnl 2C 124
BB12: Padi 1J 123
PR1: Prest 9G 114
Spa Well La. PR26: Cros 7K 171
Speakmans Dr. WN6: App B 6F 212
Speedie Cl. BB2: Blackb 8L 139
Speedwell Cl. FY5: T Clev 7F 54
Speedwell St. BB2: Blackb 6J 139
Speke St. BB2: Blackb 6J 139
Spelding Dr. WN6: Stand 8N 213
SPEN BROOK 9B 84
Spenbrook Rd. BB12: Newc P 8A 84
Spen Brow Rd. LA2: Tat 8H 19
Spen Bus. Pk. FY4: Blackp 1J 109
Spencer Ct. FY1: Blackp 3C 88
Spencer La. L40: Ruff 1E 190
OL11: Roch 8J 203
Spencers Dr. PR4: Tarl 7E 150
Spencers La. L31: Mell 8D 222
L39: Hals 1J 207
WN5: Orr 4G 221
WN8: Skelm 3M 219
Spencer St. BB4: Craws 8M 143
BB5: Acc 2C 142
BB10: Burnl 9E 104
BL0: Ramsb 9G 181
OL13: Bac 7G 162
OL15: Littleb 8M 185
Spencers Wood BL7: Brom C 6F 198
(off Hough La.)
Spen Cnr. FY4: Blackp 9N 227 (9E 88)
Spendmore PR7: Copp 3B 194
Spendmore La. PR7: Copp 5N 193
Spen Fold OL15: Littleb 1K 205
Spen La. PR4: Newt, Trea 3C 112
Spenleach La. BL8: Hawk 1B 200
Spennymoor Cl. PR7: Buck V 1B 174
Spen Pl. FY4: Blackp 1F 108
Spenser Cl. BB10: H'wood 5N 125
Spenser Gro. BB6: Gt H 4H 121
Spenser St. BB12: Padi 2J 123
Spenwood Rd. OL15: Littleb 9J 185
Spey Cl. PR25: Leyl 7H 153
WN6: Stand 3N 213
Speyside FY4: Blackp 2D 108
Sphynx Lawn Tennis Club 1L 187
Spicer Gro. L32: Kirk 8K 223
Spindle Berry Ct. BB5: Acc 4B 142
Spindle Cl. BB1: Blackb 1N 139
Spinnakers, The FY8: L Ann 3E 128
Spinner M. L39: Orms 7M 209
Spinners Ct. LA1: Lanc 8C 228
PR7: Buck V 9A 154
Spinners Gdns. OL12: Roch 1F 204
Spinners Grn. OL12: Roch 3C 204
Spinners Sq. PR5: Bam B 9A 136
Spinney, The BB2: Blackb 9H 119
BB7: Grind 5A 74
BB12: Burnl 1B 124
BL7: Turt 3J 199
FY5: T Clev 4F 62
(not continuous)
FY6: Poul F 7L 63
L37: Form 7A 206
LA1: Lanc 2M 29
LA3: Heys 9M 21
LA5: Arn 3G 4
OL12: Roch 2A 204
PR1: Penw 5C 134
PR4: Tarl 8E 150
PR6: Chor 3E 174
WA11: Rain 3K 225
Spinney Apartments WN8: Uph 2F 220
Spinney Brow PR2: Ribb 5N 115
Spinney Cl. L39: Orms 9J 209
PR4: New L 8C 134
PR6: Whit W 9D 154
Spinney Cft. PR3: Longr 3J 97
Spinney Dr. BL9: Bury 7K 201
Spinney La. LA5: Arn 3G 4
Spinneyside BB2: Blackb 7B 226
Spinning Av. BB1: Guide 8D 140
Spinnings, The BL9: Summ 2H 201
Spire Cl. BB3: Darw 7C 158
Spires Gro. PR4: Cott 4B 114
Spirit of Sport 3G 124
Spodden Cotts. OL12: Whitw 4A 184
Spodden Fold OL12: Whitw 6N 183
Spodden St. OL12: Roch 5A 204
Spod Rd. OL12: Roch 4N 203
Spokeshave Way OL16: Roch 3F 204
Sport & Leisure Ribby Hall Village 5K 111
Sportlife Fitness Cen.
Blackburn 8L 139
Sports Barn
Blackpool 4C 88
Sportsmans Caravan Pk.
FY6: Stal 5L 55
SPOTLAND BRIDGE 5A 204
SPOTLAND FOLD 4N 203
Spotland Rd. OL12: Roch 5A 204
Spotland Stadium 5N 203
Spotland Tops OL12: Roch 4M 203
Spouthouse La. BB5: Hunc 8E 122
Spout Ho's. BB9: Blacko 3G 85
Spout La. LA2: Wen 5F 18
Spread Eagle St. BB5: Osw 3J 141
Spring Av. BB6: Gt H 3J 121
SPRING BANK 5N 221
Spring Bank LA5: Silv 8G 5
OL12: Whitw 5A 184
PR1: Prest 7G 229 (1H 135)
PR3: Gars 6N 59
WN6: App B 4F 212
Springbank BB9: Barrf 6J 85
Springbank Av. FY5: T Clev 1J 63
Spring Bank Cl. BB2: Blackb 6K 139
Spring Bank Ct. BB2: Blackb 6K 139
Springbank Gdns. BB4: Craws 6L 143
Spring Bank La. LA1: Lanc 9D 228 (9K 23)
OL11: Roch 5J 203
(not continuous)
Spring Bank Ter. BB2: Blackb 6K 139
Spring Bottom OL14: Wals 8J 165
Springbrook Av. FY5: T Clev 3E 62
Spring Brook Ho. BB5: Clay M 7M 121
(off Canal St.)
Spring Bldgs. BB4: Craws 9M 143
(off Driver St.)
Spring Cl. BL0: Ramsb 8G 181
BL8: Tott 7D 200
L33: Kirk 5M 223
PR8: Birk 9G 166
Spring Ct. BB8: Colne 6A 86
(off Derby St.)
OL12: Roch 4C 204
Spring Cres. PR6: Whit W 1G 174
Spring Cft. PR25: Far 4M 153
Springdale Rd. BB6: Langh 1C 120
Springfield BB9: Blacko 3G 85
LA2: H Ben 6M 19
LA5: Arn 1F 4
LA6: Holme 2G 6
LA6: K Lon 5E 8
WA11: Rain 9J 219
Springfield Av. BB2: Blackb 7F 138
BB5: Acc 4M 141
BB18: Earl 3F 78
OL13: Bac 4L 163
OL15: Littleb 7K 185
PR4: K'ham 4K 111
Springfield Bank BB11: Burnl 4E 228 (4E 124)
Springfield Cl. BB7: Whall 4K 101
L40: Burs 1B 210
Springfield Ct. FY3: Blackp 7E 88
OL13: Bac 4L 163
(off South St.)
Springfield Cres. LA2: H Ben 6M 19
Springfield Dr. BB4: W'foot 6C 162
FY5: T Clev 8H 55
Springfield Flats BB3: Darw 7A 158
Springfield Gdns. LA6: Neth K 4C 16
PR3: Scor 7B 46
Springfield Ind. Est. PR1: Prest 2H 229
Springfield La. OL16: Roch 2G 205
Springfield M. PR6: And 4L 195
Springfield Pk. 8L 203
Springfield Rd. BB4: Rawt 4N 161
BB6: Gt H 5M 121
BB9: Nelson 4J 105
BB11: Burnl 5E 228 (5E 124)
(Emily St.)
BB11: Burnl 4F 124
(Fairview Rd.)
BL0: Ramsb 3F 200
BL1: Bolt 6E 198
FY1: Blackp 1H 227 (4B 88)
FY8: L Ann 2E 128
L39: Aug 6E 216
PR6: Adl 5K 195
PR7: Chor 6E 174
PR25: Leyl 8G 153
Springfield Rd. Nth. PR7: Copp 4A 194
Springfield St. BB2: Blackb 5J 139
BB3: Darw 7A 158
BB5: Osw 5K 141
LA1: Lanc 9D 228 (9K 23)
LA4: Morec 4N 21
PR1: Prest 2H 229 (8H 115)
Springfield Ter. BB2: Blackb 7H 139
FY7: Flee 6G 54
LA2: H Ben 6M 19
(off Springfield)
PR6: H Charn 4K 195
Springfield Vw. BB11: Dunn 3A 144
Spring Gdns. BB3: Darw 7A 158
BB4: Craws 9M 143
(off Lord St.)
BB4: W'foot 9D 162
BB5: Acc 3B 142
BB7: Wadd 8H 73
BL2: Bolt 9M 199
BL6: Hor 9C 196
FY8: L Ann 8F 108
L31: Magh 2D 222
OL13: Bac 4L 163
OL15: Littleb 9L 185
PR1: Penw 6J 135
PR4: Frec 9N 111
PR25: Leyl 7J 153
Spring Gdns. Rd. BB8: Colne 7A 86
Spring Gdns. St. BB4: W'foot 7D 162
Spring Gdns. Ter. BB12: Padi 9H 103
Spring Gdn. St.
LA1: Lanc 7C 228 (8K 23)
Spring Gro. BB8: Colne 5F 86
Spring Hall BB5: Clay M 4M 121
SPRING HILL 3N 141
SPRINGHILL 5A 162
Spring Hill BB1: Blackb 4C 226
PR4: Frec 1B 132
Springhill OL16: Roch 9E 204
Springhill Av. OL13: Bac 7H 163
Springhill Cotts. BB4: Rawt 5A 162
Spring Hill Rd. BB5: Acc 4M 141
Springhill Rd. BB11: Burnl 4B 228 (4D 124)
Springhill Vs. OL13: Bac 7G 163
Spring La. BB2: Blackb 5J 139
(not continuous)
BB4: Hasl 3G 160
Spring La. BB8: Colne 6A 86
PR5: Sam 8J 117
Spring Mdw. BB7: Clith 2L 81
PR25: Leyl 6A 154
Spring Mdws. BB3: Darw 8D 158
BB5: Clay M 6N 121
Spring M. PR6: Whit W 9G 154
Spring Mill Wlk. OL16: Roch 3F 204
Spring Mt. OL13: Bac 6K 163
Springmount BB18: Earl 3F 78
Springmount Dr. WN8: Parb 8N 191
Spring Pl. BB8: Colne 6A 86
OL12: Whitw 3A 184
Springpool WN3: Wins 9L 221
Spring Rd. WN5: Orr 3J 221
Spring Row BB8: Colne 5F 86
Springs, The OL11: Roch 6J 203
Springsands Cl. PR2: Fulw 4A 116
Springs Brow PR7: Copp 8N 193
Springs Ct. BB6: Gt H 4K 121
SPRING SIDE 4N 161
Spring Side OL12: Whitw 2A 184
Springside BB4: W'foot 9D 162
Springside Cotts. BL7: Belm 3A 198
Springside Gdns. PR6: Whit W 1E 174
Spring Side La. OL12: Ward 7D 184
Springside Rd. BL9: Bury 5J 201
Springside Vw. BL8: Bury 6G 201
Springside Vw. Cotts. BL8: Bury 6H 201
Springs Rd. PR3: Longr 2K 97
PR6: Chor 4F 174
Spring St. BB1: Rish 7H 121
BB4: Craws 8M 143
BB5: Acc 4M 141
BB5: Osw 4L 141
BB9: Nelson 3G 105
BL0: Ramsb 7J 181
(Millett St.)
BL0: Ramsb 8G 181
(Spring Cl.)
BL6: Hor 9C 196
BL8: Bury 9E 200
BL8: Tott 6D 200
OL14: Tod 7F 146
PR25: Leyl 6L 153
Spring Ter. BB4: Craws 6L 143
BB5: Osw 4K 141
BB6: Langh 9D 100
(off Clayton Row)
BL8: Tott 6E 200
(off Spring St.)
OL11: Roch 5L 203
OL13: Bac 7H 163
Spring Ter. Sth. BB4: Rawt 5K 161
Springthorpe St. BB3: Darw 9B 158
Spring Thyme Fold OL15: Littleb 9K 185
Spring Top BB4: Craws 8M 143
SPRING VALE
BB3 8B 158
BB4 5F 160
SPRINGVALE 2L 225
Spring Vale BL7: Edgw 8L 179
Springvale BB5: Acc 4M 141
PR3: Fort 2M 45
Springvale Bus. Pk. BB3: Darw 9B 158
Springvale Cl. L32: Kirk 9J 223
Spring Vale Dr. BL8: Tott 6D 200
SPRING VALE GARDEN VILLAGE 9C 158
Springvale Mill BB4: Hasl 5F 160
Spring Vale Rd. BB3: Darw 8B 158
Spring Vale St. BL8: Tott 7D 200
Spring Vale Ter. OL15: Littleb 9L 185
(off Church St.)
Spring Vw. BB2: Blackb 3K 139
BB10: Cliv 9L 125
Spring Vs. OL14: Tod 7E 146
Springwater Av. BL0: Ramsb 2F 200
Springwood Cl. PR5: Walt D 5K 135
Springwood Dr. L40: Ruff 9E 170
PR7: Chor 9G 175
Springwood Rd. BB10: Burnl 4J 125
Springwood St. BL0: Ramsb 7G 181
Spring Yd. BB8: Colne 6A 86
Sprodley Dr. WN6: App B 2E 212
Spruce Av. LA1: Lanc 3K 29
Spruce Cl. PR2: Fulw 2M 115
Spruce Ct. BB5: Hunc 9D 122
Spruce Cres. BL9: Bury 6L 201
Spruce St. BL0: Ramsb 9F 180
(not continuous)
OL16: Roch 7E 204
Spruce Wlk. OL14: Wals 7K 165
Sprucewood Cl. BB5: Acc 2C 142
Spurriers La. L31: Mell 2H 223
Spurrier Sq. PR7: Chor 8F 174
Spurrier St. PR26: Far M 3K 153
Spymers Cft. L37: Form 6A 206
Square, The BB7: Wadd 8H 73
BB7: Whall 5J 101
BB10: W'thorne 4M 125
(off Water St.)
FY3: Blackp 8G 89
FY5: T Clev 7D 54
LA6: Burt K 6G 7
OL13: Bac 5K 163
PR3: Scor 7B 46
PR3: W'ham 5B 96
PR5: Walt D 3B 136
PR6: Birns 8A 156
PR6: Whit W 8D 154
PR25: Far 5L 153
Square Ho. La. PR9: Banks 8G 149
Square La. L40: Burs 1C 210
PR4: Catf 6K 93
Square Rd. OL14: Wals 7K 165
Square St. BL0: Ramsb 8H 181
Squares Wood Cl. PR7: Chor 8C 174
Square Vw. OL14: Wals 7L 165
Squire Rd. BB9: Nelson 2K 105
Squires Cl. PR5: Hogh 6G 136
Squires Ct. FY4: Blackp 4D 108
Squires Ga. Ind. Est. FY4: Blackp 5E 108
Squires Ga. La. FY4: Blackp, L Ann 5B 108
Squires Ga. Rd. PR2: Ash R 6F 114
Squires Gate Station (Rail) 5B 108
Squires Rd. PR1: Penw 2F 134

Stonehill Rd.—Sutton Pl.

Stonehill Rd. OL12: Roch 2L 203
Stoneholme Ind. Est. BB4: Craws 8M 143
Stoneholme Rd. BB4: Craws 8M 143
Stone Holme Ter. BB4: Craws 8M 143
Stonehouse BL7: Brom C 6H 199
Stonehouse Grn. PR6: Clay W 4D 154
Stone Ho. Rd. WN5: Wigan 2N 221
Stoneleigh Cl. PR8: Ains 9C 186
Stoneleigh Ct. LA5: Silv 8G 4
Stonely Dr. OL14: Wals 8K 165
Stonemasons Ct. FY3: Blackp 3E 88
Stone Mill Cotts. BL7: Turt 2K 199
Stonemill Ri. WN6: App B 5G 212
Stone Moor Bottom BB12: Padi 3H 123
Stone Pits BL0: Eden 3K 181
Stone Row Head LA1: Lanc 8N 23
Stones Bank Rd. BL7: Belm 9N 177
Stones La. OL14: Tod 2H 165
PR3: Catt 1A 68
Stones Rd. OL14: Tod 3J 165
Stonesteads Dr. BL7: Brom C 5G 199
Stonesteads Way BL7: Brom C 5G 198
Stones Ter. OL14: Wals 5J 165
Stone St. BB4: Hasl 5E 160
BB4: W'foot 7D 162
OL13: Bac 8F 162
OL16: Milnr 8J 205
Stone Trough Brow BB18: Kelb 9C 78
Stoneway Rd. FY5: T Clev 2E 62
Stonewell LA1: Lanc 6D 228 (8K 23)
Stoney Bank Rd. BB18: Earl 2F 78
Stoney Brow WN8: Roby M 9E 212
Stoney Butts PR2: Lea 9A 114
Stoney Ct. BB8: Foul 2B 86
Stoneycroft BB10: W'thorne 4L 125
Stoneycroft Av. BL6: Hor 9E 196
Stoneycroft Cl. BL6: Hor 8E 196
Stoneycroft Dr. LA5: Wart 4B 12
STONEYFIELD 8C 204
Stoneygate FY5: T Clev 2F 62
PR1: Prest 6L 229 (1K 135)
Stoneygate La. PR3: Know G, Ribc 1D 98
WN6: App B 2E 212
Stoney Hill OL13: Bac 6G 163
STONEYHOLME 2C 124
Stoney Holt PR25: Leyl 6A 154
Stoneyhurst Av. BB10: Burnl 4H 125
FY5: T Clev 3K 63
L10: Aint 7B 222
Stoneyhurst Height BB9: Brierf 6H 105
Stoney La. BB8: Foul 2B 86
FY6: Ham 1B 64
LA2: Gal 3L 37
PR3: Goos 8B 70
PR4: Frec 3N 131
PR5: Lost H 1M 153
PR7: Adl 9G 195
WN6: Wrigh 9N 191
WN8: Parb, Wrigh 9N 191
Stoneyroyd OL12: Whitw 5A 184
Stoney Royd La. OL14: Tod 8J 147
Stoney St. BB11: Burnl 5F 124
Stoneyvale Ct. OL11: Roch 9C 204
Stonie Heyes Av. OL12: Roch 3E 204
Stonor Rd. PR7: Adl 6H 195
Stony Bank PR6: Brind 2J 155
Stonybutts BB1: Blackb 4C 226
Stonycroft Av. FY4: Blackp 4C 108
Stonycroft Dr. LA5: Arn 2F 4
Stonycroft Pl. FY4: Blackp 4C 108
Stony Head *OL15: Littleb* 4M 185
(off Higher Calderbrook Rd.)
STONY HILL 4C 108
Stony Hill Av. FY4: Blackp 4B 108
STONYHURST 8A 80
Stonyhurst PR7: Chor 1E 194
Stonyhurst Av. BL1: Bolt 8E 198
Stonyhurst Cl. BB2: Blackb 6A 226 (4L 139)
BB12: Padi 3K 123
Stonyhurst Park Golf Course 9N 71
Stonyhurst Rd. BB2: Blackb 5A 226 (4L 139)
Stony La. OL14: Tod 6H 147
PR3: Fort 4K 45
(Ratcliffe Wharf La.)
PR3: Fort 2A 46
(Richmond Hill La.)
Stony Rake BB4: Hasl 5M 159
Stoopes Hill BB18: Earl 2F 78
Stoops Fold BB2: Mellor 6F 118
Stoop St. BB11: Burnl 4A 124
Stoops Weind *PR3: Gars* 5N 59
(off Park Hill Rd.)
Stopes Brow BB3: Lwr D 9A 140
Stopford Av. FY2: Blackp 9E 62
OL15: Littleb 1H 205
Stopford Ct. BB5: Clay M 6M 121
Stopgate La. L33: S'wood 4M 223
STOPPER LANE 4M 75
Stopper La. BB7: Rim 4M 75
Store Pas. *OL15: Littleb* 9K 185
(off John St.)
Store St. BB3: Lwr D 9A 140
BB4: Hasl 4G 161
BL6: Hor 9D 196
OL11: Roch 4J 203
Storey Av. LA1: Lanc 7A 228 (8H 23)
Storey Hall LA1: Lanc 2J 29
Storey Institute & Gallery 7B 228 (8J 23)
Stork Cl. FY5: T Clev 2F 62
STORK STREET 6D 158
Stork St. BB3: Darw 7D 158
Stormer Hill Fold BL8: Tott 5E 200
Storrs La. LA5: Silv, Yea R 8K 5
Storth Rd. LA7: Storth 2J 5
Storwood Cl. WN5: Orr 6H 221
Stott St. BB9: Nelson 2H 105
OL12: Roch 4C 204
OL16: Milnr 9J 205
OL16: Roch 2G 205
Stour Lodge PR2: Fulw 3F 114
Stourton Rd. PR8: Ains 9C 186
Stourton St. BB1: Rish 7G 121
Stout St. BB2: Blackb 6A 226 (4L 139)
Stow Cl. BL8: Bury 8J 201
Stowe Av. L10: Aint 8D 222
Straight Mile Ct. BB11: Burnl 1F 228 (2F 124)
Straitgate Cotts. BB9: Rough 6E 84
Strait La. LA2: Abb 3A 48
STRAITS, THE 5G 153
Straits BB5: Osw 4L 141
Straits, The PR5: Hogh 5J 137
Straits La. BB12: Read 8C 102
Strand, The FY1: Blackp 1H 227 (5B 88)
FY7: Flee 4C 54
Strandedge Cl. BL0: Ramsb 1H 201
Strand Rd. PR1: Prest 1G 134
Strands Farm Ct. LA2: Horn 7C 18
Strand St. W. PR2: Ash R 9F 114
Strange St. BB11: Burnl 5F 124
Strang St. BL0: Ramsb 8H 181
Stranraer Rd. WN5: Wigan 2M 221
Stransdale Cl. PR3: Gars 5M 59
Stratfield Pl. PR25: Leyl 6L 153
Stratford Av. BL9: Bury 5K 201
OL11: Roch 8B 204
Stratford Cl. LA1: Lanc 5J 23
PR8: Ains 7A 186
Stratford Dr. PR2: Fulw 5G 115
Stratford Gdns. *FY1: Blackp* 7E 88
(off Stratford Pl.)
Stratford Pl. FY1: Blackp 7E 88
FY7: Flee 9E 40
Stratford Rd. FY8: L Ann 1H 129
PR6: Chor 6F 174
Stratford Way BB5: Acc 1N 141
BB8: Colne 6C 86
Strathclyde Rd. BB1: Blackb 4A 140
Strathdale FY4: Blackp 2F 108
Strathmore Cl. BL0: Ramsb 1H 201
Strathmore Gro. PR7: Chor 7D 174
Strathmore Rd. PR2: Fulw 5H 115
Strathyre Cl. FY2: Blackp 6F 62
Stratton Ct. BB9: Nelson 4J 105
Stratton Gro. BL6: Hor 8C 196
Stratton Rd. L32: Kirk 9H 223
Stratton Wlk. L32: Kirk 9H 223
Strawberry Bank BB2: Blackb 3B 226 (3L 139)
BB5: Acc 1B 142
Strawberry Flds. PR7: Chor 3D 174
Strawberry M. LA3: Heys 8L 21
Stray, The BL1: Bolt 9H 199
Streatly Wlk. BB2: Blackb 8A 140
STREET 9F 38
Strellas La. LA5: Neth K 8N 15
Stretford Cl. L33: Kirk 5K 223
Stretford Pl. OL12: Roch 2B 204
Stretton Av. FY4: Blackp 1E 108
Stretton Cl. WN6: Stand 4N 213
Stretton Dr. PR9: S'port 6M 167
Stretton Rd. BL0: Ramsb 3F 200
BL8: Greenm 3F 200
Strickens La. PR3: Barn, Oaken 6E 60
Strickland Dr. LA4: Morec 4E 22
Stricklands La. FY6: Stal 6B 56
PR1: Penw 4G 135
(not continuous)
Strike La. PR4: Frec 9N 111
Strike Ten Bowl 9B 204
Strine, The L40: Ruff 6E 170
PR4: Ruff, Tarl 6E 170
Strines OL14: Wals 8K 165
Strines La. OL14: Wals 8J 165
Strines St. OL14: Wals 8K 165
STRONGSTRY 4H 181
Strongstry Rd. BL0: Ramsb 4H 181
Stronsay Pl. FY2: Blackp 5F 62
Stroops La. BB7: Rim 4L 75
Stroyan St. BB10: Burnl 4G 125
Strutt St. PR1: Prest 2N 229 (8L 115)
Stryands PR4: Hutt 7N 133
Stuart Av. LA4: Morec 2D 22
OL13: Bac 7H 163
Stuart Cl. BB3: Darw 6A 158
PR2: Ribb 6A 116
Stuart Pl. FY3: Blackp 1G 89
Stuart Rd. FY5: T Clev 1J 63
L31: Mell 7G 222
PR2: Ribb 6A 116
Stuart St. BB5: Acc 1A 142
BB18: Barnw 2N 77
OL16: Roch 7D 204
(not continuous)
STUBBINS
BL0 5H 181
PR3 1C 68
Stubbins La. BB7: Sabd 3F 102
BL0: Eden, Ramsb 7H 181
PR3: Clau 1B 68
Stubbins St. BL0: Ramsb 5H 181
Stubbins Vale Caravan Pk. BB7: Sabd 3F 102
Stubbins Va. Rd. BL0: Ramsb 4H 181
Stubbins Va. Ter. BL0: Ramsb 5G 181
Stubbylee La. OL13: Bac 7K 163
Stub La. L40: Burs 2M 209
STUBLEY 9J 185
Stubley Gdns. OL15: Littleb 9K 185
Stubley Holme OL14: Tod 7D 146
Stubley La. OL14: Tod 7D 146
OL15: Littleb 9J 185
Stubley Mill Rd. OL15: Littleb 1H 205
(not continuous)
Studd Brow OL12: Whitw 3A 184
Stud Farm Holiday Pk. LA3: Heat 6N 21
Studfold PR7: Chor 4D 174
Studholme Av. PR1: Penw 6H 135
Studholme Cl. PR1: Penw 6H 135
Studholme Cres. PR1: Penw 5H 135
Studley Ct. PR9: S'port 4K 167
Stump Cross La. BB7: Bolt B 7M 51
Stump Hall Rd. BB12: High 3K 103
Stump La. PR6: Chor 6F 174
PR7: Chor 6F 174
Stunstead Rd. BB8: Traw 8F 86
Sturgess Cl. L39: Orms 5L 209
Sturminster Cl. PR1: Penw 6H 135
Styan St. FY7: Flee 9G 41
(not continuous)
STYDD 6F 98
Stydd La. PR3: Ribc 6F 98
SUDDEN 9N 203
Sudden Impact Paintball 1L 109
Sudden St. OL11: Roch 9N 203
Sudell Av. L31: Magh 9E 216
Sudell Cl. BB3: Darw 6C 158
Sudell Cross BB2: Blackb 3C 226
Sudell La. L31: Lyd 5C 216
L39: Aug 5C 216
Sudell Nook BB1: Blackb 8C 140
Sudell Rd. BB3: Darw 6A 158
Sudellside St. BB3: Darw 6B 158
Sudley Rd. OL11: Roch 8N 203
Sudlow St. OL16: Roch 3E 204
Sudren St. BL8: Bury 9E 200
Suffolk Av. BB12: Burnl 3M 123
Suffolk Cl. PR25: Leyl 9H 153
Suffolk Ct. PR7: Buck V 9B 154
Suffolk Rd. FY3: Blackp 8G 89
PR1: Prest 2M 229 (8K 115)
PR8: Birk 5G 186
Suffolk St. BB2: Blackb 6K 139
OL11: Roch 7C 204
Suffton Pk. L32: Kirk 9H 223
Sugar Ho. All. LA1: Lanc 6D 228
Sugar Stubbs La. PR9: Banks 2H 169
Sugham La. LA3: Heys 8L 21
Sulby Cl. PR8: Birk 2F 186
Sulby Dr. LA1: Lanc 1K 29
PR2: Ribb 4B 116
Sulby Gro. LA4: Morec 2E 22
PR2: Ribb 4C 116
Sulby Rd. BB2: Blackb 7M 139
Sullivan Dr. BB2: Blackb 7A 140
Sullom Side La. PR3: Barn 7F 60
Sullom Vw. PR3: Gars 6N 59
Sulphur Wells BD23: Brou 6M 53
Sultan of Lancaster Art Gallery 7D 228
Sultan St. BB5: Acc 2B 142
Sulyard St. LA1: Lanc 7D 228 (8K 23)
Summer Brook BB9: Nelson 3G 104
Summer Castle OL16: Roch 6D 204
Summerdale Dr. BL0: Ramsb 3G 200
Summerer Gro. PR4: Weet 4D 90
Summerfield BD23: T Crav 9J 53
PR25: Leyl 4J 153
Summerfield Cl. PR5: Walt D 6L 135
Summerfield Dr. LA2: Slyne 1J 23
Summerfield Rd. OL14: Tod 2M 165
Summerfield Rd. W. OL14: Tod 2M 165
Summerfields FY8: L Ann 9C 108
PR7: Copp 6B 194
Summerfield Wlk. *PR7: Buck V* 9B 154
(off Waltham Rd.)
Summerhill LA2: H Ben 7L 19
Summer Hill Cl. BL1: Bolt 7D 198
Summerhill Dr. L31: Magh 3E 222
Summers Barn PR2: Fulw 3A 116
SUMMERSEAT 3H 201
Summerseat La. BL0: Ramsb 2F 200
Summerseat Station
East Lancashire Railway 3H 201
Summersgill Rd. LA1: Lanc 6H 23
Summer St. BB9: Nelson 3G 105
BL6: Hor 9C 196
OL16: Roch 6D 204
WN8: Skelm 9K 211
Summerton Wlk. *BB3: Darw* 5A 158
(off Winterton Rd.)
Summer Trees Av. PR2: Lea 6A 114
Summerville FY4: Blackp 3C 108
Summerville Av. FY3: Stain 5K 89
Summerville Caravan Pk. LA4: Morec 4A 22
Summerville Wlk. BB2: Blackb 3B 226 (3L 139)
Summerwood Cl. FY2: Blackp 1D 88
Summerwood La. L39: Hals 3B 208
SUMMIT 4N 185
Summit, The BB18: Salt 5M 77
BD23: T Crav 9J 53
Summit Cl. BL9: Bury 9D 202
Summit Dr. PR4: Frec 2A 132
Summit Works BB11: Burnl 7C 124
Sumner Av. L39: D'holl 8M 207
Sumner Cl. PR7: Chor 8F 174
Sumner Gro. *L33: Kirk* 5L 223
(off Mossdale Rd.)
Sumners La. PR26: Cros 7K 171
Sumner St. BB2: Blackb 7B 226 (5L 139)
(not continuous)
PR25: Leyl 6K 153
Sumpter Ct. PR1: Penw 6J 135
Sumpter Cft. PR1: Penw 6H 135
Sunacre Ct. LA3: Heys 6M 21
Sunbank Cl. OL12: Roch 3A 204
Sunbury Av. PR1: Penw 5G 134
Sunbury Dr. PR8: Ains 9B 186
Suncliffe Rd. BB9: Brierf 6H 105
Suncourt PR8: Birk 8F 166
SUNDERLAND 7D 26
Sunderland Av. FY5: T Clev 8E 54
Sunderland Dr. LA3: Morec 6A 22
Sunderland Pl. WN5: Wigan 2N 221
(not continuous)
Sunderlands Av. FY6: Ham 1C 64
Sunderland St. BB12: Burnl 3N 123
Sun Dr. OL15: Littleb 9M 185
Sunfield Cl. FY4: Blackp 2G 108
Sunfield Vw. PR9: Banks 3F 168
Sun Ga. OL15: Littleb 4J 205
Sunnindale Av. BB4: W'foot 6E 162
Sunningdale PR4: Woodp 7F 94
Sunningdale Av. FY4: Blackp 8G 88
FY7: Flee 5D 54
LA2: Hest B 8H 15
Sunningdale Cl. PR4: K'ham 5M 111
Sunningdale Ct. FY8: L Ann 2G 129
Sunningdale Cres. LA2: Hest B 9H 15
Sunningdale Dr. FY5: T Clev 3K 63
PR7: Buck V 9N 153
Sunningdale Gdns. BB10: Burnl 6H 105
Sunningdale Pl. PR4: Inskip 2G 93
Sunny Av. BL9: Bury 8L 201
Sunny Bank PR4: K'ham 4L 111
(not continuous)
Sunnybank BB4: Craws 8M 143
Sunny Bank Av. FY2: Blackp 7C 62
PR4: Newt 7E 112
Sunny Bank Cl. BB4: Hasl 9F 160
Sunny Bank Cotts. BB4: Hasl 1E 180
Sunnybank Dr. BB5: Osw 6J 141
Sunny Bank Farm Ind. Est. FY6: Ham 2C 64
Sunny Bank Gdns. BB2: Blackb 7M 139
Sunny Bank Rd. BB2: Blackb 7L 139
BB4: Hasl 1E 180
(not continuous)
Sunnybank Rd. LA5: Bolt S 4L 15
Sunnybank St. BB4: Hasl 4F 160
Sunny Bank Ter. OL14: Tod 7E 146
SUNNY BOWER 8B 120
Sunny Bower Cl. BB1: Blackb 8B 120
Sunny Bower Rd. BB1: Blackb 8B 120
Sunny Bower St. BL8: Tott 7E 200
Sunny Brow PR7: Copp 3C 194
Sunny Dr. WN5: Orr 5J 221
Sunnyfield Av. BB10: Cliv 9L 125
LA4: Morec 2E 22
Sunnyfield La. BB3: Hodd 6F 158
Sunnyfields L39: Orms 7M 209
WN3: Wins 9M 221
Sunnyhill PR2: Fulw 4M 115
Sunnyhill Cl. BB3: Darw 5L 157
SUNNYHURST 5M 157
Sunnyhurst Av. FY4: Blackp 3D 108
Sunnyhurst Cl. BB3: Darw 5L 157
Sunnyhurst La. BB3: Darw 5L 157
Sunnyhurst Pk. FY4: Blackp 3D 108
Sunnyhurst Rd. BB2: Blackb 5A 226 (4L 139)
Sunnyhurst Wood 5L 157
Sunnyhurst Wood Vis. Cen. 5L 157
Sunny Lea St. BB4: Rawt 2L 161
Sunnymead Av. BL1: Bolt 9F 198
Sunnymede Dr. L31: Lyd 8C 216
Sunnymede Va. BL0: Ramsb 2F 200
Sunnymere Dr. BB3: Darw 5M 157
Sunny Rd. PR9: S'port 4N 167
Sunnyside L39: Aug 4H 217
LA2: H Ben 6L 19
OL14: Tod 2K 165
PR8: Birk 2F 186
Sunnyside Av. BB1: Wilp 2A 120
BB2: Blackb 8F 138
BB7: B'ton 6H 101
PR3: Ribc 7E 98
PR4: Wart 2J 131
Sunnyside Camping & Caravan Site
LA3: Morec 6A 22
Sunnyside Caravan Pk. PR3: Bils 7C 68
Sunnyside Cl. BB4: Rawt 1M 161
LA1: Lanc 8A 228 (9J 23)
PR4: Frec 1N 131
Sunny Side Cotts. OL12: Roch 3F 202
Sunnyside Ct. PR9: S'port 5J 167
Sunnyside La. LA1: Lanc 8A 228 (9H 23)
Sunnyside Ter. FY6: Pree 1B 56
Sunny Top BL8: Hawk 3B 200
Sunny Vw. PR6: Withn 5D 156
Sunnywood Cl. BL8: Tott 7E 200
Sunnywood Dr. BL8: Tott 7F 200
Sunnywood La. BL8: Tott 7F 200
Sunrise Vw. OL15: Littleb 5N 185
Sunset Cl. *L33: Kirk* 5M 223
(off Freckleton Dr.)
Sunset Pk. FY6: Ham 8C 56
Sun St. BB5: Osw 4L 141
BB8: Colne 6B 86
BB9: Nelson 2G 104
BL0: Ramsb 7G 180
LA1: Lanc 6C 228 (8K 23)
Sun Ter. OL14: Tod 7E 146
Sun Vale Av. OL14: Wals 8L 165
Superbowl
Accrington 2A 142
Super St. BB5: Clay M 5L 121
Surgeon's Ct. PR1: Prest 6J 229 (1J 135)
Surma Cl. OL16: Roch 8E 204
Surrey Av. BB3: Darw 4N 157
BB12: Burnl 2N 123
Surrey Cl. PR9: S'port 1B 168
Surrey Rd. BB1: Blackb 3D 140
BB9: Nelson 9H 85
Surrey St. BB5: Acc 1C 142
OL14: Tod 1L 165
PR1: Prest 9M 115
Sussex Av. BB5: Chur 1M 141
Sussex Dr. BB1: Blackb 6G 226 (4A 140)
BB4: Hasl 7G 160
PR3: Gars 4M 59
Sussex Pl. PR7: Buck V 9B 154
Sussex Rd. BB1: Rish 8F 120
FY3: Blackp 4E 88
L31: Magh 3C 222
PR8: S'port 8K 167
PR9: S'port 7J 167
Sussex St. BB9: Nelson 1J 105
BB11: Burnl 5F 124
BB18: Barnw 2N 77
OL11: Roch 7C 204
PR1: Prest 2L 229 (8K 115)
Sussex Wlk. BB1: Blackb 4A 140
Sustainability Way PR26: Far M 3J 153
Sutch La. L40: Lath 9F 190
Sutcliffe Bldgs. *BD24: Sett* 3N 35
(off Castlebergh La.)
Sutcliffe St. BB10: Brierc 7K 105
BB11: Burnl 2C 228 (3D 124)
OL13: Bac 7N 163
OL15: Littleb 8L 185
PR7: Chor 7F 174
Sutcliffe Ter. BB1: Belt 1E 158
Sutherland Cl. BB1: Wilp 2A 120
Sutherland Pl. PR7: Buck V 9B 154
Sutherland Rd. FY1: Blackp 3C 88
Sutherland St. BB8: Colne 7N 85
Sutherland Vw. FY1: Blackp 3C 88
Sutton Av. BB10: Burnl 8H 105
PR4: Tarl 7E 150
Sutton Cres. BB5: Hunc 8E 122
Sutton Dr. PR2: Lea 9A 114
Sutton Fold PR6: Adl 4J 195
Sutton Gro. PR6: Chor 2H 175
Sutton La. PR4: Tarl 1D 170
PR6: Adl 5K 195
(Fielding Pl.)
PR6: Adl 4J 195
(Stoneacre Dr.)
Sutton Pl. FY1: Blackp 4L 227 (6C 88)

308 A-Z Lancashire

Sutton's La.—Tetbury Cl.

Sutton's La. L37: Gt A .1E 214
Sutton St. BB2: Fenis .8E 138
PR4: Weet .4D 90
Swainbank St. BB11: Burnl .4F 228 (4F 124)
Swaine St. BB9: Nelson .2G 105
Swainson St. FY1: Blackp .1K 227 (4C 88)
FY8: L Ann .5M 129
Swain St. OL12: Roch .4B 204
Swaledale LA2: Gal .2M 37
Swaledale Av. BB10: Reed .6F 104
Swalegate L31: Magh .9B 216
Swallow Av. PR1: Penw .4H 135
Swallow Bank Dr. OL11: Roch .9M 203
Swallow Cl. FY3: Blackp .7H 89
FY5: T Clev .8G 54
L33: Kirk .3K 223
Swallow Ct. LA3: Heys .1L 27
PR6: Whit W .6E 154
Swallow Dr. BB1: Blackb .2D 226 (2M 139)
BL9: Bury .9N 201
OL11: Roch .6K 203
Swallowfield PR4: Much H .4J 151
Swallowfields BB1: Blackb .9L 119
PR4: Cott .4B 114
Swallowfold PR2: Grim .9F 96
Swallow Pk. BB11: Burnl .4A 124
Swallow Wharf LA1: Lanc .7L 23
(off Troutbeck Rd.)
Swanage Av. FY4: Blackp .3B 108
Swanage Cl. BL8: Bury .7H 201
Swanage Rd. BB10: Burnl .9G 104
Swan All. L39: Orms .7K 209
(off Burscough St.)
Swan Cl. L40: Scar .4G 188
Swan Courtyard BB7: Clith .3L 81
(off Castle St.)
Swan Delph L39: Aug .1H 217
Swan Dr. FY5: T Clev .2F 62
Swan Farm Cl. BB3: Lwr D .9N 139
Swanfield Ct. BB8: Colne .6D 86
Swanfield Ter. BB8: Colne .6D 86
Swan Hey L31: Magh .3D 222
Swan La. L39: Aug .5D 216
Swan Mdw. BB7: Clith .2K 81
Swanney Lodge Rd. BB4: Rawt .6L 161
Swan Pl. BB8: Colne .6B 86
(off Market St.)
Swanpool La. L39: Aug .2H 217
Swan Rd. BL8: Greenm .3E 200
Swansea St. PR2: Ash R .8F 114
Swansey La. PR6: Whit W .6E 154
Swan St. BB2: Blackb .8D 226 (5M 139)
BB3: Darw .9B 158
PR1: Prest .9M 115
Swan Wlk. L31: Magh .3D 222
Swan Yd. LA1: Lanc .8E 228 (8L 23)
Swarbrick Av. PR2: Grim .9F 96
Swarbrick Cl. FY1: Blackp .3D 88
Swarbrick Ct. PR3: Longr .3K 97
Swarbrick St. PR4: K'ham .5M 111
SWARTHDALE .3H 17
Sweet Briar Cl. BB5: Clay M .5L 121
OL12: Roch .3B 204
Sweet Briar La. OL12: Roch .3B 204
Sweet Clough Dr. BB12: Burnl .3L 123
Sweetlove's Gro. BL1: Bolt .8E 198
Sweetlove's La. BL1: Bolt .8E 198
Sweetstone Gdns. BL1: Bolt .8F 198
(off Stonyhurst Av.)
Swift Cl. BB1: Blackb .3E 226 (3N 139)
FY3: Blackp .8H 89
PR6: Whit W .6E 154
Swift Gdns. LA3: Heys .2L 27
Swift Rd. OL11: Roch .6K 203
Swifts Fold WN8: Skelm .3H 219
Swilkin La. FY6: Stal .6D 56
Swill Bk. La. PR1: Prest .2M 135
SWILLBROOK .9M 93
Swinburne Cl. BB5: Bax .6D 142
SWINDEN .3D 52
Swinden Hall Rd. BB9: Nelson .9J 85
Swinden La. BB8: Colne .9L 85
Swinderby Dr. L31: Mell .7G 222
Swindon Av. FY4: Blackp .1D 108
Swindon St. BB11: Burnl .4B 124
Swine Mkt. LA6: K Lon .6F 8
(off Mill Brow)
Swineshead La. OL14: Tod .4L 165
Swineshead Rd. OL14: Tod .4K 165
Swinless St. BB10: Burnl .9F 104
Swinnate Rd. LA5: Arn .2G 4
Swinnel Brook Pk. BB4: Hasl .6E 160
Swinshaw Cl. BB4: Craws .6M 143
Swinshaw Cotts. BB4: Craws .6M 143
Swinside PR4: Cott .5A 114
Swire Cft. Rd. BD23: Garg .3M 53
Swiss St. BB5: Acc .2M 141
Switch Island L30: N'ton .5A 222
Swithemby St. BL6: Hor .8B 196
(off Mary St. W.)
Swordfish Cl. L40: Burs .9N 189
Sword Meanygate PR4: Tarl .1N 169
Sybil St. OL15: Littleb .8K 185
Sycamore Av. BB9: Nelson .2L 105
BB12: Burnl .2M 123
FY4: Blackp .4F 108
OL14: Tod .9K 147
OL16: Milnr .9K 205
PR3: Gars .4M 59
PR7: Eux .3N 173
Sycamore Bungs. BB7: Gis .9B 52
Sycamore Cl. BB1: Blackb .9N 119
BB1: Rish .9H 121
BB12: Burnl .3A 124
L40: Mawd .3N 191
OL15: Littleb .9J 185
PR2: Fulw .3M 115
PR4: Elsw .1M 91
PR9: Banks .9G 148
Sycamore Ct. PR7: Chor .9D 174
Sycamore Cres. BB4: Rawt .6L 161
BB5: Clay M .4N 121
LA2: Brookh .2J 25
Sycamore Dr. BL9: Bury .7L 201
L33: Kirk .7L 223
PR1: Penw .5H 135
Sycamore Dr. PR4: Wesh .2L 111
WN3: Wins .9L 221
WN8: Skelm .1J 219
Sycamore Gdns. BB8: Foul .2A 86
LA3: Heys .1K 27
Sycamore Gro. BB3: Darw .5B 158
BB5: Acc .5D 142
LA1: Lanc .8H 23
Sycamore Ho. PR7: Chor .8B 174
Sycamore Ri. BB8: Foul .2A 86
BB9: Brierf .5H 105
Sycamore Rd. BB1: Blackb .9N 119
BL8: Tott .8E 200
LA2: Brookh .2J 25
PR2: Ribb .7A 116
(not continuous)
PR3: Bils .6D 68
PR6: Chor .4F 174
Sycamores, The BB18: Earl .3D 78
Sycamore Trad. Est. FY4: Blackp .4E 108
Sycamore Way BB18: Barnw .3L 77
Syd Brook La. L40: Mawd .6A 172
PR26: Cros .6A 172
Sydenham Ter. OL12: Roch .2A 204
Sydney Av. BB7: Whall .5K 101
Sydney Gdns. OL15: Littleb .5M 185
Sydney St. BB3: Darw .8B 158
BB3: Hodd .6F 158
BB5: Acc .2B 142
BB5: Clay M .8N 121
BB12: Burnl .1C 228 (3D 124)
FY8: L Ann .2F 128
Sydney Ter. BB8: Traw .8F 86
SYKE .1C 204
Sykefield BB9: Brierf .5E 104
Syke Hill PR1: Prest .7M 229 (1K 135)
Syke Ho La. PR3: Goos .9A 70
Sykelands Av. LA2: Halt .1C 24
Sykelands Gro. LA2: Halt .1C 24
Syke La. OL12: Roch .1C 204
Syke Rd. OL12: Roch .1C 204
OL15: Littleb .3M 205
Sykes Cl. BB18: Salt .4B 78
Sykes Ct. OL16: Roch .7E 204
(off Sykes St.)
SYKE SIDE .6H 161
Sykeside Ct. BB4: Hasl .6H 161
Syke Side Dr. BB5: Alt .3D 122
Sykes St. OL16: Milnr .9K 205
OL16: Roch .7E 204
Syke St. BB4: Hasl .6H 161
PR1: Prest .7L 229 (1K 135)
Sylvancroft PR2: Ingol .4D 114
Sylvan Dr. BB11: Burnl .5M 123
Sylvan Gro. PR5: Bam B .6C 136
Sylvan Pl. LA3: Heys .1K 27
Sylvester St. LA1: Lanc .8A 228 (9J 23)
Symonds Rd. PR2: Fulw .6H 115

T

Tabby Nook PR4: Mere B .5L 169
Tabby's Nook WN8: N 'urgh .3L 211
Tabley La. PR4: H Bart .9A 94
Tabor St. BB12: Burnl .2B 124
Tadema Gro. BB11: Burnl .7D 124
Tag Cft. PR2: Ingol .4C 114
Tag Farm Ct. PR2: Ingol .4C 114
Tagg Wood Vw. BL0: Ramsb .9F 180
Tag La. PR2: Ingol .3C 114
PR4: H Bart .3C 114
Tailor's La. L31: Magh .2D 222
Talaton Cl. PR9: S'port .1N 167
Talbot Av. BB5: Clay M .7M 121
TALBOT BRIDGE .7C 72
Talbot Bri. Rd. BB7: Bas E .9B 72
Talbot Cl. BB4: Rawt .7K 161
BB7: Clith .4M 81
PR6: Chor .4G 175
Talbot Ct. BL1: Bolt .9F 198
FY4: Blackp .9B 88
(off Waterloo Rd.)
FY8: L Ann .9G 109
Talbot Dr. BB10: Brierc .8K 105
PR7: Eux .4N 173
PR8: S'port .8H 167
Talbot Gro. BL9: Bury .7M 201
Talbot Ho. PR7: Chor .4E 174
(off Lancaster Ct.)
Talbot Rd. BB5: Acc .9N 121
FY1: Blackp .1H 227 (5B 88)
FY3: Blackp .5B 88
FY8: L Ann .4B 130
PR1: Penw .3H 135
PR1: Prest .1G 135
PR25: Leyl .5H 153
Talbot Rd. Ind. Cen. PR25: Leyl .5H 153
Talbot Row PR7: Eux .5N 173
Talbot Sq. FY1: Blackp .1H 227 (5B 88)
Talbot St. BB1: Rish .8J 121
BB8: Colne .5A 86
BB10: Brierc .8K 105
BB11: Burnl .1F 228 (3F 124)
OL11: Roch .7C 204
PR2: Fulw .6G 114
PR3: Chip .5G 70
PR6: Chor .5G 174
PR8: S'port .9G 166
Talbot Ter. FY8: L Ann .5A 130
Tallarn Rd. L32: Kirk .8G 223
Tall Trees LA1: Lanc .4K 23
Tamar Cl. PR25: Leyl .8L 153
Tamar St. PR1: Prest .9A 116
Tamar Way OL10: Heyw .9E 202
Tame Barn OL16: Milnr .8M 205
Tame Barn Cl. OL16: Milnr .7K 205
Tamneys, The WN8: Skelm .2K 219
Tamworth Dr. BL8: Bury .8H 201
Tancaster WN8: Skelm .2J 219
Tanfield Nook WN8: Parb .2N 211
Tanfields WN8: Skelm .2K 219
Tanglewood PR2: Fulw .4L 115
Tan Hill Dr. LA1: Lanc .5K 23
TANHOUSE .2A 220
Tanhouse LA2: Gal .2L 37
Tan Ho. Cl. WN8: Parb .1N 211
Tan Ho. Dr. WN3: Wins .9M 221
Tan Ho. La. BB6: Gt H .2J 121
WN3: Wins .9M 221
WN8: Parb .2N 211
Tanhouse La. PR6: Heap .9H 155
Tanhouse Rd. WN8: Skelm .3N 219
TANNERS .8G 180
Tanners Cft. BL0: Ramsb .8G 180
Tannersmith La. L40: Mawd .9C 172
PR7: Hesk .9C 172
Tanner St. BL0: Ramsb .8G 180
Tanner St. BB11: Burnl .2C 228 (3D 124)
Tanners Way FY8: L Ann .1K 129
Tan Pit Cotts. WN3: Wins .9N 221
Tanpit Cotts. OL10: Heyw .9H 203
Tan Pit La. WN3: Wins .9N 221
Tanpits La. LA6: Burt K .5G 7
Tanpits Rd. BB5: Chur .2L 141
Tansley Av. PR7: Copp .4N 193
Tansley Sq. WN5: Wigan .6N 221
Tansy La. PR3: Fort .1K 45
Tanterton Hall Rd. PR2: Ingol .3C 114
Tanyard Cl. PR7: Copp .4N 193
Tan Yard La. PR3: Longr .2L 97
Tan Yd. Rd. PR3: Catt .1N 67
Taper St. BL0: Ramsb .8G 180
Tapestry St. BB2: Blackb .7L 139
Tarbert Cres. BB1: Blackb .4D 140
Tarbet St. LA1: Lanc .8F 228 (9L 23)
TARDY GATE .8H 135
Tardy Ga. Trad. Cen. PR5: Lost H .8K 135
TARLETON .9E 150
Tarleton Av. BB11: Burnl .5F 124
Tarleton High School Sports Hall .8E 150
TARLETON MOSS .8N 149
Tarleton Office Pk. PR4: Tarl .2E 170
Tarleton Rd. PR9: S'port .6N 167
Tarleton St. BB11: Burnl .5G 228 (5F 124)
TARLSCOUGH .4A 190
Tarlscough La. L40: Burs .4A 190
Tarlswood WN8: Skelm .2K 219
Tarnacre Hall M. PR3: St M .2H 67
Tarnacre La. PR3: Catt, St M .2H 67
Tarnacre Vw. PR3: Gars .6N 59
Tarn Av. BB5: Clay M .5M 121
Tarnbeck Dr. L40: Mawd .2N 191
Tarnbrick Av. PR4: Frec .1A 132
TARNBROOK .2C 48
Tarn Brook Cl. BB5: Hunc .8E 122
Tarnbrook Cl. LA5: Bolt S .7K 15
LA5: Carn .9N 11
Tarnbrook Ct. LA4: Morec .3B 22
Tarnbrook Dr. FY3: Blackp .3G 89
Tarnbrook Rd. LA1: Lanc .6H 23
LA3: Heys .8L 21
Tarn Brow L39: Orms .9H 209
Tarn Cl. PR1: Penw .4C 134
Tarn Ct. FY7: Flee .3D 54
Tarn Hows Cl. PR7: Chor .9D 174
Tarn La. LA5: Yea R .7D 6
LA6: Burt K .7D 6
Tarn Rd. FY5: T Clev .4K 63
Tarnside FY4: Blackp .9H 89
Tarnside Cl. OL16: Roch .2F 204
Tarnside Rd. WN5: Orr .5H 221
Tarnsyke Rd. LA1: Lanc .6H 23
Tarnwater La. LA2: Lanc, Stodd .7H 29
Tarnway Av. FY5: T Clev .3K 63
Tarradale PR4: Longt .7K 133
Tarragon Dr. FY2: Blackp .7F 62
Tarrant Cl. WN3: Wins .9N 221
Tarry Barn La. BB7: Pend .8N 81
Tarves Wlk. L33: Kirk .8L 223
Tarvin Cl. BB10: Brierc .7K 105
PR9: S'port .1C 168
Taskers Cft. BB7: Wis .2M 101
Tasker St. BB5: Acc .2B 142
Tate Fold PR6: Chor .6H 175
TATHAM .6E 18
Tatham Ct. FY7: Flee .3C 54
Tatham Gro. WN3: Wins .9N 221
Tatham St. OL16: Roch .6D 204
Tatlocks Grange L39: Orms .6J 209
Tatterhorn Rd. LA2: H Ben .6M 19
LA6: Ingl .6M 19
Tattersall Sq. BB4: W'foot .4D 162
Tattersall St. BB2: Blackb .6C 226 (4M 139)
BB4: Hasl .1G 161
BB5: Osw .4K 141
BB12: Padi .1J 123
Tatton St. BB8: Colne .8M 85
Taunton Av. OL11: Roch .6M 203
Taunton Dr. L10: Aint .8D 222
Taunton Rd. BB2: Blackb .3J 139
Taunton St. FY4: Blackp .9D 88
PR1: Prest .8N 115
Tavistock Dr. PR8: Ains .7B 186
Tavistock St. BB9: Nelson .2K 105
TAWD BRIDGE .4N 219
Tawd Rd. WN8: Skelm .3N 219
Taxi Service Rd. OL11: Roch .7C 204
(off Lwr. Tweedale St.)
Taybank Av. FY4: Blackp .2D 108
Taylor Av. BB2: Blackb .9K 139
BB4: W'foot .5D 162
L39: Orms .7M 209
OL11: Roch .5K 203
Taylor Cl. BB2: Blackb .7A 226 (5L 139)
Taylor Ct. BB4: Hasl .4F 160
Taylor Gro. LA4: Morec .2F 22
Taylor Holme Ind. Est. OL13: Bac .7F 162
Taylor Ho. BL8: Bury .7H 201
Taylor's Bldgs. BB6: Langh .9C 100
Taylors Cl. FY6: Carl .6J 63
Taylors Ind. Est. PR3: Pill .8K 43
Taylor's La. PR3: Pill .7J 43
PR4: Tarl .3B 170
Taylor's Meanygate PR4: Hesk B, Tarl .7L 149
Taylors Pl. OL12: Roch .4C 204
(off Taylor St.)
Taylor St. BB2: Blackb .8A 226 (5L 139)
BB3: Darw .7A 158
BB4: Hasl .1G 160
BB4: Rawt .4M 161
BB7: Clith .3M 81
Taylor St. BB9: Brierf .4F 104
BB10: Burnl .1E 124
BB18: Barnw .2L 77
BL6: Hor .9C 196
(off Emmett St.)
BL9: Bury .9L 201
OL12: Roch .4C 204
OL12: Whitw .6A 184
PR1: Prest .2G 135
PR7: Chor .9D 174
WN8: Skelm .2G 219
Taylor St. W. BB5: Acc .2A 142
Taylor Ter. OL15: Littleb .9M 185
(off Beswicke St.)
Taymouth Rd. FY4: Blackp .3G 108
Tay St. BB11: Burnl .4B 124
PR1: Prest .2G 135
Taywood Cl. FY6: Poul F .7M 63
Taywood Rd. FY5: T Clev .8G 55
Teal Cl. BB1: Blackb .9L 119
FY5: T Clev .8G 54
L39: Aug .1H 217
PR25: Leyl .8G 152
WN3: Wigan .7L 221
Teal Ct. FY3: Blackp .4H 89
OL11: Roch .6K 203
Teal La. FY8: L Ann .1L 129
Teanlowe Cen. FY6: Poul F .8K 63
Tears La. WN8: N 'urgh .4K 211
Teasel Wlk. LA3: Morec .6B 22
Tebay Av. FY5: T Clev .8D 54
PR4: K'ham .4A 112
Tebay Cl. L31: Magh .9E 216
Tebay Ct. LA1: Lanc .4J 23
Tedder Av. BB12: Burnl .3N 123
PR9: S'port .7N 167
Teenadore Av. FY4: Blackp .2E 108
Teenley Cft. BD23: Wig .10N 35
Tees Ct. FY7: Flee .2D 54
Teesdale LA2: Gal .2L 37
Teesdale Av. FY2: Blackp .2D 88
Tees St. OL16: Roch .7E 204
PR1: Prest .7M 115
Teil Grn. PR2: Fulw .3A 116
Telegraph Way L32: Kirk .8K 223
Telford St. BB12: Burnl .2A 124
Tellcom Bus. Cen. FY4: Blackp .9H 89
Telletholme Ind. Est. L40: Burs .1N 209
Tell St. OL12: Roch .6A 204
Temperance St. PR6: Chor .6G 174
Temple BB3: Hodd .9F 158
Temple Cl. BB1: Blackb .4B 140
Templecombe Dr. BL1: Bolt .7D 198
Temple Ct. BB1: Blackb .4D 226 (3M 139)
LA5: Yea R .6A 6
PR1: Prest .6K 229
Temple Dr. BB1: Blackb .4B 140
BL1: Bolt .9C 198
Templefields PR6: Heap .3J 175
Temple La. OL15: Littleb .5M 185
Templemartin WN8: Skelm .1K 219
(off Thorpe)
Temple Rd. BL1: Bolt .9C 198
Temple St. BB8: Colne .5B 86
BB9: Nelson .2K 105
BB10: Burnl .3F 228 (4F 124)
BB11: Burnl .3F 228 (4F 124)
FY1: Blackp .2H 227 (5B 88)
Templeton Cl. BB3: Darw .5A 158
Temple Way PR6: Chor .2E 174
Tems Side BD24: Gig .3N 35
Tems St. BD24: Gig .3N 35
Tenby WN8: Skelm .1J 219
Tenby Cl. BB1: Blackb .1M 139
Tenby Gro. OL12: Roch .4N 203
Tenby Rd. PR1: Prest .8M 229 (2K 135)
Tenby St. OL12: Roch .4N 203
Tennis St. BB10: Burnl .1E 124
Tennyson Av. BB5: Osw .4J 141
BB12: Padi .2K 123
BB12: Read .8C 102
FY5: T Clev .9G 54
FY8: L Ann .4C 130
OL14: Tod .1N 165
PR4: Wart .2J 131
PR7: Chor .8E 174
Tennyson Cl. LA5: Bolt S .4L 15
Tennyson Dr. FY2: Blackp .5F 62
L39: Orms .6J 209
WN5: Bill .9G 220
Tennyson Mill Ct. PR1: Prest .8N 115
Tennyson Pl. BB6: Gt H .5H 121
PR5: Walt D .6N 135
Tennyson Rd. BB8: Colne .6N 85
FY3: Blackp .2F 88
FY7: Flee .9G 40
PR1: Prest .8N 115
(not continuous)
Tennyson St. BB10: Brierc .7K 105
BB11: Burnl .4B 124
BB12: Hapt .5H 123
OL11: Roch .8D 204
Tennyson Way L32: Kirk .9J 223
Ten Row LA2: Glas .1C 36
Tensing Av. FY2: Blackp .6D 62
Tensing Rd. L31: Magh .1C 222
Tentercroft OL12: Roch .5B 204
Tenterfield St. BB4: W'foot .7D 162
PR1: Prest .5K 229 (9J 115)
Tenterheads BB4: W'foot .8D 162
Tenterhill La. OL11: Roch .3H 203
Terance Rd. FY4: Blackp .1E 108
Tern Cl. L33: Kirk .3K 223
OL11: Roch .6K 203
Tern Gro. LA3: Heys .2L 27
Terrace, The BD24: Sett .3N 35
(off Duke St.)
LA2: L Ben .6J 19
(off Greenfoot La.)
Terrace Row BB7: B'ton .6J 101
Terrace St. PR1: Prest .8M 115
Terra Cotta Bldgs. BB4: Water .7E 144
(off Burnley Rd.)
Terry St. BB9: Nelson .9L 85
Tetbury Cl. BB2: Blackb .8F 138
WN5: Wigan .2N 221

Victoria Rd.—Warren Gro.

Victoria Rd. FY6: Poul F 7L 63
FY8: L Ann 3F 128
L38: Ince B 8E 214
L39: Aug 9H 209
OL14: Tod 1L 165
PR2: Fulw 6H 115
PR4: K'ham 4L 111
PR5: Walt D 2M 135
Victoria Rd. E. FY5: T Clev 2F 62
Victoria Rd. W. FY5: T Clev 1C 62
(not continuous)
Victoria Sq. FY5: T Clev 1D 62
Victoria St. BB1: Blackb 3D 226 (3M 139)
BB1: Rish 8H 121
BB3: Darw 6A 158
BB4: Hasl 4F 160
BB4: Rawt 6A 162
BB4: W'foot 7C 162
BB5: Acc 3A 142
BB5: Chur 2L 141
BB5: Clay M 7M 121
BB5: Osw 5K 141
BB6: Gt H 4K 121
BB7: Clith 4K 81
BB9: Barrf 8H 85
BB9: Nelson 2G 105
BB11: Burnl 2C 228 (4D 124)
BB18: Earl 2E 78
BL0: Ramsb 8G 181
BL8: Tott 6D 200
FY1: Blackp 2H 227 (5B 88)
FY7: Flee 8H 41
FY8: L Ann 5B 130
L40: Burs 8C 190
LA4: Morec 3A 22
LA5: Carn 9A 12
OL12: Roch 4C 204
OL12: Whitw 6N 183
OL13: Bac 7H 163
OL14: Tod 7F 146
OL15: Littleb 9L 185
PR1: Prest 3G 229 (8H 115)
PR3: Longr 3J 97
PR5: Lost H 8L 135
PR6: Wheel 8J 155
PR7: Chor 7F 174
PR9: S'port 6H 167
WA11: Rain 3K 225
Victoria Street Stop (Tram)
Blackpool 2H 227 (5B 88)
Fleetwood 8H 41
Victoria Ter. BB2: Mellor 6D 118
BB3: Tock 5G 157
BB7: B'ton 6G 101
(off Whalley New Rd.)
LA2: Glas 1D 36
OL10: Heyw 9G 202
OL16: Milnr 8K 205
PR3: Cald V 4H 61
PR5: Lost H 8K 135
(off Watkin La., not continuous)
PR6: Chor 5F 174
PR6: Wheel 8J 155
(off Victoria St.)
PR6: Withn 5C 156
PR25: Leyl 7K 153
Victoria Vs. BB1: Rish 7H 121
Victoria Way BB4: Rawt 5A 162
PR8: S'port 7F 166
Victoria Wharf *LA1: Lanc 7J 23*
(off St George's Quay)
Victoria Works Ind. Est. BB11: Burnl 4N 123
Victor St. BB5: Clay M 6M 121
Victory Av. PR9: S'port 7N 167
Victory Blvd. FY8: L Ann 5C 130
Victory Cen., The BB9: Nelson 2J 105
Victory Cl. BB9: Nelson 2J 105
Victory Pk. 8E 174
Victory Rd. BB18: Barnw 2N 77
FY1: Blackp 1M 227 (4C 88)
Victory Wharf PR2: Ash R 9E 114
Victrex Rd. FY5: T Clev 8K 55
Viewfield M. *BB2: Blackb 3J 139*
(off Waverley Pl.)
View Rd. BB3: Darw 2M 157
View St. PR7: E'ton 7F 172
Vihiers Cl. BB7: Whall 4J 101
Viking Cl. PR8: Birk 1G 187
Viking Pl. BB10: Burnl 2E 124
Viking St. OL11: Roch 5N 203
Viking Way LA3: Heys 2L 27
Village, The FY6: Sing 1D 90
Village Cl. WN8: Skelm 3H 219
Village Ct. *FY6: Poul F 8K 63*
(off Hardhorn Rd.)
OL12: Whitw 5N 183
Village Cft. PR7: Eux 3N 173
Village Dr. PR2: Ribb 7B 116
Village Grn. La. PR2: Ingol 3C 114
Village Nook L10: Aint 8D 222
Village Row PR8: Ains 8C 186
Village Walks FY6: Poul F 8K 63
Village Way FY2: Blackp 6D 62
L38: Hight 7A 214
WN8: Skelm 3H 219
Villas, The PR4: Cott 4B 114
Villas Ct.
LA1: Lanc 9B 228 (9J 23)
Villas Rd. L31: Magh 1G 222
Villa Way PR3: Gars 6N 59
Villiers Ct. PR1: Prest 7H 115
Villiers St. BB11: Burnl 4A 124
BB12: Padi 2J 123
BL9: Bury 9M 201
PR1: Prest 1G 229 (7G 115)
(not continuous)
Vincent Ct. BB2: Blackb 8L 139
Vincent Rd. BB9: Nelson 2K 105
Vincent St. BB2: Blackb 8L 139
BB8: Colne 5C 86
LA1: Lanc 9F 228 (9L 23)
OL15: Littleb 8K 185
OL16: Roch 8D 204
Vincent Way WN5: Wigan 3N 221
Vincit St. BB10: Burnl 1F 124
Vine Ct. *FY2: Blackp 1C 88*
(off Gosforth Rd.)
OL16: Roch 6E 204
Vine Pl. OL11: Roch 8C 204
Vinery, The PR4: New L 8C 134
Vines Pk. PR4: Wart 4H 131
Vine St. BB5: Acc 2N 141
BB5: Osw 5J 141
BB9: Brierf 5F 104
(off Cross St.)
BL0: Ramsb 1F 200
LA1: Lanc 1K 29
PR1: Prest 9G 115
PR7: Chor 5E 174
Vineyard OL12: Whitw 1B 184
Vineyard, The PR5: Walt D 4N 135
Vineyard Cl. OL12: Ward 7F 184
Vineyard Cotts. OL12: Ward 7F 184
Vineyard Ho. *OL12: Ward 7F 184*
(off Knowl Syke St.)
Viola Cl. L33: Kirk 5J 223
WN6: Stand 2N 213
Violet Ct. BB1: Blackb 2F 226
Violet Gro. PR3: Gars 5M 59
Violet St. BB10: Burnl 9E 104
Virgin Active
Walton-le-Dale 3M 135
Virginia Av. L31: Lyd 8C 216
Virginia Gro. L31: Lyd 8B 216
Virginia St. OL11: Roch 9B 204
PR8: S'port 8J 167
Virginia Way WN5: Wigan 3M 221
Viscount Av. BB3: Lwr D 1A 158
Viscount Dr. LA1: Lanc 3J 29
Viscount Rd. WN5: Wigan 3N 221
Vitalia 1J 193
Vivary Way BB8: Colne 7M 85
Vivian Dr. PR8: Birk 3G 186
Vivian St. OL11: Roch 8B 204
Voce's La. L39: Bick 8N 217
Vue Cinema
Accrington 2A 142
Blackburn 6D 226 (4N 139)
Cleveleys 9C 54
Lancaster 6C 228 (8K 23)
Southport 6F 166
Walton-le-Dale 3M 135
Vulcan Ct. PR9: S'port 7J 167
Vulcan Rd. PR4: Frec 8N 111
WN5: Wigan 3N 221
Vulcan St. BB9: Nelson 1K 105
OL14: Wals 6K 165
PR9: S'port 7J 167
Vulcan Ter. *OL15: Littleb 9J 185*
(off Spenwood Rd.)

W

Wackersall Rd. BB8: Colne 8M 85
Wadden Hall Nth. LA1: Lanc 9F 228 (9L 23)
Wadden Hall Sth.
LA1: Lanc 9F 228 (1L 29)
WADDICAR 6G 222
Waddicar La. L31: Mell 7F 222
WADDINGTON 8H 73
Waddington Av. BB10: Burnl 3H 125
Waddington Ct. FY8: L Ann 2J 129
Waddington Rd. BB5: Acc 1C 142
BB7: Clith 1K 81
BB7: West B 7K 73
FY8: L Ann 1H 129
PR2: Ribb 7C 116
Waddington St. BB12: Padi 1J 123
BB18: Earl 2E 78
Waddow Grn. BB7: Clith 3J 81
Waddow Gro. BB7: Wadd 8J 73
Waddow Vw. BB7: Wadd 8H 73
Wade Brook Rd. PR26: Leyl 9C 152
WADE HALL 8G 153
Wades Ct. FY3: Blackp 1F 88
Wades Cft. PR4: Frec 2A 132
Wade St. BB12: Padi 9J 103
Wadham Rd. PR1: Prest 8N 229 (2L 135)
Wadsworth Av. *OL14: Tod 4K 165*
(off Weir St.)
Wadsworth Cl. BB3: Darw 6A 158
Wagg Fold OL15: Littleb 7J 185
Wagon Rd. LA2: Dolp 6E 38
Wagstaffe Cl. BB2: Blackb 8K 139
Waidshouse Cl. BB9: Nelson 4J 105
Waidshouse Rd. BB9: Nelson 4J 105
Wain Ct. BB2: Blackb 4J 139
Wainfleet Cl. WN3: Wins 9N 221
Waingap Cres. OL12: Whitw 6A 184
Waingap Ri. OL12: Roch 1B 204
Waingap Vw. OL12: Whitw 7A 184
Waingate PR2: Grim 9E 96
Waingate Cl. BB4: Rawt 4N 161
Waingate Ct. PR2: Grim 9E 96
Waingate La. BB4: Rawt 4N 161
Waingate Rd. BB4: Rawt 4N 161
Waithlands Rd. OL16: Roch 7E 204
Waitholme La. LA5: Burt K 5D 6
Wakefield Av. LA4: Morec 2D 22
Wakefield Dr. LA1: Lanc 3L 29
Wakefield M. BL7: Bolt 6F 198
Wakefield Rd. FY2: Blackp 7E 62
L30: N'ton 8A 222
Walden Rd. BB1: Blackb 5N 119
Waldon St. PR1: Prest 8A 116
Waldorf Cl. WN3: Wins 9N 221
Waldron WN8: Skelm 3H 219
Walesby Pl. FY8: L Ann 3K 129
Wales Rd. BB4: W'foot 6D 162
Wales St. BB4: W'foot 5D 162
Wales Ter. BB4: W'foot 6D 162
Walgarth Dr. PR7: Chor 7C 174
Walk, The OL16: Roch 6C 204
PR4: Hesk B 3A 150
PR8: Birk 1G 186
Walkdale PR4: Hutt 6A 134
Walkden Barn Cotts. BB5: Osw 7G 140
Walkden St. OL12: Roch 4C 204
Walker Av. BB5: Acc 4N 141
WALKER FOLD
BB7 7M 71
BL1 8L 197
Walker Fold Rd. BL1: Bolt 9L 197
Walker Gro. LA3: Heys 8L 21
Walker La. PR2: Fulw 2D 114
Walker Office Pk. BB1: Guide 8C 140
Walker Pk. BB1: Guide 8C 140
(not continuous)
Walker Pl. PR1: Prest 6N 229 (1L 135)
Walker Rd. BB1: Guide 9C 140
WALKER'S HILL 2G 109
Walker's Hill FY4: Blackp 2G 108
Walker St. BB1: Blackb 6E 226 (4N 139)
BB7: Clith 3M 81
FY1: Blackp 4B 88
OL16: Roch 6D 204
PR1: Prest 4J 229 (9J 115)
Walker Way FY5: T Clev 8H 55
WALK MILL 8J 125
Walk Mill Cl. OL12: Roch 1G 204
Walk Mill Pl. BB10: Cliv 8J 125
Wallace Hartley M. *BB8: Colne 6A 86*
(off Lancaster St.)
Wallace La. PR3: Fort 9M 37
WALLBANK 7M 183
Wallbank Dr. OL12: Whitw 7M 183
Wall Bank La. OL12: Whitw 7M 183
Wallcroft St. WN8: Skelm 3J 219
Walleach Farm Caravan Pk. BL7: Edgw 8L 179
Walleach Fold Cotts. BL7: Edgw 8L 179
Walled Garden, The PR6: Whit W 9D 154
Wallend Rd. PR2: Ash R 1A 134
Waller Av. FY2: Blackp 6C 62
Waller Hill BB8: Foul 2A 86
Walletts Rd. PR7: Chor 8D 174
Walletts Wood Ct. PR7: Chor 9C 174
Wallgarth Cl. WN3: Wins 9N 221
Wallhead Rd. OL16: Roch 6G 204
Wallhurst Cl. BB10: W'thorne 4M 125
(not continuous)
Wallings La. LA5: Silv 7F 4
Wallis Av. OL16: Roch 8F 204
Wall La. PR3: Lit E 6K 65
Wallstreams La. BB10: W'thorne 4M 125
Wall St. BB4: W'foot 5C 162
FY1: Blackp 3C 88
WALLSUCHES 9F 196
Wallsuches BL6: Hor 9G 196
Wallwork Cl. OL11: Roch 4J 203
WALMER BRIDGE 2K 151
Walmer Ct. PR8: Birk 1F 186
Walmer Grn. PR4: Wal B 2K 151
Walmer Rd. FY8: L Ann 9F 108
PR8: Birk 2G 186
WALMERSLEY 6K 201
Walmersley Golf Course 5N 201
Walmersley Old Rd. BL9: Bury, Ramsb 5L 201
Walmersley Rd. BL9: Bury, Ramsb 3K 201
Walmsgate BB18: Barnw 3M 77
Walmsley Av. BB1: Rish 9G 121
OL15: Littleb 2J 205
Walmsley Bri. La. PR3: Clau, Inglew 2H 69
Walmsley Brow BB7: B'ton 6H 101
Walmsley Cl. BB5: Chur 2L 141
PR3: Gars 5N 59
Walmsley Cotts. BB1: Rish 8H 121
Walmsley Ct. BB5: Clay M 8M 121
Walmsley Dr. WA11: Rain 5L 225
Walmsley St. BB1: Rish 8H 121
BB3: Darw 5B 158
BB6: Gt H 4J 121
BL8: Bury 9G 201
FY7: Flee 9G 41
Walney Cl. PR2: Lea 8N 113
Walney Gdns. BB2: Blackb 7N 139
Walney Pl. FY3: Blackp 3G 89
Walney Rd. WN3: Wins 9N 221
Walnut Av. BB4: Hasl 4H 161
Walnut Cl. PR1: Penw 5E 134
Walnut Gro. L31: Mell 7F 222
Walnut St. *BB1: Blackb 1A 140*
(off Whalley New Rd.)
OL13: Bac 4K 163
PR8: S'port 1J 187
Walpole Av. FY4: Blackp 4B 108
Walpole St. BB1: Blackb 6E 226 (4N 139)
BB10: Burnl 9F 104
OL16: Roch 6D 204
Walro M. PR9: S'port 3N 167
WALSDEN 6K 165
Walsden Gro. BB10: Burnl 3G 125
Walsden Ind. Est. OL14: Wals 8L 165
Walsden Station (Rail) 6K 165
WALSHAW 9E 200
Walshaw Brook Cl. BL8: Bury 9E 200
Walshaw La. BB10: Burnl 8H 105
BL8: Bury 9E 200
Walshaw Rd. BL8: Bury 9E 200
Walshaw St. BB10: Burnl 1F 124
Walshaw Wlk. BL8: Tott 8E 200
Walsh Fold BL7: Turt 3L 199
Walsh St. BB2: Blackb 9C 226 (6M 139)
BL6: Hor 9C 196
Walter Av. FY8: L Ann 7G 108
Walter Pl. FY8: L Ann 7G 108
Walter Robinson Ct. FY3: Blackp 4D 88
Walter St. BB1: Blackb 6G 226 (4A 140)
BB3: Darw 1B 178
BB5: Acc 2N 141
BB5: Hunc 7D 122
BB5: Osw 5K 141
BB9: Brierf 6F 104
WN5: Wigan 5N 221
Waltham Av. FY4: Blackp 4D 108
Waltham Cl. BB5: Bax 5D 142
Waltham Ct. LA2: Halt 1B 24
Waltham Rd. PR7: Buck V 9B 154
WALTHEW GREEN 9F 212
Walthew Ho. La. WN5: Wigan 2L 221
Walthew La. WN5: Wigan 1M 221
Waltho Av. L31: Magh 1D 222
Walton Av. BD23: Garg 3L 53
LA4: Morec 3E 22
PR1: Penw 5E 134
Walton Cl. BD23: Garg 4L 53
OL13: Bac 6L 163
Walton Cres. BB2: Blackb 7A 140
Walton Dr. BL9: Bury 5K 201
Walton Fold BL7: Edgw 3G 179
OL14: Tod 1N 165
(off Cross Stone Rd.)
PR3: Longr 4K 97
Walton Grn. PR5: Walt D 4N 135
Walton Gro. LA4: Morec 3F 22
Walton La. BB9: Nelson 9K 85
WALTON-LE-DALE 5N 135
Walton-le-Dale (Park & Ride) 3M 135
Walton's Pde. PR1: Prest 7H 229 (1H 135)
Walton St. BB5: Acc 8N 121
BB8: Colne 6A 86
(not continuous)
BB9: Barrf 7J 85
BB9: Nelson 1J 105
PR7: Adl 7J 195
PR9: S'port 6J 167
WALTON SUMMIT 9C 136
Walton Summit Ind. Est. PR5: Bam B 9D 136
Walton Summit Rd. PR5: Bam B 1C 154
Walton Vw. PR1: Prest 9N 115
Walverden Av. FY4: Blackp 1D 108
Walverden Cres. BB9: Nelson 2K 105
Walverden Rd. BB9: Brierf 5H 105
BB10: Brierc 6M 105
Walverden Ter. BB9: Nelson 3K 105
Wandales La. LA6: Cast 5G 9
Wanes Blades Rd. L40: Lath 9J 191
Wanes Fold PR7: E'ton 7E 172
Wango La. L10: Aint 9D 222
Wanisher La. L39: D'holl 7N 207
Wanless BB18: Salt 6A 78
Wansbeck Av. FY7: Flee 2D 54
Wansbeck Ho. FY7: Flee 2E 54
Wansfell Rd. BB7: Clith 4J 81
Wanstead Cres. FY4: Blackp 9E 88
Wanstead St. PR1: Prest 9A 116
WAPPING 3L 77
WARBRECK 9D 62
Warbreck Ct. FY2: Blackp 1B 88
Warbreck Dr. FY2: Blackp 1B 88
Warbreck Hill FY2: Blackp 1E 88
Warbreck Hill Rd. FY2: Blackp 2B 88
Warburton Bldgs. BB4: Hasl 5E 160
Warburton St. BB4: Hasl 6E 160
Warbury St. PR1: Prest 8A 116
Warcock La. HX7: Black H 4N 147
OL13: Bac 4M 163
Ward Av. BB5: Osw 5J 141
FY5: T Clev 9D 54
Ward Grn. La. PR3: Longr, Ribc 2A 98
WARDLE 8F 184
Wardle Ct. PR6: Whit W 9E 154
Wardle Dr. FY5: T Clev 9F 54
Wardle Edge OL12: Roch 2E 204
WARDLE FOLD 7F 184
Wardle Fold OL12: Ward 7F 184
Wardle Gdns. OL12: Roch 2F 204
Wardle Rd. OL12: Roch 9F 184
Wardle St. OL13: Bac 7H 163
OL15: Littleb 8K 185
Wardleys Caravan Pk. FY6: Ham 9N 55
Wardley's La. FY6: Ham 8N 55
Wardleys Marine Yacht Club 1A 64
Wardley St. WN5: Wigan 6L 221
Wardlow Av. WN5: Orr 6K 221
Ward's End PR1: Prest 6L 229 (1K 135)
Ward's La. LA2: H Ben 8M 19
Ward St. BB6: Gt H 4J 121
BB9: Nelson 2J 105
BB11: Burnl 2A 228 (3C 124)
BL7: Belm 9K 177
FY1: Blackp 9J 227 (9B 88)
PR4: K'ham 5M 111
PR5: Lost H 9L 135
PR6: Chor 7G 174
Wareham Cl. BB5: Acc 8A 122
Wareham Rd. FY3: Blackp 1F 88
Wareham Rd. Ind. Est. FY3: Blackp 1F 88
Wareham St. BB1: Blackb 1A 140
Warehouse Apartments, The PR1: Prest 3G 229
Warehouse La. BB8: Foul 2A 86
Waring Dr. FY5: T Clev 9G 55
Warings, The BB9: Nelson 4J 105
PR7: Hesk 1G 193
Warkworth Ter. *OL13: Bac 4L 163*
(off Venture St.)
WARLAND 1N 185
Warland Ga. End OL14: Wals 1N 185
Warley Av. LA3: Morec 5E 22
Warley Dr. LA3: Morec 4E 22
Warley Rd. FY1: Blackp 2B 88
FY2: Blackp 2D 88
Warley Road Stop (Tram) 2B 88
Warley St. OL15: Littleb 8L 185
Warley Wise La. BB8: Lane B 9K 79
BD22: Cowl 9K 79
Warmden Av. BB5: Acc 5D 142
Warmden Gdns. BB1: Blackb 1A 140
Warminster Gro. WN3: Wins 9N 221
Warncliffe St. WN5: Wigan 6N 221
Warne Pl. LA1: Lanc 7H 23
Warner Rd. PR1: Prest 8N 115
Warner St. BB4: Hasl 4G 160
BB5: Acc 3B 142
War Office Rd. OL11: Roch 7J 203
Warper's Moss Cl. L40: Burs 8D 190
Warper's Moss La. L40: Burs 8D 190
Warren, The BB2: Blackb 1H 139
PR2: Fulw 3A 116
Warren Av. Nth. FY7: Flee 9F 40
Warren Av. Sth. FY7: Flee 9F 40
Warren Cl. LA2: Slyne 9J 15
Warren Ct. PR8: Birk 9E 166
Warren Dr. BB9: Barrf 8G 84
FY5: T Clev 3D 62
LA2: Slyne 9J 15
OL13: Bac 7N 163
Warren Fold BB7: Hurst G 1N 99
Warren Gro. FY5: T Clev 3E 62
LA3: Heys 2K 27

Warrenhouse Rd.—Wentworth Cres.

Warrenhouse Rd. L33: Kirk 6M 223
Warrenhurst Rd. FY7: Flee 9G 40
Warren Mnr. FY5: T Clev 3E 62
Warren Rd. LA3: Heys 1K 27
PR9: S'port 6N 167
Warrenside Cl. BB1: Blackb 5A 120
Warren St. FY7: Flee 8H 41
Warrington St. BB1: Blackb 9A 120
Warrington Ter. *BB7: Barr* 2K 101
(off Whiteacre La.)
Warth La. LA6: Ingl 3N 19
Warth Old Rd. BB4: W'foot 7C 162
Warth St. BB4: W'foot 7C 162
WARTON
LA5 5A 12
PR4 2K 131
Warton Aerodrome 4K 131
Warton Av. LA3: Heys 1K 27
Warton Crag Nature Reserve 4N 11
Warton Crag Quarry Local Nature Reserve 5M 11
Warton Pl. PR7: Chor 6C 174
Warton Rd. LA5: Carn 7A 12
Warton St. FY8: L Ann 5B 130
PR1: Prest 2G 135
Wartonwood Vw. LA5: Carn 9A 12
Warwick Av. BB3: Darw 4M 157
BB5: Acc 1N 141
BB5: Clay M 6M 121
(not continuous)
FY5: T Clev 8F 54
LA1: Lanc 2L 29
LA4: Morec 2F 22
Warwick Cl. BB2: Blackb 9C 226 (6M 139)
BB5: Chur 1M 141
BL8: Bury 9G 200
BL8: Greenm 4F 200
PR2: Fulw 5H 115
PR8: S'port 1H 187
Warwick Ct. BB2: Blackb 9C 226
Warwick Dr. BB7: Clith 1M 81
BB9: Brierf 5H 105
BB12: Padi 2J 123
BB18: Earl 3C 78
Warwick Ho. PR1: Prest 8M 229 (2K 135)
Warwick Pl. FY3: Blackp 2H 89
FY7: Flee 8G 41
Warwick Rd. BB2: Blackb 9C 226 (6M 139)
FY3: Blackp 3D 88
FY8: L Ann 2F 128
PR5: Walt D 4N 135
PR7: E'ton 7F 172
PR25: Leyl 8H 153
Warwick St. BB4: Hasl 4G 161
BB5: Chur 1M 141
BB9: Nelson 3J 105
BL1: Bolt 9E 198
OL12: Roch 3E 204
PR1: Prest 4J 229 (9J 115)
PR3: Longr 3J 97
PR7: Adl 7H 195
PR8: S'port 1H 187
Wasdale Av. BB1: Blackb 5C 140
L31: Magh 9E 216
Wasdale Cl. BB12: Padi 9H 103
PR25: Leyl 9L 153
Wasdale Gro. PR3: Longr 5H 97
Wasdale Rd. FY4: Blackp 1G 108
Washbrook Cl. BB7: Barr 1K 101
Washbrook Way L39: Orms 8K 209
Wash Brow BL8: Bury 9G 200
Washburn Ct. LA3: Morec 6F 22
Wash Fold BL8: Bury 8G 200
Washington Av. FY2: Blackp 9E 62
LA4: Morec 2B 22
Washington Cl. LA1: Lanc 9H 23
Washington Ct. FY2: Blackp 9E 62
Washington Dr. L33: Kirk 4J 223
LA5: Wart 4B 12
Washington La. PR7: Eux 4A 174
Washington St. BB5: Acc 2B 142
Wash Ter. BL8: Bury 8G 200
Wasp Mill Dr. OL12: Ward 8F 184
Waste La. LA2: Abb 8J 39
Wastwater Dr. LA4: Morec 4E 22
Watchwood Dr. FY8: L Ann 3A 130
Watchyard La. L37: Form 9A 206
WATER 8E 144
WATERBARN 7E 162
Waterbarn La. OL13: Bac 7F 162
Waterbarn St. BB10: Burnl 9F 104
Watercroft OL11: Roch 4H 203
Waterdale FY2: Blackp 6E 62
WATERFALL 6K 139
Waterfall Ter. BL7: Belm 9K 177
Waterfall Trade Pk. BB2: Blackb 5K 139
Waterfield Av. BB3: Darw 9B 158
Waterfield Cl. BL9: Bury 6L 201
Water Fold BB4: Water 8E 144
WATERFOOT
BB4, Haslingden 5F 160
BB4, Newchurch 7C 162
Waterfoot Av. FY3: Blackp 4E 88
PR8: Ains 1B 206
Waterfoot Bus. Cen. BB4: W'foot 5D 162
Waterford Cl. PR2: Fulw 4M 115
PR6: H Charn 4J 195
Waterford St. BB9: Nelson 1K 105
Waterfront BB1: Blackb 7F 226
Waterfront Marine Bus. Pk. FY8: L Ann 4D 130
Watergrove Reservoir Vis. Cen. 5E 184
Water Head PR2: Fulw 6E 114
Waterhead Cres. FY5: T Clev 5C 62
Waterhouse Cl. OL12: Ward 9F 184
Waterhouse Grn. PR6: Whit W 8D 154
Waterhouse Nook BL6: Blackr 8J 195
Waterhouse St. OL12: Roch 5C 204
Watering Pool La. PR5: Lost H 6L 135
Water La. BL0: Ramsb 4J 181
OL16: Milnr 8K 205
PR2: Ash R 8F 114
PR9: S'port 1C 168
Waterleat Glade FY6: Poul F 2L 89
WATERLOO 8J 139
Waterloo BB5: Acc 1A 142
Waterloo Cl. BB2: Blackb 8J 139
Waterloo Rd. BB7: Clith 3M 81
BB11: Burnl 4F 228 (4F 124)
(Oxford Pl.)
BB11: Burnl 5F 124
(Smalley St.)
BB18: Kelb 6D 78
FY4: Blackp 9K 227 (9B 88)
PR2: Ash R 7E 114
PR8: Birk 3E 186
Waterloo Road Stop (Tram) 9B 88
Waterloo St. BB5: Clay M 8N 121
PR7: Chor 5E 174
Waterloo Ter. PR2: Ash R 8F 114
Watermans Cl. BL6: Hor 9D 196
Waterman Vw. OL16: Roch 5F 204
Water Mdws. BB2: Blackb 9L 139
Watermede WN5: Bill 8H 221
Watermill Cl. OL16: Roch 7G 205
Watermillock Gdns. BL1: Bolt 9F 198
Waters Edge BB1: Blackb 7E 226 (5N 139)
BB7: Whall 6J 101
PR2: Ingol 6C 114
Watersedge Dr. L40: Ruff 1G 191
Waters Edge Grn. PR3: Gars 6N 59
Watershed Mill Bus. Cen.
BD24: Gig 2N 35
WATERSIDE
BB3 4E 158
BB8 7B 86
BB9 4D 104
Waterside BB5: Acc 3A 142
FY2: Blackp 9D 62
LA1: Lanc 5C 228 (7K 23)
Waterside Bus. Pk. L40: Burs 8N 189
Waterside Cl. PR3: Gars 5M 59
Waterside Ind. Est. BB8: Colne 7B 86
Waterside La. OL16: Roch 5E 204
Waterside M. BB12: Padi 1H 123
Waterside Pl. LA4: Morec 5B 22
Waterside Rd. BB4: Hasl 5F 160
BB8: Colne 7A 86
BL9: Summ 3G 201
Waterside Ter. BB3: W'side 4E 158
OL13: Bac 4K 163
(off Myrtle Bank Rd.)
Waterslack Rd. LA5: Silv 5J 5
Waters Reach FY5: T Clev 9C 54
FY8: L Ann 5K 129
Water St. BB4: Craws 8M 143
BB4: Water 8E 144
BB5: Acc 2B 142
(not continuous)
BB5: Clay M 4M 121
BB6: Gt H 4J 121
BB8: Colne 6B 86
BB9: Barrf 7H 85
BB9: Nelson 2J 105
BB10: W'thorne 4M 125
BB12: Hapt 5H 123
BB18: Earl 2E 78
BD23: Garg 3M 53
(off Hellifield Rd.)
BL0: Ramsb 9G 180
BL7: Eger 3D 198
LA1: Lanc 5C 228 (7K 23)
OL12: Whitw 6N 183
OL14: Tod 2L 165
OL16: Milnr 7J 205
OL16: Roch 6C 204
PR3: Ribc 7F 98
PR5: Bam B 6B 136
PR6: Brind 2H 155
PR6: H Charn 1L 195
PR7: Adl 7J 195
PR7: Chor 6E 174
Waterview Cl. OL16: Milnr 9L 205
Waterway Av. L30: N'ton 7A 222
Waterworks Rd. L39: Orms 6M 209
Watery Ga. La. PR3: Crossm, Gt E 9B 66
Watery La. BB3: Darw 9B 158
BD24: Gig 4M 35
LA1: Lanc 5H 23
LA6: Barb 2G 9
PR2: Ash R 9D 114
PR3: Barn 3B 60
Watery La. Ind. Est. BB3: Darw 9B 158
Watford St. BB1: Blackb 2D 226 (2M 139)
Watkin Cl. L30: N'ton 9A 222
Watkin La. PR5: Lost H 8K 135
Watkin Rd. PR6: Clay W 7D 154
Watkins Cl. BB9: Brierf 6G 105
Watkin St. OL16: Roch 9D 204
Watling Cl. LA3: Morec 5E 22
Watling Ga. *BB6: Old L* 4C 100
(off Gleneagles Dr.)
Watling St. BL8: Aff 3M 199
Watling St. Rd. *PR2: Fulw* 5M 115
(off Churchill Rd.)
PR2: Fulw, Ribb 6H 115
Watson Ct. FY4: Blackp 2D 108
Watson Gdns. OL12: Roch 3A 204
Watson Rd. FY4: Blackp 2B 108
Watson St. BB2: Blackb 6J 139
BB5: Osw 5L 141
Watton Beck Cl. L31: Magh 9E 216
Watts Cl. L33: Kirk 6M 223
Watts St. OL12: Roch 5D 204
Watt St. BB7: Sabd 3E 102
BB12: Burnl 2A 124
Watty Hole OL14: Tod 4J 165
Watty La. OL14: Tod 4J 165
Watty Ter. OL14: Tod 4J 165
Wavell Av. PR9: S'port 7A 168
Wavell Cl. BB5: Bax 7E 142
PR9: S'port 7A 168
Wavell St. BB12: Burnl 3A 124
WAVERLEDGE 5J 121
Waverledge Bus. Pk. BB6: Gt H 5H 121
Waverledge Rd. BB6: Gt H 5H 121
Waverledge St. BB6: Gt H 5J 121
Waverley *OL12: Roch* 5B 204
(off Sheriff St.)
WN8: Skelm 2H 219
Waverley Av. FY1: Blackp 2C 88
FY7: Flee 1D 54
Waverley Cl. BB9: Brierf 5H 105
BB12: S'stone 9C 102
Waverley Ct. WN3: Wins 8N 221
Waverley Dr. PR4: New L 9C 134
PR4: Tarl 9D 150
Waverley Gdns. PR2: Ribb 7A 116
Waverley Pl. BB2: Blackb 3J 139
Waverley Rd. BB1: Blackb 4E 140
BB1: Ramsg 5M 119
BB5: Bax 5D 142
BL1: Bolt 9E 198
PR1: Prest 8N 115
Waverley St. BB11: Burnl 3C 124
PR8: S'port 7G 167
Waves Water Fun Cen. 4B 226 (3L 139)
Waxy La. PR4: Frec 1A 132
Way, The LA3: Morec 5F 22
Wayfarers Arc. PR8: S'port 7H 167
Way Ga. FY5: T Clev 7D 54
Wayman Rd. FY3: Blackp 1N 227 (4D 88)
Wayoh Cft. BL7: Edgw 8K 179
Wayside FY6: K Sea 8K 41
Weald, The PR4: Cott 4A 114
Weasel La. BB3: Tock 4H 157
PR5: Hogh 6N 137
Weatherhill Cres. BB9: Brierf 5J 105
Weaver Av. L33: Kirk 4L 223
L40: Burs 8D 190
Weaver Dr. BL9: Bury 5L 201
Weavers Brow PR6: H Charn 8H 175
Weavers Cl. FY8: L Ann 1K 129
Weavers Ct. BB2: Blackb 3A 226 (3K 139)
BB8: Traw 9E 86
PR3: Scor 7B 46
PR7: Buck V 9A 154
Weavers Cft. BB7: B'ton 6G 100
Weavers Fold BB2: Mellor 6G 118
PR26: Breth 1K 171
Weavers La. L31: Magh 4E 222
PR3: Cab 7N 45
Weavers M. BB3: Darw 6N 157
Weavers Pl. BB6: Gt H 3K 121
Weavers' Triangle, The 3B 228 (4D 124)
Weavers' Triangle Visitor Centre, The
3C 228 (4D 124)
Webber Ct. BB11: Burnl 6M 123
Webber Rd. L33: Know P 9N 223
Web Complex, The L33: Know P 9A 224
Weber St. BB4: Rawt 6B 162
Webster Av. FY4: Blackp 2E 108
Webster Dr. L32: Kirk 8K 223
Webster Gdns. PR4: Wal B 3L 151
Webster Gro. LA4: Morec 2G 22
Webster St. PR2: Ash R 8F 114
Wedgewood Cl. OL16: Roch 7F 204
Wedgewood Ct. FY8: L Ann 1G 129
Wedgewood Dr. WN6: Stand 9N 213
Wedgewood Rd. BB5: Hunc 8E 122
Weedon St. OL16: Roch 5E 204
WEETON 8D 90
Weeton Av. FY4: Blackp 4E 108
FY5: T Clev 9D 54
FY8: L Ann 9G 108
WEETON CAMP 5E 90
Weeton Pl. PR2: Ash R 8B 114
Weeton Rd. FY6: Sing 2D 90
PR4: Gt P 2E 110
PR4: Weet 2D 90
PR4: Weet, Wesh 8E 90
Weets Vw. BB18: Barnw 1N 77
Weind, The PR3: Gt E 6N 65
WEIR 9L 145
Weir Bottom OL13: Weir 9L 145
Weir Cl. BB12: Padi 1H 123
Weirden Cl. PR1: Penw 7F 134
Weir La. OL13: Weir 9L 145
Weir Rd. OL16: Milnr 6H 205
Weir St. BB2: Blackb 6C 226 (4M 139)
OL14: Tod 4K 165
Welbeck Av. BB1: Blackb 9B 120
FY4: Blackp 9E 88
FY7: Flee 9F 40
OL15: Littleb 8K 185
Welbeck Cl. OL16: Milnr 7H 205
Welbeck Cres. PR5: Bam B 7A 136
Welbeck Gdns. FY7: Flee 1F 54
Welbeck Ho. *FY7: Flee* 1F 54
(off Welbeck Gdns.)
Welbeck Rd. OL16: Roch 9E 204
PR8: Birk 1F 186
Welbeck Ter. PR8: Birk 1G 186
Welbourne WN8: Skelm 3H 219
Welburn Cl. WN5: Orr 6H 221
Welburn St. OL11: Roch 8C 204
Welburn Wlk. FY5: T Clev 1K 63
Welbury Cl. BB18: Earl 2E 78
Welby Cragg Caravan Pk. LA2: Ell 9E 30
Welch Wlk. PR7: Buck V 9B 154
Weldale Ho. *PR8: Birk* 1F 186
(off Chase Cl.)
Weld Av. PR7: Chor 9E 174
WELD BANK 9E 174
Weldbank La. PR7: Chor 9E 174
Weldbank St. PR7: Chor 9E 174
Weld Blundell Av. L31: Lyd 7A 216
Weldon Dr. L39: Orms 8L 209
Weldon St. BB11: Burnl 4C 124
Weld Pde. PR8: Birk 1F 186
Weld Rd. PR8: Birk 9E 166
Welland Cl. FY2: Blackp 7E 62
WELL BANK 4F 160
Wellbank Ct. BL8: Tott 7E 200
Wellbank St. BL8: Tott 7E 200
Wellbank Vw. OL12: Roch 4K 203
Wellbrow Dr. PR3: Longr 2K 97
Well Brow Ter. OL12: Roch 4A 204
Well Ct. *BB7: Clith* 2M 81
(off Well Ter.)
Wellcross Rd. WN8: Uph 5E 220
Wellesley St. BB12: Burnl 3L 123
Wellfield BB5: Clay M 7N 121
PR4: Longt 7K 133
WA11: Rain 6L 225
Wellfield Av. L32: Kirk 9K 223
PR25: Leyl 6J 153
Wellfield Bus. Pk. PR1: Prest 9G 114
Wellfield Dr. BB12: Burnl 1A 124
Wellfield La. L40: W'head 9A 210
Wellfield Pl. OL11: Roch 8D 204
Wellfield Rd. BB2: Blackb 2K 139
PR1: Prest 9G 115
PR5: Lost H 9K 135
Wellfield St. OL11: Roch 8D 204
Wellfield Ter. OL14: Tod 3L 165
Well Fold BB7: Clith 3M 81
Wellgate BB7: Clith 3L 81
Wellhead BB8: Wine 7E 86
Well Head Rd. BB12: Newc P 1M 103
Well Hill *BD24: Sett* 3N 35
(off Castlebergh La.)
Wellhouse Rd. BB18: Barnw 1M 77
Wellhouse Sq. *BB18: Barnw* 2M 77
(off Wellhouse Rd.)
Wellhouse St. BB18: Barnw 2M 77
Wellington Av. PR25: Leyl 7L 153
Wellington Cl. L10: Aint 7B 222
WN8: Skelm 3B 220
Wellington Ct. BB5: Acc 3B 142
BB10: Burnl 3G 228 (4F 124)
LA6: K Lon 6E 8
(off Dodgson Cft.)
Wellington Fold *BB3: Darw* 6A 158
(off Market St.)
Wellington Lodge *OL15: Littleb* 8L 185
(off Lodge St.)
Wellington M. BL7: Turt 1K 199
Wellington Pl. OL16: Roch 5D 204
PR5: Walt D 6N 135
Wellington Rd.
BB2: Blackb 8A 226 (5K 139)
BL7: Turt 1J 199
FY1: Blackp 8H 227 (8B 88)
LA1: Lanc 2L 29
OL14: Tod 1L 165
PR2: Ash R 8E 114
Wellington St. BB1: Blackb 2B 226 (2L 139)
BB5: Acc 3B 142
BB5: Clay M 7M 121
BB6: Gt H 5J 121
BB9: Nelson 1H 105
BB18: Barnw 3M 77
FY8: L Ann 4C 130
OL12: Roch 4C 204
(not continuous)
OL15: Littleb 9L 185
OL16: Milnr 7K 205
PR1: Prest 9G 114
PR4: K'ham 4L 111
PR7: Chor 5E 174
PR8: S'port 8G 167
Wellington Ter. LA4: Morec 3B 22
OL15: Littleb 9L 185
(off Lodge St.)
Well i' th' La. OL11: Roch 8D 204
Well La. L39: Bart 6L 207
LA5: Wart 5B 12
LA5: Yea R 8B 6
LA6: H Cas 6G 9
LA6: K Lon 6C 8
OL14: Tod 2L 165
PR3: Larb 5J 65
PR6: Birns 8A 156
Wellogate Gdns. FY4: Blackp 3D 108
Well Orchard PR5: Bam B 2D 154
Wellow Pl. FY8: L Ann 3J 129
Wells Cl. FY5: T Clev 1G 62
LA3: Morec 6B 22
Wells Fold Cl. PR6: Clay W 6E 154
Well Springs BB3: Darw 6C 158
Wells St. BB4: Hasl 4G 161
PR1: Prest 8M 115
Well St. BB1: Rish 7H 121
BB4: W'foot 4D 162
BB12: Padi 9G 103
OL11: Roch 8D 204
OL14: Tod 3L 165
Well St. Nth. BL0: Ramsb 4H 181
Well St. W. BL0: Ramsb 9G 180
Well Ter. BB7: Clith 2M 81
Welsby Rd. PR25: Leyl 7G 153
Welwyn Av. PR8: Ains 7E 186
Welwyn Pl. FY5: T Clev 2E 62
Wembley Av. FY3: Blackp 2E 88
FY6: Poul F 8L 63
PR1: Penw 3E 134
Wembley Rd. FY5: T Clev 8H 55
Wemyss Cl. LA3: Heys 9K 21
Wendover Rd. FY6: Carl 5G 63
Wenlock Cl. BL6: Hor 7D 196
Wenning Av. L31: Magh 9D 216
LA2: H Ben 7L 19
Wenning Ct. LA3: Morec 6F 22
Wenning Pl. LA1: Lanc 6J 23
Wenning St. BB9: Nelson 3K 105
WENNINGTON 5F 18
Wennington Rd. LA2: Wray 8E 18
PR9: S'port 6M 167
(not continuous)
WN3: Wigan 7M 221
Wennington Station (Rail) 6F 18
Wensley Av. FY7: Flee 3E 54
Wensley Bus. Pk. BB2: Blackb 4J 139
Wensley Cl. BB11: Burnl 6C 124
Wensleydale Av. FY3: Blackp 3G 89
Wensleydale Cl. FY5: T Clev 3K 63
L31: Magh 9A 216
Wensley Dr. BB5: Acc 2C 142
LA1: Lanc 5K 23
WENSLEY FOLD 5A 226 (4K 139)
Wensley Pl. PR2: Ribb 5N 115
Wensley Rd. BB2: Blackb 5A 226 (4J 139)
Wensley Way OL16: Roch 7F 204
Wentcliffe Dr. BB18: Earl 3E 78
Wentworth Av. BL8: Bury 9G 200
FY7: Flee 5D 54
PR4: Inskip 2G 93
Wentworth Cl. PR1: Penw 2D 134
PR8: Ains 9C 186
Wentworth Ct. PR4: K'ham 5M 111
Wentworth Cres. LA3: Morec 6B 22

Wentworth Dr.—Wheelwright Dr.

Wentworth Dr. FY5: T Clev 3K 63
LA1: Lanc 9N 23
PR3: Brou 7F 94
PR7: Eux 2N 173
Wentworth M. FY8: L Ann 2G 129
Wentworth Pl. PR3: Brou 7F 94
Werneth Cl. PR1: Penw 7J 135
Wervin Rd. L32: Kirk 9J 223
Wescoe Cl. WN5: Orr 6H 221
WESHAM 2L 111
Wesham Hall Cl. PR4: Wesh 3M 111
Wesham Hall Rd. PR4: Wesh 3M 111
Wesham Pk. Dr. PR4: Wesh 3L 111
Wesleyan Row BB7: Clith 3L 81
Wesley Cl. LA2: H Ben 6L 19
OL12: Roch 2E 204
Wesley Ct. BL8: Tott 7D 200
FY7: Flee 8H 41
OL15: Littleb 2J 205
Wesley Dr. LA3: Heys 9L 21
Wesley Gro. BB12: Burnl 2B 124
Wesley Ho. BL8: Tott 6D 200
LA1: Lanc 7D 228
Wesley M. FY4: Blackp 2G 108
Wesley Pl. OL13: Bac 6J 163
Wesley St. BB1: Blackb 1F 226 (1N 139)
BB5: Chur 2M 141
BB5: Osw 3L 141
BB7: Sabd 2E 102
BB9: Brierf 4F 104
BB12: Padi 1J 123
BL7: Brom C 5G 198
BL8: Tott 6D 200
OL12: Roch 2E 204
OL16: Milnr 7H 205
PR5: Bam B 8B 136
PR8: S'port 7H 167
WN5: Wigan 7N 221
Wesley Ter. *OL13: Weir* 8L 145
(off Heald La.)
Wessex Cl. BB5: Hunc 9D 122
Wessex Rd. WN5: Wigan 2N 221
Westall Gdns. BB3: Darw 5B 158
West Av. BB18: Barnw 2M 77
OL12: Roch 2F 204
PR2: Ingol 3D 114
West Bank PR7: Chor 6E 174
W. Bank Av. FY8: L Ann 5L 129
Westbank Av. FY4: Blackp 2G 108
West Beach FY8: L Ann 5M 129
Westboro Cl. LA3: Heys 7L 21
Westbourne BB4: Hasl 7F 160
Westbourne Av. BB11: Burnl 5B 124
FY1: Blackp 9K 227 (9C 88)
PR4: W Grn 6G 111
Westbourne Av. Sth.
BB11: Burnl 6C 124
Westbourne Ct. FY6: K Sea 8K 41
Westbourne Dr. LA1: Lanc 9H 23
Westbourne Gdns. PR8: Birk 1D 186
Westbourne Pl. LA1: Lanc 7A 228 (8H 23)
Westbourne Rd. FY5: T Clev 7C 54
FY6: K Sea 8K 41
LA1: Lanc 7A 228 (9G 23)
LA3: Midd 5M 27
LA5: Wart 6N 11
PR7: Chor 8D 174
PR8: Birk 1D 186
Westbourne Road Stop (Tram) 7D 54
WEST BRADFORD 7L 73
W. Bradford Rd. BB7: Clith 8M 73
BB7: Wadd 8H 73
Westbrook Cres. PR2: Ingol 6D 114
Westbury Av. WN3: Wins 9N 221
Westbury Cl. BB10: Burnl 8J 105
FY5: T Clev 4C 62
Westbury Gdns. BB1: Blackb 4C 140
WESTBY 5D 110
Westby Av. FY4: Blackp 4E 108
Westby Cl. FY4: Blackp 2K 109
Westby Ct. FY6: Poul F 9K 63
Westby Gro. FY7: Flee 8H 41
Westby Pl. PR2: Ash R 8C 114
Westby Rd. FY8: L Ann 9E 108
PR4: Lit P, Westby 3C 110
Westby St. FY8: L Ann 5A 130
Westby Way FY6: Poul F 9K 63
West Cliff PR1: Prest 8G 229 (2H 135)
West Cliffe FY8: L Ann 5B 130
Westcliffe BB6: Gt H 3H 121
Westcliffe Ct. PR8: Birk 9F 166
Westcliffe Dr. FY3: Blackp 3E 88
LA3: Morec 6A 22
Westcliffe Dr. Caravan Site LA3: Morec 6A 22
Westcliffe Gro. Residential Pk. Homes
LA3: Heat 6A 22
Westcliffe Ho. OL12: Roch 1G 204
Westcliffe Rd. BL1: Bolt 7F 198
PR8: Birk 9E 166
Westcliffe Wlk. BB9: Nelson 3H 105
W. Cliff Ter. PR1: Prest 8H 229 (2H 135)
(not continuous)
West Cl. Av. BB12: High 5L 103
West Cl. Rd. BB18: Barnw 1M 77
Westcombe Dr. BL8: Bury 9H 201
Westcote St. BB3: Darw 9B 158
Westcott Cl. BL2: Bolt 8L 199
Westcott Dr. WN3: Wigan 7M 221
West Ct. FY5: T Clev 7C 54
W. Craven Dr. BB18: Earl 1E 78
West Craven Sports Cen. 3N 77
West Cres. BB5: Acc 9A 122
PR3: Brou 7F 94
Westcroft PR4: Much H 4J 151
Westdene PR9: S'port 5L 167
WN8: Parb 2M 211
West Dr. BB7: Whall 3G 100
BL9: Bury 8K 201
FY5: T Clev 9D 54
LA1: Lanc 6H 23
PR4: Inskip 2G 92
PR4: Wesh 2K 111
PR25: Leyl 4N 153
West Drive Stop (Tram) 9D 54
West Dr. W. FY5: T Clev 9D 54
WEST END
BB5 3J 141
LA4 5A 22
West End PR1: Penw 2D 134
PR3: Gt E 6M 65
Westend Av. PR7: Copp 4N 193
West End Bus. Pk. BB5: Osw 3H 141
West End La. PR4: Wart 2G 130
Westend Residential Pk. PR4: K'ham 4J 111
West End Rd. LA4: Morec 4N 21
West End Ter. *PR8: S'port* 7G 167
(off West St.)
Westerdale Dr. PR9: Banks 1G 168
Westerham Cl. BL8: Bury 6H 201
Westerlong PR2: Lea 8A 114
Western Av. BB11: Burnl 5C 124
PR7: Buck V 8N 153
Western Ct. OL13: Bac 7G 162
Western Dr. PR25: Leyl 6G 152
Western Rd. OL13: Bac 7G 162
Westfield BB9: Nelson 1H 105
PR5: Lost H 8K 135
Westfield Av. BB12: Read 9C 102
FY3: Blackp 1F 88
FY3: Stain 3H 89
FY7: Flee 2E 54
Westfield Cl. BB7: Whall 3F 100
OL11: Roch 4K 203
Westfield Ct. FY5: T Clev 8H 55
Westfield Dr. BB7: West B 6L 73
LA5: Bolt S 3L 15
PR2: Ribb 5N 115
PR4: Wart 3L 131
PR5: Hogh 7F 136
PR25: Leyl 6G 153
Westfield Gro. LA4: Morec 4A 22
Westfield Hamlet LA5: Neth K 7N 15
West Fld. Rd. BB18: Barnw 10F 52
Westfield Rd. FY1: Blackp 8M 227 (8D 88)
Westfields PR26: Cros 4L 171
Westfield Wlk. L32: Kirk 8G 223
West Gdns. *OL13: Bac* 7F 162
(off Waterbarn La.)
Westgate BB11: Burnl 2A 228 (3C 124)
BB12: Read 9B 102
BB18: Barnw 3L 77
FY7: Flee 9D 40
LA3: Morec 5A 22
LA4: Morec 5A 22
OL12: Whitw 7M 183
PR2: Fulw 4G 115
PR25: Leyl 7J 153
WN8: Skelm 2H 219
Westgate Av. BL0: Ramsb 3F 200
LA3: Morec 6B 22
Westgate Caravan Pk. LA3: Morec 6A 22
Westgate Cl. OL12: Whitw 7M 183
Westgate Dr. WN5: Orr 6G 221
Westgate Health & Fitness 3H 219
Westgate Ind. Est. WN8: Skelm 3H 219
Westgate La. LA6: W'ouse 1M 19
Westgate M. *WN8: Skelm* 2H 219
(off Westgate)
Westgate Pk. Rd. LA4: Morec 5C 22
Westgate Rd. FY8: L Ann 5C 108
Westgate Trad. Cen. BB11: Burnl 2A 228
WEST GILLIBRANDS 3G 219
Westgrove Av. BL1: Bolt 7E 198
West Hall La. LA6: Whit 9C 8
Westham St. LA1: Lanc 9E 228 (9L 23)
Westhaven Cres. L39: Aug 2H 217
WESTHEAD 8C 210
Westhead Av. L33: Kirk 8L 223
Westhead Cl. L33: Kirk 9M 223
Westhead Rd. PR26: Cros 4L 171
Westhead Wlk. FY7: Flee 2E 54
L33: Kirk 8L 223
West Hill BB9: Barrf 7H 85
OL11: Roch 7B 204
PR8: S'port 8G 166
Westholme Ct. PR9: S'port 5J 167
Westhoughton Rd. PR7: Adl, H Charn 4H 195
WESTHOUSE 2M 19
West Ing La. BD23: Hort 7C 52
W. Lancashire Investment Cen.
WN8: Skelm 5K 219
West Lancashire Light Railway 5D 150
West Lancashire Yacht Club 5G 167
Westland Av. BB3: Darw 7N 157
Westlands PR26: Leyl 8F 152
Westlands Ct. FY5: T Clev 3H 63
West La. BB7: D'ham, Wors 9F 74
Westleigh M. PR4: Lea T 5N 113
W. Leigh Rd. BB1: Blackb 9K 119
Westleigh Rd. PR2: Ash R 8C 114
WEST MARTON 7H 53
West Meade L31: Magh 9A 216
West Mdw. PR2: Lea 6B 114
Westminster Av. LA4: Morec 4N 21
Westminster Cl. BB3: Darw 4N 157
BB5: Bax 5D 142
BB12: S'stone 9C 102
LA3: Morec 6B 22
Westminster Dr. PR8: Ains 9A 186
Westminster M. LA3: Heys 5M 21
Westminster Pl. PR4: Hutt 7A 134
PR7: E'ton 6D 172
Westminster Rd. BB3: Darw 4M 157
BL1: Bolt 8E 198
FY1: Blackp 2C 88
LA3: Heys, Morec 5M 21
LA4: Morec 5M 21
PR7: Chor 7E 174
Westminster St. OL11: Roch 8A 204
Westmoor Gro. LA3: Heys 2K 27
Westmoreland Rd. PR8: S'port 9J 167
Westmoreland St. BB9: Nelson 2G 105
Westmorland Av. FY1: Blackp 6L 227 (7C 88)
FY5: T Clev 8D 54
Westmorland Avenue Stop (Tram) 8D 54
Westmorland Cl. BB3: Darw 9C 158
PR1: Penw 4E 134
PR25: Leyl 8H 153
Westmorland Dr. OL12: Ward 8G 184
Westmorland St. BB11: Burnl 4B 124
W. Moss La. FY8: L Ann 7K 109
West Mt. WN5: Orr 5J 221
Weston Av. OL16: Roch 9E 204
Weston Gro. L31: Magh 4C 222
Weston Pk. WN6: Stand 9N 213
Weston Pl. FY1: Blackp 9L 227 (9D 88)
Weston St. OL16: Milnr 7H 205
(not continuous)
PR2: Ash R 9G 115
Westover Av. LA5: Wart 5B 12
Westover Cl. L31: Magh 1B 222
Westover Gro. LA5: Wart 5B 12
Westover Rd. L31: Magh 1B 222
LA5: Wart 5B 12
Westover St. LA4: Morec 3B 22
West Paddock PR25: Leyl 7H 153
West Pk. PR9: S'port 5K 167
West Pk. Av. PR2: Ash R 7B 114
West Pk. Cl. WN8: Skelm 3H 219
West Pk. Dr. FY3: Blackp 6E 88
West Pk. La. PR2: Ash R 7D 114
West Pk. Rd. BB2: Blackb 2A 226 (2K 139)
W. Pennine Bus. Pk. OL13: Bac 2K 163
WEST PIMBO 7A 220
Westridge Ct. PR9: S'port 6K 167
West Rd. FY5: T Clev 8J 55
LA1: Lanc 6A 228 (8H 23)
(not continuous)
PR2: Fulw 6J 115
Westside FY4: Blackp 1F 108
West Sq. PR4: Longt 8L 133
West Strand PR1: Prest 9F 114
West St. BB4: W'foot 7C 162
BB6: Gt H 5J 121
BB8: Colne 7B 86
BB9: Nelson 1H 105
BB10: Burnl 1G 124
BB12: Padi 1G 123
BD23: Garg 3M 53
BL0: Ramsb 9G 180
FY1: Blackp 1H 227 (5B 88)
LA1: Lanc 2K 29
LA3: Morec 4M 21
OL14: Tod 1K 165
OL15: Littleb 9M 185
OL16: Roch 5D 204
(Buckley St.)
OL16: Roch 6G 205
(Cross St.)
PR7: Chor 7E 174
PR8: S'port 7G 167
WESTVALE 8H 223
West Vw. BB1: Belt 1F 158
BB2: Blackb 4J 139
BB3: Hodd 6F 158
(off Carus Av.)
BB4: Hasl 8F 160
(Laburnum Rd.)
BB4: Hasl 3G 160
(Spring La.)
BB4: W'foot 6D 162
(off Pleasant Vw.)
BB5: Osw 4L 141
BB7: Clith 4K 81
BB7: Grind 4A 74
(off Main St.)
BB10: Cliv 9L 125
BD24: Langc 2N 35
(off Stainforth Rd.)
BD24: Sett 3N 35
(off High Hill Gro. St.)
BL0: Ramsb 4H 181
BL6: Hor 8F 196
FY1: Blackp 5K 227 (7C 88)
L39: Orms 7L 209
LA2: Glas 1C 36
LA5: Carn 6A 12
OL13: Bac 7F 162
OL14: Tod 1L 165
OL15: Littleb 9M 185
PR1: Prest 7M 115
PR4: Longt 8L 133
PR4: Wesh 2L 111
PR5: Bam B 9A 136
PR6: Wheel 8J 155
WN8: Parb 2M 211
West Vw. Av. FY1: Blackp 8J 227 (8B 88)
West View Leisure Cen. 7M 115
West Vw. Pl. BB2: Blackb 2J 139
West Vw. Rd. BB4: Lumb 3D 162
LA4: Morec 3A 22
West Vw. Ter. BB3: Tock 5H 157
BB5: Alt 3D 122
BB7: B'ton 6G 100
BB12: Padi 2H 123
PR1: Prest 9F 114
West Wlk. BL7: Eger 3D 198
Westward Ho OL16: Milnr 7J 205
West Way BL1: Bolt 9H 199
PR7: Chor, Eux 5B 174
Westway BB11: Burnl 3B 124
FY7: Flee 5C 54
L31: Magh 9B 216
PR2: Fulw 5K 115
PR4: Frec 2M 131
Westway Ct. PR2: Fulw 5K 115
Westwell Gro. FY1: Blackp 3K 227 (6C 88)
Westwell Rd. PR6: Chor 5F 174
Westwell St. BB3: Darw 3M 157
BB6: Gt H 4J 121
Westwood Av. BB1: Rish 8G 121
FY3: Blackp 6E 88
FY6: Poul F 8L 63
FY7: Flee 1E 54
Westwood Cl. PR8: S'port 2L 187
Westwood Ct. BB1: Blackb 2A 140
Westwood M. FY8: L Ann 5N 129
Westwood Rd. BB12: Burnl 1A 124
FY8: L Ann 5N 129
PR5: Bam B 3E 154
PR25: Leyl 5K 153
Westwood St. BB5: Acc 1A 142
Wetherall St. PR2: Ash R 8G 114
Wetherby Av. FY4: Blackp 4B 108
Wetherfield Cl. LA1: Lanc 4L 23
Weybourne Gro. BL2: Bolt 9H 199
Weymouth Rd. FY3: Blackp 7F 88
Weythorne Dr. BL1: Bolt 9F 198
BL9: Bury 8D 202
WHALLEY 5J 101
Whalley Abbey 5J 101
Whalley Av. OL15: Littleb 8K 185
WA11: Rain 4K 225
WHALLEY BANKS 7J 101
Whalley Banks BB2: Blackb 6A 226 (4L 139)
Whalley Banks Trad. Est.
BB2: Blackb 6A 226 (4L 139)
Whalley Cl. OL16: Milnr 7H 205
Whalley Ct. *BB3: Darw* 6A 158
(off Burton Cl.)
Whalley Crematorium BB7: Whall 2H 101
Whalley Cres. BB3: Darw 6B 158
FY3: Stain 5L 89
Whalley Dr. BB4: Rawt 3M 161
L37: Form 1A 214
L39: Aug 3H 217
Whalley Gdns. OL12: Roch 4M 203
Whalley Golf Course 5M 101
Whalley Ind. Pk. BB7: Barr 2K 101
Whalley La. FY4: Blackp 1G 108
Whalley New Rd.
BB1: Blackb, Wilp 1F 226 (6M 119)
BB6: Langh 1C 120
BB7: B'ton 8E 100
Whalley Old Rd. BB1: Blackb 1F 226 (2N 139)
(not continuous)
BB1: Blackb, Rish 8B 120
BB6: Langh 1E 120
BB7: B'ton, Langh 9E 100
Whalley Pl. FY8: L Ann 2H 129
Whalley Range BB1: Blackb 2D 226 (2M 139)
Whalley Range Bus. Pk. BB1: Blackb 1E 226
Whalley Rd. BB1: Wilp 5N 119
BB2: Mellor B 6D 118
BB5: Acc, Clay M 8N 121
BB6: Gt H 1M 121
BB6: Langh 8D 100
BB7: Barr, Clith, Pend 6K 81
BB7: Gt M, Hurst G, S'hurst 2N 99
BB7: Sabd 5A 102
BB12: Padi, Read, S'stone 8M 101
BL0: Eden, Ramsb 5K 181
LA1: Lanc 4K 23
OL12: Roch 4M 203
PR5: Sam 8K 117
PR7: Hesk 1G 193
WHALLEYS 7M 211
Whalleys Rd. WN8: Skelm 7L 211
Whalley Station (Rail) 4H 101
Whalley St. BB1: Blackb 1D 226 (2M 139)
BB7: Clith 3K 81
BB10: Burnl 9E 104
PR5: Bam B 6B 136
PR7: Chor 7E 174
Whalley Ter. BB3: Tock 1J 157
Whalley Valley Vis. Cen. 5J 101
Whalley Villa Caravan Pk. FY4: Blackp 1G 109
Wham Bottom La. OL12: Roch 1A 204
Wham Brook Cl. BB5: Osw 3H 141
Wham Hey PR4: New L 9D 134
Wham La. PR4: Lit H 3N 151
PR4: New L, W Stake 9D 134
Whams La. LA2: Bay H 7N 37
Wharf Cott. Holiday Pk. PR3: Cab 8L 45
Wharfe Ct. LA3: Morec 6F 22
Wharfedale FY4: Blackp 2F 108
LA2: Gal 2M 37
Wharfedale Av. BB10: Reed 6F 104
FY5: T Clev 9H 55
PR2: Ribb 4A 116
Wharfedale Cl. BB2: Blackb 9E 138
PR25: Leyl 8K 153
Wharfedale Ct. FY6: Poul F 8J 63
Wharfedale Rd. LA1: Lanc 8H 23
Wharfside BL8: Bury 9J 201
Wharf St. BB1: Blackb 4F 226 (3N 139)
BB1: Rish 8J 121
FY8: L Ann 5B 130
OL14: Wals 6K 165
WHARLES 6D 92
Wharton Av. FY5: T Clev 2K 63
Whave's La. PR6: Withn 2M 155
Wheatacre WN8: Skelm 3J 219
Wheatcroft Av. BB12: Fence 2B 104
Wheatfield PR26: Leyl 7D 152
Wheatfield Cl. BL9: Bury 6L 201
FY5: T Clev 4F 62
L30: N'ton 7A 222
Wheatfield Ct. LA1: Lanc 7B 228
Wheatfield St. BB1: Rish 7H 121
LA1: Lanc 7B 228 (8J 23)
Wheathead La. BB9: Blacko 3D 84
Wheathill St. OL16: Roch 9D 204
Wheatholme St. BB4: Rawt 5N 161
Wheatlands Cres. FY3: Blackp 8J 89
Wheat La. L40: Lath 1E 210
Wheatley Cl. BB12: Burnl 2B 124
BB12: Fence 3B 104
Wheatley Dr. PR3: Longr 2K 97
Wheatley Gro. BB9: Barrf 8G 84
WHEATLEY LANE 2C 104
Wheatley La. BB12: High 3A 104
Wheatley La. Rd. BB9: Barrf 3B 104
BB12: Fence 3B 104
Wheatsheaf Av. PR3: Longr 3J 97
Wheatsheaf Cen., The OL16: Roch 5C 204
Wheatsheaf Wlk. *L39: Orms* 7K 209
(off Burscough St.)
WN6: Stand 3N 213
Wheat St. BB5: Acc 2N 141
BB12: Padi 2J 123
Wheeler Dr. L31: Mell 7G 222
Wheel La. PR3: Pill 8F 42
WHEELTON 8J 155
Wheelton La. PR25: Far, Leyl 5K 153
PR26: Far M 5K 153
Wheelwright Cl. *BB7: Gis* 9A 52
(off Bentlea Rd.)
OL11: Roch 9M 203
Wheelwright Dr. OL16: Roch 2F 204

A-Z Lancashire 315

Wheelwrights Wharf—Willow Dr.

Wheelwrights Wharf L40: Scar .9E 188
Whelan Cl. BB2: Blackb .9L 139
Whelmar Ho. WN8: Skelm .2N 219
Whelpstone Gro. *BD24: Sett* .*3N 35*
(*off Mill Cl.*)
Whernside FY4: Blackp .2F 108
Whernside Cl. BB18: Barnw .2L 77
Whernside Cres. PR2: Ribb .4N 115
Whernside Gro. LA5: Carn .8C 12
Whernside Rd. LA1: Lanc .5H 23
Whernside Way PR25: Leyl .6M 153
Whewell Row BB5: Osw .3J 141
Whimberry Cl. PR6: Chor .5G 175
Whimbrel Dr. FY5: T Clev .8G 54
Whin Av. LA5: Bolt S .3M 15
Whinberry Av. BB4: Rawt .6M 161
Whinberry Dr. L32: Kirk .9J 223
Whinberry Vw. BB4: Rawt .5N 161
Whin Dr. LA5: Bolt S .3M 15
Whinfell Dr. LA1: Lanc .4L 29
Whinfield Av. FY7: Flee .2E 54
PR6: Chor .5F 174
Whinfield La. PR2: Ash R .9C 114
Whinfield Pl. BB2: Blackb .2H 139
PR2: Ash R .9C 114
Whinfield St. BB5: Clay M .8N 121
Whin Gro. LA5: Bolt S .3M 15
Whin La. PR3: Out R .3F 64
WHIN LANE END .3F 64
Whinney Brow La. PR3: Fort .2N 45
Whinneyfield La. PR4: Woodp .8N 93
Whinney Fold LA5: Silv .9F 4
Whinney Gro. E. L31: Magh .4B 222
Whinney Gro. W. L31: Magh .4B 222
Whinney Heys Rd. FY3: Blackp .4G 88
Whinney Hill Rd. BB5: Acc, Hunc .8N 121
Whinney La. BB2: Blackb, Mellor .7H 119
BB6: Langh .9D 100
PR7: Eux .2A 174
WHINNY HEIGHTS .7A 140
Whinny La. BB7: Wadd .5E 72
FY6: K Sea .9L 41
Whinnysty La. LA3: Heys .7L 21
Whinpark Av. FY3: Blackp .4G 88
Whins, The BB7: Sabd .3D 102
Whinsands Cl. PR2: Fulw .4N 115
Whins Av. BB7: Sabd .3D 102
Whinsfell Vw. LA4: Morec .3B 22
Whins La.
BB12: Padi, Read, S'stone .8B 102
PR6: Wheel .7J 155
Whipney La. BL8: Hawk .3C 200
Whipp Av. BB7: Clith .4K 81
Whirlaw Av. OL14: Tod .9K 147
WHIRLAW COMMON .8L 147
Whirlaw La. OL14: Tod .8K 147
Whitaker Grn. BB4: Rawt .5K 161
Whitakers La. BB7: West B .5M 73
Whitaker St. BB5: Acc .1A 142
Whitbarrow Sq. LA1: Lanc .6E 228
Whitburn WN8: Skelm .2H 219
Whitburn Dr. BL8: Bury .8H 201
Whitburn Rd. L33: Kirk .6M 223
Whitby Av. OL10: Heyw .9G 202
PR2: Ingol .4C 114
PR9: S'port .9C 148
Whitby Dr. BB2: Blackb .7N 139
Whitby Pl. PR2: Ingol .4C 114
Whitby Rd. FY8: L Ann .8G 108
LA4: Morec .3C 22
Whitby St. OL11: Roch .8D 204
Whiteacre WN6: Stand .2K 213
Whiteacre La. BB7: Barr, Wis .2K 101
White Acre Rd. BB5: Bax .6E 142
Whiteacres Cl. BB11: Burnl .5C 124
White Ash BL9: Bury .8C 202
White Ash Est. BB5: Osw .4J 141
White Ash La. BB5: Osw .5K 141
White Ash Ter. BL9: Bury .7C 202
Whitebeam Cl. FY5: T Clev .7F 54
L33: Kirk .4L 223
OL16: Milnr .9K 205
PR1: Penw .5E 134
Whitebeck La. LA6: Prie H .1F 12
WHITEBIRK .2C 140
Whitebirk Cl. BL8: Greenm .3E 200
Whitebirk Dr. BB1: Blackb .9B 120
Whitebirk Ind. Est. BB1: Blackb .8C 120
(not continuous)
Whitebirk Rd. BB1: Blackb .2D 140
White Bull St. *BB12: Burnl* .*3A 124*
(*off Keith St.*)
White Carr La. BL9: Bury .4M 201
FY5: T Clev .4F 62
PR3: Fort .2B 46
PR4: Trea .7A 92
WHITECHAPEL .4N 69
Whitecoats Dr. FY8: L Ann .4C 130
WHITE COPPICE .3M 175
White Creek Caravan Site LA5: Arn .3B 4
Whitecrest Av. FY5: T Clev .8F 54
Whitecroft Av. BB4: Hasl .5G 160
Whitecroft Cl. BB4: Hasl .5G 161
Whitecroft La. BB2: Mellor .7F 118
Whitecroft Mdws. BB4: Hasl .5G 160
White Cft. Rd. BB5: Osw .7H 141
Whitecroft Vw. BB5: Bax .6D 142
White Cross Ind. Est. LA1: Lanc .8D 228 (9K 23)
White Cross St. LA1: Lanc .8D 228 (9K 23)
WHITEFIELD .2G 105
Whitefield Av. OL11: Roch .5K 203
Whitefield Bus. Cen. BB9: Nelson .2G 105
Whitefield Cl. L40: Ruff .2G 190
Whitefield Dr. L32: Kirk .8G 223
Whitefield Mdw. PR5: Bam B .6B 136
Whitefield Pl. LA3: Morec .6C 22
Whitefield Rd. PR1: Penw .4D 134
Whitefield Rd. E. PR1: Penw .4D 134
Whitefield Rd. W. PR1: Penw .4D 134
Whitefield St. BB12: Hapt .5H 123
Whitefield Ter. *BB11: Burnl* .*5F 124*
(*off Somerset St.*)
Whitefriar Cl. PR2: Ingol .4D 114
Whitefriars Ct. *BD24: Sett* .*3N 35*
(*off Church St.*)
Whitegate LA3: Morec .6D 22
OL15: Littleb .1H 205
Whitegate Cl. BB12: Padi .2K 123
Whitegate Dr. BL1: Bolt .8F 198
FY3: Blackp .2N 227 (5D 88)
Whitegate Fold PR7: Char R .2A 194
Whitegate Gdns. BB12: Padi .2K 123
Whitegate Lodge *FY3: Blackp* .*7E 88*
(*off Whitegate Dr.*)
White Gate Mnr. OL10: Heyw .9H 203
Whitegate Mnr. FY1: Blackp .7E 88
Whitegates *BL7: Eger* .*4E 198*
(*off Turnerford Cl.*)
White Gro. BB8: Colne .5N 85
Whitehalgh La. BB6: Langh .9B 100
Whitehall Av. WN6: App B .4H 213
Whitehall La. BB7: Grind .3N 73
Whitehall Rd. BB2: Blackb .1J 139
BB3: Darw .1A 178
Whitehall St. BB3: Darw .1B 178
BB9: Nelson .1K 105
OL12: Roch .4C 204
OL16: Roch .5C 204
Whitehall Ter. BB3: Darw .9B 158
White Hart Fold *OL14: Tod* .*2L 165*
(*off Station App.*)
Whitehaven Cl. BB2: Blackb .7A 140
PR8: Ains .1B 206
Whitehaven St. BB11: Burnl .4C 124
Whitehead Cl. FY3: Stain .5K 89
Whitehead Cres. BL8: Bury .7H 201
Whitehead Dr. PR26: Far M .4H 153
Whitehead St. BB2: Blackb .3K 139
BB4: Rawt .4M 161
OL16: Milnr .7H 205
Whitehey WN8: Skelm .3J 219
Whitehey Island WN8: Skelm .3J 219
Whitehey Rd. WN8: Skelm .3J 219
White Hill Cl. OL12: Roch .1A 204
White Hill Cotts. BL1: Bolt .7D 198
White Hill La. BD20: Loth .3N 79
Whitehill La. BL1: Bolt .7D 198
Whitehill Rd. FY4: Blackp .4K 109
Whitehills Dr. FY4: Blackp .2K 109
WHITEHOLME .4E 62
Whiteholme Dr. FY6: Carl .5H 63
Whiteholme Pl. PR2: Ash R .8B 114
Whiteholme Rd. FY5: T Clev .5E 62
(not continuous)
White Horse Cl. BL6: Hor .8D 196
White Horse La. PR3: Bart .1A 94
Whitehough Pl. BB9: Nelson .1M 105
Whitehouse Av. L37: Form .9A 206
White Ho. La. L40: Scar .4H 189
PR3: Gt E .7B 66
Whitehouse La. L37: Form .9A 206
Whitehouse Res. Pk. Homes PR3: Cab .7N 45
White La. PR3: Pill .1E 56
White Lea PR3: Cab .3N 59
Whiteledge Rd. WN8: Skelm .4M 219
White Lee Av. BB8: Traw .9F 86
White Lee La. PR3: Whitec .9L 61
Whitelees M. OL15: Littleb .9K 185
Whitelees Rd. OL15: Littleb .9K 185
Whitelees Way FY6: Poul F .9K 63
Whitelegge St. BL8: Bury .9G 201
Whitelens Av. PR2: Lea .8N 113
Whiteley Av. BB2: Blackb .7H 139
White Leys Cl. BB18: Salt .3C 78
Whiteley's La. L40: W'head .1B 218
Whiteleys Pl. OL12: Roch .5B 204
Whiteley St. BB4: Hasl .6H 161
Whitelow Rd. BL9: Bury .8K 181
WHITE LUND .6C 22
White Lund Av. LA3: Morec .6C 22
White Lund Ind. Est. LA3: Morec .6E 22
(Middlegate)
LA3: Morec .6D 22
(Whitegate)
White Lund Rd. LA3: Morec .6C 22
White Lund Trade Pk. LA3: Morec .6E 22
Whitely Gro. L33: Kirk .4M 223
White Mdw. PR2: Lea .6B 114
WHITE MOSS .4J 219
Whitemoss OL12: Roch .3M 203
Whitemoss Av. FY3: Blackp .3H 89
Whitemoss Bus. Pk. WN8: Skelm .5J 219
White Moss La. FY6: Ham .8D 56
White Moss Rd. WN8: Skelm .3G 219
White Moss Rd. Sth. WN8: Skelm .4G 218
Whitendale LA1: Lanc .6G 23
Whitendale Cres. BB1: Blackb .8F 226 (5N 139)
Whitendale Dr. LA5: Bolt S .7K 15
PR5: Bam B .8B 136
Whitendale Hall PR1: Prest .3J 229 (8J 115)
Whitendale Rd. BB7: Dun B .3J 49
Whitepits La. LA2: Tat .9K 19
Whiteplatts St. OL14: Tod .1L 165
Whiterails Dr. L39: Orms .6J 209
Whiterails M. L39: Orms .6J 209
Whiteray Rd. LA1: Lanc .6H 23
White Rd. BB2: Blackb .2J 139
Whiteside Fold OL12: Roch .4L 203
Whiteside St. FY1: Blackp .4C 88
Whiteside Way FY5: T Clev .9D 54
White Slack Ga. OL14: Wals .1J 185
WHITE STAKE .8E 134
Whitestocks WN8: Skelm .3J 219
White St. BB8: Colne .8M 85
BB12: Burnl .3N 123
WN5: Wigan .5L 221
Whitethorn Cl. PR6: Clay W .5C 154
Whitethorne M. FY5: T Clev .3H 63
Whitethorn M. FY8: L Ann .7G 108
Whitethorn Sq. PR2: Lea .8A 114
Whitewalls Cl. BB8: Colne .8L 85
Whitewalls Dr. BB8: Colne .8L 85
Whitewalls Ind. Est. BB8: Colne .8L 85
BB8: Nelson .8K 85
WHITEWELL .2K 71
WHITEWELL BOTTOM .3D 162
Whitewell Cl. OL16: Roch .5F 204
PR3: Catt .9A 60
Whitewell Dr. BB7: Clith .4J 81
Whitewell Pl. BB1: Blackb .1E 226
Whitewell Rd. BB5: Acc .9C 122
BB7: Cow A .4L 71
BB7: Dun B .8K 49
Whitewell Va. *BB4: W'foot* .*5D 162*
(*off Burnley Rd. E.*)
Whitewood Cl. FY8: L Ann .4L 129
Whitfield Brow OL15: Littleb .7M 185
Whitfield Dr. OL16: Milnr .8H 205
Whitley Av. FY3: Blackp .1N 227 (5D 88)
FY5: T Clev .7E 54
Whitley Rd. WN8: Roby M, Uph .9F 212
Whitmoor Cl. LA4: Morec .3B 22
Whitmore Dr. PR2: Ribb .7C 116
Whitmore Gro. PR2: Ribb .7C 116
Whitmore Pl. PR2: Ribb .7C 116
Whitpark Gro. BB12: Burnl .2B 124
Whitsters Hollow BL1: Bolt .9B 198
Whitstone Dr. WN8: Skelm .4A 220
WHITTAKER .1N 205
Whittaker Av. FY3: Blackp .3D 88
Whittaker Cl. BB12: Burnl .1N 123
Whittaker Dr. OL15: Littleb .3J 205
Whittaker Golf Course .1N 205
Whittaker La. OL11: Roch .4H 203
OL15: Littleb .1N 205
Whittaker St. BB2: Blackb .3A 226 (3K 139)
OL11: Roch .4J 203
Whittam Av. FY4: Blackp .9E 88
Whittam Ct. *BB10: W'thorne* .*3M 125*
(*off Showfield*)
Whittam Cres. BB7: Whall .4H 101
Whittam Rd. BB7: Whall .4G 101
PR7: Chor .9D 174
Whittam St. BB11: Burnl .3B 228 (4D 124)
WHITTLEFIELD .1B 124
Whitters La. PR3: Winm .1G 58
Whittingham Dr. BL0: Ramsb .1H 201
Whittingham Hospital Grounds
PR3: W'ham .5A 96
Whittingham La. PR2: Grim, Haigh .7D 96
PR3: Brou .7G 94
Whittingham Rd. PR3: Longr .3H 97
WHITTINGTON .8E 8
Whittle Brow PR7: Char R, Copp .4M 193
Whittle Cl. BB7: Clith .2M 81
Whittle Ct. BB12: Burnl .2C 124
WN3: Wins .9N 221
Whittle Dr. L39: Orms .5K 209
Whittle Grn. PR4: Woodp .7B 94
Whittle Hill BL7: Eger .2E 198
PR4: Woodp .7B 94
Whittle La. WN6: Wrigh .8B 192
WHITTLE-LE-WOODS .8D 154
Whittle Pk. PR6: Clay W .5D 154
Whittles St. OL13: Bac .7M 163
Whittles Ter. OL16: Milnr .9L 205
WHITTLESTONE HEAD .3F 178
Whittle St. BB4: Hasl .5F 160
BB4: Rawt .4M 161
BL8: Bury .9H 201
OL15: Littleb .9J 185
Whittlewood Cl. L33: Kirk .6L 223
Whitton M. *BL6: Hor* .*9C 196*
(*off Wright St.*)
Whittycroft Av. BB9: Barrf .5J 85
Whittycroft Dr. BB9: Barrf .5J 85
Whitwell Av. FY4: Blackp .4C 108
Whitwell Cl. WN6: Stand .2N 213
Whitwell Gdns. BL6: Hor .8C 196
WHITWORTH .5N 183
Whitworth Dr. PR7: Chor .7C 174
Whitworth Leisure Cen. .4A 184
Whitworth Mus. .5N 183
Whitworth Rake OL12: Whitw .6A 184
Whitworth Rd. OL12: Roch .1A 204
Whitworth Sq. OL12: Whitw .6A 184
Whitworth St. OL16: Milnr .7J 205
OL16: Roch .3F 204
PR4: Wesh .3L 111
Whitworth Water Ski Cen. .4N 183
Whitworth Way BB18: Barnw .10G 52
Wholesome La. L40: Scar, Burs .3H 189
PR4: Longt .1B 152
Whorleys La. LA5: Bolt S .3B 16
Whytha Rd. BB7: Rim .6A 76
Wicken Gro. BB4: Craws .8M 143
Wickentree Holt OL12: Roch .3L 203
Wicken Tree Row BB12: S'stone .7E 102
Wickliffe Pl. *OL11: Roch* .*7C 204*
(*off Henry St.*)
Wickliffe St. BB9: Nelson .1J 105
Wicklow Av. FY8: L Ann .3D 130
Wickworth St. BB9: Nelson .3K 105
WIDDOP .2K 127
Widgeon Cl. FY5: T Clev .8F 54
Widow Hill Ct. BB10: Burnl .9H 105
Widow Hill Rd. BB10: Burnl .9G 105
Wigan La. PR7: Adl, Chor, Copp, H Charn .7E 194
Wigan Lwr. Rd. WN6: Stand .8M 213
Wigan Rd. L39: Orms .7L 209
L40: W'head .8C 210
PR5: Bam B .2N 153
PR7: Eux .1M 173
PR7: Eux, Leyl .8M 153
PR25: Leyl, Clay W .8M 153
WN6: Shev, Stand .6L 213
WN8: Skelm .2K 219
Wigeon Row FY8: L Ann .1L 129
Wiggins La. L40: Holmesw .9M 169
WIGGLESWORTH .10M 35
Wight Moss Way PR8: S'port .2K 187
Wignall St. PR1: Prest .8M 115
Wigston Cl. PR8: Ains .9B 186
Wigton Av. PR25: Leyl .8G 153
Wilbraham St. PR1: Prest .8M 115
Wilby Cl. BL8: Bury .9J 201
Wilcove WN8: Skelm .2K 219
WILDERSWOOD .8D 196
Wilderswood Av. BL6: Hor .9D 196
Wilderswood Cl. PR6: Whit W .5E 154
Wilderswood Ct. BL6: Hor .8D 196
Wildhouse Ct. OL16: Milnr .6J 205
Wild Ho. La. OL16: Milnr .6J 205
Wilding's La. FY8: L Ann .9H 109
Wild La. FY4: Blackp .4K 109
Wildman St. FY3: Blackp .3D 88
PR1: Prest .1G 229 (7H 115)
Wild Oaks Dr. FY5: T Clev .3K 63
Wilds Bldgs. OL16: Roch .6G 205
Wilds Pas. OL15: Littleb .1H 205
(Oakley St.)
OL15: Littleb .4N 185
(Roberts Pas.)
Wilds Pl. BL0: Ramsb .9G 181
Wildwood Cl. BL0: Ramsb .1F 200
Wild Wood Ri. *OL14: Tod* .*7F 146*
(*off Burnley Rd.*)
Wilfield St. BB11: Burnl .3C 124
Wilford St. FY3: Blackp .3E 88
Wilfred Dr. BL9: Bury .9N 201
Wilfred St. BB5: Acc .4B 142
BL7: Brom C .6G 198
Wilkesley Av. WN6: Stand .4N 213
Wilkie Av. BB11: Burnl .7C 124
Wilkin Bri. BB7: Clith .3L 81
Wilkinson Av. FY3: Blackp .6E 88
Wilkinson Ho. *OL14: Tod* .*8H 147*
(*off Harley Wood*)
Wilkinson Mt. *BB18: Earl* .*2E 78*
(*off Aspen La.*)
Wilkinson Rd. BL1: Bolt .8D 198
Wilkinson St. BB4: Hasl .3G 160
BB9: Barrf .8G 85
BB10: Burnl .7H 105
BB11: Dunn .4N 143
BB12: High .5L 103
PR5: Lost H .8L 135
Wilkinson Way BB1: Blackb .7C 140
FY6: Pree .8M 41
Wilkin Sq. BB7: Clith .3L 81
Willacy La. PR4: Catf .7J 93
Willacy Pde. LA3: Heys .7L 21
Willard Av. WN5: Bill .8G 221
Willaston Av. BB9: Blacko .3J 85
Willbutts La. OL11: Roch .5N 203
William Griffiths Ct. *BB2: Blackb* .*6J 139*
(*off Mill Hill Bri. St.*)
William Henry St. OL11: Roch .8D 204
PR1: Prest .9M 115
William Herbert St. BB1: Blackb .1E 226 (2N 139)
William Hopwood St. BB1: Blackb .4A 140
William Roberts Av. L32: Kirk .8H 223
Williams Av. LA4: Morec .2G 22
Williams Dr. BB2: Blackb .7A 140
Williams La. PR2: Fulw .2M 115
Williamson Gallery, The .*9M 23*
(*within Ashton Memorial*)
Williamson Pk. .9M 23
Williamson Pk. Butterfly House .9M 23
Williamson Rd. LA1: Lanc .7E 228 (8L 23)
Williams Pl. BB9: Nelson .2K 105
Williams Rd. BB10: Burnl .9F 104
William St. BB2: Blackb .9D 226 (6M 139)
BB3: Darw .6A 158
BB5: Acc .1B 142
BB5: Clay M .8N 121
BB8: Colne .7B 86
BB9: Brierf .4F 104
BB9: Nelson .1J 105
BB18: Earl .3E 78
BL0: Ramsb .5H 181
BL6: Hor .9B 196
FY3: Blackp .3E 88
LA5: Carn .7A 12
OL11: Roch .7C 204
OL12: Whitw .5N 183
OL13: Bac .7N 163
OL15: Littleb .9K 185
OL16: Roch .1G 205
PR5: Lost H .8K 135
William Walton Cotts. *BB9: Nelson* .*1L 105*
(*off Broadway Pl.*)
William Young Cl. PR1: Prest .7M 115
Willingdon Cl. BL8: Bury .6H 201
Willis Rd. BB2: Blackb .6G 139
Willis St. BB11: Burnl .4A 228 (4C 124)
Willoughby Av. FY5: T Clev .1D 62
Willoughby St. BB1: Blackb .2C 226 (2M 139)
Willow Av. BB4: Rawt .3M 161
L32: Kirk .7H 223
Willow Bank BB3: Darw .9A 158
L40: W'head .8C 210
OL14: Tod .1L 165
PR3: Bils .6D 68
PR9: Banks .*3J 169*
(*off Main Av.*)
Willowbank FY3: Stain .4J 89
FY8: L Ann .1E 128
Willowbank Av. FY4: Blackp .4E 108
Willowbank Ct. FY6: Carl .7H 63
Willowbank Holiday Home & Touring Pk.
PR8: Ains .2B 206
Willow Bank La. BB3: Darw .6N 157
Willow Brook BB5: Acc .2A 142
L39: Hals .7N 187
Willowbrook Dr. WN6: Shev .5L 213
Willow Cl. BB5: Clay M .6L 121
BB9: Barrf .1F 104
FY5: T Clev .2K 63
FY6: K Sea .7N 41
PR1: Penw .4D 134
PR3: Fort .2M 45
PR5: Hogh .7G 136
PR5: Lost H .8K 135
PR6: And .5L 195
Willow Coppice PR2: Lea .6B 114
Willow Ct. FY5: T Clev .2K 63
Willow Cres. L40: Burs .7D 190
PR2: Ribb .7N 115
PR4: Frec .3M 131
PR25: Leyl .4N 153
Willowcroft Dr. FY6: Ham .2A 64
Willowdale FY5: T Clev .2K 63
Willowdene FY5: T Clev .2E 62
Willowdene Cl. BL7: Eger .5F 198
Willow Dr. BB7: Barr .2K 101
BB9: Nelson .2L 105
FY6: Poul F .2K 89
PR3: Gars .3N 59
PR4: Frec .3M 131

Willow Dr.—Woodcock Hill Rd.

Willow Dr. PR4: W Grn 5H 111
PR4: Wesh 2N 111
PR7: Char R 2N 193
WN8: Skelm 2J 219
Willow End L40: Burs 9D 190
Willow Fld. PR6: Clay W 4E 154
Willowfield Chase PR5: Hogh 6K 137
Willowfield Rd. LA3: Heys 9M 21
Willow Grn. L39: Orms 7L 209
(off School Ho. Grn.)
L40: Ruff 2E 190
PR2: Ash R 9D 114
PR9: S'port 2B 168
Willow Gro. BB7: West B 5K 73
FY3: Blackp 1G 88
FY6: Ham 1A 64
L37: Form 8A 206
LA1: Lanc 8M 23
LA4: Morec 2F 22
PR3: Goos 4N 95
PR3: Gt E 6M 65
PR8: S'port 7L 167
PR9: Banks 2F 168
Willowgrove Pk. FY6: Pree 8A 42
Willow Hey BB4: Hasl 6E 160
BL7: Brom C 6J 199
L31: Magh 3D 222
PR4: Tarl 8E 150
WN8: Skelm 2K 219
Willowhey PR9: S'port 2M 167
Willow La. LA1: Lanc 9G 23
Willow Lodge FY8: L Ann 1J 129
Willowmead Pk. FY8: Moss S 7E 110
Willowmead Way OL12: Roch 3L 203
Willow Mill LA2: Caton 3H 25
Willow Mt. BB1: Blackb 6N 119
Willow Pk. BB5: Osw 6J 141
PR8: S'port 9G 166
Willow Pl. PR4: Elsw 1L 91
Willow Ri. L33: Kirk 7L 223
OL15: Littleb 2J 205
Willow Rd. PR6: Chor 4G 174
PR26: Leyl 9C 152
Willow Rocks BB18: Salt 5M 77
Willows, The BB2: Mellor B 6D 118
FY8: L Ann 5L 129
L40: Mawd 3N 191
OL12: Whitw 9N 183
(off Market St.)
PR3: Bils 6C 68
PR7: Chor 2D 194
PR7: Copp 5A 194
PR8: S'port 8F 166
(off Beechfield Gdns.)
Willows Av. FY5: T Clev 2E 62
FY8: L Ann 5L 129
Willows Cotts. OL16: Milnr 7H 205
Willows La. BB5: Acc 3N 141
(not continuous)
OL16: Roch 7G 205
PR4: K'ham 4L 111
Willows Pk. La.
PR3: Longr 2K 97
Willow St. BB1: Blackb 1A 140
BB3: Darw 6N 157
BB4: Hasl 4G 161
BB4: W'foot 7C 162
BB5: Acc 2A 142
BB5: Clay M 6L 121
BB6: Gt H 5J 121
BB12: Burnl 1A 228 (3C 124)
FY7: Flee 9G 40
Willow Ter. FY3: Stain 4J 89
Willow Tree Av. BB4: Rawt 5K 161
PR3: Brou 7G 94
Willow Tree Cres. PR25: Leyl 6G 152
Willow Tree Gdns. FY5: T Clev 2K 63
Willow Tree Ho.
FY1: Blackp 1L 227
Willow Trees Dr. BB1: Blackb 9K 119
Willow Wlk. WN8: Skelm 8M 211
Willow Way FY3: Blackp 8J 89
(off Newholme Res. Pk.)
PR4: New L 9C 134
Wills Av. L31: Magh 9B 216
Willsford Av. L31: Mell 7G 222
Willshaw Rd. FY2: Blackp 1B 88
Willy La. LA2: C'ham 9H 37
Wilmar Rd. PR25: Leyl 5M 153
Wilmcote Gro. PR8: Ains 9B 186
Wilmers OL15: Littleb 4N 185
Wilmore Cl. BB8: Colne 6N 85
Wilmot Rd. PR2: Ribb 6A 116
Wilmslow Av. BL1: Bolt 8E 198
WILPSHIRE 4N 119
Wilpshire Banks BB1: Wilp 5N 119
Wilpshire Golf Course 3N 119
Wilpshire Rd. BB1: Rish 4C 120
Wilsham Rd. WN5: Orr 6H 221
Wilson Cl. OL14: Tod 9K 147
PR4: Tarl 8D 150
Wilson Dr. PR4: Elsw 1M 91
Wilson Fold BB12: Burnl 3N 123
Wilson Gro. LA3: Heys 8K 21
Wilson Sq. FY5: T Clev 4D 62
Wilson St. BB2: Blackb 9A 226 (6L 139)
BB7: Clith 4K 81
BB8: Foul 2A 86
BL6: Hor 9B 196
OL12: Roch 5C 204
Wilson Ter. BB2: Blackb 9A 226
Wilton Cl. BB2: Blackb 9G 119
LA1: Lanc 4L 23
Wilton Ct. BB2: Blackb 9G 119
Wilton Gro. PR1: Penw 4D 134
Wilton Pde. FY1: Blackp 3B 88
Wilton Parade Stop (Tram) 3B 88
Wilton Pl. PR25: Leyl 6L 153
Wilton Rd. BL1: Bolt 8E 198
WN6: Shev 6K 213
Wilton St. BB9: Barrf 8H 85
BB9: Brierf 5F 104
BB10: Burnl 9F 104
BL1: Bolt 9F 198
Wilton Ter. OL12: Roch 5B 204
Wiltshire Av. BB12: Burnl 2N 123
Wiltshire Dr. BB4: Hasl 7G 161
Wiltshire M. PR4: Cott 4A 114
Wiltshire Pl. WN5: Wigan 5M 221
Wilvere Cl. FY5: T Clev 4C 62
Wilvere Dr. FY5: T Clev 3C 62
Wilworth Cres. BB1: Blackb 8M 119
Wimberley Banks BB1: Blackb 1D 226
Wimberley Gdns.
BB1: Blackb 1C 226 (2M 139)
Wimberley Pl. BB1: Blackb 1C 226 (2M 139)
Wimberley St.
BB1: Blackb 1C 226 (2M 139)
Wimbledon Av. FY5: T Clev 5D 62
Wimbledon Ct. FY5: T Clev 5D 62
(off Wimbledon Av.)
Wimbledon Dr. OL11: Roch 8A 204
Wimborne Rd. WN5: Orr 3K 221
Wimbourne Pl. FY4: Blackp 3B 108
Wimbrick Cl. L39: Orms 8J 209
Wimbrick Cres. L39: Orms 9J 209
Winby St. OL11: Roch 8D 204
Wincanton Dr. BL1: Bolt 6D 198
Winchcombe Rd. FY5: T Clev 4E 62
Winchester Av. BB5: Acc 1B 142
FY4: Blackp 9M 227 (9D 88)
L10: Aint 7C 222
LA1: Lanc 2M 29
LA4: Morec 2D 22
PR7: Chor 2G 194
Winchester Cl. BL8: Bury 6H 201
LA3: Morec 6B 22
OL11: Roch 6L 203
WN5: Orr 4J 221
Winchester Dr. FY6: Carl 6G 63
Winchester Rd. BB12: Padi 3J 123
WN5: Bill 9G 221
Winchester St. BB1: Blackb 5A 140
Winchester Way PR3: Gars 5M 59
Winckley Ct. PR1: Prest 7J 229 (1J 135)
Winckley Gdns. PR1: Prest 7J 229 (1J 135)
Winckley Rd. BB5: Clay M 7M 121
PR1: Prest 2G 135
Winckley Sq. PR1: Prest 7K 229 (1J 135)
Winckley St.
PR1: Prest 6K 229 (1J 135)
Winder Gth. LA6: Over K 9G 12
Winder La. PR3: Fort 4M 45
Windermere Av. BB5: Hunc 8C 122
BB7: Clith 4J 81
BB8: Colne 5C 86
BB10: Burnl 8E 104
FY7: Flee 4D 54
LA4: Morec 4D 22
PR25: Far 4K 153
Windermere Cl.
BB1: Blackb 2F 226 (2N 139)
Windermere Ct. LA4: Morec 4D 22
(off Windermere Av.)
Windermere Cres. PR8: Ains 1C 206
Windermere Dr. BB1: Rish 8G 120
BB3: Darw 4C 158
BL0: Ramsb 7H 181
L31: Magh 9D 216
L33: Kirk 6J 223
PR6: Adl 4K 195
WA11: Rain 9K 219
Windermere Rd. BB12: Padi 9H 103
FY4: Blackp 1C 108
L38: Hight 7A 214
LA1: Lanc 7G 228 (8M 23)
LA5: Bolt S 4L 15
LA5: Carn 1B 16
OL13: Bac 4L 163
PR1: Prest 8C 116
PR2: Fulw 5M 115
PR6: Chor 7G 174
WN5: Orr 3J 221
Windermere Sq. FY8: L Ann 7F 108
Windermere St. OL12: Roch 3C 204
Windfield Cl. L33: Kirk 4M 223
Windflower Dr. PR25: Leyl 5A 154
Windgate PR4: Much H 5J 151
PR4: Tarl 1E 170
WN8: Skelm 3K 219
Windgate Fold PR4: Tarl 1E 170
Windham Pl. LA1: Lanc 5G 22
Windham St. OL16: Roch 2F 204
Windhill La. BB7: Rim 5L 75
Windholme LA1: Lanc 6G 22
Windle Ash L31: Magh 9B 216
Windle Cl. FY4: Blackp 5B 108
Windmill Animal Farm 1N 189
Windmill Av. L39: Orms 7L 209
PR4: K'ham 5A 112
Windmill Cl. FY3: Stain 5L 89
L33: Kirk 5K 223
Windmill Ct. LA1: Lanc 4L 29
OL16: Roch 7E 204
Windmill Hgts. WN8: Uph 3D 220
Windmill Ho. PR9: S'port 3M 167
Windmill La. PR6: Brind 9K 137
Windmill Mobile Home Pk.
FY4: Blackp 1L 109
Windmill Pl. FY4: Blackp 3F 108
Windmill Rd. WN8: Uph 4C 220
Windmill Rdbt. WN8: Skelm 4C 220
Windmill St. OL16: Roch 7E 204
Windmill Vw. PR4: Wesh 3M 111
Windrows WN8: Skelm 2K 219
Windrush, The OL12: Roch 1N 203
Windrush Av. BL0: Ramsb 3F 200
Windsor Av. BB4: Hasl 6F 160
BB4: Newc 6C 162
BB5: Chur 9N 121
BB7: Clith 4J 81
FY4: Blackp 1B 108
FY5: T Clev 1H 63
LA1: Lanc 2M 29
LA4: Morec 5N 21
PR1: Penw 5F 134
PR2: Ash R 7E 114
PR3: Longr 3H 97
PR4: New L 7D 134
PR7: Adl 7H 195
Windsor Cl. BB1: Blackb 5B 140
BB12: Read 8C 102
BL8: Greenm 4F 200
L40: Burs 1C 210
PR7: Chor 7D 174
PR25: Leyl 8G 153
Windsor Ct. FY6: Poul F 8L 63
L39: Aug 1J 217
PR8: Birk 1E 186
Windsor Dr. PR2: Fulw 3G 115
PR6: Birns 7N 155
Windsor Gdns. PR3: Gars 5M 59
Windsor Gro. LA4: Morec 5A 22
Windsor Lodge FY8: L Ann 4K 129
Windsor Pk. Rd. L10: Aint 7D 222
Windsor Pl. BB18: Barnw 1A 78
FY7: Flee 8H 41
Windsor Rd. BB1: Blackb 3E 140
BB2: Blackb 2J 139
BB3: Darw 4N 157
BB6: Gt H 4K 121
BL7: Brom C 6G 198
FY3: Blackp 3H 89
FY8: L Ann 3G 128
(St James Lodge)
FY8: L Ann 4K 129
(Woodlands Rd.)
L31: Magh 2B 222
LA3: Morec 5N 21
OL14: Tod 1K 165
PR3: Gars 5M 59
PR4: K'ham 4L 111
PR5: Walt D 5N 135
PR7: Chor 7D 174
PR7: E'ton 7F 172
PR9: S'port 8K 167
WN8: Uph 3D 220
Windsor St. BB5: Acc 2B 142
BB8: Colne 6B 86
BB9: Nelson 3K 105
BB12: Burnl 3A 124
OL11: Roch 8D 204
Windsor Ter. FY7: Flee 8H 41
OL16: Milnr 7H 205
(off Moorhouse Farm)
OL16: Roch 6F 204
Windy Bank BB8: Colne 6B 86
WINDY HARBOUR 8M 155
Windy Harbour Holiday Pk. FY6: Sing 6E 64
Windy Harbour La. BL7: Brom C 5H 199
OL14: Tod 7L 147
Windy Harbour Rd. FY6: Sing 7F 64
PR8: Birk 6E 186
Windy Hill LA2: H Ben 6N 19
Windyhill LA1: Lanc 7C 228 (8K 23)
Windy St. PR3: Chip 5G 70
Winery La. PR5: Walt D 3M 135
WINEWALL 7F 86
Winewall La. BB8: Wine 6E 86
Winewall Rd. BB8: Wine 6E 86
Wingate Av. FY5: T Clev 3D 62
LA4: Morec 5C 22
Wingate Pl. FY5: T Clev 3D 62
Wingate Rd. L33: Kirk 6L 223
Wingates PR1: Penw 5F 134
Wingate-Saul Rd. LA1: Lanc 7A 228 (8J 23)
Wingate St. OL11: Roch 4J 203
Wingate Wlk. L33: Kirk 7M 223
Wingfield Vs. OL15: Littleb 7M 185
Wingrove Rd. FY7: Flee 2F 54
Winifred Av. BL9: Bury 9D 202
Winifred La. L39: Aug 2F 216
Winifred St. BL0: Ramsb 9G 181
OL12: Roch 4M 203
WINMARLEIGH 9J 45
Winmarleigh Hall Adventure Activities 1H 59
Winmarleigh Rd. LA1: Lanc 5L 29
PR2: Ash R 8E 114
Winmarleigh St. BB1: Blackb 4C 140
Winmarleigh Wlk. BB1: Blackb 4B 140
Winmoss Dr. L33: Kirk 5L 223
Winnipeg Cl. BB2: Blackb 9J 119
Winnipeg Ct. FY2: Blackp 8E 62
Winnipeg Pl. FY2: Blackp 8D 62
Winscar Wlk. FY6: Poul F 8H 63
Winsford Cres. FY5: T Clev 3C 62
Winsford Dr. OL11: Roch 8K 203
Winsford Wlk. BB11: Burnl 4N 123
Winsham Cl. L32: Kirk 9L 223
Winslow Av. FY6: Carl 6H 63
Winslow Cl. PR1: Penw 6H 135
Winsor Av. PR25: Leyl 7L 153
WINSTANLEY 9N 221
Winstanley Gro. FY1: Blackp 1K 227 (5C 88)
Winstanley Rd. WN5: Bill 7H 221
WN8: Skelm 3K 219
Winstanley Shop. Cen. WN3: Wins 9N 221
Winstanley Tennis Club 7J 221
Winster Cl. PR5: Hogh 4G 136
Winster Ct. BB5: Clay M 7L 121
Winster Ho. WN5: Wigan 4M 221
(off Helvellyn Rd.)
Winster Pk. LA1: Lanc 6G 22
Winster Pl. FY4: Blackp 9K 89
Winsters, The WN8: Skelm 2K 219
Winster Wlk. LA1: Lanc 6G 22
Winston Av. FY5: T Clev 1F 62
FY8: L Ann 2H 129
OL11: Roch 7J 203
Winston Cres. PR8: S'port 3L 187
Winston Rd. BB1: Blackb 1B 226 (1L 139)
Winterburn Av. BL2: Bolt 7H 199
Winterburn La. BD23: Esh 1M 53
Winterburn Rd. BB2: Blackb 9K 139
Winterbutlee Gro. OL14: Wals 6K 165
Winterbutlee Rd. OL14: Wals 6K 165
Winter Gap La. BD20: Loth 4L 79
Winter Gdns. Arc. LA4: Morec 3A 22
Winter Gdns., Opera House & Empress Ballroom
2J 227 (5B 88)
Winter Hey La. BL6: Hor 9C 196
WINTER HILL 3G 197
Winter Hill Cl. PR2: Ribb 2E 116
Winter Hill Vw. BL7: Eger 2D 198
Winterley Dr. BB5: Hunc 8D 122
Winterson St. BB5: Acc 3M 141
Winterton Rd. BB3: Darw 5A 158
Winthorpe Av. LA4: Morec 4D 22
Winton Av. FY4: Blackp 9G 88
PR2: Fulw 3J 115
WN5: Wigan 6N 221
Winton St. OL15: Littleb 9L 185
Winward Cl. BB3: Lwr D 1N 157
Wirral Dr. WN3: Wins 9M 221
Wiseman Cl. LA4: Morec 4C 22
Wiseman St. BB11: Burnl 2A 228 (3C 124)
Wisp Hill Gro. LA2: Halt 1C 24
Wisteria Dr. BB3: Lwr D 9A 140
WISWELL 3M 101
Wiswell Cl. BB4: Rawt 3M 161
BB10: Burnl 8J 105
Wiswell La. BB7: Whall, Wis 4K 101
Witham Cl. WN6: Stand 3N 213
Witham Rd. WN8: Skelm 2H 219
Withens New Rd. OL14: Tod 4N 165
(not continuous)
Withens Rd. L31: Lyd 8C 216
Witherslack Cl. LA4: Morec 5B 22
Withers St. BB1: Blackb 5F 226 (4N 139)
WITHGILL 5C 80
Withgill Fold BB7: Withg 4D 80
WITHIN GROVE 8C 122
Within Gro. BB5: Hunc 8C 122
Withington La. PR7: Hesk 3H 193
Withinlea PR5: Bam B 8A 136
Withins Fld. L38: Hight 8A 214
Withins La. L38: Gt A 4F 214
WITHNELL 6B 156
WITHNELL FOLD 4L 155
Withnell Fold PR6: Withn 4L 155
Withnell Fold Old Rd. PR6: Birns 7A 156
PR6: Birns, Withn 5N 155
Withnell Gro. PR6: Chor 5G 175
Withnell Rd. FY4: Blackp 1B 108
Withy Ct. PR2: Fulw 6H 115
Withy Gdns. PR5: Bam B 7B 136
Withy Gro. Cl. PR5: Bam B 7B 136
Withy Gro. Cres. PR5: Bam B 7B 136
Withy Gro. Rd. PR5: Bam B 7B 136
Withy Pde. PR2: Fulw 5H 115
Withy Trees Av. PR5: Bam B 8B 136
Withy Trees Cl. PR5: Bam B 7B 136
Witley Rd. OL16: Roch 6E 204
Witney Av. BB2: Blackb 8F 138
Wittlewood Dr. BB5: Acc 8A 122
WITTON 5J 139
Witton Av. FY7: Flee 3E 54
Witton Country Pk. 4G 139
Witton Country Pk. Vis. Cen. 5G 139
Witton Gro. FY7: Flee 3E 54
Witton Outdoor Leisure 5H 139
Witton Pde. BB2: Blackb 5K 139
Witton St. PR1: Prest 9L 115
Witton Way WA11: Rain 3K 225
Woborrow Rd. LA3: Heys 9K 21
Woburn Cl. BB5: Bax 5D 142
OL16: Milnr 7H 205
Woburn Grn. PR25: Leyl 5L 153
Woburn Rd. FY1: Blackp 3C 88
Woburn Way PR3: Catt 1B 68
Wold, The PR6: Heap 3J 175
Wolfenden Grn. BB4: W'foot 7D 162
Wolfhouse Gallery 1G 11
Wollaton Dr. PR8: S'port 2M 187
Wolseley Cl. PR25: Leyl 7K 153
Wolseley Pl. PR1: Prest 7L 229 (1K 135)
Wolseley Rd. PR1: Prest 9G 229 (3H 135)
Wolseley St. BB2: Blackb 7L 139
LA1: Lanc 6E 228 (8L 23)
OL16: Milnr 9L 205
Wolsey Cl. FY5: T Clev 9E 54
Wolsley Rd. FY1: Blackp 9J 227 (9B 88)
FY7: Flee 9F 40
Wolstenholme Av. BL9: Bury 7L 201
Wolstenholme Coalpit La. OL11: Roch 3F 202
WOLSTENHOLME FOLD 3G 203
Wolstenholme La. OL12: Roch 3G 202
Wolverton WN8: Skelm 3K 219
Wolverton Av. FY2: Blackp 9B 62
Wolvesey OL11: Roch 7B 204
(off Boundary St.)
Woodacre Hall M. PR3: Scor 1B 60
Woodacre Rd. PR2: Ribb 7C 116
Woodale Laithe BB9: Barrf 8G 85
Woodale Rd. PR6: Clay W 3D 154
Wood Bank BB4: Hasl 9E 160
PR1: Penw 5F 134
Woodbank OL14: Wals 1N 185
Woodbank Av. BB3: Darw 5M 157
Woodbank Dr. BL8: Bury 9H 201
Woodbank Rd. OL15: Littleb 2K 205
Wood Beech Gdns. PR6: Clay W 3D 154
Woodberry Cl. L33: Kirk 4L 223
Woodbine Gdns. BB12: Burnl 2N 123
Woodbine Pas. OL15: Littleb 9K 185
(off Featherstall Rd.)
Woodbine Rd. BB2: Blackb 2J 139
BB12: Burnl 3A 124
Woodbine St. OL16: Roch 8D 204
Woodbine St. E. OL16: Roch 8E 204
Woodbine Ter. OL14: Tod 7E 146
Woodbridge Gdns. OL12: Roch 3N 203
Woodbrook Dr. WN3: Wigan 7N 221
Woodburn Cl. BB2: Blackb 9H 119
Woodburn Dr. BL1: Bolt 9B 198
Woodburn Gro. PR1: Penw 7F 134
Woodbury Av. BB2: Blackb 6L 139
BB12: Fence 3B 104
Woodchat Ct. PR7: Chor 9B 174
Wood Cl. BB9: Rough 6E 84
L32: Kirk 8J 223
LA5: Arn 1F 4
Woodclose Caravan Pk. LA6: H Cas 6F 8
Wood Clough Platts BB9: Brierf 5E 104
Woodcock Cl. FY5: T Clev 7G 54
OL11: Roch 6K 203
PR5: Bam B 6C 136
Woodcock Est. PR5: Lost H 1L 153
Woodcock Fold PR7: E'ton 7F 172
Woodcock Hill Rd. BB2: Pleas 5C 138

Woodcock La.—Wynotham St.

Woodcock La. PR7: Hesk 1H 193
Woodcock's Ct. PR1: Prest 6K 229 (1J 135)
Woodcote Cl. L33: Kirk 6M 223
Wood Cotts. OL14: Tod 5K 165
Woodcott Bank BL1: Bolt 9E 198
Woodcourt Av. BB11: Burnl 6B 124
Woodcrest BB1: Wilp 4N 119
Woodcroft WN6: Shev 6H 213
WN8: Skelm 3K 219
Woodcroft Av. BB4: Rawt 2L 161
Woodcroft Cl. PR1: Penw 6F 134
Woodcroft St. BB4: Rawt 2L 161
Wooded Cl. BL9: Bury 8L 201
Wood End BB12: Reed 7D 104
PR1: Penw 7F 134
Woodend Av. L31: Magh 3B 222
Wood End Bus. Pk. L40: Burs 6N 189
Woodend La. OL12: Ward 8G 185
Wood End Rd. PR6: Clay W 4C 154
Woodend Rd. BB12: Reed 5A 104
Woodfall PR7: Chor 5D 174
Woodfield PR5: Bam B 1E 154
Woodfield Av. BB5: Acc 5C 142
FY1: Blackp 8H 227 (8B 88)
OL12: Roch 3B 204
Woodfield Cl. PR1: Penw 4E 134
Woodfield Rd. FY1: Blackp 8H 227 (8B 88)
FY5: T Clev 2K 63
L39: Orms 9J 209
PR7: Chor 5E 174
WOOD FIELDS 9K 201
Woodfields BB7: S'hurst 8B 80
BB12: S'stone 7D 102
Woodfields Ter. BL9: Bury 9K 201
Woodfield St. *OL14: Tod* 1K 165
(off Buckley Vw.)
Woodfield Ter. BB9: Brierf 5G 104
Woodfield Vw. BB7: Whall 5J 101
Wood Fold BL7: Brom C 7J 199
Woodfold PR1: Penw 5E 134
Woodfold Cl. BB2: Mellor B 6D 118
Woodfold Hall BB2: Mellor 1B 138
Woodfold La. PR3: Cab 8N 45
Woodfold Pk. Farm BB2: Mellor 9C 118
Woodfold Pl. BB2: Blackb 3J 139
Woodford Copse PR7: Chor 7B 174
Woodford St. WN5: Wigan 5L 221
Woodgate LA3: Morec 6F 22
Woodgate Av. BL9: Bury 9B 202
OL11: Roch 7L 203
WOODGATE HILL 9B 202
Woodgate Hill Rd. BL9: Bury 9A 202
(Ferngrove East)
BL9: Bury 9B 202
(Woodgate Av.)
Woodgate Pk. LA3: Morec 6F 22
Woodgates Rd. BB2: Blackb 3F 138
Wood Grn. PR25: Leyl 5H 153
Woodgreen PR4: Wesh 2N 111
Wood Grn. Dr. FY5: T Clev 3F 62
Wood Grn. Gdns.
WN5: Wigan 2L 221
Woodgrove Rd. BB11: Burnl 5F 124
Woodhall Cl. BL8: Bury 8J 201
Woodhall Cres. PR5: Hogh 4G 136
Woodhall Gdns. FY6: Ham 1B 64
Woodhart La. PR7: E'ton 9F 172
WOOD HEAD 1E 158
Woodhead Cl. BB4: W'foot 6E 162
BL0: Ramsb 1H 201
Woodhead Rd. BB12: Read 8C 102
WOODHEY 2G 200
Wood Hey Gro. OL12: Roch 1C 204
Woodhey Rd. BL0: Ramsb 2F 200
Woodheys Rd. OL15: Littleb 3K 205
WOODHILL 9J 201
Woodhill Av. LA4: Morec 5A 22
Woodhill Cl. BL8: Bury 9J 201
LA4: Morec 5A 22
Woodhill Fold BL8: Bury 9J 201
Woodhill Ho. LA4: Morec 4A 22
Woodhill La. LA4: Morec 4A 22
Woodhill Rd. BL8: Bury 9J 201
Woodhill St. BL8: Bury 9J 201
Woodhill Va. BL8: Bury 9J 201
WOOD HOUSE 4B 50
Woodhouse OL14: Tod 2N 165
Woodhouse Ct. OL14: Tod 1N 165
Woodhouse Dr. WN6: Wigan 9N 213
Woodhouse Farm Cotts.
OL12: Roch 3H 203
Woodhouse Gro. OL14: Tod 2N 165
PR1: Prest 1H 135
Wood Ho. La. BB7: Slaid 3A 50
Woodhouse La. OL12: Roch 3H 203
Woodhouse Rd. FY5: T Clev 3L 63
OL14: Tod 2N 165
Woodhouse St.
BB11: Burnl 5F 228 (5F 124)
Woodhurst Dr. WN6: Stand 3N 213
Woodland Av. FY5: T Clev 1H 63
L40: Scar 6E 188
OL13: Bac 2K 163
Woodland Cl. FY6: Ham 2C 64
PR4: W Grn 6G 111
Woodland Ct. BB3: Darw 7D 158
Woodland Cres. FY6: Pree 7N 41
Woodland Dr. BB5: Clay M 4M 121
FY6: Poul F 1L 89
WN6: Stand 2N 213
Woodland Grange PR1: Penw 5G 135
Woodland Gro. BL7: Eger 3D 198
FY3: Blackp 4N 227 (6E 88)
PR1: Penw 3E 134
Woodland Mt. OL13: Bac 7G 162
Woodland Path L37: Ains, Form 3A 206
PR8: Ains 3A 206
Woodland Pl. BB3: Lwr D 9N 139
Woodland Rd. L31: Mell 6F 222
Woodlands, The BB6: Old L 4C 100
BL8: Bury 8J 201
L40: Burs 1E 210
PR2: Ash R 8B 114
PR3: Gars 4M 59
PR8: Ains 8C 186
Woodlands Av. BB2: Blackb 7F 138
OL11: Roch 7L 203
OL14: Tod 1L 165
PR1: Penw 5G 135
PR2: Ribb 7A 116
PR4: K'ham 4L 111
PR5: Bam B 6C 136
Woodlands Caravan Pk. PR4: Mere B 6M 169
Woodlands Cl. BB1: Blackb 4B 140
BB4: Newc 6B 162
BB7: West B 5K 73
L39: Orms 8M 209
PR4: Newt 6D 112
PR9: S'port 6K 167
Woodlands Cnr.
BB1: Blackb 1A 226 (2L 139)
Woodlands Country Pk.
PR3: Eng H 6D 58
Woodlands Ct. FY8: L Ann 4K 129
Woodlands Cres. PR3: Bart 5E 94
Woodlands Dr. BB7: West B 5K 73
BB7: Whall 5J 101
LA3: Heys 6M 21
LA5: Silv 7G 5
PR2: Fulw 1H 115
PR4: Wart 3H 131
PR4: Wesh 2N 111
PR25: Leyl 6J 153
WN6: Shev 8J 213
Woodlands Gro. BB3: Darw 5L 157
BB12: Padi 1G 122
BL8: Bury 9G 201
LA3: Heys 6M 21
PR2: Grim 9G 96
Woodlands Mdw. PR7: Chor 2E 194
Woodlands Pk. BB7: Whall 5K 101
Woodlands Rd. BB9: Nelson 2K 105
BL0: Ramsb 4J 181
FY8: L Ann 4K 129
LA1: Lanc 4L 23
OL16: Milnr 8H 205
Woodland St. OL12: Roch 3D 204
Woodlands Vw. FY8: L Ann 3K 129
LA6: Over K 1F 16
OL16: Roch 5F 204
Woodlands Way PR3: Bart 5E 94
PR4: Longt 8K 133
Woodland Ter. OL13: Bac 3K 163
Woodland Vw. BB6: Gt H 3J 121
BL7: Brom C 5H 199
OL13: Bac 3K 163
PR4: Wesh 2K 111
PR6: Birns 8A 156
Wood La. BL0: Ramsb 4J 181
L37: D'holl, Gt A 2J 215
L40: Lath 8J 191
L40: Mawd 9A 172
PR7: Hesk 1G 193
WN6: Wrigh 1G 193
WN8: Parb 2A 212
Woodlark Cl. OL13: Bac 5M 163
Woodlark Dr. PR7: Chor 9B 174
Wood Lea OL14: Tod 8H 147
Wood Lea Bank *BB4: W'foot* 7D 162
(off Wood Lea Rd.)
Woodlea Chase BB3: Darw 3C 178
Woodlea Cl. PR9: S'port 1C 168
Woodlea Ct. LA1: Lanc 9N 23
Woodlea Gdns. BB9: Brierf 5H 105
Wood Lea Rd. BB4: W'foot 7C 162
Woodlea Rd. BB1: Blackb 4B 140
PR25: Leyl 7J 153
Woodlee Rd. PR4: Hesk B 5D 150
Woodleigh Cl. L31: Lyd 6A 216
Woodley Av. BB5: Acc 4B 142
FY5: T Clev 2K 63
Woodley Pk. Cen. 8M 211
Woodley Pk. Rd. WN8: Skelm 8M 211
Woodley Rd. L31: Magh 4B 222
Woodmancote PR7: Chor 4D 174
Woodman Dr. BL9: Bury 7K 201
Woodman La. LA6: Cow B, Neth B 9F 8
Woodmoss La. L40: Scar 3C 188
WOODNOOK 4A 142
Wood Nook BB4: Craws 9M 143
Woodnook Rd. WN6: App B 4H 213
Wood Pk. Rd. FY1: Blackp 9N 227 (9E 88)
WOODPLUMPTON 8B 94
Woodplumpton La. PR3: Brou 7E 94
Woodplumpton Rd. BB11: Burnl 7D 124
PR2: Ash R, Fulw 5E 114
PR4: Woodp 6B 94
Woodridge Av. FY5: T Clev 3C 62
WOOD ROAD 4H 201
Wood Rd. La. BL8: Bury 5G 201
BL9: Bury 5G 201
Woodrow WN8: Skelm 3J 219
Woodrow Dr. WN8: N 'urgh 3K 211
Woodruff Cl. FY5: T Clev 7F 54
Woodrush LA4: Morec 2F 22
Woodrush Rd. WN6: Stand 9N 213
Woods, The OL11: Roch 9N 203
Woods Brow BB2: Bald 4M 117
PR3: Ribc 4B 98
Woods Cl. L39: D'holl 8M 207
Woods End PR1: Prest 8N 229 (2L 135)
Woodsend Cl. BB2: Blackb 8A 140
WOODSFOLD 4J 93
Woods Green PR1: Prest 9H 229 (3H 135)
Woodside BB4: Hasl 5H 161
FY4: Blackp 2L 109
OL16: Milnr 8M 205
PR7: Chor 1G 195
PR7: Eux 3M 173
PR25: Far 3M 153
Woodside Av. BB1: Rish 9F 120
PR2: Fulw 5H 115
PR2: Ribb 6A 116
PR4: New L 9C 134
PR6: Clay W 6D 154
PR8: Ains 1B 206
Woodside Bank BB3: Darw 6N 157
Woodside Cl. BB5: Hunc 8E 122
WN8: Uph 3F 220
Woodside Cres. BB4: Newc 6B 162
Woodside Dr. *BL0: Ramsb* 9F 180
(off Hillside Rd.)
FY3: Blackp 5G 88
Woodside Gro. BB2: Blackb 8H 139
Woodside Pk. Caravan Pk. FY6: Pree 3B 56
Woodside Rd. BB5: Hunc 9D 122
(Brown Birks Rd.)
BB5: Hunc 8E 122
(Woodside Cl.)
BB12: S'stone 8D 102
Woodside Ter. BB9: Nelson 2G 105
Woodside Way BB5: Clay M 5M 121
L33: Kirk 5L 223
Woods La. PR3: Eng H 5E 58
PR4: Inskip 3J 93
Woodsley St. BB12: Burnl 4N 123
Woods Pas. OL15: Littleb 9J 185
Woodstock Av. FY5: T Clev 3J 63
Woodstock Cl. PR5: Lost H 8M 135
Woodstock Cres. BB2: Blackb 8F 138
Woodstock Dr. BL8: Tott 6C 200
PR8: Birk 5F 186
Woodstock Gdns. FY4: Blackp 2B 108
Woodstock St. OL12: Roch 4N 203
Wood St. BB3: Darw 5N 157
(Alexandra Rd.)
BB3: Darw 6N 157
(Hope St.)
BB5: Chur 3L 141
BB6: Gt H 4L 121
BB8: Colne 7B 86
BB9: Brierf 5F 104
BB10: Burnl 1E 124
BB12: Hapt 5H 123
BL0: Ramsb 9G 180
BL6: Hor 9D 196
FY1: Blackp 1J 227 (5B 88)
(not continuous)
FY6: Poul F 8M 63
FY7: Flee 4E 54
FY8: L Ann 2E 128
LA1: Lanc 6C 228 (8K 23)
OL14: Tod 1L 165
OL15: Littleb 9L 185
OL16: Milnr 9M 205
OL16: Roch 7D 204
Wood Ter. BB7: Chatb 7D 74
BB12: S'stone 8E 102
WOOD TOP 7K 161
Wood Top *BL0: Ramsb* 7G 180
(off Glen St.)
Woodtop *BB11: Burnl* 4B 124
(off Harcourt St.)
Wood Top Av. OL11: Roch 8K 203
WOODVALE 1C 206
Woodvale BB3: Darw 6N 157
PR26: Leyl 7D 152
Woodvale Ct. PR9: Banks 1F 168
Woodvale Rd. PR8: Ains 2C 206
Woodvale Sidings PR8: Ains 3D 206
Wood Vw. BB2: Blackb 7G 139
LA6: Bur L 3K 19
(off High St.)
OL10: Heyw 9G 203
Woodview WN6: Shev 6L 213
Wood Vw. La. FY6: Stal 5B 56
Woodville Ct. PR1: Penw 6F 134
Woodville Rd. BB1: Blackb 1A 140
BB9: Brierf 4F 104
PR1: Penw 6G 134
PR6: H Charn 4H 195
PR7: Chor 6E 174
Woodville Rd. W. PR1: Penw 6F 134
Woodville St. LA1: Lanc 6E 228 (8L 23)
PR25: Far 4L 153
Woodville Ter. BB3: Darw 9B 158
FY8: L Ann 5M 129
Woodward Cl. BL9: Bury 8L 201
Woodward Rd. L33: Know P 6A 224
Woodway PR2: Fulw 5F 114
Woodwell La. LA5: Silv 1G 11
Wookey Cl. PR2: Fulw 3N 115
Wooley La. BB5: Bax 5E 142
WOOLFOLD 9G 201
Woolfold Trad. Est. BL8: Bury 9G 201
Woolman Rd. FY1: Blackp 4L 227 (6C 88)
Woolpack BB8: Colne 8B 86
Woolwich St. BB1: Blackb 3B 140
Woone La. BB7: Clith 5K 81
Worcester Av. BB5: Acc 1N 141
LA1: Lanc 2M 29
PR3: Gars 5M 59
PR25: Leyl 7L 153
Worcester Gdns. PR4: Cott 4A 114
Worcester Pl. PR7: Chor 2G 195
Worcester Rd. BB1: Blackb 3C 140
FY3: Blackp 7F 88
Worcester St. BL8: Bury 9J 201
OL11: Roch 9B 204
Worden Brook Cl. PR7: Buck V 9A 154
Worden Cl. PR25: Leyl 8J 153
Worden Hall
(Worden Arts & Crafts Cen.) 9J 153
Worden La. PR6: Withn 4N 155
PR25: Leyl 8K 153
Worden Pk. 8J 153
Worden Rd. PR2: Ash R 6G 114
Wordens, The *PR25: Leyl* 8L 153
(off Glendale Cl.)
Wordsworth Av. BB12: Padi 2K 123
FY3: Blackp 8H 89
FY5: T Clev 1F 62
FY8: L Ann 4C 130
LA5: Bolt S 4L 15
PR4: Wart 2K 131
WN5: Bill 9G 221
WN5: Orr 5J 221
Wordsworth Cl. BB5: Osw 4J 141
L39: Orms 6J 209
Wordsworth Cres. OL15: Littleb 3J 205
Wordsworth Dr. BB6: Gt H 4H 121
Wordsworth Gdns. BB3: Darw 6B 158
Wordsworth Pl. PR5: Walt D 6N 135
Wordsworth Rd. BB5: Acc 5N 141
BB8: Colne 6A 86
Wordsworth St. BB10: Brierc 8K 105
BB12: Burnl 3A 124
BB12: Hapt 5H 123
Wordsworth Ter. PR6: Chor 4F 174
Wordsworth Way OL11: Roch 7J 203
Wordworth Ct. FY8: L Ann 4J 129
Workshop Rd. LA3: Midd 5L 27
Worrall St. OL12: Roch 3A 204
Worsicks Cotts. FY6: Sing 1D 90
Worsley Av. FY4: Blackp 2C 108
Worsley Cl. FY6: K Sea 8K 41
WN5: Wigan 6M 221
Worsley Ct. BB5: Osw 4L 141
Worsley Grn. WN5: Wigan 6L 221
Worsley Pl. OL16: Roch 6E 204
Worsley Rd. FY8: L Ann 3J 129
Worsley St. BB5: Acc 4C 142
BB5: Ris B 9F 142
BL8: Tott 6D 200
OL16: Roch 6E 204
WN5: Wigan 6L 221
Worsten Av. BB2: Blackb 7K 139
WORSTHORNE 4M 125
WORSTON 1C 82
Worston Cl. BB4: Rawt 3M 161
BB5: Acc 4M 141
Worston La. BB6: Gt H 3L 121
Worston Pl. *BB2: Blackb* 3J 139
(off Ribblesdale Pl.)
Worston Rd. BB7: Chatb 9B 74
Worswick Cres. BB4: Rawt 5M 161
Worswick Grn. BB4: Rawt 5N 161
Worthalls Rd. BB12: Read 9C 102
Worthing Cl. PR8: Birk 2F 186
Worthing Rd. PR2: Ingol 5D 114
Worthington Rd. FY4: Blackp 5G 109
Worthy St. PR6: Chor 7G 174
Wove Ct. PR1: Prest 7H 115
Wragby Cl. BL8: Bury 8J 201
Wraith St. BB3: Darw 7A 158
WRAMPOOL 5N 43
WRANGLING, THE 6A 226 (4L 139)
Wrath Cl. BL2: Bolt 8H 199
WRAY 8E 18
Wray Ct. LA1: Lanc 4J 23
Wray Cres. PR4: W Grn 5H 111
PR26: Leyl 9C 152
Wray Gro. FY5: T Clev 3D 62
Wray Pl. OL16: Roch 7F 204
WRAYTON 3F 18
Wraywood Ct. FY7: Flee 3C 54
Wrea Brook La. PR4: Wart 1H 131
WREA GREEN 6G 110
Wrekin Dr. L10: Aint 8D 222
Wren Av. PR1: Penw 3H 135
Wrenbury Cl. WN5: Wigan 6L 221
Wrenbury Dr. BL1: Bolt 7F 198
OL16: Roch 9F 204
Wren Cl. FY5: T Clev 3J 63
FY6: Carl 7G 63
WN5: Orr 2L 221
Wren Dr. BL9: Bury 9N 201
Wren Grn. OL16: Roch 7F 204
Wren Gro. FY3: Blackp 8E 88
Wrennalls La. PR7: E'ton 1D 192
Wren St. BB9: Nelson 2K 105
BB12: Burnl 3A 124
PR1: Prest 1N 229 (7L 115)
Wren Way OL16: Roch 7F 204
WRIGHTINGTON 9F 192
WRIGHTINGTON BAR 6J 193
Wrights Fold PR25: Leyl 7M 153
Wrights Ter. PR8: Birk 2H 187
Wright St. BL6: Hor 9C 196
OL13: Weir 9K 145
PR4: Wesh 3L 111
PR6: Chor 6G 174
PR9: S'port 7H 167
Wright St. W. *BL6: Hor* 9C 196
(off Julia St.)
Wrigley Pl. OL15: Littleb 2J 205
Wrigleys Cl. L37: Form 7A 206
Wrigleys La. L37: Form 7A 206
Written Stone La. PR3: Longr 1N 97
Wroxham Cl. BB10: Burnl 8H 105
BL8: Bury 8J 201
Wroxton Cl. FY5: T Clev 4F 62
WUERDLE 1H 205
Wuerdle Cl. OL16: Roch 2H 205
Wuerdle Farm Way OL16: Roch 1H 205
Wuerdle Pl. OL16: Roch 1H 205
Wuerdle St. OL16: Roch 1H 205
Wycherley Rd. OL12: Roch 3M 203
Wychnor PR2: Fulw 2E 114
Wycollar Cl. BB5: Acc 4B 142
Wycollar Dr. BB2: Blackb 2H 139
Wycollar Rd. BB2: Blackb 2H 139
WYCOLLER 8K 87
Wycoller Av. BB10: Burnl 4H 125
Wycoller Country Pk. 8K 87
Wycoller Rd. BB8: Traw 7G 86
Wycoller Vw. BB8: Lane B 5H 87
Wycombe Av. FY4: Blackp 3B 108
Wyder Ct. PR2: Ribb 4C 116
Wye Wlk. BL8: Bury 7F 200
Wyfordby Av. BB2: Blackb 1G 139
Wyke Cop Rd. PR8: S'port 1C 188
PR9: S'port 1C 188
Wykefield Ct. PR3: Gars 4N 59
Wykeham Gro. OL12: Roch 4M 203
Wykeham Rd. FY8: L Ann 4A 130
Wyke La. PR9: S'port 6B 168
Wyke Wood La. PR9: S'port 6E 168
Wyllin Rd. L33: Kirk 8M 223
WYMOTT 9C 152
Wymundsley PR7: Chor 5B 174
Wyndene Cl. PR3: Longr 2L 97
Wyndene Gro. PR4: Frec 2N 131
Wyndham Gdns. FY4: Blackp 3D 108
Wyndham Pl. LA4: Morec 2F 22
Wynfield PR5: Bam B 6B 136
Wyngarth Ct. LA1: Lanc 8C 228
Wynnstay Av. L31: Lyd 8C 216
Wynnwood Av. FY1: Blackp 1C 88
Wynotham St. BB10: Burnl 9F 104

SAFETY CAMERA INFORMATION

Safety camera locations are publicised by the Safer Roads Partnership which operates them in order to encourage drivers to comply with speed limits at these sites. It is the driver's absolute responsibility to be aware of and to adhere to speed limits at all times.

By showing this safety camera information it is the intention of Geographers' A-Z Map Company Ltd., to encourage safe driving and greater awareness of speed limits and vehicle speed. Data accurate at time of printing.

Printed and bound in the United Kingdom by Polestar Wheatons Ltd., Exeter.

HOSPITALS, HOSPICES and selected HEALTHCARE FACILITIES covered by this atlas.

N.B. Where it is not possible to name these facilities on the map,
the reference given is for the road in which they are situated.

ACCRINGTON VICTORIA COMMUNITY HOSPITAL
....1A **142**
  Haywood Road
  ACCRINGTON
  BB5 6AS
  Tel: 01254 263555

ASHWORTH HOSPITAL 8G **216**
  Parkbourn
  LIVERPOOL
  L31 1HW
  Tel: 0151 473 0303

BEARDWOOD BMI HOSPITAL 2H **139**
  Preston New Road
  BLACKBURN
  BB2 7AE
  Tel: 01254 507607

BIRCH HILL HOSPITAL 9H **185**
  Union Road
  ROCHDALE
  OL12 9QB
  Tel: 01706 377777

BISPHAM HOSPITAL REHABILITATION UNIT
....5F **62**
  Ryscar Way
  Bispham
  BLACKPOOL
  FY2 0FN
  Tel: 01253 655901

BLACKPOOL VICTORIA HOSPITAL 4G **89**
  Whinney Heys Road
  BLACKPOOL
  FY3 8NR
  Tel: 01253 300000

BMI GISBURNE PARK HOSPITAL 8A **52**
  Gisburne Park Estate
  CLITHEROE
  BB7 4HX
  Tel: 01200 445693

BMI LANCASTER HOSPITAL 9E **228** (9L **23**)
  Meadowside
  LANCASTER
  LA1 3RH
  Tel: 01524 62345

BRIAN HOUSE (HOSPICE) 9E **62**
  Within Trinity Hospice
  Low Moor Rd.
  BLACKPOOL
  FY2 0BG
  Tel: 01253 358881

BURNLEY GENERAL HOSPITAL 8G **104**
  Casterton Avenue
  BURNLEY
  BB10 2PQ
  Tel: 01282 425071

CALDERSTONES HOSPITAL 3F **100**
  Mitton Road
  Whalley
  CLITHEROE
  BB7 9PE
  Tel: 01254 822121

CASTLEBERG HOSPITAL 3M **35**
  Raines Road
  CRAVEN
  BD24 0BN
  Tel: 01729 823515

CHORLEY & SOUTH RIBBLE DISTRICT
  GENERAL HOSPITAL 4E **174**
  Preston Road
  CHORLEY
  PR7 1PP
  Tel: 01257 261222

CLIFTON HOSPITAL 3H **129**
  Pershore Road
  LYTHAM ST. ANNES
  FY8 1PB
  Tel: 01253 306204

CLITHEROE COMMUNITY HOSPITAL 1N **81**
  Chatburn Road
  CLITHEROE
  BB7 4JX
  Tel: 01200 427311

DERIAN HOUSE (HOSPICE) 3D **174**
  Chancery Road
  CHORLEY
  PR7 1DH
  Tel: 01257 271271

EAST LANCASHIRE HOSPICE 7M **139**
  Park Lee Road
  BLACKBURN
  BB2 3NY
  Tel: 01254 733400

EUXTON HALL PRIVATE HOSPITAL 5M **173**
  Wigan Road
  Euxton
  CHORLEY
  PR7 6DY
  Tel: 01257 276261

FAIRFIELD GENERAL HOSPITAL 9C **202**
  Rochdale Old Road
  BURY
  BL9 7TD
  Tel: 0161 6240420

FLEETWOOD HOSPITAL 8H **41**
  Pharos Street
  FLEETWOOD
  FY7 6BE
  Tel: 01253 306053

FULWOOD HALL PRIVATE HOSPITAL 4M **115**
  Midgery Lane
  Fulwood
  PRESTON
  PR2 9SZ
  Tel: 01772 704111

FYLDE COAST SPIRE HOSPITAL 3F **88**
  St Walburgas Road
  BLACKPOOL
  FY3 8BP
  Tel: 01253 394188

GUILD LODGE 5B **96**
  Guild Park
  Whittingham
  PRESTON
  PR3 2JH
  Tel: 01772 406600

HESKETH CENTRE 5J **167**
  51-55 Albert Road
  SOUTHPORT
  PR9 0LT
  Tel: 01704 383110

HIGHBANK PRIORY CENTRE
  (EATING DISORDERS) 3K **201**
  Walmersley Road
  BURY
  BL9 5LX
  Tel: 01706 829540

HIGHBANK PRIORY REHABILITATION CENTRE
  (ELTON UNIT) 9E **200**
  Walshaw Road
  Elton
  BURY
  BL8 3AL
  Tel: 01706 829540

HIGHFIELD BMI HOSPITAL 8A **204**
  Manchester Road
  ROCHDALE
  OL11 4LZ
  Tel: 01706 655121

LONGRIDGE COMMUNITY HOSPITAL 3J **97**
  St Wilfrid's Terrace
  Longridge
  PRESTON
  PR3 3WQ
  Tel: 01772 777400

NHS WALK-IN CENTRE
  (KNOWSLEY - KIRKBY) 8K **223**
  St Chad's Clinic
  57 St Chad's Drive
  LIVERPOOL
  L32 8RE
  Tel: 0151 244 3180

NHS WALK-IN CENTRE (ROCHDALE) 4C **204**
  90 Whitehall Street
  ROCHDALE
  OL12 0ND

NHS WALK-IN CENTRE (SKELMERSDALE) ...2M **219**
  116-118 The Concourse Shopping Centre
  SKELMERSDALE
  WN8 6LJ
  Tel: 01695 554260

NHS WALK-IN CENTRE (TODMORDEN) 2M **165**
  82 Halifax Rd.
  Lwr. George St.
  TODMORDEN
  OL14 5QJ
  Tel: 01706 811106

ORMSKIRK AND DISTRICT GENERAL HOSPITAL
....8M **209**
  Wigan Road
  ORMSKIRK
  L39 2AZ
  Tel: 01695 577111

PARKWOOD 5G **89**
  East Park Drive
  BLACKPOOL
  FY3 8PW
  Tel: 01253 306980

PENDLE COMMUNITY HOSPITAL 1J **105**
  Leeds Road
  NELSON
  BB9 9SZ
  Tel: 01282 425071

PENDLESIDE HOSPICE 6E **104**
  Colne Road
  BURNLEY
  BB10 2LW
  Tel: 01282 440100

PRESTON PRIORY HOSPITAL 9L **93**
  Rosemary Lane
  Bartle
  PRESTON
  PR4 0HB
  Tel: 01772 691122

QUEENSCOURT HOSPICE 1M **187**
  Town Lane
  SOUTHPORT
  PR8 6RE
  Tel: 01704 544645

QUEEN VICTORIA HOSPITAL 3B **22**
  Thornton Road
  MORECAMBE
  LA4 5NN
  Tel: 01524 411661

RENACRES PRIVATE HOSPITAL 8A **188**
  Renacres Lane
  Halsall
  ORMSKIRK
  L39 8SE
  Tel: 01704 841133

RIBBLETON HOSPITAL 7B **116**
  Miller Road
  Ribbleton
  PRESTON
  PR2 6LS
  Tel: 01772 401600

RIDGE LEA HOSPITAL 7N **23**
  Quernmore Road
  LANCASTER
  LA1 3JT
  Tel: 01524 586200

ROCHDALE INFIRMARY 4B **204**
  Whitehall Street
  ROCHDALE
  OL12 0NB
  Tel: 01706 377777

ROSSALL HOSPITAL REHABILITATION UNIT
....4C **54**
  Westway
  Rossall
  FLEETWOOD
  FY7 8JH
  Tel: 01253 655101

ROSSENDALE HOSPICE 5N **161**
  161 Bacup Road
  Rawtenstall
  ROSSENDALE
  BB4 7PL
  Tel: 01706 253633

ROYAL BLACKBURN HOSPITAL 6B **140**
  Haslingden Road
  BLACKBURN
  BB2 3HH
  Tel: 01254 263555

ROYAL LANCASTER INFIRMARY
....9C **228** (1K **29**)
  Ashton Road
  LANCASTER
  LA1 4RP
  Tel: 01524 65944

ROYAL PRESTON HOSPITAL 3J **115**
  Sharoe Green Lane North
  Fulwood
  PRESTON
  PR2 9HT
  Tel: 01772 716565

ST CATHERINE'S HOSPICE 9M **135**
  Lostock Lane
  Lostock Hall
  PRESTON
  PR5 5XU
  Tel: 01772 629171

ST JOHN'S HOSPICE 4J **23**
  Slyne Road
  LANCASTER
  LA2 6ST
  Tel: 01524 382538

SOUTHPORT AND FORMBY
  DISTRICT GENERAL HOSPITAL 1L **187**
  Town Lane
  SOUTHPORT
  PR8 6PN
  Tel: 01704 547471

TRINITY - THE HOSPICE IN THE FYLDE 9E **62**
  Low Moor Road
  BLACKPOOL
  FY2 0BG
  Tel: 01253 358881

WRIGHTINGTON HOSPITAL 2G **213**
  Hall Lane
  Appley Bridge
  WIGAN
  WN6 9EP
  Tel: 01942 244000

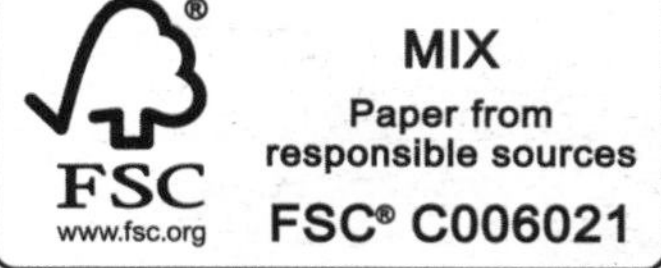